The Encyclopedia of Religion

The Encyclopedia of Religion

Mircea Eliade

EDITOR IN CHIEF

Volume 12

MACMILLAN PUBLISHING COMPANY
New York

Collier Macmillan Publishers
London

MACMILLAN PUBLISHING COMPANY
866 Third Avenue, New York, NY 10022

Collier Macmillan Canada, Inc.

Library of Congress Catalog Card Number: 86-5432

PRINTED IN THE UNITED STATES OF AMERICA

printing number
1 2 3 4 5 6 7 8 9 10

Library of Congress Cataloging-in-Publication Data

The Encyclopedia of religion.

Includes bibliographies and index.
1. Religion—Dictionaries. I. Eliade, Mircea, 1907–1986. II. Adams, Charles J.
BL31.#46 1986 200'.3'21 86-5432
ISBN 0-02-909480-1 (set)
ISBN 0-02-909830-0 (v. 12)

Acknowledgments of sources, copyrights, and permissions to use previously published materials are gratefully made in a special listing in volume 16.

Abbreviations and Symbols Used in This Work

abbr. abbreviated; abbreviation
abr. abridged; abridgment
AD *anno Domini,* in the year of the (our) Lord
Afrik. Afrikaans
AH *anno Hegirae,* in the year of the Hijrah
Akk. Akkadian
Ala. Alabama
Alb. Albanian
Am. *Amos*
AM *ante meridiem,* before noon
amend. amended; amendment
annot. annotated; annotation
Ap. *Apocalypse*
Apn. *Apocryphon*
app. appendix
Arab. Arabic
ʿArakh. *ʿArakhin*
Aram. Aramaic
Ariz. Arizona
Ark. Arkansas
Arm. Armenian
art. article (pl., arts.)
AS Anglo-Saxon
Asm. Mos. *Assumption of Moses*
Assyr. Assyrian
A.S.S.R. Autonomous Soviet Socialist Republic
Av. Avestan
ʿA.Z. *ʿAvodah zarah*
b. born
Bab. Babylonian
Ban. Bantu
1 Bar. *1 Baruch*
2 Bar. *2 Baruch*
3 Bar. *3 Baruch*
4 Bar. *4 Baruch*
B.B. *Bava' batra'*
BBC British Broadcasting Corporation
BC before Christ
BCE before the common era
B.D. Bachelor of Divinity
Beits. *Beitsah*
Bekh. *Bekhorot*
Beng. Bengali
Ber. *Berakhot*
Berb. Berber
Bik. *Bikkurim*
bk. book (pl., bks.)
B.M. *Bava' metsiʿa'*
BP before the present
B.Q. *Bava' qamma'*
Brāh. *Brāhmaṇa*
Bret. Breton
B.T. Babylonian Talmud
Bulg. Bulgarian
Burm. Burmese
c. *circa,* about, approximately
Calif. California
Can. Canaanite
Catal. Catalan
CE of the common era
Celt. Celtic
cf. *confer,* compare
Chald. Chaldean
chap. chapter (pl., chaps.)
Chin. Chinese
C.H.M. Community of the Holy Myrrhbearers
1 Chr. *1 Chronicles*
2 Chr. *2 Chronicles*
Ch. Slav. Church Slavic
cm centimeters
col. column (pl., cols.)
Col. *Colossians*
Colo. Colorado
comp. compiler (pl., comps.)
Conn. Connecticut
cont. continued
Copt. Coptic
1 Cor. *1 Corinthians*
2 Cor. *2 Corinthians*
corr. corrected
C.S.P. Congregatio Sancti Pauli, Congregation of Saint Paul (Paulists)
d. died
D Deuteronomic (source of the Pentateuch)
Dan. Danish
D.B. Divinitatis Baccalaureus, Bachelor of Divinity
D.C. District of Columbia
D.D. Divinitatis Doctor, Doctor of Divinity
Del. Delaware
Dem. *Demaʾi*
dim. diminutive
diss. dissertation
Dn. *Daniel*
D.Phil. Doctor of Philosophy
Dt. *Deuteronomy*
Du. Dutch
E Elohist (source of the Pentateuch)
Eccl. *Ecclesiastes*
ed. editor (pl., eds.); edition; edited by
ʿEduy. *ʿEduyyot*
e.g. *exempli gratia,* for example
Egyp. Egyptian
1 En. *1 Enoch*
2 En. *2 Enoch*
3 En. *3 Enoch*
Eng. English
enl. enlarged
Eph. *Ephesians*
ʿEruv. *ʿEruvin*
1 Esd. *1 Esdras*
2 Esd. *2 Esdras*
3 Esd. *3 Esdras*
4 Esd. *4 Esdras*
esp. especially
Est. Estonian
Est. *Esther*
et al. *et alii,* and others
etc. *et cetera,* and so forth
Eth. Ethiopic
EV English version
Ex. *Exodus*
exp. expanded
Ez. *Ezekiel*
Ezr. *Ezra*
2 Ezr. *2 Ezra*
4 Ezr. *4 Ezra*
f. feminine; and following (pl., ff.)
fasc. fascicle (pl., fascs.)
fig. figure (pl., figs.)
Finn. Finnish
fl. *floruit,* flourished
Fla. Florida
Fr. French
frag. fragment
ft. feet
Ga. Georgia
Gal. *Galatians*
Gaul. Gaulish
Ger. German
Giṭ. *Giṭṭin*
Gn. *Genesis*
Gr. Greek
Ḥag. *Ḥagigah*
Ḥal. *Ḥallah*
Hau. Hausa
Hb. *Habakkuk*
Heb. Hebrew
Heb. *Hebrews*
Hg. *Haggai*
Hitt. Hittite
Hor. *Horayot*
Hos. *Hosea*
Ḥul. *Ḥullin*
Hung. Hungarian
ibid. *ibidem,* in the same place (as the one immediately preceding)
Icel. Icelandic
i.e. *id est,* that is
IE Indo-European
Ill. Illinois
Ind. Indiana
intro. introduction
Ir. Gael. Irish Gaelic
Iran. Iranian
Is. *Isaiah*
Ital. Italian
J Yahvist (source of the Pentateuch)
Jas. *James*
Jav. Javanese
Jb. *Job*
Jdt. *Judith*
Jer. *Jeremiah*
Jgs. *Judges*
Jl. *Joel*
Jn. *John*
1 Jn. *1 John*
2 Jn. *2 John*
3 Jn. *3 John*
Jon. *Jonah*
Jos. *Joshua*
Jpn. Japanese
JPS Jewish Publication Society translation (1985) of the Hebrew Bible
J.T. Jerusalem Talmud
Jub. *Jubilees*
Kans. Kansas
Kel. *Kelim*

Ker. *Keritot*
Ket. *Ketubbot*
1 Kgs. *1 Kings*
2 Kgs. *2 Kings*
Khois. Khoisan
Kil. *Kil'ayim*
km kilometers
Kor. Korean
Ky. Kentucky
l. line (pl., ll.)
La. Louisiana
Lam. *Lamentations*
Lat. Latin
Latv. Latvian
L. en Th. Licencié en Théologie, Licentiate in Theology
L. ès L. Licencié ès Lettres, Licentiate in Literature
Let. Jer. *Letter of Jeremiah*
lit. literally
Lith. Lithuanian
Lk. *Luke*
LL Late Latin
LL.D. Legum Doctor, Doctor of Laws
Lv. *Leviticus*
m meters
m. masculine
M.A. Master of Arts
Ma'as. *Ma'aserot*
Ma'as. Sh. *Ma'aser sheni*
Mak. *Makkot*
Makh. *Makhshirin*
Mal. *Malachi*
Mar. Marathi
Mass. Massachusetts
1 Mc. *1 Maccabees*
2 Mc. *2 Maccabees*
3 Mc. *3 Maccabees*
4 Mc. *4 Maccabees*
Md. Maryland
M.D. Medicinae Doctor, Doctor of Medicine
ME Middle English
Meg. *Megillah*
Me'il. *Me'ilah*
Men. *Menaḥot*
MHG Middle High German
mi. miles
Mi. *Micah*
Mich. Michigan
Mid. *Middot*
Minn. Minnesota
Miq. *Miqva'ot*
MIran. Middle Iranian
Miss. Mississippi
Mk. *Mark*
Mo. Missouri
Mo'ed Q. *Mo'ed qaṭan*
Mont. Montana
MPers. Middle Persian
MS. *manuscriptum*, manuscript (pl., MSS)
Mt. *Matthew*
MT Masoretic text
n. note
Na. *Nahum*
Nah. Nahuatl
Naz. *Nazir*
N.B. *nota bene*, take careful note
N.C. North Carolina
n.d. no date
N.Dak. North Dakota
NEB New English Bible
Nebr. Nebraska
Ned. *Nedarim*
Neg. *Nega'im*
Neh. *Nehemiah*
Nev. Nevada
N.H. New Hampshire
Nid. *Niddah*
N.J. New Jersey
Nm. *Numbers*
N.Mex. New Mexico
no. number (pl., nos.)
Nor. Norwegian
n.p. no place
n.s. new series
N.Y. New York
Ob. *Obadiah*
O.Cist. Ordo Cisterciencium, Order of Cîteaux (Cistercians)
OCS Old Church Slavonic
OE Old English
O.F.M. Ordo Fratrum Minorum, Order of Friars Minor (Franciscans)
OFr. Old French
Ohal. *Ohalot*
OHG Old High German
OIr. Old Irish
OIran. Old Iranian
Okla. Oklahoma
ON Old Norse
O.P. Ordo Praedicatorum, Order of Preachers (Dominicans)
OPers. Old Persian
op. cit. *opere citato*, in the work cited
OPrus. Old Prussian
Oreg. Oregon
'Orl. *'Orlah*
O.S.B. Ordo Sancti Benedicti, Order of Saint Benedict (Benedictines)
p. page (pl., pp.)
P Priestly (source of the Pentateuch)
Pa. Pennsylvania
Pahl. Pahlavi
Par. *Parah*
para. paragraph (pl., paras.)
Pers. Persian
Pes. *Pesaḥim*
Ph.D. Philosophiae Doctor, Doctor of Philosophy
Phil. *Philippians*
Phlm. *Philemon*
Phoen. Phoenician
pl. plural; plate (pl., pls.)
PM *post meridiem*, after noon
Pol. Polish
pop. population
Port. Portuguese
Prv. *Proverbs*
Ps. *Psalms*
Ps. 151 *Psalm 151*
Ps. Sol. *Psalms of Solomon*
pt. part (pl., pts.)
1 Pt. *1 Peter*
2 Pt. *2 Peter*
Pth. Parthian
Q hypothetical source of the synoptic Gospels
Qid. *Qiddushin*
Qin. *Qinnim*
r. reigned; ruled
Rab. *Rabbah*
rev. revised
R. ha-Sh. *Ro'sh ha-shanah*
R.I. Rhode Island
Rom. Romanian
Rom. *Romans*
R.S.C.J. Societas Sacratissimi Cordis Jesu, Religious of the Sacred Heart
RSV Revised Standard Version of the Bible
Ru. *Ruth*
Rus. Russian
Rv. *Revelation*
Rv. Ezr. *Revelation of Ezra*
San. *Sanhedrin*
S.C. South Carolina
Scot. Gael. Scottish Gaelic
S.Dak. South Dakota
sec. section (pl., secs.)
Sem. Semitic
ser. series
sg. singular
Sg. *Song of Songs*
Sg. of 3 *Prayer of Azariah and the Song of the Three Young Men*
Shab. *Shabbat*
Shav. *Shavu'ot*
Sheq. *Sheqalim*
Sib. Or. *Sibylline Oracles*
Sind. Sindhi
Sinh. Sinhala
Sir. *Ben Sira*
S.J. Societas Jesu, Society of Jesus (Jesuits)
Skt. Sanskrit
1 Sm. *1 Samuel*
2 Sm. *2 Samuel*
Sogd. Sogdian
Soṭ *Soṭah*
sp. species (pl., spp.)
Span. Spanish
sq. square
S.S.R. Soviet Socialist Republic
st. stanza (pl., ss.)
S.T.M. Sacrae Theologiae Magister, Master of Sacred Theology
Suk. *Sukkah*
Sum. Sumerian
supp. supplement; supplementary
Sus. *Susanna*
s.v. *sub verbo*, under the word (pl., s.v.v.)
Swed. Swedish
Syr. Syriac
Syr. Men. *Syriac Menander*
Ta'an. *Ta'anit*
Tam. Tamil
Tam. *Tamid*
Tb. *Tobit*
T.D. *Taishō shinshū daizōkyō*, edited by Takakusu Junjirō et al. (Tokyo, 1922–1934)
Tem. *Temurah*
Tenn. Tennessee
Ter. *Terumot*
Ṭev. Y. *Ṭevul yom*
Tex. Texas
Th.D. Theologicae Doctor, Doctor of Theology
1 Thes. *1 Thessalonians*
2 Thes. *2 Thessalonians*
Thrac. Thracian
Ti. *Titus*
Tib. Tibetan
1 Tm. *1 Timothy*
2 Tm. *2 Timothy*
T. of 12 *Testaments of the Twelve Patriarchs*
Ṭoh. *Ṭohorot*
Tong. Tongan
trans. translator, translators; translated by; translation
Turk. Turkish
Ukr. Ukrainian
Upan. *Upaniṣad*
U.S. United States
U.S.S.R. Union of Soviet Socialist Republics
Uqts. *Uqtsin*
v. verse (pl., vv.)
Va. Virginia
var. variant; variation
Viet. Vietnamese
viz. *videlicet*, namely
vol. volume (pl., vols.)
Vt. Vermont
Wash. Washington
Wel. Welsh
Wis. Wisconsin
Wis. *Wisdom of Solomon*
W.Va. West Virginia
Wyo. Wyoming
Yad. *Yadayim*
Yev. *Yevamot*
Yi. Yiddish
Yor. Yoruba
Zav. *Zavim*
Zec. *Zechariah*
Zep. *Zephaniah*
Zev. *Zevaḥim*

* hypothetical
? uncertain; possibly; perhaps
° degrees
+ plus
− minus
= equals; is equivalent to
× by; multiplied by
→ yields

P

(CONTINUED)

PROCESSION is the linearly ordered, solemn movement of a group through chartered space to a known destination to give witness, bear an esteemed object, perform a rite, fulfill a vow, gain merit, or visit a shrine.

Some processions, such as the Via Dolorosa procession in modern Jerusalem, constitute major rituals in their own right. Others, such as the "Little Entrance" of Christian Orthodox tradition (in which the Gospels are carried to the front of the sanctuary) or the procession of a bridal party down a church aisle, are only facilitating gestures—formalized comings and goings. The most familiar settings for processions are civil ceremonies (such as coronations, military fanfares, and enthronements), weddings, funerals, initiations, and fertility rites. Major processions seem most widespread in agricultural or urban cultures or those in transition from the one to the other. In hunting, nomadic, and industrial cultures, processions are likely to decline in frequency or significance and thereafter function only as minor gestural tributaries to other rituals.

The ritual space of a procession is linear. When it is completed by a subsequent recession, one might speak of it as "bi-linear." By virtue of its linearity, procession differs from circumambulation. Processual action is not movement *around* a sacred object but *to* a special place. Even when a procession returns to its beginning point, its circuit is not generally continuous. The movement is oriented toward a destination rather than a center. Processants do not occupy centralized sacred space. Instead, they carry their "center" with them. The usual places of honor in hierarchically ordered processions are at the head or end of the line. Whereas circumambulation usually sanctifies or protects the place bounded by its circumference, a procession normally links different spatial orders, for instance, civic and sacred or urban and rural space. The rhythms of processing and recessing establish a corridor between a nucleus of sacred space and adjacent, nonsacred zones, or satellite shrines beyond these zones. Distances traversed in processions are usually moderate. One of the longer ones, held during the Greek Eleusinian festival, was fourteen miles. Others, such as the chorus's entrance *(parados)* and exit *(exodos)* to ancient Greek theater, were only a few yards long. Robigalia, the ancient Roman procession intended to avert blight and later adapted by early Christianity into its Rogation processions, was five miles, a more typical distance.

Walking meditation in Zen Buddhism is called *kinhin*. This practice falls between procession and circumambulation. *Kinhin* is not directed *to* any place, so it is not strictly a procession. And although its course is usually around a meditation hall, there is no centralized object of attention. Instead, practitioners' eyes are on the floor, and their attention is directed to the way of walking itself.

The solemn or meditative tone of a procession differentiates it from the expansive, celebrative ethos of a parade or the martial, aggressive one of military marches, picketing, or conquests (such as Don Diego de Vargas's *entrada* into Santa Fe, New Mexico, in 1692). When Joshua brings down Jericho's walls, he is not processing so much as circumambulating in the service of conquest. Unlike mere invasion, conquest, now an obsolete military tactic, is akin to ritual because of its obvious stylization and emphasis on symbolic, rather than strategic, ordering. Examples of ritual elements that might distinguish conquest from invasion include carrying flags, playing drums, wearing uniforms, singing, chanting, and marching in columns. These activities sometimes retain their symbolic value long after their practical military values are lost.

The usual distinction between processions and parades identifies the former as sacred, the latter as profane. The distinction is minimally useful because processions often try to link these or other classificatory domains. Perhaps we should consider parades and processions as celebrative and solemn versions, respectively, of the same basic type of action. Consequently, speaking of a "religious parade" or an "academic procession" is no contradiction in terms. The pace of a procession is typically slower than that of a parade, and its rhythms are more deliberate than that of ordinary walking (or driving if, say, chariots, pageants, floats, or automobiles are employed to transport participants).

Participation in processions is more restricted than in parades. There seems to be a persistent tendency for every procession gradually to relax its exclusivity and become a popular parade in which bystanders can join. Since processing is group movement, it contrasts with running races, which is ritualized, for example, in the Olympic Games and among some modern-day Pueblos. A race is agonistic, setting one person in competition with another. The object of a race is to arrive ordinally (first place, second, third, and so on), not corporately or simultaneously. Perhaps the best term to appropriate if we wish to speak of an "individual procession" is *quest*. "Quest," however, is probably better treated as individualized pilgrimage.

Since a procession's destination is known, it is distinct from ritualized hunting, divination-directed migration, religious wandering (of the Hebrews in the desert, for example), and wayfaring (a common practice in medieval China and Japan). Whereas essential elements of these perambulatory rituals include becoming disoriented, abiding in unprotected places, and having to invent or discover one's destination, in processions there is no doubt where to begin and end, and little need for concern about personal safety.

Dancing has no destination; processing does. Processional dances such as the medieval European Dance of Death or the Hasidic dance with the Torah, are borderline instances. Dance presupposes not only rhythm but, typically, music. When dancing arises in a procession, as it does in Rio's Carnival, perhaps we should speak of the event as a parade. And when dancing shifts from circularity and symmetry to linearity and asymmetry, the religious climate is likely to shift from prophetic criticism to priestly conservatism.

The space through which a pilgrim passes may be mapped, but, unlike a procession path, it is not chartered. Pilgrims pass through what Victor Turner calls liminal ("threshold") zones as they go from near to far. Whereas pilgrims tread ways they may not recognize or cross borders that make them subject to foreign authority, processants pass down ways specially cleared, decorated, and authorized for their arrival. Toward the end of certain pilgrimages—for instance, to the shrine of Guadalupe in Mexico City—one may sometimes join a procession. The chartered quality of procession paths is usually emphasized by the use of stations along the *via sacra;* at these, processants stop, rest, and oftentimes perform ancillary rites.

Even priestly processants may have little to say about the intentions of their actions. Processions, unlike initiation rites or sacrifices, evoke little codified commentary, so scholars usually have to infer intentions. The most obvious one is to display what Erving Goffman might have called a "with": these people "go with" that god. By walking with a god, processants gain merit by association and give witness that sacredness is not geographically restricted to one spot but capable of annexing, even if temporarily, other places. Both a territorial imperative and a hierarchy of gods or sacred places is implied in most processions. Being seen, particularly in postures of homage before elevated, but proximate, sacred objects, legitimizes bonds and often establishes these *sacra* as a group's own. Far from having an inversion effect, as a Mardi Gras parade might, public processions confirm established hierarchies and sacralize ownership and order. For example, one of the oldest known processions was part of the Great Akitu festival held in Babylon in honor of Marduk. The first day of the new year was set aside for a solemn procession in which Nabu and other gods (carried in boats), kings, and subjects were seen visiting and paying homage to Marduk in his "chamber of fates." Royalty was allowed to take the hand of the god, as if inviting him down an elaborately paved procession way, in order to confirm and renew the divine kingship. At an earlier time Marduk may have been obligated to go in procession to Nabu. Whichever deity was made the goal of a procession was by implication at the pinnacle of the pantheon.

The display of venerated objects, such as the Host during Christian Corpus Christi processions, or symbols of power, such as weapons in Roman triumphal entries, is a common motive for processing. Lustrations, or gestures of purification, are sometimes enacted to ensure that such objects do not come to be contaminated or regarded as common because of overexposure.

The ritual form most akin to procession is pilgrimage. Though both are styles of symbolic journeying, they differ in essential respects. While pilgrimage is more goal-oriented (the return is usually anticlimactic), processions may be more focused on a carried object than a goal, and recessing may be as significant as processing. In contrast to pilgrims, processants do not usually eat, sleep, or suffer together, nor do they endure long periods of solitude. Furthermore, processants are usually the objects of spectating, while such is not the case with pilgrims. For these reasons processions tend more strongly toward social conservatism. Ironically, however, the more popularly successful a procession becomes, the more likely it is to become a ritual of inversion.

[*For related discussions, see* Circumambulation *and* Pilgrimage, *overview article.*]

BIBLIOGRAPHY

In the 1910s A. E. Crawley wrote—in his article "Processions and Dances" in the *Encyclopaedia of Religion and Ethics,* edited by James Hastings, vol. 10 (Edinburgh, 1918)—that no comprehensive or scientific work on processions had yet been written. His observation is still largely true. His article, like B. I. Mullahy's in the *New Catholic Encyclopedia* (New York, 1967) and Lawrence J. Madden's in the *Encyclopaedia Britannica* (Chicago, 1973), draws from scant comparative data and depends largely on Christian, specifically Roman Catholic, categories (functional, ordinary, and extraordinary processions) for its analyses and definitions. Rare is the book that includes a chapter, section, or even an index entry on processions.

Presently, data on processions are still largely to be found in works on the religion and ritual of a particular area or tradition or, more specifically, their festivals and pilgrimages. Such works are Herbert William Parke's *Festivals of the Athenians* (Ithaca, N.Y., 1977) and J. M. C. Toynbee's *Death and Burial in the Roman World* (Ithaca, N.Y., 1971).

In *Symbol and Conquest: Public Ritual and Drama in Santa Fe, New Mexico* (Ithaca, N.Y., 1976), pp. 62–74, I have written more fully on the distinctions among processions, pilgrimages, and parades.

Since processing and dancing are so often linked, Eugène Louis Backman's *Religious Dances in the Christian Church and in Popular Medicine,* translated by E. Classen (London, 1952), is still helpful, as is Lillian B. Lawler's *The Dance in Ancient Greece* (London, 1964).

RONALD L. GRIMES

PRODIGIA. In Roman religion *prodigia* (sg., *prodigium*) are portents, normally witnessed in Roman territory, with dangerous implications. They required the intervention of the state. Eclipses, rain of stones or of blood, earthquakes, mysterious voices, plagues, thunder, fires, birth of monsters, and phantoms were the most usual *prodigia.* A military defeat or the unchastity of a Vestal Virgin could in itself be considered a *prodigium.*

By initiative of the magistrates, normally of the consuls, the Roman Senate took cognizance of the *prodigia* and questioned witnesses. The pontiffs and other priests were consulted. If action seemed to be required, the Sibylline Books were examined for advice, and haruspices were summoned from Etruria to give their opinion on the meaning of the portents and on the remedies to the menace, if any. The Senate had the ultimate responsibility of deciding what one had to do to expiate and eliminate the *prodigia.* This operation, called *procuratio,* was basically a purification of the city and might involve processions, sacrifices, banquets to gods *(lectisternia),* special prayers *(supplicationes),* games, and even the introduction of new gods. Some *prodigia,* such as a rain of stones, had a standard *procuratio.*

The intervention of the Roman state in the matter of *prodigia* declined notably during the empire. The *prodigia* were officially registered in the annals of the pontiffs and consequently in the annals of the historians, as shown by Livy (see his characteristic remark of 43.13.1) and by Tacitus. Books listing *prodigia* circulated. One, the *Prodigiorum liber* by Julius Obsequens (probably fourth century CE), has survived. In the extant, not complete, form it collects *prodigia* (mainly derived from Livy) between 190 and 11 BCE. Vergil is atypical insofar as he registers propitious *prodigia* in the *Aeneid.*

BIBLIOGRAPHY

Aumüller, Ernst. "Das Prodigium bei Tacitus." Ph.D. diss., Johann Wolfgang Goethe-Universität Frankfurt, 1948.

Bloch, Raymond. *Les prodiges dans l'antiquité classique (Grèce, Étrurie et Rome).* Paris, 1963.

Fowler, W. Warde. *The Religious Experience of the Roman People from the Earliest Times to the Age of Augustus.* London, 1911.

Grassmann-Fischer, Brigitte. *Die Prodigien in Vergils Aeneis.* Munich, 1966.

Handel, P. "Prodigia." In *Real-Encyclopädie der classischen Altertumswissenschaft,* vol. 46, cols. 2283–2296. Stuttgart, 1959.

ARNALDO MOMIGLIANO

PRODIGIES. *See* Portents and Prodigies.

PROKOPOVICH, FEOFAN (1681–1736), Russian Orthodox archbishop. Prokopovich collaborated with Peter the Great to subordinate the administration of the Russian Orthodox church to the imperial government. The instrument of subordination was the Dukhovnyi Reglament (Ecclesiastical Regulation), Prokopovich's most famous writing, which Peter had proclaimed on 25 January 1721.

The Ecclesiastical Regulation achieved the subordination of the church's administration to the tsarist state until the tsardom collapsed in 1917. It abolished the patriarchate of Moscow, replacing it with an Ecclesiastical College modeled on the collegial system that had just been introduced into the civilian administration of the Russian empire. The Ecclesiastical College immediately and successfully sought to rename itself the

Most Holy Governing Synod. The change in name symbolized the beginning of a nearly two-hundred-year struggle by churchmen and supporters of the church to regain administrative autonomy for the church.

One of the more burdensome features of the Ecclesiastical Regulation was the subjugation of the clergy to police supervision. Priests were obliged to witness against their penitents or face severe legal sanctions. The regulation had the immediate effect of strengthening the Old Believer schism and the long-term effect of alienating the clergy from their flocks.

Prokopovich's career signified a secularizing and protestantizing development within the Russian church. Like Peter, Prokopovich believed that the concept of *symphonia*, which defined church and state as two autonomous but interrelated phenomena, served to weaken political authority, to encourage Old Believer intransigence, and to foster political disloyalty.

Raised by his uncle, Prokopovich studied in Jesuit colleges in the Polish Ukraine and in Rome, where, of necessity, he converted to (Uniate) Catholicism. In Kiev, he reconverted to Orthodoxy; he was appointed rector of the Kiev Theological Academy (1711), bishop of Pskov (1718), and archbishop of Novgorod (1720).

When the tsar died in 1725, Prokopovich came under attack from traditionalist churchmen determined to restore canonical equilibrium between church and state. Prokopovich counterattacked. He was a key supporter of the candidacy to the Russian throne of Anna Ivanovna of Kurland (r. 1730–1740), thereby becoming instrumental in bringing upon the Russian church the so-called German yoke.

Prokopovich's final years found him in the anomalous situation of defending the traditional hierarchical organization and the apostolic succession of the Orthodox church against further reforms of the Kurlander administration. A collection of Prokopovich's religious and political works titled *Words and Speeches* (Saint Petersburg, 1765) appeared posthumously.

BIBLIOGRAPHY

Cracraft, James. *The Church Reform of Peter the Great.* Stanford, Calif., 1971.

Curtiss, John S., ed. *Essays in Russian and Soviet History in Honor of Geroid Tanquary Robinson.* New York, 1963.

Muller, Alexander V., ed. *The Spiritual Regulation of Peter the Great.* Seattle, 1972.

Smolitsch, Igor. *Geschichte der russischen Kirche, 1700–1917.* Leiden, 1964.

Wittram, Reinhard. *Peter I, Czar und Kaiser: Zur Geschichte Peters des Grossen in seiner Zeit.* 2 vols. Göttingen, 1964.

JAMES W. CUNNINGHAM

PROMETHEUS was one of the Titans of the generation of gods prior to the Olympian Zeus. According to Hesiod, he became the major benefactor of the human race by introducing them to crafts, fire, and sacrifice. The ambiguous position that he occupied during the rule of the Olympians around Zeus is hinted at in his name of "forethinking one" and the fact he had a twin brother, Epimetheus, the "one who thinks too late." Together they seem to form one personality, as Kerényi (1956) has pointed out.

Prometheus is the major mediator between the world of the gods and that of mankind. His original encounter with the Olympian Zeus shows his ambivalence as benefactor and bringer of evil to the human race. He challenges Zeus to a duel of wits, as Zeus had similarly challenged Kronos, his father, and Kronos still earlier had challenged his own father, Ouranos. Prometheus divides an ox into two parts, one of which Zeus is to choose; one part hides the bones under an appetizing layer of fat, while the other part hides the meat under the unappetizing layer of the animal's stomach. Zeus, despite his all-encompassing foreknowledge (obtained by swallowing the goddess Metis, or Wisdom), fulfills Prometheus's expectation by choosing for himself the heap of bones. Furious over Prometheus's "trickery," Zeus deprives mankind of fire, which Prometheus must then steal to enable mankind to lead a civilized life and cook meat instead of eating it raw. For this second misdeed by Prometheus, the Olympians punish mankind with the gift of the first woman, Pandora (fashioned by Hephaistos and endowed with sexual desirability by Aphrodite), who, in spite of her inviting allure, brings mankind a box filled with all evils but also containing hope.

The structural opposition between surface appearance and true meaning or essence, between good that is hidden under evil, and evil that comes from well-intentioned deeds, is paradigmatically depicted in this myth of Prometheus who, like all the Titans, seems to straddle divine and human nature through his mediatory position: his thinking is called *ankulomeitas* ("crooked of counsel, wily"); he is the one who "snares himself in his own trickery." While trying to challenge Zeus for sovereignty through sacrificial partition, he establishes one of the main features of civilized life, namely those sacrifices that, while opening a channel of communication to the divine world, fix forever the separation of the human and the divine spheres: man has to eat cooked meat, whereas the gods sustain themselves on the mere vapors of burned bones and fat. While Prometheus wants to benefit mankind by introducing fire, an element indispensable for sacrifices and civilization, he also brings about mortality for mankind, for Pandora is the gods' poisoned countergift to men for a gift to the gods, sacrifice, that hid its true nature, bones, under an appealing exterior. Since receiving this countergift from the gods, mankind has had to labor in the fields for sustenance, plant seeds in the earth and in womankind, and tend the fire to perform such tasks as smithery, pottery, cooking, and sacrifices.

Prometheus thus becomes the archetype of the ambivalent and ambiguous trickster-god, who through the themes of theft and deception is structurally equivalent to such figures as Loki in Germanic mythology. In this respect Prometheus is also akin to figures like Athena, Hermes, and Hephaistos, deities of crafts and craftiness. He removes mankind from the state of innocence as well as from barbarism (the eating of raw meat) by introducing knowledge and crafts, but he brings mortality as well.

[*See also* Tricksters.]

BIBLIOGRAPHY

Dumézil, Georges. *Le festin d'immortalité.* Paris, 1924. One of the first works of Dumézil tracing Indo-European parallels, in particular the theme of theft and immortality, but still short on theoretically proven propositions about the complexity of each separate tradition.

Dumézil, Georges. *Loki.* Paris, 1948. An extension of the Indo-European parallelism with concentration on one divinity of the Germanic pantheon. Dumézil stresses the impulsive intelligence of the trickster figure through comparison with Syrdon of the Ossetes and thus indirectly with Prometheus.

Kerényi, Károly. "The Trickster in Relation to Greek Mythology." In *The Trickster,* by Paul Radin, with commentaries by Károly Kerényi and C. G. Jung, pp. 173–191. New York, 1956. Kerényi's most incisive treatment of Prometheus, supported by a comparison to tribal myths from North America. It stresses the tricksterlike qualities of the mediator and the crooked thinking of the Titans.

Koepping, Klaus-Peter. "Absurdity and Hidden Truth: Cunning Intelligence and Grotesque Body Images as Manifestations of the Trickster." *History of Religions* 24 (February 1985): 191–214. A recent treatment of Prometheus from a comparative perspective, emphasizing the theme of the trickster as deceived deceiver. Prometheus is shown to be one instance of the ambiguity and ambivalence of the mediator as culture hero, a theme that continues in the European literary tradition, as seen in the dialectic between the wisdom and folly of the picaro, or rogue.

Vernant, Jean-Pierre. *Myth and Society in Ancient Greece.* Atlantic Highlands, N.J., 1980. See the chapter titled "The Myth of Prometheus in Hesiod." An exemplary analysis of Hesiod's account through philological and semantic investigation, leading to a demonstration of the structural logic of the myth, with no hint of the trickster qualities.

KLAUS-PETER KOEPPING

PROOFS FOR THE EXISTENCE OF GOD.

Early generations of Christian thinkers accepted God's existence as a given that needed no proof and was surmised on the basis of immediate evidence in an act that did not clearly distinguish faith from reason. The dominant exponent of this approach was Augustine (d. 430), who posited, for instance, an awareness of God as "first truth" in the intuition of truth as such that occurs in the depths of human consciousness. Bonaventure (d. 1274) was a legitimate heir of Augustine in the medieval period, as was Blaise Pascal (d. 1662) in the modern era. Nicolas Malebranche (d. 1715), by contrast, promoted an ontologism, in which "God" is made the first innate idea implanted in the human mind, of which all other ideas are modifications.

The Ontological Argument. Those who have sought God's existence by deploying the processes of reasoning have done so in one of two ways: either *a priori* or *a posteriori.* The first approach derives God's existence from an idea of him in the consciousness of the knower. The original formulation of this argument is that of Anselm of Canterbury (d. 1109); it describes God as "that than which a greater cannot be conceived." Such a notion demands, for Anselm, God's real existence (*Proslogion* 2), and indeed entails it as something necessary (*Proslogion* 3). Various versions of this argument appear in the works of René Descartes (d. 1650), who argues that God cannot be conceived as nonexisting *(Third Meditation),* and Gottfried Wilhelm Leibniz (d. 1716), who, echoing John Duns Scotus (d. 1308), declares that if God is possible, he exists (*New Essays concerning Human Understanding* 4.10). Among the contemporary defenders of the ontological argument are Norman Malcolm, Alvin Plantinga, and Charles Hartshorne. Its two most trenchant critics are Thomas Aquinas (d. 1274), who views it as making an unfounded move from the ideal to the real order (*Summa theologiae* 1.2.1–2), taking Anselm's idea of God to include the concept of real existence but not the actual exercise thereof; and Immanuel Kant (d. 1804), who insists that existence is not a predicate included in any concept and so can only be encountered empirically ("Of the Impossibility of a Cosmological Proof of the Existence of God," *Critique of Pure Reason* A592/B620 ff.). Conceived religiously rather than logically, however, Anselm's idea of God apparently originates in a religious experience of transcendence at once objective and beyond the reach of unaided reason. It would seem gratuitous to deny that such experience can, in the lived and concrete order, convey the real existence of the transcendent, without, however, demonstrating that existence in a logically cogent way.

The Cosmological and Teleological Arguments. An alternative position repudiates any *a priori* approach on the ground that nothing antecedes or explains God's beingness. Finite entities of the world, however, are not the explanation of their own reality but rather are the effects of a transcendent creative cause. This explains *a posteriori* the mere existence at least of a primal cause, which Christians have identified materially with God. In the language of Thomas Aquinas, arguments of this kind are not designated "proofs," but five "approaches" or "ways" *(viae)* to God that function as "prerequisites to faith" *(praeambula fidei)* in the God of revelation. The starting points of all such arguments are facts readily observable in the world of ordinary experience: motion, causality, contingency of existence, grades of ontological perfection, and intrinsic finality. The nerve of the thought process is causality: efficient, exemplary, and final. An infinite regress in any series of such causes is deemed unintelligible as long as the ordering is an essential and not merely an accidental one. The rational intelligence is thus led to postulate the existence of God as primal or ultimate cause—not as the first member of the series but as the analogical cause of the series as such. The lineaments of such a procedure were not original with Christian thinkers but were already to be found in Plato, Aristotle, Ibn Sīnā (Avicenna), Ibn Rushd (Averroës), and Moses Maimonides. Significantly, Thomas himself never refers to these movements of thought as establishing God's existence, only as justifying the judgment that "God is"; all that is claimed, then, is the legitimacy of using the copula "is" of God in a transsubjective sense.

The Moral Argument. This conviction within Christian thought, of an intrinsic intelligibility at the heart of reality bespeaking a transcendent ground to the real order, reached its clearest expression in the thirteenth century but began to erode into skepticism with the rise of nominalist theology in the fourteenth century, especially with William of Ockham (d. 1349). Immanuel Kant, in the late eighteenth century, insisted in his *Critique of Pure Reason* that human understanding has no access whatsoever to any possible realm of meaning beyond the phenomenal, which is given immediately to consciousness and structured further by categories innate to the subjectivity of the knower. God is thus, for Kant, a regulative idea formed by the mind to legitimate the ethical order. Thus, ethics becomes the grounding principle for postulating God's existence, rather than vice versa, as had been the case in the past. Moral imperatives mean, simply, postulating one who imperates; any question of a real referent to that concept outside consciousness lies beyond the competency of human reason.

Judaism and Islam. Jewish thought eschews all efforts to prove God's existence, seeing this as established beyond dispute in the prophets, whose concern is God's moral governance. Philo Judaeus (d. circa 50 CE), however, under the stimulus of Greek and Arabic thought during the Hellenistic period, integrated rational reflection on the world with what the scriptures teach. Maimonides (d. 1204), in the medieval period, advanced two forms of the cosmological argument: one from motion and one from the contingency of existence. Among moderns, Moses Mendelssohn (d. 1786) stresses the role of reason in those areas in which revelation appears unnecessary, while Franz Rosenzweig (d. 1929) argues that the existential encounter dispenses with rational inquiry and itself constitutes revelation. This position accords with Martin Buber's (d. 1965) way to God as the eternal Thou in man's dialogue with every finite thou.

Islamic thought did not employ reason on things divine that were taught in the Qur'ān until medieval times, when Ibn Sīnā (d. 1037), distinguishing essence from existence, argued for God as the necessary existent. Ibn Rushd (d. 1198), integrating Islamic tradition with his understanding of Aristotle, maintained that the metaphysician can demonstrate the revealed truth about God available to believers in metaphorical language. Ibn Rushd's influence, in the form of Latin Averroism, extended to the University of Paris in the thirteenth century and to the universities of Bologna and Padua until the mid-seventeenth century.

Modern Atheism. G. W. F. Hegel (d. 1831) returned to the ontological argument; he maintained that finite consciousness was a "moment" in the self-enactment of Absolute Spirit, which thus assumed prerogatives formerly ascribed to divinity. Ludwig Feuerbach (d. 1872) explicitly launched atheism against Christian thought by inverting Hegel's thinking and reducing all references to the infinite to mere projections of finite spirit confronted with its own seemingly inexhaustible resources and aspirations. This tendency soon manifested itself as psychological atheism with Sigmund Freud (d. 1939), as socioeconomic atheism with Karl Marx (d. 1883), as ethical atheism with Jean-Paul Sartre (d. 1980) and Albert Camus (d. 1960), and as anthropological atheism with Maurice Merleau-Ponty (d. 1961), thereby pervading much of modern Western thought.

The Post-Atheistic Age. Reactions against this denial of any accessible signs of God's existence began with Friedrich Schleiermacher (d. 1834), who postulated, below the level of either reason or will, a feeling *(Gefühl)* or immediate awareness of the utter dependence of consciousness upon the sustaining reality of the transcendent whole, amounting to a God-consciousness within mankind. Roman Catholic thought, for its part, in the constitution *Dei filius* approved by the First Vatican Council in 1870, repudiated a "traditionalism" on the one hand and a "semirationalism" (in which, after a revelation from God, reason is able on its own to understand the pure mysteries of God that form the content of such revelation) on the other, opting instead for the possibility of a natural knowledge of at least God's existence. Paul Tillich (d. 1965) set a new tone in analyzing existential encounter, as opposed to metaphysical reflection; what he called disclosure experiences enable mankind to posit questions of ultimacy that are then answered in correlation to the revelatory act of a self-manifesting God. Wolfhart Pannenberg has recently argued, in reaction to Karl Barth's neoorthodoxy, which makes all acknowledgment of the true God a matter of religious faith, that history in its universality, open to human reason, offers hypothetical grounds for the reality of God. The available "proofs," then, are simply anthropological ways of formulating the question with precision and urgency—the question which man himself is. Since history has not yet run its course, all answers are provisional in kind, based upon anticipating the consummation of history in the resurrection of Christ.

Karl Rahner (d. 1984) and Bernard Lonergan (d. 1984) have attempted a rehabilitation of Thomas Aquinas's five "ways," viewing them as reflective and logical formulations of a prereflective, unthematic dynamism of finite spirit. This transcendental structure of human consciousness, which actualizes itself in the historical and categorical order, is described by Rahner as a pregrasp *(Vorgriff)* of God himself under the formality of holy mystery. In a radically different vein, Alfred North Whitehead (d. 1947), originating a movement loosely called process thought, views God as a coprinciple with the world in a universe ultimately not of being but of creative becoming. This argument for the existence of God arises from the need to explain novelty in a self-creative universe without making God an exception to, rather than the prime instantiation of, the metaphysical schema. Here God "lures" the world forward, even as it in turn supplies data for God's own creative advance into novelty (*Process and Reality*, 1929, 5.2).

Present Status of the Proofs. Much of modern thought, especially that indebted to analytic philosophy, tends to dismiss all talk about proofs for God's existence as meaningless, since no verifiable content can be given to the very idea of God. *De facto*, neither theism nor atheism is considered to be either demonstrable or refutable by reason. The affirmation of God is taken to be a matter of faith (religious or otherwise) rather than of reason—but one which, once made, may manifest itself as entirely reasonable.

[*See also* Attributes of God; Scholasticism; Nominalism; Enlightenment, The; Doubt and Belief; Atheism; *and biographies of theologians and philosophers mentioned herein. For further discussion of reflection on God in scripture and tradition, see* God. *For further discussion of the place of proofs in philosophical reflection on God, see* Philosophy, *article on* Philosophy of Religion.]

BIBLIOGRAPHY

Cobb, John B., Jr. *A Christian Natural Theology.* Philadelphia, 1965. Chapters 4 and 5 contain an exposition of the argument from Alfred North Whitehead by one committed to its validity.

Dupré, Louis. *A Dubious Heritage.* New York, 1977. Incisive studies of the ontological, cosmological, and teleological arguments in the light of post-Kantian thought.

Gardet, Louis, and M. M. Anawati. *Introduction à la théologie musulmane.* Paris, 1948. A basic survey from a Christian perspective.

Goichon, Amélie-Marie. *La philosophie d'Avicenne et son influence en Europe medièvale.* Paris, 1944.

Guttmann, Julius. *Philosophies of Judaism: The History of Jewish Philosophy from Biblical Times to Franz Rosenzweig.* New York, 1964.

Hick, John, ed. *The Existence of God.* New York, 1964. Critical appraisals including the moral and religious arguments in light of present discussions.

Kenny, Anthony. *The Five Ways.* New York, 1969. A rejection, scholarly and moderate in tone, of each of the "five ways" as based ultimately on an outmoded cosmology.

Küng, Hans. *Does God Exist?* Garden City, N.Y., 1980. Contemporary argument against atheism and nihilism based on experiencing the trustworthiness of human existence.

Mackie, J. L. *The Miracle of Theism: Arguments for and against the Existence of God.* Oxford, 1982. Largely rejections of the traditional and contemporary arguments, with emphasis on the negating power of evil in the world.

Maritain, Jacques. *Approaches to God.* New York, 1954. Detailed defense of the "five ways" of Thomas Aquinas, plus a prephilosophic approach and one based on the dynamism of the intellect.

Mascall, E. L. *The Openness of Being: Natural Theology Today.* London, 1971. A survey of arguments including those of transcendental Thomism, of process thought, and of empiricism; basically a defense of a metaphysical approach to the question of God against Anglo-Saxon positivism.

Plantinga, Alvin, ed. *The Ontological Argument, from St. Anselm to Contemporary Philosophers* (1940). New York, 1965. An expository and critical exploration of the argument in its varied forms; does not include Plantinga's own ingenious formulation of the argument he presents later in chapter 10 of *The Nature of Necessity* (Oxford, 1974).

Smith, John E. *Experience and God.* New York, 1968. Critical assessments of the ontological, cosmological, and teleological arguments from a pragmatist's point of view. See especially chapter 5.

WILLIAM J. HILL, O.P.

PROPHECY. [*This entry consists of two articles:* An Overview *and* Biblical Prophecy. *The first article treats the prophet as a type of religious specialist found in various religious traditions. It is followed by a study of prophecy in Judaism and Christianity. For discussion of prophethood in Islam, see* Nubūwah; *for discussion of Iranian prophetic traditions, see* Zoroastrianism *and* Manichaeism.]

An Overview

The term *prophecy* refers to a wide range of religious phenomena that have been manifested from ancient to modern times. The Greek term *prophētēs* is the etymological ancestor of the English word *prophet,* and it has cognates in most European languages. The indigenous Greek *prophētēs* was a cultic functionary who "spoke for" a god; that is, the *prophētēs* delivered divine messages in association with a sanctuary where the god had made its presence known. However, the word *prophētēs* influenced European languages primarily because early Jewish and Christian writers used the term in translations of the Hebrew Bible and in the New Testament to refer to religious specialists in Israelite, Jewish, and Christian traditions. Today comparativists use *prophecy* to describe religious phenomena in various contexts on analogy with the activity of ancient Hebrew prophets and other figures who had a similarly pivotal role in founding world religions in Southwest Asia.

Ancient Prophecy. In antiquity it was commonly believed that gods controlled events in the world and made their intentions known to human beings in various ways. The earliest written records tell of religious functionaries whose responsibility it was to interpret signs or deliver messages from the gods in order to supply information useful in the conduct of human affairs. In early tribal societies the clan leader often carried out these duties, or perhaps some other individual who used a variety of divinatory and visionary techniques to gain access to special knowledge about divine intentions. These activities usually included intercessory functions, whereby the leader or "prophet" petitioned spirits or a god or gods for special favors for their group.

However, our picture of such figures (like the *kāhin* of pre-Muslim Arabia or the *kohen* of patriarchal, presettlement Israel) is only inferential. They were active in nonliterate societies that left no linguistic records of themselves except by the transmission of oral traditions that eventually were written down by later, literate generations. The groups that did leave us written records had more complex forms of religious and political organization, suggesting that adepts in religious knowledge had correspondingly more specialized functions.

From the records of ancient cultures in Mesopotamia and the Mediterranean region we know of a large number of religious specialists who sought out and interpreted messages from the gods. Their access to the world of the gods came through two different means. In the first place, there were diviners who practiced a variety of studied techniques to interpret symbolic messages in the natural world. [*See* Divination.] Some techniques were manipulative (such as the casting of lots, the incubation of dreams, and the examination of the entrails of sacrificial animals); others were more purely observational (such as the interpretation of animal movement and the cataloguing of auspicious, often horrible, events). Second, the gods were also believed to communicate their will through oracles, that is, in human language through the mouth of an inspired person. [*See* Oracles.] The behavior of these divine spokesmen is often thought to have been ecstatic, frenzied, or abnormal in some way, which reflected their possession by the deity (and the absence of personal ego) at the time of transmission. Some groups used divination to test the accuracy of oral prophecies (e.g., prophecies at Mari), while others gave priority to oral prophecy, with only marginal appeal to divination (e.g., in Israelite religion).

Within general categories the nature and function of divine intermediation was diverse. Oracles and signs could appear without request; but more commonly, especially in the Greco-Roman world, cultic officials provided answers to specific questions asked to the sanctuary's god. Ecstatic oracular behavior seems to have been the most common form of intermediation among figures not connected with recognized sanctuaries (e.g., the Akkadian *muhhu*), but it was also acceptable among those who did have such official legitimacy (e.g., the Akkadian *apilu* and various Greek mantic figures). The terminology applied to intermediaries is often ambiguous or vague, as with the Greek term *prophētēs,* which at times denotes the oracular mouthpiece for divine speech and at others refers to the official interpreter of divinatory signs within a sanctuary. The diversity is immense. But it is clear from the complexity that the need for knowledge about divine activity was perceived at various social levels; ancient societies often maintained a large and varied staff of religious functionaries to keep such knowledge alive.

Prophetic Founders of Religious Tradition. Throughout ancient Israel's history as an independent state (c. 1000–586 BCE), the religious orientation of a large segment of its population was polytheistic, and as such, it shared in the general worldview of its neighbors. But even in the monotheistic elements of Israelite culture, there were different functionaries who transmitted the will of the same god, Yahveh, to the people. During the earliest part of this history, it appears that the Yahvists relied on at least three different figures for divine communication: (1) cultic officers who performed certain techniques (like casting lots), maintained cultic implements (like the Ark), and occupied sacred space; (2) seers (Heb., *ro'eh* and *ḥozeh*), whose function is rather unclear, but may be designations from different periods of visionaries and diviners (cf. *1 Samuel* 9:9); and (3) ecstatics (Heb., *navi'*, commonly translated as "prophet"), whose unusual behavior was stimulated when Yahveh's spirit came upon them. As Yahvism evolved, the *navi'* came to be its predominant intermediary, though as this occurred the activity of the *navi'* came to include functions that were previously within the province of the other two specialists. Accordingly, the *nevi'im* depended less exclusively on ecstatic oracles for their identity, and many came to be (in some cases) cultic functionaries and inspired interpreters of ancient tradition. The evidence indicates, however, that prophetic legitimacy depended primarily on their acceptance within a given group as oracular vehicles for the communication of Yahveh's word, regardless of whether the *navi'* was an ecstatic, a cultic official, an independent critic, or some combination of these roles.

By at least the eighth century BCE the Hebrew prophets or their scribes commonly wrote down their oracles, and the prophetic writings of the Hebrew Bible (Old Testament) contain, in part, a modest literary residue of this extensive oracular activity. Historians have reached no consensus about why this development took place, nor about how these writings in particular came to be accepted among later generations as eternally authoritative. Yet, that oracular revelation came to be regarded as having an enduring value, and that followers of prophets could disseminate their written oracles among various groups with whom the prophets originally had no connection, was a major change in the history of religions. Within the religious worldview that permeated the time of the first Hebrew prophets, messages from the gods were seen as portentous for only the particular audience, time, and place attendant to the moment when they had been revealed on earth. Thus, it was necessary to maintain a retinue of religious specialists to prophesy anew and interpret messages that regularly came from the gods. As certain specified written oracles came to be accepted in Israel as the repository of normative divine instruction, the nature of prophecy itself began to change, as did the character of religious tradition.

What happened among the Hebrew prophets occurred more generally within several religious traditions in Southwest Asia. The following figures can be classed with the Hebrew prophets as intermediaries whose oracles became, at least in part, the revelational basis of a major world religion. Zarathushtra (Zoroaster), a Persian prophet of the late second millennium BCE, was the founder of Zoroastrianism (Boyce, 1975). Jesus appears in many respects as a prophet, even though Christianity has traditionally portrayed him as a unique messiah. Mani, a Babylonian born in 216 CE, founded Manichaeism, which gained a large following in countries from India to the western Mediterranean. Finally, Muḥammad, like no other, established a believing community around himself as divine messenger, and succeeding generations of Muslims have accepted the oracles written down in the Qur'ān as the unparalleled expression of divine communication.

Defining precisely what these individual prophets share in common is not a simple matter. The social location of their activity differs in each case, and the success of each prophet in gaining a following during his lifetime varied widely, from Muḥammad, who led armies and established a moderate-sized empire by the time of his death, to Jesus, who died an ignominious death on a cross. Moreover the message of each prophet, if examined in detail, depends more on the particular traditions to which it was heir and the historical-cultural setting of the prophet's activity than upon a transcendent ideal that applies to every member of the group. Nonetheless, five features are common to all.

1. *They all conceived of their activity as the result of a personal divine commission.* They thought that their supreme deity had appointed them individually to bear a specific revealed message to the human (or some more narrowly defined) community, and this message usually consisted of oracular speech and writing. Even Jesus, who frequently did not use traditional forms of prophetic speech, seems to have regarded his words and actions as communicating the message he was commissioned to bear.

2. *Religious traditions arose that regarded some oracles of these prophets as uniquely heaven-sent, sacred, and binding upon people in perpetuity.* In such cases, the prophets' words became part (or the substance) of a scriptural canon that was regarded as the repository of revealed knowledge; each sacred canon became, in turn, the standard by which the tradition judged all later religious pronouncements and activity. For prophets whose speech or writing was formally oracular (e.g. the Hebrew prophets and Muḥammad), the scripture became, at least in part, a collection of those oracles. Stories about the symbolic activities and miraculous deeds performed by these prophets also found their way into the canons (note particularly the Gospels and the prophetic narratives in the Hebrew Bible), and the members of each tradition regarded this material as having paradigmatic importance.

Whether these prophets were themselves the founders of traditions is not a question to be answered easily. Both Muḥammad and Mani organized the early Muslim and Manichaean communities, respectively, and they promoted their own writings as perpetually relevant revelation. But in the other three cases (Zoroastrianism, Judaism, and Christianity), the historical prophets had little or no influence on the organization of the later religious tradition, and others determined the content and organization of the sacred scripture. In fact, the authors and compilers of the Hebrew Bible shaped the words and actions of Moses to such a degree that his biblical portrait probably has little in common with the historical person. Nonetheless, because these prophets all had an important role in founding religious tradition, and especially because later generations revered them as the fountainheads of divine revelation, we shall call this group the "founding prophets."

3. Though the content of their messages differs significantly from one prophet to the next, depending on historical circumstance and inherited tradition, *all of the founding prophets proclaimed what their later tradition regarded as universal truths.* The theological development of these prophetic, revealed religions tended toward conceptions of a deity or deities (Zoroastrianism and Manichaeism) that transcended tribal, geographical, national, and cultic boundaries. While it would be too ambitious to attribute to these prophetic figures alone the creation of universal religious claims, the writings of such prophets as Amos, so-called Second Isaiah, and Muḥammad are among the most radical innovations in the history of religious thought.

4. *The founding prophets were, in their own individual ways, social critics,* even though their ideas about society were quite different from one another. Muḥammad, for example, seems to have been a great deal more concerned with the structures of society on this earth than Mani, who addressed social issues primarily in order to help promote gnosis (the salvific knowledge of ultimate things). Still, all of them considered moral behavior to be central in complying with the wishes of their supreme deity. Particularly in the Judeo-Christian and Muslim traditions, prophetic teachings have been seen as attempts to denounce injustices practiced against the weak and powerless. In the prophetic writings of these traditions questions of social morality have such prominence that scholars have often characterized the religion of the prophets as "ethical monotheism."

5. Finally, *the founding prophets helped both to maintain and to reform religious tradition.* They regarded their demands for change as having a basis in ancient tradition, but they insisted that their contemporary religious situation be reshaped in accordance with that tradition. Naturally, these demands met stiff resistance from those contemporaries of the prophets who wanted to maintain other traditions or the status quo. As a result each of the founding prophets suffered indignities, sometimes even torture and death. Typically, prophets who met with resistance saw popular rejection as proof of their legitimacy, since earlier prophets had been similarly despised.

Just as these prophets constitute a group because of their mutual similarites, they are also distinct from other figures in the history of religions. They are different from the various intermediaries who preceded them in that the revelation they communicated has an enduring relevance in religious tradition and remained intimately connected with their individual personalities. Revelation had previously been relevant only for a limited time, and, with a few minor exceptions, the personality of the prophet had been of relatively little significance in the mediation of divine messages. The roles of these prophets often stood in sharp contrast with priestly functions. The innovative and reforming messages of the prophets were accepted within the religious community and tradition on the basis of their personal charisma. Priests, however, are typically those who maintained the dominant, received tradition by virtue of their position within an established religious institution.

Finally, the founding prophets are distinct from others who founded major religious traditions (such as Buddhism, Jainism, Confucianism, and Taoism). The founders of these traditions originating in India and China were not divinely chosen messengers bearing a revealed message to humankind, but rather teachers and sages who had developed new philosophic insight and practical discipline as a way of addressing religious problems. These teachers, like the prophets, were often missionaries and social critics, but the basis of their words was the perfection of their own intellectual, spiritual, and moral talents, rather than their election by a deity to bear a specific message.

Prophecy under the Influence of Canon. One of the most outstanding features of the founding prophets was the special importance that their personal communication of revelation had for succeeding generations of their religious communities. Just as the Hebrew prophets and Zarathushtra were influenced by the traditions that preceded them, so too were the prophets who came later. But for Jesus, Mani, and Muḥammad the traditional inheritance included the message of the Hebrew prophets (and Zarathushtra), as well as the model they had established as prophets whose messages were canonized within scripture. [*See* Canon.]

It was rarely easy for a person bearing revelation to effect basic reforms in the structure of religious life. Among the biblical prophets themselves, the active mediation of fresh revelation had been an accepted part of religious life. However, once prophecy became written and canonical, the revelation of these same prophets attained a special status that inevitably lessened the importance and limited the scope of active mediation generally. The guardianship and transmission of prophecy—now newly conceived as the substance of prophetic oracles within the canon—moved from the ecstatics and visionaries who originally created it to the inspired sages, priests, and scribes who maintained and passed along the scriptures.

The evolution of Hebrew prophecy into received written tradition became the cornerstone upon which all subsequent prophetic constructions were built. By 350 BCE the last of the canonical prophetic writings to find acceptance in the Hebrew Bible had been written. And by the time of Jesus' ministry (c. 25–30 CE) the preeminence of these canonical prophets was generally accepted within Judaism, even among prophets such as Jesus. Within the context of this religious tradition it became necessary for contemporary prophets who did not consider their calling subordinate to any earlier prophet to claim a special status for themselves. Therefore, Jesus on occasion appears as an eschatological prophet who proclaimed the imminent arrival of the "kingdom of God." In this way his message and character could fit the traditional conception of prophets in early Judaism, where it was believed—in certain quarters, at least—that God would send prophets (who would be of equal stature with their canonical predecessors) to announce the end of the world.

By the time of Mani (216–276) and Muḥammad (580–632), several canonical religions had come to prominence. Both these prophets understood themselves explicitly as successors to a line of prophets that included (though variously) Abraham, Moses, Elijah, other Hebrew prophets, Zarathushtra, Jesus, and even the Buddha. Moreover, they each wrote down their oracles as a self-conscious attempt to form a canon that would be authoritative for their own communities. Indeed, early Muslims distinguished between two terms for prophet: *nabī*, a generic Arabic term denoting anyone who has a vision or audition of God, and *rasūl*, the Arabic word referring only to those special "messengers" (such as Moses, Jesus, and Muḥammad) who founded a religious community and transmitted their messages with a sacred book. In Islam "religions of the Book" are the highest form of religious expression.

As the words of these historical prophets attained reverential status within scriptural canons, the book replaced the living religious specialist as the primary agent of revelational mediation. The history of surviving religious traditions with a prophetic scripture (now Judaism, Christianity, and Islam) has depended in no small measure upon this development. Exegetes of various sorts replaced prophets as the maintainers of the revelational tradition, and often those who safeguarded the sanctity and purity of the written scriptures were suspicious of, even hostile to, those who claimed to have visions not mediated through the scripture. Since textual interpretation has gained the dominant socio-political position within all three traditions (probably because this mode of religious inquiry responded better to the increasingly complex social organization within which the traditions flourished), the ecstatic elements common to the earliest prophetic activity played a diminished role in later tradition. Since Muḥammad there has been no prophet to form a religious tradition with a stature equaling that of Judaism, Christianity, or Islam.

Even so, while contemporary prophetic inspiration lost influence at the center of religious authority, it was never eliminated entirely. Throughout history, in pre-Christian Judaism, in early Christianity, and in pre-Muslim and early-Muslim Arabia, prophetic figures were active alongside (though often in competition with) the rationalized institutions of canonical religion. Within the exegetical tradition itself inspirational interpretation has been a perennial source of innovation in theological thinking. In early Judaism, some of those who collected and arranged sacred writings within the Hebrew Bible conceived themselves to be prophets, for example, the levitical priests Koraḥ and Asaph, who claimed prophetic inspiration for their hymnology and arranged the psalter in a structure that gives special prominence to a prophetic interpretation of psalms. And later, during the medieval period, qabbalist interpretation of the Bible elevated not only the revelational experiences of the biblical authors, but also the necessity for inspiration among exegetes. Similar attitudes are present among Christian (e.g., Jerome and Bonaventura) and Muslim (e.g., al-Hallāj) interpreters.

More generally we can speak of mysticism within Judaism, Christianity, and Islam as being analogous with prophecy in earlier tradition. Insofar as mystics define religious knowledge as the immediate (i.e., unmediated) perception of the divine, the nature of their experience and epistemology is similar to earlier prophets. However, their activity is to be distinguished sharply from earlier prophecy, since the canonical traditions had no recognized need for specialists in mediating divine revelation. Each tradition accommodated spontaneous outbreaks of inspirational, ecstatic, visionary behavior, but each also maintained strict controls, lest the ultimate authority of canonical revelation be undercut.

Sufism (Muslim mysticism) first appeared within one hundred years of Muḥammad's death. While some Ṣūfīs who quietly made claim to personal revelation or mystical vision could coexist peaceably with those nearer the center of religious power, others met violent repression when they threatened the structure and cohesion of the Muslim community. So, while Abū Yazīd, a Persian Ṣūfī (d. 875), encountered some opposition for his claims of achieving unity with God, it amounted to his being labeled an eccentric. He died peaceably, and afterwards his tomb became the object of some veneration. However, al-Hallāj was executed (in 922) when he translated his visions and miracles into a political following that threatened the dominant order.

Within European Christianity (from the time of Constantine, at least, until well into the modern period) the orthodox were closely connected with the ruling political groups. Christian mystics, like their Muslim counterparts, were accepted by the orthodox as long as their revelational claims were subordinated to the authority of the church and Bible (e.g., Francis of Assisi and Teresa of Ávila). Yet, wherever claims of fresh revelation threatened the ecclesiastical and political power structure, the authorities responded—and violently, as with Joan of Arc, whom the English burned for heresy when she transformed her revelational claims into a potent military force. It is easy to understand why few Christians claimed to be prophets, and why, at the same time, accusations of false prophecy were leveled at those whose voices one wanted to silence.

Since fairly early in the common era, Jews have been outside the dominant power structure in cultures where they lived. Only if the prophetic claims of a messianic hopeful threatened the dominant social order of the host society was there any likelihood of political repression. Such was the case with Shabbetai Tsevi (1626–1676), whose messianic movement was perceived as a threat by his Turkish (Muslim) overlords. Tsevi recanted under threat of death. Otherwise, tensions between the more rationalist orthodoxy and mystical visionaries was something to be settled among Jews. Since Jewish orthodoxy had no power greater than rational persuasion, its ability to control mystical elements was minimal. Hence the Besht (Yisra'el ben Eli'ezer, 1700–1760) was able to generate a massive following despite the detraction of his orthodox opponents.

In no case, however, could visionaries or mystics claim for themselves a mediational status equal with the founding prophets without subverting revealed canons and the traditions that rested upon them. Those who made such claims founded new traditions (i.e., Jesus, Mani, and Muḥammad) or failed in the attempt. Otherwise prophetic and mystical vision was subordinated to the revelation that had already been canonized. In all three traditions the canonical revelation, once defined, resisted internal challenges and remained the touchstone of religious truth for well over a thousand years.

Prophecy in Modern Times. During the modern period in Europe public recognition of biblical prophecy has dwindled along with certain other aspects of European religion that had supported its primacy. The importance of prophets as the mediators of revealed truth declined sharply as the Enlightenment demolished confidence in the truth of revelation generally and enshrined a new standard of knowledge arrived at on the basis of observation and critical reasoning. At first these changes affected only the intellectual elite who had considered the impact of philosophical developments upon conceptions of God, religious truth, and divine mediation. Some philosophers (such as Hume) denied altogether the importance of revelation (and, therefore, prophetic mediation) as a source of knowledge. Others tried to accommodate revelational truths within a philosophical framework (e.g., Descartes and Kierkegaard). But others, such as Blake and Nietzsche, considered themselves to be prophets, though in their writings it is clear that they had redefined concepts related to inspiration, revelation, and truth to suit the needs of people living in post-Enlightenment civilization.

The discussion of such ideas among philosophers, scientists, and literati was contained within a minuscule portion of European culture, and the effects of their writings upon the general population materialized only very slowly. Of greater significance for popular religious culture was the diminished authority of the church. In some cases the reduction in ecclesiastical power was a direct outgrowth of Enlightenment thinking, as in the United States, where religion was consciously and explicitly separated from the centers of political power. But for the most part it seems that reductions in the power of the church to enforce its dogmas allowed for greater religious diversity (as during the Reformation), so that Enlightenment thinkers, and others, could express their religious views openly. Within this religious environment a new set of prophets arose to proclaim themselves as messengers bearing the divine word, and some have found success in founding new sects that revere their writings as sacred canon. Joseph Smith (1805–1844), for example, established the Church of Latter-Day Saints upon the claim that he had received revelations from Jesus Christ and from an angel who entrusted him with the *Book of Mormon.* Those who profess Christian Science regard the writings of Mary Baker Eddy (1821–1910) as sacred and inviolable. Others, notably the members of the international Pentecostal or the later charismatic movements, are modern ecstatics who consider themselves capable of receiving the spirit and speaking as divine agents.

As Europe exported culture during its colonialist expansions, it came to affect and discover religious traditions elsewhere. Among Muslims, for example, critical thinking about the status of Muḥammad has had some impact under the influence of and on analogy with Western reflections about religious origins. However, more important for the study of prophecy has been the impact of imperialism and modern Western culture on the indigenous tribal societies of the Americas, Africa, and maritime colonies (see bibliography, especially the entries on the ghost dance among Native Americans and cargo cults in Melanesia). As colonists encroached on territory inhabited by tribal peoples, they often found among the native religious specialists figures who showed a marked similarity to the traditional image of prophets within the major Western canonical religions. Anthropologists and comparative religionists have studied such modern prophets and their religious environment, where truths revealed through the mouths of inspired speakers remain a dominant influence in all aspects of social and personal life. Through direct observation of such religious systems we now understand the dynamics of prophecy with some specificity, and detailed research has dispelled various myths about its nature. We know, for example, that ecstatic behavior among religious specialists can help maintain the structure of society, whereas scholars had long thought that ecstasy destabilized social order through its irrational influence. Likewise, the widespread opinion that ancient prophets were individualists crying to deaf ears from the loneliness of the desert now seems to be a romantic ideal. Rather, groups tend to support prophets who express their interests, while prophets acting entirely on their own rarely find a significant audience.

Conclusion. Though comparative theorists working with modern evidence have not yet established a single dominant interpretation of prophecy, a variety of complementary approaches now challenges the exclusivistic confessional interpretations that characterized the earlier period. Some scholars (e.g., I. M. Lewis—see bibliography) consider ecstatic religious behavior a means of expression used by disenfranchised groups who find standard channels of communication closed to them. Those studying religious behavior among shamans, Pentecostals, and other modern prophetic figures have found "deprivation theory" useful in showing how ecstatic persons support the position and structure of groups whose position in society is outside the normal channels of power and influence. Others (e.g., Victor Turner—see bibliography) interpret prophecy within a framework of social evolution. These scholars see prophets as appearing in periods of transition between societies organized along lines of kinship and clan affiliation and those structured according to more highly complex groupings that accompany the rise of states, class stratification and institutional religion. Either interpretive model applies consistent evaluative criteria to both the ancient evidence and the modern anthropological data without elevating the status of any one religious tradition over another. In this they are distinctively modern interpretations of prophecy, in contrast with canonical views, which persist in granting special recognition to the prophet(s) of a single confessional tradition.

BIBLIOGRAPHY

For the background of mediation between gods and human beings within world religions, Mircea Eliade's *Shamanism: Archaic Techniques of Ecstasy*, rev. & enl. ed. (New York, 1964), remains unsurpassed for its breadth. Works about the founding prophets normally contain a general discussion and bibliography concerning their specific precursors. Such are Robert R. Wilson's *Prophecy and Society in Ancient Israel* (Philadelphia, 1980); David L. Petersen's *The Roles of Israel's Prophets* (*Journal for the Study of the Old Testament*, supp. 17; Sheffield, 1981), which surveys the evidence for Israelite intermediation in the ancient Near East, and David E. Aune's *Prophecy in Early Christianity and the Ancient Mediterranean World* (Grand Rapids, Mich., 1983), which gives a thorough discussion of Greco-Roman prophecy as well as its forms among the first Christians. Many critical works on Hebrew prophecy approach the subject from within the confessional community of Jews (e.g., Martin Buber's *The Prophetic Faith*, New York, 1949, and Abraham Joshua Heschel's *The Prophets*, New York, 1962) or Christians (e.g., Gerhard von Rad's *The Message of the Prophets*, London, 1968). Most treatments of prophecy ignore the significance of Zarathushtra and Mani, since they both have few, if any, modern followers to proclaim their value. Mary Boyce's *A History of Zoroastrianism*, 2 vols. (Leiden, 1975–1982), and Kurt Rudolph's *Gnosis* (San Francisco, 1983) provide useful bibliographies and discussions of the life and time of these prophets, respectively. The books on Muḥammad are many; the most readable and intelligent is Maxime Rodinson's *Mohammed* (New York, 1971), which contains a critical evaluation of the works that preceded it. Toufic Fahd's "Kāhin," in *The Encyclopaedia of Islam*, new ed., vol. 4 (Leiden, 1978), pp. 420–422, is a short, peculiarly lucid account of the difficulties inherent in reconstructing Arab divination during the pre-Islamic period.

Regrettably, no book discusses prophecy within a framework as broad as that suggested in this article. Hence, we suggest that the reader consult other articles within this encyclopedia for detailed bibliographies on such topics as mysticism, ecstasy, canon, scripture, and the Enlightenment, as well as on individuals that we have mentioned in the text.

Among works that may not be listed in other articles is the anthropological literature on prophecy. Max Weber's work has had a seminal influence on the field; see both *Ancient Judaism* (1922; Glencoe, Ill., 1952) and *The Sociology of Religion* (1922; Boston, 1963). I. M. Lewis's *Ecstatic Religion* (Harmondsworth, 1971) is a sociology of ecstatic behavior based on a broad range of comparative evidence, and though it does not address prophecy per se, it has influenced others (viz. Wilson, cited above) that do. Victor Turner's "Religious Specialists: Anthropological Study," in the *International Encyclopedia of the Social Sciences*, edited by David L. Sills (New York, 1968), vol. 13, pp. 437–444, offers analytical categories useful in distinguishing prophets from other religious personnel. A number of books describe the activity of prophets in modern cultures: Peter Worsley's *The Trumpet Shall Sound: A Study of "Cargo" Cults in Melanesia* (1957; New York, 1968); E. E. Evans-Pritchard's *Nuer Religion* (Oxford, 1956) and *The Sanusi of Cyrenaica* (Oxford, 1949); James Mooney's *The Ghost-Dance Religion and the Sioux Outbreak of 1890* (1896; abr. ed., Chicago, 1965); and Vittorio Lanternari's *The Religions of the Oppressed: A Study of Modern Messianic Cults* (New York, 1963).

Finally, Kenneth Cragg's *Muhammad and the Christian: A Question of Response* (New York, 1984) is a valuable beginning for the dialogue between Muslim and Christian conceptions of prophetic revelation.

Gerald T. Sheppard and
William E. Herbrechtsmeier

Biblical Prophecy

Throughout much of the history of Western thought, the biblical prophets have been understood as unique figures whose sudden appearance in ancient Israel had a profound impact on the development of Judaism and Christianity. They have been considered ethical and moral innovators whose views decisively shaped later Jewish and Christian theology. Particularly in Christian tradition, they have been seen as revealers of the future whose oracles predicted the coming of Jesus and whose words may still contain unrecognized clues to the course of world history.

This understanding of the biblical prophets continues to exist today. However, during the past century the traditional view has come under increasing attack from biblical scholars, who have reexamined the biblical evidence and then proposed a number of alternative and often conflicting theories about the nature and functions of Israelite prophecy. Rejecting the common notion that prophecy is concerned only with the future, scholars have portrayed the prophets variously as creators of a highly intellectual form of ethical monotheism, as ecstatics scarcely in control of their own actions, as religious officials with regular duties in the Israelite cult, as shrewd political advisers, as isolated mystics, and as guardians of Israel's religious traditions. The Hebrew Bible contains evidence to support all of these interpretations, and for this reason the scholarly debate on the nature of prophecy continues with no sign of an emerging consensus.

However, scholars have increasingly recognized that an adequate understanding of Israelite prophecy can be achieved only by using extrabiblical evidence to supplement the narratives about prophetic activity and the words of the prophets that have been preserved in the Bible. The most important extrabiblical evidence comes from two different sources. The first source provides additional documentary evidence on the nature of prophecy in antiquity. During the past century archaeologists have uncovered a number of ancient Near Eastern texts that challenge the traditional notion that the Israelite prophets were unique religious figures in antiquity. In the Mesopotamian city of Mari on the Euphrates, excavators have found letters from the eighteenth century BCE describing the activities and messages of several different types of oracle givers who bear some resemblance to the later Israelite prophets. The Mari oracles come from various gods and do not seem to have been solicited by the person to whom they are addressed. Some of the oracle givers described in the letters are ordinary individuals, but others have special titles, which indicates that these figures exhibited characteristic behavior and filled a recognized religious role in the society of Mari. Among the specialists mentioned are the "answerer" *(apilu)*, the "ecstatic" *(muhhu)*, the "speaker" *(qabbatum)*, and a member of the cultic personnel of the goddess Ishtar, the meaning of whose title *(assinnu)* is uncertain. Later texts from the time of the Assyrian kings Esarhaddon (r. 680–669 BCE) and Ashurbanipal (r. 668–627 BCE) record the oracles of Assyrian contemporaries of some of the Israelite prophets. In addition to the ecstatic, the texts mention the "shouter" *(raggimu)*, the "revealer" *(shabru)*, and the "votary" *(shelutu)*.

Religious specialists resembling the biblical prophets also existed outside of Israelite territory in other areas of Palestine. Inscriptions from the eighth and ninth centuries BCE refer to a "message giver" *(ʿdd)* and a "visionary" *(ḥzh)*, a title also given to some of the biblical prophets. This evidence suggests that prophetic activity was going on elsewhere in the ancient Near East before and during the time when prophets were active in Israel. Furthermore, the apparent diversity of these non-

Israelite specialists suggests that prophecy in Israel may have been a more complex phenomenon than scholars have previously thought.

This suggestion is reinforced by extrabiblical evidence from the second source, the studies that sociologists and anthropologists have made of contemporary oracle givers. These specialists form a highly diverse group that includes various types of mediums, diviners, priests, and shamans, but like the biblical prophets they all see themselves as intermediaries between the human and divine worlds. In spite of obvious differences, these figures often exhibit similar behavioral characteristics and interact with their societies in much the same way. This interaction has been analyzed extensively by anthropologists and shown to be highly complex. By delivering messages from the divine realm, oracle givers are capable of bringing about changes in their societies, but at the same time societies play a direct role in accrediting oracle givers and shaping their behavior.

The modern anthropological evidence indicates that the phenomenon of prophecy can be adequately understood only when the dynamic relationship between prophet and society is fully explored. This means that any account of prophecy in ancient Israel (c. 1200–200 BCE) must see the prophets in particular social contexts rather than treating them as ideal figures abstracted from their historical settings. For this reason it is necessary to avoid making too many statements about biblical prophecy in general. Each prophet occupied a unique place in the history of Israel and was part of a complex interaction between prophecy and society in a particular time and place. The history of Israelite prophecy is the history of a series of such interactions. However, once the uniqueness of each prophet is recognized, it is possible to outline some general features that characterized Israelite prophecy as a whole and to isolate some characteristics that were peculiar to particular groups of prophets.

The Prophetic Experience. Direct information about Israelite prophecy comes from two sources: the oracles of the prophets themselves, now preserved primarily in the fifteen prophetic books of the Hebrew Bible, and the narratives describing prophetic activity, found mainly in the books of the Deuteronomic history (*Joshua, Judges, 1* and *2 Samuel, 1* and *2 Kings*). Both of these sources are difficult to interpret because of their unusual character. At least until the exile (587/6 BCE), the prophets seem to have composed and delivered their oracles orally. Only later were their words collected, written down, and finally arranged in small collections, or books. This work was done either by the prophets themselves or by their disciples. Some of the written collections were then further edited by later generations of writers and editors, who were interested in preserving and above all interpreting the prophets' original pronouncements. As a result of this long process of transmission and composition, it is often difficult to separate genuine prophetic material from the interpretive work of later editors. A similar sort of problem exists in the case of the prophetic narratives of the Deuteronomic history. Some of the stories, such as those concerning Elijah and Elisha (*1 Kgs.* 17–*2 Kgs.* 9), probably circulated individually or as collections in oral tradition before being incorporated in the written work of the historian. As part of the incorporation process, the stories were edited at least once, and perhaps several times, in order to express the political, social, and religious views of the writers. For this reason, it is sometimes difficult to use the narratives for historiographic purposes.

Because of the nature of the sources from which a description of prophecy must be derived, any attempt to reconstruct a picture of prophetic activity must necessarily involve a great deal of interpretation, and the results will often be incomplete and tentative. This is particularly true of attempts to describe the prophets' supernatural experiences, which by their very nature were private and not open to public scrutiny. The prophets say very little about their experiences and even in recounting their "calls" to prophesy rarely describe more than the initial vision that they saw (*Is.* 6, *Ez.* 1–3) or the words that they heard (*Jer.* 1:4–10; *Am.* 7:15). Instead, the texts concentrate on the messages that the prophets received during their encounters with God.

However, enough clues exist to suggest that Israel conceived of the prophetic experience as one that occurred when individuals were possessed by the spirit of God. "The hand of the Lord" fell upon them (*1 Kgs.* 18:46; *2 Kgs.* 3:15; *Jer.* 15:17; *Ez.* 1:3), or the spirit of God "rested on them" (*Nm.* 11:25–26) or "clothed itself" with them (*Jgs.* 6:34) so that they were no longer in control of their own speech and actions. As is typical in cases of spirit possession in a number of cultures, Israel interpreted the words that the prophets spoke during possession not as human words but as the words of God. The prophets were simply the channels through which the divine word came to the world. Once the prophets were possessed by God, they felt compelled to deliver the message that God wanted to communicate (*Am.* 3:8). The divine word was perceived as a "burning fire" that gnawed at them until it was delivered (*Jer.* 20:9).

Because of the loss of personal autonomy associated with divine possession, the prophets did not usually view the experience positively. In the accounts of their initial call, they sometimes speak of trying to avoid becoming prophets (*Jer.* 1:6), and some of them report that they repeatedly sought release from their prophetic roles (*Jer.* 11:18–12:6, 15:15–21; cf. *Ez.* 2:1–3:15). However, such attempts at resistance were always futile, and in the end the compulsion to prophesy could not be thwarted.

Although the prophets themselves were apparently reluctant to describe the process through which they received their oracles, additional information on the nature of the prophetic experience can be deduced from the various titles given to these individuals and from the descriptions of their characteristic behavior. This evidence suggests that the prophetic experience was not the same for all prophets and that the prophets' characteristic behavior and social functions varied enough to require more than one title or role label.

Prophetic titles. The English word *prophet* is ultimately derived from the Greek *prophētēs,* a noun that means both "one who speaks forth" or "one who proclaims" and "one who speaks before" or "one who speaks of the future." The Greek translators of the Hebrew Bible used this word to render several Hebrew titles and apparently understood it to be a general term capable of being applied to various types of religious specialists. However, in ancient Israel the different types of prophetic figures bore distinctive titles, although the understanding and usage of these titles varied with the group that used them and the time in which they were used.

The most common prophetic title used in the Hebrew Bible is *navi'*. Extrabiblical occurrences of the word are extremely rare, and its etymology is uncertain, although scholars normally relate it to the Akkadian verb *nabu,* "to call, to announce, to name." The title may thus mean either "one who calls" or "one who is called," but this etymology sheds little light on the precise characteristics of the figure so designated. In preexilic times the label *navi'* was particularly common in northern Israel (Ephraim), where it was a general term for any prophetic figure and was the only title given to legitimate prophets. In Israelite literature produced in the north or influenced by traditions originating there (the Deuteronomic history, *Hosea, Jeremiah*), the *navi'* played a central role in religious life and was associated with the preservation of ancient theological traditions. To the south, in Judah and particularly in Jerusalem, the title was also in use as a general role label, but it appears much less frequently in Judahite literature and is often used in negative contexts. After the exile *navi'* was used by all biblical writers as a general prophetic title and seems to have no longer been recognized as a distinctive role label.

While *navi'* was the most common prophetic title in the north, in Judah and particularly in Jerusalem the term "visionary" *(ḥozeh)* was the preferred designation. This role label appears primarily in texts originating in the south *(Amos, Micah, Isaiah, 1* and *2 Chronicles),* and when it does not, it refers to figures located there. Judahite historical traditions suggest that visionaries were particularly active during the period of the early monarchy (during the reigns of David, Solomon, and Rehoboam), when some of them were part of the royal court in Jerusalem, but references to them in the writing prophets indicate that they persisted at least until the exile (1 *Chr.* 21:9, 25:5, 29:29; *2 Chr.* 9:29, 12:15, 19:2, 29:25, 30; cf. *2 Sm.* 24:11). The title "visionary" clearly refers to the distinctive means by which these figures received their revelations, and indeed three of the Judahite prophetic books explicitly speak of the visionary origin of their oracles (*Am.* 1:1; *Mi.* 1:1; *Is.* 1:1), while a fourth *(Ez.)* contains numerous descriptions of revelatory visions. This particular mode of divine-human communication was apparently not well regarded in the north, where prophets preferred to speak of their oracles as the words that they heard rather than the visions that they saw (*Hos.* 1:1, *Jer.* 1:1–4). In some circles outside of Judah, visions may have been considered an inferior form of revelation (*Nm.* 12:6–9; cf. *Dt.* 13:1–6), a fact that may help to explain the northern priest Amaziah's derisive characterization of the Judahite prophet Amos as a professional visionary (*Am.* 7:12–15).

In addition to the *navi'* and the *ḥozeh,* the biblical writers mention three other prophetic titles, which were apparently not widely used. In *1 Samuel* 9:9 Samuel is called a "seer" (*ro'eh;* lit., "one who sees"), a title that the writer tells us was already archaic. If the old story in this chapter is historically accurate, then the seer was a specialist in communicating with the divine world, presumably through visions, dreams, or divination. People who wanted to request information from a deity could go to the seer, who in exchange for a fee would transmit the petitioner's request and return an answer. In the north this particular function was later asigned to the *navi',* while elsewhere various diviners and priests were the agents of intercession (*1 Sm.* 9:9, *Dt.* 18:9–22). Late references to the seer may be archaisms (*2 Ch.* 16:7, 16:10), and it is probable that the title ceased to be used in the early monarchical period.

Better attested is the title "man of God" *(ish ha-Elohim,)* which appears in northern sources, particularly in the old prophetic legends of the Elijah-Elisha cycle in the Deuteronomic history (*1 Kgs.* 17–2 *Kgs.* 10). This label may have originally been applied to people who were thought able to control divine power and use it in various miraculous ways, but its usage was eventually broadened to include anyone who had a special relationship to God. When the designation "man of God" became an honorific title, any specifically prophetic connotations that it may have had were presumably muted or lost.

In addition to titles normally applied to a single individual, the biblical writers also apply the label "sons of the prophets" *(benei ha-nevi'im)* to members of prophetic groups. The title is attested only in the Elijah-Elisha stories and seems to have been used for a relatively brief period in northern Israel (c. 869–842 BCE). The sons of the prophets were clearly members of a prophetic guild that had a hierarchical structure headed by a leader with the title "father." On the death of the leader, the title was transferred to another prophet (*2 Kgs.* 2:12, 6:21, 13:14). Members of the group sometimes lived together and shared common meals (*2 Kgs.* 4:1, 4:38–41, 6:1). It has been suggested that the sons of the prophets were ecstatics, but there is no evidence of such behavior in the narratives about them.

Prophetic behavior. In ancient Israel, as in every society, the behavior of divinely possessed individuals followed certain stereotypical patterns, although these patterns varied somewhat depending on the historical, geographical, and social setting of the prophets' activities. There are two reasons for the existence of this behavior. First, Israelite society set definite limits on the kinds of behavior that its prophets could exhibit. In most social situations violent or uncontrolled actions were not tolerated, and when they occurred, they were considered a sign of mental illness or possession by evil powers. Prophets who wished to be considered genuine therefore had to keep their behavior within recognized boundaries or risk being considered insane. Second, members of social groups in which prophets operated had to face the problem of determining when divine possession was actually present. They needed to have some grounds for assigning a prophetic title to a particular individual. One of the ways in which they solved this problem was to examine the behavior of people in the past who were known to have been genuine prophets of God. Individuals who wished to be accredited as prophets were thus subtly pressed to conform to the group's picture of genuine prophetic behavior.

Prophetic actions. Biblical writers rarely describe behavior indicative of possession, but the existence of stereotypical prophetic actions can be inferred from the Bible's occasional use of the verb *hitnabbe'*, which seems to mean "to act like a prophet, to exhibit the behavior characteristic of a *navi'*." This verb refers to both prophetic words and deeds, but the texts give it no specific definition. It is clear, however, that the prophet's characteristic behavior was evaluated positively by some groups but negatively by others. In some cases it was seen a a sign of divine legitimation and favor (*Nm.* 11:11–29, *1 Sm.* 10:1–13), while on other occasions it was considered an indication of madness or possession by an evil spirit (*1 Sm.* 18:10–11, 19:18–24; *1 Kgs.* 18:26–29; *Jer.* 29:24–28).

It is likely that some of Israel's prophets were ecstatics. The word *ecstasy* is usually understood to refer to a type of trance behavior marked by psychological and physiological symptoms such as a reduction of sensitivity to outside stimuli, hallucinations or visions, a garbled perception of surrounding events, and an apparent loss of conscious control over speech and actions. The intensity of ecstasy and its specific characteristics vary depending on the individual being possessed and the group in which possession occurs. The actions of an ecstatic prophet may range from apparently uncontrolled physical activity to completely normal physical activity, and his speech may range from unintelligible nonsense syllables to perfectly coherent discourse. Sometimes ecstatic behavior in Israel was incapacitating or dangerous (*1 Sm.* 19:18–24, *1 Kgs.* 18:26–29), but at least in the case of those prophets who wrote, ecstasy appears to have involved controlled actions and intelligible speech (*Jer.* 4:19, 23:9; *Ez.* 1:1–3:15, 8:1–11:25). [*See* Ecstasy.]

As part of their characteristic behavior, some of Israel's prophets accompanied their oracles with symbolic acts, although this practice was by no means common even among the prophets who employed it. In most cases these acts seem to have been designed to provide the background for an oracle or to dramatize the prophet's words. Thus Hosea and Isaiah gave their children symbolic names that foretold the fate of the nation (*Hos.* 1:4–9; *Is.* 7:3, 8:1–4). Isaiah reportedly walked naked through the streets of Jerusalem for three years to drive home the point that the Assyrians would lead the Egyptians into captivity (*Is.* 20). Jeremiah smashed a pot before his listeners to dramatize the destruction what would soon occur in Jerusalem, and he later wore a wooden yoke before the king to reinforce an oracle counseling surrender to the Babylonians (*Jer.* 19:1–15, 27:1–28:17). A few of these acts seem to move beyond symbolism into the realm of magic. When Elisha commanded the Israelite king Joash to strike the ground with his arrows, the number of times that the king struck the ground determined the number of victories that Israel would have over Syria (*2 Kgs.* 13:14–19). Similarly, Ezekiel's elaborate drawing of the besieged Jerusalem actually seems to bring the siege into existence (*Ez.* 4:1–8). However, in spite of these examples of sympathetic magic, the working of miracles was not normally a component of prophetic behavior in Israel.

In addition to performing certain characteristic actions, some of Israel's prophets wore distinctive clothing and bore a special mark that identified them as prophets or as members of a prophetic guild (*1 Kgs.* 20:35–41, *2 Kgs.* 1:8, *Zec.* 13:4). However, this practice does not seem to have been widespread.

Prophetic speech. As part of their characteristic behavior, some prophets may have used stereotypical speech patterns and shaped their oracles in certain traditional ways. The existence of a distinctive northern oracle pattern is suggested by the fact that the Deuteronomic history and the prophetic literature dependent on it *(Jeremiah)* often quote prophetic oracles that have a tripartite structure. The oracle begins with the commissioning of the prophetic messenger and then moves to an accusation against an individual who has violated Israel's covenantal law. Following the accusation, an announcement of judgment is addressed directly to the accused. The announcement is usually introduced by a stereotypical "messenger formula," such as the following: "Thus says the Lord"; "Therefore, thus says the Lord"; or "For thus says the Lord" (*1 Sm.* 2:27–36, 13:11–14, 15:10–31; *2 Sam.* 12; *1 Kgs.* 11:29–40, 13:1–3, 14:7–14, 17:1, 20:35–43, 21:17–22, 22:13–23; *2 Kgs.* 1:3–4, 1:6, 20:14–19, 21:10–15; *Jer.* 20:1–6, 22:10–12, 22:13–19, 22:24–27, 28:12–16, 29:24–32, 36:29–30, 37:17). If this pattern is not simply a literary convention of the Deuteronomic authors, then what is often called the "announcement of disaster to individuals" may have been a characteristic feature of the speech of Ephraimite prophets. Other Israelite prophets also announced disaster to individuals and to the nation as a whole, but their oracles did not conform to rigid patterns.

Judahite prophets may have once used stereotypical forms of speech, but if so, the patterns had broken down by the time the oracles were recorded in writing. Early Judahite writing prophets such as Amos, Micah, and Isaiah seem to have favored distinctive judgment oracles beginning with the cry "alas" (Heb., *hoy*) and followed by one or more participles describing the addressee and specifying his crime. This introduction was followed by an announcement of disaster in various forms (*Am.* 5:18–20, 6:1–7; *Is.* 5:8–10, 5:11–14, 5:18–19, 5:20, 5:21, 5:22–24, 10:1–3, 28:1–4, 29:1–4, 29:15, 30:1–3, 31:1–4; *Mi.* 2:1–4). However, even if the "alas oracles" were once characteristic of southern prophetic speech, they were later used by prophets outside of that tradition.

The Hebrew word *massa'*, traditionally translated "burden," may have once designated a specialized type of Judahite oracle against foreign nations (*Is.* 13:1, 14:28, 15:1, 17:1, 19:1, 21:1, 21:11, 21:13, 22:1, 23:1, 30:6; *Na.* 1:1; *Hb.* 1:1; *Zec.* 9:1, 12:1; *Mal.* 1:1). However, if so, the original characteristic form of the oracle has not been preserved, and its distinctive function has been lost.

In addition to using speech patterns that seem to be primarily prophetic, Israel's prophets employed specialized language drawn from various spheres of Israelite life. For example, from the courts they took legal language and formed trial speeches that mirrored judicial proceedings (*Is.* 1; *Mi.* 6; *Jer.* 2; *Is.* 41:1–5, 41:21–29, 42:18–25, 43:8–15, 43:22–28, 44:6–8, 50:1–3). From the Temple they took priestly instruction and liturgical fragments and incorporated them into prophetic oracles. However, scholars have not usually succeeded in uncovering widespread structural patterns in oracles of this sort, and it is probably best not to understand them as characteristic of the behavior of prophetic possession in general.

Prophecy and Society. In the past there has been a tendency to portray the Israelite prophets as isolated individuals who appeared suddenly before a particular group, delivered an uncompromising divine message, and then disappeared as quickly as they had come. It was assumed that this individualism set them at odds with their society and inevitably brought them into conflict with rival religious professionals, particularly the priests. However, more recently scholars have recognized that the prophets were integrally related to the societies in which they lived. These individuals played many social roles, not all of which were related to their prophetic activities. Because in ancient Israel there were apparently no restrictions on the type of person who could be possessed by God's spirit, and because possession was not a constant experience for any given person, many of the prophets participated fully in other areas of communal life. Thus, for example, Jeremiah and Ezekiel were both priests who were possessed and transformed into prophets (*Jer.* 1:1, *Ez.* 1:3). Some priests may have delivered prophetic oracles as part of their regular cultic activities, while in the postexilic period Levitical singers in the Temple also had prophetic functions (*1 Chr.* 25:1–8; *2 Chr.* 20:1–23, 34:30). Some prophets, like Gad, seem to have earned their living through prophecy and were members of the royal court (*1 Sm.* 22:1–5, *2 Sm.* 24:1–25), while others, like Amos, engaged in other occupations and prophesied only occasionally (*Am.* 1:1, 7:14–15).

Prophetic authority. Discussions of prophetic authority normally focus on the prophetic-call narratives (*Is.* 6, *Jer.* 1, *Ez.* 1–3) and on the "charisma" that these extraordinary individuals are thought to have possessed. It is assumed that because the prophets were endowed with supernatural power, they were automatically accorded authority and viewed as divinely chosen leaders.

To be sure, the prophets did sometimes cite their initial experiences of possession in order to gain support for their message, and they may be accurately described as charismatics, although they were certainly not the only ones in Israelite society. However, these two factors must not be stressed at the expense of recognizing the role that Israelite society played in creating and sustaining prophets.

The process by which ancient Israel recognized and accepted the authority of genuine prophets was subtle and complex, but at least some of its elements can be identified. One element concerned a prophet's conformity to certain standards of behavior. At least those Israelites who created and carried the biblical traditions recognized as authoritative only those prophets who stood in a recognizably Israelite prophetic tradition. This meant above all that the only legitimate prophets were those who were possessed by Yahveh, the God of Israel. Prophets possessed by other deities were not to be taken seriously, and the Deuteronomic writers went so far as to decree the death penalty for prophets who spoke in the name of other gods (*Dt.* 18:20). However, outside of these circles, possession by other gods was accepted, and for a brief time prophets of Baal and Asherah were part of the religious establishment in the northern kingdom of Israel (Ephraim) (*1 Kgs.* 18:19–40).

Prophets who wished to be considered legitimate also were pressed to make their behavior conform to what various Israelite groups recognized as traditional prophetic behavior. Canons of acceptable behavior varied from group to group within Israel, and for this reason prophets who were considered legitimate by one group might not be considered legitimate by other groups. Thus, for example, shortly before the fall of Jerusalem to the Babylonians, Jeremiah and the group that supported him condemned those prophets who predicted the salvation of the city, even though they were accepted as legitimate prophets by powerful groups within the royal court. In the eyes of Jeremiah and his supporters, these prophets were illegitimate because the form and content of their oracles and the means by which they received them did not conform to the patterns that Jeremiah's community accepted (*Jer.* 23:9-40). Isaiah and his disciples, too, had rejected the authority of some of the prophets in Jerusalem because of their aberrant behavior (*Is.* 28:7–10), and in Babylonia the exilic community of Ezekiel denied legitimacy to those prophets who were still active in the Temple in Jerusalem (*Ez.* 13:1–23).

A second element involved in the process of prophetic authentication was the degree to which the prophet fitted into a recognized Israelite theological tradition. This did not mean that the prophet was not free to innovate or criticize the tradition, but he had to remain rooted in it. Thus, for example, in Deuteronomic tradition any prophet who advocated the worship of other gods was considered to have placed himself outside of the tradition by violating its overarching monotheistic principle, and the prophet not only was considered unauthentic but, like the prophet who spoke in the name of another god, was to be put to death (*Dt.* 13:1–5).

Because Israel's theological traditions were not always in agreement with each other at every point, what was acceptable prophetic behavior in one tradition might not be acceptable in another. When such theological disagreements occurred, a particular prophet might be an authoritative figure in his own tradition but would not be taken seriously elsewhere. Clear cases of this phenomenon can be seen in some of the writing prophets. The prophet Amos, a native of Judah and presumably standing in the tradition of the theology developed by the royal theologians in Jerusalem (which saw the establishment of the northern kingdom of Israel as a revolt against the Davidic dynasty), prophesied against the north and predicted the destruction of the Ephraimite royal sanctuary at Bethel. Such behavior was not acceptable in the north, and Amaziah, the priest of Bethel, accused Amos of treason and refused to recognize his prophetic authority (*Am.* 7:10–13). A later case is that of the prophet Jeremiah, who was influenced by Deuteronomic tradition that saw as conditional the election of Jerusalem as the dwelling place of God. He delivered oracles in the Jerusalem Temple that predicted the destruction of the city and the Temple unless the people reformed their conduct and obeyed God's covenantal law. To the officials of the royal court and the Temple, who believed that God had chosen Jerusalem as an eternal dwelling place, such words were treasonous and deserved the death penalty (*Jer.* 26). Although Jeremiah was not killed, many of the officials of Jerusalem refused to recognize his prophetic authority and considered him to be insane (*Jer.* 29:24–28).

A final element involved in the process of accrediting prophets can be seen most clearly in the Deuteronomic literature, which held that authentic prophets were those whose words always came to pass. This was particularly true of prophets said to be "like Moses," a special class of prophets in Deuteronomic theology. These prophets had more direct communication with God than did ordinary prophets and for this reason were more effective intercessors and gave more reliable oracles. The words of a Mosaic prophet would inevitably come true, according to the Deuteronomists, and when these figures appear in the Deuteronomic history, the fulfillment of their oracles is always noted (*Nm.* 12:1–8;

Dt. 18:15–22; *1 Kgs.* 11:30–39, 12:15, 14:7–11, 15:27-30, 16:1–4, 16:9–13; *2 Kgs.* 1:15-17). This criterion for recognizing authentic prophets was not always useful, for oracles might only later be fulfilled, in the distant future, and the reliability of a particular prophet's predictions could not always be determined.

Once a prophet was considered authentic by a particular group in Israel, he seems to have been at least tolerated by the rest of the society. Some of the prophets had free access to the king, the royal court, and the Temple and could carry out their activities without being harassed. Prophets were generally not held responsible for their words or actions because they spoke a divine word and not their own (*Jer.* 26:12–16). However, there were some limits to this freedom, particularly when the prophet criticized the king and the priesthood, and some of the prophets were killed because of their oracles (*Jer.* 26).

Because of the way in which prophetic authority was assigned, prophetic conflicts were common. When a prophet supported by one group gave oracles that conflicted with those of a prophet supported by another group, the conflict was often resolved only when one group simply refused to recognize the authority of one of the other group's prophets. Thus, for example, Jeremiah fought his prophetic opponents not by attacking their theological position but by accusing them of being false prophets (*Jer.* 23:9–32, 28:1–17, 29:15–32; cf. *Ez.* 13:1–23). When false prophecy led to the imposition of the death penalty, as was the case in Deuteronomic law, such accusations were effective tools for social control, whether they were used by the prophets themselves or by a government seeking to suppress troublesome critics.

Social locations and functions. In ancient Israel prophets carried out their activities in all parts of the society. However, because the prophets' functions to a certain extent depended on their social location, it is useful to identify prophets according to their relationship to the society's centers of social, political, and religious power. At the center of the social structure were prophets who may be identified as "central prophets." They carried out their activities in the context of the royal court or the central sanctuary, and individually or as part of a prophetic group they performed the functions considered necessary by the establishment. Because of their central social location, they enjoyed a certain amount of prestige and were considered authoritative by Israelite leaders. At the other end of the social spectrum were prophets who were located away from the centers of power and carried out their activities on the fringes of society. They were considered authoritative only by the small groups of supporters who shared their social location and theological views. Peripheral prophets were usually dispossessed individuals who were tolerated by the religious establishment but enjoyed little social status or political power. In Israel prophets were located at various points on the continuum that stretched between the society's center and its periphery, and some prophets changed their position on the continuum when there were alterations in the social structure.

Locating a particular prophet in the social spectrum was sometimes a subjective process, particularly in the case of peripheral prophets. Because prophets with small support groups and little status had minimal power, they could easily be classified as peripheral by the establishment, and their messages could be ignored. However, to the members of the prophets' support groups they played the crucial role of articulating group values and concerns. For this reason the prophets could be considered central by the groups that supported them. Biblical views on the social location of prophets thus often depended on the social location of the people articulating those views.

All Israelite prophets shared a single basic task. They were to deliver to individuals and groups the divine messages that had been transmitted during their possession experiences. In addition, Deuteronomic prophets served as intercessors who were responsible for communicating the people's questions and requests to God. Beyond these primary tasks, however, the prophets' social functions varied somewhat depending on their social location. Central prophets were normally concerned with the orderly functioning of the society. If they were active in the cult, they were responsible for providing oracles whenever the religious, political, or social occasion required them. They also represented God in state affairs and in general helped to preserve public morality. Such prophets were interested in maintaining and preserving the existing social order. They felt free to criticize existing conditions and structures, but they were generally opposed to radical changes that might make the society unstable.

In contrast, peripheral prophets by definition represented positions that were at odds with the majority views and practices of the society. Being possessed by God and becoming prophets gave marginal individuals an authority that they did not previously have and allowed them to bring their messages to the attention of the political and religious establishment. Peripheral prophets normally advocated basic reforms in the social structure and thus served as agents of rapid social change. Their reform programs often aimed at restoring older religious and social values and practices that the society as a whole had rejected. At the same time, the prophets were concerned with improving their marginal social position and moving their support groups closer to the centers of power. However, there were limits on the degree to which they could advocate major social changes. Up to a point, their views were tolerated, but if they became too vocal in their demands, then they ran the risk of being considered enemies of the society and having their activities brought to a halt through accusations of false prophecy or legal sanctions that would physically remove them.

Prophecy in Israelite History. Because most of Israel's prophets were active during the monarchical period (c. 1020–587/6 BCE), it is sometimes argued that prophecy and monarchy were coeval and interdependent. However, biblical traditions coming from northern Israel speak of the existence of prophets well before the rise of the monarchy, and there is no reason to doubt their accuracy. Similarly, prophets played a role in Israel's restoration after the exile (c. 538–400), so it is probably safe to suppose that prophecy played a role in Israelite society from its origins to about 400 when, according to orthodox Jewish tradition, prophecy ceased. Prophets certainly existed in Israelite society in later times and played a minor role in early Christian communities, but they do not seem to have had major social functions and have left few traces in the biblical record.

Although prophecy existed in Israel for a fairly long period of time, it is impossible to trace a comprehensive history of the phenomenon. Earlier attempts to trace an evolutionary development from "primitive" ecstatic prophecy to the high ethical principles of the writing prophets are now generally discredited. However, it is possible to describe the complex roles that prophets played at various points in Israel's political and religious development.

Premonarchical period. The Elohist traditions of the Pentateuch and the Deuteronomic history suggest that prophets were at work in Israel before the rise of the monarchy (c. 1020). Although the narratives describing the activities of these early figures have certainly been colored by later prophetic ideology, there is no reason to deny the existence of prophecy in early Israel. Prophetic phenomena are attested elsewhere in the ancient Near East in the second millennium in roughly the same areas as those thought to have been occupied by Israel's ancestors. There is no evidence to suggest that early Israelites borrowed prophecy from elsewhere, but it may well have appeared spontaneously in some of the tribes that later joined together to form Israel.

The nature and functions of these early prophets are unclear. Biblical references to the prophetic activities of Abraham and Moses are probably retrojections from later times, and certainly the Moses stories were used by Deuteronomists to support their distinctive views of prophecy (*Gn.* 20:7, *Nm.* 12, *Dt.* 18:9–22). In addition to these traditional figures, Miriam and Deborah are both said to have been prophetesses (*Ex.* 15:20–21, *Jg.* 4:4–10), and an unnamed prophet is said to have been sent during the period of the judges to explain why the people were oppressed (*Jg.* 6:1–10). If these references are in any way indicative of the role that prophets actually played in early Israel, then it would appear that prophets had a position in the central social structure and had important functions in the conduct of warfare.

It is more certain that prophecy was well established in northern Israel in the period shortly before the rise of the monarchy. A band of prophets was part of the cultic personnel at the sanctuary at Gibeah (*1 Sm.* 10:9–13), and there are numerous traditions about the prophetic activities of Samuel. He had prophetic, priestly, and governmental roles at several northern sanctuaries and was clearly a central prophet of major importance (*1 Sm.* 3:1–21, 7:1–12:25). People came to him in order to obtain information from God (*1 Sm.* 9:6–10), and he represented God among the people. Although traditions differ about Samuel's role in the rise of the monarchy, the Deuteronomists saw him as the religious official responsible for anointing and legitimating Saul as Israel's first king (*1 Sm.* 9:15–10:8).

Monarchical period. Throughout the history of the Israelite monarchy, prophets played important religious roles both inside the royal court and on its periphery. The tradition of prophetic participation in government began with Samuel, who continued to advise Saul on cultic matters during his reign. However, Saul's disagreements with Samuel and Samuel's northern support groups over the extent of royal authority eventually broke into open warfare, and Samuel stripped the kingship from Saul and anointed David as the new king (*1 Sm.* 13:1–16:13). The presence of prophets in the royal court continued during David's reign. The court prophet Nathan delivered to David an oracle promising the king an eternal dynasty in Jerusalem and designating Jerusalem as the divine dwelling place forever (*2 Sm.* 7). This oracle became the cornerstone of the Jerusalem royal theology, and it was cited as authoritative by later royal sources (*Ps.* 89, 132). Later in David's reign his royal visionary, Gad, legitimated the building of a temple in Jerusalem (*2 Sam.* 24). David is also said to have installed prophets as religious officials in the central sanctuary (*1 Chr.* 24). Although this report undoubtedly reflects the Temple administration of the Chronicler's own time, it may well be that prophets had central cultic functions in Jerusalem during the monarchical period.

Prophecy does not seem to have been prominent during Solomon's reign, but it emerged in a new form in the time of his successor, Rehoboam. In response to general Ephraimite dissatisfaction with the growing power of the Jerusalem monarchy, the prophet Ahijah, from the old northern sanctuary at Shiloh, established the dissident northern tribes as an independent kingdom by delivering an oracle legitimating Jeroboam as king of Ephraim (*1 Kgs.* 11:29–40). Ahijah was clearly a peripheral prophet representing interests that were not connected with the royal court in Jerusalem, and his newly created state may have been intended to restore his supporters to positions of power. If so, his intentions were thwarted when Jeroboam created in Ephraim a syncretist religious establishment that horrified the Deuteronomic historians. According to the Deuteronomists, Ahijah was the first of a series of peripheral prophets who attempted to reform the northern political and religious establishments (*1 Kgs.* 13–16).

Prophetic opposition in the north reached its height during the time of Elijah and Elisha (c. 869–815), when groups of peripheral prophets appeared to denounce the Ephraimite kings and the heterodox worship that they permitted in the land. This inevitably brought the peripheral prophets into conflict with the prophets of Yahveh, Baal, and Asherah, who were part of the religious establishment in the north (*1 Kgs.* 18, 22). The peripheral prophets finally prevailed and succeeded in overthrowing the northern dynasty and bringing about cultic reforms (*1 Kgs.* 17–*2 Kgs.* 10). However, by the time of the prophets Amos and Hosea (c. 760–746), Baal worship had been firmly reestablished in Ephraim. Both of these prophets, from Judah and Ephraim respectively, continued the activities of their predecessors and predicted the destruction of the evil kingdom. The prophecies were finally fulfilled with the destruction of the northern capital, Samaria, in 721, an event that the Deuteronomic historians traced to the failure of the kings and the people to listen to the warnings that God had sent through the prophets (*2 Kgs.* 17:7–18).

Little is known of prophecy in Judah during the period of the divided monarchy until the very end of that period, when the prophets Isaiah and Micah began their activities. Both reflect an acceptance of elements of the royal theology of Jerusalem and both may be examples of prophets who were more central than periphral. Isaiah in particular seems to have had access to the court (*Is.* 7:3, 8:2, 22:15–16), and he may have played an official role in resolving the crisis caused by the Assyrian invasion of 701 (*Is.* 36–39). However, he was certainly capable of criticizing the abuses of the royal theology and advocated judicious social change to preserve traditional religious values.

Most of the remaining preexilic prophets in Jerusalem were much more supportive of the government than were Isaiah and Micah. Nahum and Habakkuk have both been linked with the Jerusalem cult, and both may have had an official part in it. Both deliver oracles against Israel's enemies and in general behave like typical central prophets.

Toward the end of the monarchical period, peripheral prophecy reappeared in a mild way with the writings of Zephaniah, but it did not become a major force until the work of Jeremiah and Ezekiel (c. 627–571). Jeremiah, a priest who seems to have been heavily influenced by the Deuteronomic movement, launched a series of increasingly harsh attacks on the king and the people, urging them to repent in order to avoid the punishment that God had decreed against Jerusalem. In the final days before the destruction of the city in 587/6, he advocated surrender to the Babylonians, a policy that brought him into conflict with the royal court and the central prophets, who still advocated the old theology of the eternal election of Jerusalem. Jeremiah narrowly escaped with his life, but when the city fell, his prophecies were vindicated. At about the same time, Ezekiel, a priest who had been exiled to Babylon in 597, advocated major modifications of the Jerusalem royal theology held by most of his fellow exiles, but his words had little effect.

Exile and its aftermath. The fall of Jerusalem and the destruction of the Temple in 587/6 created serious authority problems for Israel's prophets. The political and religious institutions that sheltered the central prophets disappeared with the conquest, and those prophets who supported the traditional Jerusalem theology were tragically wrong in their predictions. Peripheral prophets, such as Jeremiah and Ezekiel, gained new credibility because of the fall; but in their latter days they also gave oracles of promise, and as the exile continued, these oracles too seemed to be false.

The prophets of the exilic and postexilic periods faced this problem of authority in several ways. First, they turned away from oral prophecy and adopted writing as the means of circulating their words. Written prophecies were apparently thought to have more authority because of their concreteness. Second, they often attached their prophecies to those of preexilic prophets in an attempt to borrow the authority of their predecessors. Finally, these last representatives of Israelite prophecy turned increasingly toward the divine world for solutions to Israel's overwhelming problems, a move that brought prophecy closer to apocalyptic. Instead of advocating the reform of human behavior in order to cure Israel's religious and social ills, as earlier prophets had done, the postexilic prophets often looked instead to God's direct intervention in history on behalf of those who waited faithfully for God's plan for Israel's salvation to be realized. Some of these postexilic solutions to the problem of prophetic authority can be seen in the postexilic books of Zechariah, Haggai, Joel, and Malachi, and all of them are visible in the writings of the anonymous prophets ("Second Isaiah" and "Third Isaiah") responsible for the last part of the *Book of Isaiah*.

After the exile, central prophecy was briefly restored in the reconstructed Judahite state, and Zechariah and Haggai in particular had roles in shaping the restored community. However, after Ezra's mission to Jerusalem toward the end of the fifth century, officially recognized prophecy was restricted to Levites with specific duties in the cult of the Second Temple (*1 Chr.* 25). [*See* Levites.] After this point, other types of prophecy disappear from the biblical record.

[*Prophecy is also discussed at length in the entry on* Israelite Religion, *and Amos, Ezekiel, Hosea, Isaiah, Jeremiah, and Micah are the subjects of independent entries.*]

BIBLIOGRAPHY

The most thorough general treatment of ancient Israelite prophecy is still Johannes Lindblom's *Prophecy in Ancient Israel* (Philadelphia, 1962), although the comparative evidence and the scholarly bibliography on which the book is based are now out of date. More recent, although not so comprehensive, is Joseph Blenkinsopp's *A History of Prophecy in Israel* (Philadelphia, 1983). A good, nontechnical introduction is provided by Klaus Koch's *The Prophets*, 2 vols., translated by Margaret Kohl (Philadelphia, 1982–1984). Koch gives an overview of biblical prophecy and then treats the major prophets individually. Some of the older literature still contains valuable observations, although many of the points of view expressed in these works have been rejected or modified by modern scholars. See in particular Theodore H. Robinson's *Prophecy and the Prophets in Ancient Israel* (London, 1923) and A. B. Davidson's *Old Testament Prophecy* (Edinburgh, 1903).

A specialized study of the difficult area of postexilic prophecy may be found in David L. Petersen's *Late Israelite Prophecy* (Missoula, Mont., 1977). Aubrey R. Johnson has mounted a strong case for the cultic involvement of most of Israel's prophets. Although few scholars would accept all of Johnson's conclusions, he has produced a valuable survey of the available evidence. See in particular his *The Cultic Prophet in Ancient Israel* (Cadiff, 1962) and *The Cultic Prophet and Israel's Psalmody* (Cardiff, 1979). The fundamental study of the literary patterns in the prophets' oracles is Claus Westermann's *Basic Forms of Prophetic Speech*, translated by Hugh Clayton White (Philadelphia, 1967), although Westermann's work needs to be set in a broader perspective, such as the one provided by W. Eugene March's article "Prophecy," in *Old Testament Form Criticism*, edited by John H. Hayes (San Antonio, 1974), pp. 141–177.

The sociological dimensions of biblical prophecy have been treated comprehensively in my *Prophecy and Society in Ancient Israel* (Philadelphia, 1980). Note also the more specialized study of David L. Petersen, *The Roles of Israel's Prophets* (Sheffield, 1981). A useful synthesis of anthropological evidence on spirit possession is provided by I. M. Lewis's *Ecstatic Religion* (Harmondsworth, 1971). Several illuminating case studies have been collected in *Spirit Mediumship and Society in Africa*, edited by John Beattie and John Middleton (New York, 1969).

A detailed study of the theology of the prophetic traditions has been made by Gerhard von Rad in the second volume of his *Old Testament Theology*, translated by D. M. G. Stalker (New York, 1965). A popular treatment of the same subject may be found in Walter Brueggemann's *The Prophetic Imagination* (Philadelphia, 1978). For two classic studies of prophetic thought, see also Martin Buber's *The Prophetic Faith*, translated by Carlyle Witton-Davies (New York, 1949), and Abraham Joshua Heschel's *The Prophets* (New York, 1962).

ROBERT R. WILSON

PROPHETHOOD, ISLAMIC. *See* Nubūwah.

PROSELYTISM. *See* Missions, *article on* Missionary Activity, *and* Conversion.

PROSTITUTION. *See* Hierodouleia.

PROTESTANTISM. [*This entry provides an overview of the Protestant branch of Christian religion. The historical origins of Protestantism are examined in* Reformation. *Particular manifestations of Protestantism are discussed in* Denominationalism *and in numerous entries on Protestant churches and biographies of Protestant leaders.*]

Protestantism is a worldwide movement that derives from sixteenth-century reforms of Western Christianity. As a movement it is both a set of church bodies and a less well defined ethos, spirit, and cultural achievement. Thus, one speaks of Reformed or Methodist churches as being Protestant, just as one may speak of a "Protestant ethic" or a "Protestant nation."

Through the years different needs have occasioned a variety of attempts to determine the definitional boundaries of Protestantism. Sometimes there may be theological or liturgical motives for restricting these boundaries. Some Anglicans, or members of the Church of England, for example, who stress how closely they are identified with the ancient catholic tradition, often resent being classified as Protestant at all. So do Lutherans of similar outlook, even though the term *Protestant* was first applied in 1529 on Lutheran soil. At another extreme, many Protestants refuse to include movements like the Jehovah's Witnesses or Mormons in their ranks, even though these new nineteenth-century religious traditions flourished on Protestant soil and kept something of the Protestant impulse in their church life.

Four Protestant Clusters. For demographic purposes, David B. Barrett in his *World Christian Encyclopedia* (1982) tries to bring some order to definitional chaos by classifying the non–Roman Catholic and non-Orthodox part of the Christian world into five families, or blocs, which he calls "Protestant," "nonwhite indigenous," "Anglican," "marginal Protestant," and "Catholic (non-Roman)." All but the last of these have some sort of Protestant ties. The mainstream Protestant category includes long-established Northern Hemisphere churches such as the Congregationalist and Baptist. The Anglican family includes plural, low church, high church, evangelical, Anglo-Catholic, and central (or Broad church) traditions. The category of marginal Protestants includes Jehovah's Witnesses, Mormons, Religious Science, and Unitarian, Spiritualist, and British-Israelite churches.

The existence of the fourth category, nonwhite indigenous Christianity, "a whole new bloc of global Christendom," Barrett speaks of as "one of the more startling findings" documented in his survey. Its existence has been long known, but few, says Barrett, realized that by 1980 it numbered eighty-two million. For all their independent rise and growth, however, nonwhite indigenous forms of Christianity still derive from missionary efforts by classic Protestants. They share many of the doctrines and practices of the Western parentages. In almost all cases they also share the familiar names Baptist, Lutheran, Anglican, and the like. Therefore, while attention to them may be secondary, these younger churches do belong in any encyclopedic coverage of the longer Protestant tradition.

Location of Old and New Protestantism. At the end of the twentieth century, after more than 450 years, worldwide Protestantism is entering a new phase, because of this shift of power to nonwhite indigenous versions. Classically the movement was strongly identified with northwestern Europe and Anglo-America. Philosopher Alfred North Whitehead once spoke of the Reformation itself as a family quarrel of northwestern European peoples. From the early sixteenth century until well into the nineteenth, the vast majority of the heirs of this Reformation did remain in Europe and its North American colonies. The Latin American nations were almost entirely Roman Catholic in makeup. Around the turn of the nineteenth century, this older Protestantism underwent vast expansion through missionary efforts to convert people in all nations and to establish churches everywhere. It was in the mid-twentieth century that the inventive and often autochthonous character of the nonwhite indigenous groups became evident, particularly in sub-Saharan Africa, parts of Latin America, and the Pacific island world.

The power shift from northwestern Europe, where established Protestantism consistently lost power in the face of secularizing forces, to the vibrant world of the Southern Hemisphere portended great changes in the Protestant ethos as well. For centuries Protestant religion had been seen as an impetus toward capitalist economies, yet the new growth came in portions of the world where capitalism had little chance and few promoters. This religious emphasis in Europe had characteristically been established in coordination with the state. However, in the new nations of Africa or in Latin America, where Catholicism was first established but where anticlerical revolutions later barred privilege to any Christian bodies, nonwhite indigenous Protestantism had to make its way as a movement independent of state establishment or privilege.

Other changes came with the shift. Historically the Protestantism of Europe relied on thought patterns that depended upon and connected with older Catholic philosophies. The Protestant reformers of the sixteenth century protested against some uses Catholics made of, for example, Platonic or Aristotelian philosophies through the centuries. Yet soon they were themselves developing theologies that relied on the mainline Western philosophical synthesis. In the new area of growth, however, leaders of nonwhite indigenous flowerings of Protestantism did not have the luxury of exploring these philosophical schools. They saw no need to relate to them and often explicitly rebelled against them.

All these changes make generalizing about Protestantism far more difficult at the end of the twentieth century than at the end of the nineteenth. Often one must fall back on definitions from the classic period, the first three or four centuries, keeping in mind the exceptional new developments as a subtheme. In any case, much of the plot of Protestantism after its period of expansion has revealed the dialectic of adaptation and resistance on the part of both missionary agents and the missionized. The agents of the West often arrived along with merchants or military forces, and they had to choose between being openly identified with their purposes or establishing an, at least, subtle detachment from them. Inevitably they were bearers of Western national values, but they could choose to keep their distance from uncritical embrace of these values. On the other hand, those who accepted Christianity at the hands of the missioners also had the choice of adopting as much of Western culture as possible or picking and choosing those elements of Protestantism that they could most easily or advantageously graft onto their old culture and ways.

Protestant Diversity and Coherence. The first perception of both old and new Protestantism has always been its diversity. Barrett claims that the one billion and more practicing Christians of the world belong to 20,780 distinct denominations. While more than half the Christians are Catholic, the vast majority of these 20,780 denominations would be classed as part of the Protestant movement. Thus, in classic Protestantism, in 1980 there were almost 345 million people in 7,889 of these distinct bodies in 212 nations. The nonwhite indigenous versions, almost all of them Protestant, were located in 10,065 distinct bodies. There were also 225 Anglican denominations and 1,345 "marginal Protestant" groups. Indeed, this diversity and this fertility at creating new, unrelated bodies were long used as a criticism of Protestantism by Roman Catholicism, which united under the Roman pope, and by Orthodoxy, which was divided more into national jurisdictions but saw itself as united in holy tradition.

It is possible to move behind this first perception of the chaos of unrelated bodies to see some forms of coherence. Great numbers of Protestant bodies, along with many Orthodox ones, are members of the World Council of Churches, established in 1948, which has a uniting confessional theme around the lordship of Jesus Christ. In many nations there are national councils or federations of cooperating churches, which allow for positive interaction even where there is not organic unity. World confessional families of Lutherans, Reformed, Baptists, and others throughout the twentieth century have brought into some concord these churches that have family resemblances. Finally, there have been significant mergers of Protestant churches both within families, such as Lutheran with Lutheran, Presbyterian with Presbyterian, and across family lines, as in America's United Church of Christ, which blended a New England Congregationalist tradition with a German Reformed heritage.

Whoever chronicles Protestant diversities and coherences also has to recognize that significant differences appear within each group and that important elements of concord transect the groups. Liberal Episcopalians and Methodists may have more in common with each other on many issues and in numbers of practices than either of them has with conservative members of their own communion. It is probably the better part of discretion not to seek rigid categories in classifying Protestant bodies; the concept of something like "zones" is more fruitful. Thus across the Protestant spectrum one may begin with "high church" Anglican zones, where many formal practices of Catholicism prevail, the liturgy is extremely complex, and worship is highly adorned (with icons, incense, and artifacts or gestures). At the opposite end of the spectrum and at least as securely in the orbit of sociological Protestantism is a "low church" zone, where groups may have rejected as much as possible from the Catholic past; for example, the Quakers seek utter simplicity and silence in worship and make no use of the sacraments of Catholic Christianity at all.

Some Protestant Elements Held in Common. To accent only Protestant diversity, as demographers or critics may be tempted to do, does not take into account the fact that the word *Protestant* arose to cover a distinct set of phenomena. In the minds of those who use the term, it may denote something fairly specific. The easiest way to put a boundary around Protestantism is to deal with it negatively and say that it is the form of Western Christianity that rejects obedience to the Roman papacy. Such an approach is an immense clarifier, since Protestants do reject the papacy. The only remaining element of confusion in this negative definition comes from the fact that Western (non-Roman) Catholic Christians also reject the papacy. In 1980 this group, including the Catholic Apostolic, Reformed Catholic, Old Catholic, and Conservative Catholic churches, numbered 3,439,375, as against 344,336,319 old- and new-style Protestants.

While the resistance to papal claims is a uniting factor, it is not likely that many people ever choose to remain loyal to Protestantism on such marginal and confining grounds alone. One is Protestant for many reasons; one *then* differentiates one's faith and practice from Roman Catholicism in nonpapal-versus-papal terms. That issue was strong in the sixteenth century at the time of the Protestant break with Rome, and it became a subject of intense controversy late in the nineteenth century, when papal infallibility was declared. The controversy remains to plague Catholic-Protestant ecumenical relations. But in the daily life of believers, the rejection of the papacy has little to do with churchly commitments. One must seek elsewhere for the positive elements and accents of Protestantism, even if it shares many of these with Catholicism.

The first common mark of Protestantism is historically clear and clean: virtually all Protestant groups derive from movements that began in the sixteenth century. When later groups were formed, as were the Disciples of Christ in nineteenth-century America, they may not have seen themselves as working out the logic of earlier Protestantism; yet historians at once traced the roots of this typical new group to various older Presbyterian and Baptist forms, among others.

A very few Protestant groups can also trace their lineage back to pre-Reformation times. Modern Waldensians, for example, are heirs of a movement begun under Pierre Valdès (Peter Waldo) in the twelfth century, and some modern Czech churches are heirs of traditions that go back to the Hussite Jednota Bratrská (Society of Brethren, known in Latin as Unitas Fratrum) of the fifteenth century. [*See* Waldensians *and the biography of Jan Hus.*] Yet the Waldensians, the Czech groups, and others began to be recognized as something other than illicit sects on Roman Catholic soil as a result of the Protestant breakthrough. At another point on the spectrum is the Church of England, or Anglicanism. Most of its articulators stress that they remain the church Catholic as it has been on English soil since the christianization of England. Although it has kept faith in the apostolic succession of bishops and has retained many pre-Reformation practices, the Anglican communion as it has existed since the break with Rome under Henry VIII in the sixteenth century is vastly different from the Catholic church under Roman papal obedience in England before and since the Reformation. In short, the Waldensians, the Czech groups, and the Anglicans alike were, and were seen to be, part of the Protestant revolt from both the viewpoints of Roman Catholic leadership and historical scholarship ever since.

To have undergone formal separation from the papally controlled church or to have been transformed by the fact that one's tradition changes through such separation are the major historical marks of Protestantism. Individual groups may have parentage in the Middle Ages or may have sprung up late in the twentieth century, yet the sixteenth-century breach in Christendom is the event by which Protestant existence is somehow measured. Beyond the normativeness of that breach, Protestants begin to share elements of Catholicism. That certain elements are shared in no way diminishes their importance in Protestant definition. They tend to acquire a special color when viewed through the prism of Protestant experiences.

God in Protestantism. All Christian movements, unlike some other religions, focus finally on their witness to God. Protestantism is theistic. There have been momentary expressions by theological elites of a "Christian atheism," but these have been dismissed by the Protestant public as idiosyncratic, personal forms of witness or philosophical expression. Then, too, some prophets and observers have pointed to a "practical atheism" among Protestants who in their ways of life seem to ignore the claims of God upon them. Yet such practical atheism is unself-conscious, reflexive. When called to their attention, it is usually vigorously dismissed by the people to whom it is applied, a sign that they regard theistic belief to be focal.

At the left wing of marginal Protestantism, as Barrett clarifies it, stand some former Protestant groups that have retained certain elements of the Protestant tradition. Among these are Unitarianisms of humanistic sorts and Ethical Culture movements, which grew up on Jewish soil in America but acquired some Protestant traits. [*See* Ethical Culture.] It is significant that such groups are dismissed by the vast cohort of Protestants precisely because they are humanistic, or because they exclude themselves from Protestantism, usually on grounds of theism.

If Protestants are not humanistic or atheistic, they also are not pantheistic. Individual pantheists may exist as mystics, and there have been pantheistic Protestant heresies, so regarded both by those who have innovated with them and by those who have excluded their advocates. In some formal theological circles, one sometimes hears advocated teachings that seem to verge on pantheism, the proposition that the world and God are coextensive, identical. Yet articulators of such teachings usually take pains to distance themselves from pure pantheism, for example, through panentheisms, which speak both of identity and distance. Marginal Protestants such as the Mormons teach doctrines that look pantheist to mainstream Protestantisms. Here, as so often, it is their departure from theism that is at issue in the principles of exclusion.

Protestantism on occasion has had deistic proponents, agents of a natural religion that made no room for a personal God, special revelation, or reasons to pray to an unresponsive, divine, originating, but now absentee force. In eighteenth-century England there were Anglican Deists, and in the continental Enlightenment one heard of equivalents. In practice, many Protestant believers may act as though they are deistic in their prayer life, which means that they somehow believe in a divine force but see no reason for prayerful intercourse with it. Yet deism has consistently in due course been seen as a deviation from, not a part of, the Protestant impulse. [*See* Deism.]

The God of the Bible and Trinitarianism. The freedom that belongs to the Protestant ethos has made room for the enterprising and innovating philosopher of religion, but the determining element in Protestant concepts of God has been some form of adherence to the biblical witness. The God of Protestants is the God of Abraham, Isaac, and Jacob. Along with Catholics, Protestants believe in the God revealed in the Hebrew scriptures, which Protestantism has taken over intact from Judaism and made its own. This God, Yahveh, is the

God of Israel and the God of the prophets. Protestantism thus relies on God as creator and sustainer of the universe, existent though hidden, being and not nonbeing, somehow an agent in history. Although not all Protestants speak of a "personal" God, most conceive of God as personal and thus addressable.

Protestant theologians spoke of the Protestant intention as one directed to what H. Richard Niebuhr called "radical monotheism." This intention has meant that Protestants share the concern of Hebrew prophecy to distance believers from "many gods" and false gods alike. The Protestant impulse, sometimes directed even against itself by its own prophets, has been iconoclastic. Pioneers of the movement such as John Calvin saw the natural human mind as an instinctive idol maker, always busy serving either the true God or gods of its own making, who must be smashed. It would be impossible to say that Protestant believers have been more successful at being radical monotheists than have others; yet reflective Protestantism has been so nervous about icons or images that might be construed as having identity with the divine or divinized figure they represent that the iconoclast always has a privileged place in Protestant arguments.

The battle against icon and idol in Protestantism may sometimes continue on the abstract planes of philosophical discourse or theological definition, but the iconoclastic position is usually stated most forcefully when Protestants explain the biblical account of Israel's witness to Yahveh, the one God. The God to whom Protestants point is one who, although hidden, exists, acts, and speaks through a divine word. This God is in every case a God of judgment and mercy, wrath and love, holiness and forgiveness.

While some Protestants have been unsure about the meaning of the covenant with Israel in the Old Testament, few have doubted the witness to God in the New Testament. The God of Israel is present in a special way in Jesus of Nazareth. Some forms of liberal Protestantism were reluctant to speak of Jesus as partaking uniquely in the divine nature associated with the one he called Father. When they showed this reluctance, this was in the interest of radical monotheism. When most other forms of Protestantism remained content with or became emphatic about classic creeds that associated Jesus Christ with God, they did so in conscious reference to the fact that this in no way detracted from monotheistic faith. Protestant interpretation of philosophies of history have always seen this God of Israel as somehow active in history.

At the same time, Protestantism is a Christ-focused faith. Here again one may speak in the language of H. Richard Niebuhr about a tendency that he saw as less compatible with true Protestantism and that, indeed, was a heresy on any terms. Some forms of evangelical, Christ-centered Protestantism, he charged, were guilty of a "Unitarianism of the Second Person" of the Trinity. This meant that just as earlier theistic Unitarians believed only in the divinity of the one God whom Jesus called Father, at the expense of the Son and the Holy Spirit, these gospel-minded people, without usually meaning to, identified Jesus almost exclusively with God and had little to say or do about God apart from witness to Jesus.

Not all Protestants have been ready to use the inherited language of the preexistent Logos, or Word, that became incarnate in the historical Jesus. They have, however, found ways to witness to the bond between Jesus and God. In his best-known hymn, "A Mighty Fortress," Protestant pioneer Martin Luther spoke of Jesus Christ as "the Lord of hosts" and then burst forth with the assertion "And there's no other God." There is no other God than the one revealed in Jesus Christ. Such witness led to radical expressions that verge on the ancient heresy of patripassionism, the claim that God the Father suffered with the Son on the cross. In this spirit Martin Rinkhart offered a line in a Good Friday hymn to the effect that in the death of Jesus "our God is dead." Nineteenth-century critics, especially left-wing Hegelians, seized on incautious lines like these to claim that the death of Jesus meant the death of God, even on orthodox soil. Rinkhart and the Protestants were not ready for such consequences or corollaries, but they left themselves open to this claim, so eager were they to proclaim the divinity of Jesus Christ. Protestants in the main have been so Jesus- or Christ-centered that they are more willing to take such risks than to side with humanistic or minority liberal Protestants who broke up notions of the Trinity and saw Jesus as a distinctive but not unique human.

As for what the creeds describe as the Third Person of the Trinity, the Holy Spirit, one despairs of pointing to a distinctive witness held by almost all Protestants. Negatively, again as a corollary to the nonpapal witness, Protestants have refused to identify the Holy Spirit with the tradition, the magisterium or official teaching, or the papal authority of the Roman Catholic church. Most have been more at home seeing the Holy Spirit connected with revelation and authority as the inspirer of the text of the Bible. Some left-wing reformers of the sixteenth century and their heirs down to twentieth-century Pentecostal Protestants have been ready to speak of revelation from the Holy Spirit direct to the individual, apart from scripture. Yet it is significant that in their minds, this revelation occurs alongside and not in antagonism toward or independent of what is heard in the inspired Bible.

This witness to God in three persons, historically as Father, Son (Jesus Christ), and Holy Spirit, has added up to a Protestant trinitarianism. Once the term *Trinity* is introduced, it is difficult to see what distinctions remain. True, a few Protestants, especially among the Pentecostals and others who resist Catholic creeds and dogma, reject the trinitarian approach because the word does not appear in the Bible and because it points to human formulations. Yet without using the term, they tend to reproduce the substance of trinitarian faith even while rejecting its formulations.

In sum, the distinctive characteristics of Protestantism emerge from the variety of models that Protestants endorse in forming their churches. Because of their diversity, Protestant churches have been less likely or less able to converge on the basis of each other's witness than have churches in the more homogeneous Eastern Orthodox and Roman Catholic traditions. As a result, Protestants are thrown back more on story than on dogma, more on biblical narrative than on creedal formulation, yet for the most part without rejecting dogma or creed. And they have been pressed to develop special ways of understanding how God is mediated and present in human affairs and, specifically, in the circle of believers and the church. Urgent on its agenda for centuries, then, has been the concept of mediation in formal authority and structure. [*See* God, *article on* God in Postbiblical Christianity; Jesus; *and* Trinity.]

Authority and Structure: The Scriptures. If the believer on Protestant soil is to be responsive to God as creator (or, sometimes, Father), Son, and Holy Spirit, questions arise. Who says so? How is this God to be known? What are the boundaries of witness to such a God? Eastern Orthodoxy and Roman Catholicism stress the authority of tradition, magisterium, apostolic succession of bishops (as do Anglicans and some Lutherans), and, uniquely to Catholicism, the Roman papal office. They also testify to God's revelation in scripture, but Protestantism is thrown almost wholly on scripture. Since the end of the nineteenth century, however, more and more Protestants have been willing to see a relationship between the Bible and tradition. They have become contextual thinkers who see that the Bible reiterates the tradition it grows out of. Yet for their ancestors in faith the Bible held a special status, and tradition or papal authority could never match it. So emphatic was this Protestant emphasis that critics from within, such as the Enlightenment-era Protestant Gotthold Ephraim Lessing, complained that Luther substituted the Bible as a "paper pope" for Protestants to match the authority of Catholicism's human pope.

The Bible of Protestantism is the canon of the Old and New Testaments, and almost never the Apocrypha, which has special status in the Orthodox and Catholic traditions. The canon is theoretically open; it is conceivable that a book could still be added to it. So teach most Protestants. It is difficult to imagine the circumstance in which the many Protestant church bodies could agree on a later-discovered and apparently canonical-level writing, yet, for thoughtful Protestants, the openness of the canon is a partial safeguard against making an icon or idol of the Bible.

While the Bible has become the only document used and useful for uniting Protestant witness or helping determine Protestant theological argument—it provides at least something of the genetic programming of Protestantism, or the ground rules for their games—there is here as so often a very broad spectrum of approaches to its authority. Most Protestants have accepted the Luthern mark *sola scriptura*, that the Bible alone is the authority; but this formula tells all too little about how to regard the book.

At one extreme, conservative Protestants who have resisted modern historical criticism of biblical texts stress that the Bible is somehow not only inspired but infallible and inerrant. The inerrancy applies not only to revelation in matters of faith but also in all details of history, geography, and science, at least as would apply to the original autographs. Some of the originators of Protestantism often used language of biblical authority that was so confident of biblical truth that it gave reasons for later theologians to build elaborate theories of this inerrancy. In later centuries, some dogmatic teachers went so far as to propound mechanical or dictation theories, in which the author of a biblical writing was a kind of conduit or secretary for God, at the expense of personal inspiration and independent style. Most proponents of inerrancy, however, have been less extreme. They have tended to build on the basis of various Aristotelian or Baconian philosophies, stressing syllogisms in which a perfect, hence inerrant, God chooses to engage lovingly in revelation, hence taking care to assure that readers receive no error or ambiguity. These inerrantists have engaged in heated polemics against all, no matter how high their view of biblical authority, who have not found inerrancy to be a biblical or theologically defensible concept.

At the other end of the spectrum are a minority of Protestants, chiefly in academic centers, who have completely adopted post-Enlightenment views of biblical criticism. They have thus treated the biblical text as they would any other ancient literary text. They grant no special status to the inspiration of biblical authors. For them the Bible still has authority as a document that both reflects and promotes the norms of the Christian community. Many schools of interpretation, even among those who have immersed themselves in historical and literary criticism, find that the Bible "discloses," or potentially discloses, what God would reveal. This disclosure or revelation, it is contended, can occur even if the Bible includes grammatical inaccuracies, historical misstatements, and scientific concepts long proven wrong and rendered obsolete. The polemic of these contenders is against the inerrantists, who, they claim, do make the Bible into a quasi-papal authority or turn it into an icon at the expense of radical monotheism.

The spectrum is visible in another way when one considers how different Protestants regard the reader of the Bible. At one end, there are those who contend that "the right of private judgment" is the Christian mark of distinctiveness. Thus Martin Luther was said to have challenged the emperor in 1521 to convince him that he, Luther, was wrong on the basis of the Bible and reason. One cannot go against conscience for the sake of authority. In a sense, the conscience and intelligence of the individual in such a case take priority over claims of the community. At the other end of the spectrum, there is as much concern as in any other part of Christianity for Christian community and the nurturing of the word in the context of congregation or church. In these cases, the church is credited with preserving the Bible, seeing that it is embodied in people who effectively display its power in their lives, and calling people to belief on the basis of biblical texts that are turned into calls of faith by living people. In all cases, it is fair to speak of Protestants as being especially "people of the Book." [*See* Biblical Exegesis, *article on* Christian Views.]

The Authority of the Church. Lacking paper authority as they do, and unwilling as they are for the most part to yield to bishops as having a determinative role in dispensing tradition, how do Protestants see the authority of the church? The vast majority of Protestants in all ages, though they be churched and faithful, have rendered secondary to the Bible all other church authority, creeds, confessions, and forms of polity. When they are serious and are seriously confronted, most Protestants characteristically will say that they get authority for teaching and practice from the Bible alone.

Despite this claim, reflective Protestants will also admit that over the centuries they have spilled much ink in treatises on churchly authority. As much as Catholics, they may have exacted sweat and blood from people who ran afoul of church authorities, who tested the bounds of orthodoxy, or who came under ecclesiastical discipline. Protestantism, in other words, may seem chaotic to the outsider who sees its many groupings and varieties, but to most confessors and members the chaos is minimized, because they are ordinarily touched only by the authority system of which they are a part, that of their own church.

Once one insists on making churchly authority secondary, other values come to be dominant in association with the church. The church on Protestant soil is a fellowship, a congregation of people who have like minds or similar purposes. The church may be seen as "the body of Christ" or "the communion of saints" before it is an authority to compel conformity in teaching or practice. Yet once one assigns values to the group, even in forms of Protestantism that accent the right of private judgment or go to extremes of individualism, there must be and in practice have been many subtle ways to assert authority and to effect discipline. A small congregation's authority on Baptist or Congregational soil can be felt more immediately, for instance, than might Catholic authority asserted from the distance between Rome and India by a not always efficient and always pluralistic church. Democracies can turn authoritarian. Ambiguity about authority can often lead to expressions of arbitrary discipline. So polity and authority have been nagging questions in Protestantism.

First, there has been ambiguity about the lay-clerical distinction. Theologian Hendrik Kraemer, in *A Theology of the Laity* (1958), accurately pointed out that Protestantism was a revolt against authoritarian and overly hierarchical clericalism. Yet almost all Protestantism retained a professional and ordained clergy, somehow setting it aside with sacred sanctions and for special functions. The "somehow," however, became problematic. Protestantism wanted to engage in a leveling of ranks by insisting that all believers were priests, that they could all intercede for one another at the altar, symbolically before the throne of God. Then what were these ordained "priests," or whatever Protestants called their ministry or clergy, and how did they hold power?

Kraemer, historian Wilhelm Pauck, and others have shown that authority (in all but Anglicanism, the Lutheran Church of Sweden, and other "high" episcopal bodies) resides chiefly in the word of God and in the responsive congregation. The minister has tended to become the person called and set aside to be the more expert preacher and expounder of the word. Yet Protestantism was unwilling to say that the laity could not be expert at speaking the word, which was accessible to all. It was also easy to demonstrate that the succession of faith in congregations that were responsive to the word was vulnerable to faithlessness and error or heresy. To claim that ministry consisted in the clergy's unique right to administer the sacraments or holy ordinances was something that not all Protestants were eager to do. They did not want the sacramental life to seem in any way magical. As a result, in almost all cases they retained a specially sanctioned clergy, ascribed great authority also to the laity, and left the status of both ambiguous and thus problematic. [*See also* Church; Priesthood, *article on* Christian Priesthood; *and* Ministry.]

Confessions and Creeds. Church authority is not only an issue of clergy and laity. It must also concentrate on the substance or content of the faith that holds people together and finds them members of one Protestant confession and not another. Of course, heredity, accident of birth, and many casual factors based on aesthetics, personal choice, or marriage across denominational lines have played their parts. But thoughtful Protestantism has also insisted that its members are not only "believers" but "believers in" and in some ways, necessarily, "believers that" something or other is true. Whether or not they call these creeds or confessions, and whether these statements are formal or informal, there tend to be some common expressions that give clarity to faith and that establish boundaries between one set of beliefs and others.

Most Protestant bodies display their distinctiveness by resorting to documents from the times of their origins. In their first or second generation, leaders of groups were called upon or felt impelled to define themselves and to witness to their truths. For Lutherans the instrument was chiefly the Augsburg Confession; for the Reformed, the Heidelberg Catechism; for Presbyterians, the Westminster Confession; and for Anglicans the Thirty-nine Articles. Even loose bodies such as seventeenth- and eighteenth-century New England Congregationalism in America produced enough creeds and confessions to make up large anthologies. These documents have attracted various levels of respect and authority. Some came to be neglected or even rejected by huge parties. Yet the ecumenical movement, in which these churches had to find out who they and their counterparts were, exposed to view these ancient documents and showed their enduring power.

By some Protestants their originating confessions were believed *quia* ("because"), that is, because they were held to be simply and perfectly congruent with biblical witness. Others held to them *quatenus* ("insofar"), that is, insofar as they witnessed to biblical truth in later times and special circumstances. At times the claim was much more informal than either of these, and in some cases it is not possible to point to a church confession at all. For many Protestants a confession says "This we believe" as a hearty declaration to the world; for others it comes across as "This you must believe" and is used to rule out heresy or to provide a basis for polemics. [*See* Creeds, *article on* Christian Creeds.]

Protestant Church Polities. As with confession, so with structure, or polity: Protestantism presents a broad spectrum of often mutually incompatible polities. Again, they can be inclusively categorized according to what they negate. They all resist the notion that the Roman papacy is the best, or only, conduit of divine revelation and that the guardianship of the Christian church must rest in the hands of the pope as the vicar or representative of Christ on earth. Beyond that, most Protestant churches have preserved elements of the polity that came with their birth, transformed by exigencies of local, contemporary demands and, in the modern world, adjustments to the managerial and bureaucratic impulse. Yet even in the last and most practical case, the Protestant impulse is to see some legitimation for polity in the Bible and in the experience of the early Christian church.

On one end of this spectrum are churches like the Anglican church or the Lutheran church in Sweden, which insist on apostolic succession in an episcopacy that is of the essence (displays the *esse*) of the church. Elsewhere, as in Methodism and much of Lutheranism, bishops belong to the *bene esse* of the church; they are beneficial for its order but theoretically could be replaced in a different polity. Many Reformed churches rely on synodical or connectional and associational patterns under the rule of presbyters or elders. From the days of the radical reformation in the sixteenth century through various later Baptist and Congregational witnesses into modern times, and especially in burgeoning nonwhite indigenous Protestantism, the authority and even the autonomy of the local congregation is asserted.

Those Protestants at the "catholic" end of the spectrum, who regard bishops as of the *esse* of the church, have been least ready to see their polity as negotiable in an ecumenical age. Presbyterian, synodical, and congregational bodies, while emphatically cherishing and defending their polities, have shown more signs of flexibility. A safe generalization suggests that even Baptist and Congregationalist groups, who find biblical rootage for congregationalism, have adopted enough bureaucratic instruments that they have functional polities that transcend mere congregationalism. Yet they would find it a part of their Protestantism to be suspicious of bishops.

Civil Government. Alongside church confession and internal polity has been the issue of the authority of the church or religious realm in or alongside the state or governmental and civil realms. Here one can speak of a long trend, based on Protestant latencies, to move from church establishment toward disestablishment and a celebration of voluntarism.

It is historically inaccurate to say, based on the record of American celebration of "separation of church and state" with Protestant concurrence, that Protestantism has always been voluntaristic. It would be more fair to say that the sixteenth-century Reformation carried with it some potential for voluntarism—seeds that broke open, sprouted, and grew from two to four centuries later.

In the late twentieth century, most of the new nations in which nonwhite indigenous Protestantism prospered had undergone experiences of modernization that, whatever else these meant, provided no room for fusion of church and state or an interwoven pattern of religious and civil authority. Similarly, it was on the soil of largely Protestant nations such as the United States that the greatest degree of constitutional separation between the two authorities first occurred. Yet political philosopher Hannah Arendt is correct to chide Protestants for claiming that modern democracy with its religious freedom is simply a Christian invention. Some Christians have found it easy to reach into their repository of options to find impetus for supporting republicanism based on Enlightenment principles and practical support of equity and civil peace whenever pluralism has been strong.

Historical Protestantism in almost all its mainstream and dominant forms first simply carried over authority patterns from medieval Catholicism. In the Church of England, the Presbyterian church in Scotland, the Lutheran churches of Scandinavia, the Lutheran and Reformed churches of Germany, Switzerland, and the Netherlands, and wherever else leaders had the power to do so, they naturally clung to establishment. They simply broke from Roman Catholic establishment to form Protestant versions. Martin Luther supported a "territorial church" with princes as bishops. Elsewhere, monarchy and legislative bodies gave establishment power or privilege to the favored church and forced disabilities on others.

Only the left-wing, or Anabaptist, churches of the first generations were independent of the state, and they tended to be harassed as much by Protestant establishments as by Catholic establishments. Where they became powerful, as did the Puritans from England who founded New England, they reversed themselves and became the new established monopoly church. Even in much later republics, where no form of Protestantism ever came to dominance, Protestants were tempted to reassert power by looking for legal privilege.

Despite all these establishmentarian dimensions, it is also fair to say that Protestantism did contain the seed that helped disestablishment and separation of church and state develop. A religion of the word, Protestantism called for that word to separate people from attachment to the culture as it evoked decision. So the boundaries of the church and the state could not be coextensive, as they aspired then to be in Catholicism. Whatever "the priesthood of all believers," "the right of private judgment," and the call to conscience in biblical interpretation meant theologically, they had as their practical consequence an honoring of individualism and personal profession of faith. Both of these would become confined were there an official and authoritative church.

Another way to describe this individualism is in terms of modern theologian Paul Tillich's famed "protestant principle" of prophetic protest. This principle calls believers to question all structures and institutions, also and especially those of their own state and church. Naturally, Protestants have not found it any easier to do this than have others, since seldom does one wish to give up ease and privilege and to share power voluntarily. Yet, in contrast to much Orthodox and Roman Catholic theology, Protestant theology at least had a legitimating principle for criticizing church structure and its bond with human governmental authority. Protestantism, then, has lived with a heightened dialectic. On the one hand, it called for support of government, in the terms of Paul's biblical letter to the Romans, chapter 13, as God's instrument. On the other hand, it was critical, along the lines of *Revelation* 13, of civil and ecclesiastical government as being especially subtle and potent concentrations of power, symbols, and capacities for self-idolization and the oppression of others. [*See* Church and State.]

Personal Experience as Authority. A word should be said about personal experience as authority in Protestantism. From the first its "spiritualists," "mystics," and "enthusiasts," who claimed that God spoke directly to and through them, have been both recognized and under suspicion. Those who carry these claims to extremes, as did many of the Quakers, or Friends, the seventeenth-century Puritan sect, and some modern Pentecostals, know that they are "on the margin," out of step with mainstream Protestantism. Their own protests and the way the rest of Protestantism unites against them reveal this.

At the same time, few Protestants have been willing to resist going further than Orthodox and Catholic teachers in granting much authority to individual assent in the grasp of faith. Calvin spoke of the inner testimony of the Holy Spirit in the heart and mind of the believer who hears the word of God or reads the Bible. Luther's possibly apocryphal cry at the Diet of Worms in 1521, a cry against emperor and pope, state and church, "Here I stand!" has acquired mythical dimensions as an act of Protestant heroism. There is always at least the theoretical possibility that the individual may be right and the church wrong, a possibility that both nagged and inspired Luther and other reformers.

In the end, most Protestantism asks the Christian who claims to have had an experience of God or a direct revelation and a call to individual conscience to subject these claims to the responsibilities of the congregation or church at large. There may be great suspicion by fellow believers of such claims, and the individuals who make them may suffer liabilities and persecution. Yet on the other hand, Protestantism honors "heart religion," insists on heartfelt response to the word and the claims of God upon the mind, and thus it sees experience as an authority alongside the Bible and the church. [*See* Christian Spirituality.]

Protestant Substance. Original or classic Protestantism was more ready to see itself as distinctive in the content of faith than is modern pluralist Protestantism. In the sixteenth century, late medieval Catholicism presented what to Protestant eyes was an egregious violation of God's system of approach to human beings. Catholicism had generated, or degenerated into, a system that progressively depended more and more upon human achievement. Key words were human *merit* or humanly gained *righteousness*. Elaborate schemes, for example, the sale of indulgences to help make up the required number of merits to assure salvation, had been devised. These led to abuses, which contemporary Catholic reformers and later historians have agreed made Protestant revolt plausible.

Protestantism across the board held to generally extreme views of human finitude, limits, "fallenness," and need. Mainstream and marginal reformers alike were not convinced by claims that human beings retained enough of the image of God upon which to build so that their own works or merits would suffice to appease a wrathful God. They exaggerated the way Catholicism had diminished the role of Jesus Christ as giver of a gift or imparter of grace upon the wholly undeserving. Once again Paul Tillich from the twentieth century can be called in as witness to what Protestantism affirmed: that God "accepts the unacceptable." Because of the sacrifice of Jesus Christ, God does not wait for sinners to become acceptable through their efforts.

In the sixteenth century, there were many variations on this theme, and Martin Luther's proclamation of "justification by grace through faith," while at home in all of Protestantism, was not necessarily the chosen formula for all Protestants. Yet all did accent divine initiative, human limits, the gifts of God in Jesus Christ, and the new condition of humanity as a result of divine forgiveness. The variations from the first included some new Protestant ways of propping up the moral quest. Not all were as sure as Luther was that the law of God, as revealed in the Ten Commandments or the Sermon on the Mount, played no positive guiding role in salvation. They often feared "antinomianism" or lawlessness. The grace-proclaimers protected themselves against this by insisting that faith must be active in love, that works must follow grace, that "sanctification" is an inevitable consequence and correlate of "justification."

Where such resorts to human claims and achievements were not part of original Protestantism, they did develop later. An example of this was a revision on Dutch and then English soil in a movement named after one Jacobus Arminius and called Arminianism. This system proclaimed the benevolence of a God who gave humans more capacity for benevolence on their own. In some Unitarianism this teaching became a kind of philosophical or moral system that moved to the edges of Protestantism. In Wesleyan Methodism it remained "evangelical," gospel-centered, but picked up on the themes of sanctification and the quest for perfection. In the latter case, it did not make the sacrifice of Christ or the imparting of grace as a gift unnecessary or even secondary. Somehow, then, Protestants have concentrated on faith and grace in distinctive ways. Modern Catholicism, however, has undergone such a revitalizing of faith in similar approaches to grace that the distinctively Protestant note has become compromised—a trend that most Protestants profess to welcome enthusiastically. Protestantism has considered the church always to be reforming, never reformed; Catholicism and Protestantism alike, many would say, stand in need of being reformed, and from time to time they move past rigid, older identities and formulas. Such moves are not incongruent with the Protestant ethos and spirit.

The Protestant Response to God. To speak of Protestant creeds and a Protestant substance or content does justice to the cognitive dimensions of its faith. At the same time, one can easily exaggerate these elements. In the lives of most people called Protestant, behavioral factors are at least as vivid and more easily grasped, if defined with more difficulty. One can readily consult a dogmatics text to see what Protestants believe or are supposed to believe. It takes more subtle observation, more willingness to risk generalization, to observe their response in practice. [*See* Worship, *article on* Christian Worship, *and* Sacraments.]

Protestantism has honored the rites of passage through life. Few Protestants would call their ordinances "rites of passage," yet most can easily be led to see that their sacraments and ceremonies do relate the individual to cosmos and community in patterns that match those observed on other soil by historians of religion. They may not see themselves classified with "the primitives" with respect to initiation, fertility, or funerary rites, but there are parallels. [*See* Rites of Passage; Initiation; Baptism; Marriage; *and* Funeral Rites.]

Thus, almost all Protestants—Quakers chiefly excepted—see the need for a rite of initiation. With so few exceptions that they do not merit pointing to, this rite is "water baptism," something shared with the rest of Christianity. Most Protestants retained infant baptism, as either an instrument of grace (as in Lutheranism) or an expression of covenantal life (as in most of Reformed Protestantism). Yet Protestants, when called to reflect, also resisted what they saw to be Catholic notions of *ex opere operato,* which Protestants regarded as a "magical" application of human elements in sacramental life. This left those who baptized infants with the burden of showing how faith can be active among children who can have no rational conception of what is going on. How to explain the decision that was still called for in response to gifts of grace in faith, or the expectation that some disciplined life must follow?

Many mainstream Protestants compensated by accenting reaffirmation of baptism in some version of a rite of confirmation. Others saw each act of repentance and each day's conscious Christian affirmation as a new death of "the old Adam" and a "being born again" as a new being in Christ. These ideas have held the imagination of millions and made it possible for the rite of initiation to occur very early in human life.

At the same time, the logic of Protestantism and the impulse to connect rites of initiation with conscious response to the word of God led many Protestant branches to grow restless about infant baptism and to move closer to locating initiation in or after adolescence, as so many other religions have it. This meant a further move from seeing water baptism as an instrument of grace to seeing it as a human response based on decision. The new evangelizers or converters, then, called for a decision that issued in repentance and faith and then initiation. "Adult baptism" as a sign of response, usually dramatized in baptism by immersion, better exemplified the sense of ordeal and the passage across a "liminal" or threshold stage to new community. As a result, whole church bodies became "Baptist," and the baptist forms of Protestantism came to prevail progressively in the modern world, where the demand for choice and identity grew more intense. Most of fast-growing nonwhite indigenous Protestantism stressed this form of passage.

Marriage, regarded on Orthodox and Roman Catholic soil as a sacrament with an imparting of grace, distinctively stopped being that on most Protestant soil. The reformers tended to regard it as essentially a civil act, with the church serving merely as an agent to bless the couple and to hear their vows. The church was the custodian and record-keeper of the state's work until the modern secular state took over the recording functions. One could, at least in theory, be validly married without the blessing of the church and clergy. In practice, however, the impulse of people to see their acts of bonding and fertility sacralized has won out. On most Protestant soil, whatever the theology of the marriage ceremony and act, people have seen to the development of elaborate churchly rites at times of nuptials. Yet it is distinctively Protestant to prevent notions of grace-giving or sacramental character from developing in most places.

Protestantism has not encouraged distinctive funeral traditions, but almost everywhere its churches have been participants in memorial or mourning rites. Again there occurred the negation of the Catholic notion that a sacrament was involved at the point of passage to a life to come. Some Protestants use oils for symbolic purposes associated with prayer for healing but assign them no sacramental or instrumental significance. When death comes, there is much reflection upon the event and its meaning. Almost always a cleric holds rites of the word that accent the gospel of what God has done in and for the deceased person and assure that God's love is stronger than death. These rites may occur in the sanctuary of a church or in a mortuary, and burial (whether of a body or ashes) can occur on church cemetery grounds or in public burial places. Here Protestantism offers few consistent words except that we see the life of the believer wrapped up in divine beneficence despite human frailty.

Alongside baptism, then, the only act seen as sacramental in the vast majority of Protestantism is the sacred meal. Such meals are common in religions, and Protestants often have failed to see theirs in a larger context. Yet they have almost unanimously—the Salvation Army and the Quakers being the nearly sole exceptions—taken over the Catholic sacrament of this meal and put their stamp on it. For centuries the Mass, in which the laity received bread and the clergy partook of bread and wine, was the repeated event in which Jesus Christ was made really present through priestly act, the word of God, and faith. [*See* Eucharist.]

Lutheranism, as an expression of a conservative Reformation, came closest to keeping the sacramental worldview with its implications for the bread and wine *as* body and blood of Christ. But even Lutheranism rebelled against *ex opere operato* concepts and did not want to see a change in the visible elements, a transubstantiation, of any sort. This could lead to what Lutherans saw to be superstitious or magical reverence. Most other Protestants sided with the Reformed tradition. They did not see the Lord's Supper or Holy Communion as an occasion for seeing God in Christ as present or for regarding Christ as sacramentally experienced in assemblies. Instead they located the Lord's Supper in a system of grace as a human response, to which people brought their faith and their intentions in response to a command of God.

Whatever their doctrinal attitude toward the rite, these Protestants took the meal seriously. For example, the nineteenth-century Protestant movements associated with the Disciples of Christ, which were attempts to restore primitive Christianity, rejected Catholic and Lutheran sacramental views. Yet, more than most Protestants, they kept the frequent, indeed weekly, practice of sharing the sacred meal, which usually takes place during the formal Sunday observance of congregations, although usually with less frequency than in the sacramental and Catholic churches. Communicants receive both bread and wine (or, in some temperance-minded bodies, unfermented grape juice) from a central table, either at that table or in the pew. The event occurs in a spirit of great solemnity, after there have been preaching and examination of hearts.

The Role of the Word. While baptism and the Lord's Supper as sacraments, and marriage, confirmation, and funeral rites as practices, receive much attention, Protestantism is supremely a religion of the word. By this most believers mean not simply the word of the Bible but the *logos* of God, the expression of God. God creates the universe by a word, pronounces sinners forgiven by a word, speaks the word to heal them, builds community through the word.

This has necessarily meant dissemination of the word. Protestantism was born early in the age of Johann Gutenberg during a revolution in printing that made literacy necessary and the spread of words possible. Some modern critics have seen Protestantism as so identified with Gutenberg's invention of movable type and a great impulse to use it that they predict its demise as print gives way to the competition from electronic and visual disseminations. However, Protestantism also makes much of the oral word and sees voice as a summons for belief. Its leaders have long quoted the Pauline notion that "faith comes by hearing" and hearing by the word of God. This has meant that most Protestant revitalizations have occurred as theologies of the word or, for the people, as enhanced preaching.

Protestantism came on the scene after the great tradition of Catholic preaching was over, and there was little new attention being given to homiletics. For Protestants, the preached word or sermon, expounding the word and applying it to the needs of people in a new day, became a challenge to the Mass as the focal act of worship. This vast majority of Protestants measure the effectiveness of worship by reference to the preaching. It is the scriptural word that gives power to baptism and the Lord's Supper, whether as instruments of grace or as human response. The word shapes prayer; people use the word in teaching and conversation. In times of crisis, it is the word that inspires intercessory prayer. Most Protestant healing involves no herbs, potions, or exercises—only spiritual direction under the word. There are as many theories about why faith comes from hearing and believing the word as there have been theologies, Protestant bodies, or movements and ages in Protestantism. Given the complexity of human psychology, the variety of social contexts, and the pluralism of philosophical options, it is difficult to picture a final definition. Despite the lack of a unitary position on the power of the word, Protestants are united in believing that somehow theirs is a religion of the word.

Protestant Worship. In describing baptism (whether sprinkling of infants or immersion of adults), the Lord's Supper, and the act of preaching and the uses of the word, the outlines of Protestant worship become generally clear. To these should be added that Protestants characteristically have gathered for worship in buildings set aside for that purpose. While they believe that the gathered community may effectively baptize, eat and drink, hear and pray under the sky or in secular buildings, they have had an impulse to set aside and consecrate a sacred space, which symbolically, not actually, becomes a house of God.

The building may be of almost any architectural style. Original Protestant churches tended to be slightly stripped-down Catholic churches that had been taken over by Protestants. In general, the concept of being "stripped down" is appropriate; when Protestants build churches, they tend to be somewhat simpler than Orthodox or Catholic churches. Rejecting icons and minimizing the sacral role of statues and painting, Protestants have tended to use pictorial art for purposes of teaching, reminder, or inspiration. This approach has led to direct and simple expressions, with the exception of a very few periods in which Protestants did revert to ornate Gothic expressions. [*See* Basilica, Cathedral, and Church *and* Iconography, *article on* Christian Iconography.]

The sacred space usually accents a place for preaching, a baptismal font or pool, and a table or altar for the Lord's Supper. Around these the people gather, in pews or on chairs. The gathering occurs to recognize the presence of God, to follow divine commands to congregate for purposes of praise, to build the morale of the group for purposes outside the sanctuary, and to celebrate the seasons of the church year, the events of the week, and the passages of life.

With few exceptions, Protestantism is also a singing religion. It took the act of praising in song, which had become largely a preserve of clergy and choir, and enlarged it to include the congregation. There may be chorally apathetic Protestantism, but in practice Protestants honor the word of God in song. Most of their revivals—Luther's and Charles Wesley's are but two examples—have been promoted through distinctive song.

Except in Seventh-day Adventism, Protestant worship almost always occurs on Sunday, the Lord's Day, the Day of Resurrection, although believers are urged to worship at any time or place. Most Protestants observe the inherited Catholic church year but have purged it of many of its occasions. That is, they annually follow the life of Christ from Advent and Christmas, with its birth rites, through another season of repentance and preparation, Lent, on the way to a climax at Good Friday and Easter weekend, and then a festival of the Holy Spirit at Pentecost. [*See* Christian Liturgical Year.] The more Puritan forms of Protestantism, however, saw something "papist" in these seasonal observances and did away with almost all of them, sometimes including Christmas itself. The rest of Protestantism, which kept the church year of observances, also honored biblical saints like Paul and John on special days but rejected most postbiblical saints. It was believed that honor directed to them distracted from worship of God in Christ. In many places a new church year tied to national and cultural events has emerged. Thus in the United States many observe a Thanksgiving Day, Mother's Day and Father's Day, Stewardship Sunday, Lay Sunday, and the like. The impulse to ritualize life is strong even on the purging, purifying, and simplifying soil of Protestantism.

The Way of Life. How, it may be asked, can one speak of a Protestant way of life when the ways are so varied? What do a wealthy American high church Anglican executive, a Latin American Pentecostal, and a black under oppression in South Africa have in common as a "way of life"? It would be foolish to impose a single ideal, force a straitjacket, or overgeneralize a vision, but something can and must be said about Protestant styles of behavior. Sometimes activities are so obvious that no one bothers to note them, and this is the case with some Protestant commonalities.

First, most overlooked and yet obvious on a second glance, is the widespread assumption that the life of grace to which Protestants witness by faith must issue in some form of personal ethic. This seems unremarkable, but by no means have all religions of the world made much of this moral notion. Many have centered themselves more on matters of rites and mores than on matters of conscience and morals. Protestantism has almost always been stereotyped as moralistic in intention and outlook. Catholic Christians have dismissed some of their own heresies, such as Jansenism, as being like "grim Calvinism" or dour Protestantism. Others have rebelled against the Protestant impulse to reform the world, to rearrange by law or example or injunction the lives of others, or to convert the experience of grace into severe new legalisms. While these rejections of Protestantism may be based on exaggerations or partial misperceptions, there is enough consistency in Protestantism to warrant elaboration of the theme.

Catholic Christianity has stressed personal ethics and produced people of impressive moral conviction and achievement. Yet often it has implied that participation in the Mass and the act of having a soul saved are paramount, and that the faithful as a group are the moral agents. Protestantism, through its tendency toward individualism, expects more of an internalization and personal application of the message of the church.

Protestantism has often been impelled to be critical of the sexual mores of its day and to ask its people for restraint in expressions of sexuality. Partly under the impetus of sixteenth-century reformers who, as clerics, had been celibate but who later married, established families, and lived in "parsonages," Protestants chose to affirm sexuality in familial contexts. Scorning monasticism most of the time, and speaking of the vocation to propagate where that was possible, Protestants became champions of the family. Their critics see Protestantism as being so familial that it tends to adopt the norms of bourgeois families wherever these appear, without sorting out what is temporary cultural expression from what is integral to the faith or biblically based. Sometimes, despite Protestant individualism, the individual who is not vividly involved in family life has felt left out by the norms of preaching and teaching that see the family as a basic unit of revelation, nurture, and discipline.

It is not easy to strain all the Protestant impulses for personal ethics and morals into a single mold. In general, Protestantism has called not just for applying the faith within the Christian community but for taking it into the world as well. The line between the sacred and the secular calling and sphere was supposed to be a fine one, whether it turned out to be so in practice or not. Some Protestant ethics have been legalistic, a somber response to the commands of God in the divine law. Yet more frequently reformers have insisted that Protestantism is an issuing of faith in forms of love that seek to serve as conduits of God's *agapē*, which is a spontaneous, unmotivated love. This understanding, it has been claimed, is more liberating than those Catholic forms that stress almsgiving or doing good to obtain merit and thus would be partly self-serving. Similarly, Protestant ethicists have often criticized Catholics for using models of human desire and friendship or natural love, not the *agapē* that exemplifies the initiative of divine love.

Protestant response often generates an ethic of attention to the life of the church. Lacking the appeal of the sacramental presence of Christ in the reserved communion Host, or bread, or the understanding that something happens uniquely in the sanctuary, Protestants have often had to work strenuously to provide reasons for attending worship regularly. "Go to church" becomes a large part of the ethic, and the quality of Christian life is often measured by faithfulness in participation on church premises.

Public Life. As for social ethics, Protestantism includes several strains. There has been a denial of the world of a sort that, in H. Richard Niebuhr's terms, pits Christ *against* culture or sees Christ to be too pure and lofty to be stained in society and thus sees Christ *above* culture. There have been constant temptations for Protestantism, where it prevails, simply to baptize the surrounding culture in forms of a Christ *of* culture. Then all lines between the Christian and the world on some terms or other are obscured.

Two other types have tended to dominate wherever Protestants have been reflective and self-critical. One of these would be called by observers and critics a form that keeps transforming culture with a millennial or utopian tinge. In this version, Protestants pick up biblical witness to the always-coming kingdom of God. Proclaiming this coming kingdom involves a prophetic denouncing of the world as it is, the vision of a better world, and some sort of program for reaching it. This transforming strain of Protestantism tends to prevail in times when progressivism is plausible in the culture and calls forth a buoyant, activistic kind of response. On its soil there have been genuine efforts to change the structures of society, to promote more justice. Many Reformed and especially Puritan and later moderate evangelicalisms have been dedicated to such models.

This form of approach tends to call forth common action by the church. Either through movements, demonstrations, or the issuance of teaching and prophetic proclamations, church bodies ask for corporate wrestling with issues. The church as church takes some stand in society and tries to work for change that will make the empirical world look like or realize some dimension of life in the kingdom of God. Then the accent on personal morality is not secondary, but it becomes specialized. It works in some aspects of life but not in others.

The other main Protestant stream also asks for engagement with culture, but it is more individualistic and relies less on progressivist models. Although the kingdom of God may be wholly eschatological, coming or to come only after human history as now known is exhausted, the individual Christian is not relieved of responsibilities of citizenship. But he or she is now a more isolated representative who does not wait for and may not agree with joint Christian efforts. In this school there is more accent on the perduring element of the demonic in human history. People are seen as more intransigent, as less malleable to change. The task of the church is more otherworldly, and salvation is seen in individualistic and spiritualizing terms. There are instincts to be more conservative, to support the status quo at its best, to honor the government and the authorities or powers that be as ordained of God.

In either case, Protestantism has been culturally productive. Whether on corporate or individual terms, this movement, in the eyes of many social thinkers, including Max Weber, took advantage of new economic opportunities that arose during and after the Reformation era in western Europe and Anglo-America. By turning its ascetic and self-denying powers from the search for salvation, as in the monastery, to the search for productive life in the secular setting, Protestants produced new motives and energies. They were ready to work hard and long. They wanted to be stewards of the earth and its resources. They would not waste and wished to save. Consequently, as they took risks with capital and invested, they developed a "Protestant ethic," which spread wherever Protestantism did.

More recent sociologists have questioned Weber's thesis. There seems to have been capitalism, as in fifteenth-century Venice, before there were Protestants. There is an equivalent to the Protestant ethic in nations such as Japan, where there have never been many Protestants. Motivations for capitalist venture were too broad to be clustered under a "this-worldly ascetic" motif. Yet the Protestants, for the most part, in Europe and now in nonwhite indigenous circles, have been great promoters of individual work and responsibility. The use of leisure, the concept of siesta and fiesta, is not dealt with so consistently where Protestants dominate. They would live out a divine-human drama in the workaday world, one that calls for them to be productive and busy.

Theology. Only with broadest brush strokes need one show how Protestantism issues in a variety of thought patterns. It goes almost without saying that as a religion of the word it must connect with other patterns of word use, other systems of thought. While it could inherit much of Catholic theology and convert it to embody the new or renewed Protestant concepts, Protestantism also placed on individuals more burden for formulation than did Catholicism, where more was inherited through the tradition. Since Protestantism also induced variety and pluralism, it became important for each group or profound thinker to formulate what was special about his or her locale, context, public, and program. The freedom that Protestantism professed to bring was a mandate and a license to be enterprising in theological form-building.

By contrast, in reaction to the Reformation, Roman Catholicism through the Council of Trent tended to freeze theological development. Experiment was downgraded, and innovation was a subject that induced suspicion. The theologian became the reformulator, the custodian of assured truths. Developmental or modernist thought was formally condemned, and the papacy came to elevate Thomistic scholasticism to privileged—indeed, virtually monopolistic—status. Protestantism also engendered scholasticisms and orthodoxies but was unable to suppress the experimental tendencies it had opened up.

Protestant theology saw the Bible as its basic set of texts and, often, the only norm and source for theology. Many thinkers, with their churches, were ready also to accept the main themes and modes of early Christian orthodoxy from the creed-making period. To these they added the statements of faith from the first or second generation of each Protestant expression. Finally, there was room for individual witness and ingenuity dependent upon available philosophy and urgent cultural necessity. Protestantism was born not in episcopal residences or monasteries but, for the most part, in universities and academies. This meant that the new formulators were uncommonly exposed to rival and alien—but also sometimes alluring—patterns of thought.

Protestant thought has moved through a number of epochs. The first generation tended to be open, explosive, rich in dialectic, ready for ambiguity, indulgent with paradox. A second period led to reaction and scholastic impulses to nail everything down, to be secure and neat, to defend propositions of faith. Later, in most of the older Protestantism, new movements of the heart, new pietisms, forced changes in thought patterns. These were quickly supplanted by the rationalisms of the Enlightenment, which colored Protestantism almost everywhere. Then came a crisis of historical consciousness, a readiness to see everything in the Christian scheme colored by accident and contingency in history. In the twentieth century, among the explosion of options, there has been some embrace of existentialist and personalist outlooks. To the non-Protestant Christian, this has all meant individualist irresponsibility. To the churched forms of Protestantism it has been both a challenge and a threat, as theologians applied Protestant witness in varied thought patterns in changing cultures. In nonwhite indigenous Protestantisms new patterns are emerging. [*See* Theology, *article on* Christian Theology.]

Protestant Expression. That Protestants chose preaching, hymnody, architecture, and the like for cultural expression and economics or reform for social expression can be inferred from preceding passages. In general, Protestantism has been less fertile than Catholic Christianity in affirming the literary and artistic worlds. Sometimes this has resulted from a certain suspicion about the validity of the earthly venture for the sake of salvation. Tillich balanced his "protestant principle" with "Catholic substance," the ability to relish and invest in the sights and sounds of human endeavor, which was often lacking in Protestantism. Sometimes moralism has prevented Protestants from literary expression, since literature often pushes at the edges of moral convention. The tinge of iconoclasm in much of Protestantism has kept it from being free for artistic expression.

All this has meant that Protestantism seemed most productive in the field of music, perhaps because the kinetic character of music seemed to be congruent with a word-centered, iconoclastic tradition. One thinks here of the musical poets of Protestantism, most notably the composer Johann Sebastian Bach. In literature there have been John Milton and John Bunyan, but in the contemporary world Protestantism has seldom helped produce anything approaching modern classics. In the visual arts geniuses like Lucas Cranach or, supremely, Rembrandt, have given expression to their evangelical sympathies and Protestant outlook. But this artistic tradition is no match for Catholic versions. The Protestant movement, then, has concentrated on other fields and still awaits substantial aesthetic articulation. [*See* Music, *article on* Religious Music in the West; Poetry, *article on* Christian Poetry; *and* Literature, *article on* Religious Dimensions of Modern Literature.]

The Future. Protestantism has been in decline in its heartland, western Europe and the British Isles. The old establishments there survive, but languidly, and churches are nearly empty in much of secular western Europe. In North America the picture is more complex, varied, and promising. While mainstream Protestantism as an heir of establishment has been languishing, revitalized conservative movements, more worldly than their antecedents, prosper. The greatest growth is in nonwhite indigenous Protestantism, especially in sub-Saharan Africa. Following present trends in the Southern Hemisphere, Christianity, and Protestantism with it, is on the way toward becoming numerically dominant. What it will choose to retain from the missionary forms of Protestantism and where it will choose to innovate are not yet determined. As the two clusters come together, the result will help determine the future of Protestantism wherever that form of Christianity propagates itself.

[*For discussion of the dispersion of Protestantism, see regional surveys under* Christianity. *For discussion of particular manifestations of Protestantism, see* Anabaptism; Anglicanism; Baptist Churches; Christian Science; Hutterian Brethren; Lutheranism; Mennonites; Methodist Churches; Moravians; Mormonism; Pietism; Presbyterianism, Reformed; Puritanism; Quakers; Salvation Army; Seventh-day Adventism; Shakers; *and* Unitarian Universalist Association. *See also* Christian Social Movements; Modernism, *article on* Christian Modernism; Neoorthodoxy; Evangelical and Fundamental Christianity; Pentecostal and Charismatic Christianity; *and* Ecumenical Movement.]

BIBLIOGRAPHY

One of the more ambitious histories of Protestantism is Émile G. Léonard's *Historie générale du protestantisme,* 3 vols. (Paris, 1961–1964), translated as *A History of Protestantism* (London, 1965–1968). Most Protestant history is simply incorporated as half of the latter third of general church histories, such as Kenneth Scott Latourette's *A History of Christianity* (New York, 1953). The most extensive easily accessible bibliography is in my own *Protestantism* (New York, 1972). One way to approach Protestantism is through its root experience in the Reformation era; on the thought of the period, see Wilhelm Pauck's *The Heritage of the Reformation,* rev. ed. (Oxford, 1968); Harold J. Grimm's *The Reformation Era, 1500–1650,* 2d ed. (New York, 1973), is especially useful for its bibliographies.

Louis Bouyer's *The Spirit and Forms of Protestantism* (London, 1956) is an informed view by a Calvinist turned Catholic. Einar Molland's *Christendom: The Christian Churches, Their Doctrines, Constitutional Forms, and Ways of Worship* (New York, 1959) is especially interesting for its comparison between Protestant and other forms of Christianity. Few scholars have attempted to discern the genius of Protestantism as a whole, but there are good reasons to consult an imaginative attempt by Robert McAfee Brown, *The Spirit of Protestantism* (Oxford, 1961), or George W. Forell's *The Protestant Faith* (Englewood Cliffs, N.J., 1960); for a European view, see Karl Heim's *The Nature of Protestantism* (Philadelphia, 1963). John B. Cobb, Jr., in *Varieties of Protestantism* (Philadelphia, 1960), treats modern theology. There is a lively treatment of the historical development in John Dillenberger and Claude Welch's *Protestant Christianity Interpreted through Its Development* (New York, 1954).

MARTIN E. MARTY

PROVIDENCE. *See* Chance; Fate; Free Will and Predestination; *and* History.

PRZYLUSKI, JEAN (1885–1944), Buddhologist. Although less well known than Sylvain Lévi and Louis de La Vallée Poussin, Przyluski was one of the most productive scholars belonging to the so-called Franco-Belgian school of Buddhology. Polish by birth, Przyluski enjoyed an energetic publishing career that spanned several decades and produced nearly fifty major publications.

If there is to be found an enduring theme in the writings of Przyluski, it is his abiding interest in unraveling several of the mysteries of early Indian Buddhist history. In this regard, he is perhaps best remembered for his masterful *Le Concile de Rājagṛha.* Utilizing his formidable philological skills, Przyluski presented a tabulation of the accounts of this important Buddhist council as found in the records of various early Indian Buddhist sects. Published in Paris between 1926 and 1928, this work was preceded by major articles on early Buddhist India ("Le nord-ouest de l'Inde dans le Vinaya des Mūlasarvāstivādins et les textes apparentés," *Journal asiatique,* 1914), Buddha's *parinirvāṇa* ("Le Parinirvāṇa et les funérailles du Bouddha," *Journal asiatique,* 1918–1919), and a study of Aśoka *(La légende de l'empereur Aśoka,* 1923). This latter text is critically important for its pioneering work on the *Aśokāvadāna* in Indian and Chinese texts. Przyluski was also the editor of the series "Buddhica: Documents et travaux pour l'étude du bouddhisme," which began publication in 1925.

Despite his lifelong interest in Buddhism, Przyluski published articles on a wide variety of Indological topics, including totemism, mythology, and symbolism and extending to such areas as Tantric Buddhism in Bali and Iranian influences on Indian religion. His studies remain valid today; indeed, it is virtually impossible for a contemporary reader to begin any serious research on early Indian Buddhist topics without a thorough grounding in the works of Przyluski. His are basic contributions to modern scholarship, for they have inspired numerous ancillary studies that have gradually begun to dispel the haze surrounding the early Indian Buddhist community.

BIBLIOGRAPHY

Appreciative notices of Przyluski's life and work appear in *Revue archéologique* 35 (January 1950): 101–102 and in *Isis* 41 (1950): 302. For a complete bibliography of his works, see A. W. Macdonald and Marcel Lalou's *L'œuvre de Jean Przyluski* (Paris, 1970).

CHARLES S. PREBISH

PSALMS are ancient Hebrew songs addressed to or invoking the deity; the Hebrew Bible, or the Old Testament in the Christian scriptures, includes a book of 150 of these religious songs. In ancient and later Jewish tradition, the book is known in Hebrew as *Tehillim* ("Praises"), although only one of the songs (Psalm 145) is so designated within the biblical text. The English title *Psalms* derives from the Greek rendering of the Hebrew *mizmor* (a song accompanied by string plucking), a label that introduces fifty-seven of the Hebrew psalms. In Christian circles, the *Book of Psalms* is often referred to as the Psalter, a name taken from the psaltery, a stringed instrument that accompanied the singing of many of the psalms. Use of the word *psalter* also implies that the *Book of Psalms* has been used as a hymnal, an official collection of religious songs, since ancient times.

In the Jewish canon, *Psalms* is the first book in the third section of the Hebrew Bible, the Writings. In the Christian canon, *Psalms* appears among the so-called wisdom books, between *Job* and *Proverbs*.

Apart from the canonical psalms, which seem to have been accorded official status in the second century BCE, we have many other ancient Hebrew songs of the psalm type. Within the Hebrew Bible are the song of triumph in *Exodus* (15:1–18), the prayer of Hannah in *1 Samuel* (2:1–10), the song of thanksgiving in *2 Samuel* 22 (which is nearly identical with Psalm 18), the prayer of Hezekiah in *Isaiah* (38:10–20), the thanksgiving psalm in *Jonah* (2:3–10), and the prayer of *Habakkuk*. The *Psalms of Solomon* in the Pseudepigrapha, dated to the first century BCE, comprises eighteen hymns, personal pleas for salvation in particular, which resemble certain biblical psalms. Although only versions in Greek and Syriac are extant, the pseudepigraphical psalms clearly reflect Hebrew originals.

In addition, seven noncanonical psalms have been recovered among the Dead Sea Scrolls. They appear interspersed with a number of canonical psalms in the large manuscript of psalms from Qumran cave 11. Of these seven, one is included as Psalm 151 in the Septuagint (the ancient Greek translation of the Hebrew Bible), one is contained in the apocryphal *Book of Ben Sira*, and two have been preserved in ancient translations. A fifth appears in another Dead Sea Scroll, so that only two of the seven compositions are "new." As many as four Dead Sea psalters, dating from no later than the first century CE, include noncanonical psalms; this suggests that ancient hymnals were not restricted to the biblical *Book of Psalms*. A lengthy Dead Sea composition, the *Hodayot* (Songs of Praise and Thanksgiving), contained over forty hymns patterned after and drawing phrases from the *Book of Psalms*. The canonical psalms, then, served as models for ancient Jewish hymnody. At least two psalms within the New Testament, the Magnificat of Mary (*Lk.* 1:46–55) and the Benedictus of Zechariah (*Lk.* 1:68–79), similarly drew upon and emulated canonical prototypes.

Formation of the Psalter. In its canonical form, *Psalms* comprises five sections or "books": Psalms 1–41, 42–72, 73–89, 90–106, and 107–150. The first four books end with a doxology, or call to praise the Lord, and the fifth ends with an entire psalm (Psalm 150) that constitutes a doxology. It has been noted that books 1, 4, and 5 tend to employ the unvocalized personal name of God in the Hebrew Bible, YHVH (traditionally and in this article rendered as 'the Lord'), while books 2 and 3 refer to God as Elohim, suggesting that divergent theological traditions, or schools, may have compiled the different books.

There are a number of indications that the psalms had formerly been organized differently. Psalm 135 concludes with a doxology, and Psalm 72 ends with an attribution to a special collection of "David." These two, then, may have once designated the close of earlier collections. A number of psalms are attributed in their titles or openings to various types or collections: the psalms of David (*Ps.* 3–9, 11–32, 34–41, 51–65, 68–70, 86, 101, 103, 108–110, 124, 133, 138–145—a total of seventy-two); the psalms of the sons of Koraḥ (*Ps.* 42, 44–49, 84, 85, 87, 88); the psalms of Asaph (*Ps.* 50, 73–83); the psalms of *ma'alot*, usually rendered "ascents" (*Ps.* 120–134); and the "halleluyah" psalms (*Ps.* 104–106, 111–113, 115–117, 135, 146–150). Because psalms of similar attribution generally occur in blocks, because very similar psalms appear in more than one collection (*Ps.* 14 and 53; parts of 40 and 70; 57 + 60 and 108), and because the attributions seem to refer to liturgical compilations (Koraḥ and Asaph were eponymous names of priestly guilds) or functions ("ascents" and "halleluyah" psalms), it is likely that the canonical books were formed from earlier groups of psalms, with psalms from one group interpolated into sets of psalms from other groups.

Evidence from the Dead Sea psalters suggests that books 1 and 2 were standardized by the second century BCE but that the order of psalms in the last three books remained flexible as late as the first century CE. At that time, the canonical Psalter was fixed within the Jewish community of ancient Judaea.

Attribution of the Psalms. Most psalms bear headings that serve either to attribute them to certain authors or collections (David, Koraḥ, Asaph, Moses, Solomon), to describe their type (accompanied song, chant, prayer), to prescribe their liturgical use (Psalm 92 is assigned for Sabbath worship), or to direct their musical performance.

Nearly half the canonical psalms are attributed to

David, king of the Israelite empire in the tenth century BCE. Few of the psalms, however, are dated by scholars to so early a period. The attributions to David are generally held to stem from a later attempt to enhance the authority of the psalms by ascribing their origin to Israel's most famed singer and psalmist, David. David is represented as a musician in *1 Samuel* 16, and within the narrative of *2 Samuel* he is credited with three songs: an elegy for Saul and Jonathan (*2 Sm.* 1:17–27), a psalm of thanksgiving for his having been delivered from enemies (*2 Sm.* 22), and a reflection on the covenant between YHVH and David (*2 Sm.* 23:1–7). Some of the psalm headings place the following psalm in a specific situation in the life of David. For example, Psalm 34 begins: "Of David, when he feigned madness before Abimelech, and he chased him out, and he went." (This ascription is clearly inauthentic, however, for it was Achish of Gath, not Abimelech, who chased out David; see *1 Sm.* 21:10–16.) The attribution of psalms to David manifests a later interest; in fact, the ancient Greek translation inserts references to the life of David where the Hebrew has none.

Large groups of psalms are attributed to Koraḥ and Asaph. According to *Chronicles*, *Ezra*, and *Nehemiah*, they were the ancestral heads of the priestly functionaries in the Second Temple in Jerusalem (c. 515 BCE–70 CE), the Levites. *Chronicles* further credits David with establishing the Levitical functions in the Temple (see *1 Chr.* 15–16). It would seem, then, that the attributions to David, Koraḥ, and Asaph refer historically to collections of psalms among Second Temple personnel. The fact that *1 Chronicles* 16 incorporates a psalm virtually identical with Psalm 105 supports this conclusion.

Beginning in the second century BCE with the apocryphal *2 Maccabees* (2:13), Christian and Jewish sources (e.g., *Heb.* 4:7; B.T., *B.B.* 146) attribute the entire *Book of Psalms* to David. A noncanonical composition toward the end of the large Psalms Scroll from Qumran cave 11 credits David not only with the 150 canonical psalms, but with a total of 4,050 (150×3^3) psalms and songs. Jewish and early Christian tradition ascribe all the laws to the classic biblical lawgiver, Moses; the wisdom books, *Proverbs*, *Ecclesiastes*, and *Song of Songs*, to Solomon, a king celebrated for his sagacity; and, accordingly, the sacred songs to David. Although certain Christian and Jewish savants in the Middle Ages questioned the Davidic authorship of all the psalms, it was not until the writing of Barukh Spinoza in the seventeenth century and that of critical scholars in the nineteenth century that David was no longer held to have composed even those psalms ascribed to him in the Bible. Fundamentalists continue to believe in the Davidic authorship.

Date and Provenance of the Psalms. Although modern scholarship has abandoned the belief that David authored all the psalms, their date and provenance has been variously determined. Nineteenth-century scholars tended to date the composition of the psalms to the period in which their use was first explicitly attested, following the return of Judahites from the Babylonian exile in the fifth century BCE and later. Similarities between the psalms and the prophetic literature were explained as the influence of the prophets on the psalmists. A number of factors have led twentieth-century scholars to conceive earlier datings. One was the discovery of hymns and prayers from ancient Egypt, Hatti (in Asia Minor), and Mesopotamia, which often display themes, motifs, and formulas similar to those of the biblical psalms. Likewise, the recovery of Ugaritic (northern Canaanite) texts shows that they exhibit a language and prosodic style similar to that of the psalms. Since psalmody is attested in the ancient Near East as early as the third millennium BCE, there is no reason to think Israel did not develop it until a late stage in its history. A second factor is thematic. If most psalms are postexilic or from the period of the Second Temple, it is surprising that they are not preoccupied with the return from the exile and the restoration of a Davidic king. A third factor is cultic or liturgical. If, as most scholars believe, many psalms functioned in the Temple cult, it is likely that a large number had already served such a function in the First, preexilic, Temple (see further below).

Because the psalms contain within them few historical references, the most scientific method for establishing the date and provenance of the individual psalms is linguistic. Psalms, like liturgical literature generally, tend to archaize. Even taking this into account, texts such as Psalms 18, 29, 68, 132, and others appear, by dint of their somewhat primitive content, affinities to Canaanite literature, and outmoded linguistic features, not merely to archaize but to be old. On the other hand, Psalms 103, 117, 119, 124, 125, 133, 144, 145, and, perhaps, others betray distinctively postexilic linguistic characteristics, making their Second Temple dating reasonably certain. Psalm 137 relates directly to the experience of exile, but most others cannot with certainty be dated before or after the sixth-century BCE exile. As regards provenance, as will be suggested below, certain psalms manifest clear origins in the ritual cult, some appear to have been commissioned by the monarchy, and others probably derive from scribal or unofficial circles.

Types of Psalms. Before discussing the ancient and later uses of the psalms, it will be helpful to describe their types. The prosodic form of the psalms, their language, and their motifs are for the most part highly conventional, suggesting they were composed according to typical patterns.

Their predominant form is comprised of parallelism—the formation of couplets and, occasionally, triplets of lines, through the repetition of syntactic structure and/or semantic content. For example, *Psalms* 92:2–3:

> Good it is to give thanks to the Lord,
> and to make song to your name, O one on high:
> To tell in the morning of your devotion,
> and of your faithfulness in the nights.

Several phrases and lines, such as "Give thanks to the Lord, for his devotion is eternal," "Chant to the Lord a new chant," "Do not in your wrath reprove me," "He has saved me from the enemy," and the like, abound in *Psalms*, such that most psalms appear contrived of common vocabulary and images. A number of psalms are arranged by artificial devices such as the alphabetic acrostic (Psalms 25, 34, 119, 145, and, more or less, others).

Many of the most common themes in the psalms also appear in the hymns and prayers of other ancient Near Eastern cultures. Psalm 104, for example, in which the deity's all-encompassing wisdom is compared to the sun and manifested in creation, bears striking similarities to the fourteenth-century BCE Egyptian hymn to Aton (the sun disk) as well as to a Babylonian hymn to Shamash, the sun god. The Israelite victory hymn in *Exodus* 15 shares a number of motifs with the thirteenth-century Egyptian song of the pharaoh Merneptah. Both exalt the deity among the other gods; both describe the submission of other peoples witnessing the triumph. Prayers of Egypt, Hatti, and Mesopotamia praise the gods, as the Hebrew psalms praise YHVH, for protecting and upholding the poor, the feeble, the widow, and the orphan. All fear the god turning away his (or her) compassionate face; all ask undeserved forgiveness for the suppliant's sins; all assert that the righteous will prevail, that evildoers will stumble; all ask vengeance on enemies. As in *Psalms* 27:4, an Egyptian prayer seeks acceptance by the deity, the opportunity to gaze upon the image, or presence, of the god. The Hebrew psalms even share the typical outcry, "How long, O Lord," with Babylonian supplications. Although no ancient Canaanite hymns or prayers have yet been discovered, the biblical psalms attest divine titles, such as "rider of the clouds" (*Ps.* 68:5), and entire verses, such as *Psalms* 92:10 and 145:13, which vary little from mid-second-millennium BCE Canaanite (Ugaritic) lines of epic. Considering these and many other parallels, and the Phoenician locale and archaic Canaanite style of Psalm 29, it would seem that Israelite psalmists drew upon, perhaps even borrowed, common Canaanite material and patterns for their own hymns and prayers.

The conventional nature of so many biblical psalms and their relations to ancient Near Eastern hymnody in general have led scholars to delineate specific types of psalms and to associate those types with specific social or cultic circumstances in which they were presumably used in ancient Israel. In the early twentieth century, Hermann Gunkel isolated five major, as well as some minor, psalm types:

1. *Hymns,* liturgical songs of praise to the deity, sometimes beatifying God's power in nature (e.g., *Ps.* 29, 33, 34, 92, 100, 104, 105, 111, 114, 134–136, 145, 146)
2. *Personal songs of praise or thanksgiving,* similar to hymns but ostensibly offered by individuals (e.g., *Ps.* 18, 30, 32, 34, 41, 56, 116, 118, 138)
3. *Communal laments* (e.g., *Ps.* 28, 86, 106, 115)
4. *Individual laments or supplications* (e.g., *Ps.* 6, 25, 26, 38, 41, 91)
5. *Songs for the king* (e.g., *Ps.* 2, 20, 21, 45, 72, 101, 110, 132)

Several psalms mix different types; Psalm 18, for example, is both a royal song and an individual thanksgiving. Some psalms recount God's redemptive acts in Israelite history in the context of a hymn or other psalm type (e.g., *Ps.* 78, 105, 106, 136). Among the minor psalm types are didactic songs which teach piety and divinely favored conduct (e.g., *Ps.* 1, 19, 37, 49, 73, 112, 119, 127, 128, 133); meditations (e.g., *Ps.* 23, 27, 90); and communal thanksgivings (e.g., *Ps.* 67, 124).

Each of the psalm types exhibits certain characteristic traits. Within the most common type of psalm, the individual supplication, for example, in both the biblical and the extrabiblical specimens we find most of the following features: a description of the suppliant's ailment; a characterization of the suppliant as somehow disadvantaged in society; a plea for divine succor, often accompanied by a vow to the deity; and praise for the deity and/or an expression of trust that the deity will heed the plea. It is also widespread in this type for the suppliant to refer both to a physical distress and to mortal foes, on whom the suppliant seeks retribution. Note, for example, these excerpts from Psalm 6 (vv. 3, 6, 8, and 9):

> Show grace, O Lord, for languishing am I,
> Heal me, O Lord, for my limbs have been trembling. . . .
> For in death there is no mind of you.
> In She'ol [the netherworld] who will praise you? . . .
> My eye from vexation has grown sore,
> It has pined from all my adversaries.
> Turn away from me, all evildoers!
> For the Lord hears my crying voice.

The stereotyped nature of so many psalms suggests they may have been composed to fit into a particular, probably liturgical, function.

The Settings of the Psalms. Some of the psalms cannot readily be associated with any specific historical or cultic setting. This is especially so for didactic and meditative compositions. In many other cases, the content of the psalm suggests a likely usage. Psalm 24, for example, does seem like an appropriate text for a ceremony in which the Ark was conveyed to Jerusalem. Psalm 45 sounds like an ode to be chanted at the wedding of a king. Psalms 114 and 136 pertain to the Exodus from Egypt and would have served well as texts for the spring festival of Pesaḥ (Passover), which celebrates Israelite freedom from Egyptian bondage.

There are a number of reasons for thinking that many, if not most, of the biblical psalms functioned within the daily and special occasional rituals of the Israelite Temple cult. It is likely that the later use of psalms in Jewish and Christian worship continued ancient practice. Ritual literature from ancient Near Eastern societies outside Israel, such as Babylon, prescribe the recitation of prayers and hymns similar to those of the Bible within various cultic ceremonies. One may infer that the biblical psalms served a similar function.

Indeed, references and statements within *Psalms* and elsewhere in the Bible suggest a liturgical usage. This is clear in Second Temple times, as *Ezra* (3:10–11) and *Chronicles* (*1 Chr.* 16:8–36) cite the singing of Psalms 117, 96, 105, and 106. Some psalms speak of chanting psalms in the sanctuary (*Ps.* 11:4, 134:2, 150:1), and several allude to worship in the sanctuary (e.g., *Ps.* 17:15, 18:7, 23:6, 26:8, 27:4). Psalms 66 and 135 display a liturgical nature, and the numerous references to singing and musical accompaniment in *Psalms* bespeak a liturgical usage.

Preexilic biblical texts such as *Isaiah* 30:29 and *Amos* 5:23 link music to worship. Not only do many psalms describe instrumental accompaniment (e.g., *Ps.* 43:4, 71:22, 81:2–4, 92:3, 150:3–5), but several psalm headings also appear to direct the method of chanting or playing the psalm. Several psalms are introduced by the ascription *la-menatseaḥ*, which, on the basis of *1 Chronicles* 15:21, refers to the conductor of stringed instruments in the liturgy. Psalms 57, 58, 59, and 75 were to be chanted to the tune of a popular song, "Destroy Not"; Psalms 45 and 80, to the tune of "Roses"; Psalm 22, to "Gazelle of Dawn"; and Psalm 56, to "Dove of the Distant Terebinths." A number of the headings appear to prescribe the manner of, or instruments for, playing a psalm, although the precise meaning of the terms cannot be defined: *neginot* (stringed instruments?); *sheminit* (on the octave?, eight-stringed instrument?); *ʿalamot* (soprano?); *neḥilot* (reed pipe?); and *gittit* (vintner song?).

Psalms 42–43 (which comprise a single piece) and 107 feature refrains that may well have served as responses for a chorus, and Psalm 136 presents the same phrase after each new line, suggesting a choral or congregational response. The fact that the refrain "Blessed is the Lord and blessed is his name forever and ever" follows each verse of Psalm 145 in the Dead Sea Scroll from cave 11 supports the view that at least some, if not most, of the psalms played a role in the Temple liturgy.

What role they played in First Temple times can only be surmised. It is often assumed that, as in the postexilic period, psalms were chanted in conjunction with the daily cult of animal offerings and on Sabbaths and festivals. Individuals may have recited psalms privately, as *1 Samuel* 2 represents of Hannah and *Jonah* 2 of Jonah. Many psalms are indeed spoken by a first-person singular "I." Such psalms, however, frequently refer to the speaker's enemies as "the nations" (e.g., *Ps.* 44, 60, 66, 74, 89, 94, 102, 118), which suggests that the "I" of these psalms is not an individual but the entire people of Israel. How many psalms served as texts for private prayer is, therefore, unclear.

In general, the psalms deal with broad themes of human anguish and need, the deity's grandeur and pathos, and the virtues and pleasures of piety. Many psalms touch on an array of themes. The nonspecific nature of so many psalms makes them, theoretically, applicable to a variety of occasions without limit to a particular time and place. For this reason, it is difficult, and perhaps inconsistent, to define the historical setting or function of any psalm in narrow fashion. Nevertheless, the presence of striking motifs in various series or groups of psalms has led some scholars to try to find for them a common ancient setting.

A number of psalms (e.g., *Ps.* 47, 93, 95–100) speak of the kingship of the biblical god, YHVH. On the basis of festivals in Egypt (Min) and Babylonia (Akitu) in which the chief god is celebrated for vanquishing the god(s) of chaos and establishing order and is then enthroned and acclaimed as king, Sigmund Mowinckel and other twentieth-century scholars have hypothesized that ancient Israel acclaimed YHVH as king at the fall New Year, on Sukkot (Tabernacles, Feast of Booths). As many as forty psalms have been presumed to have been recited as part of this "enthronement" festival. During this festival, the primeval triumph of YHVH over the forces of chaos and his creation of the world would be recounted, YHVH would be declared king, his defeat of Israel's historical enemies would be anticipated, and he would be ensconced in his temple and adulated. Psalm 103, for example, ends with an exaltation of YHVH as king over all (v. 19), and it is followed by Psalm 104, which beatifies YHVH's majestic dominion over the entire world of nature. It has been held that such juxtapositions of theme are appropriate to an enthronement festival.

The hypothesis that ancient Israel had a fall New Year celebration of YHVH's kingship may be supported by the fact that early Judaism made the acknowledgment of the Lord as king an integral part of its New Year (Ro'sh ha-Shanah) liturgy. Without an explicit textual reference to such an enthronement festival, the use of psalms on such an occasion will remain conjectural. The wide use of psalms in later Jewish and Christian worship, however, does make their earlier liturgical use fairly assured.

Use of Psalms in Jewish Liturgy. In addition to the few, above-mentioned references in the later books of the Hebrew Bible, the use of psalms in Second Temple worship is attested in the Dead Sea and early rabbinic literature. At least thirty psalters have been discovered among the Dead Sea Scrolls—more than any other text, which suggests that a collection of psalms served the Jewish sectarians as a hymnal. The late second-century CE rabbinic code, the Mishnah, states that a specific psalm was chanted in the Temple each day (*Tam.* 7.4). According to Jewish tradition, the psalms corresponded to the order of creation as delineated in *Genesis* 1. On Sunday, the first weekday, the psalm we know as Psalm 24 was chosen, as it praises God's command of all creation; on the second day, Psalm 48, which exalts God for dividing the waters; on the third, Psalm 82, which refers to God's sitting as judge over the land; on the fourth, on which the sun, moon, and stars were created, Psalm 94, for it seeks vengeance on Israel's star-worshiping persecutors; on the fifth, Psalm 81, in which the marvels of creation evoke praise; on the sixth, Psalm 93, in which the wondrous creation of humankind elicits awe at God's majesty; and on the Sabbath, Psalm 92, which is assigned to that day by its title. Traditional Jewish liturgy to this day includes the recitation of these daily psalms.

On the basis of their content, Psalm 135 was prescribed for Pesaḥ; Psalm 81, for Ro'sh Ḥodesh (the New Moon); and Psalms 120–134, songs of "ascent," or pilgrim songs, for Sukkot, the joyous pilgrimage of the fall harvest. Psalm 136, the so-called Hallel ha-Gadol ("the great praise"), was recited on festive days, and Psalms 113–118 comprised a varied series of halleluyah-songs for all festivals. The juxtaposition of these psalms in the Psalter may reflect their joint liturgical function. A number of other psalms form part of the daily morning service, Psalm 145 opens the afternoon service, and certain psalms are recited for penitence and in mourning. Altogether, some eighty-four of the biblical psalms form a regular part of the Jewish liturgy. Owing to their blending of praise and petition, the psalms are also traditionally recited on behalf of the seriously ill and dying.

Use of Psalms in Christian Worship. Since ancient times, the psalms have held a prominent place in Christian hymnals. Early churches inherited the regular recitation and chanting of psalms from the Jewish synagogue. The ancient church fathers, however, pointed to Jesus' quotation of *Psalms* 22:2 when he was crucified (e.g., *Mt.* 27:46) and assumed as a matter of course that Jesus recited psalms. Christian practice would accordingly emulate Jesus by making *Psalms* central to its liturgy. Jerome, for example, in the late fourth century attests to the chanting of psalms in Latin, Greek, and Syriac at funeral processions.

In the Middle Ages, *Psalms* formed the larger part of all regular worship. Psalm 119, the longest in the canon, was recited daily by clerics, who were required to memorize the entire Psalter; over the course of a week all the psalms were systematically recited. The psalms functioned both as devotion and as guides to piety and inspiration.

Various Christian churches and denominations utilize different texts of the Psalter, most of them adapted for public worship from the Latin of Jerome. Many English versions today stem from revisions of the Great Bible produced in 1539–1541. In addition to public worship, modern Christians have recited psalms in school and at home for meditation and for insight into God's ways.

The Psalms as Revelation. Although the psalms have been understood in Jewish and Christian tradition to embody the reflection and devotion of David, that is, as the expression of human spirit, they have also been taken to contain divine revelation of the future of the pious, on the one hand, and of the wicked, on the other.

An early rabbinic *midrash* on *Psalms* says: "Rabbi Yudan states in the name of Rabbi Yehudah: All that David said in his book [i.e., *Psalms*], he said with respect to himself, with respect to all Israel, and with respect to all times" (*Midrash Tehillim* 18.1). The fact that *Psalms* speaks in very general terms of the righteous and pious, who are favored by God, and of their enemies, the wicked, whom God will ultimately destroy, facilitates the traditional interpretation of *Psalms* as predictive of the respective fates of the good and the bad. Thus the Dead Sea sectarians, in their commentaries on *Psalms*, see themselves as the righteous and their personal opponents as the wicked; the gentile nations that God will overturn, they, like the early rabbis, identify as the Romans. Christians see themselves as the true Israel, as the devotees of the Lord in the psalms. *Acts* 4:23–28, for example, interprets *Psalms* 2:1–2 to refer to the Romans and Jews as enemies of Jesus. Jesus is said, according to *Luke* 24:44, to have told his disciples: "Everything written about me in the Law of Moses and the Prophets and the Psalms must be fulfilled."

Jews and Christians have found in a number of psalms (e.g., *Ps.* 2, 18, 67, 72, 75, 100) predictions of an eschatological age at which the legitimate, anointed king (the Messiah) would be reinstated or vindicated. Church fathers and rabbis adduced verses from *Psalms* in support of various doctrines, and in the Middle Ages Jewish and Christian clerics disputed doctrines, such as the authenticity of Jesus as the Messiah and the trinitarian character of the deity, on the basis of the psalms and other canonical texts. While Christians would seek in the psalms clues to the coming of the eschaton, Jews would more often find consolation in the assurances that the righteous would be saved and the Jewish Diaspora ended.

Theology of the Psalms. Historically, various psalms date from diverse periods and provenance, so that one finds in them a variety of perceptions of God and religious concerns. In Psalm 18, for example, the Israelite God responds to the outcry of his worshiper by flying down from the sky amid wind and cloud, casting out lightning bolts, and bellowing thunder. In Psalm 104, God as controller of all nature spreads the sky out as his tent, wraps himself in celestial light, and makes a chariot of the clouds. He dispatches the winds to push the waters back from covering the entire land. These bold naturalistic images contrast sharply with the more abstract God of Psalms 1 and 119, the source of wisdom and moral guidance.

In the Psalter as a whole, one encounters a deity who is here transcendent and awesome, there immanent and caring. Ultimately, the conception of God one will find in any given psalm depends upon the type and function of that psalm. In psalms of praise and thanksgiving, for example, one is apt to find a powerful creator god whose marvelous dominion even the phenomena of nature adore (e.g., *Ps.* 19:2). In psalms of supplication, however, the petitioner must express his confidence in a compassionate deity who listens to the prayers of his devotees. The worshiper may adduce a traditional doctrine of God's pathos (*Exodus* 34:6 is quoted in *Psalms* 86:15, 103:8, and 145:8), and he may allude to his God's saving acts for his people in the past. He may, as in Psalm 77, invoke the deity's prehistoric show of power by vanquishing the primordial forces of chaos and setting the world as we know it in order.

It is everywhere posited that God is just and, accordingly, shows special concern for the just and righteous. The occasional successes of the wicked, therefore, dismay the pious, but psalms such as Psalm 37 repeatedly affirm that God will confound the wicked:

> The wicked plots against the righteous,
> and he gnashes his teeth against him;
> But my Lord smiles at him,
> for he sees his day [of doom] is coming.
> (37:12–13)

The pious trusts that God will "repay a man according to what he does" (*Ps.* 62:13). Nevertheless, out of an apparent impatience with the prosperity of the wicked and the foes of Israel, psalms often appeal to the deity to take vengeance on the enemies of Israel and its pious (e.g., *Ps.* 5:11, 31:18, 35:4, 40:15, 58:7, 104:35, 139:19). Such imprecations, which have disturbed many Christian theologians in particular, evince a frustration with God's temporary inaction:

> O God of vengeance, Lord,
> O God of vengeance, appear!
> Raise yourself up, O judge of the earth,
> Turn retribution on the arrogant!
> How long will the wicked, O Lord,
> How long will the wicked celebrate?
> (*Ps.* 94:1–3)

The psalmists hope that the deity's care for the world and its creatures, and the indigent and weak especially, will redound to them, that God will want them to live so as to acknowledge and praise their creator. The psalms present not a systematic theological picture but a confluence of themes and interests, of which Psalm 146 is an example:

> Let me praise the Lord as I live,
> let me make song to my God while I am.
> Trust not in princes,
> in a human who has not saving.
> When his spirit leaves, he returns to the land,
> on that day his deliberations vanish.
> Happy is he whose aid is the God of Jacob,
> whose succor is the Lord his God,
> Maker of heaven and earth,
> of the sea and of all that is in it,
> faithful guardian forever;
> Doing justice for the oppressed,
> giving bread to the hungry . . .
> The Lord loves the righteous . . .
> but the path of the wicked he will pervert.
> Let the Lord reign forever,
> your God, O Zion, in every generation.
> Halleluyah! (146:2–10)

The interplay of the individual and the people Israel, on the one hand, and of the transcendent and immanent deity, on the other, is fairly typical of many psalms, and of the Psalter in general.

Psalms as Literature. Owing to their liturgical origins and functions, many psalms display the sorts of stereotyped forms and wording, as well as the frequent refrains and repetitions, that characterize formal hymn singing and prayer. Their conventionality makes them easy to join; their repetitive rhythms and phrases can, when chanted, produce a *mantra*-like drive and intensity. When read as poems rather than prayers, many psalms do not feature the sophisticated configurations of words and deployment of tropes that are usually associated with poetry. The liturgical power of *Psalms* has, however, often been praised by readers, and certain of the psalms do exhibit artful arrangements of language and memorable images. A celebrated example is Psalm 23:

> The Lord is my shepherd;
>   I shall not lack.
> In pastures of grass he has me lie down;
>   along waters of stillness he leads me.
> My spirit revives.
> He guides me on just courses
>   for his name's sake.
> Even when I walk in a vale of darkness
>   I fear no evil,
>   for you are with me.
> Your rod and your staff—
>   they comfort me.
> You set before me a table
>   opposite my adversaries.
> You anoint with oil my head;
>   my cup overruns.
> Aye, good and love will pursue me
>   all the days of my life;
> And I shall dwell in the house of the Lord
>   for a length of days.

The recurrent rhythm of short, asymmetrically balanced couplets, the contrast of the idyllic pasture and the confrontation of enemies, the fear of danger mitigated by the support of the divine shepherd—these and the psalm's various tropes have made this poem a classic statement of confidence.

[*See also* Biblical Literature, *article on* Hebrew Scriptures, *and* Music, *article on* Music and Religion in the Middle East.]

BIBLIOGRAPHY

A comprehensive discussion and summary of modern scholarship on the psalms, with treatments of the Psalter as a whole and the individual psalms, is Leopold Sabourin's *The Psalms: Their Origin and Meaning,* rev. ed. (New York, 1974). Studies that treat the psalms from a liturgical perspective as well are W. O. E. Oesterley's *A Fresh Approach to the Psalms* (New York, 1937) and Laurence Dunlop's *Patterns of Prayer in the Psalms* (New York, 1982). For a detailed summary of the critical study of *Psalms,* see Otto Eissfeldt's *The Old Testament: An Introduction,* translated by Peter R. Ackroyd (Oxford, 1965), pp. 88–127, 444–454; and for the *Psalms of Solomon* and the Dead Sea *Hodayot,* see pages 610–613 and 654–657, respectively. On the cave 11 Psalms Scroll from Qumran, see James A. Sanders's *The Dead Sea Psalms Scroll* (Oxford, 1965). The canonical shape of the Psalter is discussed in Brevard S. Childs's *Introduction to the Old Testament as Scripture* (Philadelphia, 1979), pp. 504–525, with excellent, selected bibliography. The literary history of the canonical Psalter has been most thoroughly analyzed in Gerald H. Wilson's *The Editing of the Hebrew Psalter* (Chico, Calif., 1985). Important commentaries or studies of the psalms are Hermann Gunkel's *The Psalms,* translated by Thomas M. Horner (Philadelphia, 1967); Sigmund Mowinckel's *The Psalms in Israel's Worship,* 2 vols., translated by D. R. Thomas (Oxford, 1962); Artur Weiser's *The Psalms,* translated by Herbert Hartwell (Philadelphia, 1962); and Peter C. Craigie's *Psalms 1–50* (Waco, Tex., 1983). On the relation of the psalms of lament to biblical prophecy, see W. H. Bellinger, Jr.'s *Psalmody and Prophecy* (Sheffield, 1984). For ancient Near Eastern literary parallels to the psalms, as well as specimens of liturgical texts, see *Ancient Near Eastern Texts relating to the Old Testament,* 3d ed., edited by James B. Pritchard (Princeton, 1969).

EDWARD L. GREENSTEIN

PSELLUS, MICHAEL (1018–1078?), Byzantine statesman, philosopher, theologian, and historian. Born in Constantinople, Psellus's talents, broad learning, and eloquence soon made him the favorite in the emperor's court, in which he served simultaneously as head of the chair of rhetoric and philosophy (at the University of Constantinople) and as grand chamberlain. He subsequently served as secretary of state, prime minister, and diplomat. As a patriot and philosopher in an often corrupt political setting, he may justly be compared to Francis and Roger Bacon, who had similar political roles and literary careers. His extensive knowledge in philosophy and rhetoric earned him the coveted title "consul of the philosophers." After thirty years, however, Psellus abruptly abandoned the court, frustrated by the incompetence of his favorite student, the emperor Michael VII Ducas. He died a poor and forgotten man.

Psellus's most important works are commentaries on the Greek philosophers and theologians. He also wrote poetry, funeral orations, historical treatises, and works on ancient Greek topography, alchemy, and astrology. In addition, five hundred of Psellus's letters are known to us.

Psellus's task was to interpret the Greek spirit in a conspicuously Christian setting. He soon became controversial and was almost excommunicated from the church. Nevertheless, he insisted in his teaching and writings that philosophy and theology ought not be seen as two different disciplines but as one. The former lays the intellectual foundations upon which the latter builds its spiritual mansions—philosophy is not a handmaiden of Christian theology, but a collaborator. Psellus was convinced that philosophy and theology, or science and faith, in unison could give humanity the answer to its perennial questions.

By reviving the pursuit of philosophy and learning in Constantinople, Psellus single-handedly renewed the spirit of excellence patterned on that of ancient Athens. This revival of classical study had longstanding effects, for Psellus is considered the forerunner of the Italian Renaissance. Two examples suffice to show the influence he had, not only among his own, but abroad: Giovanni Pico della Mirandola and Marsilio Ficino were two of Psellus's spiritual heirs.

BIBLIOGRAPHY

The works of Psellus are available in *Patrologia Graeca*, edited by J.-P. Migne, vol. 122 (Paris, 1864). Two works on Psellus are Christos Zervos's *Un philosophe néoplatonicien de l'onzième siècle: Michael Psellos* (Paris, 1920) and my doctoral dissertation "The Philosophical Trilogy of Michael Psellos, God-Cosmos-Man" (University of Heidelberg, 1970), written in English. I also recommend Joan M. Hussey's *Church and Learning in the Byzantine Empire, 867–1185* (Oxford, 1937) and *The Byzantine World*, 3d ed. (London, 1967); and Petros Periklēs Iōannou's *Christliche Metaphysik in Byzanz: Die Illuminationslehre des Michael Psellos und Johannes Italos* (Ettal, West Germany, 1956).

GEORGE KARAHALIOS

PSEUDEPIGRAPHA. *See* Biblical Literature, *article on* Apocrypha and Pseudepigrapha.

PSEUDO-DIONYSIUS. *See* Dionysius the Areopagite.

PSYCHEDELIC DRUGS. A great variety of substances affect the workings of the mind, and the effects they produce are often described as religious experiences. The word *psychedelic* (from the Greek *psuchē*, "soul," and *dēloun*, "to manifest"), coined by Humphry Osmond, has been widely accepted as a term referring to such materials. It can be used as a noun ("the psychedelics") or as an adjective ("the psychedelic drugs," "a psychedelic experience"). These substances range from very simple molecules, such as nitrous oxide, ether, and ethyl alcohol, to quite complex ones, such as lysergic acid diethylamide, or LSD. The plants that contain psychedelic substances belong to widely separated botanical groups. Some are fungi *(Amanita muscaria, Psilocybe mexicana);* the rest belong to various families of flowering plants. Some of these plants are highly poisonous (e.g., members of the *Solanaceae*, such as henbane or deadly nightshade). Others—hemp, for example—are relatively nontoxic, so that it is almost impossible to kill oneself by taking an overdose.

In this account I shall deal both with the crude botanicals and with purified, chemically refined substances either derived from plants or made synthetically. It was once thought that the use of chemicals whose structures are known might help to explain precisely how psychedelics affect the mind. This has not happened. We are still very much in the dark about the mode of action of the psychedelics. All we can do is describe their effects and ask whether these effects can be regarded as genuine religious experiences.

Legacy of the Aztec: The Peyote Cult. When the Spanish conquistadores arrived in Mexico they discovered that the Aztec worshiped three plants, called *teo-nanacatl*, *ololiuqui*, and *peyotl*. *Teo-nanacatl* was a mushroom; *ololiuqui* was a vine belonging to the morning-glory family; *peyotl*, or *peyote*, as the Spanish called it, was an insignificant-looking cactus. Of the three plants, peyote was the most important; it was represented by the Aztec as a divine substance, the "flesh of the gods." The Spanish priests, who had their own ideas about God's flesh, called peyote the devil's root, banned its use, and persecuted all who used it, thereby effectively driving the practice underground.

The worship of peyote remained an obscure cult until the middle of the nineteenth century, when Quanah Parker, half white, half Comanche, was saved from death by a *curandera* (a woman who heals with herbs, prayer, and magic). After he had been cured, Parker, who felt himself to be spiritually more Comanche than white, left his Texas family and returned to the Comanche, taking with him a supply of the cactus that had been used to cure him. The herb woman had informed him that this was a special plant. It was never to be eaten for the feeling of well-being it could bring but was only to be used for healing or in religious ceremonies.

Quanah Parker heeded these words. He taught the peyote ritual to the Plains Indians, whose way of life had been totally destroyed by the white man and who desperately needed a new faith. For the Indians who use it the peyote cactus is a sacred plant. "Almost one cannot speak about it," said a Huichol shaman who described the gathering of the cactus to a visitor. Even the quest for the cactus was sacred. One went quietly, one did not speak, one walked slowly and with great care. When the cactus was spotted the shaman raised his bow and shot an arrow into the base of the plant. "All venerate," said the shaman. "It is very sacred, very, very. It is a beautiful thing to see" (Myerhoff, 1974).

Does the peyote cult involve genuine religious experience? According to the Huichol shaman, from the moment when the gatherers of the cactus set off in search of the plant, the whole enterprise is suffused with a sense of the sacred. The peyote ritual itself is conducted by the Plains Indians in a tipi with the door facing east, a fire in the center, and a crescent-shaped altar to the west of the fire. "Father Peyote," in the form of a sack of dried slices of the cactus, is placed in the center of the altar. The meeting is presided over by the "roadman," the cedar chief, the fire chief, and the drum chief. The roadman knows everything that is going on in the meeting and is responsible for keeping it organized. The cedar chief controls the cedar smoke, which gives blessing; the fire chief scrupulously tends the fire, periodically cleans the altar and floor, and looks after those who need attention; the drum chief provides the "heartbeat" of the meeting. The highly formalized rite lasts all night; at dawn the peyote woman brings water and a ceremonial breakfast of corn, fruit, and boneless meat. By the dawn light she prays and gives thanks, reminding those present where everything comes from. Through the peyote woman the earth speaks.

The anthropologist J. S. Slotkin, who studied peyotism among the Menomini Indians of Wisconsin, defined the peyote religion as Christianity adapted to traditional Indian beliefs and practices. According to these beliefs, the Great Spirit created the universe and controls the destiny of everything therein. The Great Spirit put some of his supernatural power into peyote, which he gave to the Indians to help them in their present lowly circumstances. By eating peyote under the proper ritual conditions a person can incorporate some of the Great Spirit's power, just as a white Christian absorbs that power from the sacramental bread and wine.

The traditional Indian practice was to fast in seclusion until a vision was obtained. This was later replaced by the collective all-night vigil of the peyotists. Revelation often took the form of the unification of one's immediate experience with the Great Spirit itself. Alternatively, the Great Spirit would reveal some religious truth to the peyotist, teaching him how to live rightly.

The Indians, Slotkin found, did not value the purely visual effects that peyote tends to produce in certain people. The "thick, glorious fields of jewels, solitary or clustered" that so fascinated Havelock Ellis when he took peyote were regarded by Indian peyotists merely as distractions. Their aim was to communicate with the Great Spirit, and anything that interfered with that communication was to be avoided.

The amount of peyote the Indians took varied. Slotkin found it impossible to eat more than ten of the dried mescal buttons, which are extremely unpleasant to the taste and tend to produce nausea. Most of the Indians, he states, seemed satisfied with this number, but some ate as many as thirty or forty buttons. (Weston La Barre, in his book *The Peyote Cult*, describes Indians who ate as many as a hundred buttons.) As for the condition of the Indians during the ceremony, they were neither stupefied nor drunk. Each individual was sufficiently aware of what was going on to be able to sing or drum when his turn came. The participants never fell out of rhythm or fumbled their words; they were all quiet, courteous, and considerate of one another; and none acted in an unseemly manner. Wrote Slotkin: "I have never been in any white man's house of worship where there is either as much religious feeling or decorum."

Does the spirit in the cactus reveal its secrets only to American Indians? The psychiatrist Humphry Osmond attended a "peyote night" under the direction of Frank Takes Gun, president of the Native American Church of North America. The ceremony was held in a tipi illuminated only by firelight. After partaking of the sacred cactus Osmond directly experienced the tragedy of the Indians. He sensed the daily challenge Indian hunters had faced in the old days as they tracked the buffalo armed only with stone-tipped spears, confronting drought, cold, furious blizzards, and constant danger. As he watched a young Indian weeping, "shedding tears on mother earth that the Universal God might take pity on him," he experienced directly the young man's anguish. The Indian longed for a meaningful life, a life of action, danger, suffering—anything other than the humiliating emptiness of his present life. But the drumming told him he could not go back. The way of life of his ancestors was gone forever. "It is sad to be a warrior from generations of warriors with nothing warlike to do, an Achilles without Troy, staying at home among his mother's spinning women" (Osmond, 1970, p. 78). [*For more detailed treatment of the peyote ritual, see* North American Indians, *article on* Indians of the Plains.]

Aldous Huxley and Mescaline. The religious experiences produced by peyote depend very largely on set and setting. American Indians seated around the fire in a tipi will interpret their visions as gifts or lessons offered by the Great Spirit. Sympathetic participants from the white man's world, such as Weston La Barre, Stewart Brand, and Humphry Osmond, tended under such conditions to receive communications "in the Indian mode."

When peyote or its chief alkaloid, mescaline, was

taken by non-Indians in a non-Indian setting, the material perceived was of a very different nature. This was clearly demonstrated in 1953 when, "on a smogless May morning in Hollywood," Aldous Huxley swallowed three hundred milligrams of mescaline and sat down to await its effects. The result of that experiment was detailed in his book *The Doors of Perception*.

Aldous Huxley is often thought of as the intellectual's intellectual, one who was equally at home in the realms of science, art, philosophy, and religion. He was an artist with words, a writer who could portray with equal skill the sterile horrors of *Brave New World* and the spiritual profundities of *The Perennial Philosophy*. But upon taking mescaline, Huxley found himself confronted by a world in which words played no part. The effect of the drug was to strip away from his perceptions that fog of verbiage that prevents most of us from seeing "the thing in itself." It was for this reason that, trying to summarize his experience, he selected a passage from Willliam Blake's *Marriage of Heaven and Hell*: "If the doors of perception were cleansed, everything would appear to man as it really is, infinite."

The power of mescaline to cleanse the doors of perception manifested itself soon after Huxley ingested the drug. His attention was captured by a glass vase containing three flowers: a Belle of Portugal rose, a cream-colored carnation, and "the bold heraldic blossom of an iris." The simple flower arrangement, seen when the doors of perception had been cleansed by mescaline, became what Adam had seen on the morning of his creation—"the miracle, moment by moment, of naked creation."

It was not primarily the intensification of the colors that impressed Huxley, although, like most mescaline takers, he did perceive colors as raised to a higher power. Not only the flowers but also the books in his study glowed with an inner light. He saw books like rubies, emerald books, books of white agate and aquamarine, lapis lazuli books. But the brilliant colors were of less importance than the direct perception of being, the quality Meister Eckhart had called *Istigkeit*, "isness."

That quality of "isness" lay beyond the reach of verbal definition. The "being" of Platonic philosophy came close to describing that perception, but Plato had made the mistake of separating being from becoming. Thus Plato could not have perceived what the flowers so intensely signified to Huxley under the "cleansing" influence of mescaline. This was nothing more and nothing less than a transience that was yet eternal life, pure being that was, at the same time, a perpetual perishing.

Looking at the flowers, Huxley understood for the first time the meaning of the Sanskrit term *sat-chit-ānanda* ("being-awareness-bliss"). But the understanding evaded verbal expression. To express it at all, one had to resort to the subterfuge of a Zen master, as when the bewildered novice enquired, "What is the Dharma-body of the Buddha?" and the master would answer, "The hedge at the bottom of the garden," or "A golden-haired lion."

"The urge to transcend self-conscious selfhood," wrote Huxley, "is a principal appetite of the soul." He went on to quote H. G. Wells, who had described as "Doors in the Wall" all those ways men and women have found to escape for a while from the poor, limited, monotonous world of ordinary life. Art and religion, carnivals and saturnalia, dancing and listening to oratory all provided publicly sanctioned Doors in the Wall. For private use there were the chemical intoxicants that had been known and used by human beings from time immemorial.

As a Door in the Wall, mescaline, in Huxley's opinion, had much in its favor. It was relatively nontoxic; it did not harm the heart and lungs as did cigarettes; and, unlike alcohol, it did not destroy coordination or drive the user into the sort of uninhibited action that results in brawls, traffic accidents, and violent crimes. Takers of mescaline quietly minded their own business. Confronted with the colossal figures of the world of archetypes or revelations such as those experienced by Huxley, they felt no need to relate to others, either creatively or destructively.

Huxley admitted that this tendency of the peyotist to be completely wrapped up in his inner world might produce effects that were not entirely advantageous. How, he asked, could the cleansed perception and the inward-directed state that mescaline induced be reconciled with a proper concern for human relations? What of the necessary chores and duties of life? What of charity and practical compassion? Mescaline had revealed to Huxley the meaning of the word *contemplation*, but it was a contemplation that was incompatible with action, with the will to action, even with the very thought of action.

This effect was likely to confront the mescaline taker with the age-old conflict between the active life and the contemplative life, between the followers of Martha and the followers of Mary. The quietist, serenely contemplating the wonders of his own inner world, can certainly be trusted to stay out of mischief. He will not become a gambler, a drunkard, or a procurer. He will not preach intolerance or make war, nor will he find it necessary to rob, swindle, or grind the faces of the poor. But opposite the quietist stands the saint, ready to descend from the seventh heaven to bring a cup of water to a sick beggar. Opposite the *arhat*, who retreats from the world of appearances into *nirvāṇa*, stands the *bo-*

dhisattva, dedicated to the liberation of all sentient beings. Mescaline, said Huxley, could never resolve the conflict between activity and contemplation. It could only pose it, apocalyptically, for those to whom it had never before presented itself.

Although he himself was favorably impressed by the effects of mescaline, Huxley admitted that the drug was not for everybody. "Along with the happily transfigured majority of mescaline takers there is a minority that finds in the drug only hell and purgatory" (p. 65). Taken under the wrong conditions or by someone with whose personal chemistry it failed to agree, the drug could easily induce a state resembling that of schizophrenia. The schizophrenic, said Huxley, "is like a man permanently under the influence of mescaline" (p. 56). Confronted by a world he is not holy enough to bear, he is frightened into interpreting its unremitting strangeness as the manifestation of human or cosmic malevolence. The threat he feels calls for desperate countermeasures ranging from murderous violence to catatonic immobility.

Sacred Mushrooms. The second gift of the Aztec, *teonanacatl*, never attained as widespread use as did peyote. R. Gordon Wasson and his wife, Valentina, in their book *Mushrooms, Russia, and History*, have suggested that Indo-European peoples can be separated into two camps: the mycophiles and the mycophobes. For the mycophiles, fungi are fascinating, exciting, delectable, and sometimes sacred. For the mycophobes, fungi are dangerous, expressions of parasitism and decay, and associated with demons. The Spaniards who conquered the Aztec were evidently mycophobes, and they persecuted the mushroom eaters so thoroughly that the use of the sacred mushroom was forgotten by most of the inhabitants of Mexico. In 1915 a reputable botanist even insisted that such mushrooms did not exist.

In fact, the sacred mushrooms belong to several genera. *Psilocybe mexicana*, *P. zapotecorum*, *P. caerulescens*, and some species of *Paneolus* and *Stropharia* are hallucinogenic. The eater of the sacred mushroom need not go to Mexico to obtain the fungus. *Paneolus papilionaceus*, found in Maine, was described as hallucinogenic by two persons who ingested it accidentally. Similar properties are reported for *Pholiota spectabilis*, which is quite common in North America. Presumably the mycophobia that prevails in this part of the world has prevented the emergence of a mushroom cult comparable to those that have developed in Mexico and Guatemala.

The cult of the sacred mushroom is centered in the state of Oaxaca. The fungus is used by several tribes of Indians, including the Mazatec, Chinantec, Chatino, Zapotec, Mixtec, and Mixe. That the cult is ancient is suggested by the "mushroom stones," artifacts carved in the form of mushrooms, roughly a foot high, that have been discovered in archaeological sites in Guatemala. According to Gordon Wasson, the cult may have been in existence as early as 1500 BCE. It still existed in Mexico in 1936, when a Mexican engineer, Roberto J. Weitlander, became the first non-Indian to see the sacred mushrooms, in the tiny Oaxacan village of Huantla de Jimenez. In 1953 the Wassons undertook a search for the fungi in the Sierra Mazateca, Oaxaca. "We found a revelation, in the true meaning of that absurd word, which for the Indians is an everyday feature, albeit a Holy Mystery, of their lives."

The pattern of use of the sacred mushroom varies among the Indians. In some tribes the ritual is performed only by *curanderos*. In others people take the mushrooms alone or with one other person present as an observer. The mushrooms are used particularly for the purpose of divination: to help find lost objects, animals, or people; to get advice on personal problems; or to find a diagnosis and cure for some intractable disease. The cult is still surrounded by a veil of secrecy; Maria Sabina, the *curandera* who performed the mushroom ritual for Gordon Wasson (who then proceeded to describe the event in an article in *Life* magazine), found herself in trouble for having revealed tribal secrets.

The *curanderos*, having partaken of the mushrooms, wait for the power to seize hold of them, then chant to the Almighty, imploring the spirit to descend and answer the prayers of those present. The *curanderos* are called by God to follow their vocation. They are, Wasson informs us, shy and reclusive and usually live apart from the rest of the tribe. They are not organized into a hierarchy; each one practices his calling on his own.

Among the Mazatec the *curandera* takes twice as many mushrooms as the other participants. Her energies govern the proceedings. Throughout the session she sings a thread of continuous song, the words of which mix Christian and Indian mythologies. Her utterances elicit responses from the other participants, the whole building up into a swaying antiphonal chant. At times the *curandera* will rise and engage in complex clapping and slapping of different parts of her body, rotating to different cardinal points of the compass. Every twenty or thirty minutes this performance reaches a climax, after which the singing stops and the mushroom "speaks."

Does this ritual involve a genuine religious experience? For Gordon Wasson it did. "The ceremony we attended in southern Mexico was a true agape, a love-feast, a Holy Supper in which we all felt the presence of God." Nor was Wasson the only North American to react this way. Timothy Leary received seven sacred mushrooms from a scientist at the University of Mexico and ate them one sunny afternoon in the garden of a

Cuernavaca villa. During the next five hours, he tells us, he was whirled through an experience that was without question the deepest religious experience of his life. The mushrooms revealed to him that the human brain possesses an infinity of potentialities and can operate in unexpected space-time dimensions. This discovery left him feeling exhilarated, awed, and convinced that he had awakened from a long ontological sleep. He called the sudden flash of awakening "turning on." It formed the first of the three steps in the new religion he later propagated: "turn on, tune in, drop out."

The cult of the sacred mushroom was not confined to countries of central America. According to Gordon Wasson, there are peoples in Siberia who have worshiped a certain kind of mushroom from antiquity to our own time. This mushroom is the fly agaric, *Amanita muscaria*. Use of this mushroom, Wasson believes, was known to the Aryans who descended on the valley of the Indus in the second millennium BCE. The Aryan priests deified a plant called *soma*, which has never been identified, but which was used to induce visions and was regarded as a divine inebriant. The juice was extracted from it and forthwith drunk by the priests. Some students of the subject have suggested that *soma* was either alcohol or hashish, but Wasson insists that the evidence points to fly agaric.

The fly agaric produces effects quite unlike those produced by the sacred mushrooms of Mexico. It begins to act in fifteen or twenty minutes, and the effects last for some hours. The first effect of the fungus is soporific. The sleep it induces lasts about two hours, and in this state colored visions are sometimes experienced. After waking, subjects enjoy a feeling of elation that may last three to four hours; in this state they are capable of unusual physical feats. Finally, as in Mexico, the spirits of the mushroom speak to those who ingest it.

The Mexican mushrooms contain two substances to which their effects can be attributed, psilocybin and psilocyn. The fly agaric does not contain these hallucinogens. It probably exerts its effect through muscimol, an unusual amino acid. The active principle of the fly agaric is excreted unchanged in the urine.

Sacred Plants of the Amazon Region. An entirely different group of psychedelic plants is used by various tribes of South American Indians living in the jungles of the Amazon. These plants include *Piptadenia peregrina* and *Virola callophylloidea* (both of which are used for the preparation of psychedelic snuffs called *cohoba* and *epena*) and *Banisteriopsis caapi*, from which an intoxicating drink is made that is known variously as *ayahuasca, caapi*, or *yagé*. All these preparations are used to provide contact with the spirit world. Both the snuffs and the drink have rather drastic physical effects, which include sweating and vomiting. Their psychological effects have several features in common, chiefly visions of jungle animals, particularly the jaguar and the anaconda. Both macropsia (seeing everything on a giant scale) and micropsia (seeing everything dwarfed) occur with these preparations.

The drugs are used both by ordinary Indians and by medicine men or witch doctors. Among the Jivaroan headhunters *yagé* is used to kill enemies with sorcery, to cure diseases inflicted by other sorcerers, and to consult the spirits regarding various tribal problems. The Jivaroan people are unique among South American Indian tribes in believing that only in dreams is true reality revealed. Waking life is considered an illusion, but agents of the spirits, acting as friends and advisers, reveal the truth in dreams. Although ordinary dreams occurring in natural sleep may have some prognostic significance, *yagé*-induced dreams give the precious power of divination, which the Indians prize above all. Only under the influence of *yagé* can the Jivaroan shaman develop enough power to control the spirits. By means of this control he can force the spirits either to cure fellow members of his tribe or to afflict his enemies. The Jivaroan shaman thus lives almost constantly under the influence of *yagé*. The training process is severe and takes its toll. As a result of his chronic consumption of *yagé*, the shaman is reserved and taciturn, and his eyes are dull and veiled. His closest friend is the anaconda demon, the fearsome snake who rises from the river and gives to the shaman the magic arrow that endows its possessor with the power either to kill or to cure.

The psychedelic effects of these preparations appear to depend on the presence of either dimethyltryptamine (DMT) or various harmala alkaloids, particularly harmaline. DMT, which is not absorbed if taken by mouth, is probably the active principle of the snuffs *cohoba* and *epena*. The intoxicating drink prepared by boiling the inner bark of *Banisteriopsis caapi* contains the alkaloids harmine and harmaline. Claudio Naranjo, who has studied the effect of these substances on humans, states that harmaline is more hallucinogenic than mescaline, in terms of the number of images it produces and their realistic quality. Several of his subjects believed that the scenes they had witnessed had really happened, that they had been disembodied witnesses of them in a different time and place. This would explain the insistence by the Jivaroan shaman that his visions had actually occurred in the real world.

The Kava Ceremony. The religious use of *kava* (called *yagona* in Fiji) was widespread among the islanders of the South Pacific before the advent of the white man. It is still so used in Samoa and has recently undergone a revival in, among others, the islands of Tanna and Tongariki in Vanuatu (New Hebrides). Its resurgence in these islands goes hand in hand with rising resentment toward the white man, especially toward missionaries.

The *kava* drink is prepared from the roots of *Piper methysticum*, and its preparation is governed by rituals, some of which relate to the original *kava* ceremony. According to the Polynesian myth, the ceremony was brought to mortals by Tagaloa Ui, the first high chief, said to be a child of the Polynesian great god Tangaroa (Tagaloa) and a Samoan girl called Ui. Tagaloa Ui demonstrated the ceremony to Pava, the first mortal to see it. But Fa'alafi, Pava's small son, misbehaved during the ceremony and so was cut in half by Tagaloa Ui. The ceremony was begun again and this time proceeded without interruption. When the new *kava* was ready Tagaloa Ui poured some on the severed halves of the child and cried, "Soifua" ("May you live"). The two halves came together again, and the boy lived. Pava was happy and clapped his hands. Tagaloa Ui said, "Pava, do not let children stand and talk while *kava* is being prepared for high chiefs, for the things belonging to the high chiefs are sacred."

In both Polynesia and Melanesia, those who watch the sacred *kava* ceremony (women and children) are expected to remain silent and motionless. Indeed, in Fiji in the old days anyone, even a child, who made a noise during the ceremony was promptly clubbed. In Samoa children and unauthorized persons may not even attend the ceremony. The placement of the *kava* bowl and the positions of the paramount high chief, the high chief, the talking chiefs, and the lesser chiefs are precisely determined. In Samoa the ceremonies are usually held in the house that serves as the meeting place of the village council. An attitude of reverence prevails as the chiefs enter and take their places. Body ornaments of all types must be laid aside, and nothing may be worn above the waist. The attendants are silent or speak in whispers.

In the old days *kava* was prepared by mastication; chunks of the root were chewed by adolescents and deposited in the *kava* bowl, where they were mixed with water. This method is still employed on the island of Tongariki. In Samoa the dried root is pulverized in a stone mortar. The powdered *kava* is steeped in water, then freed from pieces of root by being put through a strainer made of hibiscus fibers. The talking chief watches the proceedings. When the *kava* is nearly ready, he begins a poetic recitation recounting the mythical origins of the drink or describing kava ceremonies held by the ancient Samoan gods.

The recitation is timed to end at the same moment as the *kava* is completely free of fibers. If the drink appears to be satisfactory in color and consistency the assembly indicates its approval by clapping several times. The *kava* is then served, first to the highest chief in the village. Before drinking he pours a few drops on the floor mat and offers a short prayer: "May God be with us today," "May God be our leader for today," or "Let God drink *kava* that this gathering may be pleasant." Following the prayer the high chief raises his cup and says, "Soifua" ("May you live"), to which the company replies, "Manuia" ("May the gods bless you").

Unlike peyote and *yagé*, *kava* does not produce startling visions, nor does it provoke such unpleasant side effects as headache, nausea, or vomiting. Indeed, the *kava* as prepared in Samoa is so weak that it produces hardly any effects. As prepared on Tongariki, using the green root and the method of premastication, the drink is much stronger. Those who drink the full contents of a coconut shell fall into a *kava*-induced stupor, which is not true sleep. Those who frequently use the drug experience a feeling of heaviness and weakness in their extremities. D. Carleton Gajusek, a European visitor who took *kava* on Tongariki, described its effect as "a pleasant, relaxing, paresthesia-enjoying, refreshing state of somnolence without mental dulling which eventually leads to sleep."

It is not correct to call *kava* a psychedelic agent; rather, it is a fairly effective muscular relaxant. It contains no active alkaloids. Its effects are produced mainly by dihydromethysticin, a substance similar to those that produce nutmeg intoxication.

Hemp Drugs. It has been known for centuries that hemp *(Cannabis sativa)* produces psychedelic effects. These effects can involve religious experiences, and the drug has been used by various cults for this purpose. One of these cults has a fascinating, if poorly documented, history. It was called Ḥashīshīyun (whence the English word *assassin*), and its motto ("Nothing is true, everything is allowed") greatly intrigued the philosopher Friedrich Nietzsche. The founder of the order, Ḥasane Ṣabbāḥ, was born in Qum, Persia, in the middle of the eleventh century CE. In 1072 he joined the Ismāʿīlī sect, whose center was in Cairo. He returned to Persia to make war on the hostile Sunnīs who at that time were the dominant faction in Islam. To do this he installed himself in a fortress on the craggy peak of Alamut. From this fortress he sent out his followers to assassinate various Sunnī leaders. As the representative of the imam, who, the Ismāʿīlīyah believed, held the secrets to divine understanding, Ḥasane Ṣabbāḥ possessed complete authority to lead his followers to the truth. The command to assassinate an infidel was highly regarded by the latter, for to kill an unbeliever and be killed in turn meant immediate entry into Paradise.

That Ḥasane Ṣabbāḥ used hashish to drug his followers and give them a foretaste of Paradise was first asserted by Marco Polo in the thirteenth century. That traveler described marvelous walled-in gardens in which one could find everything to satisfy the needs of the body and the caprices of the most exacting sensuality. The Grand Master of the Ḥashīshīyun, Marco Polo reported, would intoxicate his followers with hashish, then secretly transport them to the pleasure gardens to enjoy the ministrations of young boys and girls said to resemble the *ḥūrīs*, inhabitants of the Paradise promised to believers by the prophet Muḥammad. Later, Ḥasane's followers were assured that they could enjoy such delights perpetually if they would take part in the war against the infidels.

That hashish can arouse religious emotion has been stated by many observers. The most eloquent of these was Fitz Hugh Ludlow, whose book *The Hasheesh Eater* was first published in 1857. Ludlow took a very large dose of the drug and was at first terrified by its effects. His heart pounded so violently that he thought it must surely burst, and his sense of the passing of time became so changed that he seemed to have entered a state of eternity. When he lay down, a vision of celestial glory burst upon him. A white temple of unblemished purity rose up before him. Inside the temple he heard celestial chords blending into such a symphony as was never heard elsewhere. Ludlow felt as if he were melting. His soul, dilating with the swell of that transcendent harmony, bore him aloft on the glory of sound. He felt himself attaining oneness with the deity, being confronted with truths whose full meaning words could not express.

His consciousness of an ever-present and all-pervading harmony convinced Ludlow that he was a reincarnated member of the school of Pythagoras. That school, which had flourished in Greece twenty-seven hundred years earlier, had been much concerned with the musical scale and the concept of a universal harmony. Ludlow's appreciation of the teachings of Pythagoras was so greatly enhanced by hashish that he felt sure Pythagoras himself must have used the drug. Certainly it was known to the ancients and may even have been the nepenthe described by Homer, although nepenthe is generally thought to have been opium.

The use of hemp in any of various forms known as bhang or charas has been widespread for centuries among certain groups of Indian holy men, particularly devotees of the goddess Kālī. An account of the effects of hemp, taken in an Indian setting, has been given by the British anthropologist Colin Turnbull (in *The Drug Experience*). Turnbull was living in Banaras (present-day Vāranāsi) at the time, in the ashram of the holy woman Anandamai, and his drug experience was unintentional. It was the feast of Holī, a lively festival that falls in March, commemorating the god Kṛṣṇa and including the reenactment of the more licentious episodes in the life of the young god. It involves much spraying of brightly colored water and the consumption of drinks and sweetmeats laced with bhang. Turnbull consumed rather large amounts of these delicacies. Returning to the ashram, which overlooked the river Ganges, Turnbull found himself floating out of his body. He had a strong visual image of an aerial view of the Ganges, of the terrace of the ashram, and of Anandamai surrounded by her devotees. He then found himself floating through clouds, soaring above them, noting their woolly surfaces. Finally, he saw the peaks of the Himalayas, white against the dark blue sky. Rivers of clear water ran through rocky gorges and by following one of these he came to the frozen source of the sacred river Ganges, which emerged from a black cavern at the foot of a glacier.

During this trip he saw no sign of human life, but the whole world around him seemed more full of life than it had ever been before. It seemed particularly full of those qualities that the Hindu scriptures proclaim to be the highest of all: goodness, beauty, and truth. He returned through the same clouds to the ashram terrace and rather reluctantly reentered his body. Later he described the experience to Anandamai, assuring her that it had not resembled a dream or a fantasy but that it had seemed a very real and therefore not very extraordinary experience. Anandamai told him that what he had seen was real and that it had been good for him to see it. Many Hindu sages and aspirants, she said, used bhang to separate the mind from the body, but the practice was dangerous. Far safer was the traditional way of training mind and body together, until the demands of one or the other became minimal.

In Africa, as in India, drugs made from hemp are traditionally used for religious purposes. This use has recently been revived among the Rastafarians of Jamaica. This cult, best known for its reggae music, refers to hemp as "*ganja*, the mystic herb." They insist that its use is divinely sanctioned and claim that the "herb yielding seed" mentioned in *Genesis* 1:11–12 is hemp.

Among the Rastas, ganja is smoked in "spliffs," which are similar to but larger than American "joints." Smoking *ganja*, the Rastas insist, is a sacred right, a means of attaining illumination and divine inspiration. *Ganja* uplifts, they claim, whereas alcohol, which they avoid, only degrades its users.

The Psychedelic Cult of the 1960s. The cult that developed in the United States among the "Flower Children" of the 1960s had some features that distinguished it from the older cults of peyote and *teo-nanacatyl*. First, the drugs used were mainly synthetic; second, the founders of the cult were white Americans—physicians and psychologists—whose interests in the phenomena observed were scientific as well as religious.

The spiritual forefather of the movement was William James, whose studies of the effects of anesthetics on consciousness are described in *The Varieties of Religious Experience* (1902). It was James who declared that both nitrous oxide and ether, when sufficiently diluted with air, "stimulate the mystical consciousness in an extraordinary degree." It was James who made the statement, so often quoted by the high priests of the psychedelic cult, that "our normal waking consciousness, rational consciousness as we call it, is but one special type of consciousness, whilst all about it, parted from it by the filmiest of screens, there lie potential forms of consciousness entirely different."

James concluded that no account of the universe in its totality could be final if it disregarded those other forms of consciousness. He thought that drugs could open a region but that they failed to give a map. Anesthetics, including alcohol, could lead the explorer into that region, but the insights they offered might not be trustworthy. Nitrous oxide, for instance, might seem to reveal "depth after depth of truth to the inhaler," but the truth tended to fade at the moment of awakening. Alcohol, lifeblood of the cult of Dionysos, was the great exciter of the "yes function" in man and brought its votaries "from the chill periphery of things to the radiant core." James found it part of the mystery and tragedy of life that "whiffs and gleams of something we recognize as excellent should be vouchsafed only in the opening phases of what in its totality, is so degrading a poisoning."

The spiritual descendants of William James did not have much faith in either nitrous oxide or alcohol. For the most part they worked with synthetic psychedelics such as psilocybin, mescaline, and LSD. Their approaches ranged from manic enthusiasm (coupled with the feverish urge to proselytize) to cool scientific detachment. They did not limit themselves to investigating responses that could be defined as religious. The drugs were supposed to exert therapeutic effects quite apart from the religious emotions they aroused, and in various experiments psychedelics were given to prison inmates, neurotics, psychotics, and alcoholics, as well as to those who were dying of cancer. Indeed, it seemed for a while that the psychedelics might be a modern version of the universal panacea.

Timothy Leary was the leader of the more aggressive segment of the psychedelic cult. Witty, charming, and erudite, he possessed an extraordinary capacity to inflame the paranoid tendencies of those solid citizens who collectively constituted "the establishment." His own conversion to the psychedelic religion, a result of his having eaten seven sacred mushrooms, left him with an irresistible urge to proselytize. His new religion, summarized in the three commandments "turn on, tune in, drop out," was firmly linked to the use of psychedelics.

Psychedelics and Religious Experience. There was no doubt in Leary's mind that the effects the psychedelics produced were true religious experiences. To support his opinion he quoted the results obtained by Walter Pahnke, in an experiment described in the press as "the miracle of Marsh Chapel." This experiment involved twenty theology students who had never taken psychedelic drugs and ten guides with considerable psychedelic experience. The students were divided into five groups of four, with two guides assigned to each group. After attending the Good Friday service in the chapel two students in each group and one of the guides received thirty milligrams of psilocybin. The others received a placebo containing nicotinic acid, which produces a tingling sensation but no psychedelic effect. Neither guides nor students knew who had received the psychedelic and who the placebo. Nine subjects who had received psilocybin reported having had what they considered to be religious experiences. Only one of those receiving the placebo made such a claim.

Leary, of course, had gathered much experimental material of his own. In the early 1960s, until he was forced to resign from Harvard, he and Richard Alpert had given psychedelics to a variety of people including psychologists, priests, students, and criminals. Their results indicated that when the setting was supportive but not spiritual between 40 and 75 percent of psychedelic subjects reported intense, life-changing religious experiences; when the set and setting were supportive and spiritual, from 40 to 90 percent of the experiences were revelatory and mystico-religious.

Leary's attempts to organize a religion around the use of LSD or psilocybin took various external forms: the International Federation for Internal Freedom (IFIF), 1963; the Castalia Foundation, 1963–1966; and the League for Spiritual Discovery, 1966. The aim of this work was to provide conditions in which the state of *ecstasis*, or the expansion of consciousness, could be experienced. In an article entitled "Rationale of the Mexican Psychedelic Training Center," Leary, Alpert, and Ralph Metzner (in Bloom et al., 1964) described the psychedelic experience as a means of attaining *ecstasis* provided the set and the setting were appropriate.

Set and setting were important. In fact they could make the difference between an uplifting religious experience and a terrifying descent into a personal inferno. The authors also stressed the importance of preparation. The psychedelic experience, they said, was a tool, like a telescope or microscope, that could bring other space-time dimensions into focus. People had to be trained to use the tool, after which they would use it not once but whenever a situation arose that called for the examination of other dimensions of reality. The Mexican program was the first to provide a series of guided psychedelic sessions for prepared volunteer subjects. Subjects were encouraged to plan their own sessions. They might, at a certain time, arrange to listen to a particular reading, view an object that would open up a line of association, or hear a certain piece of music.

Special use was made by Leary's group of the Tibetan *Book of the Dead,* which was regarded not only as a guide for the dying but also as an aid to the living. It was "a manual for recognizing and utilizing altered states of consciousness and applying the ecstatic experience in the postsession life." To make the book more relevant to their subjects' psychedelic sessions Leary and company retranslated it from the scholarly style of W. Y. Evans-Wentz into "psychedelic English."

Leary confronted the problem of what constitutes a real religious experience and solved it to his own satisfaction: "The religious experience is the ecstatic, uncontrovertibly certain, subjective discovery of answers to seven basic spiritual questions." All issues that did not involve the seven basic questions belonged, in Leary's opinion, to secular games. Liturgical practices, rituals, dogmas, and theological speculations could be, and too often were, completely divorced from spiritual experience.

The "seven basic spiritual questions" listed by Leary were the Power Question, the Life Question, the Human Being Question, the Awareness Question, the Ego Question, the Emotional Question, and the Escape Question. The list covered the entire field of scientific inquiry, from atomic physics to the highest levels of psychology. If science and religion addressed themselves to the same basic questions then what, Leary asked, was the distinction between the two disciplines? He answered by saying that science concerned itself with the measurement of energy processes and sequences of energy transformations; it answered the basic questions using objective, observed, public data. Religion, however, involved a systematic attempt to answer the same questions subjectively, in terms of direct personal experience.

It is interesting to compare Leary's definition of the religious experience with that given earlier by William James. James devoted two chapters in *The Varieties of Religious Experience* to that condition of being he called "saintliness." It was, he declared, "the collective name for the ripe fruits of religion." A group of spiritual emotions in the saintly character formed the habitual center of personal energy. Saintliness was the same in all the religions, and its features could easily be described. They involved

1. a feeling of being in a wider life than that of the world's selfish little interests and a direct conviction of the existence of an ideal power
2. a sense of the friendly continuity of this power with our life and a willing self-surrender to its control
3. a feeling of elation and freedom resulting from the escape from confining selfhood
4. a shifting of the center of emotions toward loving and harmonious affections; a move toward yes and away from no

These characteristics may strike an objective observer as being closer to the essence of religion than Leary's "seven basic spiritual questions," which are really scientific (concerned with knowing) rather than religious (concerned with being). The aim of the religious life is to raise the level of being of its practitioner. Expansion of consciousness is one of the signs of a raised level of being. Indifference to possessions, a capacity for impartial, objective love, indifference to physical discomfort, and a complete freedom from fear of death are other fruits of this raised level. Furthermore, the saintly character does not fluctuate. Its possessor is not saintly today and demonic tomorrow. There is a stability in such a character, an inner consistency, a permanent set of values. There is also an awareness of the presence of the power that some religions call God, and such awareness is a source of repose and confidence.

Of all the fruits of the religious life, the capacity for objective love, for compassion, is the most highly esteemed. The apostle Paul defined this all-important emotion in a well-known passage: "Though I speak with the tongues of men and of angels, and have not charity, I am become as sounding brass, or a tinkling cymbal" (*1 Cor.* 13:1). What would Paul have said about Leary's seven basic spiritual questions? "Though I . . . understand all mysteries, and all knowledge: and though I have all faith, so that I could remove mountains, and have not charity, I am nothing." Nor is Paul alone in extolling charity as the choicest fruit of the spiritual life. The concept of the *bodhisattva,* who regards with compassion all sentient beings, puts the same emphasis on charity as we see in Christian teachings.

In light of such considerations, it would seem reasonable to ask not whether psychedelic drugs help those who take them to answer Leary's seven questions, but whether they enable the drug taker to attain a permanently higher level of being according to the criteria listed by James. The most that can be said for the psychedelic experience is that sometimes it helps.

R. E. L. Masters and Jean Houston, in their book *The Varieties of Psychedelic Experience*, described the range of subjects' reactions to LSD. They were less naive and dogmatic than Leary and were careful to distinguish what they called "nature mysticism" from real religious experience. The important question was whether, as a result of the insights obtained during the psychedelic experience, the subject really underwent a change equivalent to a religious conversion. One of their subjects, a highly intelligent but devil-obsessed psychologist, did show behavioral changes of a positive character, which suggested that a permanent transformation had occurred. Many other subjects found the experience useful in that it revealed to them unsuspected heights and depths in themselves. On the whole, however, the psychedelic experience did not transport the subjects to a permanently higher level of awareness.

Richard Alpert, who worked closely with Leary at Harvard and later in Mexico and at Millbrook, New York, was also compelled finally to admit that the psychedelic experience led nowhere. He had certainly tried everything: LSD, psilocybin, mescaline, hashish. He had even, on one occasion, locked himself and five other people in a building for three weeks and taken 400 micrograms of LSD every four hours, a total of 2,400 micrograms a day. (One hundred micrograms is enough to produce a strong reaction in anyone unaccustomed to the drug.) "We were very high," said Alpert, describing the experience. But they walked out of the house at the end of three weeks, and within a few days severe depression set in, which was hardly surprising. The orgy of drug taking had left the participants so drained that it was surprising that they could function at all.

Alpert later went to India and found his guru in the foothills of the Himalayas. The guru amazed him by swallowing 915 micrograms of Alpert's "White Lightning," a special batch of high-quality LSD. That much LSD, taken by one unaccustomed to the drug, would constitute an enormous overdose, but the guru showed no reaction whatever. "All day long I'm there, and every now and then he twinkles at me and nothing—nothing happens! That was his answer to my question."

That demonstration of the power of mind over matter was enough for Alpert. He finally stopped trying to obtain results with psychedelics and took up a serious study of yoga. He returned to America transformed into Baba Ram Dass and wrote a book called *Remember: Be Here Now*, a very lively and honest account of his researches. In a section entitled "Psychedelics as an *Upaya*" (the Sanskrit term *upāya* is generally translated as "skillful means") he conceded that psychedelics might help a person break out of an imprisoning model of reality created by his own mind. But no matter how high a person soared on the wings provided by such drugs, he would always come down, and coming down could bring despair.

How the Psychedelics Work. The psychedelic drugs, which range from simple chemical compounds to highly complex ones, have no single feature in common. The "anaesthetic revelation" so thoroughly explored by William James could be produced by substances as simple as nitrous oxide or ether. Details of molecular composition strongly affect psychedelic action, however. For example, cannabinol, a major component of the hemp resin, appears to produce no effect on the human psyche, but the closely related Δ-9-tetrahydrocannabinol is highly active. Lysergic acid diethylamide is the most powerful psychedelic presently known, but a very small change in the structure of this molecule is sufficient to render it inactive.

Aldous Huxley, whose experiences with mescaline I described earlier, was inclined to attribute the action of this drug to its effect on brain enzymes. Enzymes, he declared, regulate the supply of glucose to the brain cells. Mescaline inhibits the production of these enzymes and thus lowers the amount of glucose available to an organ that is in constant need of sugar. Slowed by its lack of sugar, the brain ceases to function effectively as a reducing valve, making it possible for the possessor of that brain to make contact with Mind at Large, a concept Huxley had borrowed from the Cambridge philosopher C. D. Broad.

Broad's theory suggested that the function of the brain and nervous system is eliminative rather than productive. Each person, said Broad, is capable at each moment of remembering all that has ever happened to him and of perceiving everything that is happening everywhere in the universe. The brain acts as a reducing valve to protect us from being overwhelmed and confused by a mass of useless and irrelevant knowledge. In consequence, although each of us is potentially Mind at Large, what we actually perceive is a mere fraction of what we could perceive. The brain's reducing valve cuts down to a mere trickle the profusion of Mind at Large, leaving the individual free to concentrate on the problem of how to stay alive on the surface of the planet.

Aldous Huxley suggested that in some people a kind of bypass circumvents the reducing valve or that temporary bypasses may be developed as a result of spiritual exercises, through hypnosis, or from the use of drugs. Through these bypasses human beings make contact with certain elements of Mind at Large outside of the carefully selected material that our individual minds regard as a complete picture of reality.

This theory is beyond the reach of science, for it postulates the existence of an entity (Mind at Large) that no physical instrument we possess can detect. But the assertion that mescaline acts by reducing the capacity of the brain to utilize glucose is not likely to be correct. More effective ways of reducing the glucose supply to the brain are known and were formerly employed in the treatment of schizophrenia. The chief of these methods is insulin shock treatment, which certainly cuts down the brain's sugar supply, resulting in convulsions and loss of consciousness by the patient. If Huxley's theory were correct, the schizophrenics who received this treatment should have experienced, before losing consciousness, the sort of effects that are produced by mescaline. There is no evidence that they did so.

To discover how the psychedelics work it would seem that we must postulate something other than oxygen starvation or glucose starvation of the brain. Oxygen starvation does produce strange effects on the brain, as is evident from the experiences of people who have been clinically dead but were later revived. (Their stories have been chronicled by such noted researchers as Elizabeth Kübler-Ross.) It seems probable that such experiences form the basis of the various visions described in the Tibetan *Book of the Dead*. It is also possible that yogins who have mastered *prāṇāyāma*, which allows them to reduce their oxygen intake, can experience after-death states without actually dying. It would be too simple, however, to assume that all the psychedelics operate by reducing the brain's oxygen consumption. The fact is that we really do not know how these substances produce their effects.

Legal, Social, and Spiritual Questions. The abuse of drugs is so widespread in the United States that calm discussion of the religious aspect of certain drug experiences is next to impossible. The general public hysteria regarding drugs reaches a climax when the subject under discussion is the effect of drugs on the young. Young people, the argument goes, are innocent and must be protected. Laws are therefore passed making it a criminal offense to possess even such a relatively harmless weed as *Cannabis sativa*.

But it is exactly the young who are most likely to seek the psychedelic experience. There are several reasons for this. The young are often rebellious and attracted by forbidden fruit; they are enormously curious and want to explore all aspects of the world; finally, they often have religious impulses that are not satisfied by the standard forms of religion. These religious impulses arise from a deeply rooted craving to experience altered states of consciousness, a craving that becomes particularly powerful during adolescence. The modern teenager—rebellious, confused, and often defiant of authority—may feel particularly fascinated by drugs that offer, or seem to offer, new and strange experiences.

Some thinkers have imagined a society in which supervised psychedelic experience is provided those members, young and not so young, who seek to expand their awareness, but neither our own nor any other industrialized society has yet institutionalized such a practice. It was precisely this idea of the "guided trip" that underlay Leary's ill-starred efforts to found a new religion based on the psychedelic revelation. Given the hostility to drugs that prevails in American official circles, his attempts were bound to fail. He made that failure all the more inevitable by openly defying "the establishment" and taking every opportunity to provoke its wrath. Even two very cautious physicians, John W. Aiken and Louisa Aiken, were unable to win official permission to use peyote in their Church of the New Awakening. They argued that if Indian members of the Native American Church could legally use peyote for religious purposes, members of other races should enjoy the same right. But this logic was not accepted by the authorities.

Prohibition, however, has not prevented the use of psychedelics any more than it prevented the use of alcohol. The results of prohibitory legislation have been to ensure that those who do obtain these drugs pay outrageous prices, are often sold adulterated materials, and, because of lack of guidance and prevailing paranoia, often have bad trips. As long as alcohol and tobacco can be obtained legally, laws prohibiting the possession of substances such as marijuana and peyote will remain unenforceable.

The question that both legal and social prohibitions fail to confront is why some people want to use, or feel they need to use, psychedelic substances. To ask this question is to be open to the understanding that the problems lie not with drugs but with people. These problems are the result of a growing sense of futility that has afflicted our society. More and more occupations are taken over by automated machinery and computerized robots. More and more people confront the fact that they will probably never find employment in a society dominated by automation. Under these circumstances, it is not surprising that millions experience what Paul Tillich in *The Courage to Be* called "the abyss of meaninglessness." To escape from that experience, they may stupefy themselves with alcohol, blunt their sensibilities with barbiturates or heroin, or attempt to get high with the aid of psychedelics.

Those who have experimented with psychedelic drugs

and had what they consider to be authentic religious experiences are likely to fall into two groups. In the first are people who understand that the drugs act by using up certain vital energies of the body and that those energies must be replaced. For this reason, they will use drugs rarely and only under special conditions. They will also seek other, less destructive, ways of getting the same results, such as meditation or yoga postures. Sooner or later members of this group will probably abandon the use of psychedelics altogether.

In the second group are those who make the drug experience the center of their spiritual lives, failing to realize that using the drug is robbing them of strength and damaging their health. People in this group inevitably find themselves in trouble not because they have broken man-made laws but because they have broken the laws governing their own spiritual development. Inevitably, the psychedelic used becomes less and less effective and larger doses must be taken. Finally, the drug ceases to have any effect. But the drug user's reliance on his drug may have so weakened his will by that time that serious spiritual efforts become virtually impossible.

This is the main objection to the overuse of psychedelic drugs: they weaken the will, they substitute a dream world for the real world and a dream of religious experience for the real thing. But only personal experience with these drugs can bring this truth home to their votaries.

[*See also* Visions. *For religious traditions in which the use of psychedelic drugs is central, see* Shamanism, *article on* South American Shamanism; North American Indians, *articles on* Indians of the Plains *and* Indians of California and the Intermountain Region; Quechua Religions, *article on* Amazonian Cultures; *and* Huichol Religion. *For discussion of a related phenomenon, see* Beverages.]

BIBLIOGRAPHY

A long chapter entitled "Effects of Psychedelics on Religion and Religious Experience" in *Psychedelics*, edited by Bernard Aaronson and Humphry Osmond (New York, 1970), provides much useful material. Many firsthand accounts of religious experiences induced by psychedelics (chiefly LSD) are given in R. E. L. Masters and Jean Houston's *The Varieties of Psychedelic Experience* (New York, 1966). More general reviews of the subject will be found in *The Drug Experience*, edited by David Ebin (New York, 1961), and in *Drugs and the Mind*, rev. ed., edited by Robert S. de Ropp (New York, 1976). The efforts of Timothy Leary and his coworkers to provide the "guided trip" through the psychedelic realm are described in *Utopiates: The Use and Users of LSD-25* (New York, 1964) by Richard Bloom and his associates; in *The Politics of Ecstasy* (New York, 1968) by Leary himself; and in *Remember: Be Here Now* (San Cristobal, N.M., 1971) by Richard Alpert. For early studies on religious experiences induced by anesthetics, see William James's *The Varieties of Religious Experience* (New York, 1902).

For accounts of the religious use of peyote by various tribes of American Indians, see J. S. Slotkin's *The Peyote Religion* (1956; reprint, New York, 1975), Weston La Barre's *The Peyote Cult* (Hamden, Conn., 1964), and Barbara G. Myerhoff's *Peyote Hunt: The Sacred Journey of the Huichol Indians* (Ithaca, N.Y., 1974). The religious effects of mescaline on a highly sophisticated Westerner are described by Aldous Huxley in *The Doors of Perception* (New York, 1954).

The effects of various psychedelic snuffs and those of *ayahuasca, caapi*, and *yagé* are described by various authors in *Ethnopharmacologic Search for Psychoactive Drugs*, edited by Daniel H. Efron (Washington, D.C., 1967). This book, the proceedings of a symposium published by the U.S. Public Health Service, also contains an article by Carleton Gajdusek on the use of *kava* in the New Hebrides and articles by R. Gordon Wasson and I. I. Brekhman on the religious effects produced by *Amanita muscaria*. A fuller account of the effects of this fungus and its probable identity with the Vedic *soma* will be found in *Mushrooms, Russia, and History* (New York, 1957), by Valentina Pavlovna and R. Gordon Wasson. Use of psychedelic mushrooms by the Mazatec Indians is described in *Maria Sabina and Her Mazatec Mushroom Velada* (New York, 1975) by R. Gordon Wasson and others.

Religious effects produced by hashish are detailed in Fitz Hugh Ludlow's *The Hasheesh Eater: Being Passages from the Life of a Pythagorean* (1857; reprint, Upper Saddle River, N.J., 1970). Colin Turnbull's experience with bhang is described in "While I Was Always Conscious . . . ," his essay in *The Drug Experience*, mentioned above.

Material about the inborn hunger for altered states of consciousness can be found in Andrew Weil's *The Natural Mind: A New Way of Looking at Drugs and the Higher Consciousness* (Boston, 1972).

ROBERT S. DE ROPP

PSYCHOLOGY. [*This entry consists of three articles:*

Psychology of Religion
Psychology and Religion Movement
Psychotherapy and Religion

The first article traces the development of the discipline of psychology of religion and examines some of its major concerns. The second article surveys the growth of psychology and religion as an intellectual movement in the United States from the late nineteenth century to the present day. The third article focuses on the relations between religion and psychotherapeutic practice, particularly psychoanalysis and its progeny, in the twentieth century.]

Psychology of Religion

The psychology of religion, as understood today, owes its existence to the coincidence of the birth of comparative religion in nineteenth-century Europe with the birth of two other disciplines initially unrelated to religion: depth psychology, which appeared within medical science as the first systematic pursuit of a theory of the unconscious mind for the purposes of healing mental illness, and psychophysiology, which grew out of physiology as an attempt to replace the philosophical moorings of perceptual theory with concrete measurement and experimentation. Despite the extraordinary breadth of learning and the broad-minded approach in the work of the early pioneers of the psychology of religion, this dual ancestry started the discipline off with two fundamentally opposing orientations that eventually produced the whole spectrum of approaches that characterize psychology of religion at present.

Neither the notion of an unconscious dimension of the psyche and its importance to the stability of the personality nor the application of such insights to religious phenomena were new. Both Eastern and Western civilizations had known centuries of philosophical debate on the psyche and a wide variety of religious methods for healing spiritual disorders. This fact has led those at the extreme of the empirically oriented branch of the discipline to complain that depth psychology's contribution to the psychology of religion represents little more than a gathering together and reassembling of insights scattered throughout intellectual history under the somewhat suspicious mantle of psychotherapeutic practice.

Meantime, the introduction of scientific methods modeled after the physical sciences into the study of the psychological dimensions of religion must be seen as one link in a long chain of attempts, reaching back to the origins of philosophy itself, to explain religion in rationalistic terms. Critics of the psychophysiological approach to religion would argue that the very fact that religion has survived to serve as the subject matter for this newest attempt of rationalist investigation and shows no signs of weakening under the pressure of its discoveries should give experimental researchers cause to consider how far those aspects of religion that they are able to dissect and quantify are in fact from the core of religious experience.

Fortunately, most contemporary psychology of religion has mellowed as the mass of research being carried on from a variety of approaches continues to accumulate, and regularly makes use of both measurement and introspective techniques. Given its origins, however, the whole process remains a construct of Western academia. To be sure, the discipline is steadily making inroads into Asian cultures, but even so it is still an analytical method seen as foreign to non-Western traditions and that can at best be applied to these traditions as a heuristic structure for rereading them. Systematic attempts to produce psychologies of religion based on non-Western models of philosophy, religion, and medicine are all but nonexistent.

In what follows an attempt will be made first to sketch out the broad history of the birth and development of the psychology of religion, indicating some of its major theoretical architects, and second to outline some of its chief defining characteristics.

History and Development. Although the use of the terms *psychology* and *religion* to denote particular fields of scientific endeavor first arose in nineteenth-century Europe, the phenomena that these terms refer to as their subject matter are as old as humanity itself and reflection about them reaches back to the dawn of recorded history. That the same should be true of the branch of study known as the psychology of religion is hardly to be wondered at. Indeed the word *psychology* ("the science of the soul") already implies some relationship with those dimensions of human experience that had long been spoken of as religious. Yet when the word first gained currency in Europe during the eighteenth century (it seems to have been coined two centuries earlier), it did so as part of philosophical tradition dealing with theories of perception and was only remotely related to matters of theology or religion. As the study of perception was drawn further and further away from the *a priori* approach of transcendental epistemology to be replaced by a more "scientific" psychology based on the methods of biology and physics, the ties of psychology to religion weakened still further. The way from psychology to religion was not, therefore, the familiar and clearly lighted path that might be imagined from a glance at the situation in current scholarship.

Psychophysiology. The birth of the psychology of religion can hardly be attributed to the work of any single individual or group of thinkers, nor did it unfold naturally out of any particular tradition. In fact, it is hard to speak of it as having been "born" at all. It rather arose out of a particular intellectual climate in which scientific method and the study of religion had matured to the point that they were bound to rub against one another again and again as both approached a number of different questions. In this sense the psychology of religion was as much a new stimulus to the study of religion as it was to the science of psychology. Only the hindsight of a later generation has allowed certain key contributions to this encounter to be singled out as the beginnings of the discipline itself, though even here there is no universal agreement.

The nineteenth century, it should be remembered, was witness to the first great flowering of nonsectarian, disciplined approaches to the study of religious phenomena in the West. Stimulated by the discovery, translation, and editing of Eastern religious and philosophical texts, as well as by new rigors brought to the anthropological study of primitive societies, the study of religion quickly produced methods and models for comparing various traditions and relocating Western religious traditions on a wider and more objective field.

It was against this general background that Wilhelm Wundt (1832–1930) carried on his work in experimental psychology. In contrast to "psychophysics," which grounded the science on a quantifiable relationship between stimulus and sensation (a position exemplified in the work of Gustav Theodor Fechner, 1801–1887), Wundt favored a psychophysiology aimed at establishing patterns of parallelism between the psychical facts of human consciousness and their accompanying physical phenomena. From the start his aim was to ground psychology as a "natural science" in introspection tempered by experimentation. His interest in the higher processes of the psyche or "apperception" turned him further and further away from concrete psychological research and out into the broad reaches of social history. It was in this context that he made use of comparative methods and evolutionary models circulating in anthropology to offer his own functional approach to the origins of religious behavior. Thus Wundt distinguished four stages in the history of consciousness, each of which represented a distinctive manifestation of the struggle of the human spirit to assert its identity in the world of nature: primitive ritual, totemism, myths of heroes and gods, and humanism. The laboratory for experimental psychology that he set up in Leipzig in 1879—credited as the first of its kind in the world—inspired similar efforts from others, including those who wanted to pursue his study of cultural and religious consciousness. Given the blend of the philosophical and the scientific in Wundt's methods, it is not surprising that his influence here was of two sorts. On the one hand, his work led to new efforts to bring greater objectivity to the science; on the other, it led to the attempt to introduce introspection into the laboratory. [*See the biography of Wundt*.]

The key figure in this latter tendency of "thought psychology" was Oswald Külpe (1862–1915), whose so-called Würtzburg school (after the University of Würtzburg where it was founded) introduced the use of questionnaires, interviews, and autobiographical records into the study of religious phenomena. The opposition between the individual-oriented introspectionism of the Würtzburg school and the psychocultural orientation of the mature Wundt was partly influenced by and partly influential in shaping the ideas of Franz Brentano and Wilhelm Dilthey, whose reaction against objectivist psychology spread into the phenomenological and existentialist strains of Western philosophy, including their attitudes to religion. Indeed, much of the psychological flavor one senses in the works of such scholars of religion as Gerardus van der Leeuw, Rudolf Otto, Nathan Söderblom, and Friedrich Heiler has to be seen in the context of this storm over introspective psychology. Karl Girgensohn (1875–1925) and Werner Grühn (1887–1961) carried on Külpe's investigations into the empirical foundations of religion, arguing against the pursuit of a single elementary "religious emotion" in favor of a complex structure of thought and feeling constellated in the religious personality.

Early American contributions. If Europe gave the psychology of religion its initial impetus, it was in the United States that it first took roots as an independent venture. G. Stanley Hall (1844–1924), who had studied with Wundt in Leipzig, founded a psychological laboratory in the United States where he was the first to carry on empirical research into the psychology of religion. As early as 1881 he began lecturing at Harvard University on affinities between pubescence and religious conversion, and by 1904 he had founded *The American Journal of Religious Psychology and Education*. Among his students were James H. Leuba (1868–1946) and E. D. Starbuck (1866–1947), both of whom pursued lifelong careers as psychologists of religion.

Whereas his teacher had depended on the more "objective" survey, the Swiss-born Leuba used personal interviews to obtain data. From the first he insisted that religious consciousness, including mystical experience, is not qualitatively different from ordinary consciousness. On this basis he studied the origins, growth, and function of key religious concepts in the psyche, tracing belief to two major sources: the penchant of the mind for causal explanations and the need to maintain one's psychic equilibrium in the midst of life's struggles. Science, he thought, would eventually prove its superiority to religion on both counts. [*See the biography of Leuba*.]

Starbuck's *The Psychology of Religion* (1899) was the first book-length study to be published in the discipline. It outlined the results of five years of research on descriptive coincidences between pubescence, *dementia praecox*, and religious conversion. Not surprisingly, his efforts met with opposition from the theological community. While anthropologists were just beginning to study the genesis of the idea of God among primitive peoples, Starbuck approached the question in terms of the development of individual personality, for which purpose he followed a carefully articulated method of gathering autobiographical and introspective material through questionnaires, which he classified, analyzed, and interpreted. Although as devoted as Leuba to the aim of finding order and regularity in the workings of emotional life, Starbuck never lost his sense of religion as a mystery that can never be exhausted by science. [*See the biography of Starbuck.*]

George A. Coe (1862–1951) is best remembered for his introduction of the typology of "temperaments" into the analysis of religious conversion. Although the sampling on which he based his findings was relatively small, his method of composing and scaling the results of his questionnaires anticipated many of the projective and personality tests commonly used by psychologists today. Coe also conducted interviews with friends and family to balance strictly private, introspective reports of the subjects in his sampling, took into account dreams, hallucinations, trances, and automatic behavior, and even used hypnosis to test the suggestibility of individual subjects. Avoiding the reductionism of Leuba, he looked to the fruits of conversion in moral life as the final test of the worth of such experiences.

The first great watershed for the psychology of religion, however, came in 1901–1902 with the Gifford Lectures of William James (1842–1910), published under the title *The Varieties of Religious Experience* (1902). Before distinguishing himself as a philosopher, James had taught experimental psychology and, like Wundt, had directed numerous young academics into empirical studies of perception. By the time he turned to the psychological study of religion, however, James had broken completely with the fallacy of reducing states of mind to organic states or dispositions. He was aware of the importance of taking into account subliminal and unconscious factors (though not at the time through any extended contact with European "depth psychology"), and he was determined, as he wrote in his diaries as he prepared for the Gifford Lectures, "to argue to the conclusion that a man's religion is the deepest and wisest thing in his life." His approach was less experimental than it was clinical. Although he made ample use of the data gathered by many of his contemporaries, he shifted the focus away from statistical analysis and the search for general patterns to concentrate on the uniqueness of religious and moral experiences. Like Coe, James saw "the consequential fruits of life" as the critical pragmatic test for the authenticity of religious experience. No less than Wundt, James helped to crystallize the tension between scientific empiricism and introspective analysis that remains one of the distinguishing marks of the psychology of religion. [*See the biography of William James.*]

In addition to the greater precision and objectivity that came to statistical and quantitative analysis in the human sciences in general and in the psychology of religion in particular, the rise of behaviorism has not been without its impact. While much of the work on conditioned reflexes was simply operating under premises that excluded interest in religion as such, James Watson (1878–1958) set a tone for this form of objective psychology that was openly antagonistic to "spiritualistic" tendencies. This tone has continued to this day, most notably in B. F. Skinner's neobehavioristic repudiation of religious values as agents of psychological change and in his and other behaviorists' attempt to reduce all forms of religious consciousness to epiphenomena of environmental conditioning. No less devoted to strict scientific method, Wolfgang Köhler and other advocates of Gestalt psychology, anxious to preserve a holistic view of perception, produced neurological and behavioral studies of their own to argue for the importance of the element of subjectivity in understanding personality. Although Gestalt psychology did not produce a psychology of religion of its own, its impact on psychological theory in general earns it mention at least as an indirect shaper of the psychology of religion's current empirical methods.

Depth psychology. The same intellectual climate in Europe that led Wundt to carry his research on sensation over into the study of higher psychical states and from there into the field of religion also wrought similar effects on medical science and its attitude to psychic abnormalities. Here, too, the revolt against the excesses of mechanistic approaches first came from within the circles of those using the scientific method.

The first important figure in this regard is Pierre Janet (1859–1947), whose experiments with hypnosis and work on the cathartic cure of neuroses led him to adopt theories of a "subconscious" (a word of his own coinage) dimension of personality, which included the pathogenetic theory based on the notion of fixation of ideas, and also to develop a method of psychological analysis and synthesis. At the height of his career, he also used his explanatory models to examine religion in general, a subject that had interested him from the start. Though focusing on the genesis and function of the idea of God, which he considered the core of all religion, he studied a range of religious phenomena from ordinary conversion to ecstasy and spirit possession. While recognizing the role of religion in producing the moral ego that can organize and suppress human desires, he foresaw the demise of religion with the advances of science and philosophy, and he saw the need to promote new alternatives such as scientific psychotherapy on one hand and the worship of progress through the cultivation of self-confidence on the other.

Much of Janet's mature work overlapped with and was overshadowed by that of Sigmund Freud (1856–

1939), whom he criticized for taking the credit for his own insights. Although Freud himself acknowledged a greater debt to Fechner for the formation of the theoretical structure of psychoanalysis, Janet's complaint is not altogether unfair, particularly in the area of the psychology of religion. At the same time, it is hard to imagine Janet's work having stimulated the same revolution in psychology that has come to be associated with Freud.

Freud began his scientific training in medicine with intensive studies in the natural sciences, but his attraction to the work of the famous French neurologist Jean-Martin Charcot (1835–1893)—whose work on hypnosis, hysteria, and traumatic neurosis, as well as his theories regarding unconscious "fixed ideas," had influenced Janet—proved decisive. In Charcot's work the young Freud found the stimulus to produce his first paper on hysteria, the controversy over which both isolated him from his teachers and launched the career that eventually led to his formulation of the psychoanalytic method and its accompanying models of the psyche and its workings. Almost as soon as he had conceived his first versions of psychoanalytic theory Freud's interests spread out into the areas of sociology, culture, art, literature, and religion. Quite early on in his career he had the idea to compare religious rituals and creeds with the obsessive, compulsive symptoms of neurotics and to characterize religion as a "universal obsessional neurosis," a position that he expanded and developed over the next twenty years in a variety of contexts.

Quite apart from the different models of the psyche that Freud developed over the course of his career, his basic approach to religion consisted in viewing all religious beliefs and rituals as covert projections of the same intrafamilial conflicts that determine the position of the individual ego in society into a transcendent realm where they can be resolved. Religion was thus seen to function as a system of "illusions" aimed at repressing and containing antisocial desires, the prototype of which was the Oedipal sexual desire of the sons for the mother. On these grounds Freud argued that religion began with the murder of the father figure who was restored in the form of an authoritarian deity; that religious sacrifice represented a release from the guilt of parricide; that incestuous drives needed to be met in primitive societies with religious taboos in order for these to be controlled effectively; and that the common family history of the human race passes on to each individual in the modern world as part of the general inheritance of our common mass psyche. For all the benefits that religion has provided for the psychic health of civilization, Freud left no doubt that he believed that it was time to encourage greater education to reality and resignation to our common human fate, and to overcome the infantile fixations of religion. [*See also the biography of Freud.*]

Of all of Freud's students, two are remembered for breaking away and establishing psychological schools of their own, Alfred Adler (1870–1937) and C. G. Jung (1875–1961). Adler's contributions to the psychology of religion were minimal and theoretically unsustained, but Jung distinguished himself in contrast to Freud for his positive and far-reaching concern with the psychology of religious phenomena. While Janet's intellectual pedigree shows clear ties to the Enlightenment, Jung, like Freud, turned to the Romantic movement for his major philosophical preoccupation. It was not so much Jung's initial interest in religion, myth, and esoteric symbolic traditions that alienated him from Freud, but his positive assessment of religion as revelatory of dimensions of the psyche deeper and more comprehensive than the sexual drive that Freud had made the psyche's pivot. In Jung's own assessment, it was his study of alchemy that provided him with a positive link between psychology and religion by revealing the common ground between them: a process from unconsciousness, to consciousness, to the full unity of the two in the "individuated Self." There, too, Jung found confirmation of his theory of primordial "archetypes," the universal patterns that govern symbolic expression at the level of the "collective unconscious" and provide the basic models for religious ritual, belief, and imagery. In addition to its therapeutic value, Jung's theory of archetypes allowed him a way to avoid addressing the question of the metaphysical status of religious beliefs—and hence to hold fast to his image of himself as a scientist—and at the same time to demonstrate the role that religion can play in psychic well-being when it is grounded on firsthand experience of the archetypes that we inherit at birth and is freed from the rigors of "dogmatizing" religion. Even more than Freud, Jung made bold attempts to lay his map of the psyche over the wider reaches of religion throughout both Eastern and Western history.

There is no doubt that of all the early pioneers of depth psychology none has had such a positive and powerful influence on the world of religious studies as Jung. Scholars of religion from all areas have found in his ideas a psychology sympathetic to many of their fundamental concerns, while critics of the darker sides of religion and its effects on the individual and society have found Freud more supportive of their complaints. Meanwhile, there has been no want of critics who reject Jung's work as inimical to the cause of religion and who turn instead to Freud for his stricter adherence to scientific method, which in any case religion claims eventually to transcend.

It should be noted here that both Freud and Jung, as well as Adler, attracted disciples among the clergy who carried their work over into the *cura animarum*, in fulfillment of a prediction that Janet had made for the future of the new psychology. In general the more conciliatory syntheses of psychology and religion—though often the least rigorous in terms of theory and method—stem from the practical efforts made in this regard.

Other trends. Despite the revolution that the psychoanalytic movement and its subsidiary currents brought to the psychology of religion, it did not succeed in changing the direction given by other pioneering efforts in the field. George M. Stratton (1865–1957) believed religion to be grounded in personal and social conflict, a view that he developed at more or less the same time that psychoanalysis came to America. Others, like James B. Pratt (1875–1944) and R. H. Thouless (1894–1980) recognized the importance of the movement but tried to see its religious implications in a wider framework. [*See the biography of Pratt.*] The same is true of Gordon Allport (1897–1967), whose main concerns were to argue for the primacy of the individual subject over quantitative analysis or abstract theory and to encourage new and more adequate scientific methods for studying the rational structures of religious experience. In Europe the work of Richard Müller-Freienfels (1882–1949) sidestepped the psychoanalytic movement and grounded a psychology of religion on the philosophy of Immanuel Kant, making use of comparative religious material from the field of anthropology. The work of Jacob Levy Moreno (1892–1974) also deserves mention here for its introduction of psychodrama and group therapy based on a theory of interpersonal relations drawn from religion. Moreno's work directly influenced Martin Buber's dialogic view of the religious subject. Among early attempts in Great Britain to develop sound theoretical foundations for the psychology of religion, notable are the works of W. B. Selbie (1862–1944) and Laurence William Grensted (1884–1964), both of whom were critical of psychoanalysis and favorably disposed to religion.

Perhaps the most outstanding of Freud's disciples in terms of a contribution to the psychology of religion has been Eric H. Erikson, whose theory of the stages in the life cycle combine Freud's theory of libidinal development with something akin to Jung's theory of the process of individuation to give a more positive assessment of the role of religion in psychic health. In the Jungian camp, some of the most creative advances have come with James Hillman, who has taken Jung's work a step further by arguing against the bias of monotheism that Jung built into archetypal psychology in consequence of his notion of the central "Self." Hillman sees the soul as fundamentally "polytheistic" in its generation and use of religious imagery. Among those who separated from Adler to found their own schools, Victor Frankl should be singled out for his religiously oriented "logotherapy," which took over many of the ideas and methods associated with "existential psychiatry." Frankl's theories rank among those that have been welcomed with the greatest enthusiasm by those seeking to see psychology as complementary to the pastoral aims of organized religion.

Major Concerns. From even this brief account of the history of the discipline, it should be clear that the term *psychology of religion* serves as a classifying device for too wide a spectrum of methods and theoretical models to allow for any comprehensive definition that would mark it off sharply from other human and physical sciences. Indeed, even to identify in the various strands of the discipline the common concern with describing religion in terms of the processes of the psyche one must gloss over the logical problem of isolating a particular field of phenomena for study. At the same time, it is possible to single out certain key elements that, while not all central to everyone working in the psychology or religion, protect it from being absorbed into its neighboring disciplines.

In terms of religious phenomena, the critical element has surely been the notion of a transcendent referent to religious sentiments, which Western academia is accustomed to abbreviate with the word *God*. In order to sustain any degree of empirical objectivity, the psychology of religion must in theory refuse to pronounce on the ontological status of particular transcendent referents and focus its attention merely on the fact that such publicly unverifiable beliefs are entertained and serve as focal points for certain patterns of thought and behavior. In practice, the force of particular theories commonly rests on their ability to translate some or all transcendent referents into the functioning of psychic processes.

Regarding methodology, both the speculative and the empirical approaches would seem to be crucial to the advance of the psychological description and explanation of religion. There can be no doubt that, unlike the controlled conditions that behavioral and animal psychology allow for, much psychological investigation—in particular that of depth psychology—depends heavily on introspective data and almost totally eludes validation by prediction. In formulating a logic and method to manage these data, it commonly tiptoes around the borderlands of philosophy, anthropology, sociology, history, and the other human sciences without finding itself a home in any of them. This means not only that it is able to bring together an extraordinarily wide range of insights but that problems of defining its procedures continue to resist every attempt at resolution and to lead naturally to a great amount of free and subjective speculation. Consequently, the greater objectivity that psychological methods of a more statistical and behavioral stamp have made to the study of religion can hardly be dismissed as irrelevant. Indeed without the slower, more disciplined, but less dramatic attempt to quantify the variables among religious phenomena, social conditions, and personality development, it is doubtful that the more fertile general schemes would have survived the passage through the twentieth century.

Finally, there are three nodal points—origins, transformations, and health—around which psychological theories about religion tend to cluster and that define the discipline's problematics.

Psychogenesis. Underlying all psychological theory that attempts to provide a general account of the roots of religion in the psyche are two interrelated assumptions: that the human psyche is possessed of a fundamentally stable and invariant structure and that as a psychological phenomenon religion shows patterns common to all people at all times and places. In addition, the most widely circulated theories of the psychogenesis of religion—including those dispersed throughout the history of philosophy—regularly include some version of the principle of projection.

Simply put, religious projection refers to an imaginative leap from excessively overpowering and rationally unmanageable emotions to belief in a world of transcendent forces controlling personal destiny. In order to be used as a genetic principle, it is necessary to presuppose that at some point in the primitive human community there was something like a collective transposition of the structural conditions of the psyche into the external world.

The contrast between Freud and Jung here shows how widely differing appreciations of religion can emerge from the same basic idea. For Freud the universality of religion was to be traced back to the universality of incestuous desires whose unconscious repression led primitive peoples beyond animism to the irrational and illusory projection of divinely established taboos. For Jung the projections of religion can be traced back to a natural predisposition of the psyche for wholeness, a predisposition that the primitive mind was able to express once it had achieved the requisite consciousness to form symbols and that the modern psyche can rediscover only by probing beneath the doctrines of organized religion to the archetypally patterned, spontaneous products of the unconscious mind.

In general psychology has followed anthropology and sociology in curing itself of the simplistic biases of the projectionist approach, though even today many who seek grounds for the birth of religion in psychological reactions to hallucinations, mystical or ecstatic experiences, visions, parapsychological phenomena, or even some elemental human "need," assume the validity of extrapolating general historical explanations from these reactions. Abraham Maslow's (1908–1970) attempt to link religion to "peak experiences," Erich Fromm's (1900–1980) case for religion as a response to authentically felt needs that are manifest in what he calls "x experiences," and S. G. F. Brandon's (1907–1971) tracing of religion to the internalization of the sense of time typify the many variations on the argument from projection still in force.

Aside from the somewhat loosely controlled and controversial experimentation with drug-induced states offered as data to support the link between religious imagery and "higher states of consciousness," little empirical work has been devoted to the proof of projection theories as such. For one thing, early psychological arguments seeking to ground religion in a single emotion after the manner of Lucretius's famous dictum "Deos fecit timor" ("The gods are made by fear") or to isolate a specifically "religious type" of personality—as found in the work of Eduard Spranger (1882–1963)—were soon abandoned in favor of a comprehensive understanding of the psychic dimension of religion or the religious dimension of personality. For another, the historical dimension of these theories precludes statistical studies and dictates a heavy dependence on anthropological data gathered among existing primitive peoples. The focus of psychogenetic theories has shifted clearly in the direction of more empirically oriented research into the ties between religious behavior and personality structure, as for instance with the work of Allport and of Milton Rokeach.

Psychomorphosis. Concern with describing the process by which religious beliefs and attitudes reach consciousness and the transformations they undergo from childhood to adulthood has been central to the psychology of religion from the start. Depth psychology was able to transfer its notions of the psychogenesis of religious history writ large to the history writ small of psychomorphosis, or personal development, and then to exchange new information and insights between them by adopting the nineteenth-century biological principle that ontogeny recapitulates phylogeny. In this way study of the changes of a religious nature observed in the growth process of the individual from childhood to adulthood could be enlightened by and in turn enlighten study of the ascent of the human race from a primitive to a scientific mentality. Even today, long after the principle has fallen from grace in biology and empirical data on religious conversion has introduced new cultural and social variables into the process of psychic development, the idea is not without its appeal in more speculative circles of depth psychology, particularly among those of a strong Jungian stamp.

The first notable empirical work done on the psychomorphosis of religion was that conducted by Americans in the final decades of the nineteenth century on the conversion process, the phenomenon of being "twiceborn," as William James put it. Although the models of psychic growth have changed over the years, the use of surveys, interviews, personality inventories, and general sociological statistics is still very much in evidence, and is indeed one of the most common links between organized religion and psychological science.

Erikson's "epigenetic" theory of psychic growth is one such model that has inspired numerous studies of religious identity. Basically it presents an eightfold life cycle, each stage of which represents a crisis of human relationships that generates corresponding virtues and vices, affects the progress of later stages, and is reflected in some dimension of religious behavior. Erikson has also applied his model to the controversial project of writing "psychohistories" of religious figures such as Martin Luther and Mohandas Gandhi.

Important research on the morphosis of the image of God in children began in 1913 with the work of Henri Clavier, who noted a progression from anthropomorphism to spiritualization; research was later refined from a number of different perspectives in the empirical studies of psychologists such as Ronald Goldman, J.-P. Dechonchy, Ana-Maria Rizzuto, and Antoine Vergote. Vergote founded the Center for Religious Psychology at the University of Louvain, which has carried on important research into the relations between parental images and images of the deity, the development of moral consciousness, and the levels of symbolic and ritual understanding in children. In addition to psychoanalysis, Jean Piaget's (1886–1980) studies of child psychology have exerted great influence on this work.

Psychotherapy. The study of the correlation of religion and therapy should be understood as a bilateral enterprise, embracing not only the way in which religious traditions can function prophylactically and positively to promote psychic health and development, but also the way in which psychological traditions can serve to purify religion of its psychically harmful effects. Both a great deal of the opposition and of the support that psychologists of religion of all persuasions have encountered from organized religion in the past and continue to meet today stems from this double-edged critical function.

Scholars among the clergy, such as Hans Schär, Oskar Pfister, Ernst Jahn, and Anton Boisen were among the first to recognize the importance of psychology for pastoral care and theological reflection. Already before the middle of the twentieth century a flurry of pastoral theologies grounded in a variety of different psychological theories had ushered in specialized journals, associations, university programs, and counseling and research centers devoted to the subject throughout Europe and the United States. In general, this trend represents a shift away from the concern with abnormal psychology, mystical states, esoteric rituals, "supernatural" healings, and primitive practices, which figured prominently in much early work in the psychology of religion, to a concern with promoting normal religious development in prayer, worship, conversion, and community involvement. Not unrelated to this, the critical functions of this approach have proved more helpful than threatening to organized religion, and its theoretical contribution has suffered from widespread neglect among those pursuing more classical or scientific approaches.

Psychological studies of Eastern spiritual traditions, in particular Zen Buddhism and yoga, have attempted to show how such things as rhythmic breathing, centered meditation, and the practice of *kōan, mantras*, and the like not only anticipate many of the most common psychotherapeutic techniques but can also be more effective. In much the same way that Judeo-Christian ideas inspired Western psychotherapies, attempts have been made in the East to draw on native religiosity. In Japan, for instance, the influence of Zen is evident in what is known as "Morita therapy"; and ideas drawn from the True Pure Land sect of Buddhism have been formative in *naikan* ("inward-looking") therapy, begun in the 1950s by Yoshimoto Inobu for work with prison inmates and later adopted for use in the moral education of children and adolescents and for the treatment of certain mental disorders. While a certain amount of neurological data and statistics have been gathered in support of the claims of this method's therapeutic success, it is still widely ignored by the psychotherapeutic establishment. Similar researches related to Western religious practices took place too close to the sources of the psychology of religion to generate the same interest, even though the literature is more voluminous.

From the time of its origins, the psychology of religion has never been without those proclaiming a sweeping censure of religion as damaging to mental health and full human development, based both on particular case histories and on general epistemological assumptions. At the same time, psychologists working from within particular religious traditions have frequently made use of similar ideas to decry the abuses of religion and argue for the superiority of certain religious traditions vis-à-vis other traditions, primitive religious practices, new movements, cults, and the like. What is lacking, however, is anything like a set of objective and nonsectarian criteria for distinguishing the wholesome from the sick in particular religious practices and beliefs, which might then be adopted as guidelines for directing religion in the future in the same way that philosophical, political, and theological ideas direct elements internal to organized religions today.

BIBLIOGRAPHY

Of the many general and specialized bibiliographical sources available for the psychology of religion, the most useful is that prepared by Donald Capps, Lewis Rambo, and Paul Ransohoff under the title *Psychology of Religion: A Guide to Information Sources* (Detroit, 1976). Entries cover the years 1950 to 1974 and are divided into sections dealing with general works (including other bibliographies) and the mythical, ritual, experiential, dispositional, social, and directional dimensions of religion. Their work should be consulted as a complement to William W. Meissner's earlier *Annotated Bibliography in Religion and Psychology* (New York, 1961), which brings together more than twenty-nine hundred annotated entries, including a selection of classical sources and works written from 1950 to 1959, mostly gleaned from the pages of *Psychology Abstracts* and tidily arranged in forty-seven categories.

Unfortunately, no comprehensive historical account of the psychology of religion in all its phases exists. Spotty but reliable overviews listing the major primary sources of the figures reviewed in this essay can be found in Georges Berguer's *Traité de la psychologie de la religion* (Lausanne, 1946), Laurence William Grensted's *The Psychology of Religion* (Oxford, 1952), Paul E. Johnson's *Psychology of Religion* (Nashville, 1959), Walter Houston Clark's *The Psychology of Religion* (New York, 1958), G. Stephens Spinks's *Psychology and Religion: An Introduction to Contemporary Views* (Boston, 1965), Wayne E. Oates's *The Psychology of Religion* (Waco, 1973), Paul W. Pruyser's *A Dynamic Psychology of Religion* (New York, 1968), and *The Psychology of Religion: Historical and Interpretative Readings*, edited by Orlo Strunk (Nashville, 1971). Each of these works also attempts to outline the major methodological and theoretical issues in the psychology of religion.

Henri F. Ellenberger's massive and impressive study of the origins of depth psychology, *The Discovery of the Unconscious* (New York, 1970), gives special attention to developments in the psychology of religion, presenting an unusually fair and unbiased approach to the diversity of opinion from Janet to Jung. Philip Rieff's *Freud: The Mind of the Moralist*, 3d ed. (Chicago, 1979), contains one of the most authoritative and exhaustive introductions to Freud's psychology of religion to be found anywhere. An essay by Paul W. Pruyser, "Sigmund Freud and His Legacy: Psychoanalytic Psychology of Religion," which appeared in *Beyond the Classics? Essays in the Scientific Study of Religion*, edited by Charles Y. Glock and Phillip E. Hammond (New York, 1973), pp. 243–290, provides considerable supplementary bibliographical material on the aftermath of Freud's ideas on religious studies; in this same regard, see also Peter Homans's *Theology after Freud* (Indianapolis, 1970). Representative of the relatively few attempts to apply Adler's ideas directly to religion is Rudolf Allers's *The Psychology of Character* (London, 1939). For a comprehensive historical study of Jung's psychology of religion, see my book *Imago Dei: A Study of C. G. Jung's Psychology of Religion* (Lewisburg, Pa., 1979); I have also prepared an extensive listing of secondary sources under the title "Jung and Theology: A Bibliographical Essay," *Spring* (1973): 204–255. J. Eugene Wright's *Erikson: Identity and Religion* (New York, 1982) represents the first general study of Erikson's work from the viewpoint of the psychology of religion. See also here James W. Fowler's *Stages of Faith: The Psychology of Human Development and the Quest for Meaning* (San Francisco, 1981). *Psychohistory and Religion* is a collection of essays edited by Roger A. Johnson (Philadelphia, 1977) presenting the conflict surrounding Erikson's analysis of Luther.

A collection edited by H. Newton Malony under the title *Current Perspectives in the Psychology of Religion* (Grand Rapids, Mich., 1977) contains good historical treatises, an assessment of recent empirical work, and a look at more recent trends. *Research in Religious Behavior*, compiled by Benjamin Beit-Hallahmi (Monterey, Calif., 1973), brings together seventeen empirical studies based principally on psychological models. For a good sourcebook of selected readings ranging widely over research past and present, see *Psychology and Religion*, edited by L. B. Brown (Harmondsworth, 1973). Antoine Vergote's *The Religious Man* (Dublin, 1969), provides a good overview of empirical studies in religious attitudes. For contrasting developmental studies done on the formation of the God-image, see Ana-Maria Rizzuto's *The Birth of the Living God: A Psychoanalytic Study* (Chicago, 1979) and Antoine Vergote and Alvaro Tamayo's *The Parental Figures and the Representation of God: A Psychological and Cross-Cultural Study* (The Hague, 1980). Both works include considerable reference material and brief historical surveys of the field. See also Daniel C. Bateson and W. Larry Ventis's *The Religious Experience: A Social-Psychological Perspective* (Oxford, 1982) for an example of recent cross-fertilization of sociological and psychological methods for gathering data on religion, in this case leaning heavily on the work of Freud and Allport. A general account of the relation between drug-induced states and religion, and its related research can be found in R. E. L. Masters and Jean Houston's *The Varieties of Psychedelic Experience* (New York, 1966), pp. 247–313; see also Walter Houston Clark's *Chemical Ecstasy* (New York, 1966).

A dialogue between D. T. Suzuki, Erich Fromm, and Richard De Martino on *Zen Buddhism and Psychoanalysis* (New York, 1960) attempts a theoretical comparison and contrast of the two ways. For a brief historical account of the use of Zen for therapy in Japan, see Ikenaga Isamu's *Zen-teki shinri ryōhō no susume* (Tokyo, 1976). Also helpful here are a series of essays published by K. Sato in *Psychologies* between 1957 and 1965 on Morita therapy, *naikan* therapy, and Zen in relationship to religion and Western psychology. Terry V. Lesh has prepared a brief bibliography in Western languages, "Zen and Psychotherapy: A Partially Annotated Bibliography," *Journal of Humanistic Psychology* 10 (Spring 1970): 75–83.

The Dialogue between Theology and Psychology, a collection of essays edited by Peter Homans (Chicago, 1968), offers a solid introduction to the theoretical issues involved in the meeting of the two disciplines. The works of Seward Hiltner, particularly *Pastoral Counseling* (New York, 1949) and *Preface to Pastoral Theology* (New York, 1958), present a balanced treatment of the early history and major concerns of pastoral psychology, particularly if read together with the works of Pruyser, Oates, and Johnson mentioned earlier.

JAMES W. HEISIG

Psychology and Religion Movement

In this essay, "psychology and religion" will refer to an intellectual movement that began in the 1880s and extends into the present. As such, "psychology and religion" should be distinguished from "psychology of religion," the "dialogue between psychology and theology," and "religious psychology."

Definition and Context

When attempting to understand the topic "psychology and religion" it is essential to clarify at the outset the meaning of the terms *psychology* and *religion.* They are not cognate or parallel terms. *Psychology* denotes a science or method for the study of subjective states. On the other hand, *religion* refers to a series of historical and cultural expressions or phenomena and not to a method or science. An analogy can further clarify these two terms. *Politics* refers to a social and cultural expression, whereas *political science* denotes the correct method for the study of politics. Although politicians do study things, politics is not, strictly speaking, a method or a science. So, *politics* and *religion* are cognate, or parallel, terms, as are *psychology* and *political science.* But *politics* and *psychology* are not parallel terms, nor are *psychology* and *religion.*

This distinction between method (or science) and cultural expression (or phenomenon) can be clarified still further. Theology can be thought of as the rational reflection upon religious expressions from within the institutional context of a sacred community, and as such is a method, like psychology. Psychology also can reflect on religious phenomena, and it often does so within the institutional context of a university, which is a secular and not a sacred community. When this is done, one speaks of the psychology *of* religion, and just as easily and correctly of the sociology of religion, the philosophy of religion, and the history of religion. In like fashion, one can speak of the theology of culture, or of religion, or, for that matter, of politics or personality. It is necessary to recognize that the first set of inquiries occurs under the auspices of a secular institution, whereas the second occurs within the institutional context of a church, seminary, or university divinity school.

Once these distinctions are made, however, it is possible to understand the designation "psychology *and* religion" and to recognize that it refers to an extremely important aspect of the contemporary understanding of religion. It does not refer to a particular method for the study of religious expressions. Often the term is used by those who wish to avoid a subordination of religion to psychology and who prefer a dialogical model: "psychology and religion," therefore, is an intellectual movement in which different disciplines are mixed. Some psychologists, theologians, ministers, and religious intellectuals have participated in it, and each participant has sought to clarify his or her own particular goals in relation to those of others. So viewed, the psychology and religion movement becomes one of the most important features of the study of religion in the twentieth century, taking its place alongside the theology of culture movement and the history of religions movement.

Development of the Movement. The notion of an intellectual movement suggests that men and women come together in order to understand and share specific ideas, that such activities begin in definite academic-institutional contexts, that the ideas migrate to other contexts from time to time, and that they sometimes even move out of strict intellectual enclaves into society at large. As such, an intellectual movement consists of a body of changing ideas that are grounded in an identifiable and in principle ever-widening social context. These ideas, their contexts, and the different periods of the movement can all be described.

The psychology and religion movement has been concerned with two sets of ideas that have formed what can be called its central intellectual tension. On the one hand, there is the tradition of Christian thought and practice that has pervaded American society and higher education, especially in such areas as classics, literature, and philosophy. On the other hand, there is the new science of psychology that arose in the American university, at the end of the nineteenth century. This brash, young discipline quickly separated itself from its parent disciplines, philosophy and theology, and defined itself after the fashion of the already-emergent natural sciences, in the tradition of the Enlightenment. According to one of the central principles of Enlightenment thought, science gradually removes religion from the cognitive sphere. These two strands—the religious and the scientific—which earlier had repeatedly clashed in American and European history, are vigorously represented throughout the various periods of the psychology and religion movement. At times, the clash has been open and central; at others, it has given way to creative attempts at reconciliation. In all cases, it has led to shifting definitions and redefinitions of psychology, personality, religion, the religious, theology, religious experience, human growth, and the like. Each period has had its own particular resolution to the tension.

But the ideas that constituted the psychology and religion movement had a variety of cultural contexts. In this sense it was no different from, say, the psychoanalytic movement or, for that matter, the civil rights movement. The first and most obvious context has already been mentioned: psychology and religion were anchored in the university and the churches, respectively. A third structure, the clinic, did not really appear until the second period of the movement, when psychoanalysis and behaviorism had replaced American functional psychology as the dominant psychologies. At various times, these three—the church, the university, and the clinic—have taken on very different degrees of influence.

Surrounding the ideas and their intellectual-institutional base was the distinctive political and economic ethos of each period. The psychology of religion, during the first period, was nurtured by late nineteenth-century political isolationism; the dialogue between theology and psychology, in the second period, by the aftermath of World War II; the breakdown of the dialogue, in the third period, by political radicalism; and the most recent phase by political and economic conservatism. Whether a specific ethos actually created what was distinctive in each period remains a moot point.

It is important to note the distinctively American character of the psychology and religion movement, for no European nation became nearly as excited about either religion or psychology as did the Americans, to say nothing of becoming excited about putting the two together. Beneath this national trend lies the most pervasive historical theme of the West, the secularization and persistence of traditional religion in modern, industrializing society. Industrialization and urbanization created a pluralized social world that made psychological thinking especially necessary, and these forces also shaped the personalizing and privatizing of life to which religious leaders and thinkers adapted. Finally, one cannot omit such sweeping civilizational issues as the influx of ideas from non-Western societies, both ancient and primitive, either by way of the findings of anthropology and the history of religions or through political internationalism. In what follows, only the first two of the movement's contexts—institutional-academic base and political-economic ethos—will be thoroughly discussed, although occasional reference must be made to the others as well.

Historical Overview of the Movement. The psychology and religion movement began in the 1880s and therefore spans almost exactly one hundred years. During this time, it has gone through four distinct periods, and while each period is distinct, it is possible to identify the elements in each that are common to all. Each period had its leading figures and influential books, which espoused a particular version of psychology and of religion and which centered on a special problem. This problem expressed the central intellectual tension of the time and provided coherence to the period as a whole. In addition, social circumstances created specific kinds of role patterns and conflicts for the different practitioners of psychology and religion (theologians, religious intellectuals, psychologists, etc.).

The science of psychology began in the mid-1880s as a functional psychology, and in the hands of G. Stanley Hall (1844–1924) and William James (1842–1910) it quickly turned to religious experience. The focus was on the various forms of Protestant faith, and in particular on conversion experiences. But writers also addressed such phenomena as prayer, worship, mystical states, and religious education. Religious philosophers quickly entered the scene and the "psychology of religion" came into being. By 1930, however, it had begun to decline. Several explanations will be offered for this.

During the 1930s and 1940s, economic depression and world war absorbed the energies of both psychologists and churchmen, and it was not until the 1950s that two European movements—psychoanalysis and existentialism—entered the American religious scene and the dialogue between theology and psychology was born. Paul Tillich (1886–1965) was among the several leaders of this phase of the movement; their central concern was the relationship between developmental factors that had been discovered by Freud and existential factors, such as freedom and decision, that were proposed by theologians influenced by European existentialist philosophers. Despite the freshness of this thinking during this phase, its continuity with the first period needs to be recognized.

For a great many complex social and intellectual reasons, the creative tension between two discrete entities, theology and psychology, broke down at the end of the 1960s and gave way to a pluralism in psychology and theology, producing what could be called a transitional period with a variety of orientations. This was a time of great creativity and experimentation, and it is probably the most difficult of the four periods to characterize.

Periods of plurality and structurelessness rarely last

long, and the transitional period began to consolidate into yet another pattern in the 1970s. The central feature of this period has come to be segmentation, in which theological, historical-anthropological, and social scientific orientations coexist within their own clusters of allied disciplines and subdisciplines. In this period, very different writers with very different audiences work simultaneously in very different institutional settings.

The Four Periods of the Movement

The psychology and religion movement consists of men and women sharing ideas about psychology and religious expressions, over a period of almost exactly one hundred years. Each phase of the movement has its major figures, representative works, central issue, role patterns and social conditions.

Psychology of Religion, 1885–1930. Less is known of this period and less significance is attributed to it than to any of the others, but most of the major ideas that characterize the psychology and religion movement as a whole were set forth at this time. The period is rightly associated with William James's famous study, *The Varieties of Religious Experience* (1902). Other psychologists wrote in similar ways about similar topics, but this is less often recognized, and, in fact, there was much continuity between their work and that of James.

In the last quarter of the nineteenth century, the science of psychology emerged in American universities and colleges. It modeled itself on the exact sciences by embracing the methods of empirical observation and positivistic measurement, thereby dissociating itself from theology and philosophy. Mindful of already existing studies in the sociology of religion and in the work of anthropologists on primitive religions, some workers in the new field turned to the study of religion. But unlike the sociologists and the anthropologists, the psychologists studied religious beliefs, practices, and experiences in their own society. They were therefore confronted with pressure to reconcile their scientific findings with the truth-claims of religious people. In many cases the psychologist himself was unable to escape this conflict as it appeared in his own life.

G. Stanley Hall was one of this first period's most energetic figures. President of Clark University, he founded the Clark School of Religious Psychology and published two influential books, *Adolescence* (1904) and *Jesus, The Christ, in the Light of Psychology* (1917). J. H. Leuba (1868–1946) studied under Hall at Clark and then taught at Bryn Mawr College. He wrote *A Psychological Study of Religion* (1912) and *The Psychology of Religious Mysticism* (1925). E. D. Starbuck (1866–1947) studied with James at Harvard University and also with Hall at Clark, and was known for his highly empirical work on the new subject. He published *The Psychology of Religion* (1899). In addition to these books, many of the psychologists of religion set forth their ideas and findings in *The American Journal of Psychology* (1887–), *The Psychological Bulletin* (1904–), and in Hall's own *Journal of Religious Psychology, Including its Anthropological and Social Aspects* (1904–1915).

While these psychologists wrote on a great variety of subjects, such as revival phenomena, normal religious growth, and the influence of adolescence upon religious life, they were—especially those associated with the Clark school—generally united in sharing a common view of psychology, of religion, and of the central problem in the psychology of religion. In one way or another, these psychologists used a functional psychology, which postulated that the purpose or function of the organism, both biologically and psychologically, was adaptation to the social order. William James's famous textbook, *The Principles of Psychology* (1890), served as a major statement of this point of view. Consequently, religion was understood as a higher power or force that existed beyond the reach of consciousness and of conscious will or choice and to which consciousness had to adapt itself. These psychological and religious viewpoints came together quite naturally around the privileged subject matter of the movement, the conversion experience.

When seen in the light of these considerations, James's *Varieties* becomes the representative text of this period. James collected a great many different religious experiences from a variety of published and unpublished sources. Although he discussed many topics, his unifying thread was the fact that as a result of coming into contact with religious realities, people's lives changed for the better. When coupled with the predominantly Protestant character of James's sources, this change-inducing fact made his book essentially a study of conversion (understood in a very broad sense). Religious experience was the felicitous adaptation of consciousness to a higher power. Religious experience converted a divided inner life into one that was harmonious and whole. In so concluding, James was able to offer to his colleagues—and to his age—an especially cogent solution to the movement's central intellectual tension. That is, the science of psychology could hardly contradict society's reverence for religious beliefs if those beliefs in fact facilitated psychological adaptation.

The psychology of religion had an academic-institutional base that created role patterns and role conflicts. The first psychologists were for the most part located in college and university departments of psychology. In most cases, they had been raised in religious—often Protestant—homes. Their scientific explorations of religion called into question the personal and intellectual truth-claims of their own traditions, which were represented by ministers in the society. So the new role of professor and scientist clashed with the older roles of philosopher, theologian, and minister. It was often the case that professors of psychology also taught moral philosophy; they were sometimes deans and were responsible for the moral guidance of the younger generation, a role that had traditionally belonged to the clergy. (Among these scholars, Hall was one of the few who actually had been educated for the ministry.)

Social circumstances of a broader and more sweeping sort also shaped the psychology of religion. Burgeoning industrialization and consequent urbanization tended to fragment the sense of wholeness and well-being usually associated with rural life. The psychologists joined sociologists, physicians, and clergy in expressing alarm about the new forms of nervous disease—"hysteria" in women and "neurasthenia" in men—that made their appearance at the time, and both psychology and religion were seen as resources for healing the mental ills of the modernizing society. As one who himself suffered periodically from debilitating nervous ailments, and as a psychologist deeply interested in abnormal mental states, William James was surely a man of his time. In speaking of "the divided self," he called attention to the close relation between suffering, psychology, and religion (1902). Political and cultural isolationism kept European thought and sensibilities at bay, and supported the characteristically American search for innocence and purity. The psychologist of religion worked largely with American ideas and American forms of religious experience.

By 1930, interest in the psychology of religion had begun to wane. Historians of psychology have offered many reasons for this decline. Benjamin Beit-Hallahmi (1974) finds its cause in the fact that the psychological theory of the psychology of religion lacked a sophisticated theoretical base into which both empirical findings and abstract formulations could be integrated. Perhaps for this reason behaviorism supplanted functional psychology in the early 1910s and enhanced the impression that an interest in religion was unscientific. To these internal issues was added external pressure from the religious community at large, which sensed in the work of the psychologists a threat to the truth-claims of religion. (All the second-generation psychologists of religion—such as G. A. Coe, James B. Pratt, and E. S. Ames—were theologians, though of the liberal sort.) The observation should be added that the movement had no general sociological theory of culture to explain aspects of religion that went beyond the experiences of the individual. Nor did functional psychology have a developmental dimension, something that seems so essential today. Many of these deficiencies were remedied, however, when the next phase of the psychology and religion movement began. [*For further discussion of the major figures of the first period, see the biographies of Hall, James, Leuba, and Starbuck; see also the biography of Pratt.*]

Dialogue with Theology, 1930–1960. In very different ways, the Great Depression and World War II deflected energies from the psychology and religion movement, which has always required the luxury of economic and political stability. But the war prepared the soil for the renewal of the movement. American psychology "went to war," as it were, by responding to the demand for such services as the psychological testing of recruits and the psychological treatment of those afflicted with war-induced psychopathology. Throughout this period, new and radical psychological ideas were also migrating across the Atlantic from Europe—as in fact did some famous psychologists, such as Erich Fromm, Erik Erikson, and Heinz Kohut, among others. The depression and the war managed to disillusion the optimism of religious liberalism, which had been so congenial to the psychology of religion, and prepared the way for the theological neoorthodoxies of Karl Barth and Rudolph Bultmann.

By 1950, American religious thought was aswarm with European psychoanalytic and theological ideas and the second phase of the psychology and religion movement, that is, the dialogue between psychology and theology, was well under way. Of course, the second phase recognized that psychoanalysis had entirely repudiated the truth-claims of religious thinkers, and that the new and lofty theologies had split revelation and faith from such psychological processes as experience and reason. But workers in this phase of the movement were also committed to the truth of both sides, and therefore sought a dialogue between them. In so doing, they once again took up the movement's central intellectual tension.

Tillich and his influence. By far the most outstanding figure of this period was the Christian theologian Paul Tillich (1886–1965), who immigrated from Germany to the United States in the early thirties. Tillich attempted to synthesize the sweep of Christian tradition with modern attacks on it by Marxism, psychoanalysis, and atheistic existentialism. In addition to writing books integrating psychoanalysis and theology, such as *The Dynamics of Faith* (1957) and *The Courage to Be* (1952), Tillich also included psychoanalytic insights in his theological works. The deeply religious Jewish philosopher Martin Buber (1878–1965) published a religio-philosophical discussion of social and psychological relationships, *I and Thou* (1923). Rollo May, both a practicing psychoanalyst and a former student of Tillich, synthesized the insights of Søren Kierkegaard and Freud in his *The Meaning of Anxiety* (1950). Though of lesser significance, the work of theologians David Roberts and Albert Outler, who sought to untangle Christian and psychoanalytic theories of the person in their books *Psychotherapy and a Christian View of Man* (1954) and *Psychotherapy and the Christian Message* (1953), is also worthy of mention.

As in the case of the psychology of religion, the dialogue between theology and psychology consisted of a dominant view of psychology and a dominant view of religion, both of which were organized around a central issue. Sometimes called "dynamic psychology" or "depth psychology," the psychology of the period was psychoanalytic. In its essence it consisted of four premises: (1) the existence of an unconscious dimension of the mind or psyche, (2) the grounding of unconscious wishes or processes in childhood or early developmental experience, (3) a conflict between unconscious processes and conscious thinking, and (4) the view that society and culture are the arena in which unconscious wishes are embodied, transformed, and disguised. This psychology differed radically from the earlier functional psychology and so called for a different approach to religion.

The religious part of the dialogue did not center upon religious experience but rather upon theological existence, faith, and self-understanding. The focus was the self, or man, or—as one would say today—the person. Drawing from the introspective traditions in Christian theology as set forth by Paul, Augustine, Luther, Pascal, and Kierkegaard, theological existentialism emphasized the tensions between conscious choice, decision, responsibility, identity, freedom, and responsibility on the one hand, and guilt, anxiety, despair, sin, and determinism on the other hand.

These psychological and theological perspectives converged in various ways around a central problem: the relationship between developmental factors and forces in life, which were described by psychoanalytic psychology, and the existential issues described by theology. The dialogue raised questions. What are the relations between lawful factors of growth and the perennial religious problems of freedom and choice? What is the relationship between neurosis and sin, between psychological health and redemption? Persons progressed, so the theologians argued, from a largely unconscious and deterministic developmental matrix into a wider and largely conscious historical and existential context of freedom and choice. It is possible to view this progression from the developmental to the existential as a new rendering, in entirely fresh language, of the earlier religious conversion experience.

Tillich's book *The Courage to Be* (1952) set forth many of the preoccupations and ideas of the dialogue in a representative way. In it he argued that anxiety, or dread, is a human or existential state produced by the awareness that one's life or existence is in a fundamental sense finite and arbitrary. In the face of such existential anxiety, the person can readily surrender to various authorities: the family, the state, or the church. Put in another way, anxiety about his finitude can lead a person to depend upon preliminary rather than ultimate realities. Neurosis—that is, neurotic conflict and neurotic anxiety, which Freud had described developmentally—is a means of avoiding the full or existential awareness of one's freedom, which Tillich called "the courage to be." In such fashion Tillich created a two-level theory in which both developmental and existential factors were related. In doing so, he gave his own creative solution to the movement's central tension.

Emerging roles. It was no accident, therefore, that Tillich was also the theoretician of pastoral psychology. After the war many pastors were confronted with the confusion brought about by rapid social and political change, and consequently they turned to depth psychology for help in understanding their parishioners'—and their own—lives. They also turned to writers like Tillich and May for a theological rationale to explain what they were doing. Psychoanalytic and existential ideas flowed through the books of such pastoral writers as Seward Hiltner, Wayne Oates, and Carol Wise, and a new role emerged for the minister: the minister as pastoral psychological counselor.

More than any other theologian, Tillich helped create a virtually new socioacademic role, that of the religious intellectual. Such persons identified professionally with the university rather than the church, eschewing the emotional, and often severe, religiosity of their childhood; but they continued to identify personally with the values of their Christian traditions, albeit in more rationalized and intellectualized forms. This spreading and recombination of values was further facilitated by the appearance of the academic study of religion and of departments of religion in colleges throughout the nation. The emergence of the psychologist (or psychoanalyst) as healer added the institutional context of the clinic to those of church and university. Four role patterns therefore formed the composite institutional base of the dialogue: the psychologist, the church theo-

the religious intellectual, and the pastoral counselor. All were in varying degrees grounded in or cut off from the church, the university, and the clinic.

At a deeper and more complex social level, the ideas of the dialogue were shaped by two widely shared sentiments: profound guilt and anxiety over the ravages of World War II and, especially, of the Holocaust, and intense confidence in the possibility of a better world. Many people turned for guidance to psychoanalysis, with its twin emphases on unconscious aggression and guilt and on the possibility of healing. But they also turned to theological existentialism's perception that freedom could be achieved through the recognition of sin and pride. At a still deeper level, urbanization and industrialization, so encouraged by the war effort, continued to create that sense of ambiguity and anonymity that made psychological thinking seem even more necessary and commonplace than before.

Once again, the United States had become a psychological society, and once again many Americans expected their psychologization to be complemented by a religious framework. On the whole, the religious intellectual and the psychologically oriented minister are creations of American culture. Neither has ever existed on the same scale in European nations. By embracing the tragic ideas of European psychoanalysis and existentialism, Americans had come of age; but only a distinctly American impulse could wish, in all innocence, that the two be wedded once again by religion. [*See also the biography of Tillich.*]

Breakdown of the Dialogue. The peculiarly American concern with psychology *and* theology, which reached a kind of peak in the late 1950s, was also highly nonpolitical, even though the war had brought international politics to the fore of American consciousness. The self of theological existentialism, anguished in the face of an unresponsive social order, and the alienated ego of psychoanalysis, struggling against the harshness of the cultural superego, had existed in a political vacuum. But the politicization of American society brought about the civil rights movement, the growing opposition to the Vietnam War, the youth culture, and the women's movement, and in one stroke rendered superfluous the dialogue's isolated and nonpolitical self; and so the dialogue broke down.

Coincidental with this shift in social ethos were two major intellectual changes that also supported the formation of a third model for the psychology and religion movement. The prestige of psychoanalysis waned. It had failed to deliver on its grandiose therapeutic claims and had instead ossified into ego psychology, a kind of psychoanalytic scholasticism. Advances on other fronts—sophisticated research in behavioral psychology, in cognitive psychology, and in psychopharmacology—further discredited it. But the more important intellectual shift was the waning of theological existentialism's obsession with Protestant issues of transcendence and faith, in the face of a new idea—that religion was a universal phenomenon, and that Christian faith was but one instance of it. While such a concept was of course not new, support for it crystallized around Mircea Eliade and others within the history of religions movement. As a result, the men and women who had identified with the psychology and religion movement began to explore new versions of the religious, new psychologies, and the new, special problems called forth by these.

History of religions. Eliade's work widened the dialogue's intense drive to render Protestant faith rational and plausible by introducing its participants to Eastern and primitive traditions, and by insisting that religion was essentially irrational. He therefore rejected the rationalism of both theology and psychoanalysis. The migration of these ideas into the psychology and religion movement helped to create fluidity and plurality, so that no single new model replaced the old one. The third phase of the movement actually consisted of four identifiable orientations, each with its own specific version of religion and psychology and each with its special problem. But, in an overall sense, most workers at this time sought to explore in one way or another a humanistic psychology, a view of religion as the sacred, and the problem of a universal religious consciousness and its possible structure—*homo religiosus,* as it were. During this period, the central intellectual tension once again became diffuse, as it had been in the first period.

While Eliade's books provoked fresh approaches, his work also allowed for continuity between the second and third periods. His own personal religious orientation (Eastern Orthodox Christianity), his readiness to speak of the historical and temporal uniqueness of Western monotheism, and his desire to renew modern secularity with a religious dimension made him appealing to the theologically inclined. Eliade's appreciation of the works of Freud and Jung—he in fact spoke of the history of religions as a meta-psychoanalysis—attracted many of those partial to psychoanalysis. His works were also responsible for reintroducing Jung's psychology into religious discussion. Eliade himself adopted a number of Jungian ideas, such as the collective unconscious, the psyche, and the archetype. It was perhaps for this reason that Joseph Campbell's elegant elaboration of Jung's thought into a universal psychology of world mythology, *The Hero with a Thousand Faces* (2d ed., 1968), received fresh attention. [*See also the biography of Eliade.*]

Death-of-God theology. Death-of-God theology, or "secular theology," was also a prominent blend of psychology and religion in the 1960s. It proposed not so much the death of God as the death of theology. In his book *Mircea Eliade and the Dialectic of the Sacred* (1963), Thomas Altizer used Eliade's religious concept of the sacred and Freud's psychological concept of the unconscious to explain the distant, remote, and awesome God of the theologians. By virtually identifying the unconscious with the sacred, Altizer was able to claim that the mystery of theological faith could not be completely separated from human consciousness and was, in fact, a property of man. The theologian's faith was, he therefore insisted, part of man's universal religious being and, as such, was also deeply psychological. The death of the God of the theologians coincided with the birth of the more psychological gods of the historians. This line of thinking permitted some theologians to address human, psychological phenomena more directly, by writing about the theology of hope, of play, and even of fantasy.

Humanistic psychology. A second approach was developed by humanistic psychology. Unsatisfied by Freud's emphasis on the unconscious, sexuality, stages of development, and the illusory character of religion, humanistic psychologists chose to speak out about the individual, the individual's freedom from childhood determinisms, and the values of active, conscious choice, decision, and action. They proposed that the religious is the epitome of human growth and fulfillment. Though published a decade before the opening of the third phase of the psychology and religion movement, *The Individual and His Religion* (1950) by the Harvard psychologist Gordon Allport was extremely influential, as was, to an even greater degree, Abraham Maslow's *Religions, Values, and Peak Experiences* (1964). By identifying religion with private rather than institutional experiences, and by attempting, in Maslow's case, to define religion in terms of the furthest reaches of human consciousness, these widely read books reintroduced a distinctly Jamesian flavor into the third period.

Humanistic psychology itself became a jumping-off point for yet another creative effort. In *Transpersonal Psychologies* (1983), edited by Charles T. Tart, and in Robert E. Ornstein's *The Psychology of Consciousness* (1975), one finds attempts to devise fresh approaches to the nature of psychological method and to the religious phenomena such revisions might properly address. In the first case, scientific study was directed away from the narrowness of Western methods and toward specific states of consciousness achieved through meditation, drugs, or religious practice, especially Eastern techniques such as Zen and yoga. The latter sought not only rational but also irrational modes of knowing, such as were thought to exist in more intuitive approaches to the human activities of perception and cognition. Both works emphasized spirituality as a universal personal reality rather than a specific institutional given. "Altered states" and "the nature of consciousness" became designations for a psychological approach to the human being's essentially spiritual nature. In these probes, "spiritual" did not mean "pious" but rather any higher form of consciousness that nevertheless could be studied scientifically.

Return to Freud. As if to reverse the mounting disapproval of psychoanalysis so characteristic of the third period, the last of the four orientations actually returned to Freud. While the works comprising this orientation appealed to a wide audience, their fresh approach to religious issues makes them especially valuable to students of psychology and religion. The classicist Norman O. Brown, in his *Life against Death: The Psychoanalytic Meaning of History* (1959), the sociologist Philip Rieff, in his *Freud: The Mind of the Moralist* (1959), and the philosopher-theologian Paul Ricoeur, in his *Freud and Philosophy* (1970), discussed Freud's works as a whole. They sought to assess the significance of Freud's corpus, not for a general theory of religion, but for its place in the sweeping development of Western Christian history. Each concluded, in different ways, that Freud was to be placed alongside Marx and Nietzsche as one of the major architects of the modern period. Further, they argued that the key to this perception lay in understanding Freud's persuasive analysis of the religious traditions of the West, especially Christianity.

These writers reintroduced into the third period theological themes common to the second—suffering, guilt, and the bondage of the will—and interlaced them with Freud's tragic vision of man's entrapment in unconscious processes. But they also produced an entirely new perspective: religion was to be understood as a significant historical matrix, and psychology as a fresh body of ideas arising out of that matrix. Although published in 1958, another seminal study, Erik H. Erikson's *Young Man Luther: A Study in Psychoanalysis and History,* which used psychoanalytic ideas to explore Luther's life, also belongs to this period. Erikson portrayed Protestantism as an anticipation of psychoanalysis. This reconception of psychology and religion along historical lines set the stage for the fourth and current period of the psychology and religion movement, by making possible the segmentation of its central tension.

Little change in the movement's social context occurred in the third period, beyond a further weakening and spreading of those roles already established. The church, the university, and the clinic all continued to offer their support to some extent. Under the influence of the history of religions movement, theologians and religious intellectuals became more concerned with non-Western traditions and tended to migrate into departments of religious studies. The clinical-psychoanalytic base spread to include university-situated psychologists who espoused humanistic psychology and transpersonal psychology. The formerly well-defined professional identity of the pastoral counselor became more diffuse as new and more explicitly value-laden therapies entered the marketplaces. Increased role diffusion was the price of innovation. Workers in this period were characterized by a looser attachment to their formerly more clearly defined institutional bases and, consequently, suffered more from sociointellectual anxiety.

Segmentation of the Movement, 1970s and 1980s. At the close of the third period, Philip Rieff proposed that the relations between psychoanalytic psychology and religion were not primarily dialogic at all, but were instead historical. He spoke, in *The Triumph of the Therapeutic* (1966), of traditional Christian culture giving way to a new and modern psychological culture, in which the new and typical occupant, "psychological man," would replace Christian man. In so saying, Rieff called attention to the social context of the movement's central intellectual tension. As this perception became more and more widely shared, it served to formulate and ground the fourth period, in which the central intellectual tension of the movement segmented into two coexisting orientations. The first orientation approached religion historically and humanistically, so as to be indifferent to its truth-claims. The second also recognized the antagonism between the two cultures, but viewed the new psychological culture through the lens of the older Christian tradition.

But this segmentation did not occur in a vacuum. In the early 1970s, American society rapidly took up a conservative mood, both economically and politically. This shift was accompanied by a gradual but sustained religious revival. Andrew Greeley, the priest-sociologist, was the first to note this phenomenon, in his book *Unsecular Man: The Persistence of Religion* (1972). Others like him spoke of the "myth" of secularization. Furthermore, a depression in the academic field created extremely high unemployment, forcing religious intellectuals to conform their interests to existing needs of departments. Finally, the fear of nuclear war exacerbated other trends. Together these conditions produced a mood of caution that workers in the psychology and religion movement could not entirely escape.

These intellectual and social shifts accompanied important realignments in the academic study of religion and in the definition of the role played by the religious intellectual. Throughout the first three periods, some major theologians took an interest in psychology; but in the fourth period theology returned to the church, and many who might formerly have been religious intellectuals became theologians or church intellectuals instead. None of the major Protestant theologians of this period—for example, Van A. Harvey, Harvey Cox, and Schubert M. Ogden—have shown substantial interest in psychology, nor have their Catholic counterparts, such as David Tracy.

Segmentation appeared in several different and very distinct trends. Taking the baton from the theologians, a new group of workers developed a fresh series of explorations, thereby displaying once again the seemingly inexhaustible capacity of psychology to enrich religious visions of life. Among the better-known examples are Walter Lowe's (1983) use of psychoanalytic theory to enhance the theological analysis of the problem of evil; James Fowler's use of Jean Piaget's studies of cognition and structural psychology in the service of a theological theory of stages of faith (in *Stages of Faith,* 1981); and Don S. Browning's *Pluralism and Personality: William James and Some Contemporary Cultures of Personality* (1980), in which Browning uses Jamesian psychology to build a religio-ethical mode of thinking and a new discipline of practical theology.

In the second trend of this phase of the psychology and religion movement, history of religions continued to gain momentum and to exercise greater and greater influence on departments of religion, where it struggled to meet the challenges of an increasingly psychoanalytic anthropology and a more empirical historiography. To the work of Clifford Geertz and Victor Turner, so sympathetic to psychoanalytic, structural, and phenomenological theories of religion, other important single studies have been added, such as Robert Paul's *The Tibetan Symbolic World: Psychoanalytic Explorations* (1982) and Gananath Obeyesekere's *Medusa's Hair: An Essay on Personal Symbols and Religious Experience* (1981). Among historians of religions, Wendy O'Flaherty (1980) has built on Eliade's systematic integration of both Freudian and Jungian theory in devising a morphology of religious expressions in order to make a series of phenomenon-specific interpretations.

In the third trend, some psychologists, historians, and sociologists have approached Western religious experiences as historical phenomena. Richard Sennett, in *The Fall of Public Man* (1974), and Christopher Lasch, in *The*

Culture of Narcissism (1978), worked psychoanalytic ideas into their historical method in order to analyze the secularization in contemporary society of Protestant thought and experience. My own study (Homans, 1979) of the religious, social, and psychological forces that shaped C. G. Jung's life and thought also belongs here. Working entirely with psychoanalytic materials, Charles Ducey (in *The Shaman's Dream*, 1978) and Sudhir Kakar (1982) studied healing in primitive societies and in India, respectively. John Lofland's *Doomsday Cult* (1977) and Irving Zaretsky's *Religious Movements in Contemporary America* (1978) are psychologically sophisticated studies of cults in America. Two psychologists, C. Daniel Batson and W. Larry Ventis, further developed the work of Allport on the qualitative social-psychological study of religion in their book *The Religious Experience* (1982).

Because at the time of this writing the fourth period is still defining itself, little should be said about it beyond noting the segmentation of its central intellectual tension and its role patterns. While workers in each of the three current trends are often aware of each other's work and may even use similar materials, they also tend to be indifferent to one another's major agendas. The central tension is not engaged directly, but rather in terms of the methodologies and ideologies of each of the trends. So, as one moves from the first, to the second, to the third trend, problems of certitude and faith decline, and problems of historical and psychological specificity increase. Formerly, workers in the movement were granted the luxury to "float," so to speak, above this segmentation, organizing diverse theories and methods into the movement. But the emergence of segmentation has deprived the movement of much of this luxury. Its future would seem to depend, more and more now, on the creativity and ingenuity of those workers explicitly committed to religious values, and less and less on the influence of psychological theories of religion.

BIBLIOGRAPHY

Altizer, Thomas J. J. *Mircea Eliade and the Dialectic of the Sacred.* Philadelphia, 1963. A bold scholarly attempt to blend Protestant theology, the psychoanalytic theory of religion, and Eliade's works on religious cosmology.

Beit-Hallahmi, Benjamin. "Psychology and Religion, 1880–1930: The Rise and Fall of a Psychological Movement." *The Journal of the History of the Behavioral Sciences* 10 (1974): 84–90. The best historical survey and interpretation of the movement's first period.

Browning, Don S. *Generative Man: Psychoanalytic Perspectives.* Philadelphia, 1973. An articulate appreciation of Erikson's leading ideas. Browning also argues the value of Erikson's moral vision for the rapid social changes of contemporary Western society.

Campbell, Joseph. *The Hero with a Thousand Faces* (1949). 2d ed. Princeton, 1968. A masterful discussion of the world's mythologies that is grounded in a sophisticated use of Jung's analytical psychology.

Eliade, Mircea. *Myths, Dreams and Mysteries.* New York, 1960. The most psychological of Eliade's many books. It evaluates the strengths and weaknesses of Freud's and Jung's psychologies as applied to the phenomenological study of the religions.

Erikson, Erik H. *Young Man Luther: A Study in Psychoanalysis and History.* New York, 1958. A psychobiographical study of the founder of Protestantism that is rich in historical references and psychological nuance. Erikson discusses and illustrates many of the leading ideas of the psychology and religion movement as a whole.

Freud, Sigmund. *Civilization and Its Discontents* (1932). London, 1961. Freud's major statement of the interplay between culture, society, and personality, and of the psychoanalytic meaning of religion as a source of the ideals, values, and meanings that shape the cultural and the individual superego.

Homans, Peter, ed. *The Dialogue between Theology and Psychology.* Chicago, 1968. Informative essays on psychology by theological scholars. This book captures well the major ideas and issues, as well as the spirit, of the movement's second period.

Homans, Peter. *Jung in Context: Modernity and the Making of a Psychology.* Chicago, 1979. Uses psychoanalytic and sociological theories to analyze the genesis of Jung's life and thought and his creative attempts to wed Freud's modern psychological ideas with those of the Christian tradition.

James, William. *The Varieties of Religious Experience.* New York, 1902. Proposes that religious experience can be studied psychologically. Admired for its thoroughness, stylistic elegance, and tolerance, it is the best-remembered work of the first period.

Jung, C. G. *Modern Man in Search of a Soul* (1933). New York, 1964. Clear and readable essays on most of the subjects thought to be of central importance by the famous Swiss psychologist.

Kakar, Sudhir. *Shamans, Mystics and Doctors: A Psychological Inquiry into India and Its Healing Traditions.* New York, 1982. A careful clinical study, by an Indian psychoanalyst, of religious healing in India, comparing it to healing in modern psychoanalytic psychotherapy. This work contains valuable discussions of the secularization of religious traditions that is proposed by psychoanalytic theory.

Lowe, Walter. *Evil and the Unconscious.* Chico, Calif., 1983. A series of reflections on the theological problem of evil, making substantial use of psychoanalytic ideas.

May, Rollo. *The Meaning of Anxiety* (1950). Rev. ed. New York, 1977. Develops a theory of anxiety by drawing together the many ideas of Kierkegaard and Freud. May's book is admired for its clarity and thoroughness.

O'Flaherty, Wendy Doniger. *Women, Androgynes, and Other*

Mythical Beasts. Chicago, 1980. Draws together the psychoanalytic ideas of Freud and Jung, as well as historical and philological studies, to create a general approach to the symbols and metaphors of Indian mythology.

Rieff, Philip. *Freud: The Mind of the Moralist* (1959). 3d ed. Chicago, 1979. A major exposition of Freud's works, taken as a whole. Rieff contrasts their modern character with traditional, Christian views of the moral life.

Tillich, Paul. *The Courage to Be.* New Haven, 1952. Historical, philosophical, and religious reflections on the human capacity for courage form the basis for a religious answer to the question of neurotic suffering, described by psychoanalysis.

PETER HOMANS

Psychotherapy and Religion

Historically, the relationship between psychotherapy and religion has been a strained one and has turned on the concept of "illusion." On the one hand, influenced as it is by the psychobiological origins of psychoanalytic theory, psychotherapy traditionally has considered religion an "illusion" in a strictly pejorative sense. Only relatively recently have many psychotherapists come to understand that "illusion" is a psychological need and that, as such, it can be healthily enjoyed in a socially beneficial way or distorted into pathology, just as any need can be. On the other hand, religion has defensively reacted to psychoanalysis's largely negative consideration of it by campaigning against psychoanalysis, ignoring it altogether, or prematurely incorporating its theory. Understandably, religion has bridled at being considered merely illusory, for this consideration inherently denies the reality of religious experience. Often the psychotherapeutic consideration of religious material has used a methodology that, because of its own assumptions, makes objective study impossible. Fortunately there have been positive developments in the relationship between psychotherapy and religion: psychotherapy has begun to appreciate the psychological and cultural role of religion, and religion has begun to utilize psychotherapy more appropriately and less defensively. This article will examine the main features of this developing relationship.

Psychoanalytic Theory. Any consideration of the relationship between psychotherapy and religion must start, of course, with the work of Sigmund Freud. And here the difficulties also begin.

Freud and "illusion." It is a testament to Freud's greatness that we are frustrated with him for his shortcomings, which are nowhere more evident than in his consideration of religion. Regardless of his greatness, the limitations of his era's scientific methodology—especially its psychobiology—and his own prejudice against and ambivalence toward religion combined to make it impossible for him to study religion objectively. Freud was able to see clearly the religious pathology in individual cases of neurosis and the social hypocrisy that probably has always been a feature of organized religion, but it is a deep irony that the man who cleared the way for us to see the developmental interrelation of pathology and health was not able to apply his own discovery to religious experience.

In numerous works, but nowhere as clearly as in his *The Future of An Illusion* (1927), Freud considers religion an "illusion." He contends that religion originated in early humanity's (and continues to originate in the child's) primordial fears and need for help. The idea of God is the psyche's projection onto the cosmos of infantile, unconscious wishes for omnipotence and protection, an effort to control the cosmos's impersonal harshness by personalizing it as a father god. God is therefore only a psychic phenomenon, the product of wishful thinking—in short, an illusion. For Freud, then, illusion is a pejorative concept, an adaptation that—if possible—should be overcome in favor of facing reality illusionlessly. Although Freud does distinguish between delusion and illusion (the former definitely a false belief and the latter a belief that, whether true or false, is arrived at independently of rational means), it is nonetheless the case that by the strictures of the nineteenth-century scientific paradigm that Freud employed, religion is false because it is not real.

Psychoanalysts and other psychotherapists whose practice has been influenced by Freud, then, would have little use for religion, seeing it as a defense the maladapted ego has formulated against the harsh realities of the world. In all likelihood, given a patient with a strong enough ego, such a therapist would work to encourage the patient to see that this defense is not needed. There would be some latitude here, since psychoanalytic theory has adherents at all stages of its development. There are "Freudian" psychoanalysts and also institutes that represent the full range of Freudian thought from psychobiology to pre-ego psychology. Typically, however, the faculties of these institutes come from backgrounds in psychiatry or clinical psychology and therefore are little influenced by religious perspectives.

Transitional figures. Few psychoanalysts after Freud were as concerned as he was with religion. Freud's pronouncements on religion receded from controversy and became the status quo in psychoanalysis until theoretical developments necessitated their being questioned. Psychoanalytic theory developed into two broad, interrelated "groups," one continuing Freud's psychobiological interests and focusing on mechanistic descriptions of psychodynamics and the other pursuing the more holistic study of the experiential psychic life of the person. In the first group, Anna Freud (1885–1982) and others contributed to the shift in psychoanalysis (a shift that had actually already been begun by Freud himself) toward the study of the ego and its defense mechanisms. In this way, the older view of the adaptation to "reality" at all costs began to be modified. In the second group, Melanie Klein (1882–1960) and others began to study the earliest development of the person in terms of what have come to be called object-relations. In psychoanalytic theory, an "object" is the psychological representation of a person in the most elementary terms—as a "good object," one which is nurturing, or as a "bad object," one which is persecutory. (Klein thus laid the groundwork for D. W. Winnicott's study of transitional phenomena, as well as for self-psychology and the study of narcissism, discussed below.) Both theoretical groups unwittingly undermined Freud's attitude toward religion: the first came to appreciate less stringent adaptations to reality than had been advocated by earlier analysts, and the second prepared the way for examining the methods—including illusion itself—that the psyche necessarily uses to come to grips with reality.

Two other psychoanalytic theorists who should be mentioned in a discussion of psychotherapy and religion are Eric Fromm (1900–1980) and Victor Frankl, not so much because they contributed in a fundamental way to the development of psychoanalytic theory, nor even because they advanced the psychoanalytic understanding of illusion, but because they took religion seriously on its own terms and thus began to break away from Freud's reductionistic methodology in studying religion. Fromm, as a representative of the first group of psychoanalytic theorists mentioned above, saw religion's value from a broad cultural perspective, while Frankl, as a representative of the second group, appreciated religion's psychological function in assisting the individual's search for meaning. The work of Erik H. Erikson must also be considered in the psychoanalytic examination of religion. Erikson, popularly known for his study of the "identity crisis," pioneered the discipline of psychohistory. With *Young Man Luther* (New York, 1958) and *Gandhi's Truth* (New York, 1969), Erikson studied what he called *homo religiosus,* that is, the person whose nature and historical circumstance demand a religious existence—a kind of life that, Erikson insists, can be psychologically healthy. Erikson treats the religious quests of both men with dignity, humaneness, and compassion. Even two decades before, it would have been unheard of for an analyst of Erikson's stature to psychoanalytically examine a religious figure without reducing him to a case study in psychopathology.

Winnicott and transitional phenomena. As the first pediatrician to be trained as a psychoanalyst, the Englishman D. W. Winnicott (1896–1971) was in a unique position to study the psychological development of infants and children, as well as the relationship between parents—particularly mothers—and their offspring. Winnicott's primary theoretical interest was the psychological emergence of the infant into the social world. In Winnicott's view, the bridging of these two worlds is accomplished through the presence of "good enough mothering" and the child's use of "transitional objects." For Winnicott, a "good enough mother" is concerned about her child and sensitive to his needs, but she does not err either by psychologically impinging upon the child or by traumatizing him with inconsistent care. She sees her child as progressively separate from herself; psychologically as well as physically, she weans her child carefully. In weaning, she often allows the child "transitional objects": physical objects such as teddy bears and blankets that, through their association with the mother, help to ensure the infant's own psychological continuity. As such, they ward off insanity, which Winnicott saw as psychological discontinuity.

Winnicott's central theoretical breakthrough is his study of how transitional objects are used by the child as a bridge from the child's inner reality to the outer reality of the adult world. By studying these phenomena he became the first psychoanalyst to study illusion systematically, and thus also to study the psychoanalytic correlate of religion. In his 1951 paper "Transitional Objects and Transitional Phenomena" (republished in *Playing and Reality,* London, 1971), Winnicott placed the antecedent of religious development in the period of transitional phenomena, and in this way illustrated the object-related nature of religious experience. (He did not, however, trace the development of the representation of God.) For Winnicott, transitional phenomena are located in the psychological space he calls "intermediate space" or "potential space." In successful psychological development, this "space" becomes the location of all cultural experience, including religion, which he also ties to "good enough mothering": "Here where there is trust and reliability is a potential space, one that can become an infinite area of separation, which the baby, child, adolescent, adult may creatively fill with playing, which in time becomes the enjoyment of the cultural heritage" (ibid., p. 108).

What was pejorative illusion for Freud becomes for Winnicott positive "potential space" or "the location of cultural experience." Winnicott redeems the idea of illusion in psychoanalytic theory and thereby redeems the psychoanalytic study of religion. Whereas Winnicott fully recognizes pathological illusion, he contends that illusion per se is by no means pathological. For Winnicott, although illusion is not real, that does not mean it is untrue. The psychologically healthy person is one who can use the transitional phenomenon of illusion in a healthy way. As he writes, "We are poor indeed if we are only sane" (Winnicott, *Collected Papers,* London, 1958, p. 150, n. 1).

An excellent example of the application of object-relations theory to religion can be found in Ana-Maria Rizzuto's *The Birth of the Living God: A Psychoanalytic Study* (Chicago, 1979). Rizzuto develops Winnicott's idea of transitional objects and applies it to religion in a systematic way by focusing on what she calls the "God-image." (In this way she avoids argument about the "reality" of religious experience.) Rizzuto argues that the God-image is a necessary and inevitable part of the human psyche (whether it is used "for belief or not"), and she traces its origins from the infant's earliest object-relations. The God-image is a special object, she states, because it is formed not through experience or reality-testing, being instead created out of "imaginary materials." Further, she argues that even though the God-image may be subject to repression, it can never be fully repressed. Instead, it is evoked at crucial times of life, such as the transitions between major stages of development. Rizzuto's contribution is especially important in two ways. First, departing from Freud and aligning herself with Winnicott's positive appreciation of illusion, she comes to the conclusion that religious belief is not a sign of immaturity, let alone pathology. Rather, she asserts it is simply a part of the psyche's development. Second, by tracing the personal development of the God-image, she points up the differences between the "official God" of religious doctrine and the "living God" of personal experience. She implies that, in order for religion to continue to be a living force, the personal, living God must be recognized and incorporated into organized religion.

In general, psychoanalysts and psychotherapists influenced by the work of Winnicott—and their number is likely to increase as the profound importance of his work continues to be recognized—will appreciate the importance of transitional objects of all kinds, including religion and religious beliefs. The aim of such a therapist would be to provide a "good enough" therapeutic environment (through the therapeutic relationship), and not simply to interpret unconscious conflicts, so that the client's natural ability to develop transitional objects can emerge and he can become his own resource for bridging the psychological and social worlds. In part, this bridging can result from playing, a kind of activity that Winnicott devoted considerable theoretical effort to understanding and an activity—like the arts and religious ritual and experience—that is in the intermediate area between inner and outer realities. The correlation of play and religious practice may well be an area explored in future applications to religion of psychoanalytic thought as influenced by Winnicott.

Self-psychology. As they have in the past, champions of religion look to new developments in psychoanalytic theory to justify religion against the historical onslaught started in part by psychoanalysis itself. Self-psychology, a discipline developed by Heinz Kohut (1913–1981) and related to psychoanalysis, seems likely to be yet the latest of these developments used in this way. Like Winnicott, Kohut was not directly concerned with religion. He worked with patients suffering from narcissistic personality or behavior disorders, conditions classical psychoanalytic theory considered unable to be analyzed because such patients could not be engaged in treatment, as they were unable to relate to others. Kohut was able to analyze the narcissistically disturbed because he saw value in narcissism and engaged these patients by communicating this value to them. In contrast to traditional psychoanalytic theory, including that of his contemporary Otto Kernberg, with whom he disagreed in theoretical arguments about narcissism, Kohut held that narcissism in adults has an independent line of development, so that the extreme self-love of primitive narcissism is not transformed by maturation into object-love but develops instead into mature narcissism. Although Kohut's work is just beginning to be explored by pastoral psychotherapists, its value seems to lie in the treatment of those so self-invested and self-referential that they are unable to relate to others as others. This inability to relate to others includes the otherness implied in religious experience; in this consideration, narcissists may be unable to be fully religious because they are unable to experience the Other of all religious experience.

Psychoanalysis, then, has moved from considering "illusion" in a pejorative to a positive light, but many disciplines—considered in the rest of this article—start from the experiential basis of "illusion."

Analytical Psychology (Jungianism). In a consideration of the relationship between psychotherapy and religion from the perspective of the concept of illusion, a unique position is held by analytical psychology (popularly called "Jungianism," after its founder, C. G. Jung). Jungianism has been outside the mainstream of psychoanalytic theory since the early decades of the twentieth century, a divorce that has impoverished both psychoanalysis and Jungianism itself. The isolation of Jungianism has slowed the humanization of classical psychoanalytic theory, narrowing its field of study by excluding the consideration of many common human phenomena, and it has isolated Jungians to the extent that, with a few exceptions, their vocabulary and model of the psyche has little relation to the rest of psychoanalytic theory. Moreover, the separation of Jungianism from classical psychoanalysis has had the effect of further dividing the disciplines that make use of these two camps of psychoanalytic theory. Freud has been used primarily by the social sciences, whereas Jung has been seen as the "good guy" by the arts and humanities, especially theology and religious studies.

Theology's kinship with Jungianism can be explained by Jung's refutation of the classical psychoanalytic correlation of religion and illusion. The Jungian position on "illusion" is represented by Jung's concept of the "psychological fact" (see Jung, *The Collected Works*, vol. 11, Princeton, 1969, pp. 3–105): Jung states that all psychic products—including visions, dreams, and hallucinations—are "facts" that should be considered as having the same basis in reality as other facts, including physical facts. There is, therefore, almost no such thing as "illusion" in Jungian psychological theory. It is almost an illusionless psychology. Jung was reductionistic, but his reductionism was unlike Freud's religious reductionism. Jung was able to see religion more clearly on its own terms as a human activity that, while it could often be contaminated by social hypocrisy or personal pathology, could nonetheless be based on a reality of experience irreducible by psychological method to other unconscious motives. Here Jung makes an important methodological point: it is not the business of psychology to prove or disprove the existence of God. Psychology can discuss the psychic effects of the God-image and its mythic antecedents but not the existence of God apart from the human psyche. The insistence on the reality and importance of religious experience was a position Jung held to the end of his life. When more than eighty years old, he was asked in a BBC interview if he believed in God. "I don't have to believe," he replied, "I *know*."

The religious was deeply important to Jung. In part, this was the result of his own personal history. His father was a clergyman, as were a number of his uncles. But it was also a consequence of his experience as a psychotherapist. In fact, in "Psychotherapy or the Clergy" (ibid., pp. 327–347) he went so far as to state, "Among all my patients in the second half of life—that is to say, over thirty-five—there has not been one whose problem in the last resort was not that of finding a religious outlook on life" (p. 334). He went on to add, "This of course has nothing whatever to do with a particular creed or membership of a church" (ibid.). Jung's experience as a psychotherapist informed and was informed by his work as an analytic theorist. It was his theory that the psyche is composed of "archetypes" in a "collective unconscious." That is, Jung held there was an unconscious aside from the personal unconscious of the individual's repressed past, and this was the "collective unconscious" whose contents are archetypes (typical images and patterns of human behavior, but not predestined behavior, that endlessly recur and are found in the psyche precisely because it is human). The most important and central of the archetypes is the Self (similar to, but not the same as, the self in Kohut's self-psychology). Jung thought the psychological purpose of the second half of life was for the personal ego to come to terms with the Self, the apersonal center of the collective unconscious (see *Aion*, in *The Collected Works*, vol. 9, part 2, Princeton, 1968). Jung has often been criticized by less religiously inclined psychoanalysts for projecting religious meaning onto the Self and thus, his critics claim, for advocating a religious psychology. He believed he was simply an empirical scientist.

Two movements within current Jungianism should be mentioned in a discussion of psychotherapy and religion. The first movement is a somewhat formally organized schism of Jungianism called "archetypal psychology." Led by James Hillman, archetypal psychology can be thought of as even more Jungian than Jungianism, with its extreme concentration on the archetypes of the collective unconscious almost for their own sake. Polytheism is studied by this group. The second movement is marked by the rise of interest in "the goddess" among some Jungians. Shunning what they see as the patriarchal bias of modern consciousness and, even more specifically, modern religion, a number of Jungian analysts and writers have focused on studies of the historical goddess religions and sometimes urged a return to religious focus on "the goddess" in the lives of modern individuals.

The psychoanalyst or psychotherapist who has been influenced by Jung and by developments in Jungian psychology will necessarily be respectful of a client's religious issues. From the beginning, Jungian institutes have welcomed the religiously trained. The reality of religious experience is therefore appreciated in a way that is unusual among psychoanalytic institutes. Jungians are also trained to differentiate psychologically healthy from psychologically unhealthy religion. Yet an often-heard criticism of Jungian psychology applies here:

clients are not necessarily encouraged to reintegrate their religious experience back into already-established religious groups. The individualistic aspect of religious experience is prized in the Jungian system in a way that is not always productive.

Religious Counseling. In the relationship between psychotherapy and religion, religious counseling, in contrast to psychoanalytic theory, takes as its foundation the legitimacy of religious experience. Religious counseling has two major forms: pastoral counseling (and its relation to seminary education) and Clinical Pastoral Education (CPE).

Seminary education and pastoral counseling. Two interrelated factors have influenced the development of religious counseling: the need for seminarians to be taught counseling and the development of the discipline of pastoral counseling. The first factor is important because, according to opinion polls, more people in the United States will consult clergy before other professionals for help with personal problems. Yet an already-crowded seminary curriculum does not typically allow for in-depth training in counseling (let alone psychotherapy), and when it does the counseling tends to be based not on psychological insight but on biblical precepts, which are culturally bound and which can be overly punitive. As religious conservatism continues to grow and to become institutionalized, psychology and psychoanalysis are likely to become even less influential in pastoral counseling. Nonetheless, some authors have recognized the disparity between pastoral counseling and psychotherapy and have written useful guides detailing for religious workers when to take on the work of counseling and when to make referrals to psychological professionals. Two examples are Paul W. Pruyser's *The Minister as Diagnostician* (Philadelphia, 1976) and Wayne E. Oates's *When Religion Gets Sick* (Philadelphia, 1970).

Very broadly, the character of a seminary education is formed by the denominational affiliation of the seminary, by the intellectual climate of its geographic locale, and in part by whether or not it is associated with a university. In the northeastern United States, psychology programs in seminaries reflect the psychoanalytic and history of religions approaches of the area. In the Midwest, scholars have been trying to establish a methodology of pastoral care. In the West, the influence of humanistic psychology and the psychologies arising from the counter-culture of the late 1960s and early 1970s are evident in the writing of those at the consortium of seminaries near San Francisco. However, despite all these efforts, pastoral counseling as a discipline has yet to establish a clear identity and methodology, caught as it is between the widely disparate perspectives of psychotherapy and psychoanalytic theory, on the one hand, and religious institutions and experience, on the other.

Clinical Pastoral Education (CPE). Although first organized in 1925, Clinical Pastoral Education (CPE)—a formalized system to clinically train seminarians and ministers to work with persons in hospitals, mental institutions, and prisons—had a number of antecedents. These movements had in common the urge to study spirituality scientifically, as well as a discontent with the theological education of the time, which was perceived as too concerned with theological doctrine and not concerned enough with the reality of the emotional life of the person. The development of CPE is usually attributed to Anton T. Boisen (1876–1965), a Congregational minister. Boisen had suffered a breakdown with psychotic features in the early 1920s and was consequently institutionalized. He graphically depicted his efforts to find meaning in his experience in his book *Out of the Depths* (New York, 1960), a work that still makes interesting reading. Boisen was the first to put together many of the elements now seen as central to CPE: the use of case histories and "verbatims" (written accounts of interactions with patients) and an emphasis on the presentation of this written work before the trainee's peers and supervisor for didactic supervision, as well as the first attempts to study what Boisen called "the laws of spiritual life." Slowly, Boisen and others were able to establish an ongoing, organized, and specifically trained ministry for people in hospitals, prisons, and mental institutions. A powerful speaker who used his own experiences, Boisen was able as a chaplain to engage in therapeutic relationships with the most disturbed patients at the Worcester (Massachusetts) State Hospital, the same hospital in which he had been institutionalized. The chaotic and amusing experiences of the seminarians who comprised the first group of CPE trainees are recorded by Doris Webster Havice in *Roadmap for a Rebel* (New York, 1980). The growing influence of CPE, as well as closer cooperation between CPE and various denominations, led to the formation in 1967 of the Association for Clinical Pastoral Education from several smaller organizations.

A psychotherapeutic practicioner influenced by CPE essentially functions as a pastoral counselor, balancing a clinical perspective on psychodynamics with his own religious belief and, typically, with his client's religious belief as well. It is possible that CPE will have trouble surviving the changing economics of hospitalization, as rising hospital costs and advances in medical technology combine to decrease the length of hospital stays.

Social Work. In considering the relationship between psychology and religion, social work is especially important: in the United States in 1985, social workers provided more psychotherapy than members of any other profession. The historical development of social work is intimately tied both to psychoanalytic theory and to religion and thus might be expected to be caught in the middle of the conflict between the two. This is not at all the case, however; with few exceptions, social-work schools have opted to align themselves with psychoanalytic theory, academically and professionally the more powerful of the two approaches, and to eschew any religious connections.

Social work developed in urban areas in the United States from the recognition on the part of many clergy that, following the Judeo-Christian obligation to be charitable, there was a dire need for social services and that these services required organization in order to be effective. The work of individual clergymen such as Joseph Tucker (a Unitarian minister who organized charity for the poor in early nineteenth-century Boston), Stephen Humphreys Gurteen (whose Charity Organization Society in Rochester, New York, gave rise to community welfare councils and to agencies serving families), and Charles Loring Brace (whose "orphan trains" relocated large numbers of poor urban children to the midwestern and western United States), as well as the efforts of religious organizations such as the Young Men's Christian Association and the Salvation Army, has prompted William J. Reid, in an article on sectarian agencies, to write that "the Christian church is the 'mother of social work'" (*The Encyclopedia of Social Work*, 17th ed., Washington, D.C., 1977, p. 1245).

Despite these historical associations, however, the three major religious traditions involved in social work in the United States do not directly tie religion into their social services. They vary in how they relate religion to the services they deliver, as Reid has recognized. Protestantism's decentralized structure has led to the secularization of the social services it delivers. Roman Catholicism, on the other hand, with its hierarchical structure, has tended to develop social agencies that are under church auspices. Jewish social services fall between these two extremes, offering services with a religious affiliation but without direct religious supervision. In part, this lack of a direct link between religion and the delivery of services is mandated: these agencies are prohibited from proselytizing since their programs often receive federal government funding.

The training social workers receive also increases the separation between religion and the delivery of services, especially psychotherapy. This is true even though a growing number of graduate schools of social work award joint degrees with seminaries. (In part, this movement toward joint degree programs is motivated by economic and not intellectual concerns: both seminaries and schools of social work have seen a steady decline in enrollments since the mid-1970s.) In spite of the association between graduate schools of social work and seminaries, however, the individual student is often left to integrate the two curricula on his own, and the demands of both degree programs often mean that the seminary's own curriculum is slighted. Schools of social work typically do not include the religious dimensions of psychotherapy in their curricula to compensate for this shortcoming, which is compounded by the fact that, especially during the early period of its development as a discipline, social work was heavily influenced by psychoanalytic theory. Psychotherapy offered from within the constraints of social work practice or training is likely to consider religious issues from an earlier, more sheerly Freudian psychoanalytic perspective that does not appreciate the positive values of "illusion."

Conclusion. This article has traced the history of the relationship between psychotherapy and religion from its development in psychoanalysis as pejorative "illusion" in Freud, to the positive "potential space" in Winnicott, through Jung's denial of the illusory character of the religion, to the religiously based disciplines of pastoral counseling and CPE, and ending with the studiously nonreligious discipline of social work. It is only to be hoped that the modern disciplines springing from psychoanalytic theory will mature to the point of accommodating themselves to the powerful and lasting influence of religion on human life. As I have attempted to show, this accommodation is well under way.

BIBLIOGRAPHY

An excellent short conceptual introduction to the development of psychoanalytic theory from Freud to Winnicott is Harry J. S. Guntrip's *Psychoanalytic Theory, Therapy, and the Self* (New York, 1971). The interrelationship between religion and the work of numerous psychoanalysts and depth psychologists is discussed in *Religion and the Unconscious* by Ann Belford Ulanov and Barry Ulanov (Philadelphia, 1975). A general introduction to Erikson's work is Robert Coles's book *Erik H. Erikson: The Growth of His Work* (Boston, 1970). *Boundary and Space: An Introduction to the Work of D. W. Winnicott*, by Madeleine Davis and David Wallbridge (New York, 1981), and the introduction by M. Masud R. Khan to *D. W. Winnicott, Through Paediatrics to Psychoanalysis* (New York, 1975) provide the best overviews of the work of this British psychoanalyst.

A special issue of the *Journal of Supervision and Training in Ministry* (Madison, Wis.) 5 (1982) examines the relationship between religion and the self-psychology of Heinz Kohut. No single volume is a good introduction to the meaning of religion in the work of C. G. Jung. However, both Barbara Hannah's *Jung:*

His Life and Work (New York, 1976) and Marie-Louise von Franz's *C. G. Jung: His Myth in Our Time* (New York, 1975) are good starting-points, while Ann Belford Ulanov's *The Feminine in Jungian Psychology and in Christian Theology* (Evanston, Ill., 1971) has several chapters that pertain specifically to religion. The best initial introduction to pastoral counseling is *Pastoral Care in Historical Perspective*, by Charles R. Jaekle and William A. Clebsch (Englewood Cliffs, N.J., 1964).

MICHAEL D. CLIFFORD

PSYCHOPOMP. *See* Spiritual Guide.

PTAH was the creator god of Memphis who conceived a thought in his mind (heart) and brought it forth by speaking it with his tongue. Because the founding of Memphis and the erection of a temple to Ptah at that site were accomplishments of the first king of a united Egypt, Menes, the cult of Ptah must date at least to the beginning of Egyptian history. The text that best describes the Memphite theology, however, is preserved in a very late copy dating from the twenty-fifth dynasty (c. 700 BCE). The original text may not have been much older, but it is a very interesting document, not only for its description of the creation, but also for its handling of the other two major creation myths. In this text Ptah is identified with the last pair of the Hermopolitan ogdoad—that is, Nun and Naunet, who represent the watery abyss from which the creator god comes forth. The creator god who is thus created by Ptah is Atum, who proceeds to create the other gods of the Heliopolitan ennead and all else. In this way the theologies are all connected, and Ptah as an anthropomorphic creator god is given precedence by being placed between the chthonic, precreation cosmic aspects known as the ogdoad and the old creator god, Atum.

Almost nothing remains of the temple of Ptah at Memphis, even though it was one of the three largest and best endowed of ancient Egypt. Smaller temples (such as those at Gerf Hussein and Karnak) were dedicated to Ptah in many locations, and statues of him are plentiful. His image is that of a tightly cloaked man holding a composite scepter before him. Ptah became identified, at least to some extent, with the local mortuary god of Memphis, Sokar, and also with Osiris. His consort was Sekhmet, the powerful lioness, who was the mother of his son, Nefertem, the lotus god.

BIBLIOGRAPHY

The most extensive study available is *The God Ptah* (Lund, 1946) by Maj Sandman-Holmberg.

LEONARD H. LESKO

PTOLEMY (c. 100–170), Alexandrian astronomer, geographer, and mathematician. The last of the great astronomers of antiquity, Claudius Ptolemaeus (Ptolemy) compiled works that remained the standard astronomical textbooks until the Copernican revolution in astronomy in the sixteenth century. Almost nothing is known of the details of Ptolemy's life. His *Hē mathēmatikē syntaxis* (Mathematical Compilation) was written about 150 CE; the title by which this work is better known, the *Almagest*, is a medieval Latin derivation from an Arabic corruption of the Greek title under which the work came to be known in later antiquity, *Ho megale syntaxis* (The Great Compilation). The *Almagest* sums up the mathematical astronomy of the ancient world; it became the basis of Latin and Arabic astronomy.

Ptolemy's work follows in the Greek philosophical tradition, in which the sacred nature of the heavens is expressed by the incorruptibility of the celestial realm, the divinity of the heavenly bodies, and the perfection of their motions (uniformly circular, because the circle was considered the most perfect of figures and motion around a circle was eternal). The fact that the motions of the sun, moon, and planets are evidently not circular provided a formidable challenge to thinkers within this tradition; especially challenging were the planets' periodic reverses, or retrograde motions. Drawing upon the work of his Greek predecessors, Ptolemy was able to "save the appearances" of celestial motion by using circles in his geometry of the heavens. By employing Greek and Babylonian observational data, he was able to adjust his theoretical solutions to observed celestial positions and to predict them with a precision unmatched until the work of Johannes Kepler in the seventeenth century. The geometrical devices that Ptolemy used—the eccentric, the epicycle, and the equant—were never thought to possess a physical reality, as he makes clear in the preface to the *Almagest*. But it was just for this reason that astronomy had a religious value. Astronomy developed the correspondence between the order of divine celestial things and the order of mathematical propositions.

Its science Aristotelian and it format Euclidean, the *Almagest* describes a stationary, spherical earth surrounded by concentric spheres carrying the sun, moon, planets, and stars. Motion is described geometrically by arrangements of several kinds of circles: (1) *eccentrics*, which are not centered on the earth; (2) *epicycles*, which orbit other circles that are centered on the earth; and (3) *equants*, in which the motion of the body on the circle is variable in relation to the center of the circle but uniform in relation to some noncentral point within the circle. The *Almagest* includes a star catalog and a table of observations later revised and expanded in Ptolemy's *Prokheiroi kanones* (Handy Tables).

Ptolemy's work on geometry, the *Planisphaerium*, of which only a distorted Greek title survives, *Exaplōsis epiphaneias sphairas* (Unfolding of a Spherical Surface), details the theory of the astrolabe, the chief astronomical instrument of antiquity and the Middle Ages. Ptolemy's *Hypotheseis tōn planōmenōn* (Planetary Hypotheses) suggests that the spheres of the planets nestle within one another. The astrological complement to Ptolemy's astronomy is his *Tetrabiblios*. Ptolemy also wrote works on optics and music, as well as a *Geography* (Gr., *Geographikē hyphēgēsis*), which gives directions on how to map the spherical earth on a flat surface and provides tables of longitude and latitude for generating maps. Because of a lack of precise longitude, Ptolemy's map of the known world was severely distorted, even where descriptive information abounded.

Ptolemy's works present an interrelated whole dominated by the successful application of mathematics to complex technical problems. For example, the determination of terrestrial latitude in the *Geography* is achieved through calculations based on astronomy. This in turn specifies the astrological character of the inhabitants of various parts of the earth. His cartography employs the mathematics of his optics and of the *Planisphaerium*. Ptolemy's authority in applied mathematics was undisputed for more than a millennium.

Ptolemy went to great lengths in his texts to provide procedures whereby his technical achievements could be reproduced. He thus laid the foundation for other civilizations to assimilate his work, become expert at it, and progress beyond it. Such cultural innovation is invariably associated with religious creativity, though not in a predictable fashion. For example, though Ptolemy's astronomy was used to corroborate the religious view that the earth was at the center of the universe, no one was ever convinced of this view *because* of the astronomy of eccentrics, epicycles, and equants. However, becoming technically expert in these devices did allow the accurate prediction of religious feasts. Although the Jewish philosopher Maimonides (Mosheh ben Maimon, 1135/8–1204) criticized Ptolemy, he did incorporate some of the astronomer's techniques for determining the date of Passover.

The translation of Ptolemy's work into Arabic in the ninth century was a catalyst for the flowering of Islamic culture. Refined astronomical tables were created, such as the *Toledan Tables* of al-Zarḳālla (c. 1080). This served as the basis for the *Alfonsine Tables*, which was compiled circa 1252 by some fifty astronomers assembled for that purpose by Alfonso X of Castile, and which predicted the dates of the Easter moon. New theories of optics were proposed by the Arab heritors of Ptolemy; new geographical values were established. The Islamic appropriation of Hellenistic natural philosophy inspired the Christian Middle Ages. A desire for the *Almagest* brought the greatest of medieval translators of Arabic, Gerard of Cremona (1114–1187), to Toledo. The merits of a true physical astronomy and of "saving the appearances" by geometry were argued in medieval universities, where Ptolemaic astronomy became part of the curriculum. Although the celestial bodies were no longer thought of as gods by medieval Europeans, their movement was believed to exhibit God's will (and their order his wisdom), and hence Ptolemy's astronomy continued to provide for the intellectual contemplation of the divine celestial order. Dante drew upon Ptolemy for the cosmology of his *Commedia* (1321).

When the *Geography*, with its techniques of projection, was first translated into Latin in fifteenth-century Florence, it contributed to the rediscovery of linear perspective and to the development of cartography during the voyages of exploration. Because the distortions of Ptolemy's map of the globe bore the prestige of his mathematics, Columbus and others were convinced that it would be quite easy to reach Asia by sailing west. When Renaissance astronomers finally became truly competent in Ptolemy's astronomy, their dissatisfaction with his accuracy and methods culminated in the Copernican revolution that established modern cosmology. The Jesuit mission to China in the seventeenth century used the predictive precision of Ptolemaic astronomy to enhance the value of their religious teaching at the emperor's court. Thus it was ironic that Ptolemy's science and technology were helping to introduce Christianity to the Far East at the same time that Copernican astronomy was making Ptolemaic astronomy obsolete in the West. And well after Ptolemy's cosmos was superseded by the physical universe as defined by Copernicus, Newton, and others, the *Tetrabiblios* remained an astrological standard. It was translated into English and published in 1701, the second edition in 1786.

BIBLIOGRAPHY

A translation of Ptolemy's *Almagest* was done by R. Catesby Taliaferro in *Ptolemy, Copernicus, Kepler*, vol. 16 of the "Great Books of the Western World," edited by Robert Maynard Hutchins (Chicago, 1952). The inclusion of the *De revolutionibus* by Copernicus in the same text facilitates the comparison of these two all-important works in the history of astronomy. A scrupulous new translation of the *Almagest* is provided in G. J. Toomer's *Ptolemy's Almagest* (London, 1984). Frank E. Robbins translated the *Tetrabiblios* for the "Loeb Classical Library" (Cambridge, Mass., 1940). An English translation of the Latin *Geographia* is found in Edward Luther Stevenson's *Ge-*

ography of Claudius Ptolemy (New York, 1933). An exhaustive technical account of the *Almagest* and its historical antecedents is provided in Otto Neugebauer's *A History of Ancient Mathematical Astronomy*, vol. 1 (New York, 1975). G. J. Toomer, in his article "Ptolemy, Claudius," in the *Dictionary of Scientific Biography* (New York, 1970–1980), gives a concise description of Ptolemy's science with an up-to-date bibliography. A very readable discussion of the problems posed by observational astronomy and the Greek solutions to them, as well as of their cultural context, is provided in Thomas Kuhn's *The Copernican Revolution: Planetary Astronomy in the Development of Western Thought*, rev. ed. (New York, 1959).

MICHAEL A. KERZE

PUER AETERNUS. *See* Child.

PŪJĀ. [*The forms of worship known as* pūjā *are common to both Hinduism and Buddhism, although practices vary in each tradition. Discussion is presented here in two articles:* Hindu Pūjā *and* Buddhist Pūjā.]

Hindu Pūjā

From ancient times, Hinduism has known two preeminent methods of approaching divinity in ritual: (1) the method of *yajña*, which conveys offerings to a distant god by consigning them to an intermediary fire, and (2) the method of *pūjā*, which extends offerings to a present divinity by placing them before, or applying them to, the god's symbol or image. The *yajña* appears in the earlier records; it was the principal ritual method of the ancient Aryan peoples whose priests produced the collection of texts known as the Veda. The *pūjā* is first mentioned in texts supplementary to the Veda that are known as *sūtra*s (composed around 600–400 BCE). It first became prominent in India as a result of the god-centered devotional movements that spread throughout India during the early centuries of the common era. The method of *pūjā* now predominates in Hindu practice, although the *yajña* remains important to priestly and domestic ritual.

Origins and Etymology. Scholarly opinion is divided regarding the origins and etymology of *pūjā*. Many scholars have argued that *pūjā* was initially a Dravidian practice native to India and point to the sharp distinction traditionally drawn between *pūjā* and *yajña*, the refusal of the strictest Vedic priests to participate in *pūjā*, the long-standing prevalence of *pūjā* in village cults, and the long role of low-caste (and hence non-Aryan) hereditary priests in village *pūjā*s. But no clear-cut Dravidian derivation has been established for the term *pūjā;* the best-known attempt at a Dravidian etymology is that of Jarl Charpentier (1927), who proposed to derive *pūjā* from Tamil *pūcu* or Kannada *pūsu*, "to smear," a reference to the applications of sandalwood, turmeric, or vermilion pastes that are common in *pūjā* offerings.

Alternatively, the Sanskritist Paul Thieme proposed in 1939 that the term *pūjā* is derived from the Sanskrit (and hence Aryan) *pṛc*, "to mix," a reference to the *madhuparka*, or mixture of honey and water that was commonly offered to guests in ancient Indian times. Analyzing the uses of the term *pūjā* in *sūtra* and epic literature, Thieme concluded that it had once referred primarily to a ritual of guest worship. The offerings and gestures characteristic of *pūjā* are in fact still utilized in India to honor distinguished guests, as well as other meritorious persons, sacred plants and animals, and occasionally also weapons or tools. Furthermore, elements from ancient guest ritual such as offering a seat and washing the feet still play a significant role in conventional *pūjā*s. However, traces of guest ritual are rarer in village practice and in *pūjā*s of heterodox (i.e., Buddhist and Jain) traditions; hence the question of the term's origin remains open.

Types. *Deva-pūjā*s (i.e., *pūjā*s for the gods) are offered in four sorts of settings: (1) at shrines maintained for family *(kula)* and/or "chosen" *(iṣṭa)* divinities within the Hindu home; (2) at temples devoted to pan-Indian deities such as Śiva and Viṣṇu; (3) during the course of festivals, which may be sponsored either by temples or by local communities; (4) at shrines or temples of localized village divinities. *Pūjā*s in any of these contexts may be quite freely structured, consisting of little more than gestures of reverence *(namas)* and minimal offerings. Or they may follow conventional patterns, which vary only slightly according to the devotional sect of the performer and the deity who is honored.

Pūjā at the home shrine. Most Hindus maintain a home shrine for one or more divinities honored within the household. Ideally, the home shrine is located in a small room of the house that is set aside solely for worship *(pūjāśālā)*. The shrine itself may consist of pictures of gods set up on a table or low platform, or images may be housed in a wooden shrine-cabinet, whose doors are opened only during the service. Images housed in such shrines may be Śiva-*liṅga*s, small cast-metal statues of various gods, or the stones sacred to Viṣṇu that are known as *śālagrāma*. A single family representative generally offers the *pūjā;* other household members enter at the close of the rite to offer prostrations and/or sip the water in which the image has been bathed. Worshipers of Viṣṇu will also eat the food *(prasāda)* that the god has sanctified by his taste, and may append to their *pūjā* special offerings of homage for the family's *ācārya*, or religious teacher. An ambitious household *pūjā* may incorporate all or several of sixteen traditional *upacāras*, "attendances," which also form the core of traditional temple services. (The following list varies slightly in different textual sources.)

1. *Āvāhana* ("invocation"). The god is invited to be present at the ceremony.
2. *Āsana*. The god is offered a seat.
3. *Svāgata* ("greeting"). The worshiper asks the god if the journey has gone well.
4. *Pādya*. The worshiper symbolically washes the god's feet.
5. *Arghya*. Water is extended so that the god may cleanse his or her face and teeth.
6. *Ācamanīya*. Water is offered for sipping.
7. *Madhuparka*. The god is offered the water-and-honey drink.
8. *Snāna* or *abhiṣekha*. Water is offered for symbolic bathing; if submersible, the image may literally be bathed and then toweled dry.
9. *Vastra* ("clothing"). Here a cloth may be wrapped around the image and ornaments affixed to it.
10. *Anulepana* or *gandha*. Perfumes and/or ointments are applied to the image.
11. *Puṣpa*. Flowers are laid before the image, or garlands are draped around it.
12. *Dhūpa*. Incense is burned before the image.
13. *Dīpa* or *āratī*. A burning lamp is waved in front of the god.
14. *Naivedya* or *prasāda*. Foods such as cooked rice, fruit, clarified butter, sugar, and betel leaf are offered.
15. *Namaskāra* or *pranāma*. The worshiper and family bow or prostrate themselves before the image to offer homage.
16. *Visarjana* or *udvāsana*. The god is dismissed.

Temple pūjās. A full *pūjā* of sixteen *upacāras* is in effect a miniaturized temple ritual; the daily worship, or *nitya pūjā*, in a major temple differs from it principally in scale and in the number of times that the *pūjā* is repeated (three to six times daily for the temple ritual). Temple officiants are usually brahmans; however, brahmans who are temple priests enjoy lesser status than those who perform Vedic rituals. In non-Śaiva temples *pūjās* are usually addressed to anthropomorphic images, but in temples of Śiva the central "image" is always the nonanthropomorphic *liṅga*. A sequence of temple *pūjās* may actually involve two images, for a moveable image stands in for the permanently fixed central symbol when it becomes necessary to manipulate or transport the divinity.

The god of a major temple is more of a resident than a guest. Segments of the daily *pūjā* will vary accordingly; hence the god is "awakened" rather than "invoked" in the morning, and may quite literally be aroused from a bed where his or her moveable image was laid the night before. Furthermore, the temple god is royal; the temple is his or her palace, and its priests are palace servants. Hence the god's "seat" is a throne, and ornaments affixed to the image may include a crown; furthermore, the "ruler," in the form of the moveable image, is carried each day in procession around the temple grounds, much as local rulers in India formerly processed through their territories. Temple *pūjās* differ slightly according to sect and region. Thus temples of Śiva in South India once featured performances by dancing girls *(devadāsīs)* maintained as part of the temple staff. Śaiva *pūjās* also incorporate many Tantric elements; for example, an officiating priest begins his *pūjā* by summoning Lord Śiva into his own body. Devotional hymns are often sung during *pūjās* at Vaiṣṇava temples; while images of Vaiṣṇava saints are honored as well as images of Viṣṇu.

Daily temple *pūjās* are not communal performances; as in the home, one person (here, the temple priest) acts for the benefit of all. Individuals may, however, make special requests of the gods by means of special offerings. This practice is known as *kāmya pūjā*, "the *pūjā* undertaken by choice." Such optional *pūjās* are most often performed at the small shrines that dot a major temple's grounds. The intended worshiper commissions a priest to place his or her offerings before or onto the image.

Festivals. All major temples sponsor festivals. A frequent type is the *ratha yātrā*, or "car festival," in which the moveable image is mounted on a large (sometimes multistoried) cart and pulled through the town on a set processional path. The devotee thus receives an opportunity for *darśana*, or "sight," of the god; he or she may toss flowers, break coconuts, or sprinkle the image with water as the cart progresses. Communities may also sponsor festivals in which public display and celebration of images is a central feature. Community associations or families may commission elaborate and expensive clay images for such festal *pūjās*. The images are feted with music and entertainments, then paraded to a river and left to dissolve in its waters. *Pūjā* festivals of this type are especially popular in the state of Bengal, in northeastern India.

Village pūjās. Among the major Hindu divinities, only the fierce goddess Kālī regularly receives blood sacrifices (goats) in the course of her daily worship. However, blood sacrifices have been more common in the *pūjās* of village divinities *(gramādevatā)*, which differ in several respects from *pūjās* of the urban-based pan-Indian deities. Such divinities associated with specific locales have been reported from ancient times, not only in Hindu, but also Buddhist and Jain writings. The cult of village gods is now most prominent in South India, where the village divinity is often a goddess whose name is a compound of *amma*, "mother." The *amma*'s shrine may be minimal; sometimes it is just a bare enclosure outside the boundaries of the village proper. The "image," if any permanent image exists, may be a rock or an earthen pot or lamp. The hereditary shrine priest, or *pūjāri*, is of low caste, often a potter. Village *pūjās* are not necessarily maintained on a regular basis, nor do they commonly follow the *upacāra* model; coconuts, bananas, margosa or betel leaves, turmeric, and cooked rice are the most common nonbloody offerings. Village gods may possess their *pūjāris* or other mediums during the course of *pūjās*; festivals feature such possession experiences, as well as processions, sometimes fire walking, and sacrifices of sheep, goats, fowls, or buffalo.

[*See also* Worship and Cultic Life, *article on* Hindu Cultic Life; *and* Rites of Passage, *article on* Hindu Rites. *For further discussion of domestic* pūjā, *see* Domestic Observances, *article on* Indian Practices.]

BIBLIOGRAPHY

Sources cited for proposed etymologies of the word *pūjā* are Jarl Charpentier's "Über den Begriff und die Etymologie von pūjā," *Beiträge zur Literaturwissenschaft und Geistesgeschichte Indiens: Festgabe Hermann Jacobi*, edited by Willibald Kirfel (Bonn, 1926), pp. 276–297; also Paul Thieme's "Pūjā," *Journal of Oriental Research* 27 (1957–1958): 1–16. For a summary of precepts governing *pūjās* in classical Sanskrit literature, see Pandura Vaman Kane's *History of Dharmaśāstra: Ancient and Medieval Religious and Civil Law in India*, vol. 2, pt.1 (Poona, 1941), pp. 705–740. Detailed descriptions of *pūjās* in South India are available in Carl Gustav Diehl's *Instrument and Purpose: Studies on Rites and Rituals in South India* (Lund, 1956); however, this volume can be quite difficult for the nonspecialist to follow. Jan Gonda offers a more readable summary of *pūjās* in Śaiva and Vaiṣṇava temples in his *Viṣṇuism and Śivaism* (London, 1970), pp. 75–86. The richest source on village ritual is still Henry Whitehead's *The Village Gods of South India* (1921), 2d ed., rev. & enl. (Delhi, 1976). Ákos Östör's *The Play of the Gods: Locality, Ideology, Structure and Time in the Festivals of a Bengali Town* (Chicago, 1980) provides a detailed and valuable analysis of a Durgā-*pūjā* performance in Bengal.

Nancy E. Auer Falk

Buddhist Pūjā

Even the oldest Buddhist texts refer to acts of reverence (*pūjā*) addressed to the Buddha. Within a few centuries after the Buddha's final *nirvāṇa*, this "reverence" had become a full-blown cult of the departed master. The cult's practice drew upon an ancient formula of veneration, also utilized by the cult of pre-Buddhist divinities called *yakṣas*. With accompanying gestures of reverence and circumambulations, the practitioner offered flowers, incense, and perfumes and sometimes music, burning lamps, decorative cloths, banners, and umbrellas.

It is said that the Buddha himself first authorized such *pūjās*. For example, in legendary accounts of the final *nirvāṇa* (e.g., *Mahāparinibbānasutta* 5.11–12) he instructs the Mallas of Kuśinagara to honor in this way the stupa, or monument that will contain his relics. Legendary accounts of the emperor Aśoka such as the *Aśokāvadāṇa* assert that Aśoka redistributed relics throughout his realm, establishing their stupas and appropriate *pūjās* in each populated territory. Aśoka's support of the Buddhist community and promotion of Buddhist teachings very likely played a major role in the spread of the cult throughout India. Missionaries, pilgrims, and diplomatic missions carried beyond India the cult's relics, images, and rootings from Bodhi Tree branches along with the Buddhist ordination and teachings.

During the earlier centuries of the cult's development, *pūjā* was offered primarily to bodily relics (*śarīras*) of Buddhas and outstanding disciples; to items that the Buddha had touched or used *(paribhogika)*, such as the Bodhi Tree or the begging bowl; and to the stupas, which sometimes housed relics, but were sometimes erected solely for commemorative purposes. Later the cult was extended to images of Buddhas and *bodhisattvas*.

The most striking feature of the Buddhist cult was the stupa. Early forms of this monument were constructed of brick or stone. Its basic components were an axial pillar embedded in a dome, which was mounted on a raised base and surmounted by a boxlike superstructure; gates in a surrounding fence or appended niches oriented the stupa to the cardinal directions, while umbrellas crowned the protruding tip of the pillar. A North Indian variation constructed of wood evolved into the familiar pagoda of East Asia. Such monuments have been called symbols of the Enlightenment, or "*nirvāṇa* bodies"—architectural stand-ins for the departed Buddha; alternatively, Buddhist writings sometimes interpret them as images of the Enlightenment Path.

When relics were inserted in a monumental stupa, they were permanently embedded deep within its mass. But certain famous relics, as well as images of the Buddha, were housed in monastery shrine-rooms or temples *(caityas)* where worshipers could approach them more directly.

Buddhist *pūjās* were shaped by popular religiosity rather than professional priesthoods; consequently they tended to remain free in form. Even regulations for the stupa cult included in sectarian Vinayas (writings on the monastic rule) define permissible behavior and offerings rather than fixing liturgical patterns. Individual temples, communities, and sectarian groups evolved their own procedures for *pūjās*. Thus the Chinese pilgrim Fa-hsien (traveled from 399 to 413) described an elaborate daily ritual at the temple of the Buddha's skull-bone in northwestern India. At the climax of the ritual, the local ruler lifted the relic and placed it on the top of his own head. The treasured tooth relic of Sri Lanka received for centuries elaborate thrice-daily *pūjās* much like those of Hindu temples.

Monastic communities have evolved their own patterns for daily and festal *pūjās*: reported versions feature circumambulations and chanting of *sūtras* (Buddhist scriptures). Chanted *sūtras* and formulaic recitations of the "Homage to Amida Buddha" are prominent in the *pūjās* performed at temples and home shrines by devotees of Pure Land sects of Japan and China. *Pūjās* to Tibetan and Nepali Vajrayāna divinities commonly include multiple prostrations, chanting of *mantras* (power syllables), and complex internal visualizations.

The soteriological status of Buddha-*pūjā* has been problematic for Buddhist thinkers, because the practice seems to imply that the Buddha is present in his relics and symbols. Conservative Buddhist schools denied such presence, maintaining that the Buddha had totally exited from the world at the time of his final *nirvāṇa*. Performing *pūjās* was of value only as an elementary aspect of self-discipline: venerating the Buddha helped one call to mind the Master's virtues and example, while *pūjā* offerings were a form of *dāna*, the generous giving that shows one's nonattachment to possessions. The Theravāda tradition has been least comfortable with its *pūjās*, officially maintaining that only laity should engage in such actions.

According to Mahāyāna teachings, however, the Buddha nature suffuses the whole of existence; hence it *is* present in the relics and stupas and images, but to no greater degree than it is present elsewhere. Therefore here, too, the greatest import of the *pūjā* lies in its effect on the performer and its ability to sustain his intention toward salvation. *Pūjā* became central only to Tantric practitioners, who transformed its symbols, gestures, and offerings into complex techniques of meditation.

[*Buddhist* pūjā *in particular regions is discussed in* Worship and Cultic Life, *articles on* Buddhist Cultic Life in East Asia, Buddhist Cultic Life in South and Southeast Asia, *and* Buddhist Cultic Life in Tibet. *For the veneration of relics and stupas, see* Relics *and* Stupa Worship.]

BIBLIOGRAPHY

Resources on Buddha-*pūjā* are rare. For materials on early Indian practice, see my work "The Study of Cult, with Special Reference to the Cult of the Buddha's Relics in Ancient South Asia" (Ph.D. diss., University of Chicago, 1972). André Bareau has summarized Chinese Vinaya sources on the stupa cult in an invaluable article, "La construction et le culte des stūpa d'après le *Vinayapiṭaka*," *Bulletin de l'École Française d'Extrême Orient* 50 (1960–1962): 229–274. Arthur M. Hocart's *The Temple of the Tooth in Kandy* (London, 1931) includes a detailed description of *pūjās* at the temple. Robert B. Ekvall's *Religious Observances in Tibet* (Chicago, 1964) is rich in materials on Tibetan *pūjās*; Stephan Beyer's *The Cult of Tārā: Magic and Ritual in Tibet* (Berkeley, 1973) affords excellent insight into the role of *pūjā* in a Vajrayāna cult.

NANCY E. AUER FALK

PUNISHMENT. *See* Heaven and Hell; Judgment of the Dead; *and* Revenge and Retribution.

PURĀṆAS. The Sanskrit word *purāṇa*, in its earliest use, means "old narrative and ancient lore" and, in this sense, is found in the *Atharvaveda* (11.7.24), in the *Śatapatha Brāhmaṇa* (13.4.3.13), and in various other *śruti* ("revealed") texts. The term is often associated with *itihāsa* ("so indeed it was," i.e., traditional or historical accounts), and both *purāṇa* and *itihāsa* have been used sometimes with separate senses and at other times with the same sense. Gradually, *purāṇa* came to designate a body of works, encyclopedic in scope, incorporating legends, myths, and customary observances.

While many works may bear the name *Purāṇa*, only eighteen are traditionally acknowledged. The famous Arabian traveler Albīrūnī (c. 1030 CE) gives two lists. The first comprises the *Ādi, Matsya, Kūrma, Varāha, Narasiṃha, Vāmana, Vāyu, Nārada, Skanda, Āditya, Soma, Samba, Brahmāṇḍa, Mārkaṇḍeya, Tārksya, Viṣṇu, Brahma,* and *Bhaviṣya Purāṇa*. The second list, however, includes the *Brahma, Padma, Viṣṇu, Śiva, Bhāgavata, Nārada, Mārkaṇḍeya, Agni, Bhaviṣya, Brahmavaivarta, Liṅga, Varāha, Skanda, Vāmana, Kūrma, Matsya, Garuḍa,* and *Brahmāṇḍa Purāṇa*. This second list, which must be the more recent one, is commonly accepted and is given in each one of the texts, so that it is recognized as the set of eighteen Mahāpurāṇas (major Purāṇas); works not included in this list, although called Purāṇas, are considered as Upapurāṇas (minor Purāṇas). There is no agreement about the titles of the eighteen minor Purāṇas, however, for any religious text could be called an Upapurāṇa or be declared part of a Mahāpurāṇa. This is the case with the numerous *māhātmyas*, or "glorifications" of *tīrthas* ("places of pilgrimage").

The earlier Purāṇas might have been composed, in their present form, during the first centuries of the common era; this date is suggested by M. Winternitz, in his *History of Indian Literature* (translated by V. Srinivasa Sarma, Delhi, 1981), on the basis of a comparison of Buddhist Mahāyāna texts of that period. Each Purāṇa shows, however, different historical strata, having undergone various redactions and revisions; many have several common, and often almost identical, portions, so that some scholars (e.g., Willibald Kirfel) have postulated a single original Purāṇa having the *pañcalakṣaṇas* (i.e., the five main characteristics): *sarga* ("creation"), *pratisarga* ("new creation"), *vaṃśa* (genealogy of gods and *ṛṣis*), *Manvantara* ("the great periods of a Manu," i.e., an age that has a Manu as ancestor), and *vaṃśanucarita* (the history of the dynasties whose origin is traced back to the sun and the moon). From this original pattern all the other texts are purported to be derived, each one adding variations and supplementary myths. Although the hypothesis of one original Purāṇa is no longer believed, the philological comparison of parallel sections of several Puranic texts has revealed clear similarities in basic structure. No precise chronology can be given for individual Purāṇas, although the *Bhāgavata Purāṇa*, which falls between Albīrūnī's time and the Vaiṣṇava *bhakti* movement in South India, can be considered the most recent.

The importance of Puranic texts derives from the fact that they have been and still are media of mass education with very conspicuous religious, cultural, and social functions. The Purāṇas have, first, a metaphysic derived partly from old cosmogonic accounts and partly from Sāṃkhya. This metaphysic belongs to anonymous sources as well as the entire corpus of myths and legends, although the Purāṇas are generally attributed to Vyāsa. From the metaphysical point of view, the oldest portions of the texts suggest an antagonism between theism and nontheism. But the recent strata point to the existence of sectarian influence, for there is evidence of a personal deity considered as the highest Absolute. From about the fourth or fifth century CE, the opposition between theism and nontheism is replaced by theism represented by the gods Brahmā, Viṣṇu, and Śiva. In a theistic sense they are worshiped separately by distinct sects, but metaphysically they are considered as a *trimūrti* or a trinity, that is, one God in his functions of creating, maintaining, and destroying the world.

The Purāṇas have been classified as dedicated to Brahmā (the *Brahmāṇḍa, Brahmavaivarta, Mārkaṇḍeya, Bhaviṣya, Vāmana,* and *Brahma Purāṇa*), to Viṣṇu (the *Viṣṇu, Nārada, Bhāgavata, Garuḍa, Padma,* and *Varāha Purāṇa*), and to Śiva (the *Matsya, Kūrma, Liṅga, Śiva, Skanda,* and *Agni Purāṇa*). But this classification is artificial, for none of the Purāṇas is exclusively dedicated to one deity; rather, each bears traces of different cults, even if oriented mainly to the glorification of a sectarian god.

Viṣṇu is a god who is variously described: he is often glorified as the one and only god, as the creator and preserver of the world; even the nondualistic doctrine of the Upaniṣads is combined with Vaiṣṇava devotion. But the more recent Purāṇas, the *Nārada, Varāha,* and *Garuḍa,* and the last portion *(uttara-khaṇḍa)* of the *Padma Purāṇa* teach that Viṣṇu has to be worshiped mainly by rites, pilgrimages, and festivals.

Viṣṇu is, above all, celebrated in his *avatāras* ("descents"). The doctrine of *avatāra,* as such, was a good method of incorporating ancient popular gods into the supreme deity; in fact, the oldest *avatāras*, in animal form, derive from ancient cults and, in earlier writings, were manifestations of Prajāpati ("the lord of creatures") and Brahmā. But as Vaiṣṇava *avatāras* they receive wider symbolic significance, for they are related to theological doctrines of salvation. The fish incarnation *(matsya avatāra)* is connected to the old transcultural myth of the great flood and gathers a number of soteriological symbols: Viṣṇu takes the form of a fish with a great horn to which is tied the boat that rescues Manu, the progenitor of the human race, together with the seven sages *(sapta ṛṣayaḥ)* and the seeds of all existing things. In the *Bhāgavata Purāṇa* it is said, moreover, that Viṣṇu assumed the form of a fish to save the Vedas (holy scriptures) after they had been stolen by the demon Hayagrīva during one of the nights of Brahmā, when the worlds were submerged in the ocean. This myth, although it is not homogeneous, includes such ancient and universal soteriological symbols as the flood (chaos), the ship (order and safety), the fish (the savior), and the demon who stole the Veda (the enemy of religion).

The *kūrma avatāra,* or incarnation of Viṣṇu as a tortoise, appears in the legend of the churning of the ocean. Here, the old cosmogonic symbol represented by the tortoise is combined with a myth of salvation: on the *kūrma* rests the great mountain Mandara; the gods and two classes of demons (the *daityas* and the *dānavas*) twist the great serpent Vāsuki around the mountain and thus churn the ocean, out of which comes *amṛta,* the ambrosia of immortality; from the *amṛta* emerges Lakṣmī, goddess of beauty and fortune, consort of Viṣṇu. In the *Kūrma Purāṇa* Lakṣmī is identified with the *śakti* ("creative force") of God. The objects recovered from the ocean—the jewel *(kaustubha),* the bow *(dhanus),* the conch *(śankha),* and the celestial tree *(pārijāta)*—and personages described in the myth—such as the goddess of wine (Surā), the moon (Candra), the nymph (Rambhā), the archetypal horse (Ucchaiḥśravas), the cow of plenty (Surabhī), and the elephant (Airāvata)—are all symbols of prosperity, victory, and joy, with the exception of the poison *(viṣa),* which also comes out of the churned sea and probably means that on this earth the good is always mixed with a bit of evil. Another *avatāra* related to waters is the boar incarnation: Viṣṇu assumes the form of a boar to rescue the earth, which has been dragged by a demon to the bottom of the sea. This is an old legend of the *Śatapatha Brāhmaṇa* that, adapted to a Vaiṣṇava perspective, presents the tension between demon and god, between chaos and order, and holds both cosmological and soteric significance.

The fourth *avatāra,* Narasiṃha, half man, half lion, represents the shape taken by Viṣṇu in order to deliver the world from the demon Hiraṇyakaśipu, who had become invulnerable and persecuted his son Prahlāda for worshiping Viṣṇu. Indestructible by gods, men, or beasts, the demon ultimately was slain by Narasiṃha ("man-lion"), who was neither man nor animal.

It is believed that the four incarnations noted above appeared in the first age of the world *(satya-* or *kṛtayuga).* In the second age *(tretayuga)* Viṣṇu appeared before the *daitya* king Bali as a dwarf. Bali had acquired the dominion of the three worlds (heaven, earth, and the infernal regions), and even the gods were afraid of his power, but the dwarf, offered a boon, asked of Bali only the space of ground that he could cover in three strides. Vāmana-Viṣṇu measured the earth with his first step and the heavens with his second; only the nether worlds were left to Bali. The source of this legend of the three steps of Viṣṇu is found in the *Ṛgveda,* where Viṣṇu takes three steps over earth, heaven, and the lower regions, representing the immensity of God. In the legend of the *vāmana avatāra,* he embodies vast opposites: great and minute size, transcendence and immanence, the high and the low. Even the *daitya* Bali is not opposed to Viṣṇu but is allowed by him to govern the underworlds.

The most important *avatāras* are, of course, the human ones, in particular Rāma, whose story is summarized in various Puranic sections, and Kṛṣṇa, who is considered by many devotees to be the perfect manifestation of Viṣṇu. To Rāma is dedicated the *Adhyātmarāmāyaṇa,* a poem that is taken as part of the *Brahmāṇḍa Purāṇa.* In this composition, which no doubt is one of the most recent Puranic texts, Rāma is identified with the *ātman* of the Upaniṣads and Sītā is considered the same as Lakṣmī and Prakṛti ("original nature").

Kṛṣṇa is celebrated in the fifth book of the *Viṣṇu Purāṇa,* which contains his life story and his adventures, and in the fourth book of the *Brahmavaivarta Purāṇa,* where Kṛṣṇa is exalted as the god above all gods, the creator of the world. His favorite wife, Rādhā, is described not as a separate being but as Kṛṣṇa's *śakti.* The best description of Kṛṣṇa's life is given in the tenth book of the *Bhāgavata Purāṇa;* here Kṛṣṇa's incarnation, which is enumerated as the twenty-first, is followed by that of the Buddha and of Kalkin, the *avatāra* of the future. In the *Bhāgavata Purāṇa* the life of Kṛṣṇa is related with many touching details, from his earliest days to his childhood and youth. The fascination of the Kṛṣṇa legend lies in Viṣṇu's adoption of the roles of boy and lover, similar to any child and any youth and, at the same time, different because of his inner light and his supernatural charm. Kṛṣṇa's incarnation is supposed to belong to the *dvāparayuga,* whereas the Buddha's and Kalkin's *avatāras* are in the *kaliyuga;* Kalkin is to appear at the end of the *kaliyuga,* the fourth and most degenerate age of the world.

Even Śiva has his own incarnations, but they are not so important as those of Viṣṇu; in the *Liṅga Purāṇa* and in the *Kūrma Purāṇa* (1.51) are listed twenty-eight *avatāras* of Śiva, the first of which is the Śveta incarnation and the last that of Nakulīśa. All the *avatāras* pertain to the *kaliyuga.*

The second part of the *Kūrma Purāṇa* contains an *Īśvaragītā* in which Śiva is described as the one with a thousand forms, as the great cause of creation, protection, and destruction of the universe, as the lord who has to be meditated on by yogins, as the lord of yogins. Only those who have completely subdued their minds can see him dancing in the sky, luminous as a million suns, full of bliss, the abode of eternal powers. The last part of the *Vāyu Purāṇa* states that yogins who have been meditating on Śiva arrive at the city of Śiva (Śivapura), which is shining with great splendor.

More often, in a widespread and popular way, Śiva is worshiped in the form of a *liṅga,* an ancient symbol, probably older than the Aryan culture, originally meaning a potency, or divine power, beyond form, and later on becoming a figure of fertility. The *Liṅga Purāṇa* is the most important text for the worship of Śiva in the *liṅga* symbol. The text includes a thousand names of Śiva (*Liṅga Purāṇa* 1.65), a list compiled on the pattern of the thousand names of Viṣṇu, already known in the epics.

Similarly, Śiva's *śakti* ("power") is conceived of as a female deity. Her name is Śakti, but she is worshiped and invoked under 1,008 names (*Kūrma Purāṇa* 1.11):

Śiva is one of her names, and Śiva is said to be the possessor of Śakti. The other Śaktis and possessors of *śaktis* ("powers") are born of the Śakti of Śiva. The Goddess, variously called Śivā, Satī, Maheśvarī, or Pārvatī, is the refuge of those who are desirous of liberation, for she is able to destroy the afflictions of the world. The *Matsya Purāṇa* (13) enumerates the 108 names under which Śiva's wife, or the Goddess, is to be praised; and here again she is regarded as a mother, a savior, a refuge in distress.

The most encyclopedic Purāṇas contain not only theological ideas and hymns of praise in honor of the greatest divine manifestations but also sections on astronomy, astrology, geography, medicine, grammar, metrics, and poetics, and even instructions for house building and for a variety of daily activities. The Purāṇas thus inform us, in a broad way, about the history of Hinduism.

Throughout the Purāṇas the most important theme is *bhakti*, or devotional religion, a theme that reflects the cultural and social changes in Hindu society during the centuries in which the Purāṇas were composed. The *bhakti* religion reflects a great difference from the traditional ceremonies and attitudes based on the Vedas (the holy scriptures of Brahmanism), although the authority of the Vedas is never denied. Some of the most recent texts even stress the independence of *bhakti* from all other means of salvation. In some Puranic sections, as mentioned above, yogic meditation is cited as the highest religious achievement, but in general, Puranic texts propose *bhakti* as the best way to reach union with God, whether called Brahmā, Śiva, Viṣṇu, Rāma, Kṛṣṇa, or the various names of the Goddess.

In the religion of the Bhāgavatas, as taught especially in the *Bhāgavata Purāṇa*, *bhakti* is conceived of also as a way of life, as selfless dedication to Kṛṣṇa; a *bhakta* ("devotee") has to be free from any pride in birth, wealth, and so on, and he should recognize no distinction between himself and others. This implies that a person's birth and caste have no significance for salvation. It seems that there is even an opposition between wealth and devotion, to such an extent that, according to the *Bhāgavata Purāṇa* (10.88.8–9), God removes the wealth of those whom he favors. Priests (*brāhmaṇas*) devoted to Lord Kṛṣṇa are said to be the highest of men, but they must be persons free from jealousy, falsehood, envy, injury, and pride (10.7.13). Indeed, pride, hypocrisy, and arrogance are considered to be the characteristic defects of those who reject *bhakti*. The social and ethical teachings of the Bhāgavatas may be summarized in the following two features: praise of poverty and compassion for those who are distressed, despised, and persecuted (11.22.59). Many of the *bhakta*s were poor or of low castes; some even became poor through renunciation.

One must also remember that the establishment of image worship, temple ceremonies, and the practice of pilgrimages and festivals as described in the Purāṇas must have helped greatly to bring people of the lower classes into the *bhakti* religion. Even from earliest times *bhakti* has been regarded as a way to salvation open to all; since the time of the Purāṇas, religious festivals and pilgrimages have increasingly become occasions of intercaste fraternization, and a sort of "model" of a return to an original unity.

The Sanskrit of the Purāṇas, which is similar in many ways to that of the Indian epics, shows the influence of Prakrit languages and contains grammatical irregularities as well as expressions of popular idiom, suggesting that the authors of the texts did not belong to the most cultivated circles. Puranic compositions may be, occasionally, full of poetry but here and there they show the mark of stylistic uncertainties. In contrast, the *Bhāgavata Purāṇa* is relatively free of impurities, for it is written in an archaic style that attempts to "brahmanize" or "sanskritize" *bhakti* religion and Kṛṣṇa legend; in other words, the author of the *Bhāgavata* tried to use a language similar to that of the Vedic seers in order to reconnect the *bhakti* tradition to a sacred past.

[*See also* Avatāra *and* Indian Religions, *article on* Mythic Themes. *Many of the deities and mythic heroes mentioned herein are the subjects of independent entries.*]

BIBLIOGRAPHY

The All-India Kashiraj Trust has undertaken the task of publishing critical editions of all the Mahāpurāṇas. The first critically edited text is the *Vāmana Purāṇa*, edited by Anand Swarup Gupta and translated by Satyamsu M. Mukhopadhyaya (Varanasi, 1968), with Hindi and English translations in separate volumes. The *Kūrma Purāṇa* (Varanasi, 1971) and the *Varāha Purāṇa* (Varanasi, 1982) were edited by Anand Swarup Gupta and translated into English by Ahibhusan Bhattacharya. The others will follow and will be published at Varanasi. Translation of all the Mahāpurāṇas is currently under way in the Motilal series "Ancient Indian Tradition and Mythology" (1977–). The French translation of the *Bhāgavatapurāṇa* by Eugène Burnouf (1840) has been reprinted in Paris (1982).

Various other older translations in English are still useful. These include the *Agnipurāṇam*, 2 vols., translated by M. N. Dutt (1901; reprint, Varanasi, 1967); the *Brahma-vaivarta Purāṇam*, 2 vols., translated by Rajendra Nath Sen (Allahabad, 1922); the *Garuḍapurāṇam*, translated by M. N. Dutt (1908; reprint, Varanasi, 1968); the *Mārkaṇḍeya Purāṇa*, translated by F. Eden Pargiter (1888–1904; reprint, Delhi, 1969); and the *Viṣṇu Purāṇa*, translated by H. H. Wilson (London, 1840) and issued in a second edition with an introduction by R. C. Hazra (Calcutta, 1961). A one-volume *Purāṇic Encyclopaedia* has been compiled by Vettam Mani (1964) and translated into English

(Delhi, 1975). This work is a dictionary of proper names, with many references to myths and legends contained in Indian epic as well as Puranic literature.

Among the studies on the Purāṇas it is worth mentioning R. C. Hazra's *Studies in the Puranic Records on Hindu Rites and Customs* (1940; reprint, Delhi, 1975); Achut Dattatraya Pusalker's *Studies in the Epics and Puranas* (Bombay, 1955); Paul Hacker's *Prahlāda: Werden und Wandlung einer Idealgestalt*, 2 vols. (Wiesbaden, 1960); Adalbert J. Gail's *Bhakti im Bhāgavata purāṇa* (Wiesbaden, 1969); *Krishna: Myths, Rites, and Attitudes*, edited by Milton Singer (Honolulu, 1966); and Siddheswar Bhattacharya's *Philosophy of Srimad Bhāgavata*, 2 vols. (Santiniketan, 1960–1962).

CATERINA CONIO

PURE AND IMPURE LANDS. In Mahāyāna Buddhism, a "Pure Land" is a purified land where Buddhas and *bodhisattvas*, the future Buddhas, dwell. In contrast, the realms inhabited by ordinary sentient beings are called "Impure Lands," for they are tainted by blind passion.

In Chinese Buddhism, two technical terms, *ching-t'u* and *hui-t'u*, are used to refer to Pure and Impure Lands, respectively. The concept behind these terms, however, is attested to in Indian Buddhist texts by such terms as *buddhakṣetra-pariśuddhi* ("the purification of the Buddha land") or *pariśuddhaṃ buddhakṣetram* ("purified Buddha land"), as in the *Aṣṭasāhasrikā-prajñāpāramitā Sūtra* (edited by Rajendralala Mitra, Calcutta, 1888, pp. 362–363), and *apariśuddhaṃ buddhakṣetram* ("unpurified Buddha land") or *kliṣṭaṃ buddhakṣetram* ("tainted Buddha land"), as in the *Karuṇāpuṇḍarīka Sūtra* (edited by Yamada Isshi, London, 1968; vol. 2, pp. 52, 81). It was in accordance with such usage that *ching-t'u* and *hui-t'u* were established in Chinese as technical terms.

The notion of a "Buddha land" (Skt., *buddhakṣetra;* Pali, *buddhakkhetta*) derives from the period of early Buddhism. According to the Theravāda interpretation, the *buddhakṣetra* is the realm in which the teachings of Śākyamuni Buddha prevail. However, in Mahāyāna Buddhism numerous Buddha lands are said to exist in order to accommodate the numerous *bodhisattvas* who become Buddhas; or rather, the merit accumulated by these *bodhisattvas* through their long spiritual careers goes toward creating a purified realm responsive to their influence. In other words, because of the basic Buddhist premise that no two Buddhas can preside over the same Buddha land, the "new" Buddhas are forced to emerge, as it were, in lands far distant from that of Śākyamuni, which is called the Sahā Land. These are located variously in the ten directions (the eight points of the compass, the zenith, and the nadir) of the cosmos. It is among these "distant" Pure Lands, described as "numberless as the sands of the River Ganges," that we find Amitābha (Amitāyus) Buddha's Sukhāvatī (to the west), Akṣobhya's Abhirati (to the east), and Bhaiṣajyaguruvaiḍūryaprabha's Vaiḍūryanirbhāsā (also to the east).

The best-known of these Pure Lands is Sukhāvatī. This Pure Land is described in detail in three *sūtras*, the *Larger Sukhāvatīvyūha Sūtra*, the *Smaller Sukhāvatīvyūha Sūtra*, and the *Kuan wu-liang-shou ching*. Of these, the first two *sūtras* are believed to have been compiled in northwest India around 100 CE. Modern scholarship is in general agreement, however, that the main body of the *Kuan ching* was compiled in Central Asia, and that accretions were made during the course of its translation into Chinese. But while the conditions surrounding the compilation of these *sūtras* differ, all three texts share in depicting the splendor of the Pure Land and the majestic appearances of Amitābha (Amitāyus) and his disciples and attending *bodhisattvas*. These depictions undoubtedly reflect ideal perceptions of the Buddha land, Buddhas, and *bodhisattvas* of the period when each of the *sūtras* was compiled. The ideal depiction of Sukhāvatī can be viewed as a symbolic and hypostatized representation of Mahāyāna Buddhist enlightenment. A Pure Land is a "purified land," that is, a realm that came into existence by "purifying the land." To "purify the land" means that the Mahāyāna *bodhisattvas* purify everything in the land in which they will appear upon becoming Buddhas; this "purification" includes leading all sentient beings to Buddhahood. Of course, such acts entail nothing less than the fulfillment both of the *bodhisattvas*' cultivation of the *pāramitās* ("perfections") and of his vow to benefit all beings. As such, the Pure Land can be regarded as hypostatized representation of the Buddha's enlightenment. For example, even though Sukhāvatī is described as a realm that exists to the west, it is in reality a realm that transcends space. While it is said to exist beyond billions of Buddha lands, this is actually nothing but a symbolic expression for infinite distance; what is originally beyond space was expressed in the context of space.

By means of such descriptions, the Pure Land *sūtras* succeeded in capturing the imagination of ordinary people. Consequently, the practice of contemplating the Buddha (*buddhānusmṛti;* Chin., *nien-fo*), a relatively easy form of religious practice leading to birth in the Pure Land and eventual enlightenment (Buddhahood) there, gained wide popularity among Buddhists. In the same vein, the name Sukhāvatī ("realm of bliss"), which originally denoted a realm of absolute religious bliss, also acquired connotations of relative, this-worldly happiness. Given its popular appeal, Sukhāvatī quickly became the object of the most dominant form of Buddhist devotion in East Asia. Hence, "Pure Land" in Chinese Buddhism came to be regarded as synonymous with Amitābha's Pure Land. In following this practice, the Japanese Buddhist sects that are based on the worship of Amitābha (Jpn., Amida) Buddha are called Jōdoshū (the Pure Land sect) and Jōdoshinshū (the True Pure Land sect).

In Mahāyāna Buddhism there are also other kinds of Pure Lands different in nature from the "distant" Pure Lands discussed earlier. The *Vimalakīrtinirdeśa Sūtra* espouses the idea that when *bodhisattvas* purify their mind this Sahā world itself becomes a Pure Land. This view of Pure Land was advocated in China and Japan by the Ch'an and Zen sects respectively and led to the development of the concept of the "mind-only Pure Land." The *Lotus Sutra* contains elements that lead some to regard Gṛdhrakūṭa—the Vulture's Peak where Śākyamuni Buddha preached the *Lotus Sutra*—as a Pure Land. The Japanese Nichiren sect later came to view this mountain as an ideal realm and espoused the notion of "Vulture's Peak Pure Land." The *Avataṃsaka Sūtra* speaks of Vairocana's Padmagarbha, a Pure Land in which the entire world is enveloped in a lotus flower, a notion that the Chinese Hua-yen and Japanese Kegon sects have made an integral part of their doctrine. Finally, the *Ghandhavyūha Sūtra* speaks of a Ghandhavyūha realm. Later, the Japanese Shingon sect came to regard this realm as the Pure Land of Mahāvairocana Buddha and to identify it with our present Sahā world. In Chinese and Japanese Buddhism the Tuṣita Heaven, where the *bodhisattva* Maitreya now dwells, and the Potalaka Mountain, where the *bodhisattva* Avalokiteśvara dwells, are both sometimes referred to as Pure Lands and have been the objects of large devotional followings.

In response to such views, the *Karuṇāpuṇḍarīka Sūtra* emphasized the great compassion of Śākyamuni Buddha, who appeared in this Impure Land, rather than the Buddhas of the "distant" Pure Lands such as Amitābha and Akṣobhya. This text developed in opposition to the notion of "extra-worldly" Pure Lands but never wielded much influence. The same *sūtra* explains that our Impure Land is characterized by the "five corruptions" (*pañca kaṣāyāḥ:* the corruptions of the times, of views, of blind passion, of sentient beings, and of life). However in later periods, especially in Japan, it became customary to explain the Impure Land as coextensive with the "six destinies" (*ṣaḍ gatayaḥ:* the destinies of hell, of hungry spirits, of beasts, of *asuras*, of humans, and of heavenly beings) as seen, for example, in Genshin's *Ōjōyōshū.* In this case also, the Impure Land was posited in contradistinction to Amida's Pure Land. Here the Impure Land was characterized as something that one grows weary of and wishes to leave behind in favor of birth in Sukhāvatī.

[*See also* Amitābha; Ching-t'u; Jōdoshū; *and* Jōdo Shinshū.]

BIBLIOGRAPHY

Fujita Kōtatsu. *Genshi jōdo shisō no kenkyū.* Tokyo, 1970. A comprehensive examination of the formation of Pure Land texts and doctrines. Contains a brief summary in English.

Suzuki, D. T. "The Development of the Pure Land Doctrine in Buddhism." *The Eastern Buddhist* 3 (1925): 285–326. Reprinted in *Collected Writings on Shin Buddhism,* edited by The Eastern Buddhist Society (Kyoto, 1973), pages 3–31. Although limited in focus to Japanese Buddhism, this work provides an excellent introduction to the Pure Land tradition.

FUJITA KŌTATSU
Translated from Japanese by Kenneth K. Tanaka

PURIFICATION. Concepts of pollution and purity are found in virtually all the religions of the world. While some religions recognize subtle distinctions of relative pollution, others place less emphasis upon the social and religious categories that determine pollution. The range extends from cultures like that of the Pygmies, who place almost no emphasis on concepts of pollution and purity, to hierarchical systems like Hinduism, with its highly developed mechanisms for transforming impurity from a dangerous category to a meaningful structuring principle of the Indian cultural system.

It is impossible to understand religious pollution and purification as separate phenomena; these two inseparable categories of religious experience are locked into a dynamic complementarity. Rules governing religious pollution imply a corollary code for ameliorating the condition. The purification of religious pollution is a major religious theme because it forges a path of expiation, healing, renewal, transcendence, and reintegration, establishing harmonious triangular links among the individual, the cosmos, and the social structure.

The range of activities or events considered to be polluting is vast, and there is an equally impressive range of purification rituals. In Tibetan Buddhism, for instance, pollution may be associated with trivial situations, such as crowds where polluted persons may lurk (this deters no one from being in a crowd); or it may lead to very serious conditions of impurity, as in the case of big game hunting, when pollution can cause famine or drought (Keyes and Daniel, 1983). While some pollution may be due to deliberate acts that violate social or religious norms, pollution may be accidental or unintended by the agent, as in the case of menstrual or death pollution. This distinction is important because the specific corrective rite of purification may differ depending on whether the state of pollution was attained deliberately or accidentally. Shintō, for instance, is permeated with purification rites that can be traced back to origin myths according to which the god Susano-o committed offenses against the divine order through ignorance and error. Consequently, in the Shintō religion general rites of purification must be performed periodically to resacralize the world. This contrasts with more specific occasions for purification rites, which are associated with the deliberate breaking of taboos by individuals.

Virtually all aspects of life may be surrounded by notions of pollution and purity. Not only must sins and devils be purged in annual purification ceremonies celebrated as rites of renewal; pollution rules are also applied to the ordinary products of human physiology, regulating human behavior in relation to contact with blood, vomit, excreta, cooked foods, hair clippings, and so on. The critical rites of passage associated with major transitions in life (birth, adolescence, marriage, and death) are usually governed by rules of pollution and purity, since these are times when humans are most vulnerable to attacks by evil spirits. There is no clear pattern of cross-cultural uniformity in these concepts of pollution and purity; in some societies menstruation or death may be considered especially dangerous and surrounded with elaborate rites of purification, while other cultures particularly fear pollution from eating certain foods or from contact with members of lower classes. Yet, despite this cultural diversity, there remain a number of consistent patterns that yield important insights about the nature of religious experience.

The literature on religion is replete with concern about the symbolism of purification. Nineteenth-century figures like James G. Frazer, Robertson Smith, Émile Durkheim, and Lucien Lévy-Bruhl attempted in various ways to explain principles of defilement and purification in primitive religions. Anthropologists of religion in the early twentieth century paid little attention to the subject. However, field work among African cultures and in South Asia during the 1960s challenged anthropologists to develop theoretical explanations for the increasingly complex data associated with concepts of pollution and purity in the cognitive structures of different religions. In 1966 Mary Douglas presented her extensive analysis of the topic in the classic volume *Purity and Danger*. That same year Louis Dumont published his controversial treatment of pollution and purity norms in Hinduism under the title *Homo Hierarchicus*. Since that time, symbolic anthropologists, structuralists, and religion specialists have elaborated on this theme in many different religions and cultures.

Purity and Danger is a landmark in the study of religious symbolism because it systematizes divergent information in an elegant analytical framework. For Mary Douglas, religious pollution is a property of the "betwixt and between" in human cultures; whatever falls between the social categories developed by human religious systems to comprehend and impute a sense of order and reality is considered to be impure (Parker, 1983). The concepts of pollution and purity in a particular religion make no sense without reference to a total structure of thought. Thus, along with other scholars, Douglas emphasizes the analysis of rituals and sacred texts in order to reveal semantic categories that determine mechanisms by which different peoples divide the world into domains of relative pollution or purity. Fortunately, this more systematic approach to purification has restored the concept as a major theme in the study of world religions.

Forms of Religious Pollution. The range of human activities related to religious pollution is immense. However, it is possible to isolate three general categories of pollution associated with (1) bodily functions, (2) social bonding, and (3) the maintenance of boundaries of the "holy" or "sacred." The categories of pollution presented here are artificial devices developed to facilitate analysis; they are not meant as descriptive categories to characterize the phenomenon. It should be remembered that these categories overlap and form a continuum, and that emphasis on different sorts of pollution varies greatly from one religio-cultural context to another.

Pollution associated with bodily functions. Ideas about dirt are linked into complex symbolic systems in virtually every society. One of the most widespread concepts of pollution is associated with emissions from the human body. Urine and feces are particularly impure, partly because of their odor, but also due to their more general association with putrefaction and death. In India, the left hand, used for cleansing after defecation, is forbidden to be used when touching other people or sacred objects. Other bodily secretions, such as saliva, vomit, menstrual blood, and afterbirth, are also considered to have polluting qualities. In some traditions, even sperm is polluting outside the sanctified context of marriage. All of these bodily excretions have social significance; they are usually surrounded with heavy ritualization to ensure that they will be contained within a specific religious, cultural, temporal, or spatial context. Since they are natural physiological functions, the resulting pollution is focused not on preventing their occurrence but rather on providing boundaries for control and purification.

Anything that enters the human body may be a source of pollution. Thus, air, liquid, and food are potentially polluting agents that must be carefully controlled. Contamination by polluted food is a widespread danger, involving elaborate rules of avoidance. In some religions, dietary laws are very strict. Orthodox Judaism, with its emphasis on kosher foods, carefully articulated in the Hebrew scriptures, sets the Jews apart as a holy people who are considered to be clean and consequently prepared to receive the blessings of God, along with the heavy responsibilities that accompany this covenant. Hindus are also known for their strict dietary laws. The ascendent principle operative in Hinduism is the concept of *ahiṃsā* ("nonviolence"). Hindu dietary laws stress pure vegetarianism as an ideal. Pollution from food intake, particularly meat, has serious consequences. Thus, the highest castes strive to be strict vegetarians, while meat is allowable only to lower castes and untouchables.

In many parts of the world, food is carefully preserved to avoid putrefaction. Food must be protected from contact with impure persons who can transmit their contamination to it. Thus, in many societies menstruating women, sick people, and the lower classes are prohibited from involvement in the preparation of foods. Nobles, priests, and other persons of high status are particularly vulnerable to food pollution. Due to their magnified social visibility and influence, they must be especially vigilant to avoid pollution through careful control of food intake. While most food in rural Greece is prepared by women, men cook meals to be consumed on ceremonial occasions because they are not tainted by women's general pollution. India has an extensive system of strict rules of avoidance about interdining between different castes; the leftovers of higher castes may be consumed by lower castes, but the reverse results in contamination.

Bodily pollution, in its most extreme form, results in illness or even death. Before the emergence of the germ theory to account for biotic disorders, illnesses were universally explained as the invasion of evil spirits, the curse of the evil eye, or the result of broken taboos. Even in modern societies, illnesses may be attributed to spiritual causes. Elaborate rituals to ward off pollution from evil spirits that cause human sickness are found throughout the world. Among the Inuit (Eskimo), illness was attributed to pollution associated with breaking taboos. The shaman entered a trance, then took a spiritual journey to the abode of the goddess Sedna under the sea; there he would ask her to forgive the sins of his people. This ritual act involved confessions by community members, resulting in the possibility of a cure. The Indian goddess of smallpox, Śītalā, could be angered easily and subsequently needed to be "cooled" through various rituals of purification. The innocent, the vulnerable, the aged, and those individuals who have transgressed religious and social norms are all potential victims of illness. It is widely believed that the human body can best be equipped to fight illnesses by avoiding pollution, such as the ingestion of unclean foods, contact with menstrual blood, the performance of prohibited sexual relations, neglect of proper rituals to placate deities, and lack of bodily cleanliness.

Pollution and social bonding. The intense socialization of natural bodily functions is another aspect of purification. Birth, adolescence, marriage, and death are linked to physiological stages that are highly controlled and ritualized to ensure protection from the dangers of pollution. [*See* Rites of Passage.] These life crisis events demarcate major points of transition, critical both for individuals and the community. Failure to attain these transitions would threaten the survival of human culture.

The danger of childbirth is often accompanied by rigorous rituals designed to bring about a healthy outcome for both mother and child. Consequently, the whole process of birth, in some cases including pregnancy, requires special rites of purification. The pregnant woman may be expected to observe food taboos, take daily baths, and perform only a few restricted household chores. Impurities connected with childbirth are usually associated with the afterbirth; these impurities extend to the fragile bond between mother and child and to other family members. Pollution is attributed to the invasion of evil spirits that thrive on vulnerable individuals during crisis events. Often mother and child are placed in seclusion for a period of time, then ritually welcomed into the larger community after rituals of cleansing have taken place.

The transition to adulthood is considered the proper time for prophylactic rites of purification. These rites protect the initiate from pollution during his state of liminality. In some societies uncircumcised males are considered intrinsically polluted. Among the Ndembu people of northwestern Zambia, an uncircumcised boy lacks "whiteness" or "purity" and is permanently polluting; his presence can threaten the luck of hunters. An uncircumcised Ndembu man is polluted because of the dirt beneath his foreskin. He is considered "white" or "pure" only when the glans of his penis is exposed through circumcision (Turner, 1967).

Menstruation is one of the functions most widely seen as polluting, second only to death. Menstrual impurity may apply only during menses, or it may be more generalized as a kind of gender pollution, rendering women permanently impure due to their sexuality. Menstrual pollution is usually controlled by dietary restrictions, isolation in separate huts or parts of the household, and avoidance of either cooking or the performance of ordinary household tasks. Also, women are debarred from participation in religious ceremonies during menstruation. Gender pollution appears to be related, at least partially, to male dominance and the demarcation of clear male spheres of influence; thus, the very presence of women causes dangerous pollution (Douglas, 1975). In many tribal societies, women, under the threat of death, are kept away from men's houses where sacred masks are carved and the secrets of the ancestors are kept. Some Mediterranean and Near Eastern cultures elaborate gender pollution to the point of associating women with all kinds of dark forces (such as the evil eye, the world of ghosts, and magical occult powers). Unattached women in these societies must be watched carefully because they are a great source of pollution: women are believed to be shameful creatures who can upset the entire social order by threatening the lines of distinction between separate gender domains.

Marriage and human sexuality are surrounded by elaborate pollution/purity norms in many parts of the world. Sexual relations outside culturally prescribed rules are generally treated as potential sources of pollution. These rules vary greatly from one society to another. Premarital sexual relations, for instance, are not considered to be polluting in some societies. In other parts of the world, women, in particular, who engage in premarital sex are considered to be polluted by their loss of virginity. While pollution norms surrounding sex and marriage vary, many societies consider adultery a source of defilement. Incest is a more serious offense and is universally taboo. Incestuous activities are so thoroughly polluting as to pose serious threats to the community as a whole. Consequently, persons who have committed incest are either killed or permanently banished.

The most widespread source of pollution is death and the putrefaction of bodily decay. Death breaks fragile social bonds, and the bonds that remain must be rearranged so that death pollution can be prevented from becoming a generalized condition of social disorder or chaos. The corpse and the possessions of the deceased are highly dangerous. Even though death is the most polluting social event, not all religions treat it uniformly. In some religions, as in Christianity, dead human bodies are allowed into sacred shrines or even buried there. This contrasts dramatically with Hinduism, where corpses are never allowed near a sacred shrine; even an accidental death that occurs inside a Hindu temple requires the performance of elaborate purification rites.

Funeral rituals have three general purposes: (1) the transformation of dead spirits into ancestors; (2) the placement of the ancestors in the proper realm of the afterlife (heaven, hell, or a new life via reincarnation); and (3) a restoration of both social and cosmic order from the disorder caused by death pollution (Nielsen et al., 1983). Thus, funerals are designed to accomplish a number of important tasks necessitated by the wound of death. Not only do they provide a ritual context for disposing of the pollution linked with the dead body, they also activate, contain, and assist in the resolution of grief.

Since death represents a rending of the social fabric, its pollution has far-reaching effects. In India, death pollutes the whole family, requiring strict rites of purification during prescribed periods of mourning, the length of which is determined according to the degree of kinship to the deceased. In Japan, death is believed to result in harmful and contagious pollution that can be transmitted through social contact. The idea that death pollution is communicable can be found throughout the world. The Polynesians abandoned any house where death had occurred. After the death of a Samoan chief, his house could not be entered and fishing in the lagoon was prohibited (Steiner, 1956). However, not all ceremonies surrounding death are designed to prevent the contagion of pollution; some of these rites help mourners to participate in the condition of death itself. According to Robert Parker, in ancient Greek religion death pollution was a kind of temporary participation in the condition of the dead man, who was, through the decay of the corpse, "foul" *(miaros)*. "Pollution is a transposition of this sympathetic befoulment to the metaphysical plane. 'Being polluted' is a kind of metaphysical suit of mourning" (Parker, 1983, p. 64). In the Parsi religion, contact with dead bodies pollutes family, community, and even the natural elements of air, fire, water, and earth. Consequently, earth burial and cremation are forbidden among the Parsis. They resolve the problem of contaminating the natural elements by exposing the deceased on a *dakhma* ("tower of silence") to be devoured by vultures. In this extreme case, death pollution is so highly contagious that unless contained it extends to all nature.

Violent death is the most polluting of all, for both the victim and the perpetrator of the crime. The pollution generated by violent death is exceedingly dangerous because it may activate a revenge cycle. Among headhunters in New Guinea and other parts of the world, the ghost of an individual who has been murdered is considered extremely dangerous unless it is appeased by taking another head. In some societies both the murderer and the victim of violent death are refused ordinary funeral rites; in some cases these corpses are denied burial in community cemeteries.

Pollution and purity norms are related to social rank, particularly in complex societies with strong social boundaries established by ascription. People who break conventional rules of behavior in hierarchically oriented societies by crossing lines of class or caste are considered polluted by their transgression. In Polynesia the person of the chief was highly charged with *mana*, a kind of sacred energy that could be lost through touching people of lower rank. The Hindu social system, with its strict endogamous tradition for establishing social status, is even more rigid about the link between rank and pollution; Hindu castes involve strict rules requiring marriage within subcastes, prohibiting caste interdining, and restricting physical contact between members of lower and upper castes. While these rules are less rigid than in the past, they continue to thrive in contemporary India. The degree of intrinsic pollution of each caste depends on its rank in the overall system. The lowest castes are more polluted than higher ones because of their traditional occupations; the highest brahman castes are least polluted, due to their priestly duties, and the lowest castes are most contaminated because of their contact with polluting items in the environment. Untouchables, who are outside the caste system, are most polluted because they come in contact with such highly polluting substances as leather and dead bodies. Physical contact with untouchables by caste Hindus requires strong purification rites. In the past untouchables, due to their intrinsic pollution, were prevented from entering temples; this custom was banned legally by the Indian constitution (26 November 1949).

Pollution and the maintenance of sacred boundaries. The definition of religious pollution cannot be limited to social, psychological, or physiological domains alone. The definition of the "sacred" also involves issues of spiritual pollution. This is clear to individuals who have dedicated themselves to the religious life. Rules governing pollution are more stringent for the religious because they come in contact with the supernatural more directly than the laity. Anyone who approaches the divinity, either as an intermediary or in a state of deep reverence, is required to perform extensive rites of purification.

As the religious are more vulnerable to pollution, they also may be singled out to suffer its consequences more than others. The idea of being set apart for a holy purpose is exemplified by Judaism, Christianity, and Islam. Particularly in Judaism, the idea of a sanctified, priestly people becomes highly elaborated, to the point that Yahveh's chosen may become impure by worshiping other gods, consulting fortune-tellers, or coming in contact with foreigners. The same notion is expressed throughout the world in varying degrees, as people attempt to define a relationship to divinity.

The polar tension between pollution and purity is activated in pilgrimage: pilgrims enter a dialectic where pollution is dissolved by the journey to a sacred place. Thus, in the great pilgrimage traditions of Islam, Hinduism, Shintō, or Christianity, one not only attains merit, community status, and indulgences for the afterlife; one also undergoes a "spiritual bathing" that opens the eyes, transforms consciousness, and centers human focus on the sacred. Pilgrimage is often prescribed to resolve conditions of spiritual pollution. In the classical pilgrimages, the devotee's journey returned him to a place of great sacrality and prepared him to cross boundaries and to enter more deeply into the realm of the sacred.

The definition of any sacred place is contingent on its opposite, namely, the removal of polluting elements that contaminate the "holy." In Hinduism, whenever a particular place is selected for worshiping a deity, it is sanctified through elaborate purification rites so that demons, evil spirits, and the dark forces of ignorance are excluded and conditions for invoking the presence of divinity are most favorable. Thus, the locus of the holy of holies in any religion embodies that religion's ideal of purity. This is not to imply that pollution has no place in sacred centers; on the contrary, it is through the very process of purifying the impure that human life is transformed and integrated into the religious sphere.

Rites of Purification. Religious pollution always calls for specific rites of purification, which can range from the ingestion of sacraments to painful acts of purgation. There are five types of rites, involving the use of (1) fire, (2) water, (3) detergents, (4) purgation, and (5) scapegoats. Usually several purificatory mechanisms are employed together, as parts of a sacred technology, to eliminate pollution and restore wholeness to both individual and community.

Fire. Both fire and smoke are considered sources of purification. [*See* Fire.] In some parts of the world, stepping over a fire is a rite demarcating a transition from defilement. The Hindu god Agni is the personification of fire, and purified butter is poured into fire as an offering to the god. At certain times of the year, sacrifices to Agni are performed to purify the whole world. Hindus attain sacramental benefit by passing their hands over fire. The eternal fire that burns day and night in Parsi fire temples is a source of purity for worshipers, who offer bread and milk while portions of the sacred text, the Avesta, are read before it.

Incense and fumigation are employed widely in the

world's religions for purificatory purposes. [*See* Incense.] Typically, both sacred objects and the assembled worshipers are purified with incense during the recitation of prayers. According to Parker, the ancient Greeks saw fire as an important source of purity: "Torches were an indispensable part of many ceremonies, and swung vigorously, they could purify a room or a man. Normally, however, sharp-smelling substances were added to the fire when purification was needed" (Parker, 1983, p. 227). The Greeks exposed polluted objects to the pungent odor of sulphur; by contrast, sweet-smelling burnt offerings were selected to please the gods.

Water. Water, the universal cleanser, is the most widely employed means of ritual purification. [*See* Ablutions.] Often water is used with other elements, such as fire, salt, or herbs. It is a particularly potent source of purification when obtained from holy springs, wells, or other sacred bodies of water. [*See* Water.] The many holy wells of Ireland are special places of purification. A bath in the sacred Ganges river is accompanied by such a high level of purification that it is an object of pilgrimage for millions of devotees from all over India.

A widespread requirement before worship is the custom of ritual bathing, either of the whole body or parts of the body most exposed to pollution, especially the feet. In most religions the deity must not be approached unless the devotee is ritually clean. The Hindu is expected to bathe early in the morning, recite special prayers, and consecrate his day to the service of God. Water has purificatory qualities in Hinduism, not because of its intrinsic purity, but because it absorbs pollution and carries it away (Babb, 1975). Thus, the flow of water determines its purificatory efficacy.

Water also makes the sacred more accessible to devotees. Muslims clean their mouths and ears with water to sanctify their prayers and open their hearing to the will of God. Most life crisis events, such as childbirth, marriage, or death, involve the use of water to create a state of purification in which the transaction between man and divinity is encouraged and the danger of pollution is minimized. The best-known instance of ritual purification with water is Christian baptism, which washes away sin and prepares the devotee to lead a religious life. In this case, water both washes away the pollution of sin and acts as a sign that the individual belongs to an initiated group who share a common state of purified grace. The statues of deities are ritually cleansed with water in preparation for religious ceremonies. The water that supports life is a sacred source of renewal. It is the "mother of being" in opposition to the accumulation of filth, evil, defilement, and decay associated with death.

Detergents. Aside from fire and water, a variety of agents are utilized in ritual purification. These various detergents include salt water, liquid concoctions made from propitious herbs and spices, and various other sacramental substances applied to the polluted individual or space. In Africa and the Middle East, sand or dry dirt is used as a detergent when water is not available. Charcoal, mud, and clay from special sacred places are also employed to remove religious pollution. These clinging substances are daubed on a person's body to absorb defilement, then washed away. In India, ash from cow dung is widely employed as a cleansing agent. Among the Nuba of Sudan, the ash from burnt branches of the acacia tree has purificatory qualities. In this society, sacred ash is linked to success in wrestling contests, fertility of the earth, rites of initiation, death, and the afterlife. Young Nuba men, at various critical points in their lives, cover their bodies with sacred ash as a symbol of purification.

Throughout the world, cow dung is used as fuel and as mortar to build shelters. Thus, it represents an important resource for human communities. It is not surprising, therefore, that in some cultures cow dung is used as a detergent with purificatory qualities. Since cows are sacred in India, cow dung and other bovine products are considered to be extremely pure. In the case of Indian death pollution, for example, when an individual has died in a house or temple, or whenever there is a need for special acts of purification, five products of the cow (dung, milk, ghee, curds, and urine) are mixed together and applied as a detergent to clean walls or apply to human beings. In Hinduism the sacredness of the cow, mother of life, makes this mixture almost sacramental in its efficacy.

Purgation. This category subsumes a large variety of purificatory rites. The common thread is either a physical or psychological purging to eliminate pollution, often involving self-sacrifice, pain, and suffering by the devotee. Purificatory purgation, found in one form or another throughout the world, always involves a metaphysics of cleansing transformation, as natural bodily or psychic pollution is purified through rituals that alter the human condition.

One means of cleansing the human body from defilement is to shave the head, eyebrows, and other body hair. [*See* Hair.] In Hinduism, the hair and beard must not be cut until the end of the mourning period. At that time the head is shaved to demarcate the end of death pollution. Novices in some monastic traditions are shaved to signify the termination of their worldly life and their dedication to holy orders. Even the rite of circumcision, with its removal of the foreskin, is an act of purification as well as a rite of passage designed to integrate the individual into a new level of community.

Throughout the world special clothing is used in the context of sacred ceremonies; the hair may be covered, shoes removed, or new clothes required. In the case of death pollution, old clothes of the deceased may be burned. This change of clothing signifies a termination of uncleanliness. Deities in Hinduism must be approached by devotees wearing the purest possible garments. According to Lawrence A. Babb,

> as a general rule . . . the principal actor or actors in ritual must be in a purified condition before approaching or making offerings to the deity. This usually means that the worshippers will be freshly bathed and will be wearing garments appropriate to a condition of purity: a minimum of cotton, which is quite vulnerable to pollution; silk, if possible, which is more resistant to accidental pollution.
>
> (Babb, 1975, p. 47)

Throughout the world, fasting is an act of purgation, a sacrifice to honor the divinity, and a mechanism for cleansing the body. [*See* Fasting.] In Islam, the whole month of Ramadan is a time for fasting. Until recently, Roman Catholics fasted on Fridays to recall the passion of Christ. The season of Lent is a more protracted period of fasting commemorating the passion. Intense fasting as a form of purgation is widely associated with states of visionary ecstasy. Typically, the religious specialist prepares himself to receive visions by abstaining from food and drink for long periods of time; he may become emaciated, undergo symbolic death, then experience intense spiritual illumination.

Both Judaism and Islam forbid the eating of pork. No religion has a more strict set of dietary laws than Orthodox Judaism, where eating is a sacramental act. [*See* Kashrut.] The Jewish dietary laws were a sign of the holiness of God's people; they served to preserve monotheism and to set the Jews apart from surrounding pagan societies. Dietary laws are found in the books of *Deuteronomy*, *Genesis*, and *Exodus*, but they are most widely articulated in *Leviticus*. Animals that have true hoofs and chew their cud, including oxen, sheep, harts, and gazelles, may be eaten. Only a few birds are considered clean: chickens, ducks, geese, and turkeys. Fish must have fins and scales to be considered clean; thus, all shellfish are excluded. Also classified as unclean are those animals that creep, crawl, or swarm upon the earth. Animals permitted in the Mosaic dietary laws may be eaten only under certain conditions: they must be slaughtered by a man trained in Jewish law, using a sharp knife and severing the animal's throat with one continuous stroke. Even then, the meat is not kosher unless it has been properly drained of blood, prepared with salt, then washed clean (Trepp, 1982, pp. 281–284). According to Mary Douglas, Jewish dietary laws act as signs to inspire meditation on the "oneness, purity and completeness of God" (Douglas, 1966, p. 57). Observance of these laws helps the Jewish people to express their holiness at every meal and to prepare for the sacrifice in the temple.

The body may be purged of pollution by various emetics that induce vomiting or diarrhea. The peyote ritual found among Indians of Mexico and the American Southwest involves a phase of vomiting, considered to have both physical and spiritual purifying effects (Malefijt, 1968). Purgatives such as castor oil are used as purifying agents in African religions. Emetics of various kinds are prescribed by shamans to flush out evil spirits and purify the human body. Among North American Indians, the sweat bath is widely employed to cure illnesses and remove impurities.

Psychological forms of purgation are connected to the condition of the human body. Various forms of physical torture have been employed in the world's religions to bring about a psychological state of penance and humility in the presence of the supernatural. Mortification of the flesh includes various forms of flagellation, walking on nails, lacerations, suspension on hooks driven through the skin, the wearing of hair shirts, and sleeping on rough surfaces. These painful acts of self-sacrifice are not reserved only for religious specialists; in many religions with strong pilgrimage traditions, self-denial is an act of purification for laymen. [*See* Mortification.] At the great pilgrimage shrine of Our Lady of Guadalupe in Mexico City and at numerous Marian devotions in Europe, pilgrims may be seen crawling on their bleeding knees toward the sanctuaries. Pilgrimages to Mecca, the medieval shrines of Europe, and the great pilgrim centers of Hinduism are associated with danger, hardship, and self-denial, which are believed to be purificatory. The ultimate form of purgation occurs when the pilgrim dies along the journey; in Hinduism it is considered highly auspicious to die on pilgrimage, an act equivalent to dying near the sacred Ganges River.

Another form of physical and psychological purification is sexual abstinence or celibacy. In some religions, the highest spiritual experiences can occur only for individuals who have given up all worldly pleasures. Sexual abstinence is believed to place the individual in a state of grace where he can concentrate on the supernatural. [*See* Celibacy.] In some respects, strong marriage vows prohibiting extramarital sexual activity are designed to ensure the purity of sex within the marriage contract. The transgression of sexual boundaries is an act of pollution that may require intense rites of purification.

Confession of misdeeds appears in one form or another in most religions. [*See* Confession of Sins.] The public or private recitation of transgressions purges the individual of guilt and acts as an antidote to both the personal and the collective pollution resulting from the breaking of taboos. The Inuit custom of group confession, particularly practiced during times when seal hunting is unsuccessful, is an example of corporate purgation through confession. It is believed that when the hair of the great goddess Sedna, who lives under the sea, has become dirty because of human sins (like secret miscarriages and various breaches of taboos) she angrily holds back the sea animals. During a trance, the shaman appeases Sedna, then calls for a group confession so that hunting may be plentiful (Eliade, 1964). Confession often results in a flood of tears, self-mortification, or other acts intended to express sorrow for transgressions. Thus, confession removes the stain of sin through a psychological act of expiation and purification.

Contact with holy items, such as relics of saints, sacraments, and statues of deities, is an important source of purification. The utterance of prayers also has cleansing value. In Hinduism, mantras may be used either as agents to combat evil or as foci for concentration leading to spiritual awakening. Rituals of purification in Buddhism are metaphors for inner transformations and mystical enlightenment. Prayer and meditation, particularly by ascetics, purify the soul, rendering it a fitting receptacle for God-consciousness and the spiritual life. Here purgation is followed by the contemplation of sublime spiritual visions.

Substitution and catharsis. The use of substitutions to remove pollution is a widespread purificatory custom. The sick human body may be rubbed with sticks, stones, or other objects to which the pollution is transferred. A means of curing mental disorders in Nigeria is to remove the person's clothes and rub his body with a sacrificed dove, which absorbs the evil spirits. In the American Indian peyote cult, individuals are purified by being rubbed with sagebrush. The institution of kingship is widely accompanied by the purificatory anointing of the king's body. The annual Ch'ing-ming ceremony in China involves a tradition of sweeping clean the graves of the ancestors. This rite of purification renews the whole community. Shintō priests transfer their pollution to a special wand, which is then thrown away so that they may perform sacred ceremonies in a state of ritual purity.

There are numerous instances of transferring pollution to either human or animal scapegoats. Specially selected individuals may be whipped, beaten, and then expelled from a community to rid it of pollution. [*See* Scapegoat.] In Fiji, the polluted person is washed in a stream; he then wipes his hand on a pig or turtle to remove pollution. At one time among the Maori of New Zealand, when an epidemic disease raged in the community, a man was selected as a temporary scapegoat; a fern stalk was attached to his body, he was submerged in a river, and the fern stalk was allowed to float downstream. The epidemic was transferred to the scapegoat (the fern stalk), then washed away by the river. Sometimes scapegoats are institutionalized corporately, so that a whole social class takes on the burden of pollution. Thus, Indian untouchables have been singled out to bear the suffering associated with pollution; consequently the other social castes may be at least relatively free of pollution.

Community catharsis, through substitution and the use of scapegoats, is most widely practiced in the form of ritual sacrifice, where the animal's head is exchanged for that of a human who is spiritually polluted (Preston, 1980). Sacrifice is a widespread custom in the world's religions; although it is performed for many different purposes, one major reason is to purify both the individual and community of defilement. Consequently, the dramatic shedding of blood is typically surrounded with a milieu of powerful ritual catharsis. Among the cattle-keeping Nuer tribe of the Sudan, sacrifices are performed as atonements for breaking taboos. The ancient Greeks employed blood sacrifices as rites of absorptive purification, transferring defilement to despised animals (Parker, 1983). Cattle, sheep, goats, chickens, and pigs are the animals most widely employed as scapegoats in ritual sacrifices. While human sacrifice occurred widely in the past, this form of expiation has mostly disappeared. However, in its symbolic form cathartic human sacrifice has been retained in the passion of Christ, where Jesus of Nazareth takes on the "sins of the world," becoming the "perfect offering" to cleanse the world of its collective pollution.

Secular forms. The symbolism of purification is not confined to the religious sphere. Modern secular societies continue to utilize powerful symbols of pollution and purity. Even though the religious content has been removed from much of this symbolism in technological societies, some of it lingers. The wide array of soaps and other chemicals used for cleansing the bodies and living habitats of modern peoples cannot be understood merely as extensions of scientific insights about health stemming from germ theory. Much of the preoccupation of American hospitals with white walls, antiseptics, and unstained clothing is suspiciously reminiscent of Puritan notions of religious cleanliness.

Fire, water, detergents, purgation, and substitutions remain important sources of both religious and secular purification rites in the modern world. However, the most noteworthy addition would be an array of chemicals added to this set of purificatory devices for removing pollution. Also significant is the tendency to perceive both pollution and purity in materialistic terms. Even though religious pollution is not an extinct concept in modern societies, it has often been isolated and compartmentalized away from the material world. Thus, today diseases such as smallpox are not usually thought to be related to sin or the breaking of taboos; nor are the cures of these diseases sought by performing religious purification rites. Still, some illnesses and critical life crisis events that have escaped the control of the rational scientific method remain, in many quarters, mysterious enough to require both religious and secular rites of purification. This is particularly true for some types of cancer, which remain mysterious and defy ingenious medical technologies born of the modernist world view.

Religious Meaning. Rites of purification are rarely isolated or discrete events. Usually they are linked together as sequences of rites within the larger semantic network of purity symbolism in a particular religious or cultural context. Among the Ndembu of northwestern Zambia the unifying symbol is the color white. This compound image of purity permeates every aspect of Ndembu religion. Water is regarded as white because it cleanses the body of dirt. After a funeral the widower is anointed with oil, shaved, washed, given new white cloth, and adorned with white beads. According to Victor Turner, "Behind the symbolism of whiteness, then, lie the notions of harmony, continuity, purity, the manifest, the public, the appropriate, and the legitimate" (1967, p. 77). Rites and symbols of purification have no meaning unless they are interpreted as part of a larger religious language.

We have not exhausted the range of purificatory rites available in the world religions; other mechanisms of purification that could be added to this list include the application of sandalwood paste to the skin, bleeding the little finger, chewing hot chiles, touching sacred relics, eating or drinking sacraments, and making loud noises (as in the Chinese custom of setting off firecrackers). The important question is what all this means in terms of human religion. What is the relationship of the social categories of pollution and purity to the religious impulse itself?

Pollution/purity norms serve clear sociological and psychological purposes, reinforcing the boundaries of the community, ensuring the survival of the group, reinforcing principles of health, and assisting individuals to cope ritually with life crises. Still, the relationship of people to the supernatural remains the focal point of purification rites throughout the world. In Confucianism, a state of purity is necessary to establish a channel of communication between living men and the spiritual world. The Hindu performs yoga only after purification; higher levels of consciousness may be blocked by painful impurities unless the devotee manages to overcome them. The loving God of Christianity helps his people to transcend impurities by sending his son and offering salvation through the Eucharist. In all these cases, channels of communication with the divinity are made possible through the establishment of boundaries between domains of pollution and purity, the identification of a situation of defilement, the performance of appropriate purificatory rites, and the experience of a new encounter with the ultimate supreme being.

Mary Douglas and other structuralists have noted correctly that pollution/purity norms impose order on the untidiness of life experiences: "Reflection on dirt involves reflection on the relation of order to disorder, being to non-being, form to formlessness, life to death" (Douglas, 1966, p. 5). Yet categories of pollution and purity represent more than ideological or social systems. Defilement represents our failure to attain perfection, to realize our godlike nature, while purification is the human expression of divine aspirations.

BIBLIOGRAPHY

Babb, Lawrence A. *The Divine Hierarchy: Popular Hinduism in Central India*. New York, 1975.

Douglas, Mary. *Purity and Danger*. New York, 1966. This landmark volume has had a profound effect on our understanding of religion. Pollution and purity are analyzed in different religious systems to reveal underlying structural similarities. The author stresses the need to understand concepts of pollution and purity in the context of a total structure of thought.

Douglas, Mary. "Deciphering a Meal." *Daedalus* 101 (Winter 1972): 61–81. An elegant structural analysis of the meaning of the sacred meal with particular reference to Jewish laws regarding purification and diet.

Douglas, Mary. *Implicit Meanings: Essays in Anthropology*. Boston, 1975. A collection of excellent essays, some of which expand on the author's earlier structural analysis of purity norms.

Dumont, Louis. *Homo Hierarchicus*. Translated by Mark Sainsbury. Rev. ed. Chicago, 1980. A classic study of Hinduism, with particular emphasis on structural oppositions, including notions of pollution and purity as manifested in the caste system.

Eliade, Mircea. *Shamanism: Archaic Techniques of Ecstasy.* Rev. & enl. ed. New York, 1964.

Lichter, David, and Lawrence Epstein. "Irony in Tibetan Notions of the Good Life." In *Karma: An Anthropological Inquiry*, edited by Charles F. Keyes and E. Valentine Daniel. Berkeley, 1983.

Malefijt, Annemarie De Waal. *Religion and Culture*. New York, 1968.

Nielsen, Niels C., et al. *Religions of the World*. New York, 1982.

Parker, Robert. *Miasma: Pollution and Purification in Early Greek Religion*. Oxford, 1983. An excellent, thorough analysis of pervasive purity norms in ancient Greek religion.

Preston, James J. *Cult of the Goddess: Social and Religious Change in a Hindu Temple*. New Delhi, 1980.

Steiner, Franz. *Taboo*. New York, 1956.

Trepp, Leo. *Judaism: Development and Life*. Belmont, Calif., 1982.

Turner, Victor. *The Forest of Symbols: Aspects of Ndembu Ritual*. Ithaca, N.Y., 1967.

JAMES J. PRESTON

PURIM ("lots") is a minor Jewish festival (one in which work is not prohibited) that falls on the fourteenth day of Adar. It celebrates the deliverance, as told in the *Book of Esther*, of the Jews from the designs of Haman, who cast lots to determine the date of their destruction. According to some historians, the events recorded in *Esther* are fictitious, the festival probably having its origin in a Babylonian festival. But there is evidence that Purim was celebrated as a Jewish festival from the first century BCE. Purim was observed also as a reminder to Jews that God often works "behind the scenes" in order to protect his people. Medieval thinkers found a basis for this idea in the absence of God's name in *Esther*, the only book in the Hebrew Bible in which the divine name does not appear.

The central feature of Purim is the reading of the Megillah (scroll), as the *Book of Esther* is called, in the form of a parchment scroll, written by hand and occasionally profusely illustrated. This public reading takes place on the night of Purim and again during the morning service in the synagogue. During this service the passage in the Torah concerning the blotting out of the name of Amalek (*Ex.* 17:8–16) is read because Haman was a descendant of Amalek. Based on this is the practice, frowned upon by some Jews, of making loud noises with rattles and the like whenever the name of Haman is mentioned during the reading of the Megillah.

Esther 9:22 speaks of sending portions to friends and giving alms to the poor. Hence the rabbinic rule is that each person must send a gift of at least two items of food to a friend and give at least one donation to two poor men. From the reference in *Esther* 9:17 to "days of feasting and joy," the rabbis further established the Purim festive meal, at which there is much imbibing of wine. A Talmudic statement has it that a man must drink until he is incapable of telling whether he is blessing Mordechai or cursing Haman.

As part of the Purim jollity, undoubtedly influenced by the Italian Carnival, people dress up, and children, especially, produce Purim plays in which they assume the characters mentioned in the Megillah. Rabbis objected to men dressing up as women and vice versa since this offends against the law in *Deuteronomy* 22:5, but Meir of Padua in the sixteenth century defended the practice as a harmless masquerade. In some communities it is the practice to appoint a "Purim rabbi" whose duty it is frivolously to manipulate even the most sacred texts.

The Jews of Shushan (*Est.* 9:18) celebrated Purim on the fifteenth day of Adar. To pay honor to Jerusalem, it was ordained that cities that, like Jerusalem, had walls around them in the days of Joshua should celebrate Purim on the fifteenth. Consequently, the citizens of Jerusalem today keep the festival and read the Megillah on Shushan Purim, the fifteenth of Adar, while for other Jews Purim is on the fourteenth of the month.

[*See also* Purim Plays.]

BIBLIOGRAPHY

N. S. Doniach's *Purim* (Philadelphia, 1933) is a competent survey in English of the origins, rites, and ceremonies of Purim in which both the critical and the traditional views are fairly stated.

LOUIS JACOBS

PURIM PLAYS. Known in standard Yiddish as *purimshpiln* (sg., *purimshpil*), the Purim plays, presented during the holiday of Purim, were the most common form of folk drama among eastern and western Jews up until the Holocaust. The earliest written accounts of such plays are from the middle of the sixteenth century. They describe single-actor performances in Yiddish of *purimshpiln* based on nonbiblical themes that took place in Venice, Italy, and Brest Litovsk (in the Belorussian S.S.R.). In the eighteenth century, more full-fledged plays with troupe performances were produced in various communities by *yeshivah* students, musicians, artisans, and apprentices; they were enacted in synagogues and in the homes of the well-to-do, where the actors received small sums of money. Examples of especially popular biblical stories that were performed were those of Esther and Ahasuerus (main characters in the *Book of Esther*), Joseph and his brothers, the binding of Isaac, and David and Goliath—all these plots emphasized redemption from impending destruction.

Today, most well-known traditions of *purimshpiln* occur in several Hasidic communities, of which the best known are the Reb Arele Ḥasidim (known also as Toledot Aharon), who came to Jerusalem from Hungary during World War I; the Vizhnitzer Ḥasidim, who came to Bene Beraq (in Israel) from Romania during World War II, and the surviving members of the Bobover Ḥasidim of Poland, who established themselves in Brooklyn, New York, after World War II.

In addition to the religious events of the common Jewish calendar, the Ḥasidim have established their own traditions; to a great extent these were inspired by the sixteenth- and seventeenth-century qabbalists of Safad. The qabbalists elevated the status of Purim to that of a major festival. Playing on the Hebrew word *kippurim* ("atonements," an alternate name of Yom Kippur), reading it to mean "like Purim" *(ki-Purim)*, the Purim holiday thus placed in importance alongside Yom Kippur, the most solemn of all Jewish holidays.

Like their forefathers, contemporary Ḥasidim draw on the message of Purim, particularly as it is dramatically presented through the *purimshpil*, as a means of strengthening their ideology and tradition. On both Yom Kippur and Purim, a central theme is that repentance is requested and granted; the Ḥasidim believe that God is more attentive to supplication on these days. [*See* Hasidism, *overview article*.]

The *purimshpil* has assumed the role of sacred work; the *rebe* (spiritual leader of the community) uses it to bring members of the community closer to God. The first evidence of the *purimshpil* as an element in Hasidic ritual is attributed to Aryeh Leib (1725–1813) of Shpola, a city in Russia. He believed that the performance of a play on Purim could influence the course of events, a phenomenon known to anthropologists as "sympathetic magic." Folk belief has it that when a decree was issued against Jews, Aryeh Leib suggested to his followers that they act in a play, the plot of which described a reversal of such a feared situation. Other stories are told of how these *purimshpiln* were instrumental in offsetting specific disasters. The quality of inversion is inherent in the original Purim text, the *Book of Esther*. A central idea underlying the *Book of Esther* is *ve-nahafokh hu'* (Heb., "and it was reversed," *Est.* 9:11). Accordingly, Haman, the king's vizier who wanted to hang Mordecai, is hanged himself, and Mordecai becomes a minister of the court. The Jewish community is avenged of its enemies rather than harmed by them.

Themes nowadays are also drawn from biblical sources, East European folklore, and issues of day-to-day life. In the Bobover repertoire, for example, the *Book of Daniel* serves as the background for the *Play of Nebuchadnezzar*. Similarly, a Hasidic legend retelling the wonder of a pious Ḥasid has been dramatized as the *Three Revenges*. Consistent with the *Purim-Kippurim* notion, the plays are always serious and didactic despite the comic overlay, depicting central themes in Jewish experience—survival, martyrdom, and redemption.

The production of the *purimshpil* by the community replaces the sermon the *rebe* would otherwise deliver. The *purimshpil* is incorporated into the *rebe*'s *tish* (table) on the midnight of Purim. The *tish* is a central ritual in the life of Hasidic men, who assemble around their *rebe*'s table in their prayer hall on festivals to share a communal meal, dance, and sing together. The *purimshpil* may last all night, and women may be part of the audience. The production of the play is considered sacred work rather than "entertainment," and the manner in which it is performed is as carefully monitored by those involved in the production as the content since the performance itself and the texts used may appear to be in contradiction to Jewish law. Making fun of God and misquoting biblical phrases, for example, are forbidden and could result in God punishing the actors. Therefore, it is important that the themes of Jewish belief are accurately followed.

Usually the spiritual elite of the community, the married male students and teachers, take part in the production, writing, selection of music and costume, and painting of backdrops. The comic elements are incorporated into the play during both rehearsals and the performance itself. The actors suggest jokes, which may be accepted or rejected for particular scenes. The time allocated for the preparation of the production is limited because it is viewed as taking the men away from their primary function, studying Torah.

The *purimshpil* more than any other event in the Hasidic festival calendar engages the members of the community in ludicrous, playful behavior antithetical to everyday conditions. During the performance, men become actors, wear costumes and makeup, and assume both male and female roles. In the audience, the division between male and female is also relaxed; women speak with men across the *meḥitsah* (the separation between the women's and the men's sections in the synagogue, a division mandated by religious law), which has been drawn aside. Thus, the prayer hall is converted from a house of study and prayer into a theater. In fact, the Purim play is one of the rare occasions during the year for the community to view theater: the Hasidic way of life prohibits the participation in, and viewing of, movies or plays.

Inspired by the male production of *purimshpiln*, Hasidic women have started to perform their own versions of the Purim plays for mainly female audiences during the week of Purim. Referred to by the women as "Purim musicals," the texts have sources similar to those of the male *purimshpiln* but are more influenced by musicals and modern stage effects.

World War II for the most part brought an end to the folkways of Ashkenazic Jewry. Traditions of Yiddish song, music, literature, and drama, which were integral parts of Jewish life in Europe, were brutally destroyed. The revitalization of the *purimshpil* in the latter half of the twentieth century exemplifies how traditional art forms may survive physical and spiritual catastrophes. The annual performance of the *purimshpil*, once an all-encompassing Ashkenazic Jewish tradition, has evolved among Ḥasidim into a continuation ritual, dramatizing their need to remember the past, thereby connecting that past to the present.

BIBLIOGRAPHY

Almost all the literature on the Purim plays is in Hebrew. Among works in English are Philip Goodman's *The Purim Anthology* (1949; reprint, Philadelphia, 1960), which has a musical supplement, and my doctoral dissertation, "The Celebration of a Contemporary Purim in the Bobover Hassidic Community" (University of Texas, 1979). A videotape of the play described in my work is available at the YIVO Institute in New York (*Purimshpil*, R–70–54–11 and R–80–54–29). The Purim play is also discussed in the context of Hebrew drama in Israel Abraham's *Jewish Life in the Middle Ages* (1896; reprint, New York, 1969), pp. 260–272. Following is a list of a few of the works available in Hebrew.

Moskowitz, Zvi. *Kol ha-kattuv le-Ḥayyim*. Jerusalem, 1961/2. This volume discusses "everything attributed to Ḥayyim," who is Ḥayyim Halberstam (1793–1876), of the city of Nowy Zanz (southeastern Poland), the originator of the Bobover Ḥasidim. See especially pages 84–87.

Rosenberg, Yehudah. *Tiferet MaHaR'el: Mi-shpi'lei ha-niqra' "der shpaler zayde."* Peyetrekow, 1912; reprint, 1975. A selection of the miraculous deeds of Rebe Aryeh Leib of Shpola. See especially pages 38–53.

Shmeruk, Chone. *Maḥazot miqra'iyyim be-Yiddish, 1697–1750*. Jerusalem, 1979. This is one of the best reference books in Hebrew available on the history and origin of the *purimshpil*. Also included are early texts of plays as well as a bibliography of manuscripts and printed books.

Shifra Epstein

PURITANISM. In its most common historical usage *Puritanism* refers to a movement within English Protestantism in both the British Isles and colonial America. Some historians, identifying the essence of Puritanism as a reaction to the tardy pace of the English Reformation, date it from the activities of William Tyndale (1495–1536) and John Hooper (d. 1555) in the formative years of the Church of England. But its major impact was felt during the century between the coming of Elizabeth I to the throne in 1558 and the death of Oliver Cromwell in 1658. For most of that period Puritanism had no institutional identity of its own. Puritans sought to purge the existing English church of its Catholic remnants rather than to set up a rival church. Because their goal was reform, the line that separated them from their non-Puritan brethren was often unclear, a situation to the advantage of those clergy and laity who wished to use the institutions of the church to effect an ultimate change in the ecclesiastical structure and beliefs of the nation.

The first stirrings of Puritan reform came in the reign of Elizabeth from a group of former Marian exiles, clergy and laity who had fled to Protestant centers on the continent to escape the persecutions of the Catholic queen Mary I (1553–1558). These believers had been radicalized by their experience at Geneva and elsewhere and were dissatisfied with the conservative nature of the Elizabethan settlement. That settlement was a *via media* between the demands of Catholicism and those of extreme reform. A compromise that many returning exiles could and did accept, it was unpalatable to many who saw no grace in an accommodation with sin. Initial protests focused on outward signs and ceremonies of the church such as the wearing of vestments, the physical position of church furnishings, and matters of nomenclature. The usage of the establishment, in the view of its critics, symbolized belief in a sacrificial priesthood, a real presence of Christ in the Eucharist, and other elements of Roman Catholic faith and practice.

Clerical opposition to the dictates of the queen and her archbishop of Canterbury, Matthew Parker (1559–1575), caught the public's attention. But while the position of the clergy forced them to make public displays of their conformity or nonconformity, the movement they represented was not simply a clerical protest. Puritanism drew the support of laity as distinguished as members of the queen's Privy Council and tapped deep wells of popular support in town and village, so much so that in some cases of the nonuse of vestments it was lay pressure that strengthened the will of a Puritan clergyman rather than pressure from a clergyman stirring up popular discontent.

Puritan hopes for early reform were bolstered when Edmund Grindal (1519–1583) succeeded Parker as archbishop of Canterbury in 1575. A progressive bishop, although not a Puritan, Grindal was less concerned than

Parker with enforcing practices that had caused friction in the church. He promoted efforts to upgrade the education of the clergy and to reform ecclesiastical abuses, positions strongly supported by Puritans but advocated by progressive members of the establishment as well. When Grindal refused to carry out the queen's desire to suppress prophesyings (clerical conferences designed to promote the continuing education of the participants), Elizabeth suspended him, and the division within the church widened.

Frustrated throughout Elizabeth's reign by the resistance of the episcopal hierarchy, Puritans sought other methods of reforming English religion. *An Admonition to Parliament* (1572) urged the Parliament of 1572 to take responsibility for the church. While some members of that body showed sympathy, the queen was able to block their efforts. Other clergy and laity began to discuss and advocate an alternative system of church government. Presbyterianism, first advocated by Thomas Cartwright (1535–1603), was not universally popular among Puritan reformers, most of whom were able to work with the church hierarchy on a wide range of issues. Some Puritans, however, began to despair of reforming the church. Under the leadership of men such as Robert Browne (c. 1550–1633), Henry Barrow (1550–1593), and John Greenwood (d. 1593), they broke apart from the church and organized Separatist congregations.

In the last years of Elizabeth's reign and during the rule of James I (1603–1625), a new generation of religious thinkers began to articulate their theologies. One group, which would eventually rise within and then dominate the episcopal hierarchy, was represented by Richard Hooker (1554–1600), Richard Neile (1562–1640), and William Laud (1573–1645). This strain in Anglican thought reflected an accommodation to the views of the Dutch theologian Jacobus Arminius (1559–1609), who had sought to temper the rigidity of Calvinistic predestinarianism. The Arminians in the church also stressed the authority of king and bishops, the efficacy of the sacraments in the process of salvation, and the return to a more elaborate use of liturgical ceremony. In contrast to this evolving "new orthodoxy," John Preston (1587–1628), William Perkins (1558–1602), and William Ames (1576–1633) spelled out the essentials of Puritan belief that would characterize the seventeenth-century history of the movement in England and in the New England in America. The lines of demarcation between "orthodox" and Puritan members of the church became more sharply defined, and compromise became less likely.

The starting point for Puritan theology was an emphasis on the majesty, righteousness, and sovereignty of God. God created and maintained the universe by exercise of his will and directed all things to an intelligent end. The awe-inspiring Puritan image of the Father drew heavily on the Old Testament. In contrast was the Puritan concept of man. Scripture, their social surroundings, and an intense personal introspection all persuaded the Puritans that human beings were depraved sinners incapable of earning merit in the eyes of God. But although Adam's sin had led to this fallen state and thus precluded humankind from using the Adamic covenant of works to earn its way to heaven, a benevolent and loving God predestined some of his fallen creatures for the gift of salvation included in the covenant of grace. In emphasizing humankind's sin-diminished faculties and inability to bridge the gap separating us from the creator, the Puritan stood in increasing contrast to the orthodox Anglican point of view.

In their speculation about the means whereby God reached out to elect certain souls for the gift of salvation, the Puritans developed elements of traditional Calvinism. Puritan theologians, William Perkins in particular, made concepts of the covenant central to their evangelism and moralism. Believing in predestination, they explained that all human beings were pledged by the covenant of works to adhere to the divine law and were justly condemned for failure to adhere to it. They also wrote and preached an evangelical message of hope centering on the free gift of saving grace to the elect. For those saved from the consequences of their actions by this gift, the law still remained the standard of behavior according to which they tried to live lives expressive of gratitude to their savior.

The covenant of works depended on human action, while the covenant of grace required a faith that God himself enabled the elect to grasp. This emphasis on contractual relationships became a controlling metaphor for Puritans in their social as well as their religious thought.

If the idea of the covenant was to be found in the Reformed roots of Puritanism, so was the language of conditionality that the Puritans employed in their discussion of the doctrine. While, in the words of a foremost student of covenant theology, the ministers "from the standpoint of high Calvinism . . . were solid on election but soft on perseverance," they were still within the main current of that tradition. This nuance in their thought was revealed most clearly in their tracing of the normal path of the elect to salvation.

Most Puritan preachers developed a complex morphology of conversion, identifying stages in that process such as election, vocation, justification, sanctification, and glorification. Election signified God's choosing of those to whom the grace of salvation was to be offered.

Vocation was the Holy Spirit's offer to humankind of the grace enabling us to seek contrition, faith, and cooperation with that grace. Puritans developed an extensive literature on man's preparation with God's help for the next and pivotal stage, justification. God provided natural means such as the scripture, the sacraments, and the sermons of godly preachers to facilitate the process of salvation. By grasping hold of these means sinners could not save themselves, but the elect could cooperate with the Spirit's transforming work on their souls.

For the blessed, justification—the soul-wrenching, born-again experience of conversion—represented a passage from sinner to saint, from a vile and loathsome creature to a being embraced by God. Justification placed the stamp of election on the saint and rehabilitated, though it did not perfect, human faculties. Sanctification was the life of grace lived by the saint, a life of endeavoring to show gratitude to the divine author of one's salvation by living as God's law prescribed. Because of human frailty, assurance of one's state was sometimes in doubt. Glorification was the unification of the soul with God after death, the final resolution of doubt, and the gathering of the elect into the communion of saints.

In his pilgrim's progress to the celestial kingdom the Puritan constantly encountered the moral law. Perhaps the simplest explanation of the rule by which the Puritan sought to live is the statement by Richard Baxter (1615–1691) that "*Overdoing* is the most ordinary way of *undoing*." The Puritan life was a life of vigorous involvement in the world without excessive or abusive use of the natural order. Some later commentators and contemporary critics have sought to blame Puritans for all that they themselves perceive as repressive in Protestant culture. But contrary to the image painted by their detractors, Puritans were not killjoys or prudes. They dressed as befitted their social class, participated in lotteries, drank alcoholic beverages, and approached sex as more than a mere obligation.

Puritans did, however, scorn what they viewed as the libertine excesses of many of their peers, condemning not the drink but the drunkard, not the expression of sexual love between husband and wife but extramarital sex. They felt called to vocations that were social, economic, and civic as well as religious. They rejected the monastic ideal of separation from the world and embraced a vision of total Christian involvement in the creation. As one of the elect the Puritan was called to use fully all the talents God provided without overstressing any one call; in early Massachusetts the civil magistrates had occasion to gently remind the clergy that even sermonizing could be overdone when the number of lecture days began to interfere with the task of community building. While some Puritans such as Michael Wigglesworth (1631–1705) allowed their fears of sin to become obsessions that made them walking parodies of Puritanism, the ideal of the Puritan moral life was one of sober moderation.

The Puritans' moral stance and belief that their role in history was that of a chosen people called to create a New Jerusalem and usher in the millennium made Puritans, on both sides of the Atlantic, culturally distinct from their peers. The elect envisioned themselves as a group apart, a saved and saving remnant. Their lifestyle was different enough to symbolize their uniqueness. Their effort to give God his due by spending the Sabbath reading the scriptures rather than indulging in sport or dance, their rejection of set prayers for spontaneous expressions, their disdain for the ritualization of the liturgy, their coming together in New England on designated fast days and days of thanksgiving—all of these reinforced the Puritans' sense of being apart from yet responsible for saving their native land.

The task of redeeming England seemed more difficult than ever as the reign of James I gave way to that of Charles I (1625–1649). Puritans had wielded considerable influence at Oxford and Cambridge and from those universities a brotherhood of reformed preachers had spread the Puritan message throughout the realm. The patronage of sympathetic gentry and of some borough officials secured pulpits for the Puritans. A group of lay and clerical leaders called the Feofees for Impropriation solicited donations to fund the purchase of numerous church livings that would be controlled by the movement. But the rise of William Laud symbolized the growing determination of the king and his chief counselors to root out dissent. Puritan clergymen were haled before ecclesiastical courts, deprived of their livings, and harried out of the land.

Having failed to reform England by their written or spoken word, some Puritan leaders conceived the idea of persuading their countrymen by the example of a model Puritan community. This was the goal of many who joined in the Great Migration to New England in the 1630s. As John Winthrop (1588–1649), the first governor of Massachusetts, expressed it: "We shall be as a City upon a Hill." Massachusetts and her sister commonwealths of Connecticut (founded in 1636) and New Haven (1637) and the moderate Separatist colony of Plymouth represented an orthodoxy that was designated the New England Way. Their social and political fabric was knit from ideas of Christian organicism owing much to English rural traditions as well as to the corporate strain in Puritan thought. In matters of religion the orthodox developed a congregational church structure with all residents required to attend service but with full membership and its privileges reserved for those who could persuade their peers that they had experienced saving grace.

The achievement of this orthodoxy was not without struggle. Puritans who migrated from England left the status of dissenting minority within the structure of the state church to cope with the challenge of translating their general principles into institutional practice and statements of faith. Various individuals offered their perspectives, and through the efforts of clergymen such as John Cotton (1584–1652), Richard Mather (1596–1669), Thomas Hooker (1586–1647), John Davenport (1597–1670), and Thomas Shepard (1605–1649) a consensus emerged that would be articulated in the Cambridge Platform (1648). Some Puritans found themselves outside these emerging boundaries of acceptable belief. Many responded by conforming, but Roger Williams (1603–1683), Anne Hutchinson (1591–1643), and others who would not bend were excluded; some, including Williams and Hutchinson, took up residence in Rhode Island, forming a society that rapidly achieved notoriety as a haven of radicalism.

In England Puritans who had stayed at home were at the forefront of the coalition that formed in opposition to the king's foreign policy, religious innovations, forced loans, and use of prerogative courts. The civil wars that erupted (1642–1648) pitted Parliament against the king, and so heavily was the House of Commons dominated by the reformers that the struggle also earned the name of the Puritan Revolution. During the course of the conflict Puritan reformers sought to construct a new Church of England. The same tensions that had threatened Puritan uniformity in New England appeared and the circumstances of the war made controlling them impossible.

Although most Puritans could agree on the doctrines contained in the Westminster Assembly's Confession of Faith (1647), many rejected the Presbyterian ecclesiastical structure that that reform convocation recommended to Parliament. Presbyterians, Congregationalists, and Baptists became distinct groups within the movement, while hosts of radical sects found sustenance in the excitement of the times. While political stability was provided by the rise of Oliver Cromwell (1599–1658) as lord protector in 1649, religious diversity did not come to an end. Cromwell did, however, make progress toward the establishment of a Puritan state church uniting moderate Congregationalists such as Thomas Goodwin (1600–1680) and John Owen (1616–1683), moderate Presbyterians such as Stephen Marshall (1594–1655), and moderate Baptists such as Henry Jessey (1601–1663).

The return of the Stuart monarchy with the Restoration of Charles II (1660–1685) in 1660 saw the casting out of Puritanism from the Church of England. What had been a reform movement within Anglicanism became nonconformity in the shape of Presbyterian, Congregational, and Baptist denominations. Across the Atlantic, Puritan values still dominated, but the institutional separation from the Church of England that had always been a fact of colonial life was accepted in theory as well, and New Englanders adopted the denominational badges of their brethren in England.

The story of Puritanism merges into the story of the denominations it spawned, but as a cultural movement it continued to have relevance. In England the poems of John Milton (1608–1674), the devotional writings of Richard Baxter, and the *Pilgrim's Progress* of John Bunyan (1628–1688) were fruits of the Puritan outlook. In America the literary offerings of Anne Bradstreet (1612–1672), Michael Wigglesworth, and Edward Taylor (1662–1729) and the range of writings of Cotton Mather (1663–1728) betokened the vitality of Puritanism. When Jonathan Edwards (1703–1758) spoke to the people of the Connecticut valley in the 1730s, there was sparked a great awakening not only of religious enthusiasm in general but of a distinctively Puritan outlook on the universe, its creator, and the sinners who inhabit it.

[*See also the biographies of Browne, Bunyan, Edwards, Richard Hooker, Thomas Hooker, Hutchinson, the Mather family, and Williams.*]

BIBLIOGRAPHY

My book *The Puritan Experiment: New England Society from Bradford to Edwards* (New York, 1976) is an introductory survey to the English origins and American development of Puritan ideas and practice. *The Puritan Tradition in America, 1620–1730*, edited by Alden T. Vaughan (New York, 1972), is the best single-volume anthology of Puritan writings. For those interested in the origins of the movement, the works of Patrick Collinson, especially *The Elizabethan Puritan Movement* (Berkeley, 1967), are indispensable. Barrington R. White's *The English Separatist Tradition: From the Marian Martyrs to the Pilgrim Fathers* (Oxford, 1971) is an excellent analysis of that important offshoot from mainstream Puritanism. The seventeenth-century evolution of Puritanism in England is well surveyed in Michael R. Watts's *The Dissenters: From the Reformation to the French Revolution* (Oxford, 1978). The starting point for an understanding of the faith of New England Puritans remains the classic studies by Perry Miller, especially *The New England Mind: The Seventeenth Century* (New York, 1939). Puritan polity is skillfully examined by Edmund S. Morgan in *Visible Saints:*

The History of a Puritan Idea (New York, 1963). Many key facets of Puritan theology are unraveled in E. Brooks Holifield's *The Covenant Sealed: The Development of Puritan Sacramental Theology in Old and New England, 1570–1720* (New Haven, 1974). The devotional aspects of Puritan life are the subject of Charles E. Hambrick-Stowe's *The Practice of Piety* (Chapel Hill, N.C., 1982).

FRANCIS J. BREMER

PURUṢA is a Sanskrit word meaning "person" or "a man." Throughout Indian intellectual history, however, the term has acquired the independent meanings of "the first man, self," and "consciousness." The development of the concept of *puruṣa* therefore overlaps with the development of the concepts of *ātman* ("self"), *brahman* ("universal self"), and *kṣetrajña* ("knower"). The interrelationships among these concepts can be traced through the literature of the Upaniṣads and the epics, in the work of Buddhist writer Aśvaghoṣa, in the medical work of Caraka, and in the texts of the Sāṃkhya school.

Puruṣa first occurs in the oldest extant book of Vedic hymns, the *Ṛgveda* (composed toward the end of the period from 1500 to 900 BCE). Hymn 10.90 refers to the first man from whose bodily parts sprang the different groups of society *(varṇas)* based on the division of labor. In the oldest Upaniṣads (900–700 BCE), the term still refers to the first man, whose essence, however, is entirely self *(ātman):* "In the beginning this world was self *(ātman)* alone in the form of a Person *(puruṣa)*" *(Bṛhadāraṇyaka Upaniṣad* 1.4.1). When Puruṣa first came into existence he became aware of himself and exclaimed, "I am" (1.4.1).

Both *ātman* and *brahman* inherited the function of creation from the original *puruṣa,* the first man. Such examples in the case of *ātman* are found in *Bṛhadāraṇyaka Upaniṣad* 1.4.1–10, and in the case of *brahman* in *Bṛhadāraṇyaka Upaniṣad* 1.4.11–16. Various creation myths took up the descriptions of how the "one," desiring to be many, multiplied itself, forming a new creation.

The concepts of *ātman* and *puruṣa* as the original entities are first replaced by *brahman* in a verse of the *Bṛhadāraṇyaka Upaniṣad:* "Verily, in the beginning this world was *brahman,* one only" (1.4.11). The fully articulated concept of *brahman,* according to the Upaniṣads, refers to the cosmic entity, an omnipresent self that holds the whole universe within itself. It is this universal self *(brahman)* that is a counterpart to the individual self *(ātman).* The aim of the Upaniṣadic teachings was to realize the identity of these two principles through mystical experience.

The concept of *puruṣa* cannot be uniformly understood as self or consciousness. In its development it underwent such functional transformations that at times it took on opposing functions. This development can be seen, for example, in the description of *brahman* as having two aspects: "There are, indeed, two forms of *brahman:* the formed *(mūrta)* and the formless, the mortal and the immortal, the moving and the motionless" (*Bṛhadāraṇyaka Upaniṣad* 2.3.1).

Change and creation were not the primary functions of the concept of *puruṣa;* eventually *puruṣa* took on other functions, while that of creation came to be associated with *prakṛti* (materiality). Thus, although *puruṣa* served at one time as the foundation of the whole universe it was also instrumental in establishing materiality, an opposing concept set forth by the Sāṃkhya school. Together, *puruṣa* and *prakṛti* constituted the essential entities of Sāṃkhya. This separation of *prakṛti* from *puruṣa* is reflected in the term *kṣetrajña.*

Kṣetrajña ("knower of the field," i.e., knower of materiality) is a term used to describe *puruṣa* as consciousness (cf. *Maitri Upaniṣad* 2.5). A section of the twelfth book of the *Mahābhārata* called the *Mokṣadharma* employs *kṣetrajña* as a synonym for *puruṣa,* while the *Buddhacarita* of Aśvaghoṣa uses *kṣetrajña* for consciousness in its descriptions of Sāṃkhya teachings (e.g., *Buddhacarita* 12.20).

The *Sāṃkhyakārikā* (c. 350–550 CE) of Īśvarakṛṣṇa, the only independent extant work of the Sāṃkhya school, is regarded as the classic statement on Sāṃkhya thought. According to this work, *puruṣa* is a contentless consciousness distinct in every respect from materiality. Consciousness *(puruṣa)* is, in fact, said to be the exact opposite of materiality or *prakṛti* (*Sāṃkhyakārikā* 19). For example, consciousness is uncaused and is not itself a cause; it is eternal, without space, without motion, without complexity, without substratum, without parts, independent, differentiated, and unproductive. The purpose of consciousness is to lend, so to speak, consciousness to materiality at the time of knowledge and thus to justify the existence of materiality.

By its mere presence, consciousness is the "passive witness" *(sākṣin)* of materiality. Consciousness is also the beneficiary of the activities of materiality, and finally, because it is different from all ordinary experience, *puruṣa* makes this ordinary experience meaningful by being different from it, by being conscious, and by making the experience a *conscious* experience.

Originally, *puruṣa* was spoken of as one, just as *brahman* and *kṣetrajña* are one. Yet in classical Sāṃhkya *puruṣa* came, like *átman,* to be considered plural or many. This plurality of consciousnesses served to explain differences in existence, such as different births and different deaths. If, according to classical Sāṃkhya, there were only one consciousness, it would follow that when any one person attained liberation all individuals would attain liberation at the same time.

Under the influence of the dominant philosophical school of Vedānta, the Sāṃkhya-Yoga teacher Vijñānabhikṣu (sixteenth century) attempted to reconcile the plurality of consciousnesses with the one universal self of Vedantic thought. Vijñānabhikṣu claimed that it is possible for consciousness to be many under certain conditions. This, however, was not to be considered a contradiction to the claim that there is only one consciousness, since, he maintained, the plurality of *puruṣa* is ultimately only a matter of convenience for the purposes of discourse.

In Sāṃhkya, as in most Indian philosophical schools, consciousness is instrumental in accomplishing the highest aim of Sāṃkhya philosophy, namely, liberation. Liberation, according to Sāṃkhya, comes from that knowledge whereby one distinguishes between two entities—contentless consciousness *(puruṣa)* and materiality *(prakṛti)*—as essentially different things. Recognition of this distinction is the truth that grants liberation.

[*The concept of* puruṣa *within the context of Indian philosophy is treated in* Sāṃkhya. *See also* Prakṛti *and* Brahman.]

BIBLIOGRAPHY

A minute analysis of the formative stages of the concepts of *puruṣa* is found in Erhardt Hanefeld's *Philosophische Haupttexte der älteren Upaniṣaden* (Wiesbaden, 1976). For the beginnings of the development of the concept, see E. H. Johnston's *Early Sāṁkhya: An Essay on Its Historical Development according to the Texts* (1937; reprint, Delhi, 1974). A detailed study of the Sāṃkhya school is provided in the forthcoming *Sāṃkhya: A Dualist Tradition in Indian Philosophy* by Gerald James Larson and Ram Shankar Bhattacharya, the third volume of the *Encyclopedia of Indian Philosophies*, edited by Karl H. Potter (Princeton and Delhi).

EDELTRAUD HARZER

PUSEY, EDWARD BOUVERIE

PUSEY, EDWARD BOUVERIE (1800–1882), along with John Keble and John Henry (later Cardinal) Newman, a leader of the Oxford Movement (sometimes called Tractarianism), a high church development in the Church of England that flourished between 1833 and 1845. Pusey was educated at Eton and at Christ Church, Oxford, and was a fellow at Oriel before becoming regius professor of Hebrew and canon of Christ Church. Newman said of Pusey, "He at once gave us a position and a name." With Newman's defection to Roman Catholicism, Pusey became the primary leader of the movement until his death. [*See the biography of Newman.*]

Pusey was among the first English scholars to become acquainted with the modern critical approach to scripture emerging in Germany, but throughout this exposure he maintained a quite conservative posture. His influence on the religious life of England can be seen in several areas: his tracts and sermons gave popular impetus to a revival of medieval piety in England, he was a friend and mentor of the nineteenth-century monastic revival, and the practice of private confession to a priest in modern Anglicanism can be traced to his sermon on the subject in 1846.

Extreme rigor characterized his personal piety, and his theology left little room for the forgiveness of sins after baptism. His long and diligent work on the subject of baptismal regeneration suffered from his failure to define the meaning of the term. As a whole, his scholarship lacked the subtle, seminal, and lasting quality of Newman's, or the poetic warmth of Keble's.

Pusey's life seemed characterized by defeats or disappointments: the appointment as regius professor of divinity of the liberal theologian Renn Hampden over Tractarian protests; the promulgation of the doctrine of papal infallibility; his censure by the university for his sermon on the real presence in the Eucharist; the departure from Anglicanism of Newman and others; and the Privy Council's overruling of the Ecclesiastical Courts on the Gorham case, and others like it, which seemed to Pusey to be an unwarranted intrusion of the state into the affairs of the church. However, his prestige, loyalty, and steadying influence within the Oxford Movement and subsequent Anglo-Catholicism marked a permanent change in direction within Anglicanism.

BIBLIOGRAPHY

Good collections of Pusey's writings are *Spiritual Letters*, edited by J. O. Johnston and W. C. E. Newbolt (New York, 1901), and *The Mind of the Oxford Movement*, edited by Owen Chadwick (Stanford, Calif., 1960). Useful biographical matter can be found in *Life of Pusey*, 4 vols., edited by Henry P. Liddon (London, 1884–1887), which includes an extensive bibliography of Pusey's published works in volume 4.

C. FITZSIMONS ALLISON

PYGMY RELIGIONS

PYGMY RELIGIONS. African Pygmies comprise a variety of ethnic groups who dwell as hunter-gatherers in the rain forest of central Africa. Because they live as nomads in a demanding and inaccessible environment, few serious studies have been done on them. Most studies of Pygmy life have been concerned with how they relate to the history of religions. According to Wilhelm

Schmidt (1868–1954), an ordained priest and ethnologist interested in the origin of religion, the Pygmy peoples represented humanity in its childhood; they were a living equivalent of one of the earliest stages of human culture. Since early evidence seemed to indicate the existence of monotheistic belief in primitive societies, Schmidt engaged his colleagues to explore Pygmy religious life. Hence, for years the Pygmies were studied by Catholic missionaries seeking to support the idea that monotheism (rather than animism or fetishism) was the earliest form of religion. [*See the biography of Schmidt.*]

This article discusses three Pygmy groups that are better known through recent fieldwork: the Aka, located in the southern region of the Central African Republic; the Baka of eastern Cameroon; and the Mbuti of the Ituri rain forest of Zaire. Other more sedentary and less documented groups such as the Gyeli of western Cameroon and the Twa of central Zaire and Rwanda are not included.

Aka Pygmies. According to Aka cosmology, a creator god named Bembe made the world, including the sky, earth, forest, and animals. He then fashioned the first male and female couple, Tole and Ngolobanzo. He later added a younger brother, Tonzanga. Bembe gave all worldly knowledge and goods to Tonzanga, but Tole subsequently stole them from his brother to ensure the survival of the family as a totality. Because of this theft, Bembe withdrew into the sky where he now lives without paying further attention to the world he created.

The primary twin couple, Tole and Ngolobanzo, gave birth to two children whose union later engendered the rest of humanity. Since that time, the three original beings created by Bembe have continued to live in a parallel world that represents the ideal to which human society should conform. The ghosts of human beings *(edio)* live in the forest where they lead an endless existence under the rule of humanity's two ancestral spirits, Ezengi and Ziakpokpo. Ghosts are neutral toward human beings and act either benevolently or malevolently depending on how well humans treat one another and whether they show respect for the ghosts themselves. However, it is believed that those areas outside the forest (forest edge, villages, and rivers) are inhabited by foreign malign spirits. In Aka thought, the village is a nonhuman (bad) world, the forest a realm of ghosts, and the campsite the only fully human realm.

The forest is impregnated with vital principles; from these, either by initiation or by inheritance, an individual may appropriate the spiritual power *(kulu)* that will assist him by blessing his various endeavors. However, malign spirits *(kose)* are attracted by malevolence and slander among human beings. The evil that individuals may wish upon each other is the cause of human misfortune because it provokes the wrath of the spirits.

Aka religious rituals fall into two types: large festivals that concern the entire community and small rites undertaken for more private purposes. All Aka rituals relate to three fundamental functions: propitiation of supernatural powers (ghosts or the forest god Ezengi) so as to bring about abundance and fertility; divination of the cause of disorder or the likely result of a prospective action; and the propitiation of irritated spirits, whether they are ancestor ghosts during a period of social conflict or shortage or animal spirits after a "murder" (the death of an animal during a hunt).

Rituals are performed before undertaking a journey. In Aka thought (which relies upon the juxtaposition of camp, village, and forest with all their other associated values), any passage from one world to the next is potentially dangerous and requires ritual action. While every adult male may be in contact with certain familiar spirits, it is the function of various specialists (an elder, chief hunter, or diviner-healer) to meet major spirits such as Ezengi or the elephant spirit.

The Aka obtain most of their food by hunting, and insofar as it is a highly dangerous activity with unpredictable results, it is surrounded by rites of various natures: rites of individual and collective propitiation, rites of divination, rites thanking the ghosts with offerings, and a rite of collective expiation vis-à-vis the game spirit. A period of successive hunting failures calls for a divination and propitiation ceremony that includes the appearance of ghosts in the form of leaf masks. When men are absent on extended hunting forays, women perform particular songs and dances asking not only that the men come back with large amounts of game but also explicitly asking for the resumption of sexual relations.

The value the Aka place on human fertility and human life in general is even more apparent in the Mokondi ceremony, a large festival devoted to Ezengi. During Mokondi, a figure wearing a raffia-cloth mask dances inside a throng of people who are segregated by sex into concentric circles. The ceremony is performed every night for an entire month to mark the settlement of a new camp after the death of a community member. It is intended to restore the welfare of the community by obtaining the benevolence and protection of the supreme being.

The last salient Aka ritual is connected with honey gathering. Mobandi, an annual rite linked to the flowering of a particular tree, is a collective purification ritual that involves "flagellation"; by gently beating their bodies with leafy boughs, the Aka hope to expel malign forces *(kose)* from the community. Moreover, as honey stands as a sexual symbol for the Aka, the Mobandi ritual corresponds to the periodic regeneration of the world.

Baka Pygmies. Certain religious conceptions held by the Baka are similar to those of the Aka. Several terms are also employed by both groups but are used to designate different aspects of their religious life. According to Baka cosmology, the god Komba created the world and all its creatures. He is part of a divine family that includes his sisters, a culture hero named Waito, and various offspring. In this complicated mythology, all of these creatures function as a many-faceted hermaphroditic entity that is self-engendering and productive of all humanity, including Pygmies as well as tall Africans.

Waito, who stole from Komba such goods as game and fire for the benefit of humanity, is the figure who introduced women and sexuality into human culture. Komba, on the other hand, brought death into the world. While Komba remains distant in the sky, it is his spirit, Ezengi, who gives Baka youths knowledge of the world and of social existence during initiation ceremonies. Ezengi protects humans and rules over their death and rebirth as ghosts in the forest. Communication with either the forest god Ezengi or the ghosts is the concern of a specialist (the diviner-healer), or of initiated adult males during the collective dances, and is achieved by means of songs, charms, offerings, or at times, with a fire.

The function of ritual among the Baka is akin to that of the Aka: prediction of the future, propitiation of the spirits so as to ensure a successful hunt, restoration of normal life after times of trouble, and procurement of Ezengi's continued benevolence toward the community. Before beginning on a spear hunt for large game, a divination session will be performed, followed by a women's ritual that includes yodeling and dances to entice the animals. A death requires two ceremonies. The night the death occurs, a masked spirit (symbol of life against death) performs a dance, insulting the audience and making obscene jokes. Following the burial, the deceased soul dances in the camp but is then chased off with firebrands and driven into the forest. Once the campsite is deserted, a large festival begins in order to restore the normal existence of the community. At this point, Ezengi appears in the form of a raffia mask. Because women are not allowed to participate, each family is represented in the ritual by an adult male. The ceremony, involving a large number of people, is also the culmination of the initiation of pubescent boys that generally lasts for several weeks. Through such pervasive participation, this ritual, which is marked by the collective singing of polyphonic songs, provides an occasion to reaffirm group unity after a serious crisis.

Mbuti Pygmies. The Mbuti Pygmies of the Ituri rain forest are the most well known of the various Pygmy ethnic groups. According to Paul Schebesta (1950), the Mbuti believe that God created the universe (that is, the forest) and all its creatures and forces. He then retired into the sky, ending his participation in earthly affairs. The first man, a culture hero named Tore, became god of the forest; he gave the Mbuti both fire and death and is seen as the source of game, honey, and protection. Essentially a benevolent god, Tore is thought to be particularly offended by evil. According to this version of the story, both humans and animals are endowed with vital forces *(megbe)*. Furthermore, it is believed that the shadow of a deceased man becomes a forest spirit, part of an invisible people who mediate between humans and the forest god Tore.

Colin Turnbull (1965) disagrees with this account of Mbuti cosmology. According to him, there is no creator god; instead, the Mbuti worship God as a living benevolent being personified by the forest. To them, God *is* the forest. Turnbull also diverges from Schebesta's account of the mediating forest spirits, for he views the Mbuti as a practical people who have a direct relationship with the forest as sacred being.

The Mbuti Pygmies lack both ritual specialists and divination practices. Communication with the forest is achieved through fire and smoke, offerings, whistles, wooden trumpets, and polyphonic songs. As with the Aka and the Baka, rituals surround hunting, honey gathering, food shortages, puberty, and death.

The onset of puberty in women is celebrated by an initiation festival known as Elima. At the time of the first menstruation, a girl goes into seclusion together with all her young friends. Staying in the Elima hut for several weeks, the girls receive instruction concerning motherhood and various ritual responsibilities from a respected older female relative. They are also taught how to sing the songs of adult women. Elima also functions as a means for choosing a mate.

Although Elima functions as an initiation into adult life for both girls and boys, there is a separate initiation rite, known as Nkumbi, exclusively for males. During Nkumbi, the Mbuti boys are circumcised together with the young males of the neighboring peoples who live in fixed agricultural settlements outside the forest. Nkumbi is primarily a way for the Mbuti boys to gain status in village society, but it also works to cement ties between the Mbuti and their village neighbors.

The first killing of game marks a further initiation rite for young Mbuti men. Until he has accomplished this, a young man is not allowed to participate in the most important Mbuti ritual, Molimo, which takes place after a crisis in the community (usually a death) and lasts for an entire month. The Mbuti believe that because God is benevolent, death or similiar misfortunes cannot occur unless the forest has "fallen asleep." Hence, the purpose of the Molimo is to wake up the forest with songs and to thereby restore the normal life of the community. During this rite God sings through a wooden trumpet with the whole community. The Molimo fire is kindled each day by taking embers from the hearth of each family, emphasizing the collective nature of the celebration. As a reaction to crisis and a means of seeking the regeneration of the world through polyphonic song, Molimo represents a perfect form of communication with the spiritual world.

BIBLIOGRAPHY

On the Aka, the basic reference is the *Encyclopédie des Pygmées Aka: Techniques, langage et société des chasseurs-cueilleurs de la forêt centrafricaine,* edited by Serge Bahuchet and Jacqueline M. C. Thomas (Paris, 1981–). Volume 1, *Les Pygmées Aka* (1983), and volume 2, *Dictionnaire Aka-Français* (1981), of the projected fifteen volumes have already appeared. See also Bahuchet's *Les Pygmées Aka et la forêt centrafricaine* (Paris, 1985), which presents detailed chapters on the Aka worldview and Aka rituals. On the Baka, see Robert Brisson and Daniel Boursier's *Petit dictionnaire Baka-français* (Douala, 1979) and Brisson's *Contes des Pygmées Baka du Sud-Cameroun,* 4 vols. (Douala, 1981–1984). On the Mbuti, see Paul Schebesta's *Die Bambuti-Pygmäen vom Ituri,* vol. 3, *Die Religion* (Brussels, 1952), and his *Les Pygmées du Congo Belge* (Brussels, 1952); the documentation in these two works is rich but is notably difficult to use because data from various sources are mixed. Colin Turnbull's *The Forest People: A Study of the Pygmies of the Congo* (New York, 1961) is an intimate account of daily life and ritual among the Mbuti. Two other works by Turnbull deserve attention: *The Mbuti Pygmies: An Ethnographic Survey* (New York, 1965) and *Wayward Servants: The Two Worlds of the African Pygmies* (New York, 1965). The first is a valuable synthesis of previous work, including that of Schebesta, and the second, despite its materialistic emphasis, is a classic study of the Ituri peoples.

In the study of the history of religions, Wilhelm Schmidt's *Die Stellung der Pygmäenvölker in der Entwicklungsgeschichte des Menschen* (Stuttgart, 1910) remains useful. Although dated, Schmidt's work provides interesting insights into the evolutionary school of religious analysis.

For ritual music, the following recordings can be recommended: Simha Arom's *Anthologie de la musique des Pygmées Aka* (Paris: OCORA, 1978), Simha Arom and Patrick Renaud's *Baka Pygmy Music (Cameroon)* (Paris: UNESCO Musical Atlas, 1977), and Colin Turnbull and Francis S. Chapman's *The Pygmies of the Ituri Forest* (New York: Folkways, 1958).

SERGE BAHUCHET and
JACQUELINE M. C. THOMAS

PYRAMIDS. [*This entry comprises an overview and a discussion of Egyptian pyramids. For related discussions, see* Temple, *articles on* Mediterranean Temples *and* Mesoamerican Temples. *See also* Tombs.]

An Overview

The structure of the pyramid may unite the two religious monuments of the burial mound and the elevated altar. Because these functions are not mutually exclusive but rather are in many cases complementary and combined with yet other functions, modern archaeologists often face serious difficulties of interpretation. This problem becomes especially evident when they attempt to situate the monuments in their original contexts.

On the one hand, the pyramid can be a logical derivation of the burial mound, with the primary function of concealing the tomb of a prominent ruler while exalting his often-deified memory (see figure 1). The Egyptian pyramid, with its wonderfully refined form, is the perfect embodiment of this initial phase. It is, in addition, the only monument that can be considered a true pyramid in the geometric sense of the word (excluding, of course, the oldest example, in Saqqara, built with trunk-pyramidal elements).

On the other hand, the pyramid can constitute the monumental culmination of the elevated altar, an ex-

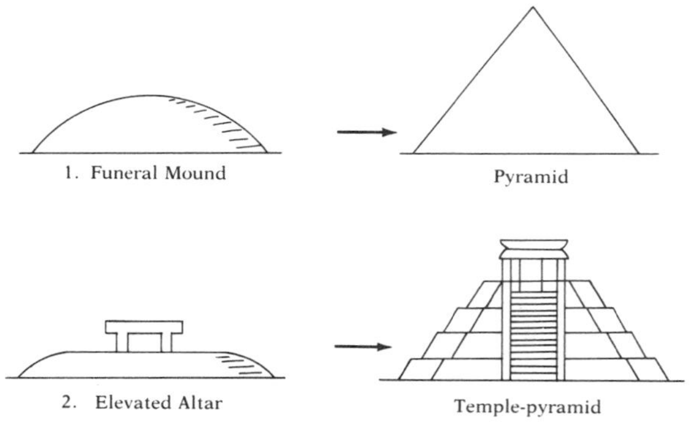

FIGURE 1. *Derivations of Egyptian and Mesoamerican Pyramids.* (1) The form of the Egyptian pyramid, which was used for burial, as derived from the funeral mound. (2) The form of the Mesoamerican pyramid-temple as the culmination of the elevated altar.

treme manifestation of the "cult of height." Overwhelmed by the sacred, the simple mortal tends to place everything that relates to that sphere at a higher level, whether they be effigies, images, or altars, whether visible or invisible. The most outstanding forms of this genre are the ziggurats in Mesopotamia and the temple-pyramids of pre-Columbian America (particularly those of Mesoamerica and, on a lesser scale, those of the Andean region).

Chronologically, the Mesopotamian buildings are older; they date from the fourth millennium BCE. The temples, such as those of Uruk (modern Warka, Iraq), are placed on high, artificial platforms accessible by staircases or ramps. From the third millennium BCE these develop into massive ziggurats, which were usually composed of terraced blocks on a square foundation (see figure 2). The terraced blocks, perpendicular or parallel to the foundation, ascend in broken patterns, either directly or in spans. Archaeologists believe that a sanctuary usually crowned the last platform, but total destruction of the upper parts of the monuments makes confirmation of this thesis difficult. In profile such monuments present a terraced succession of vertical or near-vertical shapes. Their cubical appearance is often counterbalanced by great flutings that alternate rhythmically with the buttresses to animate the exterior facings and cast elongated shadows accentuating the vertical over the horizontal.

Even more versatile than the Mesopotamian pyramid is that of Mesoamerica, which originated between 1200 and 900 BCE among the Olmec of San Lorenzo and La Venta on the Gulf Coast of Mexico and continued to develop until the sixteenth century CE. The Mesopotamian pyramid often has a quadrangular foundation, but occasionally it is circular, as in the main pyramid at La Venta or that of Cuicuilco; it can also be semicircular, as in some of the *yácatas* ("mounds," "pyramids") in Michoacán or the temples dedicated to the wind god Quetzalcoatl-Ehécatl that were part of the Aztec political expansion just before the Spanish conquest.

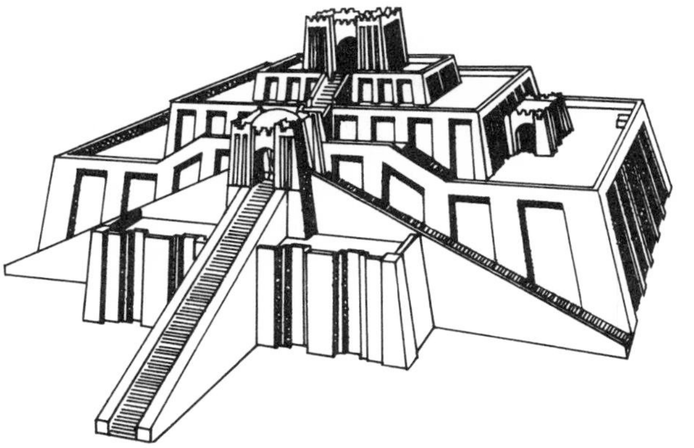

FIGURE 2. *Ziggurat at Ur.* Like the Mesoamerican pyramid-temple, the Mesopotamian ziggurat is thought to have served as the base for a sanctuary.

Conceived as a single truncated block—or, more commonly, formed by a series of terraced blocks—and generally having one staircase, the Mesoamerican pyramid almost invariably presents ornamentation in talus form, an intuitive adaptation of the natural sloping angle of its solid earth fill. A formal element that works to define the principal volumes and to differentiate regional, local, and other styles is the talus panel *(tablero-talud* or *talud-tablero)* with its salient moldings that produce well-marked shadows. The pyramid, usually crowned by a temple (single or, in certain cases, twin), tends to be complemented by plazas, esplanades, and other open spaces. These, together with stairways and altar-platforms, make up a nearly inseparable whole. This type of pyramid was conceived to satisfy the needs of a form of worship that, in its community aspects, took place outdoors.

BIBLIOGRAPHY

For a general approach to the pyramids of Egypt and Mesopotamia see *World Architecture*, edited by Trewin Copplestone (New York, 1963) and *Le grand atlas de l'architecture mondiale* (Paris, 1982). For information on the pyramid in pre-Columbian America, George Kubler's *The Art and Architecture of Ancient America* (New York, 1982) can also be consulted.

PAUL GENDROP

Translated from Spanish by Gabriela Mahn

Egyptian Pyramids

Egyptian pyramids are essentially royal tombs. Throughout the centuries their great size and architectural excellence have led to several alternative explanations for their existence, such as the medieval notion that they were granaries built by Joseph during the seven good years mentioned in the Bible (*Gn.* 41), but such theories are quite fanciful. There is a connection, however, between the origin of pyramid building and the idea of a staircase; one such stairway, which must be symbolic, was found incorporated in a mud-brick bench-shaped tomb dating from the end of the first dynasty (c. 2900 BCE) at Saqqara, south of modern Cairo, but it is far from certain that this was a royal monument. The first pyramid, however, is the Step Pyramid, also at Saqqara, consisting of six such bench tombs arranged on top of one another in the form of a stairway

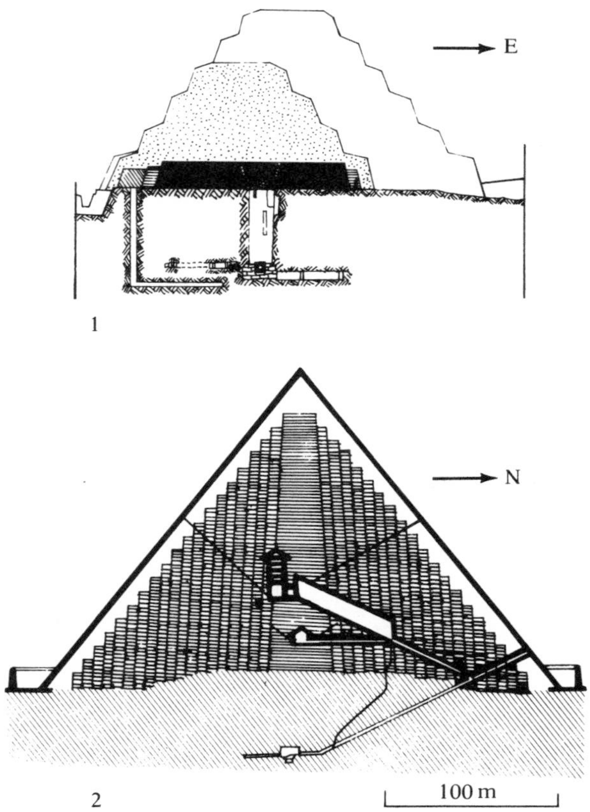

FIGURE 1. *Sections of Two of the Large Pyramids of the Old Kingdom.* (1) Zoser's Step Pyramid at Saqqara, showing the successive building phases. (2) The Great Pyramid at Giza, showing conjectural internal buttress walls.

(see figure 1). This is the earliest known monumental stone building (2700 BCE), and it has earned its architect, Imhotep, a place in history which was recognized by the ancient Egyptians themselves. Subsequent step pyramids, although unfinished, show increasing confidence in the use of stone, and they developed rapidly, replacing the step structure with something closer to a true pyramid.

The Age of the Great Pyramids. The apogee of pyramid building was reached at the beginning of the fourth dynasty, with the two massive pyramids at Dahshur built by Snefru and the Great Pyramid at Giza, the work of his son Cheops (2600 BCE). Each successive king seems to have at least planned a pyramid for himself (over eighty are known), down to the end of the Middle Kingdom (1600 BCE), when the concept was abandoned in favor of a less conspicuous burial place. Later royal pyramids are known from the Sudan, and smaller imitations are common in private tombs of the New Kingdom (c. 1569-1085 BCE) at Thebes. One such example was discovered at Memphis in 1980. Here the idea seems to have been borrowed directly from the royal prototype. The earliest pyramids show frequent changes of plan in their interior corridors, either for religious or architectural reasons or a combination of both. Pyramids of the fifth and sixth dynasties show a regular plan and are effectively standardized. Middle Kingdom pyramids have labyrinthine passages within them to provide for greater security from tomb robbers.

The Pyramid Texts. Beginning with the reign of Unas, the last king of the fifth dynasty (2350 BCE), the sarcophagus, burial chamber, antechamber, and parts of the descending corridor were inscribed with hieroglyphic texts in vertical columns. These so-called Pyramid Texts are undoubtedly our major source on the religious ideas underlying the architecture. [*See also* Egyptian Religion, *article on* The Literature.] The Pyramid Texts make it clear that the dead king, himself a god, was thought to ascend to heaven, either by a staircase or via the sun's rays; the form of the pyramid itself clearly embodies both concepts. Some texts also hint at a primeval mound, the site of the original creation, and it is possible that a pyramid also symbolizes this idea. Other notions of the next world are explored in the Pyramid Texts as well. The most common is that of a fusion with the sun god—joining in his voyage through the night, repelling his enemies, assuming his identity; this idea is so pervasive that pyramids were in effect solar symbols to the ancient Egyptians. An alternative concept is a stellar one: the king's soul or *bai* joins the "imperishable ones," the circumpolar stars which never set in the northern sky. The king's death is seen as an event of the night, ideally taking place at the end of a season in the year, and his rebirth to new life is epitomized in the sunrise. The orientation of pyramids reflects these astronomical ideas: they were built to face the points of the compass, usually with remarkable accuracy, and the entrance was invariably placed in the middle of the northern face, at least before the Middle Kingdom; the descending passage of the Great Pyramid was oriented toward the celestial north pole (see figure 1). In the southern sky, the constellation of Orion was explicitly identified with the resurrected king.

A very interesting analysis sees in the position of the texts within the pyramid a clue to the organization of the funeral ceremonies and in the use of walls and ceilings a symbolic "map" of the netherworld. While this is not unlikely, it is important to remember that the texts themselves were published in an arbitrary order, and that only one pyramid has in fact been treated as a coherent whole.

Pyramid Complexes. It is a mistake to imagine pyramids in isolation. Even the Step Pyramid was designed as the center of a stone palace, intended for the spirit of the dead king. This idea was soon abandoned, but a classic later pyramid would have a mortuary temple at its eastern side for the daily cult of the dead king and a valley temple at the edge of the floodplain where rites of embalming were carried out and cult regalia stored. Both temples would be richly decorated. The two were connected by a covered causeway, also decorated, which could be up to seven hundred meters long. Subsidiary pyramids and a series of solar or funerary boats also adorned the complex. The three pyramids at Abusir, south of Giza, dating from the fifth dynasty (c. 2400 BCE), show these features well. As much work could have gone into this part of the architecture as into the pyramid itself; the mere size of a pyramid tells us little about the power or ambition of its owner. The existence of a population relatively idle during the months of the Nile flood made such building projects easier; it may even have made them necessary, as a means of gratifying popular expectations.

Other Pyramidal Structures. Pyramid-like structures also exist in Mesopotamia; these are better known as ziggurats. They were not funerary at all but seem to have been exclusively religious, and they were the objects of a cult. In two cases temples have been found on their summits, and it is tempting to believe that the ziggurats represented either heavenly mountains or celestial stairways between gods and humans, but their function is surprisingly obscure. It is possible that Egyptian pyramids were influenced vaguely by ziggurats, or vice versa, but their purposes were markedly different. The same is even more true of the pyramid structures of Central America, which were quite different in design and function, being more like gigantic sacrificial altars. There is no reason to assume any link with Egypt, especially as the Central American "pyramids" were built two or three thousand years later. An underlying feeling that the world of the gods is elevated from that of humans and that this gap needs bridging is probably enough to explain the similarities.

BIBLIOGRAPHY

Most of the essential information on Egyptian pyramids is contained in the series of articles written by Dieter Arnold and Hartwig Altenmüller in *Lexikon der Ägyptologie,* vols. 4 and 5 (Wiesbaden, 1982-1983). Walter B. Emery's *Archaic Egypt* (Baltimore, 1967) is essential for the origins of royal tombs. Ahmed Fakhry's *The Pyramids,* 2d ed. (Chicago, 1969), is clear and well illustrated; Eiddon Edwards's *The Pyramids of Egypt* (1961; reprint, Harmondsworth, 1980) is informative, and Kurt Mendelssohn's *The Riddle of the Pyramids* (London, 1974) challenges some accepted notions. The best edition of the Pyramid Texts is by Raymond O. Faulkner, *The Ancient Egyptian Pyramid Texts* (Oxford, 1969), but the reconstructed order is best seen in the light of Jean Leclant's "Les textes des pyramides," in *Textes et langages de l'Égypte pharaonique,* vol. 2 (Cairo, 1972), pp. 37–52. Texts from a single pyramid are collected in *The Pyramid of Unas,* edited by Alexandre Piankoff (Princeton, 1968). Essential studies on the interpretation of these texts are those of Winfried Barta, *Die Bedeutung der Pyramidentexte für den verstorbenen König* (Munich, 1981), and Herbert W. Fairman in *Myth, Ritual, and Kingship,* edited by S. H. Hooke (Oxford, 1958). Babylonian ziggurats are dealt with by André Parrot in his *Ziggurats et Tour de Babel* (Paris, 1949).

J. D. Ray

PYTHAGORAS (c. 570–c. 500 BCE), Greek mystic and philosopher. There is little that can be said without qualification about the life and teachings of Pythagoras. Pythagoras wrote nothing and, as Porphyry stated in his *Vita Pythagorae:* "What Pythagoras said to his associates there is no one who can tell for certain, since they observed a quite unusual silence." The traditional sources on Pythagoras, while plentiful, are for the most part quite late, and are cast in the distorting light of hostile polemic or religious veneration; only Aristotle's writings, and some of the fragments of the fifth-century Pythagorean Philolaus are generally regarded as reliable, direct sources. Modern scholarship on the subject is, finally, a maze of divided opinions, claims, and counterclaims; Pythagoras has been depicted as everything from a religious wonder-worker with little or no scientific or philosophical understandings to the initiator of scientific, rational, and critical philosophical inquiry. Anyone interested in even a summary knowledge of Pythagoras should be cautioned to read widely, without expecting to reach definite conclusions.

What is known of the history and chronology of Pythagoras's life is limited but fairly straightforward. Pythagoras was born on the Ionian island of Samos in 571/70 BCE and lived there until his late thirties; according to the least unreliable sources, he migrated to the Achaean city of Croton in Magna Graecia (southern Italy) in 532/31, soon after the defeat of the city at the hands of its neighbors the Locrians. Pythagoras died sometime toward the close of the sixth century in the city of Metapontum, where he had moved for what were most probably political reasons.

In connection with the revival of Croton in the years following the Locrian defeat of the city, Pythagoras organized there a loose political and religious society, an antidemocratic *hetaireia* (association) that gradually assumed titular control of governmental functions and that, as a religious group, practiced ritual purification and held to a strict code of secrecy. The Pythagorean society continued, and spread its influence and organization throughout southern Italy, during the first half of the fifth century; its political hegemony was decisively broken about 454 BCE, after which time Pythagoreanism became an increasingly disparate movement that had died out or merged with other groups and schools by the late fourth century. Periodic revivals of Pythagoreanism occurred throughout late antiquity; in these, however, the emphasis was more on developing the Pythagoras legend and the Pythagorean mystical vision of the world than on establishing a formal group.

Quasi-historical and legendary accounts about Pythagoras need to be mentioned along with the historical reports: they stand as the oldest layer of the Pythagoras tradition; more importantly, they force the recognition that Pythagoras was experienced by his followers as being not a discoverer of theoretical truths, but a semidivine person (a *theos anēr*), and, to the limited extent that the term is applicable in sixth-century Greek culture, a shaman. It was said that Pythagoras was called the "Hyperborean Apollo" by the Crotoniates, that at the same time on the same day he was seen both in Croton and in Metapontum, and that, as he was crossing the river Casas, the river spoke to him, saying "Hail, Pythagoras." It was also said that, either at the theater or the games, Pythagoras revealed his golden thigh. In a different vein, Pythagoras was credited with the correct prediction of several events. Finally, it was said that he could remember his past lives, that he had a mastery over animals, and that his house was inviolate, like a sanctuary of the mysteries.

These legends do more than just depict the founder of the Pythagorean movement. They also provide a portrait and lived expression of the teachings of Pythagoras and of the promise and possibilities in a life lived under the Pythagorean rule. What Pythagoras taught was that the truth of the human was an occult self: the soul, or *psuchē*, was not, for Pythagoras, merely the life or spirit of the body; rather, it was a separate, in many ways opposing force to the physical self. Concomitant to this notion of a separate and distinct soul was a belief in transmigration, reincarnation, and the kinship of all things. As the true self was finally independent of its specific embodiment, so that self persisted, until purified, through successive incarnations. Finally, this view of the soul as the true self allowed for an upward revision of human life and worth and provided a bridge between the heretofore separated realms of the human and the divine: the soul of the individual was, if freed from physicality, capable of immortality; the realm of the divine, which here meant a power over the forces of contingency, was at least potentially within the reach of the human.

These religious beliefs were not unique to Pythagoras; they can be traced to reasonably definite non-Pythagorean sources, in this case to northern and Indo-Iranian cultures; similar notions had a general currency in the late sixth-century Greek world. Pythagoras was original in his formalization of these notions and, perhaps more importantly, in his development of a practical life based upon them. This way of life and practice can be described first in terms of the Pythagorean precepts or *akousmata* ("oral instructions"), that consisted of magical-ritual prohibitions and commandments the adherence to which would advance the soul on its route to liberation from the rounds of bodily existence. Pythagorean *akousmata,* which began as customs and reached a stage of full development in the fifth century, ranged from specific formulas, dietary rules, and practical duties to general statements about the divine status of the society's founder; they expressed an *askēsis,* or pattern of daily actions, based on avoiding pollution and the snares of physical life and on respecting those forms of life in which soul may be embodied.

Corresponding to the ascetic pattern of life according to precept was an avowal of the therapeutic value of a broadly defined life of inquiry. Here is the religious dimension to the doctrines that constituted the Pythagorean cosmology and cosmogony: the harmony of the spheres, limit *(peras)* and the unlimited *(apeiron)* as the generating principles of all things, and number and ratio as the fundamentals of the world order. Philosophical investigation gave a means to develop right relations with the world and its governing order; as with ritual practice, inquiry was a way of purification and hence, ultimately, of salvation. Pythagoreanism, which was not just a social movement but also a mystical world vision of the attunement and correspondence of all things, had its meaning and its end in an effort to assimilate existence to the divine, immortal life. In the late fifth century, however, the links between the originally complementary "acusmatic" and philosophical practices became tensions, and there appeared two Pythagorean schools—the *akousmatikoi* and the *mathēmatikoi.* The *akousmatikoi* were noted for their religious practices and way of life, while the *mathēmatikoi* were noted for their philosophical understanding and theories.

Pythagorean beliefs about the soul stand as the movement's specific contributions to the development of religious thought; Pythagoras and his followers, whether original or not, were the first in the Greek world to articulate fully and successfully to advance the understanding of a self beyond the empirical personality. Of greater significance than the Pythagorean conception of the soul, however, is the more general Pythagorean understanding about the ways and means of salvation, and about the possibilities of and the religious bindings on human life. With Pythagoras emerged the recognition that freedom was to be gained in a realm apart from a this-worldly existence, that the route of salvation was away from life and involved a process of disentanglement from the world's historical conditions. Pythagoras stood against the prevailing notion of his age that an afterlife was a lesser life; according to Pythagoras, and for good and ill concerning the subsequent development of Greek religious understanding, the religious "more" to life was not more life in the world but a liberation to a life in another world.

BIBLIOGRAPHY

The best source book in English containing the texts and fragments about Pythagoras is Cornelia J. de Vogel's *Greek Philosophy: A Collection of Texts,* vol. 1, *Thales to Plato* (Leiden, 1950). Two excellent background works, which place Pythagoras within the context of Greek religious thought, are E. R. Dodds's *The Greeks and the Irrational* (Berkeley, 1951) and Walter Burkert's *Greek Religion* (Cambridge, Mass., 1985). Edwin L. Minar's *Early Pythagorean Politics in Practice and Theory* (Baltimore, 1942) offers a summary of the Pythagorean *hetaireia.*

Interpretations about the meaning and significance of Pythagoras's thought are legion; what follows are texts representative of the basic interpretations with which the student of Pythagoras and Pythagoreanism should be familiar. Francis M. Cornford's "Mysticism and Science in the Pythagorean Tradition," *Classical Quarterly* 16 (1922): 137–150, is very good on defining the religious vision of Pythagoras, less so on Pythagorean "atomism"; J. E. Raven gives a controversial account of the development of Pythagorean thought in the fifth century in *Pythagoreans and Eleatics* (Cambridge, 1948). W. K. C. Guthrie's account of Pythagoras in *A History of Greek Philosophy,* vol. 1, *The Earlier Presocratics and Pythagoreans* (Cambridge, 1962), can be considered the standard general assessment on the subject. Other important works on Pythagoras are Walter Burkert's *Lore and Science in Ancient Pythagoreanism* (Cambridge, Mass., 1972), and James A. Philip's *Pythagoras and Early Pythagoreanism* (Toronto, 1966). Burkert offers probably the most detailed analysis of the Pythagorean religious understandings and practices. Philip, conversely, sees little evidence for a religious organization in early Pythagoreanism. Charles H. Kahn's "Pythagorean Philosophy before Plato," in *The Pre-Socratics,* edited by Alexander P. D. Mourelatos (Garden City, N.Y., 1974), pp. 161–185, provides a good summary of modern interpretations of Pythagoras, and a balanced overview of Pythagoras's religious and scientific holdings.

BENNETT RAMSEY

Q

QABBALAH. The term *Qabbalah* is derived from the Hebrew root *qbl,* which means "to receive"; in early medieval texts, *qabbalah* commonly signified "reception," namely a received tradition, mainly concerning halakhic matters. Since the early thirteenth century it has become the main term for Jewish mystical traditions, which deal almost exclusively with (1) a theosophical understanding of God combined with a symbolic view of reality and the theurgical conception of religious life, and (2) the way to attain a mystical experience of God through the invocation of divine names. These two traditions had much earlier roots, but the term *Qabbalah* refers in general to Jewish mysticism from the twelfth century onward. The following presentation will discuss the history of Qabbalah and its phenomenological aspects.

Historical Survey. The first written evidence of the existence of theosophical and theurgical thought in Judaism comes from Provence, in southern France, in the second half of the twelfth century. A series of well-known halakhic authorities, beginning with Avraham ben David of Posquières and Ya'aqov the Nazirite and later including Moses Nahmanides and his principal student, Shelomoh ben Avraham Adret, were full-fledged qabbalists, though their literary output in Qabbalah was minimal compared to their voluminous halakhic writings. Doubtless this situation is the result of a deliberate policy to keep Qabbalah an esoteric lore limited to a very small elite. However, at the beginning of the thirteenth century, the veil of esotericism began to disappear. Yitsḥaq Sagi Nahor (Yitsḥaq the Blind), Avraham ben David of Posquières's son, is known as the teacher of several qabbalists, of whom the best known are Yitsḥaq's nephew Asher ben David and 'Ezra' of Gerona. They committed to writing the first qabbalistic documents, which consist of commentaries on the cosmogonical treatise *Sefer yetsirah* and on *ma'aseh bere'shit* (the biblical account of creation), and explanations of the rationale for the commandments. During the same period, an important treatise called *Sefer ha-bahir* (The Book of Brightness), falsely ascribed to Neḥunya' ben ha-Qanah, a second-century mystic, began to circulate among Yitsḥaq's students. Although the qabbalistic doctrines incorporated into these works are presented in a fragmentary and obscure manner, it seems highly reasonable that they reflect more complex systems whose sources predated them by decades and even centuries.

In the middle of the thirteenth century, more extensive works were produced by Spanish qabbalists, who continued the major trends of their predecessors; the most important among them were 'Azri'el of Gerona and Ya'aqov ben Sheshet. After flourishing briefly in Catalonia, the center of qabbalistic creativity passed to Castile, where it underwent a renaissance. In Castile a circle of anonymous qabbalists produced a series of short treatises, known as the *'Iyyun* (speculation) literature, that combined ancient Merkavah literature (commentaries on the chariot vision in *Ezekiel*) with a Neoplatonic mysticism of light. Another group became interested in the theosophy of evil and described in detail the structure of the "other side," the demonic world. This circle included the brothers Ya'aqov and Yitsḥaq, the sons of Ya'aqov ha-Kohen; Mosheh of Burgos; and Ṭodros Abulafia. The quintessential ideas of these qabbalistic schools appear in the most important work of

Qabbalah, the *Zohar,* a collection of mystical writings that was circulated among the Castilian qabbalists beginning in 1280. Subsequently, between 1285 and 1335, the qabbalists produced many translations, commentaries, and imitations of the *Zohar,* mainly extant in manuscript, that contributed to the eventual acceptance of the *Zohar* as a canonic book.

Because of fierce controversy between the representative of the more conservative form of Qabbalah that preserved and transmitted older traditions, Shelomoh ben Avraham Adret, and Avraham Abulafia, the most important exponent of ecstatic Qabbalah, the creative and anarchic elements peculiar to the latter were rejected by adherents of Spanish Qabbalah, a fact that contributed to its overt stagnation in the latter part of the fourteenth century and most of the fifteenth century.

The expulsion of the Jews from Spain and Portugal in 1492 and 1497 respectively caused an exodus of important qabbalists from the Iberian peninsula to North Africa, Italy, and the Levant, thereby contributing to the dissemination of Qabbalah in those regions. Fifteenth-century Spanish Qabbalah, with the *Zohar* as its nucleus, became more and more influential in the new communities that were established by the expelled Jews and gradually developed into an important spiritual factor in Jewish life by the middle of the sixteenth century. The literary output of the first generation after the expulsion is remarkable, and several outstanding qabbalistic works were composed before the middle of the sixteenth century, including Yehudah Hayyat's *Minḥat Yehudah* in Italy and Me'ir ibn Gabbai's *'Avodat ha-qodesh* in the Ottoman empire. This generation of qabbalists was interested in preserving the esoteric traditions they had inherited in Spain; hence the eclectic nature of their writings. However, there were efforts to build up comprehensive speculative schemes in which the whole theosophic and cosmic chain of being was described. This work was undertaken by some Spanish qabbalists who systematically arranged older esoteric traditions, and by Italians such as Yoḥanan Alemanno, who combined philosophy, magic, and Qabbalah.

After the expulsion, a growing stream of qabbalists began arriving in Palestine. At the very beginning of the sixteenth century, Jerusalem became an important center of qabbalistic studies; its most famous members were Yehudah Albotini, Yosef ibn Saiaḥ, and Avraham ben Eli'ezer ha-Levi. Beginning in the 1540s, the small Galilean village of Safad rapidly acquired a dominant place in qabbalistic activity. For half a century, Safad was the arena of crucial developments in the history of Qabbalah. The arrival of two central figures from Turkey, Yosef Karo and Shelomoh ha-Levi Alkabets, prompted the establishment of mystical groups that formed the nuclei of intensive qabbalistic activities. Karo, the major halakhist of his time, produced a mystical diary dictated by a *maggid,* an angelic messenger who spoke from Karo's throat. Karo represents a Spanish qabbalistic trend that was primarily interested in incubational techniques to induce revelations in dreams. Alkabets, who had been close to Karo before their arrival, was aware of the philosophical perceptions of Qabbalah presented in David Messer Leon's work *Magen David* and seems to have been one of the major channels of the infiltration into Safad of Qabbalah developed by the Jews of the Italian Renaissance. However, the first towering qabbalist in Palestine was Mosheh Cordovero (1522–1570), the author of the *Pardes rimmonim* (1548), the most comprehensive exposition of all previous types of Qabbalah. He combined Spanish Qabbalah with ecstatic Qabbalah that was already flowering in Jerusalem. His clear and systematic presentation of all the major qabbalistic doctrines contributed to the immediate dissemination of his views, which remained influential for centuries, both in the Qabbalah of Isaac Luria and in Hasidism. Cordovero's main disciples, famous qabbalists themselves, were Ḥayyim Vital, Eliyyahu de Vidas, and El'azar Azikri. Through their literary activities—especially their moralistic works, which were intended for the public at large—they contributed to the further propagation of their master's doctrines.

A crucial development in qabbalistic theosophy occurred after Cordovero's death when one of his former students, Isaac Luria, rapidly moved to the center of the qabbalist community in Safad, where he became a profound influence through his saintly behavior, occult powers, and exposition of a novel type of theosophy. Luria's doctrines, commonly delivered orally to his disciples, elaborated upon some elements that had previously played a rather marginal role in the qabbalistic system. According to Luria, the initial movement in the process of creation consisted of the withdrawal of the all-pervading godhead into itself, leaving a point in which the world would come to exist. This withdrawal, or contraction *(tsimtsum),* made possible the elimination of "evil" elements inherent in the godhead. (The evil elements that left the godhead during *tsimtsum* formed the "material domain.") This cathartic event was followed by a series of emanations from the godhead that were intended to constitute the created world. As the emanations proceeded from their divine source, a catastrophic event occurred—the breaking of the vessels that carried them. Sparks of the divine light fell into the material domain where they were imprisoned in shells of matter. The task of the qabbalist was to liberate the sparks in order to reconstitute the divine configuration, the primordial man *(adam qadmon)*, a goal with eschatological overtones.

The success of Luria's thought was instantaneous; his theosophy was accepted unanimously by the former disciples of Cordovero, and his Qabbalah was regarded as superior to the Cordoverian system. With the premature death of Luria in 1572 his disciple, Ḥayyim Vital, committed Luria's views to writing, but Vital limited their dissemination to the small circle of qabbalists who recognized his leadership. In comparison to other authentic disciples of Luria, notably Yosef ibn Ṭabul and Mosheh Yonah, Vital was highly prolific; his best-known work was *'Ets ḥayyim* (Tree of Life). A rather different version of Luria's Qabbalah was brought to Italy during the 1590s by Yisra'el Sarug, a qabbalist who considered himself a disciple of Luria. He disseminated it through intensive oral and written activity, recruiting disciples from among former Cordoverian qabbalists. The most important exponent of the Sarugian version of Lurianism was Menaḥem 'Azaryah of Fano. Sarug's success was partly due to the speculative interpretations given by Sarug himself and by his disciple Avraham Herrera, who used Neoplatonic philosophy in his *Sha'ar ha-Shamayim* and *Beit Elohim.* Both Neoplatonic and atomistic views of Lurianic Qabbalah appeared in the work of Yosef Shelomoh Delmedigo of Kandia, another of Sarug's disciples.

During the seventeenth century, there was a clash between adherents of Vital's version of Lurianic Qabbalah and adherents of Sarug's version. Among the qabbalists, Vital's views prevailed in the compilations of Shemu'el Vital, Me'ir Poppers, and Ya'aqov Tsemaḥ.

The following centuries saw the development of various mixtures of Cordoverian and Lurianic doctrines. The theosophy of the followers of the seventeenth-century mystic and false messiah Shabbetai Tsevi was influenced mainly by Sarug's trend of thought; the theologies of eighteenth-century Polish Hasidism represented a revival of some of Cordovero's views, such as his view of prayer, at a period when Lurianic Qabbalah failed to supply appropriate answers.

Some central figures of the eighteenth century, were known as qabbalists; the most important among them were Eliyyahu ben Shelomoh Zalman, known as the gaon of Vilna (Vilnius) (1720–1797) and Ya'aqov Emden (1697–1776), who continued the Lurianic tradition, though not without some reservations. In the nineteenth century, major systematic presentations of Lurianism were composed by Yitsḥaq Eiziq Haver and Shelomoh Elyashar.

The dominant brand of Qabbalah in the modern qabbalistic *yeshivot* (traditional Jewish academies) is the Lurianic system. It is studied according to the interpretations offered by Mosheh Ḥayyim Luzzatto, by Eliyyahu ben Shelomoh Zalman, by Habad, the Lubavitch Hasidic movement, and by the Sefardic qabbalists of the Beit El Academy in Jerusalem. Avraham Yitsḥaq Kook (1865–1935) offered a pantheistic and mystical version of Qabbalah that tried to explain the secularism of many modern Jews as part of a larger scheme of religious evolution; his views had great influence. After the establishment of the state of Israel, and especially after 1967, the messianic overtones in Kook's thought were stressed by his son Yehudah Kook. David ha-Kohen the Ascetic (ha-Nazir), the most important figure in Kook's entourage, developed a peculiar type of mysticism in his *Qol ha-nevu'ah* that leaned heavily on the oral aspects of Jewish tradition. Some interest in Avraham Abulafia's ecstatic Qabbalah has been recently discerned in Hasidic circles.

Christian Qabbalah. Although Qabbalah was considered to be an esoteric lore that dealt with the secrets of the Law *(sitre Torah)* and was therefore peculiar to the Jewish people, it found its way into Christian thought. The first steps in the infiltration of Qabbalah were accomplished by converts to Christianity, of whom the most important were Abner of Burgos (Alfonso de Valladolid), who lived at the beginning of the fourteenth century; Paulus de Heredia, who lived in the second half of the fifteenth century; and Flavius Mithridates, who had by far the greatest impact. A teacher of the fifteenth-century Italian Christian humanist Giovanni Pico della Mirandola, Flavius translated a voluminous body of qabbalistic literature into Latin. His translations, which he intentionally distorted, represented the most important source for Pico's *Theses*, the first qabbalistic composition written by a Christian. Although he was the initiator of this new current of Christian thought, Pico did not write lengthy treatises on Qabbalah, but presented it as an ancient Jewish theology that foreshadowed, in a veiled manner, Christian tenets. He divided Qabbalah into a high form of legal magical lore and a low form of demonic magic. Besides these Christian and magical interpretations of Qabbalah, which owe much to the distorted translations of Mithridates, Pico interpreted Qabbalah philosophically, mainly using Neoplatonic sources previously translated into Latin by his friend Marsilio Ficino, as well as Hermetic Zoroastrian or Chaldean sources. These three perceptions of Qabbalah had a profound impact on the views that were developed by Pico's followers. Johannes Reuchlin, who studied Qabbalah under Pico's influence, produced in his *De arte cabalistica* the first systematic descriptions of Christian Qabbalah to be presented to the European public. In the early sixteenth century, theologians such as Egidio de Viterbo and Francesco

Giorgio expanded the philosophical and christological views of Qabbalah in influential treatises. The magical interpretation of Qabbalah reached its peak in Henri Cornelius Agrippa of Nettesheim's *De occulta philosophia.* Through the writings of these Italian and German authors, as well as artwork of Dürer, Qabbalah entered French and English literature and art in the second half of the sixteenth century. In the seventeenth century, Christian Knorr von Rosenroth's *Cabbala denudata,* a compendium of translations of important qabbalistic texts, was widely read by the European intelligentsia and it remained for a long time, together with John Pistorius's earlier *Artis cabalisticae,* the main source of the influence of Jewish esotericism on European thought. Philosophers like G. W. Leibniz and the Cambridge Neoplatonists in the seventeenth century, and writers like G. E. Lessing, Emanuel Swedenborg, and William Blake in the following century, absorbed qabbalistic ideas. The occult groups that flourished in eighteenth century central Europe were influenced by qabbalistic and Shabbatean thought. The impact of Zoharic Qabbalah is especially evident in the works of the nineteenth-century Theosophist H. P. Blavatsky. In the twentieth century, traces of Qabbalah can be found in the fiction and poetry of Franz Kafka, Yvan Goll, and Jorge Luis Borges, and in the cultural criticism of Walter Benjamin and the literary criticism of Harold Bloom and Jacques Derrida.

Phenomenological Survey. During the long history of Qabbalah, its adherents developed a variety of theosophical doctrine, symbolic systems, and methods of textual interpretation, some of them contradictory and paradoxical.

Qabbalistic theosophy. The Talmud and Midrash speak of two crucial attributes, the attribute of mercy *(middat ha-raḥamim)* and the attribute of stern judgment *(middat ha-din).* These divine qualities are believed to exist in a dynamic balance and to have been instrumental in the creation of the world and in its governance. In other texts, ten creative *logoi* or creative words (Heb., *ma'amarot)* are mentioned in this context; in *Sefer yetsirah,* the ten *sefirot* have a similar function. Pleromatic entities are also evident in the Merkavah literature. However, no detailed and systematic Jewish theosophy is extant before the composition of qabbalistic works at the beginning of the thirteenth century. Most qabbalists viewed the divinity as consisting of two layers: (1) the innermost, supreme godhead, Ein Sof (literally "the endless"), which is sometimes described in terms borrowed from the Neoplatonic negative theology and sometimes described in explicitly anthropomorphic terminology; and (2) the Sefirotic realm emanating from within the godhead as a pleromatic structure, that was said to be comprised of ten aspects, known variously as attributes *(middot),* potencies *(koḥot),* degrees *(ma'alot),* or, most frequently *sefirot* (literally "numbers"). These divine powers were conceived of as forming a supernatural man, or tree, that represents the revealed as well as the creative God. Figure 1 shows the commonly accepted set of names for the *sefirot,* although slight differences are known among qabbalists.

In some post-Lurianic texts, an additional *sefirah* was discussed, Da'at ("knowledge"), which is situated between the second and the third *sefirot,* and which plays a role similar to that of Tif'eret or Yesod, namely, a balance between two higher poles.

There were two main ideas of the nature of the *sefirot* among the qabbalists. The view expressed in the main body of the *Zohar* and by important qabbalists was that the *sefirot* constitute the essence of God and therefore are purely divine manifestations. Since the beginning of

FIGURE 1. *The Ten Divine Aspects, or Sefirot, in Their Symbolic Configuration*

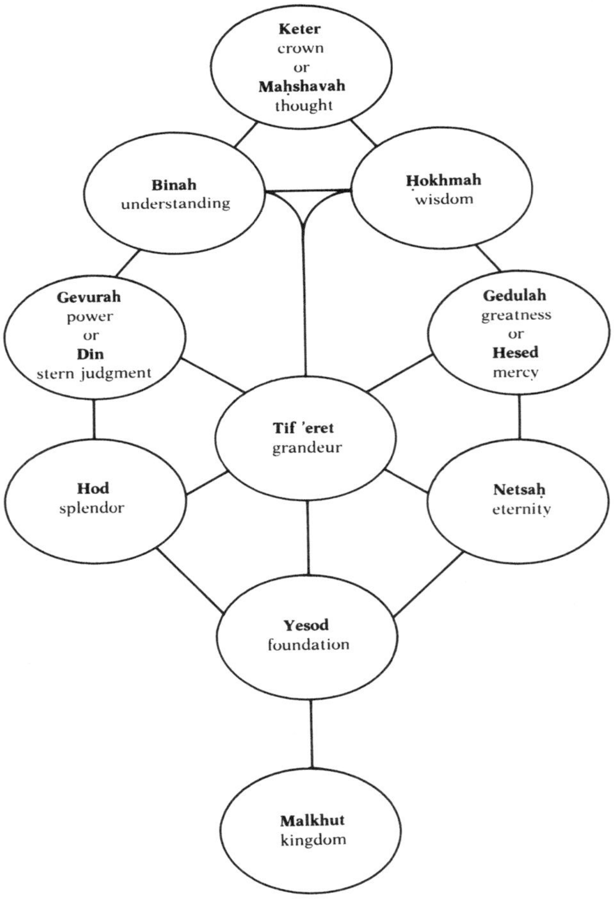

the fourteenth century, some qabbalists viewed the *sefirot* as vessels created by God to contain the divine efflux; according to a proximate view they are the instruments by which God created and governs the world. Mosheh Cordovero combined these two views, speaking of divine *sefirot* that are inherent in the external *sefirot*, with the latter functioning as vessels for the former. This approach became prevalent in later Qabbalah. Lurianic Qabbalah also developed a representation of the divine realm according to five anthropomorphic configurations *(partsufim)*, each composed of ten *sefirot*. Attempts were made in the Middle Ages to interpret the *sefirot* as symbols of human spiritual powers, and this tendency was adopted and strengthened by eighteenth century Hasidic masters.

Qabbalistic cosmogony recognized the existence of four worlds or realms of existence: the *sefirot*, called the world of emanation *('olam ha-atsilut)*; the world of creation *('olam ha-beri'ah)*, consisting of the divine chariot and higher angels; the world of formation *('olam ha-yetsirah)*, in which the angels are found; and the world of action *('olam ha-'asiyyah)*, the celestial and terrestrial material world. Under the impact of Sufism, some qabbalists mentioned a fivefold division that includes the world of images *('olam ha-demut)*.

Qabbalistic theurgy. One of the most important tenets of mainstream Qabbalah is the view that man can influence the inner structure of the godhead. By performing the commandments with the proper qabbalistic intention, man is capable of restoring the lost harmony between the lesser *sefirot*, Tif'eret and Malkhut, making possible the transmission of the divine efflux from the higher *sefirot* to our world. Moreover, man can draw this efflux from Ein Sof, the hidden divinity, downward to the *sefirot*. According to some early qabbalists, the very existence of the revealed divinity in the *sefirot* is the result of man's observance of the commandments, which, by drawing the efflux downward, counteracts the "natural" movement of the *sefirot* upward in their desire to return to their primordial status within the godhead. Qabbalistic observance of the commandments constitutes a theurgic activity, since its aim is the restructuring of God.

This view of the commandments represents a sophisticated presentation of an ancient trend in Jewish thought that found its earliest expression in Talmudic and Midrashic literature, in which God is sometimes presented as requesting Moses' blessing, desiring the prayer of the righteous, and even increasing or decreasing his power in accordance with the fulfillment or nonfulfillment of the commandments by Israel. With the emergence of Lurianic Qabbalah, the emphasis was transferred to the extraction of the divine sparks *(nitsotsot)* from the material, demonic world as a progressive eschatological activity whose ultimate aim is to restore the primeval anthropomorphic configuration of the divinity. This theurgy has obvious affinities to Manichaean theology and is phenomenologically different from Neoplatonic theurgy, which was focused mainly upon the performance of rituals intended to attract the gods to descend into statues from which they could deliver divinatory messages. In the same manner, qabbalistic theurgy differed from magical ceremony in both its means and its aims. The Qabbalah used biblical commandments to effect its goals rather than magical devices; and whereas magic is chiefly directed toward attaining material results needed by certain persons, qabbalistic activity was primarily intended to restore the divine harmony, and only secondarily to ensure the abundance of the supernatural efflux in this world.

These phenomenological differences notwithstanding, Neoplatonic types of theurgy, as well as various types of magic, infiltrated into qabbalistic systems at different stages of their development, although their influence never became dominant. An interesting blend of qabbalistic and Neoplatonic theurgies with magical practices was evident in late-fifteenth-century Spain where Yosef della Reina, a Faustian figure, attempted to facilitate the arrival of the messianic aeon by means of theurgico-magical activities.

Mystical techniques in Qabbalah. After the middle of the thirteenth century, qabbalists produced a series of treatises that discussed techniques for reaching ecstatic experiences and described such experiences. The most important representative of this trend was Avraham Abulafia (1240–c. 1291). In his numerous works, almost all of them still in manuscript form, he focused on complex devices for uniting with the Agent Intellect, or God, through the recitation of divine names, together with breathing techniques and cathartic practices. Some of Abulafia's mystic ways were adapted from the Ashkenazic Hasidic masters; Abulafia may also have been influenced by Yoga and Sufism. Taking as his framework the metaphysical and psychological system of Moses Maimonides (Mosheh ben Maimon, 1135/8–1204), Abulafia strove for spiritual experience, which he viewed as a prophetic state similar to or even identical with that of the ancient Jewish prophets. Furthermore, he perceived his attainment of such a state as an eschatological event, because he thought of himself as the Messiah. This spiritual and highly individualistic conception of salvation adumbrated the later Hasidic view of spiritual messianism. Abulafia's messianic pretensions led him to undertake such exploits as his unsuccessful attempt to discuss the true nature of Judaism with the pope.

Abulafia's prophetic and messianic pretensions prompted a sharp reaction on the part of Shelomoh ben Avraham Adret, a famous legal authority who succeeded in annihilating the influence of Abulafia's ecstatic Qabbalah in Spain. In Italy, however, his works were translated into Latin and contributed substantially to the formation of Christian Qabbalah. In the Middle East, ecstatic Qabbalah was accepted without reservation. Clear traces of Abulafian doctrine are evident in the works of Yitsḥaq ben Shemu'el of Acre and Yehudah Albotini. In Palestine, Abulafia's ideas were combined with Ṣūfī elements, apparently stemming from the school of Ibn Arabi; thus Ṣūfī views were introduced into European Qabbalah. After the expulsion of the Jews from Spain, Spanish theurgical Qabbalah, which had developed without any significant impact from ecstatic Qabbalah, was integrated with the latter; this combination became, through the book *Pardes rimmonim* by Mosheh Cordovero, part of mainstream Qabbalah. Ḥayyim Vital brought Abulafian views into his *Sha'arei qedushah*, and the eighteenth-century qabbalists of the Beit El Academy in Jerusalem perused Abulafia's mystical manuals. Later on, mystical and psychological conceptions of Qabbalah found their way directly and indirectly to the Polish Hasidic masters. The influence of ecstatic Qabbalah is to be seen in isolated groups today, and traces of it can be found in modern literature (e.g., the poetry of Yvan Goll), mainly since the publication of Gershom Scholem's researches.

Unio mystica. Theurgical Qabbalah assumes an independent and forceful human existence whose ritual activity can influence the sphere of divinity, though man and God remain, in principle, distinct and apart. However, even among the theurgical qabbalists the idea of a mystical union between man and God was known—as, for example, in the writings of 'Ezra' of Gerona—although it never came to the forefront. In the writings of Nahmanides and his followers, a distinction was made between the preliminary cleaving of reason to God *(devequt ha-da'at)* and the final cleaving of the soul to God. In contrast, nontheurgical Qabbalah of Avraham Abulafia focused upon the fusion of the human and the divine intellects as the supreme goal of the mystic; extreme literary expressions of this ideal used Hebrew forms of the Ṣūfī formula Huwa Huwa (he is he) or even *anokhi anokhi* ("I I"), which symbolized the complete union of God and man. Sometimes the qabbalists referred to mystical union with the Active Intellect, thereby giving a mystical interpretation to the psychology developed by the Islamic philosopher Ibn Rushd. They also borrowed Aristotelian concepts of intellect, intellection, and intelligibles (which form a unity during the act of thinking) to describe mystical union. Explicit unitive phenomena were reported in the writings of Yitsḥaq of Acre, and under the latter's influence and that of Abulafia expressions of *unio mystica* were included in Safadian texts, which turned out to be one of the most important sources for the eighteenth-century Hasidic masters in their search for union with God.

Eschatology. Qabbalah developed eschatological themes considerably. Traditional messianic views contributed only marginally to qabbalistic eschatology. Under the influence of Neoplatonic or Aristotelian psychologies, the qabbalists regarded individual salvation as the ultimate spiritual achievement. Under the influence of Islamic sources, they developed the idea that cosmic processes operate in cycles of seven thousand *(shemiṭṭah)* and forty-nine thousand *(yovel)* years, with each cycle culminating in a thousand years of total rest; each millennium—or, according to other sources, seven millennia—is governed by a separate *sefirah* that influences the processes taking place during this span of time. These qabbalistic views were integrated into the well-known work *Dialoghi d'amore* by Judah Abravanel (Leone Ebreo), through which they entered general European culture. Lengthy discussions on various types of metempsychosis *(gilgul)*, or the transmigration of souls, are found in Qabbalah from the very beginning. Metempsychosis was regarded mainly as an opportunity given to a sinner to amend his former sins and rarely as a purgative period.

Qabbalistic hermeneutics. Two major methods of interpretation used in Qabbalah are the symbolic and the mathematical. The former is paramount in theurgical and theosophical Qabbalah, which considered the scriptures, the phenomena of nature, and the events of history to be symbols for the dynamic and continuous changes taking place within God. The symbolization of the whole of reality enabled the qabbalists to give theosophical significance to virtually every event and, through the "intentional" performance of the commandments, to participate mystically in the divine life. The various possibilities of symbolic interpretation changed the scriptures into an "open text" pregnant with infinite meanings. With the appearance of the *Zohar*, symbols referring to the erotic union of Tif'eret and Malkhut, and those pointing to the demonic world (the *siṭra' aḥra'*), became more central. Since the late thirteenth century, a fourfold division of interpretation has been accepted by qabbalists.

Under the influence of Ashkenazic Hasidism of the thirteenth century, the ecstatic Qabbalah used such hermeneutical devices as gimaṭriyyah, the calculation of the numerical value of letters; *notariqon*, the use of letters as abbreviations for whole words; and *temurah*, the interchanging of letters. Abulafia developed a sevenfold system of hermeneutics that culminated in an ecstatic experience.

Literary Genres. Qabbalah, like other bodies of Jewish literature, produced exegetical genres. Qabbalists tended to comment upon the traditional canonic texts, although they chose to discuss issues peculiar to the Qabbalah.

The qabbalists produced more than 150 commentaries on the *sefirot* containing lists of symbols that referred to each of the ten divine potencies. These commentaries were handbooks intended to instruct novices in the relations between all the elements of reality—canonic texts, human life, and the supernatural forces. This genre flourished from the thirteenth to the sixteenth centuries. Qabbalistic commentaries on the Pentateuch had a great impact on the propagation of Qabbalah. Tens of these commentaries are extant. The most important are those of Nahmanides, Baḥye ben Asher, Menaḥem Recanati, Avraham Saba, and Ḥayyim ben Attar. Almost every important qabbalistic school produced its own commentary on the daily liturgy, thereby introducing novel theoretical elements into the common religious activity. This vast body of literature, which is partly extant in manuscripts, still requires an extensive critical analysis.

Since its beginning, Qabbalah expressed itself through numerous commentaries on the rationale for the commandments, the most important of which are still unpublished. The qabbalists also produced commentaries on *Sefer yetsirah*, commentaries on the *Zohar*, and works of moralistic literature that were deeply influenced by Cordovero's views and that contributed to the infiltration of the qabbalistic *via mystica* among the Jewish masses. The greater part of the extant qabbalistic literature, including thousands of folios, has not been examined in detail and has not been the subject of critical analysis.

External Influences. Some modern scholars, such as Naḥman Krochmal in the early nineteenth century and Gershom Scholem in the twentieth, viewed Qabbalah as having been influenced by gnostic concepts, although no hard evidence has been adduced to substantiate this assumption. The influence of Islamic and Christian Neoplatonism on early Qabbalah is indeed evident and was recognized by such opponents of Qabbalah as Eliyyahu Delmedigo and Yehudah Aryeh Modena (Leone de Modena) as early as the Renaissance period. The thesis proposed by Shulamit Shahar about the influence of Catharism on *Sefer ha-bahir* and Avraham Abulafia has not been confirmed by further studies. The qabbalistic view of evil seems to stem from older texts whose ultimate source was probably Iranian, perhaps Zurvanian. Renaissance Neoplatonism influenced the philosophical interpretation of Qabbalah in the early seventeenth century, but that trend remained without major influence on Jewish Qabbalah.

Although Qabbalah was flexible enough to enrich itself through the acceptance of external ideas, the latter never became dominant factors in its spiritual physiognomy. Through the process of absorption, the alien elements were adapted to the peculiar need of the comprehensive ideological system.

Philosophical Interpretation of Qabbalah. An important tendency in some qabbalistic writings is the philosophical interpretation of its theosophical and theurgical concepts. This tendency is evident from the middle of the thirteenth century in the works of ʿAzriʾel of Gerona and Yitsḥaq ibn Latif. It came to the forefront in the middle of the fourteenth century, when an array of Spanish authors formed a rather homogenous intellectual current into which Qabbalah was blended by means of concepts derived from the Islamic philosophers Ibn Rushd and Ibn Sīnā. The most important figures of this trend were Yosef ibn Vaqar and Shemu'el ibn Motot. However, from the beginning of the fifteenth century this philosophical Qabbalah was rejected by the Spanish qabbalists, who now focused their interest on the "pure" theurgical views of the *Zohar*. In the last decades of that century, the philosophical interpretation of Qabbalah became prominent in northern Italy, mostly in the writings of Yoḥanan Alemanno, David Messer Leon, Yitsḥaq of Pisa, and Isaac Abravanel and his son Judah. The influence of this philosophical interpretation can be discerned in the Ottoman empire, Safad, central Europe, and eastern Europe. At the end of the sixteenth century and early in the seventeenth, important authors such as Avraham Herrera, Avraham Yagel, Yosef Delmedigo, and Menasseh ben Israel made extensive use of ancient texts translated during the Renaissance in order to interpret Cordoverian and Lurianic Qabbalah. Through the works of Menasseh ben Israel and the Latin translation of Avraham Herrera's *Shaʿar ha-shamayim*, this qabbalistic trend found its way into Christian Qabbalah and thus influenced European philosophy. The latest important repercussions of this trend are to be found in the period of the Enlightenment, in the writings of Salomon Maimon and Isaac Satanov, and later on in the works of modern Jewish theologians such as Franz Rosenzweig.

This type of Qabbalah commonly mitigated or even totally nullified the mythical elements that are paramount in mainstream Qabbalah, including the theurgical nature of the commandments, processes by which God's internal life unfolds, and messianic eschatology.

For this reason, representatives of philosophical Qabbalah never became influential in Jewish theology.

[*For further discussion of two basic qabbalistic works, see* Sefer Yetsirah *and* Zohar. *On movements affected by Qabbalah, see* Ashkenazic Hasidism; Hasidism; *and* Messianism, *article on* Jewish Messianism. *See also the biographies of Shabbetai Tsevi, leader of a sixteenth-century messianic movement, and of such major qabbalistic figures as Shelomoh ben Avraham Adret, Isaac Luria, and Moses Nahmanides. The great historian of Qabbalah, Gershom Scholem, is also the subject of a separate entry.*]

BIBLIOGRAPHY

Altmann, Alexander. *Studies in Religious Philosophy and Mysticism.* Ithaca, N.Y., 1969. Pioneering studies in qabbalistic history of ideas.

Altmann, Alexander. *Panim shel Yahadut.* Tel Aviv, 1983. Contains a major contribution to the phenomenology of Qabbalah.

Ben-Shlomo, Joseph. *Torat ha-elohut shel R. Mosheh Cordovero.* Jerusalem, 1965. The most extensive analysis of the thought of an important qabbalist.

Dan, Joseph, and Frank Talmage, eds. *Studies in Jewish Mysticism.* Cambridge, Mass., 1982.

Gottlieb, Efraim. *Meḥqarim be-sifrut ha-Qabbalah.* Edited by Joseph Hacker. Tel Aviv, 1976. On the history and phenomenology of early Qabbalah.

Idel, Moshe. "Kitvei R. Avraham Abulafia u-mishnato." 2 vols. Ph.D. diss., Hebrew University of Jerusalem, 1976. A study of ecstatic Qabbalah.

Scholem, Gershom. *Major Trends in Jewish Mysticism.* 3d ed. New York, 1961. Includes chapters on the various phases of Jewish mysticism and Qabbalah, with an extensive bibliography.

Scholem, Gershom. *On the Kabbalah and Its Symbolism.* New York, 1965. Indispensable for understanding qabbalistic phenomenology.

Scholem, Gershom. *Les origines de la Kabbale.* Paris, 1966. Discusses the first manifestations of Qabbalah in Europe.

Scholem, Gershom. *The Messianic Idea in Judaism.* New York, 1971. Important for the history of messianism.

Scholem, Gershom. *Kabbalah.* New York, 1974. Summary of Scholem's numerous studies, with a full bibliography.

Tishby, Isaiah. *Torat ha-ra' ve-ha-qelippah be-qabbalat ha-Ari* (1942). Jerusalem, 1984. Most important for understanding Lurianism.

Tishby, Isaiah. *Netivei emunah u-minut.* Tel Aviv, 1964. Studies in later Qabbalah and its phenomenology.

Tishby, Isaiah. *Ḥiqrei Qabbalah ve-shiluḥoteyah: meḥqarim umeqorot,* vol. 1. Jerusalem, 1982. Studies in central events of early and later Qabbalah.

Vajda, Georges. *Recherches sur la philosophie et la Kabbale dans la pensée juive du Moyen Age.* Paris, 1962. Major contribution to the analysis of neglected material.

Vajda, Georges, ed. and trans. *Le commentarie de Ezra de Gérone sur le Cantique des Cantiques.* Paris, 1969. Important for understanding of early Qabbalah.

Werblowsky, R. J. Zwi. *Joseph Karo: Lawyer and Mystic.* London, 1962. Analysis of the mystical component of a central figure of Jewish culture.

Wirszubski, Chaim. *Sheloshah peraqim be-toledot ha-Qabbalah ha-notsrit* and *Mequbbal notsri qore' be-Torah.* Jerusalem, 1975 and 1977. Two booklets that include pioneering researches into Pico della Mirandola's Qabbalah.

MOSHE IDEL

QĀḌĪ. A *qāḍī* is a judge responsible for the application of Islamic positive law *(fiqh).* The office originated under the rule of the first Umayyad caliphs (AH 40–85/661–705 CE), when the provincial governers of the newly created Islamic empire, unable to adjudicate the many disputes that arose among Muslims living within their territories, began to delegate this function to others. In this early period of Islamic history, no body of Islamic positive law had yet come into existence, and the first *qāḍīs* therefore decided cases on the basis of the only guidelines available to them: Arab customary law, the laws of the conquered territories, the general precepts of the Qur'ān, and their own sense of equity. During the later Umayyad period (705–750 CE), a growing class of Muslim legal scholars, distinct from the *qāḍīs,* busied themselves with the task of supplying the needed body of law, and by the time of the accession to power of the Abbasid dynasty in 750 their work could be said to have been essentially completed. In constructing their legal doctrine, these legal scholars took as their point of departure the precedents already established by the *qāḍīs,* some of which they rejected as inconsistent with Islamic principles as these were coming to be understood, but most of which they adopted, with or without modification. Thus the first *qāḍīs* in effect laid the foundations of Islamic positive law. Once this law had been formed, however, the role of the *qāḍī* underwent a profound change. No longer free to follow the guidelines mentioned above, a *qāḍī* was now expected to adhere solely to the new Islamic law, and this adherence has characterized the office ever since.

A *qāḍī* continued, however, to be a delegate of a higher authority, ultimately the caliph or, after the demise of the caliphate, the supreme ruler in a given territory. This delegate status implies the absence of a separation of powers; both judicial and executive powers were concentrated in the person of the supreme ruler (caliph or otherwise). On the other hand, a certain degree of autonomy was enjoyed by a *qāḍī* in that the law that he applied was not the creation of the supreme ruler or the expression of his will. What a *qāḍī* owed to the supreme ruler was solely the power to apply the law, for which sanctions were necessary that only the supreme ruler as head of the state could guarantee.

The qualifications that a *qāḍī* must possess are stated in the law, although the law is not uniform on this subject. The minimal requirement upon which all the jurists agree is that a *qāḍī* possess the same qualifications as a witness in court, that is, that he be free, sane, adult, trustworthy, and a Muslim. Some require that he also possess the qualifications of a jurist, that is, that he be well versed in the law, while others regard those qualifications as simply preferable, implying that a person may effectively discharge the duties of the office without being well versed in the law. This latter position presupposed that a *qāḍī* who is not learned in matters of law would consult those who are before reaching a decision. Indeed, consultation was urged upon the learned *qāḍī* as well, since even the learned are fallible and can profit from the views of others. Those consulted did not, however, have a voice in the final decision making. The Islamic court was a strictly one-judge court and the final decision rested upon the shoulders of a single *qāḍī*.

The jurisdiction of a *qāḍī* was theoretically coextensive with the scope of the law that he applied. That law was fundamentally a law for Muslims, and the internal affairs of the non-Muslim, or *dhimmī*, communities living within the Islamic state were left under the jurisdictions of those communities. Islamic law governed *dhimmī*s only with respect to their relations to Muslims and to the Islamic state. In actual practice, however, the jurisdiction of a *qāḍī* was hemmed in by what must be regarded as rival jurisdictions, particularly that of the *maẓālim* court and that of the *shurṭah*. The former was a court (presided over by the supreme ruler himself or his governor) that heard complaints addressed to it by virtually any offended party. Since Islamic law did not provide for any appellate jurisdiction but regarded the decision of a *qāḍī* as final and irrevocable, the *maẓālim* court could function as a kind of court of appeals in cases where parties complained of unfair decisions from *qāḍī*s. The *maẓālim* judge was not bound to the rules of Islamic law *(fiqh)*, nor for that matter was he bound to any body of positive law, but was free to make decisions entirely on the basis of considerations of equity. The *maẓālim* court thus provided a remedy for the inability of a *qāḍī* to take equity freely into account. It also made up for certain shortcomings of Islamic law, for example, the lack of a highly developed law of torts, which was largely due to the preoccupation of the law with breaches of contracts. In addition, it heard complaints against state officials. The *shurṭah*, on the other hand, was the state apparatus responsible for criminal justice. It too provided a remedy for a deficiency in the law, namely the incompleteness and procedural rigidity of its criminal code. Although in theory a *qāḍī* exercised a criminal jurisdiction, in practice this jurisdiction was removed from his sphere of competence and turned over entirely to the *shurṭah*, which developed its own penalties and procedures. What was left to the *qāḍī* was a jurisdiction concerned mainly with cases having to do with inheritance, personal status, property, and commercial transactions. Even within this jurisdiction, a particular *qāḍī*'s jurisdiction could be further restricted to particular cases or types of cases at the behest of the appointing superior.

The principle of delegation of judicial powers not only allowed the supreme ruler to delegate these powers to a *qāḍī*; it also allowed *qāḍī*s to further delegate them to others, and there was in principle no limit to this chain of delegation. All persons in the chain, except for the supreme ruler or his governor, bore the title *qāḍī*. Although in theory the appointment of a *qāḍī* could be effected by a simple verbal declaration on the part of the appointing superior, normally it was accomplished by means of a written certificate of investiture, which obviated the need for the appointee to appear in the presence of the superior. The appointment was essentially unilateral rather than contractual and did not require acceptance on the part of the appointee in order to be effective. It could be revoked at any time.

The Abbasids created the office of chief *qāḍī* *(qāḍī al-quḍāh)*, whose holder acted primarily as adviser to the caliph in the appointment and dismissal of *qāḍī*s. Later Islamic states generally retained this office, while granting to its holder the authority to issue appointments and dismissals in his own name. The Mamluk state, which ruled Egypt and Syria from 1250 to 1516 CE, introduced the practice of appointing four chief *qāḍī*s, one for each of the Sunnī legal schools (*madhhab*s).

Although the primary responsibility of a *qāḍī* was a judicial one, he was generally charged with certain nonjudicial responsibilities as well, such as the administration of religious endowments (*waqf*s), the legitimization of the accession or deposition of a ruler, the execution of wills, the accreditation of witnesses, guardianship over orphans and others in need of protection, and supervision of the enforcement of public morals *(ḥisbah)*.

BIBLIOGRAPHY

Schacht, Joseph. *An Introduction to Islamic Law.* Oxford, 1964.
Tyan, Emile. "Judicial Organization." In *Law in the Middle*

East, vol. 1, edited by Majid Khadduri and Herbert J. Liebesny, pp. 236–278. Washington, D.C., 1955.

Tyan, Emile. *Histoire de l'organization judiciaire en pays d'Islam.* 2d ed. Leiden, 1960.

BERNARD G. WEISS

QARĀMIṬAH (sg., Qarmaṭī) is the name applied to a dissident Muslim group that broke away from the parent Ismā'īlī movement. At first, this name referred to the followers of Ḥamdān al-Qarmaṭ, an Ismā'īlī *dā'ī* (missionary) in the rural district of Kufa, who was given the surname Qarmaṭ (meaning either that he was short-legged or red-eyed). Later the term was used in a wider and derogatory sense to include all the Ismā'īlīyah.

Background. The missionary activities of Ḥamdān, who was converted to the Ismā'īlī cause by the *dā'ī* Ahwāzī, began around 873. He was assisted by his deputy and brother-in-law, 'Abdān. In 899, because of change in the central leadership of the Ismā'īlī movement and the doctrinal issue involved in this change, Ḥamdān severed his relations with the leadership. Shortly thereafter he disappeared, and 'Abdān was murdered by his subordinate *dā'ī* Zikrawayh, who at first showed loyalty to the central leadership. When Zikrawayh was threatened with revenge by 'Abdān's followers he went into hiding. In 902 Zikrawayh's son succeeded in winning the support of tribes in the Syrian desert and attacked and pillaged several cities in Syria. Two years later he was captured and executed. After several unsuccessful attempts at organizing revolts, Zikrawayh himself came out of hiding in 906 and defeated the Abbasid army, but the following year he was routed and killed, and the Qarmaṭī revolts in Syria came to an end.

The split of the Ismā'īlīyah into two factions profoundly affected the loyalty of the various *da'wah* (mission) groups to the central leadership. The *da'wah* in Syria-Mesopotamia and western Persia refused to recognize the Fatimid claims to the imamate and instead supported the Qarāmiṭah. The *da'wah* in Yemen at first remained loyal to the central leadership, but in 913 'Alī ibn al-Faḍl renounced his allegiance to the Fatimids and began waging war against his companion Manṣūr al-Yaman, who had remained loyal to them. Because of internal strife the political power of the Qarāmiṭah disintegrated rapidly. The *dā'īs* in Rayy, who were successful in gaining the support of the Daylamīs and some rulers of the Musafirid dynasty, maintained their contacts with the Qarāmiṭah.

Qarāmiṭah of Bahrein. Abū Sa'īd al-Jannābī, the founder of the Qarmaṭī state in Bahrein (the coastal area of eastern Arabia between Basra and Oman, embracing the oases of al-Qaṭīf and Hajar/al-Ḥasā), who was sent by Ḥamdān al-Qarmaṭ and 'Abdān, began his missionary activity in 886/7. Following the murder of 'Abdān, he sided with the rebels against the central leadership and plotted the murder of the *dā'ī* Ẓamāmī, who had been sent to Bahrein before him by Manṣūr al-Yaman from Yemen and who had remained loyal to the central leadership. He himself was murdered in 913. In 923, under the leadership of Abū Ṭāhir, the son of Abū Sa'īd, the Qarāmiṭah launched devastating attacks on southern Iraq and raided pilgrim caravans. Then, interpreting the conjunction of Jupiter and Saturn in 928 as a sign indicating the end of the Islamic era and the beginning of the final era, Abū Ṭāhir predicted the appearance of the Mahdi (messiah) in the near future. In 927–929 he led new attacks on southern Iraq and threatened the Abbasid capital of Baghdad itself. In 930 he attacked the holy city of Mecca during the pilgrimage season, committed slaughter, and carried away the Black Stone of the Ka'bah, thus demonstrating the end of the Islamic era. The following year he handed over his reign to a Persian youth from Isfahan in whom he recognized the expected Mahdi, but events took an entirely unexpected turn when the Persian ordered the cursing of all the prophets and instituted the worship of fire. When the Persian encouraged certain extravagant abominations and executed prominent Qarmaṭī leaders, Abū Ṭāhir plotted his murder and admitted that he had been duped by the youth. This episode demoralized his followers. Consequently, the Iraqi Qarāmiṭah, who had escaped from the Abbasid army and had joined Abū Ṭāhir, left Bahrein. Many apostatized, disclosing their secrets, and some tribal leaders joined the army of the Sunnī rulers. Abū Ṭāhir nevertheless continued to raid southern Iraq until his death in 944.

After the death of Abū Ṭāhir his brothers ruled jointly, and in 951 they returned the Black Stone for a high sum paid by the Abbasids. The Fatimid caliph al-Mu'izz li-Dīn Allāh (953–975) failed in an effort to bring the Qarāmiṭah of Bahrein back to the Ismā'īlī/Fatimid fold. Open hostilities broke out after the Fatimid conquest of Egypt, when their army advanced to northern Syria, provoking the Qarāmiṭah, who had their own interests in Syria. Temporary alliances were formed when the Qarāmiṭah were aided by the Buyids of Baghdad and the Hamdanids of Syria against the common enemy, the Fatimids. Subsequently, the Qarāmiṭah threatened the Fatimid capital of Cairo, but they were defeated both times. As their relations with Baghdad became strained they renewed their attacks on southern Iraq. In 988 the Abbasid army inflicted a crushing defeat on the Qarāmiṭah; their capital, al-Ḥasā, was besieged; and al-Qaṭīf was pillaged. When they were defeated and reduced to local power they renewed their nominal allegiance to the Fatimids in return for a tribute, but these relations did not last long. Gradually, the Qarmaṭī communities outside of Bahrein were either absorbed by the Ismāʿīlīyah or disintegrated. In 1067 they lost the island of Uwāl, and soon thereafter al-Qaṭīf was lost. Finally, in 1077–1078, after a long siege al-Ḥasā was lost to an emerging local tribe that was aided by the Seljuks of Baghdad, thus ending the Qarmaṭī rule of almost two centuries.

Teachings. The basic tenet of Qarmaṭī doctrine was the appearance of Muḥammad ibn Ismāʿīl as the seventh *nāṭiq* ("apostle" of God), the Mahdi, al-Qā'im (the Redeemer), who would abrogate the *sharīʿah* (Muslim canon law) and promulgate the *bāṭin* (inner truth of religion). The doctrine carries an antinomian tendency. The reports of historians that the Qarāmiṭah dispensed with Islamic ritual and law are therefore correct, but other accusations, of licentiousness and libertinism, are not true. Abū Ḥātim al-Rāzī (d. 934/5), Abū al-Ḥasan al-Nasafī (d. 943), and Abū Yaʿqūb al-Sijistānī (d. after 971) are some of the illustrious *dāʿīs* who have elaborated Qarmaṭī doctrine.

The Qarāmiṭah drew a fundamental distinction between the *ẓāhir* ("exoteric") and the *bāṭin* ("esoteric"), the two aspects of religion. The former consists of external aspects of religion as laid down in the religious law and explains the apparent meaning of the Qur'ān. The *ẓāhir* changes, therefore, with each prophet in accordance with time and circumstance. The *bāṭin* is comprised of the inner, true meaning of the law and the Qur'ān. It remains unchanged.

The Qarāmiṭah formulated a new synthesis of reason and revelation based on Neoplatonic cosmology and Shīʿī doctrine. Thus, they offered a new world order under the imam, who resembles Plato's philosopher-king. The classic formulation of this synthesis is found in the well-known encyclopedic work entitled *Rasā'il Ikhwān al-Ṣafā'* (Epistles of the Brethren of Purity). The Qarāmiṭah viewed history as a developmental process that progresses through seven major cycles, each containing seven minor cycles. The length of these cycles varies. In conjunction with the cyclical view of the Qarāmiṭah history also had a notion of different epochs, according to which the seven major cycles progress through three different epochs: *dawr al-kashf* ("epoch of unveiling"), *dawr al-fatrah* ("epoch of langor"), and *dawr al-satr* ("epoch of occultation"). During the first epoch good prevails, hence there is no need for external law, and the *bāṭin* is promulgated openly. This is followed by the second epoch, during which goodness loses its hold over the people and religion becomes corrupted. At the end of this period begins the third epoch, when the prophet receives the revelation and lays down the law. The prophet then appoints his successor, known as *waṣī* ("plenipotentiary"), who promulgates the *bāṭin*. The imams during this epoch remain hidden. At the end, when the people are ready, al-Qā'im appears and abrogates the law; he thus becomes the first imam of the following epoch of unveiling. These cycles are repeated until all souls are emancipated from matter and return to the Universal Soul.

Historical and Social Significance. The Qarāmiṭah were a powerful movement that shook Sunnī Islam, threatened the Abbasid caliphate, and terrorized southern Iraq. They had such an enormous influence in the region that during the Buyid supremacy in Baghdad the Qarāmiṭah had their own customhouse in the port of Basra alongside that of the Abbasid government. Their representatives resided in Baghdad, Kufa, and Jaʿfarīyah and wielded considerable influence. Sunnī Muslim authors considered them a heretic group led by people of the faiths superseded by Islam in order to undermine the latter from within. The general accusation against them that they practiced communism of goods and women is false; however, the shift in their opponents' arguments from theological issues to economic ones does indicate that they were perceived as a social threat.

The Qarāmiṭah constituted a messianic movement promising a better future with the rule of justice and equity; hence the social character of their preaching is undeniable. The famous historian al-Ṭabarī (d. 923) observes that the Qarāmiṭah consisted mainly of peasants and tillers. Their support came from rural areas and from the bedouin. Although the backbone of the army consisted of ablebodied Qarāmiṭah who were trained militarily, bedouin tribesmen joined them regularly for military campaigns. Some tribes, such as Banū Kilāb and Banū ʿUqayl, were integrated into the Qarmaṭī community. They did experiment with communal ownership of property, but those experiments remained peripheral. Their concern for the welfare of their community produced a unique experiment in the state of Bahrein. Its order and justice even evoked the admiration of non-Qarmaṭī travelers. Ibn Ḥawqal, who visited Bahrein in the latter half of the tenth century, makes interesting observations on its political structure. According to his account, the Qarmaṭī state was very much like an oligarchic republic. The ruler was not absolute and ruled with the aid of a ruling council comprised of important government officials and his own close associates. Following Abū Ṭāhir's death, the leadership was held collectively by his brothers.

Ibn Ḥawqal also describes the various taxes and tolls by which the state raised its revenue, and the distribution of these revenues among the ruling council. Income from grain and fruit estates was assigned to the Qarmaṭī community, while the revenues from customs on the island of Uwāl were allocated to Abū Sa'īd and his descendants. All other revenues from taxes, tribute, protection fees paid by the pilgrim caravans, and booty from military campaigns were disposed of in agreement with the ruling council after setting aside one-fifth for the Mahdi.

Nāṣir-i Khusraw, a Persian Ismā'īlī who visited Bahrein in the eleventh century, makes the following observations. There were in al-Ḥasā more than twenty thousand inhabitants capable of bearing arms. Though the inhabitants acknowledged the prophethood of Muḥammad, they observed neither fasts nor prayers. The ruling council ruled with equity and justice; it owned thirty thousand black slaves who did agricultural labor. No taxes were paid by the inhabitants, and any impoverished person could obtain a loan without interest. New artisans arriving there were given loans to establish themselves. Repairs for poor homeowners were done by the state. Grain was ground free of charge in the mills owned by the state. There were no mosques, but a foreign merchant was allowed to build a mosque for the use of Muslim visitors. People did not drink wine.

The fourth century of Islamic history, known for the flowering of Islamic civilization, witnessed a dramatic Shī'ī ascendancy to power, with the Fatimids in North Africa and Egypt and the Buyids in Baghdad. It was during this period that the Qarāmiṭah, representing a powerful, radical revolutionary movement, also succeeded in establishing their state in Bahrein. This state exemplifies their rule of justice and equity.

BIBLIOGRAPHY

The surviving fragments of Qarmaṭī writings from early historical works are collected, along with extracts from later works, in *Ta'rīkh akhbār al-Qarāmiṭah*, edited by Souhayl Zakkar (Beirut, 1971). The best modern studies are by Wilferd Madelung, S. M. Stern, and Vladimir A. Ivanov. Madelung's article "Ḳarmaṭī" in the new edition of *The Encyclopaedia of Islam* (Leiden, 1960–) contains an excellent bibliography.

ISMAIL K. POONAWALA

QIYĀS ("analogy") is a method of reasoning that entails the extension of a precedent to an essentially similar situation. One of the four principal sources of law among Sunnī Muslims, *qiyās* was the last to gain explicit recognition, and then only after a fierce controversy that has left its mark on the history of Islam. The expansion of the territorial domains of Islam after the great conquests raised an increasing variety of issues not covered by the Qur'ān or the *sunnah* (tradition of the prophet Muḥammad). Islamic jurists, therefore, felt the need to have recourse to reason, logic, and opinion. Their freedom was, however, limited. In a society committed to the authority of the revelation, the use of personal opinion *(ra'y)* in religious and legal matters evoked opposition. In theory, the Qur'ān contained a complete revelation and, supplemented by the *sunnah*, was considered to respond to all eventualities. To admit any source of law other than the Qur'ān and the *sunnah* meant the renunciation of the ideal of founding the individual and collective life of Muslims exclusively on divine revelation. To overcome this difficulty, the theory of *qiyās* was elaborated with a view to restricting and setting formal limits on the use of *ra'y*.

The argument in favor of *qiyās* is based on the juristic premise that divine prescriptions follow certain objectives and have effective causes that can be ascertained and applied to similar cases. The opponents of *qiyās*, however, challenged this view by emphasizing that divine prescriptions have no causes except when these are specifically indicated. Besides, distinguishing the effective cause of a ruling involves doubt, and legal rules must not be based on doubt. In the view of the challengers, the proper conduct in response to the divine prescriptions is to accept them with devotion and without attempting to determine causes. It was on the strength of these arguments that the Ẓāhirīyah and the Akhbārī branch of the Twelver Shī'ah rejected *qiyās* altogether, and the Ḥanābilah permitted its use only in cases of dire necessity.

Neither the Qur'ān nor the *sunnah* refers directly to *qiyās*. The jurists have resorted to both, however, in supporting their arguments for or against *qiyās*. Its opponents argued that *qiyās* is alien to the Qur'ān, which says "We have sent to you the Book as an explanation for everything" (16:89) and "In whatever you differ, the verdict therein belongs to God" (42:10). They also contended that analogy is a conjecture and that "surely conjecture avails not aught against truth" (53:28). They concluded that *qiyās* is not legal evidence and that action upon it is null and void.

The defenders of *qiyās* argued that the Qur'ān stipulates "As for these similitudes, we cite them for mankind, but none will grasp their meaning save the wise" (29:43) and "Learn a lesson, O you who have vision to see" (59:2). They held the view that *qiyās* is essential to appreciate and evaluate the similitudes. Furthermore, on two occasions, when Muḥammad sent Mu'ādh ibn Jabal and Abū Mūsā al-Ash'arī as judges to the Yemen, the Prophet is reported to have sanctioned the exercise of *ra'y* in the absence of guidance in the Qur'ān and the *sunnah*.

Although *qiyās* as a technical formula was elaborated

in the second century AH (eighth century CE), evidence suggests that the companions of the Prophet approved of it in principle. For example, the caliph ʿUmar's directive to Abū Mūsā al-Ashʿarī reads "Know the similitudes and weigh the cases against them." Again, when ʿUmar consulted the companions on the penalty for the wine drinker *(shārib)*, ʿAlī drew an analogy between the *shārib* and the slanderer *(qādhif)* and suggested the same penalty (of eighty lashes) for both. ʿAlī reasoned thus: "When a person drinks he becomes intoxicated; when he is intoxicated he raves; and when he raves he accuses falsely."

During the second and third centuries AH, *ra'y* and *qiyās* became the focus of a controversy between the party of tradition *(ahl al-ḥadīth)* and the party of opinion *(ahl al-ra'y)*. Mālik and Ibn Ḥanbal, the leading jurists of Medina and Mecca, the original seat of Islam, laid particular emphasis on tradition, which they adopted as their standard in deciding legal issues. The situation was different in the conquered territories. Iraqi jurists, for example, who were farther removed from the birthplace of tradition, had used *ra'y* and *qiyās* extensively. The leading figure in this controversy was Abū Ḥanīfah, who openly declared *qiyās* to be a valid source of law. But the person credited with ending the controversy is al-Shāfiʿī, who came out squarely in favor of *qiyās* by including it among the four roots of law, though he was very careful to state that *qiyās* must be based strictly on the revealed sources and on consensus *(ijmāʿ)*.

In its technical sense, *qiyās* is the extension of the value of an original case *(aṣl)* to a subsidiary case *(farʿ)* by reason of an effective cause *(ʿillah)* that is common to both. For example, when a legatee slays a testator, the former is precluded from the latter's will. This prohibition is based on the tradition that "the killer does not inherit" *(lā yarith al-qātil)*. Although this ruling refers to intestate succession only, through analogy it is extended to bequests by reason of a common effective cause, namely the prohibition on hastening the realization of a right before it is due.

The cause in analogy must be intelligible to the human mind and it must be clearly identifiable. *Qiyās* is thus not applicable in matters of worship *(ʿibādāt)*, such as the number of daily prayers, where the mind cannot understand the value in question (the command to pray five times a day rather than twenty times has no identifiable cause). A further restriction in the use of *qiyās* concerns the exercise of caution in the application of penalties. Thus, under Ḥanafī law, prescribed penalties *(ḥudūd)* may not be analogically extended to similar offences. The Shāfiʿīs and some jurists from other schools are in disagreement on this point, for they consider that the basic rationale of the *ḥudūd* is ascertainable with a reasonable degree of certainty in the Qur'ān and the *sunnah*. A total ban on the use of analogy concerning the *ḥudūd* is, therefore, not warranted. But the Ḥanafī ruling, which favors caution in the enforcement of penalties, has wider support among jurists.

There are three other conditions governing the validity of *qiyās:*

1. The value extended to a new case should be established in the Qur'ān, *sunnah*, or consensus but not in another *qiyās*.
2. *Qiyās* should not result in the altering of a prescription *(naṣṣ)*. For instance, the Qur'ān (24:4) renders false accusation *(qadhf)* a permanent bar to the acceptance of one's testimony. Al-Shāfiʿī, however, compares the false accuser to the perpetrator of other grave sins *(kabā'ir)* and argues that since punishment and repentance absolve the latter and entitle him to be a witness, this exemption should also apply to the false accuser. The Ḥanafīyah have replied that this conclusion would amount to altering the divine prescription on the basis of personal judgment.
3. The value in question should not be expressly limited to the original case. Thus, while the Prophet exceptionally accepted the testimony of Khuzaymah as legal proof (the standard being two witnesses), *qiyās* may not be used to justify accepting the testimony of another single individual as legal proof.

BIBLIOGRAPHY

Textbooks on Islamic jurisprudence *(uṣūl al-fiqh)*, which are mainly in Arabic, normally devote a section to *qiyās*. There is a wide selection of both classical and modern works in Arabic. Among the best are Sayf al-Dīn al-Āmidī's *Al-iḥkām fī uṣūl al-aḥkām* (Cairo, 1914) and Muḥammad al-Khuḍarī's *Kitab uṣūl al-fiqh*, 3d ed. (Cairo, 1938). Comprehensive information on Shīʿī law can be found in Sayyid Muḥammad Asghari's *Qiyās va sayr-i takvīn-i ān dar ḥoqūq-i Islām* (Tehran, 1982). The best single book in English that devotes a section to *qiyās* remains Nicolas P. Aghnides's *Muhammadan Theories of Finance* (New York, 1916). A more condensed but accurate summary of *qiyās* can be found in S. R. Mahmassani's *The Philosophy of Jurisprudence in Islam*, translated by Farhat Ziadeh (Leiden, 1961), which also contains a very useful bibliography. Interesting information on *qiyās* can also be found in Joseph Schacht's *The Origins of Muhammadan Jurisprudence* (London, 1950) and Noel J. Coulson's *A History of Islamic Law* (1964; reprint, Edinburgh, 1971).

M. HASHIM KAMALI

QUAKERS. The Quakers, or the Religious Society of Friends, arose in seventeenth-century England and America out of a shared experience of the Light and

Spirit of God within each person. This source of worship, insight, and power they identify as the Spirit of Christ that also guided the biblical prophets and apostles. Quakers also affirm each person's ability to recognize and respond to truth and to obey the Light perfectly through the leading of an inner witness, or "Seed," called by some Quakers "Christ reborn in us" and by others "that of God in every man," out of which transformed personalities can grow. They therefore ask of each other, and of human society, uncompromising honesty, simplicity of life, nonviolence, and justice. Quakers have often been sensitive to new forms of social evil and creative in their programs to overcome them. Their worship has been based on silent waiting upon God without outward ritual.

The early Friends, as Quakers were named (from *Jn.* 15:5) by their first leader George Fox, arose in England during the Puritan Commonwealth under Oliver Cromwell, manifesting an inward intensification of radical and spiritual forms of Puritanism; they were influenced by uncompromising Baptists, quietist Seekers, antinomian Ranters, and theocratic militants; and these were in turn influenced by English Lollards, by European Anabaptist Mennonites who rejected both the state and class inequality, and by mystics like Jakob Boehme and the Familists. Unlike their predecessors, Quakers held distinctive ideas on the purely inward nature of true baptism and Communion, on the ministry of all laymen and women, on God's power judging and working within hearts and history, and on the need for biblical events to be fulfilled within each person's life-story; but many of these ideas simply carried further those trends, already active in the mainstream of Protestant doctrine, that had turned English Christians from Catholics into Anglicans, and then into Presbyterians or radical Puritans. Indeed, many Quakers had fought in the Puritan armies of the English Civil War and had turned back from the futility of merely military millennia.

A regional mass awakening in the English Northwest, which had not been strongly reached by Puritanism or any other vital religious movement, sprang up in 1652 around George Fox and the Quaker preachers inspired by him. From open-air meetings on the Yorkshire, Westmorland, and Cumberland moors, groups were gathered who were "convinced" to sit under the Light, largely in silence, for months of anguished self-searching of their motives and habits. The name *Quaker* reflected the physical impact of their inner struggles to yield all self-will to the judgments and guidance of the Light until they could live purely and speak entirely by its "leadings." Only then would joy and love come.

The early Quaker mission throughout England, in 1654–1656, was presented as the "Day of Visitation" by the Lord to each town or region; newly transformed Friends spoke in markets and parish churches despite mobbing and arrests. In New England, Quakers challenging the "biblical commonwealth" were banished on pain of death, and Mary Dyer and three men were hanged in Boston. The pope and the sultan of Turkey had been visited but not converted. To Quakers, Puritan apocalyptic hopes for God's cosmic victory over evil seemed fulfilled as through their work the spirit of Christ conquered the world nonviolently in "the Lamb's war" (*Rv.* 19:11–15). Outward violence they saw as only the devil's distraction, injuring God's good physical creation. All early Quaker ethical standards were part of the crucial inward war of truth against human pride and, thus, were sure to arouse anger; among them were the use of "thee" and "thou" to individuals, the making of true statements without oaths, the refusal of titles such as "sir," "doctor," and "my lady," and the refusal of "hat honor" and of tithe taxes to state churches.

To persecution for these offenses under the Puritans was added, after the restoration of Charles II, mass arrests—due to the Anglicans' Conventicle Acts of 1664 and 1670. Out of fifty thousand Friends, five hundred died in jail. Quaker courage won over to Quakerism such leaders as William Penn, the mystic Isaac Penington, and the theologian Robert Barclay. Quaker ethical "testimonies" of speech and dress and the continuing of silent Meetings for worship were increasingly stressed as badges of loyalty and as the fruits of the Spirit guiding "the sense of the Meeting."

The formal network of Quaker Meetings for Business, held monthly for a town, quarterly for a county, or yearly for a state or nation, was set up to replace reliance on individual leaders. The duties of these Meetings were to register births, marriages, and burials and to aid prisoners, widows, and poor Friends. Fox insisted after 1670 on independent Women's Meetings for Business throughout Quakerism. The monthly Meeting for Sufferings in London and local Meetings recorded imprisonments, oversaw publication of Quaker books, and disowned actions untrue to Quaker norms, disavowing those who so acted until they renounced their acts. Later, Yearly Meeting Epistles and Queries became regular parts of Quaker "books of discipline."

Quaker theological writings began with 461 wordy "debate tracts" poured out by Fox and all other major Quaker leaders to answer the charges made by anti-Quaker writings; Penn wrote more systematically on the universality of the saving Light; Robert Barclay's 1678 *Apology* became the most-read statement of Quaker beliefs and worship, presenting the Bible as testimony to authentically inspired experience, parallel to that of the Friends'. In Barclay's words, the death of Jesus atones for past sins, but the power of the Spirit can purify from sinning in the present. The cross stands for self-renunciation. The essence of the sacraments is inner washing, nurture, and Christ's real presence in worship; outward water, bread, and wine are needless. Ministry and even prayer must wait for and result from direct divine leading.

Toleration was always a concern for Friends: their arguments early turned from protests against persecution of God's messengers to moral, rational, and pragmatic appeals. Penn spoke for increasing groups of Englishmen convinced of the need to allow "dissenting" or "nonconformist" worship outside the national Anglican church, which led both to the Toleration Act of 1689 and the tradition of liberal Protestant reformers; he made moral appeals to all consciences, advising nonviolence and "loyal opposition" to government policies and people in power.

Quaker governments were set up in 1675 and 1682 by Edward Billing and Penn in their new colonies of West New Jersey and Pennsylvania; the charters of these governments mandated toleration and political and legal rights for all men including the Delaware Indians. Yet even after Quakers had become a minority in these colonies, all citizens' consciences were expected to concur with the Quakers' in rejecting forts and arms, oaths, most capital punishment, and the slave trade. England's wars with France forced increasingly unacceptable compromises on Pennsylvania Quaker legislators, most of whom resigned in 1755–1758. By tender persuasion, John Woolman and others led Quakers also to make collectively the harder decision to liberate their slaves and disown Quaker slave owners. Friends were jailed and fined throughout America in the wars of 1755–1763 and 1812 and during the Revolution; the few Friends who joined or paid for the militias were disowned by their Meetings.

Friendship with the American Indians was a Quaker policy: a Quaker committee shared in peace negotiations in 1756–1758 and 1763–1768, and others set up schools and mediation for the New York Senecas and for the Shawnees and other tribes evicted from Ohio and sent to Oklahoma after 1830. In the 1870s, President Grant asked Friends to administer the Indian Agencies of Kansas-Nebraska.

The antislavery work of British and American Quakers and their allies helped to end legal slave trade in both countries in 1807, but tension piled up against Quakers such as the poet John Greenleaf Whittier, Lucretia Mott, and the Grimke sisters (pioneers also in the women's rights movement) who advocated immediate national abolition of slave-owning. Many Quakers felt driven for the first time to break laws secretly in order to protect fugitive slaves through the Underground Railroad. During the American Civil War, southern Quakers suffered much; northern Friends were inwardly torn; some enlisted to fight. In England, John Bright sacrificed his parliamentary career to oppose both England's entry into the Crimean War and cotton mill owners' support for the American Confederacy.

Change and growth characterized Quaker activities during the eighteenth and nineteenth centuries. Eighteenth-century English industry, banking, and science were increasingly led by the interbred Quaker families of Darbys, Barclays, Lloyds, and Gurneys, who (notably Elizabeth Fry) also pioneered in reforming prisons, mental hospitals, and education for Quaker youth and the poor. Philadelphia Friends emulated them. Quaker worship, watchful against self-will, rationalism, and emotionalism had turned quietist. Among non-Quaker partners in trade or philanthropy, an evangelical orthodoxy that returned to the Bible and Christ's atonement was resurgent and began after 1800 to shape the experience of urban Quakers such as banker Joseph John Gurney, who wrote theology and traveled in America. Community revivals and regional awakenings further stimulated evangelicalism in both the creed and the experience of fifty thousand Friends who between 1795 and 1828 had been drawn to the American frontier in Ohio and Indiana from Virginia, the Carolinas, New England, and Pennsylvania by the promise of open land and freedom from slave-owning neighbors.

The 1827–1828 separation was initiated by the preaching of quietism and the urging of a boycott of slave-made products by Elias Hicks, the patriarchal farmer from New York State. The breach was widened by the influence of evangelical English Quakers traveling in America and disciplinary acts of evangelical urban elders. Friends from older close-knit rural Meetings who withdrew in protest from the Philadelphia Yearly Meeting did not foresee that the split would extend to Yearly Meetings and most Monthly Meetings, as well as to schools and committees in New York, Baltimore, Ohio, and Indiana, and that it would continue permanently.

New methods of revivalism begun after 1830 by Charles G. Finney in midwestern America seemed to the Rhode Island Quaker John Wilbur to be reflected in Gurney's Bible study methods. Rural Wilburite Friends, evangelical in doctrine but rejecting evangelism, were driven in 1846 into a second split, followed by like-minded Friends in Ohio and Canada and later in Iowa and Carolina.

The word *holiness*, in midwestern revivals and Bible conferences after 1858, came to mean a sudden "second work of grace" totally purifying the hearts of already-converted Christians. This experience predominated in Quaker Holiness revivals in Ohio, Indiana, and Iowa after 1867 led by John Henry Douglas and David Updegraff and others close to non-Quaker revivalists. Simultaneously, evangelical Friends were aroused to foreign mission projects in India, Japan, China, Jamaica, Cuba, Mexico, Kenya, Guatemala, Bolivia, and among both Indians and Inuit (Eskimo) in Alaska.

Quaker organization and worship, not greatly changed since 1690, were now centered in the American Midwest on revivals and hymns and hence on pastors and superintendents, led by Douglas in Iowa and Oregon. By 1898 half the Meetings, even in Indiana, supported pastors and programmed worship with sermons and hymns and biblical Sunday schools. The Richmond Conference of 1887 gathered all orthodox Friends to look at these new patterns and to restrain Updegraff's advocacy of water baptism. The Richmond Declaration of Faith reaffirmed evangelical orthodoxy. Concern for unity led in 1902 to a formally gathered Five Years Meeting, which since 1960 has been called Friends United Meeting, and is still centered in Richmond, Indiana; it currently includes seven Orthodox (evangelical) American Yearly Meetings (mostly midwestern); the reunited Baltimore, Canadian, New England, New York, and Southeastern Yearly Meetings; three Yearly Meetings in Kenya; and one each in Cuba, Jamaica, and Palestine arising from missions. Their total 1983 membership was 59,338 in North America and about 100,000 overseas. The year 1902 also saw the gathering of Hicksite Yearly Meetings (now numbering ten) into the Friends General Conference, centered in Philadelphia, with a 1981 membership of 26,086, including Yearly Meetings of "silent Meeting Friends" in western and midwestern cities and colleges. The three Wilburite or Conservative Yearly Meetings had shrunk by 1981 to a membership of 1,832. Intensifying of the biblical and Holiness concentration, however, drove evangelical Yearly Meetings of Ohio, Kansas, and Oregon out of the Richmond network and led in 1961 to their forming the Evangelical Friends Alliance, to which were added other "Friends Churches," some begun by Quaker missions in Asia and Latin America. In 1985, there remained 18,500 Friends in England and Scotland, 1,750 in Ireland, 2,000 in English communities in Australia, New Zealand, and South Africa, and 20 to 400 each in eight post-1918 Yearly Meetings in nations of continental Europe.

Quaker universalism and mysticism were replacing quietism as the central religious experience of many Hicksite and British Friends even before Rufus Jones, student and teacher at Haverford College, Pennsylvania, drew on Emerson and European mystics to make normative for their language "positive" or "ethical mysticism" and the experience of the soul's unity with "the divine in every man." Quaker education and service programs became linked to these humanitarian or humanist ideas. Rufus Jones channeled the service of Quaker conscientious objectors in World War I by helping to found the American Friends Service Committee, which then joined with the older British War Victims Relief and Friends Service Council in feeding two million German children and many victims of the 1922 Russian famine. The 1929–1939 Depression and World War II prompted Quaker interest in their own nations' unemployed and then in issues of world peace. In 1943 the Friends Committee on National Legislation was formed to coordinate and lobby for Quaker ideals in American policy. Quaker schools of all levels moved away from the guarded education of a purist sect towards a humanism aimed at developing the whole person. American colleges of Quaker origin (Haverford, Guilford, Earlham, Swarthmore, Bryn Mawr, et al.) and the famous Quaker secondary boarding schools on both continents increasingly draw brilliant students of all faiths and none. Graduate study centers have been set up at Woodbrooke by the Cadbury family and at Pendle Hill near Philadelphia. The Earlham School of Religion trains all branches of Friends for ministry of all kinds.

New patterns of unity and division have emerged since the 1960s. Conferences, international visits, and sharing of theological concerns are sponsored by the Friends World Committee for Consultation. Increasingly periodicals such as *Friends Quarterly* and *The Friend* in England and *Quaker Life, Friends Journal,* and *The Evangelical Friend* in America transcend Quaker divisions. Reunion of Yearly Meetings and local Meetings from the Hicksite separations have occurred in Philadelphia, Canada, New York, and Baltimore. Young Friends, who have often led Quakers into new ways, are concerned now with nuclear arms, communes, and "new foundations" in theology.

[*See the biographies of Fox and Penn. See also* Puritanism *and* Quietism.]

BIBLIOGRAPHY

The *Journal* of George Fox, edited by Thomas Ellwood (1694; reprint, Richmond, Ind., 1983); John Woolman's *Journal* (1774; reprint, New York, 1971); Robert Barclay's *Apology* (1676; reprint, Newport, R.I., 1729); and William Penn's *No Cross, No Crown* (London, 1669) remain the central classics of the Friends. *The Papers of William Penn* (Philadelphia, 1981–) and photocopies of *The Works of George Fox*, 3 vols. (1831; New York, 1975), and *A Collection of the Works of William Penn*, 2 vols. (1727; New York, 1974), are in print. Other primary sources are in *Early Quaker Writings, 1650–1700*, edited by me and Arthur O. Roberts (Grand Rapids, Mich., 1973).

Joseph Smith's *Descriptive Catalogue of Friends Books*, 2 vols. (London, 1867), remains the most complete bibliography, but see also Donald Wing's *Short-Title Catalogue of Books . . . 1641–1700*, 3 vols. (New York, 1945–1951). Leonard Hodgson's *Christian Faith and Practice* (Oxford, 1950), with topical selections from all periods, and *Church Government*, rev. ed. (London, 1951), together make up the London Yearly Meeting's *Book of Discipline*; those of other Yearly Meetings are less complete.

William C. Braithwaite's *The Beginnings of Quakerism* (1912; 2d ed., Cambridge, 1955) and *The Second Period of Quakerism* (1919; reprint, Cambridge, 1961), together with Rufus M. Jones's studies entitled *The Later Periods of Quakerism*, 2 vols. (1921; reprint, Westport, Conn., 1970), and *The Quakers in the American Colonies* (1911; reprint, New York, 1962) were designed to form the normative "Rowntree Series," based on documentary work by Norman Penney. A. Neave Brayshaw's *The Quakers* (London, 1921) combines history and ideas, as do Howard Brinton's study of Quaker mysticism entitled *Friends for Three Hundred Years* (New York, 1952) and John Punshon's *Portrait in Grey* (London, 1984). Each is an outstanding interpretation. Elbert Russell's *The History of Quakerism* (1945; reprint, Richmond, Ind., 1980), centered on America, with Efrida Vipont Foulds's *The Story of Quakerism* (London, 1954) are good one-volume histories.

Each Yearly Meeting has a printed history, and biographies have been written of most key Quakers. On early Quaker history, see various works by Edwin Bronner and Frederick Tolles; on the eighteenth century, by Sydney James and Arthur Raistrick; and on the nineteenth, by J. Ormerod Greenwood, Elizabeth Isichei, and Philip Benjamin. On Quaker ethical outlooks and doctrines, especially for the early periods, Richard Bauman's *Let Your Words Be Few: Symbolism of Speaking and Silence among Seventeenth Century Quakers* (Cambridge, 1983), Melvin B. Endy, Jr.'s *William Penn and Early Quakerism* (Princeton, 1973), J. William Frost's *The Quaker Family in Colonial America* (New York, 1973), and works by me, Lewis Benson, Maurice Creasey, Christopher Hill, and Geoffrey Nuttall give solid data and a variety of insights. Thomas R. Kelly's *A Testament of Devotion*, 6th ed. (New York, 1941), remains beloved as inspiration.

HUGH BARBOUR

QUATERNITY, or a fourfold structure (together with its multiples—eightfold, twelvefold, etc.), expresses symbolically the nature of the divine and, by extension, describes the structure of the world that mirrors that divinity. Like the other great numerical symbols in its class, quaternity is impersonal; it may stand alone, or it may be associated with the attributes of a personal god. God is one, says Plotinus, and so is the truth of this world. The divine is dual, say the Zoroastrians, and thus we must choose between truth and falseness. Christians say that God is a trinity, a perception that explains for Augustine the threefold nature of human love. Yet others have experienced the divine mystery as a quaternity, and its reality can be dimly perceived in the world's four cardinal directions, the four seasons, the four elements, and the four temperaments of classical thought.

Something of this symbol's power can be seen in the boyhood vision of Black Elk, the Oglala visionary. He heard voices: "Behold him, the being with four legs!" The divine quadruped was a horse that turned in the four directions to reveal four sets of twelve horses of four different colors. These forty-eight beings went into formation, four abreast, and introduced the boy to the four Grandfathers, who were the powers of the four quarters of the world. Two other Grandfathers, the dual powers of sky and earth, were also present. This experience lasted twelve days, and for twelve days thereafter Black Elk felt homesick for his extraordinary "other world" (described in John G. Neihardt's *Black Elk Speaks*, Lincoln, Nebr., 1979). In this vision, the fourfold structure orders the religious experience and provides an image for the order of divine things.

It is, therefore, something of a surprise to learn that this North American medicine man disparages the square, a fourfold geometrical figure—especially in light of the fact that the Navajo Indians use squares, and quaternities generally, in the healing pictures called sand paintings. But Black Elk contrasts the square with the circle, which he finds more natural and thus more compatible with deity. The Navajos integrate the image of the circle with its geometrical "opposite," the square. The same is true for Tantric Buddhists, who make meditative use of an image called a *maṇḍala*. Tantric devotees imagine that the gods—often numbering a multiple of four, such as the thirty-two deities of the *Guhyasamāja Tantra*—reside in a square "palace" with four gates in the four directions; their residence, however, is surrounded by a "circle" (i.e., a *maṇḍala*). Confucius, in his *Analects* (7.8), describes the proper way to teach a religious truth through an image that appears to be a square: "If I hold up one corner and a man cannot come back with the other three, I do not continue the lesson." Here, a whole truth is symbolically fourfold; further, there lies inside the fourfold structure of truth a distinction between three of its parts and a fourth. Navajo sand paintings are often bordered on three sides only; the eastern fourth side is left open, since evil cannot enter there.

Ezekiel's vision of God's chariot in the Hebrew scriptures contains a fourfold image that inspired Judeo-Christian symbolism. The prophet saw Yahveh—the four consonants of whose name, incidentally, comprise the mystical tetragrammaton of Judaism—supported by "four living creatures." They had four wings and also four faces, three of which were those of animals (the ox, lion, and eagle) and the fourth the face of a man. Their "spirits" were in the chariot's four wheels, which seem to have been intersected by four other wheels permitting them to move in four directions (*Ez.* 1). In the apocalyptic vision of the New Testament, God's throne is encircled at a distance by twenty-four other thrones; "round the throne, on each side of the throne, are four living creatures"—like an ox, a lion, an eagle, but also like a man (*Rv.* 4). Irenaeus stated in defense of Christianity (*Against Heresies* 3.11.7–9): "The Gospels could not possibly be either more or less in number than they are," namely, four. He argued that the *Gospel of Matthew* is like a "man" while the other three are like an "ox," a "lion," and an "eagle." Perhaps we should note that, symbolism aside, these four fundamental documents of the Christian religion naturally divide themselves into a set of three—the so-called synoptic Gospels—and the very different *Gospel of John,* which became the favorite of gnostic heretics. Structurally, something similar can be said for the fundamental teaching of Buddhism called the Four Noble Truths, the fourth of which is the Eightfold Path. Three of these truths describe conditions in the phenomenal realm of *saṃsāra,* but the "truth of cessation" alone describes the goal of *nirvāṇa.*

When Vedic seers of ancient India perceived the divine as an enormous person (Puruṣa), he was a quaternity: "All creatures are but one-fourth of him, three-fourths have eternal life in heaven" (*Ṛgveda* 10.90). Their vision lay behind the later and more impersonal view of the ultimate expressed by Upaniṣadic sages as *ātman* or *brahman.* According to the *Chāndogya Upaniṣad* (3.18.2), the divine has "four feet" or quarters—speech, breath, eye, and ear. But the *Māṇḍūkya Upaniṣad* develops the point psychologically and describes the *ātman* or self as comprised of four states of mind, three of which are waking, dreaming, and dreamless sleep; the mysterious "fourth" *(turīya)* state is the unity of the other three. When these matters are expressed in later Hinduism by anthropomorphic deities like Brahmā and Śiva, the gods often have four heads as an optimum number. It is said that Brahmā once had a single stag's head when he lusted for his daughter; he was properly punished and lost his head, but then he was given the four heads one often sees in art. Or, he once had five heads but was too proud, so the number was reduced to four (*Skanda Purāṇa* 3.40.1–59; *Śiva Purāṇa* 3.8.36–66). Śiva, on the other hand, was not punished when he lusted after a celestial nymph who danced seductively; he had one head but, in order to see more, he increased the number to four (*Mahābhārata* 1.203.15–26). Perhaps the nymph's dance was the "dance of *māyā,*" or phenomenal life, which the Indian Buddhists say must be seen fully if one is to become emancipated. For that to happen, say the Mahayanists, one has to experience the "twelve acts" of a Buddha, which include the critical "four visions" (of a sick man, an old man, and a dead man; but also of a monk). Then, on the night of one's enlightenment, one must have a dream that four birds of four different colors fly from the four directions, fall at one's feet, and turn completely white (*Mahāvastu* 2.136).

[*See also* Geometry *and* Numbers; *for examples of quaternity in religious symbolism, see* Architecture; Calendars, *article on* South American Calendars; Cosmology; *and* Maṇḍalas.]

BIBLIOGRAPHY

The quaternity image is so important to Carl Jung's *Collected Works,* 2d ed., edited by Herbert Read, Michael Fordham, and Gerhard Adler (Princeton, 1968–), that one should consult them for materials and also for a psychological interpretation. On the problem of "three and four," however, Edward F. Edinger's essay on the Trinity in *Ego and Archetype* (New York, 1972) is exceptional. Wendy Doniger O'Flaherty's *Śiva: The Erotic Ascetic* (Oxford, 1981) relates the head symbolism in Hinduism to phallic symbolism. Alex Wayman's neat essay "Buddhism," in *Historia Religionum,* edited by C. Jouco Bleeker and Geo Widengren, vol. 2, *Religions of the Present* (Leiden, 1971), gives ample evidence of quaternities in the Buddhist religion.

GEORGE R. ELDER

QUECHUA RELIGIONS.

[*This entry consists of two articles on the religious systems of Quechua-speaking Indians and other South American peoples with whom the Quechua are, culturally, intimately related. The first article,* Andean Cultures, *treats the Quechua- and Aymara-speaking Indians of the highland regions of Peru, Bolivia, Ecuador, and Colombia. The second article,* Amazonian Cultures, *treats the Canelos Quechua and Achuar Jivaroan peoples of Amazonian Ecuador.*]

Andean Cultures

The Quechua and Aymara Indians of the Andes mountains are the largest group of Indians still existent in the New World. Approximately twenty-eight million Indians and mestizos (persons of mixed Spanish and Indian descent) live along the Pacific coast and in the Andean highlands. About one-fourth of these Indians live and speak as they did before the Spanish conquest in the sixteenth century. Six million speak Quechua and approximately one million speak Aymara. For the purposes of this article, the religious systems of both the

Quechua and the Aymara will be treated together, and both groups will be referred to, collectively, as "Andeans."

Although some Andeans have moved to large urban centers, such as La Paz, Bolivia, and Lima, Peru, the majority live in small communities (from twenty to five hundred families) scattered throughout the Andes, with a population density of three hundred persons per square kilometer of habitable and arable land. Indians live in rectangular, single-family, adobe huts with thatched gable or hip roofs. The Aymara group their huts in extended-family compounds surrounded by a wall with a central patio. For both Aymara and Quechua, marriage is monogamous, with trial marriages lasting several years. Residence is patrilocal, with bilateral inheritance among the Quechua and patrilateral inheritance among the Aymara.

Andeans practice intensive agriculture using crop rotation, irrigation, dung fertilization, and terracing of fields. They cultivate more than fifty species of domesticated plants, in a number of ecological niches: potatoes, quinoa, and oca are grown at the highest levels of cultivatable land; corn (maize) at lower levels; and beans, squash, sweet manioc, peanuts, peppers, fruit trees, and cotton in the deep valleys and along the coast. Herders graze alpacas, llamas, and sheep on fallow fields and in high, nonarable tundra regions (14,000–17,000 ft.). Although Andeans live dispersed over wide areas, resource exchange unifies the people of different communities. The ecological band narrows as the altitude increases, so that there are many distinct communities, each utilizing the natural resources characteristic of its altitude. Because of ecological specialization, exchange of resources is very important. Andean civilization arose through these efforts to utilize many vegetational zones to furnish communities with a variety of resources.

Andeans have also adapted to this mountainous region by means of a religion that is essentially a system of ecological symbols. They use their ecological setting as an explanatory model for understanding and expressing themselves in mythology and ritual. Andeans are very close to their animals, plants, and land. Their origin myths tell how in times past llamas herded humans; in present times humans herd llamas only because of a linguistic error when llamas misplaced a suffix in Quechua, saying "Humans will eat us" instead of "We will eat humans." Andeans consider coca *(Erythoxylum coca)* a divine plant: "The leaves are like God. They have wisdom." Diviners learn about nature by chewing coca and reading its leaves. Andeans see themselves as part of nature, intrinsically affected by its processes and intimately linked with plants and animals. Moreover, Andeans believe they originated in the earth and will return to it.

Pachamama and Achachilas. Earth and mountains provide two principal Andean symbols, Pachamama and the *achachilas*. *Pachamama* means "mother earth," but *pacha* also refers to time, space, and a universe that is divided into heaven, earth, and a netherworld. For Andeans, time is encapsulated in space. *Pacha* is an earth that produces, covers, and contains historical events, and Pachamama symbolizes the fertile nature of the earth, which provides life. Pachamama is a universal deity, referring to all the earth and the universe because she represents the principle of nature that recycles life from death, and death from life. Pachamama is unlike the *achachilas*, the mountain spirits who represent certain peaks.

Ritually, Andeans libate Pachamama with drops of liquor before drinking and present her with three coca leaves before chewing coca. The husband places coca leaves daily into the male family members' earth shrine, an indentation within the adobe bench surrounding the inside of the patio, and the wife puts leaves under her household shrine, a table within the cooking house, so that Pachamama will provide the family with food. Diviners also offer ritual meals *(mesas)* to Pachamama during August, before Andeans begin planting. Andeans believe that the earth is open at that time and needs to be given food and drink.

Roman Catholic missioners attempted to replace Pachamama with the Blessed Mother, but this resulted in beliefs that associate the Blessed Mother with the bountifulness of the earth. For example, two major pilgrimage sites in the Bolivian Andes are La Virgen de Copacabana and La Virgen de Urkupiña. Nominally, these shrines refer to the Blessed Mother, but Andeans associate them with Pachamama and the earth (Urkupiña means "rock hill"). People travel to these shrines in August to feed Mother Earth and thus ensure an abundant harvest and an increase in flocks, offspring, or, more recently, money. This illustrates how Catholicism became syncretized with the ecological symbols of the Andean religion.

Achachilas are mountain spirits, indistinct from the mountains themselves, who are the masculine protectors of the earth and ancestors of the community. Diviners feed *achachilas* with ritual meals. Every Andean community has certain bordering mountains that are considered sacred: for example, the *achachilas* of La Paz, Bolivia, are the snow-crested mountains (16,000–20,000 ft.) of Illimani ("elder brother"), Mururata ("headless one"), and Wayna Potosi ("youth-Potosi"). A more traditional Aymara community, Cacachaqa, near Oruro, Bolivia, has eleven *achachilas* that together encircle it and separate it from neighboring communities. Each peak symbolizes an aspect of nature—a mineral, plant, animal, bird, or person—that is suggested by its shape and its particular resources and natural environment. Condo, a neighboring community north of Cacachaqa, shares with Cacachaqa two *achachilas*, which shows how neighboring communities are united by *achachilas*.

Throughout the Andes, there are hierarchical relationships among the *achachilas*. Ancestral *achachilas* are related to tutelary peaks of the community, the community's tutelary peaks to the region's, and the region's to the nation's. Traditionally, the metaphor for this relationship is a kinship pyramid: at the apex is the chief of the clan, followed by the heads of the major lineages and then the leaders of the local lineages. Although clans are no longer found in the Andes, lineages are important, and Andeans refer to *achachilas* in kinship terms—*machula* ("ancestor"), *apu* ("leader"), *awqui* ("grandfather"), and *tío* ("uncle"). In sum, mountains exhibit a hierarchy that is analogous to social and political systems. The worship of these mountains, then, made Andeans conscious of social, political, and natural systems.

Earth Shrines. Diviners are responsible for naming and feeding earth shrines *(huacas)*, which are pre-Columbian in origin and are still ritually important. Earth shrines are natural openings or small holes dug into the ground through which the earth is ritually fed. They are found near passes, water holes, knobs, and rocks. Alongside the hole is usually a rock pile, where Indians place their coca quids before fresh leaves are put inside the hole. A shrine's many names may express history, humor, geography, and social relationships. For example, one earth shrine is called Jilakata's Recourse, because it was once a rest stop for Indian officials on their journey to pay tribute to the Spanish. This shrine's knob suggests its other names: Goat Corral, Bachelor's Haven, Coitus, and Chicha (corn beer) Bubble. Another earth shrine was formed, according to legend, when a certain leader expelled his sister-in-law from his land and set her upside down alongside the road. She became a rock shaped in the form of buttocks and a vagina. Today, Andean travelers place coca in the crotch of this earth shrine. Other earth shrines are dedicated to irrigation canals, agricultural fields, and livestock. An *apacheta* is an earth shrine at a mountain pass, that is, the highest point of the trail. Travelers rest at these sites, discard their coca, and pray, "With this quid may my tiredness leave me, and strength return."

Earth shrines are stratified according to ecological levels, social groupings, time, and historical epochs. Individuals have their own earth shrines; an Andean baby receives an earth shrine at birth, and he must reverence it throughout his life. If he moves from his natal village, he will periodically return to pay homage to his shrine, which continually beckons for his return until he dies and is buried with his ancestors near his sacred mountain. The patrilineage has its household shrines dug into the inside and outside of the house; the community has its shrine corresponding to its level on the mountain; and the *ayllu*, an economically and religiously related group of communities, has its shrines up and down the mountain. Certain irrigation canals have earth shrines that are associated with the Inca civilization, and, in many villages, the chapel in the plaza is often interpreted as another earth shrine, reminiscent of the Spanish conquest. Yet the earth is the center that perdures through time, and that unifies the different places and earth shrines.

Ritualists. Ritual specialists of the Andes fall into two categories: diviners and sorcerers.

Diviners. Andeans frequently consult with diviners, the principal ritualists of the Andes. All Andean communities have diviners. Although they are identified from within the group by being associated with some extraordinary natural event (commonly, a bolt of lightning), they are selected as individuals for their divining skills. A typical diviner reads coca leaves by first selecting twelve perfect leaves. He marks them with insect-like bites and designates the significance of each: good luck, bad luck, community, road, a person's name, enemies, or whatever concerns the person paying for the divination. He then casts the leaves, like dice, upon a cloth to see which leaves pair with good luck and which with bad luck. If the cast is unfavorable, the participants often argue about the outcome and require another cast. Because coca leaves usually do not fall in a conclusive way, diviners are free to suggest their insights. There are many kinds of diviners: some read the signs of nature and predict when to plant and harvest, others are skilled in social dynamics and redress conflicts, and still others understand human problems and treat mental illnesses. A few possess mystical knowledge and can reveal the inner nature of the Andean universe. Such people are highly esteemed, and Andeans travel long distances to seek them out.

Diviners conclude divinations with ritual meals *(mesas)*, which are the basic rituals of the Andes. Although *mesas* vary regionally, they follow a similar pattern. A diviner sets a table *(mesa)* with a ritual cloth and scallop shells for plates, each of which is assigned an *achachila* and an earth shrine. He places a llama fetus at the head of the table for Pachamama. Next, the diviner places white llama wool, coca, llama fat, carnation petals, and animal blood on the scallop shells, beseeching the invited deities to accept the offerings. The participants imitate the diviner. There are other ritual foods, depending upon the ecological zone, but the three principal foods are coca, which symbolizes knowledge, fat, symbolizing energy, and blood (preferably from the llama), symbolizing vitality. Finally, the diviner wraps the food with the wool to make about twelve bundles *(kintos)* and ties them to the back of the llama fetus. The diviner places this in an earth shrine, and burns it, which symbolizes the consumption of the food. Andeans say that if the fire sparkles and crackles, then Pachamama and the *achachilas* have enjoyed the meal and will repay them with a good harvest.

Sorcerers. Sorcerers are different from diviners. Diviners are usually male and feed the earth shrines with llama fat, llama fetuses, and white llama wool at specific times—Wednesday and Thursday nights. They are ritualists for *achachilas*, Pachamama, and earth shrines. In contrast, sorcerers are often female and feed the wind and river with pig fat, rat fetuses, and black sheep wool on Tuesday and Friday nights. They are ritualists for the *supaya*, a term that has often been equated with the Spanish concept of the devil, although it actually refers to certain of the dead who either have not completed something in this life or have died in a strange fashion. The *supaya* belong to the netherworld of the dead *(ura pacha)*, but they act in the world of the living *(kay pacha)* as living shadows. *Supaya* enter the world of the living to gather companions for the netherworld. Symbolically, they represent the consumptive forces of nature, such as death and decay, which are necessary to renew life. When someone is sick and a *supaya* is implicated, sorcerers attempt to appease him by killing and substituting the life of a llama for that of the sick person. They also offer pig fat and rat fetuses at *mesas de contra* ("misfortune tables"), so called because the ritual items are contrary to those employed by diviners in a *mesa de suerte* ("good-luck table") or *mesa de salud* ("health table"). Pig fat is inferior to llama fat because Andeans consider the pig a tropical animal that lives on fecal matter and garbage. Rat fetuses, symbolizing destructive rodents, are inferior to llama fetuses, which symbolize an animal very beneficial to Andean society.

Andeans select sorcerers by their reputation for either removing or inflicting misfortunes. Some sorcerers claim responsibility for as many as seven deaths, but others are secretive about their reputation because sorcerers are occasionally killed in revenge by victims of unsuccessful sorcery. Sorcery takes many forms in the Andes, but one way sorcerers curse people is by placing nail filings or hair of the victim inside the skulls of a cat and a dog, whose teeth are locked as if in battle, which symbolizes that husband and wife are fighting. (The breakdown of the household is a major tragedy in the Andes because it is the unit of production and subsistence.) The sorcerer hides the skulls inside the thatched roof of the victim. If the victim is aware of this, he can remove the curse by having another sorcerer perform a *mesa de contra*. Sometimes the victim has the sorcerer brought before the magistrate, who fines her and makes her take an oath not to do it again. Sorcery is taken seriously and is often the attributed cause for loss of livestock, crops, money, health, and even life.

The Ayllu and Its Earth Shrines. The *ayllu* is basic to Andean social organization. Although *ayllu*s are often based on kinship ties, they are also formed by religious, territorial, and metaphorical ties. One contemporary example is Ayllu Kaata of the Qollahuaya Indians, who live in midwestern Bolivia. Ayllu Kaata is a mountain with three major communities: Niñokorin, Kaata, and Apacheta. The people of Niñokorin are Quechua speakers who farm corn, wheat, barley, peas, and beans on the lower slopes of the mountain (10,500–11,500 ft.). The people of Kaata, who also speak Quechua, cultivate oca and potatoes on rotative fields of the central slopes (11,500–14,000 ft.). In the highlands (14,000–17,000 ft.), the Aymara-speaking people of Apacheta herd llamas and sheep. The three communities use the metaphor of the human body to understand their *ayllu:* Apacheta corresponds to the head, Kaata to the trunk, and Niñokorin to the legs. Just as the parts of the human body are organically united, so are the three levels of Ayllu Kaata.

The thirteen earth shrines of Ayllu Kaata are understood in relation to the body metaphor and to ecological stratifications. The three community shrines are Chaqamita, Pachaqota, and Jatun Junch'a. Chaqamita, a lake located to the east near the legs, is related to the sun's birth, fertility, and corn, making it a suitable shrine for Niñokorin, whose Corn Planting rite reverences this site. This lower lake is also a shrine for Curva and Chullina, neighboring *ayllu*s. Earth shrines, when shared by several *ayllu*s, religiously unite separate mountains, and so Qollahuaya Andeans claim that they are one people because they worship the same shrines. Pachaqota, a large lake at the head of the mountain, is the "eye" into which the sun sinks; it symbolizes death, fertilization, and llamas. On the shores of the lake, the herders of the highland community of Apacheta celebrate the All Colors rite for the increase of llamas. Pachaqota is also associated with the lakes of *uma pacha* (at the top of a mountain), from which animals and humans derive their existence and to which they return after death.

The Great Shrine (Jatun Junch'a), associated with the

liver and the central community of Kaata, is a major shrine of Ayllu Kaata because of its central location and physiography. The Great Shrine rests on a spur, which rises from the slopes and resembles a small mountain. The Great Shrine is nourished at the rite of Chosen Field, in the middle of the rainy season, and it is also the site of a mock battle *(tinku)* between the elders and clowns during Carnival. The clowns, who sprinkle people with water, are symbolically put to death by the elders slinging ripe fruit at them.

Similar ritual battles are fought throughout the Andes: the Aymara of the Bolivian Altiplano, for example, wage theatrical warfare between the upper and lower divisions of the community. *Tinku* emphasizes the importance of contrasting pairs, and in the Andes almost everything is understood in juxtaposition to its opposite. Earth shrines, also, have meanings corresponding to binary opposition. Chaqamita and Pachaqota, for example, correspond to life and death, as well as to the rising and setting of the sun, and each term explains the other; moreover, each leads to the other.

The highlands, central altitudes, and lowlands of Mount Kaata have community shrines reflecting their ecological zones, but from the viewpoint of the *ayllu,* the community shrine is only one part of the body of the mountain. In some way every level must feed all the mountain's shrines during the *allyu* rites, such as the New Earth rite. The people of Apacheta, Kaata, and Niñokorin come together during New Earth to re-create the mountain's body. The upper and lower communities send leaders to Kaata for this rite, each bringing his zone's characteristic product: a llama or some chicha (corn beer). The llama's heart and bowels are buried in the center fields, and blood and fat are sent by emissaries to feed the earth shrines of the mountain. The body awakes to become the new earth.

The New Earth rite is one illustration, of which there are many others throughout the Andes, of how Pachamama, the *achachilas,* and earth shrines are holistically understood in terms of metaphor, ecology, and *ayllu.* The New Earth rite expresses how levels of land are understood in terms of a body with a head, heart, bowels, and legs, through which blood and fat circulate when ritualists feed the earth shrines. Specific earth shrines not only refer to specific ecologial zones but also symbolize parts of the body that holistically constitutes the *achachila* and symbolizes the social and political unity of Mount Kaata. Andeans experience the solidarity of their mountain and *ayllu* similarly to the way they experience the organic unity of their corporeal bodies. The individual's corporeal life is dependent on environmental life. Thus, the New Earth rite assures the individual's organic life by awakening Mother Earth to provide a good harvest.

Ritual Calendar. Andeans insert themselves by ritual into the cycles of nature—not to control them, but to experience them and be in harmony with them. New Earth, for example, is the second of three rites dedicated to the rotative field of the year. Through these three rites the earth is gradually awakened. One year before planting, the community leaders study the fertility of the fields lying fallow to see which one is ready to begin another growth cycle of potatoes, oca, and barley. A diviner observes nature's omens and asks the neighboring mountains *(achachilas)* for their assistance. Once a field is picked, the people of the *ayllu* celebrate the rite of Chosen Field (Chacrata Qukuy) in the middle of the rainy season. Leaders dance across the field's terraces to the music of flutes, and they offer a llama fetus to the earth shrine of the selected field. The fetus brings new life to the soil, and thus the field becomes the anointed land for the year. Andeans later fertilize their plots by spreading sheep dung along the furrows where they will plant potatoes.

The rains continue to soak the anointed field, and near the end of the rainy season, in April, Andeans prepare to plow. But before the earth can be entered, it must be nurtured by the sacrifice of a grown llama during the rite of New Earth. With this rite the land is vitalized; it is opened for water, air, dung, and blood, until the time of Potato Planting, when it is covered over again. Potato Planting (Khallay Papa Tarpuna), in mid-November, is the field's final ritual, celebrated after the Feast with the Dead. According to Andean legends, the dead push the potatoes up from the inside of the earth. Also in November, people of lower levels celebrate Corn Planting (Khallay Sara Tarpuna), and at Christmastime herders sponsor their herding rituals, All Colors (Chajru Khallay). Although each rite is concerned with the animal and plant life of its zone, collectively the rites influence the corporate life of the *ayllu* and region, and leaders from the various communities participate in all of the rituals of the *ayllu* and the region.

Between the cycle of the seasons there is a day when ancestors return to the community—2 November, the Feast with the Dead. Ancestor worship remains an important part of Andean religion. Prior to the conquest, Andeans mummified the dead by wrapping them in cloth and seating them in *chullpas,* which are rock monuments above subterranean cists. The Incas dressed the mummies of their kings in fine textiles and kept them in the Temple of the Sun in Cuzco, where they were arranged in hierarchical and genealogical relationships. Today, Andeans dress the dead person for a journey, provide him with coca, potatoes, corn, and a candle, and bury him in a cemetery near the community. Traditionally, many Andeans believe that people originate from and return to the highland lakes of the mountain. They compare death to the eclipse of the sun: death is ecliptic, hiding the dead within the earth, where they journey with the movements of the sun, seasons, and land.

The Feast with the Dead is an annual rite of passage from the dry to the wet season and from the activity of the dead to that of the living. The dry season connotes resting; the wet season, growth. The living invite the dead to a meal when the harvest and festive times have ended and planting rituals begin. At this pivotal point in the Andean year, the dead visit the living, and then they are sent on another year's journey with their share of the harvest.

At noon on 1 November, the leader of the community awakens the dead with dynamite, and for twenty-four hours the dead are served food on tables that usually have three tiers, symbolizing highlands, central altitudes, and lowlands. The arrival of a fly or the flickering of a candle signals to the living that the dead are present. The living and dead share in a meal and communicate with each other by laments and prayers. At noon the next day, everyone returns to the cemetery to place more food near the graves. Relatives of the deceased distribute food to friends, who pray for the dead relatives. Later the same afternoon, the fiesta ends with a meal and drinking.

Cosmology. For Andeans, the finality of death is alleviated by their ecology. During life, Andeans become part of the land that they work: as their bodies get older, their land increases. When they die, they enter into the mountain, journey upward, and have access to the land of the dead. Moreover, the decay of their bodies enriches the land of the living. The visible levels of the living are only half of the mountain; the other half consists of the subterranean waterways of the dead.

The Andeans' worldview is an extension of the three mountain levels; they divide their universe into the heavens *(janaj pacha)*, this world *(kay pacha)*, and the netherworld *(ura pacha)*. Each place has an ancient, a past, and a present time, to which specific beings correspond. The heavens are where the elders of lightning, sun, and stars have dwelled since ancient times; where God, Jesus, and Santiago have roamed since past times; and where dead baptized babies are descending to the *uma pacha* in present times. By their permanent and cyclical features, the heavens suggest origination and restitution, whereas the experiences of this world are temporal and consecutive. The three times of this world are symbolized by *chullpa*s, the cross, and the graveyard, which refer respectively to the ancestor mummies, Jesus, and the recent dead (those who have died within three years). The ancestor mummies and the past and recent dead journey to the highlands within the subterranean waterways of the netherworld, which is the recycling area between death and life. The *supaya* are dead unable to travel because of some unfinished business. They bridge the gap between the netherworld and this world. The earth shrines denote being, space, and time, our metaphysical concepts for the universe, which are intertwined in each of the three gradient levels; thus the mountain serves as an expression of Andean cosmology.

The *uma pacha* is the point of origin and return for traditional Andeans. The highlands are the head *(uma)* of the *achachila*. Bunchgrass grows near the summit of the mountain, as hair on the head. The wool of the llamas that graze on this grass resembles human hair. As human hair grows after cutting, so llama wool and bunchgrass grow continually in the highlands. In a manner similar to the regeneration of hair, humans and animals originate in the highland lakes, or the eyes *(nawi)* of the *achachila*. The sun dies into these eyes of the highlands, but from the reflections within the lake come all living creatures. The lake's reflections *(illa)* are the animals and people returning from inside the earth to this world.

Animals and people originate in and return to the head of the mountain. It is the place of origin and return, like the human head, which is the point of entry and exit for the inner self. The dead travel by underground waterways to the mountain's head, the *uma pacha*, from whose lakes they can arise to the land of the living. The living emerge from the eyes of the mountain (the lakes of the *uma pacha*), journey across its head, chest, trunk, and legs (high, center, and low levels), and die in the lowlands. They are buried and return with the sun to the *uma pacha*, point of origin and return.

Sickness and Health. Western medicine ascribes sickness to internal disorders of the body or to the malfunctioning of organs within it, whereas Andean curing looks outside the body to the malfunctioning of the social and ecological order. Bodily illnesses are signs of disorders between the person and the land or between the person and his lineage. The diviner's role is to reveal this conflict and to redress it by ritual, which resolves the dispute or reorders the land. Diviners cure not by isolating the individual in a hospital, away from his land, but by gathering members of a sick person's social group for ritual feeding of the earth shrines of the *achachila*, because if their lineage and mountain are complete, then their body will also be complete (healthy). Community and land are inextricably bound to the physical body, and disintegration in one is associated with disorder in the other.

One illustration of how diviners interrelate environmental and social factors with sickness is the *mesa de salud* ("health table"), a commonly performed ritual in the Andes. This ritual begins with a preliminary divination session in which the diviner casts coca leaves to determine the causes of an illness. Relatives of the sick person attend and contribute to the analysis of the causes. Diviners then redress social conflicts within the lineage. If the sick person, for example, has fought with her mother-in-law, the diviner delves into the cause of this conflict and instructs the patient to gather some ritual item from the mother-in-law's household. The participants then spend several days gathering ritual items symbolic of the various altitudinal levels: *chicha* (corn beer) and carnations from the lowlands, potatoes from the central lands, and llama fat and a fetus from the highlands. The gathering of the ritual items reinforces the concept that health is related to the utilization and exchange of resources from different levels. Indirectly, the ritual affects health by reinforcing the need for a balanced diet. In this way, Andean ritual promotes holistic health rather than merely removing disease.

Traditionally, Andeans distinguish between *curanderos,* who cure with natural remedies, and diviners *(yachaj),* who cure with supernatural remedies. Andeans have many classes of *curanderos,* revealing a striking knowledge and classification of anatomy and an enormous list of medical paraphernalia. Because they have excelled in the practice of native medicine, Andeans have adapted to an environment that produces many stresses (hypoxia, hypothermia, malnutrition, and epidemics). Qollahuaya herbalists, for example, use approximately one thousand medicinal plants in curing. Andeans visit both diviners and herbalists for treatment of a disease, because both kinds of specialist are needed to deal with all the physical, social, spiritual, and ecological factors involved.

Christianity. Andeans have incorporated Catholicism into their traditional way of life by stratifying it according to place and time and thus allowing it to function in ways analogous to the function of an earth shrine. For many Andeans, Catholicism is a state religion that replaced the Inca religion. Every Andean community has a chapel with a statue of a saint who is the patron protector of the village. Sculptors mold a realistic statue from plaster of paris, and seamstresses dress it with velvet and gold cloth. These statues appear almost alive, like waxworks. For some Andeans, the saint represents a white rock; for others, the saints are transformations of the dead ancestors whom they venerated during Inca times.

Annually, each village celebrates a fiesta to its saint, whose statue is paraded around the four corners of the plaza while brilliantly costumed groups dance to the music of flutes, drums, and trumpets. The official sponsor, the *preste,* walks alongside the saint, for which privilege he provides the participants with alcohol, coca, and food. Ritual and natural kin, as well as people in debt to the *preste,* contribute supplies and sponsor dance groups. For the first day or two, the fiesta is a celebration of great beauty and festivity, but by the third day it often degenerates into drunkenness and brawling. One reason is that during recent times raw alcohol has replaced the traditional beverage, *chicha,* which has a much lower alcohol content. However, alcohol and coca also relax the participants, making them susceptible to the liminal meanings of the fiesta—the basic Andean meanings being expressed in the dance, music, and ritual. These elements are highly structured and communicate underlying symbolic patterns important to Andean culture.

Although the cult of the saints reflects the importance of Catholicism in contemporary Andean culture, Andeans are only nominal Catholics: they baptize their babies primarily to prevent hailstorms and to obtain *padrinos* ("godfathers"), who provide social and political connections. Sometimes couples marry in the church, but only after a trial marriage *(iqhisiña)* to see whether the wife is fertile. Catholic catechists and Protestant missionaries have recently been converting Andeans to an evangelistic Christianity opposed to earth shrines, fiestas, and traditional Andean beliefs. Many evangelistic Protestants emphasize literacy and the reading of the Bible. Protestantism cannot be incorporated into the traditional Andean system because it tends to be comparatively barren of symbols and ritual. Consequently, converts to certain Protestant sects have radically changed their traditional cultural patterns. In sum, Catholicism has been adapted peripherally to traditional Andean religious practices, whereas evangelistic Protestantism has been very effective in changing traditional belief systems. This is because many Andeans see traditional religious practices, which reflect verticality, resource exchange, *ayllu* solidarity, and ecology, as being unimportant to modernization, with its emphasis on literacy, horizontal links, competition, and individuality.

Nevertheless, the traditional religion retains a strong hold on Andeans, who continue to look to earth and nature for their identity. Their land and their mountains continue to be their deities—not as abstract symbols but as real entities with whom they live and work and with whom they share important relations of reciprocity. For these reasons, the Andeans built a high civilization in a mountainous land that they came to worship.

BIBLIOGRAPHY

Allen, Catherine J. "Body and Soul in Quechua Thought." *Journal of Latin American Lore* 8 (1982): 179–195. Explores the conceptual basis of "animistic" ideology, focusing on attitudes toward death and the custom of "force feeding." Excellent description of relationship between ancestors and the living.

Allpanchis Phuturinqa (Cuzco, 1969–). Published by the Instituto de Pastoral Andina, this review was founded to educate pastoral agents about Andean culture and includes many articles on Andean religion.

Arguedas, José María. *Deep Rivers.* Translated by Frances Horning Barraclough. Austin, 1978. Noted Peruvian novelist describes conflict within mestizos caught between the Andean and Spanish cultural systems. Shows how myth bridges the gulf between the magico-religious world of the Andean and the social reality of mestizo life. A penetrating book.

Arriaga, Pablo Joseph de. *The Extirpation of Idolatry in Peru* (1621). Translated by Horacio Urteaga (Lima, 1920) and L. Clark Keating (Lexington, Ky., 1968). An extirpator's manual accurately describing Andean religious practices of the sixteenth and seventeenth centuries, many of which are still found in the Andes. Shows how missioners suppressed Andean religion and attempted to replace it with Catholicism—and how Christianity got off to a bad start in the Andes.

Bastien, Joseph W. *Mountain of the Condor: Metaphor and Ritual in an Andean Ayllu.* Saint Paul, 1978. A description and analysis of rituals performed by Qollahuaya Andeans, whose diviners are famous throughout the Andes. Rituals provide the context for understanding the metaphorical relationship of Andeans with their land.

Bastien, Joseph W., and John N. Donahue, eds. *Health in the Andes.* Washington, D.C., 1981. First part contains three articles on how rituals are used to cure sick Andeans. Other parts contain environmental information concerning Andeans.

Cuadernos de investigación (La Paz, 1974–). Pamphlets on Andean culture and religion published by the Centro de Investigación y Promoción del Campesinado. Especially insightful are those by Javier Albo, Tristan Platt, and Olivia Harris.

Isbell, Billie Jean. *To Defend Ourselves: Ecology and Ritual in an Andean Village.* Austin, 1978. Describes marriage, hydraulic, harvest, and fertility rituals in the village of Chuschi, Ayacucho Department, Peru. Treats the relationship between ecology and ideology through the observation and analysis of rituals.

Lewellen, Ted. *Peasants in Transition: The Changing Economy of the Peruvian Aymara.* Boulder, 1978. Analyzes the impact of Protestantism on social and economic factors of an Aymara community.

Millones Santa Gadea, Luis. *Las religiones nativas del Peru: Recuento y evaluación de su estudio.* Austin, 1979. A review of studies concerning Andean religion. Very useful for early studies on Andean religion.

Núñez del Prado, Juan Victor. "The Supernatural World of the Quechua of Southern Peru as Seen from the Community of Qotobamba." In *Native South Americans,* edited by Patricia J. Lyon. Boston, 1974. Delineates the structure of the supernatural world in southern Peru from the mythology and ethnographic data of two Quechua communities.

Orlove, Benjamin S. "Two Rituals and Three Hypotheses: An Examination of Solstice Divination in Southern Highland Peru." *Anthropological Quarterly* 52 (April 1979): 86–98. Describes two solstice divinations in Peru. Illustrates how Andeans weigh alternatives and make decisions.

Ossio, Juan M., ed. and comp. *Ideología mesiánica del mundo andino.* Lima, 1973. Compilation of articles by anthropologists and historians concerning messianism among Andean peasants. Many authors employ structuralist interpretations of Andean religion.

Paredes, M. Rigoberto. *Mitos, supersticiones y supervivencias populares de Bolivia* (1920). 3d ed., rev. & enl. La Paz, 1963. A reference book for religious practices of the Aymara.

Sharon, Douglas. *Wizard of the Four Winds: A Shaman's Story.* New York, 1978. Documents a modern shaman's view of the world. Describes *mesas* performed by a shaman in Trujillo Valley in the northern Andean highlands. A well-written and insightful book about Andean shamanism.

Taussig, Michael T. *The Devil and Commodity Fetishism in South America.* Chapel Hill, N.C., 1980. Discusses the social significance of the devil in the folklore of contemporary plantation workers and miners in South America. The devil is a symbol of the alienation experienced by peasants as they enter the ranks of the proletariat.

Tschopik, Harry, Jr. "The Aymara of Chucuito Peru." *Anthropological Papers of the American Museum of Natural History* 44, pt. 2 (1951):137–308. Examines how ritual establishes social equilibrium among the peasants of Chucuito, Peru. Includes detailed description of ritual paraphernalia.

Urton, Gary. *At the Crossroads of the Earth and Sky: An Andean Cosmology.* Austin, 1981. Examines the astronomical system of Misminay, Peru, to understand celestial cosmology of modern Andeans. Shows how celestial formations interrelate with the agricultural and ritual calendars.

Valdizán, Hermilio, and Angel Maldonado. *La medicine popular peruana.* 3 vols. Lima, 1922. An encyclopedia of minerals, plants, and animals used in healing and ritual.

Wachtel, Nathan. *The Vision of the Vanquished: The Spanish Conquest of Peru through Indian Eyes, 1530–1570.* Translated by Ben Reynolds and Siân Reynolds. New York, 1977. An account of the structural disintegration of Inca society and culture during the early years of the conquest. Illustrates how a present-day fiesta in Oruro, Bolivia, enacts this drama.

JOSEPH W. BASTIEN

Amazonian Cultures

Persistent confusion permeates the comparative study of the religious beliefs and practices of the peoples of Upper Amazonian rain forests that abut the foothills of the Andes mountains. This is because Quechua-speaking peoples of that region and Quechua-speaking people of the Andes share a religious complex, which, in turn, is also shared with Jivaroan-speaking and Zaparoan-speaking peoples of the Upper Amazonian region. This article deals with some commonalities of Quechua and Jivaroan religious concepts. The Quechua language has long been associated with the Andes mountains and with the Inca conquest of the Central Andean peoples radiating out of Cuzco in the late fifteenth century. Jivaroan peoples have long been associated with the Upper Amazonian rain forests and with resistance to Inca conquest, and, thereby, to the permeation of the conquest religion borne by the Inca northward to what is now Colombia and southward into what, today, is Bolivia.

In Ecuador and Peru, Jivaroan and Quechua-speaking peoples of the Upper Amazonian rain forest share not only many core beliefs but also variants of the same terms for these beliefs, even though their languages are completely unrelated. The specific people referred to here are the Canelos Quichua and the Achuar Jivaroans of Ecuador. (*Quichua*, pronounced *Kichua*, is one proper spelling of the name for speakers of northern Quechua dialects.) The Canelos Quichua inhabit the region drained by the Bobonaza and Curaray rivers and the regions that radiate out of urban Puyo, Ecuador. The Achuar discussed here are those who inhabit the regions of the Copataza, Capahuari, and Conanbo rivers and also those who live in the vicinity of urban Puyo, including those living on the Llushín River. Many Achuar and Canelos Quichua people intermarry. Many of the Achuar are fluent in Canelos Quichua and in Spanish, and many of the Canelos Quichua are fluent in Achuar and in Spanish. Cultural congeners who speak Jivaroan include the Aguaruna, Huambisa, and Achuar (including Maina-Achuar) of Peru; the Shuar of Ecuador; and the Murato Candoshi and Shapra Candoshi of Peru. The two latter Candoan-speaking people may or may not speak Jivaroan, but their cultural and religious systems are virtually the same as the Jivaroans and Canelos Quichua. Zaparoans of Peru and Ecuador (including Andoa-Shimigae, Záparo, Iquitos, and Arabela) also share this religious complex, though there is no known linguistic relationship between Zaparoan, Jivaroan, and Quechua languages. The Quijos Quichua and Napo Quichua of Ecuador, the Inga of Colombia, and the Napo Quichua of Peru also share segments of this complex.

The history of the Canelos Quichua intertwines with the history of Catholic mission expansion in a manner distinct from the history of the Achuar. Nonetheless, the primary streams of traditional culture and the primary emphases of contemporary ethnic affiliation that constitute modern Canelos Quichua culture stem from Achuar, Zaparoan, early Canelos Quichua, and Quijos Quichua peoples. The Canelos Quichua, in myriad ways, provide ample evidence by which to refute the spurious but pervasive dichotomy made by many scholars between cultural orientations and religious-cosmological structures of the "Andean," or highland, regions and the "Amazonian," or lowland, regions of western South America.

Control of power and recognition of the devastating consequences of its release are fundamental to Canelos Quichua and Achuar Jivaroan cultures. Concepts of such control are embedded in a paradigm centered on knowledgeable ones: shamans for men, potters for women. Strong shamans and master potters continuously increase their knowledge of spirit forces that exert control in human affairs. Spirit forces configure—especially for the Canelos Quichua—into three dominant images: Amasanga, forest spirit master; Nunkwi, spirit master of garden dynamics and of pottery clay; and Tsunki, spirit master of water, or the hydrosphere. Whereas Tsunki and Nunkwi are dominant images in all or most of the aforementioned cultures, Amasanga is specific to the cosmogony of the people addressed in this article.

The concepts of these dominant spirit beings *(supai)*, each with a soul *(aya)* and life force *(causai)*, evoke mythic and legendary imagery to illuminate the known and unknown cosmos and to relate cosmic networks of souls, spirits, beings, forces, and events to contemporary and past quotidian life. Each dominant image evokes and indexes a myriad of spirit beings specific to various natural and supernatural domains. For example, imagery of Amasanga not only evokes the spirits of thunder and lightning above and within the rain-forest canopy but also the spirit of the mighty trees that dominate sectors of the forest.

The imagery of Amasanga (called Amasank in Achuar) also includes principles of transformation, called *tucuna* in Canelos Quichua. For example, for a given group of Canelos Quichua speakers, Amasanga represents the master spirit force of their own territory. One powerful transformation of Amasanga is that of the feared spirit Jurijuri (called Jirijri in Achuar). Jurijuri is the master of monkeys. All monkeys are associated with other peoples. But Jurijuri is not a "separate" spirit, he/she is a transformation of Amasanga, a transformation from "ours," who protects, to "theirs," who harms. Jurijuri spirits dwell in hillside caves and move under the forest's surface. As the shaman of the forest, Amasanga sits on an iguanid or tortoise seat of power; his/her corporeal manifestation is the black jaguar, and he appears in humanlike form in deep purple garb wearing a red and yellow toucan headdress.

Tsunki evokes spirits of the water world—the entire hydrosphere of airborne and undersoil moisture—which must be kept under spirit or human control if catastrophe is to be avoided. Tsunki is chthonic in association with dwelling sites under rivers or lakes; aquatic in association with waterfalls, rapids, and whirlpools of rivers and with quiet lakes; celestial and radiating in association with the rainbow and, tenuously, with the sun. As first shaman, Tsunki sits on the Amazon turtle *(charapa)* as his seat of power; his/her corporeal manifestation is the mighty anaconda (*amarun* in Quichua, *panki* in Jivaroan). He sometimes appears as one dressed in rainbow colors, or as a naked white man. (Anaconda symbolism permeates the cosmography of power in the rain-forest territories of Upper Amazonia, Central Amazonia, the Northwest Amazon, the Guianas, and beyond).

Nunkwi is associated with feminine dynamics of undersoil and leaf-mat-root-fungi systems by day, and with growth and renewed fecundity of manioc (cassava) by night. Her corporeal manifestation is the black coral snake with mouth too small to bite. She may appear to women as one garbed in deep purple who dances with hopping steps while tossing her hair to and fro.

Knowledge *(yachana)*, which is fundamental to the control of power, derives from ancient cultural mythology and historical legend. It is shaped by strong shamans and by master potters to resonate with immediate historical events and current activities. Knowledge of the cosmos (bound to the concept *yachana*, "to know, to learn") provides the basis by which knowledge from the experiential world (bound to the concepts *ricsina*, "to experience, to perceive, to comprehend," and *yuyana* or *yuyarina*, "to think, to reflect") is shaped by all individuals. Such shaping is bound to another concept, *muscuna* ("to dream, to perceive"). *Muscuna* and *yachana* are, in turn, closely associated with the spirit-master images Amasanga and Nunkwi, both of which are thought to be from datura *(Datura suaveolens)*, a narcotic plant of the nightshade family.

When a man or woman ingests datura (called *huanduj* in Quichua, *maikua* in Jivaroan), he or she "perceives" and "knows" human self, human soul, human substance, others, spirits, and all entities and beings in existence. Domains and boundaries that are part of everyday life dissolve in a datura trip as the questing individual enters mythic time-space, called *unai* in Canelos Quichua. Reincorporation into the world of humans, souls, spirits, and beings takes place through reordering by the individual of the relationships previously characterized in his or her life. For example, after taking datura the individual may "know" that someone he thought was his trading partner and true kin is, in this newly found reality, an enemy who seeks to harm him. Accordingly, the domains of kinship and trade are reordered by the individual, who now "sees" the entire kinship network and relations of trade in a new light. Such reordering of domains spreads to other domains, as well. For example, if an individual now perceives another as his enemy rather than his friend, then the powerful shaman who is father or uncle to the new-found enemy becomes a major threat to the health of the questing individual's kinship system, rather than, as previously thought, one of its buttressing ancestors. As the individual continues to reorder the relationships within such domains as kinship, economics, and shamanic protection and harm, his thought patterns and convictions continue to branch out to others both near and far, extending the effects of domain reordering further and further.

A successful datura trip gives the questing individual a sense of power. This sense is derived from knowledge of control of spirit, soul, life force, body, and visionary or imagined features of cosmic beings and events in mythic time-space, and in various past times. For example, a Jivaroan seeks the vision of an ancient being *(arutam)* in such quests and may acquire, thereby, a second soul that "locks in" his own immortal soul. If a person correctly perceives the image-vision, the lock-in mechanism prevents his death, so long as he tells no one of the vision of the acquired soul. Such a lock-in of one's soul gives to others in association with the individual a sense of pending power that must be controlled.

As a questing individual and his or her immediate associates seek to control the power rising from the datura experience, they maintain a sense of religious community in the face of, or in the midst of, possible chaos. To the extent that a person speaks of, or otherwise releases, such newly acquired power, he or she loses control of the knowledge manifest in a successful quest; the results of such release and consequent loss can be devastating. For example, increased shamanic activity aimed at harming those perceived to be enemies, and/or physical violence against such enemies, may erupt from such a release. This eruption causes social and political upheaval that can alter quotidian life and cosmic networks sufficiently to produce a historical marker.

Knowledge derived from cultural mythology and historical legend is fundamental to Quichua and Jivaroan senses of "ours" and "others'." Figure 1 illustrates how, from Canelos Quichua perspectives, knowledge of "our" culture is juxtaposed to knowledge from "other" cultures. Here the *yachaj*, or more properly *sinchi yachaj* (*uwishin* in Achuar) has attained a level of control such that he is sufficiently strong to balance his knowledge with his visions, to relate his visions to cultural knowledge, and to relate his thoughts and reflections to his knowledge and his visions. He acquires the ability to cure by sucking out magical substances *(tsintsak)* and to harm others by blowing projectiles into them. Shamanic performances take place at night, while the sha-

FIGURE 1. *Canelos Quichua Perspectives on "Our" Culture and "Other" Cultures*

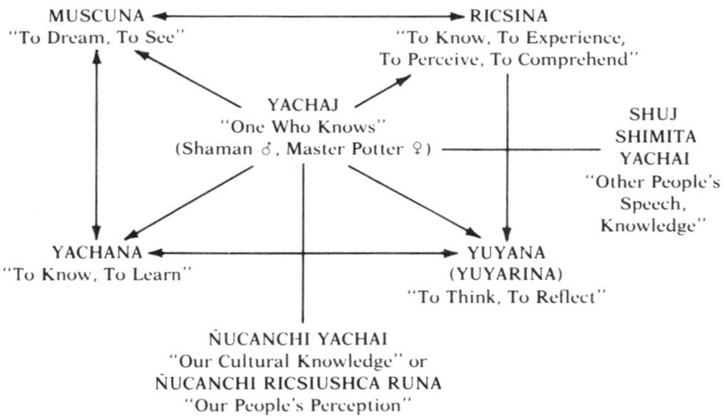

man is in self-induced trance aided by *ayahuasca* (soul vine). Among the Canelos Quichua the soul vine is *Banisteriopsis caapi*. Juice from the vine is brewed with the leaves of another *Banisteriopsis* vine, or with *Psychotria viridis* leaves, to produce the chemical bonding necessary for visionary experience. The shaman, seated on a turtle seat of power, is visited by spirits as he—the shaman—visits spirits seated on their seats of power.

To know more about that which is within, the shaman must increasingly know more about that which is without. The shaman becomes a *paradigm manipulator*. His knowledge of the cosmos and his perceptions derived therefrom are stronger than the knowledge and perceptions embodied in other minds and psyches. He moves into a shaman's class *(yachaj sami)* of humans, which parallels a similar class of spirits. He continuously reproduces cultural knowledge, continuously transforms that very knowledge, and imbues it with novel insights. He also maintains the contrast between "our culture" and "other cultures" (from Quichua and Jivaroan perspectives) while transcending the very boundaries that he enforces.

The work of the shaman must, in part, be based on his experience with other peoples who speak other languages; this kind of contact gives the shaman "other-speech knowledge." The shaman maintains Canelos Quichua and/or Achuar paradigms while expanding the paradigms by drawing from his knowledge of other cultures. The shaman controls the process of syncretism. In this control lies the interface between cultural continuity (or reproduction) and cultural change (or transformation).

Among the Canelos Quichua, master potters, all of whom are women, do the same thing. Working with designs that signal the anaconda, the Amazonian turtle, the tortoise, and the iguanid—all representing imagery of shamanic power—master potters produce an array of decorated ceramic containers for storing and drinking manioc porridge. The designs on the containers link cosmic networks to quotidian events, the general to the specific, the ancient to the present, the mysterious to the mundane. A female paradigm-manipulator may, in Canelos Quichua, be called *sinchi muscuj huarmi* ("strong image-shaping woman"), or even *yachaj huarmi* ("woman who knows").

Among the Canelos Quichua, every master potter is related closely to a strong shaman. In some cases the shaman is a father, in some cases a father-in-law. In many cases there is a complex of shamanic males and master-potter females. Cultural transmission is parallel: female paradigm-manipulators pass their skills to women, male paradigm-manipulators transmit to men. But men and women are conversant with the altergender paradigm and, upon the death of a strong shaman, a wife may assume the shamanic activities of her deceased husband.

Male shamanic performance and female ceramic manufacture draw in a parallel way on certain concepts that are fundamental to religious convictions and insights. One of these is that everything is sentient and that, accordingly, everything has a soul *(aya)*. Another is that differential power imbues various objects in manners relatively analogous to the ways by which differential power of humans vis-à-vis one another is organized. Inasmuch as power is shaped and organized into various hierarchies by different humans, human groups, spirits, and beings, there is no single power-pyramid; rather, there are many overlapping and interfacing power-pyramids through which humans, spirits, beings, and the souls of each may move.

Another fundamental concept of Canelos Quichua and Achuar Jivaroan religion is that all life exists on different planes of existence at the same time. For example, in the thought of the Canelos Quichua, *unai* refers to mythic time-space. In *unai* everything was (or is) human, and people (like those in present time-space) crawled on their hands and knees like babes and spoke only in a two-tone hum: $^{mm}{}_{mm}$ $^{mm}{}_{mm}$. One enters different planes of existence through dreams associated with sleep, through insight, through conscious imagery constructed deliberately or accidentally, through imagery induced by the ingestion of *Banisteriopsis* or datura hallucinogens, through shamanic instruction, through fatigue, through accident or by shamanic (human or spirit) design, and recently by drinking alcohol. In the transformation from *unai* to ancient times, spirits, animals, trees, celestial bodies, colors—everything—underwent reformulation to something other than human.

Today, in the worldview of the Canelos Quichua, it is not altogether certain that people speaking other languages emerged fully "human" from *unai.*

The sentient power of breath (*samai,* in Canelos Quichua) is another key Jivaroan and Quichua religious concept; the powers embodied in breath must be carefully controlled. In the transformation from *unai* to ancient times, once-human beings blew on one another and on other beings and spirits, causing them to "stay that way," to be as human beings know and perceive them today. Male shamans breathe gently onto polished stones to "see" whether the stone "lives." Female potters breathe on their pottery-burnishing stones for the same purpose. A strong shaman must have the inner ability to sing his shaman's song well enough to control the spirit defenses needed to thwart incoming shamanic projectiles from rival shamans, which all shamanic songs invoke. Similarly, a master potter must control the breath of fire that releases the souls imparted to, and the spirits associated with, her ceramics, or retribution from the imparted and subsequently liberated souls may result. A man must also control the sounds of spirits that come from *unai* to pass outward on his breath when he plays a flute or musical bow, while women control analogous sounds that come to them from *unai* when they sing songs. The specific knowledge of songs comes to them from other forebear women in other times and places.

Male/female parallelism in cultural transmission is enacted annually by the Canelos Quichua in a ceremony that expands the universe to include all spirits, souls, beings, and people. Enactment takes place only in hamlets with a Catholic church or chapel, where the chaotic and destructive merger of "outside" foreigner's force and "inside" native power may merge. All facets of Canelos Quichua cosmology are enacted as, for three days and nights, celebrants pass back and forth from the male festival house (ritual enclosure of the Moon) to the female festival house (ritual enclosure of Moon's sister-lover, the whippoorwill-like potoo). The ceremony ends with a powerful and palpable ritual reversal. In this enactment, which the Canelos Quichua call Dominario (from the Spanish word *dominar,* "to control"), the mighty anaconda is brought from the water to move on the land.

In Canelos Quichua thought, the anaconda (*amarun,* or *amaru,* as in the Andes) only comes on land to devour humans. In the Dominario, the anaconda, corporeal representative of master-spirit Tsunki, is borne on the back of four men who represent jaguars, corporeal representatives of Amasanga. Instead of controlling Tsunki's domain (the hydrosphere), Amasanga releases it. Instead of the externally imposed social control *(dominario)* represented by the church, indigenous power becomes an embodied apotheosis of stylized resistance. As the Dominario begins, an outsider, downriver (deeper Amazonian), powerful shaman gently plays a combination of flute and drum associated with Andean masked ceremonies. The melody itself is a skillful blend of his private Amazonian shaman's song *(taquina)* and a public Andean ceremonial melodic motif. As the four men come forth bearing a bamboo pole with four copal fires burning within it (the stylized anaconda brought from the water), festival participants begin dancing through arches constructed for the Catholic mission. Then the transformation, called *tucuna,* begins. The pole, as *amarun* (anaconda), Tsunki's corporeal form, is carried in a lurching, going-out-of-control manner. It becomes destructive; the bearers and the pole crash right into and through the church, slamming, falling, rising again, running, frightening everyone, going completely out of control while still in a cultural domain characterized by Catholic mission control, or domination.

Acting against such domination within a domain of domination, the festival reaches a crescendo that is, quite literally, terrifying to the participants. Women dance with their hair flying to and fro, their sideways motion being the analog of the male-performed two-tone hum of shamanic chanting that evokes the imagery of mythic time-space *(unai).* Men beat snare drums, circling and circling while producing a resonating pulse-tremolo signifying Amasanga's rumble of approaching thunder. All souls and spirits and beings are indiscriminately summoned. As escalating chaos reigns, the church is said to be destroyed in one great transformation of the world of forest and garden and earth and mire into an encompassing, rushing, surging, eastward-flowing sea. When performing this event, the Canelos Quichua say that they fear *tucurina,* which derives from *tucuna* ("transformation"), and means "ending everything." The concept of *tucurina* is one of the most powerful ones in Canelos Quichua thought, particularly when applied reflexively to one's own group. It means, in this sense, that to truly destroy the dominating authority of the church by the invocation of the ultimate power of Tsunki, as devouring anaconda, the Canelos Quicha may also destroy themselves, embedded as they are—in a revelatory manner through the vehicle of this ritual—in that very domination.

The festival sketched here embodies and syncretizes many elements of Andean and Amazonian symbolism, as well as wide-flung Catholic and indigenous symbolism. The controlled analysis of its structure and enactment in terms of Andean/Amazonian religions and Christian/animistic religions should take the comparative study of religion far toward dissolving such rigid polarities by establishing new, more productive bases for deep and meaningful comparative understanding.

BIBLIOGRAPHY

Bottasso B., Juan. *Los Shuar y las misiones: Entre la hostilidad y el diálogo.* Quito, 1982. An accurate portrayal of the historical relationships between the Shuar Jivaroans of Ecuador and the Salesian mission.

Brown, Michael Forbes. "Magic and Meaning in the World of the Aguaruna Jivaro of Peru." Ph.D. diss., University of Michigan, 1981. A highly readable doctoral dissertation that seeks to understand the cosmology of the Aguaruna together with the ecological imagery that such a cosmology organizes.

Chumap Lucía, Aurelio, and Manuel García-Rendueles. *"Duik Múun . . .": Universo mítico de los Aguaruna.* 2 vols. Lima, 1979. A splendid two-volume rendition of Aguaruna mythology.

Harner, Michael J. *The Jívaro: People of the Sacred Waterfalls.* 2d ed., rev. Berkeley, 1983. Pioneering ethnography of the Ecuadorian Shuar with an easy-to-read description and analysis of the famous *arutam* (ancient image) and *tsantsa* (human trophy head) complex.

Karsten, Rafael. *The Head-Hunters of Western Amazonas: The Life and Culture of the Jibaro Indians of Eastern Ecuador and Peru.* Helsinki, 1935. A weighty tome that deals with the Canelos Quichua, the Achuar, and the Shuar of Ecuador. Oscillations between firsthand data and speculations are disconcerting, as is the excessive lumping together of data apparently gleaned from bilingual Achuar-Canelos Quichua at Canelos and other Bobonaza River sites with those from a non-Jivaroan informant in Sucúa about the Shuar. This book must be used with care, and information in it must be cross-checked against other sources.

"Mundo Shuar." Quito, 1976–. Series F is devoted to monograph-length publications on key Shuar images, including *Arutam* (no. 1) and *Tsunki* (no. 2), and on shamanism, as in *El Uwishin* (no. 3).

Reeve, Mary-Elizabeth. "Identity as Process: The Meaning of *Runapura* for Quichua Speakers of the Curaray River, Eastern Ecuador." Ph.D. diss., University of Illinois at Urbana-Champaign, 1985. The history and identity system of the Canelos Quichua of the Curaray River region are portrayed from indigenous and Catholic mission perspectives. Convincingly demonstrates close relationships between Canelos Quichua, Zaparoan, and Achuar cultures and identity systems, as well as the striking parallels between Andean Quechua and Canelos Quichua social structure and ritual enactment.

Taylor, Anne-Christine. "God-Wealth: The Achuar and the Missions." In *Cultural Transformations and Ethnicity in Modern Ecuador,* edited by Norman E. Whitten, Jr., pp. 647–676. Urbana, Ill., 1981. A sensitive portrayal of Achuar cosmological transformations in the face of radical social, economic, and political change.

Whitten, Dorothea S. "Ancient Tradition in a Contemporary Context: Canelos Quichua Ceramics and Symbolism." In *Cultural Transformations and Ethnicity in Modern Ecuador,* edited by Norman E. Whitten, Jr., pp. 749–775. Urbana, Ill., 1981. A penetrating look at the symbolism embedded in Canelos Quichua ceramics not only in terms of traditional cosmology but also by reference to radical social change.

Whitten, Dorothea S., and Norman E. Whitten, Jr. *Our Beauty, Our Knowledge: The Expressive Culture of the Canelos Quichua of Ecuador.* Urbana, Ill., 1985. Script of a thirty-minute video documentation of the key concepts set forth in this article, thoroughly and dramatically illustrated through Canelos Quichua art and music.

Whitten, Norman E., Jr., with the assistance of Marcelo Naranjo, Marcelo Santi Simbaña, and Dorothea S. Whitten. *Sacha Runa: Ethnicity and Adaptation of Ecuadorian Jungle Quichua.* Urbana, Ill., 1976. Definitive ethnography of the Canelos Quichua culture area based on modern techniques of description and analysis.

Whitten, Norman E., Jr. *Sicuanga Runa: The Other Side of Development in Amazonian Ecuador.* Urbana, Ill., 1985. Deals extensively with the cosmological underpinnings of remarkable endurance in Canelos Quichua culture. Relationships between women's art and male shamanic performance profusely illustrated by over 150 plates, drawings, photographs, and other illustrations.

Norman E. Whitten, Jr.

QUESTS. The Ojibwa Indians tell the story of the boy Wunzh and his vision quest. Having reached the appropriate age for the ritual search for totem spirits, Wunzh is left alone in the great forest. After several days of fasting, he retires exhausted to the lonely hut provided for him and waits for the dreams he hopes his guardian spirits will send. There he prays for advice on how his family and tribe might more efficiently obtain food. Wunzh takes to his mat and soon has a vision of a strange young man dressed in yellow and green with feathers on his head. As he descends from the sky, the young man announces that he comes from the Great Spirit to answer Wunzh's prayer. "I will teach you to help your people," he says, "but first you must wrestle with me." Weak from fasting, the boy nevertheless does as he is told and holds his own in the match. "Enough!" cries the spirit. "I will return tomorrow." On the next day, the spirit returns. The boy is, of course, weaker than before but feels that he has gained an inner strength, and he fights well. Again the spirit cries, "Enough! I will return tomorrow." On the third day, the boy is weaker still, but his inner strength has grown proportionately. He fights so well that the spirit concedes defeat and begins to instruct him. "Tomorrow, because it will be the seventh day of your fast, your father will come and offer you food. You must not eat until you have wrestled with me one more time. Then, if you defeat me, strip me and bury me in the ground after clearing a spot and loosening the earth. In the weeks that follow, you must remove the weeds from my grave and keep the earth soft. If you do exactly as I say, you will learn something of great value to your people." Wunzh's father does bring food and begs the boy to eat. The boy asks his father to leave him and promises to return home by sundown. The spirit appears at the usual hour, and the boy, now full of supernatural power, easily defeats his adversary, kills, strips, and buries him as instructed, and returns to his father's lodge to eat. During the spring, Wunzh visits the grave of the spirit regularly and tends it with care. Soon the green plumes of the sky visitor's headgear begin to push through the ground. In late summer, the boy asks his father to accompany him to the spot of his fasting, and there he reveals the grave from which has sprung a fine plant with great yellow tassels. "This is my sky friend Mondawmin, the spirit of maize. If we do as the spirit has taught, we can have food from the ground. The Great Spirit has answered my prayer; my fast has been rewarded."

The story of Wunzh and Mondawmin is but one mask of a basic pattern to be found in the stories of any number of culture heroes and in the rituals of various cults. The story would not be foreign to the young San or Australian Aborigine initiate. The newly confirmed Christian, the Jew who has just become *bar mitsvah*, or the newly circumcised Muslim might feel inklings of familiarity with it. The process by which inner strength grows at the expense of physical strength during a period of self-denial and searching is as familiar to the reader of Hindu, Buddhist, Christian, Islamic, or Jewish scripture as it is to the American Indian on his vision quest.

At its most basic level the quest is a phenomenon inherent in existence itself. In a universe in which all things must ultimately be defined in terms of their relation to the dominant pull toward energy dispersal or entropy, simply to exist is to be part of the great quest for survival. For the human being another dimension is added by virtue of the existence in us of consciousness, specifically, consciousness of linear time. To see a beginning, a middle, and an end is to see a "road of life," and to see such a road is to see a potential quest. We cannot, in fact, be human without being to some degree questers, and this fact is the source of the power of the quest story to speak to us wherever and whoever we are.

Not surprisingly, then, the quest myth is inexorably associated with the figure of the hero, the human metaphor for the all-encompassing chaos-to-cosmos creation process by which entropy is held at bay. The quest, of course, takes many forms. The hero's nature, motives, and goals derive from the particular legend of which he is a part and the society he represents. The hero might be a knight, a sage, or a prince and the goal a golden fleece, a princess, or a pot of gold. The earliest quest stories, like the earliest religious systems, must have reflected a society concerned primarily with fertility and physical survival in the face of a hostile environment. We sense the vestiges of this in the many tales in which a prince seeks and finds a princess and through union with her brings prosperity to a kingdom.

One of the best known of the European quests is that of the Holy Grail. It was Jessie Weston in her classic *From Ritual to Romance: An Account of the Holy Grail from Ancient Ritual to Christian Symbol* (Garden City, N.Y., 1957) who pointed out that although the grail legend was an outgrowth of medieval Christianity and chivalry, it had deeper roots in ancient fertility cults. The ostensible quest of the grail knights is for the cup used by Christ at the Last Supper. A less conscious but more profound objective is the renewal of a society represented not only by the infertile kingdom of the Fisher King but by the somewhat complaisant order of the Round Table. The quest of the knights for the Holy Grail is analogous to—and a metaphor for—the Christian's quest for the kingdom of God in life and in the ritual of the holy elements. Life renewal is always the ultimate goal of the quest, and life renewal is both a spiritual and a physical process.

For example, one of the world's greatest quest stories, one that influenced nearly all narratives that followed it, is Homer's *Odyssey*. While Odysseus's goal seems to be a purely secular one—he wishes to return to his wife and his child—it is also true that his adventures depict a process by which a "lost soul" is reconciled with the cosmos, which is represented by the gods. The trials he undergoes, culminating in a visit to the land of the dead, are the means by which, with Athena's help, he is able to regain his proper place in the gods' order of things. Odysseus's quest is not altogether unlike that of another famous Greek, Oedipus, who can release Thebes from the bondage of infertility only by discovering himself, by finding an answer to the ultimate spiritual question: who am I?

The essentially religious aspect of the quest is perhaps most obvious in those traditions that stress mystical values. The image of the Buddha under the Bodhi Tree or that of the Hindu ascetic in deep contemplation are as much true masks of the quest as is the story of the Holy Grail, the myth of Jason and the Golden Fleece, or the account of the Magi seeking the Christ child. Literal movement from one place to the other is not necessary to the quest; the point is that the Buddha under the Bodhi Tree seeks enlightenment as actively in his own way as Gawain seeks the Holy Grail. Whether the hero gallops off to faraway lands or sits under a tree, his quest involves a journey to and often beyond the boundaries of human experience and knowledge. In this sense, the story of the quest is always what the Hindu might call a search for the Self or what the psychiatrist Carl Jung called the process of individuation. In short, the quest is a metaphor for the spiritual journey, our own potential spiritual journey represented by that of the hero.

The Ur-hero and the Ur-myth that emerge from a comparison of the world's many quest stories, then, reveal what can be called a universal ritual of re-creation. The ritual requires certain steps. First, like the priest in any ritual, the hero must be properly vested; he must be clearly recognizable and ordained for his task, a task—the realization of our humanity—that is a matter of life and death for us all. So it is that the quester's heroism has been preliminarily established by a miraculous conception and/or birth, a divine sign of some sort, or by an extraordinary childhood deed. Before his ordeal, Oedipus is recognized as a savior-hero by virtue of his defeat of the sphinx that had plagued Thebes. His abandonment in the wilderness as a child marks him as well, placing him in a sacred order, as it were—one that includes Moses, Siegfried, and the Indian Karṇa, as well as the Phrygians Cybele (the Great Mother) and Attis. Herakles and the *avatāra* Kṛṣṇa are marked by their defeat of evil monsters while still in infancy. Jesus' nature is indicated by the circumstances of his conception and birth and by his extraordinary intelligence, as demonstrated in the Temple when he is twelve. He also receives a sign from God at his baptism. The Buddha, as a white elephant, is the agent of his own conception and, like the Toltec-Aztec Quetzalcoatl, further proves his nature by possessing adult qualities at birth. Sir Gawain and the other Arthurian questers are eligible for the grail search by virtue of past "adventures" and because of their association with Arthur as knights in the sacred society of the Round Table.

The hero, having been proclaimed, is ritually called to the quest. The call might come through a natural object: Moses is called by Yahveh in the burning bush; the Magi are called by the star; and the grail knights, by the Holy Grail itself, appearing in their midst at Pentecost. Angels or other supernatural heralds are common, and often the herald remains as a guide. The Buddha is called when, driven about by his charioteer, he is made to witness several forms of suffering humanity "fashioned" magically by the gods. Another important charioteer-herald or guide is found in the *Bhagavadgītā*, part of one of the great Indian epics, the *Mahābhārata*. In this work, the god Kṛṣṇa in the guise of a charioteer urges Prince Arjuna on to battle and to higher values.

However the call is made, it signals the necessity of an awakening to destiny in the face of an individual or societal malaise. A renewal is called for, and the hero either responds to the call immediately or at first refuses it. A natural enough reaction of any individual faced with a serious psychological, spiritual, or physical task is to withdraw from the field. Prince Arjuna at first refuses the call to battle; Kṛṣṇa must convince him to fight. Even the most "religious" of heroes express their common humanity with us by their reluctance. "No, Lord, send whom thou wilt," is Moses' answer to God's call. And Jesus, in the garden of Gethsemane on the eve of his crucifixion, prays to God, saying, "My Father, if it is possible, let this cup pass me by." A particularly dramatic example of this category is the story of Jonah, whose refusal results in an unwanted voyage in the belly of a whale. The Buddha's father might be said to have attempted to refuse the call for his son when he so desperately tried to isolate him from the real world. Occasionally the call itself is a test, and the refusal one of omission rather than commission. For instance, Parzival fails to ask certain ritual questions while being entertained at the castle of the Fisher King and misses his chance to free the king and his land of the ancient curse.

In ultimately accepting the call, however, the hero undertakes a series of trials; these adventures reflect the agonies involved in confronting the inner realities that we glimpse in dreams or periods of disorientation. In the context of the spiritual journey, the monsters, demons, and impossible tasks that confront the hero are all those factors that would imprison us in the barren world of egocentricity. They would prevent us from attaining renewal—the spiritual vitality represented by the attainment of the Golden Fleece, the elixirs of life, the Holy Grail, and the rescued princesses toward which the heroic adventures lead.

So it is that in the Hindu epic the *Rāmāyaṇa*, the demon king Rāvaṇa kidnaps Rāma's wife, Sītā, setting up a quest that is a struggle between the forces of love and union and those of violence and disintegration. And the figures that stand between Odysseus and his reunion with the faithful Penelope are such nightmarish beings as the one-eyed Cyclops; the witch Circe, who turns men into beasts; and the bewitching Sirens. The Babylonian-Sumerian epic hero Gilgamesh must overcome Huwawa, the monster of death, and Ishtar in her form as seductress. Jesus is tempted in the wilderness by the devil, who offers tangible worldly achievements as a substitute for the intangible ones inherent in the quest for the kingdom of heaven. The Buddha is tempted similarly by Māra the fiend, who attempts to dislodge the Great One from his position under the tree by reminding him of the more ordinary values of human life. Māra assumes the form of a messenger who informs Siddhartha that his father's kingdom has been usurped and his wife taken, and that he must return home. When this approach fails, he resorts to violence, to theological argument, and finally to sexual temptation, all to prevent the renewal of life that is the hero's goal.

The penultimate test of the hero is the descent into the underworld and confrontation with death itself. Only by, in some sense, dying to the world can the hero be resurrected as "eternal man" renewed. Only by going down can the sun hope to arise. Odysseus, Theseus, Herakles, Jesus, the Egyptian Osiris, and Dionysos all journey to the land of the dead. And the more mystical questers such as John of the Cross (the Spanish poet-monk of the sixteenth century) and Julian of Norwich (an English mystic of the fourteenth century) or "psychological" ones such as Carl Jung take equivalent journeys, "night journeys" or "dark nights of the soul," which are characterized by agonies and fears that necessarily mark a journey into the spiritual or psychic underworld. In such journeys as these, we sense the real purpose of the descent in general as one having to do with the retrieval of a lost self. Odysseus and Aeneas seek their destiny among the dead. Jesus, the "second Adam," descends to retrieve the "lost" Adam. The sun king Gilgamesh descends to find eternal life but also hopes to retrieve his friend and double, Enkidu. In one of the oldest quest stories—if not the oldest—we know of, the Sumerian mother goddess Inanna descends into the underworld to find her lost lover, Dumuzi; the lost lover, of course, is the other half without which significant wholeness—what the Chinese would call the oneness of *yin* and *yang*—is not possible.

It should be pointed out that what heroes do in the old quest stories, flesh and blood human beings act out through the medium of religious ritual and related disciplines. The Muslim who journeys to Mecca is given the special title of *ḥājj* for having followed in the steps of the Prophet. The shaman, whether American Indian or Siberian, journeys ritually and psychically to the "other world" to confront the spirits who would deprive an individual or tribe of health or life. And tribal initiation at puberty often involves a quest, as our story of Wunzh and Mondawmin indicates. Even the ordinary worshiper becomes a real quester in the physical realm. A Hindu, Buddhist, or Christian who enters a place of worship undertakes a re-creative journey in microcosm from the chaos of the world to the cosmos of ultimate reality or primal cause. Reminders of the hero journey are frequently in evidence in these temples of worship. Gargoyle monsters guard the doorways—the thresholds—as if to say, "Enter here at risk." Indeed, the true religious quest, like the shaman's descent, can be a dangerous affair.

The symbolism of the quest sometimes literally determines the place of worship. Such is the case with the traditional church building. Having passed by the monsters over the doorway, the Christian voyager in the great medieval cathedral confronts the font that represents his baptism, the spiritual rebirth that he now reaffirms by making the sign of the cross with holy water. He enters the church proper, where he will participate in the Mass, itself a complex representation of the journey of Christ through death, descent, and resurrection—a journey that the worshiper shares and literally acts out by moving eventually to the altar at the far end of the church in order to participate in the eucharistic sacrifice before reentering the world as a renewed being. A secular modern version of this spiritual journey takes place on the psychiatrist's couch, where renewal involves a quest of self-discovery by means of a process of recalling—literally, remembering.

The most obvious expression of the quest is in literature. As has been suggested, anything that has a beginning, a middle, and an end, in the manner that plot does, is likely to be in some sense a quest. Odysseus seeks reunion with Penelope, Aeneas looks for a new Troy, Dante's and John Bunyan's pilgrims journey toward the kingdom of God, Tom Jones hopes to become worthy of his Sophia, and Anton Chekhov's three sisters long for Moscow.

A type of literature in which the quest motif is particularly unveiled and, therefore, particularly open to observation is the fairy tale. A good example is one that appears in many parts of the world and takes its most familiar form as *The Water of Life* in the Grimm brothers' collection. As the title indicates, it is a story in which the spiritual goal of life renewal is only barely masked.

"Once upon a time, there lived a king who was desperately ill." The beginning of this tale—and of most fairy tales—involves the ritual placing of a situation in time. It is one half of a framework that will be completed in the "happily ever after" ending, releasing the hero of the tale from his temporal trials by placing him in a state of wholeness that is eternal. In the first image of *The Water of Life,* the king, like nearly all kings, represents the kingdom of man on earth brought into conflict by our universal nemesis, mortality. That which was once whole—in harmony with the absolute—is now unwhole. The king's mythical and literary relatives are such figures as the Fisher King of the grail romance and Shakespeare's Lear. The sick old king constellates the theme of salvation or renewal, which is the religious essence of the quest.

The king has three sons, who weep in the palace garden at their father's plight. As potential saviors, the children must remind us of the knights of the Round Table. The symbolic nature of numbers in fairy tales, as in religious ritual and theology, is such that the presence here of three children is significant. The number four represents the quaternity, which symbolizes balance and wholeness, and four brothers would mean a common effort. Three, on the other hand, tends to suggest the discord of two against one.

In the garden an old man appears to the sons to tell them that their father might be cured by the water of life: "One drink of it and he will be well, but the water is difficult to find." As we have seen, the guide is a familiar figure in quest tales. His function is to point to the solution of the insoluble problem, to establish the means of salvation by interjecting the "other" into the limited world of time and space. His way invariably involves a difficult quest.

The oldest son goes to his father to request permission to attempt the search for the water of life. Refused at first, he perseveres so that the king finally agrees, the prince thinking all the while, "If I find the water, my father will give me his kingdom." Soon after setting off, the prince meets a dwarf, who inquires as to his destination. When he answers back in an insulting manner, the dwarf imprisons him on horseback between two mountains that magically converge upon him. When the first son fails to return, the second son makes the same request of his father, is answered in the same way, and, like his brother, dreams of inheriting the kingdom. Upon meeting the same dwarf, he is asked where he is going, and he gives the same insulting answer. Needless to say, his punishment is the same as his brother's. The identical formula used in connection with the first two sons suggests a ritual purpose: the two older sons act out the negative aspect of a pattern in which the son who is an honest and unsullied quester for Self contrasts with the sons who embody a corrupt unreceptiveness to the call.

When his brothers fail to return, the youngest son begs for and obtains his father's reluctant permission to set out on the same quest. But, unlike his brothers, he thinks only of the welfare of his father. Where the others are motivated by hope for material gain—by egotism—and are appropriately punished by their imprisonment in a narrow ravine, the young son is motivated by love, which is the proper attitude on the path to salvation. His meeting with the dwarf is, therefore, very different from that of his brothers.

"Where are you going?" asks the dwarf, following the ritual pattern. "I am seeking the water of life to cure my ailing father" is the humble reply. The dwarf, pleased, instructs the boy on how to achieve his goal: "The water runs from a fountain in an enchanted castle. Take this iron wand, and knock three times to open the castle door. And take these two loaves of bread to quiet the lions who guard the door. Only be sure that you obtain the water and leave the castle before the clock strikes twelve, or you will be imprisoned there for life."

The dwarf, like the old man in the garden, is a personification of the spiritual guide. Here, he takes the form of the shaman-teacher, who trains the good prince in magic and provides the paraphernalia necessary to release the healing forces—the water of life. The instructions he gives make no rational sense but, as in the case of all rituals, must be performed on faith, just as the ugly little dwarf himself must be accepted on faith. Only the young son has such faith; only he passes the test. The old dwarf is to him what the fairy godmother is to Cinderella or Athena to Odysseus. He is the small voice in the dark that shows the path to the essential religious experience, the goal of which is the overcoming of death. The dwarf, as an agent of the other world, is not subject to mere physical law; for this reason, he possesses magic.

Arriving at the castle, the young prince follows the ritual instructions. The iron doors are overcome by the iron rod; the lions are quieted with the bread. Inside the castle, the prince finds a sword and a loaf of bread and several enchanted princes. A beautiful princess greets him as her liberator and promises to give herself to him in marriage if he will return in a year. The princess now leads the prince to the water of life and reminds him to be sure to leave the castle before the clock strikes twelve.

Many of the elements of the hero's descent into the underworld and of the psychological and spiritual process it represents are operative in these events. The prince embodies, as do all heroes of the quest, our potential journey into the unknown, which is the locked and enchanted castle. The hero always descends to redeem those imprisoned by the darkness. Jesus brings back Adam and Eve; Orpheus almost liberates Eurydice. In this case, the retrieved one is the princess, who, like the enchanted Sleeping Beauty, is the deeper, lost half of the unredeemed Self longing to be released, an embodiment of the divine wisdom, or Sophia, apart from whom the Logos cannot be made flesh. The lions, overcome by the magic of supernatural power, are the bestial deterrents to the journey within.

In the princess's promise of marriage there is no question of realistic love. The relationship is ritualistic; the hero and heroine act in a way that is archetypal and symbolic rather than sentimental. The marriage of the future is established as the prince's ultimate goal after the curing of his father. The sword and the bread, symbols of power and nourishment and potential good deeds, are to be magical aids to that goal. It is the princess who leads the prince to the magical water, because, as Divine Wisdom, she is the proper guardian of the symbol of eternal life to be gained from the eventual emergence of the Self. Her repetition of the dwarf's interdiction concerning the hour of the prince's departure from the castle is an indication that she and the dwarf are of one and the same power, the universal creative impulse by which the continuing evolution symbolized by the quest itself is made feasible. In terms of the Christian culture in which the Grimms discovered this tale, the princess takes on meaning in the context of the Virgin cult. The Virgin is the earthly form of the mother of God, but as the church—the castle freed from enchantment—she is also God's bride. In this role as both mother-guide and wife, she reaches back to the most ancient traditions of the Great Goddess herself.

When the princess leaves him, the prince comes upon a fine bed that he finds irresistible, and he lies down to sleep. In so doing, he conveys ritually his brotherhood with all the offspring of the primordial fallen parents. Like Christ in the garden of Gethsemane, he demonstrates his human nature. Only the sound of the clock striking midnight awakens him. He quickly draws water from the fountain and escapes through the closing doors, losing only a piece of his heel, which signifies his having almost ignored the interdictions of the dwarf and the princess. In this incident we are reminded not only of Cinderella and her glass slipper but of the fact that the journey is fraught with many temptations and dangers, any of which could prevent success. Perhaps the loss of a part of the body also ties the prince to the many dismembered man-gods of the Near Eastern fertility cults. It seems evident, as the prince's mishap is never mentioned again in the story, that this is a ritual event with symbolic rather than narrative significance.

The prince is now ready for the trials that, if accomplished, will lead him back to a final reunion with the princess. Journeying homeward, he again meets the dwarf, who informs him of the magical powers contained in the sword and the loaf of bread found in the castle. The sword can be used to defeat whole armies; the bread can feed the hungry indefinitely. The religious significance of the sword as God's righteous justice and of the bread as the bread of life is clear. Much of this symbolism is traceable to the Christian tradition, in which much is made of the Christ's coming with both bread and the sword. But the ultimate source of the symbolism very likely lies in much older traditions.

The young prince now emerges more clearly as a savior figure when he begs the dwarf to release his sinful brothers. The dwarf, in his ancient wisdom, warns the boy of the danger in this course, but to no avail. The attempt to redeem them must be made; the road to reunion with the Self must involve direct dealings with the dark forces represented by the brothers. And when the brothers are released the prince—foolishly, from a practical point of view—tells them of his quest and of his prospects for the future. The three brothers travel on together, and three kingdoms are saved by the sword and the bread. It is not surprising that the older sons betray their brother at the earliest possible opportunity. One night as he sleeps, they steal the magic fluid and substitute salt water for it. The betrayal by siblings is an ancient and recurring motif found, for example, in the biblical story of Cain and Abel, the Egyptian story of Seth and Osiris, and any number of familiar fairy tales. Goodness in its mercy is by nature vulnerable to evil, which is itself by nature aggressive. It is as if the hero must, as a part of his trials, allow himself to be placed in the position of the ritual sacrificial victim.

The king is given the false water by the young prince, and his health worsens. The older sons accuse their brother of attempting to murder the king and produce the real water, claiming that it is they who have found it. The father is immediately cured. The young son, remaining silent—again, as if this were necessary for the inevitable ritual process—is exiled, and an old hunter is given instructions to slay him in the forest. The hunter, like the one in the story of Snow White, cannot bear to carry out his orders: the simple man can recognize innocence where the king cannot. He releases the prince to wander in the woods. Mythically, this period points to the hero's withdrawal into the wilderness, a symbolic death during which he must undergo the ultimate separation that will render him transcendent. It is the period of preparation for the final step in the discovery of Self—an initiation rite that will transfer him from a state of mortality to one of immortality, from immaturity to wisdom.

During this period several things happen. Three cartloads of treasure arrive at the king's palace from the three kings saved by the sword and bread of the good prince. The king begins to suspect that his son might be innocent: "How I wish he were not dead," he laments. Then comes the ritual cry from the huntsman: "He lives! He lives!" Meanwhile, the princess of the castle has prepared one final test. A path of gold is laid before her door, and her servants are told to admit only the knight who rides to the castle upon this path. The two evil brothers, remembering what their brother has told them, approach the castle but will not allow their horses to ride over the gold path, for they value the precious metal more than the object of the quest. Hence they are turned away: evil is unable to attain to divine wisdom. Only those whose priorities extend beyond material gain can enter into the absolute. The young prince, his mind only on the princess, rides on the path without even noticing it and is greeted again by the sacred maiden. The ritual separation is ended; the goddess receives the reborn son.

Like the ascent to paradise in myth, the ritual marriage that ends this and many quest tales expresses the achieved goal of wholeness. The masculine principle is joined to the feminine, and in that union of *yin* and *yang*, the Self is discovered, at which time the present becomes eternity; life can be lived "happily ever after." The joy we feel at the end of the fairy tale and other quest stories is more than a sentimental one. It results from our having gained a vision of the achieved goal of individual growth and human evolution. We glimpse ourselves literally awakening into the permanent consciousness that is self-knowledge. In this sense, the quest tale is always a creation story in which the hero emerges from chaos as re-created God in man.

[*See also* Heroes.]

BIBLIOGRAPHY

The most lively analysis of the hero's quest is still Joseph Campbell's classic study *The Hero with a Thousand Faces* (1949; reprint, Princeton, 1968). C. M. Bowra's "The Hero," in *The Hero in Literature*, edited by Victor Brombert (New York, 1969), is an important essay on the subject. A collection of mythic stories illustrating and representing the heroic monomyth is found in my *Mythology: The Voyage of the Hero* (New York, 1980).

The best treatments of the quest motif in literature, particularly in romance, and of the motif's overall importance for literary criticism are Northrop Frye's *The Anatomy of Criticism* (Princeton, 1957) and "The Archetypes of Literature" and "Quest and Cycle in *Finnegans Wake*," in his *Fables of Identity* (New York, 1963). One of the best and most accessible versions of the Arthurian story is *King Arthur and His Knights: Selected Tales by Sir Thomas Malory*, edited by Eugene Vinaver (Oxford, 1975). On the grail myth, see Henry Kahane and Renée Kahane's *The Krater and the Grail: Hermetic Sources of Parzival* (1965; reprint, Urbana, 1984). The grail myth is one important source for what is perhaps the most famous twentieth-century quest poem, *The Waste Land* by T. S. Eliot. Eliot's *Four Quartets* (New York, 1943) is also a poetic quest, one that owes much to both Occidental and Oriental quest mythology.

For a psychological approach to the quest as a search for self in the modern world, see C. G. Jung's *Modern Man in Search of a Soul* (1933; reprint, New York, 1964). For the best study of the shamanic quest, see Mircea Eliade's *Shamanism: Archaic Techniques of Ecstasy* (New York, 1964). Versions of the Buddhist and Hindu quest stories are found in *Myths of the Hindus and Buddhists* by Ananda K. Coomaraswamy and Sister Nivedita (Margaret E. Noble) (New York, 1967) and in Coomaraswamy's *Buddha and the Gospel of Buddhism* (London, 1928). Any work by Coomaraswamy on the religions of the East is likely to contain useful information on the quest as a mystical spiritual journey. Thomas Merton's writings offer a moving record of a Christian's mystical quest. See, for example, *A Thomas Merton Reader*, edited by Thomas P. McDonnell (Garden City, N.Y., 1974).

David Adams Leeming

QUETZALCOATL was one of the most powerful and multifaceted gods in Mesoamerican religions. The cult of Quetzalcoatl, the "quetzal-feathered serpent," was prominent in central Mexico from at least the time of Teotihuacán (100–750 CE) to the collapse of the Aztec capital of Tenochtitlán in 1521. He was called Kukulcan in the Postclassic Maya culture that developed from 1000 to 1521, and he played a prominent role in the organizing of the capitals of Chichén Itzá and Mayapan. In the more than seventy painted, written, and archaeological sources that carry the elements of the Quetzalcoatl tradition, he appears both as a major celestial creator god and as intimately identified with the paradigmatic priest-king Topiltzin Ce Acatl Quetzalcoatl, whose great kingdom of Tula, or Tollan, flourished between 900 and 1100, and who is remembered as a primary source of culture, political order, and religious authority in Mesoamerica. The archaeological and ethnographic records show that Quetzalcoatl was the symbol of effective organization and sacred authority in a series of capital cities that dominated the history of Mesoamerican religions for almost fifteen hundred years.

In the cosmogonic episodes of the early sources known as *Historia de los Mexicanos por sus pinturas*, the *Anales de Cuauhtitlán*, and the *Leyenda de los soles*, Quetzalcoatl, one of the four sons of the androgynous creator god Ometeotl, plays a number of creative roles: he generates the universe (together with his brother, Tezcatlipoca), rules over various cosmogonic eras, assists in the discovery of maize and pulque, creates fire, participates in the great sacrifice of the gods that leads to the creation of the fifth cosmic age, or Fifth Sun, and becomes transformed into the morning-and-evening star, Venus.

In a number of instances, this creative activity reflects the symbolic design of the Mesoamerican universe as a world divided into five major parts (four cardinal sections around a central space). For instance, in the elaborate cosmology of the *Historia de los Mexicanos por sus pinturas*, Quetzalcoatl and Tezcatlipoca, Lord of the Smoking Mirror, revive the broken universe and set the stage for the fifth age by dispersing the water of chaos and restoring dry land by carving four roads to the center of the earth, from which they raise the sky to create a living space for human beings. Coincidentally, in a number of primary sources that depict the capital city of Tollan, the ceremonial centers are shown divided into five sections with four temples and mountains surrounding the central mountain or temple where the priest-king Quetzalcoatl ruled.

In another series of sources Quetzalcoatl is depicted as the inventor of agriculture, the arts, and the calendar and the restorer of human life through a cosmic dive into the underworld, Mictlan, where he outwits the lord of the dead, Mictlantecuhtli, to recover the bones of the ancestors. In this story, Mictlantecuhtli prepares a death trap for Quetzalcoatl. Quetzalcoatl falls to his death, but then he revives himself to escape Mictlan, meanwhile revitalizing the bones of the dead.

Quetzalcoatl also took the form of Ehécatl, the wind god. As depicted in Fray Bernardino de Sahagún's *Historia general de las cosas de la Nueva España* (compiled 1569–1582; also known as the Florentine Codex), Ehécatl announces the coming of the fertilizing rains and, in one episode, blows the sun into its cosmic orbit, thereby starting the fifth age. Furthermore, a number of sources reveal Quetzalcoatl's close association with the cycles and hierophany of Venus (Tlahuizcalpantecuhtli), one of the major astronomical bodies influencing ritual, architecture, and the calendar in Mesoamerica. The cycles of Venus were a central part of Quetzalcoatl's cult in the city of Chollolan (100–1521 CE), and the *Leyenda de los soles* depicts the self-sacrifice of Ce Acatl Quetzalcoatl following the fall of the kingdom of Tollan, which ends with his heart rising into the sky to become the Morning Star.

Historically, the god Quetzalcoatl was the patron deity of the Toltec empire centered in Tula-Xicocotitlán, also called Tollan. Some scholars, such as H. B. Nicholson, have identified in the primary sources a sacred history of Tollan that relates the seven stages of the priest-king Topiltzin Quetzalcoatl's exemplary human career, including his miraculous birth after his mother swallowed a precious green stone, his teenage revenge of his father's murder, his training for the priesthood, his years as a warrior, his ascension to the throne, the fall of his capital, his flight from Tollan, and his promise to return one day in the future to restore the kingdom. The Tollan of the primary sources is a kingdom secure in agricultural resources, rich in artwork, ritual innovation, and technological excellence, and the birthplace of astronomy and of cardinally oriented ceremonial structures. This world of stability and creativity collapsed through the magical attacks of the magician, Tezcatlipoca, whose cult in some sources was said to depend on human sacrifice. The long-range significance of Quetzalcoatl's Tollan in Mesoamerican history is attested to by the identification of five other capitals—Teotihuacán, Xochicalco, Chichén Itzá, Chollolan, and Tenochtitlán—as places replicating Tollan and the cult of Quetzalcoatl.

In Aztec Mexico, Quetzalcoatl was the patron god of the schools of higher learning, the *calmecac*s, and the model for the office of the high priesthood at the Templo Mayor in Tenochtitlán, in front of which his round temple was apparently located.

When Cortés arrived and began his assault on Tenochtitlán, a number of sources state unequivocally that Moctezuma Xocoytzin (Moctezuma II) identified him as Quetzalcoatl returning to reestablish his kingdom in Mexico.

BIBLIOGRAPHY

Carrasco, Davíd. *Quetzalcoatl and the Irony of Empire: Myths and Prophecies in the Aztec Tradition.* Chicago, 1982. This study places the evidence of Quetzalcoatl's multivalence within the context of urban structure and history in central Mesoamerica. It utilizes the history-of-religions approach to interpret the paradigmatic sacred authority of Quetzalcoatl and Tollan as the sources for empire and destruction in the Aztec capital.

López Austin, Alfredo. *Hombre Dios: Religion y política en el mundo nahuatl.* Mexico City, 1973. The best Spanish-language interpretation of the historical development in pre-Hispanic times of the mythic structure of Quetzalcoatl and its impact on paradigmatic leadership and political ideology in pre-Aztec and Aztec Mexico.

DAVÍD CARRASCO

QUIETISM. Although some of the important insights of Quietism can be found in medieval devotion, in sixteenth-century Spanish spirituality, and in various mystical sources, both Christian and Buddhist, the usual meaning of the word is restricted to the late seventeenth-century devotional movement in the Catholic church in Italy and France. The main figure in the history of Quietism was Miguel Molinos (1628–1696), a Spanish priest who settled in Rome at the end of 1663. He became an enormously popular spiritual adviser, especially among nuns and women of high society. His new contemplative way of Christian perfection was summed up (without some of its esoteric aspects) in a book he published simultaneously in Spanish and Italian: *Guida Spirituale, che disinvolge l'anima e la conduce per il interior camino all'acquisito della perfetta contemplatione e del ricco tesoro della pace interiore* (1685), often referred to as his *Spiritual Guide.*

Though supported by a number of theologians and, for a time, probably by Innocent XI, the *Guide* was soon attacked by the Jesuits for its total disregard of meditation, spiritual asceticism, vocal prayers, and, implicitly, the cults of Jesus and of the Virgin. The criticism ended with the arrest of Molinos on the order of the Holy Office, a long trial, and his condemnation in May 1687. He spent the rest of his life in prison. On 20 November 1687 the papal bull *Coelestis pastor* anathematized sixty-eight of his statements. The material of the condemnation was taken not only, and not mainly, from his published works, but also from about twelve thousand of his letters and from his oral teaching; in addition to the enumerated theological errors, it included the charge of sexual licentiousness—something Molinos inferred from his own doctrines and apparently frequently practiced with his penitent women.

The new devotion (the word *Quietists* had been used since the early 1680s by the enemies of Molinos) was based on the belief that any Christian can achieve an entirely disinterested insight into God; this insight is permanent, internally undifferentiated, and free from images and affects, and it involves a previous destruction of one's own will and consciousness; it is the work of divine grace, which, after the self has emptied itself, totally fills the void and becomes the sovereign owner of the higher part of the soul; as a result, the animal part of the soul as well as the body are no longer the responsibility of the person. This state of perfectly passive contemplation is not only the highest form of religious life, but makes other, more specific forms of worship—the cults of Jesus and of the saints, the acts of repentance and hope, confession, mortifications, prayers, and even concern about one's own salvation—either useless or even harmful insofar as they divert the soul from union with God. And although contemplation is at the beginning inspired by the love of God, it eventually abolishes love, desires, will, and all separate affects. What remains is not an affect, but God himself present in the soul. While it is God's gift, this contemplation is in fact given to everybody who makes a sufficient self-destructive effort, and it does not depend on education, sex, or status. Once acquired, it is effectively permanent. Since it involves a total separation of the soul from the body, the acts of the latter do not disturb it; in fact the devil often inflicts violence on the body of a contemplative and compels it to perform "externally" sinful acts, in particular, of a sexual character, but those acts cannot break the union with God, as they do not affect the soul. Sexual permissiveness is thus justified. The contemplative, being absolutely devoid of his will and transformed into God, cannot do good works on his own initiative or have any intention to help his neighbors; he can perform such works only on a direct order from God.

Molinos's doctrine was obviously unacceptable to the church not only because of its suspect moral consequences, but because it practically abrogated the entire "external" cult, along with discipline, intellectual effort, and the variety of virtues, merits, and religious acts. It reduced the religious life to one habitual act for which the mystic no longer needs the church and which is proclaimed to be the only genuine way of union with God. Further, although Molinos did not consider himself a rebel, but rather a reformer within the church, his devotional program, especially since it was not confined to monasteries but was also propagated among the laity, undermined the role of the church as a mediator between God and man.

Molinos had a few less well-known predecessors, such as the Spanish mystic Jean Falconi (1596–1638), the blind theologian from Marseilles, François Malaval (1627–1719), and the bishop of Jesi, Pier Matto Petrucci (1636–1701), all of whom preached the superiority of passive and unreflective contemplation over meditations and vocal prayers, none of whom, however, extended the theory of mystical kenosis to the acceptance of "diabolic violence" or to the point of advising that we should not fight against temptations.

The more philosophically elaborated variety of Quietism arose on French soil, thanks to the works of Jeanne Marie de la Mothe Guyon (1648–1717) and François Salignac de Fénelon. Guyon had already been trained in mystical devotion when she met, in 1680, the Barnabite father François La Combe, who had been converted in Rome to Molinos's way of perfection. She lived in Paris after 1686, having previously organized small conventicles of mystics in various places. Among her many works, amounting to over forty volumes in the collected writings, the most popular were *Moyen court et très facile de faire oraison* and *Les torrens spirituels*. With highly developed prophetic claims, Guyon believed that God had entrusted her with the mission of a total renewal of Christianity. The contemplative devotion in her description involves all the previous Quietist tenets except for the theory of diabolic violence, but adds some metaphysical ideas. A totally passive contemplation, implying the absolute annihilation of the self, is said to be the only proper way of Christian life. At the highest stage the soul loses everything that is personal or human (*laisser agir Dieu*) and is transformed into God, like a river after reaching the ocean. The self, indeed the very fact of separate existence, is the source of evil, or rather is evil itself, and, after the annihilation, the soul attains the status of God before the act of creation. The soul returns to the original source of being where no place is left for differentiation: "At the very beginning one has to die to everything by which we are something." And this form of being cannot be lost; the deification is inalienable. Indifference to everything other than God, to sin, to the past and to the future, to life and death, to one's own and others' salvation, indeed to divine grace, all this naturally accompanies the blessed state of *theōsis*. The entire variety of religious worship, both external and internal, is done away with once the soul reaches perfection. Priests and the visible church are nothing but obstacles.

Accused of spreading heretical doctrines, Guyon was imprisoned at the beginning of 1688, but she was released after a few months. She then experienced a period of celebrity, during which she enjoyed the friendship of Fénelon and Mme. de Maintenon. The attacks did not stop, however, and a special committee headed by the influential prelate Jacques Bossuet organized a campaign against the Quietist doctrine. Although both Fénelon and Guyon signed the articles confirming the church's traditional doctrine in points where it seemed to be incompatible with the Quietists' devotion, the debates, accusations, pamphlets, and intrigues continued. They ended with the formal condemnation, in a breve (1699) of Innocent XI's, on twenty-three erroneous statements on contemplation and *caritas pura* (disinterested love of God, with no regard to one's salvation) taken from Fénelon's book *Explication des maximes des saints sur la vie intérieure*. Fénelon immediately bowed to the verdict. Guyon was imprisoned from 1695 to 1702.

The Quietist mysticism was certainly incompatible with the teaching and educational system of the Roman church; implicitly, and sometimes explicitly, it questioned the very need of the visible church. The condemnation of Molinos and Fénelon, however, had a negative impact for many decades on the development of mystical spirituality in the Catholic world.

[*See also the biography of Fénelon.*]

BIBLIOGRAPHY

Brémond, Henri. *Apologie pour Fénelon*. Paris, 1910.

Cognet, Louis. *Crépuscule des mystiques: Bossuet, Fénelon*. Tournai, Belgium, 1958.

Dudon, Paul. *Le quiétiste espagnol, Michel Molinos, 1628–1696*. Paris, 1921.

Guerrier, Louis. *Madame Guyon: Sa vie, sa doctrine, et son influence*. Orléans, 1881.

Knox, Ronald A. *Enthusiasm*. Oxford, 1950.

Kolakowski, Leszek. *Chrétiens sans église*. Paris, 1969.

Petrocchi, Massimo. *Il quietismo italiano del seicento*. Rome, 1948.

Schmittlein, Raymond. *L'aspect politique du différend Bossuet-Fénelon*. Bade, 1954.

LESZEK KOLAKOWSKI

QUIRINUS. The nominal adjective *Quirinus* is connected with *Quirites*, as the ancients realized (Varro, *De lingua Latina* 5.73). Modern philology confirms this viewpoint: *Quirinus (*Covir-ino-)* signifies the god of the "community of citizens," **covir-ium*. More specifically, this adjective refers to citizens in time of peace, as *Quirites*, in contrast with citizens enrolled in the army *(exercitus)*. This contrast is evident in the ancient document of the *Commentarii consulares* (see Varro, 6.88).

Quirinus occupies the third place in the archaic triad Jupiter-Mars-Quirinus. He was served by a particular priest, the *flamen Quirinalis*, and stood as a kind of figure symmetrical to Mars, from a threefold point of view. From an ethnic and topographic point of view: he was regarded as being Sabine in origin and possessed a small shrine near the Porta Quirinalis on the Quirinal (Varro, 51). In his "historical" role he was patron of the twelve Salii Collini (Dionysius of Halicarnassus, 2.70.7, 3.32.4), who constituted half the Salian college, and he received the third share of the *spolia opima*, the spoils awarded a Roman commander who had personally slain the enemy commander in battle (Festus, ed. Lindsay, 1913, p. 204 L.). In his specific function, he presided over production and economic prosperity. His feast, the Quirinalia, on 17 February, coincided with the last day of the Fornacalia, dedicated to the torrefaction of grain. This economic competence, which legend presented as the specialty of the Sabines, enabled the *flamen Quirinalis* to intervene in different cults within this sector, thus serving Robigo, the divinity of wheat blight (Ovid, *Fasti* 4.910 ff.) and Consus, the god of storage (Tertullian, *De spectaculis* 5).

The profile of the archaic god was blurred during the historical epoch by certain ambiguities. Owing to the legend of coexistence sanctioning the reconciliation of the Romans with the Sabines, ancient scholars were hard put to define the attributes of a Quirinus who paradoxically had become a tranquil Mars. An example of this is given by Servius (*Ad Aeneidem* 1.292): "Mars, when he rages [*saerit*] is called Gradivus; when he is tranquil [*tranquillus*], Quirinus." Further, the custom of deifying the founders of their nation and city inclined the Romans later to assimilate Quirinus into Romulus lifted up to heaven (Cicero, *De natura deorum* 2.62), as Aeneas was identified with Jupiter Indiges (Livy, 1.2.6).

BIBLIOGRAPHY

Dumézil, Georges. *La religion romaine archaïque*. 2d ed. Paris, 1974. See page 161, note 3, on the etymologies of *Quirinus* and *Vofionus*, and pages 257–283 for a general treatment of the topic. This work has been translated from the first edition by Philip Krapp as *Archaic Roman Religion*, 2 vols. (Chicago, 1970).

Schilling, Robert. *Rites, cultes, dieux de Rome.* Paris, 1979. Pages 244–260 treat Mars Gradivus and Janus Quirinus.
Wissowa, Georg. *Religion und Kultus der Römer.* 2d ed. Munich, 1912. See pages 153–161.

ROBERT SCHILLING
Translated from French by Paul C. Duggan

QUMRAN. *See* Dead Sea Scrolls.

QUR'ĀN. [*This entry focuses on the scripture of the Muslim community. It consists of two articles:*

The Text and Its History
Its Role in Muslim Piety

The first article gives a general history of the collection, standardization, and dating of the Qur'ān, including an overview of the literary structure and teachings of the text. The second article deals with the Qur'ān's language and style and its special place in Muslim piety.]

The Text and Its History

The Qur'ān is the scripture of the Muslim community. It comprises the revelations "sent down" to the prophet Muḥammad over a period of approximately twenty-two years (from 610 to 632 CE); these ecstatic utterances were collected, ordered, and made into a book sometime after Muḥammad's death. Muslims look upon the Qur'ān as the very words of God himself, which convey a divine message of saving guidance for those who submit. In consequence the Qur'ān has a place of unparalleled importance at the very center of Muslim religious life and practice. Qur'anic teachings are the guide both to personal and social life and to religious responsibility. Indeed, it may be claimed that all Muslim religious thought and activity, and much else besides, are but extended commentaries on the Qur'anic revelation and on the life of the Prophet, who was the agent of its delivery. The Qur'ān has shaped the values and the worldview of the Islamic community as has no other force. It continues to be a powerful living factor in the contemporary world just as it was a fundamental formative element of the Islamic culture of the past. Along with the Bible the Qur'ān must be reckoned as one of the most widely read, most studied, most revered, and most influential books in all of human history.

The Prophet and the Qur'ān

The Qur'ān and the Muslim understanding of it are both inextricably interwoven with the experience of the Prophet through whom the holy book was delivered. It was solely the fact of being chosen as a messenger *(rasūl)* to humankind (to deliver the Qur'ān) that constituted Muḥammad's prophethood; he had no other claim to authority and obedience. The experience of receiving the Qur'anic revelations transformed Muḥammad from an ordinary citizen of Mecca into a religious visionary who subsequently became not only the leader of his people but one of the most influential individuals in all of history. It is important, therefore, to give attention to the prophetic experience through which the Qur'ān came to be.

The Call to Prophethood. By temperament Muḥammad was a reflective person with a strong disposition toward religiosity. Tradition records that prior to his prophetic call he cultivated the habit of retiring into isolation in the hills surrounding Mecca to practice *taḥannuth,* or devotional exercises, including perhaps prayer, vigils, fasting, and mild austerities. Some scholars believe him to have been much influenced in these practices by Jewish and Christian ideas, which were well known in Arabia, although it is unlikely that he had any direct personal knowledge of the scriptures of these monotheistic religions. However that may be, there is no question that he was extraordinarily sensitive to religious impulses and deeply aware of the spiritual and intellectual climate of his native Mecca, whose people, formerly nomads, were struggling to accommodate themselves to the changed values and economic and social conditions in a prosperous commercial city. Himself an orphan, Muḥammad had experienced the bitter results of the breakdown of the time-honored tribal values that emphasized solidarity of the clan and the protection of its weakest members.

During one of his night vigils in about his fortieth year, according to tradition, Muḥammad experienced the call to prophethood. In the traditional account the call came as the vision of the angel Gabriel, who said, "O, Muḥammad, thou art the Messenger of God," and commanded Muḥammad, "Recite." At first Muḥammad replied, "I cannot recite" (or "What shall I recite?" according to the way one understands the words). Thereupon, Gabriel seized him and squeezed him violently three times until, in one version of the story, Muḥammad "thought it was death," and again the angel ordered "Recite in the name of thy Lord." Muḥammad then recited the verses that constitute the first part of surah (chapter) 96 of the Qur'ān:

> Recite in the name of thy Lord who created
> Created man from a clot
> Recite; thy Lord is most generous,
> Who taught by the pen
> Taught man what he knew not.

On the basis of this account most Muslim scholars have

considered surah 96 to be the first revelation given to Muḥammad; there are others, however, who assign the first place to other passages. In any event, once the revelations began, they continued to come with more or less frequency throughout Muḥammad's lifetime except for a short period early on in his career (known as the *fatrah,* or pause) that caused him much soul-searching and doubt.

The fragmentary nature of the revelations, the fact that they came in bits and pieces, rather than all at once, is among their most notable features. The Qur'ān is not a straightforwardly organized treatise; rather it moves without transition from one subject to another, often returning after many pages to a subject discussed earlier; it is repetitious, and it leaves many matters of great importance quite incomplete. The fragmentariness may be explained in terms of the Prophet's responses to the circumstances and problems that he and his community faced: as new situations arose, posing new questions or difficulties, the revelation provided guidance and answers. The lack of unity, however, proved of some embarrassment to Muḥammad when his enemies demanded why the revelation was not sent to him all at once (25:32). The piecemeal aspect of the revelations, which is well attested in both the Qur'ān itself and tradition, must also be reconciled with the several Qur'anic statements that the Qur'an was sent down in a single night in the month of Ramaḍān or, alternatively, on the "Night of Power" (Laylat al-Qadr). Muslim commentators have solved this problem by holding that the Qur'ān as a whole was sent down to the lowest heaven on the Night of Power and was then brought piecemeal to the Prophet.

The traditional view. Islamic religious tradition is clear about the nature of the revelatory experience; the message sent (the Qur'ān) came from God; the recipient was the Prophet, and the intermediary between the two was the angel Gabriel. The words of the revelation are considered to have been taken from a heavenly book, a "guarded tablet," which is the "mother of the book," the source of all genuine scripture both in the past and at present. The coming of the revelation involved both visions and the spoken word, as in the story of the prophetic call above, although the spoken word had much the greater role. In the usual conception, Gabriel is said to have articulated the divine words into the Prophet's ear while the latter was overcome with ecstasy, so that Muḥammad was later able to recite what he had been told. The role of the Prophet in the revelatory process was thus entirely passive, much like that of a telephone instrument that transmits the sounds spoken into it; neither the content of the message nor the words in which it was couched were his. In the Qur'ān, therefore, the Muslim community considers that it possesses the very words of God himself, not merely the intellectual content of a divine message cast into a relative mold of words supplied by Muḥammad, but the original and genuine form of the message. To recite or read the Qur'ān is, thus, to stand in the presence of the divine, to be confronted with all the awesomeness of an eternal truth. Muslims of the present day also hold that the revelations have been preserved precisely as given to the Prophet without so much as a single vowel or punctuation mark having been changed or lost. Such, however, was not always the position of the community.

To emphasize the extra-Muhammadan character of the revelations, the tradition has always insisted that Muḥammad was illiterate, able neither to read nor to write, so that he could not possibly have borrowed the contents of the Qur'ān from Jewish or Christian scriptures as some of his opponents accused him of doing. In surah 7:156–157 the words *al-nabī al-ummī* ("the *ummī* prophet") are interpreted to yield the meaning of illiteracy. Modern scholarship has shown convincingly that there was a high likelihood of Muḥammad's having had at least some ability to read and write since those skills must have been widespread among the merchants of Mecca. It has shown also, from the use of the word elsewhere in the Qur'ān, that *ummī* refers to those peoples who have not previously been given a scripture, rather than to illiteracy. The matter at issue in the traditional doctrine of Muḥammad's illiteracy, however, is not historical accuracy but the desire to buttress the divine origin of the Qur'ān and the Prophet's instrumental role with respect to it.

The traditional view finds much support in the Qur'ān itself. There are, for example, numerous verses or passages introduced by the command "Say" *(qul),* presumably given by the angel to the Prophet. The implication of this literary form for Muslims is that the angel dictated a formula of words that Muḥammad was to repeat. Clearly, in such circumstances the words could not have been Muḥammad's own but were given to him. In another interesting verse (75:16–19) God appears to reprimand the Prophet for taking some initiative in the revelations and reminds him that the revelation is God's responsibility: "Move not thy tongue that thou mayest do it quickly; ours it is to collect and recite it; when we recite it, follow thou the recitation; then ours it is to explain it." In response to doubters and Muḥammad's detractors the Qur'ān also offers repeated assurances that the prophetic words were truly a revelation from the Lord of the Worlds and not the babblings of a poet *(shāʿir)* or the declarations of a soothsayer *(kāhin),* both of which Muḥammad resembled in some degree.

Much the same significance is derived from the terms used to designate the nature of Muḥammad's prophethood. He is variously called *rasūl,* "messenger"; one of the *mursalīn,* "one who has been sent"; a *nabī,* "informer"; a *bashīr,* "bearer of good tidings"; a *nadhīr,* "warner"; and a *mudhakkir,* "one who reminds." All of these terms assume the complete humanity of Muḥammad, and they also point unmistakably to his subordination to a greater power for whom he acts. Muḥammad's significance is not personal, nor does it derive from special qualities and abilities he may have possessed; rather it is purely the result of his being chosen *(al-muṣṭafā)* by the sovereign creator, Lord of the universe. Two of the terms in particular, *rasūl* and *nabī,* also tie him to the long line of messengers and prophets who had appeared in the past, thus reinforcing the idea of a single, eternal, divine truth that has from time to time been sent down through the divine mercy for the benefit of humanity.

The Muslim traditions also record reports about the modes of the revelation, the different manners in which it was experienced: it came sometimes like the ringing of a bell in the Prophet's ear, at others through Gabriel in the form of a man, twice through Gabriel in his true form, or by the action of the Holy Spirit in Muḥammad's heart. There was also revelation from God personally, either directly, from behind a veil, or in heaven (the reference is to the Miʿrāj, the Prophet's night journey to the heavens). Although there is theological disagreement on the modes of revelation among Muslim authorities, all are at one in emphasizing that Muḥammad was not the author of the revelation, only its agent. The great majority is agreed as well on the decisive role of Gabriel as Muḥammad's link with God.

There are also reports that describe the physical accompaniments of the revelation experience. It is said that when Muḥammad received the revelation he underwent a kind of seizure in which foam appeared at his mouth, his head sank down upon his chest, and his face became pale or deep red. Often he fell to the ground. At times he would cry out, or the sweat would stream from his brow, even in cold weather. On the basis of these reports nineteenth-century Western scholars described Muḥammad as an epileptic or as subject to hysteria and thus explained away his claim to revelation. These views are no longer tenable, however, in view of what is known of Muḥammad's personality, the single-mindedness of his purpose, and his transforming effects upon those who heard and followed him. From the Muslim perspective these stories underline the special and unusual nature of Muḥammad's state at the times of revelation. He was not his normal self, was oblivious to his surroundings, and appeared to have been possessed by an outside power. His state is thus taken as an evidence that what he proclaimed was, indeed, a revelation from his Lord.

The Qur'anic view. The description of the revelation in the pages of the Qur'ān is somewhat more complex than that set out in the scenario of the traditional account. While it confirms much of the tradition, especially Muḥammad's conviction of receiving a genuine revelation and his complete sincerity with respect to his mission, the Qur'ān also differs from the tradition in important ways. The differences may be accounted for by the efforts of commentators and theologians over the centuries to achieve a uniform and consistent doctrinal position.

One example of the differences has to do with the role of Gabriel as the intermediary in the revelation and is, in turn, related to the matter of the Prophet's visions. Two prophetic visions are mentioned in the Qur'ān, both in surah 53 (1–12 and 13–18), but in neither case does the name of Gabriel appear. The text uses only a pronoun ("He saw him") to indicate the being whom Muḥammad saw. This leaves the way open to interpret the visions to mean that Muḥammad saw God himself, and many Muslims have understood them precisely in this way. Their view is supported by verse 53:10, "He revealed to his servant what he revealed," where the word *ʿabd* ("servant") is an appropriate and customary term for expressing the nature of human beings in relationship to God. Other passages of the Qur'ān, however, particularly 6:104, "Vision comprehends him not . . . ," provide evidence against Muḥammad's having seen God directly. In another verse, "It is not fitting that God should speak to any mortal except by inspiration [*waḥy*] or from behind a veil . . ." (42:51), the Qur'ān also denies direct oral communication between God and humans. These verses have buttressed the traditional view that the being in Muḥammad's visions, the one who first gave the command "Recite," could not have been God. In the light of verse 2:97, "Say: Who is an enemy to Gabriel! For he it is who hath revealed it to thy heart by God's leave," the majority of Muslim scholars have taken the visions to refer to Gabriel. By common agreement, however, verse 2:97 belongs to a late period in Muḥammad's life when he was well established in Medina, and not to the early parts of the Qur'ān.

It is likely, therefore, as W. Montgomery Watt contends, that Muḥammad's understanding of the revelation changed and grew with the passage of time, that what he at first thought to be a vision of God he later recognized as the vision of an angel. Thus the verses that refer to the revelation being brought by a "spirit" (26:193, 42:52, 16:102) to the heart of Muḥammad are also taken to refer to Gabriel. The matter is complicated by the fact that Gabriel is mentioned but three times in the Qur'ān, and only in the instance cited above is he associated with the revelation. Further, as Alford Welch has observed, Gabriel is not specifically identified in the Qur'ān as an angel, nor does the Qur'ān present the angels generally as bearers of revelation. Even among the modes of revelation that tradition records it is to be noted that revelation does not always depend upon the mediation of Gabriel. Neither is the Qur'ān strictly consistent about who is speaking when the revelations are delivered. At times God himself seems to speak directly to the Prophet; in other passages Muḥammad appears to be the speaker, and in still others, either the angels or the believers. Further, there are prayers in the Qur'ān that represent believers addressing God, the most notable being the Fātiḥah, the opening surah. In other respects as well there is basis to question whether the Qur'ān gives evidence for the firm stand of tradition, as we shall see shortly.

The Process of Revelation. The term employed in the Qur'ān to describe the revelation process is *waḥy*, a noun, or *awḥā*, a verb. Muḥammad is commanded: "And recite that which has been revealed [*mā ūḥiya*] to thee of the Book of thy Lord" (18:27). This word, which may be translated in a general sense as "inspiration," occurs often in the Qur'ān. *Waḥy* eventually became the specific term employed by Muslim theologians to designate the messages that the angel brought to the Prophet, but it is not used exclusively in this sense. God is said to "inspire" aspects of nature to act as they do (16:68), just as he "inspired" previous prophets such as Noah and Moses to follow certain courses of action. Even the *jinn* and Satan are said to be capable of "inspiring" false ideas in one another's minds (6:112). *Waḥy* is thus a broad term for inspiration of many kinds.

Following Richard Bell, Montgomery Watt has argued that *waḥy* should be understood as meaning something like "suggestion." When it is said that God revealed certain things, this statement may be taken to mean that God "suggested" these things to the Prophet or infused them into his mind. The key to Muḥammad's prophetic experience would, therefore, be the occurrence from time to time of ideas or "suggestions" implanted in his mind. The implication is that the "suggestions" came suddenly without previous conscious preparation, much as the solution of a longstanding problem or an insight may leap unexpectedly into one's consciousness. These "suggestions" may very well have taken the form of words that could later be recited, though they do not necessarily imply the auditory experience described by the tradition. Arthur Jeffery, in fact, wished to distinguish *waḥy* from *tanzīl* (see below) by saying that *waḥy* involved the appearance of an idea in Muḥammad's mind without the form of words, while *tanzīl* represented a type of revelation that came in audible and verbal form. The psychological process that unfolded may not be unlike the descent of the muse upon a poet or the inspiration that comes to an artist. The analogy with poets must not be pushed too far, however, since the Qur'ān defends Muḥammad against the accusation of being only another poet like those well known to the Arabs. Rather, it assures him with great firmness that his was not an inspiration like theirs but truly a revelation from his Lord. [*See also the biography of Muḥammad and the discussion of prophethood in* Nubūwah.]

The Names of the Revelation. Several different terms are employed in the Qur'ān as names or designations of the revelations. It is of some importance to consider these terms for the light they throw on the Muslim holy book.

Qur'ān. We may begin with the word *qur'ān* itself. As used in the text it is clear that the word cannot refer to the structured book that we know today by that name, since the revelations came at intervals, bit by bit, over a period of more than twenty years and were not complete until they ceased with Muḥammad's death. Further, the historical tradition is unanimous in holding that the Qur'ān (the book) did not achieve its final form until some time after the Prophet's demise. It follows that when it occurs in the text as a name for the revelation, *qur'ān* must refer to only a part or parts of the Muslim scripture. This is borne out by the fact that in certain instances (e.g., 10:61) separate portions of the revelation are clearly referred to as *qur'ān*s. The word *qur'ān*, thus, is used in at least two distinct senses: (1) within the text, as the designation for a portion or fragment of the revelation, and (2) as the name of the entire collected book that we know as the Muslim scripture. The revelations or *qur'ān*s were drawn from the heavenly book that is the origin of all true scripture; the heavenly exemplar, however, is not exhausted by the revelations that came to Muḥammad, for some passages imply that only portions of it have been sent down, with the remainder presumably still in the possession of God.

The noun *qur'ān* is normally said to be derived from the Arabic verb *qara'a*, meaning "to read" or "to recite." Like its English counterpart the Arabic word is ambiguous: it can mean to read in order to understand something written, or it can mean to read aloud, to recite. Both meanings are found in the text, but the sense that predominates is that of "recite." Most often it is Muḥammad who recites, and what he recites is the *qur'ān* (i.e., the recitation). In other cases, however, God recites the revelations to Muḥammad as in the instance of verse 75:17.

Scholars generally have accepted the view that *qur'ān* is non-Arabic in origin, deriving from a Syriac word that means a scripture lesson or reading, something to be recited in connection with worship. Hence, such statements as "Behold, we have made it [the Book] an Arabic *qur'ān*" (43.3) and "We have sent it down as an Arabic *qur'ān*" (12:2) were likely understood by Muḥammad and his contemporaries as signifying that he was bringing to the Arabs a body of verbal formulas that might be recited or read in a liturgical context just as other communities, notably the Christians and Jews, possessed scriptures that they used in this way. Indeed, the word is employed in certain passages that clearly indicate a liturgical setting for the recitation. Among Western scholars Richard Bell in particular has emphasized the connection between *qur'ān* and material suitable for liturgical purposes.

It must be remembered that in the first instance the Muslim community knew the revelations only in an oral form. Although, as we shall see, Muḥammad may have caused portions of the revelations to be written down, it is unlikely that he wrote them for himself: his primary function was to recite what had been made known to him in the revelation experiences. He also urged the recitation of the revelations upon others as an expression of piety, associating the recitation with prayer. Recitation, therefore, was a means of preserving the revelations and a way of conditioning the community to their significance as well as one of the most praiseworthy acts of submission to the divine will. The role played by recitation of the revelations in the community's early life has continued through the centuries as a fundamental element of religious expression.

In later times, when Muḥammad's revelatory utterances had been collected and ordered into a book, it became customary for scholars to see references to the canonical collection in the text's use of *qur'ān*. It is clear from the foregoing, however, that the sense of the word in the pages of the book is quite complex and not so readily to be equated with the later canonical scripture.

Kitāb. Another word for the revelation that often occurs in conjunction with *qur'ān* is *kitāb*, which is found more than 250 times in the Muslim scripture. Literally, it means something written, any piece of writing, such as a letter or a document, and there are instances of this use in the text. The word also occurs in connection with the Final Judgment when each person will be given his *kitāb*, the book or record of his deeds (17:71 et al.), in his right or left hand or behind his back according to the moral quality of his life. In perhaps the most general sense the term conveys God's knowledge and control of all that will happen; the destinies of human beings and the world are decreed and written down beforehand in a book. "Naught of disaster befalleth in the earth or in yourselves but it is in a Book before we bring it into being." (57:22). The Qur'ān thus mentions several *kitāb*s of different kinds. Arthur Jeffery has made much of this variety in *The Qur'ān as Scripture.*

The most frequent use of *kitāb* is in conjunction with the idea of scripture, both the scripture given to Muḥammad in the revelations and that given to others in previous times, the "peoples of the book." In this sense the *kitāb* is identical with the revelation. Further, the scripture given to Muḥammad is confirmed in the scriptures of these other religious communities and in its turn confirms them; all, therefore, originate from God. *Kitāb* as scripture in one sense also appears to be synonymous with *qur'ān* inasmuch as both are revelation, but in certain passages *kitāb* is a broader term, *qur'ān* being only those parts of the heavenly *kitāb* that have been sent down to Muḥammad in Arabic.

Both Richard Bell and Montgomery Watt argue for what they call a "Book period" in Muḥammad's life. It is to be distinguished from the "*qur'ān* period" that preceded it and is thought to have begun about the time of the Battle of Badr or that of Muḥammad's break with the Jews in Medina. The theory is based on the fact that the notion of the Book occurs most often in passages that these scholars date to the latter part of Muḥammad's life, while the term *qur'ān* is used there but rarely. *Qur'ān,* however, is the most common designation of the revelation in the early, so-called *qur'ān* period. It is suggested that Muḥammad's rivalry with the Jews and Christians in Medina, the clear delineation of Islam as a religion separate from Judaism and Christianity that then occurred, and the changed situation in Medina made it imperative that Muslims possess a book such as these other communities had. There is strong evidence from the text to show that in Medina Muḥammad began to see his mission no longer simply as the provision of material that might be recited in worship, but as the production of a book that was different from the scriptures of previous peoples. This book presumably included the revelations of the *qur'ān* period and the other revelations that preceded them, and there must also have been a considerable amount of rearranging and editing of Qur'anic materials to bring the whole into acceptable order. There is also here the implication of an evolution in Muḥammad's understanding of revelation, determined largely by circumstances, that climaxed with the idea of the book, or scripture.

Certain verses of the Qur'ān (56:77–79, 85:21, 43:1–4, and others) make reference to a mysterious heavenly book that Muslim thinkers have understood to refer to the divine original of the earthly Qur'ān. For example, the text mentions the *kitāb Allāh* ("book of God"), a "well-preserved tablet," a "concealed book" that only the pure may touch, and the *umm al-kitāb,* or "mother of the book." In addition there is much other mention of writing: Muḥammad swears "by the reed pen and what it writes," and surah 96 speaks of man being "taught by the pen." These phrases are extremely difficult to interpret, although Muslim thinkers have tended to take them literally as referring to an actual heavenly book, parts, though not all, of which were sent down to the Prophet. Many Western scholars, including Jeffery, have concurred that these Qur'anic references point to an actual book in heaven, but Alford Welch fails to find clear evidence in the text for the belief in a literal heavenly exemplar of the Qur'ān.

Other names. Other words used to indicate the revelations are *tanzīl, dhikr,* and other forms of the same root, *furqān, mathānī, ḥikmah, sūrah,* and *āyah. Tanzīl* is the verbal noun from the verb *nazzala,* "to send down" or "to cause to send down"; *tanzīl* may be rendered, therefore, either as "sending down" or as "something sent down." The noun and the related verbs are used many times in the Qur'ān; they eventually became technical words for the delivery of revelation through the agency of the angel. Perhaps no other term conveys so vividly the image of a heavenly book, parts of which are excerpted and brought to Muḥammad in the revelatory experiences. Thus, the Qur'ān refers to the "*tanzīl* of the Book wherein there is no doubt, from the Lord of all being" (32:2), and reference is also made (using verbal forms) to the "sending down" of the *qur'ān* (76:23) and the "sending down" of the *dhikr* (15:9). There is mention also, however, of the "sending down" of other things, such as the rain.

Dhikr means either "mention" or "reminder," and its significance as a name of the revelation is to indicate that the revelation is an admonition and a warning; the point is underlined by references to Muḥammad as an admonisher. [*See* Dhikr.] It is much more difficult to give an adequate explanation of *furqān,* which many commentators wish to derive from Arabic *faraqa,* "to distinguish" or "to separate," thus arriving at the meaning of norm or criterion. In the text itself the coming of the *furqān* is associated with the Battle of Badr, and Alford Welch has suggested that the designation became current because it was at about that time that the Muslims first began to differentiate clearly between their community and scripture and those of the Christians and Jews. The *furqān* would thus have been understood as the basis of the distinction between Muslims and these others.

Mathānī is another exceedingly difficult term that has long puzzled students of the Qur'ān. Etymologically, its sense is that of something folded or doubled, or by extension, perhaps something often repeated. The word occurs only twice in the Qur'ān, in one instance where God speaks of having given Muḥammad "seven *mathānī* and the wondrous *qur'ān*" (15:87), and in the other where there is reference to the *mathānī* "at which the skins of those who fear their Lord do creep" (39:23). Bell and Watt both take the *mathānī* to refer to the stories of punishment visited upon previous peoples for their unbelief or their mistreatment of the prophets. Muslim commentators, however, paying attention especially to the number seven, usually see in the term either a reference to the seven verses of the first surah, the Fātiḥah, or to the seven longest surahs of the Qur'ān.

Ḥikmah, from the verb "to judge," is most often translated as "wisdom." *Ḥikmah* is very often spoken of in conjunction with the book, as in 2:231, "the Book and the wisdom he has sent down on you." References of this sort have supplied the basis upon which later Muslim thinkers, particularly mystics, have distinguished an esoteric truth in the Qur'ān (the *ḥikmah*) from the evident exoteric truth (the book). The other two terms for the revelations, *sūrah* and *āyah,* I shall discuss briefly below.

Formation of the Text

The first question that must be faced in studying how the Qur'ān of the present day, the structured book, came to be formed is that of the state of the revelations at the time of Muḥammad's unexpected death in 632 CE, whether and to what degree they had been collected and ordered. One thing is quite certain: there was no firm written text of the Qur'ān that bore the Prophet's stamp of approval. It is inconceivable that had such a text existed, the community would not have preserved it and adhered to it, or that the tradition would be of one voice in insisting that the Qur'ān was collected and formed by Muḥammad's successors, the caliphs. It is almost equally certain, however, that there were written collections of Qur'anic material that the Prophet had had a part in creating and ordering. Bell's suggestion of a "Book period" in the Prophet's life may imply the compilation of written materials, and certain Qur'anic verses carry the same implication. Historical tradition takes notice of a variety of individuals who are said to have done writing or acted as amanuenses for the Prophet, and it also records (in the *Itqān* of al-Suyūṭī and elsewhere) instructions given by Muḥammad to these amanuenses to include specific portions of the revelations in the surah bearing such and such a name.

Not only does this kind of report clearly indicate a concern for seeing the Qur'anic revelations in written form, but it also implies that the structure of chapters and their names had been determined while Muḥammad was still living and that he used them to make an ordered record of the revelation. What is less clear is whether or not Muḥammad himself wrote down any of the materials. Despite the theological doctrine of his illiteracy, tradition speaks of several occasions on which the prophet wrote something with his own hand, and as noted earlier, writing must in any event have been a not-uncommon accomplishment among the Meccans with their fairly highly developed commercial institutions. If portions of the Qur'ān were written down under Muḥammad's direction, this activity also provided the opportunity for the arranging and rearranging of the revelatory material, as Bell has speculated; it would have been through this process that the revelations of the earlier periods would have been incorporated into the book. Here also might lie some at least of the explanation for the frequent mixing of materials from the Meccan and the Medinese periods in the same chapter. Unfortunately, given the paucity of the evidence, no firm conclusion is possible about the state of the Qur'ān when Muḥammad died.

Collection under Abū Bakr. The story of the collection of the Qur'ān accepted by the Islamic tradition is found, with variations, in several early historical sources. It divides the process of establishing the consonantal text into two phases that are difficult to reconcile.

The initial collation. The first phase of the collection process reportedly occurred during the caliphate of Abū Bakr, Muḥammad's first successor, after the Battle of Yamāmah (fought against the supporters of Musaylimah, the false prophet) when ʿUmar ibn al-Khaṭṭāb came to the caliph to point out that a number of Qur'ān reciters had fallen among the slain. Fearing that some of the Qur'ān would be lost, he urged the caliph to take steps to preserve it. After hesitation Abū Bakr agreed and succeeded in persuading a reluctant Zayd ibn Thābit, who had been one of Muḥammad's amanuenses, to undertake the task. Zayd then collected all of the Qur'anic materials he could find, many of them written on crude materials such as scraps of leather, the ribs of palm leaves, or the shoulder blades of animals, but also from the "hearts of men." Zayd used what he had collected to write out the entire Qur'ān on separate sheets or *ṣuḥuf*. The Qur'an thus assembled was given to Abū Bakr, and when he died shortly after, passed into the possession of ʿUmar, the second caliph. Upon ʿUmar's death it became the private property of his daughter, Ḥafṣah. There is no mention of other copies of Zayd's collection being made or distributed among the community at large. There are also a number of variants of the story having to do particularly with the person who first suggested a collection be made; in addition, some versions give the credit to Abū Bakr and still others to ʿAlī, the fourth caliph and the first imam of the Shīʿah.

This story has been severely criticized, especially by Theodor Nöldeke, the doyen of modern critical Qur'anic studies, in his famous *Geschichte des Qorans.* In the first place, the caliphate of Abū Bakr lasted only a short time, something just over two years, and there was scarcely time between the Battle of Yamāmah and his death for so great a task to have been accomplished. Further, the names of a number of those who fell at Yamāmah are known from history, and they do not include many people close to Muḥammad or those who would have been in a position to have much of the Qur'ān in their possession in whatever form. The most telling point, however, is what happened to the collection once it was made. The two most important and powerful men of the community, its leaders, were allegedly associated with Zayd's collection, yet it was treated as a piece of private property and not used to achieve the purpose for which it was supposedly undertaken. It is unthinkable that a text could have been formed under such auspices with nothing following from it or that it could simply have been passed on in ʿUmar's family. Moreover, the story, as Welch observes, says nothing about written materials originating with Muḥammad, although they almost certainly existed.

The story should perhaps be dismissed as not being credible at all, and the key to it may lie in the differing accounts of who should receive credit for first conceiving the all-important enterprise of collecting the Qur'anic text. Since the second phase in the received account gives the primary role in that process to ʿUthmān, the third caliph, it has been suggested that the entire account is an effort by ʿUthmān's enemies, of whom he had many, to deny him the honor of making the collection. The story would thus be seen as a species of early Islamic political polemic like numerous others. There may have been other motives for it as well, such as the desire to take the collection of the Qur'ān back as near as possible to Muḥammad's death.

Subsequent efforts. The second phase of the story of the collection of the Qur'ān makes the *spiritus movens* a certain general, Ḥudhayfah, who led Muslim troops against the Armenians in Azerbaijan. Quarreling had broken out among his Muslim soldiers from different areas about the correct reading of the Qur'ān, and Ḥudhayfah went to the caliph, now ʿUthmān ibn ʿAffān, to urge that proper steps be taken. ʿUthmān thereupon chose the same Zayd ibn Thābit to prepare an official text. Zayd was to take the leaves *(ṣuḥuf)* in the possession of Ḥafsah bint 'Umar and with the help of a committee of three natives of Mecca prepare a text that would be faithful to the language of the Quraysh, the Prophet's tribe. The work was done, and copies of the new version were sent to the principal cities of the caliphate, Damascus, Basra, and Kufa, while a copy was kept in Medina. Orders were also given that all other versions of the Qur'ān should be destroyed, and they were carried out everywhere except in Kufa where the populace preferred the version by Ibn Mas'ūd to which they were accustomed.

The story also is subject to criticism. First, it takes no account of the original Qur'ān collection mentioned in phase one or of Zayd's part in it. There is also wide disagreement about the function of Zayd's commission as well as its membership. According to some versions the commission was nothing more than a group of scribes whose task was to make multiple copies as Zayd dictated. It is difficult to accept that the purpose of the commission was to cast the Qur'ān into a dialectal form of Arabic. By general agreement Qur'anic Arabic is not a dialect, and were it so, the effect would have been to lessen its appeal to Arab tribal groups other than Quraysh. The number of persons on the commission varies from three to twelve in different versions of the story. Some names of non-Qurayshis appear, people who could not have helped to verify authentic Qurayshi Arabic; also included are names of persons who were among 'Uthmān's enemies, a most unlikely happening; there is even the name of a person known to have died before the events in question took place. Watt considers that the *ṣuḥuf* of Ḥafṣah were unsuitable as the basis of a canonical text and that the commission must have been concerned also to collect as much of the Qur'ān as possible from other sources.

Despite the difficulties with the traditional accounts there can be no question of the importance of the codex prepared under 'Uthmān. It established the basic consonantal form of the text that has endured to our day. Almost without exception Muslims consider that the Qur'ān we now possess goes back in its text and in the number and order of the chapters to the work of the commission that 'Uthmān appointed. Muslim orthodoxy holds further that 'Uthmān's Qur'ān contains all of the revelation delivered to the community faithfully preserved without change or variation of any kind and that the acceptance of the 'Uthmanic Qur'ān was all but universal from the day of its distribution.

The orthodox position is motivated by dogmatic factors; it cannot be supported by the historical evidence, which shows there to have been a great deal of flexibility in Muslim attitudes toward the text in the early years and a slow evolution toward uniformity and the achievement of a *textus receptus ne varietur.* Ignácz Goldziher has pointed to the apparent pride of Muslims in early times that the Qur'ān was *dhū wujūhin,* "possessed of many aspects," which is to say that it had a variety and richness of forms. The concern for a uniform text upon which all would agree developed only with time and did not reach its climax until the fourth Islamic century.

Standardization of the Text. There are three matters that throw light on this evolution: the development of the writing system for Arabic, the existence of variant versions of the Qur'ān, and the variant readings of the text.

The writing system. During Muḥammad's lifetime and for long afterward it was impossible to write the Arabic script with precision. The Qur'ān was at first written in a *scripta defectiva* that had signs for consonants only. This script made it impossible to distinguish some consonants from others with similar forms because of the lack of the dots that distinguish these letters in modern Arabic; it provided no indications of pronunciation and lacked other modern diacritical marks such as that for a doubled consonant. In such circumstances it was easy for mistakes to occur; words could be read with the wrong vocalization, and one consonant could readily be substituted for another. The imperfect state of the writing system is one of the arguments advanced to dispute that the task of Zayd's commission was to put the Qur'ān into the dialect of the Quraysh. At the time the means did not exist to indicate the subtle differences that would differentiate one dialect from another. Had it not been that the early Muslims depended very heavily upon memorization for their access to the Qur'ān and were thoroughly familiar with the text, the written versions would have been difficult to use; they certainly did not provide the base for a uniform text on which all could agree.

Some traditions point to an indifference toward the written text; when a mistake in writing was pointed out to 'Ā'ishah, the Prophet's wife, she is reported to have said that the Arabs would correct it with their tongues, thus indicating the primacy of oral transmission. With time, however, the need to improve the script began to be felt, and by the late ninth century CE the present-day *scripta plena* was perfected and in wide use. Credit is sometimes given to a certain al-Du'alī as the author of the system that made possible a fully voweled and pointed text, but it is far more likely that the improvements developed gradually over a period of time rather than being put into place all at once by a single man. In any case the emergence of a proper writing system was a necessary precondition for a firmly fixed text.

Variant versions. When the 'Uthmanic codex of the Qur'ān was assembled, there were already a number of other versions of the Qur'ān associated with some of the Prophet's companions in circulation among the Muslims. Some of these codices continued to be used and preferred until the fourth Islamic century, when the 'Uthmanic codex finally won out over them and came to be accepted as canonical. Some of these early written collections were preferred in particular cities or regions of the Muslim domains. Three of the best known among them, the versions of Ibn Mas'ūd, Ubayy ibn Ka'b, and Abū Mūsā, for instance, are associated with Kufa, Syria, and Basra respectively. As the story of the origins of 'Uthmān's Qur'ān shows, it was disagreement among Muslim troops from different regions about the reading of the text that provoked 'Uthmān's action.

Although Muslims of the present time generally have forgotten the very existence of these variant versions of the Qur'ān, in the early days they were a lively focus of interest, and the differences among them produced a considerable literature. In his *Materials for a History of the Text of the Qur'ān* Arthur Jeffery has listed fifteen primary codices (i.e., from the companions) and a large number of secondary ones (i.e., from the generation after the companions). The abundance of the material leads one to imagine a situation in which a number of the companions had put together a body of Qur'anic material known to them personally and which they would have used for their own purposes and taught to others. Far from there being any danger of losing the Qur'ān, the problem was rather to decide which, if any, of these many versions was the authentic Qur'ān. It has been suggested that 'Uthmān's collection was finally accepted as canonical perhaps because it represented the tradition of Medina where the Prophet had lived the latter part of his life and was therefore considered closer to the original revelations.

The variant versions exhibited differences among themselves and from the 'Uthmanic version in the reading of particular verses and in the number, names, and order of the chapters. Most notable perhaps is the absence of the Fātiḥah from Ibn Mas'ūd's version. That fact, together with peculiarities of language and its character as a prayer, has led some scholars to see the Fātiḥah as a later addition to the corpus. Some versions also lack the last two chapters in the 'Uthmanic Qur'ān; other versions (e.g., Ubayy) include chapters not found there. On the whole, however, despite their differences from the received 'Uthmanic version, the variant codices of the Qur'ān tend to support its authenticity and prophetic character.

Recent views. In recent times two scholars in Britain, John Wansbrough and John Burton, have attacked the entire body of the traditions relative to the formation of the Qur'ān and the variant versions as fabrications from whole cloth. Burton believes that Muḥammad himself prepared and sanctioned a complete written Qur'ān, which he left behind him. In his view, the Muslim lawyers *(fuqahā')* found themselves deprived of flexibility in their rulings by the need to honor this text, and in response they invented both the variant versions and the story of 'Uthmān's collection as a means to suppress it. Wansbrough sees these traditions from a polar opposite but no less negative point of view. He considers the Qur'ān not to have achieved a final form until the third Islamic century, since the prior period was too fluid to yield any agreement among the Muslims. He holds that the traditions were fabricated after the formation of the text in order to push it back into an earlier period and give it greater authenticity. Neither of these scholarly views has won wide support among students of the Qur'ān since they involve the wholesale rejection of the Muslim historical tradition with all of the problems that this raises.

Variant readings. In the variant versions of the Qur'ān there were a large number of differences among particular verses. Although the codices themselves have not survived, we have abundant information on the subject from Qur'ān commentators such as al-Ṭabarī or from historical sources. Very many of the differences were insignificant and in no way affected the meaning of the text. Some had to do only with orthography, which is somewhat peculiar even in the 'Uthmanic version. Others involved vocalization and pronunciation or the substitution of synonyms for words in the text. So small a thing as reading a word with an accusative ending rather than a genitive ending could determine the nature of the ablutions before prayers as in one famous case (5:6). As Goldziher has shown in his *Richtungen der Islamischen Koranauslegung*, some of the variant readings reflected the theological preferences of different groups among the Muslims. It must be emphasized that far from there being a single text passed down inviolate from the time of 'Uthmān's commission, literally thousands of variant readings of particular verses were known to the Muslims in the first three centuries AH. These variants affected even the 'Uthmanic codex, making it difficult to know what its true original form may have been. It is not unfair to say that by the third century a state of confusion began to obtain because of the number of variant readings and the continued preference of some Muslims for codices other than the 'Uthmanic.

The seven readings. Under these circumstances pressure began to build to achieve a single uniform text; the refinement of the writing system had now made a far more exact record of the Qur'ān possible. The person with whom the ordering process is usually most closely associated is Ibn Mujāhid (d. 935), whose book, *The Seven Readings,* provided a scheme that in due course was accepted by virtually all Muslims. Ibn Mujāhid and those after him who adopted his views base themselves on a famous tradition of Muḥammad in which, in reply to questions about why he sanctioned different readings of the Qur'ān, he replied that it had been revealed in seven *aḥruf.* Although *aḥruf* is the plural of the word meaning a letter of the alphabet, it was taken to mean seven versions of the Qur'anic text. There are other traditions of the Prophet that also support flexibility in reading the Qur'ān; their import seems to be that the form does not matter as long as the meaning is not changed: "so long as punishment is not converted into reward."

There were other scholars after Ibn Mujāhid who accepted ten readings rather than seven and still others who recognized fourteen readings as legitimate. In effect Ibn Mujāhid's list of seven itself provided fourteen possibilities since each of the readings was traced through two different transmitters. What appears to have happened in this instance is that the community, being unable to agree on a single reading, accepted diversity as the norm and proclaimed all of the seven (or ten or fourteen) to be correct. This situation might be imagined to generate considerable confusion, theological questioning, and continued conflict among Muslims, but in fact such was not the case. Although Muslim savants have devoted much attention to the seven readings, one reading has come to be preferred over all the others, that of ʿĀṣim (d. 744) through the transmitter Ḥafṣ (d. 805). In modern times the influence of the official Egyptian edition of the Qur'ān (1924), which follows the reading of ʿĀṣim, has been a major factor in accounting for this preference.

It is of some importance to call attention to a possible source of misunderstanding with regard to the variant readings of the Qur'ān. The seven *aḥruf* refer to actual differences in the written and oral text, to distinct versions of Qur'anic verses, whose differences, though they may not be great, are nonetheless real and substantial. Since the very existence of variant readings and versions of the Qur'ān goes against the doctrinal position toward the holy Book held by many modern Muslims, it is not uncommon in an apologetic context to hear the seven *aḥruf* explained as modes of recitation *(tilāwah);* in fact, the manner and technique of recitation are an entirely different matter. [*See* Tilāwah.]

Completeness of the Qur'ān. One last question remains to be answered concerning the formation of the Qur'anic text: does it contain all of the revelations given to Muḥammad or has some portion been lost? Three considerations have been advanced to argue that portions of the Qur'ān may, indeed, have been lost. First, there is the fact that we do not know when the revelations first began and whether Muḥammad may have experienced an unknown number of revelations before he began to proclaim them publicly. It is entirely possible that the Prophet may have experienced revelations for some time before his calling became clear enough to him for him to enter on his public ministry. Thus, if one accepts either the first part of surah 96 *(The Clot of Blood)* or that of surah 74 *(The Enwrapped)* as the first revelation recorded in the Qur'ān, either could be interpreted as the command to enter upon a public mission rather than as the absolute beginning of the revelation experience. In view of the doubts that Muḥammad entertained about what had happened to him, about his own sanity, and about the source of his revelations, it is not inconceivable that he initially kept his unusual experiences to himself. With no more evidence than is available, it is impossible to reach a firm judgment on this matter.

Second, there is the fact that the Qur'ān mentions the possibility of revelations being forgotten (87:6–7) and at another place states that this has actually happened, although God never fails to send another verse that is similar or better (2:106). It also speaks of the substitution of one verse for another (16:101) and of divinely dictated changes (22:52). The Qur'ān thus affirms both the forgetting of revelations and their replacement, though the replacement is not necessarily in the same form as that which was lost.

Verse 2:106 (above) is the basis for the well-known doctrine of the *nāsikh* and the *mansūkh,* the "abrogating" and the "abrogated." It is notable that despite their abrogation, the no-longer applicable verses remained in the text as part of the divine word. It might be thought that the doctrine of abrogation also would raise theological difficulties for Muslims, but this has not been the case. The abrogated verses are explained as temporary injunctions that later had to be adjusted to changed circumstances. The early Muslims were much concerned to know which verses had been set aside and which were to prevail in their place; the question was of particular interest to jurists whose rulings on points of doctrine and practice were directly affected by abrogation. In consequence there is an enormous literature on the subject, which is concerned both to know what is abrogated and in what sense it is abrogated, whether only in its form or in its content or both. According to tradition some early Muslims, such as ʿAlī ibn Abī Ṭālib, held mastery of the *nāsikh* and *mansūkh* to be essential for any true knowledge of the Qur'ān.

In addition, one verse often commented upon admits the possibility of words that were once part of the Qur'ān being eliminated from the text altogether (22:52f.). The verse speaks of Satan's influencing the declarations of the prophets and of God's abrogating what Satan had caused to be introduced into their pronouncements. This passage has usually been held to refer to the well-known story of the "Satanic verses" in which Muḥammad allegedly made concessions to the Meccans by acknowledging their deities al-Lāt, al-'Uzzā, and al-Manāt (the verses were supposedly inserted into surah 53). Even though the concessions improved his relations with the Meccans, after some time he withdrew them under the inspiration of revelation. Most modern scholars have held that the story must be true since they think it inconceivable that such a tale, which reflects unfavorably on the Prophet, could have been invented or would have been passed on by the historians if it lacked a strong basis. (For reasons that are too technical to be considered here, Welch and others, however, consider it to be false.)

Third, tradition also records stories that imply the loss of parts of the Qur'ān. Muḥammad himself and such other important personages as his wife 'Ā'ishah and his companion 'Umar are all made to refer to verses that had been forgotten or that were missing from the Qur'ān as they heard it recited. Nonetheless, while there is no firm guarantee that no small part of the revelation has been missed, it does not seem likely that any considerable portion of the Qur'anic material known to the community failed to find its way into the 'Uthmanic codex. It must be remembered that there were a number of written collections of greater or lesser length compiled by respected companions of the Prophet. Further, Zayd worked with written materials. At the time when Zayd was active many companions of the Prophet who had committed portions of the revelation to memory were still alive. This is to say that the 'Uthmanic version was prepared in an environment that would have invited criticism and revision if it had gone seriously astray. Since the historical sources do not reflect criticism of this kind or, indeed, great controversy of any kind arising over the 'Uthmanic Qur'ān, it may safely be concluded that the *textus receptus* is faithful to the revelation as it was known to those who had personally known the Prophet.

Chronology of the Qur'ān

There are many reasons other than a general historical interest why it is important to establish the chronology of the revelations. In making decisions about the abrogating and abrogated verses, for example, the dating of passages and individual verses is essential. Likewise, a reliable chronology would be an invaluable aid for the historian in tracing the development of the prophetic consciousness and the outlook of the early community.

The question of chronology is an exceedingly difficult one, however, for the Qur'ān is not a book of history concerned to give dates or to preserve a record of what happened, although it is unquestionably closely tied to the historical circumstances of Muḥammad's life and the experience of his community. As noted above, the fact that the revelation came in piecemeal fashion over a long period of time is universally acknowledged and also affirmed in the Qur'ān itself. It is also acknowledged by both Muslim and non-Muslim scholars that the present order of the Qur'ān does not represent the sequence in which the revelations were given to the Prophet. Although the traditional commentaries often record information about the occasion for the delivery of a particular revelation (the science of *asbāb al-nuzūl*, "occasions of revelation") and thus relate it to an event in the Prophet's life, the information offered can but seldom be relied upon. As with almost every other matter in early Islamic history, writers differ about the "occasions of revelation"; further, a close analysis of the purposes that the "occasions" serve suggests that the motives range from the legal and the literary to pure entertainment. In addition, no "occasion" at all is suggested for many verses. The only fruitful approach to the problem of chronology lies in close attention to the Qur'anic text in order to search out any relevant internal evidence that it may present. Such a study, however, is very technical, and it is impossible to pursue such matters here. We shall be content with a summary of the major lines scholarship has followed and the results it has achieved.

Muslim Dating. First, attention should be called to the existence of a traditional Muslim dating of the chapters of the Qur'ān. In printed versions there is customarily a heading for each chapter which, among other information, indicates that the chapter is either Meccan or Medinan. This division reflects a Muslim view that goes very far back into history and about which there has been some dispute. At the same time Muslim scholars recognize that some chapters of the Qur'ān are composite, that they may contain material from different periods with Meccan material sometimes being inserted in the midst of a largely Medinan chapter and vice versa. There are also traditional lists of the order in which the chapters are assumed to have been revealed. All of these Muslim datings rest upon traditions reported of Muḥammad or traditions that relate to the *as-*

bāb al-nuzūl. This dating system, like that devised by Western scholars, also assumes the framework of the Prophet's life as it is known from the *Sīrah,* or biographical literature, of such writers as Ibn Isḥāq (d. 768). Although one cannot hope to obtain precise dating of any particular passage or verse from this traditional scheme, its divisions of the material into Meccan and Medinan chapters has, with only few exceptions, been borne out by modern scholarship.

Modern Dating. The leaders in modern study of Qur'anic chronology have been Theodor Nöldeke and Richard Bell. In his *Geschichte des Qorans* Nöldeke, following Gustav Weil, argued that the chapters of the Qur'ān fall into four discernible periods, three in Mecca and one in Medina. He mounted his argument on the basis of internal evidence from the Qur'ān including both style and subject matter. Assuming that Muḥammad's prophetic inspiration would have been at its most intense in the beginning of his career, Nöldeke held that the short chapters, which exhibit great force of expression and strong emotion and have a marked rhythm and rhyme, must have been the first to come to the Prophet. Other chapters that are longer, more prosaic in character, lesser in intensity, and with only irregular occurrence of rhythm and rhyme, he reasoned, must belong to a later time when the prophetic inspiration had become somewhat routinized and Muḥammad's personal circumstances had changed. Particularly in the Medinan situation, where Muḥammad had all the responsibilities of rule, the revelations would have been characterized by attention to practical matters and been more expository in nature.

Nöldeke also called attention to certain features of the content of the revelation in each period that he distinguished. The Meccan chapters of the first period, for example, frequently contain oaths much like those used by pagan soothsayers; they were presumably means to demonstrate the supernatural origin and authenticity of the revelations. These oaths, which provoked accusations that Muḥammad himself was nothing but another soothsayer, disappear in the second period. The second period chapters, however, have peculiar features of their own, for instance, the use of the name al-Raḥmān ("the merciful") for God, and so on. Medinan chapters may be recognized, among other things, by the use of different modes of address for different groups of people. It was only in Medina that Muḥammad came into close relations with Jewish tribes; thus the address, "O Children of Israel" and what follows must belong to the Medinan period. Nöldeke, however, like the Muslim scholars before him, did not carry his analysis of dating beyond dealing with entire chapters, although he was well aware of the composite nature of many of them. Since some of the chapters are quite long (chapter 2, for example, contains 286 verses), his was at best a rough breakdown of the Qur'anic materials.

The Scottish scholar Richard Bell, in his *Introduction to the Qur'ān,* sought a more delicate instrument for determining the sequence of the Qur'anic revelations. Against the view that the entire chapter was always the basic unit, he believed that the revelations were given in much smaller units, often consisting of only a verse or two or three. A proper dating of the revelations, he reasoned, should concern itself with these smaller units, and he set out to divide the chapters as they presently exist into what he considered to be their component parts. By a complex process of analysis he then attempted to give a date to each of the pericopes into which he had divided the text. In some instances he found portions of what he thought to be a single revelation widely separated and inserted into different chapters. This finding was in accord with his view that the Qur'ān had been subjected to extensive rearrangement and revision. He also thought portions of the Qur'an had perhaps been written on the backs of slips of paper that contained other portions, and that the insertion of material into contexts where it did not belong could be explained by the actions of scribes who copied these slips in mechanical fashion without paying attention to the sense of the passages.

Bell rearranged the text in its supposed chronological sequence, and the whole was printed in his translation of the Qur'ān. As we have already seen, the result of this procedure was Bell's theory that the materials of the Qur'an fall into three broad periods, an early one where the revelations point to God's bounty and call people to obedience to him, a *qur'ān* period where the chief interest was the provision of material for liturgical recitation, and a Book period in which a scripture similar to that of the Christians and Jews was assembled. Despite Bell's minute verse-by-verse consideration of the Qur'ān, he could not assign precise dates to a majority of verses, and there is uncertainty about numerous others. The entire question of the dating of the revelations remains, therefore, undecided, and there has been but little interest in the problem among critical scholars in the most recent times.

External Characteristics of the Qur'ān

The Qur'ān is a book of medium size divided into 114 chapters, or *sūrah*s, each of which is further divided into a number of verses, or *āyāt.* Traditionally, the chapters and verses of the Qur'ān are known by names that they bear; in more recent times it has become customary, especially among Western scholars, to assign numbers to both and to cite them by these numbers as in the case of the Bible. The chapters of the Qur'ān, after the short Fātiḥah ("opening"), are arranged roughly in descending order of length; there are numerous exceptions to this rule, however. Although this arrangement has the disadvantage that the shorter surahs, which were likely among the first in chronological sequence, come only at the end, it has the sanction of history. The arrangement is common to the ʿUthmanic version and to the other variant versions that we know, although these versions differ with respect to the names of the surahs and the precise order in which they appear. It is not known why the surahs are arranged in this fashion; one can only speculate.

Not only does the arrangement disregard chronology; it also makes no effort to present the subject matter in systematic fashion by bringing together and organizing all of the material that may bear upon a given subject. On the contrary, to the reader who comes to it for the first time, the Qur'ān may give the impression of having little or no logical structure at all. It goes from subject to subject without apparent reason, its discussion of many important matters is fragmentary, and verses that deal with one and the same issue may be widely separated in its pages. This aspect of the book has been the frequent subject of negative comment by critical scholars, and it has stimulated many Muslim efforts to demonstrate that an order truly does exist, both in each surah of the Qur'ān and in the revelation as a whole. In any case, given the piecemeal fashion in which it was received, and the fact that individual revelations were geared to the needs and questions that arose in particular circumstances, the Qur'ān is most definitely not a composed book such as we are familiar with, the result of extensive forethought and planning. Rather it is a collection of separate utterances arising from the depths of the religious consciousness; it shows all the fervor of the prophetic experience and all the particularity of religious declarations that are relevant to the immediacies of life.

It is also important to recall in connection with the question of order in the Qur'ān's pages that the revelations were given orally and in the beginning were preserved primarily by means of oral recitations; they were meant to be heard, not read. If one accepts Bell's theory about a book period in Muḥammad's life, this assertion might have to be modified in some respects, but even so, the contents of the book were delivered by the prophet orally, and their recitation or oral expression was an essential part of the community's worship. In short, whoever was responsible for the order of the materials in the Qur'ān, whether the Prophet himself or someone after him, may not have been thinking in terms of a text that reads smoothly or that conveys ideas clearly and in structured manner, but in terms of a text for recitation. Such a point of view would seem to be supported by Bell's analysis of many surahs where he insists that the introduction of what seems to be alien material into a given context can be explained by the desire to preserve the rhythm or the rhyme scheme of the passage. The fact is that we do not know why and how the Qur'anic text came to be arranged as it is, and it would be wrong to judge the arrangement too harshly without knowledge of the motives and factors that determined it.

Surah. Each of the major divisions or chapters of the Qur'ān is called a *sūrah*. This word and its plural *suwar* appear ten times in the text itself where, like *qur'ān*, it is used as one of the names of the revelation. For example, the Qur'ān speaks of "a *sūrah* that we have sent down" (24:1) and in several other verses refers to the sending down of *sūrah*s. From this usage it is apparent that the surah is a unit of the revelation. Among the most interesting uses of the word is a passage where the Qur'ān mocks those who accused Muḥammad of composing the revelation himself, saying: "Let them come then with a *sūrah* like it" (10:38). In another verse (11:13) the opponents are challenged to bring ten sūrahs like those that have been sent down. Traditionally Muslim thinkers have understood these verses to refer to the miraculousness *(iʿjāz)* of the Qur'ān, the belief in its inimitability as literary expression. [*See* Iʿjāz.] In later centuries scholars lavished minute attention upon the details of the text in order to demonstrate its uniqueness and its excellence, thus creating an extensive literature on the *iʿjāz*. Among the best-known commentators, al-Bayḍāwī (d. 1286?) in particular is notable for his interest in the matter. It seems improbable, however, that these verses were an invitation to a literary contest. They might better be understood as referring to the divine and inspired origins of the revelations; the challenge would be, therefore, to produce materials of a similar nature and from a similar source, and the Qur'ān expresses confidence that the critics will not be able to do so (2:24). Such an interpretation of these verses is supported by the fact that the challenge in another place (28:49) is put in terms of bringing "a *kitāb* from the presence of Allāh." It would seem, thus, that *sūrah* is equivalent to *kitāb*, or scripture. The view is bolstered also by the Qur'anic reference to the miraculousness of God's *āyāt*, as we shall see below.

As already indicated, each of the surahs has a name or title by which it is commonly known; some have two names both of which have continued in use until our time. Surah 9, for example, is known either as *al-*

Barā'ah (from its first word) or more customarily as *al-Tawbah* (Repentance). How the names came to be chosen is uncertain; they are drawn in each case from some word that occurs in the text, perhaps a particularly striking word or an unusual one. Surah 2, for instance, is called *al-Baqarah* (The Cow) because of Moses' command to his people in verses 67 and following that they should sacrifice a cow. There are several lists of the surahs preserved in early Islamic sources with names diverging from those employed in the present-day Qur'ān. This fact seems to indicate flexibility about the naming and suggests that the customary names are the contribution of the Prophet or of scholars and collectors of the Qur'ān, not part of the original revelation.

At the beginning of every surah except surah 9 stands the Basmalah, the formula "Bismillāh al-raḥmān al-raḥīm" ("In the name of God, the compassionate, the merciful"), which is considered to be part of the revelation. It attests to the nature of what is to follow as coming from God; therefore, it seems to serve as the mark of the beginning of a unit of revelation. In the one instance where the formula is lacking, several explanations have been offered for its absence. Citing the continuity of style and subject matter between the end of surah 8 and the beginning of surah 9, many scholars have contended that they were originally one. Montgomery Watt, however, believes that there is no Basmalah at the beginning of surah 9 because it is not needed: the surah opens in such a way that its provenance and nature are sufficiently proclaimed without this usual formula.

Mysterious letters. Another peculiarity of certain surahs is the occurrence at their beginning, immediately after the Basmalah, of one or more letters of the Arabic alphabet that do not constitute words but are read as separate letters. This phenomenon of the "mysterious letters," as they are called, is found in twenty-nine surahs. Muslim commentators have been unanimous in affirming that the mysterious letters are part of the revelation given to Muḥammad, but there is little agreement among them about what these letters may mean. The situation is no different with modern critical scholarship. The mysterious letters have been seen as abbreviations for the names of the chapters concerned or as the initials of, or symbols for, those from whom particular surahs were collected when the Qur'ān was compiled. Still others have sought a mystical import in the mysterious letters or interpreted them numerologically, but none of the arguments is convincing. W. Montgomery Watt has called attention to the fact that surahs with the same prefixed letters normally occur together and form distinctive blocks of Qur'anic material (e.g., *ḥ-m* before surahs 40-47); he goes on to suggest that the groups marked in this way may have existed before the final compilation of the Qur'ān and simply have been incorporated, as blocks, into the text.

Headings. In editions of the Qur'ān it is customary also to include a kind of heading that provides some useful information at the beginning of each surah. In addition to giving the name of the surah, the heading also indicates whether it was revealed in Mecca or Medina and gives the number of verses. For all except the last thirty-five surahs (for the reason that they are very short) the heading also gives the number of *rukūʿ* or sections into which the surah is divided. Thus surah 2, *The Cow,* is said to be Medinese, to contain 286 verses, and to be divided into 40 *rukūʿ*. The printed Egyptian edition of 1924 (called the "royal edition" because of the sponsorship of King Fū'ād), now virtually standard throughout the Islamic world, provides still further information such as the number of the surah in the chronological order of delivery and indications of the verses that are considered exceptions to the designation of the surah as Meccan or Medinese. These headings are obviously not part of the revelation but have been added by later scholars.

Āyah. Each surah of the Qur'ān is further subdivided into a number of *āyāt* (sg., *āyah*), usually called verses in English, which are naturally separated from one another by the occurrence of rhythm, rhyme, or assonance. Although later scholars almost always use the word *āyah* to refer to a verse in the Qur'ān, this is not its principal meaning in the text itself. *Āyah* literally means a "sign" or "wonder," and it is among the most frequently used terms in the Qur'ān. Humanity has been given signs of God's creative sovereignty and his goodness in many aspects of nature and in its own life. The foremost of these is God's very creation of the heavens and the earth and that with which he has filled them. Everything in the universe about us bespeaks the reality, power, beneficence, and majesty of the divine sovereign. There are also signs of the divine judgment and retribution for sinners and for those who cry lies to God's signs or deny them in the histories of previous prophets; these prophets have also been given signs to confirm the truth and divine origin of their messages. A demand for such signs, presumably of a miraculous nature, was made also of Muḥammed by his opponents and detractors. The Qur'ān, however, insists that only God, and not the Prophet, has the power to give signs; in any event, even were Muḥammad to bring a sign (30:58), his opponents would not believe. The real signs of Muḥammad's authenticity as a prophet and of the truth of his messages were the revelations that came to him. These were miraculous events not to be explained in mundane terms. Here the concept of *āyah* is seen as virtually equivalent to the revelation, an idea that is borne out elsewhere when the Qur'ān speaks of one *āyah* being substituted for another or mentions "a surah in which we have sent down *āyāt*." Thus *āyah* was a name for one of the units of the revelation, and it carries that sense even when it refers to a verse of the Qur'ān.

It is not altogether appropriate, however, to translate *āyah* as "verse" since the Qur'ān is composed in a kind of rhyming prose and does not exhibit the uniform observance of a metrical system of any kind. Stylistically the Qur'ān does not follow the well-established formal rules of Arabic poetry. Some of the *āyāt* are quite short, consisting of only a few words, while others are lengthy, comprising a number of lines. There is also disagreement among authorities about the precise divisions of the *āyāt* from one another, a problem that is created by uncertainty over the points at which rhyme or assonance may be thought to occur. In consequence there is more than one scheme for numbering the *āyāt* of the Qur'ān. Gustav Flügel in his edition (1834) employed a division and numbering of the *āyāt* that is not used by any standard Muslim authority, but it was the system employed in the West for many years. Since the appearance of the 1924 Egyptian edition, however, it has become customary for most scholars, in those instances where the Flügel numbering differs from the Egyptian, to use both numbers in the citations of particular *āyāt*, with the Egyptian number coming first and the Flügel second.

Other Divisions and Signs. In addition to the division into surahs and *āyāt* the Qur'ān is also divided for purposes of recitation. One division marks out thirty approximately equal parts *(ajzā'*; sg., *juz')* that permit the whole Qur'ān to be completed during the month of Ramaḍān by reciting one part per day. Each part is further subdivided into two units called *ḥizb*, which are each subdivided in turn into four quarters *(rubʿ al-ḥizb)*. A different division of the text into seven *manāzil* (sg., *manzil)* envisages the recitation in the course of a single week. Some or all of these divisions for liturgical purposes are normally indicated in the margin of the text by words, signs, and numbers.

In comparison with the printed versions of ordinary Arabic texts, the Qur'ān is distinguished by the presence of a full complement of diacritical marks that give precise guidance for the vocalization of each word. These marks result in a much "busier" text than is normally the case. It is customary to write and print only the consonants in Arabic, since vocalization (therefore, the vowels) is looked upon not as an essential element of a word but only as the "movement" given to the consonants. It falls upon the readers to supply the vocalization as they read, according to their understanding of the sentence and the relationship of its various parts. Were the text not fully pointed, numerous possibilities for error would arise, especially for those readers who do not know the language well. Since the Qur'ān is looked upon as the very words of God himself, error in its reading and recitation is not acceptable. For this reason the Qur'anic text is invariably printed fully pointed.

Still other signs that are usually printed in the text between the lines or at the end of an *āyah* have to do with instructions for recitation. They are intended as helps to the reciter, who must observe an elaborate set of rules concerning the pronunciation of certain letters and combinations of letters. There are, for example, signs that indicate where a stop is mandatory in order to preserve the meaning, others where a stop is permitted but not mandatory, others where a stop is forbidden, and so forth. Indications are also given through signs of places where it was customary for the Prophet to stop while reciting, as well as indications of places where the angel Gabriel had the habit of stopping. All of these matters form constituent elements of the body of learning known to Muslims as the *ʿulūm al-Qur'ān* ("sciences of the Qur'ān").

In the case of some fourteen or fifteen surahs where it is mentioned that the creation and God's servants bow before their Lord, it is considered mandatory to perform a prostration when one recites these surahs or hears them recited. At the appropriate points the word *sajdah* (prostration) is, therefore, printed in the margin.

In Arabic editions of the Qur'ān, though often not in translations, it is also usual to print a prayer *(duʿā')* after the last surah; this is known as the "Prayer upon the Completion of the Qur'ān." The reciter begs God's mercy in the name of the Qur'ān, prays that the scripture may be a light and guidance, and beseeches God's aid in learning, remembering, and reciting the Qur'ān continually.

The Teachings of the Qur'ān

The Qur'ān contains many different kinds of materials that range from narrative to prescriptions and prohibitions of a quasi-legal nature and exhortations to fear God. Although its teaching is not developed in a systematic way, it is nonetheless possible to extract from the Qur'ān a summary of its worldview. The Qur'ān's principal concern is the divine relationship with humanity; indeed, its very purpose is to summon mortals to recognize the sovereignty of God over their lives and to invite them to submit (do or make *islām*, "submission") to his will. In consequence it has a great deal to say about the natures of both God and humankind.

Doctrine of God. There is no attempt in the pages of the Qur'ān to prove that God exists; his being and his existence are simply assumed. Although some of those whom Muḥammad addressed may have lacked such an idea, it seems likely on the basis of the Qur'ān and the pre-Islamic poetry that a high god, known as Allāh, was generally recognized among the Arabs. Despite his being the highest, however, he was but one god among others in a polytheistic system. Muḥammad's mission was to call for acknowledgment of that deity as the exclusive arbiter of human destiny and for devotion to him alone. Thus, the Qur'ān lays emphasis upon God's *tawḥīd*, his unity, singularity, or uniqueness. "God, there is no god but he" (2:255, 3:2, and numerous other places), proclaims the Qur'ān, or alternatively, "There is no god but God" (3:62 et al.), words equivalent in meaning to the first portion of the Islamic Shahādah, or short creedal statement. [*See* Shahādah.]

The sense of these words is not that Allāh is the apex of a hierarchy but that he is absolutely supreme in a manner that deprives all his possible rivals of any true reality. Among all things Allāh alone is worthy to be spoken of as truly "being." "That which you worship apart from him is nothing but names you have named, yourselves and your fathers" (12:40). Similarly, the Qur'ān pours scorn on the idols of the Arabs, things made with their own hands that can neither profit nor hurt them (25:55 et al.), mocks those who take angels as their Lord, and makes Jesus deny that he ever urged his followers to take him and his mother as lords (5:116). The Qur'anic world is thoroughly and uncompromisingly theocentric: it owes its very existence to Allāh, who created it and sustains it and with whose signs it is filled. The greatest wrong of which human beings are capable is "association" *(shirk)* of another being with God in the supremacy and uniqueness that are properly his alone. "Serve God, and associate nothing with him" (4:36) is the heart of the Qur'ān's message to humanity.

The Qur'ān does, however, recognize several classes of other supernatural beings, namely angels, *jinn*, and demons, but they are all subordinate to God. All, further, are created beings, the *jinn* and the angels having as their purpose to serve and worship God, while the demons are given freedom to tempt humans to go astray until their final punishment overtakes them.

The Qur'ān characterizes God through a number of epithets *(All-Mighty, All-Wise, Knowing, Willing, Seeing,* etc.). These descriptive terms, as well as the verbal forms that set out the divine actions, are the basis of the list of the ninety-nine Most Beautiful Names of God that have figured so prominently in Muslim theology and mysticism. In the Qur'ān the epithets should be taken as simple descriptions of the divine being who gave the revelations to Muḥammad. The chief divine characteristics that emerge from them are those of omnipotent creator (13:16 et al.), bountiful benefactor, and stern judge. God has brought the heavens and the earth and what lies between them into existence through his creative word, "Be" (40:68 et al.), and it is he who controls events in human lives and in the cosmos more generally: "He is powerful over all things." It is God who sends down rain that causes the pastures and the crops to grow, and he who created the cattle, horses, and mules that serve and benefit humankind. From his hand also arises the bounty of the sea as well as all other things that give pleasure, sustenance, and fulfillment. "And if ye would count the favor of Allāh, ye cannot reckon it" (16:18). In the earliest days of Muḥammad's mission to the Arabs the beneficence of Allāh was the central theme of his message. The bountiful, merciful, and forgiving God, however, is also the upholder of stern and unrelenting justice. For those who do evil, refuse his prophets, reject the revelations, or cry lies to God, judgment and a terrible punishment are sure to follow, while for his faithful servants there will be the reward of bliss. [*See* Attributes of God, *article on* Islamic Concepts; *and* God, *article on* God in Islam.]

One aspect of the divine mercy frequently emphasized in the Qur'ān is God's communication with humanity. God does not stand aloof from the world but involves himself in its affairs and in the lives of mortals. From the divine side communication has occurred through God's numerous signs in the creation and through the prophets who have been sent with guidance. The Qur'ān speaks of a series of prophets who include some, such as Abraham, Moses, David, and Jesus, from the biblical tradition and others, such as Ṣāliḥ and Hūd, apparently of old Arabian origin. It is notable, however, that among the biblical prophets none of the great writing prophets of the Old Testament is mentioned. To some prophets books have been given, all bearing the same message to humankind; these include the Torah of Moses, the Psalms of David, and the Evangel of Jesus, to which must be added the *kitāb* vouchsafed to Muḥammad who is the seal of the entire series of prophets. Other prophets were not bearers of books but served as guides, warners, and admonishers to the errant.

Those who have previously received scripture, principally the Jews and Christians, the "peoples of the book," share a common tradition with the Muslim *ummah*, or community, all three stemming from Abraham. The Christian scripture confirms the Torah, and the Qur'ān confirms them both. At the same time, however, the Qur'ān particularly charges the Jews with having "corrupted" or "altered" their scripture or with having "concealed" parts of it. It seems clear that in the beginning of his career Muḥammad expected to be warmly received by the two previous scriptural communities, but this was not to be, and his relations with Jews and Christians steadily worsened. Of the three only the Muslims have proved to be the true followers of Abraham and, therefore, of the original divine message.

From the human side also the communication with God may be both verbal and nonverbal. In its verbal aspect it is represented by the *du'ā'*, which is a private, individual conversation with God, either an outpouring of deep piety or a desperate cry for help when believers find themselves in imminent danger, as in the case of shipwreck (10:22) or when confronted with the terror of the final judgment. Such prayers are individual and deeply felt, even though the person may forget his or her dependence upon God when the danger has passed. Nonverbal communication with the divine takes the form of the ritual *ṣalāt*, or worship that the Qur'ān enjoins upon Muslims to render daily to their Lord. The *ṣalāt* includes bodily postures and prostrations and also some verbal formulas which are, however, fixed in their form and not spontaneous. [*See* Ṣalāt.]

Doctrine of Humankind. In the Qur'anic view human nature stands in sharpest contrast with that of God. Humans are creatures, brought into being by God, though they occupy a special position in the cosmic hierarchy somewhat higher than the angels, whom God commanded to bow down to Adam to whom he had taught the names of things (2:31–33). All did so save Iblīs, who arrogantly refused, becoming the enemy of mankind. The proper human attitude toward the Sovereign Creator Lord is that of humble, meek, and self-abasing surrender. Allāh is Lord, and the human being is his slave *('abd)* with all that this implies of subservience and dependence. This relationship is most clearly expressed in the word *islām*, which signifies the inner act of self-relinquishment into the hands of God that is required of all people. Mere outward conformity to the practices of the Muslim community is not enough; there must also be *taqwā* (fear of God), *taṣdīq* (involvement of the heart), and *īmān* (faith). Those who haughtily refuse, who do not acknowledge the signs of God and his bounty, are *kāfirs*, usually translated as "unbelievers," though its Qur'anic meaning is closer to "ingrates."

The Qur'ān lays great emphasis upon the absoluteness of God's power over human lives, to the extent at times even of suggesting that all human activity is the direct result of the divine will and initiative. This point is clearly made in such verses as 9:51, "Nothing will befall us except what God has decreed for us," and 6:125, "If God wills to guide someone, he enlarges his breast for Islam, and if he wills to lead someone astray, he makes his breast narrow and contracted." In spite of such passages, however, the Qur'ān in general maintains the freedom of human will and, indeed, emphasizes the need for people to decide and commit themselves, positively or negatively, with respect to its teaching. The seeming contradiction between these passages is probably to be explained in terms of the audiences being addressed and the rhetorical demands of the peculiar circumstances in which these revelations came. For the fiercely independent and haughty bedouin of the desert, for example, it would have been important to underline in the strongest terms that they were subject to the control of a higher power and, like it or not, subservient to a universal moral order. In other circumstances a stronger stress on the ability to choose would have been appropriate. [*See* Īmān and Islām *and* Free Will and Predestination, *article on* Islamic Concept.]

Eschatology. One of the major themes of the Qur'anic teaching is the coming Judgment when all people shall be made to answer before God for their lives. The Judgment (the Day of Religion, the Day of Resurrection, the Last Day) is the climax of history, a catastrophic and terrifying event that will leave none untouched. Some of the most powerful passages of the Qur'ān describe the cosmic upheaval and turmoil that will occur on that day; nature will disintegrate as the seas boil over and the mountains crumble into dust, and the graves will give up their dead. When that day will come no one knows save God, but come it shall and suddenly. People shall be called, each one individually, the living and the resurrected, before God's throne with the angels standing about in ranks, and each shall be required to read from the book of the record of his or her deeds. There will be naught to avail one on that day and none to intercede, not even powerful kinsmen. The Qur'ān speaks of the Judgment being made by the weighing of deeds in a scale to determine whether the good or the ill preponderates. In another passage the Judgment is rendered by a person's book being handed over in either the right or left hand or behind the back. There is no mention, however, of the bridge stretched over Hell or of the lake of fire, and no clear reference to punishment in the grave, all of which belong to the medieval elaboration of Islamic eschatological teaching.

Once judgment has been rendered, people are consigned either to the torment of Hell or the bliss of Paradise, to remain there forever. Hell is supervised by angels appointed for that purpose, and its inhabitants, in addition to the fire, are made to suffer the agony of eating bitter fruit and drinking hot water while calling to no avail on their friends in Paradise for assistance. The fortunate dwellers of Paradise by contrast live amid beautiful gardens, with flowing streams, and enjoy many luxuries and pleasures, among them reunion with earthly spouses restored to full youth. There is also the company of wide-eyed houris, unblemished maidens of great beauty. In addition the faithful in Paradise have the blessings of peace and forgiveness and, most important of all, are granted the beatific vision of their Sovereign Lord.

The Qur'anic eschatological teachings were among the most difficult for the pagan Arabs to accept, which perhaps accounts for the great emphasis they receive in the Qur'ān. The resurrection from the dead was an especially sharp point of controversy between Muḥammad and his incredulous critics, who demanded to know how bones and flesh once turned to dust could live again. The answer lay in God's omnipotence; he who had made people live, then made them die, could make them live once again. Even for those long dead there was to be no escape from the terrible Day of Reckoning. [*See* Eschatology, *article on* Islamic Eschatology.]

Legal Elements. The Qur'ān is no more a book of law than it is a book of theology, but it does contain a number of specific commands and prohibitions that commended themselves to legally minded people in later times as the elements of a legal system. They became the basis of the highly elaborated Islamic law or *sharī'ah.* These regulations are often referred to as the "laws of the Qur'ān." The first category of such commands relates to the religious duties of a Muslim with respect to prayer, observance of the fast of Ramaḍān, the pilgrimage, and the payment of the alms-tax or *zakāt;* Islamic law knows this category of regulations as the *'ibādāt* or duties that believer as slave (*'abd*) owes to the Lord. Other regulations have more to do with the life of the community or with the relationship among people. The principal groups in this category are (1) rules governing relations between the sexes, including marriage, divorce, adultery, and fornication as well as the norms for modest conduct; (2) rules regulating the relations of parents and children, comprised of their duties toward one another, as well as the rule of adoption; (3) rules relating to criminal acts, especially murder, theft, and retaliation; (4) rules relating to inheritance; (5) rules for the control of commercial relations: such things as contract, debt, usury, and justice in business dealings; (6) rules relating to slaves and their treatment; and (7) rules relating to food and drink, including the prohibition of wine. Numerous other regulations of lesser importance for the community's life are also suggested by the Qur'ān from time to time, such as, for example, the distribution of booty after a raid or relations with religious minorities living under the community's domination. [*See* Islamic Law *and* Worship and Cultic Life, *article on* Muslim Worship.]

The Qur'ān in Muslim Life

The evidences for the religious meaning of the Qur'ān and the reverence paid to it are too numerous to catalog in detail, but some broad indications may be given. Among the most striking is the vast effort devoted to the study of the Qur'ān and especially to the composition of commentaries on its text. There are literally thousands of commentaries (*tafsīrs*), many of them of massive size, in which the sacred text is deliberated upon verse by verse and phrase by phrase in order to elicit its meaning. In spite of the rich store of such works from the past, the production of commentaries continues in the twentieth century in all of the principal languages that Muslims speak. [*See* Tafsīr.]

If one considers the systematic expression of Islamic faith in the form of theological treatises and creedal statements, the role of the Qur'ān is once again central. The major themes of Islamic theology all reflect the Qur'anic teachings, and it was Qur'anic statements that both posed the basic problems for the theologians and supplied the most fundamental and authoritative materials for their solution. Such issues as the relation between the divine attributes and the divine essence or the problem of free will and predestination derive immediately from verses in the Qur'ān that invite contemplation and require clarification. One of the most intense of the theological discussions in the early centuries revolved about the Qur'ān itself and the sense in which it might be considered to be the "speech of God." There were those (the Jahmīyah) who held that God was a speaker and the Qur'ān his speech only in a figurative sense. The majority, however, looked upon speech as one of the essential attributes of God like his knowing, willing, seeing, and so forth. Speech they held to be a quality of God inherent in his nature. Since God is unchangeable, it follows that he has eternally been a speaker of his word. Thus arose the doctrine of the "uncreatedness" of the Qur'ān, which eventually triumphed in the community in spite of the powerful opposition of some of the Abbasid Caliphs who favored the sect known as the Mu'tazilah with its belief that the Qur'ān was created. The position of Muslim orthodoxy is put succinctly by al-Naṣafī (d. 1142) in his well-known creedal statement (Elder's translation):

> He (God) speaks with a kind of Speech which is one of His attributes, from all eternity, not of the genus of letters and sounds. It is an attribute incompatible with silence and defect. Allah speaks with this attribute, commanding, prohibiting, and narrating. The Qur'ān, the Speech of Allah, is un-

created and it is written in our volumes, preserved in our hearts, recited by our tongues, heard by our ears, [yet] is not a thing residing in them.

The import of this statement is that the Qur'ān is coexistent with God throughout all of eternity, a truth beyond and prior to the whole of created being. That truth lives and is communicated in the scripture of the Muslim community; indeed, it is the awareness of its inexpressible divine nature which makes the Qur'ān the scripture. [*See* Creeds, *article on* Islamic Creeds, *and* Muʿtazilah.]

The Muslim attitude toward translation of the Qur'ān may also be considered in this connection. The vast majority of Muslims in the world are not Arabophones, and the Qur'ān in its original language is, thus, not readily accessible to them. Nevertheless, learned Muslims have traditionally resisted the translation of the Qur'ān into other languages on the ground that the words delivered to and by the Prophet were Arabic words. Any other words are simply not the Qur'ān: they may convey its literal meaning, but they lack the divine aura of the original. With the passing of time, however, perhaps as early as the ninth century, translations into other languages began to be made. In the case of translations meant for the use of Muslims it has been customary to present the translation in interlinear form with the original Arabic not only present but given the place of prominence. Thus, the contact with the original divine message is maintained and cultivated, even though the worshiper may require assistance in the vocabulary of another language to appreciate much of what is being said. The same sensitivity toward translation is shown in many English renderings; one of the well-known Muslim translators, Marmaduke Pickthall, has called his translation not the Qur'ān, but *The Meaning of the Glorious Qur'ān*. When the Qur'ān is recited in connection with religious or public ceremonies, however, it is invariably recited in Arabic and never in translation.

There can be no more eloquent testimony to the place accorded the Qur'ān in Muslim hearts than the effort that many pious individuals make to internalize the scripture by memorizing it in its entirety. To commit the scripture to memory is thought to be an especially pious act, and all over the Muslim world there are not only numerous persons who have accomplished this considerable feat but also thousands of Qur'ān schools (*kuttāb*s) where the chief activity is teaching the text to young children, especially to boys. Memorization of the text is striven for even in those countries where Arabic is neither spoken nor understood, and there are many who can repeat the sacred words without, however, understanding what they mean. A person who has thus memorized the complete text is known as a *ḥāfiẓ*, one who guards or keeps the Qur'ān in his heart.

Perhaps the most powerful mediator of the Qur'ān in Muslim religious life and practice is its frequent and repeated recitation. Attention was called above to the role of Qur'anic recitation in the time of the Prophet and his companions, and that role has continued through the centuries down to the present time. For the vast majority in Islamic lands there is no other access to the divine book than that provided by its recitation; it must be remembered that literacy is limited in the countries of Asia and Africa, and, furthermore, Arabic is not the tongue of the majority of Muslims. The revelations, however, continue to be recited in the midst of the community that has formed about them, and there is no more powerful symbol or evocation of the Islamic worldview than the divine words. The Qur'ān or parts of it are recited on many different occasions. For example, a pious Muslim who faithfully observes the five daily prayers mandated by the *sharīʿah* will recite the Fātiḥah a minimum of seventeen times each day in addition to other passages of the Qur'ān. All of the great events of life, the so-called rites of passage, in the Muslim world are marked by the recitation of the Qur'ān as an essential part of the observances. The holy book is an element of the rites of marriage and of funerals. It is recited at birth, in connection with the naming of a child, and at the time of circumcision. A great enterprise of any kind, whether in public or private life, is likely to be launched with the blessings that come through recitation of the Qur'ān. In some Muslim countries it has become the custom to begin every public meeting or gathering with Qur'anic verses. In recent times, since the introduction of electronic media of communication to the Muslim world, Qur'anic passages, often beautifully recited, are regularly broadcast. Also of importance is the place of Qur'ān recitation in the celebration of the great calendrical feast days of the Muslim community such as ʿĪd al-Fiṭr and ʿĪd al-Aḍḥā, and as noted earlier, it is a special mark of piety to recite the whole of the Qur'ān during the thirty days of the fast of Ramaḍān. In short, the Qur'ān is invariably associated with the crucial occasions of Muslim life in an immediate way through the recitation of the revealed words. Its significance is not limited to these paramount events, however, but penetrates into virtually every aspect of daily life as well by virtue of its role as one of the formative forces of Islamic culture.

Evidence of this same reverence may be seen in the aesthetic embellishments given to the text of the Qur'ān by generations of calligraphers, illuminators, and bookbinders. The flowing cursive script of Arabic with its many styles of writing readily lends itself to assuming elaborate and exquisite forms. Nowhere has the art of the calligrapher been more beautifully or carefully exercised than in the presentation and decoration of the Qur'anic text, as a visit to any major collection of Islamic art will quickly show. The writing out of the text, like its memorization, is a work of devotion, and it is doubly so when the result is a thing of beauty and compelling attraction. Often no less lovely are the embossed and decorated covers within which the text is enclosed. Qur'anic verses, sometimes in a monumental size and always in beautiful forms, also appear as architectural decorations on mosques, *madrasahs*, and other public buildings. The appearance of Qur'anic inscriptions on religious buildings in particular serves as a peculiarly effective symbol of the purposes for which the building was erected and, therefore, of the divine presence in the world.

There is also an elaborate etiquette observed in the community for approaching and handling the sacred text. It is never to be approached lightly or with disrespect. Anyone who would read or recite should be in a state of ritual purity, having performed the ablutions customary before prayer, and all intentions must be pious. Care must be taken that the Qur'ān does not come into contact with any filthy substance, and it is never to be laid upon the ground or recited in situations that would conduce to its being ridiculed.

It would be difficult if not impossible to overstate the role of the Qur'ān in the religious life of the Muslim community. In no other major religious tradition does the scripture have the centrality or the significance that it commands in Muslim piety. The "book-centeredness" of Islamic faith is a response to the Muslim apprehension of the Qur'ān as the living presence of the divine word in the midst of the community and the world. Through it God continues to communicate with those who fear him and acknowledge his signs; the Qur'ān is thus revered as a transcendent reality and an eternal truth accessible to all who care to read or recite it.

[*See also the biographies of the principal scholars and historical figures mentioned herein.*]

BIBLIOGRAPHY

There are numerous English translations of the Qur'ān, the most successful being that of A. J. Arberry, *The Koran Interpreted* (New York, 1955), which captures much of the flavor of the original Arabic in addition to representing the best of critical scholarship. *The Meaning of the Glorious Koran: An Explanatory Translation* by M. M. Pickthall (New York, 1930), an English convert to Islam, is based upon the most authoritative Muslim commentaries and may be held to represent the understanding of the Qur'ān held by most Sunnī Muslims. The rendering by ʿAbdallāh Yūsuf ʿAlī, entitled *The Holy Qur'ān, Text, Translation and Commentary*, 3d ed. (New York, 1946), also has merit. The foremost French translation is that of Régis Blachère: *Le Coran: Traduction selon un essai de reclassement des sourates*, 3 vols. (Paris, 1947–1951), the first volume of which is an introduction to the Qur'ān. In German the work of the late Rudi Paret, *Der Koran* (Stuttgart, 1963–1966) has earned wide admiration.

The basic work for the critical study of the Qur'ān is Theodor Nöldeke's *Geschichte des Qorāns*, originally published in 1860, greatly revised and enlarged in a second edition by Friedrich Schwally, two volumes of which appeared in the early decades of this century. A third volume on the history of the text was prepared through the efforts of Gotthelf Bergsträsser and Otto Pretzl (Leipzig, 1909–1938). The entire three volumes of the revised and completed work are most readily available in an edition made in Hildesheim in 1964. The best English statement of the issues and problems of Qur'anic study is *Bell's Introduction to the Qur'ān*, revised by W. Montgomery Watt (Edinburgh, 1970). This volume is comprehensive in its treatment but succinct in its expression, and it contains some highly useful appendices. Also to be commended is Alford Welch's "Kur'an" in *The Encyclopaedia of Islam*, new ed. (Leiden, 1960–). Although it is necessarily compressed, it covers the major matters and offers a number of critical judgments of the author's own. Ignácz Goldziher's *Die Richtungen der islamischen Koranauslegung* (1920; reprint, Leiden, 1970) in its earlier sections deals with the history of the Qur'anic text before going on to discuss the variety of commentaries that history has produced. This book is one of the foundation stones of Western Islamology. An approach to Qur'anic study that diverges from the pattern established by Nöldeke and his successors may be seen in the books of John Wansbrough, *Quranic Studies* (Oxford, 1977) and *The Sectarian Milieu* (Oxford, 1978). Wansbrough has applied some of the methods and conceptual apparatus of Biblical studies to the Qur'ān and, as indicated above, reached revolutionary conclusions. A Muslim response to Western critical studies of the Holy Book is available in Labib al-Said's *The Recited Koran*, translated by Bernard Weiss, M. A. Rauf, and Morroe Berger (Princeton, 1975).

The most compelling exposition of Qur'anic teachings in English is Fazlur Rahman's book *Major Themes of the Qur'ān* (Chicago, 1980); the work also deals with many of the issues raised by critical scholarship. It is especially remarkable for its combination of deep learning and profound reverence for the Qur'anic message. Also outstanding is the work of Toshihiko Izutsu, especially *The Structure of the Ethical Terms in the Koran* (Tokyo, 1959) and *God and Man in the Koran* (Tokyo, 1964). These works pursue a method of semantic analysis that illuminates basic Qur'anic concepts with unique clarity. Also worthy of mention is the sympathetic study of Kenneth Cragg, *The Mind of the Qur'an* (London, 1973); it is accompanied by a basic introduction to the Qur'ān called *The Event of the Qur'ān* (London, 1971).

The most useful reference tool for the English reader to gain access to the Qur'ān is Hanna E. Kassis's *A Concordance to the Qur'ān* (Berkeley, 1982). Not only does this volume enable one to find any word of interest in the text, but its unique organization provides a key to the interrelationship of key Qur'anic terms and concepts.

CHARLES J. ADAMS

Its Role in Muslim Piety

The Qur'ān is a unique phenomenon in religious history. It is a historical document reflecting the socioeconomic, religious, and political situation of seventh-century Arab society, but it is at the same time a book of guidance and a code of conduct for millions of men and women who live by its injunctions and find in it the meaning and fulfillment of their lives. For them, the Qur'ān is the eternal word of God which entered human time and history through revelation, a light illuminating the way of the faithful from this world to the next.

As the written text declares, its original form remains with God, "a glorious Qur'ān preserved in a well-guarded tablet" (surah 85:21–22). Thus, although it took on the form and character of human speech, the Qur'ān remains in its essence a celestial archetype free from the limitations of human sounds and letters. It was communicated to the prophet Muḥammad by Gabriel, the angel of revelation, in human words, words which were subsequently written down and memorized by the pious and finally codified by them into an official book *(muṣḥaf)* "contained within two covers." Yet the Prophet himself, we are told, received the Qur'ān in humanly unintelligible sounds like those of ringing bells; like Gabriel, he received it directly from God. This dimension, the essence of the earthly Qur'ān, which God "sent down on the night of determination" (*laylat al-qadr*, 96:1) into Muḥammad's heart (26:94), enabled the Prophet to share in the power and transcendence of the divine word. As a result, the relationship between the human plane of existence and the transcendent word of God has given the Qur'ān a quasi-human personality, indued with feelings and emotions, ready even to contend on the Day of Resurrection with those who abandoned it in this life and to intercede for those who have lived by its teachings.

For more than fourteen hundred years, Muslims of all schools of thought have interiorized the Qur'ān as the transcendent word of God, infinite in meaning and significance for all times and places. Its status in the Muslim community is strikingly depicted in a prophetic tradition related on the authority of ʿAlī, the cousin and son-in-law of the Prophet. When ʿAli was told by the Prophet, "There shall be a great sedition after me," and he asked how such a calamity could be averted, the Prophet replied:

> By means of the book of God! In it is the report concerning those who were before you, the narrative of what is to come after you, and the criterion of judgment among you. . . . Whoever seeks guidance in anything other than it, God shall cause him to go astray. It is the rope of God; it is the "wise remembrance" (3:58) and the "straight way." With it, hearts shall not swerve nor tongues utter confusion. The learned shall never be sated of it. It shall not wear out from constant use, nor will its marvels ever be exhausted. . . . Whoever utters it speaks truth, and whoever abides by it shall have his rich reward. Whoever judges by it shall judge justly, and whoever calls others to it shall be guided to the straight way.
> (cited in Ayoub, vol. 1, p. 10)

The Qur'ān has thus permeated every facet and stage of the life of Muslim society and that of every Muslim believer. It is, however, particularly evident in Shīʿī piety, since much of Shīʿī theology is based on a hagiography in which the Qur'ān as well as the imams figure prominently. With its words, the newborn child is welcomed into the world, as the father utters certain popular verses into its ear. In traditional Muslim societies, a child learns the opening surah when it begins to speak and goes on to memorize other, longer surahs and in some cases the entire Qur'ān. The completion of this sacred task then becomes a festive occasion for the family and the larger community. As the sixth Shīʿī imam, Jaʿfar al-Ṣādiq, declared, "Whoever recites the Qur'ān while yet a youth and has faith, the Qur'ān becomes intermingled with his flesh and blood" (Ayoub, vol. 1, p. 12).

Language. The Qur'ān addresses Muslims in various styles and on various levels of eloquence. Its brief and cryptic verses present in sharp contrasts the portents, fears, and torments of the Day of Judgment and the bliss and pleasures of Paradise. Its longer and more didactic verses address the day-to-day life of the community—its social relations, political loyalties, and legal problems. The Qur'ān encourages the people of faith by comparing them to exuberant plants which would please cultivators (48:29) and reproaches the stubborn rejectors of faith by comparing them to dumb beasts (8:22).

Qur'anic language is at times rhapsodic. The opening verses of surah 36 (*Yāsīn*, the names of two Arabic letters), for instance, move rapidly and with great dramatic force in relating unknown stories of bygone ages and the dramatic encounter of human beings with God on the Day of Judgment; its awe-inducing power is such that it is recited over the dead. In other places the language is smooth and calming, as in surah 55 (*al-Raḥmān*, The Merciful), which describes the flowing rivers of Paradise, only imperfectly realized on earth, and which has been recognized to have hypnotic qualities. A good Qur'ān reciter often has the power to carry his listeners into moods of excitement or transports of bliss as they become totally engrossed in the words.

Among the most popular and most frequently repeated passages of the Qur'ān, recited by Muslim men and women in times of crisis, fear, or uncertainty, are the Fātiḥah (the opening surah), the throne verse (2:255), and the surah of sincere faith (112). It is a widespread custom, for instance, that when the parents of a young man and woman agree on uniting their children in marriage, the agreement is sealed with the recitation of the Fātiḥah; business deals and other transactions are blessed in the same way. The Fātiḥah is the basic Muslim prayer, for the Prophet declared: "There is no prayer except by the opening of the Book." It is composed of seven brief verses which present two distinct but closely related themes: in the first half, thanksgiving, praise, and recognition of God's mercy ("In the name of God, the All-merciful, the Compassionate/Master of the Day of Judgment/You alone do we worhsip"), and in the second half, a plea for guidance ("and you alone do we beseech for help/Guide us on the straight way/The way of those upon whom you have bestowed your favor, not of those who have incurred your wrath or those who have gone astray").

The throne verse and the surah of sincere faith both, in different ways, declare the majesty, sovereignty, and eternity of God. The throne verse is a complete and self-contained statement of God's eternal sovereignty, his great power and majesty, declaring that he is "the Ever-living, the eternal Sovereign. . . . His throne encompasses the heavens and the earth, and the preservation of them does not burden him. He is the most high, the most great." The surah of sincere faith or divine Oneness is considered by Muslims the essence of the Qur'ān, the creed of Islam and a source of blessing and great power against evil. It declares that God is "the eternal refuge," dependable in times of hardship and adversity. He is not subject to processes of birth and death: "He did not beget nor was he begotten." He is unique in his oneness: "Nor is there anyone equal to him." This surah is often recited along with the Fātiḥah in prayers; it is reported in the traditions that the Prophet recommended its recitation a hundred times a day if possible.

Power. The Qur'ān is possessed of great powers for protection and harm alike. We read, for example, that "were we to cause this Qur'ān to descend on a mountain you would see [the mountain] humbled and torn asunder in awe of God" (59:21), and indeed, tradition reports that when the fifth surah was sent down to the Prophet while he was traveling on a she-camel, the beast fell to the ground, unable to support the sacred words. Yet this Qur'ān, which even the mountains cannot sustain, is also a source of tranquillity and peace for the hearts of those of faith. Muslims consider this quality in itself a divine gift of mercy; as Qurṭubī asserts, "Had God not fortified the hearts of his servants with the ability to bear it, . . . they would have been too feeble and distraught before its great weight" (Qurṭubī, vol. 1, p. 4).

The powers of the Qur'ān have been used in Muslim folklore to heal and to inflict harm, to cause strange natural occurrences, and even to charm snakes and find lost animals. In amulets it serves to protect a child from the evil eye or any other mishap and to strengthen or break the bond of love between two people. Qur'anic verses are similarly inscribed on vehicles, shops, and entrances to homes or public buildings to guarantee protection against evil and to express gratitude for God's bounties. Qur'anic words, phrases, or entire verses are often written or uttered in combination with unintelligible words or syllables as formulas against magic. According to the sixth imam, "If a man of faith were to recite any one hundred verses of the Qur'ān he wished and then invoke the name of God seven times, he could ask for hard rocks to be split and his prayer would be answered" (Majlisī, vol. 89, p. 176).

In times of sickness and adversity, believers turn to the Qur'ān as a source of "healing and mercy for the people of faith" (17:82); the Fātiḥah in particular is called *al-shāfiyah* (the surah of healing). Since tradition has tended to take the Qur'ān literally whenever possible, it was recommended on the authority of Mujāhid, one of the earliest Qur'anic authorities, that a sick person drink the water in which a parchment inscribed with a portion of the Qur'ān has been soaked; this pious custom has persisted down to the present in many areas of the Muslim world, often with unfortunate results. Qurṭubī asserts that in veneration of the Qur'ān, a person seeking such a cure must invoke the name of God in every breath he or she takes while drinking and must be sincere in prayerful attention because his or her reward would depend upon that sincerity. The power of the Qur'ān to heal (10:57) or to reform the human character has also been recognized since the first generation of Muslims. It is related on the authority of the fifth Shīʿī imam, Muḥammad al-Bāqir, that "Anyone afflicted with a hard heart must inscribe surah 36 [*Yāsīn*] on a cup with saffron and drink from it (Qurṭubī, vol. 1, p. 31).

Comfort. The Qur'ān also serves as a source of strength and reassurance in the face of the unknown. For the pious, the Qur'ān provides the means of controlling future events or mitigating their outcome through *istikhārah*, seeking a good omen in the text. *Istikhārah* represents the choice of what God has chosen; it is carried out by averting the face, opening the book, and letting it speak directly to one's need or condition. The action is usually accompanied by elaborate prayers and rituals. A simple but typical procedure is described by Jaʿfar al-Ṣādiq, who is said to have reproached his followers for failing to consult the Qur'ān to resolve problems "with God's help." According to the instructions he gave for accomplishing this aim, a person must recite the Fātiḥah and other popular portions of the Qur'ān three times each, including the verse declaring "for with him are the keys of the unknown" (6:59). Such a person must then turn to God in prayers by means of the Qur'ān saying "O God, I come to you with the great Qur'ān from its opening to its end, for in it is your great name and your complete words. O you who hear every sound, encompass every event, and revive every soul after death—O you whom darkness cannot obscure and who is not confused by the similarity of voices—I beg you to choose for me the best course concerning a problem which I cannot resolve. For you alone know everything known and unknown." The seeker must then pray in the names of the prophet Muḥammad, ʿAlī, Fāṭimah, and their two sons, Ḥasan and Ḥusayn, as well as the rest of the twelve Shiʿī imams. Finally, he or she must open the book and count a certain number of pages and lines and read the text, which would be as though revealed in answer to the problem (Majlisī, vol. 88, pp. 244–245).

The Qur'ān is a source of blessing and comfort to the dead as well as the living. Often before a pious person dies, he or she stipulates that the Qur'ān be recited at the grave for three days to ensure the rest of his or her soul. Whenever a deceased person is remembered by friends or family, the Fātiḥah is recited; it is considered a gift to the dead, a fragrant breeze from Paradise to lighten the great hardship of the grave. It is, however, the portions of the Qur'ān learned in this world which will bring believers great merit in the hereafter. As a consolation for the followers *(shīʿah)* of the family of the Prophet, Imam Jaʿfar al-Ṣādiq promised that "Any one of our Shīʿah, or those who accept our authority *(wilāyah)*, who dies without having attained a good knowledge of the Qur'ān shall be taught it in his grave, in order that God may raise his station in paradise, because the number of stations in paradise is equal to the number of the verses of the Qur'ān" (Majlisī, vol. 39, p. 188). Indeed, the Prophet is reported to have said, "It shall be said to the bearer of the Qur'ān, 'Recite and rise [to a higher station]. Chant now as you did in the world, for your final station shall be at the last verse you recite'" (Qurṭubī, vol. 1, p. 9).

Recitation. Because the Qur'ān is an object of great reverence, we are told, no one should touch it unless he is pure (56:79), nor should anyone recite it unless he is in a state of ritual purity. Before beginning to recite, he must clean his teeth and purify his mouth, for he will become the "path" of the Qur'ān. The Qur'ān reciter must put on his best attire, as he would when standing before a king, for he is in fact speaking with God.

Likewise, because the Qur'ān is the essence of Islamic prayer, the reciter should face the *qiblah*, or direction of prayer toward Mecca. Anyone who begins to yawn in the course of reciting is obliged to stop, because yawning is caused by Satan. Normally, recitation begins with the formula of refuge: "I take refuge in God from the accursed Satan." It is therefore deemed necessary that the reciter seclude himself so that no one comes to interrupt him or speak to him, since that speech would then be mixed with the word of God, and the reciter would lose the power of the formula of refuge with which he began his recitation (see Qurṭubī, vol. 1, p. 27).

In a tradition related on the authority of Anas ibn Mālik, the bearers of the Qur'ān are described by the Prophet as those who are specially favored with the mercy of God because they are the teachers of his word: "Anyone who befriends them befriends God, and anyone who shows hostility to them shows hostility to God." The tradition goes on to assert that God protects those who listen to the Qur'ān from the afflictions of this world and protects its reciters from the trials of the world to come (Ṭabarsī, vol. 1, p. 32). The prophet is said to have further asserted that God would not torment a heart in which he had caused the Qur'ān to dwell. In a *ḥadīth qudsī* (divine utterance) related on the authority of Abū Saʿīd al-Khudrī, God says, "He who is occupied with the Qur'ān and with remembrance of me so that he has no time to pray for his needs, to him will I give the best of that which I grant to those who pray" (Qurṭubī, vol. 1, p. 4). All obligations of worship *(farā'iḍ)* shall cease with death except recitation of the Qur'ān: it shall be the delight of the people of Paradise.

The Qur'ān is not a book with a beginning, middle, and end. Every portion, or even every verse, is a Qur'ān, as the entire book is the Qur'ān, properly speaking. Thus reciting the complete text over a period of days, weeks, or months may be considered a journey through an infinite world of meaning, a journey in and with the Qur'ān. The primary purpose of this sacred journey is to form one's character and life according to the word of God, to achieve true righteousness *(taqwā)*. The task of reciting the Qur'ān is in itself a source of blessing. A man is reported to have asked the Prophet, "What is the most excellent deed?" He was told, "Be a sojourning traveler!" The man then asked, "Who is the sojourning traveler?" The Prophet answered, "It is the man of the Qur'ān, he who journeys from its beginning to its end, then returns again to its beginning. Thus he stops for a brief sojourn, then departs" (Qurṭubī, vol. 1, p. 30).

The Qur'ān guides its bearers to the eternal bliss of

Paradise. It will pray on their behalf, and God will bestow upon them the crown of glory and will be pleased with them. Indeed, those who have interiorized the sacred text through memorizing its verses and who recite it and teach others the art of recitation have occupied a special place in Muslim piety. They are described in a prophetic tradition as "the people of God and his elect" (Qurṭubī, vol. 1, p. 1). According to another prophetic tradition, the best of men is he who studies the Qur'ān and teaches it to others. In a tradition related on the authority of Abū Hurayrah, the Prophet is said to have declared: "There are no people assembled in one of the houses of God to recite the book of God and study it together but that the *sakīnah* (divine tranquillity) descends upon them. Mercy covers them, angels draw near to them, and God remembers them in the company of those who are with him" (Ayoub, vol. 1, pp. 8–9). Indeed, the highest merit for which a person can hope in the world to come is that of engaging with others in the study of the Qur'ān.

Literary legacy. In its written form, the Qur'ān has set the standard for Arabic language and literature as the proper and indeed the highest expression of literary Arabic. Its style of storytelling, its similes and metaphors have shaped classical Arabic literature and have even had their influence on the modern writers. It was the demand for absolute correctness in studying, writing, and reciting the Qur'ān which provided the basis for Arabic grammar and other linguistic sciences. Qur'anic words and phrases have permeated all the languages of the Muslim world. Even daily conversation, whether on weighty or mundane matters, is interspersed with Qur'anic words and phrases, and Qur'anic verses are beautifully calligraphed to decorate mosques, schools, and the homes of the pious.

The Qur'ān is the basis of unity in an otherwise highly diverse religious community and civilization. Its impact on the life of pious Muslims may be summed up in a prayer attributed to ʿAlī and intended to be offered at the completion of a Qur'ān recitation: "O God, relieve with the Qur'ān my breast; occupy with the Qur'ān my entire body; illumine with the Qur'ān my sight, and loosen with the Qur'ān my tongue. Grant me strength for this, so long as you allow me to remain alive, for there is neither strength nor power except in you" (Majlisī, vol. 89, p. 209).

BIBLIOGRAPHY

The role of the Qur'ān in Muslim piety, although crucial, has been largely neglected in Western scholarship. Muslim scholars also have neglected this aspect, concentrating instead on a rationalist and moral and political approach. The researcher is therefore left with the classical Muslim tradition for primary source materials.

The basic sources dealing with the place of the Qur'ān in Muslim piety fall into the genre of *faḍā'il al-Qur'ān* ("excellences of the Qur'ān"). Such discussions are often prefixed or appended to many of the standard *tafsīr* works; see for example the work by Ibn Kathīr (d. 1373) entitled *Faḍā'il al-Qur'ān* and appended to volume 7 of his Qur'ān commentary, *Tafsīr al-Qur'ān al-ʿaẓīm*, 7 vols. (Beirut, 1966). They also form a part of most major *ḥadīth* collections; see for example the chapter on *faḍā'il al-Qur'ān* in *Ṣaḥīḥ Bukhārī*, translated by Muhammad Muhsin Khan, *Translation of the Meanings of Sahih al-Bukhari*, 9 vols. (Beirut, 1979), in volume 6.

The sources used in this article are representative of the general literature on the subject. Abū ʿAbd Allāh Muḥammad al-Qurṭubī (d. 1273) was a noted commentator and jurist. The introduction to his work *Al-jāmiʿ li-aḥkām al-Qur'ān* (Cairo, 1966), is an excellent example of works treating the Qur'ān in all its aspects, including its excellences. Abū ʿAlī al-Faḍl ibn al-Ḥasan al-Ṭabarsī (d. 1153), an important Twelver Shīʿī jurist, theologian, and commentator, is the author of the *Majmaʿ al-bayān fī tafsīr al-Qur'ān* (Cairo, 1958), a reference work treating all points of view in Islamic exegesis with unusual objectivity. The introduction to this work also includes a discussion of the excellences of the Qur'ān. Mullā Muḥammad Bāqir al-Majlisī (d. 1699) was one of the most prolific Shīʿī authors of Safavid Iran. His encyclopedic work *Biḥār al-anwār*, 110 vols. (Beirut, 1983), deals with the biographies of the Shīʿī imāms, *ḥadīth*, hagiography, and popular lore. Volume 89 is devoted to the Qur'ān, including its excellences.

The only work in English thus far dealing with the place of the Qur'ān in popular piety is the introduction to my study *The Qur'ān and Its Interpreters* (Albany, N.Y., 1984).

MAHMOUD M. AYOUB

QURRAT AL-ʿAYN ṬĀHIRAH

QURRAT AL-ʿAYN ṬĀHIRAH (c. 1818–1852), Bābī preacher, poet, and their first woman martyr. Both *Qurrat al-ʿAyn* ("solace of the eyes") and *Ṭāhirah* ("the pure") were given as honorifics, and her original name has fallen into oblivion.

The daughter of a prominent Shīʿī mullah in Qazvin, she was married to her first cousin, the son of another important mullah. She was a highly intelligent woman and early studied the works of Shaykh Aḥmad Aḥsāʾī, who spoke of the imminent coming of the Bāb. After corresponding with Aḥsāʾī's disciple, Sayyid Kāẓim-i Rashtī, she took the decisive step of leaving her husband and children in order to join his circle in Karbala; but he died shortly before she performed the pilgrimage there in 1843. During her three years' stay in Karbala, Ṭāhirah preached the new doctrine with fervor and success and was accepted by the Bāb (whom she never met) as one of his eighteen disciples known as Ḥurūf-i Ḥayy ("the letters of the living," i.e., the letters that make up the word *ḥayy*). It was from the Bāb's description of her as Janab-i Ṭāhirah ("her excellency, the pure") that she became known as Ṭāhirah or, among Bahāʾīs, Ṭāhirih.

Her preaching made the authorities suspicious, and in 1847 she was put under surveillance in Baghdad. After the shah's Jewish physician became a convert to Babism during a visit there, Ṭāhirah and her followers were expelled from Iraq. Upon her return to Qazvin, she was divorced from her husband, who opposed the new teachings of the Bāb. The assassination of her uncle (her former father-in-law), also an adversary of the Bābīs, resulted in the first persecution of the adherents of the new faith, and she went to Tehran and stayed as a guest of Bahā' Allāh, whom she hailed as the awaited leader of the community. During a Bābī conference in Badasht in 1848, the beautiful young woman is said to have preached without a veil, an action that is taken as the first attempt to win freedom for Persian women. When Nāṣir al-Dīn Shāh ascended the throne later that year, Ṭāhirah was placed under arrest. After a Bābī attempt to assassinate the shah, she was executed, probably by strangulation, in August 1852.

Ṭāhirah is considered the first Iranian woman to preach equality of the sexes and religious freedom; E. G. Browne called her appearance in Iran "a prodigy—nay, almost a miracle." Her Persian poems are of great beauty; one of them is included in Muhammad Iqbal's *Javīd-nāmah* (1932), where the Bābī heroine appears as one of the "martyrs of love."

BIBLIOGRAPHY

The only biography of Qurrat al-ʿAyn is Martha L. Root's brief *Tahirih the Pure, Iran's Greatest Woman* (1938; reprint, Los Angeles, 1980). See also Edward G. Browne's sympathetic accounts in his *Materials for the Study of the Babi Religion* (Cambridge, 1918) and his *A Traveller's Narrative Written to Illustrate the Episode of the Bāb*, 2 vols. (Cambridge, 1891), which is the translation of a memoir by Abbas Effendi, Bahā' Allāh's son.

ANNEMARIE SCHIMMEL

R

RA. *See* Re.

RABBAH BAR NAḤMANI (d. around 330 CE), a third-generation Babylonian amora, rabbinical colleague of Yosef bar Ḥiyya' and Ḥisda'. Rabbah studied with Huna' and several other Babylonians, including Yehudah bar Yeḥezqe'l and, some modern scholars argue, with Yoḥanan bar Nappaḥa' in Palestine. After Yehudah's death, Rabbah began a twenty-two-year career as the head of a circle of students and a court in the city of Pumbedita. Serving as a judge, he had authority to impose rabbinic law in the marketplace and in various civil, property, and communal matters (B.T., *Ḥul.* 43b; Neusner, 1969).

Rabbah taught his disciples Torah, including everyday practical advice, lectured to them in the *kallah* gatherings (B.T., *B.M.* 86a), and, in his court, trained them as apprentice judges. His support for rabbinical privileges such as a tax exemption apparently brought him into conflict with the exilarch (lay leader considered to be of Davidic descent) (Neusner, 1969). His devotion to Torah study (see, e.g., B.T., *'Eruv.* 22a) and his sinless character reportedly gave him special access to the divine—the ability to call upon God to revive the dead (B.T., *Meg.* 7b), to receive teachings from Elijah, and to be protected from demons (B.T., *Ḥul.* 105b). Perceived as a strict follower of the law who reproved the community, he was reportedly disliked in certain circles (B.T., *Shab.* 153a).

Some stories regarding Rabbah's life apparently served to counter less flattering accounts. For example, one text describing Rabbah's death after government agents had pursued him for inciting mass tax evasion justifies his early death: miraculously protected from malicious humans, Rabbah died early in life only because he was needed in the heavenly study session to resolve a dispute (B.T., *B.M.* 86a).

Rabbah was noted for the dialectical sharpness with which he analyzed and supplemented received teachings (B.T., *Ber.* 64a). To render the Mishnah smoothly, he emended it or read in elliptical language (Epstein, 1964). Similarly, on the basis of his own views, he revised *baraitot* (texts purporting to represent extra-Mishnaic tannaitic teachings) and other earlier traditions that students cited before him. Although he treated numerous halakhic (legal) topics from ritual, civil, and even purity laws no longer in effect, few of his preserved dicta deal with aggadic (non-halakhic) matters.

[*For discussion of the circle of sages to which Rabbah belonged, see* Amoraim.]

BIBLIOGRAPHY

A comprehensive treatment and bibliography of Rabbah and his teachings can be found in Jacob Neusner's *A History of the Jews in Babylonia,* 5 vols. (Leiden, 1966–1970), esp. vol. 4. Noteworthy, too, are Jacob N. Epstein's *Mavo' le-nusaḥ ha-Mishnah,* 2 vols. (1948; reprint, Jerusalem, 1964), pp. 363–368, and David M. Goodblatt's *Rabbinic Instruction in Sasanian Babylonia* (Leiden, 1975).

BARUCH M. BOKSER

RABBINATE. From late antiquity to the present day the rabbinate has provided intellectual and spiritual leadership for the Jewish community. The term *rabbi-*

nate derives from the Hebrew title *rabbi* ("my master, my teacher"), which came into use in the first century of the common era.

Late Antiquity. According to a famous letter of Rav Sherira' Gaon of Babylonia (tenth century), the title *rabbi* was not used before the destruction of the Second Temple in the year 70 CE: "The designation rabbi came into use with those who were ordained then [after the destruction of the Temple]: Rabbi Tsadoq and Rabbi Eli'ezer ben Ya'aqov. The practice spread from the disciples of Rabban Yoḥanan ben Zakk'ai." Before that time, great sages (like Hillel the Elder) were cited without honorific. In about the first century CE, the title *rabban* (Aram., "our master") was accorded to the patriarch and other especially distinguished sages. The term *rav* was later employed in Babylonia as equivalent to *rabbi* in Palestine.

Rabbinical ordination is a ceremony of doubtful historical authenticity, although tradition holds that from the time of Moses there has been an unbroken succession of "laying on of hands" that conferred rabbinical status. Even Moses is referred to frequently as "our rabbi." But we have no instance of anyone being designated rabbi in a specific ceremony of ordination in ancient times, nor is the rabbinate decisively connected with the two Hebrew roots that designated the putative ceremony of ordination, *smkh* and *mnh*.

In the New Testament, the term *rabbi* is not often encountered in the synoptic Gospels *(Matthew, Mark,* and *Luke),* although *Matthew,* in particular, seems eager to distinguish Jesus from the "scribes and Pharisees" who hypocritically flaunt a religion they do not understand and "who like to be called rabbi by men," a term that Jesus denies to his followers (*Mt.* 23:1ff.). The term *rabbi* is, however, used particularly in the *Gospel of John:* in 1:47ff., Nathanael calls Jesus "rabbi"; in 3:1, Nicodemus says to Jesus, "Rabbi, we know you are a teacher come from God"; and in 1:38, the people refer to him by the same honorific. Perhaps no technical title is implied in these passages, but only the equivalent of any teacher of disciples. The variant *rabboni* is found in *John* 20:16.

Rabbis during the Talmudic period, roughly the first four and a half centuries of the common era, performed crucial functions in traditionally reconstructing classical Judaism. They were, above all, teachers and interpreters of the Torah. Basing themselves on a doctrine of oral law equal in religious authority to written Scripture, they became its authorized spokespersons. The only Bible that Jews came to possess was the Bible of the rabbis, and no text could be understood until and unless the rabbis, in particular the rabbis of the Talmudic age, explicated its meaning. There were, of course, innumerable debates about interpretations, but rabbinical consensus did somehow emerge on most legal issues and on some theological issues.

The rabbis of these centuries created the Jewish calendar out of biblical materials and ensured that the Jewish calendar would be a kind of temporal catechism. Before astronomical skills achieved precision and times of holidays could be predicted without direct inspection of the phases of the moon, the rabbis constituted the corporate body that intercalated months and precisely fixed days of obligation and festivity. Even in the Jewish Diaspora their calendar was final, as were their decisions in many other crucial religious matters. [*See* Jewish Religious Year.]

The rabbis of Erets Yisra'el (the Land of Israel) supervised Diaspora communities, collected funds from them, and, in general, kept them close to the motherland as a sacred focus of religious obligation.

These same rabbis fixed the biblical canon and the synagogue liturgy, which, in earlier generations, had a fluidity and spontaneity that became less and less possible. They judged their people in civil and in more technically religious matters, acknowledging Roman or other gentile law only grudgingly and only in part. They were also responsible for the self-definition of the Jewish community during periods of heresy and sectarianism. As against Jewish Christians, agnostics, and a mixed bag of dissidents whom the rabbis termed *minim,* the Jewish community became unified and distinguished through rabbinic definitions and "fences."

The Middle Ages and Early Modern Period. By profession the Talmudic rabbi was a woodsman, a farmer, a shoemaker, a shepherd, or the like. He worked for a living and served as a rabbi only in his spare time. Not until the Middle Ages was the rabbinate decisively professionalized. By the twelfth century, and despite the explicit opposition of Moses Maimonides (Mosheh ben Maimon), the greatest philosopher, legalist, and physician of that century, the paid rabbi was a universal Jewish phenomenon. Geographical differences and ambiguity of roles were important, but almost everywhere the rabbi, then often called *rav,* received a specified stipend for his services. Even the Karaites, who otherwise opposed rabbinism on scriptural grounds, used the same title and the very same methods of payment. [*See* Karaites.]

Some rabbis had written contracts (often for three years, in principle renewable) with specific salaries. Others received fees for services rendered. Occasionally a wealthy family would endow an important rabbi-scholar. A whole community might provide a home; even the civil government would occasionally offer perquisites, like housing or tax rebates.

This payment was in partial imitation of the Christian "doctor"; even that term was occasionally borrowed. Jewish communities usually wanted their own spiritual leaders to be treated as well as the Christian clergy. In the East, as the Cairo Genizah discloses, the *rav* was the virtual equivalent of the Muslim *muftī*, an authoritative scholar and quasi cleric. His salary often came from a community tax on meat and wine or rents. Sometimes his school provided him a more adequate living.

The increasingly professional rabbi confronted the organized Jewish community leadership as colleague, employee, and/or competitor. The rabbi was, after all, in a sense a layman, since he possessed no sacramental or charismatic advantage, yet his role increasingly led to a collision course with the lay establishment in his town. Wealthy lay leadership often chose the judiciary, dominated weak rabbis, and threatened strong ones. Lay leadership kept rabbis from other communities out, sometimes on the grounds that they might give uninvited collegial support to the local incumbent. Rabbi and laity struggled for control of cemetery burials and synagogue honors (which were sold to the highest bidder, despite frequent rabbinical objection), and rabbis battled with scholars over the curriculum of the Jewish schools. There were even some private chapels with family retainers serving as house rabbi.

The rabbis were not without their own discrete powers. They supervised the ritual life of the community and had prerogatives as authors and educators. They had the final weapon of excommunication, a sword better and more often sheathed than recklessly employed. But they were often torn between various lay factions, and they had to face the practical issues of tenure and dismissal.

The civil government regularly intervened in rabbinical placement and function. It sometimes tried to control ordination, to transform Jewish burial into a civil matter, and, generally, to make the rabbinate both its creature and its weapon against the lay Jewish establishment. The Jewish community slowly and steadily achieved increasing autonomy from the Middle Ages until the eighteenth century, but this strengthened the power of laymen, who had their own agenda and their own ambitions, often at the expense of the rabbinate.

The rabbi was generally honored and respected during the Middle Ages. He was called *morenu*, "our teacher," when invited to the Torah reading, and he had a seat of honor in the synagogue. Everyone rose when he entered a room, no matter how young he was. He was often the *ro'sh yeshivah*, headmaster of the local school, and he invited or excluded visiting rabbis and lecturers. Rabbis did not usually hand on their powers to their sons; nepotism was not prevalent in any Jewish community, where meritocracy was the common way to honor and privilege.

Prominent rabbis often constituted a court of appeal for decisions made by lower, lay-controlled judiciaries, and rabbis gave permission for Jews to utilize otherwise forbidden secular courts. They also delivered a kind of *nihil obstat* to authorize publication of books.

Rabbis served even in smaller communities, and in the large ones there were usually many rabbis. In Castile, in 1432, forty families were required to hire a rabbi and to pay him enough so that he would not have to beg. In Frankfurt, in 1694, 414 households supported eight rabbis rather well. The rabbi was admittedly the servant of the community and often, to his own displeasure, the servant of the rich. But he was also a model citizen, a teacher of the young, and the real if not always acknowledged leader of the people, *primus inter pares*, the spiritual center of an essentially egalitarian Jewry.

Rabbinical duties in the Middle Ages were both the same as and different in nuance from those of the Talmudic period. The rabbi taught, judged, and officiated at marriages and funerals. He slaughtered animals according to ritual standards (a function earlier performed by the laity under rabbinical supervision). The rabbi was a scribe and often a secretary (taking minutes for community meetings, since he was the most literate, though never the only literate, professional). He circumcised newborn boys and preached at least twice a year and, in some communities, more regularly. He sometimes administered burial societies and poor funds. One of the rabbi's chief responsibilities was private study. Sometimes a rabbi was dismissed simply because his community thought he was not studying long or hard enough.

There were naturally some unworthy incumbents in rabbinical posts, as we know from the *responsa* of their colleagues. Some were proud, partisan, or pseudointellectual. Some took bribes in court cases, sought publicity, or plagiarized. Some bought their incumbency or married into the elite for the sole purpose of a good living.

In the Middle Eastern communities, the *rav* or *ḥaver* ("colleague"; a lesser title), or even a person who had no title but still served as a kind of rabbi to the community, taught and decided cases, answered questions both formal and informal, and worked with people of all kinds on personal and community problems. Some Middle Eastern rabbis preached, produced books on homiletics, and supervised social services. Both in the Middle East and in Europe, there were a few rabbis who were famous from one end of the Jewish world to the other. A layperson could hardly expect that kind of reputation, no matter how wealthy or decent he was. It was the rabbi, above all, who symbolized to Jew and gentile alike what the community at its best signified.

The Modern Period. In modern times, pressures to establish a professional rabbinate continued to grow. The community nominated, and the government named, chief rabbis in Britain and France, as well as in British-mandated Palestine. No real precedent for this office can be found in Jewish history. While the British chief rabbi is not the equivalent of the archbishop of Canterbury, he remains the only British Jewish clergyman with the official title "rabbi"; all others under his supervision are called "minister."

Since the beginning of the nineteenth century, Jewish religion has lost even the semblance of uniformity that it once had. Reform, or Liberal, Judaism appeared as an early reaction to modern thinking and citizenship in western European countries, followed quickly by what came to be called Conservatism and Neo-Orthodoxy. In each of these denominations, the rabbi took on, more and more, the characteristics of a Protestant minister. There were already some Jewish precedents for pastoral responsibility (particularly in the Hasidic *rebe*), for regular preaching, and for administrative roles. Scholarship was marshaled to prove the antiquity of the Jewish sermon, and necessity validated rabbinical competence to organize and lead communal functions. Salaries of rabbis tended to rise; the status of the rabbi often paralleled that of his Christian clerical counterpart, who was also, in a new sense, his colleague.

The older functions of the rabbi—teaching, learning, judging, and the like—remained crucial in Orthodoxy. The more liberal movements produced not a few university-trained scholar-rabbis, but for them learning meant primarily *Wissenschaft des Judentums*, the modern "science of Judaism." Jewish learning had always been the rock on which rabbinical authority rested, but the notion of learning now broadened to include all of modern culture, Jewish history, and vast areas of study that the congregational rabbi could hardly be expected to master, given his busy schedule and the many lectures and sermons expected of him. For the Orthodox, Talmud and codes have remained central, but even they have usually thought it important to speak the vernacular well and to know its literature, as well as to study at least something of medieval Jewish philosophy and poetry in addition to the legal corpus.

New kinds of learning did not prevent the modern rabbi from suffering a crisis of authority. His medieval predecessor, embattled and sometimes isolated, was protected by skills and rituals of which he was the only master. But the modern rabbi could not claim to be a sole, or even a principal, authority in his milieu. His knowledge of psychology or pastoral techniques might win him admirers and supporters, but his legitimacy depended on almost wholly subjective congregational attitudes. In some countries, the community hired rabbis to serve a whole town or a designated part of it. But in America, for instance, rabbis are almost always hired by individual congregations, thus finding themselves in the anomalous position of being the employees of the very people they are expected to lead. As religious concerns diminished in Western countries, the modern rabbinate has become uniquely vulnerable. It has not only survived, however, but, more often than not, has also flourished.

At the present time there are new as well as many old issues of rabbinical function. The Reform, Reconstructionist, and Conservative movements have begun to ordain women, to the dismay of Orthodoxy. Traditionally, a woman cannot serve as a witness or judge, but there is no halakhic reason why she cannot preach or teach or administer a congregation. It seems likely that modern taste will permit, or even require, equal access by women to rabbinical office. The ambivalence over women rabbis demonstrates how divided modern Jewish communities remain beneath the surface.

The modern rabbi is the true inheritor of a millennial tradition but is also very much a product of the modern world. He or she must take orders from Sinai and Yavneh but must also speak to modern intellectuals who have been taught to prefer secular thinking. He or she must obey the Torah but must also become a kind of living Torah for all the people. The rabbi is thus caught between the old and the new in a special way. The ambiguity of the role of the rabbi is a symptom of the Jewish present and a challenge to a Jewish future, whose outline we can as yet only vaguely discern.

[*For further discussion of the role of the rabbi in various movements within Judaism, see* Reform Judaism; Orthodox Judaism; Conservative Judaism; Reconstructionist Judaism; *and* Hasidism, *overview article. Related articles include* Synagogue, *article on* History and Tradition, *and* Yeshivah, *which discusses one of the main institutions for the education of rabbis.*]

BIBLIOGRAPHY

Alon, Gedaliah. *The Jews in Their Land in the Talmudic Age, 70–640 C.E.* Translated and edited by Gerson Levi. Jerusalem, 1980. The standard history of the early centuries of the common era, by a learned Talmudic historian.

Assaf, Simha. "Liqorot ha-rabbanut." In *Be-ohelei Ya'aqov*, pp. 26–65. Jerusalem, n.d. A classic study of the rabbinate in eastern Europe during the late Middle Ages.

Baron, Salo W. *The Jewish Community*, vol. 2, *Its History and*

Structure to the American Revolution. Philadelphia, 1942. Still unsurpassed as a synopsis of leadership in the Jewish community before modern times. See especially pages 52–245.

Baron, Salo W. *A Social and Religious History of the Jews.* 18 vols. 2d ed., rev. & enl. New York, 1952–1983. See the index for a list of references to rabbis and the rabbinate in this encyclopedic history.

Ben-Sasson, H. H. *Hagut ve-hanhagah.* Jerusalem, 1959. A great Israeli historian on the role of Jewish religious leadership in Poland during the late Middle Ages. See especially pages 160–228.

Cohon, Samuel S. "Authority in Judaism." *Hebrew Union College Annual* 11 (1936): 593–646. See especially pages 612ff. A reliable, conservative summary of Talmudic and post-Talmudic rabbinic procedure.

Kohler, Kaufmann, et al. "Rabbi." In *The Jewish Encyclopedia.* New York, 1905. A brief, but not yet outdated, summary history of the rabbinate. More up-to-date encyclopedias are more complete but hardly as eloquent.

Stevens, Elliot L., ed. *Rabbinic Authority.* New York, 1982. A series of papers presented to the Central Conference of American Rabbis in 1980. Note especially the essays by Hoffman, Cook, and Saperstein.

Wolf, Arnold Jacob, ed. "The Future of Rabbinic Training in America." *Judaism* 18 (Fall 1969): 387–420. A controversial debate on the mission and training of the American rabbi by professors, practitioners, and even a student or two.

ARNOLD JACOB WOLF

RABBINIC JUDAISM IN LATE ANTIQUITY.

In its formative period, 70–640 CE, rabbinic Judaism forged a synthesis between two antithetical phenomena in the religion of Israel: first, the messianic movement, with its stress on history's meaning and end, and second, the priestly component, with its interest in enduring and ahistorical natural life, celebrated in the cult. Starting with the Mishnah, the systematic expression of the priestly viewpoint, composed in the aftermath of the two great messianic wars against Rome (66–73 and 132–135), the rabbis of late antiquity so reconstructed the Mishnah's system of law and theology as to join to that system the long-standing messianic and historical emphases. Rabbinic Judaism thus presents a way of life of order and regularity, lived out beyond the disturbances of one-time events of history, but in which Jews looked forward to the end of time and the coming of the Messiah. That is, as a result of their adhering to that same, permanent, holy way of life, the Messiah would come. The thesis of historical and teleological messianism generated its antithesis, the Mishnaic system of the everyday celebration of eternal things, which then fused into the rabbinic synthesis, legal-messianic Judaism as it has been known from late antiquity to our own times.

Definitions. By *Judaism* we mean a worldview and way of life held by a group of Jews, defining the holiness of their people. Any kind of Judaism will draw upon the Hebrew scriptures (the "Old Testament"), usually called Tanakh, an acronym standing for *Torah* (Law), *Nevi'im* (Prophets), and *Ketuvim* (Writings). Every kind selects and interprets a particular part of the Hebrew scriptures.

By *late antiquity* we mean the first six centuries of the common era, from the destruction of the Jerusalem Temple in 70 CE to the Muslim conquest of the Near and Middle East about 640 CE. The countries in which rabbinic Judaism took shape and flourished were the Land of Israel (Erets Yisra'el, i.e., "Palestine") under Roman, then Byzantine, rule (from before the first century CE to the Muslim conquest nearly seven centuries later) and Babylonia, part of the western satrapies of the Iranian empire (to about 225 under the Parthians, an Iranian people of the northeast; from about 225 to the Muslim conquest, under the Sasanids, an Iranian dynasty from the province of Fārs). [*See map accompanying* Judaism, *overview article.*]

As to sources, rabbinic Judaism is known to us from documents created in the period under discussion: the Mishnah (c. 200 CE) and the two Talmuds (one produced in Babylonia about 500 CE, the other in the Land of Israel a century earlier), which in form constitute commentaries to the Mishnah. Other important rabbinic documents of the time include commentaries on parts of the Hebrew scriptures—in particular *Mekhilta'*, for *Exodus; Sifra'*, for *Leviticus;* and *Sifrei*, for *Numbers* and *Deuteronomy*—and *Bere'shit Rabbah* and *Vayiqra' Rabbah,* compilations of exegeses on *Genesis* and *Leviticus.* The Jewish prayer book *(siddur)* and certain mystical writings come down from this same period. They clearly relate to the larger rabbinic form of Judaism. But the precise definition of that relationship has not been fully clarified.

The adjective *rabbinic* before the noun *Judaism* tells us that we deal with a kind of Judaism named after its principal kind of leader, a rabbi, a supernatural sage. The definition of *rabbi* shifts in ancient times. The title itself was originally quite neutral, and not unique to Jews. It means simply "My lord," and hence no more than *Monsieur* or *Mein Herr.* When Jesus was called "rabbi," the term was equivalent to *teacher* or *master, Sir.* Rabbis in the Mishnah, figures of the first and second centuries, generally give opinions about trivial legal matters; they were considered sages but were never represented as wonder-workers. Representations of rabbis in documents from the third century onward, including discussion of first- and second-century figures in those later documents, by contrast present the rabbi as a supernatural figure. The rabbi then emerges as a lawyer-magician, or supernatural judge-sage-mystic. Accordingly, through the centuries the title *rabbi* has come to refer solely to a distinctive amalgam, within the Jewish nation, of learning, piety, and holiness or supernatural power, associated with the sages of the Talmud and related writings.

"Rabbinic Judaism," then, is the worldview and way of life applied to the Jewish nation by rabbis. The Judaism under discussion also is called "Talmudic," after its principal literary documents. It may be called "classical" or "normative" in reference to its definitive character from its own day to today. In Talmudic times, however, the conception of a systematic *-ism*, a Judaism, is not attested in the rabbinical literature. Outsiders, coming after the fact, identify and name a religion. That an abstract system was perceived and named is not likely. We cannot isolate a word, or a concept to be presented by a single word, for "Judaism." The closest verbal symbol for this kind of Judaism is *Torah*. A sage became a rabbi because he knew Torah in the right way, having learned under proper auspices and having given ample evidence of accurate mastery and correct interpretation of the Torah.

It follows that the definitive trait of rabbinic Judaism is stress upon Torah. In fact, we may define the character of this kind of Judaism within three elements: holy faith, holy man, holy way of life. Thus, first is emphasis upon the doctrine of the dual revelation to Moses at Sinai, a written Torah (the Pentateuch) and an oral Torah. Second comes belief in the leadership of the sage, or rabbi (in context, "My lord"). Third, we find stress upon doing the will of God through study of Torah under the guidance of sages and upon living the holy way of life laid down in the Torah as interpreted by rabbis.

The Myth. Let us now consider in detail the definitive symbolic structure of rabbinic Judaism, as it emerges from late antiquity. The central myth of classical Judaism is the belief that the ancient scriptures constituted divine revelation, but only a part of it. At Sinai God had handed down a dual revelation: the written part known to one and all, but also the oral part preserved by the great scriptural heroes, passed on by prophets to various ancestors in the obscure past and finally, and most openly and publicly, handed down to the rabbis who created the Talmuds. The "whole Torah" thus consisted of both written and oral parts. The rabbis taught that the "whole Torah" was studied by sages of every period in Israelite history from Moses to the present. It is a singular, linear conception of a revelation preserved only by the few but pertaining to the many, and in time capable of bringing salvation to all.

The Torah myth further regards Moses as "our rabbi." It holds that whoever embodies the teachings of "Moses, our rabbi," thereby conforms to the will of God, and not to God's will alone but also to his *way*. In heaven God and the angels study Torah just as rabbis do on earth. God dons phylacteries like a Jew. He prays in the rabbinic mode. He carries out the acts of compassion called for by Judaic ethics. He guides the affairs of the world according to the rules of Torah, just as he does the rabbi in his court. One exegesis of the creation legend taught that God had looked into the Torah and therefrom had created the world.

The myth of Torah is multidimensional. It includes the striking detail that whatever the most recent rabbi is destined to discover through proper exegesis of the tradition is as much a part of the way revealed to Moses as is a sentence of scripture itself. It therefore is possible to participate even in the giving of the law by appropriate, logical inquiry into the law. God himself, studying and living by Torah, is believed to subject himself to these same rules of logical inquiry. If an earthly court overrules the testimony, delivered through miracles, of the heavenly one, God would rejoice, crying out, "My sons have conquered me! My sons have conquered me."

Before us is a mythical-religious system in which earth and heaven correspond to one another, with Torah as the nexus and model of both. The heavenly paradigm is embodied upon earth. Moses "our rabbi" is the pattern for the ordinary sage. And God himself participates in the system, for it is his image that, in the end, forms that cosmic paradigm. The faithful Jew constitutes the projection of the divine on earth. Honor is due to the learned rabbi more than to the scroll of the Torah, for through his learning and logic he may alter the very content of Mosaic revelation. He is Torah, not merely because he lives by it but because at his best he forms as compelling an embodiment of the heavenly model as does a Torah scroll itself.

The final and generative element in the rabbinic Torah myth concerns salvation. It takes many forms. One salvific teaching holds that had Israel not sinned—that is, disobeyed the Torah—the scriptures would have closed with the story of the conquest of Palestine. From that eschatological time, the sacred community would have lived in eternal peace under the divine law. Keeping the Torah was therefore the veritable guarantee of salvation. The opposite is said in many forms as well. Israel had sinned; therefore, God had called the Assyrians, Babylonians, and Romans to destroy the Temple of Jerusalem; but in his mercy he would be equally faithful to restore the fortunes of the people when they, through their suffering and repentance, had expiated the result and the cause of their sin.

So, in both negative and positive forms, the Torah myth tells of a necessary connection between the salvation of the people and of the world and the state of Torah among them. For example, if all Israel would properly keep two Sabbaths, the Messiah would come. Of special interest here is the rabbinic saying that the rule of the pagans depends upon the sin of Israel. If Israel would constitute a full and complete replication of "Torah"—that is, of heaven—then pagan rule would come to an end. When Israel makes itself worthy through its embodiment of Torah—that is, through its perfect replication of the heavenly way of living—then the end will come.

The Mishnah's Layer of Rabbinic Judaism. The history of the Judaism expressed in this Torah myth is obscured by the superficially uniform character of the rabbinic compilations of late antiquity. All of them, early and late, appear to wish to say pretty much the same thing. It goes without saying that each rabbinic document finds in scripture ample precedent for its own viewpoint. That is why they all look alike. The documents, moreover, are collective, bearing the names of many authorities in common. Accordingly, when we turn to the sources for the viewpoint just now outlined, we find it everywhere. So it is difficult to trace the history of the ideas shared in common by them. Yet that is not entirely the case, for there is one rabbinic document of late antiquity, the Mishnah, that stands apart from the rest. It ignores scripture and the need for proof-texts, on the one side, and it omits reference to the Torah myth as the critical symbolic element, on the other.

The Mishnah is the first document of rabbinic Judaism, and it constitutes the foundation for the two Talmuds and the law of Judaism thereafter. The Mishnah rarely cites a scriptural proof-text for any of its propositions, even when the laws simply rephrase in the Mishnah's own language the facts supplied by scripture. Except for the tractate *Avot*, distinct in language and character, the Mishnah finds no room in its definitive construction—that is, in the formation of its principal divisions, let alone in its subdivisions (tractates) and their chapters—for extended discussion on the matter of the study of Torah, the place of the sage in the heavenly-earthly continuum, and those other propositions definitive of the Judaism that rests upon the Mishnah.

That is not to say the Mishnah knows nothing of the priority of learning. On the contrary, here and there we find explicit statements that the sage takes precedence. But the issue is this-worldly, not a matter of supernatural consequence, as is the case in equivalent allegations in Talmudic and later writings. An instance of the Mishnah's phrasing of the matter is in *Horayot* 3.5, followed by the Tosefta's gloss of the passage:

> A priest takes precedence over a Levite, a Levite over an Israelite, an Israelite over a *mamzer*, a *mamzer* over a *natin*, a *natin* over a proselyte, a proselyte over a freed slave.
>
> Under what circumstances?
>
> When all of them are equivalent [in other regards].
>
> But if the *mamzer* was a disciple of a sage, and a high priest was an ignoramus, the *mamzer* who is a disciple of a sage takes precedence over a high priest who is an ignoramus.

The Tosefta adds:

> A sage takes precedence over a king.
>
> [For if] a sage dies, we have none who is like him.
>
> [If] a king dies any Israelite is suitable to mount the throne. (Tosefta, *Horayot* 2.8)

What we see here is the first stage in the process by which the sage is moved from a merely earthly status as a principal authority to the supernatural position described above. Accordingly, the notion that Torah-learning enjoys priority is not alien to the Mishnah, and indeed begins there. But the Mishnah contains no hint of the view of the sage as a supernatural figure. Furthermore, the Mishnah distinguishes wonder-workers, such as Ḥoni the Circle Drawer (*Ta'an.* 3.8), from the sages, expressing disapproval of the former.

A still more striking trait of the Mishnah's kind of Judaism is the stress, within the Mishnah's system, upon enduring things and the omission of reference to one-time, historical events. The Mishnah presents a world in stasis, in which regularities and orderly patterns govern. It scarcely alludes to the coming of a messiah, the end of days, the meaning of Israel's suffering. The Mishnah offers no explanation or interpretation of Israel's history. If, therefore, we may characterize the first literary evidence of rabbinic Judaism in late antiquity, as of about 200 CE, we describe that Judaism as focused upon the ongoing life of nature, the priesthood, and the Temple, with the sage telling the priests what to do. The Mishnah's simple, descriptive laws indicate how Israelite society, revolving about the cult, is maintained in stasis.

The Talmudic Rabbis' Return to Scripture and History. Now at the other end of the period at hand, about 600 CE, that is not the Judaism that emerges. On the contrary, as we have seen, rabbinic Judaism fully revealed focused upon the meaning of Israel's history, its end in the coming of the Messiah. It was deeply engaged by one-time events and their meaning. Torah was defined by the sage as a supernatural figure who was qualified by constant reference to scripture. The contrast between the Mishnah's statements, divorced from scripture even where repeating scripture's own facts, and the later reception of the Mishnah, is seen in one fact. Both

Talmuds systematically supply to Mishnah's laws precisely those proof-texts omitted by the Mishnah's framers. Accordingly, the Talmudic authorities will cite Mishnah's passage and immediately ask, "How do we know these things?" What follows will be scriptural proof-texts.

There is further indication that, in the two centuries after the closure of the Mishnah, about 200 CE, a massive reaction against the Mishnah's formulation of an ahistorical Judaism of eternal return took place. The character of other writings produced by the rabbis of those centuries provides important evidence of a renewed interest in history and its meaning. Beyond the two Talmuds and Tosefta, centered upon the Mishnah, we have the formation of compilations of exegetical remarks, systematically laid forth for the Pentateuchal books of *Genesis* and *Leviticus*. These are generally supposed to have come into existence in the fifth century, that is, just as the Talmud of the Land of Israel had come to conclusion and the Talmud of Babylonia was coming to closure. Even more striking is the character of *Sifra'*, a systematic essay on the *Book of Leviticus*. One basic literary form of that exegetical document is the citation of a passage of the Mishnah, or of Tosefta, verbatim or nearly so. The anonymous voice of the document then asks, "Is this not a matter of [mere] logic?" The argument then will unfold to prove that logic alone cannot prove with certainty the proposition of the Mishnah that has been cited. To the contrary, the only foundation of certainty is in a cited scripture, sometimes then subjected to exegetical work to prove the proposition of the Mishnah that stands at the head of the passage. The polemic is unmistakable. The Mishnah's laws, standing by themselves, cannot endure. Only provision of exegetical bases for them will suffice.

Messianism. Beyond the emphasis upon the sage as a supernatural figure and upon scripture as the sole sound basis of truth, the third pillar of rabbinic Judaism as it emerged from late antiquity was its emphasis upon Torah as the means of reaching the messianic fulfillment and resolution of Israel's history. The authoritative expression of the messianic expectation is in the *siddur* (prayer book), emerging from late antiquity and enduring to the present day:

> Sound the great shofar to herald man's freedom;
> Raise high the banner to gather all exiles;
> Restore our judges as in days of old;
> Restore our counselors as in former times;
> Remove from us sorrow and anguish.
> Reign over us alone with loving kindness;
> With justice and mercy sustain our cause.
> Praised are You, O Lord, King who loves justice.

The restoration of the exiles to Zion and the gathering of the dispersed followed naturally by the prayer for good government, government under God's law. Then comes the concrete reference to the Messiah:

> Have mercy, O Lord, and return to Jerusalem, Your city;
> May Your presence dwell there as You promised.
> Rebuild it now, in our days and for all time;
> Re-establish there the majesty of David, Your servant.
> Praised are You, O Lord, who rebuilds Jerusalem.
> Bring to flower the shoot of Your servant David.
> Hasten the advent of the messianic redemption;
> Each and every day we hope for Your deliverance.
> Praised are You, O Lord, who assures our deliverance.

The link between the messianic hope for salvation and the religion of Torah and of rabbinic authority is expressed time and again in rabbinic writings. One example is as follows:

> Rabbah [a fourth-century rabbi] said, "When a man is brought in for judgment in the world to come, he is asked, 'Did you deal in good faith? Did you set aside time for study of Torah? Did you engage in procreation? Did you look forward to salvation? Did you engage in the dialectics of wisdom? Did you look deeply into matters?' "
> (B.T., *Shab.* 31a)

Rabbah's interpretation of the scripture "And there shall be faith in thy times, strength, salvation, wisdom and knowledge" (*Is.* 33:6) provides one glimpse into the cogent life of rabbinic Judaism. The first consideration was ethical: did the man conduct himself faithfully? The second was study of Torah, not at random but every day, systematically, as a discipline of life. Third came the raising of a family. Celibacy and abstinence from sexual life were regarded as sinful. The full use of man's creative powers for the procreation of life was a commandment. But, fourth, merely living day by day according to an upright ethic was not sufficient. It is true that people must live by a holy discipline, but the discipline itself was only a means. The end was salvation, daily expected in consequence of everyday deeds.

When we reflect upon the Talmudic teaching, already cited, that if all Israel only twice will properly keep the Sabbath (as the rabbis instruct), the Messiah will come, we see the true state of affairs. The heirs of the Mishnah took over the messianic hope, so deep in the consciousness of the Jewish nation from biblical times onward, and harnessed its power to the system we now know as rabbinic Judaism, a holy way of life taught by masters of Torah. Accordingly, as stated at the outset, in late antiquity we witness the formation on the disparate foundations of, first, the Mishnah, a law code lacking reference to history, on the one side, and, second, hope for the end of history and the coming of the Messiah, on the other, the kind of Judaism we call rabbinic.

Institutions. The institutional forms of rabbinic Judaism as we know them in particular from the Talmuds, are two. The first, not surprisingly, is the figure of the rabbi. The second is the court-school, that is, the place in which the rabbi ruled on certain matters affecting the Jewish community and also taught his apprentices, that is, disciples. Let us speak first of the figure of the rabbi as we know him in the third through the seventh century in the Babylonian Talmud.

The rabbi. The rabbis of that period conceived that on earth they studied Torah just as God, the angels, and "Moses, our rabbi," did in heaven. The heavenly schoolmen were even aware of Babylonian scholastic discussions. This conception must be interpreted by reference to the belief that the man truly made in the divine image was the rabbi; he embodied revelation, both oral and written, and all his actions constituted paradigms that were not merely correct but actually heavenly. Rabbis could create and destroy men because they were righteous, free of sin, or otherwise holy, and so enjoyed exceptional grace from heaven. It follows that Torah was held to be a source of supernatural power. The rabbis controlled the power of Torah because of their mastery of its contents. They furthermore used their own mastery of Torah quite independently of heavenly action. They were masters of witchcraft, incantations, and amulets. They could issue blessings and curses, create men and animals, and communicate with heaven. Their Torah was sufficiently effective to thwart the action of demons. However much they disapproved of other people's magic, they themselves were expected to do the things magicians did.

The rabbi was the authority on theology, including the structure and order of the supernatural world. He knew the secret names of God and the secrets of the divine "chariot"—the heavens—and of creation. If extraordinarily pious, he might even see the face of the Shekhinah, the presence of God; in any event, the Shekhinah was present in the rabbinical schools. The rabbi overcame the evil impulse that dominated ordinary men and was consequently less liable to suffering, misfortune, and sickness. He was able to pray effectively because he knew the proper times and forms of prayer. Moreover, the efficacy of his prayers was heightened by his purity, holiness, and other merits, which in turn derived from his knowledge of the secrets of Torah and his consequent particular observances. He could bring rain or cause drought. His blessings brought fertility, and his curse, death. He was apt to be visited by angels and to receive messages from them. He could see and talk with demons and could also communicate with the dead. He was an authority on interpretation of omens and dreams, on means of averting witchcraft, on incantations for cures, on knot tying (for phylacteries), and on the manufacture and use of amulets.

A central conception set rabbinic Judaism apart from Manichaeism, Mazdaism, Christianity, and other contemporary cults. It was not expected that the masses would assume the obligations of or attain to the supernatural skills of the Manichaean elect, Mazdean magi, Christian nuns and monks, or the religious virtuosi and cultic specialists of other groups. All male Jews, however, were expected to become rabbis. The rabbis wanted to transform the entire Jewish community into an academy where the whole Torah was studied and kept.

These beliefs aid in understanding the rabbis' view that Israel would be redeemed, the Messiah brought, through Torah. Because Israel had sinned, it was punished by being given over into the hands of earthly empires; when it atoned, it would be removed from their power. The means of this atonement or reconciliation were study of Torah, practice of commandments, and doing good deeds. These would transform each male Jew into a rabbi, hence into a saint. When all Jews had become rabbis, they then would no longer lie within the power of history. The Messiah would come. So redemption depended upon the "rabbinization" of all Israel, that is, upon the attainment by all Jewry of a full and complete embodiment of revelation or Torah, thus achieving a perfect replica of heaven. When Israel on earth became such a replica, it would be able, as a righteous, holy, saintly community, to exercise the supernatural power of Torah, just as some rabbis were already doing. With access to the consequent theurgical capacities, redemption would naturally follow.

The school. Study of Torah was just that: primarily an intellectual enterprise whose supernatural effects were decidedly secondary. The resources of the schools were knowledge of the laws and traditions that for the rabbis constituted the Torah of Moses. The actual method of learning used by the academies had nothing whatever to do with magic. The "Torah" of the rabbis was essentially no more than a legal tradition that had to be studied by the classical legal methods. The rabbis were expected to act as did other holy men, but they themselves respected legal learning and the capacity to reason about cases. Not everyone would achieve such skills of reasoning any more than everyone could make rain, and the academies doubtless attracted many who could only memorize and repeat what they knew. The whole process of learning, not merely its creative and innovative aspects, was, however, regarded as sacred, for the words themselves were holy.

The following exposition from the school of Rabbi ʿAnan exemplifies this process:

> What is the meaning of the Scripture *You that ride on white asses, that sit on rich cloths, and that walk by the way, tell of it* (*Judges* 5:10)?
>
> Those *that ride on asses* are the sages who go from city to city and from province to province to study Torah.
>
> *White* means that they make it clear as the noon hour.
>
> *Sitting on cloths* means that they judge a case truly.
>
> *And that walk* refers to masters of Scripture.
>
> *On the way,* these are masters of Mishnah.
>
> *Tell of it* refers to masters of Talmud, all of whose conversation concerns matters of Torah. (B.T., *Eruv.* 54b)

Found in the Song of Deborah, this verse about the victory of Israel over the Canaanites was explained by the rabbis as a description of the triumph of the Lord in the "wars of the Torah," a frequent image of rabbinic Judaism, and the consequent celebration by the people of the Lord. That people included many whose talents were limited but who, added all together, constituted, and celebrated, the Lord's triumph. Some, like itinerant philosophers, would wander in search of teachings. Others had great skill at clarification. Others were able and selfless judges. Still others merely knew scripture, or Mishnah, or Talmud, but spoke of nothing else. Here is the integrated, mature vision of the academies: a whole people devoted to revelation, each in his own way and according to his talent.

Rabbis and Ordinary Folk. What average Jews ordinarily did not know and the rabbis always did know was the one thing that made a common man into a rabbi: *"Torah" learned through discipleship.* It begs the question to speak of the ordinary people as "ignorant of Judaism." One does not have to exaggerate the educational attainments of the community as a whole to recognize that learning in the rabbinic traditions did not by itself separate the rabbi from other people. It would, accordingly, be a gross error to overestimate the differences separating the way of life of the ordinary Jews from that of the rabbinical estate.

In general the rabbis' merely conventional social manners or customs were deepened into spiritual conceptions and magnified by their deeply mythic ways of thinking. In the villages ordinary people regarded the rabbi as another holy man, but still as a man, heart and soul at one in community with other Jews. The rabbinical ideal was antidualistic; the rabbis believed that all Israel, not just saints, prophets, and sages, stood at Sinai. All bore common responsibilities. No one conceived of two ways of living a holy life—two virtues or two salvations—but of only one Torah to be studied and observed by all, and thus the cutting edge of rabbinical separateness was blunted. The inevitable gap between the holy man and the layman was further reduced by the deep concern felt by rabbis for the conduct of the masses. This concern led them to involve themselves in the everyday affairs of ordinary people, and it produced considerable impact upon daily life.

A review of the primary distinctive characteristics of the rabbinical school will show that the rabbis could not have created unscalable walls of social or religious difference. The sages spent a good part of their years in these schools; ordinary Jews, obviously, did not. Yet the schools were not monasteries. Disciples who left but who remained loyal to the school's way of life did not engage in ascetic disciplines of an outlandish sort, calculated to utterly divide the sages' way of living from that of normal men. They married. They ate regularly and chose edible food, not wormwood or locusts or refuse. They lived in villages, not in the wilderness. They did not make their livelihood through holy vagrancy. Their clothes were not supposed to be tattered or in rags. These differences between rabbis and other types of holy men, such as the Christian monks and the Manichaean elect, are obvious and therefore all the more important. The sages sought the society of ordinary Jews, so they lived in the villages rather than in the countryside ("wilderness"). Not engaged in begging ("holy vagrancy"), they owned property and were glad of it. They occupied important and permanent positions in the administration of communal life, and so came into constant and intimate contact with the common people. Access to rabbinical schools remained open to all, and the rabbis actively proselytized within the community to gain new candidates for their schools. Advantages of birth were minimal. In no way did the rabbis form a caste or a clan; the right marriage counted for little.

What, therefore, did the peculiarities of the rabbinical way of living amount to? A rabbi could eat with any other Jew in Babylonia because the biblical taboos about food were widely observed. Differences between the rabbis' interpretation of taboos about food and those advanced by others gradually diminished, as in time the rabbis' growing domination made their learned exegeses seem more commonplace. For example, although the rabbis said grace at meals and offered intelligible blessings for food, they were willing to teach others just what those blessings and prayers meant. Nothing in the rabbinical ritual of eating was to be kept secret. A person showed himself "ignorant" if he violated the rituals. His remedy was to go to a sage to study and learn, and this was explicitly recommended by the rabbis.

The Rabbi as Judge. What did a rabbi actually do as a community administrator? The following account gives a helpful portrait of the workday function of Rabbi Huna', head of the Sura academy about 300 CE:

> Every cloudy day they would carry him out in a golden palanquin, and he would survey the whole town. Every wall which looked unsafe he would order torn down. If the owner could rebuild it, he did so, but if not, he [Rabbi Huna] would rebuild it of his own funds.
>
> On the eve of every Sabbath, he would send a messenger to the market, and all the vegetables that remained to the market-gardeners, he would buy and throw into the river.
>
> Whenever he discovered a medicine, he would fill a jug with it, and suspend it above the doorstep and announce, "Whoever wants to, let him come and take." Some say, he knew from tradition a medicine for [a certain disease caused by eating with unwashed hands], and he would suspend a jug of water and proclaim, "Whoever needs it, let him come so that he may save his life from danger."
>
> When he ate bread, he would open his door wide, and declare, "Whoever is in need, let him come and eat."
>
> (B.T., *Ta'an.* 20b–21a)

The variety of public responsibilities carried out by the rabbi is striking. He had to prevent the collapse of mud buildings during a rainstorm. He had to ensure a constant market by encouraging truck gardeners to provide a steady supply of fresh vegetables. He had to give out medical information, to preserve public health, and to make certain that poor people could benefit from the available remedies. And he had to provide for the poor, so that no one would starve in his town.

These responsibilities reflected the different roles played by the rabbi. Only the first and second duties listed depended upon his political function. As judge he could order the destruction of dangerous property; as administrator he had to supervise the marketplace and use his funds to control supply and prices. But these roles had nothing to do with medical and eleemosynary activities. The former was contingent upon his reputation as a man of learning who had mastered the occult sciences, which then included medicine; the latter was based upon his possession of great wealth, accruing from his positions in politics, administration, and academic life.

Litigations coming before the Jewish courts were not particularly important in the evidence covering 200–500 CE. On the whole they corresponded to those likely to come before a small-claims court in modern society. Thefts involved a book or a few rams. Betrothal cases concerned the exchange of property, such as a few *zuz*, a willow branch, some onions, or a piece of silk. Settlements of marriage contracts required division of a robe of fine wool, a silver cup. A few cases of alleged adultery were recorded, all of sufficient innocence for the court to rule that no adultery had taken place. The preparation and delivery of proper divorce documents hardly amounted to weighty matters of state. Divorce litigations in any event were provoked by peculiar and exceptional circumstances; normally a man could divorce his wife without court intervention, merely with the help of a scribe who wrote out the writ of divorce in accordance with the law.

The settlement of estates entailed somewhat larger sums of money. A woman's marriage contract stipulated that if she were divorced, she would be given an alimony of four hundred *zuz*, a round number that probably represented approximately enough capital for two years' maintenance. Provisions by the court for widows (food, wine, clothing) were humble and more typical matters. Even most estate cases pertained to rather small claims, such as a few trees, a slave, or a choice plot of ground. Settlement of debts, collections of mortgages and bonds, and the like did require rulings on somewhat more substantial sums, but the real issues were still relatively inconsequential—a hundred *zuz*, or whether a pledged spoon or knife had to be returned.

Some commercial litigations were brought before the courts. Questions of contract involved a few ferrymen and sharecroppers, or devolved upon a hired ass, a purchase of wine or poppy seed, a flooded field. Some commercial disputes demanded that the courts decide about a few *zuz* worth of silk beads, some sour wine, the sale of a wine press or a field. Others concerned a damaged jar or utensil, a dead goat, a stolen purse, a broken ax or wine barrel. Property cases similarly involved alleged fraud in a relatively small plot, the claim of an option to purchase a field, the use of canal water, and, very frequently, squatter's rights over a house or field and the eviction of tenant farmers.

Cases such as these clearly reveal the real substance of issues left in the rabbis' hands. With a few exceptions, strikingly petty sums of money or barely consequential pieces of property were all that the lower classes of society brought to litigation. And it was those classes that were primarily subject to rulings by the rabbinical courts. Large commercial transactions for many thousands of *zuz* worth of silk or pearls, wine or beer; enormous property transactions involving a whole village or town; claims of a considerable number of workers against a single employer, or vice versa; the affairs of large estates, rich landowners, big businessmen, important officials—none of these appears with any frequency, if at all, in extant reports.

The rabbis surely could not have agreed, however, that the humble and petty issues before them were of no consequence. It was their view—a very old one in

Judaism—that the least and humblest affairs, as much as the largest and most weighty ones, testified to heaven about the moral state of society. If the prophet Amos had condemned Israel of old because a poor man was cheated of his shoes, then one can hardly be surprised that a later rabbi insisted upon the return of a cooking utensil given in pledge. What was important to the rabbis was that justice should prevail. They knew that if justice did not characterize the street, the trading market, the small farms and shops, then great affairs of commerce and the state would not likely be morally superior. They knew that the ethics of daily life, the life concerned with exchanges of onions and the use of water in a small canal, determined the destiny of Israel.

Summary. The history of Judaism in late antiquity can be summarized very simply. First came the Mishnah, shaped over the first and second centuries CE. Then, second, followed four hundred years in which the legal and theological system of the Mishnah was drastically reshaped into something new. Since the Mishnah's system constituted a reaction against the messianic wars of the time in which it came into being, we see a process by which the messianic "thesis" generated the Mishnah as its antimessianic antithesis, so producing the rabbinic synthesis in the Talmuds. That is to say, the messianic "thesis" rested on prophetic, historical, and apocalyptic passages of scripture. The Mishnah's "antithesis" constructed a system based on priestly and ahistorical legal passages. The Mishnah's system stood aloof both from biblical proof-texts and from the messianic interest in the meaning and end of history characteristic of its own day. Over the next four hundred years the rabbinic heirs of both the Mishnah and the scripture brought the two back into relationship. They forged them into a messianic and legal synthesis, the one "whole Torah" of "Moses, our rabbi," just as their Torah myth alleged.

[*See also* Pharisees; Tannaim; Amoraim; Mishnah and Tosefta; Midrash and Aggadah; *and* Talmud.]

BIBLIOGRAPHY

The best systematic account of the theology of rabbinic Judaism is George Foot Moore's *Judaism in the First Centuries of the Christian Era: The Age of the Tannaim,* 3 vols. (Cambridge, 1954). The same categories of historical theology are addressed by E. E. Urbach in *The Sages: Their Concepts and Beliefs,* 2 vols. (Jerusalem, 1975), translated from the Hebrew by Israel Abrahams; by Solomon Schechter in *Some Aspects of Rabbinic Theology* (1909; reprint, New York, 1936); and by E. P. Sanders in *Paul and Palestinian Judaism: A Comparison of Patterns of Religion* (Philadelphia, 1977). These three works present a categorically similar picture of rabbinic Judaism's theology. An important anthology of sources is C. G. Montefiore and Herbert Loewe's *A Rabbinic Anthology* (New York, 1974). Two collections of essays on special topics provide guidance into the principal scholarly approaches of the last generation: Jacob Z. Lauterbach's *Rabbinic Essays* (Cincinnati, 1951) and Louis Ginzberg's *On Jewish Law and Lore* (Philadelphia, 1955). A different approach to the description of rabbinic Judaism is provided in my book *Judaism: The Evidence of the Mishnah* (Chicago, 1981). On the mysticism of rabbinic Judaism the most important book is Gershom Scholem's *Major Trends in Jewish Mysticism* (New York, 1954); on messianism, Scholem's *The Messianic Idea in Judaism* (New York, 1971). On the liturgy of Judaism in this period, the two definitive books are Joseph Heinemann's *Prayer in the Talmud* (Berlin and New York, 1977) and Lawrence A. Hoffman's *The Canonization of the Synagogue Service* (Notre Dame, Ind., 1979). On the archaeology of Judaism in this period one should consult, as a start, Eric M. Meyers and James F. Strange's *Archaeology, the Rabbis, and Early Christianity* (Nashville, 1981) and Lee I. Levine's edition of *Ancient Synagogues Revealed* (Jerusalem, 1981). On rabbinic Judaism viewed historically, there is my own *History of the Jews in Babylonia,* 5 vols. (Leiden, 1965–1969).

JACOB NEUSNER

RABBINIC LAW. *See* Halakhah.

RABBITS.

The belief that a rabbit dwells in the moon is widely attested not only in Inner Asia, South Asia, and East Asia but also in North America, Mesoamerica, and southern Africa. Among the Turco-Mongol peoples of Inner Asia, the shaman hunts a rabbit in the moon during his ecstatic journey to the heavenly world. In China, as early as the Han period, the rabbit is represented on bronze mirrors as inhabiting the moon, pounding the drug of immortality with a pestle and mortar. The Japanese depict him as pounding rice cakes in the moon spots.

The Khoi and the San of the Kalahari in southern Africa also tell of a rabbit in the moon. In Khoi myths of the origin of death, the hare is presented as the careless messenger. Charged by the moon with bringing a message of immortality to mankind, he mistransmitted the good tidings as a message of death. The San have similar stories.

In North America, a rabbit is at the center of the creation myth of the ancient Algonquin. At the mythical time of beginning, the Great Hare appeared on earth and laid the foundation of the world. He instructed people in the medicine dance and other forms of life; he fought the oceanic monsters; he reconstructed the earth after the deluge, and on his departure he left it as it is today. The rabbit, as well as the hare, appears as a trickster in the Indian tales of the southeastern United States.

In ancient Mesopotamia and Syria, about the beginning of the second millennium BCE, the hare was imbued with the symbolism of death and rebirth. In Egypt it was probably associated with Osiris, the god of rebirth and immortality. The hare appears in Islam, for example, in Rūmī's poetry, as one of the animals symbolizing man's base soul.

In the Greco-Roman world, the hare was multivalent: it was widely recognized for its lubricity, it was thought to be androgynous, and its flesh was used as an aphrodisiac. It was most pleasing to Aphrodite and sacred also to Eros, who hunted the animal. However, it was especially associated with Dionysos, the god not only of love, fertility, and life but also of death and immortality. The hare was hunted, torn to pieces and eaten, and used as a love gift. It was considered a most appropriate symbol for a grave stele, because in man's basic dreams it represents the love that will conquer death. As belief in immortality became more popular, the hare was increasingly used in funerary art. Early Christians accepted this rabbit symbolism and depicted rabbits on gravestones. In modern times, the Easter Bunny, whose eggs represent the source of life, seems to be a continuation of archaic religious values associated with both the rabbit and the egg.

BIBLIOGRAPHY

On the symbolism of the rabbit in the Mediterranean world, see Erwin R. Goodenough's excellent study in *Pagan Symbols in Judaism,* volume 8 of his *Jewish Symbols in the Greco-Roman Period* (New York, 1958), pp. 85–95. See also Johannes Maringer's "Der Hase in Kunst und Mythe der vor- und frühgeschichtlichen Menschen," *Zeitschrift für Religions- und Geistesgeschichte* 30 (1978): 219–228, and Ananda K. Coomaraswamy's review of John Layard's *The Lady of the Hare: A Study in the Healing Power of Dreams* (London, 1945) in *Psychiatry* 8 (1945): 507–513. Coomaraswamy's review was also published under the title "On Hares and Dreams" in the *Quarterly Journal of the Mythic Society* (Bangalore) 37 (1946): 1–14.

MANABU WAIDA

RĀBIʿAH AL-ʿADAWĪYAH (d. AH 185/801 CE), Arab mystic, poet, and Muslim saint. Even though she attained great age and fame, little is known of Rābiʿah's personal life. Her name indicates that she was a fourth *(rābiʿah)* daughter, probably of a poor family. For some time she was a house servant in Basra, but, thanks to her amazing piety, her master released her from bondage. Her life thereafter, marked by austerity and otherworldliness, was spent largely in retirement, although her sanctity attracted many who sought her prayers and teachings. Rābiʿah of Basra is regarded as the person who introduced the concept of pure love of God into the ascetic way of life prevalent among God-seeking Muslims during the second century AH.

It seems probable that Rābiʿah met some of the well-known ascetics of her time, among them Ibrāhīm ibn Adham of Balkh (d. 770?). However, the stories that connect her with the ascetic preacher Ḥasan al-Baṣrī, and even claim that he proposed marriage to her, are pure invention, for Ḥasan (whose constant call to renunciation and fear of God certainly colored the spiritual atmosphere in Basra) died in 728, when Rābiʿah was only about ten years old.

Many legends have been woven around her. When she performed the pilgrimage, the Kaʿbah is said to have moved forward to greet her, and her donkey, which had died on the road, was miraculously revived. But Rābiʿah, faithful to the ascetic tradition, and extremely afraid of hellfire, rejected the common belief that she was capable of performing miracles. Rather, she considered such miracles as satanic temptations.

Rābiʿah's greatest contribution to the development of Sufism lay in her insistence upon pure love of God, emphasizing the Qurʾanic verse "He loves them and they love him" (surah 5:59). She expressed her feelings sometimes in short, artless poems, sometimes in beautiful prayers, for she spent long nights in intimate conversation with her beloved Lord. In daily life, she experienced remorse when her thoughts strayed from him. Her heart was filled with love of God, with no room left even for a special love of the Prophet. Asked whether she hoped for Paradise, she answered with the Arabic proverb "Al-jār thumma al-dār" ("First the neighbor, then the house"), meaning that she thought only of him who had created Paradise and Hell.

Thus arose the best-known legend about her: having been seen carrying a flaming torch in one hand and a pitcher of water in the other, she explained that this symbolic act meant that she would set Paradise on fire and pour water into Hell, "so that these two veils may disappear and nobody may worship God out of fear of Hell or hope for Paradise, but solely for his own beauty." This tale, which reached Europe in the early fourteenth century, is the basis of several short stories, mystical and otherwise, in Western literature. Other accounts, too, eventually became known in the West, at least in nineteenth-century England, as Richard Monckton Milnes's poems *The Sayings of Rabiah* prove.

In the Islamic world, Rābiʿah was highly praised by ʿAṭṭār (d. 1221) in his *Tadhkirat al-awliyāʾ* (Biographies of the Saints), where he states that a woman who walks in the path of God cannot be called merely (i.e., deprecatively) "woman." Some centuries later, however, Jāmī (d. 1492) reminded his readers that the fact that the sun is feminine in Arabic does not distract from its grandeur. Certainly, her gender never clouded Rābiʿah's renown. The legend that she refused to go out to admire nature on a radiant spring day, preferring to contemplate the beauty of the Creator in the darkness of her house, has been retold for centuries, often without mentioning her name, and her life has even served as scenario for at least one Arab movie. Her name is still used to praise exceptionally pious women.

BIBLIOGRAPHY

Modern Arabic scholars, among them ʿAbd al-Raḥmān Badawī, have devoted studies to Rābiʿah, but the only comprehensive study in a Western language is Margaret Smith's *Rābiʿah the Mystic, and Her Fellow Saints in Islam* (1928; reprint, Cambridge, 1984).

ANNEMARIE SCHIMMEL

RABINDRANĀTHA THAKŪR.

See Tagore, Rabindranath.

RACHEL AND LEAH,

or, in Hebrew, Raḥel and Le'ah; wives of Jacob and daughters of Laban. According to *Genesis*, Rachel, who was the great-granddaughter of Abraham's brother Nahor, met Jacob at a well after he had fled Canaan to escape his brother Esau. Jacob worked for Laban seven years so that he might marry Rachel, but he was deceived into marrying her older sister Leah and had to work another seven years to earn Rachel's hand.

Both women have animal names, for *Raḥel* means "ewe" and *Le'ah* "cow." Although Rachel was beautiful, Leah was more fertile. At one point Leah gave Rachel mandrakes to improve her fertility in exchange for Rachel's turn to spend the night with Jacob. Ultimately Leah produced seven children (Reuben, Simeon, Levi, Judah, Issachar, Zebulun, and Dinah); two more (Gad and Asher) were born to her slave girl Zilpah. Rachel's slave girl Bilhah bore Dan and Naphtali; later Rachel produced two sons of her own, Joseph and Benjamin.

When Jacob fled from Laban, Rachel took the family idols, sitting on them when her father came and claiming she could not rise "because the way of women has come upon me" (*Gn.* 31:35). She died after giving birth to Benjamin and was buried at the spot, between Bethel and Ephrath. Her purported tomb is venerated to this day and may have been similarly regarded in biblical times (*Gn.* 35:20, *1 Sm.* 10:2, *Jer.* 31:15). Leah apparently died in Canaan and was buried in the cave of Machpelah (*Gn.* 49:31).

Most scholars agree that these stories include personifications of Israelite tribal history. The Leah tribes may have formed an early confederation. Both the monarchy and the priesthood are ascribed to tribes descended from her sons Judah and Levi. Rachel is the mother of the Joseph tribes, which were dominant in northern Israel, and of the adjoining Benjamin tribe, from which came the first king, Saul.

BIBLIOGRAPHY

A thorough survey of the patriarchal narratives can be found in Nahum M. Sarna's *Understanding Genesis* (New York, 1972). The historical material is discussed in great detail in Roland de Vaux's *The Early History of Israel*, translated by David Smith (Philadelphia, 1978). Postbiblical traditions pertaining to biblical events are collected in Louis Ginzberg's *The Legends of the Jews*, 7 vols., translated by Henrietta Szold et al. (Philadelphia, 1909–1938).

FREDERICK E. GREENSPAHN

RADCLIFFE-BROWN, A. R.

(1881–1955), English social anthropologist. Alfred Reginald Radcliffe-Brown, as he was known formally after changing his name in 1926 (Radcliffe having been his mother's original surname), was born in Sparkbrook, Birmingham. He was educated at King Edward's School in Birmingham, at Birmingham University (where he spent a year as a premedical student), and at Trinity College, Cambridge University, from which he graduated with a bachelor's degree in mental and moral science. Among those who taught him as an undergraduate were C. H. Myers and W. H. R. Rivers (both medical psychologists who had participated in Cambridge's pioneering anthropological expedition to the Torres Strait off the northeastern tip of Australia). After graduation in 1904 Radcliffe-Brown went on to study anthropology under Rivers and A. C. Haddon (who had also been on the expedition of 1898–1899) and was sent by them in 1906 to study the people of the Andaman Islands, southwest of Burma, for two years.

Radcliffe-Brown's initial report on this expedition, "The Religion of the Andaman Islanders," published in *Folk-Lore* in 1909 (his book *The Andaman Islanders* was not published until 1922), led Trinity College to offer him a fellowship, the tenure of which (from 1908 to 1914) was for a brief period combined with a teaching position at the London School of Economics. It was in those years that he first encountered and became permanently influenced by the sociological orientation of Émile Durkheim. Radcliffe-Brown quickly became part of the rapidly developing, distinctively sociological approach to the study of primal societies, and by the 1920s he was probably this movement's most influential figure. Until well into the twentieth century this field was dominated by the ethnological approach, the practitioners of which were particularly interested in the detailed history of particular societies and the patterns of diffusion and transmission of their cultures. That style of analysis was itself still influenced by the evolutionist approach which had been strongly in evidence in the later part of the nineteenth century and had largely regarded religion as a primitive form of science. While the ethnologists of the early part of the twentieth century did not cling strongly to the latter view, they stood in contrast to the emphasis that Radcliffe-Brown, under Durkheim's influence, increasingly placed on the idea that primitive societies should be analyzed synchronically rather than diachronically. In other words, Radcliffe-Brown's work increasingly involved the claim that in order to comprehend scientifically the main features of a society one should regard it as a functioning whole; its different parts were explainable in terms of their interrelatedness and their contribution to its maintenance.

Radcliffe-Brown's impact, which grew intermittently but strongly in the 1920s and 1930s through his teaching and writing in various countries, was based primarily on his advocacy and practice of what he came to call a natural science of society, with particular reference to social structure. His attention to religion was largely confined to the study of ritual and ceremony—which was particularly evident in the book which he published on the Andaman Islanders in 1922—and the related phenomenon of totemism. In his work on ritual, Radcliffe-Brown was greatly influenced by Durkheim's argument that the primary significance of ritual is its expression and promotion of collective sentiments and social solidarity.

In his first major essay on totemism, "The Sociological Theory of Totemism," published in the *Proceedings of the Fourth Pacific Science Congress* in 1929, Radcliffe-Brown maintained that Durkheim, by arguing that a totemic object acquires its significance via its sacredness, had begged the crucial question as to why totemism in primal societies typically involves plants or animals, even though Durkheim had pointed cogently to the ways in which ritualized collective conduct in connection with totems was intimately related to social structure and social integration. Radcliffe-Brown argued that plants and animals should not be regarded simply as emblems of social groups, but rather that they are selected as representatives of groups because objects and events which deeply affect the material and spiritual well-being of a society (or any phenomenon that represents such an object or event) are likely to become what he called objects of the ritual attitude. Although there has been disagreement as to the extent to which Radcliffe-Brown's second essay on this subject ("The Comparative Method in Social Anthropology," *Journal of the Royal Anthropological Institute*, 1952) involved a substantial change of position, there can be no doubt that it exhibits a very explicit interest in a theme which was not conspicuous in the essay of 1929—namely, the various relationships between totemic objects and between these objects and the structures of the groups that maintain ritual attitudes toward them.

Some have regarded Radcliffe-Brown's work at this point as embracing a form of cognitive structuralism, which is committed to the view that while animals and plants are good to eat they are even better to "think" (that is, they constitute a highly suitable and accessible symbolic means for "talking about" central features of a society's social structure and its relationship with its environment). Others have insisted that Radcliffe-Brown did not move so far beyond his original position of maintaining that the selection of totems is based primarily upon the tangible effects which particular plants or animals are perceived to have in a society. For discussion of the debate see Milton Singer's book, *Man's Glassy Essence: Explorations in Semiotic Anthropology* (1984).

BIBLIOGRAPHY

Radcliffe-Brown's major writings on religion are to be found in *The Andaman Islanders*, 3d ed. (Glencoe, Ill., 1948), *Structure and Function in Primitive Society* (London, 1952), and *The Social Anthropology of Radcliffe-Brown*, edited by Adam Kuyper (London, 1977). Illuminating discussion of his work can be found in Adam Kuyper's *Anthropology and Anthropologists*, rev. ed. (Boston, 1983).

Roland Robertson

RĀDHĀ. The cowherd woman *(gopī)* whose passionate love for the god Kṛṣṇa has been celebrated in song and story throughout the Indian subcontinent since medieval times, Rādhā has been revered by Vaiṣṇava devotees not only as Kṛṣṇa's earthly beloved but also as his eternal consort, as one half of the divine duality. Her name may be a feminine form of the Vedic *rādhas* ("desired object"). Epitomizing the ideal of *prema bhakti* ("loving devotion"), she has herself been an object of Vaiṣṇava worship, sometimes as a mediator but often as the highest reality, surpassing even Kṛṣṇa.

Origins and History. Despite the considerable scholarly attention that has been devoted to Rādhā's origins, the matter remains veiled in obscurity. Available evidence points to possible literary beginnings, perhaps in the songs of the Ābhīrs, a cattle-herding community of North India. From our earliest source material—a succession of stray verses in Sanskrit, Prakrit, and Apabhraṃśa from roughly the third century CE that celebrate the love of Rādhā and Kṛṣṇa—it is clear that her association with him was established throughout much of the subcontinent by the close of the first millennium.

The transfiguration of Rādhā from literary heroine to object of religious devotion was a complex and gradual process. The *Gītagovinda* of Jayadeva gives evidence that already in the twelfth century she was viewed as Kṛṣṇa's eternal consort. In the succeeding centuries, especially in eastern India, she continued to appropriate designations earlier applied to such goddess figures as Devī or Durgā, notably, *śakti* (strength, power), *prakṛti* (nature), and *māyā* (the creative energy of illusion). Recent studies have revealed her kinship with Ekānaṃśā-Durgā, whose complexion is also fair, and suggested that she may be in part a transformation of Durgā. Her counterpart and possible precursor in the South, Piṉṉai, who is portrayed as Kṛṣṇa's consort and wife among the cowherds, likewise appears to have had connections with Ekānaṃśā-Durgā. Both Rādhā and Piṉṉai have also assimilated aspects of Viṣṇu's consort Śrī-Lakṣmī, especially her role as mediator between God and human souls.

Although we find references to Rādhā in the Purāṇas, the most characteristic and important arena of her development is not narrative myth but poetry, or, more strictly, song, for Hindu poetry is composed to be sung. Building on the literary tradition of the courts, the poets of eastern India (and, to a lesser extent, of the North) sensitively and feelingly portrayed every phase and mood of her love with Kṛṣṇa: her shyness and ambivalence at its first dawning, her fulfillment in union with him and her subsequent hurt and jealous anger *(māna)* when he betrays her, and her final agony of separation when he leaves the cowherd village to fulfill his destiny by slaying the demon-king Kaṃsa. Most of the poets and dramatists who developed this theme appear to have presupposed that Rādhā was already married, leaving to the theologians the awkward task of reconciling her status as a *parakīyā* heroine — one who belongs to another — with her role as consort of Kṛṣṇa, who as lord of the universe is the upholder of the moral order *(dharma)*. In one such resolution, the Bengali Vaiṣṇava Rūpa Gosvāmī (sixteenth century) explains that Rādhā and the other *gopīs* belong eternally to Kṛṣṇa; their marriage to earthly cowherds is thus an expedient designed to enhance the intrigue of Kṛṣṇa's *līlā*.

Theology and Worship. Although the *gopīs* have been depicted with Kṛṣṇa in images dating from the seventh century or even earlier, we do not know whether they were at that time themselves objects of worship. It is only much later, from approximately the time of Caitanya (1486–1533), that we find clear evidence for the worship specifically of Rādhā with Kṛṣṇa, often in the characteristic *yugala-mūrti* ("paired image," the two side by side) that can still be seen in temples in Bengal and Vṛndāvana. Rādhā's worship, however, is not confined to those communities that place her image next to his; in the main Rādhāvallabha temple in Vṛndāvana, for example, she is represented simply by a throne cushion over which hangs a golden leaf that bears the inscription of her name. Nor need her presence be marked even to that degree: members of the Nimbārka and Vallabha communities regard Rādhā and Kṛṣṇa as indistinguishable from one another, and hence a devotee worshiping Kṛṣṇa is considered to be worshiping Rādhā as well. The Nimbārkīs in fact interpret the honorific element "Śrī" in "Śrīkṛṣṇa," a title of Kṛṣṇa used throughout India, as explicitly designating Rādhā; thus, "Śrī-Kṛṣṇa." [*See also the biographies of Vallabha and Nimbārka.*] Her paramount importance for residents of Vṛndāvana is also reflected in their use of the vocative form of her name, "Rādhe," as a standard mode of greeting. Members of the Rādhāvallabha community further honor her name by writing it on vines, stones, and pieces of wood placed in certain sacred spots. Like Kṛṣṇa's name, then, Rādhā's functions as a *mantra*, a group of syllables embodying sacred power. [*See also* Vṛndāvana.]

In addition to worshiping Rādhā through her images and her name, devotees attend performances in which episodes from the love story of Rādhā and Kṛṣṇa are sung and enacted by professional and amateur performers. In Bengal, for example, where she has always been especially popular, the medieval verses celebrating her love for Kṛṣṇa are sung in a semidramatic musical form known as *padāvalī-kīrtan*. In a typical performance, the lead singer, assisted by several other singers and two or three drummers, spins out a single episode in the divine love story over the course of three or four hours, interspersing narrative and dialogue with the lyrical verses describing and reflecting on Rādhā's feelings. These songs play on the central juxtaposition of the physical and the metaphysical as well as the paradox of the human-divine encounter. Devotees respond with expressions of wonder at the intensity, depth, and steadfastness of Rādhā's love, which, while representing the heights of human passion, also symbolizes the religious ideal of selfless, unswerving devotion to God. Her unexpected triumph over the lord of the universe, which is indicated, for example, by his abject submission as he begs for her forgiveness, invariably evokes exclamations of astonishment and delight.

The chief basis for the worship of Rādhā is thus the transcendent quality of her love for Kṛṣṇa; even when the theological designation *śakti* is applied to her, its meaning shifts from its usual Tantric sense of strength and activity to one of love. That she is the personification of love is indicated by a common designation for her: *mahābhāva* ("great emotion"). So exalted has this love rendered her that many Vaiṣṇavas since the time of Caitanya have felt that one should not imitate her directly; they have chosen rather to assume in their devotion the role of a humble maidservant of hers, a *mañjarī,* who is privileged to assist her and thereby enjoy vicariously the bliss of her union with Kṛṣṇa.

Rādhā's nature contrasts with that of all other major Hindu goddesses. She is neither mother goddess nor fertility deity, neither angry and destructive goddess nor social paradigm. Worshiped solely in relation to Kṛṣṇa, she has never become an independent deity. Yet her importance for Vaiṣṇava devotion since the sixteenth century can scarcely be overestimated. In the intensity and steadfastness of her love for Kṛṣṇa, especially in her separation from him, she serves as the highest inspiration to the devotee. The strength of Rādhā and her friends and the superiority of their devotion provide a valorization of the religious capacities of women that has had social implications as well. Finally, as the embodiment of supreme love, Rādhā in her eternal relation to Kṛṣṇa represents ultimate reality, for love *(prema)* itself, in the Vaiṣṇava vision, is the highest principle in the universe.

[*See also* Kṛṣṇa *and* Līlā.]

BIBLIOGRAPHY

Two books serve as major sources for the study of Rādhā. The most comprehensive treatment of her, a work in Bengali by S. B. Dasgupta, *Śrīrādhār kramabikās darśane o sāhitye* (Calcutta, 1952), is a judicious, well-documented account of her origins and development that traces her relations to other goddesses and to Indian conceptions of *śakti.* A more recent volume, *The Divine Consort: Rādhā and the Goddesses of India,* edited by John Stratton Hawley and me (Berkeley, 1982), contains articles on the religious significance of Rādhā in various texts and traditions, together with an extensive annotated bibliography.

Two other articles, as well as portions of two books, treat particular aspects of Rādhā. In "A Note on the Development of the Rādhā Cult," *Annals of the Bhandarkar Oriental Research Institute* 36 (1955): 231–257, A. K. Majumdar surveys evidence for the worship of Rādhā. Bimanbehari Majumdar's *Kṛṣṇa in History and Legend* (Calcutta, 1969) includes two chapters documenting her importance in religious literature. In a more recent article, "Rādhā: Consort of Kṛṣṇa's Vernal Passion," *Journal of the American Oriental Society* 95 (October–December 1975): 655–671, Barbara Stoler Miller surveys early verses in Sanskrit, Prakrit, and Apabhraṃśa on the Rādhā-Kṛṣṇa theme. Finally, Friedhelm Hardy's *Viraha-bhakti: The Early History of Kṛṣṇa Devotion in South India* (Delhi, 1983) distinguishes the primarily secular early poetic traditions of the love of Kṛṣṇa and Rādhā from the epic and Puranic traditions of Kṛṣṇa and the *gopīs.*

Four recent studies contain portraits of Rādhā as she is presented in particular literary works and performance traditions. In her *Love Song of the Dark Lord: Jayadeva's Gītagovinda* (New York, 1977), Barbara Miller includes a chapter on the figure of Rādhā. My own *Drama as a Mode of Religious Realization: The Vidagdhamādhava of Rūpa Gosvāmī* (Chico, Calif., 1984) discusses and illustrates through summary and translation the treatment of Rādhā by the Bengali Vaiṣṇava theologian and playwright Rūpa Gosvāmī. Finally, two works of John Hawley throw new light on the interpretation of Rādhā in the Braj region of North India. The introductions and translations in his *At Play with Krishna: Pilgrimage Dramas from Brindavan* (Princeton, 1981) present Rādhā as she is portrayed in the *rās līlās,* and a chapter of his *Sūr Dās: Poet, Singer, Saint* (Seattle, 1984) traces the conception of Rādhā through the successive layers of the *Sūr Sāgar,* the collection of poetry attributed to the sixteenth-century poet Sūr Dās.

DONNA MARIE WULFF

RADHAKRISHNAN, SARVEPALLI (1888–1975), Indian philosopher, statesman, and president of India (1962–1967). Born in Tirutani, a small town south of Madras noted as a pilgrimage center, Radhakrishnan attended Christian missionary schools for twelve years, until his graduation from Madras Christian College in 1908. The tension between the Hindu piety he learned at home and the Christian doctrine he was taught at school generated an interest in comparative philosophy, religion, and ethics that occupied him for the remainder of his life. Both of his major works, *An Idealist View of Life* (published in 1932 on the basis of his 1929 Hibbert Lectures) and *Eastern Religions and Western Thought* (lectures delivered at Oxford University, 1939), show the interplay of Indian and Western religious thought characteristic of his entire life's work.

The scant information that Radhakrishnan disclosed concerning his personal life is contained in a brief essay, "My Search for Truth" (1937). A seventy-five-page essay, "The Religion of the Spirit and the World's Need: Fragments of a Confession" (1952), intended as an autobiographical writing, offers one of the clearest summaries of his thought but treats his personal life in a few unrevealing pages. In refusing an editor's request for a brief autobiography, Radhakrishnan insisted, in "Fragments of a Confession," that discretion prevented him from doing so, and further, that his writings were worth more than his personal life.

In 1908, at the age of twenty, Radhakrishnan published his master's thesis, "The Ethics of the Vedānta and Its Metaphysical Presuppositions," and continued publishing one or more works almost every year for the next five decades. His first full-length work, *The Philosophy of Rabindranath Tagore* (1918), reveals most of the themes that would occupy him throughout his career: the Indian sources, varieties, and ethical implications of religious and philosophical intuition. With the exception of his first original work, *The Reign of Religion in Contemporary Philosophy,* wherein he criticizes the influence of religion on philosophy, Radhakrishnan's writings are characterized by the intimate relationship between religious experience (particularly the Hindu mystical tradition) and philosophy (particularly modern Western idealism). With the publication of his next major works, *Indian Philosophy* (vol. 1, 1923; vol. 2, 1927), *The Hindu View of Life* (1926), and *An Idealist View of Life* (1932), Radhakrishnan established his case for the positive relationship between idealist philosophy and a universalist religious attitude that he later termed "religion of the spirit."

In various ways, all of Radhakrishnan's mature writings focus on three closely related concerns: his presentation and positive interpretation of classical Indian religious thought, or Vedānta, especially as found in its three fundamental scriptures, the Upaniṣads, the *Bhagavadgītā,* and the *Brahma Sūtra;* his defense of philosophical idealism, both in its Indian expression and as found in Western philosophers from Plato to Hegel and F. H. Bradley; and his critique of contemporary (and especially Western) materialist and scientific thinking insofar as it excludes religious and spiritual values. On behalf of each of these three concerns, Radhakrishnan sought to show that although *brahman* (the Absolute) is the ultimate self-sufficient reality, the world is nevertheless valuable and worthy of man's deepest commitment and dedication.

Radhakrishnan's own dedication to the affairs of the world could not have been more convincing: in addition to his positions as professor of philosophy (University of Mysore, 1918–1921; University of Calcutta, 1921–1931 and 1937–1941) and university administrator (vice-chancellor of Andhra University, 1931–1936; vice-chancellor of Banaras Hindu University, 1938–1948; chancellor, University of Delhi, 1953–1962), he served in many demanding diplomatic positions, including head of the Indian delegation to UNESCO (1946–1952) and Indian ambassador to the Soviet Union (1949–1952). He was vice-president of India from 1952 to 1962, and president from 1962 to 1967.

BIBLIOGRAPHY

In addition to *An Idealist View of Life* (1932; 2d ed., London, 1957) and *Eastern Religions and Western Thought* (Oxford, 1959), which represent Radhakrishnan's major works in philosophy and in comparative religion and ethics, respectively, three other of his works are especially to be recommended. For the Indian expression of Radhakrishnan's religious and philosophic position, the fullest account is his 240-page introduction to the *Brahma Sūtra, The Philosophy of Spiritual Life* (New York, 1960). The best introduction to his understanding of contemporary religious life and thought is *Recovery of Faith* (New York, 1955). *The Philosophy of Sarvepalli Radhakrishnan,* edited by Paul Arthur Schilpp (New York, 1952), contains twenty-three essays covering all aspects of Radhakrishnan's thought, as well as his "Replies to Critics," his semiautobiographical essay "Fragments of a Confession," and a complete bibliography of his writings through the year 1952.

ROBERT A. MCDERMOTT

RADIN, PAUL (1883–1959), American anthropologist. Born in Lódź, Poland, Radin was brought to the United States by his parents while he was still an infant, in 1884. Upon completing his studies in anthropology at Columbia University, he spent his life as a vagabond scholar, teaching at numerous colleges and universities in the United States and lecturing at most of the major universities of western Europe. Among them were the University of California at Berkeley, Cambridge University, Fisk University, the University of Chicago, Kenyon College, Black Mountain College, and Brandeis University. He was never offered, nor did he seek, tenure anywhere; devoted to his studies of the cultures of primitive societies, he was content to be institutionally rootless.

Radin was perhaps the most cultivated anthropologist in the history of the discipline. He was a man of paradox: a skeptic with a strong sense of the sacred, an agnostic who was fascinated by all religious phenomena, a Jew who disclaimed the uniqueness of the revelation contained in the Hebrew scriptures. In deconstructing the specificity of Old Testament claims, Radin's work follows that of Andrew Lang and others on the ubiquity of high gods among primitive—that is, pre-class, or stateless—peoples.

Radin was always equivocal about primitive religions. In *Primitive Religion* (1937) he argues for a Freudian explanation of religious concepts, and a "Marxist" awareness of the potential for domination in religious establishments, but he does not thereby deny the authenticity of a given faith stripped down to its core. In his arguments, Radin clearly indicates a belief in the irreducible universality of religious faith, which universality is an essentially phenomenological matter. On the other hand, he was fully aware of the exploitative potential of all significant religious figures and movements. These include the primitive shaman who could conceivably dominate others through his peculiar capacity to evoke religious states. Nonetheless, as he makes clear in *Primitive Man as Philosopher* (1927), Radin did not imagine that structures of domination, as we understand them, could be found in primitive societies. In fact, Radin's sense of the comparative deficiencies of civilization is evident throughout his work.

Radin brought to the study of religion a powerful sense of human fatality and historical contingency. It is probable that his own personality, continuously shaped by a very broad understanding of human experience, led him to focus on the ambivalent figure of the trickster, which is given free reign in primitive societies but is repressed in our own. More than any other aspect of his work, this concern—presented in *The Trickster: A Study in American Indian Mythology* (1956)—commended him to philosophers and psychologists alike. For Radin, the trickster reflected the double image of God: an androgynous figure, bursting with energy, without values, both creator and destroyer, the cosmic villain, and, at the same time, a bumbling fool. This definition of the trickster, which has become a classic, probably represents Radin's most striking contribution to the development of anthropological thinking.

Radin's interest in primitive religion covered a wide range of subjects. *The Autobiography of a Winnebago Indian* by Sam Blowsnake (1920), which Radin edited and translated, is a pioneer work that represents, presumably in the protagonist's own words, the cultistic efforts to compensate for a lost culture, and the conflicts that ensue. Radin had a particular concern for people caught between faiths.

However, it is not Radin's focus on religious matters that commands our attention, but rather the great sweep of his thinking and his powerful, indirect critique of modern secularism (see *The World of Primitive Man*, 1953) and the depths of his humanity that bound him to the primitive peoples and sacred societies he studied. If Paul Radin was the most cultivated anthropologist in the history of the discipline, he was also the most faithful, in every sense of the word.

BIBLIOGRAPHY

Besides the works cited above, most of which are available in reprint editions, the following books represent important contributions made by Radin to anthropological studies: *The Genetic Relationship of the North American Indian Languages* (Berkeley, 1919) and *The Method and Theory of Ethnology: An Essay in Criticism* (New York, 1933).

STANLEY DIAMOND

RAHNER, KARL (1904–1984), Roman Catholic theologian. The most prolific and influential Catholic theologian of the twentieth century, Rahner's bibliography comprises more than four thousand entries. Writing primarily as a dogmatic theologian, he also addressed philosophical, historical, pastoral, and spiritual questions. His work as a whole may be summarized as theological anthropology, correlating human experience and God's self-communication. His method is most often described as transcendental, inasmuch as it seeks to discover the conditions of possibility for divine salvific action, but it also has an inseparable historical dimension, inasmuch as the humanity addressed by God's word and presence is understood as always situated in a temporal world. Indeed, it may be even more accurate to see Rahner as a Catholic dialectical theologian whose career was marked not only by personal response to the religious issues of his day but also by an enduring effort to conceive human history as destined for eternal communion with God, achieved through the course of time.

Born and raised in Freiburg im Breisgau, Rahner entered the Society of Jesus in 1922. During his education in the Jesuit order he developed an Ignatian spirituality of "seeking God in all things." His formal philosophical (1924–1927) and theological (1929–1933) studies were shaped largely by the neoscholastic revival; but through the writings of the Belgian Jesuit Joseph Maréchal he entered into philosophical conversation with Immanuel Kant and later with G. W. F. Hegel and German Idealism. To these general influences on his thought must be added his intensive reading in patristic sources and in medieval mysticism. Ordained a priest in 1932, Rahner concluded his basic theological program the following year and then pursued a further year of pastoral and ascetic studies (the Jesuit tertianship).

In 1934 Rahner began a doctoral program in philosophy at the University of Freiburg, where he attended Martin Heidegger's seminars. His doctoral dissertation, a modern retrieval of Thomas Aquinas's theory of knowledge, centered on the theme of *conversio ad phantasma* (conversion to the phantasm) as the ground of all human knowledge, and it conceived human existence fundamentally as "spirit in world." When his director rejected the thesis as insufficiently traditional (it was published in 1939 as *Geist in Welt*), Rahner left for Innsbruck. After quickly completing a theological doctorate and habilitation, he began in 1937 to teach dogmatic theology. From those first years came an eloquent book of meditations, *Worte ins Schweigen* (1938), and also the publication of his Salzburg summer lectures on human history as the place where God's self-revelation must be sought, *Hörer des Wortes* (1941).

When the Nazis closed the Innsbruck faculty in 1938, Rahner moved to Vienna and served at the Pastoral Institute until 1944. From 1945 to 1948 he taught theology under straitened circumstances at Pullach bei München. Returning to Innsbruck in 1949, he was responsible for courses on grace and the sacrament of penance, topics that shaped his thought for the rest of his life. Rooted in the experience of grace as God's mysterious self-communication, Rahner's thought broke new ground in a whole range of areas: for example, the biblical understanding of God; current problems in Christology, nature, and grace; the human condition after original sin; human dignity and freedom; the meaning of church membership; existential ethics; and the pastoral situation of the church. His major essays were collected from this time on in a multivolume collection, *Schriften zur Theologie* (1954–1984).

Already in *Hörer des Wortes* it was clear that Rahner was developing a philosophy of religion on the assumption that Christian revelation had occurred, and in order to make plausible how that was possible. A theologian of grace and reconciliation, he engaged in extensive positive research, as is made abundantly clear in *Schriften*, vol. 11 (1973), with his historical essays on penance in the early church. But the special creativity of his writing showed itself in his efforts to correlate the circumstances of particular experience with the permanent "existentials" of the human condition. This interrelation of historical and transcendental moments was evident as well in the prodigious editorial labors that began in his early Innsbruck years and continued with the publication of four editions of Denzinger's *Enchiridion Symbolorum* (1952–1957) and seven editions of *Der Glaube der Kirche in den Urkunden der Lehrverkündigung* (1948–1965).

Building on the early Innsbruck period came a second phase of Rahner's thought, during which he was coeditor of the second edition of the *Lexikon für Theologie und Kirche* (1957–1965) and a leading figure in the preparation and course of the Second Vatican Council (despite efforts to disqualify his participation). His retrieval and renewal of tradition in light of contemporary perspectives had previously been achieved largely through pressing particular questions against the background of School Theology. Now he drew out the consequences of these studies and began to speak more programmatically of a theological anthropology encompassing the history of a world whose call to union with God (the "supernatural existential") evokes transcendental reflection on the structural possibilities for such salvation. In powerful essays on mystery, incarnation, theology of symbol, and hermeneutics of eschatological assertions, collected in *Schriften*, vol. 4 (1960), Rahner developed his analogy of transcendence. Facing questions posed by evolutionary science, the great world religions, and utopian views of the future, other major essays in *Schriften*, vol. 5 (1962), present the scope of the divine salvific will in more comprehensive terms and argue for the coextension of salvation history and the history of the world. Corresponding to the council's ecclesiological focus, *Schriften*, vol. 6 (1966), collects papers that present a dialogue with secularized, pluralistic society and seek to express the Christian church's new self-understanding in it. Earlier, Rahner had published a large collection of essays in pastoral theology (*Sendung und Gnade*, 1959). He gathered a new collection of essays in spirituality (*Schriften*, vol. 7, 1967), and in 1962 he cooperated in drafting a plan for the *Handbuch der Pastoraltheologie*, which subsequently appeared in five volumes between 1964 and 1972, with Rahner as one of its editors.

In 1964 Rahner succeeded Romano Guardini in the chair of Christian *Weltanschauung* at the University of Munich. As it became apparent that he would not be allowed to direct doctoral students in theology, he accepted in 1967 a call to the University of Münster, where he taught until his retirement in 1971. In these first years of Vatican II's reception within Catholicism, criticism of Rahner's thought grew in various quarters. Concerned with fidelity to the tradition and to Christian symbolism, some writers, for example, Hans Urs von Balthasar, accused him of anthropological reductionism. Others, especially his former student J.-B. Metz, drew back from what they considered an individualistic, idealistic existentialism. Rahner took the second critique more seriously and gave new emphasis to the historical concreteness of Christianity and its social responsibility. Renewing the dialectic of unity in difference with which he had from the beginning sought to understand time in its openness to eternity, he addressed basic conciliar themes with a deepened sense of faith's constructive participation in its secular context. *Schriften*, vols. 8, 9, and 10 (1967, 1970, 1972), calls for a new understanding of Jesus of Nazareth as the human way to God ("Christology from below") and reform of the church in the direction of a declericalized, more democratic, and socially critical community of service. Meanwhile Rahner had undertaken additional editorial responsibilities for the four volumes of *Sacramentum Mundi* (1967–1969) and for *Concilium* (1965–).

During the first years of Rahner's retirement in Munich, his major project was the preparation of his *Grundkurs des Glaubens* (1976), an introduction to the idea of Christianity. While not intended as a complete systematic theology, the book does present many of his basic positions on the central topics of Christian doctrine and has commonly been seen as a summation of his thought.

In the last years of his life Rahner continued to lecture and write vigorously. Four further volumes of the *Schriften* were published (vols. 13–16: 1978, 1980, 1983, 1984), two while he was still living in Munich, two more after his final retirement to Innsbruck in 1981. They were accompanied by numerous smaller works and several anthologies, one of which, *Praxis des Glaubens* (1982), may also serve as a general introduction to its author's thought. These later years are again of a piece with the whole career and include familiar themes as well as considerable repetition. Nevertheless, some significant developments occur here too: in the consolidation of a historical Christology, in the proposal of a "universal pneumatology" that might precede Christology, in pleas for ecumenical seriousness, and in arguments for a truly world church.

In these last years of his life Rahner was newly concerned with addressing the mounting relativism and skepticism he saw about him. In addition, the writings of this last phase show how thoroughly dialectical his thought was, as it sought to mediate between opposed positions in either doctrine or morals, to speak of the fruitful tension between permanent polarities of historical existence, and, above all, to understand the relation between continuity and discontinuity through the passage of time.

Rahner's future influence will depend largely on how effectively his students and readers will be able to draw on his thinking for a continuing dialogue with scientific and technological culture, the social sciences, and narrative and symbolic modes of discourse. It remains to be seen how a more biblically imagined, historically diverse, and socially responsible theology will appropriate his legacy. Many who knew him would insist that the personal witness of his life will surely endure alongside the remarkably elastic architecture of his thought.

BIBLIOGRAPHY

For a complete, chronological listing of Rahner's publications, see *Bibliographie Karl Rahner: 1924–1969*, edited by Roman Bleistein and Elmar Klinger (Freiburg, 1969); *Bibliographie Karl Rahner: 1969–1974*, edited by Roman Bleistein (Freiburg, 1974); "Bibliographie Karl Rahner: 1974–1979," compiled by P. Imhof and H. Treziak, in *Wagnis Theologie*, edited by Herbert Vorgrimler (Freiburg, 1979), pp. 579–97; and "Bibliographie Karl Rahner: 1979–1984," compiled by P. Imhof and E. Meuser, in *Glaube im Prozess*, 2d ed., edited by Elmar Klinger and Klaus Wittelstadt (Freiburg, 1984), pp. 854–871.

The core of Rahner's work is in his *Schriften zur Theologie*, 16 vols. (Einsiedeln and Zurich, 1954–1984), of which fourteen volumes have been published in English as *Theological Investigations*, 20 vols. to date (New York, 1961–). Outstanding examples of his spiritual writing can be found in *Worte ins Schweigen* (Leipzig, 1938), translated as *Encounters with Silence* (Westminster, Md., 1960), and in *Von der Not und dem Segen des Gebetes*, 4th ed. (Innsbruck, 1949), translated as *On Prayer* (New York, 1958). Key essays on charismatic gifts and existential decision are in *Das Dynamische in der Kirche* (Freiburg, 1958), translated as *The Dynamic Element in the Church* (New York, 1964). The major late work is *Grundkurs des Glaubens: Einführung in den Begriff des Christentums* (Freiburg, 1976), translated as *Foundations of Christian Faith: An Introduction to the Idea of Christianity* (New York, 1978). Karl Lehmann and Albert Raffelt have edited a fine anthology of Rahner's spiritual writings in *Praxis des Glaubens* (Freiburg, 1982), translated as *The Practice of Faith* (New York, 1983).

For further biographical information and commentary, see Herbert Vorgrimler's *Karl Rahner: His Life, Thought and Works* (London, 1966) and my collection of studies entitled *A World of Grace: An Introduction to the Themes and Foundations of Karl Rahner's Theology* (New York, 1980).

LEO J. O'DONOVAN, S.J.

RAIN. The symbolism of rain derives from its correlation with the sacred substance water, a universal metaphor for the origin and renewal of life. [*See* Water.] The primacy and awesome mystery of natural phenomena for early man, and his vital dependence on their manifestations, are reflected in his exaltation of rain as a supreme creative power and intermediary between heaven and earth. In the seasonal revival of nature and the infusion of new life, rain was seen as the dispenser of divine grace and plenty, the promise of survival; in the periodic destruction wrought by storms and floods, as the agent of divine retribution and disaster, the threat of annihilation. Rain signified the descent of heavenly influences upon the earth; at times the gods themselves descended in rain or spoke in the thunder. Like the sun's rays, "the rain from heaven" (*Gn.* 8:2) was cognate to light, illumination.

The sacrality of sky and the supremacy of rain deities are fundamental elements in the structure of the myths and religions of archaic peoples. As the "most high," sky gods were assimilated to transcendence, their very names often connoting elevation. The Mesopotamian hieroglyph for "height" or "transcendence of space" also meant "rainy sky," and thus linguistically linked rain to divinity. Baal, the chief god of the Syro-Palestinian nomads, was called "rider of the clouds" and was worshiped as the dispenser of fertility. When the Israelites reached Canaan and their prophets condemned the widespread cult of fertility gods, a conflict arose between the worshipers of Baal and those faithful to Yahveh. The ancient Hebrews conceived of rain as a reservoir of treasure in heaven, a benison bestowed in return for loving God and obeying his law, and withheld as retribution for sin. In times of abundance, the Israelites were drawn to the fertility gods, and the Lord's promise to Moses, "Behold, I will rain bread from heaven for you" (*Ex.* 16:4), was forgotten. In the New Testament, rain is the symbol of joy and fruition, the answer to prayer from a loving Father in heaven who sends rain on the just and the unjust alike.

The life-renewing, life-sustaining powers of rain have been personified in the pantheons of both primitive and higher religions. Worship of rain gods as symbols of fertility prevailed in the East, among the main branches of Aryan stock in early Europe, and in parts of Africa, Oceania, and the Americas; and many, like the Maya god Chac, were believed to be the creator of all things. The Mesoamerican moon god whose name meant "I am the dew of the heavens, I am the dew of the clouds" was the father of gods as well as of men, and represented death and resurrection.

The perennial, universal aspiration for rain is reflected in all traditions in the divine promises recorded in their sacred texts. Every Egyptian god was in some way related to water. In the *Ṛgveda,* the god Varuṇa proclaims, "I made to flow the moisture-shedding waters"; in the *Vendidad,* Ahura Mazdā pledges to "rain down upon the earth to bring food to the faithful and fodder to the beneficent cow"; in the Qur'ān, Allāh is described as "he who created the heavens and earth and sent down for you out of heaven water." The Persians conceived the tree of life as rising from a lake of rain, its seeds mingling with the water to maintain the earth's fertility. A common saying among the ancient Greeks when rain fell was "The Father [heaven] is pressing grapes." Both tribal rain gods and a national rain spirit were propitiated by the Burmese.

A dominant theme in universal mythology is the celestial marriage between Heaven and Earth, or between the fructifying sky god and fecund earth goddess. Rites and festivals of the seasonal fertilization of the earth by the penetrating rains have been celebrated since Neolithic times, when the correlations of rain and serpent, woman and vegetation, and death and rebirth were integrated into the complex of lunar symbolism. The union of the divine couple was the archetypal image of fruitfulness. Speaking in the storm, the Sumerian high god called himself the "fecund seed." Homer described the conjugal couch where Zeus lay with his spouse on Mount Ida as covered with a cloud from which rain fell, and Aeschylus wrote, "Rain impregnates the earth so that she gives birth to plants and grains." Birth and its attendant dangers are symbolized by a great storm in Vergil's *Aeneid.* In many of the prayers and tribal myths of North American Indians, the gentle rain is called "female" and the pelting rain "male."

Rites to ensure rain and fertility had their origin in remote antiquity and have been observed throughout the world. At the lower stages of civilization, sorcery and magical charms related to imitative or sympathetic magic were employed by shamans to evoke rain; later, prayer and sacrifice were combined with magico-religious rituals. A rain sacrifice rock painting from the Rusape district of Zimbabwe, now in the Frobenius Institut in Frankfurt, depicts a man standing with hands uplifted as if conjuring heaven, a female figure lying under a tree, and another bending forward above falling rain. Rainmakers were the most important members of the community and exerted enormous authority over the group. There is reason to believe that both chieftainship and kingship stemmed from the powerful position of the shaman. Ramses II of Egypt was credited with the faculty of rainmaking. The Zand Avesta, the Pahlavi translation of the Avesta with added commentaries, states that Ahura Mazdā (Pahl., Ōhrmazd) would raise the dead on the first day of the New Year with libations and purifications by water to ensure rain. Saints, especially in desert lands, were often reputed to be rainmakers, and the lives of Muslim saints abound with such miracles. The offices of the rainmaker are recorded among the Vedic rites of remote antiquity, where the sacred drink *soma* is called "son of the rain god." Water libations were celebrated by ancient Jewry as a so-called rain charm. At the Feast of Tabernacles in Jerusalem, the priest performed the ritual mixture of wine with water from the Pool of Siloam to induce rain. At a later period, Orthodox Jews practiced a rain charm that may have had its origin in fertility rites: as they recited the names of the Ten Plagues of Egypt at the Seder on Passover eve, a few drops of water were poured into a jar of wine and the mixture was cast upon the ground in front of the house. In Greece, after the participants in the Eleusinian mysteries had been purified by water, they cried out, "Let there be rain! Be fruitful!"

According to the Chinese doctrine of "like to like," similar things summon one another, which implies that the dragon, traditionally associated with rain, generates rain. Evidence of rainmaking magic on oracle bones attests to the antiquity of such beliefs. The *Li-chi* (Record of Rites) from the first century BCE chronicles the practice of ritual nakedness, a magic formula continued into late Chinese history in which even Confucian officials participated in time of drought. Buddhist priests poured water into little holes in the temple floor to symbolize rain going into the earth. Rainmaking spells are mentioned in *sūtra*s of 230 BCE.

In many parts of the East, the custom of immersing the fertility goddess, and in Europe the rite of drenching the Corn Mother, reflect earlier practices of sacrificing human victims to induce rain. In Mesoamerica, small children and birds were sacrificed to propitiate rain gods, and on the occasion of the Itzamna festival in March the hearts of certain species of wild animals were immolated. A custom among the Arabs of North Africa was to throw a holy man into a spring to end a drought, and in Russia to drench a priest or the figure of a saint for the same purpose. In societies where blood was assimilated to water, as in Abyssinia (ancient Ethiopia), human blood was the oblation offered to rain spirits. In Java, men whipped one another to draw blood, the symbolic equivalent of rain.

A milder form of rain magic was the sprinkling or scattering of water. In Lithuania, when rain was needed, people sprinkled themselves with water as they stood facing the sun at their morning prayers. The Celtic priests, the druids, bearing the image of a saint, led a procession to a sacred spring or well where water was sprinkled over special stones, which were then tossed into the air to fall to earth like rain. Pausanius left a description of the priests of Lycaean Zeus sacrificing an oak branch to a spring in time of drought, and the wizards of New Guinea and Siberia dipped branches into water and scattered the drops. Northern Dravidian tribes held an "umbrella feast" at the critical period of transplanting the rice crop, and Australian tribes performed ceremonial dances and songs around a pool to call down rain.

Rain dances figured prominently among American Indian tribes. The Omaha, members of a sacred buffalo society, filled vessels with water before they danced. Buffalo-head rituals were performed by the Plains and Woodland tribes when rain was lacking, and the Shawnee dipped a buffalo tail in water and shook it to bring rain. The Hopi and Zuni tribes depicted aquatic animals and symbolic rain clouds on their sand altars, half circles from which vertical lines depended as rain. An important feature of these rites was the bull-roarer, a sacred instrument that simulated the sound of thunder and was originally used in primitive initiations and Greek mystery ceremonies to represent the voice of God. Many of the peoples of Africa and Oceania believed that their gods spoke in the thunder. In the rites of the Oglala Lakota Indians, the water in the sweat lodge represented the thunder beings, fearsome powers that tested the warriors' strength and endurance and brought them the blessings of purification.

Rain accompanied by a thunderbolt symbolizes power or energy. In the form of a double trident, the thunderbolt is prominent in representations of the gods of ancient Sumer, Babylonia, Assyria, and Akkad. The Etruscan doctrine of thunderbolts related eleven different kinds of thunder to the powers of eleven gods. The synthesis of a sun god and a storm god connotes the energy of the pairs of opposites. An Assyrian sun god with a thunderbolt, believed to be the national deity Assur, is depicted on an alabaster wall panel from the palace of Ashurnasirpal II (c. 850 BCE), now in the British Museum. The Hebrew god Yahveh unites traits of both storm and solar god, as does Zeus, who destroyed the Titans with his thunderbolt. His Roman counterpart was believed to descend in the form of a thunderbolt and is represented on the Antonine column as the rain god Jupiter Pluvius hovering over the Roman legions with outspread wings and raining down his power upon them. This same synthesis pertains to the prehistoric Peruvian deity Viracocha, universal father and creator of all things, who as a rain god is depicted with a thunderbolt in each hand, his head surrounded by a rayed solar disk and his eyes shedding tears of life-renewing rain. The names of the Teutonic and Scandinavian war gods (Óðinn, Þórr, Donar, etc.) all mean "thunder." [*See* Meteorological Beings.]

Lightning symbolizes the action of the higher realm upon the lower, and in every culture has been assimilated either to a god, his weapon, or the manifestation of his sovereignty. At times, lightning has been construed as the salutary arrow of a god bringing deliverance or illumination to mankind, as when Mithra, the Persian god of light, pierced a rock with his arrow to end a drought by freeing the waters; at others, as the portent of his wrath or retribution. The lightning of the Vedic god Indra split the head of the dragon Vṛtra, demon of drought, to release the waters obstructed by him and regenerate the world, which had been made a wasteland. The storm god Rudra and his sons the Maruts, who shared the dual powers of their benign and destructive father, wielded their lightning bolts both to slay and to heal. The lightning god of the Indonesians was venerated as a supreme deity.

In the Hindu-Buddhist notion of the forms of divine manifestation, the *vajra*, lightning or thunderbolt, symbolizes the mystic, divine energy and the adamantine weapon of truth. As the invincible force in the sphere of transcendental reality, the *vajra* is the illusion-shattering light of spiritual illumination, which links the grace flowing into the world from the sun with the energy of the lightning bolt. In Buddhist iconography, the *vajra* is an emblem of the spiritual power of Buddhahood, an image of which is the solar Buddha, Vairocana, encircled by the halo of his emanations. The double trident wand carried by Buddhist monks is a form of the *vajra*. In early Tantrism, in which magic and science were inseparable, the Vajrayāna, doctrine of the "way of the thunderbolt," related to a form of electric energy.

Rain clouds and thunderstorms symbolized celestial activity in ancient China, and lightning was regarded with the same awe as were the thunderbolts of rain gods in other cultures. *Shen,* the pictogram for lightning, signifies divinity and the operation of the expansive forces. When the thunder ceases and rain ends, it is the work of demons and the contractive forces. These opposing forces symbolize two facets of the human spirit, the one ascending in life, the other descending in death. In the *Book of Changes,* the trigram *chen,* the Arousing, is the image of thunder and signifies tension resolved after the cloudburst, nature refreshed, deliverance. According to the *Li-Chi,* only when the two opposing forces of *yin* and *yang* are in proper harmony will the beneficent rains fall, and when they fail to come, *yin* must be activated.

As a symbol of purification and redemption, rain is associated with the dissolving and washing away of sin, followed by rebirth and renewal. Every torrential rainfall bears the implication of the archetypal flood, the creation destroyed by its creator, and mankind submerged in an initiatory ordeal or cosmic baptism preliminary to redemption and regeneration. The concept of a cataclysmic inundation of the world is found in myths of every part of the world except Egypt and Japan, and only rarely in Africa. The two major interpretations of the Deluge reflect two ways of relating to the universe. The first, for which the early Mesopotamian *Epic of Gilgamesh* is the model, characterizes man's identity with a wholly impersonal universe controlled by the cosmic rhythm or recurrent cycle of the manifestation and disappearance of the world at the turn of every aeon. Engulfing rains alternate with a world drought in the Hindu myth in which Viṣṇu rescues mankind by becoming first the sun, then wind, then fire, and finally a great cloud from which fall the restorative rains. The second concept, exemplified in the biblical story of Noah, represents the flood sent by God as a punishment for man's sins and expresses the Semitic dissociation from, and guilt toward, God, with the implication of free will.

No other natural phenomenon has been so universally associated with the Holy Spirit as the rainbow, which on every continent has been the emblem of some aspect of man's spiritual life, or some stage in the development of human consciousness. From the myths of Paleolithic and Neolithic peoples to the aborigines of Oceania and the Americas, the rainbow has been equated with the celestial serpent, the Great Father, the creator, or fertility god. The Egyptian sky mother Nut is depicted on coffins and papyri arced over the earth like a rainbow to signify the creation of the world. A representation of this figure is in the Egyptian Museum in Turin. A rainbow goddess in the identical posture appears in Navajo Indian sand paintings made to effect cures.

Like all sky phenomena, rainbows possess an ominous aspect, but for the most part have been regarded as an auspicious omen. An arc of light between earth and sky, the rainbow is a perennial symbol of the bridge linking the material world to Paradise and making possible communication between them. The rainbow was the path to the gods for the Mesopotamian, Indian, Japanese, and Hebrew peoples; for the Nordic peoples, it was the Bifrǫst, the "tremulous way" to Ásgarðr; in the Greco-Roman world, it was a sign from Zeus. To the Pygmies of equatorial Africa, the rainbow was a sign of the god's desire to communicate with them, and to the American Indian, it was the ladder affording access to the other world. The heroes of Polynesian and Hawaiian myths ascend the rainbow in order to deliver the souls of the dead to Paradise. Often construed as a prophetic sign or portent of blessings when appearing in the sky after a storm or flood, rainbows denote God's appeasement and reconciliation to mankind. Sealing his bond with Noah, God declared, "I do set my bow in the cloud, and it shall be for a token of a covenant between me and the earth" (*Gn.* 9:13). As a symbol of transfiguration and heavenly glory, rainbows are associated with the nimbus, aureole, halo, and mandorla surrounding the body of a god or saint. In Buddhism, the rainbow symbolizes the highest state attainable in the realm of *saṃsāra* before attaining to the clear light of *nirvāṇa,* and in Hinduism, the "rainbow body" is the highest yoga state. The rainbow is depicted in Christian art as the Lord's throne, and in scenes of the Last Judgment, Christ is frequently portrayed seated on a rainbow. In the *Revelation to John* in the New Testament, when the door opened in Heaven, "there was a rainbow round about the throne" (*Rv.* 4:3).

BIBLIOGRAPHY

Allen, Don Cameron. *Mysteriously Meant: The Rediscovery of Pagan Symbolism and Allegorical Interpretation in the Renaissance.* Baltimore, 1970. An exhaustive conspectus of interpretations by Renaissance authors of symbol, myth, and allegory in ancient Egypt and in pagan writers of classical antiquity. Includes an extensive bibliography.

Morley, Sylvanus Griswold. *The Ancient Maya.* 3d ed. Revised by George W. Brainerd. Stanford, Calif., 1956. A comprehensive account of the benevolent and malevolent rain gods and their personification of the struggle between good and evil in the dualistic Maya religion.

Needham, Joseph. *Science and Civilisation in China,* vol. 2, *History of Scientific Thought.* Cambridge, 1956. A fully documented account of the correlations in Chinese thought of the symbolic forms in Taoism and Tantrism as they relate to the positive and negative aspects of rain and the balance of energy in the *yin-yang* system.

Pettazzoni, Rafaele. *Dio: L'essere celeste nelle credenze dei popoli primitivi.* Rome, 1922. A history of the symbolism of rain, and of the sky and storm gods, in the belief systems of early peoples of Africa and Australia.

Reichard, Gladys A. *Navajo Religion: A Study of Symbolism.* 2 vols. New York, 1950. Both volumes are relevant: vol. 1, *An Investigation of Symbolism in Navajo Rain Ceremonies;* vol. 2, *Symbols in the Sandpaintings of the Rainbow Guardians.*

Sébillot, Paul. *Le folk-lore de France,* vol. 2. Paris, 1905. A valuable survey of rainmaking rites in southern France from pagan to modern times.

ANN DUNNIGAN

RAINBOW SNAKE (Rainbow Serpent) is an almost ubiquitous but elusive mythological figure throughout the Australian continent. To A. R. Radcliffe-Brown (1930), the Rainbow Snake was "perhaps the most important nature-deity, . . . the most important representation of the creative and destructive power of nature, principally in connection with rain and water." Writing about southeastern Australia, he notes the Rainbow Snake's association with waterfalls, as well as with smallpox, and he mentions the belief that ordinary people who approached the Snake's home site were in danger of being eaten. He adds that paraphernalia prepared for young men's initiation sequences in the Bora rites included a snakelike earth mound up to forty feet long. Although Radcliffe-Brown concludes that the *bunyip* in Victoria was not a Rainbow Snake, Charles P. Mountford (1978) includes *bunyips*, as well as other Snake-like characters, in this category of beings. Even among traditionally oriented Aborigines, the name Rainbow Snake can apply to snakes with no obvious rainbow connections. They may have quasi-crocodile shapes or just "something" about them that is dangerous or not normally visible.

Human Contact with Rainbow Snake Power. Because of the aura of danger surrounding the *idea* of Rainbow Snakes and other similar beings, certain places are taboo to ordinary people but not to Aboriginal "doctors," the men or, less often, women whose experience goes beyond cases of illness or injury to include the supernatural dimension, usually through special initiation rites involving the Rainbow Snake and perhaps spirits of the dead. According to some Kimberley and Western Desert beliefs recorded by A. P. Elkin (1945), the novice was taken up into the sky, where he underwent a ritual death and had inserted into his body quartz crystals and perhaps *maban* (sometimes called "pearl shell"), both associated with the Rainbow Snake. The crystals or shells are invisible and confer particular powers on the recipient; or he might be given "little rainbow-snakes . . . from a water-hole at the foot of the rainbow" (Elkin, 1945, pp. 32–33). A person with such powers can see Rainbow Snakes and other beings and perhaps have a personal Rainbow Snake as a spirit familiar. He can use the rainbow as a vehicle in which to travel great distances through the sky.

Actual pearl shells from the northwest coast of Western Australia, some engraved with water and rain designs, were also associated with Rainbow Snakes. Used in initiation and in rainmaking rites, they were (and are) passed on along recognized trade routes, eastward well beyond the Victoria River district and south to the Great Australian Bight.

During the wet season (the cyclone season), the northwest coast is subject to monsoon storms that deluge the whole north coast across to northern and eastern Queensland. [*See* Yulunggul Snake.] Rainbow Snake and other Snake stories are especially common throughout these potential flood areas. The Rainbow Snake of arid zones, known as Wonambi, Wanambi, and other names, is dangerous and powerful, but less dramatically so than his northern counterparts. Even inland, however, dry sandy creek beds can suddenly become raging torrents that flood the surrounding country (for example, the Tod River in Alice Springs and other rivers in northern South Australia or the usually dry Lake Eyre, which floods less often).

Along the northwestern Australian coast, for instance, summer cyclones threaten coastal towns—sometimes extending even into the southwest. For the non-Aboriginal population, the urgent questions have to do with whether a given cyclone will cross the coast, where and when it will do so, how destructive it will be, and, if it moves inland, whether it will become a rain-bearing low-pressure system, bringing water to areas that depend on the monsoon. Weather officials still regard cyclone movements as unpredictable. For traditional Aborigines, however, the matter is plain: mythic characters control the seasonal weather and tidal patterns, including cyclones, and the decisions are theirs.

Among the most important mythic characters are the *wandjina (wondjina),* well known to the outside world through cave and bark paintings. [*See* Wandjina.] In Ungarinyin territory, these spirits, which can be manifestations of Rainbow Snake, are also sometimes called Ungud. Ungud "brings down spirit babies in the rain to the waterholes" (Elkin, 1930, p. 351). Elkin adds, "The rainbow-serpent is associated with the coming of rain, the increase of natural species and the continuance of mankind." [*See* Ungarinyin Religion.] According to Phyllis M. Kaberry, in northeastern Kimberley, the Rainbow Snake known as Galeru (Kaleru) is also a life saver and sustainer, the embodiment of fertility, "the most sacred of the totemic ancestors and . . . revered as such." He is a lawgiver, responsible for such features of social organization as marriage rules and subsections, and he is "the source of magical power not only in the past but also in the present" (Kaberry, 1937, pp. 194, 200–201; see also pp. 193, 196n). Pearl shells come from him, and in some circumstances it is dangerous to dream of them (p. 206); in the creative era of the Dreaming (the *ngarunggani*), he carried inside him certain foods now subject to life-crisis or age-linked taboos; white stones used for rainmaking also belong to him (p. 207).

Here, as in many cases, the main emphasis is on the Rainbow Snake as a male being: for example, as husband to Kunapipi. [*See* Gadjeri.] In north-central Arnhem Land, Yulunggul is more often thought to be male. His Rainbow Snake identification there, less positive than it is in northeastern Arnhem Land, may have been influenced by the strong Rainbow Snake presence in western Arnhem Land. The Rainbow Snake in the west has several names—Ambidj, for instance, among the Maung of Goulburn Islands and the adjacent mainland, and Ngalyod among Gunwinggu speakers farther inland. Numereji, noted by Baldwin Spencer in 1912 as the Kakadu (Gagadju) name, has not been in use for at least forty years.

Gunwinggu speakers, especially, prefer to speak of the Rainbow Snake only obliquely, not directly by name. One everyday word for "creature(s)," edible or otherwise, is *mai*—provided it is included in the noun class that takes the prefix *na-* (which can be a masculine prefix). When *mai* is used with the indicator *ngal-*, which can be a feminine prefix, it usually refers to the Rainbow Snake. If Gunwinggu speakers had traditionally used written language, they would surely have written *Mai.* As it is, the context and the *ngal-* indicators differentiate it quite plainly. Among other such oblique names, one that depends partly on intonation and context for its maximum effect is Ngaldargid: here the prefix *ngal-* is attached to a word in ordinary use, *dargid*, meaning "living," or "alive." It could be taken in more than its ordinary sense, as in "the living one" or even, perhaps, as "the life-charged one." In other instances, such as in Ngaldargidni, it means that the Rainbow Snake is still there, still living, at a particular site. Hundreds of myths recount the events of the creative era in which the landscape was formed, and the Rainbow Snake plays an active role in the majority of them.

In one traditional western Arnhem Land view the Rainbow Snake is a creator, the first mother. She travels under the sea from the northwest, and on the mainland she eventually gives birth to the people she is carrying inside her. She vomits them out, licking them with her tongue to make them grow and scraping them with mussel shells to make their skin smooth and lighter in color. Some Gunwinggu women have told me,

> No matter what our [social affiliations], we all call her *gagag*, "mother's mother." We live on the ground, she lives underneath, inside the ground and in the water[s]. She urinated fresh water for us to drink, otherwise we would all have died of thirst. She showed us what foods to collect. She vomited the first people, the Dreaming people, who prepared the country for us, and she made us, so that we have minds and sense to understand. She gave us our [social categories and] language, she made our tongues and teeth and throats and breath: she shared her breath with us, she gave us breath, from when we first sat inside our mothers' wombs. . . . She looks a bit like a woman, a bit like a snake.

Although other creators are recognized, and other major figures had specific tasks in the creative era, the Rainbow Snake has a more conspicuous dual role as creator and destroyer.

In myth, and in recent and even present belief, the Rainbow Snake, Ngalyod, can be aroused by too much noise, such as that of a crying child, or by too much shouting, too much interference with the ground, the breaking of a taboo-rock, or a person's failure to take precautions at times when he or she is especially vulnerable (by going near water during pregnancy or menstruation or too soon after childbirth or by allowing a young baby to do so). Gunwinggu women at Oenpelli summed up the expected consequences:

> Far away, she lifts up her head and listens, and she makes straight for that place. A cold wind blows, there is a red glow like a bush fire, a great roaring sound, the ground cracks and moves and becomes soft and wet, water flows rushing, a flood covers the rocks, stones are falling, she comes up like a dream and swallows all those people. She carries them about for a while. Then she vomits their bones, and they turn into stone. They are still there today, as *djang*, eternally present: their spirits remain at [that place]. Let nobody go near [that place], where they came into Dreaming!

There are many variations of this account just as there are many distinctive rock formations in the Arnhem Land escarpment. Most of the named sites throughout the region have their specific *djang* spirits, and in almost all cases the Rainbow Snake was an agent in their transformation (see Berndt and Berndt, 1970).

On the coastal islands and nearby mainland, the Rainbow Snake is more often specifically categorized as male; the inland classification, however, is sometimes acknowledged to be partly a matter of grammatical gender, and the Rainbow Snake is occasionally described as either male or ambisexual. Moreover, in coastal and island contexts, myths often tell of parties of men who track down and kill the Rainbow Snake, cut her (him) open, and try to save the people inside. In one version they cook and eat the Snake to give them strength in the long task of pulling out the living and burying the great numbers of dead. But the Rainbow Snake is timeless, indestructible, and not limited to any one locality. Rainbow Snake manifestations can be almost everywhere or anywhere. For all the people of western Arnhem Land, the Rainbow Snake is traditionally a symbol of monsoon storms, rain, floods, *and* of danger; her (his) formal links with the sphere of the sacred are epitomized in the secret-sacred rites of the Ubar.

The Rainbow Snake as Catalyst and Symbol. Not only healers and law keepers can draw on the Rainbow Snake's power. In one western Arnhem Land myth, a man with a grievance deliberately smashes a taboo rock, knowing that when the Snake comes rushing to swallow (drown) everyone at that site he himself will die along with the people he wants to kill. Some sorcerers were believed to send their own Rainbow Snake familiars on vengeance missions.

In other areas a sorcerer could also supposedly draw on that power, for personal reasons or on someone else's behalf, to avenge a perceived wrong. When sorcery is identified as the cause of death, it is likely to be condemned as a misuse of the powers obtained from the Rainbow Snake and from spirits of the dead (e.g., Kaberry, 1937, p. 211). The argument is that such powers are directed toward selfish ends that are not socially approved, whereas directing them outside the community to avenge the death of one of its own members is assumed to have the community's approval.

Nevertheless, in many respects the Rainbow Snake is a guardian of the status quo as well as a source of power. The terror and dismay of victims in myth are sometimes a consequence of their own carelessness, sometimes a matter of fate or destiny (particularly in western Arnhem Land) or of seemingly harsh treatment for their own ultimate good. The Rainbow Snake is not necessarily a destroyer, to go back to Radcliffe-Brown's comment, but rather a symbol and a reminder of the potentially destructive and overpowering, as well as revitalizing, forces of nature, which can be fearsome as well as splendid. This constellation of cosmic imagery attracts within its orbit a host of other figures not necessarily categorized as Rainbow Snakes. Thus, according to Ursula H. McConnel, in North Queensland the deadly taipan snake is identified with the Rainbow Snake by virtue of its assumed "power . . . as arbiter of life and death" (McConnel, 1957, p. 111).

The Rainbow Snake is Our Mother, but there are other mythic mothers. In some accounts he is Our Father, but there are other mythic fathers (although fewer, perhaps, than mothers). There are other phallic symbols, as well as other storm, flood, cyclone, lightning, thunder, wind, rain, and fertility symbols. Other Snakes and other beings are associated with deep pools, waterfalls, whirlwinds, and rivers. But the rainbow in the sky and the Rainbow Snake on the ground and in the waters are somehow—directly or indirectly, explicitly or potentially—linked to any or all of these from the very beginning of time. Very few elaborate ritual sequences are devoted to the Rainbow Snake alone as a central personage, and he or she has not one localized site but rather many actual or potential sites in all parts of the continent. These are pointers to a frame of beliefs that, though partly open, has as its central core-image a wide-ranging, powerful deity of cosmic proportions, never wholly visible at any one time or place.

BIBLIOGRAPHY

Berndt, Ronald M. *Kunapipi: A Study of an Australian Aboriginal Religious Cult.* Melbourne, 1951. Discusses the Rainbow Snake in the context of rituals and associated myths.

Berndt, Ronald M., and Catherine H. Berndt. *Man, Land and Myth in North Australia: The Gunwinggu People.* Sydney, 1970. Includes discussion of myths and ritual relating to the Rainbow Snake in western Arnhem Land, including the Snake as an agent of destiny or fate in the transformation of the "First People."

Berndt, Ronald M. and Catherine H. Berndt. *The World of the First Australians* (1964). Rev. ed., Adelaide, 1985. Includes a number of references to Rainbow Snakes in the contexts of myth and ritual and of seasonal fertility.

Eliade, Mircea. *Australian Religions: An Introduction.* Ithaca, N.Y., 1973. Includes an overview and discussion of Rainbow Snake material from various parts of the continent, with critical comments and comparisons, see the sections on "The Wondjina and The Rainbow Serpent" (pp. 76–80) and "The Rainbow Serpent," pp. 113–116. Footnotes to the text cover a large range of published items on this topic.

Elkin, A. P. *Aboriginal Men of High Degree* (1945). 2d ed. New York, 1977. The John Murtagh Macrossan Memorial Lectures for 1944. Summarizes material available to that date, including his own earlier field notes and published material, on the initiation of Aboriginal "native doctors" or "clever men" in various parts of Australia.

Kaberry, Phyllis M. *Aboriginal Woman, Sacred and Profane.* London, 1939. Includes useful references to the Rainbow Snake in its (his) sociocultural context, in the Kimberley region of Western Australia, where her field research covered several different "tribal" groups. The book would have a stronger impact on present-day readers if she could have revised and updated it, compacting and reframing her data and her arguments. Unfortunately, she did not live to do that.

Mountford, Charles P. "The Rainbow Serpent Myth of Australia." In *The Rainbow Serpent,* edited by Ira R. Buchler and Kenneth Maddock, pp. 23–97. The Hague, 1978. Includes some interesting items, but needs to be read with caution. It is most useful for the quite lavish illustrations.

Radcliffe-Brown, A. R. "The Rainbow Serpent Myth in South-East Australia." *Oceania* 7 (October–December 1930): 342–347. In addition to Radcliffe-Brown's essay, this issue of *Oceania* includes articles by Ursula H. McConnel on the Rainbow Serpent in North Queensland, by A. P. Elkin on the Rainbow Serpent in northwestern Australia, and by Ralph Piddington on the Water Serpent in Karadjeri mythology. They are short, tentative statements based on some field research, and mostly expanded in later publications. Radcliffe-Brown had an earlier article on the Rainbow Serpent in the *Journal of the Royal Anthropological Institute* 56 (1926): 19–25. McConnel later included the story of "Taipan, the 'Rainbow Serpent'" in *Myths of the Mungkan* (Melbourne, 1957), pp. 111–116. She added that "the most dangerous snakes, and the water-snakes, are associated with the rainbow, and of these Taipan, the deadly brown snake of North Queensland, is the most destructive. It is therefore Taipan who goes up in the rainbow, with his sisters, and causes all these troubles"—storms and cyclonic disturbances that bring "terrors and discomforts," floods and high tides "in the low-lying Gulf County."

Stanner, W. E. H. "On Aboriginal Religion: IV, The Design-Plan of a Riteless Myth." *Oceania* 31 (June 1961): 233–258. One part of Stanner's larger study of Australian Aboriginal religion, this concentrates on a particular myth in the sociocultural setting of the Murinbata and neighboring groups in the Port Keats region, in the northwest of the Northern Territory. He analyzes various versions in some detail, exploring issues of interpretation and explanation in his usual carefully thought-out prose style and includes Aboriginal comments and differences of opinion in his assessment.

CATHERINE H. BERNDT

RĀMA, the hero of the *Rāmāyaṇa,* an epic of ancient India, is the figure most celebrated in literature, music, and art throughout India and Southeast Asia. Valmīki's *Rāmāyaṇa* is the earliest known source of Rāma's heroic biography. Many modern scholars agree that in the central part of Vālmīki's epic Rāma is depicted as a secular hero. The first and the sixth books of the Vālmīki text, however, depict Rāma as an incarnation of Viṣṇu, who comes down to the earth as a human warrior to kill the menacing demon Rāvaṇa. Medieval devotional *Rāmāyaṇas* developed this theme, making Rāma the god himself. In this view, Rāma's wife, Sītā, is the goddess Śrī, and his brother Lakṣmaṇa is perceived as the human incarnation of the snake Ādiśeṣa, on top of whom Viṣṇu sleeps. Rāma and Lakṣmaṇa are perceived as inseparable brothers, identical even in physical appearance except for their skin color: Rāma is blue, Lakṣmaṇa is golden yellow.

Rāma is described as perfect: he is self-controlled, eloquent, majestic, and capable of annihilating all his enemies. Above all, he is truthful and totally devoted to only one wife. Similarly, Sītā is described as the ideal in chastity, devoted to Rāma in thought, word, and deed.

The idealizations of Rāma and Sītā are not totally free of problems, particularly for the authors of *bhakti* texts. Several events described in Vālmīki's text tarnish Rāma's character. For instance, after his wife is abducted by Rāvaṇa, Rāma makes a pact with the monkey king Sugrīva to kill the latter's brother Vālin in return for Sugrīva's help in finding Sītā. To keep his part of the contract, Rāma, hiding behind a tree, kills Vālin. This act violates all norms of justice and valor. A second such incident occurs later, when Rāma wages a battle against Rāvaṇa. Rāma succeeds in killing the demon king, but refuses to take Sītā back because she has lived in another man's house. To prove her innocence, Sītā has to go through the fire ordeal. Later, Rāma again abandons Sītā (who is now pregnant) when the people of Ayodhyā spread vicious talk about her stay in Rāvaṇa's house.

Buddhist texts transform Rāma from a martial hero into a spiritually elevated person. In the *Dāśaratha Jātaka,* Rāma is depicted as a *bodhisattva* figure. In this version there is no mention of Rāvaṇa, and Sītā is not abducted. Indeed, Sītā is depicted as Rāma's sister. The intrigues of their stepmother make their father, Daśaratha, send Rāma, Sītā, and Lakṣmaṇa into the forest for twelve years. At the end of twelve years Rāma returns and is crowned king. He rules with Sītā for sixteen thousand years. Other Jātaka stories also incorporate the Rāma theme, with some variations.

If Buddhists made Rāma a *bodhisattva,* Jains transformed him into one of their sixty-three *śalākāpuruṣas.* In Jain retellings, prominent among which is Vimalasūri's *Paumacariya* (written in Prakrit in the early centuries of the common era), Rāma eats no meat, performs no sacrifices involving animals, and wins his battle by wit rather than by violence. Jain *Rāmāyaṇas* include the story of Rāma up to the birth of his twin sons. Other *Rāmāyaṇa* texts of the Jain community include Hemacandra's *Jaina Rāmāyaṇa* and Nāgacandra's *Rāmacandracarita Purāṇa,* both of the twelfth century. In these versions Rāma eventually enters the Jain order as a monk and finally achieves liberation through heroic mortifications.

Rāma's story is mentioned in a number of Purāṇas. The Śaiva Purāṇas, such as the *Liṅga Purāṇa* and *Śiva Purāṇa,* make Rāma a devotee of Śiva, while the *Bhāgavata Purāṇa* and other Vaiṣṇava Purāṇas describe him as an incarnation of Viṣṇu.

In about the twelfth century, the Vaiṣṇava theology, particularly that of Rāmānuja, gave rise to a cult of Rāma. Numerous Vaiṣṇava commentators on the *Rāmāyaṇa* interpret Rāma as the manifestation of the divine among human beings. In keeping with Vaiṣṇava influences, the *bhakti* Rāmāyaṇas make Rāma the god (Viṣṇu) incarnate exercising his *līlā* ("divine play") with his consort, Sītā. [*See also* Līlā.]

A late fourteenth-century text, *Adhyātma Rāmāyaṇa*, uses the narrative form to provide an *advaita* (nondualist) philosophical orientation to the teachings of the Rāma cult. In this book, presented as a conversation between Śiva and Pārvatī, Rāma is *brahman*, the Absolute itself, which takes a human shape as a pretext to accomplish his divine purposes. Sītā, in this text, is the eternal consort of the Lord. In keeping with this logic, the events leading to the abduction of Sītā, her later abandonment, the birth of her two sons Lava and Kuśa, and the final separation of Sītā and Rāma are significantly altered to represent the reuniting of the couple in Vaikuṇṭha, Viṣṇu's heavenly abode.

Tulsīdās's *Rāmcaritmānas* (composed around 1574) adopts ingenious themes to free Rāma's biography of its problems. [*See also* Tulsīdās.] In this text all the characters of the *Rāmāyaṇa*, including Rāvaṇa and all the demons whom Rāma kills, are described as Rāma's devotees. According to the devotional theory presented here, even an enmity to God is one of the means of reaching God. For human beings, however, the model of devotion is said to be set by Hanumān, the monkey servant of Rāma, who attends upon his master with intense devotion. *Bhakti* Ramayanists also borrow elements of stories about Kṛṣṇa, especially relating to the god's childhood, to describe the child Rāma.

The figure of Rāma remains prominent in many *bhakti* cults. There, devotees believe that chanting Rāma's name and reflecting upon the main incidents of his biography ultimately lead them to reach God.

[*See also* Rāmāyaṇa.]

BIBLIOGRAPHY

Bulcke, Camille. *Rāma-kathā* (1950). 2d ed. Allahabad, 1962.

Goldman, Robert P., trans. *The Rāmāyaṇa of Vālmīki*, vol 1, *Bālakāṇḍa*. Princeton, 1984.

Hill, W. Douglas P., trans. *The Holy Lake of the Acts of Rāma* (1952). Reprint, Oxford, 1971.

Smith, H. Daniel. *Reading the Rāmāyāṇa: A Bibliographic Guide for Students and College Teachers*. Syracuse, N.Y., 1983.

VELCHERU NARAYANA RAO

RAMAḌĀN. *See* Islamic Religious Year *and* Ṣawm.

RAMAKRISHNA (1834/6–1886), Hindu ecstatic and mystic, to many Hindus a "supremely realized self" *(paramahaṃsa)* and an *avatāra*, or incarnation of the divine. Through his disciple Swami Vivekananda, he became a basis for the modern resurgence of Hindu religion; and on a worldwide scale, his "gospel" of the truth of all religions has challenged other, more exclusive teachings.

Life. Born Gadādhar Chatterjee in an isolated village in Bengal, Ramakrishna belonged to a Vaiṣṇava brahman family whose primary deity was the *avatāra* of Viṣṇu, Rāma, although the family also worshiped other deities, such as Śiva and Durgā. The boy's most striking characteristic, one nurtured by the ecstatic devotion *(bhakti)* of the Bengal Vaiṣṇava tradition, was his emotional and aesthetic sensitivity and power; when overwhelmed by beauty and emotion, he would lose consciousness in an ecstatic trance.

His father's death in 1843 increased Ramakrishna's dependence upon his mother, while the role of father figure was assumed by his eldest brother, Rāmkumār, whom he followed to Calcutta in 1852. Rāmkumār became the adviser of a wealthy widow, a Śākta (a devotee of Śakti, the divine power symbolized as the Goddess) who was building a temple to the Divine Mother Kālī. The temple also included shrines to Śiva and to Rādhā and Kṛṣṇa, thus combining all the major strands of Hindu devotional religion. Rāmkumār was appointed the temple's chief priest, and Ramakrishna became priest to Rādhā-Kṛṣṇa. But Rāmkumar's health soon failed, and Ramakrishna was forced to become priest to the Divine Mother shortly before his brother's death in 1856.

Again bereft and overwhelmed by the pain of separation, Ramakrishna developed a frenzied longing for the Divine Mother. Once, as an "intolerable anguish" drove him to the brink of suicide, he lost consciousness in a vision of the Mother, submerged in waves of bliss and light, an experience that only intensified his sense of separation and his self-destructive striving for continual awareness of the Mother. As he later attested, he became "positively insane," spending several years in a state of "divine madness or inebriation" in which visions of various deities came repeatedly, while he was unable even to close his eyes.

In 1861 a wandering renunciant, a middle-aged woman named Yogeśvarī, arrived at the temple. A master of Tantric discipline, she became Ramakrishna's first *guru* and guided him through a remarkable transformation. Tantric ritual seeks to overcome all socially based distinctions, enabling one to realize in a direct, experiential manner that *all* aspects of existence are manifestations of the Divine Mother, the Śakti, the divine productive power. This discipline, which Ramakrishna underwent over a three- or four-year period, had a decisive impact upon his development, overcoming his sense of separation and transforming his self-destructive frenzies into the joyful play *(līlā)* of a child in his Mother's "mansion of mirth," as he came to call the physical universe. This Tantric transformation also provided the structure into which he integrated all of his religious experiences, realizing all divinities as forms of the Mother and desiring to participate fully in all aspects of her divine play. In such a vein, he returned to his Vaiṣṇava heritage, playing with and realizing the divine child Rāma and longing for the divine lover Kṛṣṇa.

In 1864 or 1865, Ramakrishna took instruction from another renunciant named Totāpurī, a master of Śaṅkara's absolute nondualism, which teaches the sole reality of the impersonal Absolute *(nirguṇa-brahman)* to be realized in *nirvikalpa samādhi*, a state of consciousness devoid of all conceptual forms. Ramakrishna was forced to tear his mind from the beloved form of his Divine Mother in order to plunge into this trancelike state, and for more than a year he was so preoccupied with it and so neglectful of his body that he came near to death. According to his biographers, he returned from this state only at the Mother's command and for the welfare of the world. They also maintain that his realization of the nondual Absolute was the culmination of his spiritual quest, providing the basis for his teaching of the truth of all religions as paths leading to this unifying goal. However, Ramakrishna's own teachings present a much different picture, stressing that such withdrawal from the world produces a "knower," or *jñānī*, who is negative, self-centered, dry, and monotonous. He also contrasts such a *jñānī* with his own ideal of perfection, the *vijñānī*, a "complete or full knower" who has realized the reality not only of the impersonal Absolute but also of the world as the play *(līlā)* of the Divine Mother. The following quotation, dated 23 May 1885, typifies his mature perspective upon his exploration of Śaṅkara's Vedānta under Totāpurī: "Once I fell into the clutches of a jñāni, who made me listen to Vedanta for eleven months. But he couldn't altogether destroy the seed of Bhakti in me. No matter where my mind wandered, it would come back to the Divine Mother" (Nikhilananda, 1952, p. 779).

After this experiment, Ramakrishna returned to enjoy life as a child at play within his Mother's world. During this period he expanded his religious experience beyond Hindu religion, first devoting three days to the worship of Allāh and then, some years later, four days to Christ. In both cases, he had visionary realizations that he held to be the same as those he had had of the various Hindu divinities. These brief but intense visions became the experiential basis for his claim that all religions can lead to the same realization of the divine.

In the mid-1870s he began to attract wider notice and gradually became a focal point for a Hindu resurgence among Calcutta's intellectuals, many of whom had been adopting European and Christian ways. His spiritual power and authenticity challenged them to reevaluate the worth of their own heritage. His last years were spent teaching his disciples and a stream of visitors; many of these teachings during 1882–1886 were recorded by one of his disciples.

Teachings. Crucial to Ramakrishna's lasting impact was the articulation of a widely inclusive worldview that integrated the many diverse and often conflicting aspects of Hindu religion and that offered to many the basis for a more harmonious relationship among the religions of the world. A major point of division among Hindus has been that of the relative reality and value of the impersonal Absolute, on the one hand, and of the personal God, seen as the source and ruler of the manifest universe, on the other. Ramakrishna dealt with this dispute by repeatedly asserting the reality and value of both. Striking an ancient Vedic note, he maintained that reality is one and that everything that exists is to be affirmed as a manifestation or form of that One. The formless *brahman* is real, but so is the Divine Mother, or Śakti, at play in the changing world of form. *Brahman* and Śakti are thus two sides of the same reality, "like fire and its power to burn." Ramakrishna thus affirmed the reality of the goal sought by the followers of Śaṅkara's absolute nondualism, that is, *jñāna*, or knowledge of the formless *brahman*, while also making clear that his own ideal was *vijñāna*, or full knowledge, that realizes the reality of both *brahman* and Śakti, of both the eternal *(nitya)* and the play *(līlā)* aspects of the One that becomes all. His own religious emphasis, therefore, was upon loving devotion *(bhakti)* to the personal manifestations of reality in the forms of his Divine Mother and the other deities of the Hindu pantheon and the world's religions.

For Ramakrishna, then, the "gospel" of the potential truth within all religions is not based primarily upon the belief that they all lead to the realization of the same formless Absolute, in which all difference is transcended and negated. Rather, it is based upon Ramakrishna's own experience of the truth and reality of *all* manifest forms, including the different religions and their divinities, as manifestations of the Śakti, or Divine Mother, and upon his conviction that this divine power is at work everywhere. While aware that human ignorance, lust, and greed can obscure this divine presence, he had confidence that a sincere and ardent devotee of any religion would discover the Divine Mother at work, or rather at play, leading her child to herself.

The Ramakrishna Movement. The small band of Ramakrishna's young disciples who took formal vows of renunciation became the swamis or "masters" who formed the core of the Ramakrishna Math. Around this monastic order has formed the Ramakrishna Mission, a broader movement that has spread his gospel throughout India and the world. Swami Vivekananda dramatically launched this mission at the World's Parliament of Religions in Chicago in 1893, and before his premature death in 1902 he had provided the mission with a solid organizational structure largely derived from Western religious models. This mission's emphasis upon social service was thus influenced in part by the example of Christian missions, but it was also directly inspired by Ramakrishna's dynamic and world-affirming Tantric worldview and by his message that the poor, along with all other beings, are manifestations of the Divine Mother and thus are deserving of loving devotion and service.

[*For discussion of the divine play that typifies Ramakrishna's teachings, see* Līlā. *See also the biography of Vivekananda.*]

BIBLIOGRAPHY

Although Ramakrishna left no written works, a by-all-accounts faithful record of his teachings and conversations during 1882–1886 was preserved in Bengali by Mahendranāth Gupta under the pseudonym "M" in *Śrī Śrī Rāmakrishna Kathāmṛita,* 5 vols. (Calcutta, 1897–1932); the most complete and generally reliable English translation is Swami Nikhilananda's *The Gospel of Sri Ramakrishna* (New York, 1952). The standard traditional biographies are Swami Saradanada's *Sri Ramakrishna: The Great Master,* 3d ed., translated by Swami Jagadananda (Madras, 1963), and *Life of Sri Ramakrishna Compiled from Various Authentic Sources,* 2d ed. (Calcutta, 1964). A valuable early and relatively independent biographical account is found in F. Max Müller's *Rāmakrishna: His Life and Sayings* (1899; reprint, New York, 1975). Useful more recent biographies include Ranganath Ramachandra Diwakar's *Paramahansa Sri Ramakrishna,* 2d rev. ed. (Bombay, 1964), and Christopher Isherwood's *Ramakrishna and His Disciples* (New York, 1965). Interpretations stressing the Tantric element in his religious experience and thought are Heinrich Zimmer's *Philosophies of India,* edited by Joseph Campbell (1951; reprint, Princeton, 1969), pp. 560–602; and my essay "The Transformation of Śrī Rāmakrishna," in *Hinduism: New Essays in the History of Religions,* edited by Bardwell L. Smith (Leiden, 1976). Nalini Devdas's *Sri Ramakrishna* (Bangalore, 1966) is helpful for its stress upon the centrality of *vijñāna,* and Harold W. French's *The Swan's Wide Waters: Ramakrishna and Western Culture* (Port Washington, N.Y., 1974) for its bibliographic references and treatment of Swami Vivekananda and the Ramakrishna Movement.

WALTER G. NEEVEL, JR.

RĀMĀNUJA (1017–1137), Hindu philosopher-theologian and the most influential exponent of a theistic interpretation of Vedantic philosophy that opposed the earlier monistic teaching of Śaṅkara. Within the Śrī Vaiṣṇava community Rāmānuja's importance comes from his authoritative exposition of the Vedānta, his leadership of the community in a period of formative growth that brought Tamil devotion together with Sanskrit philosophy and ritual, and, above all, his decisive mediation of divine grace to Śrī Vaiṣṇavas of all subsequent generations.

Accounts of Rāmānuja's life figure prominently in many Tamil and Sanskrit hagiographies. Two purport to be by contemporaries of Rāmānuja, but the earliest that can be dated with certainty was written more than a century after his death. Rāmānuja is presented as the last of the three great *ācārya*s, the first of whom was Nāthamuni, and second, his grandson Yāmuna. Rāmānuja just failed to meet Yāmuna before the latter's death, but during his own lifetime he was able to carry out Yāmuna's unfulfilled wishes for establishing the community on a firm footing. Yāmuna's extant writings do in fact anticipate major tenets of Rāmānuja's philosophy; they also provide a spirited defense of the Pāñcarātra system of ritual, and express in Sanskrit verse some of the sentiments of the earlier Tamil hymns of the Āḻvārs. [*See also the biography of Yāmuna.*]

Rāmānuja had to be instructed in five aspects of Yāmuna's teachings by five of the latter's disciples. The one who was to teach Rāmānuja the secret meaning of the fundamental ritual formula *(mantra)* of the community made Rāmānuja come to see him eighteen times before he swore the bright young convert to silence and disclosed the secret. The very next day, however, Rāmānuja went up onto the temple balcony and shouted down the secret to the Śrī Vaiṣṇavas below. Cheerfully acknowledging that for disobeying his teacher he would go to hell, he added, "But because of their connection with you these souls will be saved!" The teacher was so impressed with Rāmānuja's concern for the welfare of others that he recognized him as Yāmuna's successor and the new leader of the community. This well-known story, along with many other stories in the hagiographies, suggests a gradual shift in emphasis from a secret yoga passed on to a small number of disciples to a more open teaching shared with a community jointly worshiping Lord Viṣṇu and his consorts, incarnate in temple images.

Rāmānuja is responsible for many innovations in the Śrī Vaiṣṇava community. He reorganized the central Śrī Vaiṣṇava temple at Śrīrangam to accommodate his growing band of disciples, traveled widely to other temples to try to persuade them to adopt a more strictly Vaiṣṇava liturgy, and went all the way to Kashmir to consult ancient commentaries. He then composed new commentaries intended to convince brahman scholars all over India of the theistic Vaiṣṇava interpretation of the Sanskrit scriptures.

Much of the latter part of Rāmānuja's life was spent in the Hoysala kingdom to the north where he fled to escape the persecution of the Śaiva-oriented Cōḻa king. Indeed, the earliest "hard evidence" for Rāmānuja's historical reality is a stone carving and inscription showing him with the Hoysala king he is said to have converted from Jainism.

In general, the hagiographers put less emphasis on Rāmānuja's intellectual prowess than on his fervent devotion to Lord Viṣṇu, his life-long efforts to establish Yāmuna's teaching, and his skill in awakening the loyalty and utilizing the distinctive talents of his disciples and scholarly converts. The success of his efforts to persuade many of his own relatives and other brahmans to join the multicaste community of Viṣṇu worshipers had a double effect: the leadership of the community passed still more completely into brahman hands, while Brahmanic Hinduism itself was transformed so that forever after caste ranking, in principle if not always in practice, has been subordinated to the quality of devotion. The story about Rāmānuja's renouncing his wife and becoming an ascetic does not imply that it is necessary in general for devotees to leave their life in society, but in this particular case Rāmānuja's wife stood in the way of his spiritual progress. She was unwilling to subordinate caste ranking to spiritual preeminence and therefore thwarted Rāmānuja's desire to honor his lower-caste teacher.

Nine writings have consistently been attributed to Rāmānuja since the earliest hagiographies and biographical compendia. Three are commentaries on the *Vedānta Sūtra*: the famous *Śrībhāṣya* and the briefer *Vedāntadīpa* and *Vedāntasāra*. One, perhaps his earliest work, is an independent summary of his philosophical position, called the *Vedārthasaṃgraha*. A fifth is his commentary on the *Bhagavadgītā*, in which his mood is at least as devotional as polemical. The remaining four works are very much in the devotional mood and are sufficiently different from the major works that their authenticity has recently been challenged. One is a manual of daily worship called the *Nityagrantha*. The other three are hymns in prose, the *Śaraṇāgatigadya*, *Śrīrangagadya*, and *Vaikuṇṭhagadya*. The first of these has been interpreted as Rāmānuja's own conversation with the Lord during the solemn ceremony of "taking refuge" *(śaraṇāgati)*, and is taken by the tradition to provide a clear warrant for replacing the path of disciplined meditation with the path of "humble approach" or "surrender" *(prapatti)*. (The text itself seems to me not to diverge so radically from the philosophical works as either the renowned teacher Vedānta Deśika or modern critics maintain. In my opinion all these minor works are genuine.)

Rāmānuja's epistemology is hyperrealistic. The first two sources of knowledge are perception and inference, and they are trustworthy notwithstanding general human subjection to "beginningless ignorance." Knowledge is always of the real, even in dreams, and error is a disordered perception or faulty inference concerning what is really there. The third source of knowledge is the testimony of scripture, or more strictly, *śabda* ("eternal sound"), which helps to establish much that is uncertain on the basis of sense perception and inference, notably the existence and nature of the ultimate reality *(brahman)*, who is also the Supreme Person and personal Lord. In explicit contrast to Śaṅkara's doctrine of two levels of truth in scripture, Rāmānuja maintains that scriptural texts are all at the same level; apparent discrepancies or contradictions must therefore be resolved without placing one side or the other on a lower level. The emphasis on unity in some texts and duality or plurality in others is resolved by noting the synthetic principle in a third group of texts: radical distinction and inseparable connection coexist in the relation between the self (whether finite or infinite) and the body that it ensouls, and likewise in the relation between a substance and its mode.

Scripture testifies to a supreme self who is the inner self of finite selves. Thus the finite self is to the supreme self as the material body is to the finite self. This is Rāmānuja's celebrated doctrine of *śarīra-śarīri-bhāva*: the relation of the self to the body, which corresponds to the relation between grammatical subject and predicate adjective, or substance and mode. It is the special characteristic of finite selves to be a mode in relation to God and substance in relation to material things, which are their bodies or instruments. The entire finite universe of souls and material bodies is also the body of God. Thus God is the only ultimately substantial reality, and reality may be viewed as *viśiṣṭādvaita* (the later philosophical label for this school of Vedānta, not used by Rāmānuja): the nondual reality of that which is (internally) distinguished.

Rāmānuja defines the self-body relation in terms of

three subordinate relations, those between the support and the supported, the controller and the controlled, and the owner *(śeṣī)* and the owned *(śeṣa)*. It is the third relation that is most distinctive, for ownership is understood to include the obligation of the slave to serve the master and the confident expectation that the master will look after the slave. In each case it is the Supreme Self who provides the defining instance; the finite self's relation to its body is only a limited approximation of complete supporting, controlling, and owning its body.

Rāmānuja assumes that there are three kinds of reality: nonsentient matter *(acit),* sentient but finite selves *(cit),* and the Lord (Īśvara), who is the Supreme Self. The world consists of material bodies controlled by finite selves. While the particular bodies are temporary, the basic matter of which they consist and the finite selves that they embody have no beginning in time. The bondage of many finite selves to "beginningless *karman*" causes their repeated return to the world in new bodies, but the entire world of material bodies and embodied souls is intended to glorify God, that is, to express in the finite realm his power and goodness. Those who escape the ignorance induced by *karman* can see that the finite world is *now,* along with God's infinite world, a realm of glory *(vibhūti).* Despite his horror of linking God with anything defiling in the material world, Rāmānuja insists that the entire finite universe is the body of God.

Finite selves and the Supreme Self are similar but not identical in their essential natures: both have consciousness and bliss as their essential characteristics, but the finite self is limited in its power and extent whereas the Supreme Self is all-powerful and all-pervasive. Moreover, finite selves still "bound" to the material world have their secondary consciousness (that which they *possess* rather than *are*) obscured by the ignorance produced by "beginningless *karman.*"

The Vedānta is concerned with the proper knowledge of reality in order to find liberation from this bondage. In Rāmānuja's interpretation of Vedānta both performance of social and ritual duties and knowledge of reality are auxiliary means in seeking liberation, but the chief means is *bhakti* (devotion), a calling to mind of God's attributes with an attitude that should become as constant as the flow of oil, as vivid and immediate as sense perception, and so emotionally gripping that the devotee feels unable to live without the pervading presence of God.

The ultimate reality thus "remembered" in devotion is not an abstract principle but that most concrete and substantial reality who is the personal Lord, the Lord who escapes all self-confident seeking by finite selves but who chooses to become available to those who acknowledge their dependence. The Lord descends and condescends out of his great compassion to save, but those who most deeply feel their need for God's presence learn the deepest secret: the Lord also needs them. This emphasis on God's initiative along with the surprising secret that the Lord who owns everything needs his devotees' love leads to a second way of talking about the salvific process that is quite different from the first. Instead of loving devotion being the means to attaining the Lord's presence, the Lord is the means to enabling devotion that is a mutual participation of infinite and finite selves. The end has become the means, and the means has become the end. Rāmānuja seems to be able to move back and forth between the older concept of devotion as means and the implications of a radical doctrine of grace.

A century after his death, Rāmānuja was understood by his followers to have taught surrender *(prapatti)* as a preferable alternative to the path of devotion, and they were beginning to differ as to whether some human response to grace was part of this surrender. That difference would gradually split the community in two, but for both groups it was Rāmānuja's own act of surrender that gave the assurance of divine grace for all his followers, a grace then mediated through the generations by a succession of teachers. It is as if they continue to say to Rāmānuja what he is purported to have said to the teacher whose secret he made public: "Because of their [our] connection with you their [our] souls will be saved."

[*See also* Vedānta; Śrī Vaiṣṇavas; *and* Vaiṣṇavism, *article on* Pāñcarātras.]

BIBLIOGRAPHY

Buitenen, J. A. B. van., trans. *Rāmānuja's Vedārthasaṃgraha.* Poona, 1956.

Buitenen, J. A. B. van. *Rāmānuja on the Bhagavadgītā* (1953). Reprint, Delhi, 1968.

Carman, John B. *The Theology of Rāmānuja.* New Haven, 1974.

Lester, Robert C. *Rāmānuja on the Yoga.* Madras, 1976.

Lott, Eric J. *God and the Universe in the Vedāntic Theology of Rāmānuja.* Madras, 1976.

Raghavachar, S. S. *Introduction to the Vedarthasangraha of Sree Ramanujacharya.* Mangalore, 1957.

Raghavachar, S. S. *Śrī Rāmānuja on the Gītā.* Mangalore, 1969.

Yamunacharya, M. *Rāmānuja's Teachings in His Own Words.* Bombay, 1963.

JOHN B. CARMAN

RĀMĀYAṆA. Along with the *Mahābhārata,* the *Rāmāyaṇa* is the most influential epic of India. Attributed to the sage Vālmīki, it is a poem of about fifty thousand lines narrating in Sanskrit the tale of Rāma and his wife, Sītā. The core of the epic is the story surrounding Rāma's birth, his marriage to Sītā, his exile, Sītā's abduction by the demon king Rāvaṇa, the battle leading to the killing of the demon, and the recovery of Sītā.

The origins of the epic are obscure and beyond definitive recovery. The epic is available in three recensions—the Northeastern, the Northwestern, and the Southern. The recensions vary considerably; approximately a third of the text of each is not common to the other two. However, the variations, substantial as they are, do not alter the main theme of the epic.

The *Rāmāyaṇa* consists of seven books called *kāṇḍas*. The story contained in these seven books is divided into two unequal parts, the first part consisting of the first six books and the second part covered by the seventh book. The content of these books is too complicated to capture in a summary, but the main story-line is recounted here.

Daśaratha, the king of Ayodhyā, is childless. He performs a sacrifice to obtain sons. At that time the gods, who are disturbed by the atrocities of the ten-headed demon Rāvaṇa, pray to the god Viṣṇu for protection. Viṣṇu responds to their prayers and decides to incarnate himself as a human being. He will be born as Rāma, son of Daśaratha. At the end of the sacrifice Daśaratha's three wives give birth to four sons, Queen Kausalyā to Rāma, Queen Kaikeyī to Bharata, Queen Sumitrā to Lakṣmaṇa and Śatrughna. Rāma is the favorite son of the king, and Lakṣmaṇa is devoted to his elder brother Rāma. While the boys are still young, the sage Viśvāmitra takes Rāma and Lakṣmaṇa to the forest and instructs them in the use of magic weapons.

King Janaka of Videha, who has the mighty bow of Śiva in his possession, declares that the prince who can wield the weapon will be eligible to marry his beautiful daughter Sītā. Rāma wields the weapon and with his superior strength breaks it, then marries Sītā.

In Ayodhyā King Daśaratha decides to have Rāma installed as prince regent. The decision, which was made while Kaikeyī's son Bharata was away, causes Kaikeyī, on the advice of her maidservant, to rebel against the king. Kaikeyī insists that Bharata should be declared prince regent and that Rāma should be exiled to the forest for fourteen years. The king, who owes Kaikeyī two wishes, is compelled to obey her desire. Obeying his father's command, Rāma leaves the capital city accompanied by his wife, Sītā, and his brother Lakṣmaṇa. Daśaratha dies from the pain of separation from his most beloved son.

In the forest a demoness, Śūrpaṇakhā, the sister of Rāvaṇa, attempts to seduce Rāma. Frustrated in her efforts, she attempts to kill Sītā. Rāma punishes Śūrpaṇakhā by having her ears and nose mutilated. Śūrpaṇakhā complains to her mighty brother. Enraged by Rāma's action and attracted by Sītā's beauty, Rāvaṇa decides to abduct Sītā. Rāvaṇa sends his subject Mārīca to lure Rāma away. Mārīca assumes the form of a golden deer and attracts the attention of Sītā. Consenting to her request, Rāma chases the deer, leaving Lakṣmaṇa to guard Sītā. Sītā persuades Lakṣmaṇa to go in protection of his brother. Once Sītā is alone, the demon Rāvaṇa appears at her doorstep dressed as an ascetic and carries her off by force.

When Rāma learns that Rāvaṇa has abducted Sītā, he secures the friendship of the monkey king Sugrīva. Sugrīva's minister Hanumān flies across the ocean to the island of Laṅkā and locates Sītā in a forest grove. Rāma, aided by the monkey army, besieges Laṅkā, defeats Rāvaṇa's armies, kills Rāvaṇa, and brings Sītā back.

The seventh book of the *Rāmāyaṇa* describes how Rāma abandons Sītā, this time by his own choice. The inhabitants of Ayodhyā doubt the purity of Sītā's character because she has lived in another man's house. Sītā, now pregnant, is given shelter by the sage Vālmīki. In the sage's hermitage, Sītā gives birth to two sons, Lava and Kuśa. Vālmīki composes the story of Rāma and teaches the boys to sing the story.

In Ayodhyā, Rāma begins a sacrifice that Vālmīki attends with the twin boys. The boys sing the epic for Rāma, who then discovers that the boys are his own sons and that Sītā is alive. Vālmīki announces before the assembled crowd that Sītā is pure and without fault. Rāma accepts Lava and Kuśa as his sons. Sītā appears before the guests and prays that her mother, the earth, receive her as a proof of her purity. The earth breaks open, and Sītā is received on a golden throne. Rāma, saddened by the loss of his queen, gives the kingdom to his sons and returns to the world of the gods.

According to tradition, the *Rāmāyaṇa* is believed to belong to the legendary *tretayuga*, the second of the four mythic ages. Historically, the date of the epic is a matter of considerable controversy and nearly impossible to fix with certainty. Extensive scholarly work on the linguistic, stylistic, sociological, geographical, and political data narrows down the possible dates of the epic as we have it now to the period between 750 and 500 BCE.

Western scholarly opinion is fairly unanimous in agreement with Hermann Jacobi's finding that substantial parts of the first and seventh books of Vālmīki's version are later additions to the core of the five books. In the Hindu scholarly tradition, however, it is believed that the epic is the first poem *(ādikāvya)* and is composed by a single poet, Vālmīki, who is called the first poet *(ādikavi)*. Thus it is believed to predate the other Indian epic, the *Mahābhārata*. Comparative dating of these two epics is a tangled issue since both the epics evolved together, borrowing extensively from each other. Although no evidence is available to establish Vālmīki as a historical personage, the stylistic evidence suggests that the central core of the five books of the *Rāmāyaṇa* are most likely to be the work of a single author. [*See also* Vālmīki.]

The origins of the Vālmīki text are most likely to be folk oral narratives of the hero Rāma, a prince of the eastern Indian state of Kosala. Vālmīki's version itself has been sung orally for centuries by bards, known as *kuśīlava*s, before being set down in writing. Secular and heroic in quality, the Vālmīki version depicts the story of a perfect hero, steadfast in virtues and devoted to the control of his passions. The secular, heroic, and tragic messages of the *Rāmāyaṇa* have continued to influence generations of poets like Bhāsa, Kālidāsa, and Bhavabhūti, as well as a number of poets from the regional languages of India.

A major shift in the interpretation of the *Rāmāyaṇa* took place during the Middle Ages. Rāma was then identified as an *avatāra* (incarnation) of Viṣṇu. The story of Rāma was read as an allegory of the conflict between good and evil in which the good always succeeds under the leadership of God. Prominent among such devotional *(bhakti) Rāmāyaṇa*s is Kamban's *Irāmavatāram* (twelfth century), in Tamil. A further development in the devotionalization of the *Rāmāyaṇa* becomes popular with Tulsīdās's *Rāmcaritmānas*, in the sixteenth century. In Tulsīdās all the characters of the *Rāmāyaṇa*, including the demon Rāvaṇa, are Rāma's devotees. All the conflicts of the story and its tragedy are eliminated to produce a harmonious, balanced, lyrical world of God and his devotees. [*See also* Tulsīdās.]

In addition to literary *Rāmāyaṇa*s, there are a number of folk/oral versions all over India with significant variations in emphasis and messages. Folk versions of the *Rāmāyaṇa* sung by women emphasize the role of Sītā and portray her as more independent than she is in the literary versions.

[*See also* Rāma *and* Mahābhārata.]

BIBLIOGRAPHY

Bulcke, Camille. *Rāma-kathā* (1950). 2d ed. Allahabad, 1962.

Goldman, Robert P., trans. *The Rāmāyaṇa of Vālmīki*, vol. 1, *Bālakāṇḍa*. Princeton, 1984.

Jacobi, Hermann. *Das Rāmāyaṇa: Geschichte und Inhalt nebst Concordanz der gedruckten Recensionen*. Bonn, 1893.

Raghavan, V., ed. *The Rāmāyaṇa Tradition in Asia*. New Delhi, 1980.

Shastri, Hari Prasad, trans. *The Rāmāyaṇa of Vālmīki*. 3 vols. London, 1962.

Smith, H. Daniel. *Reading the Rāmāyaṇa: A Bibliographic Guide for Students and College Teachers*. Syracuse, N.Y., 1983.

VELCHERU NARAYANA RAO

RAMBAM. *See* Maimonides, Moses.

RAMBAN. *See* Nahmanides, Moses.

RAM MOHAN ROY. *See* Roy, Ram Mohan.

RASHI, acronym (RaSHI) of Rabbi Shelomoh ben Yitsḥaq of Troyes (1040–1105), the most influential Jewish commentator on the Bible and the Babylonian Talmud. Nearly nine hundred years after his death, Rashi's writings are still the standard commentaries for any serious student of the Hebrew Bible or the Babylonian Talmud, and new scholarly studies of his achievement continue to be published.

Rashi was born in Troyes, the political center of the county of Champagne, in northeastern France, but outside the close-knit rabbinical circles of the founding families of German Jewry. After pursuing his preliminary studies in Troyes, including studies with his father, he married and around 1060 traveled to the *yeshivot* of the Rhineland, then the most advanced in northwestern Europe. He studied there with the two heads of the Mainz academy, Ya'aqov ben Yaqar, whom he considered his most important teacher of Talmud and Bible, and after the master's death in 1064, his successor, Yitsḥaq ben Yehudah, for a short time. Almost immediately, he went to Worms to study with Yitsḥaq ha-Levi whose academy was superseding the Mainz school in advanced Talmud instruction. By the end of the decade he was back home, but he continued to correspond with Yitsḥaq ben Yehudah and Yitsḥaq ha-Levi.

Rashi attracted his own students in Troyes, and he served as the local rabbinical authority there. Though he wrote answers *(responsa)* to hundreds of questions sent to him, he was not a professional rabbi. He made a living some other way; however, the often repeated assertion that he was a vintner has been disputed.

Rashi had no sons. His well-educated daughters married learned men; their sons became eminent rabbinical authorities. Yokheved married Me'ir ben Shemu'el, and among their four sons were Shemu'el ben Me'ir (known by the acronym Rashbam), one of the most important commentators on the Hebrew Bible and developer of the literal method of interpretation, and Ya'aqov ben Me'ir (known as Rabbenu Tam), who dominated the new scholastic method of Talmud study in the form of additions *(tosafot)* of questions and answers to his grandfather's running gloss. Rashi's daughter Miryam married Yehudah ben Natan, whose commentary to the end of *Makkot* is printed in the standard editions of the Babylonian Talmud. In this way, Rashi created his own French rabbinical family elite.

Rashi lived through the devastation of Jewish rabbinical leadership in the Rhenish academies of Mainz and Worms caused by the First Crusade riots of 1096, and some traces of early anti-Crusade polemic have been detected in his writings. Thus he says that the Bible begins with the creation of the world and not with the first law given to the Jewish people (*Ex.* 12:1), in order to teach that the Land of Israel belongs to the Jewish people, and not to the Christians or Muslims who were fighting over it in the First Crusade. Why? Since God created the world, the entire earth belongs to him, including the Land of Israel, which he first gave to the nations of Canaan and then gave to Israel (Rashi on *Gn.* 1:1).

Rashi's major achievement was his composition of comprehensive running commentaries to most of the Hebrew Bible and Babylonian Talmud. Of the biblical commentaries attributed to him, those to *Job* from 40:25, *Ezra, Nehemiah,* and *Chronicles* are not his but may be based on his approach. Of the Talmudic commentaries, those to *Ta'anit, Mo'ed Qaṭan, Nedarim, Nazir,* and *Horayot* are not his. The gloss he began to *Bava' Batra'* was finished by his grandson Shemu'el ben Me'ir, and the one to *Makkot* was completed by his student and son-in-law Yehudah ben Natan.

In his Talmud commentary, Rashi focused on each difficult term or passage in sequence and supplied punctuation or logical transitions that were not clear from the text itself. He used his profound knowledge of the Talmud and Jewish law to help the student by briefly introducing the general topic that the text is about to discuss in detail, and he provided reasons for particular laws and mentioned historical conditions in ancient times. At times, he indicated that he preferred a particular version of a passage, and later copyists corrected the text so that there is no difference between the Talmud and Rashi's correction. His commentary became widely used from the beginning of the thirteenth century and has been printed with the Talmud from the first editions to this day.

Although Rashi based about three fourths of his commentary to the Pentateuch on earlier Midrashic works, he integrated into his work a newer method of Jewish biblical exegesis that focused on the plain meaning of the text. When an ambiguity in the text created the possibility of different interpretations, Rashi explicitly contrasted a straightforward textual interpretation *(peshuṭo shel miqra')*—which could be arrived at through (1) a literal reading of the text, (2) a contextual approach, or (3) the use of a *midrash* that explains the plain meaning of the words as written—to an interpretation which he paraphrased from a Midrashic source. This dual method of interpretation is Rashi's most characteristic innovation, but it has sometimes been misunderstood. Whereas later twelfth-century French commentators like Shemu'el ben Me'ir and Yosef ben Yitsḥaq (Bekhor Shor) developed a method of interpretation based on the systematic inquiry into the literal meaning of the text *(peshaṭ)* in preference to one based on earlier rabbinical homilies *(derash)*, Rashi himself did not explicitly distinguish between the two methods of reading; he did not use the terms *peshaṭ* and *derash* and so certainly did not prefer the former. In his glosses to the other books of the Bible, such as *Isaiah* and *Psalms,* scholars have detected explicit or implied anti-Christian polemics. While there is no evidence that Rashi read Latin, he could have heard many christological arguments and arguments derived from scriptural proof texts from Christian neighbors and introduced counterinterpretations for the benefit of his students.

From Rashi's commentaries and *responsa,* it is obvious that Jews and Christians lived in the same towns, walked the same streets, bought their household goods in the same markets, and paid for them with the same coinage. Although the medieval fairs at Troyes began only in the twelfth century, the town was already a manufacturing center and commercial depot in Rashi's day, and many travelers passed through. His commentaries include remarks about the city of Venice and about German currency. He observed firsthand in Troyes embroidery of silk with gold, soldering and engraving techniques, and the manufacture of parchment. He also comments about popular customs and street life: some women pierced their ears; butchers sometimes used their hands for scales, putting the meat in one hand and a weight in the other; the well-to-do slept in four-poster beds or else had rods constructed to support a tentlike curtain to keep flies away when they slept.

In addition to noting hundreds of such concrete references to everyday life, Rashi uses approximately a thousand medieval French terms or phrases to explain or illustrate Hebrew or Aramaic terms; these lexical items, written in phonetic Hebrew characters, have preserved important evidence about linguistic characteristics of eleventh-century French.

Apart from its value as a source for Jewish intellectual history and early French, Rashi's biblical commentary also influenced Christian biblical exegesis. Already in the twelfth century, Hugh of Saint-Victor and other Victorine scholars in Paris were interested in the Hebrew text and reflect familiarity with Rashi. But it was especially the Franciscan Nicholas of Lyra (c. 1270–1349), writing in Paris at the very time that a chair in Hebrew had been established in accordance with the Council of Vienne (1312), who made systematic use of Rashi's biblical commentary in his own running gloss on the whole Bible, the *Postilla litteralis*.

The immense influence of Rashi's commentaries in shaping the religious culture of European Judaism still awaits proper historical treatment. As a bridge between the Rhenish center of Jewish learning in Mainz and Worms and the newer dialectical methods of Bible and Talmud study that were developed in the twelfth century based on Rashi's own commentaries, his place in Jewish cultural history is secure. Through Nicholas of Lyra, Rashi also influenced subsequent Christian Hebraists down to Martin Luther and beyond.

[*For discussion of Rashi's place in the history of biblical interpretation, see* Biblical Exegesis, *article on* Jewish Views. *See also* Tosafot, *which discusses the commentary on Rashi written by Jewish scholars primarily of the twelfth and thirteenth centuries.*]

BIBLIOGRAPHY

Rashi's commentary to the Pentateuch has been translated into English by Morris Rosenbaum and Abraham M. Silbermann as *Pentateuch with Targum Onkelos, Haphtaroth and Prayers for the Sabbath, and Rashi's Commentary*, 5 vols. (London, 1929–1934).

An important interpretive sketch about him is Alexander Marx's "Rashi," in his *Essays in Jewish Biography* (Philadelphia, 1947) and the most comprehensive, if dated, biography is still Maurice Liber's *Rashi*, translated by Adele Szold (Philadelphia, 1906).

Rashi's influence on Christian Bible commentaries in the early Middle Ages is discussed in Beryl Smalley's *The Study of the Bible in the Middle Ages*, 2d ed. (1951; Notre Dame, 1964) and for the later period in Herman Hailperin's *Rashi and the Christian Scholars* (Pittsburgh, 1963). An illustration of Rashi as anti-Christian polemicist is Michael A. Signer's "King/Messiah: Rashi's Exegesis of Psalm 2," *Prooftexts* 3 (September 1983): 273–278.

Esra Shereshevsky's *Rashi: The Man and His World* (New York, 1982) is of particular interest for his compilation of data from Rashi's oeuvre about everyday life.

Rashi's methodology as Bible exegete is discussed in Benjamin J. Gelles's *Peshat and Derash in the Exegesis of Rashi* (Leiden, 1981) and assessed in a review essay by Sarah Kamin in the *Journal of Jewish Studies* 36 (Spring 1985): 126–130, based on her own sophisticated study of this tricky problem which she has summarized in "Rashi's Exegetical Categorization with Respect to the Distinction between Peshat and Derash," *Immanuel* 11 (1980): 16–32.

Ivan G. Marcus

RASHĪD RIḌĀ, MUḤAMMAD (1865–1935), Arab Muslim theologian and journalist. Born in a village near Tripoli, Lebanon, Riḍā had a traditional religious education. The writings of the pan-Islamic thinker Jamāl al-Dīn al-Afghānī and the Egyptian theologian Muḥammand ʿAbduh opened his mind to the need to reform Islam. In 1897 he settled in Cairo and from then until his death published a periodical, *Al-manār* (The Lighthouse), devoted to explaining the problems of Islam in the modern world.

His starting point was that of ʿAbduh, whom he regarded as his master: the need for Muslims to live virtuously in the light of a reformed understanding of Islam. That understanding involved drawing a distinction between the doctrines of Islam and its social morality. Doctrines and forms of worship were unchanging, laid down by the Qurʾān and the practice of the prophet Muḥammad and the first generation of his followers (the *salaf*, hence the name *salafīyah*, often used for this type of thought). He opposed what he regarded as innovations, in particular the beliefs and practice of later Ṣūfīs, and in his later years drew close to the Wahhābī point of view.

Riḍā believed that, apart from some specific injunctions, the Qurʾān and the practice of the Prophet gave only general principles of social morality and law; their implications had to be drawn out by competent Muslims in the light of circumstances. Blind imitation of past teaching led to stagnation and weakness; the changed circumstances of the present age made a new interpretation necessary, and its guiding principle should be *maṣlaḥah* (interest), a concept accepted in traditional legal theory but broadened by Riḍā so as to mean social utility. By using this principle, his aim was to create a body of modern Islamic law on which the different legal schools could agree; to this end he published a large number of rulings on hypothetical cases raising important questions of law.

Riḍā was much concerned with the question of political authority. He believed it should be delegated by the community to a combination of just rulers and men of religious learning, trained to deal with the problems of the modern world; there was a need for a caliph, not as universal temporal ruler but as the final and generally accepted authority on law. He emphasized the central position of the Arabs in the Muslim world; Arabic was the language of the Qurʾān and the religious sciences, and without the Arabs Islam could not be healthy. He played some part in the Arab nationalist movement, but the influence of *Al-manār* spread far beyond the Arab world, and some of its ideas were adopted by later movements aiming to restore Islam as the moral norm of modern society.

BIBLIOGRAPHY

General summaries of Riḍā's ideas can be found in my work, *Arabic Thought in the Liberal Age, 1798–1939,* 2d ed. (Cambridge, 1983), chaps. 9 and 11, and in Hamid Enayat's *Modern Islamic Political Thought* (London, 1982). A fuller treatment is that of Malcolm H. Kerr in his *Islamic Reform: The Political and Legal Theories of Muḥammad ʿAbduh and Rashīd Riḍā* (Berkeley, 1966). Jacques Jomier's *Le commentaire coranique du Manâr: Tendances modernes de l'exégèse coranique en Egypte* (Paris, 1954) studies the commentary on the Qur'ān which ʿAbduh and Riḍā published jointly in *Al-manār.* Riḍā's treatise on the caliphate has been translated into French and annotated by Henri Laoust in *Le califat dans la doctrine de Rašīd Riḍā* (Beirut, 1938). Of his other works, the biography of ʿAbduh, *Ta'rīkh al-ustādh al-imām al-shaykh Muḥammad ʿAbduh,* vol. 1 (Cairo, 1931), is full of information about the Islamic reformers. His legal rulings have been collected by Ṣalāḥ al-Dīn al-Munajjid and Yūsuf Q. Khūrī in *Fatāwā al-imām Muḥammad Rashīd Riḍā,* 5 vols. (Beirut, 1970–1971).

ALBERT HOURANI

RASTAFARIANS. *See* Caribbean Religions, *article on* Afro-Caribbean Religions.

RAUSCHENBUSCH, WALTER (1861–1918), Baptist clergyman and intellectual leader of the Social Gospel movement in American Protestantism. Rauschenbusch was born in Rochester, New York, received most of his schooling there, and taught at the Rochester Theological Seminary from 1897 to 1918. His father, August, a highly educated Westphalian Lutheran pastor, had gone to Missouri in 1846 as a missionary to German immigrants. After becoming a Baptist, August Rauschenbusch headed the Rochester seminary's program for German-speaking clergy. He bequeathed to his son an enduring appreciation of both evangelical piety and the Western cultural tradition.

Following his graduation from the Rochester Theological Seminary in 1886, young Rauschenbusch became pastor of the Second German Baptist Church in a tenement section of New York City. Here he was stirred by the hardships of the people: "I saw how men toiled all their life . . . and at the end had almost nothing to show for it; how strong men begged for work and could not get it in the hard times; how little children died" (*The Social Gospel in America, 1870–1920,* p. 265). He realized that his training had not equipped him to understand the powerful social, economic, and intellectual currents sweeping through American life; nor had his conservative seminary professors offered him a religious perspective adequate to cope with those currents. During his eleven-year pastorate in New York City he undertook an intense schedule of reading, discussion, and writing, much of it in collaboration with colleagues in two new organizations he helped to direct, the Baptist Congress and the Brotherhood of the Kingdom. Rauschenbusch received intellectual stimulation from a variety of authors, notably the American economist Henry George, the English theologians Frederick D. Maurice and Frederick W. Robertson, the Russian novelist Leo Tolstoy, the Italian patriot Giuseppe Mazzini, and the German sociologist Albert Schäffle.

Rauschenbusch returned to the Rochester Theological Seminary in 1897 as professor of New Testament; from 1902 until his death he was professor of church history. More than any other person in the United States, he provided a theological undergirding for the growing numbers of laity and clergy who sought to mold social and economic institutions according to Christian principles. His chief books were *Christianity and the Social Crisis* (1907), *Prayers of the Social Awakening* (1910), *Christianizing the Social Order* (1912), *The Social Principles of Jesus* (1916), and *A Theology for the Social Gospel* (1917).

Central in Rauschenbusch's message were the affirmations that the churches must recognize afresh that the kingdom of God had been Jesus' key teaching, that God intends this kingdom to reach into every realm of life, and that the competitiveness and selfishness fostered by capitalism must be opposed by persons committed to fulfilling God's beneficent will for humanity.

In the decades following Rauschenbusch's death many churches continued to address the tasks of social criticism and reconstruction, albeit not with the single-mindedness and effect for which he and other Social Gospel leaders had wished. Some influential religious thinkers in the middle third of the twentieth century judged Rauschenbusch's theological perspective to have been colored excessively by the optimism of his era. Recently, his thought has been viewed more appreciatively by persons who find richly provocative such Rauschenbuschian themes as the centering of Christianity in Jesus' proclamation of God's reign, the historical and social character of sin and salvation, and the complementarity of personal piety and social activism.

BIBLIOGRAPHY

The information contained in Dores R. Sharpe's *Walter Rauschenbusch* (New York, 1942) makes this an indispensable volume. However, it offers little historical and theological perspective, and significant gaps exist in Sharpe's presentation of Rauschenbusch's life. Perceptive analyses and important portions of Rauschenbusch's writings can be found in *The Social Gospel in America, 1870–1920,* edited by Robert T. Handy (New York, 1966). See also "Sources of American Spirituality," in *Walter Rauschenbusch: Selected Writings,* edited by Winthrop S. Hudson (Mahwah, N.J., 1984).

PAUL M. MINUS

RAV (lit., "rabbi"), epithet of Abba' bar Ayyvu (c. 155–c. 247), a first-generation Babylonian amora. Rav helped lay the foundations for rabbinic Judaism in Babylonia. He studied in Palestine with his uncle Ḥiyya' and with Yehudah ha-Nasi', from whom he reportedly received authorization to render decisions in many areas. These contacts gave him a rich reservoir of teachings, self-reliance, and the freedom to go beyond tannaitic traditions.

Later Talmudic circles considered his resettlement in Babylonia, conventionally dated to 217, a turning point in Jewish history, one presaged by natural omens (B.T., *Shab.* 108a). First dwelling in Nehardea, a city on the Euphrates River, he assisted other rabbis and served as a market administrator (J.T., *B.B.* 5.11[5]; 15a–b). He later moved to Sura, a town hitherto said to lack a rabbinical presence. There he gathered a circle of students but probably did not head an academy, as was anachronistically claimed by some post-Talmudic chronicles (Goodblatt, 1975).

Rav's prestige was enhanced by a claim of Davidic descent and by his daughter's marriage into the exilarchic family. He was perceived as a master of wisdom and practical advice (B.T., *Pes.* 113a), able to read natural signs and endowed with the power to hurl curses to maintain respect (B.T., *Meg.* 5b).

In explaining the Mishnah, he drew on Palestinian sources and patterned his teachings after the Mishnah's style and phraseology even where he disputed it (Epstein, 1964). Though later Talmudic circles considered Rav especially authoritative in ritual matters, his dicta affected the way amoraim approached issues in general. Indeed, his comments, with those of Shemu'el the amora, were subsequently reworked to form a structure around which later teachings were organized; thereby they eventually became the literary rubric for the *gemara'* (Bokser, 1980).

Rav stands out for his wide-ranging theological interests. He emphasized that God rules with supremacy and that he benevolently and with knowledge created the world (B.T., *Ḥag.* 12a). The latter belief was expressed in a Ro'sh ha-Shanah prayer, *teqi'ata' devei Rav,* selected or edited by Rav, which stresses creation (J.T., *'A.Z.* 1.2; Neusner, 1966). Describing the future, Rav distinctively suggested that the righteous will experience as a reward a spiritual nourishing analogous to what the mystic visionaries of God experience in their lifetime (Chernus, 1982). He often emphasized the importance of Torah study and the respect due to Torah students (B.T., *Ta'an.* 24a, *San.* 93b). Rav made the fulfillment of messianic hopes dependent on human repentance and good deeds (B.T., *San.* 97b). He reportedly asserted that the commandments were designed to purify *(tsaref)* people, in the sense of refining or improving (*Gn. Rab.* 44.1). His ideas, teachings, and activities thus started the process of transforming tannaitic Judaism in Babylonia into a wider social movement.

[*See also* Amoraim.]

BIBLIOGRAPHY

A comprehensive treatment and bibliography of Rav and his teachings can be found in Jacob Neusner's *A History of the Jews in Babylonia,* 5 vols. (Leiden, 1966–1970), esp. vol. 2, passim. Valuable works in Hebrew are Jacob Samuel Zuri's *Rav* (Jerusalem, 1925); Jacob N. Epstein's *Mavo' le-nusaḥ ha-Mishnah,* 2 vols. (1948; reprint, Jerusalem, 1964), pp. 166–211, on Rav's attitude to tannaitic traditions and the Mishnah; and E. S. Rosenthal's "Rav," in *Sefer Ḥanokh Yalon* (Jerusalem, 1963), pp. 281–337, on Rav's lineage and background. Works in English that include discussion of Rav are David M. Goodblatt's *Rabbinic Instruction in Sasanian Babylonia* (Leiden, 1975), my own *Post Mishnaic Judaism in Transition* (Chico, Calif., 1980), and Ira Chernus's *Mysticism in Rabbinic Judaism* (Berlin, 1982), esp. pp. 74–87.

BARUCH M. BOKSER

RAVA' (d. circa 352 CE), a leading fourth-generation Babylonian amora, based in the city of Mahoza. The son of Yosef bar Ḥama' and a student of Ḥisda', Naḥman, and Yosef bar Ḥiyya', Rava' gathered students in Mahoza after the deaths of Yosef bar Ḥiyya' (c. 323) and Abbaye (c. 338). In his work he attempts to analyze and further disseminate earlier rabbinic teachings.

Through his function as a *dayyan* (judge) and market supervisor, Rava' imposed rabbinic norms on Babylonian Jewry (B.T., *Ket.* 67a, *San.* 99b–100a). He lectured in the *pirqa'* gatherings, where aggadic and halakhic topics were discussed. These were convened on sabbaths and special occasions especially for the general public, although students were also expected to attend (B.T., *Pes.* 50a). He instructed many students who attended the *kallot* (sg., *kallah*), academic conventions that lasted several days. He trained disciples as well in his court and had them observe and emulate his personal practices (B.T., *Ber.* 6a; Goodblatt, 1975). Stories depict the students' deep involvement in learning and the insistence of Rava' that they maintain family and community ties (B.T., *Ket.* 62b).

Rava' also played an important part in transmitting earlier Babylonian teachings and possibly the third-century Palestinian traditions of Yoḥanan bar Nappaha' (Dor, 1971). With Abbaye, his fellow student and older colleague, he led in critically analyzing the logic of both sides of issues. Conventionally these discussions have been considered key building blocks of the Talmud, though recent research (by David Weiss Halivni and others) suggests they may have been shaped and especially preserved by postamoraic circles. Rava' in particular recognized that to construe the Mishnah, one might have to emend the text or posit an ellipsis (Epstein, 1964). He particularly sought the biblical basis for various Mishnaic laws and practices (B.T., *Soṭ.* 17a, *B.Q.* 92a–b)

Rava' taught the full range of halakhic, aggadic, and exegetical topics as well as practical advice. In comments such as "a person when distraught cannot be held accountable" (B.T., *B.B.* 16b), he recognized the significance of a person's mental or psychological state. He spoke of God's place in the world and, in stressing public and private study, he claimed that Torah study, even more than good deeds, can counter demons (B.T., *Soṭ.* 21a). In emphasizing the respect and privileges due to Torah students, he asserted that rabbis, like the priests and Levites of Ezra's day (*Ezr.* 7:24), should be exempt from poll taxes (B.T., *Ned.* 62b).

Rava' stands out in his generation not only for a judicial role with extensive jurisdiction, his reportedly large number of students, and his unusual methods of teaching but also, with Abbaye, for the large number of supernatural stories told about him (B.T., *Ta'an.* 21b–22a). People believed that Torah study and good deeds brought Rava' divine blessings, protection against evil and demons, and divine communications in omens and dreams (B.T., *Ber.* 56a–b). His great prestige is reflected in the Talmudic stories describing the gifts he received from the mother of King Shāpūr II and in the subsequent principle that his legal opinions should be followed in all but six cases (B.T., *B.M.* 22b).

[*See also* Amoraim *and the biography of Abbaye.*]

BIBLIOGRAPHY

A comprehensive treatment and bibliography of Rava' and his teachings can be found in Jacob Neusner's *A History of the Jews in Babylonia,* 5 vols. (Leiden, 1966–1970), esp. vol. 4, passim. Noteworthy, too, is Jacob N. Epstein's *Mavo' le-nusaḥ ha-Mishnah,* 2 vols. (1948; reprint, Jerusalem, 1964), pp. 381–391, on the attitude of Rava' to tannaitic traditions and the Mishnah. Other informative works are Zwi Moshe Dor's *Torat Erets-Yisra'el be-Bavel* (Tel Aviv, 1971); David M. Goodblatt's *Rabbinic Instruction in Sasanian Babylonia* (Leiden, 1975) and his "The Babylonian Talmud," in *Aufstieg und Niedergang der römischen Welt,* vol. 2.19.2 (Berlin and New York, 1979), reprinted in *The Study of Ancient Judaism,* edited by Jacob Neusner, vol. 2, *The Palestinian and Babylonian Talmuds* (New York, 1981); and David Weiss Halivni's *Midrash, Mishnah, and Gemara* (Cambridge, Mass., 1986).

BARUCH M. BOKSER

RAWZ̤AH-KHVĀNĪ is the Persian ritual of public lamentation over the suffering of Imam Ḥusayn and other Shīʿī martyrs. Together with the *taʿziyah* (passion play) and the Muḥarram mourning procession, known in Iran as *dastah,* it forms a part of the trilogy of the mourning observances that determines the basic popular ritual orientation in Shīʿī Islam. Similar rituals are known by different names in other countries with Shīʿī populations.

The recitation and chanting of eulogies for the Shīʿī martyrs, which has flourished in the Muslim world during the last thirteen centuries, produced a literary genre known as *maqtal* (pl., *maqātil*). It was precisely at the beginning of the Safavid period (1501), when Shīʿī Islam became the state religion of Persia, that the major Persian *maqtal* masterpiece was composed. This was the work of Ḥusayn Vāʿiẓ Kāshifī, titled in Arabic *Rawḍat al-shuhadā'* (The Garden of the Martyrs), from which *rawz̤ah-khvānī* takes its name: the second word of the Arabic title was replaced with the Persian *khvānī* ("chanting" or "recitation") to yield *rawz̤ah-khvānī,* or "garden recitation."

The public lamentation of *rawz̤ah-khvānī* is performed most often during the first two months of the Muslim calendar, Muḥarram and Ṣafar, in commemoration of the murder of Imam Ḥusayn on the tenth of Muḥarram in AH 61/680 CE. As the son of ʿAlī and the grandson of the prophet Muḥammad, Ḥusayn was the third imam of the Shīʿah, who consider his death at the hands of the caliph's troops the treacherous murder of the just and rightful ruler at the hands of an evil usurper. Mourning for Ḥusayn thus combines grief over his death with a strong condemnation of tyranny and injustice.

All classes of society participate in the *rawz̤ah-khvānī*s (popularly called *rawz̤ahs*), which can be held in black tents set up for the occasion in the public square of a town or village, in mosques, or in the courtyards of private houses. During the late eighteenth and the nineteenth century, special edifices known as *Ḥusaynīyah*s or *takīyahs* were also built for the performance, often by official patrons. Richly decorated and carpeted, they displayed black standards and flags, as well as a variety of weapons intended to recall the Battle of Karbala.

The *rawẓah* usually begins with the performance of a *maddāḥ* ("panegyrist") reciting and singing in praise of the Prophet and the saints. He is followed by the *rawẓah khvān* (also known as a *vā'iẓ*, "preacher"), who offers storytelling and songs about Ḥusayn and the other martyrs. His rapid chanting in a high-pitched voice alternates with sobbing and crying to arouse the audience to intense emotion. The *rawẓah-khvānī* ends with congregational singing of dirges called *nawḥahs*. The performances last anywhere from several hours to an entire day and well into the night, and the emotional atmosphere that is generated can result in weeping, breast-beating, and body flagellation, as in the Muḥarram parades. Through the choice of episodes and the modulation of their voices, a succession of chanters are able to excite and manipulate the emotions of their audiences so that they identify with the suffering of the martyrs, who will serve in turn as their intercessors on the Day of Judgment. At the same time, the *rawẓah khvāns* frequently make digressions into contemporary political, moral, and social issues, creating the kind of social and religious climate that is ripe for political action. There is no doubt that the religious symbolism of the just Imam Ḥusayn, martyred at the hands of a tyrannical ruler, played a major role in the Iranian Revolution of 1978–1979.

Outside of Iran, it is only in Bahrein that public lamentations for Ḥusayn and other Shīʿī martyrs follow the Persian model of *rawẓah-khvānī*. The Shīʿah of India, Pakistan, Iraq, and Lebanon, along with smaller Shīʿī communities in Turkey and the Caucasus, observe the mourning months of Muḥarram and Ṣafar according to various local traditions, although the intensity of the feelings is the same.

[*See also* ʿĀshūrāʾ *and* Taʿziyah.]

BIBLIOGRAPHY

Mahmoud Ayoub's *Redemptive Suffering in Islam* (The Hague, 1978) is an important discussion of the philosophical concept of redemption. For discussions of rituals, see my *Ta'ziyeh: Ritual and Drama in Iran* (New York, 1979); B. K. Roy Burman's *Moharram in Two Cities: Lucknow and Delhi* (New Delhi, 1966); G. E. von Grunebaum's *Muhammadan Festivals* (New York and London, 1958); and Gustav Thaiss's "Religious Symbolism and Social Change: The Drama of Husain," in *Scholars, Saints and Sufis*, edited by Nikki R. Keddie (Berkeley, 1972).

PETER CHELKOWSKI

RĀZĪ, FAKHR AL-DĪN AL- (AH 543–606/1148–1210 CE), more fully ʿAbd Allāh Muḥammad ibn ʿUmar ibn al-Ḥusayn; Muslim author, theologian, and philosopher. He was born in Rayy to a family famed for its learning and piety. He completed his education at Rayy, studied in Maragha under the philosopher Majd al-Dīn al-Jīlī, and then set out for different countries, where he debated and taught in accordance with the custom of Muslim scholars of his time. He also won the patronage of several princes and sultans.

In Khorezm he engaged in relentless disputation with the Muʿtazilah until they eventually forced him to leave; in Transoxiana he met with further opposition from some theologians; in Ghur he entered into a relationship with Shihāb al-Dīn al-Ghūrī, the ruler of Ghaznah, and his brother Ghiyāth al-Dīn. Before long, however, he had a serious confrontation with the Karrāmīyah, after which he was expelled from Ghaznah in the midst of public disorder.

Returning to Khorasan, he accepted the patronage of ʿAlāʾ al-Dīn Khwārizm-shāh Muḥammad and came to enjoy a position of great influence. A legal college *(madrasah)* was built especially for him in Herat, and many disciples gathered there. Al-Rāzī is said to have traveled further, but he finally returned to Herat, where he died in 1210.

Works. Al-Rāzī devoted his entire life to writing and study, and his works reflect his comprehensive intellectual interests. Most of his books deal with theology or philosophy, but he also wrote on jurisprudence, language, physiognomy, ethics, and medicine.

His works on theology, philosophy, and *tafsīr* (Qurʾān commentary) reflect the two conflicting trends of thought of his time, traditional Islamic doctrine and the ancient Greek philosophy that was known through translations and through the works of al-Fārābī, Ibn Sīnā (Avicenna), and others. Owing perhaps to his active and sincere participation in both traditions (which had already clashed at the hands of al-Ghazālī), al-Rāzī has remained a controversial figure among medieval and modern scholars. Thus, contemporary accounts referred to him as one who "turned away from the *sunnah* [the traditions of the Prophet] and occupied the attention of the people with the books of Ibn Sīnā and Aristotle." Ibn Khallikān reported that the lectures he held in Herat were attended by the heads of the philosophical schools, who came to pose questions and listen to his distinguished replies. At the same time, there are accounts of his great activity as an Ashʿarī theologian who defended traditional Sunnī Islam against the free rationalism of the Muʿtazilah, the rigidity of the Ḥanābilah, and the heresy of the Karrāmīyah and other sectarian groups. To some, his rationalism appeared extreme, while to others, he seemed completely sincere in his conservatism.

Theology. In his search for a positive compromise, al-Rāzī faced the usual difficulties of a synthesizer: he satisfied neither the traditionally minded Muslims, such as Ibn Taymīyah, nor the philosophically minded, such as Ṭūsī. Both sides criticized him severely. For the Ashʿarī theologians, at least, al-Rāzī opened the way for a new system in which theology became a rational philosophy of being and a science *par excellence.*

He declared himself to be an Ashʿarī theologian in many of his works, but he had a great interest in philosophical thought. In other words, he was a man of an Ashʿarī heart and Avicennian mind, and in practice he tried to put the Ashʿarī traditions into a philosophical system that could appeal to the intellectual Muslim. Through logical interpretation, al-Rāzī adapted the Muslim peripatetic theory of being to the Ashʿarī theological system. With the exception of Ibn Sīnā's doctrine of emanation, which is metaphysically associated with the notion of the eternity of the world, al-Rāzī tended to adopt the entire Avicennian theory of being as the general framework for theological speculation.

Philosophy. By advocating a rational system of theology along the line of Ibn Sīnā's philosophy, al-Rāzī presented Ashʿarī theology, a theistic philosophy of creation, as an analytic philosophy of being. On the whole, his theory of knowledge and his analysis of being constituted a theological reproduction of Aristotelian philosophy as he knew it through Ibn Sīnā and al-Fārābī. This new system of theology appealed to the intellectual Muslim of his time as a new philosophy because it assumed an identification between the dictates of reason and those of revelation. Al-Rāzī, as al-Ghazālī's Ashʿarī successor, completed al-Ghazālī's work with greater emphasis on the rational element in Ashʿarī thought and ultimately achieved what could be termed the theologization of rational philosophy in Islam. At his hands, the two systems were almost identified, so much so that thereafter the Sunnī theologian was himself the Muslim philosopher.

Al-Rāzī wrote an interpretation of the Qur'ān in which he followed the same method, but his attempt to read Qur'anic verses in the light of his knowledge of Aristotelian philosophy lacks the prophetic vision of Islam. He shows a deep appreciation of the Qur'anic teaching, which constantly reminds Muslims that they are surrounded with the evidences of divine handiwork, but he establishes his doctrine of God's existence and attributes on a theory of being that is ultimately Aristotelian.

BIBLIOGRAPHY

Boer, Tjitze J. de. *The History of Philosophy in Islam.* Translated by E. R. Jones. New York, 1967.

Kholeif, Fathalla. *A Study on Fakhr al-Dīn al-Rāzī and His Controversies in Transoxiana.* Beirut, 1966. Includes a list of al-Rāzī's writings.

Rahman, Fazlur. *Prophecy in Islam.* London, 1958.

EFFAT AL-SHARQAWI

RE, the ancient Egyptian sun god, was, for most of the pharaonic period, the chief god or at least among the chief gods. His cult center was at Heliopolis, where he seems to have displaced Atum as universal god during the fifth dynasty, and at the same time he also achieved some supremacy over Horus. In the Pyramid Texts the deceased king, who becomes identified with Osiris, joins Re in the solar bark and serves as a guide on the voyage through the day and night skies. By the First Intermediate Period (c. 2181 BCE), local monarchs and other nobles were having these same texts copied on the interior of their coffins, and thus the right to become Osiris (or join him) and the right to join Re was extended. The theology of the Re religion is known not only from mortuary literature but also from the tenth-dynasty *Instruction for King Merikare* and the later solar hymns.

Re is combined with the old Heliopolitan creator god, Atum, as Re-Atum, the supreme god of the later Old Kingdom, and he is assimilated to the Theban god Amun as Amun-Re, "king of the gods," in the Middle and New kingdoms. Representations of Re in his combined forms are very common, but Re does occur individually on Memphite stelae as a human with hawk head surmounted by a sun disk. This is also his regular appearance in the late New Kingdom, when as Preharakhte (the Re-Horus of the Horizon) he is universal lord. The sun disk itself is known as Aton, and in the eighteenth dynasty this became the object of Akhenaton's devotion at the expense of Amun-Re's cult temple at Karnak. The old Heliopolitan priesthood may have persuaded Akhenaton to transfer his allegiance, but his movement failed and he was later regarded as a heretic.

Hathor is the consort of Re and personification of the entire ennead of gods, and in this way she is also mother of Horus, the king. "Son of Re" was one of the major titles of the king beginning in the fourth dynasty. The great temple of Re at Heliopolis has not survived, but there are separate chapels to the sun god in New Kingdom mortuary temples. The great rock-cut temple of Ramses II at Abu Simbel was dedicated to the sun god in his two aspects, Re-Harakhte and Amun-Re. Re's central position in the early mortuary literature continued in the New Kingdom, when papyri of the *Book of Going Forth by Day* were available to anyone who could afford them and kings used new books that described the underworld of Sokar of Memphis, through which the deceased ruler was to guide the solar bark. The solar hymns acknowledge Re's involvement with creation and with sustaining and overseeing what he created. Other gods are described as coming from his sweat, and mankind from the weeping of his eye.

BIBLIOGRAPHY

The best single source of further information is Hans Bonnet's article "Re" in the *Reallexikon der ägyptischen Religionsgeschichte* (Berlin, 1952), pp. 626–630.

LEONARD H. LESKO

REASON is the human capacity for (or practice of) seeing, forming, and investigating cognitive relations. The use of the term ranges all the way from its application to more or less routine calculation to a supposed means for directly apprehending the ultimate nature of things. The classical rationalists of the West—Plato and Aristotle and their medieval descendants—understood everything to be accessible to reason, excepting only one "first principle" (the Good, the One, the transcendental, God) placed "beyond reason." Modern rationalists (Descartes, Spinoza, Leibniz, Hegel) take some combination of causalism (or teleology) and logicism to describe ultimate reality. This approach is challenged by philosophies emphasizing experience, will, intuition, myth, skepticism, revelation, or faith.

The term *reason,* related to Latin *ratio,* has as its nearest Greek equivalent *logos,* which also has the narrower meaning of "word" *(verbum). Reason* absorbs the meanings of "giving an account," "ordering things," or "laying things or ideas out in a comprehensible way." Among other terms it may be contrasted with are *muthos* ("tale" or "story"), *aisthēsis* ("perception"), *phantasia* ("imagination"), *mimēsis* ("imitation"), and *doxa* ("belief").

Already in Plato (and even earlier in Parmenides and Heraclitus) we find a number of the traditional uses or methods of reason: the method of definition, or looking for a common denominator; the method of dialectic, or division (often as one form of definition); the method of reduction to elements; and the method of axiomatization. The so-called Socratic method of elenchus (cross-examination) is related, if only tangentially, to eristics (debating techniques) that were developed into a rhetorical art by the Sophists and, especially, the Megarics (logicians from Megara).

Aristotle offered a systematization of rational methods, not only in the distinction he introduced between deductive and inductive reason, but in his elaboration of the principles of syllogistic logic, which monopolized the field of logic until the twentieth century, when the development of propositional, rational, modal, many-valued, and other logics broke this monopoly. Equally if not more important philosophically were two other distinctions made by Aristotle: the distinction between active and passive reason (which together constitute a two-step process enabling us to know the forms of all things) and the distinction between theoretical and practical reason (the latter extending over the entire domain of human conduct). What may be called the hegemony of reason in the Western world over both thought and action (with the consequences that this has had in the development and application of modern science) stems from these and related points of view.

In the modern scientific era the application of mathematical measures and ways of thinking to experimentally controlled situations has led to the formulation of highly successful mechanistic laws (or laws couched solely in terms of Aristotle's efficient causality). As a result, what is understood as reason has narrowed to comprise only the demand for, and expectation of, a similar type of "explanation." The limitations of this approach when applied to biology (and even more when applied to psychology, sociology, and other so-called soft sciences) have become evident only in the twentieth century, so great has been the prestige of mechanistic physics.

Since biblical religion has a revelational rather than a rational character, the relation between reason and religion in the Western world has been altogether an uneasy one. Something similar may be said about the role of reason in every religion—in particular, for example, in relation to such "liberation" experiences as *mokṣa, samādhi,* and *satori* in Hinduism and Buddhism. In religion, reason is far more often regarded as a prison or a constriction to be escaped from than as a key to the world. In this respect, the importance attributed to various types of meditation, prayer, visualization, paradox, sudden illumination, conversion, grace, charismatic gifts, and even, in some religions (Zen and Sufism), shock, "nonsense," and humor, indicates the limited role assigned to reason in religious thought. It is thus recognized that the bonds of concepts, logic, and rational explanation must be broken in order to have a genuine freedom. [*See* Logic *and* Paradox and Riddles.]

Those religions that have consciously attempted to harmonize reason and religion, even in one aspect, are in a small minority. On the other hand, the role of religion in establishing and maintaining patterns of order in a culture or a civilization is of major importance, whether for good or ill, and this has been recognized by such thinkers as Durkheim, Weber, Nietzsche, and Foucault. Even in societies committed to the separation of church and state, or where the state is actively hostile to religion, various religious practices are present in civil guise. (Here the Confucianist conception of the civil, natural, and "normal" character of religion is especially relevant.) Particularly in the Hindu, Buddhist, and Judeo-Christian traditions philosophical thinkers have formulated what amount to metaphysical and onto-theological statements of religious revelations and experiences. These are rational and doctrinal expressions of practice and belief integrating revelation and experience with a reasoned conception of the world.

There has been a marked decline in the prestige of reason in the twentieth century, due partly to a changing conception of the nature of science as well as to an increasing awareness of the conventionality of what passes for reason. But the present age does not suffer so much from a want of rationality as from a too narrow conception of what constitutes rationality. To some present-day critics, rationality has been purchased at the cost of human meaning and human understanding.

A good deal of what has been called "reasoning" will in the future be turned over to machines. One effect of this could be to make it clear that thinking no longer has to be thought of as synonymous with reasoning, or even primarily connected with reasoning. Metaphorical and analogical as well as holistic aspects of thinking are likely to become increasingly important. Rational schemes in science tend to be thought of more and more as "models" rather than as metaphysical truths. The concern with "foundations" or "grounding" is sometimes replaced by a much greater flexibility of theoretical construction. The kind of liberty that mathematicians and poets have enjoyed, and which at crucial points transcends what is ordinarily called reason, may become accessible in all sciences.

Under these conditions reason is more likely to be regarded as an instrument or a tool than as the supreme defining characteristic of human beings. The effect of this upon religion, upon spiritual practices and development, upon human maturity and the growth of sympathy, understanding, and the ability to live together remains to be seen.

BIBLIOGRAPHY

Dasgupta, Surendranath. *A History of Indian Philosophy.* 5 vols. Cambridge, 1922–1955.

Fung Yu-lan. *A History of Chinese Philosophy.* 2d ed. 2 vols. Princeton, 1952–1953.

Gilson, Étienne. *History of Christian Philosophy in the Middle Ages.* New York, 1955.

Guthrie, W. K. C. *A History of Greek Philosophy.* 6 vols. Cambridge, 1962–1981.

Hartshorne, Charles, and William L. Reese. *Philosophers Speak of God.* Chicago, 1953.

Höffding, Harald. *A History of Modern Philosophy.* 2 vols. London, 1924.

Ranade, R. D., and S. K. Belvalkar. *History of Indian Philosophy.* 8 vols. Poona, 1927–1933.

Russell, Bertrand. *Wisdom of the West: A Historical Survey of Western Philosophy in Its Social and Political Setting.* Edited by Paul Foulkes. Garden City, N.Y., 1959.

Sharif, M. M., ed. *A History of Muslim Philosophy.* 2 vols. Wiesbaden, 1963–1966.

Überweg, Friedrich. *History of Philosophy from Thales to the Present Time.* New York, 1872–1874.

Zimmer, Heinrich. *Philosophies of India* (1951). Edited by Joseph Campbell. Bollingen Series, vol. 26. Reprint, Princeton, 1969.

HENRY LE ROY FINCH

REBECCA, or, in Hebrew, Rivqah; wife of Isaac; the second of the biblical matriarchs. The name *Rivqah* is usually taken to be an animal name, like those of Rachel and Leah; it is derived from a hypothetical form *(*biqrah)* meaning "cow." According to *Genesis,* Rebecca was the granddaughter of Abraham's brother Nahor.

Abraham sent his servant to find a wife for Isaac in Mesopotamia, where he encountered Rebecca drawing water from a well, a meeting place often indicative of divine providence in the Bible. God's involvement is further evidenced by Rebecca's offer of hospitality, fulfilling the servant's stipulated sign. Rebecca subsequently consented to make the journey back to Canaan, where she met and married Isaac. Like his father Abraham, Isaac once claimed that his wife was his sister lest Abimelech, king of Gerar, have him killed in order to possess her. The ruse was discovered, however, when the king observed an amorous encounter between them.

After twenty years of infertility, Rebecca bore twins. According to a divine oracle they were to become two nations, with the descendants of the older serving those of the younger. Rebecca ensured the fulfillment of this prophecy by helping Jacob, her younger son, deceive his blind father while the elder son, Esau, was away. As a result, Isaac gave Jacob the blessing intended for Esau. According to rabbinic tradition, Rebecca instigated this deception because she recognized from her sons' behavior that Jacob would make the better leader. She later helped Jacob flee Canaan in order to escape Esau's anger. Her earlier reassurance to Jacob that the "curse will be on me [for this deception]" (*Gn.* 27:13) came to be fulfilled when she never again saw her favorite son. The Bible presents Rebecca as a strong and incisive figure, complementing the relatively weak Isaac.

BIBLIOGRAPHY

Nahum M. Sarna's *Understanding Genesis* (New York, 1972) contains a thorough treatment of all the patriarchal narratives from a modern scholarly perspective. Rabbinic traditions pertaining to these figures are collected in Louis Ginzberg's *The Legends of the Jews*, 7 vols., translated by Henrietta Szold et al. (Philadelphia, 1909–1938). An evaluation of the biblical depiction of Rebecca can be found in Christine Garside Allen's essay, "Who Was Rebekah? 'On Me Be the Curse, My Son!,'" in *Beyond Androcentrism: New Essays on Women and Religion*, edited by Rita M. Gross (Missoula, Mont., 1977).

FREDERICK E. GREENSPAHN

REBIRTH. *See* Reincarnation *and* Transmigration.

RECITATION. *For discussion of Qur'anic recitation, see* Tilāwah; *see also* Chanting.

RECLUSES. *See* Eremitism.

RECONSTRUCTIONIST JUDAISM. Reconstructionism, the youngest of the four main religious movements in contemporary Judaism, is the only one indigenous to America. Its ideology remains the creation of its founder and theoretician, Mordecai Kaplan (1881–1983); it can be summarized as an appreciation of the unifying elements of the Jewish past, a critical discontent with the present ideological and institutional responses to the posttraditional Jewish situation, and an activist resolve to advance Judaism through conscious and deliberate planning. Both the Reconstructionist ideology and movement thus grew in partial response to other Jewish movements in America.

Foundation of the Movement. In January 1922, Kaplan established in New York the Society for the Advancement of Judaism, which functioned as a synagogue center and gathering place for rabbis, educators, and laity sympathetic to Kaplan's philosophy of Judaism. The influential magazine *The Reconstructionist* was launched in 1935 in collaboration with Kaplan's closest associates Eugene Kohn, Milton Steinberg, and Ira Eisenstein, all rabbis ordained at the Conservative movement's Jewish Theological Seminary of America, as was Kaplan himself. Kaplan's magnum opus, *Judaism as a Civilization*, first published in 1934, laid the architectural frame of the Reconstructionist approach to the institutional structure, theology, and ritual of Judaism.

Kaplan remained affiliated with the Conservative movement, but late in his teaching career at the seminary, ideological differences led to the transformation of Reconstructionism from a school of thought to a fourth movement. Ira Eisenstein, who assumed the leadership of the Reconstructionist Foundation in 1959 and founded the Reconstructionist Rabbinical College (RRC) in 1968, was the driving force behind this denominational change.

Judaism as an Evolving Religious Civilization. Kaplan's social pragmatism argues for the right and obligation of a people to use its discriminating intelligence in adapting to the changing conditions that confront it. The Jewish people are a living organism whose will to live and fulfill itself often necessitates theological and institutional changes, a process that characterizes Judaism, in Kaplan's definition, as the evolving religious civilization of a living organism, the Jewish people. Kaplan's sociological and theological proposals are rooted in the matrix of the Jewish people and are responsive to its needs and aspirations. Jewish theology is responsible for the salvation, or self-fulfillment, of the Jewish people. For Kaplan, there is no paradox in maintaining that continuity requires change. The new is no less sacred than the old, and reverence for the creative innovation expresses no less a piety than does veneration of the past. Kaplan's sociological bent carries with it a pragmatic intent. His descriptive analysis of the condition of Judaism and the Jewish people lays the groundwork for his program to reconstruct.

Kaplan's social existentialism. Reconstructionism is thus an amalgam of philosophy, sociology, and ideology. As its founder and architect, Mordecai M. Kaplan functioned as both its statesman and theologian; he was concerned with preserving the identity, unity, and continuity of the Jewish people and its civilizational superstructure, Judaism. At the core of Kaplan's universe of discourse lies a social existentialism: the existence of the Jewish people is prior to any attempt to define its essence. If any characterization of Judaism can be made, it is in its overriding concern with the preservation and fulfillment of the Jewish people. The matrix out of which the civilizational complex of Judaism emerges is the Jewish people. In Kaplan's self-declared "Copernican revolution," Judaism is for the sake of the Jewish people, not the Jewish people for the sake of Judaism. His inversion of the traditionalist formulation of the relationship between people and religion entails both descriptive and prescriptive elements. The centrality of the Jewish people, consciously or not, has been the guiding motivation of Jewish thought.

The primacy of peoplehood explains the evolutionary character of Judaism, which, according to Kaplan, has passed through three major stages: the national era, while the First Temple stood; the ecclesiastical era of the Second Temple; and the rabbinic era, from then until the modern age. Judaism at the end of the eighteenth century entered the democratic state, and therein lies the uniqueness of its internal challenge. Judaism as a civilization refers to that which unites the millennial generations of Jews into one people. It is expressed through language, art, history, music, culture, ethics; the variety of sancta manifests a people's collective will to find meaning in its life. Judaism is not a set of dogmas, doctrines, or ritual prescriptions, nor is it a philosophy. It is the expression of a people's instinctual will to live, according to a postulate articulated by Aḥad ha-ʿAm (Asher Ginzberg, 1856–1927), one of Kaplan's cultural heroes, and used by Kaplan to counter a purely ideational rationale of Jewish existence. As a civilization, Judaism neither requires justification as an indispensable means to some universal good nor needs rely on claims of supernatural election and design. Aḥad ha-ʿAm could find no more meaning in the question "Why be Jewish?" than in the question why he remained his father's son. For Kaplan, as well, the ties of belonging are prior to the justification of believing. Nevertheless, "since Judaism not only exists for the sake of the Jews but has been fostered by the Jews themselves, who, for thousands of years, have devoted their best energies to its preservation, obviously the Jews are badly in need of Judaism and cannot get along without it" (Kaplan, 1967, p. 427). In this sense, the relationship between the Jewish people and Judaism, described in Kaplan's Copernican inversion, is not linear but dialectical. Judaism exists for the sake of a people who develop a sacred social heritage that, in turn, affects the character and choices of a people.

In Kaplan's analysis, the threat to the status of Jewry and the continuity of Judaism in the modern era is unique. The emancipation in the late eighteenth century offered Jews entry into a publicly neutral society, freer of economic restraints and religious barriers than any in its history. No analogy with Jewish communities in the premodern past properly applies to the condition of this old-new people who were offered citizenship in open societies. Jews who in traditional societies functioned quasi-autonomously as an *imperium in imperio* were now asked to surrender their corporate interests for the rights of individual, cultural, and socioeconomic advantages. Modern nationalism sought to melt down the cultural and ethnic individualities of minority groups and to relegate Judaism to a religion of private affairs. Postemancipation Jewish efforts to accommodate the imperatives of modern nationalism—for example, Reform Judaism, Neo-Orthodoxy, and Zionism—threatened, in Kaplan's view, to sever the organic religio-ethnic cord and result either in an inauthentic spiritualization and intellectualization of Judaism or in a nationalism devoid of all religious memory. Accompanying the threat of nationalism was the challenge of naturalism, which shook the plausibility of traditionalism shared by Muslims, Jews, and Christians alike. The supernaturalist worldview of miraculous divine intervention, literalistic divine revelation, and otherworldly reward and punishment is confronted by a this-worldly naturalism. Nationalism and naturalism present a two-pronged challenge to the status of Jewry and the continuity of Judaism.

The unity of the Jewish people in modern times cannot be retained by the imposition of uniform religious or secular ideologies. The new condition of Jewish status and the fragmentation of traditional faith requires acceptance of a voluntaristic and pluralistic Jewish society and the ideal of unity in diversity. It demands a discriminating assimilation of the values of nationalism and naturalism. The democratic character of modern nationalism, the separation of church and state, and the unprecedented opportunities offered to citizens of an open society are to be absorbed into Judaism without abandoning the fidelities and attachments to Jewish peoplehood. While extolling the values of naturalism, Kaplan warns against the reductionism, scientism, and desacralization that frequently accompany secular naturalism and humanism. The creative adaptation of the values of naturalism, pragmatism, and functionalism calls for genuine alternatives for Jews who can no longer accept the inherited presuppositions and authority of supernaturalism. The artful integration of naturalism and tradition promises to expand the circle of Jewish identity and introduce a new nexus for Jewish continuity. Kaplan's pragmatic statesmanship and theology were designed to offer no excuse for Jewish apostasy. His inclusive project aims at Jewish unity without creedal uniformity and Jewish continuity without the conceit of immutability.

God and the God idea. The major adjective characterizing Kaplan's definition of Judaism as an evolving civilization is *religious*. The Jewish religion expresses the self-consciousness of a people's quest for meaning, purpose, or salvation. The God idea of a people is the apogee of religion. The Jewish conceptualization of God does not spring from instant revelation or metaphysical speculation. The Jewish idea of God develops out of the transactions of a particular people with its historical environment. "Divinity" and "peoplehood" are correlative concepts in much the same manner that "parent" and "child" are correlative terms. To paraphrase George Santayana, to speak of religion in general is as meaningful as speaking in general without using any language in particular. Judaism is the particular language through which the Jewish people articulate their spiritual meaning. While God ideas are cultural expressions and, as such, are subject to various formulations, belief in God refers to the intuitive experiences that point to the cosmic power upon which we depend for our existence and self-fulfillment. Belief in God is not a logical but a soteriological inference. It expresses the psychic manifestation of the will to live and fulfill one's life. Belief in God, thus, is not a reasoned but a "willed" faith.

Such faith is not acquiescence to a supernatural subject who orders the world on our behalf. It is trust in the energies within the world that must be properly understood and used to transform the world in quest of salvation. This-worldly salvation is conditional. It depends upon the proper exercise of human intelligence, responsibility, and will. When physical and human nature are understood and responsibly cultivated, the salvific processes of divinity are revealed. When we are sustained in our tragic losses, find strength to overcome the paralysis of despair, and are propelled toward life, we discover the power within and beyond us that is transnatural but not supernatural. According to Kaplan, the meaning of the God idea is grasped pragmatically by observing the behavorial and attitudinal consequences that flow to it from commitment. "All we can know about God is what happens to human life when men believe in God, and how much improvement in their mode of life and thought is reflected in their belief concerning God" (Kaplan, 1948, p. 181).

Change and continuity. Kaplan's widely quoted aphorism "The past has a vote but no veto" articulates his insistence that the modern era calls for conscious choices in revitalizing Judaism and selectively assimilating those features of naturalism, humanism, and pluralism that further the advancement of Jewish life. Creative interaction between the values of tradition and modernity requires restructuring the institutions of Judaism and the reconstruction of its theological, ritual, and liturgical expressions. As religious statesman and ideologue, Kaplan was aware of the need for structure and stability. He identified the "sancta" of Judaism as those constants that Jews share together though they may be differently interpreted and celebrated: the heroes, events, places, celebrations, and commemorative holy days that function as unifying factors in Judaism. Kaplan's own liturgical reconstruction demonstrates the struggle to hold on to continuity and change in a pluralistic society.

Large public interest in Reconstructionism was not aroused through the publication of Kaplan's sociological and theological writings. The movement gained mass attention through the publication of two of its liturgical texts. The first was the *New Haggadah* (1941), edited by Kaplan, Eugene Kohn, and Ira Eisenstein, which sought to integrate the traditional and contemporary meanings of democracy and freedom and eliminated such items from the Seder as the enumeration of the Ten Plagues and the imprecation of the psalmist against the nations that do not know God and consume his people. The publication of the *Reconstructionist Sabbath Prayer Book* in 1945, edited by Kaplan and Kohn with assistance by Eisenstein and Milton Steinberg, led to its denunciation by the Union of Orthodox Rabbis. At a special meeting that year in New York, the 200 members of the Orthodox Union voted unanimously to issue a *ḥerem,* a writ of excommunication against Kaplan. A copy of the "new heretical prayer book" was placed on the speaker's table and burned by Joseph Ralbag, then rabbi of Congregation Oheb Shalom in New York.

Kaplan sought to express liturgically what he sensed many Jews believed privately. He argued that Jewish religiosity is not exhausted in its supernaturalist formulation. God is one, but God ideas are many. Accordingly, there are many ways to express one's relationship to God in prayer. Moreover, if prayer is poetry, it is poetry believed in. The compartmentalization of theological convictions and liturgical nostalgia is to be overcome by a liturgy that can be followed with both heart and mind. Those theological obstacles that blocked some Jews from serious prayers were to be either reinterpreted, replaced, or removed.

The changes in the Reconstructionist prayer book had to exhibit, in the language of the editors, the "courage as well as reverence" to set aside or modify such prayers or ideas unacceptable to moral and intellectual sensibilities of modern people. Unlike other modern prayer books, the Hebrew text was deleted or altered wherever changes were made in the English translation. Thus, the *Reconstructionist Sabbath Prayer Book* substituted prayers in praise of Jewish uniqueness for those proclaiming the exclusive divine choice of the Jewish people, omitted references to the hope for restoration of the Temple and animal sacrifices there, and deleted prayers in praise of the physical resurrection of the dead and God's reward and punishment of Israel by granting or withholding the rainfall. Prayers that discriminated against women, slaves, and gentiles were replaced by positive affirmations of freedom and the celebration of the divine image in all human beings.

It was Reconstructionism's rejection of the literal meaning of God's election of the Jewish people that created the deepest controversy. For Kaplan the idea of divine election could be explained functionally as a belief that compensates for a people's sense of isolation and persecution; but exclusivity raises questions not only about the nature of a God who chooses and rejects but about the morality of a divine favoritism, which tends to inflame rivalry among sibling religions, each contending superiority. Kaplan replaced the notion of God choosing a people with the idea of "vocation," the calling to serve God that religious civilizations claim. No religion is precluded from serving God according to its own concept of salvation.

Later Development of the Movement. In 1963, with the impending retirement of Kaplan from the faculty of the Jewish Theological Seminary of America in New York, where he had been teaching since 1909, and the reluctance of the seminary to appoint a Reconstructionist successor, Kaplan faced increased pressure to institutionalize Reconstructionism. Throughout his career, Kaplan had resisted the efforts to turn Reconstructionism into a fourth religious movement. He warned against the centrifugal forces of congregationalism and denominationalism. Reconstructionism was to transcend institutional privatism and not further fragment Jewish life. When the Reconstructionist Federation of Congregations was created in 1955, it insisted that the associating congregations retain or acquire membership in the Union of American Hebrew Congregations (the main body of the Reform movement, UAHC) or the United Synagogue (which unites Conservative congregations). But by 1968, when it became the Federation of Reconstructionist Congregations, its transdenominational character was transformed into another wing of American Judaism. Under the vigorous leadership of Ira Eisenstein, the Reconstructionist Rabbinical College was founded in Philadelphia also in that year. Under Eisenstein, its first president, men and women were accepted for a five-year program of graduate study. Reflecting Kaplan's concept of Judaism as an evolving religious civilization, the curriculum was divided into the study of five major periods of Jewish civilization: biblical, rabbinic, medieval, modern, and contemporary. In 1982, Ira Silverman succeeded Eisenstein as the college's president. In the same year, the federation was restructured as the Federation of Reconstructionist Congregations and Havurot under the guidance of its first full-time executive director, David Teutsch, and three years later numbered over fifty affiliated groups. *The Reconstructionist* magazine, first published in 1935, was renewed in 1983 under the editorship of Jacob Staub. After a decade, the members of the Reconstructionist Rabbinical Association, founded in 1975, numbered nearly one hundred and included as well a number of student members of RRC and faculty members. In 1980, the association established for the first time in Jewish history a procedure for an egalitarian *geṭ* (a Jewish divorce).

Reconstructionism, after Kaplan and his immediate successor Ira Eisenstein, evidences a "softer" naturalism, a greater hospitality to the mystical and emotional elements in Judaism. This openness and responsiveness to the changing needs of a community is compatible with the latitudinarian spirit of Reconstructionism. No one can *a priori* know precisely how the living organism of a dynamic people may express its vitality; the essence of Judaism, and of Reconstructionism, is continually redefined.

[*See also the biography of Kaplan.*]

BIBLIOGRAPHY

Berkovits, Eliezer. "Reconstructionist Theology." *Tradition* 2 (1959): 20–66.

Eisenstein, Ira, ed. *Varieties of Jewish Belief.* New York, 1966.

Eisenstein, Ira and Eugene Kohn, eds. *Mordecai M. Kaplan: An Evaluation.* New York, 1952.

Kaplan, Mordecai. *Judaism as a Civilization* (1934). Reprint, Philadelphia, 1981.

Kaplan, Mordecai. *The Meaning of God in Modern Jewish Religion* (1937). Reprint, New York, 1974.

Kaplan, Mordecai. *The Future of the American Jew.* New York, 1948.

Kaplan, Mordecai. *Questions Jews Ask.* New York, 1956.

Kaplan, Mordecai. *Judaism without Supernaturalism.* New York, 1958.

Kaplan, Mordecai. *The Greater Judaism in the Making* (1960). Reprint, New York, 1967.

Liebman, Charles S. "Reconstructionism in American Jewish Life." *American Jewish Yearbook* 71 (1970): 1–99.

Meyer, Michael A. "Beyond Particularism: On Ethical Culture and the Reconstructionists." *Commentary* 51 (March 1971): 17–76.

Schulweis, Harold M. "The Temper of Reconstructionism." In *Jewish Life in America*, edited by Theodore Friedman and Robert Gordis, pp. 54–74. New York, 1955.

HAROLD M. SCHULWEIS

REDEMPTION (from Lat. *redemptio,* derived from *red-emere,* "to buy back") literally means liberation by payment of a price or ransom. The term is used metaphorically and by extension in a number of religions to signify the salvation from doom or perdition that is wrought by a savior or by the individual himself. Like the concepts of salvation, sacrifice, and justification, the concept of redemption belongs to a cluster of religious notions that converge upon the meanings of making good, new, or free, or delivering from sickness, famine, death, mortality, life itself, rebirth, war, one's own self, sin and guilt, anguish, even boredom and nausea. [*See also* Soteriology.] Redemption bears the closest conceptual kinship to salvation, sharing with it the intentionality of the need or desire to suppress an essential lack in human existence and to be delivered from all its disabling circumstances. [*See* Salvation.] This deliverance requires various forms of divine help, succor, or intervention to be achieved, which often secures for the believer an access to the *dunamis* of the spirit and to its outpourings, thereby leading to charismatic gifts. Redemption may be of God's or of man's doing. In a certain sense, redemption makes possible a recovery of paradise lost, of a primordial blissful state. In another sense, it points to new creation or ontological newness in the future. Creation is in many religions a highly sacrificial act that requires prior destruction, as in the dismemberment of Prajāpati's body in Hinduism or the thorough destruction of the shaman's body in northern Asian religions. These acts signify reconstruction-participation in divine fecundity or, respectively, multifecundation by the god Prajāpati, equivalent to partnership in the world. To be redeemed may mean to be divinized, either by the reenactment of the primordial creative act (preceded by a descent) or through the theandric, sacrificial action of a savior *(sōtēr)*. In both cases, grace plays an important role; forgiveness also may be redemptive to the extent that it is provoked by, or calls for, repentance.

In Judaism, the psalmist's "God of my salvation" (Heb. *go'el,* "redeemer," from the verb *ga'al,* used to refer to the redeeming of relatives from slavery, of property from foreign possessions, etc.) is a savior from distress and disaster, yet sometimes is himself in need of salvation *(salvator salvandus)*. Says Job: "I know that my Redeemer liveth, and that he will at last stand forth upon the dust" (*Jb.* 19:25). And the Psalm: "Truly no man can redeem himself!" (*Ps.* 49:7). "Israel, hope in the Lord. He will redeem you from all your sins" (*Ps.* 130:7–8). In Judaism the concept of redemption is closely associated with repentance.

Liberation from exile (*Dt.* 15:15), restoration of freedom (*Is.* 62:12, 63:4), and the vision of a just society have always been signs of divine redemption for the people of Israel. Messianic Judaism projected the new heaven and the new earth, the final restoration and reintegration in peace and harmony of the people of Israel into a remote, utopian future, an ultimate event that, however, was to be preceded by apocalyptic, catastrophical changes; in this respect, the liberation of Israel from slavery in Egypt and the Sinai covenant are complementary to each other. Yet there are in the Old Testament elements of realized eschatology, of "redemption here and now," beliefs that were carried over by various sects (the Ebionites, Essenes, Nazarenes) into Christianity. While having an indubitable eschatological dimension, redemption cannot be reduced to it. And, the extent that it is involved with sacrifice, redemption shares with sacrifice either an active or a passive character. Redemption points to both liberation and repurchase.

This mystery of redemption is best illustrated in Christianity: Christ suffered on the cross in order to satisfy retributive justice. The meaning of redemption in the New Testament is chiefly that of the deliverance of man from sin, death, and God's anger, through the death and resurrection of Christ. A certain Greek influence makes itself felt through Paul, who took in the notion of ransom (*lutron,* from *luō,* "to loose") and thus pointed to the Greek custom of emancipating slaves through payment. "Jesus Christ gave himself for us, to ransom us from all our guilt, a people set apart for himself." (*Ti.* 2:14); and "that flock he won for himself at the price of his own blood" (*Acts* 20:28). Also in *1 Corinthians:* "A great price was paid to ransom you; glorify God by making your bodies shrines of his presence" (6:20); and "A price was paid to redeem you" (7:23).

Yet *lutron* must not be taken literally, as denoting a particular commercial price, a barter; it may mean any instrument of deliverance without there being a question of paying a ransom. (One must exercise prudence, as Thomas Aquinas did, and use the word *price* as that which is payable to God, not to the devil.) Going beyond the juridical notion of punishment and ransom, Paul emphasized the gratuitous aspect of redemption as an act of love: Christ's passion and death take on their supreme redemptive value due to the voluntary nature of the sacrifice, the free acceptance of suffering. Obedience to the divine Father's decree is the proof of love; *price* here equals liberating satisfaction, deliverance from the double slavery of sin and punishment. The exaltation of Christ and the sending of the Holy Spirit signify the decisive act of salvation history (*Heilsgeschichte*), which ushers in the new age proclaimed by the prophets (*Is.* 65:17). Works of satisfaction for sin—fasting, alms-giving, prayer, and works of mercy—all have redemptive value, not only for Christianity, but for other religions as well. Functional equivalents of the Judeo-Christian notion of redemption can be found in many other religions, especially in ethically oriented ones that stress the virtues of action. Salvation is of course the primary and essential goal. But to gain it many primitive cults devised severe and sometimes complicated rituals and ceremonies of redemption.

The Egyptian Pyramid Texts of 2400 BCE looked upon salvation as both a mystery and a technique. Osiris, slain by his brother Seth, is rescued by Isis and brought back to life by means of a secret and complicated ritual; he becomes the one savior from death and from its consequences. The redeeming efficacy of the mortuary ritual of embalming, in which the devotee is identified with the god, was believed to stem from Osiris' primordial experience, which, by being reenacted, made salvation possible.

The primitive vegetation-gods were redeemer gods who required the sacrifice of a symbolic part of the crop to save the whole and allow its use by humans. The agrarian sacrifices of the Romans were meant to appease the wrath of the gods and bring about plentiful crops. The sacrifice of an animal instead of a human was believed to cure illness. According to Ovid, the Romans sacrificed to the *manes,* or spirits of the ancestors. In Babylon, as in ancient Israel, the sacrifice of the firstborn or vicarious forms of it played an important role in the process of redemption by transmitting the tension and effecting the link between primordial time (*Urzeit*) and the eschaton (*Endzeit*). The idea that the sins of the fathers are visited upon the sons appears in the *Ṛgveda,* even before the notion of *karman* was unfolded. To be cleansed of paternal sin, the son has to break violently away from his past; this is viewed as a split between the ascetic and erotic parts of man, located respectively in a mental seed (above the navel), and a lower seed (below the navel). The alchemic function of yoga tends to transform animal instinct into soma, the mental type of seed. Blood functions here as mediator between semen and *soma.* The sacrifice of wild beasts as well as the taming of the cows are symbolic of this sought-for individual regeneration.

The Vedic sacrifice is more beneficial to the gods than to the individual; indeed, it strengthens the gods, but their prosperity in turn reverberates on humans; thus it is said that the gods nourish you if you nourish them. Agni, the god of fire and sacrifice, behaves like a demon and tries to burn everything down, but placated by sacrifice, he resurrects man from ashes. Hence sacrificial food is a bribe to the gods. In the post-Vedic, ascetic mythology, sacrifice becomes a two-edged sword, for Hindu mythology, even demons can be redeemed. The *bhakti* spirit generates entire cycles of its own, in which even apparently malevolent acts of God are regarded as being of ultimate benefit to mankind; hence the practice of a magic of friendship or of friendliness as means of redemption.

In Zoroastrianism, the redemption of mankind, viewed as both individual and universal eschatology, is linked with the hope of seeing that Ōhrmazd, having been released from his entanglement with darkness and evil, emerges victorious from the war over Ahriman. The *haoma* ritual, a central act of worship, actualizes such a god-centered redemption. The theological trend in Sasanid Zoroastrianism exhibits a belief in the redemption of the world through the individual's efforts to make the gods dwell in his body while chasing the demons out of it. Mazdaism admits of a cosmical redemption besides individual deliverance, which is supposed to occur at the end of time at the hand of Saoshyant, the savior.

Buddhism is a religion fully bent on salvation. In Mahāyāna Buddhism the doctrine of the Buddha and the *bodhisattva* shows the great vows required by the spiritual discipline of enlightenment to be a devotion to the principle that the merit and knowledge acquired by the individual on this path be wholly transferred upon all beings, high and low, and not jealously accumulated for one's self. This "activity without attachment" involves a free restraint from entering upon *nirvāṇa,* exercised for the sake of one's fellow beings. In Japanese Buddhism the principle of salvation by self-power *(jiriki)* is contrasted by salvation through "another" *(tariki),* that is, through the power of the Buddha Amida. In Zen, devotion, fervor, and depth are all equally redeeming inner attitudes. Some types of mysticism have been categorized as redemptive: for instance, true gnosticisms rely on the dispelling of ignorance, as, for example, the gnosticism of *al-insanal-kamil* ("the perfect human being") and the dispensers of the individual's proper spirituality in Hinduism. Some others cannot be so categorized; Hasidic mysticism, for example, is self-redemptive, noneschatological, and nonmessianic.

There are three main ways of redemption in mystical religions: through illumination, as in Zen Buddhism, or through a dispelling of ignorance of the gnostic type, as in Islam; through membership and participation in the community (the Buddhist *saṃgha,* the Christian *ekklēsia,* the Muslim *ummah*); or, in secular types of religiosity by a redirection of the libido, a reordering of the soul's powers in a harmonious use of the personality, which may mean either a widening or a narrowing of consciousness.

Ancient Mexican religions knew a variety of redemptive types, among which was a form of plain self-redemption from diseases such as leprosy, cancer, buboes, or bubonic plague, and from spiritual sins such as falsehood, adultery, or drunkenness. The Aztec religion favors redemption from existence itself during one's very lifetime, the highest aim being identification with divinity. One example of such a "perfect redemption"

(Joachim Wach) is the return of the high priest Quetzalcoatl after his beatification achieved by encounter with the divinity.

In African traditional religions, the need for redemption is expressed in myths of the Baganda peoples: terms such as *kununula* ("to buy back, to ransom, to redeem") and *kulokola* ("to save, to rescue") point to deadly misfortunes from which the spirits of the departed (*lubaale*, "deity of the below") may rescue one. Redemption is far more directed toward the reintegration of the cosmic, social, and political order in the present moment of the community than toward the afterlife, in spite of the general belief in immortality.

BIBLIOGRAPHY

Brandon, S. G. F., ed. *The Savior God.* Manchester, 1963.

Florovskii, Georgii Vasilevitch. *Creation and Redemption.* Belmont, Mass., 1976.

Knudson, Albert C. *The Doctrine of Redemption.* New York, 1933.

O'Flaherty, Wendy Doniger. *The Origins of Evil in Hindu Mythology.* Berkeley, 1976.

Przyluski, Jean. "Erlösung im Buddhismus." *Eranos-Jahrbuch* (Zurich) (1937): 93–136.

Schär, Hans. *Erlösungsvorstellungen und ihre psychologischen Aspekte.* Zurich, 1950.

Toutain, Jules. "L'idée religieuse de la rédemption." In *Annuaires de l'École des Hautes Études* (Sciences Religieuses), Section 5. Paris, 1916–1917.

Trinité, Philippe de la. *What Is Redemption.* New York, 1961.

Werblowsky, R. J. Zwi. *Types of Redemption.* Leiden, 1970.

ILEANA MARCOULESCO

REFERENCE WORKS on religion are of many kinds. Dictionaries, or one-volume encyclopedias, define terms and give basic information. They may include minimal bibliographic aid. Multivolume encyclopedias either cover the entire field of religion and religions or concentrate on a particular religion or a particular period. Articles, written by recognized authorities, are signed and usually include lengthy bibliographies that refer the reader to the basic works in the field. Specialized bibliographies that cover religion and religions are very rare. Atlases present the history and geographic distribution of religions. In the following sections devoted to these kinds of reference work, each entry will present bibliographic details and give a short characterization of the work.

One-Volume Dictionaries and Encyclopedias. The sixteen entries that are listed under this heading comprise single-volume works (and one two-volume work) that either define religious terms or provide brief articles on religion and religions. Not listed are one-volume concordances and lexicons that are commonly used for translation and exegesis of specific religious texts.

Abingdon Dictionary of Living Religions. Edited by Keith Crim. Nashville, 1981. 830 pp. Intends to be an authoritative guide to the historical development, beliefs, and peculiarities of the sometimes bewildering variety of religions in the world today. All articles are signed and cross-referenced and contain brief English bibliographies. Well illustrated.

The Concise Encyclopedia of Living Faiths. Edited by R. C. Zaehner. New York, 1959. Short-entry dictionary; minimal value.

A Dictionary of Comparative Religion. Edited by S. G. F. Brandon. London, 1907. 704 pp. Short, signed articles by British scholars. Designed to discuss religions in proportion to their significance in human cultural history. Brief bibliographies. General index and an index that groups articles under fifteen major religions. Important first reference tool.

Dictionary of Non-Christian Religions (1971). 2d ed. By Geoffrey Parrinder. Amersham, Buckinghamshire, England, 1981. 320 pp. Short entries, with illustrations. Strongest on Hinduism, Buddhism, and Islam; Christianity not treated. Basic general bibliography.

A Dictionary of Religion and Ethics. Edited by Shailer Mathews and Gerald Birney Smith. New York, 1921. 521 pp. Signed articles giving definitions of all terms used in religion and ethics; fuller discussion of terms used in primitive or ethnic religions. Recent terminology not treated, but useful for history of religions school and the Chicago sociological school.

Dictionary of Religious Terms. By Donald T. Kauffman. Westwood, N.J., 1967. 445 pp. Brief definitions of terms, symbols, rites, faiths, movements, and people in past and present religions.

Eastern Definitions: A Short Encyclopedia of Religions of the Orient. By Edward Rice. Garden City. N.Y., 1978. 433 pp. Dictionary of terminology of major and minor Eastern religions. No bibliographies.

The Encyclopedia of American Religions. 2 vols. Edited by John Gordon Melton. Wilmington, N.C., 1978. Describes all religions represented in the United States and Canada, with bibliographies.

Encyclopedia of Religion and Religions. Edited by Edgar Royston Pike. New York, 1958. 406 pp. Seeks to write without bias; articles submitted for revision to authorities in the various world religions.

An Encyclopedia of Religion. Edited by Vergilius Ferm. New York, 1945. 844 pp. Initialed articles; comprehensive; short English bibliographies for many entries.

The Encyclopedia of the Jewish Religion. Edited by R. J. Zwi Werblowsky and Geoffrey Wigoder. New York, 1966. 415 pp. Short articles; no bibliographies.

An Illustrated Encyclopedia of Mysticism and the Mystery Religions. By John Ferguson. London and New York, 1977. 228 pp. Brief articles on names, movements, and terminology of mysticism in its various forms.

Lexikon der griechischen und römischen Mythologie, mit Hinweisen auf das Fortwirken antiker Stoffe und Motive in der bildenden Kunst, Literatur und Musik des Abendlandes bis zur

Gegenwart. 6th ed. By Herbert Hunger. Vienna, 1969. 444 pp. Short-entry dictionary. Bibliographical references to later use of the themes.

Reallexikon der ägyptischen Religionsgeschichte. By Hans Bonnet. Berlin, 1952. 883 pp. Comprehensive definitions and articles on all aspects of Egyptian religion and mythology. Some bibliographical references to available source materials.

Religionswissenschaftliches Wörterbuch: Die Grundbegriffe. By Franz König. Freiburg, 1956. 956 cols. Short signed entries on the science, history, philosophy, phenomenology, and psychology of religion. Basic bibliographies, primarily of material in German.

Wörterbuch der Religionen (1952). By Alfred Bertholet and Hans Freiherr von Campenhausen. 2d rev. ed. Edited by Kurt Goldammer. Stuttgart, 1962. 617 pp. Brief articles with bibliographies.

Multivolume Encyclopedias. The following list includes encyclopedias that are written from a Christian perspective, that cover a particular religion, or that treat an aspect of ancient or past religion. No attempt is made to trace the history of theological encyclopedias. Nor will there be entries under persons or titles that are significant in the history of theological encyclopedias, such as Isidore of Seville's *Etymologiae* (1472) *Grosses vollständiges Universal-Lexikon aller Wissenschaften und Künste* (1732–1754), or Denis Diderot and Jean Le Rond d'Alembert's *Encyclopédie, ou Dictionnaire raisonné des sciences, des artes et des métiers* (1751–1780). None of the general encyclopedias will be listed (e.g., *Encyclopaedia Britannica*), though most modern works have significant articles on religion. Interested readers should consult Robert Collison's *Encyclopaedias: Their History throughout the Ages* (New York and London, 1964) and the relevant entries in Eugene P. Sheehy's *Guide to Reference Books*, 9th ed. (Chicago, 1976; supp., 1980). Standard abbreviations for these reference works are given in Siegfried Schwertner's *Internationales Abkürzungsverzeichnis für Theologie und Grenzgebiete: Zeitschriften, Serien, Lexika, Quellenwerke mit bibliographischen Angaben* (Berlin and New York, 1974).

Ausführliches Lexikon der griechischen und römischen Mythologie. 6 vols. & 4 supps. Edited by Wilhelm Heinrich Roscher. Leipzig, 1884–1937. Signed articles by leading scholars; good bibliographic coverage, which should be supplemented by the material in Herbert Hunger's *Lexikon der griechischen und römischen Mythologie* (1969) and *Der kleine Pauly* (1969–1975); richly illustrated. The basic reference work for all research on Greco-Roman mythology.

The Catholic Encyclopedia. 17 vols. New York, 1907–1922. Long the standard reference work in English on all aspects of the Catholic church. Now updated, but not completely replaced by the *New Catholic Encyclopedia.*

Dictionary of Philosophy and Psychology. 3 vols. Edited by James Mark Baldwin. New York, 1901–1905. First major encyclopedia of philosophy in English. Authoritative when issued; concise, with excellent bibliographies of material available at the end of the nineteenth century. Includes philosophy of religion.

Dictionnaire de la Bible, contenant tous les noms de personnes, de lieux, de plantes, d'animaux mentionnés dans les Saintes Écritures, les questions théologiques, archéologiques, scientifiques relatives à l'Ancien et au Nouveau Testament et des notices sur les commentateurs anciens et modernes. 5 vols. Edited by Fulcran Grégoire Vigouroux and Louis Pirot. Paris 1907–1912. Lengthy signed articles by French biblical scholars writing from a Roman Catholic perspective. Brought up to date by the *Dictionnaire de la Bible: Supplément.*

Dictionnaire de la Bible: Supplément. 10 vols. Edited by Louis Pirot, André Robert, Henri Cazelles, and André Feuillet. Paris, 1928–1983. The supplement, larger than the original encyclopedia, has extensive, signed articles on the religion of the Bible and the ancient world. Bibliographies.

Dizionario teologico interdisciplinaire. 3 vols. Edited by Luciano Pacomio. Turin, 1977.

Enciclopedia cattolica. 12 vols. Vatican City, 1949–1954. Major contemporary encyclopedia treating the life, thought, history, and general relationship of the Catholic church to other religions and systems of thought.

Enciclopedia filosofica. 2d ed. 6 vols. Sponsored by the Centro di Studi Filosofici di Gallarate. Florence, 1968–1969. Scholarly, signed articles with excellent bibliographies. Relates philosophy to tangential disciplines, including religion.

Encyclopaedia Judaica. 16 vols. Edited by Cecil Roth and Geoffrey Wigoder. Jerusalem and New York, 1971 and 1972. The basic contemporary encyclopedia of Judaism in all aspects; based on the incomplete *Encyclopaedia Judaica* that was published in Berlin from 1928 to 1934. Comprehensive signed articles with extensive bibliographies.

Encyclopaedia of Buddhism. 3 vols. to date. Edited by G. P. Malalasekera. Colombo, Ceylon (Sri Lanka), 1961–. The third volume brings the work to "Burlingame." Massive work on all aspects of Buddhism: names, literature, history, and religious and moral aspects and concepts. Some articles signed. Bibliographies of varying quality.

The Encyclopaedia of Islam. 4 vols. & supp. Edited by M. T. Houtsma and A. J. Wensinck. Leiden, 1913–1934. Scholarly and authoritative; in process of replacement by the new edition.

The Encyclopaedia of Islam. New ed. 5 vols. to date. Edited by H. A. R. Gibb, J. H. Kramers, E. Lévi-Provençal, and J. Schacht. Leiden, 1960–. Signed articles by authorities on every aspect of Islam: history, religion, science, geography, and so on. Excellent bibliographies; comprehensive cross-referencing.

Encyclopaedia of Religion and Ethics. 13 vols. Edited by James Hastings. Edinburgh, 1908–1926. The fundamental encyclopedia of religion in English until the present work. Comprehensive. Articles on religions and all their aspects, beliefs, customs, practices, mythology, personages, philosophical ideas, and so forth. Signed articles with extensive bibliographies. Illustrated. Because of its age, many articles are now outdated.

The Encyclopedia of Philosophy. 8 vols. Edited by Paul Edwards. New York, 1967. Lengthy articles designed to stress the interaction of philosophy with other disciplines, including moral reformers, religious thinkers, and so forth, from ancient to modern times. Index in last volume. More comprehensive than the *Dictionary of Philosophy and Psychology.*

Encyclopedic Dictionary of Religion. 3 vols. Edited by Paul Kevin Meagher, Thomas C. O'Brien, and Consuelo Maria Aherne. Washington, D.C., 1979. Useful, especially for its entries on Christian groups.

Evangelisches Kirchenlexikon: Kirchlich-theologisches Handwörterbuch. 4 vols. Edited by Heinz Brunotte and Otto Weber. Göttingen, 1955–1961. Stresses recent literature and developments in Protestant theology and tangential areas.

The Hindu World: An Encyclopedic Survey of Hinduism. 2 vols. By Benjamin Walker. New York, 1968. Dictionary of Hinduism, drawn from secondary sources. Bibliographies.

International Encyclopedia of the Social Sciences. 17 vols. Edited by David L. Sills. New York, 1968. (Supp. vol. 18, 1978.) Authoritative, signed articles with extensive bibliographies. Covers numerous topics in the social sciences relevant to the study of religion. Volume 17 includes index; volume 18 is a biographical supplement.

The Interpreter's Dictionary of the Bible. 4 vols. Edited by George Arthur Buttrick. New York, 1962. (Supp. vol., edited by Keith Crim, 1976). Authoritative signed articles on all aspects of ancient religion that are relevant in the Christian interpretation of the Bible.

The Jewish Encyclopedia. 12 vols. Edited by Isidore Singer. New York and London, 1901–1906. Standard authoritative work at the beginning of the twentieth century. Now replaced by the *Encyclopaedia Judaica.*

Der kleine Pauly: Lexikon der Antike. 5 vols. Edited by Konrat Ziegler and Walther Sontheimer. Stuttgart, 1964–1975. Not a mere abridgment of the great *Realencyclopädie der classischen Altertumswissenschaft,* but a new work with extensive bibliographies. The best modern encyclopedia on the classical world, including religions.

Lexikon für Theologie und Kirche. 2d ed. 10 vols. Edited by Josef Hofer and Karl Rahner. Freiburg, 1957–1967. The first edition of this ten-volume work was edited by Michael Buchberger (Freiburg, 1930–1938). An updating of the older "Wetzer and Welte" lexicon; now the standard Catholic encyclopedia in German. Authoritative signed articles, with extensive bibliographies. Covers general religious history beyond Christianity.

New Catholic Encyclopedia. 15 vols. Edited by William J. McDonald. New York, 1967. (2 supp. vols., 1974–1979.) Latest English encyclopedia of the Catholic church in English. Major contribution. Treats not only traditional Catholic topics, but movements, institutions, religions, philosophies, and scientific trends that impinge on Catholic thought and life.

The New Schaff-Herzog Encyclopedia of Religious Knowledge. 12 vols. Edited by Samuel Macauley Jackson. New York, 1908–1914. Along with the *Encyclopaedia of Religion and Ethics* and the present work, the major encyclopedic source in English on religions. Based on Herzog and Hauck's *Realencyclopädie,* it is a major revision and expansion to introduce later and non-Germanic materials. Supplemented by the *Twentieth Century Encyclopedia of Religious Knowledge.*

Paulys Real-Encyclopädie der classischen Altertumswissenschaft. 2 major series in 68 vols. and 15 supp. vols. By August Friedrich von Pauly. Edited by Georg Wissowa, Wilhelm Kroll, Karl Mittelhaus, Konrat Ziegler, and Kart Witte. Stuttgart, 1894–1978. Massive; complete; full bibliographies on every subject relating to the classical world. Basic resource for Greco-Roman religion.

Profiles in Belief: The Religious Bodies of the United States and Canada. 4 vols. to date. By Arthur Carl Piepkorn. Edited by John H. Tietjen. New York, 1977–. Extensive articles on the history, polity, and thought of the major Christian bodies. Massive documentation. Volumes 5–7 will cover non-Christian religious groups.

Realencyclopädie für protestantische Theologie und Kirche. 3d rev. ed. 24 vols. Edited by Albert Hauck. Leipzig, 1896-1913. Original edition was edited by Johann Jakob Herzog. Massive signed articles, with full bibliographies by experts. Covers much more than Protestant theology. Still of fundamental value.

Reallexikon der Assyriologie. 6 vols. Edited by Erich Ebeling, Brunno Meissner, Ernst Weidner, and Wolfram von Soden. Berlin, 1932–1983. Scholarly articles on all aspects of Assyriology, including religion. Generous bibliographies.

Reallexikon für Antike und Christentum. 12 vols. (incomplete). Edited by Theodor Klauser. Stuttgart. 1950–. Extensive authoritative articles by leading scholars on all aspects of antiquity and Christianity; extensive bibliographies. Fundamental.

Religion in American Life. 4 vols. Edited by James Ward Smith and A. Leland Jamison. Princeton, 1961. Along with Piepkorn's *Profiles in Belief,* fundamental for its understanding of the development and role of religion in America. Volume 4, written by Nelson R. Burr in collaboration with the editors, is a massive bibliography.

Die Religion in Geschichte und Gegenwart: Handwörterbuch für Theologie und Religionswissenschaft. 3d ed. 6 vols. & index vol. Edited by Kurt Galling. Tübingen, 1957–1965. The three editions of this major reference tool (first ed., 5 vol., edited by Friedrich Michael Schiele, Tübingen, 1909–1913; 2d ed., 5 vols. & index vol., edited by Hermann Gunkel and Leopold Zscharnack, Tübingen, 1929–1932) have kept this work up to date, while reflecting the changes in theological climate. The first arose out of the Religionsgeschichtliche Schule and paid much attention to the phenomena of religions. The second combined that interest with the concerns of dialectical theology. The third represents the position of critical Protestant theology. All three contain long signed articles by experts from many countries, with extensive bibliographies. The three editions are a major resource for the history of the study of religions in the West.

Theologische Realenzyklopädie. 12 vols. to date. Edited by Gerhard Krause and Gerhard Müller. Berlin and New York, 1976–. To be completed in twenty-five volumes. Signed articles, often monographic in length; extensive international bibliographies. Coverage less "denominational" than is its predecessor. Major reference work.

Twentieth Century Encyclopedia of Religious Knowledge. 2 vols. Edited by Lefferts A. Loetscher. Grand Rapids, Mich., 1955. Updates and supplements *The Universal Jewish Encyclopedia.*

The Universal Jewish Encyclopedia. 10 vols. Edited by Isaac Landman. New York, 1939–1943. Useful, but somewhat popular.

Atlases. The following titles are atlases that deal with the biblical world, church history, and the world of religion.

Atlas Hierarrchicus. Descriptio geographica et statistica ecclesiae catholicae tum occidentis tum orientis. By Heinrich Emmerich. Mödling, Austria, 1968. Contemporary Catholic church throughout the world.

Atlas of Israel. Edited by Ministry of Labour, Survey of Israel. Jerusalem, 1970. The Land of Israel considered historically, sociologically, religiously, ethnographically, and economically. Outstanding.

Atlas of the Bible. Edited by Lucas Hendricus Grollenberg. Translated by M. H. Reid and H. H. Rowley. London, 1956. Thirty excellent maps with minimal commentary printed on them. More than four hundred black-and-white photographs integrated into an excellently written text. Organized historically.

Atlas of the Biblical World. Edited by Denis Baly and A. D. Tushingham. New York, 1971. The best atlas for the geology and geography of Palestine in the context of the Middle East. Excellent maps and color plates.

Atlas of the Early Christian World. Edited by F. van der Meer and Christine Mohrmann. Translated by Mary Hedlund and H. H. Rowley. London, 1958. Covers the early church from circa 30 CE to 700 CE in pictures, text, and maps.

Atlas zur Kirchengeschichte: Die christlichen Kirchen in Geschichte und Gegenwart. Edited by Hubert Jedin, Kenneth Scott Latourette, and Jochen Martin. Freiburg, 1970. The best atlas for church history. Outstanding coverage in numerous clear maps.

Bilderatlas zur Religionsgeschichte. Edited by Hans Haas. Leipzig, 1924-1934. Ancient religions individually treated with introductory text and extensive black-and-white plates. Useful, albeit dated.

The Cultural Atlas of Islam. Edited by Isma'īl Rāgī al Fārūqī and Lois Lamyā' al Fārūqī. New York, 1986. Includes 78 maps, 260 photographs, and approximately 50 pieces of line art.

Grosser Historischer Weltatlas. 3 vols. Munich, 1953. Clear, comprehensive, useful.

Historical Atlas of the Muslim Peoples. Compiled by Roelof Roolvink. Cambridge, Mass., 1957.

Historical Atlas of the Religions of the World. Edited by Isma'īl Rāgī al Fārūqī. Maps edited by David E. Sopher. New York, 1974. Text divided into religions of the past, ethnic religions, and the world religions of Buddhism, Christianity, and Islam. Each religion is presented in written text, with minimal illustrations, and a series of maps showing its history and present distribution. This atlas has no competition that is also up to date.

The Modern Bible Atlas. Rev. ed. Edited by Yohanan Aharoni and Michael avi-Yonah. New York, 1974. Over 260 maps, with line drawing illustrations, to illustrate the political and military history recounted in the Bible.

The New Atlas of the Bible. Edited by Jan H. Negenman. Garden City, N.Y., 1969. Designed to replace Grollenberg's *Atlas of the Bible;* spectacular photographs, dramatically colored maps, but an inadequate text.

The Oxford Bible Atlas. 3d rev. ed. Edited by Herbert G. May. Revised by John Day. New York, 1984. Inexpensive, clear, accurate. The best general atlas for students.

Student Map Manual: Historical Geography of the Bible Lands. 2d ed. Jerusalem, 1984. Clearest topographical maps available in an atlas (drawn by the Survey of Israel); maps by archaeological period from prehistory to the close of the Byzantine era.

The Westminster Historical Atlas to the Bible. Rev. ed. Edited by Ernest Wright and Floyd V. Filson. Philadelphia. 1956. Focus on history; excellent explanatory text, useful pictures; archaeologically somewhat dated.

World Missionary Atlas. Edited by Harlan P. Beach and Charles H. Fahs. New York, 1925.

Catalogs and Bibliographies. The following listings are bibliographical resources in the area of religious studies. Not listed are the general bibliographical resources that have separate sections or volumes on religious books, such as *Religious Books and Serials in Print* (New York).

A Bibliography of Bibliographies in Religion. By John Graves Barrow. Ann Arbor, 1955. Comprehensive from approximately 1500 to 1955.

International Bibliography of the History of Religions. Leiden, 1952–. Annual publication, related to the journal *Numen.* Fundamental.

Missionary Research Library, New York. Dictionary Catalog. 17 vols. Boston, 1968. Major resources on world religions included.

Religion Index Two: Multi-Author Works. Chicago, 1976–. Annual bibliography of essays appearing in collected essays and polygraphs. Indexes material not covered elsewhere.

Religions, Mythologies, Folklore: An Annotated Bibliography. 2d ed. By Katherine Smith Diehl. New York, 1962.

Union Theological Seminary Library, New York. (1960). 10 vols. Boston, 1965. Alphabetical arrangement of the shelf list.

EDGAR KRENTZ

REFLEXIVITY is a potent and popular concept; it is also a problematic and paradoxical one. The term is problematic because it is so popular today; it is used in several different disciplines to refer to a wide variety of mental, verbal, and performative phenomena that nonetheless share a family resemblance. Reflexivity is a paradoxical concept because the type of self-referential activity—consciousness of self-consciousness—that it denotes involves the epistemological paradox so well discussed by Gregory Bateson (1972, pp. 177–193) and Rosalie Colie (1966, pp. 6–8), in which the mind by its own operation attempts to say something about its operation—an activity difficult both to contemplate and to describe without conceptual vertigo and verbal entanglements.

In the most general sense, the terms *reflexive, reflexivity,* and *reflexiveness* "describe the capacity of language and of thought—of any system of signification—to turn or bend back upon itself, to become an object to itself, and to refer to itself" (Babcock, 1980, p. 4). This is anything but the rarefied activity it might at first seem, for reflexivity has come to be regarded as a *sine qua non* of human communication. When, for example, Kenneth Burke defines man in the first chapter of *Language as Symbolic Action* (1966), he describes as "characteristically human" this "'second-level' aspect of symbolicity or 'reflexive' capacity to develop highly complex symbol systems about symbol systems, the pattern of which is indicated in Aristotle's definition of God as 'thought of thought', or in Hegel's dialectics of 'self-consciousness'" (p. 24).

The adjective *reflexive* first appeared in English in 1588; it was used as early as 1640 to refer to the capacity of mental operations to be "turned or directed back upon the mind itself." Regarding things grammatical, *reflexive* has been used since 1837 to describe pronouns, verbs, and their significations that are, as the *Oxford English Dictionary* says, "characterized by, or denote, a reflex action on the subject of the clause or sentence." With reference to mental operations, the adjective is frequently confused and used interchangeably with its near synonym, *reflective.* To be reflexive is to be reflective; but one is not necessarily reflexive when one is reflective, for to reflect is simply to think about something, but to be reflexive is to think about the process of thinking itself. In its present usage, *reflection* does not possess the self-referential and second-level characteristics of reflexivity. Such was not always the case, and the terminological confusion arises because Locke, Spinoza, and Leibniz, as well as subsequent philosophers, used the term *reflection* to denote the knowledge that the mind has of itself and its operations, in contrast to mere "thinking" about matters external to the mind itself.

A related confusion occurs with the term *self-consciousness,* which denotes primary awareness of self rather than the consciousness of self-consciousness characteristic of reflexivity—what Fichte described as the "ability to raise oneself above oneself," in contrast to "vain self-reflection." The latter phrase raises yet another terminological tangle and, in this instance, a negative connotation that must needs be dispensed with: the association of reflexivity with narcissism and solipsism. By definition, both involve self-reference and self-consciousness, but both are forms of "vain self-reflection" without any second-level awareness of that self-absorption. Unlike reflexivity, neither narcissism nor solipsism partakes of epistemological paradox, ironic detachment, or, hence, the ability to laugh at oneself. Reflexivity involves what Maurice Natanson defines as "methodological solipsism," that is, the examination of all experience from the perspective of the self-aware ego, in contrast to "metaphysical solipsism," which claims that the individual is the sole reality (1974b, pp. 241–243). As Merleau-Ponty pointed out in a discussion of modern painting in *Signs* (Evanston, 1964), reflexivity "presents a problem completely different from that of the return to the individual." Rather, like Husserl's concept of the transcendental ego, it involves the problem of knowing how we think and communicate, of "knowing how we are grafted to the universal by that which is most our own" (p. 52).

In Western philosophy, reflexivity has been recognized at least since Socrates as an inevitable if not always welcome companion of thought. Man is not only an animal who thinks, he also—certainly if he is a philosopher—thinks about thinking, and thinks of himself as a thinker: "to be a questioner in reality is to locate oneself as part of the questionable and also as the source of questions" (Natanson, 1974a, p. 233). Philosophers have tended to explain this paradoxical state of affairs in two related ways. The first and most familiar is "the two-in-one that Socrates discovered as the essence of thought and Plato translated into conceptual language as the soundless dialogue *eme emautō*—between me and myself" (Arendt, 1977, p. 185). While the participants in this dialogue have been variously named—me and myself, I and me, self and other, self and soul, "naked self" and "selfsame," I and Thou—philosophers from Socrates to Arendt have similarly described the dynamics of thinking as an exchange between an experiential or perceiving self and a reflexive or conceptual self. In all cases, the viewpoint of the latter is regarded as a higher form of consciousness, and it is frequently regarded as transcendent, if not explicitly divine. Hence, the second mode of explaining reflexivity and its seeming transcendence of human symbol systems—its thought-trains by which one could take one's way out of the world—is to equate it with the divine. To give but a few examples: in Platonic dialectic, a movement toward the abstract was equated with a movement toward the divine; Aristotle similarly defined God as "thought of thought"; Augustine's reflexive or "selfsame" self is the mind illuminated by God; and, for Kant and Hegel, ultimate meaning, if not divine, is nonetheless described respectively as "transcendental reflection" and "absolute knowledge." While acknowledging this affinity between reflexivity and the higher forms of consciousness in religion, philosophers since Hegel have argued that reflexivity is beyond any particular system of belief, that "thinking is equally dangerous to all creeds" (Arendt, 1977, p. 176).

More recently, phenomenological philosophers such as Schutz and Merleau-Ponty have "grounded" reflexivity by conceiving of it as embodied institution tied to temporality and situation, rather than as transcendental constitution. Far from being a philosopher's prerogative, reflexivity so conceived is nothing more nor less than the process of rendering experience meaningful—the inevitable and necessary "framing" that we all engage in. Phenomenological discussions of reflexivity as a series of exchanges between subject and object, or between individual consciousness and social reality, recall not only the Socratic conception of thought as internal dialogue but also the conception of the self as reciprocal, dialogical, and reflexive as formulated by American pragmatic philosophers and psychologists, notably Peirce, James, Mead, and Cooley.

In *Mind, Self, and Society* (1962), social psychologist George Herbert Mead defines reflexiveness as "the turning back of experience of the individual upon himself," asserting that "it is by means of reflexiveness that the whole social process is brought into the experience of the individuals involved in it" and that "reflexiveness, then, is the essential condition, within the social process, for the development of mind" (p. 134). Mead's concept of "reflexiveness" as a dialogue between a personal "I" and a social "me" is closely related to Cooley's formulation of the "looking-glass self" and to Jacques Lacan's more recent description of "le stade du miroir," for Mead indicates that the achievement of identity involves mirroring, or the assumption of a specular image; the individual "becomes a self in so far as he can take the attitude of others and act toward himself as others act" (p. 171). The self, therefore, "as that which can be an object to itself, is essentially a social structure" (p. 140); or, in Charles Sanders Peirce's terms, it is a semiotic construct: "When we think, then, we ourselves, as we are at that moment, appear as a sign" (*Philosophical Writings of Peirce,* New York, 1955, p. 233). Thus described, the self, like the world, is a text embedded in and constituted by (as well as constitutive of) interconnected systems of signs, of which the most important and most representative is language.

While Peirce asserts that reflexivity is perforce semiotic, subsequent semioticians, linguists, and philosophers have argued that *all* systems of signification are inherently and necessarily reflexive. As Fredric Jameson summarizes in *The Prison House of Language* (Princeton, 1972), "Every enunciation involves a kind of lateral statement about language, about itself, and includes a kind of self-designation within its very structure" (p. 202). Because of its descriptive usefulness, the metalinguistic or metacommunicative model has become pervasive in discussions of all forms of reflexivity. It would be wrong, however, to regard linguistic self-reference as either the cause or the explanation of reflexivity. As Robert Nozick has recently pointed out, reflexive self-knowledge is a basic phenomenon without which neither cognition nor communication is possible, and it is pointless to argue which comes first (1981, p. 82).

Both the idea that reflexivity consists of the self representing itself to itself and the notion that all forms of representation involve self-reference or reflexivity are present in the plural in the concepts of collective representations and cultural performances, as defined and discussed by sociologists and anthropologists since Durkheim. In *The Elementary Forms of the Religious Life* (1915), Durkheim defined collective representations, such as a clan's mythic ancestor, as forms in which the group "represents itself to itself," implying that the collective symbolization process as expressed in myths and rituals includes within its operations consciousness of itself. In recent decades, Claude Lévi-Strauss has argued not only that myths are sociocultural metacommentaries but that all myth is "meta-" insofar as its implicit if not explicit subject is the emergence of language or communication. In his earlier work on ritual and ritual symbols, Victor Turner (1974) suggested that liminal periods are reflexive moments when society "takes cognizance of itself" and reflects on the order of things through symbolic disordering, through the "analysis and recombination of the factors of culture into any and every possible pattern" (p. 255). In later works (1979, 1982, 1984), Turner argued that *all* genres of cultural performance (ritual, myth, theater, narrative, games, etc.) are instances of plural reflexivity because they are self-critiques and reflections *upon,* rather than simply reflections *of,* the structures and strictures of the everyday world. Clifford Geertz (1973) has similarly asserted not only that religion is a reflexive cultural system that provides "models of" and "models for" self and society but that illicit, secular cultural performances such as Balinese cockfights are stories that a group "tells itself about itself" (pp. 93, 448). While not all collective representations—verbal, visual, and performative—are religious, it is no surprise that many of them are, for as Robert Bellah states in *Beyond Belief* (New York, 1970), religion has been "the traditional mode by which men interpreted their world to themselves" (p. 246)—the "pattern of patterns" or epitome of plural reflexivity.

If, as I have already implied, it is difficult to discuss reflexivity without discussing religion, the reverse is equally true. Regardless of whether one considers religion as a system of belief and body of texts or as praxis and experience, one is concerned with the interpretation of the moral complexities and paradoxes of human social and individual life—thus, with signs about signs, with reflexive self-reference. In his myths, man not only renders an account of himself and his world, he testifies to the power of language to make a world and to create gods. In his rituals and sacred symbols, he embodies and reenacts these comprehensive ideas of order, and every time sacred words and deeds are retold and represented, these primal interpretations are interpreted and criticized yet again.

Quite apart from the metadiscourse about religion—explicit reflexivity—that has developed in the great religious traditions in the form of systematic theology, religious history, and textual hermeneutics, every religious system is implicitly reflexive. The communication of the highest truths and the most sacred order of things is invariably accompanied by the subversive self-commentary of *aporiae* (liminal disorder in such diverse forms as Ndembu monsters, Sinhala demons, Zen *kōans*, Pueblo clowns, Midrash tales, and Christ's parables). Such ambiguous and paradoxical elements generate reflexive processes that redirect thoughtful attention to the faulty or limited structures not only of thought, language, and society but of religion itself (cf. Colie, 1966, p. 7).

In addition to this ineluctable reflexivity of religion's collective representations and plural expressions, many singular religious practices are explicitly reflexive. Contemplation, meditation, prayer, and confession all have in common a withdrawal from the world and a bending back toward the self. Frequently, the reflexive character of such practices is marked by their literal or figurative association with mirrors, with *specula*, reminding us not only that mirrors reflect the essence of things and are crucial to the achievement of identity (Fernandez, 1980, pp. 34–35) but that "as in mirror images, self-reference begins an endless oscillation between the thing itself and the thing reflected, begins an infinite regress [or progress]" (Colie, 1966, p. 355). Such mirroring frequently occurs as well in language itself, for careful analysis of sacred discourse reveals a markedly higher proportion of metalinguistic verbs in contrast to everyday speech.

In sum, reflexivity is not a consequence of social complexity or the degree of religious articulateness; it is an essential and inevitable dimension of all religious experience. The power of religious consciousness that we keep trying to explain is probably not its prescriptive, descriptive, or explanatory force but its reflexiveness—religion offers a system of interpretation of existence that is itself subject to interpretation, and that is infinitely compelling.

BIBLIOGRAPHY

Arendt, Hannah. *The Life of the Mind*, vol. 1, *Thinking*. New York, 1978. Arendt's final work is a rich, challenging analysis of man's mental activity; it brings together and reflects upon the major insights of the Western philosophical tradition into the nature of thought and its reflexive and dialogic structure.

Babcock, Barbara A., ed. *Signs about Signs: The Semiotics of Self-Reference*. Special issue of *Semiotica* 30 (1980). An interdisciplinary collection of essays that examine reflexive forms and processes in a variety of genres and cultural traditions, with an introduction that summarizes the meanings and uses of reflexivity.

Bateson, Gregory. "A Theory of Play and Fantasy." In *Steps to an Ecology of Mind*. New York, 1972. This seminal formulation of the paradoxical metacommunicative or reflexive frame essential to all forms of play has inspired much subsequent work on metacommunication and framing, notably Erving Goffman's *Frame Analysis* (New York, 1974).

Colie, Rosalie Littell. *Paradoxia Epidemica: The Renaissance Tradition of Paradox*. Princeton, 1966. This stunning and comprehensive study of paradox is especially important for illuminating both the reflexive self-reference of paradoxes and the paradoxical nature of self-referential operations.

Fernandez, James W. "Reflections on Looking into Mirrors." *Signs about Signs*, special issue of *Semiotica* 30 (1980): 27–40. An especially important discussion of the African use of mirrors and a speculation on the ritual and symbolic significance of this magical object cross-culturally.

Geertz, Clifford. *The Interpretation of Cultures*. New York, 1973. A selection of this interpretive anthropologist's most important essays on the concept of culture, which are notable for their analysis of cultural systems, institutions, symbols, and performances as reflexive forms and processes.

Hofstadter, Douglas R. *Gödel, Escher, Bach: An Eternal Golden Braid*. New York, 1979.

Hofstadter, Douglas R., and Daniel C. Dennett. *The Mind's I: Fantasies and Reflections on Self and Soul*. New York, 1981. Like Hofstadter's *Gödel, Escher, Bach*, this is an important and unconventional meditation on the paradoxical and reflexive nature of thought processes and on the problem of self and self-consciousness.

Mead, George Herbert. *Mind, Self, and Society* (1934). Edited by Charles W. Morris. Reprint, Chicago, 1963. This edition of Mead's lectures presents the outlines of his system of social psychology and his classic formulation of the self as reflexive, as a social construct.

Natanson, Maurice. *Phenomenology, Role, and Reason: Essays on the Coherence and Deformation of Social Reality*. Springfield, Ill., 1974. (Cited in text as Natanson, 1974a.) This book and Natanson's article cited below are summaries of the major issues in social phenomenology, including the central conception of reflexivity.

Natanson, Maurice. "Solipsism and Sociality." *New Literary History* 5 (1974): 237–244. (Cited in text as Natanson, 1974b.)

Nozick, Robert. *Philosophical Explanations*. Cambridge, Mass., 1981. This speculation on philosophical issues contains a superb chapter, "The Identity of the Self," and the best single, summary discussion available of reflexivity.

Singer, Milton. "Signs of the Self: An Exploration in Semiotic Anthropology." *American Anthropologist* 82 (September 1980): 485–507. The single most important discussion of Peirce's conception of the self as semiotic and reflexive.

Turner, Victor. *Dramas, Fields, and Metaphors: Symbolic Action in Human Society*. Ithaca, N.Y., 1974. This collection contains several essays that summarize Turner's view of liminality and liminal symbols and their implicit reflexivity.

Turner, Victor. *Process, Performance, and Pilgrimage: A Study in Comparative Symbology*. New Delhi, 1979. Contains several essays that extend the notion of liminality beyond tribal ritual and examine the public and plural reflexivity of cultural performances.

Turner, Victor, ed. *Celebration: Studies in Festivity and Ritual*. Washington, D.C., 1982. An interdisciplinary collection of essays that explore the reflexivity of human celebrations through the medium of ceremonial objects.

Turner, Victor. "Dramatic Ritual/Ritual Drama: Performative and Reflexive Anthropology." In *A Crack in the Mirror: Reflexive Perspectives in Anthropology*, edited by Jay Ruby, pp. 83–98. Philadelphia, 1982.

Turner, Victor. "Liminality and the Performative Genres." In *Rite, Drama, Festival, Spectacle: Rehearsals toward a Theory of Cultural Performance*, edited by John J. MacAloon, pp. 19–41. Philadelphia, 1984. Like Turner's "Dramatic Ritual/Ritual Drama," this essay expands upon the concepts of liminality and reflexivity and examines a variety of genres of cultural performance as instances of and occasions for metasocial commentary, for public and plural reflexivity.

BARBARA A. BABCOCK

REFORM.

REFORM. In everyday usage, the term *reform* generally connotes advance, progress, modernization. In discussions within religious groups, the use of this word is not so limited. It occurs in the most varied contexts, with reference to a wide range of individual and social questions, as well as with regard to specifically religious matters. Proposals for reform may be directed at the actions, or even the attitudes, of a relatively few persons within a particular faith-community. In this case, unless the change that is advocated would entail either a conflict with the law of the entire community or a violation of public decency—as might, for example, a restoration of animal sacrifices—the change at issue should be of no concern to those persons outside the particular group involved. On the other hand, the reform that is urged may pertain to the entire society. In many modern situations, however, the larger society encompasses members of other religious groups and persons of no religious attachment for whom the proposed reform may seem totally undesirable and unwarranted. If this is the case, and if the reform would affect the lives of persons other than those who propose it, as would, for example, the recriminalization of abortion in the United States, then the proposed reform should become a matter of public concern, properly to be decided by public procedures.

The examples just touched on may seem to suggest that, as applied to religion, the term *reform* is always used to refer to a return to older, more traditional ways of acting. In some cases, this is so, but far more often the reform that is advocated is seen as a step forward. Its acceptance would further progress toward the realization of an ideal future; rather than signal a return to the past, it would usher in ways that never were, in actual time and place. Every world religion has called often for the moral reform of individuals, both among its own followers and among those others too unregenerate to heed its saving message. The content of the morality thus imagined has deepened with the complications of human culture and will, no doubt, change even further as the social order changes. Often, too, the political and economic conditions of a particular time and place affect the customary morality and evoke a religiously grounded demand for reform. Less often, perhaps, but with reasonable frequency, a call from within has demanded that the religion set its own house in order.

Religious Concern for Moral Reform. Religious sanctions designed to enforce the morality of a particular tribe or other small group almost certainly preceded the religious proclamation of a universal morality. But once the idea of universal morality had been broached, some time during the first millennium before the common era (the "axial age"), it was inevitable that the sovereignty claimed for a moral ideal would become as universal as the ideal itself. Just as tribal cults had maintained their own tribal moralities as sacrosanct, so the universal religions all proclaimed the sacred, and often the revealed, character of their own versions of universal morality. The Ten Commandments of Judaism and Christianity enshrine one version of such a religiously sanctioned universal moral code. Other forms, some even older, are to be found in China, in India, in Iran, in Mesopotamia, and in Egypt. These codes differ in detail but are alike in their claim to universality.

The most important issue is not which of these codes came first, nor even whether the codes had their origin in religious belief or were merely adopted by the various religious groups. The point is that, once they were accepted as partial statements of the religiously sanctioned rules of behavior, one aspect of the proper function of religion was to try to assure that these rules of moral behavior were observed, and to call attention to any failure to observe them. In this way universal morality added an important accent to the universality of religious ideas, while the emphasis on morality tended to become, increasingly, the *raison d'être* of religious life. This transformation of tribal religion into universal moral religion had what might be termed its apotheosis in the Zoroastrian tradition of Iran. There, the divine forces of good in the universe, led by the god Ahura Mazdā (Pahl., Ōhrmazd), are in eternal conflict with the comparably divine forces of evil in the universe, under the rule of Angra Mainyu (Pahl., Ahriman). The moral life of each person, if good, helps the cause of Ahura Mazdā; if evil, it aids Angra Mainyu and his cohorts. Thus individual reform has not only a moral but also a metaphysical or transcendental part to play in the age-old struggle between good and evil. In the end, during the final era of the universe, Zoroastrians believe that Ahura Mazdā will triumph. Thus, although Zoroastrianism has dualistic strains, it is not formally a theological dualism. Through its offshoot, the religion of the solar deity Mithra, Zoroastrianism's theology of moral strife reached the Occident and, through the adherents of Mithraism in the Roman legions, had some influence on both Judaism and Christianity.

In some religions, as in the tradition of Confucianism in China, the moral emphasis has been so dominant as to virtually eliminate concern for the theistic aspects of religious life. This is true also of the classical (Theravāda, or Hīnayāna) schools of Buddhism, which, although they arose in India, have remained especially vital in Southeast Asia (Sri Lanka and Burma). A like emphasis on the moral and social aspects of Christianity appears from time to time; it has given rise to such predominantly sectarian groups as the Society of Friends (Quakers) and to "religious humanist" offshoots like Unitarian Universalism. In some aspects of liberal Judaism (Reform Judaism) a similar moral emphasis has been manifest. In their major developments, however, both Christianity and Judaism have remained too theocentric to permit moral concern to become the autonomous core of religious belief and practice. Relations among people, the central theme of the moral life, have in Western religious thought been considered for the most part as relations mediated through the presence of divinity.

Consequently, the reform of the moral lives of individuals has been treated in Western religions as a means toward entering into a right relation with God, rather than as an end in itself or as a matter of right relations with one's fellow humans. This indirectness of moral consciousness does not imply greater or lesser morality in the Western world than in the Eastern. It indicates only that moral reform has been preached in Western religions on ulterior grounds. As the prophet Micah insisted, God demands of his human creations that they act justly, love mercy, and walk in ways of humility, not before priests, kings, or presidents, but only with their God (*Mi.* 6:8). Micah, like his predecessor Amos, his contemporary Isaiah, and many of his successors among the prophets, including Jesus, affirmed the centrality of moral reform among religious values over against the priestly emphasis on cultic ritual. Prophetic reform called for the moral regeneration of relations among people as the sovereign road to a revivified relation with God.

In more recent times, as a consequence especially of development in the social sciences of psychology, sociology, and anthropology, religious leaders in many faiths have come to realize that an absolute, universal moral code is by itself not enough to ensure higher levels of morality. Principles like the Golden Rule, whether in its negative ("Do not do unto others . . .") or affirmative ("Do unto others . . .") version; codified sets of rules, like the Ten Commandments; even the Kantian categorical imperative ("Act as if the maxim from which you act were to become through your will a universal law") all are far too general to give guidance for the majority of specific moral problems. In addition, their very form of expression as rules or laws is foreign to the moral context in which they are proposed as guides.

The reform of individual morality that is sought in current advanced religious thought is one grounded not in a formal rule but in a concern for one's fellows that takes into account all the individual and cultural factors that arise in each moral situation. General rules and laws are the business not of morality but of legislatures and courts of law. In ethical discourse, "right" and "wrong" must yield place to "good" and "bad." As Henry Thoreau wrote, in the mid-nineteenth century: "Absolutely speaking, Do unto others as you would that they should do unto you is by no means a golden rule, but the best of current silver. An honest man would have but little occasion for it. It is golden not to have any rule at all in such a case" ("Sunday," in *A Week on the Concord and Merrimack Rivers*). To be good is to be "good for" somebody or something other than oneself.

Thus the reform of morality is not to be achieved by

the passage of more laws, by the criminalization of more acts. Making more laws only makes more lawbreakers. Criminalizing more acts only makes more criminals. A truly religious understanding of morality would recognize that the causes of immorality are rooted in the home and family, in the educational experiences of the streets as well as the schools, in the popular entertainments, in the world of work and of play, indeed in all the social world that is the matrix within which a child grows to an adult. As these roots differ from child to child, so the development of child into adult will differ. If healthy shoots are to develop, if society is to harvest healthy fruits, then society must care for the roots. This recognition is the reason for twentieth-century religious reform's tendency to place greatest emphasis on social change, so that the soil may be prepared for the growth of a better humanity in the future. [*See* Morality and Religion.]

Religious Concern for Social Reform. When the universal religions are in complete accord with the social orders in which they are embedded, they are clearly not serving their proper function within society. They are then functioning as tribal, not as universal, religions. An important part of the obligation and of the value of any religion to society is its ability to make critical judgments of the social order from a larger and more transcendent perspective than the society can adopt in judging itself. The religious view of society and its institutions should properly be *sub specie aeternitatis* (from the point of view of eternity). In immediate, local, and temporal terms, any social order may seem to be doing very well; viewed, however, from the perspective of the larger religious demand, the demand for righteousness, it may be in very bad condition. It has been noted many times that some of the kings of ancient Israel who had the longest and, from the secular point of view, the most successful reigns are dismissed in the biblical books of *Kings* with the terse judgment that they "did evil in the sight of the Lord." Religion does not exist to glorify the current social order but as a spur to its reform.

In many periods of history, in many parts of the world, those who spoke for the religion of the place and time have been keenly aware of their obligation to criticize the social status quo and to promote its reform. The modes in which they have carried out this obligation have varied greatly. Some, especially in the Buddhist and the medieval Christian world, have done so by setting up communities of monastics whose "discipline" exemplified an approximation to the envisaged ideal form of social life. It is a measure of the humanness of human beings that these ideal communities themselves frequently needed to be reformed.

Even within these monastic communities there were differences in the degree of separation from the evils of the surrounding social world. Some monasteries were a base from which the monks made sorties into the secular world to teach, to preach, and, most importantly, to exemplify, as nearly as possible, the ideal they represented. Other monastic communities were content with complete withdrawal; this type of community served as a retreat from the evils of the social world, a passive exemplar rather than an active witness. A beautiful example of this type is described by Philo Judaeus of Alexandria in his treatise *On the Contemplative Life.* In the Buddhist tradition, in its early form, the ideal of the *arhat,* or saint, although available to anyone was thought most readily achievable by those who pursued the monastic life, that is, by those who exemplified a reformed society rather than those who preached it. On the other hand, among Protestant Christians, the impulse to social reform has tended to be expressed in many different forms of worldly intervention; the most usual, other than charitable relief, has been the formation of special bodies established for the promotion of specific reforms of great urgency, as, for example, antislavery groups in the eighteenth and nineteenth centuries, temperance groups in the nineteenth and twentieth, and "honest government" groups in every time and place.

The methods pursued by dedicated religious adherents of social-reform causes have ranged from prayer services dedicated to enlisting divine aid to the most militant forms of civil disobedience. Men and women of all religious groups have not hesitated to risk imprisonment, even execution, in their struggle to achieve social reforms that they conceived as sanctioned by their religious commitments. It must be noted, of course, that such social reforms are not always "liberal." Highly conservative and even reactionary positions are frequently defended ardently on religious grounds. Examples of such retrograde "reforms" are commonplace: the retention of the caste system in India; the persistent maintenance of an all-male priesthood in Roman Catholicism; the agitation, in many parts of the United States, for so-called voluntary prayer in public schools. Since it is of the essence of a religious position that it be a strong commitment, religiously motivated advocates of a social reform tend to become, for better or for worse, dominated by a single issue.

If religiously motivated social reform is to have a significant impact upon society in the late twentieth century, it cannot concentrate on a limited range of such matters. In the process of bearing witness to the changes that are necessary in the complexly woven fabric of modern life, many of the older simplicities must be abandoned, however reluctantly. For example, just one twentieth-century development, that of air travel, has wrought great change, bringing all the parts of the earth into relatively close proximity. Long-distance travel and its resultant interactions have become commonplace, not only between residents of one country or one continent, but between people of very different backgrounds and customs from all over the globe. The number of cross-cultural contacts has increased phenomenally within less than half a century. The more mobile of American men and women, as well as a great many American youths, have the opportunity to experience life and to meet people in countries where prevailing customs are different from those in the United States. Similar groups from other countries can now visit the United States and get to know some of its people.

It is inevitable that these multitudes of travelers will soon begin to make critical comparisons of their countries' social orders and institutions with those of countries they have visited. They will not at first be considering larger theoretical questions of politics or economics. They will look at the actual day-to-day lives of people. Their consciousness in such matters will rapidly become a world consciousness. Religious reformists must be prepared to adapt their visions of directions and goals to the concerns of this new kind of "international" public mind. Even as individual churches have had to expand the horizons of their awareness to include the concerns of a denomination, so denominations must broaden their thought to the interlocked concerns of the human world.

Religious Concern for Religious Reform. Religions are not only faiths; they are also churches. That is, they not only express a deep feeling for the mutual interrelation of humankind and the universe but are also organized groups of people who come together on specified occasions for specific purposes, groups of people who relate to the transcendent, to each other, to outsiders, to animals, and to nature in traditional, ritualized ways. In addition to those members who come together periodically for celebratory or ceremonial purposes, most of these organized groups have a professional corps of leaders with specialized educational (sometimes merely vocational) preparation and qualifications. These leadership corps go under various names (priests, ministers, rabbis, etc.). In some cases, they constitute a separate class within the larger society, such as the brahman caste in Hinduism, and they may have still, though in a reduced form in modern times, certain privileges or prerogatives, sometimes called "benefit of clergy."

While some internal reforms in religious life have been inaugurated by members of the nonprofessional group, the "laity," in most cases both the need for reform and the program for putting the reform into practice have been first recognized and then expressed by members of the professional class, the "clergy." It is scarcely to be wondered at that this should be so—that those whose lives and careers are centered in the institution, the "church," and who are, as a general rule, more fully trained for the understanding of matters of religion, should be those who see that old words, old ways, or old rules no longer serve the faith as they presumably did at an earlier time. What does surprise is that so many of the clergy, seeing this, have called loudly for reform of their institution, placing its future and its purposes above their own convenience and comfort. On the one hand, the clergy as a body is composed of those who have most to gain from not troubling the waters, from not disturbing institutional stability; on the other hand, most of the prophetic calls have come from members of the clergy and have pointed emphatically to the need for reform, for change, and, by implication, for instability.

Because there are these two internal strains in each major religious tradition, and perhaps also in the thinking of many individual members of the clergy, religions do change—although, as a rule, slowly and very cautiously. The heretic of one age is gradually transformed into the saint of a later time; the philosophy of Thomas Aquinas was forbidden reading to Franciscans for many years after his death, and some of his ideas were officially regarded as dubious even at the end of his life. But within a century he was proclaimed a saint, and his philosophy became the dominant intellectual system within the Roman Catholic church. Similarly, the roundness of the earth was acknowledged in practice long before it was accepted in religious cosmology. Step by cautious and hesitant step, reluctant at every move, religious bodies ultimately accept new moral and social ideas and are even led, in the end, to *novellae* (new theological formulations) and to revised religious practices derived from the new ideas. Characteristically, however, these novelties, on first proposal, are greeted with dismay, even with horror. The earliest formulators of the novelties may be silenced, denounced, unfrocked and expelled from their orders, even excommunicated, as were the founders of many of the more extreme Christian sects of the Middle Ages and as was so well-known a figure as Martin Luther in the early modern period. During the Protestant Reformation itself John Calvin's Geneva burned Michael Servetus at the stake for his antitrinitarian views.

Both Christianity and Judaism, in earlier times, tended to be more akin to tribal religions than to universal religions, and therefore harsher in their treatment of dissenters. In the modern Western world, most religious leaders are more ready to recognize that silencing the thinker does not silence the thought. Toleration of religious reform and religious reformers has come to be the norm in the Western world in the nineteenth and, thus far, in the twentieth centuries. Intolerance, however, has again begun to flourish in the Middle East, in the form of religio-political strife not only between Muslim and Jewish groups but also between Druze and Christian, Muslim, and Christian in Lebanon, between Muslim and Baha'i in Iran, and between Muslim and Hindu in India and Pakistan. The resurgence of conflicts such as these raises doubts whether the message of religious toleration has roots as deep as they seem to be, whether in fact mutual toleration has become as widespread as was once believed. It is surely evident that there is a need for the reform of interreligious relations, as well as for maintaining within each religion a climate hospitable to the idea of reform.

Religious Reform and Traditional Practice. There is no aspect of religion that is more important to the members of any religious group than the traditional practices to which they adhere. Truly, religious practice is the context in which the child that is latent in every adult comes closest to self-revelation. Psycholgists maintain that what people learn in early life persists longest in their memories, and the traditional practices associated with every religion are a large part of what holds the attention of young children. Some traditional practices are peculiar to a particular family and remain in use within that family for many generations. Others are traditions of a national group and are carried with the members of that group wherever they may migrate. The most persistent practices are those handed down from the founders of a religious movement or from its great leaders. Some may even be held over from the religious tradition that preceded the one by whose members it is now practiced, as some pre-Buddhist traditions have persisted in the Tibetan form of Buddhism, or as earlier Arab pagan practices were preserved in Islam. Even today, despite its explicit prohibition by the hierarchy of the Orthodox Greek church, a pre-Christian fertility rite (now called Pyrovasia), in which young men jump through a fire as a magical way to ensure good crops, is still performed in Thrace, usually with the connivance of local priests. A very similar practice is associated with the Holī, a spring festival in popular Hinduism. This festival, too, is thought to antedate the Hindu religion, which would explain why it is found only in popular Hinduism and not in the formal religion. Thus rituals and other religious practices precede, in many cases, the religions in which they are preserved; theology comes to people later in their lives and is accepted with little questioning because it comes wrapped in the haze of familiar, traditional rites and practices.

Since these rituals are so deeply embedded in people's consciousness at the most impressionable period of their lives, it would be most desirable if the advocates of religious reform could consistently retain the ancient ritual traditions. In some instances it is possible to do so without being false to the reforms advocated. There is no great virtue in withholding the experience of Christmas celebration from a Christian child on the grounds of the historical falsity of the date, or because snow in the vicinity of Bethlehem is impossible, or because there is no astronomical report of so bright a star as that in the Christmas story. Christmas is itself often reinterpreted today as the Christmas version of a far more ancient festival of the winter solstice, developed by Roman Christians as an alternative to the Mithraic Birthday of the Invincible Sun (Dies Natalis Solis Invicti), celebrated on the day in the Roman calendar equivalent to 25 December. To the Roman Christian rites of celebration there were added, as Christianity spread into northern Europe, a variety of elements more suitable to the climate of that region. Easter, too, must be recognized as a christianized and spiritualized version of the widespread festivals celebrating the arrival of spring. To acknowledge the earlier ancestry of these Christian festivals adds a universal dimension to their significance; it does not diminish their Christian poetic and symbolic value. Similarly, it is possible to take many of the festivals of other religions and, while retaining all or most of their attractive ceremonial, to refine their traditional basis. Reforming religion does not necessarily imply destroying its poetry or its myth; it requires only recognizing the difference between myth and actuality, between poetry and history.

There are other instances, however, in which ancient traditions have already had to yield to later and higher ideals, and still others in which the advocates of reform must continue the struggle to change traditional practice. The age-old Hindu practice of *satī*, immolating widows on the funeral pyres of their husbands, was forbidden by British rulers as early as 1829 in those parts of India that they controlled. In the "native states," enclaves ruled by native princes, the traditional *satī* was maintained for a time but was gradually eliminated. The theological rationale (perhaps originally an economic rationale) could not be maintained against the higher sense of women's personhood that has developed in modern Indian society. Hindu scholar-priests found no difficulty in reinterpreting the Vedic texts by which the old practice had been justified. Similarly, the Bible, the basic text of Judaism and Christianity, still presents animal sacrifice as a ritual practice divinely commanded and to be routinely carried out by the priests. Both religions have long since given up the practice literally commanded and have replaced actual sacrifice with the symbolic sacrifice of almsgiving. Other biblical injunctions, too, such as the "levirate" obligation, in which the brother of a man who died childless married the widow of his deceased brother in order to sire a son to perpetuate the dead brother's name (*Dt.* 25:5–10), have been either totally abandoned or replaced by a merely symbolic substitute.

Reform is a process that is never finished. Those who carried forward the reforms that have been mentioned, and others like them, may have thought that they had made all the changes that were necessary. But because human knowledge is always increasing, there is no point at which people can say that there is nothing left for them to learn and that all their beliefs are final. It is a continuing part of the religious reformers' obligation to carry on in their own time the unending struggle to renew tradition by bringing features of the religious systems into line with the most advanced knowledge and the most modern sensibilities of their time. There is no reason, for example, why the struggle to achieve parity for women should not, in the present age, be pursued in every religion, even though the achievement of this goal would require the overthrow of certain traditional practices and beliefs. In any area of life in which traditional religious practice comes into conflict with modern sensibility there is a frontier for religious reform. It might well be extremely difficult to eliminate the exclusively masculine language that has become traditional in speaking of God in the monotheistic faiths. But as the role of women in the formal services of these religions is increased, and as certain ritual formulas, such as ". . . who hast not made me a woman," are forced out of the prayer books by insistent and repetitive agitation, the development of a gender-neutral language for religious practice should be possible.

These examples suggest that there are two directions to follow in achieving reform of traditional religious practice. The easier of the two, for all concerned, is to reinterpret, in the light of modern understanding, the theoretical doctrine or historical principle upon which a practice is based, and thus to modify the meaning that the practice has for people today without forcing them to give up the practice itself. Wherever it is possible to do so, the goal of religious reform should be to change meaning without eliminating well-loved practice. Where this is impossible, however, where the practice itself involves a kind of behavior unacceptable in the modern world, reform must be total; the practice and the principle on which it rests must be uprooted, not merely reinterpreted. To be modern, religions must not require either practices that fail to conform to the present-day moral ideas of their environing cultures or beliefs that contradict the best knowledge available. If religions fail in either of these respects, they require reform.

[*See also* Tradition *and* Revival and Renewal *for related discussions.*]

BIBLIOGRAPHY

Most general discussions of religion concentrate on antiquity rather than modernity, on tradition rather than reform. An exception worthy of mention is a collection of essays, *Religious Movements in Contemporary America,* edited by Irving I. Zaretsky and Mark P. Leone (Princeton, 1974). Although limited in geographic scope, these articles present interesting theoretical material on marginal sectarian groups, chiefly among minorities. For our purposes, it is more useful to look at works that view particular major religious traditions in their modern development.

Hinduism. In addition to the useful collection of essays by Hindu scholars, *The Religion of the Hindus,* edited by Kenneth W. Morgan (New York, 1953), Philip H. Ashby's perceptive discussion in *Modern Trends in Hinduism* (New York, 1974) looks at recent trends with a discriminating eye. More recent, and more of a textbook, is *Hinduism: A Cultural Perspective* (Englewood Cliffs, N.J., 1982) by David R. Kinsley, an excellent resource for the reader with little previous knowledge of Hindu religion.

Buddhism. Buddhism, in its many forms, has received a great deal of attention; perhaps the most useful starting point is a collection of essays, *Buddhism in the Modern World,* edited by Heinrich Dumoulin and John C. Marald (New York, 1976). *The Buddhist Religion,* 3d ed. (Belmont, Calif., 1982), by Richard H. Robinson and Willard L. Johnson, is an extremely informative work, valuable for its broad perspective. *Buddhism: The Light of Asia* (Woodbury, N.Y., 1968) by Kenneth Ch'en is especially valuable for its material on Buddhism in China. Similarly valuable for Southeast Asia is Kenneth Perry Landon's *Southeast Asia: Crossroads of Religion* (Chicago, 1969). Buddhism and other religions in China are the subject matter of Wing-tsit Chan's *Religious Trends in Modern China* (New York, 1969). Comparable concerns in relation to the religions of Japan are presented by Joseph M. Kitagawa in *Religion in Japanese History* (New York, 1966).

Islam. Wilfred Cantwell Smith's *Islam in Modern History* (1957; Princeton, 1966) presents a sensitive and sympathetic study by a Western scholar. Unfortunately, it was published too early to take into account contemporary Islamic fundamentalism, which must still find its historian. Smith's *Modern Islām in India* (London, 1946) is a useful supplement to the work mentioned above. For those who know little of Islam, an older work by Henri Lammens, *Islam: Beliefs and Institutions* (London, 1968), provides good background material; so, too, does *Islam: A Concise Introduction* (San Francisco, 1982) by Dennis S. Roberts.

Judaism. My own work, *Modern Varieties of Judaism* (New York, 1966), deals briefly with both the Reform and the Reconstructionist movements in Judaism, as does *American Judaism: Adventure in Modernity* (Englewood Cliffs, N.J., 1972) by Jacob Neusner. The best studies of the Reform movement, however, are *The Rise of Reform Judaism* (New York, 1963) and *The Growth of Reform Judaism* (New York, 1965), both edited by W. Gunther Plaut. For Reconstructionism, consult two works by the founder of the movement, Mordecai M. Kaplan: *The Purpose and Meaning of Jewish Existence* (Philadelphia, 1964) and *Judaism without Supernaturalism* (New York, 1958).

Christianity. The literature of reform movements in Christianity is far too extensive to be listed here. For the period of the Reformation, a convenient summary with a good bibliography is provided by Roland H. Bainton in *The Reformation of the Sixteenth Century* (Boston, 1952). For the modern period in America, as good a brief exposition as one can hope for is found in the last three sections of Sydney E. Ahlstrom's magisterial *A Religious History of the American People* (New Haven, 1972).

JOSEPH L. BLAU

REFORMATION. [*This entry discusses the sixteenth-century movement within Western Christendom that led to the emergence of the several Protestant churches. For discussion of religious reformation in broader perspective, see* Reform *and* Revival and Renewal.]

The term *reformatio* (from the Latin *reformare*, "to renew") was employed in the Middle Ages to denote attempts to reform church and society; the use of the term *Reformation* in the sixteenth century indicates a sense of continuity with earlier efforts. While the term expressed the notion of turning the church from alleged worldliness and lack of proper theological emphasis, it did not, either conceptually or pragmatically, entail the notion of separation from the one church.

When it became evident in the sixteenth-century controversy over the proper interpretation of the Christian faith that the Protestant reformers in fact believed the Roman Catholic church to be in theological error rather than merely to have mistaken emphases, a major step in the direction of separation had been taken. The Catholic church, in turn, viewed the Reformation movement as rebellion and revolution. The term *Protestant*, applied to the adherents of the Reformation, stemmed from the "protest" voiced at the Diet of Speyer (1529) by the Lutheran estates against the revocation of the policy of toleration decreed at the Diet of Speyer three years earlier.

Reformation scholarship has tended to be dominated by confessional perspectives. Catholic scholars have viewed the Reformation as a religious and theological aberration and (as regards its historical significance) the cause of modern secularism. Protestant historiography, in turn, has depicted the Reformation as the restoration of authentic Christianity, with different emphases placed, according to the orientation of particular scholars, on the particular branch (Lutheran, Calvinist-Reformed, Anabaptist, Anglican) of the Reformation. Protestant Reformation historiography has generally focused on theological foci, stressing the distinctive emphases of the respective Protestant churches. [*See also* Protestantism *and separate entries on particular Protestant churches.*]

Background

The traditional view, from the Protestant perspective, has been that in the early sixteenth century, church and society were in a state of crisis. The church was seen as suffering from various moral and theological abuses and the Reformation as a necessary reaction against that state of affairs. Recent research has drawn a different picture, holding that in the early sixteenth century, church and society were essentially stable, although not without problems. Therefore, the explanation for the outbreak of the Reformation is sought elsewhere, namely in a complex interplay of an essentially stable society and powerful new forces.

The foremost political reality of the time, the "Holy Roman Empire of the German Nation," was characterized by uncertainties about its boundaries and the respective roles of the emperor and the territorial rulers. A demand for greater effectiveness in governance had begun to surface in the late fifteenth century, particularly among the territorial rulers. A call for imperial reform was variously voiced and diets (parliamentary assemblies) in 1495 and 1500 went far in reorganizing the formal institutional structures of the empire.

The territories of the empire were in a state of transition in the late fifteenth century. The territorial rulers sought to enhance their own power at the expense of the emperor, while striving for a balance with the nobility in their territories. Because of his need for increased financial resources to support more extensive governmental activities and the flourishing bureaucracies, the emperor had to rely for support on the territorial rulers, who in turn depended on the nobility. The towns, many of which, as free imperial cities, were politically autonomous, presented a similar picture of superficial power relationships. Important centers of commerce and finance were emerging, the political power of which remained restricted. Tensions between the towns and the territories in which they were located were real, since the territories depended on the fiscal resources of the towns but sought to curb their political aspirations.

The Catholic church stood in the center of society. It had extensive land holdings. It controlled education. It possessed its own legal system. It provided the ethical principles on which society was based and which were meant to guide it. Above all, the church, as the guardian of eternal truth, mediated salvation. There is no doubt that, on the eve of the Reformation, the church possessed a great vitality, especially in Germany, and that it commanded considerable loyalty and devotion. Heresy had virtually disappeared. Ecclesiastical benefactions increased in the late fifteenth and early sixteenth centuries. Pilgrimages were popular. Preaching positions in churches were established, and the newly invented printing press provided a host of devotional materials for a growing reading public.

Along with these manifestations of vitality, there were also problems. The hierarchy seemed distant and too cumbersome to deal with the spiritual needs of the people. The higher clergy, notably the bishops, were mainly recruited from the nobility and viewed their office as a source of prestige and power. This was particularly true in Germany, where many bishops were political rulers as well as spiritual rulers. The condition of the lower clergy, the parish priests, was often deplorable. Their theological learning was fragmentary and their economic circumstances marginal. Many parishes had absentee priests; as a result, clerical responsibilities were assumed by the less qualified curates.

In this setting many voices pleaded for church reform. The argument was that the church was too worldly, the papacy too far removed, the clergy too greedy, the religion of the people too vulgar. The humanists, notably Erasmus of Rotterdam, were outspoken in their opposition to scholastic theology. They argued that the simple religion of Christ should be restored. They objected to the scholastic concern over trivia, to the vulgar popular preoccupation with such matters as pilgrimages and relics, and to the pomp and worldliness of the hierarchy. The dominant theological influence emanated from Gabriel Biel, whose Ockhamism seemed a balanced treatment of the themes of human effort and divine action. An overall assessment of the theological situation on the eve of the Reformation must stress the presence of harmonious consistency. [*See also* Humanism.]

The decades before the Reformation brought the growth of "territorial church government." Political authority became increasingly involved in ecclesiastical affairs, while, quite consistently, the role of the church in society—politically, fiscally, and legally—was challenged. In the towns the municipal councils became concerned with responsibility for education, the supervision of morality, and the care of the poor, all of which previously had been the prerogative and function of the church.

When all is said, however, a survey of church and state on the eve of the Reformation fails to reveal extensive symptoms of a profound crisis. Tensions existed but were hardly fundamental, and sundry efforts were being made to alleviate them. Despite criticism and anticlericalism, the call was for change and reform, not for disruption and revolution.

Controversy over Indulgences

The Reformation originated in a controversy over indulgences precipitated by Martin Luther's Ninety-five Theses of 31 October 1517. Indulgences, originally remissions of certain ecclesiastical penalties, had by the early sixteenth century come to be understood as offering forgiveness of sins in exchange for certain payments. Luther's misgivings about a singularly vulgar sale of indulgences by the Dominican monk Johann Tetzel found expression in a probing of the theology of indulgences. In a letter to Archbishop Albert of Hohenzollern, Luther pleaded for the discontinuance of the sale. What was meant as an academic and pastoral matter quickly became a public one, however, primarily because Luther sent out several copies of the theses, and the positive response of the recipients helped to propagate them. Moreover, Luther had inadvertently touched upon a politically sensitive matter. By attacking the sale of indulgences, he had infringed upon the fiscal interests of both the papacy and Archbishop Albert. [*See also the biography of Luther.*]

The subsequent course of events that turned Luther's expression of concern into a public controversy finds its explanation primarily in the astonishing intensity and swiftness of the official reaction: by early 1518 Luther had been cited as a suspected heretic. Undoubtedly, the church still had a vivid memory of the Hussite troubles of the previous century, and its strategy was to squelch the controversy as quickly as possible. The next three years were characterized by dogged pursuit of the official ecclesiastical proceedings against Luther, culminating, in January 1521, in his formal excommunication. After much deliberation and amid unresolved legal uncertainties, a rump diet issued the Edict of Worms in May 1521, whereby Luther was declared a political outlaw.

Events between 1517 and 1521 were dominated not only by the official ecclesiastical proceedings against Luther but also by the concurrent unfolding of his public presence and the increasing echo thereof. Luther's public message was a combination of cautious anticlericalism and a call to a deepened spirituality. This message explains at once the popular response: people responded precisely because they were not called upon to break with the church or to embrace a new theology.

Beginning of the Reformation

At Luther's formal condemnation in 1521 the nature of events changed. With Luther removed from the scene (many thought him dead), the message of reform was spread by an increasing number of comrades-in-arms and supporters. By that time consequences of the new message and its call for reform were beginning to emerge. What would be the practical consequences of Luther's call for a deepened spirituality? If, as Luther had argued, monasticism was unbiblical, what was to be done about the monks and the monasteries? If clerical celibacy was wrong, should priests marry? As these questions were asked and practical answers were offered and implemented, the Reformation in the real sense of the word can be said to have begun.

The Edict of Worms proved but a scrap of paper. Most territorial states plainly ignored it in view of the widespread support for Luther, the dubious legality of the edict, and the rulers' concerns for their legal prerogatives. In the Imperial Council, which exercised the emperor's function during his absence from Germany for the remainder of the decade, the debates about the execution of the edict were lengthy and inconclusive. Nor did diets meeting in Nuremberg in 1523 and 1524 have any greater success, other than issuing plaintive pleas for the convening of a general or at least a German council.

The message that evoked such widespread support is evident in the multitude of pamphlets published between 1517 and 1525. Their themes were simple. They were concerned more with personal piety than with theological propositions. Their message was that of a religion of substance rather than form, of inner integrity rather than outward conformity, of freedom rather than rules. It was also a message of utter dependence on God's grace. At the same time, certain key slogans made their appearance: "human traditions," "works righteousness," "the pure word of God," and, once the battle lines were drawn, the fateful declaration that the papacy was the seat of the Antichrist.

The impact of the reformers was so strong because they deliberately took their arguments to the people whom they knew to be interested in the issues discussed. Abandoning Latin as the language of religious discourse, the reformers used the vernacular in their writings and preferred the brief tract, the pamphlet, to the weighty tome. The genres used for disseminating the message of the Reformation were extensive and varied—straightforward expositions, satires, dialogues, plays, even cartoons. The quantitative output was enormous. Within the first decade of the controversy, over a million copies of Reformation tracts were disseminated in Germany, with its population of roughly ten million. Many tracts were reprinted more than fifteen times.

At this point in its development, the movement was diverse and imprecise in its theological focus. The common denominator was the vague notion of the need for change and reform. Everything else was up in the air, so to speak; the only certainty was that Luther clearly occupied a position of central eminence. The issues propounded were not merely religious ones; they encompassed a wide variety of social and political concerns that made for an intertwining of religious and nonreligious motifs.

The further course of events brought a variety of issues to the fore that defined and divided the Reformation movement. Luther became engaged in controversy with several fellow reformers—among them Ulrich Zwingli, Andreas Karlstadt, and Thomas Müntzer—who challenged both his perspective and his eminence. The controversy with Zwingli, about the Lord's Supper, dominated the remainder of the decade of the 1520s. [*See also the biographies of Zwingli and Müntzer.*]

By the end of the 1520s the reform movement had firmly established itself, especially in southern and central Germany, so much so that the Diet of Speyer in 1526 concluded the impossibility of enforcing the Edict of Worms. Accordingly, the diet allowed the territorial rulers for the time being the freedom to proceed with the edict according to the dictates of their consciences and their sense of responsibility to the emperor.

Two themes were dominant in the years between the Diet of Speyer (1526) and the Peace of Augsburg (1555): the expansion of the Reformation and the pursuit of reconciliation (or coexistence) between the two sides. The theme of Protestant expansion found striking expression in the spread throughout Europe and, in Germany, of the acceptance of the Reformation by a majority of the imperial cities. The convergence of societal concerns and religious goals, characteristic of the Reformation as a whole, is clearly discernible in the cities. The cities were centers of economic power and literacy, and in many were manifest a pronounced anticlericalism and a conflict between the church and those who held political power.

Three patterns of ecclesiastical change in the cities emerged. In some, the agitation for change came from the councils, which sought to bring their quest for full control of all areas of municipal life to a consistent conclusion. In others, the Reformation became part of the political conflict between the council, the ruling oligarchy, and the guilds. The attempt to introduce the Reformation paralleled the effort to democratize. In the third pattern, the quest for ecclesiastical change came from a group of intellectuals who forced the city council to embrace the Reformation.

The second Reformation theme between 1526 and 1555, the pursuit of reconciliation between Catholics and Protestants, had both its political and constitutional aspects. At the Diet of Speyer (1529) the Catholic estates mustered a majority, which insisted on enforcement of the Edict of Worms. But this move had no discernible consequences, and Charles V convened a diet at Augsburg in 1530 to resolve the controversy. The Lutheran estates were invited to submit a confessional statement; the Zurich reformer Zwingli was deemed politically insignificant; the theologically extreme were ignored.

The Lutheran declaration of faith, known as the Augsburg Confession, argued that there was agreement in major matters and that the disagreements pertained only to minor issues, notably the married clergy and episcopal jurisdiction. The issues that had dominated the controversy—the sacraments, authority, and justification—were treated in a broad and most general fashion. This approach of stressing conciliation may have been an astute propaganda move, since there was reason to believe that the Catholics would be rigid. In fact, however, the papacy had also decided on a conciliatory policy, and the eventual failure of the discussions was in part attributable to the failure of each side to understand the other.

At the adjournment of the diet, the Protestants were given six months to rescind their ecclesiastical changes. When the deadline came, however, nothing happened. The emperor, preoccupied militarily with the Turks, was dependent on the support of all the estates, including the Protestants. Moreover, the important Protestant territories had formed the Smalcaldic League to resist any attempt to resolve the religious controversy by force. Accordingly, Charles V had to agree to the Peace of Nuremberg (1532), which afforded the Protestants legal recognition until the convening of a general council.

The 1530s brought continued Protestant expansion in Germany. At the end of the decade new attempts were made to explore the possibility of theological agreement. At the Colloquy of Worms (1539), agreement was reached concerning justification, which had been the main point of controversy between the two sides. In the end, however, disagreement prevailed, and the attempt to resolve the controversy by theological conciliation failed.

Charles V was now determined to use force. Upon concluding peace with France in 1544, he was ready to face the Protestants. War broke out in 1546 and despite a good deal of blundering, Charles emerged successful, winning the decisive Battle of Muhlberg in 1547. The victorious emperor convened a diet at Augsburg in 1548 to impose his religious settlement on the Protestants. The result was the Augsburg Interim, which afforded the Protestants two temporary concessions—use of the communion cup and the married clergy—but left little doubt about the emperor's determination to restore Catholicism fully in the end. At the same time, Charles V sought also, through an ambitious constitutional reform project, to enhance imperial power in Germany. The pairing of these two objectives proved his undoing, for once his political objectives had become clear, his military coalition promptly disintegrated. A conspiracy of territorial rulers, headed by Maurice of Saxony, almost succeeded in imprisoning the emperor.

Charles faced increasingly formidable opposition from the territorial rulers, Protestant and Catholic alike, and he had to acknowledge that Protestantism was firmly entrenched in Germany. The formal recognition of Protestantism could no longer be avoided. Lengthy negotiations conducted by his brother, Ferdinand, culminated in the Peace of Augsburg in 1555. While both sides affirmed the ideal of eventual reconciliation, the realities intimated a permanent division. The foremost provision of the peace was "Cuius regio, eius religio," by which territorial rulers were given the freedom to choose Lutheranism or Catholicism as the official religion in their territory. The emerging distribution of political power in Germany provided the framework for the settlement of the controversy. Even as political power shifted from the emperor to the territorial rulers, so was the religious countenance of Germany formed by the territories rather than the empire.

Differentiation of Reformation Views

As the Reformation movement spread, it became evident that the reformers' common opposition to the Catholic church did not entail a common theological position. Differences of views emerged, pertaining both to the timing and to the scope of reform.

The first incidence of differentiation came in 1522, when Andreas Karlstadt, a colleague of Luther's at the University of Wittenberg, publicly disagreed with Luther. Two years later Thomas Müntzer, minister at Allstedt, not far from Wittenberg, published two pamphlets in which he dramatically indicted Luther's notion of reform. He accused Luther of selling out to the political authorities by preaching a "honey-sweet Christ." In the spring of 1525, Müntzer joined the rebellious peasants in central Germany and became their spiritual leader. The pamphlets that issued from his pen were vitriolic and categorical: the true church would be realized only through suffering and by a resolute opposition to the godless rulers.

While the most famous of the peasant programs, the Twelve Articles, astutely linked peasant aspirations with the Lutheran proclamation, the connection between the reform movement and the peasants was tenuous at best. It must remain doubtful whether, given their illiteracy, the peasants were extensively touched by the Reformation. But Luther felt sufficiently implicated to publish two pamphlets against the peasants in which he expressed sympathy for their plight yet categorically declared that the gospel did not provide the justification for its amelioration and that rebellion was against the gospel. These tracts heralded a fundamental divorce of the Reformation from a major social issue of the time.

Ulrich Zwingli. The major division within the ranks of the reformers is associated with the Swiss reformer Ulrich (Huldrych) Zwingli, of Zurich. Unlike Luther, whose theological development occurred in the setting of monastery and university, Zwingli matured as a parish priest and as a theologian greatly influenced by Erasmus. In 1522, he publicly defended eating meat during the Lenten fast and in so doing precipitated a lively controversy about the propriety of the prescribed ecclesiastical practices. The Zurich city council ordered a disputation to resolve the contested issues. It took place in January 1523 and resulted in the public declaration of support for Zwingli by the council, a declaration that had the noteworthy underlying assumption that a community could itself determine the faith, regardless of established ecclesiastical authority. A new norm of religious authority was evident here.

A second disputation, in October 1523, dealt with the issues of the use of images in churches and the interpretation of the Mass. Agreement was quickly reached that both were unbiblical, but opinion differed as to the most propitious time for their abolition. From the ranks of some of Zwingli's followers came the same kind of impatience with the course of ecclesiastical change that Luther had witnessed in Wittenberg in 1522. Eventually some of these followers broke openly with Zwingli; thus was launched the Anabaptist movement.

The specific issue that was to divide the Reformation was the interpretation of the Lord's Supper. [*See* Eucharist.] Luther, while rejecting the Catholic doctrine of transubstantiation, affirmed the real presence of Christ in the elements of bread and wine, while Zwingli affirmed a spiritual presence. The controversy between the two men erupted in 1525 and continued, with increasing vehemence, for years to come. By 1529 political overtones to the theological disagreement had surfaced. Since military action against the Protestants was a possibility, the internal disagreement weakened the Protestant position. It became clear that the future of the Reformation lay in political strength. Landgrave Philipp of Hesse, the driving force behind such notions, arranged for a colloquy between Luther and Zwingli at Marburg in October 1529. Luther was a reluctant participant, not only because he had little empathy for Zwingli's theology but also because he reflected a different political perspective. Any rapprochement with Zwingli, who was seen as both anti-Habsburg and a theological radical, would make conciliation with the Habsburg emperor Charles V more difficult.

The Marburg colloquy, therefore, manifested both political and theological issues. No agreement was reached in the lengthy discussions, even though the document signed by those present skillfully buried the disagreement concerning communion in an inconspicuous sentence. The Reformation movement remained divided. Zwingli's influence was strong in Zurich, Switzerland, and even southwestern Germany even though the second of two military engagements between Swiss Catholics and Protestants in 1529 and 1531 ended with Protestant defeat and the curtailment of further Protestant expansion. Zwingli himself died on the battlefield of Kappel in 1531.

The Anabaptists. A second major division within the ranks of the Reformation pertained to a heterogeneous group whom contemporaries called "Anabaptists." This term, derived from a Greek word meaning "rebaptizer," indicated the Anabaptists' most prominent assertion: that baptism should be performed in adulthood as the outgrowth of an individual's decision. More important was the Anabaptist conviction, which echoed Thomas Müntzer, that the major reformers had been neither serious nor comprehensive in their effort to restore biblical Christianity. The Anabaptists thus placed great emphasis on the personal commitment to follow Christ (exemplified by the desire to be baptized), viewed the church as a voluntary group of believers, and held for complete aloofness from the political structures.

Anabaptism originated formally in Zurich among young humanist associates of Zwingli who, influenced by Müntzer and Karlstadt, were disenchanted with the slow progress of reform. Their attempt to impose their own vision of speedier and more comprehensive reform on the course of events proved unsuccessful. They broke with Zwingli, administered believer's baptism early in 1525, and found themselves promptly persecuted, since the authorities were unwilling to tolerate diverse forms of religion in their midst. Impatience and dissatisfaction with the course of ecclesiastical change were widespread in the mid-1520s, so that it is not possible to speak of a single point of origin for Anabaptism. Events were moving too slowly for many, and the theological atmosphere at the time was so diverse as to suggest a multiplicity of mentors and sources.

The Anabaptist movement expanded throughout Austria and Germany, chiefly through itinerant lay preachers. Small congregations developed as a result of their preaching. Both ecclesiastical and secular authorities declared the Anabaptists to be revolutionaries and pursued a harsh policy of persecution. This caused Anabaptism to become an underground movement. Its literature was sparse, since it had to be clandestinely printed and disseminated. It had no trained clergy. Despite such handicaps Anabaptism enjoyed a widespread, if modest, expansion.

The catastrophe of Anabaptism at the northwestern German town of Münster, in the early 1530s, proved to be a turning point in the history of the movement. The coming of the Reformation to Münster had prompted the town's leading minister, Bernd Rothmann, to embrace Lutheran notions and successfully secure the appointment of other reform-minded Lutheran clergy. Elections to the city council in 1533 resulted in a Lutheran majority. Subsequently, Rothmann came under Anabaptist influence, and Münster underwent a second Reformation in embracing Anabaptism. Early in 1534 representatives of the Dutch Anabaptist leader Melchior Hofmann arrived to administer adult baptism. Euphoria set in, since Hofmann had earlier prophesied that the imminent end would be preceded by the victory of the elect over the godless. The events at Münster seemed to vindicate his prophecy of the glorious things to come.

Extensive changes occurred in the city. In 1534 Jan van Leyden, who had assumed leadership, declared himself king of the New Jerusalem. Communism and polygamy were introduced, both measures forced upon the Münster Anabaptists as much by external pressures as by biblical reflection; these changes prompted Catholic and Protestant authorities to lay siege to the city. Food and other supplies were at a premium, and women vastly outnumbered men.

After Münster was captured in the spring of 1535, and this New Jerusalem came to its end, the consequences for Anabaptists proved catastrophic. The authorities concluded that their fears had been vindicated: religious dissent had indeed, as they had predicted, escalated into political revolution. The persecution of Anabaptists intensified, and their very credibility suffered disastrously.

In northern Germany and Holland, Anabaptism was significantly aided by the leadership of a former Dutch priest, Menno Simons. With sensitive theological reflection and organizational skill, he succeeded in directing the perplexed Anabaptists to the ideal of a quiet, otherworldly Christianity that removed itself from any involvement in the political structures of society and acknowledged that existing authorities could not be replaced. While the themes of nonviolence and withdrawal from society had been voiced by earlier Anabaptist leaders, Simons emphasized them as hallmarks of Anabaptism. The Netherlands became, with Switzerland, the center of the movement. [*For further discussion, see* Anabaptism *and the biography of Simons.*]

The Antitrinitarians. Although some of the intellectual roots of Antitrinitarianism can be traced to the late Middle Ages, the catalytic influence of the Reformation was paramount in the movement. The atmosphere of challenge of established opinion and the stress on the Bible as sole authority seemed to call for the repudiation of the doctrine of the Trinity. A most dramatic event, in the early 1530s, was the publication of two staunchly antitrinitarian tracts by a Spanish lay theologian and physician, Michael Servetus. Servetus's later *Restitution* of 1553 offered a detailed critique of traditional dogma. However, it was not until the second half of the sixteenth century that a new ecclesiastical tradition embracing such notions emerged, notably in Poland. In an atmosphere of toleration, a part of the Calvinist church in Poland became antitrinitarian, greatly influenced by the Italian reformers Laelius and Fausto Sozzini. [*See the biographies of Servetus and Sozzini.*]

John Calvin. An urbane French lawyer and humanist by background, John Calvin was the embodiment of both the differentiation of Reformation views and of its European dimension. Calvin had left his native country for Switzerland to arrange for the publication of his brief summary statement of Reformation theology, *Institutes of the Christian Religion.* Passing by chance through Geneva in 1536, the twenty-seven-year-old scholar was pressured into staying to take part in the reform there. His first attempt to implement reform led to conflict with the city authorities and to his expulsion in 1538. Three years later, however, he was invited to return and he remained there until his death in 1564. [*See the biography of Calvin.*]

Institutes of the Christian Religion, an originally slender volume that was many times revised and enlarged, stands as the monumental systematic delineation of reformed religion. Its basic motif, echoed in many variations, is the majesty of God, from which man's eternal destiny—predestination to salvation or to damnation—is reasoned. While Calvin always wished to emphasize God's majesty as the overarching theme of biblical religion, the concept of predestination emerged as the characteristic feature of Calvin's thought.

Calvin's notion of election to salvation made the elect the warriors for God. At the same time, Calvin consciously sought to implement the societal implications of the Christian religion. Following notions of Zwingli and the Strasbourg reformer Martin Bucer, he undertook to reform not merely the church but all of society. [*See the biography of Bucer.*] Thus Geneva, Calvin's seat of action, was to become the most famous of the towns of the Reformation.

Calvin's instrument of reform was the *Ecclesiastical Ordinances* of 1541, a comprehensive summary of the structure of the church and its place in society. The most important administrative institution in Geneva (and wherever Calvin's version of the Reformation gained a foothold) was the consistory, a body composed of both clergy and laity whose task was to supervise the maintenance of true faith and pure morals. Thus, it was not an ecclesiastical (or clerical) body, turning Geneva into an ecclesiastical tyranny. The political authorities participated fully in it in pursuit of an orderly and moral community.

Calvin's determination to implement his vision of God's law brought him into conflict with influential Genevans. There were several serious confrontations, and matters remained at an uneasy stalemate until 1553, when the trial of Michael Servetus forced the issue. Calvin, who despised Servetus for his heretical views, regarded his appearance in Geneva as part of a larger plot to undo Calvinist reforms in the city. Servetus's condemnation and execution consolidated Calvin's role. Elsewhere in Europe, notably in Poland, the Low Countries, Scotland, and especially France, Calvinism emerged as the major form of the Reformation. Lutheranism at the time was rife with internal theological controversy, leaving to Calvin and his followers the role of the dynamic force of the Reformation in the second half of the sixteenth century.

European Dimension of the Reformation

In light of the European dimension of the Reformation the question has been asked whether to view this dimension as the result of the transmission of ideas from Germany or as the emergence of simultaneous reform movements in a number of European countries. There has been support for both views, although there seems little doubt that the Lutheran controversy in Germany affected theologians and laity throughout Europe. Travelers and the printed word carried forth the message from Germany. To this German influence the native reformers added their own emphases.

The European theological themes were also uniform; they were determined by a common opposition to Roman Catholicism and a common stance concerning the authority of scripture. Moreover, the essential course of development of the Reformation in Europe hardly differed from one country to another, in that theological discussion was always accompanied by a quest for legal recognition. In each country the period of the Reformation ended with a legal pronouncement: in France with the Edict of Nantes (1598); in Poland with the Confederation of Warsaw (1573); and in Scotland with an act of Parliament (1560).

The spread of the Reformation movement was uniformly related to local political issues and to the concomitant ability of the Protestants to demonstrate that their religion could have relevance for these issues. The success of the Reformation hinged on its ability to convert king or nobility, whichever was crucial in the struggle. As events turned out, in England, Sweden, Norway, Denmark, Finland, and Scotland, the Protestants were on the winning side.

At the time the Reformation movement broke out in Germany, reform notions were already strong in France. Although Jacques Lefèvre d'Étaples had anticipated some of Luther's notions and had translated the New Testament into French, we may see the first phase of the Reformation in France as the dissemination of Lutheran ideas and pamphlets. The official reaction was that of suppression. While Francis I was himself a humanist by disposition, political prudence led him to take a Catholic and papal course. The *placard* affair of 1534, in which a Protestant poster was affixed to the door of the king's bedroom, symbolized Protestant strength in the country. Francis responded with persecution and a stern censorship of books. His successor, Henry II, continued this policy, which found embodiment in the Edict of Chateaubriand (1551).

Henry's unexpected death in 1559 precipitated a constitutional crisis over the exercise of regency during the minority of the new king, Francis II. Cardinal Guise summarily assumed the regency, but his move was opposed by the prestigious Bourbon family, which argued for a council of regency. The constitutional issue had religious overtones, since the Guises were staunch Catholics, while the Bourbons had Protestant leanings. To side with the Bourbons seemed to promise toleration for the Protestants. The constitutional uncertainty prompted the question whether royal authority was being properly exercised. This crisis saw the emergence of the issue of political resistance among French Protestants. Calvin's doctrine of the right of resistance to rulers who did not fulfill their duty served as sanction for the contention that the higher nobility had the right to oppose the king when he violated the law.

The Wars of Religion, which began in 1562, sought to resolve the issue of political power in France and saw the French Protestants (Huguenots) combine political concerns with their religious cause. The Edict of Nantes (1598) ended the struggle and brought the French Reformation to an end. It resembled the Peace of Augsburg in that the Protestants failed in their effort to win acceptance of their religion by France. They were recognized legally, however, and were given freedom of worship. In Germany only the territorial rulers possessed freedom of religious choice; in France this freedom was extended to all.

The Reformation in England. In the 1520s England underwent a period of lively agitation against the Roman Catholic church. Although this agitation was influenced by events on the continent, there were indigenous forces at work as well: anticlericalism, the tradition of the Lollard heresy, and Erasmian humanism. Henry VIII had himself participated in the initial Reformation controversy with a defense of the traditional Catholic teaching on the sacraments, for which Pope Leo X granted him the title "Defender of the Faith." The king's conservative temperament was thus on record.

This atmosphere of religious agitation was complicated by Henry's sudden desire for an annulment of his marriage to Catherine of Aragon (his deceased brother's widow) on the grounds that the marriage violated canon law. Extensive efforts to obtain a favorable papal decision proved unsuccessful, and Henry eventually chose, on the advice of Thomas Cromwell, the parliamentary route to provide legal justification for his intention. In 1533 Parliament passed the Act in Restraint of Appeals to Rome, which declared England an "empire" whose sovereign could adjudge all spiritual and temporal matters in his realm. This act kept the judicial resolution over Henry's "divorce" in England. The king had broken with the papal church. [*See also* Anglicanism.]

Concomitant ecclesiastical changes in England were initially few, however, and pertained mainly to jurisdictional and organizational matters. Despite his own Catholic temperament, Henry actively encouraged anti-Catholic propaganda throughout the 1530s. In 1534, Parliament passed several acts concerning ecclesiastical appointments and the royal supremacy: the earlier acknowledgment of the Convocation, the legislative body of the church, that the king was the supreme head of the church was transformed into a legal statute. This designation did not encompass spiritual functions but provided for the care of the external order and structure in the church. In essence, it was the conclusion of a development long antedating the Reformation and evident throughout Europe. Henry's agent until 1540 was his chief minister, Thomas Cromwell. Cromwell undertook to orchestrate the changes, subsidize a grandiose propaganda effort, and subject religious considerations to the affairs of state. A significant ecclesiastical change was the dissolution of the monasteries (1536), which had the dual consequence of increasing the king's property and of doing away with centers of Catholic propaganda. It precipitated a series of conservative Catholic uprisings known as the "Pilgrimage of Grace," which Henry suppressed with cunning and ease.

The doctrinal statement of the religion imposed by Henry came with the Six Articles of 1539. These articles were Catholic in orientation—as, for example, in espousing transubstantiation and clerical celibacy. Thomas Cranmer, archbishop of Canterbury, who was married, had to send his wife abroad. [*See the biography of Cranmer.*] Although the legal situation was restrictive, the actual situation was relatively free. The penalties imposed by the articles were rarely applied, and antipapal propaganda flowed openly. Protestant sentiment, except of the ardent kind, could be easily disseminated. Adamant Catholics were persecuted no less than adamant Protestants. The influence of Erasmian religion made itself felt in England, a religion relatively open, yet essentially Catholic in orientation.

When Henry died in 1547 religious affairs were thus in a precarious balance, neither strongly Protestant nor strongly Catholic. He had intended this state of affairs for his minor son, Edward VI, but the Council of Regency was dominated by men of Protestant sympathies. The official religion of the land veered in the direction of Protestantism. Under the aegis of Archbishop Cranmer, a new order for worship *(The Book of Common Prayer)* was promulgated in 1549. Drawing on the rich liturgical heritage of the medieval church, this order for worship, with the beauty of its language and its structure of the divine office, proved to be an immensely enriching contribution to English Christendom. The theological tone of the prayer book was conservative in that it espoused a Lutheran view of Communion. A revision of the book, three years later, embraced a Zwinglian view.

Mary, the daughter of Henry's first wife, Catherine of Aragon, who succeeded her stepbrother in 1553, attempted to restore Catholicism, with an increasingly heavy hand and, in the end, with a ruthless persecution of all avowed Protestants. In so doing, she overlooked the fact that England's ties with the Catholic church had been severed for almost a quarter of a century; what is more important, she failed to understand the danger of creating martyrs. After her reign (1553–1558), John Foxe wrote his *Book of Martyrs*, a gripping, often melodramatic description of Protestant suffering, torture, and martyrdom. Put into the context of the martyrs of the faith of all times, the book helped make Catholicism impossible in England.

The Elizabethan settlement. With the succession of Mary's stepsister, Elizabeth I, in 1558, the English situation changed dramatically. As Anne Boleyn's daughter, Elizabeth was predisposed to Protestantism and promptly set out to effect a religious settlement in that direction. She wished only for a limited restoration of Protestantism, aiming for the initial reestablishment of royal supremacy and the possibility of further religious change later. But Parliament, convening in 1559, was determined to move in a more Protestant direction. Elizabeth yielded to a settlement that restored religion as it had existed at the end of Edward's reign. An important change, however, made the section on Communion in *The Book of Common Prayer* less precise. By juxtaposing language of the 1549 and 1552 editions of *The Book of Common Prayer* with respect to Communion, it was left uncertain if Christ was bodily present in the Communion bread and wine.

In 1563 the Convocation adopted a theological statement for the Church of England. With Thomas Cranmer's Forty-two Articles of 1551 serving as the point of departure, various revisions resulted in the Thirty-nine Articles, a theologically moderate statement.

Puritanism. Before long the settlement of 1559 began to evoke opposition from those for whom it was not sufficiently Protestant. Its critics argued that too many vestiges of Catholicism remained in the English church. They wanted a "pure" church, and before long they came to be called "Puritans." The Puritans were to be a major element in English history until the second half of the seventeenth century. Puritanism underwent significant changes in the course of its lengthy history. Toward the end of the sixteenth century it became increasingly diverse and sectarian, some strands determined to break with the established church. It also became increasingly political. [*See* Puritanism.]

Until the end of the sixteenth century, England witnessed successive waves of Puritan dissent. Clerical vestments and the episcopal form of church government soon became the subject of controversy. By the 1580s some Puritans had concluded the impossibility of effecting change from within. Robert Browne's *A Treatise of Reformation without Tarrying for Any* argued for the establishment of separate congregations because the Church of England was unable to reform. In response, Richard Hooker's monumental *Laws of Ecclesiastical Polity* stated the case for Anglicanism as the perfect middle way, arguing with an impressive command of the principles of natural law and the early church. [*See the biographies of Browne and Hooker.*]

On the continent the Reformation controversies had virtually subsided by the end of the sixteenth century. In England, however, the separatist sentiment came to fruition during that time with the emergence of different groupings, of which several—Congregationalists, Baptists, and Quakers—were to become ecclesiastical traditions in Anglo-Saxon Christendom. [*See* Denominationalism.]

The Catholic Reaction

The initial reaction of the Catholic church to Luther was astoundingly swift and categorical. Undoubtedly, it was influenced by the apprehension that, if not properly handled, the conflagration would lead to another Hussite debacle. By 1520 the position of the church had been delineated: Luther's understanding of the Christian faith was declared heretical and his notion of reform rejected. It was to be of profound import for subsequent events that despite this condemnation, the Catholic church possessed neither a comprehensive policy for reform nor a clear perception of how to execute the judgment against Luther or halt the increasing defections. Moreover, the papacy had its own priorities, which were slow to focus on the Lutheran affair and the Protestant Reformation, even though there was no dearth of voices predicting disaster unless a solution was found.

The disadvantages facing the defenders of the Catholic church were obvious. They had to defend the status quo with all its shortcomings, while the reformers were able to delineate a splendid vision of an ideal church. Many of those who attacked the church did so for other than religious reasons, thus introducing an element of power politics into what purported to be a religious matter. Pope and emperor, whose concerted efforts would have been able to stem the Protestant tide, frequently were at odds with each other, working at cross-purposes, and thereby aiding the Reformation.

The question of whether a general council should be convened was undoubtedly the overriding issue during the first two decades of the Reformation. With striking unanimity Christians throughout Europe saw a council as the panacea not only for the ills of the church but also for those of society. To be sure, notions differed as to what the function of a council should be, and perhaps not much would have been accomplished had a council actually convened. But the negative stance of Pope Clement VII, who feared a resurgence of conciliarism, precluded a council in the early years of the Reformation. [*See* Papacy.]

When a council eventually convened at Trent in 1545, it was clear that it could have no other function than to sharpen the true Catholic position on a wide variety of issues. Thus the council, which met intermittently until 1563, possessed significance only for the Catholic church. Its canons and decrees were consciously anti-

Protestant and offered conciliatory views only with respect to issues contested within Catholicism. Thus the council served to revitalize the Catholic church, formulating the principles and policies that characterized an invigorated Catholicism for the century to come.

The Council of Trent gathered together the sundry strands of renewal within the Catholic church, some of which had been discernible even before 1517. The revival of monasticism, for example, antedated the Reformation. Renewal continued in the 1520s and 1530s, in many instances not influenced by the Reformation. The foremost expression of this renewal was the work of Ignatius Loyola and the Society of Jesus, which he founded. The manifestation of Catholic renewal became an instrument of reaction against the Reformation, and in one of its central forms, namely, monastic spirituality, it reiterated the traditional vehicle of Catholic reform. [*See* Trent, Council of; Jesuits; *the biography of Ignatius; and* Monasticism, *article on* Christian Monasticism.]

Significance of the Reformation

Perceptions of the significance of the Reformation have differed markedly since the sixteenth century. Generally it is the ecclesiastical persuasion of the observer that has provided the cue for the interpretation.

Protestants saw the Reformation as the restoration of biblical Christianity against a worldly and perverted church. In turn, Catholics saw the Reformation as rebellion against truth and, concomitantly, as a triumph of subjectivism. Nineteenth- and twentieth-century Catholics have argued that, because the Reformation repudiated authority, it was a direct forerunner of the French Revolution. Such stereotypes as these have largely disappeared. Catholic scholars have been willing to acknowledge the religious depth and significance of Luther, while Protestants have revised their negative assessment of the pre-Reformation church and are prepared to see greater continuity between the late Middle Ages and the Reformation. Recent scholarship has also made clear that there was great misunderstanding among the protagonists on both sides of the sixteenth-century controversy. The theological differences are nowadays seen to have consisted in divergent notions of authority and salvation: authority of the Bible and the church or of the Bible alone; salvation by works and grace or by grace alone.

Although the divergence between Catholic and Protestant historiography of the Reformation has largely disappeared, the resurgence of the interpretation first delineated by Friedrich Engels has perpetuated the tradition of divergent assessments of the Reformation. Marxist historians view the Reformation and the German Peasants' War collectively as "early bourgeois revolution." In their view the rising class of townspeople engaged in commerce and trade and holding increasing economic power, found itself in conflict with the holders of political power. In opposing this political power, the new class had to reject the ideological undergirding of medieval society, the Catholic church. Luther was the religious spokesman for economic power and a new, bourgeois mentality.

The foremost consequence of the Reformation was the division of Western Christendom into several churches. The centrality of the Catholic church was irretrievably destroyed, and the universal church gave way to national churches. While the political authorities precluded the formal recognition of more than one church, the existence of several religious perspectives (bitterly opposing one another) surely diminished the public as well as private significance of religion in Europe. This disintegrated the notion that had characterized medieval society—the oneness of this world and the next. The existence of diverse religious options did not, however, entail a sense of toleration or religious liberty. All parties clung to the notion of objective truth and the impossibility of allowing the public expression of religious error.

The masses, illiterate and living in isolation in rural areas, remained untouched by the controversies of the Reformation. In other words, the sixteenth century is not to be viewed as a time of intense popular preoccupation with religion. Evidence abounds of outright disinterest in religion, despite countless governmental mandates stipulating church attendance or religious instruction. Popular religion was a simple folk religion, little influenced by the sophisticated theological arguments that characterized Reformation controversies.

The role of the political authorities in these religious controversies has already been noted. Throughout Europe the rulers had the last word about the success or failure of the Reformation. They rarely hesitated to exercise that power, at times for religious reasons and at other times for political reasons. In exercising their power, they enhanced their political stature and enlarged the scope of their authority.

Clearly, the role of political authority in religion was more firmly established at the end of the sixteenth century than it had been at the beginning. If the Reformation thus conformed harmoniously with the new self-understanding of the political rulers, it also proved exceptionally congenial to the mentality of a new type of person, very much in evidence in the late fifteenth century—literate, self-confident, and energetic. The Reformation, after all, affirmed the priesthood of all believers, the freedom of the Christian individual, and the sanctity of the common life. The autonomy of the individual was asserted not with respect to transcendental concerns but with respect to the role and place of the church in society.

In such a setting, the Reformation provided a host of stimuli for all areas of life. The notion of vocation declared all jobs to be spiritually meaningful. This sanctity of the common life must not be defined merely by an individual sense of liberation, enabling men and women to go about their daily rounds with confidence, but also by a societal sense, embodied by statute no less than by ethos, that society did not need to be dominated by the church. All facets of life, both individual and societal, became subject to new formulations. Conceptual and practical problems of education, law, commerce, and behavior were approached with eagerness and enthusiasm. The common denominator was the notion of a lay culture, where the laity rather than the clergy played the incisive role. This did not entail the secularization of society: religion continued to be very much in the center of things, if for no other reason than that a divine order was generally agreed to govern all of life. If the genius of the medieval world had been its notion of the oneness of society under the aegis of the church, the Reformation stipulated a oneness that entailed the equality of church and society.

[*See also* Christianity, *article on* Christianity in Western Europe. *For discussion of elements of Christian theology raised herein, see* Theology, *article on* Christian Theology; Church; Grace; Free Will and Predestination, *article on* Christian Concepts; Justification; *and* Sacraments, *article on* Christian Sacraments.]

BIBLIOGRAPHY

General Surveys. The best general introductions to the history of the Reformation are G. R. Elton's *Reformation Europe, 1517–1559* (New York, 1963); *The Reformation, 1520–1559,* edited by G. R. Elton, "The New Cambridge Modern History," vol. 2 (Cambridge, 1958); Lewis W. Spitz's *The Renaissance and Reformation Movements,* 2d ed., 2 vols. (Saint Louis, 1980); and my *The World of the Reformation* (New York, 1973). The Literature Survey of the Archiv für Reformationsgeschichte (Leipzig and Berlin, 1903–) provides an annual annotated survey of all literature pertaining to the Reformation. Useful also is *Bibliography of the Continental Reformation: Materials Available in English,* 2d ed., rev. & enl., edited by Roland H. Bainton and Eric W. Gritsch (Hamden, Conn., 1972). A survey of current research emphases is *Reformation Europe: A Guide to Research,* edited by Steven E. Ozment (Saint Louis, 1982).

Specialized Studies

Blickle, Peter. *The Revolution of 1525.* Baltimore, 1982.

Brady, Thomas A. *Ruling Class, Regime and Reformation at Strasbourg, 1520–1555.* Leiden, 1978.

Clasen, Claus-Peter. *Anabaptism: A Social History, 1525–1618.* Ithaca, N.Y., 1972.

Edwards, Mark U., Jr. *Luther's Last Battles.* Ithaca, N.Y., 1983.

Elton, G. R. *Policy and Police.* Cambridge, 1972.

Goertz, Hans, ed. *Profiles of Radical Reformers.* Scottdale, Pa., 1982.

Hendrix, Scott H. *Luther and the Papacy.* Philadelphia, 1981.

Lienhard, Marc, ed. *The Origins and Characteristics of Anabaptism.* The Hague, 1977.

Lortz, Joseph. *The Reformation in Germany.* New York, 1968.

Moeller, Bernd. "Piety in Germany around 1500." In *The Reformation in Medieval Perspective,* edited by Steven E. Ozment, pp. 50–75. Chicago, 1971.

Moeller, Bernd. *Imperial Cities and the Reformation.* Philadelphia, 1972.

Ozment, Steven E. *The Reformation in the Cities.* New Haven, 1975.

Stayer, James M. *Anabaptism and the Sword.* Lawrence, Kans., 1972.

Walton, Robert C. *Zwingli's Theocracy.* Toronto, 1967.

Williams, George H. *The Radical Reformation.* Philadelphia, 1962.

HANS J. HILLERBRAND

REFORMED PRESBYTERIAN CHURCH. *See* Presbyterianism, Reformed.

REFORM JUDAISM is the branch of the Jewish faith that has been most adaptive, in belief and practice, to the norms of modern thought and society. It is also sometimes called Liberal Judaism or Progressive Judaism. By *Reform* is meant not a single reformation but an ongoing process of development. Over one million Reform Jews live in the United States and Canada, with about another one hundred thousand in Europe, Latin America, South Africa, Australia, and Israel. Internationally, all Reform congregations are united in the World Union for Progressive Judaism, which holds biennial conferences usually in Europe or in Israel. In the United States some 750 independent congregations constitute the Union of American Hebrew Congregations (UAHC), and more than 1,300 rabbis—some of them serving abroad—make up the Central Conference of American Rabbis (CCAR). Rabbis, as well as scholars, educators, community workers, and cantors, are trained at the Hebrew Union College–Jewish Institute of Religion (HUC-JIR), which has branches in Cincinnati, New York, Los Angeles, and Jerusalem. The most influential role of organizational leadership in Reform Judaism is the presidency of the UAHC, in recent years a professional position held by a rabbi.

Beliefs and Practices. Unlike more traditional forms of the Jewish faith, Reform Judaism does not hold that either the written law (Torah) or the oral law (Talmud) was revealed literally by God to Moses at Sinai. It accepts biblical and other historical criticism as legitimate, understanding scripture and tradition as a human reflection of revelation rather than its literal embodiment. While theologies among Reform Jews vary greatly, from the traditional to the humanistic, concepts of God strike a balance between universal and particular elements, with somewhat more stress upon the former than among other religious Jews. Like other branches of Judaism, Reform recognizes the close connection between religion and ethics. It especially emphasizes the prophetic message of social justice and seeks to act upon it both congregationally and as a united movement. Judaism is seen to exist for a higher universal purpose, which aims messianically at the biblical vision of world peace. Traditionally in Reform Judaism, this sense of purpose has been known as the "mission of Israel."

The doctrine that most significantly sets Reform Judaism apart from more traditional currents is the conception of progressive revelation. Reform Jews hold that revelation is ongoing with the progress of human knowledge and religious sensitivity. This represents a reversal of the Orthodox belief whereby the theophany at Sinai, as interpreted by the rabbis, constitutes the authoritative, permanent expression of God's will, which must therefore remain normative for all time. The Reform conception of progress in understanding of the divine does not necessarily imply the continuous moral advance of the Jews or of Western civilization, although Reform Judaism before the Holocaust was prone to draw that conclusion.

The freedom of the individual Jew to be selective, to draw from Jewish tradition those elements of belief and practice that he or she finds the most personally meaningful, is far greater among Reform Jews than among either Orthodox or Conservative. Religious anarchy, while always a danger, is restrained by a common though theologically diverse liturgy, general agreement on basic commitments, and a well-structured organizational framework. Reform Jews do not accept the Jewish legal tradition as binding but have always—and especially in recent years—turned to it for guidance in ritual matters. The CCAR currently issues both a manual for Sabbath observance and a guide to the Jewish life cycle.

At most Reform congregations in America the main religious service of the week is held after dinner on Friday evenings; men and women sit together, participating equally in the service. Only in recent years have many rabbis, some male congregants, and a much smaller number of women begun to wear the ritual head covering (*kippah* or *yarmulke*) during worship. In nearly all Reform synagogues (or temples, as they are often called) the liturgy is accompanied by an organ, while musical responses are led or performed by a choir and/or a cantor. Most of the prayers are spoken in English, except for those of central significance, which are rendered in Hebrew; the ratio varies from congregation to congregation. Especially under the impact of the state of Israel, the relative amount of Hebrew in the service has generally increased and its pronunciation has been altered from the Ashkenazic (central and eastern European) to the Sefardic (Spanish and Near Eastern) accent used in the Jewish state. Formality and decorum have been hallmarks of the Reform temple, but in recent years some congregations have sought to regain some of the informality and emotion of the traditional synagogue through greater congregational involvement in the service and experimentation with alternative musical instruments such as the guitar. The influence of worship services conducted in the summer camps of the National Federation of Temple Youth has been an appreciable factor in this regard.

Outside the synagogue Reform Jews practice their faith by attempting to guide their lives according to the moral precepts of Judaism. A large percentage practices some Jewish rituals in the home, especially the lighting of the Sabbath candles on Friday evening, the Passover eve ceremony, or Seder, and the celebration of Ḥanukkah. Once especially aware of their religious differences from traditional Jews, today Reform Jews emphasize to a greater extent their common ethnic identity and the faith shared by all religious Jews, limiting the significance of denominational differences.

Reform Jews remain more favorably inclined to proselytism than other branches of religious Judaism. The largest portion of converts to Judaism become Reform Jews, often as the result of marriage with a Jewish partner. Such "Jews by choice" today comprise a small but growing percentage of the membership of most Reform congregations. Reform Judaism has recently given much attention to issues concerning procedures for conversion as well as the Jewish legal status of children born from mixed marriages in which the father, but not the mother, is Jewish. According to the *halakhah* (traditional Jewish law), such children are not Jewish unless formally converted. The Reform rabbinate is unique in that some Reform rabbis will conduct weddings for mixed couples in which the non-Jewish partner does not intend to convert to Judaism. Usually in such instances, however, the couple promises to raise its children as Jews.

The Movement in Europe. Reform Jews have often pointed out that religious reform was inherent in Judaism from its beginnings. They have noted that the prophets were critics of contemporary religious practices, that the Talmud includes reforms of earlier biblical legislation, and that even later legal scholars were willing to alter received beliefs and practices. Such willingness to adjust to historical change waned only under the pressure of persecution and the isolation of the ghetto. Latter-day Jews seeking religious reform thus sought, and to a degree found, precedent for their programs in earlier layers of Jewish tradition. However, they soon became aware that most of their fellow Jews, and especially the established rabbinical leadership, did not share such views. The result was a movement for reform, originally intended to harmonize all aspects of Jewish life with the modern world into which European Jews increasingly entered beginning with the later eighteenth century. Only gradually did the movement come to focus specifically on the religious realm, and only after a generation did it separate itself as a differentiable religious current with a more or less fixed religious philosophy. In discussing origins, it is therefore more accurate to speak of the "Reform movement in Judaism" than of Reform Judaism. Even this terminology, however, requires the qualification that self-conscious awareness of being a movement with definite goals came only gradually with the coalescence of various elements of belief and practice.

Beginnings. The background for the emergence of the Reform movement is the changing political and cultural situation of central and western European Jewry in the last decades of the eighteenth century and the beginning of the nineteenth. For numerous generations Jews had been physically and intellectually excluded from the surrounding, largely Christian civilization. With occasional exceptions, they lived within their own spiritual world. Their communities possessed corporate status; they were allowed to conduct their internal affairs according to Jewish law. The curriculum of their schools was confined almost exclusively to study of traditional Jewish texts. Secular knowledge was gained only informally and only to the extent necessary for the conduct of daily affairs. This medieval situation of the Jews was undermined by two novel elements: political centralization and the universalism of the Enlightenment. As European states sought greater concentration of power, they found it necessary to remove the divisive elements of medieval corporatism. Jews were brought more directly under state control; their autonomous jurisdiction and the coercive power of their rabbis were curtailed. Hopes were raised among Jews that political integration would lead as well to abolition of political, economic, and social disabilities. At the same time a more friendly attitude to Jews, which regarded them foremost as creatures of the same God rather than as Christ-killers, began to pervade enlightened circles, drawing Jews to respond with their own broader, more universal identifications. In increasing numbers they now began to learn modern European languages, to read contemporary literature, to absorb the prevalent aesthetic sensibilities, and to regard themselves culturally as Europeans no less than religiously as Jews.

Gradually a gap was created between Jewish traditions, harmonious with medieval realities, and the new economic, social, and cultural status of a portion of western Jewry. To be sure, this modernizing process did not affect all Jews at once or to the same degree. Well into the nineteenth century most Jews in eastern Europe remained virtually untouched by the norms of modern civilization, while even in western Europe modernization among Jews was a slow process, more so in the religious sphere than in the cultural sphere. However, as early as the turn of the nineteenth century, there began, especially in Germany, a pronounced falling away from Jewish belief and observance on the part of those Jews most exposed to the currents of modernity. Fears arose that unless Jewish traditions could be brought into harmony with the intellectual canons and the social norms of the surrounding society, Judaism might find itself relegated to the dustbin of medievalism. The Reform movement arose as an attempt to reconcile Jewish religious tradition with cultural and social integration, to stem the rising tide of religious apathy and even conversion in certain circles, and to reshape Judaism in such a way as would make it viable under radically novel circumstances.

The first religious issue to arouse major controversy was burial on the very day of assumed death, as required by Jewish law. The famed Jewish philosopher of the Enlightenment, Moses Mendelssohn (1729–1786), who remained an Orthodox Jew, broke with established practice in 1772 when he advocated temporary "burial" above the ground and graveyard vigil until actual death could be determined with certainty. Mendelssohn based his view both on the precedent of an ancient custom and on current medical experience. For decades thereafter this question served as a touchstone separating traditionalists from modernists, those who held that all customary practice was sacred and inviolable from those who believed that at least in some instances criteria external to the Jewish tradition should be invoked to determine religious obligation.

A new theoretical religious position, which thereafter was largely, if not directly, absorbed by the Reform movement, first appears in a work entitled *Leviathan* (1792), by Saul Ascher (1767–1822), a Jewish book dealer living in Berlin. Ascher rejected the Mendelssohnian dichotomy between natural religion (that shared by all rational human beings) and revealed law (that given exclusively to the Jews and the basis for their separation as a religious community). For Ascher the distinguishing feature of Judaism was not its legal corpus but its unique religious faith. Thus Judaism was not dependent on political or judicial autonomy; it could take its place alongside Protestantism and Roman Catholicism, differentiated from them as one faith from another. In contrast to Mendelssohn, Ascher held that Judaism does indeed possess specific dogmas that set it apart from natural religion. These include belief in the God of love, who revealed himself to the patriarchs, who rewards and punishes, and who guides the world through divine providence. Likewise essential to Judaism are certain practices, including circumcision, observance of Sabbaths and holidays, and atonement as a way of seeking God's favor. Ascher's arbitrary selectivity marks a sharp departure from traditional Jewish thought. In the fashion of non-Jewish thinkers of the eighteenth century, it makes religion largely a means to the end of personal spiritual happiness (*Glückseligkeit*) rather than, as in Judaism, the fulfillment of God's will as expressed in divinely ordained commandments. Though Ascher's specific program remained idiosyncratic, his subjectivization of the Jewish faith and its confessionalization soon became characteristic for the Reform movement. In later literature the differentiation is repeatedly made between what is essential to Judaism and what has been added by historical accident, "the kernel and the husk." In Jewish education the concomitant to this endeavor to isolate the basic tenets and distinctive practices of the faith was the catechism, now increasingly introduced in place of, or supplementary to, traditional texts.

The reform of synagogue ritual under modern cultural influence was undertaken for the first time by the Adath Jeshurun congregation of Amsterdam in 1797. This synagogue was established in separation from the general community, following the grant of emancipation to Dutch Jewry by the French-controlled Batavian Republic the previous year. The congregation buried its dead only on the third day, shortened its liturgy, made aesthetic "improvements" in the worship service, introduced a regular sermon on a moral theme, and eliminated a prayer that asked for vengeance against those who had martyred Jews at the time of the Crusades. The congregation had existed for only about a decade when the new king of Holland, Louis Bonaparte, required it to rejoin the general Jewish community.

Although France preceded other European states in giving its Jews complete political equality at the time of the French Revolution, its Jewish community did not lead the movement for religious reform. The Assembly of Jewish Notables (1806) and the Sanhedrin (1807), called by Napoleon, committed French Jewry to the fulfillment of all civic obligations and to the official acceptance of the superiority of the law of the state over Jewish law. However, the delegates were not required to undertake liturgical reforms, to give up any religious practices, or to alter their theological conceptions. The centralized Jewish consistory system, which emerged in France shortly thereafter, militated against individual initiative in religious matters, favoring a superficially modernized official orthodoxy.

It was in the kingdom of Westphalia that a program of religious reforms for an entire Jewish community was first undertaken by an officially constituted body enjoying government support. Under the leadership of the wealthy and influential financier Israel Jacobson (1768–1828), a Jewish consistory, composed of three rabbis and two laymen, was created there in 1808. It introduced the confirmation ceremony, which it borrowed from Christianity, removed secular elements from the sacred space of the synagogue, and generally sought to impose a more dignified and decorous mode of worship. One of the rabbinical members of the consistory, Menachem Mendel Steinhardt (1768–1825), attempted to justify some of its reforms by reference to Jewish law and tradition as well as to the variant customs of Sefardic Jewry.

Some months after Jacobson moved to Berlin following the demise of the Westphalian kingdom and its Jewish consistory in 1813, he established regular weekly worship in his home for those members of the community who desired a service modeled on that of Westphalia. Like the services that Jacobson had instituted at the chapel of a school that he sponsored in the small Westphalian town of Seesen, the worship here was enhanced by the use of an organ and by a boys' choir. Later moved to larger quarters, these services attracted as many as four hundred worshipers. There were hymns and regular edifying sermons in the German language. However, the liturgy—for which a special prayer book was published—remained mostly traditional in content, if not in form. As long as the prayer gatherings remained a private venture, the Orthodox faction of the community was willing to tolerate them. However, once it seemed that some of these reforms would be introduced into the community synagogue, traditionalist opposition, combined with Prussian government hostility to religious innovations, led to a royal edict in 1823 prohibiting any and all Jewish religious reform. This was the first of many disputes and polemical exchanges between reformers and traditionalists that thereafter punctuated the history of the Reform movement.

In 1817 a "New Temple Association" was formed in the independent city of Hamburg. Its members, who represented a broad economic and social cross section of the city's Jewry, succeeded in establishing and maintaining their own synagogue, despite Orthodox opposition, on account of the more indulgent attitude of the city's senate. The Hamburg temple, which lasted until the Holocaust, remained for a generation the model for the movement. In 1819 it issued a prayer book which, for the first time, made substantial changes in the liturgy. Intensely particularist passages were removed or altered. While references to Zion were not wholly excised, the prayer book reflected the members' abandonment of the desire to return to the Land of Israel and to reestablish the ancient sacrificial service. Two lay preachers gave regular German sermons on the Christian model and prepared both boys and girls for the confirmation ceremony.

Ideologists. The next two decades may be described as a period of latency in the history of the Reform movement. The climate of political reaction in Europe was not conducive to religious innovation. Orthodox opposition, moreover, had proven to be pervasive and united. No new Reform prayer books were published between 1819 and 1840, and no new congregations were established. Aside from the Hamburg temple, Reform of any more than a minimal variety flourished only in those modern Jewish schools that, as in Berlin and Frankfurt am Main, offered a modified worship service for the children and their parents.

However, during this same period a new generation of rabbis came to maturity, some of them eager to institute religious reforms. Schooled not only in traditional Jewish texts but also at German universities, this younger rabbinical generation was able to provide spiritual leadership for what heretofore had been basically a lay movement. Gradually these men received rabbinical positions, first in the smaller Jewish communities and then in the larger ones. A number of them possessed considerable scholarly abilities and applied themselves to the task of creating a historical theology for the Reform movement. The most prominent was Abraham Geiger (1810–1874), who rapidly became the leading ideologist of the movement in Europe. Employing the new critical approach to Jewish texts, an approach known as *Wissenschaft des Judentums,* Geiger wrote scholarly studies and delivered lectures that showed Judaism as an evolving entity, subject to the forces of history. The essence of Judaism, Geiger argued, was not its legal system but its religious spirit, reflected and symbolized in its rituals. This Jewish spirit was the product of revelation, creating in turn the great literary monuments of Judaism. Geiger stressed the universal message of Judaism, setting its rational ethical monotheism into sharp contrast with Christian trinitarian dogma and pagan materialism. Under the influence of the early Romantic thinker Johann Gottfried Herder, who conceived spiritual epochs succeeding one another in nondialectical fashion, Geiger saw Judaism as a spiritual historical entity, which in the modern world was entering a new epoch in its history. It bore within it the combined heritage of previous stages of its development and was moving toward yet undetermined forms of historical existence. For Geiger it was the task of the Reform rabbi to press the wheel of history forward with a program of modernizing and rationalizing reforms.

Geiger's colleague, Zacharias Frankel (1801–1875), the rabbi of Dresden, took a more conservative position. He maintained the centrality of Jewish law, though he recognized its historical development and believed that the rabbinical leadership should rather be responsive to the present collective will and spiritual situation of the community than attempt to direct and hasten its course of development. In 1845 Frankel broke with fellow reformers on the issue of Hebrew in the worship service, and in 1854 he became the head of the new conservatively oriented rabbinical seminary in Breslau. The most prominent radical reformer in this period was Samuel Holdheim (1806–1860), who believed the revolutionary new situation of Western Jewry demanded a thoroughgoing transformation of Judaism. Holdheim favored the transfer of the Jewish Sabbath to Sunday and the abolition of all legal elements in Judaism. He regarded his own age as representing a clearly higher level of religious evolution and hence argued that contemporary Jews had the right to reshape Judaism in messianic, universal terms without overmuch regard for preserving continuity with the past. Holdheim eventually became the rabbi of a separatist Reform congregation in Berlin, which radically abbreviated and altered the traditional liturgy, retained only a minimum of Hebrew, and conducted its principal weekly service on Sunday.

Collective activity and diffusion. In the 1840s the Reform movement in Germany underwent a major revival. After considerable opposition, Geiger was able in 1840 to assume his tasks as one of the rabbis in the influential Breslau community. A year later the Hamburg temple issued a new version of its prayer book on the occasion of its move to more spacious quarters. Lay societies seeking more radical reforms sprang up in Frankfurt am Main, Berlin, and Breslau. Led for the most part by university-educated, highly acculturated German Jews, these societies proposed elimination of national symbols and ritual prescriptions from Judaism in favor of a highly spiritualized and universalized faith, anchored in a humanistic understanding of the Hebrew Bible and virtually excluding later rabbinic tradition. In their religious radicalism they paralleled similar contemporary movements in German Protestantism and Catholicism.

The rabbis inclined to religious reform now undertook a collective initiative for the first time. Three conferences were held in the years 1844–1846, in which a total of forty-two rabbis participated. Most of them were still in their thirties and possessed doctorates. Although they represented a spectrum of opinion, the tenor of these conferences reflected a middle position among German reformers, dissatisfying both conservatives like Frankel, who favored only the slightest revisions in existing law and custom, and radicals like Holdheim, who urged strict conformity to the demands of the *Zeitgeist*. Among the conclusions reached were that the use of Hebrew in the service was a subjective but not an objective necessity, that prayers for the return to Zion and the reinstitution of the sacrificial service should be eliminated from the prayer book, and that it was permissible to accompany the service with an organ even on the Sabbath. Plans for a new common liturgy and a committee report favoring equality of women were not acted upon when the annual conferences ceased after the third year, in part because of the agitated political situation preceding the Revolution of 1848.

In the second half of the nineteenth century the Reform movement in Germany continued to make inroads in the Jewish communities, but generally with less éclat and polemic than heretofore. Increasingly, the larger Jewish communities provided for modified services (with organ accompaniment and a modified liturgy) as well as traditional ones. Religious reform became institutionalized in Germany as "Liberal Judaism," one of two religious currents or trends (*Richtungen*) within the general community, and it soon won over the majority of German Jews. Synods, including laity as well as rabbis, were held to discuss further reforms in 1869 and 1871. At the end of the century a permanent union of Liberal rabbis was established, with a similar national organization for all Liberal Jews coming into existence in 1908. However, a common prayer book for the German Liberal congregations—quite traditional in character—was not issued until 1929.

While the Reform movement in Europe remained centered in Germany, which had the largest Jewish population west of the tsarist empire, it spread to other countries as well. The Vienna community as early as 1826 adopted a number of aesthetic reforms, as did some congregations in Hungary, Galicia, Holland, and Denmark. Even in Russia certain circles of *maskilim* ("enlightened" Jews) or immigrants from the West introduced decorum, choirs, and vernacular sermons. In the 1860s some Russian Jewish intellectuals argued, as did reformers in the West, that religious reform was indigenous to Jewish tradition from ancient times and that Orthodoxy in fact reflected stagnation.

In England a Reform congregation, called the West London Synagogue of British Jews, was founded in 1840. Generally conservative in character, its most pronounced reform was the abolition of the second days of certain holidays, which were celebrated only according to rabbinic, not biblical, precept. Similar congregations were established elsewhere in England. After the turn of the century a more radical religious movement emerged, which soon adopted the term *Liberal* to differentiate itself from the earlier *Reform*. British Liberal Judaism, which was patterned largely upon the American Reform Judaism of the time, sought to win back to the synagogue the large mass of English Jews who had become alienated from all religious Judaism. Its liturgy was largely in English, and men and women sat together.

In France the centralized consistory long militated against religious division. Some, mostly cosmetic, reforms were undertaken by the chief rabbis, and proposals for more radical change were aired with some regularity in the Jewish press. However, a viable, independent Reform congregation, the Union Israélite Liberale, was established only after the separation of church and state in France in 1905.

European Liberal Judaism—together with its counterpart in America—finally achieved international organizational unity with the establishment of the World Union for Progressive Judaism in London in 1926. Until World War II, the work of the Union and of Reform Judaism in Europe generally was particularly influenced by Leo Baeck (1873–1956), a Liberal rabbi in Berlin and a teacher at the seminary of the movement, the Hochschule für die Wissenschaft des Judentums, which had been established there in 1872. As a religious thinker, Baeck elaborated an antiromantic theology, greatly indebted to Kant, which stressed the revealed moral commandment that emerges out of the mystery of revelation. Under the influence of Rudolf Otto, Baeck's theology later became less rationalistic while his perspective grew more particularistic as he came to focus his attention on the unique religious history of the people of Israel.

Americanization. Reform Judaism has enjoyed its greatest success in the United States. In Europe it was repeatedly forced to assert itself against an entrenched Orthodoxy, sometimes supported by the government; in the New World it faced no such established institutions.

The United States lacked officially recognized Jewish communities, like the German *Gemeinde* with its powers of taxation and centralized control over Jewish affairs. The complete separation of church and state, the numerous Christian denominations existing side by side, and the prevalent notion that religious activity was strictly a matter of free choice created an atmosphere most conducive to Jewish religious fragmentation. Moreover, it was difficult for an immigrant Jew in nineteenth-century America to make a living while still observing all the inherited traditions. Given also the large influx of Jews from Germany in the second third of the nineteenth century—among them some who had had experience with religious reform, as well as a number of Reform rabbis—it is understandable that until the massive Jewish immigration from eastern Europe in the last decades of the century, Reform Judaism should play the dominant role in American Jewry. In the freer atmosphere of America, Reform soon took on a considerably more radical character than its counterpart in Europe.

Classical American reform. With the exception of an isolated and short-lived attempt to create a Reform congregation in Charleston, South Carolina, in 1824, somewhat on the model of the Hamburg temple, Reform Judaism took hold in the United States only toward the middle of the nineteenth century. Beginning in 1842 with Har Sinai in Baltimore, and during the next twenty years, liturgical reforms were gradually introduced into existing congregations or new Reform congregations founded in New York City, Albany, Cincinnati, Philadelphia, and Chicago. Jewish periodicals favoring religious reform made their appearance, as did new prayer books embodying various degrees of liturgical revision. When a rabbinical conference, held in Cleveland in 1855, reaffirmed the authority of the Talmud, it aroused protests from the more thoroughgoing reformers, whose influence was to increase in the following decades.

During the second half of the nineteenth century, American Reform was dominated by two immigrant rabbis representing, respectively, a consistent, separatist ideological position and a pragmatic, relatively more conservative stance, which sought to make Reform Judaism most broadly acceptable. David Einhorn (1809–1879), a rabbi in Baltimore and later in New York, stressed the priestly mission of the Jewish people and vigorously opposed mixed marriages, but he saw little value in most Jewish ceremonials and was a firm believer in the progress of Judaism beyond its ancient sacred texts. His influence was dominant at a meeting of Reform rabbis held in Philadelphia in 1869. Following debate held in the German language, this conference declared that the dispersion of Israel providentially served its universal messianic aim. It also rejected the traditional dogma of bodily resurrection in favor of belief only in the immortality of the soul.

Isaac Mayer Wise (1819–1900) was the founding father of organized Reform Judaism in the United States. Unlike Einhorn, whose intellectual stature he did not rival but whom he far excelled in practical energy, Wise sought to create an Americanized Judaism that could appeal to the widest spectrum of Jewry in the United States. Eschewing consistency, Wise sometimes took one position on religious issues, sometimes another, concerned more with momentary effect than with crystallized ideology. However, unlike the radicals, he consistently rejected pentateuchal criticism as undermining the foundations of Judaism. As a rabbi in Cincinnati, Wise came to represent the more moderate midwestern wing of Reform Judaism, which differentiated itself from the more thoroughgoing Reform of the East Coast. It was largely due to Wise's efforts that the national organizations of Reform Judaism were created: the UAHC in 1873, HUC in 1875, and the CCAR in 1889.

In 1885 Wise served as president of a rabbinical conference that formulated the Pittsburgh Platform, a document that was to represent the ideological position of American Reform Judaism for the next half century. The key figure at the conference, however, was not Wise but Kaufmann Kohler (1843–1926), a son-in-law and spiritual heir of David Einhorn, who became the movement's leading theologian and, after a short interval, succeeded Wise as president of the Hebrew Union College. Under Kohler's influence the Pittsburgh conference declared that "Judaism presents the highest conception of the God-idea as taught in our holy Scriptures and developed and spiritualized by the Jewish teachers in accordance with the moral and philosophical progress of their respective ages." It recognized in the Bible "the record of the consecration of the Jewish people to its mission as priest of the One God" but found only the moral laws of the Pentateuch to be binding, while ritual precepts were to be subjected to the criterion of their continuing capacity to sanctify life and to be harmonizable with modern civilization. Jews were defined as a religious community, not a nation, their religion as progressive, "ever striving to be in accord with the postulates of reason." A final paragraph expressed commitment to seek social justice in American society by reducing the "contrasts and evils" in its present organization.

For the next fifty years Reform Judaism adhered to the Pittsburgh Platform. During this period the movement increased in numbers, reaching a high point of about 60,000 families in 285 congregations before the Great Depression temporarily halted its growth. In 1892 the CCAR published the first edition of the Union Prayer Book, which with only relatively minor revisions remained standard in Reform Judaism until 1975. However, during this same half century the movement was forced to give up its hopes of becoming the norm for American Jewry. Increasingly it was associated specifically with the German Jewish immigrants and their descendants. Eastern Europeans, concentrated in New York, either remained Orthodox, dissociated themselves from religion entirely, or in the second generation were attracted by the more ethnic and nostalgic appeal of Conservative Judaism. Most Reform Jews until the late thirties were opposed to Jewish nationalism and saw in Zionism a retreat from the universal mission of Judaism. Nonetheless, a small percentage, especially among the rabbis, played active roles in Zionist affairs from the beginning of the century.

Reorientation. It was only in the late 1930s that Reform Judaism in the United States began to lose its identification with the German immigrants. Reform rabbis, and then increasingly the laity as well, were now coming from eastern European backgrounds. During this same decade awareness of the lot of Jews in Nazi Germany created stronger national ties among all Jews. Gradually Reform Judaism began a process of transformation from which it would emerge with a much more significant ethnic and ceremonial component than heretofore. Eventually the earlier period came to be designated Classical Reform Judaism, and while its particular emphases continue to be represented in some congregations even down to the present, a reoriented Reform Judaism began to displace or modify it at an increasing pace.

The first major indication of this shift in position was the Columbus Platform, adopted by the CCAR in 1937. This document was largely the work of Samuel Cohon (1888–1959), an eastern European Jew who served for many years as professor of Jewish theology at the Hebrew Union College. It spoke of a "living God" rather than a "God idea," described Torah, in its broad sense as both written and oral law, as enshrining Israel's "ever-growing consciousness of God," and declared that it was the task of all Jews to rebuild Palestine as a Jewish homeland, both as a "refuge for the oppressed and a center of Jewish culture and spiritual life." In contrast to the Pittsburgh Platform, it stressed the use of Hebrew in worship and the importance of customs, symbols, and ceremonies. Like its predecessor, the platform declared the movement's commitment to social justice, a dominant concern of Reform Judaism during those years of economic distress in the United States.

Developments since World War II. In the immediate postwar years Reform Judaism in the United States enjoyed remarkable growth. New congregations were established in the suburbs of major cities as increased Jewish affluence made possible higher levels of support for religious institutions both locally and nationally. The Christian religious revival of the 1950s produced renewed interest in Jewish theology. In 1951 the UAHC moved its offices from Cincinnati to New York, the center of Jewish life in the United States. From 1943 to 1973 the congregational union was headed by Rabbi Maurice Eisendrath, a talented organizer and impressive public speaker. The well-known biblical archaeologist Nelson Glueck, as president of the Hebrew Union College from 1947 to his death in 1971, was able to achieve a merger with the Jewish Institute of Religion, founded by the Zionist Reform rabbi Stephen S. Wise in 1922, and to bring about considerable expansion of the combined institution.

Reform Judaism now engaged itself vigorously with the moral issues troubling American society. Rabbis and laity participated actively in the civil rights movement and later in the organized opposition to the Vietnam War. In 1961 the UAHC established the Religious Action Center in Washington, D.C., with the intent of making a direct impact on legislation of Jewish and general religious or moral concern, as well as educating the Reform constituency as to questions under current legislative consideration. In the spirit of ecumenism, the UAHC developed a department dealing with interfaith activities, supplementing the long-standing work of individual congregations and of the National Federation of Temple Brotherhoods in this area.

Reform theology in this recent period grew increasingly diverse. A group of Reform rabbis, who became known as "covenant theologians," favored a more personalist and existential grounding of their faith. Influenced by the twentieth-century European Jewish thinkers Franz Rosenzweig and Martin Buber, they eschewed the earlier idealist theology based on progressive revelation in favor of the notion of divine-human encounter as represented both by the testimony of the Torah and by contemporary religious experience. At the same time, however, there arose a significant rationalist and even humanist faction within the movement. Its members stressed the impact of biblical criticism and psychoanalysis upon religion, as well as the difficult theological questions that the Holocaust had raised for Jewish theism.

While theological positions in Reform Judaism generally moved apart, religious practice, for the most part, became more traditional. The postwar period witnessed a renewal of interest in Jewish law, not as authoritative in the Orthodox sense but as a guide for the religious life. Over three decades Solomon Freehof of Pittsburgh, one of the most influential Reform rabbis, published half a dozen collections of Reform *responsa* on issues ranging from aspects of synagogue ritual to matters of individual observance. The publication of these *responsa*, as well as guides for religious observance, was due in part to the feelings of most of the religious leadership that Reform Judaism needed to reengage itself with traditional symbols and practices if it was not to dissipate in the absorptive social climate of postwar America. It was also prompted by a heightened ethnicism and personalism in Reform Judaism. The individual *bar mitsvah* ceremony for boys reaching the age of thirteen, and later the equivalent *bat mitsvah* ceremony for girls, were increasingly adopted by Reform congregations, preceding the group ceremony of confirmation. The rabbinical role, which in Reform Judaism had principally been that of prophetic preacher, now became more priestly, as congregants especially sought rabbis whose personal warmth would enhance life-cycle ceremonies. Reform synagogues introduced more Hebrew into the liturgy and encouraged greater congregational participation.

Jewish education among Reform Jews became more comprehensive in the 1970s. In place of the customary two hours per week of Sunday school instruction, most temples now offered twice-weekly classes, supplemented by weekends or summer sessions at a camp. A handful of Reform day schools came into existence for those children whose parents desired them to obtain more extensive Jewish knowledge and depth of Jewish commitment. The National Federation of Temple Youth introduced study programs for Reform teenagers beyond religious-school age, and rabbinical education was extended to women, the first woman (Sally Preisand) being ordained by HUC-JIR in 1972. In 1981 the UAHC published its own Torah commentary, encouraging lay study of the Pentateuch according to the liberal approach of Reform.

The commitment of Reform Judaism to Zionism deepened in the postwar period. Reform Jews welcomed the establishment of the state of Israel in 1948, shared feelings of crisis and relief during its Six Day War, and increasingly appropriated its cultural impact. Israeli melodies entered the synagogues, religious schools, and summer camps. The CCAR declared Israeli Independence Day a religious holiday, and beginning in 1970 HUC-JIR required all entering rabbinical students to spend the first year of their study at its campus in Jerusalem. Reform Jews organized the Association of Reform Zionists of America (ARZA) in order to give Reform Judaism an individual voice in the world Zionist movement.

In the state of Israel itself, the first successful Progressive congregation was established, mostly by German Jewish immigrants, in Jerusalem in 1958. It was followed by congregations in the other major cities, attendance reaching about five thousand for the High Holy Days. The congregations and their rabbis united as the "Movement for Progressive Judaism in Israel," a regular constituent of the World Union for Progressive Judaism, the latter moving its headquarters to Jerusalem in 1974. In the seventies Israeli Reform also established its first *kibbuts* (collective agricultural settlement) in the southern desert and a youth movement with groups in various cities. In 1980 HUC-JIR for the first time ordained an Israeli Reform rabbi in Jerusalem. However, Reform Judaism (and also Conservative Judaism) remained unrecognized by the Israeli rabbinate and was forced to wage a continuous, and as yet very incompletely successful, struggle for equal rights with Orthodoxy. In general, Israeli Reform emerged as considerably more traditional than its counterpart in the United States, finding the positions taken by the American radical wing on such matters as rabbinical officiation at mixed marriages and conversion procedures to be embarrassing in the Israeli milieu.

The centrality of Jewish peoplehood, symbolized by the state of Israel, found clear expression in the most recent platform of Reform Judaism. Called "A Centenary Perspective" because it was composed about one hundred years after the creation of the first national institutions of American Reform Judaism, it was adopted by the CCAR in 1976. The statement was the work of a committee chaired by Rabbi Eugene Borowitz, a professor at the New York school of HUC-JIR and one of the most influential contemporary theologians of the movement. Unlike previous platforms, it does not seek to define Judaism as a whole dogmatically, but only to give a brief historical account of Reform Judaism—what it has taught and what it has learned—and to describe its present spiritual convictions. Recognizing and affirming the diversity of theology and practice in contemporary Reform, it points to those broad conceptions and values shared by most Reform Jews. In the wake of the Holocaust and recognizing the physically precarious situation of Israeli Jewry and the assimilatory forces operative on American Judaism, the statement gives prominence to the value of ethnic survival, an element not highlighted in earlier platforms. It affirms the reality of God, without setting forth any specific theology, and defines the people of Israel as inseparable from its religion. Torah is seen as the product of "meetings between God and the Jewish people," especially, but not only, in ancient times. Rejecting the optimism of nineteenth-century Reform Judaism, the statement nonetheless reaffirms the religious significance of human history and the moral obligations of Jews, both particularly in Jewish matters and in the pursuit of universal messianic goals.

[*See also* Judaism, *article on* Judaism in Northern and Eastern Europe since 1500, *and the biographies of the principal figures mentioned herein.*]

BIBLIOGRAPHY

Although outdated in many respects, the standard work on Reform Judaism remains David Philipson's *The Reform Movement in Judaism*, 2d ed. (1931), reissued with a new introduction by Solomon Freehof (New York, 1967). W. Gunther Plaut has brought together a good selection of primary sources, abbreviating the lengthier ones and translating into English those in other languages. The material in two volumes edited by him, *The Rise of Reform Judaism* and *The Growth of Reform Judaism* (New York, 1963 and 1965), extends to 1948. More general, but valuable for the European context, are Heinz Moshe Graupe's *The Rise of Modern Judaism*, translated by John Robinson (Huntington, N.Y., 1978), and the older Max Wiener's *Jüdische Religion im Zeitalter der Emanzipation* (Berlin, 1933), translated into Hebrew (Jerusalem, 1974) but not, regrettably, into English. The specific matter of liturgical change is comprehensively treated, with extensive quotation of primary sources, in Jakob J. Petuchowski's *Prayerbook Reform in Europe* (New York, 1968). The initial phases of Reform Judaism in the United States are best understood from Leon A. Jick's recent study, *The Americanization of the Synagogue, 1820–1870* (Hanover, N.H., 1976). Sefton D. Temkin has chronicled the history of the Union of American Hebrew Congregations in "A Century of Reform Judaism in America," *American Jewish Year Book* 74 (1973), pp. 3–75, and the story of the movement's seminary is told in my article, "A Centennial History," in *Hebrew Union College-Jewish Institute of Religion at One Hundred Years*, edited by Samuel E. Karff (Cincinnati, Ohio, 1976), pp. 3–283. The more significant speeches delivered at meetings of the Central Conference of American Rabbis have been collected by Joseph L. Blau in *Reform Judaism: A Historical Perspective* (New York, 1973), while some of the more thoughtful members of the CCAR themselves reflect on various aspects of the history of their organization in *Retrospect and Prospect: Essays in Commemoration of the Seventy-Fifth Anniversary of the Founding of the Central Conference of American Rabbis*, edited by Bertram Wallace Korn (New York, 1965). The variety in Reform Jewish theology after World War II is well reflected in *Contemporary Reform Jewish Thought*, edited by Bernard Martin (Chicago, 1968). Two sociological analyses based on surveys taken at the beginning of the last decade present the state of belief and practice among Reform rabbis and laity: Theodore I. Lenn's *Rabbi and Synagogue in Reform Judaism* (West Hartford, Conn., 1972) and Leonard J. Fein et al., *Reform Is a Verb: Notes on Reform and Reforming Jews* (New York, 1972). Contemporary Reform Judaism can best be followed through its current major publications. *Reform Judaism* is a popular UAHC magazine circulated to all members four times a year; the *Journal of Reform Judaism*, a quarterly, is the official organ of the CCAR; and the occasional *Ammi* presents news of the World Union for Progressive Judaism.

MICHAEL A. MEYER

REIMARUS, HERMANN SAMUEL (1694–1768), German theologian and philosopher. Son of a scholar, grandson of a clergyman, student and son-in-law of J. A. Fabricius (one of the staunchest defenders of orthodoxy of the time), Reimarus was for much of his life a professor of Oriental languages at the Hamburg academic *Gymnasium*. He lived during the period of the German Enlightenment, amidst the evolving discussion of the relation between reason and revelation.

Reimarus's public religious views belong to that stage characterized by the philosophical synthesis of Christian Wolff: (1) revelation may be above reason but not contrary to it, and (2) reason establishes the criteria by which revelation may be judged, namely, necessity and consistency. Publicly, Reimarus argued that the demands of a natural religion of reason only and those of Christianity agree with or complement one another. Natural religion, he contended, lays the ground for Christianity. These public views were set forth most succinctly in his *Abhandlungen von den vornehmsten Wahrheiten der natürlichen Religion* (Essays on the Principal Truths of Natural Religion; 1754). At his death, a colleague would eulogize him as a defender of Christianity.

Reimarus's private views of religion were not known even to his wife. They were part of the rationalism that contended that the criteria of reason judge revelation to be false. Revelation is at odds with reason and must be displaced. Natural religion, he believed, replaces Christianity. Reimarus recorded his private views in a secret manuscript he entitled *Apologie oder Schutzschrift für die vernünftigen Verehrer Gottes* (Apology for or Defense of the Rational Worshiper of God), three copies of which remain. Of the thirty-seven works that he wrote, this one alone has brought him renown. In it he accepts Wolff's contention that the two criteria of necessity and consistency must be satisfied by any alleged revelation before its genuineness can be accepted. He then sets out to show (1) that it is possible to describe the origins of Christianity as entirely natural (not miraculous and therefore not necessary) and (2) that any supposed revelation is filled with contradictions (not logically consistent). Reason thereby undermines the claims of the alleged Christian revelation. Seven fragments of this manuscript were published by G. E. Lessing between 1774 and 1778. Of these the two most influential were the sixth, "On the Resurrection Narratives" (1777), which declares the revelation of the resurrection false on the basis of contradictions, and the seventh, "On the Intentions of Jesus and His Disciples" (1778), which draws a distinction between the message and intention of Jesus and that of the early church.

Reimarus has influenced contemporary thought indirectly through Lessing, David F. Strauss, and Albert Schweitzer. The fragments of the *Apologie* caused Lessing to break with the eighteenth-century assumption that religious truth depended on the historicity of certain alleged events in scripture. Lessing's position, in turn, influenced Kierkegaard, who maintained that Christian truth is established independently of one's estimate of the historical origins of Christianity by God's act in the moment, though history occasions that moment. The fragments also caused Lessing to come to grips with the need for source criticism of the Gospels.

The fragments played a role in Strauss's struggle to establish a mythical view of miracles. Strauss used Reimarus to show that Christianity was not supernatural. As a result, Reimarus confronts the modern reader with the question of the historicity of the miracles.

The fragments also influenced Schweitzer in his work in the area of eschatology. Schweitzer turned to Reimarus to support his view that Jesus' orientation was eschatological, that Jesus expected an imminent end of the world, and that the delay of the Parousia was the main problem of early Christian theology, beginning with Jesus himself.

BIBLIOGRAPHY

Grappin, Pierre. "La théologie naturelle de Reimarus." *Études germaniques* 6 (1951): 169–181.

Lundsteen, A. C. *Hermann Samuel Reimarus und die Anfänge der Leben-Jesu Forschung.* Copenhagen, 1939.

Sieveking, Heinrich. "Hermann Samuel Reimarus, 1694–1768." *Zeitschrift des Vereins für hamburgische Geschichte* 38 (1939): 145–182.

Strauss, David F. *Hermann Samuel Reimarus und seine Schutzschrift für die vernunftigen Verehrer Gottes.* 2d ed. Bonn, 1877.

Talbert, Charles H., ed., *Reimarus: Fragments.* Translated by Ralph S. Fraser. Philadelphia, 1970. Includes my critical introduction (pp. 1–43).

CHARLES H. TALBERT

REINACH, SALOMON (1858–1932), French archaeologist and author of more than seventy books. Reinach is most widely known for his controversial writings in the area of the anthropological-ethnological comparative study of religions. He became conservator of the Musées Nationales in 1893, director of the Musée des Antiquités Nationales in Saint-Germain in 1901, and also served from the following year onward as professor at the École du Louvre in Paris. He was coeditor of the *Revue archéologique,* and from 1896 a member of the Académie des Inscriptions.

Although he branded eighteenth-century rationalism as a "paltry doctrine" seeking "to suppress religion without knowing its essence and without any clear idea of its origin and development" (*Cultes,* vol. 2, p. xviii, my translation), Reinach expressed his admiration for Voltaire, whose ideas about religion he did not share, but whose "incomparable gifts as a narrator" greatly inspired him (*Orpheus,* Eng. ed. of 1930, pp. vi–vii) and in whose spirit he wished to wage a more effective campaign against the church. "The history of humanity is that of a progressive secularisation [*laïcisation*] which is by no means complete as yet" (*Orpheus,* p. 23).

Reinach saw his own role as that of a popularizer of what others—among them Robertson Smith, Frazer, Tylor, Lang, and Jevons—had discovered: "Mine has been a lowlier part—to grasp the ideas of my betters, and to diffuse them as widely as I might" (*Cults,* p. xi). His summary definitions of magic and religion and of totem and taboo are in many ways illustrative of his approach. Reinach described magic as "the strategy of animism," and he based his definition of religion on the Latin word *religio,* calling it "a sum of scruples which impede the free exercise of our faculties" (*Orpheus,* p. 23). On totem and taboo Reinach remarked: "The totem is inconceivable without a taboo, and the logical outcome of a generalised taboo can hardly be anything else than a totem" (*Cults,* p. ix). His admission, made during the Third International Congress for the History of Religions held at Oxford in 1908, that totemism was "an overridden hobby" of which he himself had been "one of the roughriders" was followed by the statement that he "did not yet feel disposed to apologize nor to recant," and this unwillingness seems to hold true for subsequent writings as well. Discussing, for example, the ceremonial killing and eating of a totem, he leaves the possibility open that this idea of "fortifying and sanctifying oneself by assimilation of a divine being" survived in the medieval Christian rite of the Eucharist: "If primitive Christianity, with its theophagistic practices, conquered Europe so rapidly, it was because this idea of the manducation of the god was not new, but simply the presentation of one of the most profound religious instincts of humanity in a more spiritual form" (*Orpheus,* p. 19).

BIBLIOGRAPHY

Reinach wrote extensively in the areas of classical philology, archaeology, and art history. Among his publications in these fields are *Manuel de philologie classique,* 2 vols. (Paris, 1883–1884); *Minerva,* 4th ed. (Paris, 1900); and *Apollo: Histoire générale des arts plastiques* (Paris, 1904), which has been translated by Florence Simmonds as *Apollo: An Illustrated Manual of the History of Art throughout the Ages,* 2d ed. (London, 1907).

Almost one hundred of Reinach's articles, most dealing with the comparative study of religion, were republished in *Cultes, mythes et religions,* 2d ed., 4 vols. (Paris, 1908–1913). Elizabeth Frost selected fourteen of these essays for her translation, *Cults, Myths and Religions* (London, 1912). Reinach's *Orpheus: Histoire générale des religions* (Paris, 1909) was translated by Florence Simmonds as *Orpheus: A General History of Religions* (New York, 1909), and went through thirty-eight editions before Reinach's death (the edition quoted in the text is that of 1930).

Bibliographical sources include E. Pottier's "Salomon Reinach," *Revue archéologique,* 5th series, 36 (1932): 137–154; *Bibliographie de Salomon Reinach, 1874–1922,* with supplement (Saint-Germain, 1922–1927); and *Bibliographie de Salomon Reinach,* with notes by Seymour de Ricci (Paris, 1936). This last volume also includes a biographical sketch of Reinach.

WILLEM A. BIJLEFELD

REINCARNATION. The doctrine of reincarnation concerns the rebirth of the soul or self in a series of physical or preternatural embodiments, which are customarily human or animal in nature but are in some instances divine, angelic, demonic, vegetative, or astrological (i.e., are associated with the sun, moon, stars, or planets). The concept of rebirth may also be expressed in such terms as *metempsuchōsis* (or more accurately, *metensōmatōsis,* "passage from one body to another") and *palingenesis* (Gr., lit., "to begin again").

The belief in rebirth in one form or another is found in tribal or nonliterate cultures all over the world. The notion is most dramatically evident in the native societies of central Australia and West Africa, where it is intimately associated with the cult of ancestor worship.

It is in ancient India and Greece, however, that the doctrine of rebirth has been most elaborately developed. In India, the precept is linked inextricably with the teachings and practices of Hinduism, Buddhism, Jainism, Sikhism (a hybrid synthesis of Hinduism and Islam founded in the fifteenth century by Gurū Nānak), and Sufism (the mystical branch of Islam); it even figures in the writings of such modern thinkers as Ramakrishna and Aurobindo. In ancient Greece, the idea is identified primarily with the philosophical lineages of Pythagoras, Empedocles, Plato, and Plotinus.

The doctrine of rebirth can also be found in certain ancient Near Eastern religions, for example, the royal cultus of the pharoahs in ancient Egypt and the mystery cult of Orpheus in second-century Greece. It is found in the teachings of Manichaeism, a third-century CE Persian religion founded by the prophet Mani. The concept of reincarnation also figures in such modern schools of thought as the Theosophy of H. P. Blavatsky and Annie Besant and the humanistic psychology of thinkers like C. G. Jung and Fritz Perls; it appears also in the "perennial philosophy" of Aldous Huxley.

Archaic Cultures. That the belief in reincarnation is of great antiquity in the history of the human species is suggested by the existence of the idea at the core of the belief systems of numerous nonliterate ethnic groups scattered throughout various parts of the world. It is also suggested by the fact that some archaic peoples whose physical culture (domestic architecture, implements of livelihood, etc.) is of an extremely primitive nature (e.g., the Arunta, or Aranda, people who originally inhabited the wastelands of central Australia and who may be classified as a Stone Age society) espouse the ideas of preexistence and reincarnation, which may indicate that this belief arose contemporaneously with the origins of human culture per se.

It is particularly significant that a belief in reincarnation in some form or another is to be bound in nonliterate cultures all over the world. Other primary cultural areas (besides central Australia) in which this precept is noticeably present are West Africa (among the Ewe, Edo, Igbo, and Yoruba), southern Africa (among the Bantu-speakers and the Zulu), Indonesia, Oceania, New Guinea, and both North and South America (among selected ethnic groups).

In sub-Saharan Africa, for example, reincarnation is not only viewed positively, but failure to be reborn and thereby gain yet another opportunity to improve the world of the living is regarded as an evil (as is the state of childlessness). Weighty emphasis is placed upon fertility rites and the efficacious powers of the shaman to promote the production of offspring (i.e., the rebirth of the ancestral spirits).

Among the Yoruba and Edo peoples, the belief in the rebirth of the departed ancestors remains a strong and vibrant cultural force to the present day. It is their custom to name each boy child "Father Has Returned" and each girl child "Mother Has Returned." The Zulu hold that the spirit of each person undergoes numerous rebirths in the bodies of various beasts, which range in size from tiny insects to huge elephants, until at long last the spirit enters a human body where it is fated to undergo yet another birth. Finally, after reaching the pinnacle of human existence, the soul is united with the supreme spirit from which it originated in the beginning. Here, as in other archaic cultures, the belief in reincarnation is linked directly with the veneration of ancestors, for it is the spirits of deceased ancestors that return in one or another life-form in association with the various totemic groups that form the organizational structure of the society.

For the Australian Aborigines, it is axiomatic that the spirits of human beings are periodically incarnated in animal or plant forms or even in such inanimate entities as water, fire, and wind, or the sun, moon, and stars. This belief is based upon the presupposition that the soul is separable from the body and from any other physical object it may inhabit. By virtue of its capacity to survive independently of a physical abode for at least a brief time, the soul possesses the capacity to travel from body to body and to inhabit a variety of forms ranging from stones and insects to animals and human beings. Because of the centrality of the totemic clan in Aboriginal religion, it was of utmost importance to establish the precise identity of the ancestor being reborn in each instance.

According to Australian Aboriginal religious beliefs, a deceased ancestor, after a sojourn of an unspecified length of time in the land of the dead, returns to the world of the living by entering the body of a mother at the moment of conception. The father is believed to play no direct role in impregnating the mother. Instead, the mother-to-be conceives new life by coming into the proximity of an *oknanikilla*, or local totem center, in which a spirit being *(alcheringa)* or soul of a deceased ancestor is lying in wait to be reborn.

Women who desire children travel to a sacred totem center with the intention of conceiving. The Aborigines also believe that if a woman happens to walk in the revered spots where the *alcheringa* ancestors are located, she will become impregnated without their intending it, even against their will. It is also commonly believed that when a woman conceives a child at a site sacred to a particular clan or totemic group (say, for example, the lizard totem), then that child will belong to the clan identified with the place of conception rather than with the clan of its parents. Thus, clan connections outweigh blood-relationships in cultural significance.

Hinduism. The whole of the Hindu ethical code laid down in the ancient law books (e.g., *Laws of Manu*) presupposes the survival of the soul after death and assumes that the present life is fundamentally a preparation for the life to come. According to the Hindu conception of transmigration or rebirth (*saṃsāra*, "a course or succession of states of existence"), the circumstances of any given lifetime are automatically determined by the net results of good and evil actions in previous existences. This, in short, is the law of *karman* (action), a universal law of nature that works according to its own inherent necessity. [*See* Karman.] Reward and punishment are thus not decreed by a god or gods nor by any other supernatural personage. It is a person's own actions, in conformity to the moral and cosmic law *(dharma)*, that is determinative. The law of *karman* finds synoptic expression in the Upaniṣadic assertion: "By good deeds one becomes good, by evil, evil."

As early as the Upaniṣads human destinies are assigned to two divergent pathways: the pathway of the ancestors (*pitṛs*), which is traversed by those persons who follow worldly pursuits, and the pathway of the gods (*devas*), which is taken by those who meditate with faith and austerity in the forest (*Chāndogya Upaniṣad* 4.15.5, 5.10.1–10). The former path leads to rebirth; the latter, toward brahman and liberation. After the "worldling" has resided in the postmortem realm until the effects of his previous deeds has been consumed, he returns along the same route by which he departed the world to be reborn. By contrast, those who depart by the pathway of the gods reach *brahman*, the Ultimate, and are released from the rule of *saṃsāra* forever. For them, say the scriptures, there is no returning.

The *Bhagavadgītā*, one of the most highly revered texts of Hinduism, asserts that the eternal self *(ātman)* is unaffected even to the slightest degree by the vicissitudes of finite existence. According to this text, the universal soul, or self, in its essential nature neither comes to be nor passes away, for "of the nonexistent there is no coming to be; of the existent, there is no coming not to be" (2.11–25). It is rather the body *(śarīra)* or the embodied form *(jīva)* of the self that is subject to the changing conditions of life: creation and destruction, good and evil, victory and defeat. As the eternal, unchanging, and imperishable spiritual essence of humanity, the self is invincible to alteration of any sort, whether on this side of eternity or beyond.

The succession of finite births has traditionally been regarded by Hindus pessimistically, as an existential misfortune and not as a series of "second chances" to improve one's lot, as it is often viewed in the West. Life is regarded not only as "rough, brutish, and short" but as filled with misery *(duḥkha)*. Thus, the multiplication of births within this "vale of tears" merely augments and intensifies the suffering that is the lot of all creatures. Furthermore, this painful existence continues unabated until such time as a person experiences spiritual liberation *(mokṣa*, or *mukti)*. [*See* Mokṣa.]

The root cause of this existential bondage to time, ignorance, and suffering is desire *(taṇhā)*, or avaricious attachment to objects that at best bring only limited, and often debased, pleasure. Even the life of a deity *(deva)* is governed by the law of death and rebirth. Hence, a person's only hope of escaping the clutches of rebirth is through extinguishing all desires except the desire for perfect unification with the universal self *(brahman)*. The empirical self of the liberated person "goes to the *brahman* and becomes the *brahman*." As a result, he is free from the effects of all actions, both good and evil, and from any subsequent participation in existences determined by *karman*. This state of complete union with the universal self is known as *mokṣa* ("release" or "salvation").

Opinions differ among Indian sages as to whether final liberation is attainable while still in an embodied state or only after death. At least from the time of the *Vedānta Sūtra* (second century), the sages believed that salvation could be achieved while still alive. Thus, according to the *Mahābhārata*, the *ātman* is affected by the bonds of finite existence only under the conditions of metaphysical ignorance *(avidyā)*, but once a soul is enlightened *(prakāṣita)*, the self is freed from the consequences of its good and evil deeds and thereupon becomes indistinguishably identified with the *brahman* (12.267.32–38).

Buddhism. Śākyamuni Buddha, like his philosophical and spiritual predecessors, believed that birth and death recur in successive cycles for the person who lives in the grip of ignorance about the true nature of the world. However, he undercut the Vedāntic position by denying that the world of evanescent entities is undergirded and suffused by an eternal and unalterable Self or "soul-stuff" *(ātman)*. In place of the doctrine of absolute self, he propagated the precept of "no-self" *(anātman)*, namely, that the human person, along with everything else that constitutes the empirical universe, is the offspring *(phala)* of an unbroken, everfluctuating process of creation and destruction and birth and extinction according to the principle of Dependent Coorigination *(pratītya-samutpāda;* Pali, *paṭicca-samuppāda)*. The technical formulation of this Law of Causation is as follows: "If this exists [e.g., an acorn], then that comes to be [an oak tree]." The entire universe perishes and is created afresh in every instant; nothing remains the same from one moment to the next, from a single microbe to an entire galaxy.

The human being or personality, therefore, is not to be understood essentially as an integral and enduring mind-body organism but rather as the manifestation of a highly complex succession of psychosomatic moments propelled along the temporal continuum by the force of *karman*. In the Buddhist view, the human person can be broken down into five constitutive elements, or strands (*skandhas*); it is continually changing but is always determined by its previous actions. As such, humans are never the same from moment to moment and therefore are in no sense the projection of a permanent self. Hence, a cardinal teaching of the Buddha is "there is nothing that transmigrates and yet there is rebirth."

If there is no absolute self that survives the death of one body and is reborn in a new one, then how is the doctrine of rebirth to be reconciled with that of "no-self"? The Buddha declares that this question, like other questions pertaining to the fundamental nature of reality, arises out of a misconstruing of the nature of *karman*. *Karman* is not a unified and independently existing entity that moves from life to life, as a traveler might go from place to place. Rightly understood, *karman* is the life process itself, the blending of energy and form that coordinates an unending flow of life moments. That is, the myriad clusters of factors that constitute the universe at any given moment are nothing more than the product of all its pasts. In other words, the sprout is not the temporary projection of some universal "soul-stuff" but rather a permutation of the parent seed. As one Buddhist text declares, "One hundred thousand universes conspire in the creation of the iridescent eye that graces the feather in the peacock's tail." Birth and death, then, are to be construed as nothing more than dramatic interruptions or exceptional innovations in the ongoing life process.

Therefore, neither a single entity (however subtle and rarified) nor a conglomeration of entities passes across from the old life-form to the new, yet the continuity among the phenomena is maintained. That is, all of the constitutive elements of a person's life are present from the moment of conception, just as the sprout preexists in the seed and contains the sum total of all the effects of its antecedent causal elements, at least in a state of potentiality.

According to the doctrine of *karman*, a person may be reborn successively into any one of five classes of living beings: gods, human beings, animals, hungry ghosts, or denizens of hell. Since birth as a human being occurs at the apex of the ladder of existence and is the penultimate stage to full enlightenment, it follows that all humans have undergone a birth in each of the four other orders of existence prior to the current cycle and occupy a privileged position from which to reach the ultimate goal.

While theoretically all human beings possess the capacity to achieve enlightenment and, thence, liberation from rebirth (Zen Buddhists, for example, contend that a person can experience *satori* at any moment simply by dropping off the thinking mind), in practice only those select few who forsake the life of social responsibility in the world and follow the Buddha *dharma* exclusively as monks and nuns have a realistic hope of achieving salvation in this life. [*See* Enlightenment.]

Jainism. According to the teachings of Mahāvīra (c. 599–527 BCE), the founder of Jainism, the unenlightened soul is bound to follow a course of transmigration that is beginningless and one that will persist for an unimaginable length of time. The soul becomes defiled by involvement in desire-laden actions and thereby attracts increasingly burdensome quantities of karmic matter upon itself. This polluting material, in turn, promotes the further corruption of the soul and causes its inevitable movement through countless incarnations.

The Jains conceive of *karman* as composed of innumerable invisible particles of material substance that pervade all occupied space. Actions of body, mind, and speech project waves of energy that, when combined with the antithetical passions of desire *(rāga)* and hatred *(dveṣa)*, attract karmic "dust" to the soul and weigh it down deeper and deeper in the slough of ignorance and rebirth.

Jains also distinguish between the initial awakening to an awareness of one's bondage to ignorance, suffering, death, and rebirth (the most that the layperson can hope to achieve), on the one hand, and the ultimate state of liberation, on the other. This ultimate state of bliss to which aspire all Jains (or at least the adherents of the monastic path) disperses and dissolves the load of karmic matter that encumbers the mind-body ego and transforms the practitioner into an omniscient and totally dispassionate soul.

Ancient Greece. Whether the idea of metempsychosis was imported by the ancient Greeks from the East (more specifically, India) is subject to speculation in face of the absence of conclusive evidence to support one or another view. Be that as it may, the concept of rebirth occupied a central place in Greek thought from the time of Pherecydes of Syros (sixth century BCE), the mentor of Pythagoras (c. 582–507 BCE), and came into full flowering in the writings of Plato (427–347 BCE) and Plotinus (205–270 CE).

Herodotus, the greatest of ancient Greek historians, records that the Egyptians were the first people to embrace the doctrine of reincarnation. According to his sources, the Egyptians believed that the soul is immortal (i.e., subject to rebirth after each death) and that it passes through various species of terrestrial, marine, and aerial creatures before once again becoming embodied in human form, the entire cycle being completed at the end of a period of three thousand years.

Empedocles (490–430 BCE), under the influence of the writings of the mystic-mathematician Pythagoras, asserted that nothing in the cosmos is either created or destroyed. All living things undergo transmutation in accordance with the relationships among the four basic elements (air, fire, water, and earth). The souls of the impure are condemned to transmigrate for thirty thousand years through numerous types of incarnations. In the course of this transition, various lifetimes are affected in diverse ways by each of the four elements. Escape from this dark destiny is achieved through a lengthy purification process, the primary requirement of which is the avoidance of eating the flesh of animals whose souls once may have inhabited human bodies.

Like many other religious and philosophical traditions that hold to a belief in reincarnation, Orphism, an ancient Greek mystery cult that celebrated the life, death, and resurrection of the god Orpheus, is based upon a dualistic conception of humanity. Orphic sages declared that humans are composed of an invisible soul that was originally good and pure but that has become polluted by some kind of primordial sin or error. As a consequence of this ancient transgression, the originally pure soul has become imprisoned within a physical body that is believed to be impure or evil by nature.

The ultimate aim of this mystery was to raise the soul of each devotee to increasingly loftier and purer levels of spiritual existence. The elevation of the soul was promoted by participation in the sacramental practices of the Orphic brotherhoods *(thiasoi)*. By performing these sacraments—always in secret places and often in the dead of night—the devotee received the power of the divine life. By continually cultivating this gift through meditation, prayer, and vegetarianism, he eventually gained immortality and thereby achieved release from any future reincarnations.

Orphic eschatology emphasized postmortem rewards and punishments. Because of its essentially spiritual nature, the soul could not achieve its true state of existence until after the last of a lengthy series of lives. Complete and lasting freedom from bondage to the material order could be realized only after undergoing a series of rebirths in a variety of physical forms that were determined by the merits of the previous life or lives. Supposedly it was this mystical teaching that was the heart of the revelation that was given to each novice initiated into the Orphic religion. [*See* Orpheus.]

Plato drew together and synthesized numerous strands of thought concerning the fate of the individual soul. Under the influence of Empedocles, Pythagoras, the Orphic prophets, and others, he fashioned a theory of the nature and destiny of humanity that is as complex in its philosophical makeup as it is inspiring in its poetical contents. Like the Vedāntins, he believed that the soul *(psuchē)* is immortal. The soul is the governor and indweller of all conscious beings; it descends periodically into the physical realm of existence as a result of metaphysical nescience and bondage to the passions.

Like the Vedāntins and the Buddhists, Plato declared that the soul of each human being (except for that of the "true philosopher," who is the one truly enlightened being) is entrapped by the body (and by material reality, generally) because of its attachment to the objects of transitory desire (i.e., objects of pleasure and pain). In a statement in the *Laws* (book 10) that could easily have been lifted directly from the Upaniṣads, he asserts, "Recognize that if you become baser you will go to baser souls, and if higher, to the higher, and in every course of life and death you will do and suffer what like may appropriately suffer at the hands of like."

Even the selection of a new incarnation by each soul at the beginning of a new life cycle is determined by the experiences of the former lifetime. During its journey through a series of births, the soul finds temporary abode not only in a variety of land, air, and water creatures, but, once it has achieved the status of humanity, it may pass through a number of professions of varying degrees of moral quality, ranging from that of a demagogue and tyrant at the nadir of the scale, to a lover, a follower of the Muses, and a seeker after wisdom at the apex (*Phaedrus* 248d–e).

According to Plato's famous myth of Er (*Republic* 10), those souls whose minds are governed by the baser pleasures first travel to the plain of Forgetfulness and take up residence on the banks of the river of Indifference, "where each as he drinks, forgets everything"; they then go to their respective births "like so many shooting stars."

The painful and disorienting wanderings of the soul throughout the various orders of creatures are brought to a halt, and the soul is ushered into a state of eternal and perfectly fulfilling bliss, but only after it has divorced itself completely from the pleasures of the body and the material world, placed all of its appetites and yearnings under the governance of Reason, and attained a pure and undeviating contemplation of the Absolute ("the Good"), thereby obtaining "the veritable knowledge of being that veritably is."

In the end, the liberated soul finds unending sojourn in the "place beyond the heavens" (cf. the *brahman* in Vedānta), where "true being dwells, without color or shape, that cannot be touched; reason alone, man's pilot, can behold it and all true knowledge is knowledge thereof" (*Phaedrus* 247d–e).

Conclusion. There is no question but that the twin doctrines of *karman* and reincarnation have done more to shape the whole of Asian thought than any other concept or concepts. It might be difficult to identify an idea or set of ideas that has exercised a comparable influence through the entire scope of Western thought, including the cardinal concepts in the writings of Plato and Aristotle.

Ironically, the notion of reincarnation is beginning to make inroads into contemporary Western thought (particularly in theology, the philosophy of religion, and psychology) by way of a number of circuitous routes. One of the most notable avenues along which the idea is traveling to the West is the number of Asian (primarily Indian) religious traditions that have appeared in Europe and America, along with theosophy, transpersonal psychology, and the academic study of the history of religions and comparative philosophy.

One of the most curious manifestations of the belief in reincarnation in modern times is a new approach to psychotherapy that operates in the United States under the rubric of "rebirthing analysis," which purports to help the client deal with current psychological and spiritual problems by recalling personal experiences during numerous past lifetimes with the aid of meditation, hypnosis, and in some cases, consciousness-altering drugs.

Time alone will tell whether this new imprint on the fabric of Western thought and life will endure to become an integral part of the overall design or will, in time, fade into insignificance and remain only as a vague memory of a short-lived image in Western consciousness.

[*See also* Immortality.]

BIBLIOGRAPHY

de Bary, Wm. Theodore, et al., eds. *Sources of Indian Tradition.* New York, 1958.

Ducasse, Curt John. *A Critical Examination of the Belief in the Life after Death.* Springfield, Ill., 1961.

Head, Joseph, and S. L. Cranston, eds. *Reincarnation: The Phoenix Fire Mystery.* New York, 1977.

MacGregor, Geddes. *Reincarnation as a Christian Hope.* London, 1982.

Parrinder, Geoffrey. "Varieties of Belief in Reincarnation." *Hibbert Journal* 55 (April 1957): 260–267.

Radhakrishnan, Sarvepalli, and Charles A. Moore, eds. *A Source Book in Indian Philosophy.* Princeton, 1957.

Stevenson, Ian. *Twenty Cases Suggestive of Reincarnation.* 2d ed. Charlottesville, Va., 1974.

Thomas, N. W., et al. "Transmigration." In *Encyclopaedia of Religion and Ethics,* edited by James Hastings, vol. 12. Edinburgh, 1921.

Tylor, E. B. *Primitive Culture,* vol. 2, *Religion in Primitive Culture* (1871). New York, 1970.

J. Bruce Long

REINES, YITSḤAQ YA'AQOV (1839–1915), one of the founders and first leaders of Mizraḥi, a religious Zionist movement established at the beginning of the twentieth century. Reines was born in Belorussia, studied at the leading *yeshivot* (rabbinic academies), and served as a rabbi in a variety of towns in Lithuania throughout his life. He made a major contribution to rabbinic scholarship, with emphasis on a strictly logical approach to problems in Jewish law. He published a number of important legal works, including *Ḥotam tokhnit* (1880–1881), and a homiletical work, *Nod shel dema'ot* (1891). While serving as rabbi of Sventsyany from 1869 to 1885, Reines established a *yeshivah* that combined traditional studies with secular subjects, but he was forced to close the school after several months as a result of extreme Orthodox opposition. Only in 1905 did he succeed in establishing such a *yeshivah*, in Lida. This new school became the model for religious Zionist education in the Mizraḥi movement and, following World War I, was copied throughout eastern Europe.

In addition to his legal and educational contributions, Reines was active politically. He joined the proto-Zionist movement Ḥibbat Tsiyyon at its inception in the 1880s and proposed religious agricultural settlements in the Land of Israel. Following the creation of the World Zionist Organization in 1897, he became one of Theodor Herzl's most fervent rabbinical supporters in the face of rejection by most other Orthodox authorities. In 1902, Reines published a book defending Zionism entitled *Or ḥadash 'al Tsiyyon* (A New Light on Zion).

Despite his support for Herzl, Reines was concerned that the secular leadership of the World Zionist Organization would ignore or even denigrate Jewish religious values in the struggle for a Jewish state. In 1902, he convened a conference of Orthodox Zionists in Vilna that resulted in the establishment of Mizraḥi in 1902. Reines also founded the movement's first journal, *Ha-Mizraḥi*. The movement sought to defend and inculcate traditional Jewish values while supporting the Zionist settlement in the Land of Israel. Mizraḥi established a network of schools in eastern Europe and, later, in Palestine. It became the foundation for the National Religious Party (Mafdal), which plays a critical role in Israeli politics today.

[*For further discussion of Ḥibbat Tsiyyon and Mizraḥi, see* Zionism.]

BIBLIOGRAPHY

In addition to Getzel Kressel's biographical article on Reines in *Encyclopaedia Judaica* (Jerusalem, 1971), appraisals of his life and work can be found in *Sefer ha-Mizraḥi*, edited by Y. L. Maimon (Jerusalem, 1946), pp. 83–101, and in David Vital's *Zionism: The Formative Years* (Oxford, 1982), pp. 215–224.

DAVID BIALE

REIYŪKAI KYŌDAN. A Japanese Buddhist lay organization, Reiyūkai Kyōdan was founded between 1919 and 1925 in Tokyo by Kubo Kakutarō (1890–1944) and his sister-in-law Kotani Kimi (1901–1971). As of 1982 it had roughly three million members in Japan, with branches in seventeen foreign countries. Deriving from the tradition of Nichiren, the thirteenth-century religious reformer, Reiyūkai created lay rites of ancestor worship based on daily recitation of an abridgement of the *Lotus Sutra*. Personal salvation is believed to follow upon salvation of one's ancestors, which in turn is brought about through lay rites in the home without priestly mediation. Reiyūkai represents a rare example in the history of religions of ancestor worship as the center of a voluntary association that transcends kinship boundaries. In daily life, Reiyūkai emphasizes traditionalist ethics in marriage and the family, linking these ideals to salvation of oneself and one's ancestors.

An employee of the Imperial Household Ministry, Kubo regarded himself as the Nichiren of the Taishō era (1912–1926), and like the medieval saint he set out to alert the world to the catastrophe he believed imminent. In Kubo's day, Japan was undergoing a radical social transformation, even as it had begun to gain place in international politics. Kubo saw in the massive changes about him a threat to traditional values and a need for religious response. He received religious instruction from exponents of Nichirenshugi, a nationalistic political interpretation of Nichiren's thought, but Kubo sought an understanding of contemporary events that would suggest an appropriate course of religious action for the laity. Since he regarded the Buddhist clergy as utterly incapable of providing suitable moral leadership, he set out to found a lay religious society in order to implement his understanding of Nichiren Buddhism.

Kubo believed that the world was beset with war and disaster because modern society had entrusted the rites of ancestor worship to the Buddhist clergy. He believed that social and political upheavals are actually signs of ancestral distress, reflected to the human world to inform the living that their ancestors are in need of ritual care. When descendants fail to worship them directly, ancestors in the spirit world are unable to achieve Buddhahood. Priests claim to be able to transfer merit to them through esoteric ritual, but actually, in Kubo's view, clerics have no karmic bonds with parishioners' ancestors. These are the ties of blood, filiation, and morality, which exist only among persons actually descended from common ancestors, or between spouses. A priest cannot mediate this relationship. Therefore, Kubo concluded, the ancestors' plight will continue to manifest itself as disasters in the human world until lay people perform the rites that will transfer merit effectively and until they implement in their daily lives an ethic that will "satisfy" the ancestors. The terrible earthquake of 1923 increased tremendously Kubo's sense of urgency in propagating this message.

Kubo's ideas might never have gone beyond a small circle of followers had he not been aided by Kotani Kimi. While Kubo elaborated doctrine and refined ritual, it was Kotani who gathered a core of followers. She proselytized in the poor sections of Tokyo, and by sharing the poverty of her converts, nursing them, and performing faith healing, she established herself as a pillar of the organization. Even after her death, Kotani continues to be widely regarded as a "living Buddha." In activities held at the group's mountain training center, Mirokusan, Kotani has been identified with the Buddha of the future, Maitreya.

Among the present membership, 70 percent reside in urban areas and 30 percent in rural areas. Reiyūkai is organized into a number of branches formed by the links of proselytization. A person rises in rank by converting others, and conversion forms a pyramid in which all those proselytized by the same person are considered his or her "spiritual children," and the original proselytizer the "spiritual parent." Those at the foot of this pyramid look to an original "parent" as their leader, and that person is placed in charge of a branch headquartered in a certain area. The Eighth Branch, for example, has its headquarters in Osaka, claims roughly six hundred thousand members, and on a daily basis operates independently of the Tokyo headquarters of Reiyūkai.

Reiyūkai ritual consists chiefly of daily recitation morning and evening of the *Blue Sutra,* an abridgement of the *Lotus Sutra.* The ritual is structured so as to mobilize the power of the *Lotus Sutra* for the salvation of the ancestors by simultaneously transferring merit and eliminating negative *karman* through repentence. It is assumed that men and women share equally the responsibilities of ritual, and it is considered most desirable that families unite in these observances. It is also assumed that men and women share equally in the fruits of correct ritual: a happy home, filial descendants, and personal salvation. Adherence to a prescribed ethic in marriage is the counterpart to ritual and is regarded as no less essential to salvation.

In the traditionalist family ethic advocated by Reiyūkai, the ideal of the family follows the prewar form (the *ie*). That is, members idealize a situation in which three generations live together, worship together, and if possible engage in a common economic enterprise. The idea of filial piety is central, as is respect for elders. A hierarchical principle exists between men and women, with men in the dominant position. This idea receives religious formulation in the notion that women have worse *karman* than men and therefore have a greater need for religion. A corollary of this notion holds that if women can overcome their *karman* they can achieve spiritual feats impossible for men, an ideal expressed ritually in shamanistic practices resembling spirit possession, from which men are barred.

Reiyūkai continues to engage in political activity in support of various conservative causes, such as advocating state support for the Yasukuni Shrine, formerly the official shrine of the war dead. It also supports revision of the Constitution, particularly Article 9, which renounces the use of war. It is allied with other right-wing religious groups in this and other causes and supports conservative candidates for election. The extent to which this activity accurately mirrors the sentiments of the general membership is unclear, but it seems certain that this large, well-organized group may, along with other religious groups, wield an important political influence in Japan's future.

[*See also* New Religions, *article on* New Religions in Japan.]

BIBLIOGRAPHY

For a comprehensive introduction to the organization, see my *Lay Buddhism in Contemporary Japan: Reiyūkai Kyōdan* (Princeton, 1984).

HELEN HARDACRE

REJUVENATION myths are found all over the world and in varied forms. A concern with being made young and healthy again is found not only in ancient cultures but also in contemporary society. The rejuvenation slogans of the advertising industry have an ancient heritage, as, for example, in the account of beer brewing in the Finnish epic, the *Kalevala,* which says, "The beer of Kalevala strengthens the weak, cheers the sick, and makes the old young again." Myths of rejuvenation are a part of the way humankind has responded to the fear of death and the love of life. To undo the ravages of time, to turn the clock back, has been an age-old longing.

Imitation of Nature. The earliest human cultures were close to nature, experiencing both hardship and joy in the annual change of seasons, lamenting the death of vegetation as it grew old and withered, and rejoicing at the return of spring. The waning of the sun in the west at the close of each day and its rising again to new strength the next day also suggested a rejuvenating power in nature. The Greeks and Celts had stories of a "western paradise" where the aged could obtain youth. Changing Woman, in the Navajo pantheon, transforms herself into a young girl when she becomes old; as wife of the Sun Carrier, her home is in the west. From the idea that the land of the world is surrounded by water, water became associated with the renewal of the sun, as well as with that from which life itself came.

Myths of rejuvenation that focus on the role of sleep reflect an imitation of nature. A myth of the Selk'nam of Tierra del Fuego tells of a culture hero, Kenos, and three of the ancestors who, in old age, tried to fall into a long sleep so as to be rejuvenated. Finally, after several efforts, they went north and there were wrapped in mantles and put in the ground. After a few days they began to stir and whisper, and then, upon rising, they saw that they were young again. They had succeeded in a transformation sleep.

The snake's shedding of its skin has led it to be associated with the power of rejuvenation as well as with healing and transformation. [*See* Snakes.] An Icelandic saga describes a man who shed his skin every few centuries and always emerged thirty years old. The *Ṛgveda*, an ancient scripture of India, describes a priest who in old age had been exposed to die but who was rejuvenated by two physician gods who took off his skin as one would a mantle, prolonging his life and making him the "husband of maidens." Depth psychologists report that the association of snakes with the development of a new perspective, one that is presenting itself to consciousness for the first time, is a frequent motif in contemporary dreams.

The Special Elixir. There are many accounts of special fruits, herbs, or waters that rejuvenate or provide everlasting life. [*See* Elixir.] Usually these stories are about foods of the gods, or foods in distant lands that, if humans could only obtain them, would assure the desired result. An old Norse story tells of a king grown old who heard of a distant land where there was a special water and a priceless apple that would make one young again. He sent his eldest son in quest of them, but the son was distracted by the pleasures of a strange city. So also with the king's second son. Finally, the third and youngest son, after numerous difficulties, succeeded. However, on his return journey the older brothers took from him his treasures and rejuvenated the king themselves. In a German version it is the "water of life" for which the king sent. In Japanese mythology is the story of Ningyo, the Fisherwoman, a mermaidlike creature who lives in the sea; it is said that women who were fortunate enough to eat of her flesh gained perpetual youth and beauty. In Eddic mythology, the goddess Idunn guarded the apples that the gods tasted when they began to grow old lest the giants steal them. In Celtic mythology Fraoch went in search of a tree that grew on an island in a lake. Every month it produced sweet fruit that prolonged life for a year and healed sickness. In ancient China it was believed that gold, the metal that never "grows old" (that is, never tarnishes), not only would preserve a dead body from decay but would also, when ingested in the proper way, promote longevity.

E. Washburn Hopkins sought to demonstrate in "The Fountain of Youth" (*Journal of the American Oriental Society* 26, 1905) that all the many European stories of magic springs or fountains of youth were descended originally from a story in the *Mahābhārata*, an Indian epic. In this story an old man who had married a young woman made an agreement with the Aśvins (twin physician gods) that he would make them drinkers of *soma*, the divine ambrosia, if they would rejuvenate him. They took him to the "youth place," and when he emerged from its water, he had indeed been restored to youthful vigor and appearance. In the European stories the mysterious and miraculous fount is located, usually rather vaguely, in Asia. Hopkins suggested that the Spanish explorer Ponce de León would have been aware of those stories when in the early sixteenth century he set out for India by way of the West Indies, and thus, when he heard stories in Florida of a medicinal and healing spring, he naturally interpreted it as being the famed fountain of youth. Furthermore, Hopkins disagreed with Brinton (*Myths of the New World*, New York, 1896), who contended that the fountain of youth was a universal myth that had emerged from the veneration of water as the female element. [*See* Fountains.]

The Reversal of Time. Mircea Eliade has described in *Myth and Reality* (New York, 1963) and elsewhere how health and youthfulness are obtained by a "return to the origins," by abolishing the work of time—time "the destroyer," as the Roman poet Ovid called it. The therapies for reversing time usually included a ritual reiteration of the creation of the world, thereby permitting a sick person to be born anew and to recommence existence with the health of earlier years. The ancient Taoist and other Chinese alchemists took up these traditional healing methods and applied them to the cure of the illness that results from the ravages of time, that is, from old age and death. Eliade has pointed out that there is a continuity between the early concern with health and rejuvenation and the alchemical traditions of both the East and the West. All the symbols, rituals, and techniques of these traditions emphasized a basic idea: in order to obtain rejuvenation or long life, it is necessary to return to the origin of life and recommence with the vitality that was then present.

Initiatory rituals often enact a "return to the womb" in which the initiate is placed in isolation for a period and then greeted as a newborn upon his delivery. [*See* Initiation.] In ancient China the Taoists had a technique of "embryonic respiration" in which the adept tried to imitate respiration within a closed circuit, in the manner of a fetus. This was believed to drive away old age. Myths concerning a "return to the origin" are on different levels, some more physical, some more spiritual. Eliade has pointed out a similar motif in the psychoanalytic system of Sigmund Freud that involves a "return to the beginning" in its method of healing.

A caution about tampering with time is expressed in the Japanese story of an old woodcutter who, becoming thirsty one day, drank from a stream he had not drunk from before. The water was unusually delicious, flowing clear and swiftly. He went to the pool from which the stream flowed, and as he knelt to drink some more, he saw his reflection in the pool, but his face was that of his youth. Realizing that he had drunk from a fountain of youth, he ran (which he had been unable to do for years) to tell his wife. With difficulty he persuaded her of his identity. She insisted that she must drink of the same water, for he would not want an old wife, and she hurried away. When she did not return, he went in search of her. At the pool he found a baby girl lying on the bank. In her eagerness the old woman had drunk too much from the fountain of youth.

The Realm of the Divine. Many stories of rejuvenation take place in the realm of the divine or involve gifts or rewards from the gods. In a Scandinavian legend the age of Olger the Dane is changed from one hundred years to thirty by means of a ring provided by the fairy Morgana. In Greek mythology, when Zeus heard that Prometheus had stolen fire from him and had given it to humanity, he became indignant and so gave to those who informed him about the theft a drug that was an antidote to old age. And on the return of the Argonauts, the enchantress Medea made Aeson, Jason's father, young again with herbs and incantations.

In a Navajo myth, the two sons of Changing Woman are warned by Old Age not to walk on her path, but, rather, to keep to the left of it. They forgot this counsel, however, and walked on the path. Then they began to feel heavy; they stooped, and their steps became shorter; and finally they could not move, even with the help of canes. Old Age rebuked them and, in a Navajo pattern of creating, sang a song so that in future, she said, everything should reach old age. Then, however, she made them young again and sent them on their way. In some stories continual rejuvenation is the reward for living in an especially holy place or on a blessed island. In Aztec mythology there is a holy mountain, the residence of the great mother of the gods, that one can never entirely climb, for the upper half consists of fine, slippery sand. However, whoever climbs part way, no matter how old, grows young again in proportion to the distance climbed.

Some myths explain why old age and death are inevitable. [*See* Death.] In Mesopotamian mythology, Gilgamesh is told at the end of a long journey in search of a means of avoiding death that the gods have reserved immortality for themselves. Disappointed, he is told, as a parting gift, of a plant that makes one young again. He dives to the bottom of the sea to get the plant; but on his return journey, when he stops to bathe in a pool, a snake steals the plant, sloughing its skin as it goes—thus obtaining immortality for snakes. In the Hebrew scriptures, eating of the fruit of the Tree of Life, which stood in the midst of the Garden of Eden, enabled one to live forever. After Adam and Eve disobeyed God by eating of the Tree of the Knowledge of Good and Evil they were driven from the garden, and a guard was placed there to protect the path to the tree of life.

Spiritualization of the Quest. Mesopotamian and Egyptian mythologies tended to focus on the quest for immortality or life after death, while in ancient China and Vedic India the quest was much more for rejuvenation and the recovery of youthfulness in this life. [*See* Quest.] In later Indian thought, beginning in the sixth century BCE, for both Hinduism and Buddhism the aim of life was not rejuvenation but liberation from earthly existence. Similarly, beginning in the sixth century BCE, the mystery religions of the Mediterranean world responded to a longing for cleansing and renovating the human spirit and found in nature a model for that renewal; thus their professed aim was to assure eternal life. Christianity then turned the emphasis to an inner, spiritual renewal: "Unless one is born anew, he cannot see the kingdom of God" (*Jn.* 3:3). The water in the baptismal font assured the possibility of life eternal. In one eucharistic liturgy the words of the priest at the moment of delivering the bread and wine indicate their life-giving power: "Preserve thy body and soul to everlasting life."

Implications. The desire for rejuvenation in this life, however, is still present. In the secular culture of the modern world, with its loss to a large extent of any sense of the sacred, there has been a new interest in rejuvenation, not as a gift from the realm of the divine, but as a goal for human endeavor. According to early records, priests and elders in ancient India and China consumed the sexual organs of wild animals in order to resist the effects of old age and restore their youthful vigor; similar attempts at rejuvenation have continued throughout history. In the late nineteenth and early twentieth centuries, a few surgeons in Europe and North America claimed to have achieved rejuvenation by transplanting reproductive glands from animals. The medical community in general rejected the technique and attributed to other factors the apparent results, which were, at best, temporary. Vitamins are now advocated as a means of prolonging the consequences of old age.

When the present lacks meaning, discontent expresses itself in a longing for the past. The thirst for rejuvenation may occur precisely at the point in human development when either the culture as a whole or an individual is ready to move on to a new level of understanding but is reluctant to undertake the journey and seeks instead to find meaning in the way life was before. The contemporary developmental understanding of human life as moving from stage to stage, with each stage having its own maturation task to be accomplished or wisdom to be achieved, suggests that the thirst for rejuvenation may stem from a failure to move on to the next level of development. The investigations of the history of religions as well as contemporary psychotherapy demonstrate that humans cannot stand a meaningless life. How this dilemma is to be faced, expressed, and lived out by individuals is the challenge that faces contemporary civilization, with its expanding population of old people.

BIBLIOGRAPHY

Among the numerous anthologies of myths, one that includes numerous myths of rejuvenation is *The Mythology of All Races,* 13 vols., edited by Louis Herbert Gray et al. (Boston, 1916–1932). A short essay by Mircea Eliade, "Rejuvenation and Immortality," in *Patterns in Comparative Religion* (New York, 1958), contrasts and discusses the implications of mythologies that focus on rejuvenation. In the *Forge and the Crucible: The Origins and Structures of Alchemy,* 2d ed. (Chicago, 1978), Eliade illuminates the attempts of the Chinese and Indian alchemists to accelerate the work of nature and thereby conquer time. A comprehensive collection of legends about the fountain of youth and related stories of rejuvenation is to be found in E. Washburn Hopkins's article entitled "The Fountain of Youth," *Journal of the American Oriental Society* 26 (1905): 1–67.

WALLACE B. CLIFT

RELATIVISM. The term *relativism* is applied to ethical, cultural, and religious views. Relativism contends that such views are to be evaluated relative to the societies or cultures in which they appear and are not to be judged true or false, or good or bad, based on some overall criterion but are to be assessed within the context in which they occur. Thus, what is right or good or true to one person or group may not be considered so by others.

This theory was first presented by certain Greek authors who noted the varieties of religions and moral behavior in the Mediterranean world and suggested that differing mores indicated that there were no absolute standards. Protagoras said, "Man is the measure of all things," and this was interpreted to convey that each man could be his own measure. The variations of human, social, political, and ethical behavior were worked into a basic theme of the Greek skeptics. The fact of differences in human behavior is taken to imply that no general standard can possibly apply to all peoples and cultures. Sextus Empiricus even suggested that cannibalism, incest, and other practices considered taboo are just variant kinds of behavior, to be appreciated as acceptable in some cultures and not in others. This reasoning was applied by the Greek skeptics to various religions and their practices. They urged suspension of judgment about right or wrong and undogmatic acceptance of one's own culture. [*See* Skeptics and Skepticism.]

This relativistic attitude was in sharp contrast to the dogmatic views of the Jews and Christians in the Roman empire, who insisted their revealed information assured them that their religious beliefs and practices were the only correct and acceptable ones. The christianization of the Roman empire and of pagan Europe pushed the relativistic approach aside. There could be some variations in ritual or practice, but in essential beliefs and practices anything different was heretical. [*See* Apologetics.]

The skeptical-relativist view reappeared in new and forceful ways in the Renaissance, with a rediscovery of the wide variety of beliefs and practices of ancient times, and with the discoveries of radically different cultures all over the world. The rapid development of new kinds of Christian practices resulting from the Reformation also contributed to an emerging view of differences as based on cultural factors. Contrasts with the Ottoman empire made people even more cognizant of the wide range of human beliefs and practices. Montaigne was foremost in presenting the panorama of human beliefs and implying that the fact of difference indicated that each set of beliefs and practices was culturally conditioned. He contended that most people hold their religious views as a result of custom rather than conviction. He also suggested that the religious and moral practices of the "noble savages" were at least as good as those of European Christians.

Montaigne's skepticism and cultural relativism were carried further by the French skeptic Pierre Bayle, who insisted that a society of atheists could be more moral than a society of Christians, since moral behavior results from natural causes such as custom and education and not from religious doctrines. Bayle sought to show that such biblical heroes as David, such leading Christians as Calvin and Luther, and saints and popes throughout the history of Christianity have all acted in the moral sphere because of their own human natures and not because of their religious beliefs.

Bayle's analysis was incorporated into the Enlightenment's quest for a science of man that would explain why people acted, behaved, and believed in different ways. This science would deem religious beliefs the effects of different physical and psychological conditions, which might be studied neutrally. Climate, history, customs, education, institutions, and so on would account for the fact that societies differ in their social, cultural, and religious practices. One's personal psychological conditions would account for an individual's strong or weak religious convictions. Hume's *Natural History of Religion* (1757) initiated the study of religion as a manifestation of human behavior in which religious activity is relative to individual and cultural conditions. [*See the biography of Hume.*]

This relativistic aspect of religion was identified as a crucial feature of the human condition by the German philosopher J. C. Herder, who contended that every society or culture develops from its own unique idea or character. Ethical and religious norms are part of the expression of these ideas, and no culture is inferior or superior to any other; it is simply different. Thus religion is seen to be relative to the culture in which it appears. [*See the biography of Herder.*]

Herder's relativism and the growing interest in comparative studies of language and religion led to the full-blown relativism of Alexander von Humboldt in the nineteenth century, and of many twentieth-century anthropologists. Von Humboldt stated, "There are nations more susceptible of cultivation, more highly civilized, more ennobled by mental cultivation than others—but none in themselves nobler than others. All are in like degree designed for freedom" (*Cosmos*, London, 1888, vol. 1, p. 368).

The relativist position was further reinforced by various theories of the natural causes of beliefs. The theories of Marx and Freud offered ways whereby one could account for the fact that individuals and groups adhere to beliefs without considering whether or not these beliefs are true. Scholars now began to consider instead whether various religious beliefs were beneficial or deleterious, or why a particular belief arose at a certain moment in human history. [*See the biographies of Freud and Marx.*]

The relativist position was forcefully stated by the anthropologist Edward A. Westermarck in his major work *The Origin and Development of Moral Ideas* (1906). Westermarck contended on the basis of historical, sociological, and anthropological evidence that no ethical principles are objectively valid. In *Ethical Relativity* (1932) he further argued his position on philosophic grounds.

Critics of cultural relativism have suggested, first, that evidence of cultural differences does not rule out the possibility that there exist common beliefs and attitudes held by most or all cultures and, second, that factual information about such differences does not eliminate the possibility that one belief system may in fact be better, or more true, than another. Further, philosophers are still arguing about whether causal explanations about people's beliefs evidence the value, truth, or falsity of these beliefs. Yet by the late twentieth century, cultural relativism was a rather common view among many students of ethics and religion.

[*See also* Anthropology, Ethnology, and Religion *and* Study of Religion, *article on* Methodological Issues.]

BIBLIOGRAPHY

Brandt, Richard B. "Ethical Relativism." In *The Encyclopedia of Philosophy*, edited by Paul Edwards, vol. 3. New York, 1967. A careful presentation and examination of the relativistic theory.

Freud, Sigmund. *Totem and Taboo: Some Points of Agreement between the Mental Lives of Savages and Neurotics.* Authorized translation by James Strachey. New York, 1950. A psychoanalytic interpretation of some features of primitive religion and their present form in ordinary neurotic behavior.

James, William. *The Varieties of Religious Experience: A Study in Human Nature.* New York, 1902. A classical psychological description of the role of religion in human experience.

Jarvie, Ian C. *Rationality and Relativism: In Search of a Philosophy and History of Anthropology.* London, 1984. A critical evaluation of relativism as a proper interpretation of anthropological findings.

Needham, Joseph, ed. *Science, Religion and Reality.* New York, 1925. Contains, among other essays, Bronislaw Malinowski's "Magic, Science and Religion," Charles Singer's "Historical Relations of Religion and Science," and Needham's "Mechanistic Biology and the Religious Consciousness," all pressing a relativistic interpretation of religion.

Westermarck, Edward A. *Ethical Relativity.* New York, 1932. The basic philosophical statement of relativism in the twentieth century.

Yinger, J. Milton. *The Scientific Study of Religion.* New York, 1970. A study of religion in relation to human needs, behavior, and problems. A multidisciplinary approach.

RICHARD H. POPKIN

RELICS may loosely be defined as the venerated remains of venerable persons. This should be taken to include not only the bodies, bones, or ashes of saints, heroes, martyrs, founders of religious traditions, and other holy men and women but also objects that they once owned and, by extension, things that were once in physical contact with them.

According to the principles of contagious magic, any personal possession or part of a person's body can be thought of as equivalent to his whole self, no matter how minute it may be, or how detached in time and space. Thus a bone, a hair, a tooth, a garment, a footprint can carry the power or saintliness of the person with whom they were once associated and make him or her "present" once again.

Scholars eager to discuss the "origins" of relics have often pointed to the magical use of such objects by "primitive" peoples in rituals of war, healing, rainmaking, or hunting. They have gathered examples from all sorts of ethnographies to show that fetishes and talismans, amulets and medicine bundles were sometimes made of human bones, hair, or organs. They have thereby concluded that the impulse in man to preserve and use "relics" must be very ancient indeed. They may well be correct, but it is important to try to view such examples within their individual cultural contexts, and not to generalize too quickly from them about the development of relic worship as a whole.

In fact, the veneration of relics is not equally emphasized in the various religions of the world. Highly featured in some traditions (such as Buddhism and Catholicism), it is virtually absent in others (Protestantism, Hinduism, Judaism), and found only incidentally elsewhere (Islam, ancient Greece). In this article, therefore, we shall deal primarily with the Roman Catholic and Buddhist traditions. But before doing so, it may be helpful to examine briefly some of the reasons for the other traditions' diversity.

Protestantism, Hinduism, and Israelite Religion. The Protestant reformers condemned the veneration of relics partly for theological reasons and partly because it was closely associated in their minds with the sale of indulgences and with other ecclesiastical practices of which they disapproved. From the start, their criticism was thus polemical, and, appealing to reason, it lambasted in particular the fantastic proliferation of relics that had developed in medieval Catholicism. For instance, John Calvin (1509–1564), who wrote a treatise on relics, mockingly commented that in his day the quantity of wood contained in relics of the True Cross was so great that even three hundred men could not have carried it.

In Hinduism, opposition to relic worship occurred for quite different reasons. Though Hindus commonly honor the memories of great saints and teachers and visit sites of pilgrimage associated with them, they do not generally venerate their bodily remains. On the one hand, the doctrine of reincarnation and the belief in the ultimately illusory nature of things of this world simply do not promote relic worship. On the other hand, and probably more importantly, death and things associated with it are, in Hinduism, thought to be highly polluting. For this reason, in fact, Hindu funeral customs stress the total destruction of the body, which is most commonly cremated. The ashes from the pyre and any unburned fragments of bone, though they are treated with respect for a while, are all eventually disposed of, often in a nearby river, ideally in the Ganges.

In ancient Israel, there also existed a concern for purity and for separating the dead from the living. Bodies were not cremated, but they were quickly and carefully buried in the hollowed sides of caves or burial chambers. There it was expected that they would decay, dry up, and disintegrate; thus tombs were commonly reused by family members. Pronounced rites of mourning and lamentation did take place, but, generally speaking, the tomb and the corpse were thought to be unclean, and contact with them was defiling (*Lv.* 21:1–4, *Nm.* 19:11–16). Hence, there was little room for any enthusiasm for relics.

It may also be, however, that too great a veneration of the remains of the dead—as in the occasionally mentioned practice of making food offerings in the tombs—was thought of in certain ancient Israelite circles as bordering on idolatry or paganism, and hence to be condemned.

Islam. Much the same concern can be found in Islam; certain Qur'anic scholars periodically denounced the veneration of relics, especially of the bodies of saints, as *shirk* (polytheism), that is, as treating the grave as an idol rather than worshiping God alone. Nevertheless, the cult of relics did manage to grow within the Muslim fold, and it continues to be popular today.

In addition to the various "traces" *(athar)* left by Muḥammad, such as hairs, teeth, autographs, and especially footprints, Muslims have long venerated the remains of saints. This, it should be pointed out, is a cult of bodies rather than of bones, and focuses on the tombs of holy persons that dot the countrysides of those Muslim lands where their worship plays an important role. Though ritual patterns at these tombs may vary, often believers will circumambulate the saint's enshrined coffin, leave votive offerings there, and pray for cures, for help with family problems, or more generally for "blessing" *(barakah)*. While some Muslim theologians may claim that such petitions are not technically made to the saint but through the saint to God, it is clear that, in the minds of the faithful, the saint himself is thought to be present in the tomb and able to respond effectively.

In some instances, owing to their great popularity, certain famous saints are reputed to be buried in more than one place. Thus, for example, the body of the great Shīʿī martyr, Ḥusayn ibn ʿAlī (d. 680 CE), while usually thought to be enshrined in Karbala, is also reputed to rest in Medina, Damascus, Aleppo, and a number of other places, and his head is said to be in Cairo, where it remains a popular center of piety.

Nonetheless, because of orthodox objections, the cult of relics in Islam seems never to have mushroomed in quite the way it did in Christianity or Buddhism, and it has retained a somewhat ambiguous status. This ambiguity is perhaps best summed up in the recurring legends of mausoleums that were destroyed by the very saints they entombed—the saints themselves thereby posthumously objecting to their own cult (and at the same time showing their even greater glory).

Ancient Greece. In ancient Greece, the veneration of relics was closely connected to the cult of heroes, whose reputed remains—often bones larger than life-size—were enshrined and honored in towns as a guarantee of their protection and an enhancement of their prestige. Thus Lesbos had the head of Orpheus, Elis the shoulder bone of Pelops (which had been found by a fisherman and identified by an oracle). Tantalus's bones were at Argos, while the remains of Europa were the focus of the great Hellotia festival in Crete. All of these were thought to ward off disease and famine, to encourage fertility and welfare, and sometimes to bring about miraculous cures.

Occasionally the relics of great heroes were the object of searches and, when found, had to be translated to their place of enshrinement. Plutarch, for example, describes in some detail the quest for the bones of Theseus, a hero whose armed ghost many Athenians believed to have helped them achieve their victory at Marathon. Finally, when his remains were discovered on the island of Siphnos, they were transported to Athens with considerable pomp and celebration and enshrined in the center of the city.

In addition to the bones of the heroes, weapons and other objects associated with them were honored. Thus, in a variety of temples, visitors could marvel at Orpheus's lyre, Achilles' spear, Helen's sandal, Agamemnon's scepter, the Argonauts' anchor, the stone swallowed by Kronos, even the tusks of the Erymanthian boar captured by Herakles. Such items were, perhaps, more objects of curiosity than of cults, but they served the important function of drawing pilgrims and of concretizing the myths and glories of a former age.

Early Christianity. In Christianity, we find an example of the fully developed veneration of relics. Its origins within the Christian tradition are usually traced to the cults that arose around the tombs of the early saints and martyrs. [*See* Persecution, *article on* Christian Experience.] These cults are often compared to the similar hero cults of the Hellenistic world. They stem, however, not only from a desire to venerate the memory of the departed saint, but also from a hope to partake of some of the power and blessing he or she derived from a close and ongoing relationship with God.

It was thought to be beneficial in the early church to be physically close to the saints. Hence, from the start, Christians paid visits to their tombs; there they celebrated the Eucharist on the stone slabs covering their graves. Sometimes, they even decided to settle permanently in the vicinity of these graves. In this way, tombs became altars, and whole cities arose where once had been cemeteries.

Alternatively, the bodies of the saints were sometimes brought to the faithful; they were translated from their graves to existing cities and enshrined in churches there. Thus existing altars also became tombs, and the custom of celebrating mass over the bones of the martyrs was reinforced. In fact, by the fourth century, in the Eastern church, the Eucharist could only be celebrated on an altar covered with an antimension—a cloth into which were sewn fragments of relics. And in the West, the common custom was to enclose relics in a cavity in the altar top itself—a practice that became formalized in 787 when the Second Council of Nicaea declared the presence of such relics to be obligatory for the consecration of a church.

With the toleration of Christianity throughout the Roman empire beginning in the reign of Constantine (272–327), the demand for and veneration of relics grew. Especially in the fourth and fifth centuries, not only were the known remains of martyrs venerated but lost relics of ancient saints started making their appearance. Thus the body of Saint Stephen—the first Christian martyr—was discovered as though it had been waiting for this time and was enshrined in a number of important centers.

At the same time, relics connected with Christ's passion came to be highly esteemed: the crown of thorns, the nails that pierced his hands and feet, and especially the wood of the True Cross on which Christ had died and which, according to legend, had been discovered by Constantine's mother, Helena. The cross was said to have been made of the wood of the Tree of Life, taken belatedly from the Garden of Eden by Adam's son Seth. It was, thus, a powerful symbol of both the death of Christ and the rewards of eternal life. Along with other relics, it was credited with miraculous cures, even resurrections. It was also used as a talisman for magical protection; Gregory of Nyssa's sister Macrina (c. 327–

379) always wore around her neck an amulet consisting of a splinter of the True Cross encased in a ring, and she was clearly not the only noblewoman to do so. It comes as no surprise, then, that by the middle of the fourth century, according to one account, wood from the True Cross filled the world (though miraculously the original cross itself still remained whole and undiminished in Jerusalem).

The growth of the cult of relics in the early church, however, was not without controversy and opposition. On the one hand, it was clearly an offense to traditional Roman sensibilities about keeping the dead in their proper place. For example, Julian the Apostate (r. 361–363) denounced the Christians for filling the world with sepulchers and defiling the cities with the bones and skulls of "criminals." On the other hand, even within the Christian community, there were those such as Vigilantius (early fifth century) who were very critical of the worship of relics, claiming that it was grossly superstitious and bordered on idolatry. However, Jerome, in an angry reply to Vigilantius, argued that Christians did not "worship" relics but "honored" them. Doctrinally, then, if not always in practice, a distinction was made that still stands today between the *veneratio* paid to the saints and their relics and the *adoratio* espoused for God and Christ.

Other church leaders, however, were concerned about the veritable traffic in relics that was developing in the fourth and fifth centuries, especially in the East. In 386, therefore, the emperor Theodosius passed legislation restricting the translation of dead bodies and the selling, buying, or dividing of the remains of martyrs. This, however, seems to have had little effect; at the end of the century, Augustine was still complaining of unscrupulous monks who wandered and traded in "members of martyrs if martyrs they be," and over a century later, the emperor Justinian had to issue another decree regulating the exhumation and transfer of saints' bodies.

It is important to realize the many dimensions of these practices and their larger religious and social significance. As Peter Brown has pointed out, the translations of relics that started in the fourth century helped to spread Christianity by making it more mobile and decentralizing it (Brown, 1981, p. 88). Because of this, not only local holy men but centrally important saints could be worshiped in places far away from the ancient foci of the faith. It was not necessary to journey to Palestine or Rome to honor the memory of Jesus or of the early martyrs; they could be found—present in various physical objects—more close to home, indeed in any consecrated church. In this, the translation of relics was a perfect complement to the popular practice of pilgrimage; it brought the saints to the people instead of taking the people to the saints. At a somewhat different level, the translation of relics also served to establish an intricate network of "patronage, alliance, and gift giving that linked the lay and clerical elites of East and West," which was crucial in the development of the church (Brown, 1981, p. 89). In this, the remains of saints acted as a sort of symbolic exchange commodity.

At the same time, as Brown has also pointed out, the exhumation, dismemberment, and translation of relics has played an important role in divorcing them from too direct an association with death. Precisely because relics are fragments of bones and not whole corpses, precisely because they are in altars or reliquaries and not in coffins, the connotations of death are suppressed, and in the relics the saints can be thought to be "alive."

The Middle Ages. By the time of the Middle Ages, the veneration of relics had become so widespread, popular, and intense that more than one scholar has called it the true religion of the medieval period. Especially in Europe, churches, monasteries, cathedrals, and other places of pilgrimage seemed to develop an almost insatiable thirst for relics that might add to their sanctity, prestige, and attractiveness to pilgrims. This increasing demand led, in fact, to a renewed search for the bodies of ancient saints in places such as the catacombs in Rome. Quickly, a transalpine trade in bones developed, manned by relic merchants and professional relic thieves, who were eager to supply the needs of Carolingian bishops and abbots and later of Anglo-Saxon kings. Then, with the Crusades, still new sources of relics became accessible—Jerusalem and Constantinople being the most important of these.

Throughout the Middle Ages, relics, in fact, were significant sources of revenue. Offerings made to the shrine of Thomas Becket, for example, accounted for almost half of Canterbury's annual income in the late twelfth century, and this proportion increased when special indulgences were granted to pilgrims there. It is not surprising, then, that persons in power were willing to invest considerably in the acquisition of relics. Louis IX of France (r. 1226–1270), for example, reportedly offered the count of Fondi fifteen thousand florins for the bones of Saint Thomas Aquinas, but, alas, in vain.

When relics were obtained, they were often magnificently enshrined. The reliquaries in which they were encased were some of the most richly adorned products of medieval art; sometimes entire buildings were conceived of as reliquaries, such as the splendid Sainte Chapelle in Paris, which was built to house Christ's crown of thorns.

Given such enthusiasm and piety, it is perhaps not surprising that fraudulent and false relics should also appear. Chaucer, in his *Canterbury Tales*, tells of a relic monger who in his trunk had a pillowcase that he asserted was Our Lady's veil. Other sources mention exhibitions of vials that were said to contain a sneeze of the Holy Spirit, or the sounds of the bells of Solomon's temple, or rays from the star that guided the wise men from the East. One church in Italy even claimed to possess the cross that Constantine saw in his vision.

More generally, however, piety and rival claims led to a bewildering multiplication of the remains of saints. During the Middle Ages, it was rare, in fact, for a saint's body or bones to exist in one place only. At least nineteen churches, for example, claimed to enshrine the jaw of John the Baptist. The body of Saint James was found most famously at Santiago de Compostela in Spain, where, like a magnet, it drew pilgrims from all over Europe along well-established routes; it was also venerated, however, in at least six other places, with additional heads and arms elsewhere. Saint Peter, of course, was honored in Rome, but despite (or because of) his fame there, pilgrims could also venerate significant portions of his body at Arles, Cluny, Constantinople, and Saint-Cloud. While his thumb was to be seen in Toulon, three teeth were in Marseilles, his beard was in Poitiers, and his brain was in Geneva (although John Calvin later claimed it was but a piece of pumice stone).

Relics of more minor saints—six hands of Saint Adrian, various breasts of Saint Agatha—abounded as well. The list is almost endless, and Collin de Plancy easily filled three volumes of a dictionary of relics with references to them.

As for relics of Jesus and the Virgin Mary, they, too, were extremely popular during the Middle Ages, though the doctrine of their bodily ascension to heaven presented some difficulties. In their cases, bones were, for the most part, not legitimately acceptable. Great emphasis, however, could be laid on any object that had once been in contact with their persons.

In the case of the Virgin, these relics tended to emphasize her maternal, nurturing, and domestic characteristics. Thus vials of her breast milk (spilled on various occasions) could be found in countless churches throughout Christendom, later causing Calvin to comment that, had she been a cow all her life, she could not have produced such a quantity. Almost as popular was her tunic (especially that worn at the time of the Annunciation). Threads from it were occasionally worn in protective amulets. Roland, in Spain, for example, fought with a sword in whose hilt was a piece of the Virgin's robe (along with a hair of Saint Denis, a tooth of Saint Peter, and some of Saint Basil's blood). Finally, in Loreto, in central Italy, the whole of the house in which the Virgin had raised the young Jesus in Nazareth could be visited. It was believed to have been miraculously transported there through the air from Palestine in 1296.

In the case of Jesus, the relics were of a more varied character. Some, such as his swaddling clothes and the boards of the manger in which he lay in Bethlehem, brought to mind the figure of the Christ child. Others called up more complex associations, perhaps; no fewer than seven churches claimed to possess his circumcised foreskin, and the one at Coulombs in the diocese of Chartres was venerated by pregnant women hoping for an easy childbirth. Still others simply recalled various episodes recorded in the Gospels: bread crumbs left over from the loaves he had used in feeding the five thousand, one of the pots in which he had turned water into wine, the cloth that had covered the table at the Last Supper, the towel he had used on that occasion to wipe the apostles' feet, the body of the ass on which he had entered Jerusalem.

The greatest veneration and enthusiasm, however, were reserved for relics associated with Christ's passion. Some of these, such as the crown of thorns, the spear that had pierced his side, the nails and wood of the True Cross, had long been popular. But now no detail of Christ's agony escaped attention, and in various churches, pilgrims could also venerate the pillar to which he had been tied, the reeds with which he had been whipped, Veronica's veil on which he had left an image of his face on the way to Calvary, the seamless robe that the soldiers divided, the sponge with which he was offered vinegar, the blood and water that flowed from his side, and, finally, the burial shroud in which he lay in the tomb and on which he left the full imprint of his body. This shroud, now in Turin, was perhaps the last major relic of Christ's passion to come to light. It was first exhibited in the fourteenth century and has, in recent years, become the subject of intensive debate and scientific analysis.

It is sometimes difficult to realize the fervor with which medieval man approached many of these relics. Part of their attraction, of course, lay in their reputed miraculous powers, especially in the form of cures, but there was more to it than this. Relics enabled the pious to relive—to recall experientially—events that were central to their faith. They were visible manifestations of the presence of Christ and of his saints that could, in the words of one bishop, "open the eyes of the heart." They thus provided effective focal points for religious devotion and emotion. Suger, the abbot of Saint-Denis in Paris, has described the scene there in the early twelfth century. The old church, he states, was often filled to overflowing by the faithful, who pressed in closely to implore the help of the saints and strove hard to kiss the nail and crown relics of the Lord. Women found themselves trampled underfoot or squeezed to the point of suffocation, while the brethren themselves, pressed hard by the crowd, periodically had to make their escape with the relics through the windows.

Buddhism. Christianity is but one of two major traditions in which relics have played a prominent and popular role. The other—Buddhism—became one of the great propagators of relic worship throughout Asia. Unlike Hinduism, which, we have seen, had little room for relics, Buddhism was from the start fascinated by, and preoccupied with, death. This does not mean that Buddhists did not share some of the Indian repugnance for dead bodies. They tried, however, to overcome that repugnance, meditating on the impurity and impermanence of the body, dead or alive. The remains of the Buddha and of other enlightened saints, however, were thought not to be impure but worthy of the highest veneration.

The focus in Buddhism has been by and large on the relics of the Buddha himself, even though Buddhists in ancient India did also honor the relics of his disciples, and though still today, in some places, believers will search the ashes of great monks for their *śarīradhātu* (either bits of bone or tiny pieces of what is thought to be metamorphosed bodily substance).

According to tradition, when the Buddha passed away into final *nirvāṇa,* he told his disciples who were monks not to preoccupy themselves with his physical remains but to follow his teaching. After his cremation, therefore, his relics were left to the laity. Almost immediately they became the object of a dispute among various North Indian monarchs, each of whom wanted all the physical remains of the Buddha for his own kingdom. According to the *Mahāparinibbāna Sutta,* this squabble was resolved not by the monks but by a brahman named Droṇa who divided the Buddha's relics into eight equal shares and distributed them to eight kings, instructing each to build a stupa (a domed funerary mound) over his portion.

The fate of these eight "Droṇa stupas" (as they were called) is uncertain. According to one legend, however, soon after his conversion to Buddhism, the great Indian emperor Aśoka (third century BCE) collected from them the relics, which he then redistributed throughout his empire, this time dividing them into eighty-four thousand shares and building eighty-four thousand stupas to enshrine them. Thus, the Buddha's physical body (his relics), along with his teaching (his Dharma), was spread throughout the Indian subcontinent in a systematic and ordered way. It is clear, however, that Aśoka was also using Buddhism and the relics symbolically in order to impose his own authority over the kingdom.

In addition to this legend of the eighty-four thousand stupas, there are a number of other quite different traditions concerning the fate of the Buddha's relics. These focus not so much on his ashes as on the fortune of certain of his bones and teeth. One tooth, for instance, ended up enshrined in Sri Lanka, where today it is an object of veneration by pilgrims who come to the Temple of the Tooth in Kandy to make offerings of flowers and incense. Once a year, in the summer month of Äsala, it is paraded in pomp around the city in what remains one of the chief Sri Lankan festivals.

Throughout the precolonial history of Sri Lanka, possession of the Buddha's tooth was seen as an indispensable attribute of kingship. Its cult was the privilege and duty of the legitimate ruler and was thought to ensure social harmony, regular rainfall, bountiful crops, and righteous rule. Its possession meant power. Thus, when the British finally took Kandy in 1815 and captured the tooth, they found to their surprise that resistance to them soon stopped.

The official cult of the tooth relic was and is today carried out by an entire hierarchy of priests. Several times a day, in a series of ceremonies that closely resemble the Hindu pattern of worship of the gods, they ritually entertain the tooth, bathe it, clothe it, and feed it. In this, it is quite clear that the Buddha is thought to be somehow present, despite the doctrine that he has completely transcended the realm of rebirth.

As with the saints in Christianity, this presence of the Buddha in his relics is sometimes emphasized by the occurrence of miracles. For instance, according to the *Mahāvaṃsa* (Great Chronicle) of Sri Lanka, when King Duṭṭhagāmaṇi (first century BCE) was about to enshrine some Buddha relics in the great stupa he had built, the casket in which they were kept rose up into the air; it opened of itself, and the relics came out, took on the physical form of the Buddha, and performed all sorts of miracles that had been performed by the Buddha himself during his lifetime. According to some traditions, it might be added, much the same miracle is expected to take place at the end of this present world cycle, when, just prior to the advent of the next Buddha, Maitreya, all of the dispersed relics of the present Buddha will miraculously come together again to form his body one more time, before disappearing forever into the depths of the earth.

Sri Lanka, however, was by no means the only Buddhist nation to enjoy the possession of prestigious Buddha relics. A number of hairs of the Buddha were enshrined in splendor in the great Shwe Dagon pagoda in Rangoon, Burma; and in Lamphun in northern Thailand, several relics of the Buddha became the object of great veneration and elaborate legends. In both of these places, as in many others throughout the Buddhist world, the presence of Buddha relics is closely linked to the first introduction of Buddhism into the country. In other words, the relics were not just objects of veneration for a few but were symbolic of the establishment of the faith in a whole region.

The situation was somewhat different in China, where Buddhism was always in competition with a number of other faiths and ideologies. Nevertheless, in Ch'ang-an (present-day Sian), the ancient capital of the T'ang dynasty, the emperor's periodic reception for the Buddha's finger bone relic (generally kept at a monastery outside the city) was perhaps the greatest religious festival during the ninth century.

As Kenneth Ch'en put it in his *Buddhism in China,* "Whenever this relic was put on public display, the people . . . would work themselves into such a state of religious frenzy as to belie the statement that the Chinese are rational and practical in their conduct" (Ch'en, 1964, p. 280). Devotees threw themselves on the ground, gave away all their possessions, cut off their hair, burned their scalps, and made fiery offerings of their fingers. It was, in fact, this sort of display that in 819 led the Confucian scholar Han Yü to petition the throne to put an end to such celebrations, pointing out that it was demeaning for the emperor to have anything to do with the bone of a barbarian.

Another famous relic of the Buddha in China was a tooth that was originally brought to Nanking in the fifth century and then taken to Ch'ang-an. Lost for over eight hundred years, it was rediscovered in 1900 and is presently enshrined in a pagoda outside Peking. In the late 1950s and early 1960s, the Chinese government, eager to improve its relations with Buddhist nations of South and Southeast Asia, allowed it to go on a tour to Burma and then Sri Lanka, where it was worshiped by hundreds of thousands of people.

Not all of the Buddha's relics, however, have been bodily remains. In several places in South and Southeast Asia, great stone footprints, reputed to be his, are still venerated today. In northwest India, he is said to have left his shadow or reflected image on the wall of a cave that was a popular pilgrimage site from the fourth to the eighth century. There, given the right amount of devotion and meditation, pilgrims were thought actually to be able to see the Buddha himself in his shadow. Nearby was a rock on which one could discern the pattern of the cloth in the Buddha's robe where he had set it out to dry. Also in the same region was the Buddha's begging bowl, which the Chinese pilgrim Fa-hsien saw during his trip to India (399–414). Fa-hsien recounts a legend concerning the bowl's miraculous migration over the centuries throughout the Buddhist world. According to this, at the end of the present age, it is destined to ascend to the Tuṣita Heaven, where it will be a sign for the future Buddha Maitreya that the time for him to come down to earth is at hand.

Conclusion. In both the Christian and Buddhist traditions, as well as to a lesser extent in Islam and ancient Greece, the examples of relics we have considered present a great variety of aspects and have been caught up in a whole gamut of symbolisms. In relics, believers have found the ongoing presence and power of Jesus, of the Buddha, of the saints of different traditions. Everywhere relics have performed miracles of various kinds; they have been used to ward off evil, to effectuate cures, and to ensure the prosperity of individuals, cities, and even nations; they have legitimized the rule of kings and emperors; they have helped spread and popularize religion; they have been bought, stolen, traded, and fought over, and have held social, economic, and political importance.

But for all these many functions, it must be noted that relics remain marked with a certain ambiguity. They are often objects that are normally considered to be impure—dead flesh, bones, and body parts—and yet they are venerated as holy. In this very paradox, however, we can see some of the ways in which relics work to heighten the holiness and purity of the saints; if even their impurities are venerated, how much purer and more venerable they must be themselves!

Somewhat the same reasoning can be applied to a second and more basic ambiguity found in relics. They are clearly symbols of death and impermanence; they are what is left after the saints and founders of the tradition are no more. Yet, as we have seen repeatedly, they also make manifest the continuing presence and life of these absent beings. In asserting that the saints are "alive in death," or, in the case of Buddhism, that they are paradoxically present despite their final *nirvāṇa,* relics in both traditions manage to bridge a gap that is one of the great divides of human existence.

[*See also* Bones. *For discussions of religious architecture connected with the veneration of relics, see* Architecture; Tombs; *and* Stupa Worship.]

BIBLIOGRAPHY

Surprisingly little has been written of a general comparative nature on relics. Mention should be made, however, of the two articles by J. A. MacCulloch and Vincent A. Smith: "Relics (Primitive and Western)" and "Relics (Eastern)," in the *Encyclopaedia of Religion and Ethics,* edited by James Hastings, vol. 10 (Edinburgh, 1918). They are still useful, although dated.

For the study of relics in Christianity, a number of more specialized works are helpful. Peter Brown's *The Cult of the Saints: Its Rise and Function in Latin Christianity* (Chicago, 1981) is a good place to begin, while André Grabar's *Martyrium: Re-*

cherches sur le culte des reliques et l'art chrétien antique (Paris, 1946) remains a standard and readable classic. On the True Cross, see Anatole Frolow's *La relique de la Vraie Croix: Recherches sur le développement d'un culte* (Paris, 1961) and, from an art historical perspective, the Pierpont Morgan Library's *The Stavelot Triptych, Mosan Art and the Legend of the True Cross* (Oxford, 1980) by William Voelke. For a still useful introduction to the place of relics in medieval Christianity, see chapters 6–8 of George G. Coulton's *Five Centuries of Religion*, vol. 3 (Cambridge, 1936). For a fascinating listing of various relics through the ages (but one marked by a highly prejudiced commentary), see J. A. S. Collin de Plancy's *Dictionnaire critique des reliques et des images miraculeuses*, 3 vols. (Paris, 1821–1822). This also contains, in an appendix, a reprint of John Calvin's treatise on relics. For a fine study of the medieval traffic in relics in western Europe, see Patrick J. Geary's *Furta Sacra: Thefts of Relics in the Central Middle Ages* (Princeton, 1978). Finally, among the many recent works to appear on the Shroud of Turin, mention might be made of Ian Wilson's *The Shroud of Turin: The Burial Cloth of Jesus Christ?* (Garden City, N.Y., 1978).

For the study of relics in Buddhism, several specialized sources are also available. A useful discussion of various sources concerning the division of the Buddha's relics after his death can be found in chapter 11 of Edward Joseph Thomas's *The Life of Buddha as Legend and History* (London, 1927). For a study of Aśoka's enshrining of the relics in eighty-four thousand stupas, see John S. Strong's *The Legend of King Aśoka* (Princeton, 1983), pp. 107–119. A detailed description of the rituals associated with the Buddha's tooth in Sri Lanka can be found in H. L. Seneviratne's *Rituals of the Kandyan State* (Cambridge, 1978). This work surpasses all earlier ones on this topic. A helpful introduction to the temple of the Buddha's relic in Lamphun, Thailand, is Donald K. Swearer's *Wat Haripuñjaya* (Missoula, Mont., 1976). For Buddhist relics in China, see Kenneth Ch'en's *Buddhism in China: A Historical Survey* (Princeton, 1964).

Finally, two useful works for the study of relics in Islam deserve mention: Ignácz Goldziher's "On the Veneration of the Dead in Paganism and Islam," in volume 1 of *Muslim Studies* (Chicago, 1966), and, on the cult of the saints in Egypt, Jane I. Smith and Yvonne Haddad's *The Islamic Understanding of Death and Resurrection* (Albany, N.Y., 1981), appendix C.

JOHN S. STRONG

RELIGION. The very attempt to define *religion*, to find some distinctive or possibly unique essence or set of qualities that distinguish the "religious" from the remainder of human life, is primarily a Western concern. The attempt is a natural consequence of the Western speculative, intellectualistic, and scientific disposition. It is also the product of the dominant Western religious mode, what is called the Judeo-Christian climate or, more accurately, the theistic inheritance from Judaism, Christianity, and Islam. The theistic form of belief in this tradition, even when down-graded culturally, is formative of the dichotomous Western view of religion. That is, the basic structure of theism is essentially a distinction between a transcendent deity and all else, between the creator and his creation, between God and man.

Even Western thinkers who recognize their cultural bias find it hard to escape, because the assumptions of theism permeate the linguistic structures that shape their thought. For example, the term *holy* comes from linguistic roots signifying wholeness, perfection, well-being; the unholy, then, is the fragmentary, the imperfect, the ailing. Sacredness is the quality of being set apart from the usual or ordinary; its antonym, *profane*, literally means "outside the *fane*" (ME, "sacred place"). Thus every sanctuary—synagogue, church, mosque—is a concrete physical embodiment of this separation of the religious from all else. So too, in a more general sense the sacred is what is specifically set apart for holy or religious use; the secular is what is left over, the world outside, the current age and its fashions and concerns. This thoroughgoing separation has been institutionalized in a multitude of forms: sacred rites including sacraments; sacred books and worship paraphernalia; holy days; sacred precincts and buildings; special modes of life and dress; religious fellowships and orders; and so on *ad infinitum*.

Many practical and conceptual difficulties arise when one attempts to apply such a dichotomous pattern across the board to all cultures. In primitive societies, for instance, what the West calls religious is such an integral part of the total ongoing way of life that it is never experienced or thought of as something separable or narrowly distinguishable from the rest of the pattern. Or if the dichotomy is applied to that multifaceted entity called Hinduism, it seems that almost everything can be and is given a religious significance by some sect. Indeed, in a real sense everything that is is divine; existence *per se* appears to be sacred. It is only that the ultimately real manifests itself in a multitude of ways—in the set-apart and the ordinary, in god and so-called devil, in saint and sinner. The real is apprehended at many levels in accordance with the individual's capacity.

The same difficulty arises in another form when considering Taoist, Confucian, and Shintō cultures. These cultures are characterized by what J. J. M. de Groot termed "universism": a holiness, goodness, and perfection of the natural order that has been misunderstood, distorted, and falsified by shallow minds and errant cultural customs. The religious life here is one of harmony with both the natural and human orders, a submersion of individuality in an organic relationship and in an inwardly experienced oneness with them. And Buddhism in all its forms denies the existence of a transcendent creator-deity in favor of an indefinable, nonpersonal, absolute source or dimension that can be experienced as the depth of human inwardness. This, of course, is not to forget the multitudinous godlings, *bodhisattvas*, and spirits who are given ritual reverence in popular adaptations of the high religion to human need.

There is one other important result of the Western concept and practice of religion, here alluded to in passing: the religious community, distinct and more or less set apart from the environing society. This is not absolutely unique to Western religiosity, for in almost every culture there are those individuals believed to have unusual capacities and powers—the soothsayers, shamans, witch doctors, medicine men, and other specialists who are set apart from all others by their powers and who use them in a professional manner. Likewise in most cultures there are those temporary and voluntary groups of initiates into secret or occult fellowships who take upon themselves prescribed special obligations, diets, psychosomatic disciplines, and the like.

But none of these achieves the form or distinctive qualities of the congregations of synagogue, church, or mosque. There is more and other here than the geographical togetherness of worshipers at a Hindu or Buddhist temple or the cultic togetherness of a tribal society. In one sense, a Western-style congregation is a "gathered people," a group of persons who have been divinely called to and have consciously chosen to follow this particular faith rather than other possible faiths or nonfaith. (That geographical, historical, and social factors greatly modify the actuality of the factor of choice is to be understood, but being chosen and choosing remain the ideal model.) Such groups have their chosen leaders, carry on joint worship periodically as well as other corporate activities, and evangelize for their faith among others. Thus, being a member of a body of believers—a term that betrays the Western theistic emphasis upon doctrine—separates individuals to some extent from others in the environing society. And the professional teachers and ritualists—rabbis, ministers, priests, and to some extent mullahs and imams—are by their dress and mode of life even more separated from "the world" than the devout laity are.

Again, this special type of grouping, though produced in part by many other factors as well, is a distinctive product of the Western theistic dichotomous conception of religion as a set of beliefs and practices that are different from surrounding beliefs and practices and that embody a special relation to deity, that transcendent other. The very term *religion* originally indicated a bond of scruple uniting those who shared it closely to each other. Hence *religion* suggests both separation and a separative fellowship. How, then, is religion to be conceptually handled for the purposes of thought and discussion, since the very term itself is so deeply ingrained with specifically Western cultural presuppositions?

Definitions. So many definitions of religion have been framed in the West over the years that even a partial listing would be impractical. With varying success they have all struggled to avoid, on the one hand, the Scylla of hard, sharp, particularistic definition and, on the other hand, the Charybdis of meaningless generalities. Predictably, Western-derived definitions have tended to emphasize the sharp distinction between the religious and nonreligious dimensions of culture and sometimes have equated religion with beliefs, particularly belief in a supreme being. Obviously such definitions exclude many primitive and Asian religions, if we still wish to use the term.

Such definitional usage has had its critics in the West. As early as the late eighteenth century an attempt was made to shift the emphasis from the conceptual to the intuitive and visceral in defining religion. In a very influential statement, Friedrich Schleiermacher defined religion as "feeling of absolute dependence"—absolute as contrasted to other, relative feelings of dependence. Since that time there have been others who have sought to escape formalistic, doctrinal definitions and to include the experiential, emotive, and intuitive factors, as well as valuational and ethical factors. These factors seemed to be truer to the religious person's sense of what religion is like from the inside, to include what William James called "the enthusiastic temper of espousal." Such definitions appear to be more universally applicable to primitive and Asian religions than belief-oriented ones.

This is surely the case with primitive religion where, as noted, the religious is scarcely distinguishable from the sociocultural, where custom and ritual are abundant while belief structures are scarce, where emotional realities carry more weight than statable ideas. The Asian religious traditions, too, characteristically place their prime emphasis upon the inner states of realization rather than upon the merely instrumental rite or doctrine. Indeed, this is so much the case that in some of the more radical expressions, such as Zen Buddhism and Hindu *bhakti* (devotional faith), creed and tradition are purely secondary or even valueless hindrances. Of course, it should be added that this is not quite the case in actuality. For feeling-based experience never subsists on its own exclusive resources: feeling (and love as in *bhakti*) is always feeling *about* or *toward* some object or other. Experience never happens in a complete ideational vacuum. In all these cases, be they primitive,

Buddhist, or Hindu, there is an underlying conceptual context of some sort, and its implicitness or verbal denial does not indicate its total functional absence.

With the rise of the sociological and anthropological disciplines, another factor has been projected into definition making—the social, economic, historical, and cultural contexts in which religion comes to expression. Sociologists and anthropologists rightly argue that religion is never an abstract set of ideas, values, or experiences developed apart from the total cultural matrix and that many religious beliefs, customs, and rituals can only be understood in reference to this matrix. Indeed, some proponents of these disciplines imply or suggest that analysis of religious structures will totally account for religion. Émile Durkheim, a pioneer in this societal interpretation, asserted in *The Elementary Forms of the Religious Life* (New York, 1926) that "a society has all that is necessary to arouse the sensation of the divine in minds, merely by the power that it has over them" (p. 207). Thus the gods are nothing more than society in disguise. Since Durkheim's time, sociologists have refined their methods of analysis, but some still maintain the essential Durkheimian view.

The various forms of psychology come out of the same scientific-humanistic context as the social science disciplines. The central concerns of psychology are the psychic mechanics and motivational forces that result from human self-consciousness. In some sense, psychological interpretations of religion are more akin to those that stress experiential inwardness than to those that accent intellectual and societal aspects. In the final analysis, however, psychology is more akin to the social sciences in its treatment of religion than to any intrareligious effort at interpretation. It tends, like social studies, to dissolve religion into sets of psychological factors.

It should be observed in passing that the religious person would not be satisfied with such analyses. That person's sense of what is happening in religion seems always to contain some extrasocietal, extrapsychological depth-factor or transcendent dimension, which must be further examined.

Among Western religion scholars there have been attempts to define religion in a manner that avoids the "reductionism" of the various sociological and psychological disciplines that reduce religion to its component factors. A prominent one has been the analysis of religions of varied nature in terms of the presence of an awareness of the sacred or the holy. First proposed by Schleiermacher, this approach found its most notable expression in Rudolf Otto's *The Idea of the Holy* (1917). Analyzing the biblical accounts of the experience of the prophets and saints in their encounters with God, Otto defines the essence of religious awareness as awe, a unique blend of fear and fascination before the divine. Thus Isaiah, upon becoming aware of the presence of the living God (Yahveh) in the temple sanctuary, cried out, "Woe is me, for I am undone!" Isaiah's response expresses both creaturely fear of his creator and his own sense of sinfulness before God's absolute righteousness. Yet he does not flee but remains to worship and to become the bearer of a prophetic message to his people. In Otto's terms, Isaiah and others like him sensed the *mysterium tremendum*, the "wholly otherness" of the divine being. And for Otto this was the prototype of all truly religious experience.

Otto's conception of the essential nature of religious experiences may be acceptable in the context of Western theism, though this type of religious experience seems relatively rare or else is smothered by the religious apparatus that envelops it. But even in Otto's own writings the application of this concept to primitive and Asian religions seems difficult. In primitive religions any sense of the divine in the mode of Isaiah seems missing despite the early attempt of Andrew Lang to find a "high god" tradition in primitive antiquity. Here religion is scarcely distinguishable from magic; rites seem primarily used for the fulfillment of physicial needs; and fear rather than awe predominates. *Sacred* and *profane* are inappropriate terms to apply to this cultural continuum. Of course, it must be said that the powers that are feared, placated, and used, in turn, do have their invisible and esoteric dimensions with which some rites attempt to make contact.

Nor does this definition of religion as the experience of the awe-inspiring wholly other seem to fit Asian religions. To be sure, at the popular level much religion consists of placation and use of spirits and superhuman powers and various rituals reminiscent of theism. But in their own self-definitions Buddhism and Hinduism, for example, seem to have little or no sense of a radically other and ultimate being. In fact, the basic thought and action model here is that of man's oneness with his environing universe. He seeks to live religiously in organic harmony with the ultimate, and the highest level of religious experience tends toward a mystical monism, though with Eastern qualifications. Immanence of the sacred rather than its transcendence is emphasized. Thus Hinduism, Buddhism, and Taoism characteristically find the truly transcendent within the human self itself. The divinized, exteriorized forms given to the holy in theistic religions—and in the popular forms of their own faiths—are viewed as temporary and practically expedient but essentially false means for the final enlightenment of the ignorant.

The most recent and influential formulation of sacredness as the unique and irreducible essence of all religious experience has been that of Mircea Eliade. He has refined and expanded Otto's use of the term extensively. No longer is the sacred to be sought almost exclusively in the God-encounter type of experience; it is abundantly exemplified in the symbolisms and rituals of almost every culture, especially the primitive and Asian cultures. It is embodied as sacred space, for example, in shrines and temples, in taboo areas, even limitedly in the erection of dwellings in accordance with a sense of the *axis mundi*, an orientation to the center of the true (sacred) universe. Indeed, structures often symbolically represent that physically invisible but most real of all universes—the eternally perfect universe to which they seek to relate fruitfully. This sense of sacredness often attaches to trees, stones, mountains, and other like objects in which mysterious power seems to be resident. Many primitive rituals seek to sacramentally re-peat the first moment of creation often described in myth when primordial chaos became recognizable order. Sacred time—that is, eternal and unfragmented time—is made vitally present by the reenactment of such myths. In *The Sacred and the Profane* (New York, 1951) Eliade writes, "Every religious festival, every liturgical time, represents the reactualization of a sacred event that took place in a mythical past, in the beginning" (pp. 68–69).

It is a matter of opinion whether Eliade's portraiture of the experience of the sacred, much more elaborate and extended than here stated, escapes the limitations of Otto's view and represents a viable way of defining and describing the religious mode. Sociologists and anthropologists question its verifiability in actual cases as well as Eliade's interpretation of his data. To them sacredness is an ideal construct, not a genuine cultural or experiential entity. Linguists, psychologists, and philosophers also question the identifiability of such a distinctive entity in patterns of language, experience, and thought patterns. For all of these critics the religious experience is a compound of cultural entities and experiences, not a separable thing in and of itself.

Is there no alternative to such reductions of religious experiences and structures into congeries of easily identifiable and nonmysterious psychological, social, political, and economic factors? Conversely, is there no alternative to the definition of the religious as a mystical essence that can be located in every culture by the proper methodology, like the detection of uranium by a geiger counter? The truth in the former views is that a religious awareness, wherever found, occurs in the context of and is given tangible form by cultural, economic, and social factors. Traditionally, these factors condition members of a society to perceive and experience the world in ways given as religious.

On the other hand, it is also true that there is something of a sacred otherness about religious experiences that cannot be easily dissolved or given no weight. Even though an unanalyzable, unqualifiable factor called "the holy" or "the sacred" cannot be isolated from its varied components and contexts, almost every known culture displays elements that, if not wholly other from their context, do show a certain discontinuity with it. When these discontinuous elements are spoken about or related to, there occurs at least a slight shift to another perspective, another realm of discourse, which concerns the more mysterious and indefinable areas of experience and expectation. Or these elements might be discussed in terms of a depth dimension in cultural experiences and customs that hints at the more central, serious, or ultimate concerns and values. Perhaps religions could be seen, then, as the attempt to order individual and societal life in terms of culturally perceived ultimate priorities.

It should be noted, of course, that the form, clarity, and degree of such an ordering of life vary immensely from culture to culture. Thus primitive man adds enhancing rituals and magic incantations to his tool-making and hunting skills, without clearly conceptualizing why he does so. He does not confuse the two means to his end, never substituting religio-magic for good weaponry, or chants for physical skill. Rather, he adds the magic and ritual elements to the humanly possible means in order to ensure their success; the magic and ritual elements are efforts to deal with the powerful and mysterious dimensions of existence that cannot be controlled or affected by ordinary means. This quality of other-than-ordinary also resides in the ritual paraphernalia, in the ritual specialists, and often in the secret content of the rites themselves and certain special localities. Thus even in primitive society there is a vaguely felt and inarticulate awareness of transcendence as strange, more, and different.

In Asian traditions that emphasize immanence rather than transcendence, characterized by continuums rather than discontinuities both of theory and of experience, gradations of both understanding and of experience exist nonetheless. Recognized levels of practice and attainment are buttressed by texts and incorporated into systems of praxis. "Lower" levels of attainment are not considered totally false or wrong but as less than fully true or ultimate. There is, then, a kind of transcendence by degree or stage; the highest is "other" to the lower states, and in some Buddhist and Hindu traditions (i.e., Zen and meditative Advaita) there is a breakthrough experience (*satori* and realization of *brahman*) that experientially is wholly other than or wholly transformative of ordinary awareness.

In summary, it may be said that almost every known culture involves the religious in the above sense of a depth dimension in cultural experiences at all levels—a push, whether ill-defined or conscious, toward some sort of ultimacy and transcendence that will provide norms and power for the rest of life. When more or less distinct patterns of behavior are built around this depth dimension in a culture, this structure constitutes religion in its historically recognizable form. Religion is the organization of life around the depth dimensions of experience—varied in form, completeness, and clarity in accordance with the environing culture.

Distinguishing Characteristics of Religious Experience. If religiousness is a depth-awareness coming to distinctive expression in the forms we call religion, how is religiousness distinguished from various other types of awareness such as the aesthetic and ecstatic—what Abraham Maslow (1964) calls "peak experiences" and Marghanita Laski (1961) terms "non-religious ecstasy"—and the states of "altered consciousness" produced by various psychosomatic techniques or drugs?

Indeed, there are those who would equate all such states with the so-called religious variety. For example, Maslow urges that all peak, that is, highly emotional and ecstatic, experiences should be recognized as equally valid and valuable, whatever the conditions of their occurrence or production. He criticizes religions for preempting the quality of genuineness as proof of the truth of their respective doctrines. Laski likewise fully equates the structured religious experiences of mystics with the "natural" experiences of ecstasy, transcendence, and aesthetic intensity that occur in the presence of some natural wonder, in sexual experience, in childbirth, or by other means. In the case of mystical experiences, she argues, religious "overbeliefs" have gratuitously attached to them and are erroneously considered to be causal.

There have also been many experiments, with and without drugs, in the achievement of a nonindividualized or transpersonalized consciousness. In these experiments the subject is lifted out of the usual narrow, self-oriented awareness into an awareness of the overpowering beauty of ordinary objects, colors, and sounds and of unity with the boundless infinitude of space, time, and being. Some subjects have reported the fusing of all the senses so that color has sound as well as the converse. Others report a sense of oneness with all other beings. Aldous Huxley equated these experiences with those of Christian, Muslim, Taoist, and Hindu mystics. Some practitioners have deliberately fused the use of psychosomatic techniques and drugs with religious practice—Zen, Hindu, American Indian.

However, the true significance of these experiences, misinterpreted in such views, is not found in the likeness of psychosomatic character in all such experiences, whether religious or not. That they can occur in nearly identical forms in a variety of contexts and with varied stimuli (or are they really identical?) indicates at most the similar psychosomatic nature of all human beings. The truly significant element is precisely that ideational and emotional context discarded by Maslow, Laski, and others as dispensable "overbeliefs." Such experiences in and by themselves are anonymous, miscellaneous, and trifling emotional flashes, unless they are connected with some system of ideation that interprets them in terms of meaningful concepts or other like experiences. In short, the ideational system gives the experiences an identity. And by thus having a traditional religious identity, these experiences also have power to affect the whole life—a power denied them as anonymous feeling. Thus the mystical ecstasies of Teresa of Ávila remolded her spirituality and propelled her into a life of strenuous activity in the cause of Roman Catholic Christianity. The same could be said of a Zen *satori* experience, even though it is not expressed in doctrinaire terms. *Satori* dynamically activates the total man because it validates the Zen context of tradition, thought, and values in which it occurs. It is oneness with the absolute Buddha essence; it is an experience of the Buddha mind, of organic harmony with the entire universe, of the felt unity of outer and inner worlds. These experiences are of revolutionary significance to the experiencer because of their contextual religious meaning.

In summary, it may be said that while ecstatic, transic, and intense aesthetic experiences are found both within religious and nonreligious frameworks and have many features in common psychologically, the religious experience is religious precisely because it occurs in a religious context of thought, discipline, and value.

Characteristics and Structures of Religious Life. As previously suggested, religions adopt their tangible historical forms as matrices of cultural and social elements about the depth-centers of culture. Hence the beliefs, patterns of observance, organizational structures, and types of religious experience are as varied as the matrices that give them birth, and that they in turn help form and reform. Even in the midst of this variety, however, we may distinguish certain characteristic elements and categories of structures distinctively religious.

Traditionalism. All attempts to find a primitive religion embodying the primordial form of all subsequent religions have encountered two insurmountable problems. The first is the sheer arbitrariness of seeking the origin of all types of religion in a single form. The second is that wherever religion is recognized—if one uses the above definition of religion as a depth-dimensional structure—one also encounters an existent tradition comprising stylized actions related to the pursuit of cultural goals, however meager or closely geared to survival needs. Present modes of religious activity always seem to look backward for origins, precedents, and standards. As cultures become more complex and literate, these traditions of ancient thought and practice become more elaborate and stylized.

Whatever the degree of elaboration, two things seem to be taken for granted. First, the beginnings—the original creative action, the life and words of an individual founder, even the authorless antiquity of a tradition's scriptures, as in the case of Hinduism—are taken as models of pristine purity and power, fully authoritative for all members of the group or adherents of the faith. Second, no matter how great the actual changes in a particular historical religious tradition—and sometimes this means the entire cultural tradition, more or less—the basic thrust of traditionalism is to maintain itself. Typically, religious reformers speak about a re-forming of the religion in terms of its more holy past. Thus Zen seeks to go back directly to the mind of the Buddha, bypassing all historical forms and scripturalism. Revivalist Islam speaks of returning to pure Qur'anic faith and practice. Protestantism sought a return to New Testament Christianity, eliminating all the Roman Catholic "accretions"; and the Roman Catholic church responded that its doctrine and ritual and authority were demonstrably older than anything in Protestantism, going back to Christ himself.

Myth and symbol. Religious traditions are full of myth and replete with symbol. *Myth* in most contemporary use simply means "false"; myths are the fanciful tales of primitives spun out as explanations of beginnings. Hence creation myths are rationalizations of what prescientific cultures cannot understand through other means. Though this explanatory function of myth has been important, an even more basic function has been that of symbolic source. Apparently, even the writers of myths recognized the impossibility of expressing the fundamentally indescribable nature of absolute beginnings and ultimate realities. Hence poetry and symbol were their metier. In this way, religious myths have become modes of action, mankind's way of relating to physical and environmental realities. Thus does religious man seek to grasp the actionable significance of the world and relate to it emotionally. In passing, it should be noted that all disciplines of thought and life have their mythology of guiding images and unproven assumptions. [*See* Myth.]

Symbol is the language of myth. When the crucially important but mysterious nature of ultimate reality—the basic concern of religious man—can only be seen through a glass darkly, how else can one speak of it except in symbolic forms? Ordinary language will not serve for the fullness of either the question or the answer here. Therefore religious language is rich in analogies, metaphors, poetry, stylized actions (ritual), and even silence ("Be still and know that I am God"). [*See* Silence.] For the symbol stands for something other and more than itself; it is only a finger pointing at the moon of reality. [*See* Symbolism.]

In seeking to deal with man's ultimate concerns, religions are prolific in the production, use, and elaboration of symbolic forms and objects; thus it is not surprising that religions have been the inspiration of an overwhelmingly large and diverse body of art. Indeed, in most cultures of the past, religions have been the central cultural fountainhead. To realize the importance of symbols in religion one need think only of the immense variety of rituals; of the stylized dress, manner, and speech of ritual officiants; of artifacts used in rituals; of paintings and sculptures, of shrines and sanctuaries of all levels and types. [*See* Architecture *and* Iconography.]

Finally, the tremendous tenacity of symbolic forms and their ritualized vehicles must be emphasized. Many a symbol outlives its parent religion and culture, as the lotus, for example, has lived through centuries of symbolic existence, first in Hinduism and then in Buddhism. Symbols are more lasting than their explanatory doctrinal forms because they speak to the human imagination and to human feelings, not merely to the rational sense. Religious symbols often embody what is felt to be the central religious reality involved; they are its sacramental form, which must be preserved at all costs.

Concepts of salvation. Salvation is but another name for religion. That is, all religions are basically conceived as means of saving men at one level or another. And there are always two aspects to salvation: what men are to be saved *from* and what they are to be saved *to.* It goes without saying that what men are saved from and to varies immensely from culture to culture and from religion to religion. [*See* Soteriology.]

At the primitive level of religion, salvation both "from" and "to" is achieved mainly in the realm of physical dangers and goods. The primitive seeks by his rituals to save himself from starvation, from death by storm, from disease, from wild animals, and from enemies and to sufficiency of food and shelter, to freedom from danger and disease, and to human fertility. Implicit in this context, and in the realm of mental and emotional malaise, is salvation from mysterious and even malign powers and forces of evil. The achievement of salvation in all these areas is striven for by all possible physical means with the superadded power of ritual, charm, and magic.

Of course, the development of environing cultures implies a change and expansion in the nature of religious salvation. Group values come to play a larger and more conscious role. The group—whether tribal kinship-clan or nation-state—comes to be a sacred entity in its own right, perhaps the preeminent one in some cases. Roman religion, for example, was essentially a state religion whose major purpose was the preservation (salvation) of the state in prosperity and power; a triumphal conquest was a triumph of the Roman deities. In time the emperors themselves were considered incarnate deities, as were the Egyptian pharaohs of an earlier era. Later, inner values, relatively unimportant to primitive and early nationalistic cultures, became matters of prime religious importance. Inner states of mind, the cultivation of ecstasy, and concern about the personal survival of physical death became important, sometimes almost paramount in times of social and political turmoil.

In time, this area of inner development, experiences, and values became the impetus for religious development. The "great" religious traditions of Judaism, Buddhism, Hinduism, Christianity, and Islam are all oriented toward the inner life. Their doctrines, texts, religious disciplines, and even organizations aim to cultivate the inner life of prayer, faith, enlightenment, and purity of character.

Yet the development of the inner life in religion does not completely exclude the lower level of physical-material goods. They remain as the object of perfectly acceptable religious hopes so that prayers are still made for health, safety, rain in times of drought, and sufficiency of food. And in some instances the final higher goods represent only the absolutizing or infinitizing of the physical-material ones. Thus eternal life maximizes the desire for deliverance from death—that primary human desire for survival toward which so much of primitive religion is directed. Indeed, the Greek religion of ancient times seems almost alone in portraying life after death as an unsatisfactory shadow existence. Most pure lands, heavens, and paradises are described as the perpetual enjoyment of life without pain, sorrow, or unhappiness of any sort. Similarly, the indescribable *nibbāna* of Theravāda Buddhism is conceived as the final, absolute end of the emptiness, impermanence, and pain of all embodied existence.

But even given the continuing presence of the lower-level goods sought by religious means in the higher-level religions, it is still true that the inner goals of peace, self-sacrificing love, purity of heart, and awareness of absolute goodness increasingly become central to the religious quest. When they are sought for themselves with no ulterior motives, the possibility of saintliness comes into being.

It is, of course, obvious that religious salvation is as responsive to and expressive of human needs and desires as any secular scheme of salvation. For salvation in religion is a means of fulfilling needs and desires, even when the needs and desires are revealed from "above." Yet the forms fulfillment takes express specially religious values, supplementing and sometimes opposing other, nonreligious values. And it is also evident that the varied cultural contexts of religions each represent a variant perspective on the human situation—its goods and goals, its dangers and evils. These varied perspectives greatly influence the form of religious salvation. Thus the Hindu Advaitin, the African San, the Sunnī Muslim, the Orthodox Jew, the Zen Buddhist, the Protestant, and the Greek Orthodox Christian would define religious needs and goods quite differently.

Is there then any appreciable difference between the ways in which religious and nonreligious modes of need fulfillment proceed? In other words, are there distinguishing characteristics of religious salvation? The first is that religious salvation tends to concentrate on the needs a culture defines as most fundamental, neglecting needs that a culture defines as less important. Religious means of salvation, often indirect and extrahuman, seek to use supersensible forces and powers either in addition to or in place of ordinary tangible means. The second distinguishing characteristic is that religious salvations tend to aim at total, absolute, and sometimes transcendent fulfillment of human needs. As defined by the cultural context, this fulfillment ranges all the way from the fullness of physical satisfactions to the eternal ecstasy of union with the Absolute.

Sacred places and objects. One of the striking features of historically observable religions is the presence of special religious areas and structures set apart from ordinary space by physical, ritual, and psychological barriers. Precincts, churches, mosques, synagogues, and shrines are the highly visible manifestations of religious discontinuity with the surrounding world. Various physical actions are often required of those who enter sacred areas to indicate this separation: ablutions, removal of footwear, prayers and incantations, bowing and kneeling, silence, preparatory fasting, special garb, and preliminary inward acts of contrition.

Further, particularly within the more spacious precincts, there are grades of sacredness that enshrine specially sacred objects or relics in their supremely holy areas. A classic example is the last of the Jewish temples in Jerusalem, in which there was a spatial progression from the outermost court of the gentiles to the women's court to the men's court to the court of the burnt offering to the priests' enclosure to the Holy of Holies wherein was the Ark of the Covenant and, in some sense, the special presence of Yahveh. In synagogues today the ark containing a copy of the Torah is the most sacred part. In Roman Catholic and Eastern Orthodox churches, the altar supporting the sacramental bread and wine is the focal point of sacredness. Protestant churches display a weaker form of the same principle, centered around the Bible or pulpit. Buddhist shrines in Southeast Asia commonly are pagodas containing sacred relics and/or consecrated Buddha images, which are honored by removing footwear, circumambulating with the central spire to one's right, and presenting floral offerings and obeisances. Japanese Buddhist temples usually contain large Buddha images at the rear of ornately decorated altars. Hindu temples vary somewhat in this respect; some have a holy inner sanctum into which only the ritually pure devotee may enter, while others provide relatively open access to the revered god images. Perhaps the Islamic mosque is the least set apart of religious places. Yet even here ablutions are required before entry, nonbelievers are scarcely welcome, and the semicircular alcove set in the rear wall *(qiblah)* must project toward the Muslim holy of holies, the Kaʿbah in Mecca, so that praying believers always face in that direction.

Quite logically, many of the furnishings and objects used in temples and shrines, particularly in their most sacred rituals, partake of the sacredness of the shrine itself. One thinks here of altar furnishings and utensils, sacrificial paraphernalia, baptismal water, the special garb of temple officiants, special words and gestures, incense, candles and the like. These furnishings and objects are less holy than the shrine and revered relic, which are intrinsically sacred.

But in the final analysis sacred places are sacred because of what has occurred there or may occur there. Their essence is sacramental. Sacred places are cherished and revered because they offer the possibility of directly encountering and partaking of the real in the given tradition. An unusual power has manifested itself in a natural object or taboo place either for good or ill. Or tradition tells that some primordially creative act once took place here and that power still lingers. So in both more and less developed religious traditions, past sanctity and present hope characterize sacred places, The shrine of the Virgin of Guadalupe appears to have been first a center of pagan deity worship before its adoption by the Christian faith; its religious power is centuries old, transfixing past and present devotees. This same quality is found at the Dome of the Rock in Jerusalem, from which Muḥammad reputedly made his ascent into heaven; at the places of the Buddha's birth, enlightenment, first sermon, and death in India; and at the legendary birth and death places of Jesus in Palestine.

Other sacred places and objects (images) particularly emphasize the hope of present and future blessing. The shrine at Lourdes is venerated not simply because a French peasant girl reputedly once saw a vision of the Virgin there but because of the hope of present healing. Similarly, many Buddhists expect to gain merit by praying and making offerings before Buddha images or to reap tangible benefits in the here and now by touching *bodhisattva* images. The Shintō practitioner rings the bell to summon his chosen deity and petition him or her for a specific boon. A Roman Catholic church is made sacred because of its consecrated altar at which the life-giving miracle of bread and wine transformed into the spiritual body of Christ occurs at every mass. The Protestant pulpit is the space where the word of the living God is expounded; at the very least the devout parishioner hopes for some sense of empowerment and renewal for daily living. Every functioning shrine embodies such living and sacred hopes. [*See* Sacred Space.]

Sacred actions (rituals). Just as it is impossible to think of living religions without their sacred places, so is it impossible to conceive of a religion without its rituals, whether simple or elaborate. The forms of ritual are familiar, involving the stylized saying or chanting of certain words, bowing or kneeling, offerings of various kinds including animal sacrifices, dancing and music making.

Several features are prominent in most rituals. One is the element of order. Indeed, an established ritual pattern is the ordered performance of sacred actions under the direction of a leader. This order usually develops early in the history of a given tradition. Initially the sacred actions are more or less informal and spontaneous, then, step by step, become ordered and standardized procedures, and in the end may become elaborate ritual patterns requiring a considerable quantity of equipment and personnel (ritualists, priests). In Christianity we see the beginnings of this in Paul's exhortation to the church in Corinth to conduct their worship "decently and in order" (*1 Cor.* 14:40). He had heard reports of chaotic gatherings at which all participants were under the "inspiration of the Spirit." From this order developed the classical Christian liturgies. However, perhaps the maximal degree of ritualization was achieved in another tradition, for the Brahmanic Hindu sacrificial rituals involve an almost unbelievable complexity and rigidity of pattern.

Rigidity of pattern, requiring the utmost care and precision in use of word, action, and material, points to another feature of ritual, maximized in the Hindu sacrifice but more or less present in all fixed rituals: meticulous performance. Analogies may be drawn to magic formulas and scientific experiments, and the resemblance is indeed meaningful. Just as in magic and science, where success depends upon meticulously faithful following of the given formula, so too in religious ritual the desired healing, fertility, safety, prosperity, or inward state will not result if the ritual is improperly performed. Ritual words are words of power. The Hindu sacrificial ritual mentioned above involved priests specifically appointed to cover any lapses (wrong words or incorrect actions) by ritually speaking charms. Of course, cases such as this and some primitive rituals are the extreme manifestation of this quality. In other ritual patterns aesthetic concerns and inner-personal aspirations are important; ritual uniformity also has the practical advantage of giving the worshiper or user a sense of familiarity and ease as well as identity with a given tradition and group. [*See* Orthopraxy.]

Yet deep within ritualism there is inherent the concern for accuracy and faithfulness. This is the essentially sacramental nature of ritual that arises from its nature as an ordered symbol system. Thus both symbol and ritual are perceived as intrinsic embodiments of the sacred essence, the supersensible and indescribable ultimacy of a religion. Thus ritual and symbol bring the real presence of the religious depth-dimension into the lives of its experients and in so doing become incredibly precious. This seems to apply across the religious spectrum to magic prayer rituals of the primitive, the Voodoo dance, sacrificial rituals, repetition of the Pure Land Nembutsu, Tibetan mantric *maṇḍala* rituals, and the Roman Catholic Eucharist. The preciousness of myth and symbol explains why religious groups tend to cherish and preserve their rituals more jealously and zealously than any of their doctrinal statements and why ritual patterns often survive longer than their parent traditions.

One final observation is required: ritualism in religion often produces an antiritualistic expression. Many examples could be given. Zen Buddhism was in one sense antiritualistic, as were Hōnen's and Shinran's Pure Land Buddhism. These latter substituted the easy, simple repetition of the name Amida for elaborate and often esoteric rituals. Devotional Hinduism, in which one is saved by love *(bhakti)* wholeheartedly given to a deity, protested against excessive Brahmanic ritualism. And Protestantism, in particular its radical forms, sought freedom from Roman Catholic ritualism. In all cases the motifs were simplicity and ease of access to the sacred. [*See* Ritual.]

Sacred writings. In literate societies writings are often of considerable religious importance. (Christianity calls sacred writings scriptures.) Typically sacred writings comprise the reported words of the holy men of the past—prophets, saints, founders of faiths such as Zarathushtra, Moses, the Buddha, Muḥammad, Christ, or Nanak. As such they are of prime importance as statements of the truth and expositions of the right way for believers to live. (Of course, nonliterate societies have their oral traditions that serve the same purpose.) The Hindu Vedas are considered to be without human author or known human channel of transmission.

When scriptures exist, interpreters must also exist. Successive interpretations vary greatly, for interpreters are caught between their desires to be faithful to the original sacred word and to make its exposition relevant and meaningful to their own age. A multitude of sectarian divisions based on variant scriptural interpretation is found in all the major religious traditions. Perhaps the number of writings in the Buddhist and Hindu traditions give interpreters an advantage in this regard, but Christian and Islamic sectarians have been nearly as successful with a smaller scriptural base.

Confucianism, Taoism, and Shintō can scarcely be said to have scriptures in the above sense of a corpus of inspired utterances. Their revered writings—the sayings of Confucius and Meng-tzu, of Lao-tzu and Chuang-tzu, and the *Records of Ancient Matters*—are studied more as the wise counsels of sages than as inerrant statements of truth. (In the latter the apothegms are considered precedent setting.) In general, Buddhist and Hindu scriptures can be interpreted much more flexibly than Western ones because of their greater variety and their emphasis on truth as dependent on the level of the hearer's understanding. [*See* Scripture *and* Truth.]

The sacred community. Every religion has some communal sense and structure. Ritual is essentially a group exercise, except for magico-religious rituals geared to personal desires. Hence ritual nearly always involves professional ritualists and a group bound together by its experience. But the communal bonds vary greatly in nature and extent. [*See* Community.]

Some ritual groupings are quite temporary: one thinks of the occasional, selective, and experience-based spirit groups found among some Native Americans. In other primitive cultures, the religious-ritual grouping is hardly separable from the general clan or tribal social structure and indeed might better be called a social subculture with religious elements centered on certain particular occasions and activities. In many Buddhist and Hindu contexts the religious community is little more than those in the vicinity who attend various religious ceremonies in the local temple and often come on purely personal quests. In such situations the only sacred community seems to be the priests and ritualists at a religious shrine, persons qualified for such functions by character and training.

To be sure, in most of these societies there are special groupings of a secret or semisecret nature open only to initiates. Such are the Native American spirit groups. Late Greek religion developed its "mystery" rites that sought goals and experiences beyond those offered by the ordinary temple and priesthood. Hinduism abounds in such special-interest, special-ritual groups bound together by a particular god, common pilgrimage points, and distinctive rituals; sometimes members live in separate communities built around a leader.

Buddhism and Christianity institutionalized such special-interest groups in their monastic orders. Men and women for a variety of reasons retire from the world to seek a more intensely religious way of life than that possible in ordinary secular pursuits or even as priests having everyday dealings with the laity and major liturgical duties. Some Ṣūfī communities in medieval Islam approximated the monastic life of a community apart from the wider community of believers.

Perhaps it is only in Islam and Christianity, and somewhat limitedly in Judaism, that the concept of a holy fellowship of believers, called a church in Christianity, has been created to express religious faith and practice. The prevailing ethnic qualification in Judaism prevents its description as a purely faith-gathered group. Islam represents a near equivalent to the Christian church, especially as Islamic groups have spread out into other areas than those totally Muslim in nature. Muslims, like Christians, consider themselves members of one sacred group, called out from among others by the faith and practice of their religion, ideally a unity stronger than any other bond. In the early days of Christianity, the apostle Paul could speak glowingly of the Christian community as a universal one in which there was neither Jew nor Greek, neither slave nor freeman, for all were equal in a new Christ-like humanity. Of course, in actuality both Christians and Muslims have divided along lines of race and nation. Both faiths, however, continue to cherish the ideal of the universal fellowship of faith.

It may be observed in passing that such a definition of community comes more naturally and more easily to Islam and Christianity than to most Asian religions. To a large extent this is because of the strong emphasis on doctrinal belief in Islam and Christianity: believers and nonbelievers can be clearly distinguished because religion is seen as a deliberate choice by the individual. In Asian religions, inclusive and naturalistic values predominate: experience rather than doctrine receives emphasis, rendering exclusivist religious formulations almost unknown. It may also be that the underlying Asian patterns of social organization have emphasized the group to such an extent that individual religious decision is nearly impossible.

The sacred experience. The question of whether all depth experiences, experiences of transcendence, or unusual mind-body states should be considered on a par with religious experiences, or are intrinsically religious themselves, has already been discussed. Here are considered only those experiences that occur within a declared religious context and are therefore doubly set apart, both as designatedly religious and as of special clarity and intensity even within that context.

These special experiences represent a continuum from the comparatively mild and frequent experiences to those commonly termed mystical. At the less intense end of the continuum are those instances of a sense of awe in the sacred precincts, a sense of humility before a felt presence, an unusual degree of joy or peace suddenly coming upon one, or the deep conviction of a prayer answered. Then there are those of a much more intense nature such as physical sensations of fire, electric shock, or a strong and sudden conviction of the forgiveness of one's sins such as John Wesley's "warming of the heart" at Aldersgate. Indeed, in some Christian groups special conversion or purification-of-heart experiences are made a matter of explicit emphasis and a condition of church membership. In Pentecostal groups a sudden and unexpected experience of speaking in unknown tongues is considered a sign of the "baptism of the Spirit." There are classical instances of the same phenomenon: Muḥammad hearing the voice of the angel Gabriel commanding him to recite (resulting in the Qur'ān) and Isaiah seeing the Lord high and lifted up with his train filling the temple (resulting in Isaiah's call to prophesy).

At the further end of this experiential continuum are the mystical experiences found in Judaism, Islam, Christianity, Taoism, Hinduism, and Buddhism. Those who have had such experiences (especially in Christian, Hindu, and Muslim contexts) insist that they differ in kind from all other religious experiences, including the less intense ones just discussed. Their distinctive qualities seem to be these: (1) their suddenness and spontaneity (without warning or overt preparation), (2) their irresistibility, (3) their absolute quality of conviction and realistic authority, (4) their quality of clear knowledge, not strong emotion, which is asserted even when the mystically received knowledge is conceptually indescribable. Perhaps the true and basic content of such moments is an assurance of the absolute reality of God, Kṛṣṇa, Brahmā, Dharma, or Buddha nature, that is, the ultimate reality as envisioned by the given faith. Also rather uniformly experienced is the overpowering conviction of knowing directly, climaxing in a felt encounter with the ultimate one or with the basic oneness of the universe.

In any case, these special experiences of prophets, saints, and enlightened persons have played an important role in many religious traditions. Though beyond the reach of ordinary religiosity, they have given a kind of reflected authenticity to faith at all levels, have encouraged the creation of various spiritual methodologies of devotion and meditation, and have vitalized traditions in difficult times. Mystical experiences have kept alive a sense of the reality and availability of religious power and have constantly renewed the whole corpus of ritual, doctrine, and organization. [*See* Mysticism.]

Religion and Modernity. The question whether religion, at least in its traditional forms, will survive the ongoing cultural changes of modern times is often discussed. Certainly many traditional and current formulations, and perhaps entire traditions, will radically change or even disappear. Yet it also seems that as soon as one form of religion disappears, another rises to take its place. Without asserting a religious instinct in mankind, it may perhaps be said that man is incurably religious in one way or another and that the human situation and human nature make it inevitably so. The immense mysteries and uncertainties of the world and man's own inquiring and evaluating self-consciousness make inevitable a reaching out for some sort of ultimate values and realities—which is but another name for the religious quest.

[*See also* Religious Experience; Study of Religion; Philosophy; *and biographies of the principal scholars mentioned herein.*]

BIBLIOGRAPHY

Beane, Wendell C., and William G. Doty, eds. *Myths, Rites, Symbols: A Mircea Eliade Reader.* 2 vols. New York, 1975. A well-chosen, substantial anthology of Eliade's writings on various aspects of religion.

Campbell, Joseph. *Masks of God,* vol. 1, *Primitive Mythology;* vol. 2, *Oriental Mythology;* vol. 3, *Occidental Mythology.* New York, 1959–1965. These three volumes present a richly varied portrait, penetrating analysis, and many concrete illustrations of the forms and functions of myth in these three different contexts.

Eliade, Mircea. *Patterns in Comparative Religion.* New York, 1958. The subtitle indicates the nature of this work: *A Study of the Element of the Sacred in the History of Religious Phenomena.*

Huxley, Aldous. *The Doors of Perception.* New York, 1954.

Huxley, Aldous. *Heaven and Hell.* New York, 1956. These two volumes present accounts of Huxley's experiments with psychedelic drugs and his positive interpretations of them.

James, William. *The Varieties of Religious Experience.* New York, 1902. James's Gifford Lectures (1901–1902) are among the early, classic studies of religious experience, offering numerous specific examples and his own interpretations.

King, Winston L. *Introduction to Religion: A Phenomenological Approach.* New York, 1968. A descriptive and analytic study of the various forms and structures of the religious life as expressed in various traditions.

Laski, Marghanita. *Ecstasy: A Study of Some Secular and Religious Experiences.* Westport, Conn., 1961. A thesis of this volume is that transcendent experiences are universally human and not necessarily religious.

Leeuw, Gerardus van der. *Religion in Essence and Manifestation: A Study in Phenomenology* (1938). 2 vols. Gloucester, Mass., 1967. The first major attempt to apply the phenomenological methodology to the field of religion, bracketing normative evaluations of truth and ethical considerations in the interests of describing the religious essence in its essential and characterstic manifestations.

Lessa, William A., and Evon Z. Vogt, eds. *Reader in Comparative Religion: An Anthropological Approach.* 4th ed. New York, 1979. A wide selection of significant readings on the interpretation of religion by various leading anthropologists.

Long, Charles H. *Alpha: The Myths of Creation.* New York, 1963. An anthology of creation myths from the folk tales and religions of the world, organized according to type.

Maslow, Abraham. *Religions, Values, and Peak-Experiences.* Columbus, Ohio, 1964. Maslow calls for religion to make common cause with other areas and disciplines in the constructive use of all peak experiences, whether religious or otherwise.

Masters, R. E. L., and Jean Houston. *The Varieties of Psychedelic Experience.* New York, 1966. An evaluative, critical analysis of psychedelic experiences claiming to be religious.

Noss, John B. *Man's Religions.* 6th ed. New York, 1980. A standard, college-level text describing the major religious traditions of the world.

Otto, Rudolf. *Das Heilige.* Marburg, 1917. Translated by John W. Harvey as *The Idea of the Holy* (1950; Oxford, 1970). The author's own subtitle expresses the thrust of this seminal volume: *An Inquiry into the Non-Rational Factor in the Idea of the Divine and Its Relation to the Rational.*

Pratt, James B. *The Religious Consciousness: A Psychological Study.* New York, 1921. Expressed in psychological terms no longer current but perceptive and suggestive, particularly with respect to mysticism.

Stace, W. T. *Mysticism and Philosophy.* New York, 1960. An acute philosophical analysis of the mystical experience, concluding that "something" objective is there but not quite what the mystic thinks it is.

Tart, Charles T., ed. *Transpersonal Psychologies.* New York, 1975. Analytic discussions from a psychological viewpoint of the qualities, nature, and meaning of a variety of mystical experiences and psychotherapeutic techniques.

Underhill, Evelyn. *Mysticism.* 12th ed. New York, 1961. A long-time classic, Underhill's book is a sympathetic presentation of the mystical life, mainly within the Christian context but including Muslim Ṣūfī materials.

WINSTON L. KING

RELIGIONSGESCHICHTLICHE SCHULE is the name that was given, beginning in 1903, to a group of German Protestant theologians who consistently applied the history of religions method to the interpretation of the Bible. This school of thought originated at the University of Göttingen, where a number of young theologians became known as the "little Gottingen faculty" because of their common concerns and their critical dissociation from Albrecht Ritschl, who had earlier been their teacher. The group was made up of Hermann Gunkel, Wilhelm Bousset, Johannes Weiss, Ernst Troeltsch, Wilhelm Wrede, Heinrich Hackmann, and Alfred Rahlf. After 1900, Carl Clemen, Hugo Gressmann, and W. Heitmüller joined the school, while Rudolf Bultmann and Otto Eissfeldt may be reckoned as forming a third generation. All looked upon Albert Eichhorn as the decisive influence on their work.

Development of the School. The Religionsgeschichtliche Schule drew theological conclusions from preceding developments in historical science, Orientalism, the history of religions, and ethnology. Many kinds of scholarly endeavors served as godparents for the school: Johann Jakob Wettstein's efforts to produce a complete, annotated edition of the Greek New Testament, including variants (*Hē Kainē Diathēkē*: *Novum Testamentum Graecum*, 2 vols., 1751–1752) and J. G. Herder's undogmatic and literary approach to the Bible; the discoveries made and the languages deciphered in the Near East; the rise of historical thinking in the works of such scholars as Barthold G. Niebuhr, Leopold von Ranke, and Johann G. Droysen; the discovery and decipherment of new sources from the ancient Near East; the development of literary criticism; the new science of religions as developed by F. Max Müller, C. P. Tiele, P. D. Chantepie de la Saussaye, James G. Frazer, and Nathan Söderblom; the new field of ethnology associated with Adolf Bastian, Friedrich Ratzel, and E. B. Tylor; and the antimetaphysical spirit promoted by Neo-Kantianism in Germany during the second half of the nineteenth century. Even the "Babel and Bible" discussion started by Friedrich Delitzsch, Alfred Jeremias, and Peter Jensen, which to some extent ran parallel to the Religionsgeschichtliche Schule, contributed to the rise of the latter. [*See the biography of Delitzsch.*]

Historical criticism in the form of source analysis of biblical documents had already been generally accepted and was causing difficulties for dogmatic theology. The rise of the Religionsgeschichtliche Schule meant the definitive victory of the historical-critical method, but the school supplemented this method with a deeper understanding of the historical process that lay behind the literary sources and with the application of the comparative history of religions to the Bible and Christianity. For this reason the representatives of the approach comprised primarily biblical scholars. Apart from Clemen, only Hackmann opted for the general history of religions. Strictly speaking, this method was a movement within Protestant biblical exegesis, and theologically it was of course in the liberal camp.

Though it was initially a purely academic phenomenon, its representatives attempted, as those of hardly any other theological movement of the past had done, to broadcast their view on a large scale through popular works on the history of religions and through periodicals such as *Theologische Rundschau* (1917–), *Religionsgeschichtliche Volksbücher* (1903–), and *Forschungen zur Religion und Literatur des Alten und Neuen Testaments* (1913–), and collections such as *Die Religion in Geschichte und Gegenwart* (1st ed., Tübingen, 1909–1913), *Die Schriften des Alten Testaments in Auswahl: Übersetzt und für die Gegenwart erklärt*, by Hermann Gunkel (Göttingen, 1910–1915), and *Die Schriften des Neuen Testaments neu übersetzt und für die Gegenwart erklärt*, by Johannes Weiss (Göttingen, 1906). As a result, they were soon in conflict with ecclesiastical authorities, who accused them of destructive, secularizing intentions, an accusation that the school firmly denied.

Historians see the Religionsgeschichtliche Schule as beginning its public activity in 1895, which was the publication year of Gunkel's *Schöpfung und Chaos in Urzeit und Endzeit* (Creation and Chaos in Primordial Time and End Time). But the basic ideas of the school had been clearly at work even earlier in Gunkel's *Die Wirkungen des heiligen Geistes: Nach den populären Anschauungen der apostolisch Zeit* (The Effects of the Holy Spirit according to the Popular Mind of the Apostolic Age; Göttingen, 1888). In this earlier publication Gunkel examined exotic and even irrational features of early Christianity, such as belief in the preternatural, and explained these features as due to the ideas that were popular in the period of "late Judaism." The same approach was soon adopted by Johannes Weiss in his *Die Predigt Jesu vom Reiche Gottes* (Jesus' Preaching of the Kingdom of God; Göttingen, 1892) and by Wilhelm Bousset, who in his *Die Religion des Judentums im neutestament-*

lichen Zeitalter (Tübingen, 1903) developed the idea that Judaism in the New Testament era was the real soil from which Jesus and the primitive Christian community sprang. In *Hauptprobleme der Gnosis* (Göttingen, 1907) and *Kyrios Christos* (Göttingen, 1913) Bousset also drew upon the religious history of Hellenism and late antiquity in describing the Christianity of the first and second centuries. By and large, the further work of the school followed the same general lines, though at times the emphasis differed, as in the case of the brilliant but short-lived Wilhelm Wrede, who, in his *Paulus* (Tübingen, 1904), *Das Messiasgeheimnis in den Evangilien* (Göttingen, 1901), and *Vorträge und Studien* (Tübingen, 1907) maintained what were probably the school's most radical views.

In the field of Old Testament studies Gunkel pioneered not only the religio-historical explanation of the Old Testament, especially in his *Genesis* (1901) and *Psalmen* (1926), but also the literary-historical method and, in particular, a reformulated "tradition-historical" approach that ushered in a new age of Old Testament exegesis. Hugo Gressmann followed Gunkel's lead in his *Der Ursprung der israelitisch-jüdischen Eschatologie* (Göttingen, 1905) and *Der Messias* (Göttingen, 1929).

The end of the Religionsgeschichtliche Schule after World War I was due not only to the social changes that the war brought to Germany but also to correlative radical shifts in theology, such as those produced by Karl Barth and dialectical theology, and, surely, to the early deaths of many of the school's leading representatives. Richard Reitzenstein (1861–1931), who wrote *Die Vorgeschichte der christlichen Taufe* (Prehistory of Christian Baptism; Leipzig, 1929) was one of the last champions of the school's ideas, unless one includes Rudolf Bultmann and his school as the third, most recent generation. This third generation reshaped the heritage of the Religionsgeschichtliche Schule and sought to safeguard it, especially in the area of the study of gnosticism, by new methods such as form criticism, redaction history, tradition history, existential interpretation, and demythologization.

Characteristics of the Approach. The mounting criticism, especially after World War II, of the Religionsgeschichtliche Schule and its program cannot gainsay the fact that it brought major progress in the understanding of biblical writings and their history. Questions first raised by the school, such as the role of Canaanite religion, apocalyptic thought, eschatology, pneumatology, gnosis, and Hellenistic Judaism, cultus, and piety in the formation of Christianity, are still vital and have acquired increased relevance due to new discoveries such as those at Ugarit, Khirbat Qumran, and Nag Hammadi. Biblical exegesis, theology, and religious studies cannot retreat to the scholarly situation as it was before the Religionsgeschichtliche Schule was formed. The facts brought to light by the school cannot be dismissed, even if scholars now prefer explanations other than those proposed by the Religionsgeschichtliche Schule.

Plurality of Christianity's origins. The school's members rejected interpreting the New Testament solely in light of the Old Testament. Primitive Christianity, they believed, was not a mere continuation of Old Testament history but had other roots as well.

One of these other roots was Hellenistic Judaism, represented by the thought of Philo Judaeus (d. 45–50 CE), as opposed to rabbinic Judaism, which belongs to a later period. The Hellenistic religious outlook, as expressed in the mystery religions and other Oriental religions of redemption, in gnostic groups, Hermetism, emperor worship, and magic, played an important part in the development of early Christianity. Gunkel, in his *Zum religionsgeschichtlichen Verständnis des Neuen Testaments* (Göttingen, 1903) had already spoken of the "syncretic" character of early Christianity, arguing that, from the historical viewpoint, Christianity had many links with contemporaneous religions. Bousset, though somewhat more cautious on this point, constantly rejected the artificial division between primitive Christianity and its historical environment. He explained the disjunction that appeared between the teachings of Jesus and those of the later church by citing the influence of this early environment. Behind the replacement of "Jesus the itinerant prophet" with "Christ the Lord" was the transition, beginning even before Paul, of primitive Christianity into the Hellenistic-Roman world in the form of a Hellenistic community of Christians at Antioch. The Religionsgeschichtliche Schule was concerned primarily with intellectual links, not with individual derivations or parallels. The same principle held for the Old Testament, whose historical development, the school believed, was to be understood in light of its changing milieu, to which belonged Canaan, Babylon, Egypt, and Iran.

Historical framework. The division between the New Testament and the history of the early church and its dogma, the school believed, is an artificial one. The New Testament canon is a historical product and should be studied only in the framework of a history of early Christian literature. Prominent examples of this approach are found in the works of Eichhorn and Wrede.

Concept of religion. According to the Religionsgeschichtliche Schule, the traditional focus on doctrinal concepts should be replaced by a focus on religion, the religious spirit, and piety. Theology is only one side of religion—the rational, conceptual, and systematic side. The essence of religion, as understood by the Religionsgeschichtliche Schule, is nonrational experience. This concept of religion originated in the works of Friedrich Schleiermacher (1768–1834) and became normative for the theology and philosophy of religion of the subsequent period. The school aimed at writing a history of Christianity as a religion and not simply a history of ideas, dogmas, and doctrines.

Role of religious practice. The Religionsgeschichtliche Schule was part of a current of thought that, in contrast to the overemphasis by some scholars on mythology or ideology, regarded the realm of cult and religious practice as central and as an important expression of piety. The interest in the "theology of the community," that is, the popular religion of the masses (including folk tales and fairy tales, or, in other words, the "seamier side" of religion as contrasted with the "heights" of elitist theology), was already paving the way for a sociological and psychological interpretation of religion. On the other hand, the school also stressed the innovative role of religious individuals and authorities (for example the Old Testament prophets and Jesus), who, according to the school, have a formative influence on the history of religions.

Tradition history. One of the most important but often overlooked discoveries of the school is what is known as "tradition history," which was first proposed by Gunkel. Tradition history is the attempt to get behind the written tradition (i.e., texts) to its prehistory. This approach was considered to be the only way to make texts historically intelligible. The abandonment of classical literary history and criticism for a history of preliterary "form," "genres," or "materials" is a result of the historical approach taken by the Religionsgeschichtliche Schule: a text yields its meaning through its history, its development, and the materials (its "prehistory") used to compose it. This turning of written tradition into something problematic soon became a tool of tradition criticism and made nonsense of many problems regarded as central by literary criticism. The old representatives of literary criticism, such as Wellhausen, rejected Gunkel's works, although they themselves could not avoid raising questions that involved the history of traditions. [*See the biography of Wellhausen.*]

This aspect of the school's work is another indication of its concern with "the religion of the community" as a sociopsychological category. The designation "history of traditions" was at times used by members of the school as a synonym for "history of religions." Unfortunately, the Religionsgeschichtliche Schule failed to make a clear distinction here and, more importantly, to introduce a necessary reflection on method, a step that would have spared it a great deal of trouble. Methodological clarification began only with the rise of "form criticism" in the works of Bultmann and Martin Dibelius (1883–1947). [*See the biography of Bultmann.*]

Definition of the field. Consideration of the Bible as a historical religious document that is to be investigated with the same tools as other religious texts soon led to the view that the traditional theological faculties should be replaced by departments of the history of religions. The historical disciplines associated with theology are really no longer theological, Wrede clearly saw; rather, they belong to the history of religions, since they employ the same tools as philology and all other historical sciences.

The school's "leveling down" of Christianity so that it becomes just one more subject of a general or comparative history of religions led to a certain relativism that had an important impact, especially on dogmatic and theological systems. In this situation Troeltsch, who remained faithful to a romantic and ultimately Hegelian concept of development, drew historico-philosophical conclusions that looked to the future development of Christianity in the framework of a universal history of religions. Bousset, too, sought to rescue Christianity from the maelstrom of historical relativization by reverting to the liberal theological emphasis on ethics and morality and to the idea of the irreducible personality of Jesus as a revelation of God. But Christianity cannot be rescued by the tools of historical science; at this point the assertions of faith stand alone against the power of history and critical reflection. To rescue Christianity is the task of theology, not of the history of religions.

The Religionsgeschichtliche Schule began as a movement within theology, but it ended outside theology because its methods and approach were so radical. The attempt to restore the ties connecting the school and Christian theology expresses only the personal piety, or Christian faith, of the school's representatives. Here again the Religionsgeschichtliche Schule created a dilemma, in this case one of the most difficult that the history of religions as such must face: the relation between personal conviction or faith and scientific honesty or objectivity.

[*See also* History of Religions.]

BIBLIOGRAPHY

To date there is no successful overall portrait or bibliography of the Religionsgeschichtliche Schule. A number of monographs are available on individual representatives of the school (Gunkel, Bousset, Wrede) or on special topics (gnosis, salvation history, tradition history). More recently, additional materials concerning the beginnings of the school have been published (in particular by Hans Rollman and Friedrich W. Graf). For general orientation, see articles in the first edition of the encyclopedia *Die Religion in Geschichte and Gegenwart*, 5 vols., edited by Friedrich Michael Schiele (Tübingen, 1909–1913), which work as a whole is representative of the school's aims and methods. See also Werner Georg Kümmel's *Das Neue Testament: Geschichte der Erforschung seiner Probleme* (Freiburg, 1958), esp. pp. 259–414; Hans-Joachim Kraus's *Geschichte der historisch-kritischen Erforschung des Alten Testaments von der Reformation bis zur Gegenwart* (Neukirchen, 1956); and Horst Stephan and Martin Schmidt's *Geschichte der evangelischen Theologie in Deutschland seit dem Idealismus*, 3d ed. (Berlin, 1973). The works listed below may also be fruitfully consulted.

Bousset, D. Wilhelm. *Religionsgeschichtliche Studien*. Leiden, 1979.

Clemen, Carl. *Die religionsgeschichtliche Methode in der Theologie*. Giessen, 1904.

Colpe, Carsten. *Die religionsgeschichtliche Schule*, vol. 1. Göttingen, 1961.

Gressmann, Hugo. *Albert Eichhorn und die religionsgeschichtliche Schule*. Göttingen, 1914.

Ittel, Gerhard Wolfgang. *Urchristentum und Fremdreligionen im Urteil der religionsgeschichtlichen Schule*. Erlangen, 1956.

Ittel, Gerhard Wolfgang. "Die Hauptgedanken der 'religionsgeschichtlichen Schule.'" *Zeitschrift fur Religions- und Geistesgeschichte* 10 (1958): 61–78.

Klatt, Werner. *Hermann Gunkel*. Göttingen, 1969.

Morgan, Robert, ed. and trans. *The Nature of New Testament Theology: The Contribution of Wilhelm Wrede and Adolf Schlatter*. Naperville, Ill., 1973. Includes (pp. 68–116) a translation of Wrede's *Über Afgabe und Methode der sogenannten neutestamentlichen Theologie*.

Paulsen, H. "Traditionsgeschichtliche und religionsgeschichtliche Schule." *Zeitschift für Theologie und Kirche* 75 (1958): 22–55.

Reischle, Max. *Theologie und Religionsgeschichte*. Tübingen, 1904.

Renz, Horst, and Friedrich W. Graf, eds. *Troeltsch-Studien*, vol. 1. Gütersloh, 1982. See especially pages 235–290 and 296–305.

Rollman, Hans. "Zwei Briefe Hermann Gunkel an Adolf Jülicher." *Zeitschrift für Theologie und Kirche* 78 (1981): 276–288.

Rollman, Hans. "Duhm, Lagarde, Ritschl und der irrationale Religionsbegriff der Religionsgeschichtlichen Schule." *Zeitschrift für Religions- und Geistesgeschichte* 34 (1982): 276–279.

Rollmann, Hans. "Theologie und Religiongeschichte." *Zeitschrift für Theologie und Kirche* 80 (1983): 69–84.

Sänger, Dieter. "Phänomenologie oder Geschichte? Methodische Anmerkungen zur religionsgeschichtlichen Schule." *Zeitschrift für Religions- und Geistesgeschichte* 32 (1980): 13–27.

Troeltsch, Ernst. "Die 'kleine Göttinger Fakultät' von 1890." *Christliche Welt* 18 (1920): 281–283.

Troeltsch, Ernst. "Die Dogmatik der 'religionsgeschichtlichen Schule.'" In his *Gesammelte Schriften*, 2d ed., vol. 2, pp. 500–524. Aalen, 1962.

Troeltsch, Ernst. "Christentum und Religionsgeschichte." In *Gesammelte Schriften*, 2d ed., vol. 2, pp. 328–363. Aalen, 1962.

Verheule, Anthonie F. *Wilhelm Bousset: Leben und Werk*. Amsterdam, 1973.

KURT RUDOLPH
Translated from German by Matthew J. O'Connell

RELIGIONSWISSENSCHAFT. *See* Comparative Religion *and* History of Religions.

RELIGIOUS BROADCASTING. The technological revolutions in radio and television communication and in computers have shaped forms of evangelism and worship services that reach an unseen mass audience. Use of these media by religious groups and institutions differs among countries and among traditions. Modern developments in religious broadcasting depend on at least three major factors: the liturgical orientations of particular groups that predispose them to utilize telecommunication technology, the structure of media ownership and control, and government regulations that vary from country to country. As an example of this last factor, in England the government-owned and -operated broadcasting corporation has consistently included religious broadcasts as part of its programming. Different conditions exist in other countries, such as the United States and Mexico, where the activities of church and state are clearly separated. No religious broadcasts are permitted in Mexico. In the United States, however, religious programs are aired on commercial stations as well as on those owned by religious organizations. From the perspective of the 1980s, this article examines the transformations in religious communication that have taken place in the United States since the advent of radio and television.

In the United States the basic pattern of programming for all commercial TV and radio stations evolved from the use of these media for advertising and marketing by private business and industry. Support of programs has come through revenues generated by the selling of airtime for commercials. At the same time some radio stations began to allocate free time to certain religious groups for the broadcast of formal worship services. After the Communications Act of 1934 this became a standard procedure. However, not all religious groups had access to public service time, and evangelical and fundamentalist groups outside the mainstream of American religious traditions began to buy time from amenable stations. Thus two types of sponsorship of religious programs developed in this culture. First, there were religious services aired by stations as a public service and fitted into very limited time frames, usually on Sunday morning. And, second, there were broadcasts by religious groups who bought airtime for their programs. This structure, however, was modified considerably in the 1970s and 1980s as modern religious stations emerged that were themselves profit-making institutions, owned and operated by particular religious groups.

Development of Video Evangelism. The styles of religious communication in the so-called electronic churches represent a fusion of elements inherent in the media and in liturgical forms embedded in individual religious traditions. Television is particularly well suited for those traditions that have emphasized the charismatic quality of religious leaders rather than the office of priesthood. Prior to radio and television one had to be physically present in the audience to experience the forcefulness and persuasiveness of a dynamic, spirit-filled religious leader. Written or printed words are not able to express the complex symbolic messages that come through the enlivened spoken words.

Radio was the first medium to transmit to a distant, mass audience the sense of a speaker's physical presence. In the 1940s Charles E. Fuller used the medium of radio to extend his sermons and Bible study to thousands of unseen listeners in a program entitled *The Old-Fashioned Revival Hour*. Addressing his audience as "friends in radioland," Fuller urged them to get out their Bibles and gather round to feast on the good things in Christ. Fuller's congregation heard his Bible interpretations and sermons in a church without walls. Communion depended on the listener's turn of the radio dial and correspondence by mail with the radio pastor.

Fulton J. Sheen, the Roman Catholic archbishop of New York, had a radio career in the 1940s before he was introduced to television audiences in 1952. In these appearances the conversion motif was not stressed. Instead he appealed to a wider range of reflective individuals who could appropriate his wisdom and apply it to their own human predicament. Part of his appeal lay also in the symbols of his office. Viewers saw as well as heard the signs of authority as he spoke.

Television became a particularly effective form for dramatic, persuasive preachers such as Billy Graham. His revival services all over the world became special TV programs rebroadcast for American viewers, frequently at prime time. In these broadcasts the conversion motif dominated. Graham was making an evangelical appeal for spiritual rebirth, which emphasized personal conversion and commitment to a rigorous moral life. Although Graham's broadcasts included the basic elements of an evangelical Protestant service, they portrayed worldwide revivals held in spaces that could accommodate thousands.

Survey of Contemporary Video Evangelism. Jerry Falwell, one of the most prominent electronic preachers of the 1980s, regularly telecasts the worship services of his church, the Thomas Road Baptist Church in Lynchburg, Virginia. In Falwell's program, *The Old-Time Gospel Hour*, television techniques are used to visually modify and enhance the formal elements of a free church, evangelical service. Television cameras provide a variety of angles and shots to give the viewer the sense of being present. When Falwell reads from the Bible, a camera will film an actual page, and these printed passages will fill the viewer's screen. Other modifications depend entirely upon the medium. For example, in the middle of a sermon an illustration or extended point is made by inserting a taped interview made previously by the preacher.

Frequently Falwell's sermons address national issues—social, economic, and political. And even though the sermon concludes with the invitation to come forward and profess one's faith, he exhorts viewers to take a stand to support the positions he is advocating. These shifts in emphasis point to a shift in function. National broadcasts of his views of particular social issues suggest an educational rather than sacramental function. While instruction cannot be separated from the evangelist's call for repentance, Falwell's advocacy for causes appears to play a dominant role. In this respect he does not try to use the television program as a sacramental occasion but instead as a teaching medium.

Robert Schuller's program, *Hour of Power*, originates in his Crystal Cathedral in Los Angeles, California. Schuller's program opens with views of his spectacular church and its environs, accompanied by triumphant music. Although the sermon is the most important part of *Hour of Power*, in the first part of the service Schuller usually brings in special guests who talk with him informally about their religious experiences. These testimonials and a variety of musical presentations set the stage for the sermon, which is compact, has clear, crisp points, and is sufficiently general in theological content to appeal to a wide range of religious believers. There is no urgent exhortation leading up to an altar call. Nor does Schuller confront controversial issues directly. Robed in a rich blue academic gown, a smiling, confident Schuller addresses his church and viewing audience, inviting them to rejoice. "God loves you" and "You are special" are frequent themes, and his homilies stress the importance of "possibility thinking" and "self-esteem." Although his church is affiliated with the Reformed Church in America, Schuller relies upon simplified psychological terms and easily perceived humanistic goals to enable people to "feel good about themselves." Some admirers and critics view Schuller as "pre-evangelical"—that is, as one who can perhaps bring individuals to the threshold of a more demanding and unfathomable, less neatly packaged gospel.

In contrast to Jerry Falwell and Robert Schuller, there are other evangelists whose programs do not originate in the formal worship spaces of the church. These men and women transform the broadcast studio, using stage properties, lighting, TV technology, musical groups, and visiting celebrities to produce programs that are designed expressly for viewing audiences. Oral Roberts was among the first to use the facilities of the studio in this way. The core of his program was the sermon, which had a particular emphasis upon faith healing. Standing before a simple curtain backdrop and dressed in a business suit, he preached and prayed while the cameras concentrated on his gestures and facial expressions. Although the sermon was the climax of the program, he introduced as guests nationally recognized culture heroes, such as movie stars, who shared with him and the viewing audience their own conversion experiences. There was also an orchestra and chorus dressed not in choir robes but in formal attire and stylish gowns.

Musician-evangelist Jimmy Swaggart's weekly broadcasts originate in a huge auditorium, with the audience functioning as a congregation. In these broadcasts, Swaggart is both musical star and preacher, and he shifts easily from the role of a popular performer to center stage where he reads from scripture and begins to preach. Television production techniques are used extensively to enhance the visual effects for the viewing audience. Unlike Falwell, Schuller, or Roberts, Swaggart moves vigorously and dramatically around the stage as he passionately preaches with the Bible in one hand and a microphone in the other. The hour-long program ends after the sermon and closes with taped images of Swaggart, speaking directly to the television audience about the missions and projects with which he and his staff are engaged.

Among the video evangelists, Pat Robertson has developed the most complex type of programming, with many features styled after programs appearing on commercial television. Robertson and Ben Kinchlow are cohosts of *The 700 Club*, broadcast Monday through Friday. The program, lasting ninety minutes, is composed of a variety of segments. There are interviews with guests who sit and talk informally with Robertson or Kinchlow. Those interviewed include successful businessmen and businesswomen, authors, sports heroes, movie and television celebrities, politicians, and ordinary folk who have had extraordinary religious experiences. Their common denominator is generally their testimony to the power of God in their lives. Other segments of the program include short features on health, food preparation and nutrition, investments, architectural advice for home owners, and business and industry reports. There are also special features prepared by film crews and staff on social, economic, and political crises. These include on-site filming with interviews and commentary.

Robertson, a law school graduate, will on occasion go into a detailed analysis of his views of certain political, economic, or social issues. Standing before a huge world map, he and Kinchlow may discuss a particular world crisis. Very often the discussion of the news event prepares the way for biblical and theological teaching and speculation about the event's significance for biblical prophecy, especially if the event occurred in the Middle East.

Robertson is head of the Christian Broadcasting Network (CBN), which he hopes will rival the three large national commercial networks. In addition to producing a so-called Christian soap opera, *Another Life*, and a series of commercials promoting the conversion experience, CBN has developed broadcasting operations in Japan and Lebanon. The growth and diversification that have evolved through Robertson's work in *The 700 Club* and the CBN suggest forms of communication more enduring and far-reaching than those developed by other video evangelists.

Common Themes of Video Evangelists. Although the forms of the programs differ, among the video evangelists there are common elements related to the tradition of ascetic Protestantism.

Protestant roots. Most of these preachers come out of a type of Protestantism that was suspicious of the visual arts and emphasized the verbal and musical over the visual. In American society this kind of evangelical Protestantism developed its own special culture. Unhindered by more formal liturgical traditions and practices, evangelical groups and institutions have been quick to appropriate printing, radio, television, and computers. Through modern technology these religious organizations have developed new ways of identifying membership and of communicating with their constituencies. Nationally known video evangelists, for example, use computerized lists of persons who have expressed interest in or have donated to their organization, and the evangelists are persistent in maintaining contact with such persons through standardized mailings. An unseen membership can have some sense of community participation through regular mailings of tapes, records, pamphlets, books, cards, charts, Bibles, pins, and other objects. Along with the transformation of evangelism and worship goes a transformation of devotional forms. Traditional "holy cards" and icons have been replaced by new, rationalized forms of sacramentalism.

Conversion. Another common element among the video evangelists is their emphasis upon a conversion experience—"born-again" faith. Whether teaching, preaching, informally talking, or interpreting world events, they insist that religious faith and practice must be grounded in a decisive change of heart. This emphasis upon the conversion experience is not unique to the contemporary electronic preachers nor is it exclusive to the Christian faith. Its roots, however, are deep in American religious culture. The evangelistic service differs from classical Protestant worship. In the evangelistic tradition the confession of sin has been transferred from the beginning of the service to the end. The call to confession and repentance brings an emotional and effective climax to the sermon. Similarly, the video evangelists, regardless of the type of program, assume the conversion experience to be a key to salvation and a turning point for the individual, and they construct the messages and forms of communication around that central conviction.

Charismatic leadership. A third common element is the importance of charismatic leadership. It is a type of religious leadership in which the office of priesthood and salvific role of the sacraments are de-emphasized. Instead, spiritual authority rests with the Bible, individually interpreted, and the attainment of salvation without priesthood or hierarchy. The power of the charismatic religious leader does not reside in the office but in the calling to teach, preach, and heal through the inspiration of the Holy Spirit and in accordance with biblical teachings. First radio, and later television, provided unprecedented aesthetic and technical forms to emphasize the personality and forcefulness of religious leaders who claimed biblical guidance for preaching, prophecy, and healing and who could persuasively admonish listener-viewers to confess sins, repent, and be born again.

Political concerns. In the messages of politically oriented video preachers, common themes appear. Particular moral and theological positions are constant and can be discerned, even though the individual styles and types of programs differ. One persistent theme is the categorical choice between right and wrong action with which viewers are challenged. The evangelists tend to summarize and simplify complex social, political, and economic issues—as well as religious ones—and to identify those positions that are "biblical" and "Christian" and those that are not. To a degree all religious groups, liberal and conservative, have been susceptible to this kind of categorization. Father Charles F. Coughlin, one of the first to use radio for preaching, was an outspoken advocate of particular liberal positions. He first supported Franklin Delano Roosevelt and his programs but later turned vociferously against him. Electronic evangelists associated with the "religious right" in the later twentieth century unite in their conservative fight against abortion and their advocacy of prayer in public schools. Generally speaking, they oppose the position described as "secular humanist," which they see as eroding the moral principles of contemporary American culture. The sins that are most often identified by these evangelists are sins of the flesh, attributed to individual moral blindness or corruption. Witnesses to liberation from particular sins of the flesh—addiction to alcohol and drugs, infidelity, sexual deviance—contribute to the dramatic, confessional quality of the telecast interviews and testimonials.

Good and evil. Easily recognizable, personal defections from accepted norms of behavior dominate the evangelical rhetoric, accompanied by a commensurate tendency to look with little depth and rigor on collective social evils and what might redeem them. The tendency is reinforced by the concept of an individualistic, self-willed action assisted by God's grace. The effect is a blurring of the accepted notions of "liberal" and "conservative" attitudes toward ethical action and responsibility. While the evangelical preachers have been viewed as "conservative," a careful, close reading of their attitudes about human nature suggests a very different image. For example, these preachers may frequently criticize government intervention in social and economic problems and recommend voluntary, individual acts of charity as a better solution. Converted individuals, guided by the precepts of the gospel and unfettered by government, will often respond with generosity and fairness to the less fortunate and to the victims of social ills. In this example, there is an assumption about human nature and its essential goodness that is, ironically, more characteristic of some liberal, secular humanism than of classical Christian doctrine. This optimistic assertion about the behavior of reborn individuals creeps into the social ethic of the evangelists, in spite of their use of words such as *sin* and *fall*. A genuinely conservative Judaic or Christian tradition would be much more realistic about the tendency to human greed and neglect of the neighbor, even among "reborn" individuals. And the prophetic tradition would echo the need for systemic restraints on the powerful and the support of the powerless.

The video preachers use the metaphors of warfare

and struggle with Satan to dramatize the tensions and conflicts in the moral life of both individual and society. Introspective reflections, ambiguities, endless shades of gray, and the multiple interconnectedness of human evil do not suit television timing, show business, and technology. When the personification of evil in the struggle with Satan dominates, there is a kinship with the dualistic motifs of good and evil in Manichaean theology. This dualism can be applied to the struggle of forces in human beings for health and salvation. Some evangelists will, during the time of prayer on their shows, invoke the name of Christ to drive out the power of doubt and the demons of disease.

For some evangelists the warfare in the soul between the forces of light and the forces of darkness expands to a discussion of the warfare of good and evil in the community, in the nation, and in the cosmos. On a global scale this conflict focuses primarily upon the Soviet Union and the United States, with the political and military actions of the United States representing the forces of light.

Apocalypticism. Another favorite theme of many television evangelists is prophecy regarding the final days and the coming of the millennium. In these apocalyptic interpretations the warfare metaphor is enlarged to a cosmic scale and the imminent end of history described, with its detailed scenarios of conflict between Christ and the forces of the Antichrist. TV evangelists inject apocalyptic prophecy into any kind of program—talk-show interviews, teaching, preaching, news reporting, editorial comments. These prophecies are particularly dramatic when the teacher-preacher assumes the role of news reporter and commentator. A world crisis is reported as a news story and then becomes a point of departure for speculation. Such an easy blending of reporting, editorial comment, and prophecy blurs the distinctions that most viewers expect between uneditorialized reporting and speculative commentary.

Anti-intellectualism. Prophecy, healing, preaching, judgment, and social action are rooted in a view of biblical inerrancy that holds that the original writings of scripture are without flaw in matters of science and history as well as in matters of morals and theology. Fundamentalist evangelists condemn the historical-critical methods of biblical interpretation. The video preachers understand well that there is always the possibility of a revitalization of faith through Bible reading and personal interpretation. They radicalize themes that have been a part of many Protestant communities and that center on direct personal encounters with "the Word of God." Yet, obsession with biblical literalism and immediacy of experience tends to turn the Bible into a cultic object. And the total rejection of critical methods harbors both an anti-intellectualism and a diversion from the central themes of biblical faith, dissipating the strength of scholarly traditions and the historical experience of Christian communities.

Fund raising. Finally, the successful TV evangelists have developed support for their ministries through the solicitation of funds from the viewing audience. Their "polity" or church order depends upon the latest forms of telecommunications, rather than a hierarchy of local or denominational organization. While some of the video preachers do indeed have local churches, most of their organizations are independent of mainstream religious bodies. Their funds are obtained in many ways. Viewers can write in for free literature and be placed on the mailing list. Or they may contribute money, or make pledges to the institutions. Donors can generally expect to receive tax deductions from contributions such as stocks, bonds, and property. Above all, there is a massive telephone system for viewers to call in for counseling and prayer. This combination of telecommunication forms and computerized lists of contributors is comparable to the connections that characterize denominational structures. And although many of the evangelists stress the importance of the viewer's relationship to a local church, they nevertheless compete—at least for funds—with local churches and denominations.

In mainline Protestant communities the most serious question about solicitations is one of accountability. Yet for most of the electronic evangelists there is no larger order or denomination that supervises the contributions, expenses, and investments. For some of the evangelists the financial and organizational autonomy has led to a diversification of evangelical activities—missions, hospitals, and educational institutions.

Religious Functions of Commercial Television. Limited analogies can be made between certain kinds of broadcasts on commercial television and traditional forms of religious communication. Important events televised for millions of interested viewers are ritualistic in character. These events take place at special times and in special places and are eagerly awaited by an audience who, to a degree, "participate" in that event through television. This enactment of significant events in extraordinary places and at an extraordinary time, faithfully attended by believers, constitutes a basic ritualistic structure. In traditional religious ritual, of course, the physical presence is important to the communicant, who is transformed by participation. Moreover, traditional ritual is concrete action within a community of believers. Nevertheless, in a modern technological society, particularly one as vast as the United States, commercially televised events frequently fulfill the integrative function of ritual. Analogies between traditional ritual and ritualistic events presented on television depend upon a broad, sociological definition of religion that stresses religion's integrative role in providing symbol systems to give order and value to human experience. Rather than conversion, the celebration and renewal of common values characterize commercial television's ritualization processes.

Whereas in many religions sacred stories have been told with images as well as with words, in the religious and cultural history of the United States they were more often narrated than pictured. However, over the years illustrations and movies have provided a popular, visual, narrative tradition. Television has continued this visual story telling through soap operas, situation comedies, and dramas.

Some denominations have produced programs appropriating that visual narrative tradition. Their writers have deepened the subject matter of ordinary experience so that dramas are more profound than commercial entertainment. *Insight*, produced by the Paulist Fathers, has consistently been characterized by high technical competency, professionalism, and provocative, dramatic stories. Through stories about believable, often insoluble human predicaments, the show has touched the full range of human conflict and suffering. Another outstanding series, produced by the Lutherans, *Davey and Goliath*, has been a model of what can be done by religious groups in television programs for children.

Religion and the Television Medium. Although this article has focused exclusively on religious broadcasting in the United States, certain issues can be raised that are pertinent to other countries and other religious traditions. Foremost is the question of the nature of religious experience and the relationship of the individual to the religious community. Can television communication, unaided by a particular community, sustain and nurture faith? At issue in this question is the worth attributed to the integrative function of television—commercial or religious—in a mass society where traditional mediators of value, such as family and church, have declined. While sports fans, avid followers of a soap opera, or loyal viewers of a TV evangelist can gain some sense of attunement with unseen millions who share their loyalty, how deep are the bonds between members of the "tune in" community? Can mass ritual through television go beyond the sharing of common values? Can it bring lasting redemption and hope to broken and bewildered human beings?

Traditional religious communities have shaped personal and social ethics for their members. Yet television in the late twentieth century also offers a far-reaching and powerful form through which persons, directly or indirectly, derive information about the right or the fitting action. Video evangelists are quite explicit in advocating and attempting to organize support for or resistance to certain policies. But the medium can be used by so-called liberal or conservative, reactionary or progressive individuals or groups to champion their causes. From one perspective, the medium appears to be a neutral one that can be used for a variety of causes. And, to a degree, this is correct. However, the production and management of television communication involves such large financial investments that there are many sectors of the world population that do not have the means to enter telecommunications.

For this reason radio has begun to reemerge as an important source of communication and social orientation in poorer, less developed countries, particularly in Central and South America. There the rural and urban poor are making greater use of this and other less expensive and more easily managed media. Simple audiovisual materials, newspapers, and radio systems have been developed through church, labor, and populist groups.

Commercial and religious broadcasters show a common danger of overlooking and underrepresenting the poor and powerless. The delivery of the nightly news programs, entertainment, and sports, as well as the sermons and rhetoric of electronic preachers, are all sufficiently linked to economic power bases to cover the costs of programming, management, research, polling, advertising, computers, and data banks. Commercial broadcasters and religious broadcasters could theoretically have competing visions of moral and social responsibility. If, however, the distinctions between cultural and religious values should blend or become confused, then television becomes a powerful source of indoctrination into ideology, for there is little opportunity for opposition or genuine iconoclasm through the medium itself.

BIBLIOGRAPHY

Among the most useful research tools is *Religion and Television*, 2 vols. (Philadelphia, 1984), which represents comprehensive study coordinated by the National Council of the Churches of Christ in the U.S.A., and sponsored by the NCC and thirty other religious organizations. Research for this volume was conducted by the Annenberg School of Communications at the University of Pennsylvania, and by the Gallup Organization, Inc. Jeffrey K. Hadden and Charles E. Swann's *Primetime Preachers* (Reading, Mass., 1981) provides a basic introduction to the phenomenon of the electronic church. One of the most thorough and balanced analyses of this phenomenon is Peter G. Horsfield's *Religious Television* (New York, 1984). For a treatment of the historical forces that have contributed to the emergence of American fundamentalist culture, see George W.

Marsden's *Fundamentalism and American Culture* (New York, 1980). Gabriel J. Fackre's *The Religious Right and Christian Faith* (Grand Rapids, Mich., 1982) offers an acute analysis of the theological dimensions of the television ministries. Michael R. Real's *Mass-Mediated Culture* (Englewood Cliffs, N.J., 1977) and my own *The T.V. Ritual* (Boston, 1981) analyze commercial television using religious forms of communication as analogues. Stewart M. Hoover's *The Electronic Giant* (Elgin, Ill., 1982) examines social and ethical issues emerging in telecommunication technology. *The New Christian Right*, edited by Robert C. Liebman and Robert Wuthnow (New York, 1983), is the most careful and well-documented study of the new religious right. Ben H. Bagdikian's *The Media Monopoly* (Boston, 1983) critiques the socioeconomic system of mass media in American culture. Wilson P. Dizard offers an overview of technology, economics, and politics in his *The Coming Information Age*, rev. ed. (New York, 1982). Finally, Cees J. Hamelink's *Cultural Autonomy in Global Communications* (New York, 1983) provides a critical look at the problems of cultural identity and communication in developing nations.

GREGOR T. GOETHALS

RELIGIOUS COMMUNITIES. [*This entry consists of two articles:* Religion, Community, and Society, *a general discussion of the nature of religious community in the broadest sense, and* Christian Religious Orders, *a historical treatment of specialized religious communities in Christianity.*]

Religion, Community, and Society

Religion is both a personal matter and a social reality. In dealing with the latter, we are confronted by a confusion of categories and by terminological difficulties. For example, popular references to "religious community" reflect ambiguities in the current use of the term *community*. From Webster we learn that *community*, derived from the Latin *communitas*, has many meanings, including (1) a body of people having a common organization or interests, or living in the same place under the same laws and regulations, (2) society at large, a commonwealth, a state, (3) joint relationship or ownership, and (4) a common character or commonness.

Students of society have tried to overcome such ambiguities. Under the influence of the later German Enlightenment's notion that society is a product of human will, Ferdinand Julius Tönnies (1855–1936) proposed the famous dichotomy between community *(Gemeinschaft)* and society *(Gesellschaft)*. Community embodies natural will *(Wesenwille)* and is maintained by face-to-face interhuman relationships and a sense of solidarity governed by traditional rules. Society, however, is a more complex entity reflecting rational will *(Kürwille)* and characterized by indirect and impersonal interhuman relationships motivated by rational self-interest. Émile Durkheim (1858–1917) also attempted to distinguish between primitive and archaic social groups (roughly analogous to Tönnies's community type) and more complex groups (Tönnies's society type). In Durkheim's model, the former are based on the mechanical solidarity of undifferentiated individuals who live according to the authority of the social group, while the latter are based on the organic solidarity of more differentiated individuals who relate to one another by means of the division of labor. Prior to Tönnies and Durkheim, of course, Karl Marx (1818–1883) had classified various social organizations according to modes of production and the class system, ranging all the way from primitive communism to modern capitalist society. An implicit evolutionary assumption—that the movement from what Tönnies called community to what he called society was irreversible—underlay all these typologies and classifications.

Students of religion generally apply Tönnies's notion of the community type to both archaic and contemporary tribal communities, in which religious and natural bonds coalesce. They also acknowledge that a more stratified society usually develops from community, even though smaller religious or ethnic communities may continue to exist within the framework of a larger society. Beyond this general level, however, students of religion encounter a bewildering variety of religious phenomena that defy simple categorization in terms of community and society. For example, some of the ancient states, from the Hebrew to the Japanese, considered themselves "sacred communities" embracing a number of "religious societies." In the course of time, some of these religious societies themselves developed into religious communities. Other troublesome examples stem from the classical world religions such as Buddhism, Christianity, and Islam. These three considered their fellowships to be "religious communities" or "faith communities" that united different segments with a society or even crossed ethnic, linguistic, cultural, and national lines. Here again, these larger religious communities gave birth to a variety of religious societies that often became *de facto* religious communities, even if they retained the nomenclature of "society," as in the case of the Society of Jesus (the Jesuits).

Thus, for students of religion, the category *religious community* must include at least (1) tribal communities, both natural and religious, archaic and contemporary, (2) sacred national communities, (3) founded religious communities such as the Buddhist, the Christian, and the Islamic, and (4) various religious societies-turned-communities, as for instance orders of monks and nuns. Different though these groups may be, they share what the Dutch scholar Gerardus van der Leeuw (1938) calls the sense of community. This sense "is something not manufactured, but given; it depends not upon sentiment or feeling, but on the Unconscious. It need be founded upon no conviction, since it is self-evident; we do not become members of it, but 'belong to it'" (p. 243).

Tribal Religious Communities. To avoid the misleading adjective *primitive*, many scholars now use expressions—not wholly satisfactory—such as *tribal*, *nonliterate*, and *folk* to refer to the religious forms of a wide variety of peoples who live in small social groups and who possess a simple material culture and an unwritten language. It is often assumed that there are many similarities between tribal communities in archaic or prehistoric periods and tribal communites in our own. It is indeed possible that archaic and contemporary tribal communities are in some way typologically similar, presumably owing to their simple living conditions. Still, we should not overlook the long span of time that separates them.

Archaeological excavations have unearthed a variety of material remains from the prehistoric period, but very little can be reconstructed of the social system of the peoples or the movements of the so-called tribal migrations, including the prehistoric migration of Native Americans from Eurasia to North and South America. Excavated sites of Neolithic settlements, such as Pan-p'o in Shensi, China, may give glimpses of the physical layouts of archaic tribal communities, but it is difficult to know how prehistoric food-gatherers, hunters, and agriculturalists conducted their personal, communal, or religious affairs. Even so, by piecing together evidence from archaeology, physical anthropology, philology, and other sources, we conjecture that all activities directed toward subsistence and all cultic and religious activities merged to form a single, unified community. Some scholars even speculate that the archaic tribal community was, so to speak, a "religious universe" in which living itself was a religious act.

The contemporary tribal or folk communities scattered throughout Africa, Asia, Oceania, Australia, and the Americas display a great divergence in complexity of community structure, division of labor, cultic and religious beliefs and practices, and relations with neighboring societies and cultures. Moreover, as E. E. Evans-Pritchard (1951) reminds us, these communities "have just as long a history as our own, and while they are less developed than our society in some respects they are often more developed in others" (p. 7). Different though they are in many other respects, contemporary tribal communities share one characteristic: they are held together, to quote Robert Redfield (1953), "by common understanding as to the ultimate nature and purpose of life." Each community "exists not so much in the exchange of useful functions as in the common understandings as to the ends given" (p. 12). To these communities, life's ultimate purpose is the creation of a meaningful order through imitation of the celestial model, transmitted by myths and celebrated in rituals.

Unlike their archaic counterparts, contemporary tribal communities have more complex social organizations based on locality, age, sex, and sometimes totemic affiliations. Their nucleus is the kinship system, usually with exogamous clans and local territories. Many tribal communities have secret men's societies, which usually meet in the "men's house," an institution known by different designations in different localities but serving similar purposes—a club house for bachelors, a place for community worship, a residence for young boys during their initiatory seclusion. Such societies are found in Australia, New Guinea, Melanesia, Micronesia, Polynesia, the Philippines, India, Africa, and North, Central, and South America. (For examples, see Hutton Webster's *Primitive Secret Societies*, 1932.)

Today it is becoming increasingly inappropriate to apply the designation *community* to some tribal groups. The term is still applicable to such groups as the hunting and gathering tribes of South America and Australia and to the San of southern Africa, but larger groups like the Navajo Indians, who occupy eighteen million acres in Arizona and New Mexico, and the Inuit (Eskimo), whose habitations stretch from Greenland to the Bering Strait, resemble instead huge conglomerate societies containing a series of smaller communities and subgroups and various kinds of cultic fraternities. In addition, because of the impact of surrounding societies, some tribal groups now live in permanent settlements and so have lost their sense of the traditional tribal-religious community.

Sacred National Communities. The first great civilization in the history of the world emerged around 3500 BCE on the Mesopotamian plain. It was followed by the rise of other civilizations in Egypt, Crete, India, China, Mexico (Mesoamerica), Peru (Andean), and Palestine. According to the cosmography of these civilizations, the state was more than a political entity: it constituted the sacred national community.

Understandably, different civilizations have understood the meaning of the sacred national community differently. For example, in Mesopotamia the universe as a whole was considered a sovereign state governed by the assembly of the gods. In turn, the national state—made up of many city-states, each owned by its own god and ruled by his human steward—was governed by a king, who was himself guided by the executive officer of the assembly of the gods. Thus, as part of the cosmic commonwealth directed by the united wills of the divine powers, the earthly national community was sacred.

In contrast to the Mesopotamian tradition, the Egyptian national state was considered sacred because the king himself was one of the gods. At the same time, he was the intermediary between the people and the gods, the earthly community's divine representative. He was also the one recognized priest of all the gods, and as such he ruled the nation with the help of deputies, the officials and priests.

A third type of sacred national community, one rarer than the first two, is the Hebrew concept of a community based on a covenant between a god and his people. Despite the fiction of their common ancestry from Abraham, the Israelites were a composite people. As the prophets Hosea and Jeremiah stressed, they understood the sacral character of their commonwealth to depend both on faithful adherence to the covenant and on ethical conduct.

Throughout history, many nations have defined their sacrality in terms of one of these three types—king as deputy, king as god, or covenantal/contractual community—or a combination of them. But with increasing stratification of society and political organization, and the solidification of religious traditions, national communities have eroded. They have been replaced by a variety of relationships between religion and state ranging from theocracy—reminiscent of the sacred national community—to the secular state. But the *idea* of the sacred national community has persisted in various forms into the present century, as in, for example, Japan and Tibet.

Founded Religous Communities. In contrast to the sacred national community, whose *raison d'être* and destiny depend on the corporate life of the sociopolitical entity, the founded religious community, as I am using the term, refers to a community that derives its initial impetus from the religious experience of the founder of a religion. The better-known classical examples of such founded groups are the Buddhist, Christian, and Islamic communities; lesser known but equally significant are the Jain, Zoroastrian, and Manichaean communities. The founded religious communities of recent origin, such as the Sikh, Baha'i, Mormon, and a number of contemporary new religious communities in Asia, Africa, and the Americas, generally follow a similar pattern.

For convenience of exposition, we can identify three stages in this pattern: (1) the significance of the founder, (2) the process of formation, and (3) the usual, but by no means universal, manner in which such a religious community develops.

For the most part, the actual or legendary accounts of a religious founder (accepted as authentic, of course, by the given religious community) follow—with some notable exceptions—what is often called a law or scenario of sacred biography: the founder's miraculous birth, unusual childhood, ordeal or personal crisis prior to having a decisive religious experience, successful or unsuccessful ministry, and memorable demise, implying death or a new life beyond.

Then, either during or after the founder's lifetime, a circle of disciples becomes the nucleus of an informal brotherhood or fraternity. In the course of time, this brotherhood grows into an egalitarian or hierarchical religious community, with official scriptures, liturgies, and rules of conduct as well as specialists in sacred matters: clergy, scholars, jurists, monastics, bureaucrats, and service personnel. The religious community also develops a channel of authority to coordinate the activities of its scattered branches and faithful.

Finally, the religious community must cope with the surrounding culture, society, and secular political authorities, which view it with varying degrees of positive, negative, or neutral attitudes. Internally, this community often suffers from routinization, clericalization, inertia, spiritual decay, and fossilization. In this process, various kinds of reform and protest movements arise. Whether forward- or backward-looking, they cause change, schism, or secession, or establish small societies of like-minded members within the framework of the larger religious community *(ecclesiola in ecclesia)*. The reformers and leaders of schismatic and sectarian groups often become *de facto* founders, and the groups—both inside and outside the larger religious communities—take on the characteristics of religious communities.

Significantly, the idea of the unity of the religious community tends to persist, in spite of schismatic division or the breakup of the community's empirical structure into sects or denominations or possibly both. Thus, all divided Buddhist groups recite the same threefold affirmation of the essential unity of the Buddha, the Dharma (Buddhist doctrine), and the Saṃgha (the Buddhist community); all traditions of Islam affirm the unity of its community *(ummah)*; and all divisions of Christianity accept the Christian community (church) as the one unbroken "body of Christ" that exists beneath its empirical disunity: "Credo in . . . unam sanctam catholicam ecclesiam."

Religious Societies-Turned-Communities. As mentioned earlier, a variety of small religious societies and cultic fraternities tend to emerge within the framework of "sacred national communities" and "founded religious communities." Many such groups, if not formed for limited, temporary, and specific purposes, have the potential to become religious communities. How a religious society, viewed from a sociological perspective, becomes a religious community, may be seen in the initial development of the founded religious community. For example, as E. J. Thomas astutely observes in *The History of Buddhist Thought* (1933), the Buddhist community started "not with a body of doctrine, but with the formation of a society bound by certain rules" (p. 14). But the initiation of a variety of individuals into this society reoriented it toward the corporate soteriological objective and led to a shared experience, so that the society became a religious community.

To take another familiar example, Christianity started as a charismatic society within the fold of the Jewish community. After the Pentecost, it affirmed that those who were initiated into that society, Jews and gentiles alike, became the true Israel by virtue of being grafted onto the stock of Abraham. This in turn transformed them into children of God in the Christian community by being born "not of the will of man, but of God" (*Jn.* 1:13). Similarly, gnostic groups started out as mystery societies or circles at the periphery of the Christian fold but quickly developed into full-fledged religious communities.

The intricate relationship between religious societies and religious communities just illustrated tempts one to count numerous groups of ambiguous character among religious communities. However, I shall here consider only those societies that were established for specific religious and cultic purposes within larger tribal, sacred national, and founded religious communities, and that were later transformed into more permanent and coherent religious communities possessing such characteristics as rites of initiation, private or corporate religious ceremonies and duties, and independent organizational structures. I shall give brief typological discussions of (1) secret societies, (2) mystery societies/communities, (3) cult-based communities, (4) religous orders/monastic communities/service societies, and (5) utopian communities.

Secret societies. Secret societies include a wide range of groups that initiate in secret, possess secret symbols or rituals, or transmit esoteric knowledge. In size they range from small societies in tribal religious communities to Freemasonry, whose membership on both sides of the Atlantic numbers 5.9 million. (Freemasonry's satellite groups, among them the Ancient Arabic Order of the Nobles of the Mystic Shrine—popularly known as the Shriners—and the Order of the Eastern Star, are not secret societies. The Ku Klux Klan, on the other hand, is a secret terrorist organization but not a religious society, despite its stress on white Protestant supremacy.)

In part, secret societies overlap with the next two types of society-turned-community—the mystery societies and the cult-based communities. For example, the secret societies of ancient Egypt, Greece, and Rome were in fact mystery societies, with the possible exception of the Pythagorean community, and they will be discussed under that heading. The past ten centuries of Chinese history have been sprinkled with secret societies, some of which—notably the Maitreya Society, the White Lotus Society, the White Cloud Society, and the Triad Society—were inspired by Buddhist-Taoist eclecticism. The last major Chinese secret society was the Society of Shang-ti, whose patriarch, Hung Hsiu-ch'uan, who was influenced in part by Christianity, started the Taiping Rebellion in 1848. Contrary to popular impression, the esoteric schools of Buddhism, which transmit esoteric truth, are not secret societies: though the transmission of the teaching is secret, membership is open to anyone. In Europe, despite the predominance of Christianity and the threat of the Inquisition, pre-Christian pagan legacies of witchcraft and sorcery were kept alive by secret societies such as the Călşari, while the neo-Manichaean Cathari and other persecuted heretical groups went underground and tried to survive as secret societies.

Among contemporary tribal communities, secret societies are virtually universal phenomena. According to Paul Radin in *The Winnebago* (1923), the Winnebago Indian community has the following four groups: (1) clans or natural groups, which exclude outsiders from their ceremonies, (2) religious societies limited to those who receive the blessings of a special spirit, (3) the medicine group, a mystery society, and (4) associations of warriors and other such groups. As for African secret societies, Wilfrid D. Hambly's *Source-Book for African Anthropology* (1937) depicts the following types: (1) those based on age and sex affinities, (2) those connected with initiation, (3) those concerned with political and legal matters, and (4) those based on economic differentiation. Similar admixtures of religio-cultic, economic, and social factors are found in many other secret societies of contemporary tribal communities in various parts of the world. [*See also* Secret Societies.]

Mystery societies/communities. Classical types of mystery societies or communities emerged in the Greco-Roman world and in China, where the mysteries were believed to confer immortality and eternal life. Many mystery cults, such as that of Eleusis, originated with certain families. In the course of time, various Greek mystery cults developed private mystery societies. Under Roman rule, some of these societies became more open cultic communities. Meanwhile, other mystery cults of foreign origin—for instance, the cults of the Great Mother from Asia Minor, of Mithra from Iran, and of Serapis from Egypt—penetrated Greece and Rome. In the Roman world, many joined the cultic groups of Dionysos in search of personal immortality, but the religion of Mithra was probably the most influential mystery cult. [*See* Mystery Religions.]

In China, Taoism greatly amplified the belief in immortals *(hsien)*, which was already very strong. The so-called Huang-lao cult (the cult of the legendary Yellow Emperor and Lao-tzu) attracted many immortality-seekers before the beginning of the common era. Vigorously promoted by priest-magicians, this tradition was further developed in the second century CE by Chang Ling, who inaugurated a magico-religious movement called the Way of the Five Bushels of Rice with Chang Ling himself as the Heavenly Teacher. Meanwhile, other Taoists combined Taoist philosophy with the Yin-yang school and with alchemy. In the fifith century, K'ou Ch'ien-chi systematized the Taoist community, regulating its theories and cults. Since then Taoism, also called the Religion of Mystery (Hsüan Chiao), has exerted great influence not only in China but also in neighboring countries.

Many mystical or semimystical cults, societies, and communities in the Hindu, Buddhist, Islamic, Jewish, and Christian folds exhibit external resemblances to Greco-Roman and Chinese mystery societies and communities. Opinions vary, however, as to how central the "mysteries" are to their communal life.

Cult-based communities. Like the Orgeones, a free cultic association that persisted in Greece at least until the sixth century, certain groups are united primarily by cultic devotion to one or more deities and not by clan, tribal, national, or occupational ties. In other words, their specifically religious interests cut across sectarian and denominational boundaries. Or sometimes different communities participate in common, albeit temporary, cult associations, as do Kwakiutl Indian communities in North America in wartime and during winter dances. The prototype of this category is the *sampradaya* of Hinduism, which may be characterized as a phenomenon halfway between mystery communities and sects or denominations. The members of the *sampradaya*, divided though they are in terms of caste and other affiliations, experience a ritual unity in a communal adherence to particular traditions of teachers, as illustrated by the *sampradaya*s of the deity Viṣṇu, which trace their origin to eminent teachers such as Rāmānuja and Madhva. Similarly, the different groups united in devotion to Śiva trace their origin back to various ascetics. One of the subdivisions of the cult groups of Śiva, the Liṅgāyat, numbers four million members of different backgrounds, who wear the emblem of the phallus as the symbol of their cultic unity.

Similar cult-based communities, by no means as elaborate as the *sampradaya* of Hinduism, are found in many other parts of the world, from ancient Greece to modern Japan. At times, cult seems to be a stronger bond of unity than other features of religious life.

Religious orders/monastic communities/service societies. Important among voluntary groups within larger religious communities are religious orders, which are often, but not always, identified with monastic communities, and sometimes with service societies sponsored by or affiliated with religious bodies. In common English usage, the term *religious* not only connotes "scrupulously faithful" or "devout" but as a noun also refers to those who are bound by monastic vows or devoted to a life of piety and religion, such as monks, friars, and nuns. Similarly, the term *order* signifies a society of persons bound by some common rule, especially an aggregate of separate communities like a monastic brotherhood or community. The term *religious order* could, of course, designate a variety of holy orders that may not practice a monastic form of life. In this article, however, I shall discuss only those religious orders that come under the category of monastic communities. Similarly, of all the service societies under religious jurisdiction—societies for missionary work, teaching, and philanthropy, and others as well—only those that are organized as communities will be discussed.

Students of religions recognize various kinds of religious brotherhoods, guilds of priests, and monastic communities in different traditions, as for example the Pythagorean brotherhood in ancient Greece, the Bektashī order in Islam, and the Vedanta Society of modern India. Two religious traditions that have developed elaborate systems of monastic communities, Buddhism and Christianity, deserve special attention.

Although the early Buddhist community consisted of four components—monks *(bhikkhu* or *bhikṣu)*, nuns *(bhikkhunī* or *bhikṣuṇī)*, laymen *(upāsaka)*, and laywomen *(upāsikā)*—the most central group was the order of monks. Initially, the monastic order started as an informal assembly of wandering mendicants, but soon it developed into monastic communities in which monks shared a normative discipline (Vinaya). Under the patronage of King Aśoka in the third century BCE, monastic communities played an important role as missionaries propagating Buddhism. In the course of time, great monastic communities became centers of religious and secular education and of cultural activities. Although the Buddhist community divided into Southern (Hīnayāna or Theravāda) and Northern (Mahāyāna) traditions, each with further subdivisions along doctrinal and cultic lines, it was possible for monks of different schools to live in the same monastic communities.

In the main, the Southern tradition follows an elitist model: monks leave the secular world and enter monasteries for a life of full-time spiritual striving toward their own enlightenment, while the laity receives merit by supporting monastic communities. The most elaborate monastic hierarchy developed in Thailand, where the *sangharāja,* or ruler of the monastic community, was under no other authority except that of the king. In the modern period, the traditionally otherworldly monastic communities in the Southern tradition have become more involved in the affairs of the world. In the Northern tradition, on the other hand, the paths of monastics and laity were always regarded as different but equally important vocations. Mahāyāna monastic communities, inspired as they are by the compassionate bodhisattva ideal, stress active service to all beings.

Monastic communities in the Christian tradition are many and varied. Unlike communities in Western Christendom, Eastern Orthodox communities are not divided into different orders. Having originally developed out of informal fellowships of hermits who lived a life of prayer, they were transformed in the fourth century into monastic communities with three components: those who lead a monastic life without taking vows and two grades of monastics who take permanent vows (monks of "lesser" and "greater" habits). In Western Christendom, the *Rule of Saint Benedict* (c. 540) transformed earlier, loosely organized communities of hermits into disciplined monastic communities. The Rule provided the norm of communal life based on the daily offices, as followed by the Cluniacs and the Cistercians. Meanwhile, more activist orders of friars, such as the Franciscans and the Dominicans, appeared on the European scene. They were followed by the Society of Jesus (the Jesuits), which not only championed the cause of the Counter-Reformation at home but also initiated extensive missionary activities abroad. Both Eastern and Western traditions of Christianity comprise many orders of nuns. Like their male counterparts, some nuns are contemplative while others pursue educational and philanthropic vocations. [*See also* Monasticism.]

Utopian communities. Most religious communities have what might be characterized as utopian features or ideals. Many myths of tribal religious communities reflect their notion of the idealized celestial realm or the paradigmatic activities of gods and heroes at the beginning of time. Many historic religious communities affirm the existence of an ideal state either in their golden past or at the end of history. Philosophers like Confucius and Plato have also attempted to depict the ideal society on earth.

But in a more specific sense, the term *utopia* is derived from Thomas More's *On the Highest State of a Republic and on the New Island of Utopia* (1516). More's idea of an idealized society, realizable on earth, and his critique of the lamentable state of the world, continued to stir literary and religious imagination after his time. From the seventeenth century onward, a number of utopian communities have been established on either side of the Atlantic, including New Harmony in Indiana, Brook Farm in Massachusetts, and Oneida in New York. There have also been such religious utopian communities as the Dutch Mennonite colonies in Delaware, the German Pietist settlements in Indiana and Pennsylvania, and the Bruderhof communities in Germany, England, and North America.

For the most part, utopian elements in the Islamic, Buddhist, and Chinese traditions were absorbed into millenarian and eschatological ideologies, but they did not inspire the establishment of separate communal settlements. In modern Japan, however, a number of utopian communities inspired by Lev Tolstoi and several indigenous messianic cults have emerged. Modern Jewish settlements in Palestine, many of which took the form of *kibbutsim,* exhibit an intricate homology of religious, political, and social utopian features. Most of the "hippie" communes that emerged in America in the 1960s and 1970s can hardly be classified as religious utopian communities, but an increasing number of utopian communities are being generated in North America today by Christians, Theosophists, and new religious groups of diverse origins. [*See* Utopia.]

Conclusion. Religion, then, is both a personal matter and a social reality. Throughout the history of humankind, from the prehistoric period down to our own, religion has sought fellowship either by intensifying the existing social fabric—family, clan, tribe, caste, local or national community—or by creating specifically religious communities within, above, or apart from other social and political groupings and institutions. Despite their diversity, these groups all share that unconscious sense that makes them communities to which religious persons belong.

[*See also* Community.]

BIBLIOGRAPHY

Durkheim, Émile. *The Elementary Forms of the Religious Life* (1912). New York, 1965.

Evans-Pritchard, E. E. *Social Anthropology.* Glencoe, Ill., 1951.

Frankfort, Henri, Henriette A. Frankfort, John A. Wilson,

Thorkild Jacobsen, and William Irwin. *The Intellectual Adventure of Ancient Man.* Chicago, 1946.

Kitagawa, Joseph M. *Religions of the East.* Enl. ed. Philadelphia, 1968.

Leeuw, Gerardus van der. *Religion in Essence and Manifestation: A Study in Phenomenology* (1933). 2d ed. 2 vols. New York, 1963.

Möller, Christian, and Jacob Katz. "Gemeinde." In *Theologische Realenzyklopädie,* vol. 12, pts. 1–4, edited by Gerhard Krause and Gerhard Müller. Berlin and New York, 1983.

Niebuhr, H. Richard. *The Social Sources of Denominationalism* (1929). New York, 1972.

Popkes, Wiard. "Gemeinschaft." In *Reallexikon für Antike und Christentum,* vol. 9, edited by Theodor Klauser. Stuttgart, 1973–1976.

Redfield, Robert. *The Primitive World and Its Transformations.* Ithaca, N.Y., 1953.

Ringeling, Herman. "Gemeinschaft." In *Theologische Realenzyklopädie,* vol. 12, pts. 1–4, edited by Gerhard Krause and Gerhard Müller. Berlin and New York, 1983.

Thraede, Klaus. "Gesellschaft." In *Reallexikon für Antike und Christentum,* vol. 10, edited by Theodor Klauser. Stuttgart, 1976–1978.

Tönnies, Ferdinand. *Community and Society* (1887). East Lansing, Mich., 1957.

Troeltsch, Ernst. *The Social Teachings of the Christian Churches* (1931). Chicago, 1981.

Turner, Victor. *The Ritual Process: Structure and Anti-Structure* (1969). Ithaca, N.Y., 1977.

Wach, Joachim. *Sociology of Religion* (1944). Chicago, 1962.

Waszink, J. H., Carsten Colpe, and Bernhard Kötting. "Genossenschaft." In *Reallexikon für Antike und Christentum,* vol. 10, edited by Theodor Klauser. Stuttgart, 1976–1978.

Weber, Max. *The Sociology of Religion* (1922). Boston, 1963.

Wilson, Bryan R. *Religion in Sociological Perspective.* Oxford, 1982.

Yinger, J. Milton. *Religion, Society and the Individual: An Introduction to the Sociology of Religion.* New York, 1957.

Joseph M. Kitagawa

Christian Religious Orders

Christians have used the term *religious order* in both a narrow, technical sense and a broader, more common one. Popularly, religious orders are thought to include any and all men or women who profess public vows of poverty, chastity, and obedience; follow a common rule of life; engage in a specific kind of work (e.g., teaching, nursing, missionary endeavor); and submit to the directions of superiors who may be either appointed by higher ecclesiastical authority or elected in some manner by the order's members. In this broad sense, virtually all religious communities of Christian men and women may be referred to as orders, but more technically, a religious order is qualified by certain conditions that do not necessarily affect all Christians who choose a life of prayer and service in community with others.

Three qualifications have commonly been attached to this narrower meaning of a religious order: the public profession of "solemn" (as opposed to "simple") vows; an obligation to celebrate publicly each day the Liturgy of the Hours (a pattern of psalms, hymns, scripture readings, and prayers attached to specific times of day and night), and restriction to a cloister or "enclosure" (a defined space, often identified with the physical limits of the monastery or convent, within which members live and from which all outsiders are excluded). [*See* Monasticism.] In history and practice, however, these qualifications have been neither rigid nor absolute. The Society of Jesus (Jesuits) has been regarded in Western church law as a religious order in the strict sense, even though its members have never been cloistered. Similarly, the exact distinction between solemn and simple vows, unknown before the thirteenth century, has never been entirely clear either to theologians or to experts in church law. In common theory, a solemn vow has been defined as a free, irrevocable promise made to God that binds the individual forever and renders certain actions opposed to the vows (e.g., marriage as opposed to celibacy; the ownership of property as opposed to poverty) not only illicit but null and invalid as well. A simple vow, in contrast, is regarded as having a less absolute character and may thus be made for a limited period of time (e.g., for one year or three years). In practice, however, the distinction blurs, since people may make simple vows in perpetuity, while those who have made irrevocable solemn vows may be released from them through a legal process known as dispensation.

The term *religious order* is more commonly used by Western Christians (e.g., Roman Catholics or members of Protestant communions) than by Eastern Christians (e.g., Greek or Russian Orthodox). Even within the Roman Catholic church, where attention to the precise legal status of religious vows and communities has been examined and evaluated for centuries, ambiguities still exist. Catholic members of religious orders are subject to the definitions and provisions of the Code of Canon Law (1983).

Origins. For centuries, Christian apologists have attempted to find a basis for religious orders in the historical ministry and teaching of Jesus. An early example may be seen in the *Life of Antony* by Athanasius (c. 298–373), which reports Antony of Egypt's (c. 250–355) conversion to a solitary life of prayer and asceticism after hearing Jesus' words in church: "If you would be perfect, go, sell what you possess and give to the poor . . . and come, follow me" (*Mt.* 19:21). This biography helped spread monastic ideals throughout the Roman empire and encouraged the notion that to live alone with God, apart from all human company, is the supreme Christian response to Jesus' message.

There is no clear evidence that Jesus himself observed or promoted the ascetic life, or directly invited or commanded his followers to choose a life of poverty, celibacy, and obedience to human superiors. Central to Jesus' understanding of the relation between God and humankind was the conviction that God's reign (or kingdom) could break in upon the world at any time in any place—and that this reign would guarantee blessing and happiness for those open to receive it. Significant among the traditions associated with Jesus' life and collected in the Gospels are stories that show Jesus enjoying certain events (parties, dinners) and associating with people not ordinarily linked with an ascetic way of living (sinners, prostitutes).

While the remote origins of religious orders cannot be directly assigned to Jesus, possible antecedents to Christian asceticism may be discerned in both Judaism and the Greco-Roman world. Some members of the circle that gathered around John the Baptist probably adhered to a life of strict self-denial and repentance as preparation for God's impending judgment of the world. Most notable among Jewish antecedents were the sectarians of Qumran near the Dead Sea, whose collection of writings, the Dead Sea Scrolls, was discovered in 1947. Many scholars have identified the Qumran sectarians with a Jewish ascetic group known as the Essenes, who are mentioned by Philo of Alexandria (c. 13 BC–AD 45–50), Josephus the Jewish historian (c. AD 37–100), and Pliny the Elder (AD 23–79). Their descriptions show that the Essenes not only existed during Jesus' time but had developed a highly organized manner of life, which included an arduous three-year novitiate for newcomers, sharing of goods, celibacy, and strict obedience to authorities. [*See* Asceticism *and* Essenes.]

Similar to the Essenes was an Egyptian Jewish group of ascetics called the Therapeutae, whose principal center was a hill just outside Alexandria above Lake Mareotis. Among ancient writers, only Philo describes them. If his report is reliable, the Therapeutae were distinguished from more active groups like the Essenes by their strict seclusion. Each member of the sect seems to have had a separate dwelling, within which a special room was set aside for the daily study of scripture. Weekly, on the Sabbath, members met for common worship, while once every seven weeks a solemn feast, marked by a ritual meal eaten in silence and by the wearing of white clothing, was celebrated. The Therapeutae appear to have been celibate, though persons previously married were permitted to join them. Members were also expected to abjure the use of money, share goods in common, and keep bodily needs to a minimum.

Though the Therapeutae were Jewish, they can hardly have escaped influence from Greek philosophical traditions, especially in the region around Alexandria, the intellectual center of the Hellenistic world in the first century AD. In both the first century BC and the first century AD, there were non-Jewish ascetic movements inspired by philosophers like Pythagoras (c. 580–500 BC) and the Neo-Pythagoreans. Pythagoras himself is thought to have established a quasi-religious "club" or school in Croton, Italy, which fostered secret initiation ceremonies, communal sharing of goods, vows, and a vegetarian diet. Neo-Pythagoreans were particularly interested in religious life and theology, and they probably exerted influence upon both Judaism, through Philo of Alexandria, and early Christianity, through Clement of Alexandria (150?–215?).

While the extent of Jewish and Greco-Roman influence on the origins of Christian asceticism is difficult to assess, at least some early Christian congregations are known to have prized celibacy, if freely chosen for religious motives. In the *First Letter to the Corinthians* (c. 57), Paul encourages celibacy as a means of giving undivided attention to the Lord (*1 Cor.* 7:25–35). Because in Christ the final age of salvation has dawned for the world, Paul argues, even married Christians should behave in a manner that leaves them unencumbered by the business and burdens of the world (*1 Cor.* 7:29–31). Similarly, an earlier letter of Paul's to the congregation at Thessalonica (c. 51) had encouraged all Christians to pursue constant prayer and watchfulness (*1 Thes.* 5:1–17), practices later linked to monasticism and the ascetic life.

Before the end of the New Testament period, a distinct body of persons dedicated to prayer, celibacy, and charitable service within the congregation was recognized and regulated by church leaders. The widows described in the *First Letter to Timothy* appear to have been such a body. Widows were expected to be at least sixty years old, to be married only once, to be devoted to hospitality and the care of others, and to attend faithfully regular meetings for prayer and worship. In return, they could expect to receive material support from the congregation. Once admitted to the group, widows were to remain celibate; thus younger women who lost their husbands were advised to remarry (*1 Tm.* 5:11–15).

These examples reveal that the earliest Christians did not think an ascetic way of life should involve separation from the rest of the community. The celibate widows of the *First Letter to Timothy* are organized for the edification and service of the local community; they do not take vows, nor are they set apart through a public ceremony. Neither the widows nor the virgins mentioned by Paul in *1 Corinthians* are seen as having "superiors" distinct from the ordinary local leaders of the congregation. And nowhere in the New Testament are Christians advised to withdraw into solitary isolation.

Historical Development. Despite early Christian deemphasis on an ascetic way of life separate from the community, the notion that some Christians might be called to a life of extraordinary dedication to God gained ground—and with it the related idea that such a life was more perfect than that of other believers. Both Clement of Alexandria, head of an important Christian school in Alexandria in the late second century, and his pupil Origen (c. 185–c. 254) were enthusiastic for ascetic ideals. Strongly influenced by the philosophy of Middle Platonism, both Clement and Origen spoke rapturously of the "true Christian gnostic" whose knowledge (Gr., *gnōsis*) is perfectly illuminated by faith in Christ, God's Logos (the Greek *logos* meaning both "word" and "reason"). In his commentary on the *Song of Songs*, Origen traced the stages of growth in the Christian's interior life and seemed to suggest that certain degrees of contemplative intimacy with Christ were possible only for the "perfect"—and that such perfect believers were a breed apart from the rest of the community.

Neither Clement nor Origen intended to create sectarian divisions within the church, nor did they want to pit groups of perfect Christians against less perfect ones in a battle for perfection. Still, their discussions of spiritual growth could be interpreted by less subtle thinkers as meaning that the truest Christians are celibate ascetics, while all others are innately inferior. It is not insignificant that Latin Christian writers of this period like Tertullian (c. 160?–225?) and Cyprian of Carthage (third century) also began producing works devoted to the praise of virginity as an ideal state for Christians.

By the fourth century, ascetic ideals were securely entrenched, as was the notion that Christians might legitimately withdraw from society and church in a solitary pursuit of perfection. The example of Antony has already been mentioned. Changes in the relation between church and culture after the emperor Constantine's Edict of Milan (313), which recognized Christianity as a licit religion in the empire, created a new situation. Some Christians felt that acceptance of their religion by the empire posed a serious threat to devout living and perfect union with God. Martyrdom, the oldest form of Christian heroism and a symbol of utmost dedication to God, was displaced by celibate asceticism, a spiritual sacrifice of ultimate value. Numerous ascetic movements began in the fourth century; virgins and monks became the "new martyrs" in an imperialized Christianity.

This notion of protest leads directly to the question of monastic origins. For a long time scholars assumed that Christian monasticism began as an exclusively eremitical phenomenon in Egypt, with people like Antony, and that it spread from there to other parts of the world. Cenobitic monasticism (monks living in community with other monks) was thought to have developed in a similar way, beginning with Pachomius (c. 293?–346) and his cenobitic foundation in the Thebaid near the Nile River (c. 320), but recent scholarship has shown that this hypothesis about monastic origins is untenable. A more likely theory is that monastic life, in both its eremitical and cenobitic forms, developed simultaneously in many different parts of the ancient world—Egypt, Syria, Palestine, Cappadocia, Mesopotamia. [*See* Eremitism.]

The work of Pachomius was extremely influential because it provided an organized pattern of community life for men and women who wished to devote themselves both to asceticism and to service of others. Pachomian monks met twice daily for prayer and scripture-reading, but they also worked hard, raised their own food, engaged in handicrafts, shipped grain and products down the Nile to Alexandria, cared for orphans and the elderly, and nursed the sick. When Pachomius died in 346, there were eleven cenobitic monasteries, nine for men and two for women.

Elsewhere the development of organized monastic life encountered greater difficulty. In Cappadocia, Basil of Caesarea (c. 329–379) struggled to keep Christian ascetics from both sectarian eccentricity and heretical separation from the church. In that region, the legitimacy of ascetic life had been compromised by the unbalanced views of Eustathius of Sebaste (c. 300–377), who repudiated marriage for Christians, rejected the ministry of married clergy, and encouraged ascetics to hold their own worship services apart from those of the larger church. These views were denounced by the Council of Gangra (c. 345). Through his *Moral Rules* (c. 360) and his *Longer Rules* and *Shorter Rules* (c. 370), Basil tried to root Christian asceticism in texts drawn from the Bible. Rejecting sectarianism of the Eustathian sort, Basil affirmed the necessity of ascetic principles for all Christians and insisted that ascetics should remain close to the life and worship of the local congregation. Eastern Christian monks and nuns still regard Basil's rules as the fundamental charter for their way of life.

In the fourth century in the West, interest in asceticism and monastic life flourished. Jerome (c. 347–420) informs us that a disciplined ascetic life, especially for virgins and widows, was well known in Rome and elsewhere in Italy. Bishop Ambrose of Milan (c. 339–397) is known to have consecrated virgins and also to have acted as patron for a monastery of men just outside Milan. Martin of Tours (c. 316–397), traditionally if inaccurately known as "the first monk in the West," promoted monasticism in western France, while in the south, Lérins (actually two islands just off the coast from Cannes) became an influential monastic center after Honoratus, bishop of Arles (d. 429), established a monastery there around the year 410.

In Roman North Africa, too, monasticism was expanding. Augustine of Hippo (354–430) provided advice and structural organization for communities of men and women. His rule (reconstructed from three separate documents) emphasizes such ideals as common ownership of property, communal prayer several times each day, simplicity in food and clothing, manual labor, celibacy, and obedience. At a later period, the Augustinian rule was adopted by groups known as "canons regular" (see below).

The most significant figure in Western monasticism was Benedict of Nursia (c. 480–547). Though almost nothing certain is known of his life, the rule (c. 530) that bears his name became so widely respected that it eventually supplanted most other Western monastic legislation and remains the foundation for the Benedictine order to this day. While it does not reject the eremitical life, the *Rule of Saint Benedict* clearly prefers cenobitic living and proposes a pattern that balances prayer, scripture-reading, rest, and manual labor in almost equal proportion under the government of an abbot responsible to God for the welfare of each individual in the monastery.

Benedictine monasticism, like the other ascetic movements described so far, was primarily "lay" rather than clerical in character. Many early ascetics like Pachomius and Jerome were in fact politely hostile toward the clergy, and while sixth-century documents like Benedict's rule permit ordained people to seek admission to the monastery, they include stern warnings against clerical pride and privilege. After the ninth century especially, it became common to ordain most Benedictine monks to the priesthood, but this practice was a departure from the rule and from earlier tradition.

Like many movements, Christian monasticism periodically needed reform, sometimes to correct abuse, at other times to reinvigorate or redefine ideals. In the West, especially from the time of Charlemagne (r. 768–814) onward, periodic reforms resulted in changes within monasticism and occasionally in the creation of new religious orders. Benedict of Aniane (c. 750–821) helped reorganize monasticism in the Carolingian empire by promoting exclusive allegiance to the Benedictine rule. Toward the end of the eleventh century, the reforming efforts of Gregory VII (r. 1073–1085) had two important effects: the reform of groups known as "canons regular" and the emergence of a new monastic order, the Cistercians. These latter stem from the Monastery of Cîteaux, founded in 1098 by Robert of Molesmes and made most famous by Bernard of Clairvaux, who joined it in 1112. Reacting against the wealth and prestige of Benedictine houses like Cluny (founded in 909), the Cistercians hoped to recall monks to a stricter, more primitive observance of monastic life. The Cistercian order still exists, though it was later reformed by Armond-Jean de Rancé (1626–1700) at the Abbey of La Trappe (hence the name Trappists).

The reform of canons regular, whose way of life had already been organized by Chrodegang of Metz (d. 766) in the eighth century, resulted in adoption of Augustine's rule by groups such as the Augustinian Canons (papal approval in 1059 and 1063) and the Canons of Prémontré (Norbertines, after Norbert, who founded them in 1120). Unlike monks, who were originally laity, canons were from the beginning a body of clergy who lived in common and ministered with the bishop at a diocesan cathedral. As a result of the eleventh-century reforms, canons assumed many features of monastic life (including an abbatial structure of government), much as monks had taken on many characteristics of clerical life.

It was a Spanish canon regular, Dominic (c. 1170–1221), who was largely responsible, along with Francis of Assisi (1181/2–1226), for the emergence of a new type of religious order in the West—the "mendicant friars." Unlike either canons (clergy) or monks (originally lay, but bound to one place by a vow of stability), the mendicants could move about freely to carry on tasks of teaching, preaching, studying, and serving the poor. Dominic's Order of Preachers quickly gained a reputation for scholarship, especially in the thirteenth-century universities. Thomas Aquinas (c. 1225–1274), the great theologian, was an early and brilliant exponent of Dominican ideals, while his contemporary at the University of Paris was Bonaventure (c. 1217–1274), a Franciscan. Like the Augustinian and Norbertine canons, the Dominican and Franciscan friars still exist, with members working in many parts of the world.

In 1215, the Fourth Lateran Council forbade the creation of more religious orders, though in fact new communities have continued to emerge up to the present time. Perhaps the most significant of these newer groups were the "congregations" of religious men and women that appeared after the Council of Trent (1545–1563). Some leaders at Trent appeared to agree with the Protestant reformers and sought to abolish religious orders altogether. But the work of people like Antonio Maria Zaccaria (1502–1539, founder of the Barnabites in 1530), and later of Francis de Sales (1567–1622) and Jeanne-Françoise de Chantal (1572–1641), founders of the Visitation sisters, helped convince doubters that viable new religious communities were possible. Most of these newer groups stressed active participation in church and society through works like teaching, nursing, care of orphans, and assistance to the needy.

In the nineteenth and twentieth centuries, religious orders also appeared in some Protestant communions, such as the Church of England. A monastic community of men, the Society of Saint John the Evangelist (Cowley Fathers), was founded in 1865 by Richard M. Benson while in 1907, the Sisters of the Love of God were established as a cloistered, contemplative community for women at Fairacres, Oxford. Among Roman Catholics, the Second Vatican Council (1962–1965) caused sweeping changes in religious orders. Old styles of clothing (the religious habit), government (methods of choosing superiors, their terms of office, the practice of obedience), and local customs (rules of fasting, silence, prayer) have been modernized or abandoned. For some orders these changes have brought dwindling memberships, while others have continued to grow.

[*See also* Benedictines; Cistercians; Dominicans; Franciscans; Jesuits; *and the biographies of religious leaders mentioned herein. For discussion of the architecture of Christian religious communities, see* Monastery.]

BIBLIOGRAPHY

Annuario Pontificio. Vatican City, 1716–. An annual publication available in most large libraries; includes statistics on Roman Catholic religious orders, together with further information about their founders and origins.

Brown, Peter. "The Rise and Function of the Holy Man in Late Antiquity." *Journal of Roman Studies* 61 (1971): 80–101. A seminal article that studies the complex and changing relations between structures of civil authority in the ancient world and the emerging ascetic heroes and heroines of Christianity.

Brown, Peter. *The World of Late Antiquity, AD 150–750.* New York, 1971. An excellent survey of the people and places that constituted the world within which Christian religious orders first developed, written for the nonspecialist.

Campenhausen, Hans von. "Early Christian Asceticism." In his *Tradition and Life in the Church,* pp. 9–122. Philadelphia, 1968. A penetrating study of the origins of asceticism among Christians by a respected Protestant biblical scholar and church historian.

Chitty, Derwas J. *The Desert a City.* Oxford, 1966. Examines the origins of asceticism and monastic life with special attention to developments in the Christian East.

Gribomont, Jean. "Le monachisme au quatrième siècle en Asie Mineure: De Gangres au Messalianisme." In *Studia Patristica,* vol. 2, pp. 400–415. Berlin, 1957. An important essay that reexamines and repudiates earlier hypotheses about the origins and early evolution of Christian monasticism.

Knowles, David. *The Religious Orders in England.* 3 vols. Cambridge, 1948–1959. An exhaustive study of the history of religious orders in the West, with special attention to their development in the British Isles.

Knowles, David. *Christian Monasticism.* New York, 1969. A brief and lucid exposition of the entire history of Christian monastic life.

The Rule of St. Benedict, RB 1980. Collegeville, Minn., 1980. Latin text of the Benedictine rule with English translation by Timothy Fry and extensive commentaries, notes, and essays on the history of Christian religious life by Imogene Baker, published by American Benedictine monks and nuns on the occasion of Benedict's sesquimillennium.

Southern, Richard W. *Western Society and the Church in the Middle Ages.* Harmondsworth, 1970. See pages 214–299 for a succinct but comprehensive account of the rise of newer religious orders in the medieval West.

Veilleux, Armand. "The Abbatial Office in Cenobitic Life." *Monastic Studies* 6 (1968): 3–45. An important study of government, authority, and obedience in Christian monastic life.

Veilleux, Armand. "Évolution de la vie religieuse dans son contexte historico-spirituel." *Collectanea Cisterciensia* 32 (1970): 129–154. A brilliant and comprehensive survey of all Christian religious orders, with special attention to the social and cultural conditions within which they arose.

NATHAN D. MITCHELL

RELIGIOUS DIVERSITY.

[*This entry examines the origins and differing patterns of development of the world's major religious traditions, as well as the varying patterns of interaction between these religions and the social, political, and economic frameworks with which they coexist. For discussion of philosophical problems engendered by the existence of divergent religious traditions, see* Religious Pluralism.]

Religion and religious conceptions, beyond being systems of belief and patterns of worship, constitute a central component, as Max Weber pointed out, in the construction of the basic symbolic and institutional premises of societies and civilizations. In this article I shall explore systematically the relationship between several crucial aspects of religions and the construction of institutional features of societies and civilizations.

"Pagan" and "Great" Religions. I shall concentrate on the analysis of a basic distinction between two broad types of religions: the so-called pagan religions (without, for reasons of space, going into the many differences between them) and the "great" religions (with some distinctions drawn from within the latter). I shall explore some of the major ways in which some of the basic characteristics of these religions, especially of the religious belief systems, have shaped the contours of the respective civilizations in which they were institutionalized.

The societies in which different types of pagan religions were predominant have, of course, been many, and they include all tribal or preliterate societies, as well as many so-called archaic ones such as those of the ancient Near and Middle East, South and Southeast Asia, Japan, Mesoamerica, and many others.

The civilizations shaped by the great religions were denoted by Karl Jaspers in his work *Vom Ursprung und Ziel der Geschichte* (1949), as the "Axial Age" civilizations, including ancient Israel, ancient Greece, the early Christian world, Zoroastrian Iran, early imperial China, the Hindu and Buddhist civilizations, and, though postdating the Axial Age proper, the Islamic world.

The central distinction between these two broad types of religions is focused on the nature of the perception and definition of the relationship between what is mundane, or "given," and what is "transmundane" (otherworldly).

In all human societies, the transmundane order has been perceived as somewhat different, usually higher and stronger, than the mundane one. In pre–Axial Age, pagan civilizations, this higher world was symbolically structured according to principles very similar to those of the mundane or lower one; in other words, there existed a high degree of homology between them. Relatively similar symbolic terms or connotations were used for the definitions of both gods and man and for both the mundane and transmundane orders, even if there always was a stress on the differences between them. In such societies the transmundane world was usually equated with a concrete setting, "the otherworld," which was the abode of the dead, the world of spirits, not entirely unlike the mundane world in detail.

By contrast, in the Axial Age civilizations, the perception of a sharp disjunction between the mundane and transmundane worlds developed. There was a concomitant stress on the existence of a higher, transcendental moral or metaphysical order that is beyond any given this-worldly or otherworldly reality.

On the symbolic or ideological level the development of these conceptions gives rise to the problem of salvation, to use Weber's terminology. The roots of the quest for salvation are manifest in the consciousness of death and the arbitrariness of human actions and social arrangements. The search for some type of immortality and a way to overcome such arbitrariness are universal to all societies. In societies where the mundane and transmundane worlds are defined in relatively homologous terms, the search for immortality has generally been envisaged in terms of some physical continuity; it is usually seen as conditional to the fulfillment of one's concrete obligation to one's group.

This no longer holds true for civilizations where there is an emphasis on the chasm between the transcendental and the mundane order and a conception of a higher moral or metaphysical order. While the concept of immortality in such civilizations may or may not still be tied to bodily images and to ideas of physical resurrection, the very possibility of some continuity beyond this world is usually seen in terms of the reconstruction of human behavior and personality. This reconstruction tends to be based on the precepts of the higher moral or metaphysical order through which the chasm between the transcendental and mundane orders is bridged; as Gananath Obeyesekere has put it, rebirth eschatology becomes ethicized.

Structure of Axial Age Elites. The conceptions outlined above were developed and articulated by a relatively new social element, a new type of intellectual elite, which became aware of the necessity of actively ordering the world according to some transcendental vision. The best illustrations of such elites are the Jewish prophets and priests, the Greek philosophers and Sophists, the Chinese literati, the Hindu brahmans, the Buddhist *saṃgha*, and the Islamic *'ulamā'*. These new elites, which developed in conjunction with the process of institutionalization of these visions, generally differed from the ritual, magical, and sacral specialists of the pre–Axial Age civilizations. Intellectuals and clerics alike were recruited and legitimized according to distinct criteria, and were organized in autonomous settings, apart from those of their basic ascriptive units. They acquired a society-wide status of their own. They also tended to become independent of other categories of elites and social groups and competed strongly with these others, especially over the articulation and control of symbols and media of communication. Such competition became intensive because a parallel transformation had taken place in the structure of other elites, who also developed claims for an autonomous place in the construction of the cultural and social order. They saw themselves not only as performing specific technical, functional activities, but also as the potential carriers of a distinct cultural and social order related to the transcendental vision prevalent in their respective societies. The nonpolitical cultural elites and the political elites each saw themselves as the autonomous articulators of the new order, with the other type potentially inferior to and accountable to themselves.

Moreover neither of these groups of elites was homogenous. There developed a multiplicity of secondary cultural, political, and educational elites, each of which often carried a different conception of the cultural and social order. These elites were the most active in the restructuring of the world and the institutional creativity that developed in these societies.

Construction of Axial Age Societies. Common to all these elites were several tendencies with respect to the restructuring of the world and the construction of personality, civilization, and social order according to a transcendental vision and the principles of a higher metaphysical, ethical, or sacred order.

The given, mundane order was perceived in these civilizations as incomplete, inferior, and even in need of being reconstructed according to the conception of salvation, or the bridging of the chasm between the transcendental and the mundane orders.

Personal identity was usually taken beyond the definition of man in terms of the primordial givens of human existence, beyond the various technical needs of daily activities, to be constructed around the central mode or modes of human action through which the tensions between the transcendental and the mundane order are resolved. Purely personal virtues, such as courage, or interpersonal ones, such as solidarity, mutual help, and the like, have been taken out of their primordial (i.e., given) framework and combined in different, often dialectical, modes with the attributes needed to enact such a resolution. This combination resulted in a new level of tensions in the structure of the personality.

These conceptions also had far-reaching implications for institutions. The most common has been the high degree of symbolic and ideological orientation of the major aspects of institutional structure, manifest in the construction of distinct civilizational frameworks, collectivities, and autonomous centers, as well as the growth of conceptions of the accountability of rulers and new patterns of political struggle.

Civilizational collectivities. Some collectivities and institutional spheres (for instance, political, military, or economic) were singled out as the most appropriate carriers of these attributes that were required for resolution. As a result, new types of collectivities were created, or seemingly natural and "primordial" groups were endowed with special status couched in terms of the perception of the tension between the transcendental and mundane order and its resolution. In this context, the most important innovation was the development of cultural or religious collectivities—as distinct from ethnic or political ones—even if some embryonic elements of this development existed in some of those societies where this tension had not been institutionalized. The membership of these collectivities tended to become imbued with a strong ideological orientation and to become involved in ideological struggle. An aspect of this struggle was the insistence on the exclusiveness and closure of the group, and on the distinction between inner and outer social and cultural space as defined by it. This led to attempts to structure the different cultural, political, and ethnic collectivities in some hierarchical order, which usually became a focus of ideological and political conflict.

Centers and center-periphery relations. Related to the construction of such major collectivities was the tendency toward the development of autonomous organization of the social centers and toward a relatively strong emphasis on the symbolic distinctiveness of the centers in relation to the periphery. Such centers have been conceived as the major loci of the charismatic attributes of the transcendental vision, and hence also of the construction of cultural and societal orders. These attributes of centrality became naturally related to the institutional spheres that show the closest affinity to the focus of the transcendental tension, and the centers most closely related to these spheres became autonomous and distinct from the periphery.

At the same time, the symbolic differentiation of the center gave rise to its tendency to permeate the periphery and to reorganize it according to its own, autonomous criteria. Carriers of the great traditions attempted to pull the little traditions into their orbit, and the latter tried to dissociate themselves from the great traditions, to profane them, and also, paradoxically enough, to generate their own distinct ideology.

In all these civilizations (as distinct from pre–Axial Age civilizations) there also took place a far-reaching reordering of the relationship between the political and the higher, transcendental order. The political order, as the central locus of the mundane order, was usually conceived as lower than the transcendental one; accordingly it had to be restructured according to the precepts of the latter. Above all, the political order had to reflect the perception of the proper mode of overcoming the tension between the transcendental and the mundane order (i.e., "salvation").

At the same time the nature of the rulers became greatly transformed. The king-god, who embodied the cosmic and earthly orders alike, disappeared, and a secular ruler, in principle accountable to some higher order, appeared. Thus there reemerged the conception of the accountability of the rulers and of the community to a higher authority—God, divine law, and the like. Accordingly, the possibility of calling a ruler to judgment emerged.

Autonomous spheres of law and conceptions of human rights also began to develop. These tended to be somewhat distinct from ascriptively bound custom and from purely customary law, and while their scope varied greatly from society to society, all were established according to some distinct and autonomous criteria.

Parallel developments have also taken place in the

structuring of social hierarchies and the economy, which became imbued in varying degrees and modes with broader ideological dimensions.

Dynamics of Axial Age civilizations. All these modes of reconstruction of the social and civilizational orders were not, however, static; indeed they were the focus of continuous struggle and change, and cannot be understood except in connection with the tensions inherent in the institutionalization of the tension between the transcendental and the mundane order as well as of the quest to overcome it. Such institutionalization generated an awareness of a great range of possibilities or visions of the very definition of such tensions; of the proper mode of their resolution as well as an awareness of the partiality or incompleteness of any given institutionalization of such vision. Historically, institutionalization was never a simple or peaceful process. It has usually been connected with a continuous struggle among many groups and their respective visions.

Once the conception of a basic tension between the transcendental and the mundane order was fully recognized and institutionalized in a society, or at least within its center, any definition and resolution of this tension became in itself very problematic. It usually contained strong heterogeneous and even contradictory elements, and its elaboration in fully articulated terms generated the possibility of different emphases, directions, and interpretations, all of which have been reinforced by the historical existence of multiple visions carried by different groups. Because of this, no single vision could be taken as given or complete.

This multiplicity of alternative visions gave rise to an awareness of the uncertainty of different roads to salvation, of alternative conceptions of social and cultural order, and of the seeming arbitrariness of any single solution. Such awareness has become a constituent element of the self-consciousness of these civilizations, especially among the carriers of the great traditions. This was closely related to the development of a high degree of "second order" thinking, of a reflexivity turning on the basic premises of the social and cultural orders.

Another element common to all these civilizations emerged from the combination of the conception of possible ways of salvation, alternative cultural and social orders, and the structuring of time. This element is the utopian vision: an alternative cultural and social order beyond any given place or time. Such visions contain many of the millenarian and revivalist elements that can also be found in pagan religions, but they go beyond them by realizing the necessity of constructing the mundane order according to the precepts of the higher one, and of searching for an alternative, "better" order beyond any given time and place.

The full impact of these dynamics can be understood only in connection with the nature of the social groups that were most active in the structuring of these civilizations, the major societal elites that developed within them, and the various autonomous intellectual and political elites mentioned above.

Of crucial importance for my analysis are the following facts: these elites were, as I have indicated above, heterogeneous; they were in constant competition with one another; and they were members not only of the ruling coalition, but also were the most active element in the movements of protest and processes of change that developed in these societies. They were above all involved in the construction of new sects and heterodoxies that upheld various alternative visions and conceptions of the social and cultural order and that became closely connected with the struggle among different elites, indeed often becoming the foci of such struggle. Because of this connection there emerged in these civilizations the possibility of structural and ideological linkages among different movements of protest and foci of political conflict (particularly rebellions, central political struggle, and religious or intellectual heterodoxies), and the possibility that all such movements, as well as sects and heterodoxies, would influence the center or centers of the society.

It is thus that there developed a new type of civilizational dynamics that transformed group conflicts into potential class and ideological conflicts and cult conflicts into struggles between the orthodox and the heterodox. Conflicts between tribes and societies became missionary crusades for the transformation of civilizations. The zeal for reorganization, as shaped by each society's concept of salvation, made the whole world at least potentially subject to cultural-political reconstruction. In all these new developments the different sectarian movements and heterodoxies played a central role.

Differences between Axial Age civilizations. Beyond the characteristics common to all the Axial Age civilizations, far-reaching differences developed among them. These were shaped by many conditions, two of which have been of special importance from the point of view of my analysis. One refers to variations in the basic cultural orientations, in the basic ideas or visions concerning civilizations, and their implications for institutions. The other set of conditions refers to different social arenas in which these institutional tendencies can be played out.

First of all, among the various cultural orientations there are crucial differences in the very definition of the tension between the transcendental and mundane orders and the modes of resolving this tension. There is the distinction between those cases in which the tension was couched in relatively secular terms (as in Confucianism and other classical Chinese belief systems and, in a somewhat different way, in the Greek and Roman worlds), and those cases in which the tension was conceived in terms of a distance between basic religious terms (as in the great monotheistic religions, Hinduism, and Buddhism).

A second distinction within the latter cases is that between the monotheistic religions, in which there was a concept of God standing outside the universe and potentially guiding it, and those systems, like Hinduism and Buddhism, in which the transcendental, cosmic system was conceived in impersonal, almost metaphysical terms, in a state of continuous existential tension with the mundane system.

Another closely related distinction lies in the focus of the resolution of the transcendental tensions, or, again in Weberian terms, salvation. Here the distinction is among purely this-worldly, purely otherworldly, and mixed this-worldly and otherworldly conceptions. It is probably no accident that the secular conception of salvation was connected (as in China and to some degree in the ancient world) with an almost wholly this-worldly approach, while the metaphysical, nondeistic conception of this tension (as in Hinduism and Buddhism), tended toward an otherworldly conception of salvation, and the great monotheistic religions tended to stress combinations of this-worldly and otherworldly conceptions.

These cultural orientations, as articulated by different elites, shaped to a very high degree the symbolic autonomy and characteristics of the new types of elites and ruling coalitions that characterized the post–Axial-Age civilizations. That is, they shaped the relations between them, their place in the ruling coalitions, the modes of control of the major institutional spheres effected by them, and the degree to which different ruling elites, secondary elites, and heterodoxies became involved with processes of societal change and transformation. The differences in the cultural orientations and structure of elites in various Axial Age civilizations had far-reaching impact on their institutions, structure, and dynamics—above all on the structure of centers, of center-periphery relations, and of collectivities—as well as on patterns of societal and civilizational change.

Otherworldly Axial Age civilizations. In most otherworldly civilizations there developed patrimonial regimes, to some degree similar to those that can be found in pre–Axial Age civilizations, yet with some crucial differences.

Such systems were characterized by a relatively low level of economic development, weak internal markets, a stronger orientation toward external markets, and strong extractive policies as well as, on the whole, a low degree of coalescence between the boundaries of the collectivities and the civilizational frameworks. The predominant coalitions within these systems were composed of relatively nonautonomous political and religious elites. The latter were also nonautonomous in most pagan societies, and in the post–Axial Age civilizations they were autonomous in the religious but not the political field.

In a parallel manner, the patrimonial societies were characterized by a relative lack of structural (as compared with ecological and symbolic) distinctiveness of the center from the periphery and usually by an adaptive attitude of the center toward the periphery. Within these patrimonial societies there generally developed a lower degree of society-wide class consciousness and symbolic articulation of the major types of collectivities.

The major distinction between those patrimonial regimes of the great post–Axial Age civilizations (Hindu, Buddhist, Islamic, and Latin American Catholic) and those that belonged to pagan civilizations lay first of all in the fact that the major types of elites (cultural and political alike) in the latter case were embedded in basic ascriptive frameworks, whereas in the former, the religious elites (and the political ones to a smaller degree, as in the Latin American Spanish empire) were autonomous mainly in the religious sphere. The carriers of the cultural and social order were those cultural elites that developed the great traditions and special, broader civilizational frameworks based on a strong perception of the tension between the transcendental and the mundane orders, the likes of which could not be found among the other pagan patrimonial regimes. Concomitantly, those elites created centers that were distinct from their own periphery in the religious sphere, as well as special interlinking networks between these centers and the periphery.

Hence these societies tended to develop more compact and dynamic political regimes (of which one type was the Theravāda Buddhistic gallactic polity as analyzed by Stanley J. Tambiah) while at the same time the national communities became imbued with stronger universal religious symbols. In times of crisis the religious elites also developed some autonomous activities.

Opposed to this development, in Axial Age civilizations in which a this-worldly orientation (as in China), or a mixed this-worldly and otherworldly orientation (as in the Byzantine and Russian empires and, to a smaller degree, the Abbasid and Ottoman empires) was prevalent, imperial systems, or mixed imperial and feudal ones, tended to develop. Western and central Europe are two important examples of such systems, which were characterized by highly coalescent boundaries of the major collectivities, political centralization, relatively developed economic systems, a preponderance of internal markets, and highly autonomous elites.

Most of the elites in the imperial and imperial-feudal societies tended to define themselves in autonomous terms, having their own resource bases and potential access to the center of society, and to each other. This was above all true with respect to the articulators of the cultural and social order (i.e., the cultural and religious elites), the political elite, and, to a lesser degree, the representatives of different collectivities and the economic elite.

Within these societies, moreover, a multiplicity of secondary elites developed, such as various sectarian groups in the religious sphere, or various social and political groups or movements. These elites impinged on those of the center and the periphery, and shaped protest movements and political activities within them. Each of the primary and secondary elites could constitute the starting point of movements of protest or of political struggle possessing a high level of organizational and symbolic articulation.

These elites also generated specific types of center-periphery relations, the major characteristics of which were a high level of symbolic and ecological distinctiveness from their respective centers and the continuous attempts of the centers not only to extract resources from the periphery but also to permeate and reconstruct the periphery according to their own premises. Thus, the political, religious, and cultural centers constituted the foci and loci of the various great traditions that developed in these societies as distinct from the local traditions. The permeation of the periphery by the centers was manifest in the latter's promotion of widespread channels of communication and in the attempts to break through the ascriptive ties of the periphery.

Closely connected to this type of center-periphery relationship in these societies was the development of a high level of articulation of symbols of society-wide social hierarchies, of some political consciousness of the upper strata, and of high ideological symbolization and mutual orientation among the major religious, political, and even ethnic and national collectivities. Although each collectivity tended to develop a relatively high degree of autonomy, they also constituted mutual referents for each other. For example, being a good "Hellene" was identified, in the Byzantine empire, with citizenship, and vice versa. This high degree of symbolic articulation and distinctiveness of the major institutional aspects of these imperial and imperial-feudal societies, was closely related to certain types of cultural orientations which, as we have seen, were articulated by these elites.

The most important difference between imperial and other types of regimes (such as those that were patrimonial or decentralized) was found in the structure of their ruling elites, the cultural orientations they articulated, the modes of control they exercised, and the relative autonomy of the major social strata. Differences existed between the monolithic elites, usually evincing strong this-worldly orientation, and the more heterogeneous ones, usually carrying some combination of this-worldly and otherworldly orientations. The latter patterns could also be distinguished according to the degree to which heterogeneous elites were segregated or interwoven. Both the monolithic and segregated elites tended to exercise relatively restricted modes of control. While the segregated elites were inclined to exert more intensive control than the monolithic ones, the control exercised by the more heterogeneous and closely interwoven elites was more flexible, though often also very intensive. But these possibilities became more fully developed in a political-ecological constellation in certain types of decentralization. I shall now turn to the analysis of decentralized political-ecological systems.

Religious and social dynamics in Axial Age civilizations. The different Axial Age civilizations were characterized also by patterns of religious and societal dynamics in general and by the impact of religious changes on societal ones in particular. From the point of view of my discussion the most crucial difference is between those civilizations that can legitimately be called heterodoxies and those that are more appropriately labeled sects.

The term *heterodoxy* is, of course, applicable only in cases where one can talk about orthodoxy, and this term in its turn implies certain types of organizational and cognitive doctrinal structures. Organizationally the crucial aspect is, of course, the existence of some type of organized church that attempts to monopolize at least the religious sphere and usually also the relations of this sphere to the political powers. But of no lesser importance is the organization of doctrine, in other words, the very stress on structuring clear cognitive and symbolic boundaries of doctrine.

With respect to both organizational and doctrinal aspects, the major difference among the Axial Age civilizations is that between the monotheistic civilizations (Christianity in particular) and Hinduism and Buddhism. (Confucian China constitutes a sort of in-between type.)

Within Christianity, these organizational and doctrinal aspects of orthodoxy, as well as full-fledged churches that constituted potentially active and autonomous partners of the ruling coalitions, developed in the fullest way. In Judaism and Islam these developments were weaker; there developed rather powerful but not always as fully organized and autonomous organizations of clerics.

Similarly, in Christianity, and to a smaller, but yet not insignificant, degree also in Judaism and Islam, there developed strong tendencies toward the structuring of relatively clear cognitive doctrinal and ritual boundaries.

In comparison, in Hinduism and Buddhism—despite a very strong transcendental and otherworldly orientation—the structuring of cognitive doctrines (as distinct from ritual) did not constitute a central aspect or premise. Hence, though it is not impossible to talk about something akin to church in Buddhism—albeit a much more loosely organized one than in the monotheistic traditions—it is very difficult to talk about heterodoxy. At the same time sectarianism abounds, Buddhism itself being, in a sense, a sect developing out of Hinduism.

The various Hindu sects, and Buddhism itself, did indeed have far-reaching impact on the structuring of the mundane spheres of their respective civilizations. They extended the scope of the different national and political communities and imbued them with new symbolic dimensions. They also changed some of the bases and criteria of participation in the civilizational communities, as was the case in Judaism, in the *bhakti* movement and, above all, in Buddhism when an entirely new civilizational framework was constructed.

Buddhism also introduced new elements into the political scene, above all the special way in which the *saṃgha,* usually a very compliant group politically, could in some cases become a sort of moral conscience of the community, calling the rulers to some accountability.

But this impact was of a different nature from that of the struggles between the ruling orthodoxies and the numerous heterodoxies that developed within the monotheistic civilizations. Of crucial importance has been the fact that, in these latter cases, a central aspect of the struggles was the attempt to reconstruct the political and cultural centers of their respective societies and that, because of this, these struggles became a central part of the histories of these civilizations, shaping the major contours of their development.

The impact of religion on society in China and in the Islamic world was greatly shaped by their prevalent orientations and the structure of their respective elites and heterodoxies, that is, by their respective political-ecological settings; by whether they were small or great societies; by whether they were societies with continuous, compact boundaries, or with cross-cutting, flexible boundaries; by their economic structure; and last by their specific historical experience, especially in terms of encounters with other societies (such as mutual penetration, conquest, or colonization).

The interplay between the different constellations of the cultural orientations analyzed above, their carriers, and their respective visions of restructuring the world (and the concrete arenas and historical conditions in which such visions could be concretized), have shaped the institutional contours and dynamics of different Axial Age civilizations, both in the "historical" periods as well as in the transition to modernity, and in the different modes of modernity, that have developed within them.

[*See also* Intellectuals *and* Modernity.]

BIBLIOGRAPHY

Eisenstadt, Shmuel N. *Revolution and the Transformation of Societies.* New York, 1978.

Eisenstadt, Shmuel N. "The Axial Age: The Emergence of Transcendental Visions and the Rise of Clerics." *European Journal of Sociology* 23 (1982): 294–314.

Jaspers, Karl. *Vom Ursprung und Ziel der Geschichte.* Zurich, 1949.

Obeyesekere, Gananath. "The Rebirth Eschatology and Its Transformation: A Contribution to the Sociology of Early Buddhism." In *Karma and Rebirth in Classical Indian Traditions,* edited by Wendy Doniger O'Flaherty, pp. 137–164. Berkeley, 1980.

Schluchter, Wolfgang. "The Paradox of Rationalisation." In Guenther Roth and Wolfgang Schluchter's *Max Weber's Vision of History: Ethics and Methods,* pp. 11–64. Berkeley, 1979.

Voegelin, Eric. *Order and History.* 4 vols. Baton Rouge, 1956–1974.

Weber, Max. *The Religion of China: Confucianism and Taoism.* Glencoe, Ill., 1951.

Weber, Max. *Ancient Judaism.* Glencoe, Ill., 1952.

Weber, Max. *The Religion of India: The Sociology of Hindu and Buddhism.* Glencoe, Ill., 1958.

Wisdom, Doubt and Revelation: Perspectives on the First Millennium B.C. Special issue of *Daedalus* 104 (Spring 1975).

SHMUEL N. EISENSTADT

RELIGIOUS EDUCATION. Anyone who tries to define the term *religious education* is confronted by extraordinary difficulties. No body of scholarly literature exists where the term is used with any consensus. One could plausibly argue that religious education is as narrow as what a few groups in a few places in the contemporary world are engaged in. Or, in contrast, one could make the case that religious education is broad enough to include the practices that govern people's lives in every time and every place.

This essay begins by using the term narrowly, partly

because space prevents detailed description of every religious group. In addition, however, logic and etymology suggest that we should look at the emerging use of the term in the twentieth century and then reflect on the appropriateness of broadening the term's application. Although the words *religious* and *education* long antedate the twentieth century, their conjunction in a single term with an implied single referent is quite novel. Of course, many terms in the modern study of religion are not the terms that particular groups have used to describe their respective practices. In this case, however, the ambiguities inherent in both *religious* and *education* are compounded in the creation of the term *religious education.*

Definitions. *Religious education* is a term confined mainly to places that are strongly influenced by modern Western Christianity. Even in those places, however, it is not a common term. Particular religious groups usually employ an educational language that is more specific than the generic word *religious*; for example, most Protestant Christians refer to their efforts as "Christian education." Groups that do commonly use the term *religious education* are usually outside the mainstream religions, as, for instance, in the United States, the Unitarian Universalist Association and the Unification Church. Despite all their differences, these two groups are similar in seeking an education that somehow transcends religious divisions.

Probably the clearest single usage of the term *religious education* today is in the schools of England and Wales, where the term does transcend particular religious parties and has taken on a legally established meaning. The roots of this usage can be traced to the late nineteenth century, but the term was clearly defined only in 1944, when the government made religious education compulsory in state-supported schools. The law specified that religious education meant religious instruction according to an approved syllabus and a daily assembly for worship. Since 1960, two major developments have modified this meaning: increasing doubt about the value of compulsory worship in state schools, and a greater pluralism of religion in many English schools.

As a result of these two developments, religious education has come to be nearly identical with the instructional element. At the same time, religious instruction has become more clearly distinguished from instruction in Bible knowledge or Christianity. Religious education thus comes to mean approaching the many religions of the world with an attitude of understanding and trying to convey that attitude to children. In contrast to most of the world, England by the 1970s had a clearly defined referent for *religious education,* this being the name of a subject taught in state schools.

The contrast with the United States of America could hardly be more striking. There the term *religious education* was born with the founding of the Religious Education Association in 1903. This organization shared common roots with the Progressive Education movement and the liberal Protestantism of that era. The association's intention was to be ecumenical, but its constituency was mainly the liberal denominations of Protestantism. Roman Catholics tended to be suspicious of the organization until the 1960s, at which time they became very prominent in it. Reform Jews played some part from the beginning, at least in writing for the organization's journal. In general, the conservative wings of all the religions were never involved in the movement, the association, or the journal. In the early decades of the century, there was hope of including the public schools in this movement. The nineteenth century had combined the generalized religiousness of the public schools with the denominational religion of the Sunday school. The leaders of the Religious Education Association sought to reshape this cultural alliance so as to provide a better educational ideal than the Sunday school and a more scholarly approach to religion in public and church schools.

By the 1940s, the movement seemed to have spent itself. The economic problems of the 1930s had scaled back the professionalizing of education in churches, while the resurgence of neoorthodox Protestant theology undermined the movement's liberal premises and hopes. Nor had the public schools become allies of the movement. Most Protestant writers at this time stopped referring to religious education; the seminary and congregational concern was renamed *Christian education.*

Since the 1960s, there has been some revival of the term *religious education* in the United States. U.S. Catholics had been using the term in several contexts since the 1930s, and their schools have had a tradition of "teaching religion." In the 1960s, the instruction of children outside Catholic schools came to be called religious education. Today, there is no consensus of meaning for the term within the Catholic church, though it is used more frequently by Catholics than by Protestants and Jews.

State laws in the United States seldom use the term *religious education.* However, the term *religious instruction* is used commonly to refer to sectarian programs. And since no clear distinction exists between religious education and religious instruction, writers and politicians generally assume that religious education in public schools is unconstitutional. Although the U.S. Supreme Court in its decisions of the 1960s encouraged an academic approach to religion in public schools, neither *religious education* nor *religious instruction* has been used to designate this project. Thus, in scholarly writing as well as in popular usage religious education is associated with churches and synagogues. While there has been agitation for prayer in the public schools, practically no one advocates religious education in them.

The contrast between England and the United States suggests the variety of ways in which Western countries, and countries colonized and missionized by the West, speak of religious education. Most Western European nations have worked out a relation between one or several churches and the educational apparatus of the state. For example, in Norway 95 percent of the population belong to the Church of Norway. The state schools provide compulsory instruction in religion throughout the nine years of school required by law. In the first six years, the subject is called "Christianity"; in the later years, it is called "Religion." The Church of Norway supplements this compulsory instruction with Sunday school.

West Germany provides another variation on the theme. It gives "religious instruction" in state schools with the cooperative help of the Protestant and Catholic churches. "Christian education" has been an integral part of the educational system since the eighteenth century. Religious instruction is guaranteed in the school curriculum but not required of the student. The churches supplement the school instruction with voluntary programs: children's service, confirmation classes, youth work, adult work. In West Germany as elsewhere, no single framework of religious education encompasses these diverse activities. A small number of writers in Europe, North America, and Australia have been trying to develop the theoretical basis of such a field.

Religious Education: Schooling or Lifelong Training? As indicated at the beginning of this article, the term *religious education* can be so narrowly conceived that it is barely visible, becoming meaningful only in the twentieth century when modern schooling combined with an ecumenical approach to religion. If one moves away from that clear but infrequent usage of the term, then religious education can be understood to embrace a bewildering variety of practices throughout the centuries. Even if one were to concentrate upon a single religious tradition such as Buddhism or Islam, it would not be a simple matter to draw a line between educational and noneducational practice, or between living religiously and being educated religiously.

Under the influence of modern schooling, there is a natural tendency to declare that any systematic training of the young should be called education. And since the practices can be classified as religious, one can call such activities religious education for Buddhists or Muslims, the Pueblo or the Inuit (Eskimo). The question of religious education is thus made manageable by drawing chronological lines around what the modern world calls "school age" youth. In addition, a set of instructions is viewed as a forerunner of the modern school with its focus on the study of books. Religious groups of the past are then seen as more or less fitting this pattern, with some groups having strong emphasis on preschool education and extracurricular activities.

As an example, consider the religious education of children in Aztec religion. A fairly systematic induction can be traced from about the age of three. Admonition through homilies and instruction in household duties were provided to the child. A little later, a rigorous system of corporal discipline was imposed. At about age fifteen, boys entered a kind of school called "the house of youth." A small number went to an elite school for the training of priests. Youths were taught the elements of citizenship, how to bear arms, traditional stories, and the proper observance of rituals. The boys who trained for the priesthood received extra instruction in the performance of sacred rites. Girls underwent a different training, more closely connected to the home. A girl was considered ready for marriage at about the age of sixteen. Modern commentators on this data could debate whether Aztec religious education began at age three or fifteen; whether it applied only to the elite school or to all boys; whether it involved only boys or girls and boys alike; and whether it included instruction in household chores or only instruction in performing sacred rituals.

Progress in understanding is probably not helped by giving *religious education* the widest meaning possible. Many educational reformers in the twentieth century, frustrated by confining school systems, have declared that education is all of learning and that learning is coextensive with life. But saying that education is everything can also mean that education is nothing. If no particular meaning is assigned to education, the re-forming of education is frustrated even more.

Religious history could be helpful in discussions of education because something more varied than a modern school is at issue, yet there is definite form or discipline to the activities. For a religious life, training begins well before the age of five or six. Just as important, the guidance and discipline of religious devotion continue beyond sixteen, eighteen, or any age considered normal for leaving school. To be sure, modern cultures have discovered the limits of an education acquired in youth and so have been trying to add adult education to their systems of schooling for the young. But only if one first assumes that education means something given to school-age children does one have the problem of awkwardly adding a kind of "second story" for people who want "continuing education."

Given these difficulties in modern theories of education, religious education could be understood not as a peculiar addition to real education but as a more comprehensive way to speak about education. Most religious groups offer education that is lifelong and varied. For example, the sacramental system of Roman Catholicism is a formation in religious life that extends from birth to death. The system may need constant reform to be educationally effective; nonetheless, it has been in place over many centuries and has been as important as or more important than schools for maintaining the church and passing on the tradition. Not that systematic instruction in a school should be excluded from the meaning of religious education. Rather, what is needed is a comprehensive theory within which schooling is an integral part.

Religious Education in the Great Religious Traditions. An adequate theory of religious education is probably impossible until there is both more systematic reflection on education within the "great" religious traditions and more comparison of practices across religious lines. Religions that have existed for thousands of years could learn something new from modern educational systems. At the same time, religious practice could challenge the post-Enlightenment meaning of education. To such a dialogue with contemporary education, each of the great religions would bring a distinctive voice.

Christianity and Judaism. Christianity in its post-Reformation forms had an important role in the emergence of modern schooling. An impetus toward widespread literacy was part of the attempt to reform the church on the basis of God's word in the Bible. Each individual was to read the Bible and to know the church's doctrine. Although this project was never completed, high rates of literacy were attained in much of Europe and North America. Until the nineteenth century, the Bible was a centerpiece of all education, so that a person received some religious education in the course of ordinary schooling. Only in the past century have Western countries seen a dichotomy between state-supported schools and church-influenced education.

The church's exclusion or at least segregation from modern education has led to new interest in early Christian practice. In the first centuries, new members were initiated into the Christian liturgical rites. At each stage of the initiatory process, there was a revelation of secrets and an explanation of the rites. Having been received into the church, one continued one's education by means of the family, community devotions, instruction by homily, and the practice of a moral code.

Christianity arose out of the Jewish reform movements of the first century of the common era. Judaism had by then established the synagogue, where systematic instruction was closely linked with prayer. The individual Jew was to know the details of the Law and to regulate all of life according to God's commands. There developed in Judaism an extraordinary dedication to learning, so that learning itself could be seen as a form of worship.

Since the rise of rabbinic Judaism, the home and the *yeshivah* have been the centers of Jewish religious education. Family rituals have preserved and transmitted Jewish life down through the centuries. Daily observances of prayer and dietary laws, together with the weekly celebration of the Sabbath, have guided the lifelong education of the Jew. The Talmud says that *torah* is acquired by forty-eight things, including awe, fear, humility, long-suffering, and generosity. Jewish religious history has been centered on the performance of ritual and deeds of righteousness.

The understanding of *torah* as embracing every aspect of life led to the inclusion in the Talmud of every field of human knowledge. The study of the Bible and the Talmud, as well as commentaries on the texts and an endless debate over their interpretation, have encouraged literacy and learning in Jewish communities. Jews have been in the forefront of modern secular education, while at the same time a separate Jewish system of education has flourished in countries where Jews are a small minority of the population.

Hinduism and Buddhism. Hinduism is a more sprawling example of ritual practices and social relations that constitute a kind of education. Schooling has made headway in parts of the Hindu world, but the religion has survived for millennia on myths passed down within the family and on intricate sets of rites. Ablutions, meals, and festivals provide educational guidance as to one's place in the universe. Along pathways of wisdom, devotion, and service, an individual's life is structured so as to attain the goal of spiritual release.

Hinduism has its own theory of development. As an educational ideal, it has four stages of life: student, householder, forest dweller, renouncer. While Western countries are not likely to adopt this scheme of categories, conversation across religious lines might still be illuminating. Both religious and secular educators in the West would be forced to reflect on their own stages of lifelong development and how education occurs in each stage.

Buddhism is based upon a strict discipline of morality. Instruction takes the form of stories, sayings, and discourses that are often learned by heart. Meditation is the way to the goal; the practice of mindfulness is at the heart of Buddhist meditation. The way of meditation and moral discipline leads to the realization that the self is unreal.

In traditionally Buddhist countries, education was centered in the monasteries. Instruction in both secular and religious knowledge was given by the priests. The life of the monk included a stricter moral code and greater concern with meditation. In the contemporary era, Buddhist meditation has attracted or at least intrigued a wider audience, including Western physicians and psychologists.

Islam. Islam is a religion that arose later than the other religions referred to above. Knowing the word is especially crucial in Muslim life. The child is to learn the Qur'ān and the tradition, so that the human will can be merged with the divine will. Much of the instruction is based on repetition of the teacher's words and memorization of Qur'anic passages and prayers.

There are fixed times for saying daily prayers. Together with fasting, acts of charity, and pilgrimage, this liturgical practice constitutes a continuing education for all Muslims. A more sophisticated study of the ancient texts and the history of Islam is available in Muslim educational institutions. Like the other religions, Islam is now in many places confronted by the effects of modern secular culture and of schooling as part of that culture. Muslim leaders generally remain skeptical of ecumenical conversation or the attempt to study Islam from the standpoint of a neutral observer.

Common features. One commonality across these religious traditions is the nature of teaching. In each religion, teaching means to show someone a way of life. The agent of the teaching is the community, which is represented by individuals functioning as teachers. The aim is to pass on the complex set of rites and practices that constitute the community's way of life. Movements of the body play a key role in religious teaching: thus one cannot practice Zen Buddhism without learning to breathe differently and to change one's posture.

It is within the context of bodily individuals in a community that one can understand the peculiar role that speech plays in religious teaching. The teacher often demands memorization, as noted above in reference to Islam and Buddhism. Christianity and Judaism have used the same technique throughout most of their histories. Speech in religion takes on a ritual character in the recitation of prayer, moral rules, or doctrine. Even the sermon in modern Christianity is a ritualized use of speech.

In addition to a ritual usage, speech is used in very directive ways by religious teachers. Speech is a kind of choreography for the bodily movement at the heart of religious practice. The sacred texts found in most religions are a guide to living. Individual religions, as indicated earlier, do not speak of teaching religion; rather they speak of teaching the way, whether it be that of the Christ, the Buddha, or Islam. Despite the common structure that religions seem to have, one cannot abstract a standard form of religious education into which the contents of the various traditions could be placed.

The religious form of teaching thus stands in marked contrast to modern concepts of teaching. The modern world tends to take schoolteaching as the prototypical form of teaching. The schoolteacher tries to convince by explaining and giving reasons. A teacher in a classroom is to some extent a representative of a community, but his or her authority rests largely on the clarity, rationality, and persuasiveness of evidence presented to the class. A dispassionate attitude toward the evidence is part of the ethos of classroom teaching. No religion could survive on classroom teaching alone; every religion experiences some threat of subversion when placed in a classroom environment.

The Future of Religious Education. In summary, *religious education* is a term used mainly for instruction in a few school systems (most clearly in England) and for conversations between Catholics and Protestants or between Christians and Jews. The term is not an ancient one, nor is it likely to be heard today in regions where Islam, Buddhism, or Hinduism prevail. Its future usefulness would seem to depend on developments in two opposite directions. First, in cultures where many years of schooling are compulsory, the meaning of education would have to reincorporate some nonschooling elements of education; this would make it easier to include both the very young and the adult population when one refers to education. Second, in cultures where the critical thinking of the Western Enlightenment has not been prominent, a systematic and comparative study of religious practice would have to develop. This need not mean submission of religion to Western rationality but rather an opening to academic tools and techniques.

In the past, when religions were separate from each other, existing in relative isolation, religious education did not exist. Instead, what existed were Jewish education, Muslim education, Buddhist education, and so forth. These categories will not disappear in the decades to come, but as cultures are increasingly forced to confront one another, an educational approach to religious similarities and differences will be needed. If such an approach should develop, religious education will be neither intramural training nor high-level abstraction, but will be the living out of a particular religious embodiment in a context of worldwide conversation.

[*For a treatment of the form that religious education takes in tribal and traditional cultures, see* Initiation. Yeshivah *and* Scholasticism *provide general histories of specific forms of religious education in Judaism and Christianity. For discussion of the relationship between religious education and public education in the United States, see* Law and Religion, *article on* Religion and the Constitution of the United States.]

BIBLIOGRAPHY

Bushnell, Horace. *Christian Nurture.* Grand Rapids, Mich., 1979. A recent edition of the 1861 version of this classic. Concentrating upon the family, this book is the basis for much of Protestant education in the United States.

Cenkner, William. *The Hindu Personality in Education.* Delhi, 1976. A study of key figures in modern Hindu education, including Tagore, Aurobindo, and Gandhi; helpful contrasts with secular and Christian education of the West.

Coe, George Albert. *A Social Theory of Religious Education.* New York, 1917. The main work of the leading theorist in the U.S. religious education movement. It has the strong vision and ideals of the progressive era as well as that era's limitations.

Holm, Jean. *Teaching Religion in School.* London, 1975. A good example of the trend in the English school system. It presents the rationale for addressing religion within the setting of the school curriculum.

Lynn, Robert W. and Elliot Wright. *Big Little School.* Rev. ed. Birmingham, Ala., 1980. A readable and reliable history of the Sunday school with the main emphasis on the nineteenth-century United States.

Moran, Gabriel. *Religious Education Development.* Minneapolis, 1983. A comprehensive survey of developmental theories in their relation to religious education. The book elaborates its own theory of development from the perspective of religious education.

Nipkow, Karl Ernst. *Grundfragen der Religionspädogogik.* 3 vols. Gütersloh, 1975–1982. An ambitious work that lays the foundation of religious education; its stress is on intergenerational learning.

Pilch, Judah, and Meir Ben-Horin, eds. *Judaism and the Jewish School.* New York, 1966. A collection of essays that represent the variety of perspectives in Jewish education. The volume includes essays from throughout the twentieth century.

Sherrill, Lewis. *The Rise of Christian Education.* New York, 1944. Still worthwhile as a study of early Christian history. Especially helpful is the tracing of the Jewish roots of Christian education.

Taylor, Marvin J., ed. *Changing Patterns of Religious Education.* New York, 1984. A wide-ranging survey of Catholic and Protestant writing in religious education. The issues treated are indicators of interests in the 1980s.

Gabriel Moran

RELIGIOUS EXPERIENCE. The concept of religious experience is rooted in broader concepts of experience as such and in theories of what, if anything, is distinctively religious in experience. The English word *experience* derives from the Greek *empeiria,* the Latin translation of which is *experientia.* Earliest connotations of this word reflect its origin in terms that designate the action of testing or proof by actual trial (experimenting). Later, the word expressed more generally the actual observation of acts or events considered to be the source of knowledge, or the fact of consciously being the subject of a state or condition, or of consciously being affected by an event. Standard dictionary definitions of experience, therefore, give the primary meaning as "the actual living through an event or events; actual enjoyment or suffering; hence, the effect upon the judgment or feeling produced by personal or direct impressions." Secondary meanings include, simply and broadly, "the sum total of the conscious events which compose an individual life." Fundamental to the concept is emphasis on the primacy of "actual living through" or "direct impressions," whereas its scope embraces all "enjoyments and sufferings of an individual." The accent, in these definitions, tends to fall on subjective consciousness, although various theories of experience may emphasize volitional, intentional, affective, attitudinal, or foundationally cognitive elements of experience. Theories of religious experience, in turn, have similarly emphasized one or more of these components.

The origin of the term *experience* in the Greek *empeiria* signals the emphasis on experience in those philosophical schools that consider themselves to be empirical. In classical Greek philosophy, the empirical or experiential mode was considered to be less significant for cognition and evaluation than was reason, which gave "form" to experience and expressed its "essence." Experiential cognition was called "opinion," whereas certainty lay in the dictates of reason. This view persisted through much of classical Christian philosophy. With the Renaissance and the emergence of modern scientific inquiry, however, greater attention was focused on firsthand doing and undergoing and on views claiming less than absolute certainty. The term *empiricism* came to denote either an appeal to forms of experience considered to be foundational for various human concerns; or, more broadly, to stress the experimental method; or, simply, to denote a general attitude of "tough-mindedness," or "realism," in the negotiation and appraisal of human involvement in the world. All of these factors and meanings are reflected in modern theories about religious experience and in their employment in religious philosophy and the study of religion.

Perhaps no one is more responsible for a general interest in the concept of religious experience as a key to the understanding of religion than the American philosopher and psychologist William James, whose Gifford Lectures appeared in 1902 as *The Varieties of Religious Experience.* James came to the concept and study of religious experience through his early interest in art, his later study of physiology, medicine, and the infant science of psychology, and through his engagement with contemporary philosophy. The first laboratory of scientific psychology had been established in Leipzig in 1879 by Wilhelm Wundt. The methods employed there involved a combination of physiological studies and introspective reports of the ingredients of consciousness. For the study of religious experience, James turned to classical and contemporary written accounts of a variety of experiences generally deemed to be "religious." For purposes of his inquiry, he defined religion as "the feelings, acts, and experiences of individual men in their solitude, so far as they apprehend themselves to stand in relation to whatever they may consider the divine" (James, 1902, p. 31). Reference to "feelings, acts, and experiences" reflects the many dimensions of human life that James believed to be involved in religion. The emphasis on solitude echoes the emphasis on the subjective and personal dimension that characterizes many theories of experience in the larger sense, as well as the inwardness and solitariness that may associate with the concept of religious experience. It resonates with the widely quoted definition of religion offered by Alfred North Whitehead, "what the individual does with his solitariness" (Whitehead, 1926, p. 16), though for Whitehead the philosophical framework of interpretation was somewhat different than for James. The key to the distinctiveness of religious experience, however, lies for James in the phrase "to stand in relation to . . . the divine." The relation itself may take many forms: cognitive, ritual, inspirational, transformative, and sustaining. Each of these forms may be positive or negative in total effect. Specification of reference to the divine expresses the concept of transcendence, which is generic to all widely employed theories of religious experience. Indeed, it may be said that some form of transcendental reference is the one normative factor in concepts of religious experience. The locus and character of that which is taken to be transcendent vary, however, with the religious and philosophical tradition and with the form and purpose of the particular study of religious experience.

James sought to give somewhat greater specificity to his characterization of religion by stating that not all employments of concepts of the transcendent or divine should be accounted religious. The total self is involved in the religious relation; the religious reaction to life is a "total reaction." Furthermore, there is something "solemn, serious, and tender" in the distinctively religious attitude. "If glad, it must not grin or snicker; if sad, it must not scream or curse. . . . The divine shall mean for us only such a primal reality as the individual feels impelled to respond to solemnly and gravely, and neither by a curse nor a jest!" (James, 1902, p. 38). In this informal characterization, James articulates the emphasis on reverence, or the sense of the sacred, that informs many seminal theories of religious experience. James found in his materials a few general types of religious experiences and personalities, which he labeled as the religion of "healthy-mindedness" or of "the sick soul," and of the "once-born" or the "twice-born." The depth and scope of materials relating to the "sick soul" and the "twice-born" led him to an extensive analysis of the phenomenon of conversion.

The inward and transformative, or unifying, character of a type of experience that is exemplified by representative persons in most major religious traditions is associated with the general phenomenon termed *mysticism.* James's analysis of mystical experience has been widely used. It is, he said, viewed by the mystic as finally ineffable, yet it is also believed to be in some sense noetic. It is transient and passive, yet elaborately developed techniques are employed to induce or evoke it. In the life of the mystic, there is, as William Ernest Hocking noted, an alternation of worship and work, or of meditation and nonmeditational activity (Hocking, 1912). In the life of the mystic, the culminating and foundational experience plays a uniquely authoritative role.

Underlying all the varieties of religious experience that he studied, James concluded, is a general sense that "there is *something wrong about us as we naturally stand,*" and a sense of solution, resolution, or salvation—a sense "that we are saved from the wrongness by making proper connection with the higher powers [the transcendent]" (James, 1902, p. 498). James's characterization of religious experience may appear to be minimal, imprecise, or too vernacular. Nevertheless, it may serve as a useful guide both for further exploration of theories that have developed in greater depth concerning one or more aspects of the phenomenon that James sought to define, and for further application of the concept of religious experience to the study of selected features of major religious traditions.

Any account of religious experience must recognize the fact that all experience is to some extent theory laden. The question whether there is any totally uninterpreted, or nonconceptualized, "pure" or "immediate" experience (James used the phrase "blooming, buzzing confusion") that is presuppositionless, or "given," is largely answered in the negative in current philosophical discussion. Similarly, Wilfred Cantwell Smith, in *The Meaning and End of Religion,* maintains that the concept of religion is a misleading abstraction from the actual intersection of a uniquely personal consciousness with a transcendent referent (putative or real), the nature of which is variously articulated in cumulative religious traditions. Any instance of religious experience will reflect constantly changing patterns of personal life and of the traditions through which persons relate to the transcendent. It is appropriate in analysis, therefore, to examine features of religious experience through employment of a classic expression of a specific tradition, an expression that also exemplifies many elements highlighted by one or more influential theorists. Such a classic is the *Bhagavadgītā,* perhaps the most highly prized and widely employed expression of the Hindu tradition.

The fundamental sense of the penultimate "wrongness" of life that underlies the tradition epitomized in the *Bhagavadgītā* relates to the qualities and conditions of finitude as such. The spatiotemporal world is viewed as possessing such reality as is spatiotemporally possible, but it reflects and is ultimately rooted in transcendent reality, which is the ultimate source of bliss, beatitude, and eternal meaning. Life in the spatiotemporal world of *māyā* is governed by an immutable law of cause and effect *(karman)* that regulates moral and spiritual as well as physical reality. The goal of salvation is the realization of the identity of the personal self with the transcendent Self. There are three major paths (*mārgas*) to this goal, and each of them is celebrated in the *Bhagavadgītā.*

Religious Experience as the Realization of Duty. The *Bhagavadgītā* relates to dialogue between Arjuna, a warrior, and his charioteer, who is an incarnation of the god Kṛṣṇa, on the eve of battle in a civil war. Arjuna raises the question whether, given the fact that the enemy are kinsmen, it would not be better to refuse to fight than to kill blood relations. In response, the charioteer invokes first the concept of duty, related in this tradition to the cosmically founded structures of caste. Inaction is not an option; the path to salvation for the warrior is action in accord with duty, duty performed with regard only to the roots of action, not to its fruits. Here is a religious experience of a means of salvation that finds echoes in many other traditions. Fundamental to both Hindu and Buddhist traditions is the primacy of *dharma,* the path, or way, that is uniquely fitting and obligatory for the devotee in the devotee's unique situation. In the Confucian tradition, the religious significance of acting according to *li* (an informed sense of propriety) in a carefully structured system of human relations is widely stressed. The Latin origins of the English term *religion* connote a sense of conscientiousness or dutiful devotion to that by which one is "bound." Something of this sense is perhaps continued in the use of the term *religious* in the Roman Catholic tradition to designate persons bound by vows, who exemplify religious practice in carrying out the duties and functions of special offices and vocations. When the seminal figure of modern Western philosophy, Immanuel Kant, sought to fix the nature of "religion within the limits of reason alone," he found it in the implicates of "pure practical reason," in the rationale of practice in accordance with the moral law. Religion, he said, views all duties as divine commands. Religious experience is the experience of duty as sacred obligation. Many other modern thinkers have associated religion and religious experience most closely with, if they have not asserted it to be identical with, the volitional dimensions of experience as such. When Kant went on to analyze aesthetic experience, he asserted that the experience of mathematical (the sense of the infinite) and dynamic (the sense of the uncannily powerful) sublimity evokes a sense of reverence that is closely akin to, if not identical with, that sense of reverence for the moral law that is uniquely religious. Two things, he said, "filled his soul with awe and wonder: the starry heavens above, and the moral law within."

Religious Experience as Meditational Insight. A second way of salvation celebrated in the *Bhagavadgītā* is that of unitive wisdom or insight achieved through study and meditation *(jñāna mārga).* The roots of this path lie deep in the tradition exemplified by this text. The historic movement in the tradition toward conceptualization of the transcendent emerged from the experience of ritualized worship, which engendered speculation about the character of the ultimately real and the ultimately true. The canonical term employed for the transcendent is *brahman,* some of whose roots are related to a term meaning "prayer." Just as the discipline of duty may lead to singleness of relation to the transcendent, the discipline of study and meditation may lead to the realization of identity of the individual self with the ultimately real Self. Such realization is not, of course, mere intellectual awareness or conceptual understanding. The total self is unified in attainment of salvific insight or intuition, and the unified self realizes identity of being with the ultimate Self. Paths toward attainment of this realization typically involve guidance by sages or teachers, who are farther advanced in saving wisdom. Elaborately articulated systems of meditational discipline, or yoga, may serve as aids to attain unitive insight. The term *yoga* is derived from the

Indo-Aryan root from which also comes the word *yoke* as employed in classical English (cf. the Authorized Version of a saying of Jesus in *Matthew* 11:19: "Take my yoke upon you and learn of me"). Physical, moral, and aesthetic as well as intellectual dimensions of the self are involved in disciplined concentration toward realization of unity with the One. In the *Bhagavadgītā*, Arjuna is offered instruction in, and reminded of, the saving value of this "way." The normative religious experience of this way is one that is frequently associated with the concept of mysticism.

There are those who would maintain that mystical experience is the paradigmatic religious experience. In relation to the analysis of the concept of religious experience, however, we may recall James's minimal characterization of mysticism and note that other students of the subject have offered more extensive and more highly nuanced analyses and descriptions of religious experience as mystical. These have included such suggested distinctions as that between nature mysticism and experiences of transcendence that are specific to a religious tradition. There are descriptions of experiences believed to be relatively instantaneous as well as of experiences that deepen in patterns that are believed to be shared by the mystical traditions of several religious faiths. Distinctions are also made between traditions in which the goal of the experience is believed to be the attainment of union with, or absorption in, the transcendent and traditions in which the goal is perfect communion between transformed and fulfilled self and the transcendent subject.

Religious experience as transformation through meditational insight may be considered foundational for the Buddhist tradition. The founding experience is that of Gautama, through whom came the realization of the Four Noble Truths and the Eightfold Path to the goal of *nirvāṇa*. As Buddhism developed and spread, many other elements of religious experience and practice were embraced in the tradition, but the meditational element has been of central importance throughout the history of the tradition. This is perhaps most consistently true of the Therevāda schools; in Mahāyāna, the explicitly meditational schools are of major significance. Perhaps the most arrestingly explicit of these are the Ch'an schools of Chinese Buddhism and the Zen schools of Japanese Buddhism. In each of these, the definitive form of religious experience is that which brings transforming insight issuing in authentic life: true and, therefore, liberating understanding of the natural and human realms. There would appear to be many affinities between the structure of such experiences and that of experiences that might also be called aesthetic.

There are echoes or overtones of these forms of religious experience in some forms of the Confucian tradition, especially in certain Neo-Confucian schools in which "quiet sitting" is an important part of the path to sagehood. In the classical Confucian tradition, the way toward the ideal of harmony in nature and society and harmony between the human and the transcendent *(t'ien)* is informed instruction in, and practice of, the way of K'ung-tzu (Confucius). The major source in China of emphasis on transforming insight, however, has been associated with the Taoist tradition. The ineffability of the Tao and the spontaneity of the life in tune with it have frequently been contrasted with the centrality of volitional and ethical elements in Confucian religious experience. The indigenous religion of Japan, Shintō, has cherished and displayed aesthetic and other elements of experience in interplay with the Japanese forms of the Buddhist and Confucian traditions.

In the theistic traditions of the West, in biblical Judaism and Christianity and in Islam, forms of religious experience typically called mystical have been both suspect and deeply prized and influential. Suspicion and caution stem from the fear that in such experience there may be an impetus toward obliteration of the distinction between creature and creator together with an exaltation of human experience to salvific power, which stems ultimately and solely from God. The goal of these traditions, however, is perfection of communion between the human and the divine and a fulfilling enhancement of the created order in the glory of the divine. In all three theistic traditions, therefore, certain forms of experience that incorporate elements of the mystical have been prized.

In biblical Judaism, these receive notable expression in poetry (e.g., the *Song of Songs*, in which the joy of human love is a medium for celebration of divine love) and in certain nuances of hymns in the *Book of Psalms*. Some passages in the scrolls of the prophets also echo some mystical or quasi-mystical themes. The foundational and uncompromising monotheism of basic biblical Judaism, however, is more typically articulated in expressions of divine-human encounters that employ the language of "call and response" or "command and obedience." In later Judaism, there have been various movements that seek to celebrate the richness of the created order in all of its dimensions and to prize communion with the divine through an appropriate sense of the glories of creation. Among these are the qabbalistic and Hasidic movements. Especially in the latter, there has been a prizing of warm and intimate experiences of the divine issuing a joyous affirmation of life. Perhaps no one has been a more effective interpreter of what he deemed to be the Hasidic ideal than the modern Jewish philosopher Martin Buber.

William James defined religion in terms of relation to the divine. Buber, in his widely influential book *I and Thou*, affirmed that all of life is relation—or, in his more specific understanding of relation, a "meeting." There are two basic forms of relation: I–Thou and I–It (the latter includes third-person human relations). A person as such is differently constituted and engaged in these fundamentally different relations. The I of I–It is a "me"; the other of I–It is basically an impersonal other. Engagement in an I–Thou relation is not, in Buber's terms, a matter of experience. Experience, embedded as it is in temporal sequence, belongs to the world of It. Therefore, it would be misleading to call engagement in a religiously defined relationship "religious experience." Relation with the world of It is not the source of "wrongness" in human life; the world of It is to be sanctified. The It-relation, however, does not and cannot involve all of one's being; an authentic I–Thou relation, on the other hand, can occur only when all of one's being is engaged. Such a relation cannot be brought about or achieved only by the I; there must be "meeting" or "address"; a work of grace or unmerited and nonmanipulable givenness. There are nonverbal and nonconceptual encounters with a Thou in artistic inspiration, when a form demands the work of creative materialization. There may also be a dim awareness of a Thou in relations with nonhuman creatures. A definitive I–Thou relation occurs, however, in the mutuality of encounter and response with another person, and it may be reflected in genuine human community. All lines of relation intersect in the Thou, who is always and only a Thou; all other relations offer "glimpses" of the eternal Thou: the eternal First-Person-Present. In this manner, Buber describes what others might consider a religious experience that is faithful in its nuances of intimacy and ultimacy to both the monotheism of biblical Judaism and to some features of what, in the contexts of other traditions, might be termed mystical experience.

Command, response, obedience, and personal divine-human encounter have also been central themes in Christian and Muslim forms of religious experience. In both traditions, however, there have been persons and movements whose devotion has focused on a warmer and more intimate and fulfilling sense of communion with the divine. In the Christian tradition, some of the conceptuality and discipline employed in these forms of experience originated in the Hellenistic religions and philosophies that substantially informed early Christian doctrine and spirituality. The way of the contemplative hermit was prized, and it continues to be so in Eastern Christianity. In Western Christendom, however, communal monasticism became normative, and monastic communities gave varying emphases to the life of contemplative meditation. Protestant churches, on the whole, placed less stress on such forms of religious experience, although groups like the Society of Friends and individuals within most other Protestant groups have found that elements of what could be termed mystical experience are of central importance for the life of devotion and service. In Islam some of these elements are displayed in the devotional practices of the Ṣūfīs, who seek to celebrate the glory of Allāh in vivid fervor.

Religious Experience as Personal Devotion and Worship. Reference to devotional practice brings us back to the *Bhagavadgītā* and to the third of the paths of salvation that it celebrates: the way of *bhakti*, or complete personal devotion to a personal god. It is, indeed, in its celebration of this way that the *Bhagavadgītā* has been most prized and most influential in the Hindu tradition. Although while Arjuna is instructed in the ways of duty and meditative knowledge, it is in the deeply personal experience of the divine presence and grace that he is offered a way of liberation that is open to all persons alike. The experience of this presence, however, is both shatteringly awesome and overpowering as well as inwardly transforming and liberating. In this twofold experience is reflected the root of religious experience in a life of worship, which is perhaps the sole distinctively religious activity.

In chapter 11 of the *Bhagavadgītā* Arjuna asks that he be allowed to see the divine in all the fullness of godhead. As is typical of many accounts of such theophanies, it is necessary for Arjuna to receive first a "supernatural eye" in order to "behold my mystic power as God." When this has been granted, there ensues a type of experience that Rudolf Otto calls experience of the numinous. In his influential work *The Idea of the Holy*, Otto affirms that it is the holy that is the uniquely religious referent or category, and that experience of the holy embraces both rational and nonrational dimensions. In its rational "moment," the sense of the holy is expressed in conceptual terms designed to articulate the ultimacy of the holy in being, truth, and righteousness; the holy is conceived as omniscient, omnipotent, and wholly good. If the natural is the concept of all that is only penultimately or derivatively real, the holy is supernatural. In addition to such rational expressions of the sense and reality of the holy, however, there is always a nonrational, nonconceptual dimension, or an "overplus of meaning"; this is the numinous (from the Latin *numen*). It is the *mysterium tremendum et fascinans:* that which is mystery (not "mysterious," or "problematic"), that which is overpoweringly awesome, yet also that which is the focus of deepest fascination and the source of ultimate bliss. The experience of Arjuna and the experience of Isaiah, described in the sixth chapter of the *Book of Isaiah,* are, Otto suggests, typical of numinously charged theophanies. The term *theophany* has been more widely employed by Mircea Eliade, who has sought to describe in the duality of sacred and profane the appearance of both "moments" of the holy as characterized by Otto. The sacred, says Eliade, is an ontologically primary orienting of space and time, one that is definitively and uniquely constitutive of the religious life of *homo religiosus.*

The devotional experience of Arjuna that is described in the *Bhagavadgītā* is not, however, simply an experience of intolerable or unsustainable awe of the divine. It is also an experience of deep intimacy, one in which Arjuna is told that, through the grace (unmerited favor) of the deity, an act of total worship may itself be a medium of salvation. "Through devotion he comes to know Me / What my measure is, and who I am, in very truth / Then, knowing me in very truth / He enters into me straightway" (18.55; Edgerton, trans.). An act of devotion may be such a simple thing as the wholehearted offering of water, fruits, or flowers.

It is the affective component that may be said to be the dominant ingredient in the religious experience of this type. What is perceived to be a uniquely religious "feeling" unifies and directs the volitional and cognitive elements in relation to the transcendent. Through the deeply felt and transforming sense of the divine, the will is inclined to the life of duty and the mind directed to cognitive insight. The life of worship provides the context for devotion, and the symbols and concepts of the tradition in and through which the individual devotee relates to the transcendent provide the verbal and nonverbal forms of expression.

Religious Experience and Modern Religious Thought. Variously nuanced relations of feeling to thought and action have characterized religious experience in the Christian tradition, and it is specifically from certain theological concerns of modern Christian thought, especially in its Protestant forms, that the interest in the concept of religious experience has stemmed. In the life and thought of traditional Christianity, many forms of what might later have been called religious experience played significant roles. These were primarily associated with personal and corporate cultivation of the life of faith, however, and they were not viewed as foundational to the formal enterprise of Christian theology as such. Devotional practice formed the context of religious experience, and that context was firmly embedded in a structured ecclesiastical framework. A tradition with relatively clearly defined contours provided the setting for closely articulated relations of thought to practice, and of worship to work. The sacramental system embracing the major rites of passage provided clear parameters for ritual expression and celebration of major human concerns. There was, accordingly, less occasion for self-conscious reflection on those personal and corporate experiences that would later be singled out as religious experiences. To a large extent, this continues to be the case in Roman Catholic and Eastern Christian communities.

In some forms of the Protestant Reformation, however, the centrality of what was taken to be normative religious experience was of major importance for theological reflection and reformed ecclesiastical practice. The "sola scriptura, sola fides" of Luther included a focus on personal experience of divine grace, authenticated by scriptural authority. Personal experience, in turn, provided a basis for revision of the dominant received understanding of the relations of faith to practice and of grace to good works. In the Calvinist tradition, a high sense of the divine sovereignty and providence undergirded a similar valuing of personal consciousness of grace through faith and of corporate expression of faith in the political order. Even so, many of the "left-wing" or "Anabaptist" Protestant groups felt that both Lutheran and Calvinist forms of Christianity, at least in their official theology and polity, did not stress with sufficient clarity or force the fundamental role of the religious consciousness and experience of the individual believer. In this consciousness and experience, affective elements were deemed to be of basic importance. Piety was associated with warmth of conviction, and pietism appeared as both the central theme of certain separate Protestant groups and as the basis of reform movements in certain Lutheran, Calvinist, and Anglican groups.

Theological and ecclesiastical pietism found congenial philosophical and literary counterparts in what is broadly designated the Romantic movement in German philosophy and arts, as well as in currents of thought and practice in other countries that were influenced by German romanticism. In philosophy, Immanuel Kant had sought to provide a "prolegomenon to any future metaphysics" on the basis of critical appraisal of the possibilities and limits of empirical-rational knowledge. We have noted that he found the heart of religious experience in the life of "practical reason" and the implicates of freedom established in the experience of moral law. It was, however, to the life of feeling that he turned for analysis of exemplary judgment, and in the aesthetic experience of the sublime, he found a close analogue of the sense of reverence evoked by contemplation of the moral law. Rudolf Otto, in turn, affirmed that his concept of the numinous bore "a more than accidental analogy" to the concept of the sublime as analyzed by Kant.

For Otto, however, the sense of the numinous is a particular quality of feeling, and it was in it—in conjunction with ethical, rational, and aesthetic factors—that he found the distinctiveness of the holy. In expressing this view, he acknowledged himself to be deeply appreciative, although critical, of the views of Friedrich Schleiermacher. It was Schleiermacher, more than any other thinker, who engendered an interest among liberal Protestant theologians in religious experience as the foundation of theological construction.

Schleiermacher, like Kant, was nurtured in a German pietist environment. From this background he went on to engage in critical philosophical study, in the translation of Plato, and in significant hermeneutical work as well as in theological reflection. Both a popular preacher and a recognized theological scholar, he found congenial company in a circle of literary and other artists who celebrated the life of feeling as the source of creative artistic work. They were, however, disenchanted with the Christian faith as they saw it exemplified in contemporary theological and ecclesiastical forms. They perceived Christian theology to be based on belief expressed in outmoded dogma and Christian practice to be centrally concerned with ethical conformity and unimaginative celebration. To them, in 1799, Schleiermacher presented his *On Religion: Speeches to Its Cultured Despisers.*

In this seminal volume, Schleiermacher maintained that the heart of religious faith lies in the affections, and, more particularly, in a distinctively religious feeling, that he variously termed (in this and later works) the "feeling of absolute dependence," the "sense and taste of the Infinite," and "the feeling of the Whole." From this basic feeling, he said, stems the life of religion in both its doctrinal and its cultic forms. In theological terms, the feeling is "God-consciousness." The definitive character of the Christian faith lies in the centrality of the figure of Christ, who was completely open to, and reflective of, that creating and redeeming reality that is apprehended in perfect human God-consciousness.

With the conviction that there is normative religious experience, a number of liberal Protestant theologians and philosophers (primarily in the United States) proceeded in the spirit of Schleiermacher to undertake the development of an "empirical" theology and philosophy of religion. Not all of them used the label "empirical," but all sought to provide critically defensible expositions of religious faith on the basis of the primacy of religious experience for faith. The general designation of the movement as empirical reflects the relationship of empiricism in philosophy to the primacy of experience in human life and thought and to the experimental character and "tough-mindedness" or realism of the empirical method. The movement in America was not without precedent in more traditional forms of American theological and philosophical thought. Jonathan Edwards, America's premier theologian, sought to relate certain concepts of Puritan theology that were inherited from forms of Platonism to the empirical emphases embodied in John Locke's understanding of knowledge as exemplified in Newtonian science. He maintained that the key to the practice and understanding of Christian faith lies in "the religious affections" and that the divine sovereignty as well as the worth of the created order may be best expressed philosophically in terms of the concept of beauty.

Edwards's emphasis on religious experience was echoed and magnified in American pietistic and evangelistic groups, and it was reflected in critically speculative ways in the work of some later American philosophers and theologians. Each of these brought to the appraisal and employment of religious experience a framework of theory and conviction related to specific philosophical and theological positions. Ernest Hocking, in a deeply sensitive and thoughtful study, *The Meaning of God in Human Experience,* sought to give an account of mystical experience and the relation of the life of worship to the life of work in terms of a form of absolute idealism that was tempered by critical modifications stemming from the work of James and other pragmatists. Edgar Sheffield Brightman employed the personalistic idealism of B. P. Bowne and others to interpret the significance of religious experience understood as any experience taken in relation to the whole of experience. Henry Nelson Wieman drew on the philosophies of Alfred North Whitehead and John Dewey to construct a "naturalistic theism" based on the primal experience of creativity. Douglas Clyde Macintosh, in *Theology as an Empirical Science,* maintained that a theological science may be constructed from religious experience, just as the natural and social sciences are constructed from other forms of human experience. For him, the normative religious experience was "right religious adjustment," which reflected in its components many experiential elements valued by liberal evangelical Protestantism. Nontheistic empirical philosophers also sought to describe normative religious experience. For John Dewey, the religious in experience, which may be authentically expressive of although not necessarily foundational to a "common faith," is a deep-seated and pervasive accommodation to the exigencies of life, from which may stem a commitment to adapt and reform the conditions of life in the light of ideals firmly held in imaginative vision. In the light of such conviction, he suggested, "God" may stand for the actual relation of the ideal to the real for the continuous and open-ended actualization of ideals that enhance and fructify the human and other dimensions of nature.

The concept of religious experience, then, is logically and practically complex, as well as rich in various nuances that have been stressed by those who have sought to employ it in the study of religion and in religious philosophy and theology. It reflects both general theories of experience and specific theories of religion. Further analysis of the concept may be aided by more precise reflection on the relation of religious to moral and cognitive experience, and especially on the relation of religious to aesthetic experience. [*See* Aesthetics, *article on* Philosophical Aesthetics.] Both the religious and the aesthetic modes involve apprehending and articulating reality. To the extent that the religious mode is rooted in the affections, the relation of aesthetic feeling to artistic expression as understood in aesthetic theory may be relevant to further development of theories about religion and religious experience. In each case, there are subtle and distinctive implications for pursuit of questions of truth and goodness in intellectual and moral experience.

Perhaps both the complexity and the promise of further study of religious experience are illustrated in the work of the Religious Experience Research Unit at Manchester College, Oxford University. The findings of this group, based on thousands of volunteered written accounts of experiences considered to be religious by those who proffered them, are remarkably similar to the conclusions reached by James in his study more than half a century earlier. It is interesting that Sir Alister Hardy, in his summary of the findings and their implications, states that, although a distinction between cognitive and affective elements "was originally thought to be a reasonable distinction . . . in practice, any such distinction breaks down" (Hardy, 1979). So do assumed distinctions between new and transforming forms of awareness and emotive elements from other matters previously "learnt from experience." With respect to affective elements as such, he concludes that "there can be no precise analysis of such feelings." While the varieties of occasions for the experiences and their perceived implications for life and belief could be broken down into no fewer than ninety-two categories, in all cases there is significant overlap of categories. Analysis of the concept of religious experience and of its employment in the field of religion is, therefore, clearly unfinished business.

[*See also* Mysticism; Pietism; *and the biographies of Buber, James, Kant, Otto, and Schleiermacher.*]

BIBLIOGRAPHY

Buber, Martin. *I and Thou.* New York, 1970. Highly influential account of a form of religious apprehension by a noted Jewish scholar.

Dewey, John. *A Common Faith* (1934). Reprint, New Haven, 1968. A nontheistic view of the religious in experience.

Eliade, Mircea. *The Sacred and the Profane.* New York, 1959. Succinct formulation and employment of the concept of the sacred as definitive for religious experience.

Hardy, Alister. *The Spiritual Nature of Man.* Oxford, 1979. Summary and interpretation of the findings of the Religious Experience Research Unit, Manchester College, Oxford University.

Hocking, Ernest. *The Meaning of God in Human Experience.* New Haven, 1912. A pioneering and substantial inquiry from the perspective of idealist philosophy.

James, William. *The Varieties of Religious Experience* (1902). Reprint, New York, 1963. Perhaps the most influential book to focus attention on the concept of religious experience.

Knox, Ronald Arbuthnott. *Enthusiasm: A Chapter in the History of Religion.* Oxford, 1950. A classic account of religious experience in the seventeenth and eighteenth centuries.

Macintosh, Douglas Clyde. *Theology as an Empirical Science.* New York, 1919. Theology as the science of religious experience.

Martin, James Alfred, Jr. *Empirical Philosophies of Religion.* New York, 1944. An account of some philosophers and theologians for whom religious experience is the key to understanding religious faith.

Otto, Rudolf. *Das Heilige.* Marburg, 1917. Translated by John W. Harvey as *The Idea of the Holy* (1950). 2d ed. New York, 1970. Seminal account of the nonrational dimension of religious experience.

Schleiermacher, Friedrich. *On Religion: Speeches to Its Cultured Despisers.* New York, 1955. Foundational for the emphasis on religious experience in liberal Protestant thought.

Smart, Ninian. *The Religious Experience of Mankind.* 2d ed. New York, 1976. Exposition of major classical and contemporary forms of religious experience.

Smith, Wilfred Cantwell. *The Meaning and End of Religion.* New York, 1962. Stresses the role of individual consciousness and cumulative tradition in religious faiths.

Underhill, Evelyn. *Mysticism* (1911). Reprint, New York, 1961. Early but still valuable exploration of forms of mystical experience.

Whitehead, Alfred North. *Religion in the Making.* New York, 1926. Reflections on religious experience by the major philosopher of process.

Zaehner, Robert C. *Mysticism: Sacred and Profane.* New York, 1961. Analysis of distinctive types of mystical experience.

JAMES ALFRED MARTIN, JR.

RELIGIOUS PLURALISM. Phenomenologically, the term *religious pluralism* refers simply to the fact that the history of religions shows a plurality of traditions and a plurality of variations within each. Philosophically, however, the term refers to a particular theory of the relation between these traditions, with their different and competing claims. This is the theory that the great world religions constitute variant conceptions and perceptions of, and responses to, the one ultimate, mysterious divine reality. We can approach this theory by contrasting it with its two main rivals, exclusivism and inclusivism.

Exclusivism—the view that one particular tradition alone teaches the truth and constitutes the way to salvation or liberation—is a natural initial stance for any religious movement coming into existence through a new revelatory event and seeking to establish itself in a relatively inhospitable environment. Indeed, the more hostile the environment, the more emphatic the exclusive claim to truth and salvation has normally been. Thus Christians have stressed the words attributed to Jesus in the *Gospel of John,* "No one can come to the Father, but by me" (*Jn.* 14:6), and have put forth from as early as the third century the dogma of *extra ecclesiam nulla salus* ("outside the church, no salvation"). This exclusivism became deeply entrenched, and through the assumption that only Christians can be saved came much of the motivation for the missionary movements of the eighteenth and nineteenth centuries. Likewise, Muslims in their more militant moments have exhibited a powerfully exclusivist outlook, even though such an outlook lacks any clear Qur'anic basis. And Jews cherish their ethnically exclusive identity as God's chosen people. Hindus revere the Vedas as eternal and absolute, and Buddhists have often seen Gautama's teachings as the *dharma* that alone can liberate human beings from illusion and misery.

Exclusivism is, indeed, an almost inevitable outlook for anyone brought up within a particular tradition whose boundaries are the boundaries of one's intellectual world. Criticism of the exclusivist assumption arises with an awareness of other streams of religious life and particularly through encounter with their best fruits regarding the transformation of human existence from self-centeredness to a radical recentering in the divine. It then becomes evident that the creative and value-enhancing results of the human awareness of the divine are not confined to one's own tradition, and other traditions are then likely to appear as ways, though sometimes strangely different ways, of responding to the same transforming divine reality.

This kind of perception has led to inclusivist theologies and religious philosophies, according to which one particular tradition presents the final truth while other traditions, instead of being regarded as worthless or even demonic, are seen to reflect aspects of, or to constitute approaches to, that final truth. Thus Hindus may regard other religions as so many paths to the one divine reality, but tend also to see them as ministering to different stages of spiritual development. According to Advaita Vedānta, worship of a personal god occurs at a lower level than absorption into the transpersonal *brahman.* Buddhists likewise often see aspects of the *dharma* reflected incompletely in other traditions. And Muslims have their conception of the "people of the Book," which some have extended to include religions beyond the three Abrahamic faiths. Roman Catholic theology since the Second Vatican Council (1962–1965), at least in many of its official expressions, has largely moved from its former exclusivism to the view that, while human salvation depends entirely upon the sacrificial death of Christ, all human beings are somehow united to Christ and can share in the benefits of his redeeming act (*Redemptor hominis,* 1979, par. 14). Thus, as Karl Rahner has suggested, those who truly seek God within other religions can be regarded as "anonymous Christians." Jewish thought includes the concept of the righteous of all nations, who will have a share in the world to come (*Tosefta Sanhedrin* 8.2). Such inclusivist views presume the centrality and normativeness of one's own revelation or illumination but are concerned, in a spirit of ecumenical tolerance, not to condemn those who are religiously less privileged because they have been born into other traditions.

Inclusivism, however, while practically helpful to a community as it becomes more ecumenically minded, is logically an unstable position. Explicit pluralism accepts the more radical position implied by inclusivism: the view that the great world faiths embody different perceptions and conceptions of, and correspondingly different responses to, the Real or the Ultimate, and that within each of them independently the transformation of human existence from self-centeredness to reality-centeredness is taking place. Thus the great religious traditions are to be regarded as alternative soteriological "spaces" within which—or "ways" along which—men and women can find salvation, liberation, and fulfillment. We find instances of religious vision capable of either inclusivist or pluralist development within each of the world religions, although usually not as central themes. Thus in the New Testament it is written that the Logos, which became incarnate as Jesus Christ, was "the light that lightens every man" (*Jn.* 1:9). In the Hindu *Bhagavadgītā* the ultimate Lord says,

"Howsoever men may approach me, even so do I accept them; for, on all sides, whatever path they may choose is mine" (4.11). And in the Mahāyāna stream of Buddhism, the *bodhisattva* gives himself "for the salvation of all beings" (*Śikṣāsamuccaya* 280). In the Qur'ān (2:109) we read:

> To God belong the East
> And the West: whithersoever
> Ye turn, there is the Presence [or Face]
> Of God. For God is all pervading,
> All knowing.

And the Muslim Ṣūfī poet Rūmī wrote this of the different religious traditions: "The lamps are different but the light is the same: it comes from beyond" (*Math.* 3, 1259; trans. R. A. Nicholson, *Rūmī, Poet and Mystic,* London, 1978).

How is religious pluralism to be articulated philosophically? This has yet to be done in any generally acceptable way. What is needed is a theory that fully acknowledges the vast range and complexity of differences apparent in the phenomenology of religion while it at the same time enables us to understand the major streams of religious experience and thought as embodying different awarenesses of the one ultimate reality.

Perhaps the most hopeful approach is through a distinction that occurs in different forms within each of the great traditions. Let us refer to the final object of religious concern as "the Real"—this being a universal concept, one that lies behind the Western term *ultimate reality,* the Sanskrit *sat,* and the Arabic *al-ḥaqq.* We may then distingush between the Real *an sich* (in his/her/its-self) and the Real as humanly experienced and thought. In Hinduism, this is the distinction between *nirguṇa brahman* (*brahman* beyond the scope of human concepts) and *saguṇa brahman* (*brahman* humanly experienced as a personal deity). In Christianity, it is the distinction between God in his eternal, self-existent being, independent of the creation, and God as known from within his creation as maker, judge, and redeemer. The Christian mystic Meister Eckhart distinguished between God *(deus)* and the godhead *(deitas),* and, more recently, Paul Tillich has distinguished between "God" and "the God above God." Jewish and Muslim mystics draw analogous distinctions between, on the one hand, *ein sof* (the infinite) and *al-ḥaqq* (the creative truth) and, on the other God as known concretely in religious history. Mahāyāna Buddhism includes the distinction between the *dharmatā dharmakāya* (the *dharmakāya* in itself) and the *upāya dharmakāya* (the *dharmakāya* known as the personal Amida Buddha), and, more generally, in the *trikāya* doctrine, between the *dharmakāya* in itself and as it is expressed in the heavenly *saṃbhogakāya* and (docetically) incarnated in the *nirmāṇakāya.*

To this basic distinction we must add our modern recognition (initially formulated by Immanuel Kant) of the human mind's indispensable contribution to all conscious awareness. Our environment as it impinges upon us always comes to consciousness in terms of concepts. Indeed, conscious awareness involves an interpretative activity of the mind, which operates with concepts and categorial patterns, some of which are common to the species, while others vary significantly from culture to culture. In the particular case of religious awareness, there appear to be two basic concepts through which the Real is humanly thought and experienced. The concept of deity, or of the Real as personal, presides over the theistic traditions, while the concept of the Real as nonpersonal—for which our nearest, although not wholly satisfactory, term is *the Absolute*—presides over the nontheistic traditions.

In actual religious history, however, the Real is not experienced as deity in general, or as abstract absoluteness, but always in particular concrete forms. Thus the various divine *personae* known in the history of religions—including Yahveh, Śiva, Viṣṇu, Allāh the Qur'anic Revealer, God the Father of Jesus Christ—occur at the interface between the Real and the different human communities of faith. For personality is essentially interpersonal: it exists in changing systems of personal relations. Accordingly each divine *persona* has a historical character. For example, the Yahveh of the Torah and of rabbinic Judaism exists in relationship with the Jewish people and cannot be conceived as the same divine personality outside that context. He is a part of Jewish history, and the Jewish people are a part of his history. Śiva, on the other hand, exists in relation to a different stream of religious life, that of the Śaiva tradition of India, and cannot be abstracted from this very different historical context.

In yet other traditions the Real is thought of and experienced as nonpersonal and is made concrete in a range of divine *impersonae—brahman,* the Tao, the *dharma, nirvāṇa,* the *dharmakāya, śūnyatā.* These are not "things" distinct from "persons," but are apprehensions of the Real as the ground of being, or of the universal transpersonal consciousness, or of the structure or process of the universe and the inner reality of things, that which gives meaning and joy to life.

At this point, however, one might object that in Hindu and Buddhist thought *brahman* and *nirvāṇa* or *śūnyatā* are not forms under which the Real is humanly known but are the Real itself, directly experienced in a unitive awareness in which the distinction between knower and known has been overcome. The gods may be forms in which the Real appears to particular human groups; but *brahman,* or *śūnyatā,* is reality itself directly apprehended. Nevertheless, this claim is called into question by the plurality of experienced absolutes with their differing characters—for the *brahman* of Advaita Vedānta is markedly different from the *nirvāṇa* of Theravāda Buddhism and from the *śūnyatā* of the Mahāyāna, and this very variety suggests a human contribution even to these forms of mystical experience. Distinct kinds of meditation, linked to diverse conceptualities and supported by different communities with their own scriptures and their own characteristic forms of life, seem to make possible types of religious awareness that differ in important ways. Thus the broadly Kantian thesis seems after all to apply to the nonpersonal as well as to the personal modes of awareness of the Real.

A version of another Kantian distinction, that between noumenon and phenomenon, may offer a way of conceiving the relationship between the Real *an sich* and the Real as variously thought and experienced by human beings. In one interpretation of Kant's distinction, the phenomenal world, structured in terms of human concepts, is not a "mere appearance" but is the noumenal, or real, world itself as humanly experienced. For we cannot experience the world as it exists independent of the observer. The same appears to be true of the divine reality. We never experience the Real *an sich* but always as it is finitely, inadequately, and no doubt often distortedly thought of and perceived by different human communities of faith. Hence we have the hypothesis of one infinite divine noumenon beyond the grasp of human concepts, and a range of divine phenomena constituting the Real as perceived through the lenses of different religious cultures.

But one might again object, how can any human being be in a position to affirm such a picture? Like the ancient parable of the elephant and the blind men—one of them, feeling the animal's trunk, identifies it as a huge snake; another, feeling a leg, identifies the elephant as a tree; and so on—so it is with the different religions: each identifies the Real in terms of its own partial experience of it. Yet, in order to know that this is so, one would have to be able to observe both the Real *an sich* and the different partial human awarenesses thereof, and this is clearly impossible. Such an objection, however, mistakes the nature of the pluralist hypothesis, which is arrived at inductively as a way of making sense, from a religious point of view, of the facts described in the history of religion. Naturalistic interpretations of religion view the variety of religions as proof of religion as human projection and illusion. A religious interpretation, however, will view the same phenomenon as a range of human responses to a transcendent divine reality—whether the "direction" of transcendence lies beyond or within. To postulate the divine noumenon, the Real *an sich,* as the ground of the different experienced divine *personae* and *impersonae* is to affirm that religion is not *in toto* illusion but is, however partial and inadequate its manifestations, our human response to the most real of all realities.

Perhaps the most serious objection to the pluralist hypothesis, however, is that it conflicts with the absolute claims that have been made and are still being made by each of the great religious traditions. For genuine pluralism is incompatible with any claim that there is no salvation outside the church, or outside *dār al-Islām,* or outside the *saṃgha,* or outside any other bounded human group, and it is inhospitable to any claim to sole possession of complete, definitive, and normative revelation or truth, a truth that judges all others even while perhaps also imperfectly reflected in them. Accordingly, a wider acceptance of a pluralist view of the religious life of humanity must involve developments in the self-understanding of each tradition, a modification of their claims to unique superiority in the interests of a more universal conception of the presence of the Real to the human spirit.

[*For a discussion of the many ways in which people in different traditions conceive of and perceive the Real, see* Truth.]

BIBLIOGRAPHY

There is a large literature concerning the relations between the different religious traditions and particularly concerning the relation between Christianity and the other world traditions, but there is as yet only a small number of works that specifically explore the pluralistic hypothesis. Wilfred Cantwell Smith's *The Meaning and End of Religion* (1963; reprint, London, 1978), by a distinguished Islamicist and historian of religion, is a modern classic that sets the problem of the relations between the religious traditions in a new light. Two other works by Smith, *Religious Diversity* (New York, 1976) and *Towards a World Theology* (London, 1981), are important contributions to pluralistic thinking. My own *God and the Universe of Faiths* (London, 1973), *God Has Many Names* (Philadelphia, 1982), and *Problems of Religious Pluralism* (London, 1985) advocate pluralism from a philosophical point of view. Bede Griffiths's *Return to the Center* (London, 1976), Alan Race's *Christians and Religious Pluralism* (London, 1983), and Paul Knitter's *No Other Name? A Critical Survey of Christian Attitudes toward the World Religions* (New York, 1985) explore pluralism as a Christian option. Harold G. Coward's *Pluralism: Challenge to World Religions* (New York, 1985) surveys attitudes within all the world traditions.

JOHN HICK

RELIGIOUS STUDIES. *See* Study of Religion, *article on* Religious Studies as an Academic Discipline.

REMEMBERING. *See* Anamnesis *and* Memorization.

RENAN, ERNEST (1823–1892), French Orientalist and essayist. Joseph Ernest Renan is a fragment of a mirror held up to nineteenth-century France. His life and work reflect especially the appeal of positivist science and its conflict with religion, particularly Roman Catholicism.

Born on 28 February 1823 in Tréguier, Brittany, Renan was raised a Roman Catholic and educated in seminaries until, at the age of twenty-two, he left both the seminary and the church. He wrote to his spiritual director that the church would not allow him the freedom to pursue the kind of scientific study that had increasingly fascinated him. Three years later, in 1848, he wrote *L'avenir de la science* (The Future of Science), a kind of apologia for his conversion to positivist science. In it Renan developed the ideas that would govern virtually all his later work. First, he thought that science would eventually supplant religion in developed societies. "Only science," he wrote, "can resolve eternal human problems." Second, he understood science as an inquiry that exhibits a comparative, skeptical, and nonjudgmental attitude toward its subject, and so distinguishes itself from doctrinaire religion as well as eighteenth-century rationalism.

The Future of Science was not published until 1890, two years before Renan's death; nevertheless, his attitude toward and confidence in science showed clearly in his work on Middle Eastern languages and religion. Renan's interest in the Middle East began during his seminary study in Paris, where he worked under Arthur Le Hir and Étienne Marc Quatremère. In 1848 he won the prestigious Prix Volney for his essay on the history of Semitic languages. In 1852 he was appointed an assistant to the keeper of Eastern manuscripts at the Bibliothèque Nationale in Paris, where he was in charge of Syrian, Sabaean, and Ethiopian manuscripts; this work, he once said, was the most rewarding he had done. During the same period, he published his doctoral thesis on the Arab philosopher Ibn Rushd (Averroës).

As a result of this work Renan had begun to earn a reputation as an Orientalist and so was able to secure a place on a scientific mission to Syria that was organized under the protection of the troops of Napoleon III, who were occupying Beirut. Despite the tragedy of the death of his sister, Henriette, who had always aided and supported his work and who had accompanied him and his wife to Syria, the trip was a milestone for Renan because it cemented his interest in the Middle East and set him to work on what would be the major accomplishment of his professional life, the seven-volume *Histoire des origines du christianisme* (1863–1881) and its five-volume supplement, *Histoire du peuple d'Israël* (1887–1893).

The first volume of *Origines* was the controversial and enormously popular *Vie de Jésus* (Life of Jesus). This little book, which first appeared in 1863, gave educated Frenchmen Renan's idiosyncratic portrait of Jesus. What made the book remarkable in its time, however, was its effort to draw the portrait of Jesus only along the lines roughed out by historical criticism and to project it against the larger background of the Middle Eastern religions. It showed Renan's comparative method at work, and because it failed to make or support the traditional religious claims about the divinity of Jesus or the uniqueness of Christian religion, it was widely condemned by the churches.

Renan returned to the Middle East again in 1864, this time to Egypt, Asia Minor, and Greece. It was on this trip that Renan composed the *Prière sur l'Acropole*, which expressed what he called his religious revelation that the perfection promised by Judaism, Islam, and Christianity actually existed in the Greek civilization that created science, art, and philosophy. Since religion is, in Renan's view, the way people often satisfy their craving for such perfection, he continued to pursue his research into the relationships among Judaism, Christianity, and Islam. His thesis was that Christianity adapted Judaism to the European temperament and Islam adapted it to the Arab.

Renan's historical sense was not always the best, and he clearly preferred to draw his conclusions from what he thought were psychological patterns of the races and religions he studied. He speculated a good deal more freely than scholars are accustomed to do today (for example, he described in detail the physical appearance of Paul of Tarsus), and he was ready to base his judgments on aesthetic principles as much as on historical fact. However, his prose style was provocative and so effective that he often had an impact in excess of the merits of his research. His work earned him appointment as professor of history of religions at the Collège de France in 1862 and again in 1870. In 1878 he was elected to the Académie Française. He died in Paris on 2 October 1892.

Above all, Renan has reserved a place for himself in the religious history of France because he, as much as anyone else, focused public attention on the potential and the consequences of a scientific approach to religious questions. Particularly for the group of French

Catholic scholars who followed him, he served as a challenge and a warning to their effort to modernize the church.

BIBLIOGRAPHY

Renan's works have been published in many languages. In French, his *Œuvres complètes*, 10 vols., edited by Henriette Psichari (Paris, 1947–1961), is the basic source. Among his works that have appeared in English editions, translated by various hands, are *The Future of Science, History of the People of Israel, The Life of Jesus*, and *Studies in Religious History*. Renan's two autobiographical pieces are also available under the English title *The Memoirs of Ernest Renan* (London, 1935).

The standard work on Renan in English is Francis Espinasse's *The Life of Ernest Renan* (1895; reprint, Boston, 1980), written only a few years after Renan's death. H. W. Wardman's *Ernest Renan* (London, 1964) is another English-language study. A useful bibliography can be found in Jacques Waardenburg's *Classical Approaches to the Study of Religion*, vol. 2 (The Hague, 1974), pp. 228–241.

RICHARD J. RESCH

RENNYO (1415–1499), Japanese Buddhist and eighth head priest of the Honganji branch of the Jodō Shinshū ("pure land true sect"). Under Rennyo, Honganji rose to preeminence among the branches of the Shinshū, and the foundation was laid for the most widespread and, perhaps, consequential Buddhist movement in Japanese history. Within that movement, he is revered as the "restorer" or "second founder" of the tradition acknowledging Shinran (1173–1263) as founder.

Rennyo was born at Ōtani Honganji, the site of Shinran's mausoleum in the Higashiyama district of Kyoto. There he was instructed in Shinshū and Pure Land texts by his father and grandfather; he received the name Kenju on his ordination at age seventeen. In 1457 he succeeded his father as head priest and set about expanding Honganji's base of support in the central provinces. His successes evoked the hostility of warrior-monks from the Tendai complex on Mount Hiei who destroyed Ōtani Honganji in 1465. In 1471, Rennyo shifted his proselytizing activities to the Hokuriku, a region northwest of Kyoto on the Japan Sea. For the next four years, during a period of political and social unrest, his community experienced dramatic growth. He developed "pastoral letters" *(ofumi* or *gobunsho)*, written in colloquial Japanese, as an effective instrument for instruction and exhortation. In the final decades of his life, after returning to the central provinces, he rebuilt the Honganji at Yamashina on a grand scale and established a powerful religious organization that played an active role in a series of popular uprisings known as *ikkō ikki*. A century later, Honganji was to seriously challenge the efforts of Oda Nobunaga (1534–1582) to unify Japan.

Rennyo's extant writings, *Rennyo Shōnin ibun*, include over two hundred letters held to be authentic. Eighty of these letters, collected by his grandson and known as *Gojō ofumi*, as well as several hundred of Rennyo's sayings, *Rennyo Shōnin goichidaiki kikigaki*, are found among the Shinshū sacred texts.

Rennyo's main contributions to Shinshū thought and piety can be described as follows:

1. He provided a catechetical approach to Shinshū teaching. Rennyo's letters express in colloquial Japanese the subtleties of Shinran's theological texts, which were written in Chinese. They emphasize that one is to take refuge exclusively in Amida Buddha; that faith (*shinjin* or *anjin*) given by Amida is the only means to salvation in the age of the Latter Days of the Law *(mappō)*; and that the recitation of the Nembutsu is solely an expression of gratitude to Amida.
2. He presented a critique of deviant positions. His letters identify erroneous beliefs and practices such as those based on the notion that salvation is possible through one's own efforts, or those that encouraged antinomian tendencies.
3. He set norms of conduct. Rennyo's letters list injunctions governing the behavior of Shinshū adherents. These include respect for the *kami*, other Buddhas, and *bodhisattvas*, obedience to civil authorities, and respect for members of other sects.
4. He provided an explication of the Nembutsu in six characters, "Na-mu A-mi-da Butsu," in terms of the concept *ki-hō ittai*. Under this interpretation, the characters *na-mu* symbolize sentient beings *(ki)* taking refuge; the characters *A-mi-da Butsu* symbolize the saving power of Amida Buddha or *dharma (hō)*; and their conjunction in the Nembutsu is thus expressive of the fundamental unity *(ittai)* of sentient beings and Amida.
5. His religious career served as a model for Shinshū piety. His presentation of Shinshū teaching, mirrored in the piety of his devoted follower, Dōshū of Akao, serves to define the person of exemplary faith, the *myōkōnin*.

In general, two contrasting lines of interpretation of Rennyo's place in the history of the Shinshū may be discerned. Sectarian scholars have stressed Rennyo's doctrinal continuity with Shinran, giving only minimal consideration to critical issues in social and intellectual history. Historians have focused on Rennyo's role as a brilliant political strategist during a period of social upheaval in late medieval Japan, with little attention to his religious thought.

[*See also* Mappō *and* Jōdo Shinshū.]

BIBLIOGRAPHY

Rennyo's extant writings have been critically edited by Inaba Masamaru in *Rennyo Shōnin ibun* (Kyoto, 1948), while a volume of his sayings recorded by his disciples, *Rennyo Shōnin goichidaiki kikigaki*, has been translated by Kōshō Yamamoto as *The Words of Saint Rennyo* (Tokyo, 1968).

The most useful general introduction to Rennyo's life and thought in their historical setting is Stanley Weinstein's "Rennyo and the Shinshū Revival," in *Japan in the Muromachi Age*, edited by John Whitney Hall and Toyoda Takeshi (Berkeley, 1977).

In my essay "Rennyo and Jōdo Shinshū Piety: The Yoshizaki Years," *Monumenta Nipponica* 36 (Spring 1981): 21–35, I examine Rennyo's letters written during a critical four-year period of his life at Yoshizaki, noting significant innovations in Shinshū thought and practice. My comparative study, "The Shin Faith of Rennyo," *Eastern Buddhist* 15 (Spring 1982): 56–73, argues that Shinran's and Rennyo's notions of faith express individual and communal aspects of personal faith, respectively.

For a discussion of *myōkōnin* in relation to Rennyo, see D. T. Suzuki's *Nihonteki reisei* (Tokyo, 1944), translated as *Japanese Spirituality* by Norman Waddell (Tokyo, 1972).

MINOR L. ROGERS

RENOU, LOUIS (1896-1966), French student of the religions of India and Sanskrit grammarian. Louis Renou gave to the Indological world French translations of the *Ṛgveda* and other studies that have gained central importance in the scholarly understanding of Sanskrit texts as autonomous and internally consistent literatures. His *Études védiques et pāṇinéennes* (1956–1969) and other publications on Sanskrit philology are exacting and precise studies that have elucidated for specialists the often obtuse and difficult, but fundamentally important, literatures of ancient India. His introductory works on the religions of South Asia have helped beginners gain confidence in their understanding of complicated religious systems.

Renou taught himself Sanskrit in his mid-twenties, and by the time he took a course in 1922 with Sylvain Lévi he found that he could read Sanskrit texts with ease. He was frustrated in his initial studies of the language, however, by the paucity of critical or analytical tools, and he became determined to provide such materials for others. He therefore focused his attention in his earlier works on Sanskrit philology, grammar, and literature. From these concerns he then moved into specialized studies and translations of the hymns of the Vedic Samhitās.

Generally taking issue with historical or cultural methods in the critical study of Indian religious systems, and particularly of Vedic canonical texts, Renou insisted throughout his career that the literatures and religious ideas of ancient India should not be understood either in comparison to the religions of other cultures or in their relationship to later developments in the religious systems of India itself. He was particularly assertive in his notion that the verses of the *Ṛgveda* are intentional poems in their own right and are not to be understood as Indian counterparts of Iranian religious literatures or as veiled records of or literary precursors to the Brahmanic ritual. For Renou, data relevant to a text's interpretation lay within the syntax and semantics of the text itself, not in the structures and dynamics of other religious expressions.

Since he maintained that the sacred texts of ancient India should be analyzed in their own terms, Renou's linguistic studies may be characterized as extended critical *explications du text* that eschew sociological, mythological, sacerdotal, developmental, or other contextual concerns. He therefore saw no recourse in commentaries, indigenous or otherwise (even those of the perhaps too widely accepted fourteenth-century Vedic commentator Sāyana), in his pursuit of the meaning of primary texts. His interpretive spirit was thus kindred to that of Pāṇini, a Sanskrit linguist who in the eighth century BCE wrote what many modern scholars hold to be the oldest grammar in the world and whose works Renou studied diligently.

Renou was born in Paris, but through his mother he had a long line of Alsatian ancestors. He was introduced to Indic studies while at the Lycée Janson of Sailly, where he read various articles by Auguste Barth, a family friend. He obtained the *licence ès lettres* in 1921, his studies having been interrupted by his captivity during World War I. During 1921–1922 he taught at the Lycée Corneille in Rouen and was awarded the *docteur ès lettres* in 1925, having written a principal thesis entitled "La valeur du parfait dans les hymns védique" (1925) and a secondary thesis entitled "La géographie de Prolémée: L'Inde (VII 1–4)" (1925), a critical edition and commentary.

Renou was professor of Sanskrit and comparative literature at Lyons from 1925 until 1928, when he moved to a similar positon at the École des Hautes Études in Paris. He was chosen in 1937 to head the department of Indian languages and literatures at the Sorbonne, where he succeeded Alfred Foucher as the director of the Institute de Civilisation Indienne. Renou was elected to the Académie des Inscriptions et Belles Lettres (1946) and to the Académie du Japon (1956) as well as to academic and intellectual societies in India,

Denmark, Czechoslovakia, the Netherlands, and other countries. He also was the vice president of the Société Asiatique. Renou gave a series of lectures in India in 1948–1949 and subsequently became active in the Sanskrit Dictionary Project based in Pune (Poona). In 1951 he was invited to give a series of lectures at the University of Louvain and then at the University of London's School of Oriental and African Studies. Renou accepted Franklin Edgerton's invitation to teach at Yale University for the academic year 1952–1953, and from 1954 to 1956 Renou was the director of the Maison Franco-Japonaise in Tokyo, where he developed a course on the *Atharvaveda*.

Despite his concentration on Sanskrit grammar and exegesis, no aspect of Indian culture remained foreign to Renou, and through his writing he contributed much to Indological studies on an international scale.

BIBLIOGRAPHY

From the long list of works written and edited by Renou, he is perhaps best known for the following.

La civilisation de l'Inde ancienne, d'après les textes sanskrits. Paris, 1950. Translated as *The Civilization of Ancient India,* 2d ed. (Calcutta, 1959).

Dictionnaire sanskrit-français. 3 vols. With N. Stchoupak and L. Nitti. Paris, 1931–1932.

Grammaire sanscrite. 2 vols. 2d ed. Paris, 1962.

L'hindouisme. 2d ed. Paris, 1958. Translated as *The Nature of Hinduism* (New York, 1963).

L'Inde classique. With Jean Filliozat et al. 2 vols. Paris, 1947–1953.

Les littératures de l'Inde. 2d ed. Paris, 1966. Translated as *Indian Literature* (New York, 1964).

La poésie religieuse de l'Inde antique. Paris, 1942.

Religions of Ancient India (1953). Reprint, New York, 1968.

Marie-Simone Renou
Translated from French by William K. Mahony

RENUNCIATION. *See* Fasting; Monasticism; Retreat; Silence; Sleep; *and* Spiritual Discipline. *For discussion of the Hindu concept of renunciation, see* Saṃnyāsa.

REPENTANCE. The noun *repentance* and the verb *repent* came into modern English via Middle English and Old French from the Latin verb *paenitere,* meaning "to be sorry, to grieve, to regret." As a religious term repentance denotes a change in a person's attitude, will, and behavior, sometimes accompanied by feelings of sorrow and regret for past transgressions and perhaps accompanied also by some form of restitution.

Morphology of Repentance. Repentance is a phenomenon found in some, but not all, religious traditions. When present it can range along a continuum from informal but socially recognized practices (for example, the repentance preceding conversion in modern Protestant revivalism) to very complex formal institutions (for example, the sacrament of penance in Roman Catholicism). Whether formal or informal, repentance is a ritual procedure; it exists to repair a breach in relations between the gods and an individual (or—since ritual and moral pollution are communicable—between the gods and a group). The establishment and maintenance of good relations with the supernatural order is thus a central preoccupation of religion. The interruption of these relations, when it occurs, is either inferred from the experience of misfortune (frequently thought the result of conscious or unconscious transgressions), or discovered through divination (for example, in the Roman senate, reports of prodigies could be either accepted or rejected; if accepted, some form of divination was used to discover the mode of expiation). Repentance belongs to a constellation of restorative religious techniques (for example, confession of sins, restitution, purification, expiatory sacrifice) that lie at the frontier leading from impurity to purity, from sin to salvation, from the community of the lost to the community of the saved. The primary function of these techniques is to objectify and rectify the cause of the breached relationship. Since many important human activities must be undertaken in a state of ritual and perhaps moral purity (warfare, hunting and fishing, childbirth), taboo violations as well as ritual and moral infractions are often confessed and expiated in preparation for such activities.

Confession of sin and accusation. The confession of sin, nearly always a characteristic of repentance, is the verbalization of wrongs committed and the acceptance of blame for their personal and social consequences. [*See* Confession of Sins.] Confession can be made privately (to the gods directly as a penitential prayer, or to a specially credentialed representative of the gods), or it can be made publicly. In many cultures the act of confession is inherently cathartic, the sincerity of the penitent being irrelevant. Confession and accusation are sometimes closely connected, particularly when witchcraft and sorcery are involved; in parts of Africa where the onset of witchcraft is thought involuntary (in contrast to sorcery, which is regarded as a skill to be learned), confessions of witchcraft double as accusations against those who imposed it. Among the Ashanti of Ghana, women often confessed acts of involuntary witchcraft at shrines whose presiding spirits troubled them. The Bete of the Ivory Coast think that confession of witchcraft automatically involves absolution. Among the Iroquois of New York State and Ontario who follow the Good Word religion of Handsome Lake, witchcraft is a serious offense requiring public or private confession. During the Salem, Massachusetts, witchcraft trials of 1692, many publicly accused witches acknowledged their culpability and were publicly forgiven and reintegrated into the community. Confession may be seen as self-accusation: during the revivalist movement known as the Great Awakening, which began in 1734 in New England, many people publicly accused themselves of various moral offenses (thereby avoiding accusation by others) and experienced religious conversion.

Penitential rites. Repentance may take form as a ritual presentation, made by the penitent person to observers, of outward expressions of remorse and sorrow. Penitential sorrow often takes the form of customs associated with mourning for the dead: wearing sackcloth and rags, smearing oneself with ashes or mud, self-inflicted pain, fasting, and sexual abstinence. Confession may be formalized both as a rite with its own efficacy (as among the Indian Shakers of the Pacific Northwest), and as part of a more elaborate expiatory protocol perhaps concluding with a sacrifice (as among the Nuer or the ancient Israelites). Restitution or compensation is often an integral feature of penitential rites, particularly in cases wherein others have been harmed or their property damaged or taken away. Confession is sometimes regarded as the necessary prerequisite for formalized types of expiation, such as public sacrifice or public penitential discipline.

Guilt. Repentance is an institutionally approved means of eliminating excessive guilt stemming from the awareness of having transgressed in thought, word, or deed, and thus its public and ritually prescribed protocol exists for the formal recognition and removal of guilt. In order to understand the ritual removal of guilt, it is useful to bear in mind that an anthropological distinction was formerly made between guilt cultures and shame cultures. This distinction was an attempt to reify the fact that in some (generally small-scale) societies self-control is based primarily on *external* sanctions, namely, fear of shame, ridicule, and punishment, while in other societies (often more complex and stratified) self-control is determined primarily by *internal* sanctions, in particular the desire to avoid painful feelings; this is known also as the inner value-structure of the individual conscience, a phenomenon Freud labeled "the censor."

Conversion. The word *conversion* may be defined as the voluntary entry into a religious movement having exclusive claims that are buttressed by a system of values and norms at variance with the outside world; and for conversion repentance is often a necessary precondition, for it involves abandoning the old in order to embrace the new. [*See* Conversion.] Particularly with respect to revitalistic or millenarian movements, repentance is often a necessary step for entry. After the rebellion in 1944 of the Bagasin cult of New Guinea (one of the cargo cults), its members were required to confess all past transgressions—primarily sorcery and quarrels over women—in order to demonstrate their genuine conversion to the new order. Two rebel leaders, Kaum and Dabus, had confessional services each Monday; adherents were told that when God-Kilibob was satisfied with their new intentions he would turn their skins white and send cargo through the spirits of the dead. Another cargo cult, the so-called Vailala Madness of Papua, was characterized by both public accusation and public confession as preparations for reform. (Transgressions included stealing and adultery—the established fine for each was one pig; positive injunctions included Sunday observance and the provision of feasts for ancestors.) The rite of public confession may in this instance have been adapted from Roman Catholicism; whatever its origin, it served to ritualize the embracing of the new morality and abandonment of the old. Again, emphasis on conversion to a new life characterizes the Good Word (Gaiwiio) religion, whose belief system is based on the revelatory visions received from 1799 forward by the Seneca chief Handsome Lake (Ganio'Daí Io'), and whose tenets are still maintained by half the fifteen thousand Iroquois in New York State and Ontario. The codification of these visions articulates an ethical and cultural program of accommodation between the white man and the Indian. Converts to this religion are required to abstain from drinking, gambling, witchcraft, gossip, vanity, boasting, and pride; in short they are to abandon many aspects of the past. In place of these the precepts of the code are tendered, which require the adoption of the white man's mode of agriculture (including men working in the field), the learning of English, and a respect for family life and children.

Classical Greek Traditions. Among the ancient Greeks, the causes of illness, injury, or other misfortunes were variously diagnosed as (1) the result of chance, (2) the effect of sorcery, (3) divine revenge for affronting a particular divinity's honor, or (4) a punishment for having committed ritual or moral transgressions. In the event that guilt was incurred—for which the main term was *miasma* (pollution, defilement)—a state of purity might be regained by *katharsis* (ritual purification). Consciousness of sin, that is, guilt, was rarely understood in terms of emotional suffering alone. The views of the Athenian orator Antiphon (fifth century BCE) expressed in *On the Murder of Herodes* 5.93 are a striking exception to this rule; more commonly, guilt looked not inward, but outward in anxious anticipation of the consequences of the deed, that is, physical misfortune. After the fifth century BCE the term *enthumios* ("weighing on the mind") and cognates thereof were often used of religious scruples or anxiety, but used in the sense of anticipating an evil fate to result from evil deeds. Thus Euripides interpreted the Erinyes as hypostatized projections of guilt who pursued Orestes in the form of avenging spirits, symbols of his uneasy conscience over past transgressions (acknowledged in *Orestes* 396).

For the existence of repentance and confession among the Greeks, as for the existence of inwardly directed guilt, only limited evidence can be adduced. For example, Lydian and Phrygian inscriptions of the second and third centuries CE may be cited that were dedicated by persons believing themselves punished with illness for specific transgressions (usually ritual offenses); in their belief, healing was obtained by identifying and confessing the sin. Evidence may be claimed also in Plutarch's description of the superstitious man who confesses numerous transgressions and subjects himself to various ritual expressions of repentance: wearing sackcloth and rags, rolling in mud, and using various magical means of purification (*On Superstition* 168d). However, these repentance rituals appear to be of Asian origin rather than Greek; Plutarch's example is perhaps borrowed from the cult of Dea Syria, which he is known to have held in general contempt. Again, some might cite the conclusion of the first Hermetic treatise (*Poimandres* 28), a call for repentance very similar to Jewish and Christian appeals. But the phenomenon perhaps closest to the idea of repentance is found in certain rites of purification practiced in the Greek cults, including Orphism and the Samothracian, Eleusinian, and Dionysian mysteries. It must be stressed that ritual, not moral, purity was demanded of initiates; in particular they must be free of blood guilt. Entrance to the mysteries therefore required purification rites, such as smearing oneself with mud lest one wallow in mire in the afterlife. In the mysteries of Samothrace initiates were expected moreover to confess any significant crimes (Plutarch, *Apophthegmata Laconica* 217d, 229d), a requirement involving the expiation of ritual pollution. The phenomenon of conversion existed not in cults but in philosophical schools, which were ideologically exclusivistic and thus made conversion possible. For the idea of conversion Plato uses the word *epistrophē* (*Republic* 518dff.): Cicero calls it *conversio* (*De natura deorum* 1.77). Finally, in the *Pinax* of Cebes (a philosopher of the first century CE), wherein the life of vice and virtue are described, repentance personified as Metanoia provides deliverance from the bad life (chap. 26). [*See* Purification.]

Near Eastern Traditions. Repentance is a particularly important aspect of many ancient Near Eastern religions including Mesopotamian religions, Judaism, Islam, and Christianity. Among these religions illness and misfortune were widely attributed to transgression, whether ritual or moral, deliberate or unconscious. Similarly, Akkadian and Sumerian penitential prayers enumerate ethical as well as ritual transgressions. Ancient Egyptian religion is an apparent exception, if one accepts Henri Frankfort's claim that Egyptians had no real consciousness of sin; certainly they had no conception of original sin. Chapter 125 of the Egyptian *Book of Going Forth by Day* contains a script for recital by the deceased person on entering the hall of judgment, and within this script is the very opposite of a confession of sin, that is, a declaration of innocence, using a stereotyped list of the many kinds of crimes and transgressions *not* committed. Siegfried Morenz, however, correctly insists that this display of innocence is actually funerary magic in which the deceased identifies himself with Osiris to evade judgment. The lengthy protestations of innocence provide indirect evidence of a consciousness of sin; nevertheless the phenomenon of repentance is wholly lacking. (Ceremonial avowals of innocence can be found also in the All Smoking ceremony of the Blackfeet Indians and in the Old Testament (*Dt.* 26:13–14, *Ps.* 26:4–5, *1 Sm.* 12:3).

Judaism. In ancient Israel, as in the rest of the Near East, fear existed concerning the possibility of committing unconscious sin and incurring guilt thereby (*Dt.* 29:28, *1 Sm.* 26:19, *Ps.* 19:13, *Jb.* 1:5). But the Bible deals more extensively with guilt incurred by conscious and deliberate sin, described several ways. Guilt may be a motion of the heart: *1 Samuel* 24:5 and *2 Samuel* 24:10 use the expression "David's heart smote him." Guilt may be physical suffering: in an investigation of the *asham* (guilt) offering, Jacob Milgrom has shown that the verbal root *'shm* denotes the pangs and remorse brought on by guilt and that it should be translated as "feel guilty" (cf. *Lv.* 5:24–25, *Nm.* 5:6–7). The Hebrew root *shav* ("turn, turn back") eventually came to denote repentance, that is, a turning back to God. The same root was used to denote sin or apostasy, that is, a turning away from God (*Jos.* 22:16). *Shav* meaning "repent" is emphasized by the eighth-century classical Israelite prophets (*Am.* 4:6–11; *Hos.* 3:5, 5:4; *Is.* 1:27, 6:10), and becomes more popular after the sixth century (variant forms occur twenty-seven times in *Jeremiah,* twenty-three times in *Ezekiel,* and twenty-eight times in the postexilic books). The earlier prophets addressed Israel as a whole and demanded national repentance, but later prophets like Ezekiel emphasized individual repentance (*Ez.* 18:21, 18:27, 33:9, 33:11). The Israelite prophets did not distinguish sharply between ritual and moral transgressions, but called Israel back to an earlier, better relationship to God as defined by the terms of the covenant. For the Deuteronomist historian repentance or conversion is primarily a turning away from cultic sins such as idolatry (*1 Sm.* 7:3, *1 Kgs.* 13:33, *2 Kgs.* 17:7–18).

The repentance demanded by the Israelite prophets is linked to ritual manifestations of repentance, as may be seen in *Joel* 2:12–13: "Return to me [Yahveh] with all your heart, with fasting, with weeping, and with mourning; and rend your hearts and not your garments." These manifestations accord with traditional Near Eastern rites of repentance: fasting, wearing sackcloth or mourning garb, rending one's clothes, strewing earth on one's head, sitting in ashes (*Est.* 4:16, *1 Kgs.* 21:27, *Neh.* 9:1, *Jon.* 3:5–9). These manifestations also include the offering of a sacrifice (*Mi.* 6:6–8, *Is.* 1:10–17; occasionally, as in *Jl.* 2:14, the sacrifice is a gift or blessing rather than an expiation). For the prophets forgiveness of sins is dependent on repentance, by which they mean the shunning of evil (*Is.* 33:15) and the practice of good (*Am.* 5:14–15, *Jer.* 26:13).

For sacrificial expiation to take place, there must first occur confession *(hitvaddut)*, restitution of goods to persons, and atonement *(asham)* for offense to God (*Nm.* 5:6–8). In the case of deliberate sin, moreover, remorse must be verbalized (cf. *Dn.* 9:5–20, *Neh.* 1:6–37; sacrificial expiation is not possible for the sinner who does not confess or repent (*Nm.* 15:27–31). In the wisdom literature, confession, a prerequisite for sacrificial expiation, includes admitting having committed a specific sin and accepting the blame for it (*Ps.* 32:5, 38:18; *Prov.* 28:13).

During the Second Temple period (516 BCE–70 CE), the notion of repentance or conversion (Heb., *teshuvah;* Gr., *metanoia)* was of central significance to Judaism. The conception could involve the prophetic notion of restoration as well as the conversion of pagans. The Jewish philosopher Philo Judaeus of Alexandria (d. 45–50 CE) viewed the Jewish tradition of conversion or repentance through the spectacles of Greco-Roman philosophy, whereby a proselyte *(epelus)* underwent a conversion *(metanoia)* from a life of vice to one of virtue (*On the Virtues* 175–186, *On Abraham* 17, *Questions and Answers on Genesis* 1.83.) In every age, the mark of the pious Jew is to turn continually to God. Repentance means a permanent break with sin (*Eccl.* 34:25–26, *Sibylline Oracles* 1.167–170; Philo, *On the Special Law Books* 1.93, 1.240). In rabbinic Judaism repentance *(teshuvah)* and good deeds together describe the ideals of Jewish piety (*Avot* 4.21–4.22). In modern Judaism the Days of Awe (Ro'sh ha-Shanah, followed by a week of repentance, culminating in Yom Kippur), is a period of communal contrition and confession of sins. The ritual blowing of the shofar, or ram's horn, beginning a month before Ro'sh ha-Shanah and ending on the festival day itself, comprises four symbolic sounds: *teqi'ah* (the waking call), *shevarim* (the sobbing of the contrite heart), *teru'ah* (the weeping of a heart aware of guilt), and *teqi'ah* (the awakening sound again). On Yom Kippur sins are confessed through statutory prayers recited privately and in unison publicly.

Islam. The most important theological conception in Islam is that God is compassionate and merciful. Repentance has therefore played a central role throughout the history of Islam. Throughout history messengers from God have tried with little success to call men to return to God, that is, to repent; the Arabic word for repentance, *tawbah,* literally means a "returning" to God. Those who reject the message are unbelievers (Arab., *kuffār,* literally "ungrateful ones"). Nevertheless sinners can always repent, be converted to the truth, and do good deeds (Qur'ān 6:54, 42:25–26). They are cleansed from all sins and restored to their original sinless state. Repentance must be followed by faith and good works (Qur'ān 25:70). *Zakāt* (almsgiving) is a continuing sign of repentance, which must be manifest throughout life (Qur'ān 66:5, 9:112).

Traditional Islam is not as concerned about repentance as the Ṣūfīs and the Mu'tazilah. According to the Ṣūfīs, who are the mystics of Islam, the first station *(maqāmah)* on the mystical path begins with repentance. A spiritual guide *(shaykh)* enrolls the penitent as a disciple *(murīd)* and assigns him a regimen of ascetic practices. Ṣūfīs recognize three degrees of repentance, namely, in ascending order, (1) *tawbah* (turning to God), which is motivated by fear; (2) *inābah* (returning), motivated by the desire for reward; and (3) *awbah* (returning), motivated by the love of obedience. For the Ṣūfī, life is a constant struggle against the *nafs* ("self," i.e., lower nature). The Mu'tazilah, proponents of a liberal theological view within Islam, emphasized three elements in repentance: (1) restitution, (2) the importance of not repeating the offense, and (3) continuing remorse. In most forms of Islam, repentance is a relatively informal institution.

Christianity. The religious reform movements led by John the Baptist and by Jesus of Nazareth were revitalistic or millenarian in character. Both emphasized the necessity for repentance or conversion, and took from Judaism the dual means of restoration and proselytism. Even though the activities of John have been christianized in gospel tradition, it is apparent that John summoned fellow Jews to a repentance that he sealed with a ritual bath reminiscent of the washing of Jewish proselytes (*Mt.* 3:1–12; *Lk.* 3:1–20; *Acts* 13:24, 19:4). Those who underwent this baptism were initiated into an eschatological community preparing for the imminent visitation of divine judgment. Jesus, too, is presented as summoning fellow Jews to repentance (*Mk.* 1:14–15; *Lk.* 13:1–5, 15:7), and the ritual of baptism inherited from John was perpetuated as a rite of initiation into the community of the saved. Thus this emphasis on repentance, which was to characterize many strands of Christianity throughout its history, was inherited primarily from Judaism.

There are two Greek words used in early Christian literature that convey the basic notion of repentance, namely, *metanoia* and *metameleia*. By the time of the Christian era both words had come to convey a change of attitude or purpose as well as a sorrow for past failings, whereas in non-Christian Greek texts the terms are not used in an ethical or religious sense until the late Hellenistic period.

As in Judaism, in early Christianity forms of the term *metanoia* (occurring approximately fifty times in the New Testament) continued to mean conversion to a new faith and abandonment of the old, or restoration within the new faith by confession and rejection of sins. Employing the same word, the *Revelation to John* reports a series of visions in which the risen Jesus demands repentance of Christians in Asia Minor who have made accommodations to paganism (*Rv.* 2:5, 2:16, 2:21, 3:3, 3:19); the ritual protocol involved (if any) is unstated. John uses the same term for the conversion of pagans (*Rv.* 9:20–21, 16:9–11). The ethical rigorism expressed in the *Letter to the Hebrews* (*Heb.* 6:4–6, 10:26–31, 12:14–17) reveals a problem with postbaptismal apostasy.

The ideal of moral purity in the Christian church was contradicted by reality. During the second and third centuries Christianity underwent a penitential crisis. By the second century baptism was thought to confer sinlessness as well as the forgiveness of all previous sins. Since baptism or martyrdom were the only two means of eradicating postbaptismal sin, the practice of adult baptism and deathbed baptism became common. Many reform movements arose. The prophet Elkesai (fl. 100 CE) summoned people to repent and submit to a second baptism to expiate sin. The Marcionites and the Montanists (middle of the second century) proclaimed different forms of ethical rigorism. In a complex document called the *Shepherd of Hermas* (compiled c. 100–150 CE), revelatory visions legitimate the possibility of a second and final repentance. Forms of the word *metanoia* are found therein nearly a hundred times. The prophetic author urges Christians to repent the abuses stemming from the possession of wealth and the conduct of business affairs (*Visions* 3.6.5; *Commandments* 10.1.4; *Similitudes* 9.20.1). Throughout the document there is no explicit connection of the appeal for repentance with a formalized ritual procedure. Tertullian (c. 160–225 CE), before converting to Montanism, wrote *De paenitentia,* in which he dealt both with the repentance required of candidates for baptism (chaps. 4–6) and with a single final opportunity for repentance following baptism (chap. 7), after which the penitent must never again return to sin (chap. 5). The ritual behavior of repentance described by Tertullian includes lying in sackcloth and ashes, severe treatment of the body, restricted food and drink, and weeping (chap. 9). The orthodox tradition developed the practice of auricular ("to the ear") confession to a priest as a surrogate for God. By the third century a system of public penance came to be regarded as a second baptism. Excluded from the Eucharist, the penitent went through a regimen of fasting, prayer, and almsgiving. The Council of Trent (1545–1563) reaffirmed that repentance must involve three elements, namely, contrition, confession, and satisfaction.

Traditions of Small-scale Societies. Among the Nuer of the Sudan, certain acts are regarded as bad because God punishes them. Faults *(dueri)* are against God and he is the one who punishes them. Such faults include incest and adultery as well as offense against certain prohibitions, such as eating with those with whom one's kin have a blood feud and milking one's own cow and drinking the milk. In Nuer belief the person who commits *dueri* places himself in physical danger, for moral faults accumulate and predispose the offender to disaster. Thus faults destroy a person, but they can be "wiped out" *(woc)* by sacrifice. The Nuer have a custom of confessing sin at certain sacrifices, wherein the worshiper must reveal all the resentments and grievances that he holds against others if his sacrifice is to be efficacious. (In effect he confesses the shortcomings of others.) The faults and the feelings of aggrievedness are wiped out by the blood of the sacrificial victim. Such sacrifices are regarded as effective only when accomplished with the will and desire of the sinner.

Among the Indian Shakers of the Pacific Northwest ritual confession was practiced early in the sect's history (late nineteenth and early twentieth centuries), but was later abandoned. The founder, John Slocum, emphasized the necessity of confessing sins and asking for forgiveness in order to attain salvation. Every Friday Slocum would hear the confession of individual penitents privately—though he rang a bell all the while so that he would be unable actually to hear them. Early Shakers believed that the ability to hear confessions was a gift. Louis, a Shaker leader possessing this gift, received penitents who came each carrying a bundle of sticks, a mnemonic device representing their sins. As each sin was confessed (while Louis rang the handbell), a stick was placed on the table, and all were burned at the conclusion of the confession. For the Shakers confession was a catharsis for immediate personal relief and was not connected with spiritual regeneration.

The phenomena of confession and repentance are culture traits indigenous to American Indian cultures quite apart from Christian influences. This conclusion is supported by the early character of the evidence as well as by the fact that tribal confessors are native functionaries. Examples abound. The Aurohuaca Indians of the Columbian Sierra Nevada regard all illness as a punishment for sin. When a shaman is summoned for curing, he will not treat patients until they confess their sins. The Ijca of Columbia abstain from salt and alcohol before confession. In the manner of the Pacific Coast Shakers, when they visit the priest *(mama)* they bring mnemonic devices made of corn shucks and knotted strings to help them remember each sin. Similarly the Huichol of southern Mexico confess sexual transgression on their way north in search of peyote *(híkuri)*. Women knot palm-leaf strips for each sin and throw them into the fire after reciting the name of each lover. Among the Maya of Yucatan, women in labor summon native shamans to confess their sins, particularly those of a sexual nature. The Inuit (Eskimo) are anxious lest by conscious or unconscious violation of taboos they offend Sedna, the mistress of animals, who resides at the bottom of the sea and whose displeasure might threaten the food supply. As Weston La Barre has observed, the wages of sin are starvation. If the guilty party confesses, all is well: seals and caribou are caught. If not, the shaman *(angakkoq)* must ferret out the offender and secure a confession.

[*For the relationship between repentance and restoration, see* Merit.]

BIBLIOGRAPHY

The most comprehensive study of the phenomenon of confession, which includes a great deal of information about the related notion of repentance, is Raffaele Pettazzoni's *La confessione dei peccati*, 3 vols. (1929–1936; reprint, Bologna, 1968). However, Pettazzoni's hypothesis proposing an evolutionary development of the notion of confession, from the magical to the theistic, is unconvincing. A more theoretical discussion of the phenomenon of repentance in Albert Esser's *Das Phänomen Reue: Versuch einer Erhellung ihres Selbstverständnisses* (Cologne, 1963). For a shorter discussion from a history of religions perspective, see Geo Widengren's *Religionsphänomenologie* (Berlin, 1969), pp. 258–279). For a critique of the shame-culture or guilt-culture typology, see Gerhart Piers and Milton B. Singer's *Shame and Guilt* (Springfield, Ill., 1953).

For an overview of the notions of confession, repentance, and guilt in antiquity, see Franz Steinleitner's *Die Beicht im Zusammenhänge mit der sakralen Rechtspflege in der Antike* (Leipzig, 1913). For Greco-Roman religions and philosophical systems, see Arthur Darby Nock's *Conversion: The Old and the New in Religion from Alexander the Great to Augustine of Hippo* (Oxford, 1933). An exceptionally complete study of Greek pollution and purity with full bibliography is found in Robert A. Parker's *Miasma: Pollution and Purification in Early Greek Religion* (Oxford, 1983). Still indispensable is Kurt Latte's "Schuld und Sünde in der grieschischen Religion," *Archiv für Religionswissenschaft* 20 (1920–1921): 254–298. For the Roman world, see Anna-Elizabeth Wilhelm-Hooijbergh's *Peccatum: Sin and Guilt in Ancient Rome* (Groningen, 1954).

Henri Frankfort outlines the ancient Egyptian concept of sin and sinlessness in his *Ancient Egyptian Religion* (New York, 1948), pp. 73–80. Frankfort's treatment of the topic has been corrected by Siegfried Morenz's *Egyptian Religion* (Ithaca, N.Y., 1973), pp. 130–133. For the relationship between repentance and sacrificial expiation in ancient Israel, see Jacob Milgrom's *Cult and Conscience: The Asham and the Priestly Doctrine of Repentance* (Leiden, 1976). Also important is William L. Holladay's *The Root Subh in the Old Testament* (Leiden, 1958).

One of the only detailed studies of the Christian concept of repentance within the context of Judaism, Greco-Roman sources, and subsequent patristic evidence is Aloys H. Dirksen's *The New Testament Concept of Metanoia* (Washington, D.C., 1932). A philologically oriented study of Hebrew and early Christian terms and concepts related to repentance, together with a wealth of references to primary sources, is found in the *Theological Dictionary of the New Testament*, edited by Gerhard Kittel and Gerhard Friedrich, vol. 4 (Grand Rapids, Mich., 1967), pp. 975–1008. The most important study of the second- and third-century penitential crisis is Hans Windisch's *Taufe und Sünde im ältesten Christentum bis auf Origenes* (Tübingen, 1908). For a selection of important early Christian texts on repentance in Greek and Latin with German translations, see *Die Busse: Quellen zur Entstehung des altkirchlichen Busswesens* (Zurich, 1969).

On the phenomenon of confession and repentance among small-scale societies, see Weston La Barre's well-documented "Confession as Cathartic Therapy in American Indian Tribes," in *Magic, Faith, and Healing*, edited by Ari Kiev (New York, 1964). Kiev's book contains many relevant essays. Robert I. Levy's *Tahitians: Mind and Experience in the Society Islands* (Chicago, 1973) is an important study. Bryan R. Wilson's *Magic and the Millennium: A Sociological Study of Movements of Protest among Tribal and Third-World Peoples* (New York, 1973) is an important synthetic study of revitalistic or millenarian movements.

David E. Aune

RESHEF, a West Semitic god, is attested as early as 2300 BCE, in personal names (e.g., *Ebdurasap*, "servant of Reshef"), in the recently excavated cuneiform texts at Ebla (Syria), in the literature of Ugarit (Syria) from the thirteenth century BCE, and in many inscriptions from the eighth to the third century BCE. Worship of Reshef also found its way to Egypt, where some fifty stelae have been discovered bearing his name or image.

In his Syrian homeland Reshef was a god of the underworld, associated with warfare, darkness, disease, and death. In this respect he was much like the Mesopotamian god Nergal, and one god-list from Ugarit explicitly identifies the two. This rather gloomy picture of Reshef is evident in the literature of Ugarit. In the story of King Keret, Reshef is responsible for the death of several princes, apparently by bringing plague. He is associated with Shaps, the sun goddess, as the gatekeeper of the underworld, where the sun descends at night. He is called Reshef of the Arrow, a title recalling the Greek god Apollo, with whom Reshef was later identified at Carthage and Cyprus, and who shot his plague arrows throughout the Danaan camp (Homer, *Iliad* 1.45–52).

Yet Reshef also had a positive image as protector and warrior. At Ugarit there was at least one temple dedicated to him, and his name was popular in compound personal names with such meanings as "Reshef is my father" and "Reshef is gracious." In some later inscriptions, most notably one from Karatepe in Cilicia (c. 750 BCE), Reshef is mentioned as a special patron of the local ruler.

In the eighteenth dynasty, especially under the Syrophile Amenophis II (c. 1436–1413), who chose Reshef as his personal military patron, Reshef was introduced into Egypt, and it is only from Egypt that we have an iconography of him. He is depicted on many stelae, evidently the workmanship of imported Syrian craftsmen, as a warrior and protector god, usually assuming a martial stance, holding a spear and shield in one hand and brandishing a mace-ax over his head with the other. There is often a quiver of arrows on his back. On some stelae, all from Thebes, Reshef is associated with Qudshu, a Syrian fertility goddess, and with Min, an Egyptian protector god. His Egyptian epithets are often elaborate: "the great god, lord of eternity, sovereign everlasting, master mighty amid the divine ennead" (Stela Louvre 86); "great god, lord of the sky, master of power, everlasting god" (Stela Turin 1601). These titles probably reflect more the enthusiasm of his devotees than his actual stature in the Theban pantheon.

The name *Reshef*, or *Resheph*, appears seven times in the Old Testament, although this fact is usually obscured in the translations. For the most part he has been demythologized, and *reshef* is almost a common noun, indicating some kind of flame, arrow, or pestilence—all meanings that can be traced back to the mythological roots. In *Habakkuk* 3:5 and in the Hebrew text of *Ben Sira* 43:17–18, he is a quasi demon or destructive force accompanying Yahveh in a theophany that precipitates a meteorological uproar. In *Deuteronomy* 32:23–24, *Job* 5:7, and *Psalms* 91:5–6, 78:48, he is a negative force bringing disaster. In several of these passages he is associated with Qeṭev ("disease") and Dever ("plague"), probably also of mythological origin. The plural form of *reshef* occurs in *Song of Songs* 8:6, where the reference seems to be to some sort of uncontrollable force that turns love into an unquenchable flame. Finally, *1 Chronicles* 7:25 mentions a son of Ephraim named Resheph.

By the end of the first millennium BCE the cult of Reshef had stretched across the Mediterranean as far as Ibiza in Spain, and through religious syncretism he was identified with several other gods. Reshef was assimilated to Herakles, Melqart, Shulman, and possibly the Palmyrene god Arsu as well as to Apollo.

In the scholarly literature there is frequent reference to the so-called Reshef bronzes, statuettes found in abundance in the Levant, in northern Egypt, and elsewhere. Although these may well be associated with Reshef there is no proof of this. Reshef is sometimes described as a weather god, partly because of the Old Testament theophany passages and partly because the arrow epithet suggested to some the image of lightning bolts. At most, however, any association with weather is very secondary. Some scholars have proposed that he is a fertility god because he appears with Qudshu and the ithyphallic Min on Egyptian stelae, but his iconography in Egypt is specifically martial, not sexual. Finally, some have taken "Reshef of the arrow" to refer to belomancy (divination by means of arrows) and would prefer "Reshef of (good) luck." There is little supporting evidence for this. The arrow, especially in light of Reshef's ultimate identification with Apollo, was clearly an image of plague and warfare.

BIBLIOGRAPHY

The literature concerning Reshef consists mostly of scattered monographs in learned journals. A catalog of the ancient sources, discussion of the evidence, and annotated bibliography can be found in my study *The Canaanite God Rešep* (New Haven, 1976). Mitchell J. Dahood provides much comparative material in his "Ancient Semitic Deities in Syria and Palestine," in *Le antiche divinità semitiche*, edited by Sabatino Moscati (Rome, 1958). For the Egyptian materials, most valuable is Rainer Stadelmann's *Syrisch-palästinensische Gottheiten in Ägypten* (Leiden, 1967).

WILLIAM J. FULCO, S.J.

RESH LAQISH. *See* Shimʿon ben Laqish.

REST. *See* Work. *For discussion of the Jewish day of rest, see* Shabbat.

RESURRECTION. The term *resurrection* is so intricately bound up with Christian ideas that it is extremely difficult to decide when it should be used for similar ideas in other religions. Obviously, the term should not be used to refer to the belief that there is an immortal element in man (often called "soul" or "spirit") that lives on after the destruction of the body, or to the belief in some kind of continued existence in a shadowy realm of the dead. Also excluded is the idea of reincarnation, which implies that the soul is repeatedly reborn into a new body. If we define resurrection as the revival of the body, or rather of the man as a whole, after a period of death, we find phenomena that fit this definition only in Zoroastrianism, Judaism, Christianity, and Islam, with doubtful analogies in Chinese Taoism and ancient Indian and Egyptian religions. Belief in resurrection presupposes either a monistic view of man, which implies that man as a whole disappears in death and is then revived to a new existence; or a dualistic view, according to which the body dies whereas the soul or spirit lives on and is later united with the body into a renewed being. Another phenomenon that should be discussed here is the idea of dying and rising gods, which is found in several religions, some with and some without a belief in resurrection.

Taoism. In Chinese Taoism there is frequent mention of prolonging life and strengthening the vital force, but there is no uniform doctrine on this subject. The background is the idea that man, like the universe, consists of several elements, some light, pure, and heavenly, others heavy, impure, and earthly; they are held together by the vital principle, or breath. One early report had it that a certain Po Yu managed to strengthen his life to the extent that he actually returned to life after being dead for some time. In most cases, however, we are told of various practices—meditation, use of alcoholic beverages, magical rites—through which the lower and mortal elements in man can be replaced by higher and immortal ones and the vital principle can be strengthened so as not to be separated from the body. In this way man can achieve immortality and ascend to the heavenly world. But this is hardly resurrection in the strict sense of the word.

India. The Vedic religion of ancient India offers a rich variety of beliefs concerning the dead and the life in the hereafter. There is the idea of the dead haunting the living as ghosts; there is the idea of the heavenly world of Yama, the first man, where the ancestors live; and there are hints of a dark world or a kind of hell. The dead were either buried or burned, the latter practice becoming predominant.

The Vedic language possesses several words that have been thought to denote the "soul" as an immortal spiritual substance in man: *manas* ("thought, thinking"), *asu* ("life"), *ātman* ("breath"), *tanu* ("body, self"). But the equation of any of these words with "soul" is hardly correct. That which appears as a ghost or exists in heaven or hell is not a bodiless spirit but the dead person himself with some kind of body. Any existence without a body is inconceivable. It might seem that the fire in which the corpse is burned would consume it, but in reality the corpse is supposed to be transformed into a heavenly body. In the *Ṛgveda* there are hints that at death the various parts of the body merge with natural phenomena of a similar kind: the flesh goes to the earth, the blood to the water, the breath to the wind, the eye to the sun, the mind *(manas)* to the moon, and so on. These natural phenomena then give the elements of the body back to the deceased as he ascends to heaven in the burning fire. Thus the individual is re-created in the other world as a kind of shadow that looks like his former self but that cannot be touched or embraced. Although this belief differs considerably from the Christian idea of resurrection, it may perhaps be described by this term.

In the Upaniṣads, the term *ātman* ("breath") came to denote the imperishable spiritual element in man, identical with the "spirit" of the universe, called *brahman*. This correlation opened the way to the idea of mystical union between man's spirit and the divine element in the cosmos, and also to the idea that the soul can be reborn into a new body (reincarnation). Thus the idea of resurrection was lost.

Egypt. The ancient Egyptian ideas of the hereafter are very complicated, partly beause they contain elements of differing origins and belonging to different stages of development. The Egyptian view of man presupposes two incorporeal elements, neither corresponding to any modern concept of the soul. The *ba*, usually translated as "soul," is often depicted as a bird; it can mean power or external manifestation, and it represents the ability to "take any form it likes." When a person dies, his *ba* leaves the body but hovers near the corpse. The *ka* combines the ideas of vital force, nourishment, double, and genius. The British Egyptologist Alan Gardiner suggests such translations as "personality, soul, individuality, temperament, fortune, or position." *Ba* and *ka* cannot exist without a bodily substrate. Therefore the body is embalmed to secure their existence. In addition, the funerary rites transform the deceased into an *akh*, a "shining" or "transformed" sprit. In this capacity the deceased lives on in the realm of Osiris, the god of the netherworld, who once died but was revived again as the ruler of the dead.

Other beliefs include the judgment in the hall of Osiris of the deeds of the deceased; the latter's taking part in the journey of the sun god, Re, in his bark; the warding off of monsters and other dangers in the netherworld by means of magical formulas; the happy life of the deceased in the Field of Rushes; and so on. One common idea seems to be that of absorption into the great rhythm of the universe. Osiris was, among other things, a symbol of grain; thus, when the dead join Osiris they participate in the renewal of life in the growing grain. Similarly, when the dead join the sun god they partake of the life of the sun that is renewed every morning. It is difficult to decide whether these are beliefs in resurrection or whether they should be given another name.

Zoroastrianism. The earliest documents of Zoroastrian religion do not mention the resurrection of the body but rather the soul's ascent to paradise. But in the later parts of the Avesta there is at least one reference to resurrection: "When the dead rise, the Living Incorruptible One will come and life will be transfigured" (*Yashts* 19.11). The Living One is the savior, Saoshyant (Pahl., Sōshans), who is to come at the end of the present era. Another passage (*Yashts* 13.11), which speaks of joining together bones, hairs, flesh, bowels, feet, and genitals, refers not to resurrection, as has been maintained, but to birth.

In the cosmological treatise the *Bundahishn* (ninth century CE), a doctrine is set forth in detail. Chapter 30 describes what happens at the death of a man. His soul remains near the head of his body for three nights and is then carried away. If the man has been righteous the soul meets a fragrant wind, a sleek cow, and a beautiful young girl and is brought across the Chinvat Bridge to Paradise. If he has been evil the soul meets a foul wind, a gaunt cow, and a hideous girl and is thrown from the bridge into Hell. This description should be read against the background of the ideas set forth in the Avestan fragment *Hadhōkht Nask,* where we are told that after the three nights the soul meets its *daēnā,* which, according to his works, appears either as a beautiful girl or as an ugly hag. It becomes apparent that the *daēnā* is the heavenly counterpart or double of the soul, whose character is dependent on the man's deeds in this life. As the two join together, the spritual part of man is complete and can enter eternal life.

Chapter 33 of the *Bundahishn* describes the course of the world as it evolves in subsequent periods toward the end, when evil is defeated and the world perfected. Chapter 34 deals with resurrection. At the arrival of the third and last savior, Saoshyant, the dead will be roused, first the primeval man, Gaya-maretan (Pahl., Gayōmard), then the first human pair, Mashyē and Mashyānē, and finally all mankind. Then the great gathering will take place at which everyone's good and evil deeds are revealed. The sinners will be punished and the righteous will enter the bliss of Paradise. A stream of molten metal will spread over the earth, and all men will have to pass through it: the evil will be burned (and purified), the righteous will experience it like lukewarm milk. At the end, all will be saved, and creation will be renewed.

Similar ideas are set forth in chapter 34 of the *Selections of Zatspram* (approximately contemporary with the *Bundahishn*). Here it is asked how creatures who have passed away can receive their bodies back and rise again. The first answer is that it is easier to assemble parts already existing than to create from nothing. If Ahura Mazdā was able to create them, he is also able to assemble the scattered parts again. There are five "storekeepers" that receive the bodily substance of those who have died: the earth keeps flesh and bone; the water, the blood; the plants preserve the head and the hair; the light of the firmament receives the fire; and the wind, the spirit. At the time of the rehabilitation (Frashōkereti; Pahl., Frashkart), Ahura Mazdā will assemble all these elements again then create new human beings. This account is very close to the belief expressed in the Indian *Ṛgveda.* Obviously, these later expositions present a combination of at least two ideas of different origin and character, the idea of the soul joining its counterpart in the other world and the idea of bodily resurrection. Lack of sources prevents us from following the process of amalgamation of these ideas.

Judaism. The Hebrew scriptures (Old Testament) as a whole have no doctrine of resurrection. When it is said, "I kill and I make alive, I wound and I heal" (*Dt.* 32:39), or "The Lord kills and brings to life, he brings down to She'ol [the realm of death] and raises up" (*1 Sm.* 2:7), the stress is on God as the origin and cause of everything rather than on resurrection. Usually the scriptures assert that "if a man dies, he will not live again" (*Jb.* 14:14) or that "he who goes down to She'ol does not come up" (7:9). In the *Book of Psalms* there is the general conviction that Yahveh is stronger than death and can rescue from She'ol: "You have delivered my soul from death, my eyes from tears. . . . I walk before the Lord in the land of the living" (116:8–9); "I shall not die, but I shall live . . . he has not given me over to death" (118:17–18); "God will ransom my soul from the power of She'ol" (49:15). It is never stated how this deliverance takes place; it is enough for the psalmist to know that God will not give him up to death or She'ol. It is probable that for an explanation of the mechanism of deliverance we have to look to the metaphorical language referring to healing of illness or rescue from some deadly danger. Illness or calamity is potential death, and it means being in the grip of She'ol; consequently, rescue from illness or danger is rescue from death. It is interesting to recall that when a Babylonian god is said to be "a reviver of the dead," it clearly means that he cures illness.

Ezekiel 37 reports the prophet's vision of a heap of dry bones in a valley that is revived through "the spirit." At an early stage of Judaism this text was understood as referring to resurrection (e.g., in the paintings of the synagogue at Dura-Europos), but the context indicates that the bones symbolize the Jewish nation, and the message of the vision is that just as it seems impossible for the dead bones to be revived, it also seems impossible for the nation to be restored; however, the impossible is made possible through a divine miracle.

Isaiah 26:19 reads, "Your dead shall live, their bodies shall rise." This passage evidently points back to verse 14, "The dead will not live, the shades will not rise," a reference to the enemies of Israel. It may be, therefore, that verse 19 should be interpreted along the same lines as *Ezekiel* 38: Israel is in a better position than her enemies, therefore Israel shall "live." The next line, however, reads: "Wake up and rejoice, you who sleep in the dust." This may be an early, though vague, reference to the resurrection of the dead. But the chapter belongs to the latest part of the *Book of Isaiah,* the so-called Isaiah apocalypse, and it probably dates from the third century BCE.

The only clear reference to resurrection is found in the *Book of Daniel* (c. 165 BCE). There we read: "Many of those who sleep in the dust will awake, some to eternal life, others to eternal shame (12:2). There can be no doubt: the dead are described as sleeping, and they are going to wake up from their sleep; consequently they will live again. It is not explicitly said that all the dead shall rise, although "many" *(rabbīm)* often has that connotation. Yet not only the righteous will be resurrected; others will awaken also, but to eternal shame.

It has been suggested that the idea of resurrection in Israel has its roots in Canaanite religion. There, the dying and rising of the god Baal plays a significant part in symbolizing the annual death and renewal of vegetation. But the conclusion that such a resurrection might apply to man in general is never drawn, as far as our evidence goes. It should be noted, however, that *Isaiah* 26:19 combines the revival of the dead with the falling of the dew of light, and that dew plays an important part in Canaanite mythology. It is also very probable that *Hosea* 6:2, "He will revive us after two days, on the third day he will raise us up," goes back to a Canaanite formula quoted by repenting people. The prophet, however, rejects the conversion of the people and does not accept their hope of revival. Thus, there may be Canaanite ideas in the background, but the final development of the idea of resurrection probably did not take place without Zoroastrian influence. The Judaism of the period of the Second Temple develops the idea further, without, however, reaching any consensus regarding the details. Above all, the testimonies differ as to whether resurrection means a reunion of body and soul or a renewal of man as a totality.

One of the earliest references to resurrection is found in the *Second Book of the Maccabees* (first century BCE). It shows that the idea of resurrection is bound up with belief in just retribution, especially in the case of martyrdom. Seven young brothers are tortured and killed by King Antiochus, and one young man after another confesses his belief in resurrection: "The king of the universe will raise us up to an everlasting renewal of life" (7:9). "We cherish the hope that God gives of being raised again by him, but for you there will be no resurrection to life" (7:14). Finally, their mother addresses her sons: "God will in his mercy give life and breath back to you again" (7:23). The reason for this hope is that the sons are giving their life "for God's laws," and it is repeatedly stated, especially in 7:36, that the king will receive just punishment for his arrogance. No statement is made about the *how* of the resurrection, but the mother, addressing her last son, expresses her hope "to get him back again with his brothers" (7:29), which seems to imply some kind of family life in the other world.

According to Josephus Flavius (37/8–c. 100), the Essenes believed in the immortality of the soul (*Antiquities* 17.18), whereas Hippolytus (*Against Heresies* 9.27) says that they believed in the resurrection of the body. So far no words to this effect have been found in the Qumran writings.

The clearest statements about resurrection appear in documents from the end of the first century CE; they were probably inspired by reaction to the fall of Jerusalem in 70 CE. Though several passages in *1 Enoch* (22, 90:33, 91:10, 92:3) mention the resurrection, it is only in the so-called Similitudes (chapters 37–71, which are absent from the Qumran manuscripts and probably of later origin) that the idea is clearly set forth: "And in those days shall the earth give back that which has been entrusted to it, and She'ol also shall give back that which it has received, and Hell shall give back that which it owes"(*1 En.* 51:1). It is clear from other passages (46:6, 49:9–10) that the sinners do not take part in this resurrection, which is not the joining of body and soul but the renewal of man as a whole to live on a new earth (51:5).

Similar statements are found in other documents from approximately the same periods. In *4 Ezra* 7:32 we read: "The earth shall give up those who sleep in it, and the dust those who rest there in silence, and the storehouses shall give back the souls entrusted to them." The mention of the souls seems to indicate that death is the separation of body and soul (cf. 7:78) and that resurrection means they are reunited. Similarly, the Syriac *Apocalypse of Baruch* speaks of the opening of the treasuries in which souls are preserved (30:2). The dust is told to give back what is not its own and to let everything arise that it has preserved (42:7); it is said further that the earth shall restore the dead without changing their form (50:2). This last text clearly teaches the resurrection of the body, but the context shows that the righteous will then be transformed into an angelic state. The word *soul* here seems to refer, as in the Old Testament, to man as a whole. Finally, the *Liber antiquitatum biblicarum,* falsely ascribed to Philo, says that God will "revive the dead and raise up from the earth those who sleep" (3:10); after that, judgment will be held and everybody will receive according to his work.

These texts use more or less the same formulaic language, but their view of man is not uniform. Some use *soul* to refer to man as a whole, others distinguish between body and soul. Resurrection always implies the restoration of the body and usually its transfiguration. According to Josephus and the New Testament, the Pharisees accepted the resurrection of the righteous, whereas the Sadducees denied it altogether (*Acts* 23:8, *Mt.* 22:23).

The victory of Pharisaism after the fall of Jerusalem led to general acceptance of the belief in resurrection in rabbinic Judaism. Thus in the Mishnah tractate *Sanhedrin,* chapter 10 begins with the statement that the one who denies the resurrection of the dead has no part in the world to come, and the rest of the chapter is devoted to a discussion of who is not going to rise *(qūm).*

Liturgical texts, such as the ʿAmidah, assert that God "makes the dead alive and keeps faith to those who sleep in the dust" (cf. *Dn.* 12:2), and that he "kills and makes alive and causes salvation to sprout forth" (cf. *1 Sm.* 2:6). It is interesting that on some occasions a reference to God as giving wind and rain is inserted into the prayer, which uses the verb "to sprout forth," in its literal sense referring to the growing of plants. This indicates a parallel between the life of nature and the life of man. The parallel is also suggested by Talmudic comments comparing resurrection with the growing of a grain of wheat (B.T., *San.* 90b; cf., in the New Testament, *1 Cor.* 15:36ff.) and stating that the dead "sprout forth" from the earth (B.T., *Ket.* lllb). Does this language contain a reminiscence of ancient roots in the fertility cult? One rabbinic statement explains resurrection as the reunion of body and soul: "Blessed art thou, who bringest the souls back to the dead bodies" (B.T., *Ber.* 60b). Other passages defend the possibility of resurrection by assuming that a certain part of man, the lowest vertebra or a spoonful of rotten mass, escapes corruption and serves as material for the new body.

Christianity. In primitive Christianity the resurrection of Christ was the fundamental fact; belief in it was even regarded as a prerequisite of salvation. The earliest statements, which are found in the letters of Paul, are very simple and state the fact in a credal form: "God raised Jesus from the dead" (*Rom.* 10:9); "Jesus died and rose again" (*1 Thes.* 4:14). Sometimes the significance of Jesus' resurrection is defined: "He was designated the son of God in power by his resurrection from the dead" (*Rom.* 1:4); "He was put to death for our trespasses and raised for our justification" (4:25). The choice of words and the context indicate (1) that he was dead; (2) that it was God who raised him; and (3) that his resurrection was not merely a return to normal life on earth but a transfer into an existence of a higher kind. The question of body and soul is not discussed.

Jesus' death and resurrection are mentioned together also in his predictions of suffering in the Gospels (*Mk.* 8:31, 9:31, 10:34, and parallels), and in the proclamation of the apostles in *Acts of the Apostles* (2:23–24, 10:39–40, 17:3). It is difficult to tell whether the expression "on the third day" derives from an interpretation based on *Hosea* 6:2 (see above) or is based on actual experience.

The Gospels give no detail of the resurrection itself. What we have is the report on the empty tomb (*Mk.* 16:1ff. and parallels), to which Matthew has given an apologetic touch by adding the story of the guard being bribed by the chief priests to report that the disciples stole the body (*Mt.* 28:11–13). There are, however, several reports of appearances of Jesus, some taking place in Jerusalem, others in Galilee. It is a matter of dispute whether these different geographical locations rest on independent traditions and, if not, how they are related. According to Luke the last appearance is connected with Jesus' ascension to heaven; according to Matthew it is associated with his sending the apostles to preach to all nations.

The New Testament seems to have taken over the general idea of resurrection from contemporary Judaism. *Matthew* 12:41 mentions it explicitly ("will arise at the last judgment"), and it is presupposed in many other passages (e.g., *Mt.* 7:22, 8:11, 11:22, 12:41–42). In his answer to the Sadducees, who deny the resurrection, Jesus adopts the idea of an angelic existence of the resurrected (*Mk.* 12:18–27 and parallels).

The first Christians expected the second coming of Christ (the Parousia) to happen in their lifetime. But as several Christians died without having experienced the Parousia, questions arose as to the reliability of the Christian hope. Paul answers such questions in *1 Thessalonians* 4:13–18, asserting that just as Christ died and rose again, the fellowship with him cannot be broken by death: first those who have died in Christ will rise when "the archangel calls and the trumpet sounds," then those who are still alive will be taken away to heaven to Christ. This idea of a two-step process is taken further in the *Book of Revelation,* according to which the righteous will rise at the beginning of the millennium ("the first resurrection," 20:6), the rest at its end (20:12–13). The same idea seems to be present in *1 Corinthians* 15:22–23, where we learn that "all shall be made alive in Christ . . . first at his coming those who belong to Christ; then comes the end," when all evil powers are defeated and everything is laid under his feet. Elsewhere, there is only reference to resurrection in general as one event, which is clearly presupposed in the parable of the Last Judgment in *Matthew* 25.

The question of how the resurrection is going to take place is dealt with by Paul in *1 Corinthians* 15. The body that rises is not the old body but a new one, just as a new plant comes out of a seed. Nothing is said here of an immortal soul. Man as a whole is perishable; man as a whole is re-created as a "spiritual body." Other New Testament passages seem to imply some kind of existence between death and resurrection, for example, "to be with Christ" (*Phil.* 1:23), "to be in Abraham's bosom" (*Lk.* 16:22), and "to be with Christ in paradise" (23:43). A different approach is represented by the *Gospel of John.* He who believes in Christ receives eternal life here and now (3:36, 5:24). However, other statements in the same gospel, which many exegetes ascribe to a later editor, retain the idea of a resurrection at the end of time (5:28).

Under Greek influence the early church developed the idea of an immortal soul that continues to exist after death and is reunited with the body at the resurrection. This remained the commonly accepted belief of the Christian church into the twentieth century. Modern theology now often tries to view man as a unity that is totally dissolved in death, whereas resurrection implies a total re-creation of the whole being.

Islam. Islam shares with Christianity the belief in a general resurrection followed by a judgment. The stress is rather on the latter. In the Qur'ān the last day is referred to as "the day of resurrection" *(yawm al-qiyāmah),* but also as "the day of judgment" *(yawm ad-dīn),* "the day of reckoning" *(yawm al-ḥisāb),* or "the day of awakening" *(yawm al-ba'th).* In the Qur'ān there are several very graphic descriptions of the day of resurrection, focusing on the natural phenomena that accompany it and on the outcome of the judgment—the believers entering paradise and the unbelievers being thrown into the fire of hell. It is a day "when the trumpet is blown" (cf. *Mt.* 24:31, *1 Thes.* 4:16) and men "shall come in troops, and heaven is opened and the mountains are set in motion" (surah 78:18–20; cf. 18:99), a day "when heaven is rent asunder . . . when earth is stretched out and casts forth what is in it" (84:1–4; cf. 99:1–2). After these events the dead "shall come forth from their graves unto their Lord; they shall say: Alas for us! Who roused us from our bed?" (36:51–52).

There is no reference in the Qur'ān to an immortal soul, nor is resurrection defined as the reunion of body and soul. Surah 81:7 states that "the souls shall be coupled"; some Muslim commentators take this to mean that the souls are to be joined to their bodies, whereas others think that they are to be coupled with their equals (good or evil) or that they will be divided into two groups.

When the unbelievers express doubt in the resurrection, the Qur'ān refers to God's omnipotence as the creator: "Does man think we shall not gather his bones? Indeed, we are able to shape again his fingers" (75:3–4); "Man says: Who shall quicken the bones when they are decayed? Say: He shall quicken them who originated them the first time. He knows all creation" (36:78–79; cf. 17:53, 19:68). Again, "O men, if you are in doubt as to the uprising, surely we created you of dust, then of a sperm-drop, then of a blood clot . . . and we establish in the womb what we wish, till a stated term, then we deliver you as infants. . . . And you see the earth blackened, then we send down water upon it, it quivers and swells and puts forth herbs of every joyous kind. This is because God—he is the Truth—brings the dead to life and is powerful over everything" (22:5–6). Thus God forms the child in the womb, he renews the life of vegetation, so he is also able to raise the dead. Only on one occasion is there a hint that the resurrected body will be different from the present one: "We have decreed among you death . . . that we may exchange the likes of you and make you to grow again in a fashion you do not know" (56:60–61). But the wording is not very specific here.

Later Muslim tradition has developed these ideas in several directions. A great number of signs foretelling the day of resurrection are mentioned; the blast of the trumpet has become three blasts: the blast of consternation, the blast of examination and the blast of resurrection. We also find the idea that at the resurrection the body will be raised and united to its soul, and that the lower part of the spine is preserved as a basis for the future body (as in the rabbinic idea discussed above). There are also speculations about a "punishment in the grave" (*'adhāb al-qabr*): immediately after burial the deceased is questioned by the two angels, Munkar and Nakir, and if the deceased is not able to answer the questions concerning God and the Prophet, punishment is inflicted.

Several speculations are based on an interpretation of the obscure word *barzakh* in the Qur'ān (23:100), taken by commentators to denote a bar or obstacle preventing return to the world after death. The word is now defined as the interval or space between this world and the next, or between death and resurrection, a kind of intermediary state. Ibn Qayyim al-Ǧauzīyah (d. 1350), who wrote a book about the spirit, presents various theories about what happens to the spirit between death and resurrection: the spirits are in or near the grave; the spirits of the believers only are in Paradise, or at the gates of Paradise, or in the sacred well Zamzam, or on the right-hand side of Adam; the unbelievers are in the fire of Hell, or in the well Barhūt.

A Possible Precursor. The belief in dying and reviving gods has sometimes been taken as one of the roots of the idea of resurrection. The English anthropologist James G. Frazer (1854–1941) devoted one volume of *The Golden Bough* to "the dying god," interpreting the myth as a symbol of the death and renewal of vegetation. However, the clearest example of a dying god, the Canaanite Aliyan Baal, was not known when the book was written, because the Ugaritic texts were only discovered in 1929. Baal is the god of thunder, rain, and fertility. He is killed by his enemy Mot (whose name means "death" and who represents the dry season), and vegetation withers away. However, Baal's sister Anat defeats Mot, and Baal returns to life, which also implies the renewal of vegetation. The myth probably served as the scenario of a ritual drama, whose aim was to secure the new life of vegetation and promote fertility in general. However, there is no trace of any belief in the resurrection of man based on the god's return to life.

Another example is the Sumerian god Dumuzi (the Akkadian Tammuz). According to the Sumerian myths, Dumuzi, the god of the flocks and the grain, was killed by demons and had to descend into the netherworld. There are no clear texts referring to his resurrection, but there are hints that it was decided that he spend part of the year in the netherworld and the other part on earth. This would indicate that his death and return to life represent the seasonal cycle. Here too, evidence for a belief in resurrection is lacking.

Elements from these two myths (of Baal and Dumuzi) are clearly recognized in what Greek sources report on the Phoenician-Syrian god Adonis (Phoen., *'ādōn*, "lord"). He was loved by the goddess Aphrodite and by the lady of the netherworld, Persephone; Zeus finally decided that Adonis should stay one half of the year with Aphrodite and the other half with Persephone. (It is also told that Adonis was killed by a boar and was bitterly mourned by Aphrodite.) In the case of the Egyptian god Osiris, the facts are somewhat more favorable to the theory of belief in resurrection growing out of the myth of the dying god. The myth of Osiris was known in several versions, but their essence is as follows. Osiris was a good king who was killed and dismembered by his brother Seth. His wife, Isis, mourned him, found the body, reassembled its parts, and restored it to life through a magical formula. Isis then was made pregnant and bore a son, Horus, who was recognized as the lawful successor of his father, while Osiris was made ruler of the netherworld. As a god, Osiris had clear connections with the inundation of the Nile and with grain. These connections are manifest in several rites of the Osiris "mysteries," including the burial of an effigy of Osiris made of earth and grain. Growing grain symbolizes the god's return to life. Here, for once, is a clear connection with beliefs concerning man's life in the hereafter. Every man who is properly buried becomes an Osiris in the other world and shares the life of the god.

Clearly, there are considerable differences between these dying gods, and it is doubtful whether all of them represent the same specific type of god. Great caution should be exercised in seeking to draw conclusions concerning the role played by these myths in the development of the belief in resurrection.

[*See also* Dying and Rising Gods.]

BIBLIOGRAPHY

There is no monograph on resurrection in general. Volume 5 (1965) of the journal *Kairos* has a series of articles on resurrection in different religions, supplemented by two articles on Jewish ideas in volumes 14 (1972) and 15 (1973).

Discussion of Chinese ideas can be found in Henri Maspero's *Mélanges posthumes sur les religions et l'histoire de la Chine*, 3 vols. (Paris, 1950) by consulting the index entries under *immortalité*. Indian ideas are dealt with by Helmuth von Glasenapp in *Unsterblichkeit und Erlösung in den indischen Religionen* (Halle, 1938). For Egyptian ideas, see Alan H. Gardiner's *The Attitude of the Ancient Egyptians to Death and the Dead* (Cambridge, 1935); Herman Kees's *Totenglauben und Jenseitsvorstellungen der alten Ägypter*, 2d ed. (Berlin, 1956), a classic but difficult work; and, for certain aspects, Louis V. Zabkar's *A Study of the Ba Concept in Ancient Egyptian Texts* (Chicago, 1968) and Gertie Englund's *Akh: Une notion religieuse dans l'Egypte pharaonique* (Uppsala, 1978). The only comprehensive study of Iranian conceptions is Nathan Söderblom's *La vie future d'après le Mazdéisme* (Paris 1901). It is now somewhat out of date, but is still useful, as is J. D. C. Pavry's *The Zoroastrian Doctrine of a Future Life* (New York, 1926).

Old Testament ideas have been dealt with by Edmund F. Sutcliffe in *The Old Testament and the Future Life* (Westminster, Md., 1947) and by Robert Martin-Achard in *De la mort à la résurrection . . . dans . . . l'Ancien Testament* (Neuchâtel, 1956). For further discussion, see Harris Birkeland's "The Belief in the Resurrection of the Dead in the Old Testament," *Studia Theologica* 3 (1950): 60–78, and my book *Israelite Religion* (Philadelphia, 1975), pp. 239–247. Among studies dealing with later Jewish and Christian ideas, see R. H. Charles's *A Critical History of the Doctrine of a Future Life in Israel, in Judaism, and in Christianity* (1899; reprint, New York, 1979) and Pierre Grelot's *De la mort à la vié eternelle* (Paris, 1971). For Judaism, see also H. C. C. Cavallin's *Life after Death*, vol. 1, part 1, *An Inquiry into the Jewish Background* (Lund, 1974), a comprehensive study of all relevant texts, and George W. E. Nickelsburg's *Resurrection, Immortality, and Eternal Life in InterTestamental Judaism* (Cambridge, Mass., 1972).

Of the literature on the New Testament only a few books can be mentioned: Murdoch E. Dahl's *The Resurrection of the Body: A Study of 1 Corinthians 15* (London, 1962); *Immortality and Resurrection*, 2d ed., edited by Pierre Benoît and Roland E. Murphy (New York, 1970); Robert C. Tennenhill's *Dying and Rising with Christ* (Berlin, 1967); and Geerhardus Vos's *The Pauline Eschatology* (Grand Rapids, Mich., 1961). Works in German are Oscar Cullman's *Unsterblichkeit der Seele und Auferstehung der Toten* (Stuttgart, 1963), Paul Hoffmann's *Die Toten in Christus: Ein religionsgeschichtliche und exegetische Untersuchung zur paulinischen Eschatologie* (Münster, 1978), and Günter Kegel's *Auferstehung Jesu, Auferstehung der Toten* (Gütersloh, 1970).

On resurrection in Christian theology, see Paul Althaus's *Die letzten Dinge* (1922; Gütersloh, 1956), Walter Künneth's *Theologie der Auferstehung* (1934; Giessen, 1982), and Klaus Kienzler's *Logik der Auferstehung* (Freiburg im Breisgau, 1976), a study of the theologians Rudolf Bultmann, Gerhard Ebeling, and Wolfhart Pannenberg.

For a broad discussion of dying and rising gods, see James G. Frazer's *The Golden Bough*, 3d. ed., rev. & enl., vol. 4, *The Dying God* (1912; London, 1955). On Dumuzi, see Thorkild Jacobsen's *The Treasures of Darkness: A History of Mesopotamian Religion* (New Haven, 1976), pp. 25–73. On Baal, See Arvid S. Kapelrud's *Ba'al in the Ras Shamra Texts* (Copenhagen, 1952); Werner H. Schmidt's "Baals Tod und Auferstehung," *Zeitschrift für Religions- und Geistesgeschichte* 15 (1963): 1–13; and Michael David Coogan's *Stories from Ancient Canaan* (Philadelphia, 1978). On Osiris, E. A. Wallis Budge's *Osiris and the Egyptian Resurrection*, 2 vols. (1911; New York, 1973), and J. Gwyn Griffith's *The Origin of Osiris and His Cult*, 2d ed., rev. & enl. (Leiden, 1980), may be profitably consulted.

HELMER RINGGREN

RETREAT may be defined as a limited period of isolation during which an individual, either alone or as part of a small group, withdraws from the regular routine of daily life, generally for religious reasons. Retreats are one of the commoner practices in the religious life of nearly all peoples, although they are often restricted to a determinate type or class of persons: those preparing for initiation (e. g., into the adult life of a clan, into a religious group, or into some public office of a religious nature), those undergoing a process of conversion, those in search of a religious vocation, or those seeking a periodic renewal of their spiritual lives. During this period, retreatants interrupt their ordinary routine, break off regular social relationships, and (except for those who already live in monasteries or the like) withdraw into a solitary place or to a special building set apart for such purposes. This isolation, as well as the interruption of social intercourse and ordinary life, is adopted as a condition that enables individual retreatants to enter within themselves in silence, in order to establish contact with the divinity or with the world of the spirits. [*See* Silence.] Hence, retreats often involve the use of various ascetical means, such as fasting, abstinence, prayer, meditation, and techniques aimed at inducing a revelatory dream, trance, or ecstasy.

Various forms of retreat may be distinguished, and participants may engage in retreats with varying frequency. A retreat accompanying a radical conversion of life or the discernment of a vocation may be a rare or even unique event in an individual's life; whereas that aimed at personal spiritual renewal might be repeated periodically. Retreats of initiation may follow quite diverse procedures, depending on the kind of initiation involved. Thus, one may distinguish retreats of tribal initiation; retreats of search for a revelatory dream; retreats of shamanistic or monastic initiaion; and retreats of conversion, discernment, and renewal.

Retreats of Tribal Initiation. In generic and somewhat abstract terms (since in reality quite different forms of ritual may be involved), initiation into the life of a tribe entails separating candidates from the social nucleus to which they belong as children, especially from their mother, and isolating them in a well-defined zone, protected by rigid taboos. [*See* Initiation.] There they are placed under the direction of elders chosen by the tribe. The neophytes are then subjected to certain strict disciplines (fasting, abstinence, and various taboos), are instructed by the elders in certain traditional truths and beliefs (social and sexual ethics, myths and rituals, techniques of hunting, fishing, or farming), and are forced to undergo certain more or less painful tests. At the end of this period of initiation, after passing through certain liberating rites, the neophytes, having undergone a profound transformation, return to the tribe as adults. The symbolic meaning of this period of isolation seems clear enough. Cultures that practice this kind of initiation regard it as a mutation or deep transformation of the human being: a sort of death and rebirth. Henceforth, all that had previously constituted the life of a child must be suppressed, especially the child's former dependence on its mother. The adolescent through this isolation, enters the world of the sacred, of mythic time, and is often locked in struggle with mysterious force, involving some form of bodily suffering (torture and, above all, circumcision). In this case the retreat is precisely the vehicle that allows this breaking away and entry.

Retreats of Search for a Revelatory Dream. A number of peoples, especially pre-Columbian Indians, submitted their children and adolescents to a period of isolation aimed at enabling them to enter into contact with the spirit who was to guide each of them throughout life. [*See* Quest.] This phenomenon is especially notable among certain Canadian groups, such as the Athapascans, who submitted children as young as five years old to the test. The norm commonly followed involved removing these children or adolescents from their normal world of relationships, abandoning them in a solitary place, and subjecting them to a strict fast until physical weakness induced a state of hallucination. The first image that presented itself to the child or adolescent was the spirit who would accompany and protect him until death, a sort of tutelary *numen* whom he would thenceforward invoke. The Delaware and Algonquin of the Atlantic coast observed much the same procedure with twelve-year-old girls and boys, but introduced the concept of the compassion of the spirits, whom the adolescents were required to invoke while they practiced their total fast. The spirits then put an end to the sufferings of the initiates by revealing themselves to them in a dream. After a certain length of time, the parents visited the adolescents to see whether the revelatory experience had yet occurred. If it had, they brought their offspring back to the tribe, where they were regarded as the depositories of a sacred force (Walter Krickeberg et al., *Die Religionen des Alten Amerika,* Stuttgart, 1961; see also J. Blumensohn, "The Fast among North American Indians," *American Anthropology* 35, 1933, pp. 451–469).

Retreats of Shamanistic Initiation. Mircea Eliade treats shamanism as a religious limit-experience: a form of mysticism originating in a vocation awakened by a crisis that is found in many religions (*Shamanism: Archaic Techniqes of Ecstasy,* rev. and enl. ed., New York, 1964). Here, we take shamanism in its original, strict sense, as a characteristic and primary expression of the religious life of the peoples of north central Asia. The shaman is an individual who has been suddenly overcome by a spirit and has, by that very fact, received a distinctive gift. The signs whereby this possession becomes known coincide with what the Western mind would call symptoms of epilepsy or, more generally, a form of nervous disorder. Whoever receives such a "dangerous" gift must stay in constant contact with the world of the spirits, and this the shamsn does by isolating himself. Frequently, the candidate is instructed by an old shaman, or the whole tribe may take part in his initiation by contributing to its ritual sacrifices. The future shaman learns the necessary formulas and offertory rites and then retires to the wild in order to learn the techniques of ecstasy by sitting before a fire and repeating certain formulas. At the end of his retreat, the individual is consecrated in a rite celebrated by the ancient shaman who instructed him. From this retreat the new shaman emerges endowed with special powers. He can now enter into contact with the world of the spirits, and his mediation thus becomes important for the tribe. [*See* Shamanism.]

Retreats of Monastic Initiation. Among the four exemplary stages that Hindu tradition distinguishes in the life of a man—the third, after those of student and father of a family, but before that of wandering holy man—is that of the individual who withdraws in solitude into the forest, where he (now called a *vanaptrasthin*) commits himself to meditation and to certain practices of asceticism. This retreat portends his coming to spiritual maturity and his eventual irradiation of the people who surround him, by way of his example and teaching. Since a long period of isolation is involved here, we might well classify this retreat as an experience of the eremitical life. Significantly, in the history of Western monasticism, Athanasius, in his *Life of Antony,* describes how his hero, after his conversion, first underwent a stage of basic intitation under the direction of an ascetic, after which he underwent a further stage of isolation in a necropolis, followed by a third and decisive stage of enclosure in a ruined castle, where he remained for twenty years. At the end of this stage, Athanasius tells us in terms reminiscent of the mystery cults, that Antony "came forth as from a sanctuary, initiated in the mysteries and filled with the divine spirit" (*Life of Antony* 14). Finally, after receiving the gift of spiritual fecundity, Antony accepted some disciples, although he remained with them in solitude. The parallels to Hindu monasticism are revealing: in both cases there is a retreat into complete solitude, which prepares the individuals for full spiritual maturity and confers on them a certain irradiative power. The Hindu ascetic then embarks upon an itinerant, renunciative life *(saṃnyāsa),* returning to society but not forming part of it. The Christian anchorite becomes an elder—a religious father or mother—and accepts disciples, instructing them in the spiritual life. [*See* Eremitism.]

A similar phenomenon appears in the lives of other Christian saints, who were dedicated not to monastic contemplation but rather to intense activity among people. Ignatius Loyola spent almost an entire year, from March 1522 to February 1523, in Manresa, where he devoted himself to prayer (seven hours daily), fasting, and abstinence. He emerged from this experience transformed and illumined in spirit by revelations of various kinds. Three centuries later, Anthony M. Claret (1807–1870) spent some months at San Andrés del Pruit (Girona, Spain), dedicated to prayer. He went forth from this retreat powerfully consecrated to itinerant preaching. In both cases, the retreat was one of initiation into an intense religious experience, accompanied by an outburst of apostolic irradiation. It would be easy to cite numerous other examples of this type.

A different sort of retreat of monastic initiation is represented by the novitiate, a relatively long period of trial prior to incorporation into a religious community. During the novitiate, candidates are separated from others—even from professed members of the community—and placed under the direction of a master, who instructs them and tests their vocation. The novitiate appears in the Buddhist tradition, where it is called *upasaṃpadā* ("goal, arrival"). Its aim is to prepare the novices for entry upon the way of salvation, and it ends with an anointing ceremony *(abhiṣeka),* which consecrates them. In Christian monasticism, an initial period of instruction and trial originated among the anchorites of the fourth century. It was a rather long period, which ended when the elder in charge adjudged the novice to have reached the required maturity, and invited him to withdraw into his chosen solitude. In monastic communities, the novitiate was reduced to a period of a year. At present, it lasts from one to two years, according to custom. Originally, the year of novitiate began with investiture of the novice in the habit, while it later came to be terminated with his commitment to the religious life. Besides this investiture, another feature observed in the past was a change of the novice's name, to indicate that a secular individual had died and a religious one had come to birth. The medieval Christian theology of the religious profession as a second baptism referred to this idea of a symbolic death and rebirth. [*See* Monasticism.]

Retreats of Spiritual Renewal. The practice of withdrawing for a relatively brief period of time in order to revitalize oneself spiritually seems to be evidenced in all religions that attach great importance to the spiritual experience of the individual. The retreat in the woods constitutes one of the stages of the ideal way of the Hindu. Even masters return periodically to the forest solitude, in order to encounter themselves more deeply. But it is above all in Islam and Christianity that this kind of retreat has been most popular.

Islam. The custom of devoting a period of time to prayer and fasting *(khalwah),* while withdrawing from social contacts and ordinary occupations, is amply documented in the Muslim world much earlier than in Christendom. The source of inspiration for this practice is the fact that, according to the Qur'ān, God gave the Law to Moses at the end of a retreat of forty days (surah 7:142). It is also said that Adam received his life-breath only forty days after he had been formed from the clay. The Prophet himself left an example, by going frequently into retreat. The great Andalusian mystic Muḥammad ibn al-ʿArabī (d. 1240) tells of the revelations he received during a retreat he made as a very young man in Seville (*Al-futūḥāt al-makkīyah,* Cairo, AH 1329/1911 CE, vol. 1, p. 186). Ibn al-ʿArabī also wrote a treatise on the conditions for making a retreat, the *Kitāb al-khalwah.* A century later, the Indian Sharaf al-Din Manērī (d. 1381) devoted one of his *Hundred Letters* to explaining the origin and aim of the retreat. An essential element in it is the remembrance of God, that is, the sense of God's presence and the invocation of his name. By reviving the sense of the divine presence, the retreat heals and fortifies the soul, and disposes it to continue in that presence when the retreatant returns to ordinary life.

In Ṣūfī orders, the superior of a house is obliged to go on retreat periodically. The novices, too, must make a retreat, ordinarily for forty days. This forty days' experience must be made in a solitary place or, if one is a member of a community, in a dark cell. Fasting is essential to this kind of retreat: whoever makes one must reduce his food consumption considerably throughout, and abstain completely from eating during the last three days. The lives of the Ṣūfī mystics contain numerous allusions to this practice (see Javad Nurbakhsh, *Masters of the Path,* New York, 1980, pp. 115, 117). Ibn al-ʿArabī tells us of a retreat he made with the master Abū Zakarīyā' Yaḥyā ibn Ḥassān (*Sufis of Andalusia,* Berkeley, 1971, p. 138).

Christianity. In Christianity, especially during the last few centuries, this type of retreat, aimed at the spiritual renewal of the individual through meditation, prayer, and silence, has reached a high level of development. Such a retreat is often made under the direction of a master, who engages in periodic dialogue with the individual retreatant, or else delivers instructions, when the retreat is made by a group.

It is significant that certain popular histories of the retreat begin with the episode narrated by the evangelist Mark (repeated, with amplifications, in the Matthaean and Lukan parallels), concerning Jesus' withdrawal into the desert of Judaea after his baptism and the "descent" of the Holy Spirit upon him. The Markan account (*Mk.* 1:12–13) is not only christological in content, but also exemplary in intention. Jesus, after his baptism and his anointing by the Spirit, appears as the New Adam, dwelling among the wild beasts and ministered to by angels. During this time (scholars debate whether the passage existed in the tradition prior to Mark), Jesus was tempted by the spirit of evil but, unlike the first Adam, overcame the temptation (see Vincent Taylor, *The Gospel according to Mark,* London, 1955, pp. 162–164). Of itself, the episode did not overtly attribute to Jesus the intention of devoting himself especially to spiritual exercises of prayer. The accounts of Matthew (4:1–11) and Luke (4:1–13) add that Jesus' stay in the desert lasted forty days, and that the temptation came at the end of this period.

The account of Jesus' sojourn in the desert added even richer spiritual implications to the biblical texts on the passage of the Hebrew people through the desert, before their entry into Canaan. The desert now became the symbol of a new spiritual attitude. [*See* Desert.] Origen, in his commentary on *Exodus,* speaks of the need for retreat: we must leave our familiar surroundings and go to a place free of worldly preoccupations, a place of silence and interior peace, where we can learn wisdom and come to a deep knowledge of the word of God (*In Exodum Homiliae,* Wilhelm Baehrens, ed., Leipzig, 1920, p. 167).

Drawing their inspiration from the example of Jesus, the Christian churches soon established a period of forty days dedicated to fasting, abstinence, and greater prayer, in order to prepare the faithful for the celebration of the Pascha. Two themes were interwoven in the sermons of the Fathers on Lent: that of participation in Christ's struggles and sufferings during his passion as a preparation for the celebration of the Resurrection, and that of a model projection on it, of the fast and temptations of Jesus in the solitude of the Judean desert. On this fundamental model, they occasionally superimposed the image of the wandering of the Israelites in the desert, with all the trials and temptations to which they were subjected there (see Leo the Great, "Sermons on Lent," *Patrologia Latina,* vol. 54). In addresses to the laity, the latter were not asked to go on retreat (although they are asked to prolong their prayer), but were exhorted to conversion, to charity toward the poor, and to reconciliation with enemies. Traditionally, it was also recommended that they forego diversions and entertainments.

The anonymous author of the *Rule of the Master* (central Italy, c. 500) introduced three chapters on the observance of Lent by monks, prescribing that they multiply their prayers and perform more acts of fast and abstinence (*Rule of the Master,* chaps. 51–53). Benedict (480–c. 547) reduced the rule for Lent to a single chapter, in which he echoed Leo the Great and the *Rule of the Master.* In it he added a recommendation that monks recite more numerous individual prayers and restrict their dealings with each other (*Rule of Saint Benedict,* chap. 49). Lent thus tended to become a sort of forty-day retreat spent in silence, prayer, fasting, and abstinence. From the Middle Ages on, the monastic orders began to interrupt all contact, even by way of letter, with outsiders, throughout the period of Lent. Thus, the Lenten retreat was fundamentally a retreat of spiritual renewal, in which the individual retreatant relived certain fundamental themes of Christianity, derived primarily from the passion of Christ, but secondarily from his withdrawal and fast in the desert.

It is fitting at this point to inquire into the rise, in Christian churches, of the practice of the retreat proper, that is to say, of that prayerful kind of withdrawal practiced by a person, either alone or as part of a small group, for a certain short period of time. It was precisely the celebration of Lent that suggested the first tentative steps in this direction. Around the end of the fourth century and the beginning of the fifth, Euthymius the Great, a monk of Melitene, adopted the custom of withdrawing during Lent of each year and going to a mountaintop, where he gave himself over to prayer and fasting. Later, he went with a friend each year into the desert of Koutila (see Cyril of Scythopolis, *Life of Euthymius,* edited by E. Schwartz, in *Texte und Untersuchungen,* vol. 49, no. 2, Lipsia, 1939, pp. 3–85). Jesus' stay in the Judean desert thus became a model that was imitated literally. It is quite possible—indeed, probable—that other monks followed the same norm, in an endeavor to practice a stricter eremitical life during Lent.

Yet another historical fact might be considered as a precursor of the modern retreat. Pilgrimages to shrines, which were so frequent during certain periods of the Middle Ages, involved a break with the normal situation of the individual, a going forth from one's city and family, in order to visit some usually distant holy place ("to *ferne* halwes," as Chaucer noted in his prologue to the *Canterbury Tales,* poking fun at English pilgrims who managed to get no farther than Canterbury). Palestine, the tombs of the apostles in Rome, and Compostela were among the most common goals. The deep reason behind these journeys was the desire to visit a sacred place where the presence of the supernatural was more perceptible, thanks to the presence either of the relics of a saint or of some venerable holy image. Sometimes these pilgrimages became the occasion of a process of conversion and separation from the world. It is noteworthy, for example, that the primitive nucleus of twelfth-century hermitages of Our Lady, at Mount Carmel (the future Carmelite order), were constituted by men of western Europe who had established themselves in the Holy Land. In certain cases, the pilgrimage shrine was served by a community of monks who ran a hostelry for those who wished to spend a limited period of prayer and silence nearby. This fact is documented in connection with the shrine and abbey of Einsiedeln, Switzerland, perhaps as early as the twelfth century (Ludwig Raeber, *Our Lady of Hermits,* Einsiedeln, 1961), and, somewhat later, at the shrine and monastery of Montserrat, Spain (Joan Segarra, *Montserrat,* Barcelona, 1961).

But the retreat as commonly known during the past few centuries has its roots, properly speaking, in the spiritual movement called the Devotio Moderna, initiated by Gerhard Groote (1340–1384) in the Low Countries, of which the most widely known representative is Thomas à Kempis (c. 1380–1471). Groote, converted to a fervent life in 1374, withdrew for a time to the charterhouse of Munnikhuizen, near Arnhem on the Rhine. The Brethren of the Common Life and the authors of the Devotio Moderna popularized their form of piety among the secular clergy and the laity, giving it a practical and ascetical interpretation, well suited to the clearly individualistic horizons of the spirituality of the Christian West in their day. Next came the refinement of different methods of meditation, and the compilation of various handbooks of meditations. In the early fourteenth century, the Tuscan Franciscan John de Caulibus published his *Meditations on the Life of Christ;* Gerard of Zutphen (d. 1398), in his *De spiritualibus ascensionibus,* propounded a precise method of meditations and examens, a procedure repeated later by the Dutch canon regular, John Mombaer (d. 1501), the last master of the Devotio Moderna, who used it as an instrument of reform in the monasteries of the clerks regular in France. In 1500, the reforming abbot of Montserrat, Francisco Jiménez de Cisneros, printed his *Ejercitatorio de la vida espiritual,* containing a precise method of meditations, and a plan that structured the various meditations into four successive weeks. The technique developed out of the Devotio Moderna could thus be used in a period set aside especially for prayer and meditation.

This technique culminated in the *Spiritual Exercises* of Ignatius Loyola, the founder of the Society of Jesus. It is a methodical interweaving of meditations, contemplations, and examens, more or less developed, taking place over four weeks and accompanied by a series of counsels and rules. He first sketched out the method during his own retreat at Manresa, and perfected it over the years until the definitive version was approved by Pope Paul III in 1548. Although there are points of contact between Ignatius and some of his predecessors (especially Jiménez de Cisneros, whose method he seems to have known), he is quite original in definitively tying these meditations to a retreat made under the direction of a master, with the basic aim of choosing a proper mode of life for the greater service of God—hence, the rules of discernment that accompany the *Exercises.* Starting with the first companions of the founder, the Jesuits have continued to be trained in the *Exercises* of Ignatius.

In the sixteenth century, retreat exercises according to the Ignatian method had already become popular, although they were practiced only by priests and religious at the time, not by the laity. Retreat houses were established in order to facilitate the arrangement of retreats for those who wished to make them. The first such house was opened in a villa in Siena, Italy, in 1538. This was followed by the retreat houses of Alcala, Spain, in 1553, Cologne, Germany, in 1561, and Louvain, Belgium, in 1569. In the seventeenth century this practice was adopted by the principal representatives of French spirituality. Vincent de Paul (d. 1660) is said to have directed the *Exercises* of more than twenty thousand persons. The *Exercises,* in somewhat modified and shortened form, began to be practiced by the laity in great numbers. An outstanding figure in the history of retreats was the Argentinian María Antonia de San José de la Paz (1730–1799), who organized Ignatian retreats in the course of her life for more than a hundred thousand people. However, the Ignatian retreat was gradually converted into a retreat of spiritual renewal as it came to be repeated periodically by persons who had already chosen a type of Christian life (priestly, religious, or secular) and only sought to be spiritually revitalized through a retreat.

Priests, religious, and seminarians of the Roman Catholic church commonly make eight days of spiritual exercises annually. Many members of the Catholic laity follow the same norm in our time. Some periodically make even a month's exercises. Hence one may find retreat houses in all countries where the Roman Catholic church is present. In 1836, the bishop of Viviers, France, approved the Congregation of the Sisters of Our Lady of the Cenacle, founded by Marie Victoire Thérèse Couderc and by Jean-Pierre Étienne Terme. Initially called Dames de la Retraite ("retreat ladies"), the Sisters promoted the practice of retreats among laity. They presently have retreat houses in England (since 1888), and even more exist in the United States, where they arrived in 1892. A similar end is pursued by the Retreat Sisters of the Sacred Heart, founded in 1678 in Quimper, France, by Claude Thérèse de Kermeno. Other men and women religious are dedicated to the same apostolate. In France, toward the end of the nineteenth century, the Oeuvre des Retraites de Perseverance was founded, and soon the movement spread to Italy. Its aim is to promote yearly retreats and monthly days of recollection among the laity, as a means of renewing Christian life. Besides the month-long and annual eight-day retreat forms, where the dominant influence is Ignatian, there are weekend retreats for laity, which follow many different methods: scriptural, charismatic, healing, and so forth. In the United States, the National Catholic Laymen's Retreat Conference was founded in 1928. A retreat league founded by the Sisters of the Cenacle became, in 1936, the National Laywomen's Retreat Movement.

A particular form of retreat, originally among Catholics, has been propagated by the movement known as Cursillos de Cristiandad, founded by Bishop Hervás in Majorca in 1949, whence it has spread to several other countries. A group of Christians, from almost any walk of life, retreat for a few days dedicated to community reflection, liturgy, dialogue, and private reflection. They examine and share the concrete faith-experience of their ordinary life. The *Cursillos* movement, which has existed for some years in the United States, is organized on national and diocesan levels, and has, to some extent, been practiced by other Christian groups, mainly Lutherans and Episcopalians.

Finally, some mention should be made of the monthly retreat or recollection day. Practiced mainly by religious and priests in the nineteenth century, it became almost obligatory after Pius X recommended it in his exhortation to the Catholic clergy in 1908. The Second Vatican Council, in its Decree on Priests, also recommended the practice of retreats to the clergy (*Presbyterorum Ordinis*, no. 18).

BIBLIOGRAPHY

Very little, if anything, of a general nature has been published on the topic of retreat. References to retreats, seclusion, and the like can be found in any general survey on Hindu, Muslim, and Christian mysticism, as well as in works dealing with phenomenology of religion.

Works dealing with specific traditions can, however, be recommended. For a discussion of retreat traditions in tribal societies, see Victor Turner's *The Forest of Symbols* (Ithaca, N.Y., 1969). On the role of seclusion in the Buddhist monastic tradition, see John C. Holt's *Discipline: The Canonical Buddhism of the Vinayapaṭaha* (Delhi, 1981). On retreat in the Christian tradition, the *New Catholic Encyclopedia*, vol. 12 (New York, 1967), includes a valuable article by Thomas E. Dubay. Further discussion of the topic is available in *Historia de la practica de los Ejercicios Espirituales de San Ignacio de Loyola*, 2 vols. (Bilbao, Spain, 1946–1955), by Ignacio Iparraguirre. For the role of retreat in Eastern Orthodox churches, see Catherine de Hueck Doherty's *Sobornošt* (Notre Dame, Ind., 1977). For discussion of Muslim retreats, see Muḥammad ibn al-ʿArabī's *Kitāb al-khalwah* (Aya Sofia, 1964) and letters 96 and 22 in Sharafuddin Maneri's *The Hundred Letters*, translated by Paul Jackson (New York, 1980).

JUAN MANUEL LOZANO

RETRIBUTION. *See* Revenge and Retribution; *see also* Judgment of the Dead.

REVEL, BERNARD (1885–1940), rabbinic scholar and organizer of American Jewish Orthodoxy. Born in Pren, a suburb of Kaunas (Kovno), Lithuania, where his father was the community rabbi, Revel later studied in the Telz *yeshivah* and was ordained in Kaunas at the age of sixteen. Immigrating to the United States in 1906, Revel received his master of arts degree from New York University in 1909; three years later he completed a Ph.D. at Dropsie College with a thesis entitled "The Karaite Halakhah and Its Relation to Sadducean, Samaritan, and Philonian Halakhah."

Revel first worked in the Oklahoma-based petroleum company of his wife's family, but in 1915 he accepted the presidency of New York's newly merged Yeshivat Etz Chaim and Rabbi Isaac Elchanan Theological Seminary. Under its auspices, Revel then opened the Talmudical Academy, the first such *yeshivah* high school in the United States. He also reorganized the rabbinical school, and in 1928, he continued his expansion program with the opening of Yeshiva College, later Yeshiva University (1945).

Revel guided the schools in the spirit of modern Orthodoxy, attempting to perpetuate the traditional Torah way of life within the context of American society. Yeshiva College, in particular, marked the first effort to provide traditional Talmudic study and liberal arts training under the same auspices. Despite the vigorous opposition of some rabbinical leaders, who feared for the primacy of Torah study in such an institution, Revel forged ahead and in 1937 opened a graduate department in advanced Jewish and cognate studies. In 1941 this school was renamed the Bernard Revel Graduate School in his memory.

Revel was a presidium member of the Union of Orthodox Rabbis of the United States and Canada from 1924 (later honorary president) and vice-president of the Jewish Academy of Arts and Sciences from 1927. He was an associate editor of the *Otsar Yisra'el* encyclopedia (vol. 9, 1913), and his doctoral dissertation was published by Dropsie College (1913). Despite the demands made upon his time by his manifold Yeshiva responsibilities, Revel continued his doctoral research with monographs and studies about deviant *halakhah* systems. He also produced articles of rabbinic scholarship and wrote halakhic *responsa*. His writings were published mainly in the *Jewish Quarterly Review, Yagdil Torah, Ha-Pardes,* and various Yeshiva student publications.

BIBLIOGRAPHY

Hoenig, Sidney B. *Rabbinics and Research: The Scholarship of Dr. Bernard Revel.* New York, 1968.

Poupko, Bernard A., ed. *Eidenu: Memorial Publication in Honor of Rabbi Dr. Bernard Revel* (in Hebrew). New York, 1942.

Rakeffet-Rothkoff, Aaron. *Bernard Revel: Builder of American Jewish Orthodoxy.* 2d ed. Jerusalem, 1981.

AARON RAKEFFET-ROTHKOFF

REVELATION. The concept of revelation is a fundamental one in every religion that in any way traces its origin to God or a divinity. Revelation is a divine communication to human beings. This broad description allows the phenomenologist of religion to include very different manners and degrees of revelation. In fact, the most diverse experiences, ranging from an obscure clue given by a supernatural power to the self-communication of a personal God, are possible from the standpoints of psychology, religious philosophy, and theology.

In general, religious phenomenologists use five different criteria (characteristics or factors) of revelation:

1. Origin or author: God, spirits, ancestors, power *(mana),* forces. In every case the source of revelation is something supernatural or numinous.
2. Instrument or means: sacred signs in nature (the stars, animals, sacred places, or sacred times); dreams, visions, ecstasies; finally, words or sacred books.
3. Content or object: the didactic, helping, or punishing presence, will, being, activity, or commission of the divinity.
4. Recipients or addressees: medicine men, sorcerers, sacrificing priests, shamans, soothsayers, mediators, prophets with a commission or information intended for individuals or groups, for a people or the entire race.
5. Effect and consequence for the recipient: personal instruction or persuasion, divine mission, service as oracle—all this through inspiration or, in the supreme case, through incarnation.

It is to be noted that the historians of religion derived the concept of revelation from the Judeo-Christian religion where it received its theological elaboration and then in the course of research into the history of religions was transferred in a broad and analogous sense to other religions. The answer to the question whether we may speak of revelation in the proper sense in animistic, polytheistic, and polydemonistic religions will depend on the understanding of religion maintained by a given Christian scholar. In theologian Karl Barth's view Christianity alone possesses a revelation; historian of religion van der Leeuw, on the other hand, develops a much more inclusive understanding of revelation and therefore a series of types that culminates in the Christian concept of revelation.

It is certain that revelation must be clearly distinguished from magic, since magical practices aim at power over and disposal of the divine, while revelation means in principle a free announcement by the divinity. This announcement even goes beyond hierophanies and epiphanies and involves the manifestation of something holy or the rendering apprehensible of a divine depth, inasmuch as it always clearly includes the distinction between revealing subject and revealed object, between self-revealing God and mystery made known. In any case, this fuller meaning is regularly intended by the Latin *revelatio* and the Greek *apokalupsis.*

Whether gnosis and mysticism are to be regarded as forms of revelation or, on the contrary, as the opposite of revelation depends essentially on the role assigned to divine grace (as help from and self-communication of God) in these manifestations of religious life. Whenever ultimate knowledge and the vision of supreme wisdom are regarded not as the fruit of human effort alone but as a gift from God, then, as in the experience of a profound union with God that cannot be acquired by force or produced by the human being but can only be received as a gift, a self-communication of a personal God comes into play and the concept of revelation is correctly applied.

Natural Revelations. It may therefore seem at first sight contradictory to speak of "natural revelation," since the knowledge of God derived from nature seems to involve no personal, here-and-now turning of God to human beings but to result rather from the intellectual efforts of the latter. The objection overlooks the fact that religio-philosophical statements about God can never take the form of knowledge gained by the natural sciences, which turn the object of their investigations into an object of human experience and human categories of thought. God cannot be fully grasped by human thought or defined or adequately described in concepts derived from our experience of the spatiotemporal world. This fact is reflected in "negative theology," which regards it as possible to say unreservedly of God only what he is not. Positive statements about him always fall short and are compatible with his absolute transcendence, his wholly-otherness *(totaliter aliter)* and ever-greaterness *(semper maior),* only insofar as they are made with a realization of the analogous structure of human language. In this context "analogy" does not mean mathematical similarity; it refers rather to a fundamental relation of similarity-dissimilarity, due to which every positive assertion of a formal perfection in God (being, goodness, justice, etc.) must immediately be negated. That is, it must be purified of the experienced finiteness that attaches to these concepts in the spatiotemporal world, and then applied to the trancendent God in a nonmaterial sense and in the highest possible degree of perfection. It is clear that in this three-step operation—assertion, negation, and reassertion in the mode of supereminence—negation plays the decisive role.

To make the point more simply: God is a hidden God *(Deus absconditus).* Only if he discloses himself and only to the extent that he makes himself known can he be known by human beings. This is the basic idea behind the concept of "natural revelation," which is proposed at various points in the Western tradition of philosophical theology.

The Bible. In his *Letter to the Romans,* the apostle Paul vividly states the possibility (not the actuality) of a natural knowledge of God: "The wrath of God is revealed from heaven against all ungodliness and wickedness of men who by their wickedness suppress the truth. For what can be known about God is plain to them, because God has shown it to them. Ever since the creation of the world his invisible nature, namely, his eternal power and deity, has been clearly perceived in the things that have been made. So they are without excuse; for although they knew God they did not honor him as God or give thanks to him, but they became futile in their thinking and their senseless minds were darkened" (*Rom.* 1:18–22).

The most important statement here is "God has shown it to them." This clearly brings out the revelational character of the knowledge. The cosmos is not simply *phusis* or nature in the form of an eternally self-subsisting world, such as the Greeks understood it to be; rather, it is *ktisis* or creation, that is, God's handiwork that had a beginning and that as finite nature points to the infinite God as its creator.

Ever since the creation of the world, the invisible being of God has been known by reason. Human beings understand themselves to be creatures and therefore by reason know God's power and deity.

The apostle Paul was evidently referring to a passage in the *Wisdom of Solomon,* which was probably a Jewish composition written in Egypt in the first century BCE. Rejecting Egyptian polytheism, the author says: "All men who were ignorant of God were foolish by nature; and they were unable from the good things that are seen to know him who exists, nor did they recognize the craftsman while paying heed to his works; but they supposed that either fire or wind or swift air, or the circle of the stars, or turbulent water, or the luminaries of heaven were the gods that rule the world. If through delight in the beauty of these things men assumed them to be gods, let them know how much better than these is their Lord, for the author of beauty created them. And if men were amazed at their power and working, let them perceive from them how much more powerful is he who formed them. For from the greatness and beauty of created things comes a corresponding perception of their creator" (*Wis.* 13:1–5).

In this passage myths about the origin of the world and philosophical explanations of the world as emerging from primal matter (water, air, etc.), such as were offered by the Ionian natural philosophers, are being rejected in favor of an understanding in which the beauties of this world are explained as produced by a first cause.

Philosophy of Plato. The very wording of the passage from the *Wisdom of Solomon* betrays the philosophical influence of Plato, who speaks in his dialogue the *Symposium* (178a–c) of the ascent of the soul, via the various degrees of bodily and intellectual beauty, to the primordially beautiful, that is, the idea of Beauty as such. Here as elsewhere in Plato's elaboration of his doctrine of the Ideas, his thinking takes as its point of reference the origin *(archē, prōton)* of things. Such is the case in the *Lysis,* where we find the concept of the Primordially Lovable *(philon),* and especially in the *Republic* (505–511), where Plato describes the function of the idea of the Good as such, which is the cause of being and knowledge in everything else that is. In conceiving the world as having its ground in the ideas, Plato provides the philosophical presupposition for understanding everything finite as conditioned and as sustained in being by the idea of God. The world is not intelligible in itself either ontically or noetically, either in its being or in its knowableness. Once this fundamental insight is grasped, it becomes easy to understand the viewpoint of Jewish and Christian thinkers who saw the world as a message conveying God's greatness, beauty, power, and goodness, and therefore as a revelation in the proper sense.

It is for this reason that in the passage from *Romans* Paul says human beings should have advanced from knowledge of God to acknowledgment of him and the payment to him of honor and gratitude. Even natural revelation implies and calls for existential consequences such as reverence and obedience.

Luther for his part interpreted Paul as saying in *Romans* that they are foolish who endeavor to gain a natural knowledge of God from creation as the "work" of God's power and glory. Over and against such a "theology of glory" he set a "theology of the cross" that maintains that "insofar as God's being is made visible and is turned to the world, it is represented there in suffering and the cross" (Heidelberg Disputation of 1518). But, valuable though this emphasis on God's revelation in Christ is, in Paul's view human beings are "foolish" not because they attempt to learn God's eternal power and divinity from creation but because "by their wickedness [they] suppress the truth." In general, evangelical theology still has a negative attitude toward natural theology.

Aristotle and Thomas Aquinas. In the Constitution on Faith of the First Vatican Council (1869–1870), on the other hand, the Catholic church insisted on the possibility and point of natural revelation: "God, the beginning and end of all things, can be known with certainty from the things that were created through the natural light of human reason, for 'ever since the creation of the world His invisible nature has been clearly perceived in the things that have been made' (*Rom.* 1:20)" (Henricus Denzinger and Adolfus Schönmetzer's "Enchiridion symbolorum, no. 3004," *The Christian Faith in the Doctrinal Documents of the Catholic Church*, 36th ed., no. 113, Rome, 1976). The passage goes beyond what is said in *Romans* and speaks of God as not only the ground but also the destination of creation. It is clear from this, as it is from the expression "the natural light of human reason," that the council fathers were here following the teaching of Thomas Aquinas.

In his five "ways" of obtaining knowledge of God (*Summa theologiae* 1.2.3), Thomas was basing his thought on Aristotle rather than Plato. The background of this link in the history of ideas must be briefly sketched.

Aristotle had accepted several points made by Plato: the priority of movement proceeding from within over movement initiated by what is outside *(Laws, Phaedrus);* the idea that what is first in the cosmos is an idea, or *eidos* ("spiritual entity"); and, finally, the view that first cause and end are necessarily identical. In the framework of his own theory of potency and act, Aristotle then elaborated his doctrine of God as the First Unmoved Mover *(to prōton kinoun akinēton auto),* who as self-sufficient intellectual reality *(actus purus)* is not dependent on anything outside of himself, while at the same time all other intellectual and corporeal beings have their ground in him. God is the origin and source of the world and at the same time its ultimate end, since all things strive toward him and he moves them as "that which is loved," that is, as a supreme value that draws them (*Metaphysics* A, 6–9).

All these "movements" of which Aristotle speaks are not to be interpreted in mechanistic terms but intellectually or metaphysically: they are a striving for form or fulfillment in reality or value.

Thomas Aquinas reduces these arguments of Plato and Aristotle to concise systematic form. The first three ways take as their starting point certain facts of experience: that the beings of our world are in movement (in potency); that they do not have their efficient cause in themselves (they are conditioned beings); and that they do not exist necessarily but are finite, temporal, and contingent. These three ways conclude to a First Cause that "moves" everything (in the Aristotelian sense of the word "move"), is the ground of all further causal series, and has the ground of its own being within itself, or, in other words, exists necessarily and eternally.

The inevitability of this conclusion is underscored by the consideration that an infinite regress does not offer an alternative solution and that one must abandon the endless series of causes and conditions *(ab alio)* and accept a First that is of a different kind *(a se)* if anything at all is to be explained. The idea that an infinite regress is impossible bears the clear mark of Platonic thinking, according to which something finite and conditioned is explicable only in terms of something infinite and unconditioned *(anupotheton).* Platonism thus conceived is indispensable for the philosophy of religion.

Thomas's fourth way is likewise based on the gradations of being and value that we find in the doctrine of the ideas. The ground of every goodness is located in the supreme Good as such (in Platonic terms: in the [divine] idea of the Good), which distributes of its goodness and gives a participation in it.

The fifth way concludes from the order found in the world to an orderer who possesses intellectual knowledge and who is all-powerful and so infinitely good that he can bring good even out of evil. The Aristotelian idea of God as end (destination) of the cosmos merges here with the Platonic idea that evil in all its forms is simply a lack of goodness.

If we add now the assertion that these insights (for we are not dealing here with empirical proofs as this term is used in the natural sciences) are acquired by "the light of reason," the place of this entire body of considerations in the history of ideas becomes clear once again. Just as in our material world the sun gives light and makes things knowable, so the idea of the good gives things being and the power to know (analogy with the sun in the *Republic* 508–509). Augustine therefore says that in every act by which we know the truth we are illumined by the eternal Truth, and Thomas teaches that human reason participates in "the divine light" (*Summa theologiae* 2.1.91.2).

The circle is now closed. Natural revelation means that it is possible in principle to think about the finitude of the world and our own existence and come thereby to know something of God's wisdom and creative power, because God himself makes it possible to know him through traces, reflections, and images in his creatures.

In regard to the actual fulfillment of this potentiality Vatican I showed itself rather reserved, noting that "such truths among things divine as of themselves are not beyond human reason can, even in the present condition of mankind, be known by everyone with facility, with firm certitude and with no admixture of error" because God has in fact granted a supernatural revelation (Denzinger-Schönmetzer, no. 3005; Neuner-Dupuis, no. 114). This appraisal of the situation is fully in accord with that of Thomas Aquinas (*Summa theologiae* 1.1.1), for in his view the knowledge made available by natural revelation is indeed possible for the human race in its present condition, but it is by no means easily gained or accessible to all. We are thus brought to a consideration of "supernatural revelation," which will here be called "biblical revelation."

Kant did not join Thomas in this approach. His criticism of the proofs for the existence of God is based on the principle that knowledge is valid only within the realm of sense experience and that there is no correspondence between thought and the truth as it exists in itself.

Old Testament and Judaism. Jewish theology regards it as inconceivable that human beings should know God by their own powers and apart from God making himself known, that is, revealing himself, to them. Like the rest of the Near East, Israel had certain techniques for penetrating the mysteries of God, such as soothsaying, the interpreting of omens and dreams, and the casting of lots. The Old Testament accepted some of these techniques (*Dt.* 33:8, *1 Sm.* 14) and always refused others, for example, astrology. On the other hand, God's action toward Israel in the course of its history is always understood as revelatory in the strict sense. The people experience the nearness of God through external signs and events such as thunderstorms (*Ex.* 19:16), pillars of cloud and pillars of fire (*Ex.* 14:24), and the wind (*1 Kgs.* 19:12). Descriptions of theophanies in human or angelic form (*Gn.* 16:7, 18:2, 48:16) are also found in the early stage of the patriarchal tradition; the "angel of God" *(malakh Yahveh)*, in particular, seems obviously to be a device for maintaining the transcendence of God.

As the history of salvation advanced it became increasingly important to interpret God's guidance of Israel. The result was revelation through words, taking the form of auditions and going beyond visions or else interpreting these. God's spirit filled the prophets; his hand was laid on the human beings he chose for this revelation.

Various verbs were used to express the divine act of revelation:

1. *glh* ("to uncover, unveil"). Yahveh opens the eyes and ears of human beings so that they are able to see and hear (*1 Sm.* 9:15, *Ps.* 119:18); he unveils himself (*Gn.* 35:7, *Is.* 22:14) and his mysteries (*Dt.* 29:29), his glory (*Is.* 40:15), and his justice (*Ps.* 98:2).
2. *yd*ʿ ("to proclaim, make oneself known"). The essence of revelation according to the Old Testament consists precisely in this self-communication of God to his people as he makes himself known to them (*Ex.* 6:2), speaks to them (*Ex.* 25:22), and, above all, brings them out of Egypt (*Ez.* 20:9) and enters into a covenant with them. It is for this purpose that he makes known to Israel his name (*Is.* 64:2) and his ways (*Ps.* 25:4), that is, his commandments and his law (the Torah), as well as his wisdom (*Ps.* 119).
3. *nggd* ("to report, communicate"). This is the most frequent of all the words for revelation and means to manifest something that is hidden: God's name (*Gn.* 32:30), his plan (*Gn.* 41:25), his salvation (*Is.* 42:12), and his hidden wisdom (*Jb.* 11:6). All these contexts have this in common, that God directs his word to human beings. For this reason,
4. *dvr* can frequently be used for this decisive communication on God's part. God's word to Israel is his most precious gift; in it he communicates himself: "I am the Lord" (*Gn.* 28:13; *Ex.* 6:2, 6:29) and "there is no other" (*Is.* 45:5, *Jl.* 2:27).

The word of God is spoken in a special way to Moses (*Ex.* 20:18). The people perceive only the thunder and lightning, the trumpet blast and the smoke, that accompany the word; they see the "glory" of God but receive the commandments only through a mediator who is therefore regarded as the greatest of the prophets (*Dt.* 18:15). In like manner, all the later prophets are also proclaimers of God's word. He speaks through their mouths, his spirit moves them, his word is given to them; when they speak, "It is I, Yahveh, who speak" (a frequently occurring expression).

The goal and purpose of revelation is the call of Israel to be a covenanted people. This purpose is served by the revelation of God as "the God of Abraham, the God of Isaac, and the God of Jacob" (*Ex.* 3:6), as well as by the announcement of his name, which is at one and the same time a promise of his presence as helper ("I will be there as the One who will be there"; *Ex.* 3:12) and a concealment and withdrawal of God from any control by human beings ("I am who I am"; *Ex.* 3:14). The paradigmatic saving action of God becomes a reality in the deliverance and exodus from Egypt (*Ex.* 14) and, climactically, in the conclusion of the covenant at Sinai (*Ex.* 19–20). The entire religious practice and tradition and the entire liturgical cult of Israel, as well as the attribution of all laws to Moses and the constant warnings of the prophets, all show the fundamental importance of this encounter with God. Not only does the individual Jewish believer live by the light and power of that encounter; the entire social and political life of the people also takes its direction from it.

Since history is the reduction of the covenant to practice it too acquires a theological significance. Successes and catastrophes alike are explained as having their basis in God's plan of salvation, which thus subsumes all the destinies of individuals and all events under a universal saving will that orders everything to the "day of the Lord" (*Am.* 5:18, *Is.* 2:17). That day will bring the definitive fulfillment of God's reign over all of humankind. Revelation thus has a comprehensive meaning; it looks to world history in its entirety, since it sets forth and wins recognition of God's holiness and love. For this reason a special importance is attributed to the end time (eschatology) in Jewish apocalyptic. What is to come and the one who is to come (the Messiah) take on central meaning.

The "revelation of mysteries" (a notion that occurs first in *Daniel* 2:18) becomes a commonplace in the Qumran documents. The devotees at Qumran believe that they possess a special revelation for the end time, a revelation available only to the "wise and initiated."

By contrast, the Judaism of the scribes (beginning with Ezra, fourth century BCE) shows a tendency to regard revelation as closed and to see the prophetic movement as now past. The Jewish tradition generally accepted these positions. Only Jewish mysticism (Qabbala, Hasidism) regarded not only the once-for-all historical act of divine revelation but also the repeated mystical experience of God as revelatory; the function of the latter is to bring out the implications of the historical revelation and make it intelligible.

New Testament and Christianity. Building on the Old Testament understanding of revelation, the New Testament writers see revelation as the self-communication of God in and through Jesus Christ. This communication is regarded as the supreme, final, irrevocable, and unsurpassable self-disclosure of God in history (*Heb.* 1:1f.). It is unique because, as Christians understand it, in Jesus of Nazareth, agent of revelation and content of revelation (the person, teaching, and redemptive work of Jesus) are identical and make up the sole object of revelation. The theological elaboration of the New Testament concept of revelation is to be found especially in Paul and John.

Paul. To express the idea of revelation, Paul uses above all the words *apokaluptein* ("uncover, remove from concealment") and *phaneroun* ("make apparent, show"). His basic theme is the uncovering of the mystery that has previously been hidden and is now made manifest (*Eph.* 1:9, *Col.* 1:26). Revelation, therefore, means the uncovering or unveiling of the divine plan by which God reconciles the human race to himself in Christ. Revelation is a divine creative activity, an eschatological saving deed, rather than a simple announcing of messages or items of knowledge. God is the really active one in the process of revelation. It is he who from eternity decides that in his Son he will turn in love to the human race. The incarnation of his Son in the womb of a woman (*Gal.* 4:4), this Son's expiatory death on the cross, and the recapitulation or unification of the cosmos under him as head and firstborn from the dead (*Rom.* 3:25, *Col.* 1:18) are the fulfillment of this hidden plan. In this plan Christ himself is what is revealed. The death and resurrection of Christ, and even the church as his body, are elements of this mystery of salvation.

In a derivative application of the term, the apostles also "reveal" the salvific justice of God (*Rom.* 1:17) inasmuch as they proclaim the good news brought by Jesus (*2 Cor.* 2:14). In the fullness of time (*Gal.* 1:16) the gospel is preached to all peoples (*Rom.* 1:16, 16:26), not like an esoteric doctrine of the Hellenistic mystery religions but as a message meant to profit the entire human race, provided men and women are ready to accept the scandal of the cross (*1 Cor.* 1:18–25). For it is of the very essence of revelation that it must be accepted in faith and obedience. It does not supply empirical evidence that forces acceptance; on the other hand, neither may it be accepted or rejected at whim, for it makes a claim upon its hearers and may not be rejected without resultant guilt.

In short, revelation is still incomplete within historical time. Only in its definitive stage of development at the return (Parousia) of Christ will it be complete. At that point, too, the glory promised to the redeemed will be manifested, for it will be clear beyond doubt that the redeemed are risen and that they are the children and heirs of God (*1 Cor.* 1:7; *2 Thes.* 1:7; *Rom.* 8:18–23).

The synoptics. The revelation accomplished in Jesus is extremely important to the early community as well. As a result, the statements made in the synoptic Gospels are in principle the same as those in the preaching of Paul.

There is no doubt that the Old Testament is a vehicle of revelation; nonetheless the fullness of revelation comes to us only in Christ (*Mt.* 5:17–19). Jesus differs from the other agents of revelation because not only does he claim a complete and direct knowledge of God's saving will (*Mt.* 11:27, *Lk.* 10:22), but his messianic work is also the definitive revelation and calls for an unconditional decision (*Mt.* 4:20, 8:22, 10:37–39; *Mk.* 1:18; and others).

John. The concept of revelation emerges most clearly in John, even though he almost never uses the term *apokaluptein.* He prefers the verb *phaneroun* ("make apparent, show") and likes to use pairs of concepts that were popular in the Hellenistic religious movements of his time, especially gnosticism: light and darkness, truth and falsehood, life and death. The expression "bear witness to the truth" is typical of Johannine theology.

John regards the revelatory event as the center of his message. Not only is Jesus the redeemer by means of his "work"; he is also and above all the proclaimer of God's truth and the life and light of the world (*Jn.* 1:4). God is invisible and unknowable; the Son alone knows the Father, and in him the Father is made visible and understandable (*Jn.* 1:14, *1 Jn.* 1:1). He has brought knowledge of God and borne witness to him (*Jn.* 1:18, 3:11–13); he speaks in plain words of the Father (*Jn.* 8:38). Revelation is therefore given together with the person of the Logos (the Word); it is the manifestation of the life and love of God (*Jn.* 4:7–9). Because Jesus is the only-begotten Son, he reveals the Father in what he says and does. "He who has seen me has seen the Father" (*Jn.* 14:9).

In keeping with the realized eschatology of the gospel according to John, faith, as response to revelation, can even now be described as a "seeing" (*Jn.* 6:40, 12:45, 14:19). What is revealed is already present. Yet, although revelation is essentially completed with the first coming of Jesus, John, like Paul, can speak of the "revelation of Jesus" and of the "glory of the children of God" at the return of Christ (*1 Jn.* 2:28, 3:2).

Revelation. The *Revelation to John* is a New Testament book that focuses its attention on the final age and the return of Christ. It presupposes the proclamation of salvation as achieved through the cross and resurrection of Jesus and, in John's vision on Patmos of the Apocalypse, it interprets the persecutions and sufferings endured by the communities in the light of the hope of their coming fulfillment. The book's images and symbols, taken from Jewish apocalyptic, are intended to urge the reader to perseverance and fidelity. The various hymns of the heavenly liturgy reflect the response of the church to God's judgments, which have for their ultimate purpose the salvation of his creation; this salvation will be achieved despite the terrors that are announced.

Islam. Islam's understanding of revelation comes closest to that of the Bible. *Waḥy,* or revelation, comes from God, usually through the agency of the archangel Gabriel. It is concerned with God's decrees, his mysterious will, the announcement of judgment, and his commandments, the divine law *(sharīʿah).* Revelation is given to the prophets and, in its definitive form, to Muḥammad (c. 570–632), who receives it in dreams, visions, and auditions. It is set down in the Qur'ān, the uncreated archetype of which has been taken up to the throne of God in heaven. This uncreated word is not, however, the source of God's self-knowledge (as it is in Christian theology). To this extent, the Muslim conception resembles the Jewish, while at the same time it is distinguished from the latter by the absence of any promise. In the Qur'ān the content of revelation is wisdom and guidance for living and, above all, warnings and the announcement of final judgment. Because it is divine in origin revelation may not be altered.

Zoroastrianism. Zarathushtra (seventh to sixth century BCE) was another nonbiblical prophet. He too saw revelation as having its source in the voluntary action of a unique and personal God. The dualism that is otherwise prevalent in the Iranian world is based on an original revelation to the extent that this last calls for an unqualified ethical decision. Like Ahura Mazdā, the Mazdeans opt for the good and against evil. This tension soon hardens, however, into an ontic dualism. The world is divided between good and evil and thus reflects at all cosmic levels the opposition between the virtues and their contraries. History becomes the field of a struggle that is predetermined by God and will end with judgment and transfiguration.

Hinduism. Even in Hinduism it is possible to speak of revelation as this concept is understood by historians of religion. The Vedas have the status of sacred revelation: *śruti* ("heard," i.e., revealed directly by the gods to seers) is clearly distinguished from *smṛti* ("remembered," i.e., composed by men). According to Hindu belief, the Vedic literature has existed from eternity, is supernatural in origin, and has been transmitted to human beings by unknown seers of the primordial period.

In the *Ṛgveda,* forces and elements of nature are viewed as divinities. Later on the question arises whether behind the multiplicity of divinities there is hidden an ultimate ground of the world. The Upaniṣads are concerned with the question of the identity of *ātman* and *brahman* (the principles of the individual and the cosmos respectively), and with the transcription of souls and redemption.

Notions of revelation and a consciousness of transcendence are also discernible in other religions, although often only in an obscure and confused form, despite the fact that an especially clear idea of God is evident in archaic forms of religion. Because of this last-named fact many scientists of religion in the past accepted the existence of a primordial revelation in the form of an originally given knowledge of God in the early phase of human history; today, however, this view is generally not accepted.

[*Revelation in the sense of the appearance of the divine is discussed in* Hierophany. *For treatment of different forms of revelation, see* Prophecy; Oracles; Divination; Inspiration; *and* Enthusiasm.]

BIBLIOGRAPHY

For basic information concerning the topic, entries in several reference works can be profitably consulted: "Offenbarung," in the *Lexikon für Theologie und Kirche,* 2d ed., vol. 7 (Freiburg, 1962); "Offenbarung," in *Die Religion in Geschichte und Gegenwart,* 3d ed., vol. 4 (Tübingen, 1960); and "Révélation" in the *Dictionnaire de théologie catholique,* vol. 6 (Paris, 1937). Karl Rahner's article "Revelation," in *Sacramentum Mundi: An Encyclopedia of Theology,* vol. 5 (New York, 1969), is especially valuable.

Those aspects of revelation accessible to the phenomenology of religion are summarized in Gerardus van der Leeuw's *Religion in Essence and Manifestation,* 2 vols. (1938; reprint, Gloucester, Mass., 1967), and in Th. P. van Baaren's *Voorstellingen van Openbaring, phaenomenologisch beschouwd* (Utrecht, 1951), which includes an English summary. There is also a very good discussion in Herbert H. Farmer's *Revelation and Religion: Studies in the Theological Interpretation of Religious Types* (New York, 1954). For the history of religions approach, see the standard work of Mircea Eliade, *A History of Religious Ideas,* 3 vols. (Chicago, 1978–1986).

On the treatment of the topic within Islam, see A. J. Arberry's *Revelation and Reason in Islam* (London, 1957). On Hinduism, see K. Satchidananda Murty's *Revelation and Reason in Advaita Vedānta* (1959; reprint, Livingston, N.J., 1974).

For discussions of natural revelation, see Fernand van Steenberghen's *Dieu caché* (Louvain, 1961), translated as *Hidden God: How Do We Know That God Exists?* (Saint Louis, Mo., 1966), and Johannes Hirschberger's *Gottesbeweise: Vergängliches-Unvergängliches in denkender Glaube* (Frankfurt, 1966).

The following works treat the biblical concept of revelation: H. Wheeler Robinson's *Inspiration and Revelation in the Old Testament,* 4th ed. (Oxford, 1956); Erik Voegelin's *Order and History,* vol. 1, *Israel and Revelation* (Baton Rouge, 1956); Ernest Findlay Scott's *The New Testament Idea of Revelation* (New York, 1935); and Frederick C. Grant's *Introduction to New Testament Thought* (New York, 1950). For theological discussions of revelation, see Rudolf Bultmann's "The Concept of Revelation in the New Testament," in *Existence and Faith: Shorter Writings of Rudolf Bultmann,* edited and translated by Schubert M. Ogden (New York, 1960); Romano Guardini's *Die Offenbarung: Ihr Wesen und ihre Formen* (Würzburg, 1940); Karl Barth's *Das christliche Verständnis der Offenbarung* (Munich, 1948); Paul Tillich's *Systematic Theology,* 3 vols. (Chicago, 1951–1963); Karl Rahner's *Hearers of the Word* (New York, 1969); and *Revelation as History* (New York, 1968) by Wolfhart Pannenberg and others.

JOHANNES DENINGER
Translated from German by Matthew J. O'Connell

REVENGE AND RETRIBUTION. There are actions by which human beings compensate for something—for a loss by a reimbursement, a gain by a reward, a crime by expiation, an insult by satisfaction, an advantage by a sacrifice, a defeat by a victory. These are all forms of repayment based on an essential connection made between agency and receptivity in action. That connection is tacitly assumed by human beings to be the price paid for every deed; it is an element in the performance of every deed and is the means used to ensure a particular behavior. In it lies the origin of private and public law, which allow for a retribution in which individuals settle scores for themselves, and a retribution in which they become the subject of a settling of scores. They avenge themselves and are penalized.

The instrumental character of retribution finds exemplary expression in the "law of talion," in which the penalty matches the crime, and in the Golden Rule (behave toward others as you wish them to behave toward you). Good deeds bring their reward, and evil deeds their punishment.

Opinions on revenge differ from science to science. Students of the history of law see it as a primitive form of law. From this point of view, it is an unbridled, unreflective, and arbitrary act of retribution, whereas punishment has a purpose and is administered according to laws and on the basis of a judicial sentence. The passage from thinking focused on vengeance to penal law thus represents an ethical advance.

Some ethnologists and structuralist sociologists reject this view and see revenge as moral behavior within the context of the laws of exogamy. It is an act of self-assertion by a group against an outside attacker, "an outward-directed act of solidarity." Revenge is taken exclusively on outsiders. This distinguishes it from punishment, which is imposed by a group on members who violate its order; it is an act of exclusion, "an internal sanction for a lack of solidarity." Punishment is found in primitive legal systems, just as revenge is found in more developed systems. Revenge is a problem connected with the balance between private and public agencies in every system of justice; it resists legal positivism but does not inevitably lead to anarchy.

Many historians of religion and theologians lend support to this nuanced approach. Tribal gods avenge themselves and high gods exercise retribution through rewards and punishments.

The high religions and the world religions set limits on vengefulness and move beyond it. Guilt is compensated for by punishment in a process that is cosmic (as in the Hindu idea of *karman*) or historical (as in the Christian idea of judgment). The dead are no longer agents of retribution (avenging themselves so that they may have peace of soul) but its recipients, as seen in the concepts of the transmigration of souls and the judgment on the dead. Their actions are now significant only for themselves and no longer for their tribe.

Structural differentiation in the ways of making up for guilty acts becomes an existential problem for religion. For revenge can be simultaneously a duty and a crime. Punishment takes different forms in different legal systems; hence "summum ius, summa iniuria" ("strict justice can be the height of injustice"). Greek tragedy presents the myth of unavoidable guilt and the problem of whether or not justice is really done through penal retribution.

A question arises: is there an unbreakable connection between receptivity and performance in action as such and, therefore, in redemption?

Revenge as the Archaic Form of Retribution. In a system based on vengeance, the reciprocity of sin and expiation is regulated by those directly involved. It entails an exchange of life at all levels of existence. The individual and the group are mutually accountable. Vengeance places authority, prestige, and material possessions on the same level of value. Those who avenge themselves gain prestige; they take part in the social life of the group and become respected. They represent the honor of their clan.

Retribution exercised by individuals is a problem in the anthropology and theology of religion.

Regulation of vengeance in archaic societies. Groups in which revenge is an institution are of a kinship or totemic type. They are made up of families and clans (or subclans). In them, personal existence and collective existence are regarded as interchangeable. The group is the vital sphere for the individual, and the individual is a quantity in the vital capital of the group. For individuals to be avenged means, therefore, that the group stands up for them. The group is the vehicle of individuals' right to life. It establishes an identification between what they are in themselves (their existence as persons) and what they stand for in the group (their prestige). Murder and homocide are, therefore, offenses to the family, as are rape and theft. A slander can be regarded as a crime deserving of death, and theft can be regarded as murder. Blood vengeance, substitutional vengeance, and symbolic vengeance each represent a different aspect of the identification of individual and societal life, namely, the power of blood, the property of the family, and the honor of the clan.

An example of such interchangeableness is the Australian Aborigines' custom of obtaining blood vengeance by the wounding, not the killing, of a culprit. Magical rites also provide an illustration; Lucien Lévy-Bruhl (1927) speaks of a "mystical compensation." Another example is the identification of bride-price and blood-price, since in each case there is a question not of purchasing a life but of presenting gifts that symbolize life, and, therefore, of an exchange of life. In this sense the blood-price is equivalent to life itself, just as the bride-price replaces the bride who is exchanged for it.

This explains why many languages use the same word for bride-price and blood-price. Among the Maengue of New Britain, the word *kuru* (literally, "head") means "both the human life demanded in revenge and treasures given to a bride's family at her marriage" (Verdier, 1980, p. 28). The bride herself may be a blood-price. Among the bedouin, the daughter of the nearest relative of a murderer is the price paid. She belongs to the son, brother, or father of the slain man as a substitute for the loss suffered, until she bears a son; she regains her freedom only when this child has grown up and can bear arms. "Among the Mundang of Africa the king can compensate the brother of a victim with a woman instead of cattle; when she brings a son into the world, the reparation is complete; the husband must then in turn pay a price to his parents-in-law" (ibid., p. 29). Revenge may therefore take a bloodless form and contribute to peace; the person who exercises vengeance now breathes freely and is satisfied. His act asserts the right to life and honor: "The righteous will rejoice when he sees the vengeance; he will bathe his feet in the blood of the wicked" (*Ps.* 58:11). To avenge a murder is thus to avenge honor and wipe out a disgrace. In many societies this is the decisive motive at work in revenge. "A man reviled is like a weakling. He cannot regain his honor without shedding blood" (ibid., p. 19). Among the Moussey of Cameroon, a man is judged by the enemies he has killed. When he marries, he must answer his father-in-law's ritual question: "Whom have you killed in order to win my daughter's hand?" Vengeance rests on a complex involving feelings of honor and disgrace.

The reciprocity of individual and collective existence is the source of linguistic peculiarities and helps us understand various legal provisions. The German expression that means "to pay someone back" is understood as "to take revenge on him." Among the Beti of Africa, the equivalent expression can mean "to return evil" or "to recompense someone" or "to take advantage of him"; among the two Maengue groups, "to pay a price" or "to set a price"; among the Kikuyu, "to remove someone's guilt"; among the Hausa, "to cancel his debt"; among the Kabyle, "to pay the price of a corpse," which indicates payment for a death. The wiping out of guilt for a crime and the wiping out of debts (in a business matter) are forms of making up for a loss that a possessor has suffered in each case.

These forms of wiping out are ruled by the principle of harm done, not of culpability; that is, it is the act itself, and not the responsibility for it, that evokes revenge. Moreover, the principle of collective liability, not individual liability, is operative: the group, and not the culprit, is liable; in addition, the rank of the person harmed is taken into account in the compensation. Only those acknowledged by law as persons, and not slaves, are capable of revenge.

The principle of representation also comes into play. The person harmed and his avenger, on the one hand, and the culprit, on the other, are members of different groups. Each represents the right and duties of his group and acts in its name. The duty of revenge depends on the degree of kinship with the person harmed, the order being son, brother, uncle, nephew; there can also, however, be hired representatives. The principle of representation accounts for the phenomenon of sequential vengeance, inasmuch as the representative, too, is subject to the principle of the collective liability of his kindred. The result is feuds and wars.

Revenge is taken on outsiders, not on fellow members of the same group. That is, the principle of exogamy comes into play. As a result, different persons are affected, depending on whether the society is matriarchal or patriarchal.

The rules governing vengeance also include provisions meant to prevent escalation into cycles of revenge. Among these provisions are the exclusion of damages that do not justify revenge (homicide as distinct from murder), the determination of places and times to which revenge is limited (the criminal caught in the act), an expanded range of compensations and substitutions that can replace vengeance *(wergeld)*, and the provision of sanctuaries or places where revenge is utterly forbidden (sanctuary cities, palaces, temples, churches).

The religious basis of vengeance. Guilt binds the guilty party to the debtor by means of the conscience, which accuses him, and a curse that pursues him. [*See* Conscience.] Guilt thus takes on an aspect of revenge, for conscience and the curse exercise retribution and are nevertheless agencies in the overall order of life. They are vengeance exercised by the gods. They represent the vital force of the gods and their power to prevail, the necessity directing the gods to restore their own honor and to fulfill the responsibility they have on earth. Consequently, the symbolism associated with vengeance is very closely linked to ancestor worship, the cult of the dead, belief in the soul, the ownership of land, and magical rituals. [*See* Ancestors.]

In primitive religion, the souls of the dead themselves commit acts of retribution because they have lost life and now demand it back. The living fear the vengeance of the dead because it can be undirected and therefore strike anyone at all. It is told of the Negritos of northern Luzon in the Philippines that "one who has trodden on the grave of a stranger is slain with arrows from safe ambush by the relatives of the dead person who keep watch at the grave" (S. R. Steinmetz, 1928, vol. 1, p. 337). The Manobos of Mindanao, also in the Philippines, are said to go into the forests at the death of a family member "in order to make reparation for the death, which they do by killing the first person that comes along" (ibid., p. 338). In New Zealand it used to be the custom "after a murder for friends of the slain person to go out sometimes and kill the first person, friend or foe, who came along" (ibid., p. 223). The Maori would kill someone at random after a murder. Among the inhabitants of Daghstan someone would be slain at random after a death from unknown causes, and custom demanded that the parents of a murdered man appear in front of the mosque and declare someone guilty at random. For guilt and expiation are part of life as such, and therefore revenge is taken in the name of life.

> On the one hand, fear of the souls of the dead and specifically a fear of revenge the dead may take on those who violate the social order, and, on the other hand, the hope of protection and support for those who behave in an orderly way—or, in short, belief in the retributive role played by the souls of the dead—are the basis of the ancestor worship that was so widespread among early human beings.
>
> (Kelsen, 1941, p. 12)

This fear and hope are the basis of tradition and one reason for belief in retribution generally. For we may not "overlook the fact that the concept of the soul arose out of the concept of the souls of the dead, and that the original function of the soul, its first effect as it were, is revenge" (ibid., p. 238).

Vengeance is religious in character and can be applied to everything that has life or is regarded as living. [*See* Soul.] Thus animals and plants, and also mountains and rocks, the soil, and indeed the earth in its totality can be seats of the living soul and can exercise vengeance. The existence of the dead and the retribution they exercise thus go together. An unexpiated death is like a life without honor, life as a mere shadow. Revenge, on the other hand, restores honor, wipes away disgrace, and gives the soul power. "A Bedouin seeks to wipe out his disgrace through blood vengeance or even, in the spirit of the pre-Islamic Arabs, to satisfy thereby the soul of the slain person, for after a violent death the soul is transformed into an owl that seeks unwearyingly to drink the blood of its enemy" (Joseph Chelhod, in Verdier, 1980, p. 125).

Blood is the symbol of the soul, of a family's life, and of honor itself. [*See* Blood.] When blood is shed, dangerous forces are unloosed; it cries out for revenge. It has been dishonored, and the lack of peace that afflicts it stains the earth. The spirits of blood call for compensation, for they possess the earth, and the latter cannot exist apart from the integrity of the soul that these spirits embody.

The land is a clan's living space and, therefore, the root of its being. "The ancestral land is 'therefore' often regarded as the source and refuge of life and on this score embodies a spiritual quality. Every attack on the life of a group is consequently an attack on the land" that the group inhabits and on the spirits that possess the land and are its real owners. Every conflict will be avenged on it (ibid., p. 22).

Among the Mundang of Chad, it is therefore customary to give the land on which someone has been killed to the clan to which the dead man belonged. This exchange reflects the view that the land is the possession of the blood and that the blood is the soul of a tribe. The tribe accepts possession of this land by virtue of the soul that is embodied in its blood. For among the Mundang the blood is "the root of one of the souls (*masenbyane:* God of my birth) which constitute the person; but it is also the root of a less differentiated power which may be described as a life-force and which the Mundang call *ma-zwe-su* (spirit or genius of the body)" (Alfred Adler, in Verdier, p. 83). One who sheds blood and thereby releases the interior and the exterior soul inflames the land and excites the spirits that possess it. One who effects a reconciliation creates a new existence. This process takes place in the offering of gifts. For one who gives something of his own can take something for himself. By means of the sacrifice one makes a space for himself in the area of another's life. In that area he is restored to himself. "A blood-price . . . like a bride-price consists therefore not in a transfer of wealth but in sacrificial blood by means of which the two parties recover their integrity" (ibid., p. 84). The blood is the offering and acceptance of their common will to be reconciled.

Chthonic divinities are spirits that wreak vengeance. The Greeks and Romans called them Erinyes or Furies respectively. They were "the embodiment, as it were, of the spilt blood, which, because it had turned against itself, resulted in madness. . . . For there is not yet any such thing as punishment in the modern sense: it is the power of the outraged blood itself that reacts against the murderer" (van der Leeuw, vol. 1, 1933, p. 248). Vengeful gods are demonic in many myths. They are therefore warded off and exorcised by magic.

Retribution as Punishment. Guilt is not only avenged but is also punished, for there are on the one hand offenses against life itself and on the other hand offenses against the rules that protect life and are instituted to defend life. These latter offenses are made up by punishment, which is directed not against the clan but against the offender. The principles at work here are not those of representation but of culpability (the responsible agent is punished); individual liabiity; personal responsibility; as well as the principle of endogamous sanction (that is, the sanction applies only to subjects of the group's own juridical order, not to subjects of an outside juridical order). What is reflected here is the passage from particularity to universality in the concept of religion.

The "law of talion." Retribution through punishment is regulated by bodies of law whose sets of rules describe cases, define responsibilities, and determine the kind and extent of payment. The guilty party is looked upon as a member of a juridical community and, depending on the harm he has done to this community, he suffers harm in turn and is thereby excluded from the community.

The "law of talion" is one of the oldest forms of payment for crime. The term comes from the Latin *lex talionis* ("law of retaliation") and is first documented in the Law of the Twelve Tables (451–450 BCE): "If someone breaks another's limb and does not come to an agreement on it, he shall suffer the same and equal punishment." *Talio* refers to a codified numerical equality in every punishment (for example, one eye for one eye, one hand for one hand, and so on). For a correct understanding of *talio,* one should omit the element of vengeance implied by the English term *retaliation.*

The provisions are as follows: the case in question is the destruction of a bodily member, and the injured party has a right to retribution, member for member. "If the talion exceeded the measure provided in the law, the person justified in taking talion was himself now subject to a new talion. If the injured party was unable personally to take talion, his nearest male relative was appointed to take it" (Jüngling, 1984, p. 3).

Roman law provided for talion-like punishments or analogous talion: "mirror punishments," as they were called. Under this heading came the death penalty for homicide and murder, "but especially punishments in which the culprit was punished by the instrument used in the commission of his crime (death by fire for an arsonist) or was punished in the bodily member used in the crime (by cutting off a thief's hand or cutting out a perjurer's tongue)" (ibid., p. 4). These punishments were imposed by courts. They were quite different from talion in the proper sense, and for this reason some scholars urge that they not be called talion at all.

The legal principle embodied here is found in many non-Roman legal systems as well. Among these are cuneiform law, Mosaic law, and Islamic law.

The Code of Hammurabi (c. 1795–1750 BCE) is characteristic of this principle: a slave for a slave, an eye for an eye, a broken bone for a broken bone, a tooth for a tooth. The code treats citizens differently from slaves, men differently from women. The agents who carry out the sentence are those affected by the misdeed: the plaintiff and his relatives.

In the Hebrew scriptures (Old Testament), the administration of talion is, unlike that found in Roman and Babylonian law, still a tribal matter (see *Dt.* 19:21, *Lv.* 24:20, *Ex.* 21:23–25). Talion here is a juridical principle that operates in the framework of basic legal responsibility and is not to be defined independently of the principle of just exchange and its life-enhancing character. It is a formula for giving and taking within the sphere of authority over the clan. It is located in a personal framework: "If any harm follows, then you shall give life for life, eye for eye, tooth for tooth, hand for hand, foot for foot, burn for burn, wound for wound, stripe for stripe" (*Ex.* 21:23–25).

Islam has two sources for retributive law: blood vengeance and judicial punishments. The clan has the right to kill the murderer of one of its members, provided the murderer acted on his own responsibility and deliberately. But Muḥammad limits the application even further: the right can be exercised only on the legally and morally responsible individual.

Legal punishments are imposed for offenses against religion and public order. But talion for these offenses is limited to cases in which there can be complete equality, for example, "the loss of a hand, a foot, or a tooth, etc. If the guilty party has cut off the same hand of two persons, his punishment is to lose that same hand; for the second hand he must pay a blood-price" (Schacht, 1964, p.185).

In Christianity the law of talion is inverted. It requires that evil be repaid not with evil but with good, so that the evil may be turned to good. "You have heard that it was said, 'An eye for an eye and a tooth for a tooth.' But I say to you, Do not resist one who is evil. But if any one strikes you on the right cheek, turn to him the other also. . . . Give to him who begs from you, and do not refuse him who would borrow from you" (*Mt.* 5:38–42). In this new principle retribution continues to be retribution, but it is put on a new level: the guilt of the guilty party becomes a means of conversion (see *Rom.* 12:20).

The Myth of Guilt and Retribution through Punishment. In the transition from archaic retribution through revenge to official retribution through punishment, retribution itself became problematic. A person is obliged to exercise it, yet it is forbidden; it is a right, but it also creates injustice; it is both destiny and sacrifice. This contradiction and the impossibility of avoiding it become a central theme in both Greek tragedy and the Bible. It is a basic motif in biblical myth and theology.

In Greek thought, retribution is justice in the form of punishment. It is the context in which Greek thought comes to grips with justice as regulative of revenge:

> The word *dikē* occurs in such phrases as *dikēn didonai, dikēn tinein,* literally to give, to pay, justice, which signify "to be punished." The word *tisis* means "payment," "compensation," but also "revenge," for justice and revenge are not very different, indeed they coincide when vengeance is taken for wrongdoing. A product of this kind of justice is the *ius talionis* which was usual in early times and finds pregnant expression in the saying "an eye for an eye and a tooth for a tooth." This is to be traced among the Greeks also; for them, justice is retributive justice. . . . This view was so deep-rooted that it comes out now and then in the older philosophers when they are describing the course of nature. Anaximandros of Miletos said: "The boundless is the origin of all that is. It is the law of necessity that things should perish and go back to their origin. For they give satisfaction and pay the penalty *(didonai dikēn kai tisin)* to one another for their injustice (*adikia*) according to the ordinance of Time.
> (Nilsson, 1948, pp. 35–36)

The Erinyes, or Furies, are the champions of archaic justice. They are spirits who embodied the anger of the dead, the curse of the slain on their murderers. They are among the oldest Greek divinities of justice, especially of archaic matriarchal rights but also of the rights of parents generally. The Areopagus at Athens was also known as the Hill of the Erinyes. The court that prosecuted murderers held its sessions there. At the beginning of a trial, the two opposing parties swore by these divinities that if the court condemned one who was in fact innocent, the truly guilty party would be forfeit to them, since they were the avengers of perjury. The Erinyes were regarded as the agents who defended the order of law. Heraclitus calls them the handmaids or ministers of Dike (justice).

An order of justice that includes both patriarchal and matriarchal rights is unthinkable in system ruled by the Erinyes. Aeschylus tackles this problem in the *Oresteia*, where the Erinyes do not pursue Clytemnestra, who has murdered her husband, but do pursue Orestes, who has murdered his mother. The regime under which the clan lives has confronted Orestes with an insoluble conflict: the patriarchal code demands that he avenge his father, but the matriarchal code prohibits his attacking his mother. Whichever course he chooses, he contravenes archaic law. He is trapped in the myth of guilt:

> The Erinyes who pursue Orestes because he has killed his mother appear here as divinities of an earlier time and representatives of the blood vengeance that is connected with the kinship group. They are sharply contrasted with the younger gods, Apollo and Pallas Athene, who represent the higher principle of the law of Zeus and the right of the state to pass judgment and are therefore unwilling to hand Orestes over to the vengeance of the Erinyes.
>
> (Kelsen, 1941, p. 220)

In Homer and the tragedians, the Erinyes are an agency of justice that belongs to an earlier time. Aeschylus has them say in *The Eumenides*, "That is the way of the younger gods: they alter things by violence and laugh all justice to scorn" (165). And again: "Novelty is breaking in and overturning all that is old, if guilt and the horror of matricide are victorious at the judgment seat" (466). They plead with Apollo: "You are destroying the power of the ancient divinities" (697).

The chthonic goddesses that embodied a matriarchal order were related in several ways to the Olympian gods. The shrine of Zeus at Olympia, the sanctuary of Apollo at Delphi, and Athens, the city of Athena, were all places where the chthonic goddesses were originally venerated. Daughters of Gaia, the supreme agency of justice on earth, these goddesses included Demeter (one of whose titles was Erinys) and Themis, goddess of communities and rights of assembly. Among them were also many other divinities of later derivation whose myths point to the irreconcilability of earthly justice and heavenly retribution, of divine law and earthly destiny. Nemesis, goddess of retribution, and the Moirai, goddesses of destiny, were daughters of Night (the goddess Nux). They punished hubris and took revenge on those who achieved happiness, for injustice was punished by injustice, and happiness unaccompanied by unhappiness aroused the envy of the gods.

The symbols of the court—the wolf, the serpent, and the lightning bolt—are part of the myth of guilt and punishment. They are also symbols of the soul that seeks revenge, and of the Olympian gods who represent the rights of such individuals. Apollo is defender of the rights of blood but also god of purification from blood guilt. He contracts this guilt but also purifies himself from it. He grants oracles concerning the future. He establishes norms by subjecting himself to them: "The god who forbids and punishes murder, must himself murder and be punished for it; this identification of the addressee of norms with the authority behind the norms, of the god who punishes with man who is punished, is a very ancient motif in the establishment of the efficacious norms" (Kelsen, 1941, p. 364).

There is a cycle of guilt, and there is deliverance from guilt, a pattern that constantly repeats itself. The transmigration of souls represents this mystery of life in the Orphic and Eleusinian religions.

Retribution nonetheless involves not only vengeance and punishment but also promise. But those who open themselves to a new hope must achieve deliverance from old guilt. This notion is the basis for the discussion of the concept of retribution in the Bible, and has therefore an archaic as well as an eschatological meaning. The biblical concept is one of God's acting as God. Both aspects are fundamental for the biblical concept of retribution. He who does something undergoes a fate, and he who undergoes a fate has to do something as well. Many biblical expressions contain this reciprocity: to do evil is identical with suffering misfortune, to do good is to incur blessing. The evildoer is he who finds himself in misfortune. To make oneself guilty is like declaring someone guilty; fidelity like steadiness; badness like downfall; reward like work; path of life like way of life. This reciprocity of action and result is guaranteed by Yahveh himself, the tribal God of Israel. It is he who unfolds this reciprocity fully.

The Bible is thus able to include God in the framework of retribution, since he himself exercises vengeance. When in *Genesis* 4:10 the voice of spilled blood cries out to him from the ground, he punishes the murderer by expelling him; he avenges himself sevenfold, however, on anyone who then avenges the murderer. God's clan is the entire human race, and he himself acts on behalf of the race and is its source of strength. He punishes those who attack the race and set themselves against him, and punishes any transgression, taking vengeance on those who avenge the transgression: thus he restores his own honor. Retribution, therefore, is not only a response to action but surpasses it.

[*See also* Judgment of the Dead.]

BIBLIOGRAPHY

Bowers, Fredson. *Elizabethan Revenge Tragedy, 1587–1642.* Princeton, 1966.

Coppet, Daniel de. "Cycles de meurtes et cycles funéraires: Esquisse de deux structures d'échanges." In *Échanges et communications,* edited by Jean Pouillon and Pierre Maranda, vol. 2, pp. 759–781. The Hague, 1970.

Girard, René. *Violence and the Sacred.* Translated by Patrick Gregory. Baltimore, 1977.

Hermesdorf, Bernardus H. D. *Poena talionis.* Utrecht and Nijmegen, 1965.

Jüngling, Hans-Winfried. "'Auge für Auge, Zahn für Zahn': Bemerkungen zu Sinn und Geltung der altestamentlichen Talionsformeln." *Theologie und Philosophie* 59 (1984): 1–38.

Kelsen, Hans. *Vergeltung und Kausalität: Eine soziologische Untersuchung.* The Hague, 1941. Translated as *Society and Nature: A Sociological Inquiry* (Chicago, 1943).

Koch, Klaus, ed. *Um das Prinzip der Vergeltung in Religion und Recht des Alten Testaments.* Wege der Forschung, no. 125. Darmstadt, 1972.

Kohler, Josef. *Zur Lehre der Blutrache.* Würzburg, 1885.

Kohler, Josef. *Shakespeare vor dem Forum der Jurisprudenz.* Berlin, 1919.

Leeuw, Gerardus van der. *Phänomenologie der Religion.* Tübingen, 1933. Translated as *Religion in Essence and Manifestation* (1938; 2d ed., 2 vols., New York, 1963).

Lévy-Bruhl, Lucien. *L'âme primitive.* Paris, 1927. Translated as *The "Soul" of the Primitive* (New York, 1928).

Malinowski, Bronisław. *Crime and Custom in Savage Society.* London, 1926.

Mauss, Marcel. "La religion et les origines du droit pénal d'après un livre récent." In his *Œuvres,* vol. 2, pp. 65–698. Paris, 1969.

Nilsson, Martin P. *Grekisk religiositetet.* Stockholm, 1946. Translated as *Greek Piety* (Oxford, 1948).

Onuf, Nicholas G. *Reprisals: Rituals, Rules, Rationales.* Princeton, 1974.

Pigliaru, Antonio. *Il banditismo in Sardegna.* 2d ed. Milan, 1975.

Schacht, Joseph. *An Introduction to Islamic Law.* Oxford, 1964.

Steinmetz, Sebald Rudolf. *Ethnologische Studien zur ersten Entwicklung der Strafe nebst einer psychologischen Abhandlung über Grausamkeit und Rachsucht.* 2 vols. Groningen, 1928.

Thurnwald, Richard. "Blutrache." In *Reallexikon der Vorgeschichte,* edited by Max Ebert, vol. 2, pp. 30–41. Berlin, 1925.

Thurnwald, Richard. "Vergeltung." In *Reallexikon der Vorgeschichte,* edited by Max Ebert, vol. 14, pp. 130–131. Berlin, 1929.

Tobien, E. S. *Die Blutrache nach altem Russischem Recht, verglichen mit der Blutrache der Israeliten und Araber, der Griechen und Römer und der Germanen.* Dorpat, 1840.

Verdier, Raymond, ed. *La vengeance: Études d'ethnologie, d'histoire et de philosophie,* vol. 1, *Vengeance et pouvoir dans quelques sociétés extra-occidentales.* Paris, 1980.

Weidkuhn, Peter. *Aggressivität, Ritus, Säkularisierung: Biologische Grundformen religiöser Prozesse.* Basel, 1965.

ELMAR KLINGER
Translated from German by Matthew J. O'Connell

REVIVAL AND RENEWAL. The phenomena of revival and renewal have been classified and described by various terms reflecting a wide range of analytical frameworks based on such criteria as overt purposes, main emphases or characteristics, historical period, and location. The catalog of relevant terms thus bears examination.

The terms *accommodative, acculturative, adaptive, adjustive,* and *syncretic* are largely interpretive, indicating that revival and renewal activities took place in, and as a response to, a situation in which two or more different sociocultural orders were in contact and were more or less in opposition or conflict, as, for example, in the colonial situation. The terms *denunciatory, militant,* and *nativistic* speak mainly to what seem to have been the main emphases or characteristics of revival, as, for instance, the vehement reactions to the dominant culture in the colonial process. The terms *dynamic, revitalization,* and *vitalistic* interpret revival activities as more positively creative rather than merely responsive. *Devotional* and *pious* are usually used to describe movements of renewal that occur squarely within an established religious tradition. In these cases the objective is a deeper understanding of, and closer conformity with, the perceived truths of the tradition. But since revival and renewal activities may become heterodox and refractory with the discovery of new truths, the terms belong in the general lexicon. In activities described as *reformative* and *revivalist* new truths, heterodoxy, and criticisms of the given tradition are explicit.

Utopian, more familiarly descriptive of literary works, proposals, and indirect suggestions for a better world, is often used to describe revival and renewal activities because they appear to have as their purpose an impractical state of perfection or bliss. The word *cargo* has been reserved for revival activities occurring in Oceania, particularly in the islands of Melanesia, where the overt purpose is to gain access to European manufactured goods, called in Pidgin *kago* ("cargo").

The terms *enthusiastic* and *enthusiasms* refer specifically to movements within the Christian tradition during the seventeenth, eighteenth, and nineteenth centuries. But because the activities were heterodox, antinomian, and anticlerical, and because they sought new truths in a direct relation with the godhead without the intervention of clergy and envisaged a state of comparative bliss, the terms have come into a more general usage. *Millenarian* is gaining ground as a general portmanteau term, but it specifically refers to those activities in the European medieval period whose overt purposes and emphases were grounded in an expectation of the second coming of Christ. *Adventism* carries much the same connotations as *millenarian* but is usually used to describe more recent Christian movements and sects. Although *messianic* refers particularly to the Judeo-Christian tradition, it is also used more widely for any activities hinging on the advent of a leader-redeemer. Hence the term *prophet movements* is also used. Finally, while *charismatic*, like so many other words of specific Christian reference, is now used more loosely and generally, as in "charismatic leader," within the Christian tradition it refers more precisely to a form of worship centered on the "gift of tongues," glossalalia, a supposed charism of the Holy Spirit.

The above list of labels is not exhaustive. But since the bulk of those remaining are differing forms of, or are derived from, the terms provided, it will suffice. Whether the number of terms—so many of which are synonyms of each other—indicate significant phenomenological differences or are distinctions without a difference is a moot question. Still, for the most part the labels refer to activities that are heterodox, refractory, or rebellious in relation to a given tradition and appear to anticipate the discovery of new truths and new moralities, looking forward to a more certain redemption and better or even blissful times. Hence it is perhaps permissible to consider them as millenarian-type activities and their leaders, charismatic or otherwise, as prophets.

Morphology. Briefly and generally, what happens in millenarian-type activities is that an individual, usually a man but sometimes a woman, the prophet, articulates to a given community a seemingly imperative program of action. When the program falls on deaf ears, the prophet is regarded as more or less insane or deranged. If, on the other hand, members of the community take up and pursue the program, something significant is beginning to happen even though nonparticipants may regard the collective action as insane, ill-considered, or foolish. Behind the articulation, bizarre and odd though the program may sometimes seem, has lain a period of hard thought and imaginative wrestlings, which culminate in a vivid and compelling inspirational experience. This, revelatory in nature, usually occurs in a dream, vision, or trancelike state but also in that more controlled mode in which a number of apparently intractable problems, mulled over in the mind, suddenly cohere into a resolution to act. In any case, the prophet usually disclaims personal authority except insofar as he or she is the agent of some transcendent source: God, Christ, the Holy Spirit, the Virgin Mary, the Great Spirit, an angel, an ancestor or ancestors, a figure or passage from mythology, a particularly powerful spirit or ghost in human or animal form, or passages from the sacred scriptures. There are many such sources. It suffices that the program for action has a divine warrant, usually also sanctioned by threats of imminent disaster—a destructive flood, storm, tidal wave, earthquake, volcanic eruption, holocaust, or, more simply, eternal damnation. Sometimes the disaster is muted into a life of continuing misery and helplessness. The point is that while participants will be saved or redeemed or will enjoy happiness, nonparticipants will deserve the fate reserved for them.

The general framework of revival and renewal activities may be described in terms of two phases between a prologue and an epilogue, with the caution that during the course of the action the parts of one phase may well overlap those of the other.

The prologue consists of the development of an ambience of general dissatisfaction with the way things are. People talk and gossip about their present difficulties, hark back to a time when, supposedly, all was well with them, and cast forward to a misty future when all might be well again, the heart's desires capable of being satisfied, the good life possible, and an earthly as well as a heavenly or spiritual redemption obtainable. The present appears as a kind of limbo, a transitional time of disappointment and dysphoria sandwiched between two kinds of well-being. In literate societies there is recourse to the sacred scriptures. Reinterpretations are bandied about, talked over, rethought. In nonliterate societies new meanings are pulled out of old myths; the new meanings then interact with present circumstances to form, in effect, new myths. In either case the following are the implicit questions: What is the truth of things? How may the good and moral life be lived in accordance with the truth? How is redemption to be obtained? In both cases it is thought that somewhere along the way something has gone wrong and that if it could be put right, a new age—envisaged as a new set of moral relationships in which each person will be able to satisfy his or her desires through others—will dawn. One or two in the community may already have attempted, publicly, to articulate a program to resolve present problems. Others have heard them but have rejected them as false prophets. Nevertheless, the early speakers have brought some things together and have created an expectation that someone sometime will get it right.

The development of the prologue seems essential to the effectiveness of a prophet. A particular connection—whose constituents are not easily unraveled—between prologue and revelation creates an authenticity in the prophet, sparks the revival and renewal activities, makes explicit what has been incipient and implicit in the prologue. The issues are, generally, the creation of new moralities, the construction of a new and relevant semantic environment of meaning, the transformation of a state of misery and helplessness into one of happiness, control, and the promise of redemption.

The first phase, assuming the form of a classic rite of transition, consists of a symbolic—and actual—return to first beginnings. Essentially, participants strip themselves of extant statuses, roles, and moralities to become, in effect, a noncommunity of mere selves. This is done most commonly by dancing a new dance to exhaustion; by dramatized orgies of sexual promiscuity; by the use of drugs; by the destruction of crops, animals, and property; or, in a more modern idiom, by the organization of encounter groups or mutual confessional sessions. There are other techniques. Glossalalia often occurs, for example. But whatever the mode employed, it is vital that an extant self be at least temporarily deprived of or released from its social and moral supports, that it understand itself and relate to other selves as well as to the divine outside of a sociocultural matrix that has become, by definition, intolerable. In short, to paraphrase a Christian idiom, participants are invited to die to themselves in order to put on the new person.

The second phase is the reverse or obverse of the first: a definition of the new social self both internally among the participants and externally by reference to outsiders. Special badges may be worn; exclusive modes of greeting, address, and apparel may be adopted. Gatherings of the faithful assume a distinctive, ritualized form; set procedures are carefully followed, especially when directed toward releasing the self from social constraints. Even in specifically secular movements, ritualized social observances (brushing or flossing one's teeth, practicing drills, performing the daily round of activities in prescribed ways) strengthen internal solidarities and emphasize the distinction between insiders and outsiders, the elect and the lost, the saved and the damned. The use of money—to which prophets often advert in their revelations—is strictly controlled, and narrow, rigorous moralities govern community interrelationships. Finding fault in others, at first a necessary adjunct to maintaining the new ways and moralities, becomes a major concern. Where the prologue and first phase had been informed by sentiments of love and egalitarianism and by the transcending of status barriers and competing interests, now hierarchy and close definitions of status and relative worth begin to seem more important. Although new recruits may be welcomed, they are closely examined. Backsliders are denounced and made to atone or are expelled from the community in disgrace.

The epilogue is by no means always a sad ending to hopeful beginnings. Many Christian sects and denominations—indeed, Christianity itself—have started in a variety of modulations of the way outlined and have survived. And there are many other communities which, whether regarded as part of or distinct from and independent of a larger fold, have survived in quietist and particularist modes. On the other hand, what more often occurs is that government forces intervene, either to bring an end to the activities of the first phase, because they appear to disturb the peace and seem contrary to good order, or to extirpate the movement because the new moralities are seen to have political overtones that challenge government authority. Alternatively, the activities of the prologue and the first phase may never actually cohere into a definable movement and simply evaporate as the collective will to continue dissipates in uncertainty.

Whether the prologue develops into a pious movement of renewal within an established church, the foundation of a religious order, the formation of an independent sect or denomination, or into a position wholly independent of its parents, the new community and its moralities cannot be other than syncretic, evoking the first group of terms mentioned at the outset of this article. Ideas from a variety of sources are brought together and reformulated as the prologue develops. The freshness of the new moralities lies not so much in the rituals (although these may seem peculiar enough to an outsider) as in the wider appreciations and deeper understandings brought to a novel hierarchical arrangement of what had existed before. What had once seemed intractable and intolerable is transformed into a semantic environment of relevance, an environment of meanings that guarantee the truth of things, indicate the good and worthwhile life, and assure members of the community that at the end of a good life lies redemption.

The force of the prophet's revelatory experience lies in the fact that it seems to make entirely possible the realization of what had been before in large part a kind of wish-dream. While the duration of a prologue varies greatly, and while there must always be a "first time," it is unusual for an effective prophet not to have had precursors. This indicates that the prologue may take some time to develop. Furthermore, interventions by governments aside, for a movement to be viable, the initial revelation perforce has to be developed and modified. And for this, political skills are required. Sometimes the prophet possesses such skills. More often, however, the survival of the movement depends on the managerial and political abilities of participants other than the prophet, who is shunted more usefully into an honorary, advisory position.

In principle, millenarian-type activities represent a general human proclivity realizable in any culture. Instances have occurred within Islam, Hinduism, and Buddhism. Oral traditions suggest that instances also have occurred in nonliterate societies of all types. Indeed, in an evolutionary context renewal and revival activities enable groups or communities to survive by creating more meaningful semantic environments, whereas otherwise they might have perished.

However, the incidence of recorded instances of revival and renewal shows that the vast bulk have occurred within a Christian ambience. This is not simply a function of colonialism or the European passion for recording. The nature and history of Christianity reveal it as peculiarly susceptible to millenarian-type activities. The history of Christianity in Europe is replete with instances, and as Europeans and Christian missionaries have moved into other lands, the instances have multiplied. If it seems odd to think that Christianity, variegated though it is in its denominational manifestations, yet contains within itself such a re-creative evolutionary property, it is at least a possibility not to be lightly dismissed.

The idea of an alternative sociocultural order or semantic environment informed by perfected moralities, as well as attempts to realize such orders, comprise an integral part of Christianity. From first beginnings under the coercive aegis of the Roman hegemony, Christianity developed in a variety of differing cultural milieus. Given the Christian affirmation of the world as well as of things divine, its promise of new earths as well as new heavens, two contrasting models of community became dominant. Although both spoke to the greater perfection of morality, the first model of community was egalitarian, characterized by the mutual sharing of property and goods and held together by a set of transcendent beliefs, particularly in the guidance of the Holy Spirit. The second model, derived from Plato's ideal society, was hierarchical with supposedly mathematically harmonious structures and was grounded, at least initially, in measures of physical coercion. The permutation and combination of the contraries contained in the two models continually generate possible alternative sociocultural orders. And this process, sociologically speaking, would seem to have been largely responsible not only for the multiplicity of Christian sects and denominations but also for utopian writings, the formation of secular movements intent on an ambience of more perfect moralities, and the founding of experimental and ideal secular as well as religious communities. The history of Euro-Christian, or Western, civilization teems with examples.

This is not to say that an idea of the alternative sociocultural order has been absent from traditional societies and communities outside or beyond the Christian ambience and influence. But manifestations have been only sporadic. On the other hand, as Christian-derived Western ideas have spread, so have notions of the alternative moral community; and the incidence of attempts to realize such alternatives has been increasing, particularly in Japan since the end of World War II. Traditionally, however, in spite of historical change, whatever existed in any one lifetime has had to be taken as given: the good life has had to be managed either within its terms; in spite of them, through techniques of gaining an inner spiritual peace; or by renunciation.

Interpretive Theories. Description inevitably involves interpretation, and with millenarian-type activities there are further difficulties. The evidence for what has actually occurred is rarely obtained firsthand and usually becomes accessible only through the reports of those who were unsympathetic if not actively hostile. Because it is almost impossible for a competent observer to be in the right place at the right time, only a fraction of the data that might have been available ever comes to light. Questions as to whether the prophet and participants mean what they say in a literal or a symbolic sense and how these senses relate to each other and to the activities are difficult to disentangle and form into a relatively unimpeachable statement of what is really happening. Social scientists and professional ethnographers began to investigate millenarian-type movements only in the second decade of this century, and it was not until the late forties that the activities began to be investigated more or less systematically. Even then the large bulk of the work has concentrated on activities in the colonial situation, virtually ignoring the specifically Christian inheritance and contribution. Finally, although the force of the transcendent is clearly of great significance, social scientists, whatever their personal views, must either ignore the transcendent or reduce or translate it into sociocultural factors.

In such circumstances, accounting for or having a theory about millenarian-type activities presents problems. Moreover, an adequate theory should consist of a set of integrated statements about a phenomenon that, in accounting for the positive instance, also should account for the negative. For example, the disaster theory holds that millenarian-type activities follow upon what is perceived as a disaster, the last conceived broadly and including sociocultural as well as physical circumstances. In cases where an outsider identifies such a disaster but where no revival or renewal activities occur, it is likely that the insiders have not perceived the disaster as such. That is, the identification of a disaster is dependent on the activities, and the problem becomes one of specificity about the kinds of disaster involved. At present, such specifics are lacking.

In another example, a significant difference between what are thought of as legitimate expectations or aspirations and social realities has given rise to the "relative deprivation" hypothesis. That is, where social realities hinder legitimate expectations, revival and renewal activities occur. But since legitimate expectations may be economic ("we ought to have as much wealth as . . .") or political ("we ought to deploy as much power as . . .") or religious ("we ought to have the same opportunities for spiritual redemption as . . ."), and since there are few groups that do not consider themselves "deprived" in one or another sense in relation to another group, the negative instances are legion and unexplained. While the activities define the cause, the latter fails in its effects much more often than it succeeds.

One of the first professional social scientists to consider the problem, A. C. Haddon, described the parameters neatly enough:

> An awakening of religious activity is a frequent characteristic of periods of social unrest. The weakening or disruption of the old social order may stimulate new and often bizarre ideals, and these may give rise to religious movements that strive to sanction social and political aspirations. Communities that feel themselves oppressed anticipate the emergence of a hero who will restore their prosperity and prestige. And when the people are imbued with religious fervour the expected hero will be regarded as a Messiah. Phenomena of this kind are well known in history, and are not unknown at the present day among peoples in all stages of civilization. (Haddon, 1917, p. 455)

However, with the intervention of World War I, the implications of Haddon's statement were lost for a generation and more. While Ronald Knox's (1950) study of "enthusiasms" did not go wholly unnoticed, when social scientists again addressed the problem, they turned to psychology rather than sociology and history. [*See* Enthusiasm.]

Psychological interpretations were, and to a great extent still are, centered around the notions of "cognitive dissonance" or "collective flights from reality," where proper cognitions and reality were and are taken as givens. Although from this point of view, one might suppose forms of schizophrenia, Norman R. C. Cohn (1970) identified collective paranoia as the leitmotif of medieval millenarism. Thus arises the question of whether in the light of social unrest, oppression, disasters, and relative deprivation, the paranoia reflected reality or represented an avoidance of reality—like the rabbits of Richard Adams's *Watership Down* (New York, 1972) who escaped the destruction meted out to their fellows through just such a "collective flight from reality" and after many adventures eventually realized a comparative state of earthly bliss.

If the participants in millenarian-type activities feel that something is wrong with their world that they want to put right, psychological interpretations generally move toward the view that something is wrong with or lacking in the participants. (Anthony F. C. Wallace's 1956 article on revitalization is the notable exception.) The same is true of biological interpretations, which cite brain lesions or the complexities of the interconnections and relations between the right and left hemispheres of the brain. Thus it has been suggested that leaders who are followed despite their apparently irrational demands are wont to have brain lesions. Yet, as history informs us, true leaders cannot be other than extraordinary people. Perhaps such lesions are necessary to leadership with a vision of the future. And since left-hemisphere dominance is thought to give rise to logical thought and science, whereas right-hemisphere dominance is typical of the intuitive and nonrational approach of charismatics, it is likely that prophets will be right-hemisphere-dominant. Suggestive, but waiting on a great deal of further research, biological interpretations raise questions about whether they will inform us further about what we need or want to know or, more pertinently, whether they will tell us what questions remain to be asked.

Biological and psychological interpretations must tend toward the identification of a lesion—something wrong or abnormal. Moving from the opposite premise, that there may be something reasonable and expectable rather than something amiss or lacking in millenarian-type activities, many scholars working in sociological or anthropological modes have attempted explication rather than explanation. That is, accepting that some kinds of explanation must be inherent in an explication, these scholars have not sought causes like disaster and deprivation theories but have sought to tease out and define the relevances of the phenomenon. Some examples follow.

Breaking out of the anthropological functionalism that often inhibited studies of millenarian-type activities by insisting on equilibrium, synchronic analyses, and virtual denial of historical relevances, Peter Lawrence's detailed explication of a cargo movement in Papua New Guinea (Lawrence, 1964) demonstrates in historical depth, and with particular reference to the influence of Christian missionaries, how historic events and political and economic circumstances interacted with traditional mythologies and cohered into a movement. Lawrence is particularly illuminating on the nature of the prophet involved, Yali: not mad or insane or given to wild imaginings but experienced, traveled, and particularly affected by the differences in lifestyle, power, and economic resources obtaining between black and white peoples. In a similar study (Burridge, 1960), I have done much the same as Lawrence in an adjacent area, but, lacking the detailed historical data, my study accents traditional and symbolic elements in relation to social, political, economic, and cognitive features inherent in the colonial process and missionary activity. In later and more general works I consider a variety of features, including money and interpretive modes (Burridge, 1969) and the relevances of identity, individuality, Christianity, and contrasting models of community (Burridge, 1979).

Johannes Fabian's 1971 study of the Jamaa movement, which started as a pious movement within the Roman Catholic church and whose prophet was a Roman Catholic missionary priest, emphasizes semantic and organizational changes largely through detailed analyses of what was said and done. Although the prophet's maxim was "organization kills the movement," participants began to feel the necessity to organize once church authorities had removed the prophet. Fabian shows how organization was achieved not so much purposively and directly as through what was inherent and implicit in the discussions and activities of the participants. He also shows how the process of becoming organized in itself began to move the participants into an independent position, no longer a pious movement within the church.

Peter Worsley's classic study of Melanesian cargo activities (Worsley, 1957) is both historical and developmental, framed within an analysis of the politico-economic features of the colonial process. Worsley shows how millenarian-type activities are the only way in which a generally nonliterate and subject people can, lacking other means, signal their objections to the way things are. Not only are nonrational means adopted because no rational means exist, but the people themselves, in their traditional lives, habitually make use of transcendent sources or nonrational means when what is called rationality in the European view seems to fail them. Stephen Fuchs (1965) emphasizes themes of economic disadvantage, political disfranchisement, oppression, and consequent rebellion. Vittorio Lanternari (1963) does much the same. Bryan R. Wilson (1973) has pursued the problem of the rational and the irrational, concluding that thaumaturgical desires—command of transcendent or divine forces as well as of politico-economic and social features—are the basis for millenarian-type activities, and are thus inappropriate in or to rational and industrialized society.

Whether the interpretation be biological, psychological, cultural, or sociological, studies of millenarian-type activities have converged and reached a point at which, traditional methodologies having been more or less exhausted, a phase of consolidation and rethinking has started. Over a period of fifty years or so, systematic studies have moved from virtually dismissing the activities as forms of insanity or madness to considerations of different kinds of reality, their construction and interrelations, and the implications of terms such as *rational, nonrational,* and *irrational.* Ideologies, symbolic constructs, and notions of the transcendent are coming to be viewed as not simply epiphenomenal, products of the realities of politico-economic relations and modes of production, but as themselves kinds of reality that react back on other arrangements in ways that we do not yet wholly understand. While the painting on a cave wall depicting a buffalo transfixed by a spear may be thought of as a magical and irrational way of attaining an end, it is also a means by which the hunter makes explicit to himself and fixes in symbolic terms an image of what he desires to accomplish. Similarly, the making of airplanes, radio stations, ships, and storage sheds from palm leaves and rattan (as well as many other apparently odd activities so frequently encountered in cargo movements) is now appreciated not simply as magical or irrational fantasy but as the forming of symbolic constructs of desired ends.

Studies of historical depth have made it abundantly clear that millenarian-type activities and their modulations are likely to occur in situations characterized by contradictory juxtapositions of affective and impersonal relations, particularly where differences of culture or subculture, lifestyle, modes of production, economic opportunity, and kinds of access to political control are involved—industrialized society notwithstanding. Why the problems that arise from these juxtapositions should cohere in a religious idiom, and why this should be thought irrational, are perhaps the main issues. For even in secular activities it is possible to discern a vital and essentially religious element. Too little is known about the nature of reality and about the transcendent and its relations to forms of redemption. The symbolic resonances of money—in particular its effects on moral affective and impersonal relationships—require much closer attention. Examination of the relevances of literacy—the quantum leap in symbolic and logical competence, the different kinds of effects wrought by the written and spoken word, the release from thralldom to a learned and literate clergy and secular elite—will surely provide further insights.

Finally, beyond their intrinsic human interest millenarian-type activities remain a crucial challenge to social scientists. They invite the statement through which particular actions and rationalizations, presently confined to specific situations, may aspire to a more general ontological validity. Absurd or irrational though they may seem, millenarian-type activities reveal human beings in the crisis of deciding how to be true to themselves and their future.

[*See also* Millenarianism; Reform; Syncretism; *and* Utopia. *Considerable discussion of this topic can also be found in* African Religions, *article on* Modern Movements; Australian Religions, *article on* Modern Movements; *and* North American Religions, *article on* Modern Movements.]

BIBLIOGRAPHY

A. C. Haddon's early remarks appear in "Five New Religious Cults in British New Guinea," by E. W. P. Chinnery and A. C. Haddon, *Hibbert Journal* 15 (1917): 448–463. The article is worth reading in its entirety. There are many excellent accounts of revival and renewal based on fieldwork: *The Peyote Religion among the Navaho* (New York, 1966) by David F. Aberle; my own work, *Mambu: A Melanesian Millennium* (London, 1960); *Jamaa: A Charismatic Movement in Katanga* (Evanston, Ill., 1971) by Johannes Fabian; *Rebellious Prophets* (New York, 1965) by Stephen Fuchs; and *Road Belong Cargo: A Study of the Cargo Movement in the Southern Madang District, New Guinea* (Manchester, 1964) by Peter Lawrence. *Enthusiasm: A Chapter in the History of Religion, with Special Reference to the Seventeenth and Eighteenth Centuries* (Oxford, 1950) by Ronald Knox is a brilliant study of enthusiastic movements in socio-theological perspective. Norman R. C. Cohn's *Pursuit of the Millennium*, 3d ed. (New York, 1970), and Anthony F. C. Wallace's "Revitalization Movements," *American Anthropologist* 58 (April 1956): 264–281, provide the most notable sociopsychological studies. Of the more general works, Michael Barkun presents a good analysis of disaster theory in *Disaster and the Millennium* (New Haven, 1974). A short but comprehensive survey can be found in my book, *New Heaven, New Earth* (New York, 1969), and a discussion of the implications on a wider level is provided in my later work, *Someone, No One: An Essay on Individuality* (Princeton, 1979). *The Religions of the Oppressed: A Study of Modern Messianic Cults* (New York, 1963) by Vittorio Lanternari is an excellent portrait of the political and economic aspects of the subject. Bryan R. Wilson relates thaumaturgies and religious change in his full yet compendious survey of *Magic and the Millennium: A Sociological Study of Religious Movements of Protest among Tribal and Third-World Peoples* (New York, 1973). A landmark study of colonial problems and politico-economic relations is provided by Peter Worsley's *The Trumpet Shall Sound: A Study of "Cargo" Cults in Melanesia* (1957; New York, 1968). In some ways the fullest and most rounded account, in which the actors are rabbits, is *Watership Down* (New York, 1972) by Richard Adams.

KENELM BURRIDGE

REVIVALISM. *See* Reform *and* Revival and Renewal. *For discussion of Christian revivalism, see* Fundamental and Evangelical Christianity *and* Pentecostal and Charismatic Christianity.

REVOLUTION. Throughout the course of history, religion has functioned as a source of social solidarity, and this fact is undoubtedly related to the very essence of religion, which provides a set of basic values for the regulation of man's life on earth and guidance in his search for meaning and salvation. Since in all traditional societies both nature and society were regarded as part of the same cosmic universe controlled by gods or spirits, a religious legitimation of the social order developed as a matter of course.

The integrative role of religion has been known for a very long time. The eighteenth-century rationalist Voltaire assured his noble pupil, Frederick the Great, that a "wise and courageous prince, with money, troops, and laws, can perfectly well govern men without the aid of religion," but most rulers of mankind and the wise men counseling them have preferred not to take any chances on the firmness and sway of political authority. In his *Discourses* (1517) Machiavelli called religion "the most necessary and assured support of any civil society," and he exhorted princes and heads of republics "to uphold the foundations of the religion of their countries, for then it is easy to keep their people religious, and consequently well conducted and united." The duration of empires, argued the French conservative Joseph de Maistre, writing after the French Revolution, "has always been proportionate to the influence that the religious principle has acquired in the political system." The emphasis on the importance to society of a sense of shared values endeared de Maistre to his fellow countryman, the sociologist Émile Durkheim, probably the best-known modern spokesman for the view that the primary function of religion is the preservation of social unity.

But religion has often also functioned as an agent of revolutionary mobilization. Religion involves transcendent moral standards that define an ideal against which human performance can be measured. Hence those who are dissatisfied—politically, economically, socially, or spiritually—may find in religion strong support for their attack upon the status quo. Religion can be a powerful agent pushing the thoughts of men beyond tradition; it may become the spiritual dynamic of revolution that Georges Sorel called the "social myth." As the judicious Richard Hooker observed in the sixteenth century, during a period of great religious and social upheaval, when the minds of men are once "persuaded that it is the will of God to have those things done which they fancy, their opinions are as thorns in their sides, never suffering them to take rest till they have brought their speculations into practice." Religion can provide man with the zeal of the true believer who knows that he is right and who acts with fortitude since he carries out God's will and counts on God's helping hand.

While some religious ideas, such as the conception of sacred kingship to be found in many premodern societies, have reinforced a pattern of political subservience and quietism, most religious views of rulership have not had such unequivocal political consequences. The ancient Chinese doctrine of the mandate of Heaven, for example, legitimized the rule of the emperor, the Son of Heaven, who traced his title to deified ancestors upon whom Heaven, the supreme deity, had conferred the right to rule. And yet, the mandate of Heaven was not seen as granted in perpetuity or unconditionally. Heaven demanded righteousness and good government and deposed rulers who abused their exalted office. Hence, just as the concept had apparently come into being to justify the seizure of power by the Chou dynasty (around 1028 BCE), which claimed a divine mandate for overthrowing the Shang, so the mandate of Heaven could later be invoked by new aspirants to the supreme rulership. Indeed, in Chinese a revolution is called *ko ming*—"breaking of the mandate."

The Christian ideas of divine providence and of the divine origin and sanction of rulership also have had diverse results: they have helped shore up and sanctify political authority, but they also have been used to justify rebellion. In the deterministic worldview of Augustine of Hippo, nothing could exist without divine approval. Divine providence has arranged things in such a way that every evil in the world is directed to some good. God appoints rulers according to the merits of the people, and in view of his omnipotence and justice tyrants must be considered God's retribution for the perversity of the people. Both just kings and cruel tyrants reign by God's providence; none may be resisted.

This gospel of submissiveness, a justification for a theologian desirous of obtaining secular support for the suppression of heresy or for a Martin Luther in need of assistance from the princes of the Holy Roman Empire, was a burdensome handicap for Christians eager to fight the pretensions of absolute temporal power. Hence, in the later sixteenth century, in particular, the doctrine of divine providence was reinterpreted so as to make possible certain political actions. Theodore Beza, a disciple of Calvin, conceded that nothing can exist without divine approval and that God uses the evil deeds of sinners to punish other sinners. But, he asked, why could it not be God's will that tyrants be punished by the people rather than people by tyrants? During the Puritan Revolution (English Civil War) the Christian humanist John Milton rejected the suggestion that God had put the English nation in slavery to Charles Stuart and that only God, therefore, could be relied upon to release it. If God can be said to give a people into slavery whenever a tyrant prevails over a people, he asked, why ought God not as well be said to set them free whenever people prevail over a tyrant?

But this kind of politically useful theological reasoning did not originate with either Beza or Milton. Around 1110, Hugh of Fleury had taught in his *De regia potestate* that God punishes bad princes by the insubordination of their people, and the same idea is found in Eastern Christendom. The Kievan chronicler considered a revolt of the citizens against their prince an act of God's will, punishing the prince for his misconduct. More recently a pastoral letter issued in 1967 by "Sixteen Bishops of the Third World" declared that "Christians and their pastors should know how to recognize the hand of the Almighty in those events that from time to time put down the mighty from their thrones and raise up the humble." Needless to say, the impressment of God for the cause of rebellion is today no monopoly of the political left. After the military coup of 1964 in Brazil, a group of Brazilian archbishops and bishops thanked God for having listened to their prayers for deliverance from the communist peril. Divine providence, they said, had made itself felt in a tangible manner.

Other contradictory consequences of the doctrine of divine providence must be noted. The acceptance of the omnipotent role of the deity can lead to fatalism and inaction, but it can also spur people to mighty effort because of the conviction that God is on their side. Thus the early Jewish apocalyptic writers counseled complete reliance upon God's direct intervention, which would redeem Israel, whereas the later Zealots, engaged in eschatological war against Rome, believed that God would usher in the new age of freedom and justice only if pious Jewish warriors actively participated in the realization of the divine plan. Here strong faith in the certainty of divine assistance acted to inspire superior exertion and fortitude and gave the struggle against Rome the character of a holy war. Revolutionary action merged with messianic utopianism and led to an utter disregard of Rome's overwhelming might, a realistic appraisal of which would have discouraged any hope of success.

The fact that most religious doctrines are protean in character and are open to different readings does not mean that the doctrinal content of a religion is entirely irrelevant to politics. Though all religions have both quietistic and revolutionary potentials, the relative proportions of these differing political implications vary. Considering the phenomenon of revolutionary millenarianism, for example, we see that certain religious traditions are more conducive to expectations of a coming age of bliss than others. The cyclical view of history in Hinduism and Buddhism, providing as it does for perpetual flux and endless repetition of the cosmic drama, appears to discourage millenarian ideas, just as the linear theory of history and the expectation of a final salvation of humanity in Judaism, Christianity, and Islam provide inspiration for the millenarian dream of eternal terrestrial redemption.

The leadership of religious organizations or movements is often of considerable importance in determining that group's political posture. A charismatic leader of a millenarian movement is a potent agent of radical change. As the bearer of chiliastic prophecy, he is not just a champion of felt needs or a catalyst but also a cause of the movement he is heading. The millenarian prophet's ambitious and challenging vision of what the world ought to be increases expectations and dissatisfactions, which can lead to a revolutionary situation. The limited success of *conscientização*, the attempted "raising of the consciousness" of the subservient peasant population of South America by various radical groups, shows that this enterprise encounters serious difficulties when entrusted to persons of ordinary and secular cast.

In sum, religion can be both a prop for the established institutions of society and a revolutionary force, since it includes elements for integration as well as for radical change. Religion can defuse social conflict by devaluing earthly concerns and emphasizing happiness in the world beyond, but its promise of divine intervention in human affairs can also strengthen the hope that a better life is possible here on earth. Hence many times different groups within one religion will line up on opposite sides of the barricades. God's will, when seen through the lenses of human desires and interests, can be, and in fact usually is, read in several different ways.

Whether religion discourages or promotes revolution depends on variables such as the relationship of the religious institution to the state or the presence or absence of a forceful leader. All religions known to us can assume both roles, though the intellectual and organizational traditions they hold will incline some more in one direction than in the other. Situational factors, such as the relative chances for success of a revolt, will also be important. In all there are four ways in which religion can assume a revolutionary posture:

1. *Millenarian revolts* occur (a) when situations of distress or disorientation develop, and the causes are not clearly perceived or appear insoluble by ordinary and available remedies; (b) when a society or group is deeply attached to religious ways of thinking about the world and when the religion of that society attaches importance to millenarian ideas; and (c) when an individual or group of individuals obsessed with salvationist fantasies succeeds in establishing charismatic leadership over a social movement.
2. *Militant religious nationalism* arises among colonized people in situations of awakening national consciousness. Religion supplies a sense of national identity; it becomes a symbol of self-assertion against the colonial regime, which is usually indifferent, if not hostile, to the native creed.
3. *The leaders of religious bodies with a developed ecclesiastical organization support a revolutionary upheaval* because they are sympathetic to the aims of this revolution, or because they are protecting the interests of the religious institution. These interests can be temporal or spiritual or both. They can involve the defense of worldly possessions or the protection of the mission of the religious institution as the channel of divine grace to man.
4. *Individual theologians or laymen support a revolutionary movement* to give a concrete social and political meaning to the transcendent elements of their faith, as in the Christian "theology of revolution." Such religious revolutionaries often work in concert with secular revolutionary movements and many lose their identity in them.

Just as in earlier times religion was often used to support the status quo, religion has, in many parts of the world today, become the handmaiden of revolution. The cross of Christianity, the crescent of Islam, and even the peaceful prayer wheel of Buddhism have been enlisted to shore up revolutionary movements and regimes, which are often identified with liberation, modernization, and progress, although, as especially in the case of Islamic revolutionary movements, the radical and far-reaching change instigated by revolution can entail fighting modernization and restoring the old ways. Whether this new positive relationship of religion and revolution will indeed promote human liberty and happiness is, of course, a question nobody can as yet answer. Religion has its part in this celebration of heroic ruthlessness and violence. It continues to inspire killing in Northern Ireland as much as on the Indian subcontinent and in the Philippines, demonstrating once again that religious zeal can be a powerful force for love but also an important force for hate and man's inhumanity to man. The various theologies of revolution make men slight the cruelties and the hatreds that commonly accompany revolutionary upheavals. What the theologizing of revolution cannot do is to establish the progressive character of such revolts. That judgment is reserved to future generations, who will have the opportunity to live with the consequences.

BIBLIOGRAPHY

The classic study of the integrative role of religion remains Émile Durkheim's *The Elementary Forms of the Religious Life* (New York, 1915). On the phenomenon of revolutionary millenarianism, see *Magic and the Millennium* (New York, 1973) by Bryan R. Wilson and *Millennial Dreams in Action*, edited by Sylvia L. Thrupp (1962; reprint, New York, 1970), especially the essay by Norman Cohn, "Medieval Millenarianism: Its Bearing on the Study of Millenarian Movements." For the political manifestations of Christianity, consult Ernst Troeltsch's *The Social Teachings of the Christian Churches*, 2 vols. (1911; reprint, London, 1931), and for the important sixteenth century, see John William Allen's *A History of Political Thought in the Sixteenth Century*, 3d ed. (London, 1951). For a fuller treatment of the subject of this essay and further bibliography, see my own work, *Religion and Revolution* (Oxford, 1974).

GUENTER LEWY

RICCI, MATTEO (1552–1610), Jesuit missionary. Born at Macerata, in the Papal States, Ricci studied law at Rome and entered the Jesuit novitiate in 1571. He volunteered for the missions and was sent to Portugal (1577) and then to Goa (1578). He finished his theological studies in Goa and in 1580 was ordained at Cochin, on the Malabar coast. In 1582 he went to Macao to study Chinese language and culture. The next year, with unprecedented permission from Chinese authorities, Ricci and Michele Ruggier (1543–1607) traveled to Chao-ch'ing, China. Beardless, with shaven heads, they assumed garb similar to that worn by Buddhist monks. They sought to spread Christian doctrine unobtrusively, attracting educated visitors with their world map, Western clocks, and prisms. Ricci's use of the term *t'ien-chu* ("lord of Heaven") to refer to God dates from that period. In 1588 Ricci, known in Chinese as Li Ma-tou, took charge of the mission. Ordered by local authorities to leave (1589), the group of three missionaries went to Shao-chou (modern-day Kwangtung). There they were advised by Ch'ü Ju-k'uei, an early convert who had initially been attracted by rumors of the foreigners' expertise in alchemy. It was probably he who counseled the Jesuits to present themselves as scholars rather than as monks. At Shao-chou Ricci appears to have completed a Latin translation (now lost) of the Confucian Four Books.

After a brief visit to Nanking (1595), the Jesuits settled in Nanchang (modern-day Kiangsi), appearing with hair and beards and wearing Confucian robes. At Nanchang Ricci wrote, in Chinese, *Chiao-yu lun* (On Friendship), dedicated to an imperial prince he had met, and also completed his "catechism" *(T'ien-chu shih-i)*. In 1598 the Jesuits went to Peking, but they stayed only two months, as people feared to associate with them at the time of the Chinese involvement in Japan's invasion of Korea. They settled in Nanking (1599), where the atmosphere had improved; there Ricci met many scholars, including Li Chih and Chiao Hung, and published a revised edition of his world map (1600). That same year the Jesuits left once more for Peking, reinforced with presents for the emperor, including clocks, clavichords, statues, and crucifixes. At Tientsin a eunuch confiscated some articles and held the party for nearly six months.

When the Jesuits finally reached Peking in January 1601, their gifts so pleased the emperor that he allowed them to stay on and even granted them a monthly stipend. Ricci associated there with scholar-officials including grand secretary Shen I-kuan, minister of rites Feng Ch'i, and minister of personnel Li Tai, with whom Ricci discussed science and religion. Feng Ying-ching, editor of an encyclopedia, was prevented from receiving baptism by his untimely death. Another convert, Li Chih-tsao, helped Ricci publish his world map, his catechism, and his treatise on friendship. By 1604 Ricci had also published a short treatise, *Erh-shih-wu yen* (Twenty-five Sayings), and became sole superior of the China mission, now independent of Macao. In 1608 he also published a work on ethics, *Ch'i-jen shih-p'ien* (Ten Dialogues of a Nonconformist). With Hsü Kuang-ch'i, another collaborator baptized at Nanking, who would rise to the position of grand secretary, Ricci translated the first six chapters of Euclid's *Elements* (1607) and other texts on astronomy, trigonometry, geometry, and arithmetic. He prepared a special copy of the world map for the emperor, as well as various polemics directed against Buddhism, especially the *Pien-hsüeh i-tu*. By this time the Jesuits had bought a compound inside the Hsüan-wu Gate, later known as Nan-t'ang (South Church). There they met Ai T'ien, a Chinese Jew from Kaifeng, who told them about the Nestorian presence in China. By then also, their suspicion that China was identical with the legendary land of Cathay had been confirmed. Ricci died of illness at age fifty-seven. He was buried outside the western city-gate of Peking, in Cha-la-erh. His grave, destroyed by the Boxers in 1900, was desecrated again in 1966 but was subsequently repaired; it has been open to the public since 1980.

Ricci's gentle personality, his expertise in Western science and philosophy, and his knowledge of Chinese culture made him one of the great cultural mediators of all time. He was venerated posthumously by Chinese clockmakers as their patron. His method of cultural accommodation in the China mission left its legacy of controversy. Whether Chinese converts to Christianity should still be permitted to participate in Chinese rites was a question long debated in China and Europe by missionaries and philosophers, Chinese emperors, and papal legates. Such participation was condemned as intrinsically evil by popes Clement XI (1704) and Benedict XIV (1742). Even a later papal decision in 1939 to allow a measure of "Chinese rites" did not fully rehabilitate Ricci's institutional position. His ideas were ahead of his time, although his exclusive preferences for early Confucian morals as an ally of Christianity and his opposition to Neo-Confucian philosophy and to Buddhism is not entirely acceptable to even more ecumenically minded modern missionaries.

BIBLIOGRAPHY

No satisfactory book-length biography of Ricci is available in English. Vincent Cronin's *The Wise Man from the West* (New York, 1955) is a popular work. Wolfgang Franke's scholarly entry in *Dictionary of Ming Biography, 1369–1644*, vol. 2 (New York, 1976), is short but full. R. P. Bernard's *Le Père Matthieu Ricci et la société chinoise de son temps*, 2 vols. (Tientsin, 1937), is still useful. Ricci's diary has been translated into English by Louis Gallagher as *China in the Sixteenth Century: The Journals of Matteo Ricci, 1583–1610* (New York, 1953).

Serious scholars must still consult *Opere storiche del P. Matteo Ricci*, 2 vols., edited by Pietro Tacchi Venturi (Macerata, 1911–1913); *Fonti Ricciane*, 3 vols., edited by Pasquale Maria d'Elia (Rome, 1942–1949); and the Jesuit Archives in Rome. There are two chronological biographies available in Chinese, by Li-ou and by Fang Hao, collected in *Li Ma-tou yen-chiu lun-chi*, edited by Chou K'ang-hsieh (n.p., 1971).

JULIA CHING

RICHARDSON, CYRIL C. (1909–1976), American church historian. Born in London, England, Cyril Charles Richardson emigrated to Canada in 1927 and was educated at the University of Saskatchewan (B.A., 1930) and Emmanuel College, Saskatoon (Lic.Theol., 1931). He pursued graduate study at Union Theological Seminary, New York City (Th.D., 1934) and, in Europe, at the universities of Göttingen, Dijon, and Basel. He was ordained to the priesthood of the Protestant Episcopal church in 1934 and became a naturalized American citizen in 1940. From 1934 until his death he taught at Union Theological Seminary, New York, becoming the seminary's fifth Washburn Professor of Church History in 1949 and its dean of graduate studies in 1954.

A brilliant lecturer and prolific writer, Richardson specialized in early Christian literature, patristic theology, and the history of Christian worship and spirituality. He also wrote extensively on the relationship of Christian faith to mental health, spiritual healing, and parapsychology—interests engendered by his hospitalization and successful treatment for tuberculosis from 1943 to 1945. His churchmanship, at once practical and innovative, showed itself in his lifelong concern for Christian unity and in his advocacy, already in the early 1950s, of the ordination of women to the priesthood.

Richardson viewed church history as a specifically theological discipline, whose chief aim is not to study "Christianity," understood as a phenomenon in the general history of religions, but to recount the story of the "holy community" called into being by God's saving acts. Thus church history is "the tale of redemption" and "the medium of revelation," which requires not only a critical sifting of the historical evidence but, above all, the use of symbolic language, or what Richardson referred to as "myth," to convey the ultimate meanings of events.

He is the author of five monographs: *The Christianity of Ignatius of Antioch* (1935); *The Church through the Centuries* (1938); *The Sacrament of Reunion* (1940), a historical examination of the ministry, apostolic succession, and the Eucharist as bases for Christian unity; *Zwingli and Cranmer on the Eucharist* (1949), showing Archbishop Thomas Cranmer's indebtedness to the sacramental theology of the Swiss reformer Ulrich Zwingli; and *The Doctrine of the Trinity* (1958), wherein he argues that the church's classical trinitarian dogma is an "artifical construct" that fails to resolve the profound theological problems it addresses. This pathbreaking book, which generated intense controversy in academic and church circles, typifies Richardson's scholarship, combining mastery of historical detail with acute philosophical criticism and deep religious faith.

He also edited two highly regarded volumes in the Library of Christian Classics series: *Early Christian Fathers* (1953) and, with Edward R. Hardy, *Christology of the Later Fathers* (1954). He collaborated on eleven books, including the second, revised edition of Williston Walker's widely used textbook, *A History of the Christian Church* (1959). He contributed over one hundred articles and a like number of book reviews to theological and historical journals.

Richardson's eminent abilities as a director of doctoral students and his many publications, remarkable for their chronological scope and weight of learning, earned him international repute as one of the leading church historians of the mid-twentieth century.

BIBLIOGRAPHY

To date there has been no biographical study of Richardson or full-scale appraisal of his scholarship. His understanding of the discipline of church history is summarized in his inaugural lecture, "Church History Past and Present," *Union Seminary Quarterly Review* 5 (November 1949): 1–11. He discussed the doctrine of the Trinity in numerous publications (besides his controversial book *The Doctrine of the Trinity*), including "The Enigma of the Trinity," in *A Companion to the Study of St. Augustine*, edited by Roy W. Battenhouse (New York, 1955); "A Preface to Christology," *Religion in Life* 27 (Autumn 1958): 504–514; and "The Trinity and the Enhypostasia," *Canadian Journal of Theology* 5 (April 1959): 73–78. The journal *Religion in Life* 29 (Winter 1959–1960) featured assays on the Trinity by Richardson and Claude Welch, followed by a sharp exchange of views between these two scholars ("The Doctrine of the Trinity," pp. 7–31). Richardon's liturgical scholarship is best represented by his essays, "The Foundations of Christian Symbolism," in *Religious Symbolism*, edited by F. Ernest Johnson (New York, 1962); "Worship in New Testament Times, Christian," in *The Interpreter's Dictionary of the Bible*, edited by George A. Buttrick, vol. 4 (New York, 1962); and "Word and Sacrament in Protestant Worship," in *Ecumenical Dialogue at Harvard: The Roman Catholic-Protestant Colloquium*, edited by Samuel H. Miller and G. Ernest Wright (Cambridge, Mass., 1964).

DAVID W. LOTZ

RIDDLES. *See* Paradox and Riddles.

RIGHT AND LEFT. *See* Left and Right.

RISSHŌ KŌSEIKAI (Society Establishing Righteousness and Harmony) is one of the new religions of postwar Japan. It was founded in 1938 by Niwano Nikkyō (b. 1906), at that time a minor leader of Reiyūkai, and his disciple and assistant Naganuma Myōkō (1889–1957), a woman with shamanic attributes. The school regards the *Lotus Sutra* as the ultimate source of their teachings.

Niwano Nikkyō was born into a farming household in a mountain village in Niigata Prefecture, went to Tokyo in 1923, and eventually became a shopkeeper. In his early twenties he studied systems of fortune-telling based on people's names and on rules governing auspicious and inauspicious dates *(rokuyō)* and directions *(shichishin)* derived from ancient Chinese forms. In 1934, when his daughter became seriously ill, he turned to Arai Sukenobu, a chapter leader in the Reiyūkai organization and a renowned scholar of the *Lotus Sutra*, for advice. Convinced that the *Lotus Sutra* provided answers to the problems of suffering, Niwano became active in the Reiyūkai movement. However, by 1938 his increasing doubts about Reiyūkai, especially its insistence that lectures on the *Lotus Sutra* were unnecessary, led him to form a new organization, Risshō Kōseikai.

Early in its development, Kōseikai taught that adverse karmic causes and effects caused by bad deeds in a previous existence or by the bad deeds of one's ancestors could be overcome by means of ancestor veneration in which the *Lotus Sutra* was chanted, by religious training for the improvement of one's personality, and by guiding others to the faith. This teaching, which stemmed primarily from Reiyūkai doctrine and practice, was complemented by Niwano's use of fortune-telling techniques in order to attract converts to the movement. Niwano also instituted mutual counseling sessions, known as *hōza*, designed to improve the mental outlook of practitioners.

In keeping with the doctrinal roots of the movement, the original iconographic focus of Kōseikai devotion was the Daimoku ("Hail to the *Lotus Sutra*") *maṇḍala* transmitted in the Nichiren tradition. But as Niwano became increasingly disillusioned with the Nichiren sect and the possibility of carrying on joint missionary work with it, he began his own study of the *Lotus Sutra*. In 1958, as a result of his study of the text, he declared the focus of Kōseikai devotion to be the Eternal Buddha of the *Lotus*, and an image of this Buddha was installed in the movement's headquarters in 1964. From around this time a change took place in the composition of the Kōseikai members, as an increasing number of them sought a more meaningful life rather than mere respite from worldly problems. This reflects perhaps the rising standard of living in the Japan of the 1960s. With the changing concern of its followers, and also with the emergence of second-generation members, the core of the Kōseikai doctrine shifted from the attainment of happiness by the elimination of negative karmic effects to the perfection of the personality and the realization of peace on earth.

The basic unit of membership in Risshō Kōseikai is the household rather than the individual. Kōseikai claimed a membership of about a thousand households in 1945. Since then, its membership has increased dramatically: 50,000 in 1950, 399,000 in 1960, 973,000 in 1970, and 1,640,000 in 1980. Members are not requested to end all former religious affiliations. While no clergy-laity distinction exists, the formal status of "teacher" is institutionalized; in 1980, 173,000 people had this qualification. Originally, new members were installed in the same branch as the senior member who brought them to Kōseikai (a system called *oya-ko,* literally, "parent-child"). There were nine such branches in 1945. In 1959, there was a reform in branch organization, and the *oya-ko* system was replaced by one based on propinquity, whereby a branch was made up of members living near one another irrespective of *oya-ko* relations; 138 new branches were set up by this system. A further reform instituted in 1969 defined the boundaries of a branch as coincident with those of municipalities. In 1982 there were 224 branches in Japan, with additional ones in Korea, Brazil, and the United States. These reforms promoted local Kōseikai activities, including campaign work for local and national elections and dissemination of its teachings to nonmembers. Around 1970, Kōseikai launched the Brighter Society Movement (a public-spirited movement bringing together secular, religious, and governmental organizations to create a better society) and an international movement for the attainment of world peace through interreligious cooperation. The headquarters of Kōseikai have been located in Wada, Suginami-ku, Tokyo, since its foundation. Full-time workers at the headquarters and its affiliates numbered a little over five hundred in 1980. No position is hereditary, with the exception of the presidency, which is held by lineal descendants of Niwano.

Kōseikai, the second largest new religion in contemporary Japan, is unique in a number of ways. Although it may be said to stem in part from Nichiren Buddhism, today it stresses basic *bodhisattva* practices as well as faith in the Eternal Buddha. While Kōseikai emphasizes traditional values such as reverence of ancestors, modesty, and harmony, it is neither nativistic nor nationalistic, as demonstrated by its peace movement. It is not meditation-oriented; rather it is practice- or action-oriented on the basis of inner reflection. Its organization is unlike that of other new religions in that the municipality-based local branches are linked to the highly developed bureaucracy at the headquarters.

[*See also* New Religions, *article on* New Religions in Japan.]

BIBLIOGRAPHY

Dale, Kenneth J., and Akahoshi Susumu. *Circle of Harmony: A Case Study in Popular Japanese Buddhism with Implications for Christian Mission.* Tokyo, 1975. A valuable study of *hōza,* the small mutual discussion and counseling group that is the center of Kōseikai's teaching and training activities.

Kyōdanshi Hensan Iinkai, ed. *Risshō Kōseikai shi.* 5 vols. Tokyo, 1984. A history of Risshō Kōseikai written by nonmember specialists.

Niwano Nikkyō. *A Buddhist Approach to Peace.* Tokyo and Rutland, Vt., 1977. Translated and compiled by Masuo Nezu. Based mainly on the author's *Heiwa e no michi* (Tokyo, 1972).

Niwano Nikkyō. *Lifetime Beginner: An Autobiography.* Tokyo and Rutland, Vt., 1978. Translated by Richard L. Gage. An autobiography of the founder of Risshō Kōseikai based on Niwano's two books, *Shoshin isshō* (Tokyo, 1975) and *Niwano Nikkyō jiden* (Tokyo, 1976).

Risshō Kōseikai, ed. *Niwano Nikkyō hōwa senshū.* 7 vols. Tokyo, 1978–1982. A comprehensive collection of Niwano's sermons, speeches, and essays. Very detailed biographical notes are appended to volume one.

MORIOKA KIYOMI

RITES OF PASSAGE.

[*This entry consists of five articles on the phenomena known as rites of passage:*

The first article presents a cross-cultural overview of rites of passage in various religious traditions, paying particular attention to the religions of tribal cultures but drawing examples also from the major historical traditions. The second piece consists of a few definitions that further elucidate the topic. It is followed by studies on rites of passage in Hindu, Jewish, and Muslim traditions. For discussion of rites of passage in the Christian tradition, see Sacrament, *article on* Christian Sacraments.]

An Overview

Rites of passage are a category of rituals that mark the passage of a person through the life cycle, from one stage to another over time, from one role or social position to another, integrating the human and cultural experiences with biological destiny: birth, reproduction, and death. These ceremonies make the basic distinctions, observed in all groups, between young and old, male and female, living and dead. The interplay of biology and culture is at the heart of all rites of passage, and the struggle between these two spheres asserts the essential paradox of our mortal heritage. As humans, we dwell in an equivocal world, for we belong to both nature and culture, as Claude Lévi-Strauss has pointed out. It is through rites of passage that we are able to contemplate, to formulate and reformulate, our ambivalent condition of animal and human. Biology dictates the fundamentals of our experience—birth, reproduction, and death—yet the ways in which we manipulate and modify these imperatives through cultural means are endless.

Tribal Societies. That certain physiological "facts" are as much cultural or social as biological is brought home to us time and time again if we search the vast, intricate descriptions of rites of passage in tribal societies. And the message is clear: men and women are not simply born, nor do they merely procreate and die; they are made what they are through ceremonies. An act of procreation alone cannot make a bride; a wedding must be performed. And brides who can neither copulate nor procreate can be made from infants; many years may separate betrothal from puberty. Sometimes, a female must be initiated into fertility by her society before she is allowed to mate; a girl's social definition as "woman" is provided by ceremony, whether she has begun to menstruate or not. Similarly, males frequently must satisfy certain social conditions before they are allowed to mate; for a boy, a successful hunt or the cutting of his foreskin may be required for passport into adulthood.

In rites of passage we are reminded, too, that the ages of a life are not ordained by laws of nature; most of the ages we acknowledge are socially or culturally created. As Philippe Ariès has demonstrated in *Centuries of Childhood: A Social History of Family Life* (New York, 1962), "childhood" is an invention of post-Renaissance Europe, not a distinctive, universally recognized condition. Prior to modern history, a child was treated, dressed, and regarded as a miniature adult, without special needs or privileges. In like manner, adolescence represents a recently invented, rather than a biologically ineluctable, phase of the human life cycle; G. Stanley Hall established the concept with his book *Adolescence* in 1904. Since then, all manner of social agencies, commercial enterprises, psychologists, physicians, legislators, and educators have arisen to articulate and serve the needs of teenagers. And, as Margaret Mead in *Coming of Age in Samoa* (New York, 1928) has pointed out, the menstrual cramps and discomforts that American women regard as inevitable were unknown among Samoan adolescent girls, attesting that biology is not always destiny and that physiological symptoms may result from social or cultural conditions. To be sure, we often quite forget how complex and how numerous are the cultural templates we lay over our biological essence.

Celebration of paradox. Rites of passage embody paradox, the inevitable legacy of our humanity, vividly calling our attention to, and allowing us to announce and renounce, the most profound enigma of all: that we live out our lives suspended between the borders of nature and culture. This is the essential paradox, but other paradoxes are played out as well. Because rites of passage mark distinctions in an otherwise continuous life course, they celebrate and facilitate change or disruption of standard social categories, while at the same time they preserve them. A third paradox represented reveals the conflict between our aspirations and strivings for individual ventures, and our yearnings for assurance and sustenance from our social group. In actual physiological fact, we are born and die quite alone, unique and separate, but we also do so as members of a group, a group that seeks to preserve the continuity of its values and understandings, a group that therefore defines our birth, aging, and death and that reassures us that life is meaningful.

Hence, during the performance of these life-crisis rituals, societies may inscribe their designs both literally and figuratively upon the initiate, and in doing so, life's paradoxes are proclaimed, contemplated, and dramatized. The struggle between nature and culture is evidenced in Bali, where before a young man or woman may marry, he or she undergoes a tooth-filing ceremony, in which the canine tooth, the mark of the beast, is smoothed so that the smile is less reminiscent of an animal's snarl. The theme of disruption and continuity is enacted in certain African societies, where, as Victor Turner has described, an initiate undergoing male puberty ceremonies ingests a powder ground from the burned foreskins of previous initiates, thereby incorporating into his body the vitality and power of his forebears. And James Fernandez has called our attention to the interdependence of the individual and the collectivity in "Reflections on Looking into Mirrors" (*Semiotica*, 1980) by describing an initiation ceremony in which a neophyte stares into a looking glass until the face of an ancestor appears and merges with his own.

In the extreme expression of the interdependence between the individual and his or her social group, the initiate is construed as a microcosm of society, and what is enacted by or upon the individual is thought to transform the collectivity. Rites of transition performed for divine royalty—birth, marriage, procreation, and death—are rites performed for the perpetuity of the kingdom as a whole, and in certain cultures a king has been killed annually in order to rejuvenate and ensure the fertility of the land. Moreover, certain rites of passage, such as healing rituals, may serve to resolve social problems and to perpetuate the social order directly as well as indirectly because they treat not only the sick or diseased person but also the entire society.

For all that societies use rites of passage to instill their values and configurations in the individual, they also take advantage of these ceremonies to foster the arousal of self-conscious questioning, for rites of passage are also times of what Victor Turner terms "reflexivity." Individuals (as well as the society itself) may be moved to the edge of profound self-investigation and exploration: social categories are played with, inverted, suspended; social borders are liquidated, crossed, blurred; identity symbols are stripped away and affixed anew. Such play is facilitated through the use of mirrors, masks, costumes, and other kinds of novelty. Free reign of reflexive awareness is permitted, even expedited—but only within the formal constraints of the ritual itself.

Paradox, then, lies at the heart of rites of passage. The paradoxes and conflicts in our lives as humans may produce great anxiety because they defy our desire to live in a logically consistent and comprehensible world. Ritual exposes these paradoxes and accentuates them; tension is heightened and resolution is eagerly sought. But precisely because these paradoxes are cognitively or logically irresolvable, no actual resolution can be gained. But the familiar bounds and safety that ritual provides allow us to experience their truth, and thereby to discover the intractable parameters of our fate as humans. In this way, rites of passage not only accentuate anxiety but also alleviate it.

History of study. The structure of rites of passage was clearly articulated early on in the discipline of anthropology by Arnold van Gennep, who in 1907 discerned a fundamental tripartite form inherent in all rites of passage: separation, transition, and incorporation. Van Gennep noted that a person had to be separated from one role or status before he or she could be incorporated into a new one. He thus identified not only those phases of separation and incorporation but a transitional, or liminal, one as well. Consequently, for van Gennep ritual truly represented a process, and he thus stood apart from mainstream Victorian anthropology, which emphasized evolutionary phases and the tracking down of the origins of customs. In this way, van Gennep laid much of the groundwork for the modern interest in symbolic and ritual studies.

Building on van Gennep's work, Victor Turner has generated exceptionally rich and fruitful theories for the study of ritual processes; his works articulating the concept of liminality are especially generative and far-ranging. Through Turner's work, *liminality* has been extended far beyond its original sense of an intermediate or marginal ritual phase and has taken on new meaning as an autonomous and sometimes enduring category of people who are "betwixt and between." All manner of those who inhabit and cross the edges of social boundaries and codes—tricksters, clowns, poets, shamans, court jesters, monks, "dharma bums," and holy mendicants—represent liminal beings. Not only people but also social movements, such as millenarian cults, and social principles, such as matrilaterality in patrilineal systems, may be viewed as liminal. These ideas are developed in *The Ritual Process* (Chicago, 1969) and *Dramas, Fields, and Metaphors: Symbolic Action in Human Society* (Ithaca, N.Y., 1974).

What do these persons or principles have in common with neophytes in a liminal phase of ritual transition? The point is made in many ways: the symbols used for them are similar, emphasizing innocence, rebirth, vulnerability, fertility, change, emotion, paradox, disorder, anomaly, opposition, and the like. Such people, because they dwell on and between the borders of our categories, as Mary Douglas tells us in *Purity and Danger* (London, 1966), are designated taboo or polluted simply because they are out of place. Like ritual neophytes they are neither here nor there, and like ritual neophytes they threaten our orderly conceptualizations. Yet, because they are out of place, they are mysterious and powerful; and liminal beings or phases can also be, as Turner shows, the sources of renewal, innovation, and creativity.

The liminal phase also contains another universal and critical element. Turner observes that among the neophytes living outside the norms and fixed categories of the social system a feeling of solidarity and unity emerges, and this oneness, or *communitas,* also has a structure, although its purpose is antistructural. Equality, undifferentiated humanness, androgyny, and humility characterize this condition, and neophytes are symbolically represented as a kind of *tabula rasa,* pure, undetermined possibility—the converse of social structure, which emphasizes differentiation, hierarchy, and separation. Even historical periods may be liminal, transitional times, when the past has lost its grip and the future has not yet taken definite shape. At those times, the "subjunctive" mood of the culture prevails, and play, imagination, and paradox are encouraged, all as part of a self-conscious quest for the basic truths of the human condition.

Another structuralist interpretation of initiation rites is advanced by Mary Douglas in *Purity and Danger,* in which she seeks to explain the sex and role reversals so common to these ceremonies. Douglas sees them as a reflection of the usual social symmetry. That is, the impersonation of women by boys is a statement of symmetry that echoes a fundamental social structural principle in societies in which wife exchange between two groups must articulate the symmetry and equality between the two groups.

Mircea Eliade in *Rites and Symbols of Initiation* (New York, 1958) contends that the dynamics in rites of passage provide a means through which participants may achieve religious perfection. The concepts of male and female provide a fundamental structural complementarity in the usual social order, but complementarity also fosters envy between men and women. Each is fascinated with the special attributes of the other. Because rites of passage abound with sexual symbolism, particularly evident in cross-dressing and role-play reversal between the sexes, they allow the neophyte the chance to experience the usually repressed other half. Accordingly, the neophyte can then become the incarnation of totality, can then reach perfection, and can then transcend irreducible quotidian complementarity.

Some scholars hold that rites of passage function to underscore the social importance of the group or sex that is the focus of the celebration. This stance is illustrated by Alice Schlegel and Herbert Barry in "The Evolutionary Significance of Adolescent Initiation Ceremonies" (*American Ethnologist,* 1980), in which they show that puberty ceremonies for girls predominate in those societies where female participation in food production exceeds or is more important than male contribution. They also add an evolutionary scheme by contending that as societies grow more complex, gender as a classificatory principle recedes in importance, and fewer initiation ceremonies are found altogether. A further twist on the evolutionary scheme is put forth by Martha and Morton Fried in *Transitions: Four Rituals in Eight Cultures* (New York, 1980). The Frieds examine four critical transitions (birth, puberty, marriage, death) and find that they are not crucially linked to the success of social cohesion or of social operation. They also conclude that ritual may not be a critical element in the success of social groups, for they note that ritual seems to have appeared rather late on the human scene. The evidence we have for this are the flower-strewn remains of Neanderthal humans, which date from only about 40,000 BCE.

Learning and experience through ritual. Whether or not rites of passage, or any ritual activity, is *necessary* to human existence is a debatable matter, yet rites of passage do provide for and fulfill at least one crucial task: that of inculcating a society's rules and values to those who are to become its full-fledged members. Because rites of passage occur at great moments of anxiety (life crises) and because they even provoke anxiety by vividly calling attention to irresolvable human paradoxes, they provide an atmosphere in which the neophyte is rendered most susceptible to learning. Initiates are almost always separated from society; their previous habits of acting, thinking, and feeling are stripped away. Thus cut off from their usual ways of apprehending the world—their routines and their customary ways of communicating—they are placed in a highly suggestible state for learning. But how does this learning take place? How does learning permeate the various levels of consciousness and unconsciousness so that the person is filled with motivation and desire to become what he or she must become in addition to absorbing knowledge?

One way the communication of society's arcane knowledge is achieved is through direct instruction. Sometimes secret names of deities or ancestors are revealed; sometimes the mythical history of the society is recounted in full; sometimes special incantations or creeds are taught. All of these do much to transmit the store of esoteric principles to the initiates, and they are often encouraged, if not forced, to reflect upon this knowledge.

Yet certainly this is not the only kind of teaching and learning that transpires during rites of passage. What are we to make of the masks and images that incorporate grotesque combinations and weird juxtapositions of animal and human parts; what of the bold body decorations or scarifications; what of the driving, incessant beat of the music that accompanies ritual? Symbolic experience—whether in drama, poetry, myth, the arts, or trance—holds forth its particular kind of information, eluding words but nonetheless significant and real. On other deeper, less verbal, less cognitive levels, we are moved to understand something of our lives and our place within the cosmos when we enact ritual. Because rites of passage are *performed*—that is, carried out physically and mentally—*experience*—affective and subjective as well as cognitive—may well represent the crux of ritual. Unfortunately, for the most part, anthropologists have failed to deal with the experiences of ritual participants—private, subjective, psychological, conscious, and unconscious—in their endeavors to explain ritual, and this represents an enormous barrier to an understanding of the subject.

There are notable exceptions to this truism, however. There are some who have pioneered an examination of emotion and learning in ritual. In the classic study *Religion: An Anthropological View* (New York, 1966), Anthony Wallace presents the concept of a "ritual learning process," which essentially works through what he calls the "law of dissociation." That is, because the neophyte has been placed in a stage in which he or she is radically dissociated from past knowledge before being presented with much new information, cognitive and affective restructuring is facilitated. Wallace outlines the various phases of this kind of learning: prelearning or anticipation; separation (through sensory deprivation, monotonous stimuli, extreme physical stress, and the like); suggestion (high suggestibility associated with trance or dissociation, sometimes thought of as conversion or possession); execution (achievement of a new cognitive structure); and maintenance (through repetition or reinforcement), occasionally involving a resynthesis.

We find that Jerome Frank uses a similar paradigm in *Persuasion and Healing: A Comprehensive Study of Psychotherapy* (Baltimore, 1961). However, Wallace's and Frank's work do not seem to have been utilized, at least not systematically, in subsequent studies of ritual, and it is clear that a complete comprehension of the manner in which learning takes place in ritual calls for psychologically informed theories and hypotheses.

One that stands out is cognitive dissonance theory. Leon Festinger informs us in the seminal *A Theory of Cognitive Dissonance* (Evanston, Ill., 1957) that there is a direct relationship between the degree to which persons suffer for an experience and the value that they attach to the experience. The higher the psychological price paid, the more likely are subjects to pronounce it worthwhile. It is noteworthy that rites of passage, especially rites of puberty, may be acutely painful, involving as they often do tattooing, circumcision, scarification, cicatrization, and other forms of mutilation. Yet, the application of this theory has not been systematically applied to initiation rites.

Psychologists, for their part, have not availed themselves of the opportunity to test learning theories against the vast and rich ethnographic literature on rites of passage. True enough, there has been enormous interest generated for puberty rites among psychologists, but this attention has been limited generally to the use of psychoanalytical theory in explanation. Freudians, particularly, have focused on the dramatic aspects of puberty rites, seeing in them support for the ideas that Sigmund Freud advanced in *Totem und Tabu* (1913). In his "Oedipus theory" Freud proposed that the beginning of civilization occurred when an ancestral patriarch was slain by his jealous sons because of his monopolization of the females in the group. The patriarchs in turn punished their sons for their incestuous yearnings toward their mothers and for the sons' desire to overthrow the authority of their elders. In this view, puberty rites celebrate this moment in human history by recreating these episodes, especially through circumcision or other forms of genital mutilation.

The diverse and plentiful symbols of procreation and birth in adolescent initiation rites led Bruno Bettelheim to expound another interpretation of these rituals in *Symbolic Wounds* (New York, 1954). Noting that circumcision and subincision of the penis cause bleeding and that often puberty rites stipulate that boys must move through the legs of older men (symbolizing rebirth), Bettelheim concludes that male initiation ceremonies are thus forums for the expression of envy of the procreative powers of women. Circumcision is seen as imitative of menstruation, giving birth to new life, and extreme cases of subincision are viewed as making male genitals superficially similar to those of women. Envy and emulation are thus the key messages and purposes of male puberty rites.

Another psychological view holds that male initiation rites serve to expedite the resolution of Oedipal conflicts and to establish masculine identity. This perspective, represented in Frank Young's *Initiation Ceremonies: A Cross-cultural Study of Status Dramatization* (New York, 1965), further contends that in societies where the mother-son bond is particularly strong, elaborate and painful ceremonies are needed to vigorously and decisively break a male child's identification with his mother (and hence with other women) and to install him in the psychological and social company of his father's group.

Most psychological treatments of initiation ceremonies have investigated those of male puberty; discussions of female initiation rites are scarce. In *The Drums of Affliction* (London, 1968), Victor Turner describes the girls' initiation rites observed and analyzed by him and Edith Turner while among the Ndembu of Zambia. The rites express woman's ultimate structural dominance in a matrilineal system. The central symbol, a "milk" tree, with white sap, is not merely an emblem of womanhood, it also represents the value set on matriliny as the hub around which the whole society revolves. The rites oppose women to men as a sex before they reunite them with men as joint producers of children. The great aim of initiation is to convert a girl into a fruitful married woman. Other writings on girls' initiation have emphasized the bonding between females that occurs at these times; however, they describe rites whose main function is to communicate female inferiority and the suppression of female sexuality.

As has been made clear in the foregoing paragraphs, the literature on rites of passage is profuse and much research attention has been devoted to the subject. These rituals of transition and initiation have yielded forth many distinct lines of explanation: structural, functional, religious, symbolic, and psychoanalytical, each articulating an aspect of what these ceremonial activities *tell* the participants and onlookers. Many of these interpretations have gone a long way toward analyzing the multilayered meanings contained in rites of passage. Unfortunately, however, anthropologists and other scholars have paid disappointingly little heed to what these rites *do* to people. We need to know how, in fact, culture is transmitted—not merely as a codified system of principles and messages, but as an intrinsic learning process, embracing experience so that, as Victor Turner puts it, one's duty becomes one's desire. Anthropology cannot possibly reach an understanding of the transmission of culture, of the maintenance of values, without expanding its conceptions of learning theory and symbolic processes, unconscious and conscious.

Modern, Industrial Society. When we peruse the literature on rites of passage, we find, in addition to scholarly interpretations, descriptions (and often photographs) of fantastic, elaborate masks, costumes, or other body decoration, and while these certainly may be intriguing, Westerners may be quite thankful that they do not have to endure tooth filing, circumcision, subincision, cicatrization, tattooing, and the like. Still, the impression we are frequently left with is that rites of passage are elaborate affairs occurring in small-scale societies in which every member of the community takes part. What meaning, if any, do rites of passage hold for us in the modern, industrial world? Have we lost sight of our need to move people clearly and safely from one life stage to another? Is the safety and assurance that ritual provides no longer possible, or even applicable for those of us in complex societies?

Our society may be characterized as fragmented, confusing, complex, and disorderly. We put a premium on our individuality; we pay dearly, though, for the individuality that we so cherish. The cost of our freedom is often adjustment to life's transitions quite alone, and with private, not public, symbols. Our society is so multifarious and diffuse that we must entrust our lives into the hands of experts and anonymous agencies or individuals who care for only a small part of our human needs. We are born, for the most part, in hospitals, and we usually die there. Birth and death, the irreducible entrance and exit, become merely secular affairs, matters of the most profound emotional significance that are left publicly uncelebrated.

There may well be dire consequences for our lack of public ritual. Long ago, Émile Durkheim made evident in his classic work *Suicide* (1897) that the lack of social connection, the unacknowledged existence, and the feeling of anomie may be expressed by the individual in the form of suicide. More recently, Solon Kimball remarks in the introduction to a reprint of van Gennep's *Rites of Passage* (Chicago, 1960) that one result of the strain of undergoing individualistic ritual may be mental illness.

Some scholars argue that genuine rites of passage are not possible in modern societies because of the limited, specialized, or attenuated social relations experienced in them. For example, Max Gluckman asserts in *Essays on the Ritual of Social Relations* (Manchester, 1962) that rites of passage are "sacred" and thus can exist only in societies where the social is also religious, where social relations serve multiple purposes and are charged with moral valuations.

But ritual is not synonymous with religion, and it may well be that religion operates more through conscious cognitive faculties than does ritual. The differences are informative. One of ritual's distinguishing features is that it is *performed.* One must engage more than merely cognitive processes in order to *carry out* ritualistic activity, for ritual absorbs and employs all the senses, and indeed it probably involves different centers in the brain from those of cognition. As Mircea Eliade puts it so well, one may become what one performs; hence, critical thinking may not be so essential an element here as it may be in religious belief. Rituals also incorporate paradox and conflict; problems of codification and consistency, therefore, may not be so relevant as they are in religious belief. Rituals are indeed "transformative" experiences, as Victor Turner tells us; and as Sherry Ortner observes in *Sherpas through Their Rituals* (Cambridge, 1978), we approach ritual with a cultural problem, stated or unstated, and then work various operations upon it, arriving at "solutions"—reorganizations and reinterpretations of the elements that produce a newly meaningful whole. Achieving the appropriate shift in consciousness is the work of ritual.

It is important to note that rituals are *constructed*—fabricated, built, created—for that indicates that we may then be able to create and provide them for ourselves if they are not already bestowed by our society. Studies of crises in the adult life cycle in Western society today (e.g., Roger Gould's *Transformation: Growth in Adult Life,* Louisville, Ky., 1978, and Gail Sheehy's *Passages: Predictable Crises of Adult Life,* New York, 1974) have highlighted our creation of various life phases and the various cultural and psychological problems that result from them. These works, however, have not considered the relation and importance of ritual to these junctures in our lives.

Those of us in modern Western society indeed experience numerous forms of crises and transitions: menopause, surgery, "empty nests," divorce, retirement. They are traumatic and anxiety-provoking, and yet they regularly occur uncelebrated. We do make attempts to enact rituals at several crossroads in our lives, although we usually do so alone and secluded. Burning an unfaithful lover's photograph, returning gifts from one no longer cherished, changing a hairstyle, and cleaning house are all ways to announce that one phase of life has ended and a new one is beginning.

We in Western society do not live in the same kind of world as do those in tribal or traditional societies, yet surely we experience the same anxiety and uncertainty at life's crisis points. And surely we share with them the same conceptual quandaries about life: that we are natural yet cultural beings; that our lives are marked both by disruption and by continuity; and that we are individual yet collective. These are the fundamental paradoxes that everyone everywhere experiences, and that rites of passage announce to us, instruct us about, and help us to transcend.

[*See also* Sacrament, *overview article, and, for specific rites,* Birth; Initiation; Marriage; Ordination; *and* Funeral Rites.]

BIBLIOGRAPHY

Eliade, Mircea. *Rites and Symbols of Initiation: The Mysteries of Birth and Rebirth.* New York, 1958. A classic work on initiation in its religious aspect. Eliade deals with the transcendence of sexual opposition in initiation.

Fried, Martha N., and Morton H. Fried. *Transitions: Four Rituals in Eight Cultures.* New York, 1980. A study of life-crisis rituals in a carefully varied selection of cultures.

Gennep, Arnold van. *Les rites de passage.* Paris, 1909. Translated by Monika B. Vizedom and Gabrielle L. Caffee as *The Rites of Passage* (Chicago, 1960). The essential handbook on rites of passage. Van Gennep, the pioneer in this study, laid out the three stages: separation, the transitional or liminal stage, and reincorporation.

Gluckman, Max. "Les Rites de Passage." In *Essays on the Ritual of Social Relations,* edited by Max Gluckman, pp. 1–52. Manchester, 1962. A useful commentary on van Gennep's *Les rites de passage.* Gluckman, a social anthropologist, discusses the social roles and processes involved in such rites.

Mead, Margaret. *Coming of Age in Samoa.* New York, 1928. The controversial study of the life of girls in a Polynesian culture.

Turner, Victor. "Mukanda: The Rite of Circumcision." In his *The Forest of Symbols: Aspects of Ndembu Ritual,* chap. 7. Ithaca, N.Y., 1967. A detailed account and anthropological analysis of boys' initiation among the Ndembu.

Turner, Victor. "Nkang'a." In his *The Drums of Affliction: A Study of Religious Processes among the Ndembu of Zambia,* chaps. 7 and 8. London, 1968. A detailed account and anthropological analysis of girls' initiation among the Ndembu.

Turner, Victor. *The Ritual Process: Structure and Anti-Structure.* Chicago, 1969. Turner goes beyond van Gennep in exploring the liminal domain found in rites of passage, where that domain exists in a number of different cultures and periods of history.

BARBARA G. MYERHOFF, LINDA A. CAMINO, and EDITH TURNER

A Few Definitions

[*The following notes were found among the papers of the late Victor Turner.*]

The term *ritual* denotes those aspects of prescribed formal behavior that have no direct technological consequences. If one performs Trobriand gardening ritual, for example, this will not directly cause the taro crop to grow. The "prescription," or prescribed component in the definition, is ordinarily provided by cultural tradition, but it may in some cases be a spontaneous invention of the individual. The majority of "religious" and "magical" actions are ritual in this sense, but the concept of ritual is not usefully limited to religious and magical contexts. Ritual actions are "symbolic" in that they assert something about the state of affairs, but they are not necessarily purposive, that is, the performer of ritual does not necessarily seek to *alter* the state of affairs.

For anthropologists—and ecclesiastics, for that matter—the term *ritual* always refers to *social* customs, traditionally sanctioned, but some psychoanalytic writers use the term to include prescribed and elaborated behavior that has been spontaneously invented by an individual, as by compulsion neurotics, for example.

The term *rites de passage* was first used by Arnold van Gennep in his book of that name (published in 1909 and now available in an English translation). It describes two types of rite:

1. Rites that accompany the passage of a person from one social status to another in the course of his or her life and
2. Rites that mark recognized points in the passage of time (new year, new moon, solstice, or equinox).

The term has come to be restricted (although I am not in agreement with this) to the former type, which are now sometimes called "life-crisis rites." Typical *rites de passage* in the modern sense are those that accompany birth, the attainment of adult status, marriage, and death.

Van Gennep analyzed these rites into a sequence of three stages: (1) rites of separation, (2) marginal, or liminal, rites, and (3) rites of aggregation, or, more simply, rites of entry into, waiting in, and leaving the intermediate no-man's land. The three elements are not equally marked in all *rites de passage;* according to van Gennep, the element of separation is more important in mortuary or funerary rites, that of aggregation in marriage. The marginal rites, marking the period in which an individual is detached from one status but not yet admitted into the next, are most conspicuous in those initiation ceremonies that involve the participants in a long period of isolation, cut off from their normal social contacts.

The sacralization of these crucial periods in individual life is itself a matter of sociological interest. Van Gennep drew attention to the characteristic symbolism of *rites de passage,* such as a simulated death and resurrection, or a ritualistic passing through a door or archway (hence the term *liminal,* from the Latin *limen,* "threshold"). He interpreted birth rituals as signifying the separation of the infant from the world of the dead (or the not-living) and his aggregation to that of the living. Recent ethnography has supplemented his analysis of mortuary ritual by showing how it can explicitly include the aggregation of the dead person to the society of the ancestors.

VICTOR TURNER

Hindu Rites

India is a land of many ethnic, tribal, and linguistic groups, and of numerous castes and sects, each with its distinctive customs and practices. This article does not presume to be an exhaustive survey of the rites of passage practiced by all these groups. Its scope is limited to those rites handed down in the mainstream Brahmanic tradition and described in its normative texts.

Rites of passage are defined as the rites that accompany a change of state, whether it be age or social position. This study will focus on three classifications formulated within the Hindu tradition that partly overlap and together indicate what we call rites of passage as well as the states that they initiate: *saṃskāra, dīkṣā,* and *āśrama.* I have also included rites performed at various junctures of an individual's life even though there is no change of state; the Hindu category of *saṃskāra* includes these life-cycle rites, as well as strict rites of passage.

Saṃskāra. Hindu theologians define *saṃskāra* as a rite that prepares a person or thing for a function by imparting new qualities and/or by removing taints. It consecrates and purifies. The term, therefore, covers a broad group of preparatory rites, including sacrifices and the consecration of sacrificial utensils. The texts on Hindu domestic rites (Gṛhyasūtras) and the law books (Dharmaśāstras) apply the term more specifically to rites associated with the human life cycle. "Sacrament," the customary translation of *saṃskāra,* captures only a part of its significance and is liable to cause misunderstanding.

Sources do not agree on the number or the procedures of the *saṃskāras*. Some list as many as forty, using the term broadly to cover numerous domestic rites, while others give just twelve. The medieval handbooks enumerate sixteen. The descriptions of these rites also show marked discrepancies. The texts themselves acknowledge the existence of local and caste differences and often ask the reader to consult women, the custodians of folk customs. Our account, therefore, offers only a partial glimpse of these rites as they were performed at various times and places.

Marriage. It is customary for modern accounts of *saṃskāras* to begin with the prenatal rites. The Gṛhyasūtras, however, begin with marriage, and for good reason. It is the central Hindu institution: only a married man accompanied by his wife is the complete *persona religiosa* entitled to perform the principal religious acts of sacrifice and procreation. The Vedic texts declare that a man becomes complete after securing a wife and begetting a son. Other *saṃskāras* either lead up to marriage or flow from it.

Sources contain detailed instructions regarding the selection of a partner, the marriageable age of a boy and a girl, the auspicious times for marriage, and the like. The betrothal takes place some time before the marriage: the father of the groom asks for the bride's hand and her father formally gives his consent.

The rite of marriage, more than any other *saṃskāra,* is subject to local variations. Four rites, however, form the core of the ceremony:

1. Several oblations are made into the sacred fire.
2. The bridegroom takes the bride's hand, saying: "I take your hand for happiness."
3. He guides her three times around the fire. After each circumambulation he makes her step on a stone, saying: "Tread on this stone. Be firm like a stone. Overcome the enemies. Trample down the foes."
4. He makes her take seven steps toward the northeast, saying: "Take one step for sap, two for juice, three for prospering in wealth, four for comfort, five for cattle, six for the seasons. Be my friend with your seventh step! May you be devoted to me. Let us have many sons. May they reach old age." Most authorities consider these seven steps as the essential rite of matrimony; if the bridegroom dies before this rite is performed, the bride is not considered a widow.

After the marriage rite the couple goes to the husband's home and remains chaste for three days. On the fourth day several rites are performed to ensure fertility, after which the marriage is consummated.

Prenatal saṃskāras. There are three principal rites performed before birth to promote conception and to ensure the safety of the mother and the fetus. Garbhādhāna, the conception rite, is performed between the fourth and the sixteenth day after the beginning of the wife's monthly period. Puṃsavana, which literally means "quickening of a male child," is performed in the third or fourth month of pregnancy to ensure a male progeny, and also contains ritual and medicinal safeguards against miscarriage. Sīmantonnayana, ceremonial parting of the mother's hair, is performed between the fourth and the eighth month of pregnancy to protect the fetus from evil spirits.

It is very likely that the prenatal *saṃskāras* once formed a part of the marriage ceremony to promote the fertility of the bride. Their transfer to a later time may have resulted from the progressive lowering of the marriageable age of girls. When prepubertal marriage became the custom, rites associated with intercourse and conception would have seemed inappropriate within the marriage ceremony. Some features of these *saṃskāras*, moreover, recall their original context. For example, invocations of many sons and prayers for fertility abound. Further, the conception rite, the parting of the hair, and, according to some, even the quickening of a male child are performed only for the first pregnancy. Accordingly, these rites are viewed by many Hindu theologians as directed at the purification of the mother rather than of the fetus.

Childhood saṃskāras. The largest number of *saṃskāras* belong to the period between birth and adolescence, the most precarious time of life in premodern societies. Sources differ widely regarding the number, the names, and the procedures of these rites. The most significant of them are: Jātakarman (birth rites), one of the oldest of the *saṃskāras* and performed immediately after birth; Nāmakaraṇa (naming ceremony) on the tenth or the twelfth day after birth; Niṣkramaṇa (exit from the birthing room) between the twelfth day and the fourth month from birth; Annaprāśana (first eating of solid food) in the sixth month; Karṇavedha (ear piercing) performed between the twelfth day and the fifth year; Cūḍākaraṇa or Caula (first haircutting) in the third year.

Saṃskāras of adolescence. While the childhood *saṃskāras* are aimed at protecting and nurturing the child, those of adolescence have a markedly social significance. They prepare the youth to assume the social and religious responsibilities of the adult world. They are, therefore, associated with education, and the teacher plays a central role in them.

The main *saṃskāra* of adolescence is Vedic initiation (Upanayana). It is regarded as the second birth of the initiate. The teacher who performs the initiation and who imparts the Veda is said to bear the pupil within him like an embryo and to cause him to be born again in the Veda. Thus the *brāhmaṇas*, *kṣatriyas*, and *vaiśyas*, who form the first three social classes *(varṇa)*, are called "twice-born" because they undergo initiation, whereas the *śūdras*, who are not qualified for initiation, are said to have only a single birth—the physical birth from the parents. Before initiation a child of the upper classes is not subject to the norms that minutely regulate the lives of adult Hindus, and, therefore, he is likened to a *śūdra*.

The standard age for initiation is eight years for *brāhmaṇas*, eleven for *kṣatriyas*, and twelve for *vaiśyas*, although all are permitted to undergo initiation at a younger or an older age. Men of the three upper classes who remain uninitiated after the ages of sixteen, twenty-two, and twenty-four respectively are considered sinners. Social intercourse with them is forbidden.

Before the rite the boy takes his final meal in the company of his mother. Then his head is shaved and he is bathed. He is given a girdle, a deerskin, a staff, and a sacred thread. The sacred thread consists of three cords, and each cord is made by twisting three strands. It is normally worn over the left shoulder and hangs under the right arm. Though the sacred thread is not mentioned in the earliest sources, it has come to be regarded as the central element of initiation and as the symbol of a person's second birth. Today the rite is often called the "thread ceremony." At first the thread was probably a substitute for the upper garment worn during ritual activities.

The teacher performs several symbolic acts that establish an intimate relationship between him and his new pupil. The initiatory rite reaches its climax when the teacher reaches over the pupil's right shoulder, places his hand over the pupil's heart, and says: "Into my will I take thy heart. Thy mind shall follow my mind. In my word thou shalt rejoice with all thy heart. May Bṛhaspati join thee to me." The teacher then imparts the sacred Sāvitrī formula: "That excellent glory of Savitṛ [Sun], the god, we meditate, that he may stimulate our prayers" (*Ṛgveda* 3.62.10). The centrality of these rites is pointed out by an ancient Vedic text, the *Śatapatha Brāhmaṇa* (11.5.4.12): "By laying his right hand on the pupil the teacher becomes pregnant with him. In the third night he is born a *brāhmaṇa* with the Sāvitrī." The initiate, who is called a *brahmacārin*, then puts wood into the sacred fire. This is his first encounter with the sacrifice, the central religious act of the Vedic religion.

The pupil remains for many years at the teacher's house, away from his home and family. This is a liminal period. The number of years is not determined; twelve, the number most often given, probably has a symbolic value, signifying completeness. The pupil is reduced to the level of a servant, without status, rank, or property; he obtains even his food by begging from house to house. Humility, obedience, and chastity are his main virtues.

Samāvartana is the *saṃskāra* that concludes the period of studentship. Initiation separates the boy from the social community, while Samāvartana reincorporates the youth into the adult world. The term literally means the return of the scholar to his parents' home after graduation. The central feature of the ceremony is a ritual bath. The rite, therefore, is often termed *snāna* (bath), and the young graduate is called a *snātka* (the bathed). This feature, present also in the rite that ends the period of seclusion following the consecration *(dīkṣā)* for a Vedic sacrifice, indicates that it is the concluding act of the initiatory ritual, rather than a separate *saṃskāra*. After the bath the youth discards the student's attire and puts on ornaments and fine clothes; he assumes his status in society. The young adult is now ready to get married and establish a household, and a search for a suitable bride will soon begin.

Funeral. The funeral is the last *saṃskāra*. It prepares a person for existence after death. From the earliest period of Indian history human remains were normally cremated. With the growth of sacrificial speculation in the late Vedic period, cremation came to be regarded as one's last sacrifice (Antyeṣṭi), in which one's own body is offered in the fire. From this sacrifice the deceased person is born again into a new existence in the company of his or her ancestors. Vedic texts call it a person's third birth. The funeral, therefore, is a rite of passage from the earthly existence to the world of the fathers.

Cremation, however, does not conclude the funeral; it is believed that newly deceased people pass through a liminal period lasting twelve days or one year, during which they live as ghosts (*pretas*). The dead are then dangerous, and their relatives are impure. During this time special offerings of food and water are made for the newly deceased (Ekoddiṣṭa-śrāddha). On the twelfth day, which is the current practice, or after one year, the newly deceased person is ritually united with his or her dead ancestors through a rite called Sapiṇḍīkaraṇa. Four rice balls are prepared, three for the three preceding generations of ancestors and one for the newly dead person. The latter is cut into three parts, which are then mixed with the three balls intended for the ancestors. The union of rice balls symbolizes the union of the deceased with his or her ancestors. It is the final act of the funeral. Henceforth, the dead person will participate in all the normal offerings that his or her relatives will make to their ancestors.

The Upaniṣads contain information on a rite performed by a father when he feels that his death is imminent. In it he transfers his duties and powers—his ritual persona—to his son. This rite of transmission (Saṃpratti or Saṃpradāna) by which a son succeeds his father was later assimilated into the rite of renunciation, which also results in the ritual death of the father.

A remarkable feature of the funeral as well as the other *saṃskāras* is that they do not refer at all to the common Indian beliefs of rebirth *(saṃsāra)* and liberation *(mokṣa)*. These Hindu rituals are founded on a different worldview that celebrates life and fertility, shrinks from pollution and death, and, when death comes, ritually transports the dead to the world of the fathers.

Dīkṣā. Like *saṃskāra, dīkṣā* is a preparatory rite. It is, however, more closely associated with the assumption of a new state. While *saṃskāras* are obligatory for all, most *dīkṣās* are undertaken voluntarily. It is, however, impossible to define either term precisely because they are often used as synonyms, and *dīkṣā* frequently refers to a wide variety of purificatory and other rites.

The most famous *dīkṣā* is the consecration of a man for a Vedic sacrifice. It prepares the sacrificer for the solemn act by purifying him and by transferring him to a new but temporary state similar to that of the gods. In *dīkṣā* the sacrificer is ritually transformed into an embryo and is born again with a new and more perfect body. Many elements of the rite symbolize the birthing process. The consecrated man *(dīkṣita)* is surrounded by taboos. He is sacred and dangerous: others are not allowed to touch him or to pronounce his name. At the conclusion of the sacrifice the consecratory period ends with a ritual bath, after which the sacrificer returns to his normal state.

The royal consecration is also called *dīkṣā*. It shares many common features with the sacrificial *dīkṣā*. Like the sacrificer, the new king is ritually reborn at his consecration. His period of *dīkṣā* lasts a year, during which time he is deprived of his royal prerogatives.

In the post-Vedic religions of India the most common forms of *dīkṣā* are associated with the entry into voluntary religious groups. The earliest such *dīkṣā* was probably that of ascetics. Buddhist and Jain sources indicate that at a very early period these sects developed rites of entry into their respective monastic orders. Brahmanical sources contain information on the *dīkṣā* of renouncers (*saṃnyāsins*) and forest hermits. These rites symbolically enact the death of the novice and his rebirth into the new ascetic life. Some rites include ordeals, such as pulling the hair by the roots and branding. At the conclusion of the rite the ascetic assumes a new name and the insignia of the new state: ascetic garb, tonsure, staff, begging bowl, and so forth. Initiatory rites of ascetics often assume an educational dimension in imitation of the Vedic initiation. The teacher plays an important role in them and imparts a secret formula *(mantra)* to the novice. The ascetic *dīkṣā* begins a long period of training for the novice.

Medieval Hindu sects, where admission is not limited to ascetics, devised *dīkṣās* for admitting lay members. They are patterned after the Vedic initiation and are regarded as constituting a new birth of the initiate. In some sects, such as the Vīraśaiva, the voluntary nature of *dīkṣā* is eliminated and a child is initiated at birth. Admission to each higher level or rank within a sect also entails special *dīkṣās*.

Dīkṣā introduces a new state, either temporary like the sacrificer's or permanent like the ascetic's. The term, therefore, is used as a synonym of *vrata* (vow) that often indicates a special mode of life. This meaning of *dīkṣā* is very close to that of *āśrama*.

Āśrama. By the sixth century BCE new religious ideas advocating a life of renunciation, celibacy, and poverty were sweeping the Ganges River valley. New religions, such as Buddhism and Jainism, broke with the Vedic tradition. Considering human beings as bound to an endless cycle of births and deaths, they questioned the value of central Vedic institutions such as sacrifice and marriage, and of society as such.

There were brahman thinkers at this time who advocated these new ideals but were unwilling to break with the Vedic tradition. They attempted to find theological formulas that would give scriptural legitimacy to renunciation while maintaining the religious significance of marriage and other Vedic institutions. One such formula was the system of the *āśramas*. Historically it was the most significant.

The term *āśrama* in all probability referred originally to "places of austerity" or hermitages. Its meaning was then extended to include lifestyles devoted to religious exertion. The term has the latter meaning when used within the context of the *āśrama* system. Its earliest formulation, which I shall call the preclassical, is found in the ancient law books, the Dharmasūtras, the earliest of which were composed around the fifth century BCE. The preclassical system considers the four *āśramas*—Vedic student, householder, forest hermit, and renouncer—not as temporary stages but as permanent vocations. A young adult, after completing the period of study following Vedic initiation, is allowed to choose one of these *āśramas*. It is clear, therefore, that in the preclassical system the first *āśrama* was that of a permanent student, who remained with the teacher until death. The temporary period of study following initiation, on the other hand, was not regarded as an *āśrama* but as a period of preparation for all *āśramas*.

Āśrama represents a theological understanding and evaluation of several social institutions; it cannot be equated with the institutions themselves. They existed prior to the invention of the *āśrama* system, and even afterwards continue to exist independently of that system both within and outside the Hindu tradition. Certain forms of Hindu marriage and the renunciation of women and *śūdras*, for example, fall outside the *āśrama* system. The system gives the institutions religious legitimacy. The *āśramas* are proposed as a new fourfold division of *dharma*, paralleling its older division into the four social classes *(varṇa)*, and as four alternative paths leading to the heavenly world. These institutions are thus made integral parts of *dharma* and, therefore, of the Vedic tradition.

Although it represented an important theological breakthrough for Brahmanism, the preclassical system had several drawbacks. It allowed choice in a matter of *dharma*. Choice or option was never encouraged by Brahmanic hermeneutics; even in minor matters of ritual it was used as a last resort in interpreting conflicting injunctions. Choice with regard to how one will spend one's adult life, moreover, gave rise to debates on the relative superiority of the *āśramas* and in particular eliminated the obligatory nature of marriage. Some used the Vedic theory of the three debts of man—study, procreation, and sacrifice—as an argument against the *āśrama* system: if one does not marry, one is not able to repay the debts of procreation and sacrifice. Others even suggested that the Veda authorized only one *āśrama*, namely that of the householder.

Toward the beginning of the common era a new formulation of the *āśrama* system, which I shall call the classical, gained wide acceptance. It is given in the authoritative *Laws of Manu*, composed in the early centuries of the common era. The preclassical system all but disappeared from the later Hindu tradition, and even modern scholars are often ignorant of its very existence.

The classical system conceived of the *āśramas* not as permanent vocations but as temporary stages of life through which an individual passes as he grows old. The *āśrama* system thus came to parallel the *saṃskāra* system, and the two central *saṃskāras*—initiation and marriage—became the rites of entry into the first two *āśramas*. The first *āśrama* is no longer the permanent studentship but the temporary period of study following initiation. Thus, according to Manu, a person should undergo initiation and live the first part of his life in the student's *āśrama*. After graduation (Samāvartana) he should marry and enter the householder's *āśrama*. When he is a grandfather and when, as Manu says, he sees his hair turning gray and his skin wrinkled, he should retire to the forest as a hermit. After spending some time there, he should enter the fourth *āśrama*, renunciation.

These, then, are the states that recur in the life of each individual. They are viewed as four rungs in the ladder leading up to liberation. The ladder image replaces the path image of the preclassical system. The rites of passage from one *āśrama* to the next are called *saṃskāra* and *dīkṣā* indiscriminately. The passage, however, takes place only in one direction; one is not permitted to return to an *āśrama* one has left. A person who does so—for example, a renouncer who reverts to the household life—is considered an outcaste.

The classical system eliminates choice and reaffirms the centrality of the householder. The ascetic orders are relegated to old age and retirement. The Vedic doctrine of three debts, once used as an argument against the preclassical system, is now seen as a scriptural basis for the *āśramas*. Payment of the debts is carried out by passing through at least the first two *āśramas*.

The third *āśrama* (forest hermit) had already become obsolete by the early centuries of the common era. Passage through the other three *āśramas* is today, as it probably was even during the time of Manu, an ideal rather than a reality in the lives of most Hindus. Yet the theological understanding of these four central socioreligious institutions as hierarchical stages of life that one enters and leaves through rites of passage became a cornerstone of Hindu doctrine and practice. It is this theology that has given *āśrama* a place alongside *varṇa* as the two pillars of Hinduism and made the compound term *varṇāśramadharma* the closest Sanskrit approximation to the foreign term *Hinduism*.

Women and Rites of Passage. Hinduism has always been a patriarchal religion. Women play a decidedly secondary role in it. This is especially so with regard to ritual activity. It is generally accepted that the prenatal and childhood *saṃskāras*, and of course the funeral, are performed also for women belonging to the twice-born *varṇas*. The Vedic formulas normally recited at these rites, however, are omitted, since women are forbidden to study the Veda. However, there is some evidence to suggest that in ancient times girls were allowed to be initiated and to study the Veda. By the time of Manu's lawbook this practice had been discontinued. Marriage, it was claimed, constituted initiation for women.

The position of women in Hindu sects varies considerably. The major sects follow the Brahmanic prohibition against female initiation. Many fringe and antistructural sects, such as the Vīraśaiva, however, admit women to initiation and full membership.

Women are also excluded from direct participation in the *āśrama* system. In marriage and, according to some, also in the hermit's *āśrama*, a woman participates in the *āśrama* of her husband. Female renouncers are found in Buddhism, Jainism, and in many medieval Hindu sects, and even mainstream Brahmanism acknowledges their existence. A woman's life in these institutions, however, is not theologically interpreted as constituting an *āśrama*.

Śūdras and Rites of Passage. *Śūdras*, by which I mean all the groups that do not belong to the twice-born *varṇas*, are excluded from reciting or even hearing the Veda. Thus they cannot be admitted to Vedic initiation. It is quite likely, however, that these groups did possess their own initiatory rites, although no information on them has come down to us. Regarding the other *saṃskāras*, however, there is a conflict of opinion. Some hold that no *saṃskāra* should be performed for a *śūdra*, while others allow them the prenatal and childhood *saṃskāras*, as well as marriage and funeral rites, but without Vedic formulas.

Śūdras are similarly excluded from the *āśrama* system, though some authorities recognize their marriage as an *āśrama*. Many medieval sects permit a type of *dīkṣā* for *śūdras* and admit them to membership.

Conclusion. Hinduism has no single dogma or doctrine. Its cohesion is found in its rites and observances. The central rites of Hinduism, whether it be mainstream Brahmanism or sectarian cults, have traditionally been the rites of passage.

The situation in modern India, however, is very different. The only *saṃskāras* regularly practiced today are marriage and funeral. Vedic initiation, where it is still practiced, has become the prerogative of brahmans to such a degree that the sacred thread has become the hallmark of a brahman.

The practice has changed, but the theology has remained the same: the modern Hindu villager as well as the modern Hindu theologian will, if asked, define Hinduism as *varṇāśramadharma*.

[*For further discussion of rites performed in the home, see* Domestic Observances, *article on* Hindu Practices. *A detailed overview of the Hindu* dharma *literature is provided in* Sūtra Literature *and* Śāstra Literature. *For discussion of the special rites involving the fourth and final* āśrama, *see* Saṃnyāsa.]

BIBLIOGRAPHY

Altekar, A. S. "The Ashrama System." In *Professor Ghurye Felicitation Volume*, edited by K. M. Kapadia, pp. 183–194. Bombay, 1954. A useful description of the classical system.

Bhattacharyya, N. N. *Indian Puberty Rites*. Calcutta, 1968. A comprehensive survey of male and female initiation rites using textual and ethnographic data.

Gonda, Jan. "The Sīmantonnayana as Described in the Gṛhyasūtras." *East and West* 7 (1956): 12–31. A detailed analysis of a prenatal rite with significant methodological implications for the study of other *saṃskāras*.

Gonda, Jan. *Change and Continuity in Indian Religion*. The Hague, 1965. An extensive and penetrating study of initiatory rites (pp. 315–462), pupilage (pp. 284–314), and the role of the teacher (pp. 229–283).

Kane, P. V. *History of Dharmaśāstra*, vol. 2. 2d ed., rev. & enl. Poona, 1974. The most detailed and comprehensive account available of *varṇa* (pp. 19–187), *saṃskāra* (pp. 188–415, 426–636), and *āśrama* (pp. 416–426).

Mookerji, Radhakumud. *Ancient Indian Education, Brahmanical and Buddhist.* 2d ed. London, 1951. An extensive survey of the educational institutions and practices of ancient India, including initiatory rites preceding education.

Olivelle, Patrick. "Renouncer and Renunciation in the Dharmaśāstras." In *Studies in Dharmaśāstra,* edited by Richard W. Lariviere, pp. 81–152. Calcutta, 1984. A historical account of renunciation and of the *āśrama* system.

Pandey, Raj Bali. *Hindu Saṃskāras: A Socio-Religious Study of the Hindu Sacraments.* 2d rev. ed. Delhi, 1969. A useful description of all Hindu *saṃskāras* without much historical analysis.

Sprockhoff, J. F. "Die Alten im alten Indien: Ein Versuch nach brahmanischen Quellen." *Saeculum* 30 (1979): 374–433. An extensive analysis of customs and institutions relating to old age in ancient India.

Stevenson, Margaret S. *The Rites of the Twice-Born* (1920). Reprint, New Delhi, 1971. A dated but still useful description of the rites of passage practiced by modern brahmans based on the author's personal observations.

Winternitz, Moriz. "Zur Lehre von den Āśramas." In *Beiträge zur Literaturwissenschaft und Geistesgeschichte Indiens: Festgabe Hermann Jacobi,* edited by Willibald Kirfel, pp. 215–227. Bonn, 1926. A lucid study of the historical development of the *āśrama* system.

Patrick Olivelle

Jewish Rites

Judaism has a highly developed series of rites that mark both initiatory and transformative moments in the lives of Jews. The rituals permit both the individual and the community to experience in an orderly and regulated manner the changing status of the Jew's relationship to other individuals and to society as a whole. Although some of the rites may have originated in other neighboring cultures, once adopted they were thoroughly judaized. Their meaning for the Jewish people is to be sought not in their origin but in their function in Jewish society. Some rites have changed little in the millennia since their introduction. Others have been radically transformed. In this article I describe the rites as they are currently practiced, with special emphasis on the Jewish community of North America.

In general, the rites are rooted in biblical regulations (*mitsvot*, "commandments") that were refined and standardized in the Talmudic and medieval periods. Although Jewish law *(halakhah)* defines the essential elements in each rite, local customs *(minhagim)* provide some degree of variation from community to community.

During the last century and a half, Judaism became divided into four streams, Orthodox, Conservative, Reform, and Reconstructionist, and this has created an increased divergence in the liturgy and ritual of life cycle ceremonies. The greatest divergence from standard traditional practice as defined by the Talmud and the later legal codes occurs in Reform and Reconstructionist Judaism. In addition, the growth of the feminist movement in the 1960s and 1970s has had a significant impact on life cycle ceremonies in the non-Orthodox movements: new rituals have been created specifically for women and some standard rituals have been made more egalitarian by the inclusion of women as equal participants or by the removal of sexist language.

Circumcision, Naming, Redemption of the Firstborn. The male initiatory rite is *berit milah* ("covenant of circumcision"). It involves the surgical removal of the foreskin of the penis and the recitation of prayers that welcome the infant into the Jewish people by initiating him into the covenant of Abraham (*Gn.* 17:11ff.). The rite takes place on the eighth day after birth, counting the day of birth as the first day. So significant is the eighth day that even if it falls on the Sabbath or a festival, the circumcision is not postponed.

Circumcision was practiced by other ancient Near Eastern peoples, probably as a fertility rite, but among Jews it became the physical sign of belonging to the Jewish people. [*See* Circumcision.] In the Hebrew Bible, circumcision is first mentioned in the injunction proclaimed by God to the ninety-nine-year-old Abraham, that instructed him to circumcise himself and the male members of his household:

> God further said to Abraham, "As for you, you and your offspring to come throughout the ages shall keep my covenant. Such shall be my covenant between me and you and your offspring to follow which you shall keep: every male among you shall be circumcised. You shall circumcise the flesh of your foreskin, and that shall be the sign of the covenant between me and you. And throughout the generations, every male among you shall be circumcised at the age of eight days. . . . Thus shall my covenant be marked in your flesh as an everlasting pact." (*Gn.* 17:9–13)

In Jewish law, it is the father's responsibility to circumcise his son. As a practical matter, however, it is rare for a father to perform the actual operation. Generally, he appoints a specially trained ritual circumciser, a *mohel,* to perform the rite in his stead. Jewishness does not depend on being circumcised, since any child born of a Jewish mother is a Jew. (In Reform and Reconstructionist Judaism, a Jew is anyone born to either a Jewish mother or father, who is raised exclusively as a Jew.) However, because over the millennia the rite has assumed an ethnonational significance in addition to its religious one, it is observed almost universally even by highly assimilated and secular Jews, though the latter may have their sons circumcised by a physician without any particular ceremony.

The preferred time for *berit milah* is in the morning, to demonstrate that the parents are as eager as Abraham was to fulfill the commandment. Although circumcision is never performed before the eighth day, it may be postponed or in rare cases omitted for medical reasons. If, however, the child was circumcised before the eighth day or was born without a foreskin, the ceremony of *haṭafat dam berit* (taking a drop of blood) is mandated for the eighth day.

Whereas the circumcision ceremony used to be held in the synagogue, it is now commonly held at the home of the new parents. The rite proceeds as follows: the infant is taken from his mother by the godmother and brought to the room where the circumcision is to take place. She hands the infant to the godfather, who in turn hands him to the *mohel*. As the child is brought into the room, he is welcomed by those present with the greeting (usually in Hebrew) "Blessed be he that comes." The father then formally declares his willingness to have his son circumcised in fulfillment with the divine commandments. The *mohel* takes the child and places him on the lap of the *sandaq* ("holder"). (When circumcisions were regularly performed in the synagogue there was a special chair for the *sandaq* called the Chair of Elijah. The symbolism of this chair derives from a legend based on the identification of the angel of the covenant in *Malachi* 3:1 with Elijah, according to which the prophet is present at every circumcision and is considered to be the guardian of the child as he enters the covenant of circumcision.)

The surgical procedure consists of three steps: (1) *milah,* the removal of the foreskin, (2) *peri'ah,* the tearing off and folding back of the mucous membrane to expose the glans, (3) *metsitsah,* the suction of the blood from the wound. During this procedure, the infant's legs are held firmly by the *sandaq*. In some places, the infant is placed on a surgical restraining board, which renders the *sandaq*'s role only symbolic. The *mohel* removes the foreskin and recites the blessing over the rite of circumcision. The mucous membrane uncovered, it is torn down the center as far as the corona. *Milah* and *peri'ah* may take place in a single step. After the blood is suctioned from the wound *(metsitsah),* the father recites the blessing: "Blessed are you, O Lord our God, Ruler of the Universe, who has sanctified us with your commandments and commanded us to bring our sons into the covenant of Abraham our Father." Those present respond: "Just as he entered the covenant, so may he enter into the study of Torah, into marriage, and into the performance of good deeds." A blessing is then recited over wine, and a prayer is said for the well-being of the child and his family. The child is given a little wine and is formally named, and the wine is then given to the parents. The child is returned to his mother, and the ceremony is concluded. In the Reform ritual, either parent or both parents together may take the role traditionally assigned to the father.

It is customary to name a boy at the *berit milah* ceremony and a girl in the synagogue. However, in the 1970s, Reform Judaism, in accord with its long-held principle of the equality of men and women and in response to the growing desire on the part of parents to formally initiate their infant daughters into the covenant, adopted a new rite called *berit ha-ḥayyim,* "covenant of life." It follows the liturgical outline of the traditional *berit milah* service, but involves no surgery. The ceremony, as described in the Reform movement's *Gates of the House* (1977, pp. 114–115) proceeds as follows: the infant is welcomed with the words, "Blessed is she who comes." Her mother lights a candle and recites the blessing: "Blessed is the Lord our God, Ruler of the Universe, by whose *mitsvot* we are hallowed, who commands us to sanctify life." The father then lights a candle and recites the blessing, "Blessed is the Lord, whose presence gives light to all the world." The parents both say, "Blessed is the Lord our God, Ruler of the Universe, for giving us life, for sustaining us and enabling us to reach this day of joy." After a prayer invoking the covenant is said, the child is formally named. Although only Reform Judaism has adopted a specific ritual, many individuals of the other movements have written and performed their own initiation service.

There are no normative rules regarding the naming of children in Judaism. Although it is customary among Ashkenazic Jews to name a child after a deceased relative but not after a living person, among Sefardic Jews a child can be named after a living person. Outside the state of Israel, it is common to give a child two names—a secular one, which is used for most purposes, and a Hebrew or Yiddish name, which is used for occasions of religious significance, for example, when one is invited to read from the Torah in synagogue or when a marriage contract *(ketubbah)* is written. Hebrew or Yiddish names take the following form: for a boy, name, *ben* ("son of"), father's name; for a girl, name, *bat* ("daughter of"), father's name. In non-Orthodox naming ceremonies, it is becoming common practice to include the name of the mother as well as the name of the father.

Pidyon ha-ben, the rite called Redemption of the Firstborn, takes place on the thirty-first day following the birth of a firstborn male child. To qualify for the rite, the male child must literally be the firstborn child of his mother. A child born by Cesarean section is not eligible, because he has not opened his mother's womb. The firstborn son of a *kohen* or a Levite (descendants of the ancient priestly class) is exempt from the rite, as is the firstborn son of the daughter of a *kohen* or a Levite.

The requirement to redeem the firstborn son is found in the Bible: "The first issue of the womb of every being, man or beast, that is offered to the Lord, shall be yours; but you shall have the firstborn of man redeemed. . . . Take as their redemption price, from the age of one month up, the money equivalent of five shekels by sanctuary weight" (*Nm.* 18:15–16). The present ceremony was already well established in Mishnaic times (c. 200 CE). The father makes a declaration affirming that the child is the firstborn son of the mother. A *kohen*, selected by the father, asks him whether or not he wishes to redeem his son. The father responds that he does, then holds five silver coins in his hand and recites the following blessings: "Blessed are you, O Lord our God, Ruler of the Universe, who has sanctified us with your commandments and commanded us concerning the redemption of the firstborn son. Blessed is the Lord our God, Ruler of the Universe, for granting us life, sustaining us, and permitting us to reach this occasion." The father gives the coins to the *kohen*, who passes them over the child, declaring that the coins are the price of redemption. The *kohen* then raises his hands and recites what is known in Jewish tradition as the Priestly Benediction: "May the Lord bless you and keep you. May the Lord let his countenance shine on you and be gracious to you. May the Lord lift up his countenance to you and grant you peace" (*Nm.* 6:24–26). After the rite, the *kohen* returns all or part of the money, which is then usually given to charity. In the United States, it is customary to use either silver dollars or silver medals minted in the state of Israel specially for use in the redemption ceremony. Reform Judaism has eliminated redemption of the firstborn from its standard practice, because it does not recognize a hereditary priesthood or believe that firstborn sons should be differentiated in any way from firstborn daughters. Some individuals have created a rite for firstborn daughters, but no movement has adopted such a rite.

Bar and Bat Mitsvah, Confirmation. A boy reaches religious majority, becoming *bar mitsvah,* on his thirteenth birthday according to the Hebrew calendar. A girl reaches religious majority, becoming *bat mitsvah,* on her twelfth birthday according to the Hebrew calendar. The term *bar/bat mitsvah* ("son/daughter of the commandment") means a person who is subject to the commandments *(mitsvot),* that is, a person responsible for observing them. The term also refers to the ceremony marking the child's coming of age. The ages of thirteen for a male and twelve for a female were chosen because they mark the onset of puberty. Most congregations perform the ceremony at age thirteen for both boys and girls.

For males, *bar mitsvah* is usually celebrated by the boy's formal participation in the public worship service. Usually, he is invited to read from the Torah and to recite the blessings over the Torah reading and passage from the prophets *(hafṭarah).* The boy is often assigned the *mafṭir,* the final brief reading of the weekly Torah reading. Depending on the boy's training and skill, as well as on local custom, he may be invited to conduct all or part of the service, to recite an original prayer, or to give a learned discourse on some biblical or Talmudic subject. The occasion is then usually celebrated with a festive meal or party.

In the post-World War II period, Conservative, Reform, and Reconstructionist Jews developed the celebration of a girl's becoming a *bat mitsvah* in counterpart to that of a boy's becoming a *bar mitsvah.* The exact nature of the girl's participation varies widely from synagogue to synagogue and community to community. There is a general egalitarian trend in non-Orthodox Judaism, so that in many communities *bar* and *bat mitsvah* are indistinguishable.

Among the Orthodox, where women are not counted in the *minyan* (quorum of ten) necessary for public worship, and are not permitted to lead the service or to read from the Torah at a public worship service where men are in attendance, no *bat mitsvah* celebration has developed.

In the nineteenth century, Reform Judaism in Germany instituted the ceremony of confirmation as a substitute for *bar mitsvah.* It is a group ceremony for boys and girls together, which takes place either on or near the festival of Shavu'ot. Shavu'ot was chosen because it celebrates the Jewish people's receiving and acceptance of Torah, and was seen, therefore, as an appropriate time for young people to affirm their commitment to Judaism. The age of confirmation was set at sixteen or seventeen, because at that age the confirmands are better able to understand the implications of the commitments they are affirming. In the 1950s and 1960s, as *bar* and later *bat mitsvah* were reintroduced as standard practices in Reform congregations (in addition to confirmation), many Conservative and Reconstructionist congregations added confirmation to their life cycle ceremonies.

Marriage: Qiddushin and Nissu'in. In Judaic tradition, marriage is the ideal human relationship, ordained by God in the creation narrative: "The Lord God said, 'It is not good for man to be alone; I will make him a fitting helper for him'. . . . Hence a man leaves his father and his mother and clings to his wife so that they shall be one flesh" (*Gn.* 2:18, 24). Marriage in Judaism is a legal contractual relationship. Therefore, even though it is a sacred relationship with spiritual significance, it may be dissolved through divorce.

In the Bible, the marriage ceremony is not described in any detail. In the Talmudic period, marriage took place in three stages: engagement *(shiddukhin)*, betrothal (called either *erusin* or *qiddushin*), and wedlock *(nissu'in)*. Engagement *(shiddukhin)* was a formal commitment to marry at which time a document called *tena'im* ("conditions") was drawn. It was a legally binding agreement which stipulated such things as the time and place of the wedding as well as the dowry and maintenance. Today engagement has become largely a social occasion at which the intention to marry is announced. Originally the act of betrothal and wedlock were separated by a year. They have since been joined into a single marriage ceremony and are thus enacted at the same time. In Orthodox Ashkenazic tradition, immediately prior to the formal wedding ceremony, the groom, in the presence of his and the bride's immediate families, covers the bride's face with a veil in a ceremony called *bedeken.* The officiant then says, "Our sister, may you grow into myriads" (*Gn.* 24:60), and concludes with the words, "May God make you like Sarah, Rebecca, Leah, and Rachel," and recites the Priestly Benediction. The bride and the groom are then led to the wedding canopy *(ḥuppah)* by their parents, where words of greeting are recited by the officiant. Next, two betrothal blessings are recited over wine:

> Blessed are you, O Lord our God, Ruler of the Universe, creator of the fruit of the vine. Blessed are you, O Lord our God, Ruler of the Universe, who has sanctified us by your commandments and commanded us concerning forbidden relationships, who has forbidden unto us those to whom we are merely betrothed, but has permitted us to those who are married to us by means of the wedding canopy and the sacred rites of marriage. Blessed are you, O Lord our God, who sanctifies his people Israel by means of the wedding canopy and the sacred rites of marriage.

The groom, in the presence of two witnesses, gives the bride an object, usually a ring worth at least a *perutah* (the least valuable coin of the Talmudic period) and recites the formula: "Behold, you are consecrated unto me with this ring as my wife according to the law of Moses and Israel." Next, the marriage contract *(ketubbah)*, previously signed by both partners, is read. The marriage itself proceeds with the recital of the *sheva' berakhot* (Seven Wedding Blessings) over a second cup of wine:

1. Blessed are you, O Lord our God, Ruler of the Universe, creator of the fruit of the vine.
2. Blessed are you, O Lord our God, Ruler of the Universe, who has created all things for his glory.
3. Blessed are you, O Lord, our God, Ruler of the Universe, creator of man.
4. Blessed are you, O Lord our God, Ruler of the Universe, who has made man in your image, after your likeness, and has prepared for him, out of his own being, a building forever [i.e., Eve]. Blessed are you, O Lord, Creator of man.
5. May she who was barren [i.e., Zion] rejoice and exult when her children will be gathered in her midst in joy. Blessed are you, O Lord, who makes Zion rejoice through her children.
6. Grant perfect joy to these loving companions, even as of old you gladdened your creation in the garden of Eden. Blessed are you, O Lord, who makes bridegroom and bride rejoice.
7. Blessed are you, O Lord our God, Ruler of the Universe, who created joy and gladness, bridegroom and bride, mirth and exultation, pleasure and delight, love, harmony, peace, and companionship. Soon, O Lord our God, may there be heard in the cities of Judah and in the streets of Jerusalem the voice of joy and gladness, the voice of the bridegroom and the voice of the bride, the jubilant voice of bridegrooms from their wedding canopies and of youths from their feasts of song. Blessed are you, O Lord, who makes the bridegroom rejoice with the bride.

The ceremony concludes with an address by the rabbi, and with the breaking of a glass. According to the Talmud (B. T., *Ber.* 31a), the purpose of breaking a glass is to temper the joy of the occasion and to engender proper decorum. Another explanation relates the breaking of a glass to the destruction of the First and Second Temples in Jerusalem in the years 587/6 BCE and 70 CE which reminds all assembled that the world is not yet perfect and that joy can be suddenly terminated. Today, the breaking of the glass signifies the conclusion of the ceremony and draws applause and songs of joy.

Reform Judaism omitted the two betrothal blessings and the formal reading of the marriage contract, but recently there has been a tendency to reintroduce the reading of a new, egalitarian marriage contract into the Reform ceremony. In the Orthodox ceremony, it is only the groom who acquires the bride, by presenting her with a ring and reciting the marriage formula. At Reform weddings, the bride may also present the groom with a ring, and then she, too, recites the marriage formula. The "double ring" ceremony is also used by Reconstructionist and many Conservative rabbis.

The two essential prerequisites of marriage are the mutual consent of the bride and the groom and the writing of a *ketubbah.* The *ketubbah* sets forth the obligations of the husband to his wife. By Jewish law, he is required to provide her with food, clothing, and other necessities, which include a commitment to engage in conjugal relations with her. He also stipulates a fixed amount of money that will be paid to her in the event of a divorce.

In addition to changes in the marriage contract that have been made for ideological reasons, new language has been introduced to deal with the circumstances created by the reestablishment of the state of Israel and by the changing conditions of contemporary life. For example, in order to remedy the problem of the woman whose husband refuses to grant her a Jewish divorce *(geṭ),* the Conservative movement has added a clause to the marriage contract. This clause gives the rabbinical court of the Rabbinical Assembly (the organization of Conservative rabbis) the authority to summon the husband and wife at the request of one of them, to provide counseling, and to impose sanctions if its decisions are not obeyed. Orthodox authorities have also used the addition of new language to the marriage contract to solve problems in Jewish marriage and divorce law.

Death and Mourning. In Judaism, the mourners and the mourning rites are clearly defined. Mourners are those who have an obligation to observe the rites of mourning, that is, father, mother, brother, sister, son, daughter, and spouse of the deceased. Mourning itself is divided into three clearly defined periods: (1) *aninut,* from death to burial, (2) *shiv'ah,* the seven days following burial, (3) *sheloshim,* from the end of the seven days until the thirtieth day. These are fixed periods, and they apply to all relatives for whom one is required to mourn. An additional mourning period is observed only for a parent; it extends until the year anniversary of the day of death. It is referred to simply as mourning *(avelut).* Each of these periods has its own set practices and restrictions.

From death until burial, mourners are exempt from the observance of all positive religious obligations, such as reciting morning prayers or donning phylacteries *(tefillin).* Mourners are also forbidden to engage in pleasurable activities, such as eating meat, drinking wine, attending parties, or engaging in sexual intercourse. The purpose of the exemptions and restrictions are to permit the mourners to attend to the needs of the deceased and to fulfill their obligation to make appropriate preparations for the funeral and burial. This is based on the principle of respect for the dead *(kevod ha-met)* and the Talmudic principle that one who is engaged in a religious obligation *(mitsvah)* is exempt from other religious obligations (B.T., *Suk.* 26a; B.T., *Soṭ* 44b).

The body of the deceased is prepared for burial through a process of washing (*ṭahorah,* "purification"), which is performed by members of the Jewish burial society (*ḥevra' qaddisha',* "holy society"). After the washing, the deceased is dressed in plain linen shrouds *(takhrikhim).* This practice, which levels distinctions of wealth, was established to avoid embarrassing the poor at the time of death. In addition, funerals were considered inappropriate times to display one's wealth. A man is usually buried with his prayer shawl *(ṭallit).* Reform Jews often omit the ritual washing, and they dress the deceased in street clothes. After the body has been properly prepared and dressed, it is placed in a plain wooden coffin in preparation for burial in the ground. The use of wooden caskets and burial in the ground is in fulfillment of the biblical verse, "For dust you are, and to dust you shall return" (*Gn.* 3:19). Jewish tradition prohibits both embalming (except when secular law or circumstance requires it) and cremation. Reform Judaism permits both cremation and the entombing of the deceased in a mausoleum, but burial remains normative Jewish practice.

Jewish tradition recommends that burial take place as soon as possible, preferably on the day of death. Today, this is often not possible, because members of the family may not live in close proximity to one another; therefore, burial may be delayed out of respect for the dead, to permit a mourner who lives at a distance to attend. Timely burial is still the rule, however.

Part of the mourning ritual is the rending of a garment *(qeriy'ah).* In some instances, the actual rending of a garment has been replaced by the symbolic rending of a special black ribbon, which is attached to the mourner's clothing for this purpose. The rending is done standing, and is preceded by the blessing, "Blessed are you, O Lord our God, Ruler of the Universe, Judge of Truth."

Today, funerals often take place in special funeral chapels or at graveside. In some communities, funerals are also held in synagogues. The liturgy for a funeral usually consists of the recitation of several psalms, a eulogy, and the memorial prayer El Male' Raḥamim ("God full of compassion"):

> O God full of compassion, you who dwell on high! Grant perfect rest beneath the sheltering wings of Your presence, among the holy and pure who shine as the brightness of the heavens, unto the soul of . . . [the deceased] who has entered eternity and in whose memory charity is offered. May his/her repose be in the garden of Eden. May the Lord of Mercy bring him/her under the cover of his wings forever and may his/her soul be bound up in the bond of eternal life. May the

Lord be his/her possession and may he/she rest in peace. Amen.

After the funeral, the deceased is transported to the cemetery. The casket is borne to the grave by the pallbearers, who make seven stops along the way while Psalm 91 is recited. The coffin is then placed in the grave and covered with earth. Most Reform rabbis omit the practice of stopping seven times during the procession to the grave and do not have the casket lowered and covered with earth until after the interment service is completed. The interment service consists of the recitation of Tsidduq ha-Din, which is an acclamation of God's justice; a memorial prayer; and Qaddish, which is a doxology reaffirming the mourner's faith in God in the face of death. A tradition based on a story about a condemned man's soul rescued from the punishment of Gehenna by ʿAqiva' ben Yosef's recitation of Qaddish has assigned an intercessary role to the recitation of Qaddish. After the service has concluded, the people in attendance form two lines through which the mourners pass. Those present comfort the mourners as they pass, saying, "May God comfort you among the rest of the mourners of Zion and Jerusalem."

The completion of the funeral marks the end of the first mourning period, *aninut,* and the beginning of the second period, *shivʿah.* On returning home (usually to the home of the deceased), the mourners kindle a candle, which is kept burning for the whole seven-day period. The flame is a symbol of the human soul. ("The soul of humankind is the lamp of the Lord," *Proverbs* 20:27.) Then the mourners are served a meal of consolation *(seʿudat havra'ah),* which is prepared by friends and relatives; it traditionally includes round foods such as eggs, a symbol of life and hope.

During *shivʿah* the mourners remain at home and do not attend to business or engage in social activities. Traditionally, they sit on special low benches, refrain from shaving, cutting their hair, bathing, or anointing themselves for pleasure (though they may do so for hygienic reasons). They do not wear leather shoes or engage in sexual intercourse. (Most of these practices of abstinence have been abandoned by Reform Jews.) A *minyan* (quorum of ten) gathers at the house of mourning for twice-daily services—morning and evening. During *shivʿah,* friends and relatives have an obligation to visit the mourners to comfort them. When *shivʿah* ends, the mourners return to work but continue to avoid social gatherings until the thirtieth day after burial. When one is mourning the death of a parent, the restrictions are observed for one year.

Yahrzeit, the yearly anniversary of a person's death, is observed by the mourners' lighting a memorial light, which is kept lit for twenty-four hours; by giving charity in the deceased's memory; and by attending services to recite Qaddish.

The erecting of a tombstone is an ancient custom. Usually the mourners wait one year following the death before having the monument put in place at the gravesite. A common practice is for the mourners to dedicate the tombstone in a brief ceremony, popularly called an "Unveiling," because as part of the ritual a cloth covering the tombstone is removed by the family.

Four times a year—on Yom Kippur (the Day of Atonement), on the last day of Pesaḥ (Passover), on Shavuʿot (Feast of Weeks), and on the last day of Sukkot (Tabernacles)—a memorial service, popularly called *yizkor,* is held as part of the holy day observance. A memorial light is lit at home, and the deceased is remembered at the service. (Most Reform congregations have a memorial service only on Yom Kippur and on the last day of Passover.)

Conversion. Conversion may be considered a rite of passage since through the process a person changes his or her status from being a non-Jew to a Jew. The history of proselytism in Judaism is complex and is beyond the scope of this discussion (see Bernard Bamberger's classic study, *Proselytism in the Talmudic Period,* Cincinnati, 1939). Candidates for conversion must come of their own free will without ulterior motive. Therefore, a person who comes for the purpose of marriage is automatically disqualified. However, this stricture is observed only by the Orthodox. Once the sincerity of the prospective convert is ascertained, there is a period of instruction during which the candidate is taught the basic principles and practices of Judaism. Once the prospective convert has completed this education and accepts the obligation to observe *mitsvot* (commandments), the candidate is examined by a *beit din* (a rabbinical court consisting of three rabbis or other observant Jews). Male and female converts are then immersed in a *mikvah* (ritual bath) and males are circumcised by a *mohel.* If the male had been previously circumcised by a doctor as a child, then only a symbolic circumcision *(haṭafat dam berit)* is required. The Reform movement does not require immersion or circumcision although an increasing number of Reform rabbis require the traditional rites. In addition to the appearance before the rabbinical court, immersion, and circumcision, a public ceremony of welcome has been introduced into many Reform, Conservative, and Reconstructionist congregations.

[*For further discussion of the development of Jewish law and tradition concerning these rites, see* Conservative Judaism; Orthodox Judaism; Reconstructionist Judaism; *and* Reform Judaism.]

BIBLIOGRAPHY

The best general book on Jewish rites of passage, which contains both popular practices and historical development, is Hayyim Schauss's *The Lifetime of a Jew throughout the Ages of Jewish History* (New York, 1950).

Orthodox Practice. Standard Orthodox practice is explained in H. Halevy Donin's *To Be a Jew* (New York, 1972), which has a good bibliography but lacks extensive source references. The Orthodox rabbi's manual, Hyman E. Goldin's *Hamadrikh, the Rabbi's Guide,* 2d ed. (New York, 1956), contains the liturgy and an excellent summary of the laws. The liturgy and extensive explanatory notes can also be found in Joseph H. Hertz's *The Authorized Daily Prayer Book,* 2d ed. (New York, 1963). Maurice Lamm has two extensive studies on the Orthodox view of death and marriage, *The Jewish Way in Death and Mourning* (New York, 1969) and *The Jewish Way in Love and Marriage* (San Francisco, 1980).

Conservative Practice. The most comprehensive study of Jewish practice available is Isaac Klein's *A Guide to Jewish Religious Practice* (New York, 1979). In addition to a detailed description of the practices from a traditional Conservative point of view, he provides extensive reference to the Talmud and later legal codes. The book contains an extensive bibliography. *A Rabbi's Manual,* new rev. ed., edited by Jules Harlow (New York, 1965), provides the liturgical texts for rites of passage according to Conservative Judaism's interpretation.

Reform Practice. *Gates of Mitzvah: A Guide to the Jewish Life Cycle,* edited by Simeon J. Maslin (New York, 1979), explains the Reform practice. It contains source reference notes and explanatory essays. The Reform liturgical texts are found in *Gates of the House,* edited by Chaim Stern (New York, 1977), and *A Rabbi's Manual* (Cincinnati, 1928), edited and published by the Central Conference of American Rabbis. A recent version of the liturgical texts are contained in *Ma'aglei Tsedeq,* edited by David Polish with notes by W. Gunther Plaut (New York, forthcoming).

New Rituals. *The Jewish Catalog,* edited by Richard Siegel, Michael Strassfeld, and Sharon Strassfeld (Philadelphia, 1973), and *The Second Jewish Catalog,* edited by Michael Strassfeld and Sharon Strassfeld (Philadelphia, 1976), are excellent sources for traditional and creative rituals of observance. *The Jewish Woman: New Perspectives,* edited by Elizabeth Koltun (New York, 1976), contains two essays, "On the Birth of a Daughter" by Myra Leifer and Daniel Leifer, and "On Writing New *Ketubbot*" by Daniel Leifer, which describe some of the egalitarian tendencies in non-Orthodox rites of passage.

PETER S. KNOBEL

Muslim Rites

While Muslims throughout the world emphasize the unity of Islam, they also recognize the impressive diversity of cultural and historical contexts in which Islamic civilization has been elaborated and expressed. Because of this diversity, rites of passage in the Islamic world draw equally upon ritual forms and metaphors specific to local cultural contexts and upon the more universal elements of the Islamic tradition. Some of these ritual and expressive forms existed prior to the advent of Islam in the seventh century CE and were incorporated with appropriate shifts in context and meaning into the Islamic tradition. Others developed concurrently with the Islamic tradition.

Some transitions marked by rites of passage, including birth, naming, circumcision, social puberty, betrothal, marriage, pregnancy, motherhood, fatherhood, death, and mourning, are not specific to the Islamic world. These rites show an especially wide diversity of form and content because they incorporate major elements of local belief and practice. Marriage, for instance, is a secular contract in Islam. Muslim jurisprudence specifies certain legal requirements but not the form taken by marriage ceremonies. Provided that preexisting rites of passage are not directly contrary to the more universalistic aspects of the Islamic tradition, they remain a part of accepted local practice. Likewise, socially recognized transitions considered significant in some Islamic societies may be given much less emphasis in others. Some transitions, including the completion of Qur'anic schooling and the pilgrimage *(ḥajj)* to Mecca, are specifically Islamic, yet how these occasions are ritually marked varies considerably with location.

Because of this diversity, rites of passage considered to be inherent components of the Islamic tradition in some parts of the Islamic world or by some social groups are not always accepted as having anything to do with Islam by Muslims elsewhere. For example, before departing for the pilgrimage to Mecca, many North African Muslims first circumambulate their town or village, visiting its principal shrines in the company of friends and relatives. Flags or banners associated with these shrines are carried in the procession. On their return from Mecca, the pilgrims participate in a similar procession and visit local shrines before crossing the thresholds of their homes. Modernist Muslims claim that these "local" ceremonies have nothing to do with Islam or the pilgrimage proper, but for many North Africans these practices remain an integral part of Islam as they practice and understand their faith. Modernist sentiments are even more intense against the annual festivals *(mūsims)* of some ethnic groups in North Africa, especially Morocco, in which ethnic collectivities renew their "covenant" *('ahd)* with particular saints and their living descendants through the offering of a sacrifice. Many such festivals occur annually just before the planting season and the moving of herds from summer to winter pastures. Similarly, the Alevi (Arab., 'Alawī) Muslims of eastern Turkey, Syria, and northern Iraq fast only twelve days a year, in honor of the twelve imams (leaders of the Islamic community) whom they recognize, instead of for an entire lunar month. Alevis also consider that the true *ḥajj* is carried out in one's heart, not in travel to Mecca. Their interpretation of Islamic obligations and practice is not recognized as valid by neighboring Muslims of other sects.

Although some rites of passage resemble one another in general form throughout the Muslim world, a thorough knowledge of how they are locally elaborated is essential to understanding their contextual meaning. Most of these rites derive in part from formal Islamic doctrine but are equally shaped by, and in turn shape, diverse underlying local conceptions of society. In Marrakesh, for example, the ceremonies marking birth, circumcision, marriage, and pilgrimage resemble one another because they share an underlying conception of social boundaries and social space. These conceptions are not derived from Islamic doctrine, but neither are they opposed to it. After a woman gives birth, she and her child are confined for seven days to the room in which the birth took place. Ceremonies involving only close relatives are then performed, but until the fortieth day after birth, the mother and her child refrain from crossing the threshold of the house. At the end of this period, they visit one of the principal shrines of Marrakesh. After a child is circumcised, he and his mother are likewise confined, to one room of the house for the first week, then to the entire house for another interval; finally, all restrictions on movement end after a visit to one of the major local shrines. For marriage, newly wed couples remain seven days in the nuptial chamber, followed by a few days in the house itself and finally a visit to one of the principal shrines. Returning pilgrims, once they have entered their houses, follow a similar progression to regain the full use of social space and to reincorporate themselves into ordinary society. Even with the widespread expansion of mass education in recent years, which has the effect in many parts of the world of modifying or eliminating local ritual practices, those of Marrakesh remain largely intact.

In Islamic societies, as in others, the social and cultural significance accorded to specific rites of passage becomes clear only when the rites are considered in their full social context. In some parts of the Muslim world—in Silwa, a village in Egypt's Aswan province, for example—weddings are an important marker of transition, especially for women. Upon marriage a woman leaves the residence of her own parents and becomes part of her husband's domestic group. However, the significance of marriage elsewhere—as in Atjeh, in northern Sumatra, for example—is overshadowed by a woman's first live birth. In Atjeh, when a woman becomes a mother, she also becomes an adult and takes legal possession of her house. The ceremonies associated with her becoming a mother and the naming of her child are locally regarded as much more significant than marriage itself: women claim that they are girls until they have children.

In the interior of Oman, a country in the southeastern corner of the Arabian Peninsula, marriages generally occur within the extended family and often involve a move of no more than several hundred feet for the bride, from the house of her father to that of a nearby relative. She continues to spend the better part of the day in the house of her own mother, although elsewhere in the Muslim world it is common to have a period of avoidance between a new wife and her family of birth. Marriage ceremonies in the Omani interior are such subdued, private occasions that non-family members often learn that they have taken place only after the event. In contrast, once a woman gives birth, the naming ceremony for her child is elaborate. It occasions visits from every household in the community and results in the mother's achieving full social status as a woman. The mother, not the child, is the center of attention at naming ceremonies.

Since the interpretation of rites of passage is dependent upon local cultural contexts, principal Moroccan practices are described here to illustrate a complete set of major social transitions. Examples are also provided from elsewhere in the Islamic world to indicate the range of major variation.

Birth and Naming. In Morocco, if a woman wishes to induce pregnancy or fears a difficult one, she visits the sanctuaries of marabouts (*walīs*) reputed for their efficacy in dealing with such difficulties. She will often leave a strip of cloth from her own dress as a promise that, if her childbirth occurs, she will return and sacrifice a sheep or goat, distributing its meat either to descendants of the *walī* or to the poor. Once a woman knows she is pregnant, she begins to eat special foods and to receive visits from female neighbors and relatives, practices that are common elsewhere in the Islamic world.

After she has given birth, a woman is confined to her house for a period that varies from a week to forty days. During this period she is regarded as ritually unclean and is unable to pray and fast, an indication of her marginal status. At the end of her confinement she is taken by female friends and relatives to the public bath, resumes normal activities, and is able once again to leave her house. The child is kept in its swaddling clothes during this period and is constantly guarded for fear that he or she might be exchanged for a malevolent spirit *(jinnī)*. Most women unaffected by modernist Islamic belief and practice perform a series of rituals designed to propitiate any such spirits that might be nearby.

The most important event in the child's life is the naming ceremony *(subūʿ)*, which ideally occurs a week after the birth of a child of either sex. On this day the child is named, usually by its father but in agreement with the mother and other relatives. The mother is bathed, dressed in new clothes, and painted with henna, often by the midwife who has delivered the child. The child also has henna applied to its face, hands, and feet, both because henna is thought to be pleasing to the eye and because it is thought to protect the child's spirit from harm. The mother receives visits from female relatives and neighbors on this occasion.

There is no fixed set of relatives involved in the naming of a child in Morocco. The choice is primarily a personal one and may also involve consultation with patrons or close friends. Likewise, the selection of names reflects a variety of influences and personal choices. Some persons prefer distinctly religious names such as Muḥammad (Mḥā in Berber-speaking regions) or ʿAbd Allāh ("servant of God") for men, and Fāṭimah, the name of the Prophet's daughter, for women. Other children are named after a religious feast day, such as Mulūdī for a man born on or near the Prophet's birthday (colloquially, ʿĪd al-Mulūd). Other names reflect a commitment to nationalism, as in using the name ʿAllāl, after the Moroccan nationalist leader ʿAllāl al-Fāsī. The name chosen may honor a recently deceased relative; it is a bad omen to name a child after a living relative. In non-Arabic-speaking countries, such as Indonesia and Bangladesh, the growing use of Arabic names instead of non-Islamic ones or names in local languages is a direct result of a growing commitment to reform Islam.

For boys in Morocco, the naming ceremony is always accompanied by the sacrifice of a sheep or goat, although a blood sacrifice is often omitted in the case of girls. This sacrifice is known as the *ʿaqīqah* ceremony. The male relatives and friends of the father are invited to a midday feast, the child's hair is cut for the first time, and alms are distributed to the poor. A separate feast is held for female relatives in the evening. This rite of passage is so significant that in wealthy families it is not unusual for hundreds of guests from throughout the country to attend. In many villages, each part of the sacrificed animal has a special significance and is designated for particular persons. The liver is eaten only by members of the household, and the heart and stomach fat are eaten by the mother alone. Other parts of the animal, usually including the skin and entrails, are destined for the midwife.

Moroccans consider the sacrifice for the naming ceremony to be an Islamic obligation, although of the four legal schools of Sunnī Islam only the Ḥanbalī school regards it as compulsory. The other schools merely allow the practice, although Islamic tradition ascribes the sacrifice, which has pre-Islamic antecedents, to the prophet Muḥammad (d. 632). The sacrifice, like the haircutting, is thought to avert evil from the child by offering a substitute sacrifice. At the same time, with the acquisition of a name, the child becomes a full social person.

Circumcision. Circumcision is the next major rite of passage for boys. It usually occurs between the ages of two and seven. There is no equivalent ceremony in Morocco for girls. The day before the circumcision, the boy is bathed, and his head is shaved. His mother paints henna on his hands and feet to ward off the evil eye. A sacrifice is made, and a feast is prepared for friends, neighbors, and relatives, to which the guests bring small gifts. Many households wait until ʿĪd al-Aḍḥā or a marriage in the family or arrange with other households to have their children circumcised together. On the day after the circumcision feast, the boy, dressed in fine clothes and accompanied by musicians, is led around town on a mule. In the past in some areas, his clothes would have resembled those of a bride. Elements of the circumcision ceremonies are exactly parallel to those of marriage. The boy's mother and sisters wear their hair loose, as they would for a wedding. Just before the circumcision itself, usually performed by an itinerant specialist but increasingly by medical personnel, the boy is dressed in a new, white shift, often similar to that worn by pilgrims to Mecca. The garment is another indication of the purificatory intent of the ritual.

In classical Arabic, circumcision is known as *khitān*, although in Morocco and elsewhere in the Arab world it is usually known as *ṭahārah* ("purification"), and in Turkey as *sünnet*, or the practice of the Prophet. Although not mentioned in the Qurʾān, circumcision is attributed to the Prophet and recognized as a pre-Islamic Arabian tradition; it appears to have been performed at puberty and as a preliminary to marriage. There is a modern tendency among educated Moroccans to have their children circumcised at an earlier age, sometimes even at birth, although for most families circumcision still takes place when a child, toward the age of six or seven, prepares to assume the responsibilities of an adult Muslim, including the daily prayers and the Ramaḍān fast.

In Morocco, as elsewhere in the Muslim world, the possession of reason *(ʿaql)* informed by accepted Islamic practice implies the ability of Muslims to subordinate their "natural" passions or personal inclinations *(hawa nafs)* to God's will. The concepts of *ʿaql* and *hawa nafs* occur in almost all Islamic societies. Children are said to be "ignorant" *(jāhil)* because they lack knowledge of the Islamic code of conduct and the capacity to abide by it. Thus, when circumcision occurs at the traditionally preferred age of six or seven, it marks the beginning of full participation in the Islamic community. Memorization of the Qur'ān, for those children who accomplish this feat, also sets a child apart from ordinary society through the mnemonic possession of the word of God. Like circumcision, the event is marked by a public procession and announcement of the child's new status.

Marriage. After discreet private negotiations between the families involved, a date for the wedding and the size of the marriage payment *(ṣadāq)* are set. This payment, relative to the value placed on the girl and her family, is used to buy domestic furnishings that remain the bride's property. By Islamic law, payment must be made in order for the marriage to be valid. The contract is usually signed in the presence of notaries or valid witnesses just after a ceremonial dinner at the girl's home at which her father or guardian is formally asked for her hand. Later, an engagement party is held. This is primarily a woman's party, with dancing and singing, the closing of the marriage contract, and payment of the bridewealth.

A day or two before the actual wedding, the bride's family delivers to the bridegroom's home the furnishings purchased with the *ṣadāq* money. These are publicly displayed, often on the back of a truck, and accompanied by drummers and musicians. There is often a small celebration at the woman's house before she is taken to that of her future husband. In rural areas, the groom's party may bring an animal to be sacrificed at her house. Several days later they return to carry the bride away to the groom's house, where the major ceremony is held. As the groom's party, often accompanied by the blowing of horns and drumming, approaches the woman's house, there is a mock battle between the bride's family and the groom's, at the end of which the girl is allowed to be taken away. She has been prepared by purification with water and henna.

The day before the wedding, the groom also undergoes purification. He goes to the bath, accompanied by his friends, and is treated as if he were a sultan with his court. He is often painted with henna and entertained by musicians. In the past in some regions, the groom was himself dressed like a bride for a brief period, a custom that emphasized all the more the imminent transformation of his status. Afterward, he is washed, shaved, and dressed in new clothes.

Upon arrival at the groom's house, the bride is ceremonially dressed in heavy layers of fine brocades and jewels, often rented for the occasion. After a long evening of music and feasting, the groom leaves his guests, enters the bridal chamber, lifts the bride's veil, and ceremonially offers her milk and dates. Depending upon the region of Morocco and the social class, close relatives may visit the couple briefly at this stage. Wedding gifts are publicly announced and displayed at this time. Religious specialists are invited to the wedding feast, where they recite the Qur'ān and invoke blessings upon the couple but do not play a central role. Celebrations continue until proof of the bride's virginity is brought to the guests, although Moroccans are rapidly abandoning this practice. For a week thereafter, the wife remains confined to her husband's house, receiving visits only from close female friends. So that the bride may become accustomed to new patterns of domestic authority, she is forbidden to see her father, brothers, and other male relatives for at least three months. The public nature of parts of the ceremony, the bride's change of residence, and the restrictions on her conduct formally denote the couple's change of marital status.

Death. Deaths and funeral ceremonies show the most consistency in essential features throughout the Muslim world. More so than the other rites of passage, those for death and mourning are largely common to all Muslims. If the death is expected, the Qur'ān is recited continuously in the presence of the ailing person. At the point of death, the eyes and mouth of the person are closed, and the arms are straightened alongside the body. The deceased is placed with his or her face turned toward Mecca. For the duration of mourning, regular social life is suspended for those affected. A person of the same sex who knows the prescribed ritual washing and preparation of the dead is called in. The women of the family are expected to cry and lose their composure, but men's expressions of grief are expected to be much more restrained. The deceased is wrapped in a white seamless cloth similar to that worn for the pilgrimage; in the case of those who have actually made the *ḥajj*, the seamless white garments worn while in Mecca are used. The Qur'ān is recited. Burial occurs quickly, on the same day if death occurs in the morning or early afternoon; if death occurs late in the day, burial is postponed until the next morning. Friends and relatives accompany the procession to the cemetery, where a prayer for the dead is recited by a religious specialist. On returning from the cemetery, participants in the procession are provided with a meal at the house of the deceased. In some rural areas, food is also placed over the grave for the first three days after death.

Mourning continues for three days, the period thought to be sanctioned by the Qur'ān, and consolations are received by the relatives of the deceased. Since death is ordained by God, proper conduct for a Muslim after the initial shock of grief is to accept the will of

God. The lack of forbearance and composure (*'azā'*) implies a lack of reason, in this context the capacity to adjust to an expression of God's will. A widow remains in seclusion for four months and ten days, a period prescribed by the Qur'ān and the minimum legal waiting period (*'iddah*) before she is allowed to remarry. In Morocco, it is not unusual for elaborate stone markers or enclosures to be erected around the grave, a sharp contrast with, for example, the custom of the Ibāḍīyah of Oman, who indicate the equality of all Muslims after death by marking graves with simple stones, none of which carry inscriptions.

Major Variations. If there are numerous points of resemblance among rites of passage in the Islamic world, divergences are just as pronounced. In Egyptian villages along the Nile, women visit shrines and cross the river to encourage conception; the latter practice is directly related to a wish to induce a change in the woman's status. In these practices, the parallels with Morocco are almost exact, yet divergences also become clear when overall patterns are considered. In Atjeh, for instance, an elaborate series of visits takes place between the mothers of the wife and the husband, both before and after births, accompanied by complex food restrictions. Some of these restrictions occur only for odd-numbered pregnancies. In Java, the various rituals associated with birth are timed by the Javanese calendar, in which each month has thirty-five days. Many of the rituals involve a rich mixture of Islamic, Hindu-Buddhist, and indigenous spirits, and each food and gesture associated with these rituals has a specific implication. Thus, in the small feast for household members only, which occurs just before birth, a dish of rice is served with a peeled banana in the middle, to symbolize an easy birth. The precision with which events are timed and the punctilious concern with ritual detail are alien to other parts of the Islamic world. After childbirth in Atjeh, a woman may not leave her house for forty-four days. For much of this time, she lies on a platform over hot bricks with her legs extended and her ankles together. The idea behind this "roasting" is to become as dry as possible in order to expel the aftereffects of childbirth, again a set of notions without direct correspondences elsewhere.

The obligations incurred by guests at life-crisis ceremonies and the comportment appropriate to them also show considerable range. Egyptian villagers keep punctilious written accounts of the gifts they give to other members of the community and the value of those they receive in return. By contrast, the notion of strict, explicit equality of value is lacking in the Arabian Peninsula and is there considered to be against the spirit of Islam. In Java, certain foods such as wafer-thin disks of rice are served at major life-crisis feasts. Sharing them is meant to symbolize that all guests are internally composed and free from strong emotions such as envy, hate, and jealousy, a concern not equally emphasized elsewhere.

Circumcision shows two major patterns of variation throughout the Islamic world. Although all males are circumcised, women are circumcised only in certain areas, notably in Upper Egypt, the Sudan, Somalia, Ethiopia, West Africa, and Atjeh. Circumcision for women, which occurs between the ages of six or seven (Egypt) and twelve (Atjeh), occasions a minimum of ceremony. It does not result in any significant change of status for a girl, although the operation is considered a necessary prerequisite to marriage. Unlike boys undergoing circumcision, girls are allowed and even encouraged to cry out in pain. The Islamic jurist al-Shāfi'ī (767–820 CE) argues that circumcision is obligatory for both sexes. Other jurists argue that it is merely "honorable" for women. The more extreme forms of circumcision, including infibulation, have been declared illegal in recent years by many governments, although enforcement is highly variable.

The age at which male circumcision occurs varies according to its significance in a particular cultural context. In northern Yemen, for example, circumcision until recently took place between the ages of twelve and fifteen and, despite official government bans, continues in some areas. The youth is surrounded by men and women of his village. A knife is held to his foreskin as he recites three times, "There is no god but God and Muḥammad is his Prophet." The foreskin is then cut and thrown into the crowd. The youth retrieves it and is carried on his mother's shoulders while he continues to display it proudly, leading a procession of dancers and brandishing his dagger. He is humiliated for life if he shows any sign of pain. In this context, circumcision is more a test of virility and a marker of young adult status than a point of entry into participation in the religious community, which is the case when circumcision occurs at the age of six or seven, as in Morocco. In Java, it traditionally occurred after a youth had completed religious studies, between the ages of ten and fourteen; two transitions that are kept separate elsewhere in the Islamic world were thus fused. Circumcision is also seen as a prelude to marriage, which is not the case when it occurs at a much younger age.

The vitality of the Islamic tradition is indicated in its capacity for self-renewal and transformation. The rites of passage described here for the Islamic world are inseparable from basic notions of social and cultural identity. As notions of identity shift, so do the forms of many of these rituals, even in the face of traditions previously accepted and taken for granted in specific contexts. Since the late nineteenth century, modernist and reform movements in Islam have given impetus to a reappraisal of the links between Islam and personal identity. Likewise, the abandonment or modification of practices not considered authentically Islamic, even if locally tolerated, signifies that notions of self and community are in a process of change, a process that is ongoing throughout the Islamic world.

BIBLIOGRAPHY

The relevant entries in the old edition of *The Encyclopaedia of Islam*, 4 vols. and supplement (Leiden, 1913–1938), and the new edition in progress (Leiden, 1960–) are strongest in summarizing Islamic legal thought and classical writing on rites of passage and include extensive bibliographies for these fields. W. Robertson Smith's *Kinship and Marriage in Early Arabia*, edited by Stanley A. Cook (1903; new ed., Oosterhout, Netherlands, 1966), and *Lectures on the Religion of the Semites*, 2d ed. (1894; reprint, New York, 1956), remain valuable for comparing early Islamic rites of passage with earlier Semitic practice. Christiaan Snouck Hurgronje's *Mekka in the Latter Part of the Nineteenth Century* (1888–1889), translated by J. H. Monahan (1931; reprint, Leiden, 1970), provides extensive ethnographic description. For Morocco, Edward A. Westermarck's *Marriage Ceremonies in Morocco* (1914; reprint, London, 1972) and *Ritual and Belief in Morocco*, vol. 2 (1926; reprint, New Hyde Park, N.Y., 1968), provides meticulous ethnographic detail useful to contrast with descriptions contained in studies of more recent practice.

Among modern studies, see my *Moroccan Islam: Tradition and Society in a Pilgrimage Center* (Austin, 1976). For a psychoanalytic perspective on a single ritual, see Vincent Crapanzano's "Rite of Return: Circumcision in Morocco," in volume 9 of *The Psychoanalytic Study of Society*, edited by Warner Muensterberger and L. Bryce Boyer (New York, 1981), pp. 15–36. Excellent discussions of rites of passage in other countries are included in Hamed Ammar's *Growing Up in an Egyptian Village* (1954; reprint, London, 1956); James T. Siegel's *The Rope of God* (Berkeley, 1969), for Atjeh; Clifford Geertz's *The Religion of Java* (New York, 1964); and John R. Bowen's "Death and the History of Islam in Highland Aceh," *Indonesia* 38 (October 1984): 21–38. For an excellent study of historical change in naming practices, see Richard W. Bulliet's "First Names and Political Change in Modern Turkey," *International Journal of Middle East Studies* 9 (November 1978): 489–495.

DALE F. EICKELMAN

RITSCHL, ALBRECHT (1822–1889), German Protestant theologian. Born in Berlin, the son of a pastor and bishop of the Evangelical church, he was reared in Stettin (present-day Szczecin, Poland), in the Prussian province of Pomerania. From 1839 to 1846 he studied at the universities of Bonn, Halle (Ph.D., 1843), Heidelberg, and Tübingen (where he learned the church historian's craft from Ferdinand Christian Baur). From 1846 to 1864 he taught at Bonn, and from 1864 until his death he was professor of dogmatics (systematic theology) at Göttingen.

Ritschl's teaching and writing at first concentrated on the New Testament and early church history. The views of Baur and his "Tübingen school"—which regarded late second-century Christianity ("old Catholicism") as the outcome and reconciliation of struggles between Jewish Christians ("Petrinists") and gentile Christians ("Paulinists")—informed Ritschl's first two books: *Das Evangelium Marcions und das kanonische Evangelium des Lukas* (The Gospel of Marcion and the Canonical Gospel of Luke; 1846) and *Die Entstehung der altkatholischen Kirche* (The Rise of the Old Catholic Church; 1851). The second edition of the latter book (1857) marked a dramatic personal and academic break with Baur, whose "conflict model" of early church history Ritschl now repudiated as too speculative or "Hegelian." He insisted, rather, that all the apostles proclaimed a fundamentally similar message, interpreting the ministry of Jesus in the light of its Old Testament presuppositions; that the differences between Jewish and gentile Christians were relative, not substantive, with only a few groups of Judaistic Christians opposing Paul; and that early Catholicism, far from being a Jewish-gentile "synthesis," was wholly a gentile phenomenon, the result of a gradual "de-judaization" of Christianity.

During the 1850s Ritschl's interests turned increasingly to dogmatic theology. While at Göttingen he published two monumental works, each occupying three volumes: *Die christliche Lehre von der Rechtfertigung und Versöhnung* (The Christian Doctrine of Justification and Reconciliation; 1870–1874) and *Geschichte des Pietismus* (History of Pietism; 1880–1886). These works, in tandem with numerous essays and several short monographs—notably *Unterricht in der christlichen Religion* (Instruction in the Christian Religion; 1875)—established Ritschl's international reputation as the foremost Protestant systematic theologian of his time. His disciples occupied the leading chairs in theology at the German universities well into the twentieth century. The most prominent Ritschlians were Adolf von Harnack, Wilhelm Herrmann, and (at an early stage of his career) Ernst Troeltsch.

Ritschl's paramount aim during his Göttingen years was to fashion a comprehensive interpretation of the Christian religion based on the doctrine of justification and reconciliation, as set forth by the New Testament (chiefly the letters of Paul) and by the Protestant reformers (chiefly Martin Luther in his writings of 1515–1520). In Ritschl's judgment, however, the reformers, while recovering essential components of New Testament Christianity and turning them to church-reforming effect, had failed to order their religious insights in a holistic theological system. They had neglected, not least, to correlate their fundamental teaching on justification by faith alone with the biblical teaching on the kingdom of God. Thus they left the impression that Christianity is primarily a religion of personal redemption from sin, and not equally one of corporate ethical activity directed to the moral reconstruction of society. Viewed in respect of its formal theological productions, therefore, the Protestant Reformation was unfinished.

Ritschl contended, moreover, that post-Reformation Protestantism had continued and heightened the "theological atrophy" of the Reformation era, leading to serious "deformations" of authentic biblical-Reformation Christianity—as evidenced, for example, in the intellectualism (neoscholasticism) of Protestant orthodoxy, in the emergence within the Lutheran and Reformed churches of a "half-Catholic" mysticism, in the sectarianism and "otherworldliness" of Pietism, in the rationalism ("natural religion") and eudaemonism ("self-justification") of Enlightenment theology, and in the flight from the historical Christian revelation in Hegelian speculation. To be sure, Immanuel Kant and Friedrich Schleiermacher had given significant impulses for the reconstruction of Protestant theology on the basis of Reformation religion, but their gains had soon been surrendered by their epigones.

Ritschl took it as his own vocational task, therefore, to effect a true re-formation of Protestant theology by recovering the reformers' religious root ideas through critical-historical scholarship and by articulating these ideas, with the aid of constructs supplied by Kant and Schleiermacher, in a "homogeneous" theological system. Thereby, he believed, the unfinished Reformation would be brought to theological completion; classical Protestant Christianity would be vindicated before its cultured despisers and its newly resurgent Roman Catholic foes; and the Reformation's epoch-making significance, including its immediate relevance for the modern world, would be displayed, all with the result that a debilitated Protestantism would at last be purged of "alien growths" and so would attain "maturity."

The main themes of Ritschl's doctrinal system are presented in the third volume of *Justification and Reconciliation.* God, for the sake of Christ, freely pardons sinful humanity ("justification"), thereby overcoming the sinner's fear, mistrust, alienation, and enervating consciousness of guilt, and thus making possible the individual's entrance into a new, confident relationship to God as Father ("reconciliation"). This relationship is verified, first, in the religious virtues of trust in God's providential guidance of the world, patience, humility, and prayer (whereby the believer attains "spiritual lordship over the world" and the vindication of the unique worth of spirit, or the "order of persons," vis-à-vis nature, or the "order of things"); and, second, in the moral virtues of fidelity in one's secular vocation and active love for the neighbor (whereby the kingdom of God, or "moral society of nations," is ultimately to be realized). Ritschl claimed that this doctrine was faithful to the biblical-Reformation heritage because it centered entirely on God's self-revelation as loving Father in Jesus Christ ("history")—a revelation mediated to individuals solely by and within the community of believers ("church"), and appropriated solely through lively personal trust ("faith"). This doctrine, therefore, entailed the explicit repudiation of all "disinterested" knowledge of God, metaphysical speculation, "natural theology," ahistorical mysticism, monastic-ascetic piety ("flight from the world"), ethical quietism, and unchurchly individualism.

From about 1920 to 1960 Ritschl's theology suffered an almost total eclipse. The leading representatives of the then-dominant Protestant neoorthodoxy, Karl Barth and Emil Brunner, charged Ritschl (and Ritschlianism) with egregious departures from classical Christianity, including religious subjectivism, moralism, capitulation to the cultural *Zeitgeist,* and, in sum, a return to the anthropocentrism of Enlightenment religion in its "chastened" (antimetaphysical) Kantian form. Since the 1960s, however, there has been a noteworthy Ritschl renaissance, which has defended Ritschl before his neoorthodox detractors by eschewing "criticism by catchwords," by relating his total theological program to its immediate historical context, and by taking seriously his claim to have constructed his system on biblical and Reformation foundations.

BIBLIOGRAPHY

The only biography of Ritschl is that by his son, Otto, *Albrecht Ritschls Leben,* 2 vols. (Freiburg im Breisgau, 1892–1896). Otto Ritschl also edited his father's *Gesammelte Aufsätze,* 2 vols. (Freiburg im Breisgau, 1893–1896). There are English translations of volumes 1 and 3 of Ritschl's magnum opus: *A Critical History of the Christian Doctrine of Justification and Reconciliation,* translated from the first edition by John S. Black (Edinburgh, 1872), and *The Christian Doctrine of Justification and Reconciliation: The Positive Development of the Doctrine,* translated from the third edition by H. R. Mackintosh and A. B. Macaulay (1900; reprint, Clifton, N.J., 1966). Ritschl's "Prolegomena" to *The History of Pietism, Theology and Metaphysics,* and *Instruction in the Christian Religion* have been translated by Philip J. Hefner in *Albrecht Ritschl: Three Essays*

(Philadelphia, 1972)—the best place to begin for the first-time reader of Ritschl. Valuable older studies are A. E. Garvie's *The Ritschlian Theology, Critical and Constructive,* 2d ed. (Edinburgh, 1902), and Gösta Hök's *Die elliptische Theologie Albrecht Ritschls: Nach Ursprung und innerem Zusammenhang* (Uppsala, 1942). The fullest expositions of Ritschl's relationship to Reformation thought are my *Ritschl and Luther: A Fresh Perspective on Albrecht Ritschl's Theology in the Light of His Luther Study* (Nashville, 1974), which includes a translation of Ritschl's important "Festival Address on the Four Hundredth Anniversary of the Birth of Martin Luther" (1883); and "Albrecht Ritschl and the Unfinished Reformation," *Harvard Theological Review* 73 (1980): 337–372. Four pathbreaking studies of Ritschl's theological system, offered as "correctives" to neoorthodox criticisms, are Philip J. Hefner's *Faith and the Vitalities of History: A Theological Study Based on the Work of Albrecht Ritschl* (New York, 1966), Rolf Schäfer's *Ritschl: Grundlinien eines fast verschollenen dogmatischen Systems* (Tübingen, 1968), David L. Mueller's *An Introduction to the Theology of Albrecht Ritschl* (Philadelphia, 1969), and James Richmond's *Ritschl: A Reappraisal* (London, 1978).

David W. Lotz

RITUAL. Although it would seem to be a simple matter to define *ritual,* few terms in the study of religion have been explained and applied in more confusing ways. For example, Edmund Leach, a contemporary cultural anthropologist, after noting the general disagreement among anthropological theorists, suggested that the term *ritual* should be applied to all "culturally defined sets of behavior," that is, to the symbolical dimension of human behavior as such, regardless of its explicit religious, social, or other content (Leach, 1968, p. 524). Thus we could presumably discuss the ritual significance of scientific experimental procedures, for example. For Leach, such behavior should be regarded as a form of social communication or a code of information and analyzed in terms of its "grammar." Ritual is treated as a cognitive category.

Only slightly less vast a definition, but one that covers a very different set of phenomena, is implied by the common use of the term *ritual* to label religion as such, as in "the ritual view of life" or "ritual man in Africa," the title of an article by Robert Horton (reprinted in Lessa and Vogt, 1979). Many modern theories of religion are in fact primarily theories of ritual, and study of the literature on either topic would introduce us to the other.

Another very broad but commonly encountered usage is the one favored by, for example, psychoanalytic theory, in which notably nonrational or formalized symbolic behavior of any kind is distinguished as "ritual," as distinct from pragmatic, clearly ends-directed behavior that is rationally linked to empirical goals. Here "ritual" is often contrasted to "science" and even to common sense. Without much further ado, religious rituals can even be equated with neurotic compulsions, and its symbols to psychological complexes or genetically linked archetypes. Sociologists and anthropologists who favor such a contrast between ritualistic and rational behavior are usually interested in ritual's sociocultural functions, in which religious values shrink to social affirmations. (Some social anthropologists distinguish between "ritual"—stylized repetitious behavior that is explicitly religious—and "ceremony," which is merely social even in explicit meaning.) [*See* Ceremony.] According to these theorists, the manifest religious content of ritual masks its more basic, "latent" social goals. However, there are anthropologists, such as Clifford Geertz and Victor Turner, who are interested in the explicit religious meaning of ritual symbolisms and who point out that ritual acts do endow culturally important cosmological conceptions and values with persuasive emotive force, thus unifying individual participants into a genuine community. Here ritual is viewed sociologically, to be sure, but in terms of its existential import and explicit meanings rather than its purely cognitive grammar, its psychological dynamics, or its merely social reference.

Such an approach comes closest to that adopted by most scholars in the history and phenomenology of religions. According to Rudolf Otto and Mircea Eliade, for example, ritual arises from and celebrates the encounter with the "numinous," or "sacred," the mysterious reality that is always manifested as of a wholly different order from ordinary or "natural" realities. Religious persons seek to live in continual contact with those realities and to flee or to transform the inconsequential banality of ordinary life, thus giving rise to the repetitions and "archetypal nostalgias" of ritual. In this approach, there is the attempt to define ritual by its actual intention or focus. This intentionality molds the formal symbolisms and repetitions of ritual at their origins, so that when the rituals are repeated, the experience of holiness can be more or less fully reappropriated by new participants.

For our purposes, we shall understand as "ritual" those conscious and voluntary, repetitious and stylized symbolic bodily actions that are centered on cosmic structures and/or sacred presences. (Verbal behavior such as chant, song, and prayer are of course included in the category of bodily actions.) The conscious and voluntary aspects of ritual rule out the inclusion of personal habits or neurotic compulsions in this definition, as does the stress on a transcendent focus (as Freud has shown, neurotic obsessions refer back to infantile traumas and represent contorted efforts of the self to communicate with itself: the focus of neurotic compulsion is the self).

Even more fundamentally, ritual is intentional bodily engagement in the paradigmatic forms and relationships of reality. As such, ritual brings not only the body but also that body's social and cultural identity to the encounter with the transcendental realm. By conforming to models or paradigms that refer to the primordial past and that can be shared by many people, ritual also enables each person to transcend the individual self, and thus it can link many people together into enduring and true forms of community. As a result, ritual draws into itself every aspect of human life, and almost every discipline of the social sciences and humanities has something to say about it. I shall begin this analysis of ritual, however, with an attempt to articulate its manifest religious orientation and how this gives rise to repetitious behaviors. After that I shall turn to other approaches that highlight the latent factors in ritual, such as its personal or social value. In this way I shall be able to review the major theoretical approaches to ritual.

The Religious Meaning of Ritual. Ritual appears in all religions and societies, even those that are nominally antiritualistic. Although it is common to contrast "ritualism" with "deeper spirituality" and mysticism, we find ritual especially stressed in mystical groups (Zen monasteries, Ṣūfī orders, Jewish mystical communities, Hindu yogic ashrams, etc.); in such groups ritual often expands to fill every moment of daily life. The body is evidently more important in religious experience than is often thought.

Ritual centers on the body, and if we would understand ritual we shall have to take the body seriously as a vehicle for religious experience. It is evident that without a body we would have no awareness of a world at all. The infant builds up an understanding of the world out of sensory-motor experience, and as Jean Piaget and Sigmund Freud, among others, have shown, this understanding underlies and sustains our adult experience of space, time, number, and personal identity. The self is first of all a bodily self. As a result, physical experiences and actions engage consciousness more immediately and irresistibly, and bestow a much stronger sense of reality, than any merely mental philosophy or affirmation of faith. Much ritual symbolism draws on the simplest and most intense sensory experiences, such as eating, sexuality, and pain. Such experiences have been repeated so often or so intimately by the body that they have become primary forms of bodily awareness. In ritual, they are transformed into symbolic experiences of the divine, and even into the form of the cosmic drama itself. We may therefore speak of a "prestige of the body" in ritual. In the bodily gesture, the chant, dance, and stride of participants, primordial presences are made actual again, time is renewed, and the universe is regenerated.

Ritual is more than merely symbolic action, it is hieratic. Almost all human activity is symbolic, even the most "rationally" pragmatic. People would never trouble to fix cars if cars had no cultural value; even scientific experiments would be meaningless without a tacit reference to a specific kind of world and society that validates such activities. However, ritual underlines and makes emphatic its symbolic intention. Hence the stylized manner of ritual: the special clothes, the altered manner of speech, the distinctive places and times. But above all, behavior is repetitive and consciously follows a model. Repetition, after all, is a natural way for the body to proclaim, enact, and experience the choice of true as opposed to false things and ways, and to dwell self-consciously in determinative model realities, in the "holy."

The use of model roles and identities is crucial to ritual. As Mircea Eliade has shown, ritual is shaped by archetypes, by the "first gestures" and dramas from the beginning of time, which must be represented again in the ritual and reexperienced by the participants. It is easy to stress the imaginative and mythic aspect of these dramas, and to ignore their significance specifically as bodily enactments. In ritual, people voluntarily submit to their bodily existence and assume very specific roles with highly patterned rules—rules and roles that conform the self to all others who have embodied these "typical" roles in the past. To contact reality, in short, the conscious self must sacrifice its individual autonomy, its freedom in fantasy to "be" anything.

The self is not utterly unique and self-generated, and it cannot control life as it wishes. This is no doubt one of the deepest reasons for the common resentment of ritual: it locates and imprisons us in a particular reality whose consequences can no longer be avoided. The power of ritual is wryly indicated by stories about the bride left abandoned at the altar: in the specificity of the wedding ritual and its implications, the singular and immortal youth who exulted in the eternity of romantic dreams must become merely one of many mortals who have passed this way before. The autonomous and infinitely free self is transformed ritually into "groom" (remorselessly implying the series "father," "grandfather," and dead "ancestor"). The ritual makes him take his place in the cycle of the generations. Thus it signifies human limitation, and even death. He becomes what he had always undeniably been, a bodily, mortal being. Through ritual, the self is discovered as a public, external reality, which can be known only through perspectives mediated by others and especially by transcendent others: the self is something already determined and presented, which can be understood above all and most truly in the ritual act itself. In these actions and encounters the primal beings provide the model and the source of life. The ritual participants must submit to those deeper realities. They must will their own bodies into identities and movements that stem from the ancestral past. They must be humble.

We can call this essential preliminary movement of the self "recentering": there is in a kind of standing outside of oneself, a taking up of the position of the divine "other" and acting on its behalf that is expressed explicitly as a personal submission to it and that is experienced directly as a submersion of the personal will in the divine will. The ritual comes from the ancients and was a gift from the divine; to repeat it means to receive their stamp upon the self and to make their world one's own.

In a wide-ranging study of native religions, Adolf E. Jensen (1963) has defended the thesis that the various epochs of human history have been characterized by distinctive visions of the universe. Although the details and applications of these visions vary enormously from society to society and era to era, the basic visions themselves are not numerous. Early agriculture, for example, was made culturally possible by a certain way of seeing the world and understanding life, death, and humanity, a way that transformed the "burial" of the root or seed, its "rebirth" (or "resurrection") as a plant, and its "murderous" harvesting as food into a kind of mystery, a compelling and salvific vision. The first seer to whom the divine revealed itself in this way must have had a shattering experience. Here, according to Jensen, is the fundamental origin of the rituals of the early agriculturalists: these rituals arose to induct neophytes into the mystery and to enable full initiates to reexperience the shattering revelations of the primal reality. The participants remember the creative acts that made them what they are, and thus they are able to dwell in a world that has meaning. Farming itself becomes not only possible, but necessary.

Eliade (1959) terms these primal, constitutive encounters with the sacred *hierophanies* (self-disclosures of the holy) and *kratophanies* (revelations of overwhelming power). [*See* Hierophany.] It is the underlying purpose of rituals to recall and renew such experiences of reality. These powerful visions—which are usually devoted to the mythic origins of the universe or to those aspects of the creation that hold special consequence for mankind, but which are preserved within the sacred field of ritual enactment—provide a focus and framework for living in the "profane" world of everyday activity. They even sanctify this activity, and so rescue it from the terror of inconsequentiality and meaninglessness. However, ordinary life, with its egoisms, pressures, and attractions, constantly threatens to erode a wider sense of reality. Crises arise that make the challenge acute. The regular enactment of rituals renews the experiential focus on the sacred. In the recentering process, the overall meaning of life and the reality of transcendental powers are again made paramount over merely egoistic or social concerns. The ordering that ritual effects can even be directly healing, inasmuch as many physical ailments have a significant psychosomatic component, and social crises are above all crises in accommodating individuals or groups to each other and to cultural norms.

There is a tendency among phenomenologists of religion concerned with ritual to emphasize the personal encounter with divine beings as the focus of ritual experience. Rudolf Otto, in his influential *The Idea of the Holy* (first published in 1917), was explicitly guided by Christian (and specifically Lutheran) assumptions when he described the holy, or "numinous," this way. However, there are many religions in which the focus of ritual is mostly or entirely impersonal, or in which there are no prayers or sacrifices made to divine beings. Rather, ritual action consists in repeating the primal deeds of beings not now actively present. It is the deeds, not the persons, that are important. Most Australian Aboriginal ritual fits in this category; a striking parallel can be found in the teachings of the ritual texts of late Vedic Hinduism. The *Śatapatha Brāhmaṇa*, for example, states repeatedly that the priests are to perform the sacrifices because this is what the gods themselves did to create the world; in fact, it is by performing these rites that the gods became gods and immortal. Therefore the priests re-create the world when they repeat certain actions, and all who participate in the sacrifice become gods and immortal as well.

In this view, the dynamic of reality is sacrificial; it is renewed only through sacrifice and attained only by those who sacrifice. Through sacrifice one becomes equal to the gods, or even their master, since they too depend on sacrifice. In later Hinduism, there developed a philosophy of ritual, the Pūrva Mīmāṃsā (also called the Karma Mīmāṃsā), which in some versions was explicitly atheistic: the process underlying the universe was a ritual process repeated in and sustained by Brahmanic ritual performances alone. However, the enactment of the duties (*dharma*) appropriate to one's caste, sex, and age is also a form of this ritual world maintenance, especially if done with the fully conscious intention of sustaining the impersonal ritual order of the universe. We may call this a structural rather than a personal focus to ritual action. The aim of such ritual is to enact and perhaps even regenerate the structure of reality, the deep structure that consists of a certain pattern of relationships and their dynamic regeneration. It can even be argued that this structural focus is the real or deeper one in most rituals directed to personal beings, for commonly those personal beings are addressed in ritual in order to assure the proper changing of the seasons, the fertility of the fields, the restoration of health, prosperity in business and everyday affairs, or perhaps more profoundly the general preservation of social tranquillity and universal harmony.

We need not expect to find that ritual emerges first as the result of a personal experience of encounter with a divinity, although traditional cultures often explain their rituals in this fashion. We also find rituals taking shape in conformity with a general sense of what is right and fitting to do in the context of a given situation. This structural sense of what is "right and fitting" may well lack much precision, at least on the conscious level, but despite this a preconscious (or "unconscious") awareness of the nature of the world and the way in which it relates to the ritual situation may operate to determine ritual details with great exactitude. Monographs on particular ritual systems often illustrate this vividly.

As Bruce Kapferer (1983) has shown for exorcism rituals in Sri Lanka, the details of cult can only be understood in terms of the general sense of life, and the overall existential environment, of ritual participants, although they may not be able to explain these details and simply accept them as "traditional." In fact, participants insensibly adapt rituals to specific situations, personal experiences, and training. James W. Fernandez (1982) has given us an astonishingly rich analysis of the symbolic coherence of an African religious movement that shows how conscious thought and prereflective experience interact to produce ritual behavior. At times, the conscious component may be very high: Stanley J. Tambiah's (1970) description of spirit cults in Thailand necessarily involves a discussion of Buddhist metaphysics at certain points, but even here most of the structure of the ritual conforms to unspoken but vividly present folk realities.

One of the most telling instances of the influence of a general sense of the "right and fitting" on ritual behavior, however, is described in W. Lloyd Warner's classic study of Memorial Day and other rituals in a New England community, *The Living and the Dead: A Study of the Symbolic Life of Americans* (1959). Warner describes how the celebration of the holiday was planned and carried out one spring. Many people were involved; in fact almost all groups in the community were represented. Many random factors and issues intervened, but the result can be regarded as a crystallization of the American ethos as it existed at that time and place. We have here neither the calculated imposition of ritualized ideology on underclasses by an authoritarian, hypocritical elite nor solitary ecstatic encounters with sacred beings used as models for community cult (two current theories of the origin of ritual). Instead, we find the voluntary community enactment of a felt reality, which in turn makes the common dream an actuality, at least in the festival itself. The felt reality is also a dream, an ideal, for it consists of those experienced values that at the deepest level guide members of the community, and in terms of which they understand and, on occasion, even criticize each other and themselves.

Shame and death in ritual. This phenomenon of criticism, and especially of self-criticism, is an essential part of ritual. It is part of the "recentering" that has already been mentioned, a self-transformation that is necessary if there is to be any hope of escaping personal fantasies and encountering authentic realities outside the self. For reality, which the self longs for as a secure grounding, at the same time must include other things and beings, which in turn must condition and limit the self. Encounters with these other presences will be chaotic and destructive, however, unless some harmonious and stable mode of interaction is discovered. In ritual, the bodily self enacts the true and enduring forms of relationships within a cosmic order that has a constructive place for the self. But this enactment must begin with an acceptance of personal limitation. So we commonly find that ritual sequences may begin with explicit declarations of personal flaw, shame, or guilt existing in the participants or in their world that it will be the task of the ritual to assuage or nullify. The "flaw" need not be narrowly moral, of course: it may only be, for example, that a youngster is growing into an adult without yet knowing or assuming adult responsibilities and roles. If this willful autonomy were to continue, or to become common, the sanctified social order would cease; therefore, initiation is necessary to rectify the disharmony introduced by the child-adult.

Rituals cluster especially around those primary realities (such as sexuality, death, strife, and failure) that force us to face our personal limits and our merely relative existence. In many Indo-European and Semitic languages the very word for "shame" felt before the opposite sex (especially in regard to their sexual organs) is the same as that for "respect" before the elderly, the rulers, the dead, and the gods; it is also the word for "ritual awe." This deeply felt "shame-awe" provides us with the proper stance and poise to accept our mere relativity and our limits, and thereby to restore harmony to our world. Beginning with a shamed sense of flaw and submission, one comes in the course of the ritual to perceive the self from the perspective of the holy. From this perspective and this transcendental center, one wills the ritual actions until the identification of wills results in making the ritual one's voluntary, autonomous, and bodily enactment of truth. Although ritual commonly begins in duty or submission, it generally ends in voluntary and even joyful affirmation. In this way, the dread and the enchantment that R. R. Marett and Rudolf Otto found to be two aspects of the experience of the sacred articulate also the actual structure of most ritual sequences, which begin in disequilibrium and end in harmony after confession, submission, purification sacrifice, or other ritual strategies.

Connected with this is what might be called the ritual barter of immortalities. In ritual, one inevitably and implicitly wills one's own death, since one takes on a merely partial identity as "man" or "woman," "elder" or "youth," the identity of an actual finite self existing within boundaries and under obligations, defined through relationships with others and destined to die. It is therefore both as a kind of palliative and as a necessary consequence of the search for reality that rituals of initiation, the New Year, and so on place such stress on immortality and mythic eternity. The consolation for accepting one's death is the awareness that through this one attains to another kind of eternity, as part of a larger cosmic reality. The seeming eternity of one's immediate desires and wishes are given up for an eternity mediated through the divine order, which certainly endures beyond all individuals and embodies the "otherness" that limits us.

There should be nothing surprising in this intimate mixture of personal need and ruthless objectivity, for ritual as such is constituted by the longing to place the self in enduring contact with absolute or source realities. This necessarily requires a relationship compounded of both self and other, of heteronomy and autonomy. (It would therefore be incorrect to identify ritual action with heteronomy, as Kant, Friedrich Schleiermacher, and others have done.) W. Brede Kristensen, the Dutch phenomenologist of religions, refers to this connection of self and other as the fundamental "compact," "agreement," or "covenant," "man's Law of life" that underlies all rituals, for in them humanity and the divine bind themselves together to sustain a unified and stable order of the universe.

Space and time in ritual. Through ritual, then, the self is inducted into the necessary forms of space and time, and these forms are disclosed as harmonious with the body. The space and time of ritual are organic experiences. Time, for example, waxes and wanes; like organisms it can grow and decay, and must be regenerated. [*See* Sacred Time.] Time has neither static eternity nor monotonous regularity but the rhythms of the body, even if it embraces the universe. Yearly festivals mark the moments in the "life" of the year, from birth through fertility to death. The rites of passage, including birth, initiation, marriage, and death, translate the patterns of time into the individual life cycle, giving the chief transitions of every life the authentic resonance of the sacred. Even the minor moments of ritual, ignored by participants, render an architecture in time in which the girders are ceremonial gestures, the rhythms of chant, the turn, and the stride.

Space, as well, is drawn into the ritual field of correspondences and boundaries and is given a shape that hospitably welcomes the body. [*See* Sacred Space.] The cosmos is revealed as a house and a temple, and, reflexively, the personal and physical house and temple are disclosed as the cosmos made immanent. The mountain is the "throne" of the gods, the heavens their "chamber"; the shaman's drum is his "horse," by which he ecstatically mounts through the "roof" of heaven. The Brahmanic altar is shaped in the form of a woman in order to tempt the gods to approach the sacrificial place. And if the center of the universe is brought symbolically into our midst, so too is the beginning of creation, which we can then ritually repeat in our central shrines. Ritual makes all of this immediately and bodily present. The universe itself may be embodied in the participants, so that the marriage of king and queen may at once simulate and stimulate the marriage of heaven and earth, and the slaying of slaves may accomplish the overthrow of chaos. The elementary sensory-motor experiences of up and down, in and out, and left and right, rudimentary though we may think them, are utilized in ritual, often in astonishingly systematic fashion, showing to what degree ritual is a meditation on the final and basic experiences of the body, an attempt to discover deeper meanings in them. Left and right symbolisms, for example, are everywhere in the world correlated through ritual equivalences and oppositions between male and female, day and night, order and disorder, the sun and moon, and other basic elements in experience. Robert Hertz, who first noted that rituals worldwide share these left and right symbolisms, suggested that they were rooted in the general human experience of skill and mastery in the right hand and relative weakness and clumsiness in the left, which then served to characterize and give order to a wide range of other experiences and perceptions (see essays in Needham, 1973). Ernst Cassirer (1955, pp. 83ff.) has shown how specific bodily organizations of experience of other sorts, especially of space, time, number, and self, are ritually integrated into cosmological enactments.

Certainly ritual definitively breaks up the homogeneity of space and establishes places in it for humanity. The body itself is a common model for the universe. Puranic descriptions of the universe develop this idea in astonishing detail, in schemes that are often reproduced in Hindu temples and iconography. The Hindu temple has a waist, trunk, and head. In Nepal, Buddhist stupas often have two eyes painted on the dome and are topped with a small parasol, just as the Buddha himself used to have. Such ritual symbolisms make such actions as moving through the temple a journey through the various heavens and lend shape to meditation as well. The yogin may practice visualizing his body as the temple-universe, finding within it all the gods and heavens. It is common even in folk religions to find ritual identification of the cardinal points with the four limbs, and the center of the world identified as an omphalos, or umbilicus, which may be located at the center of one's village or enshrined as the goal of religious pilgrimage. In every example, the religious motivation is to establish necessary links between the body and the world, to make these links "natural" in the very fabric of things, to make secure continuities that give the self access to transcendent and sacred life.

A major strategy employed by ritual to achieve this goal is simply to reenact with the participants' own bodies the primeval or constitutive acts by which the cosmos came into being. Mircea Eliade, who has devoted many studies to this almost universal trait in ritual, has called it "the myth of the eternal return." To exist truly is to remember, and even more to reenact, the foundational events; to forget is to dissolve the world in chaos. By repeating the primordial deeds of the gods, human beings become as the gods, posturing out their will and establishing their divine world. Precisely as bodily beings, and through the body, they enter eternity and "become" the transcendent others who control their lives. The personal distancing of the self from the self mentioned earlier permits this ritual ecstasy, which perhaps achieves its most extreme form in trances of possession or mystical union, when the sense of self is entirely blotted out. [*See* Ecstasy.] However, the ritual dialectic of self and other much more usually seeks to retain the full consciousness of both in reciprocal harmony. New Year's festivals, initiations, funerals, and coronations all show this passion for the abiding dynamic process, the eternal form of the universe.

When, in the Finnish epic *Kalevala,* Väinämöinen, the shaman hero, wishes to heal himself of a wound caused by an iron weapon, he ritually chants the myth of the first creation of iron and so is able to reverse and negate the impure and wrong unfolding of time (*Kalevala,* rune 9). The first act of Columbus when he set foot on the soil of the New World was to hold a religious service, praying to God and drawing this new and alien territory into the same universe of dedication that contained God, sovereign rulers, and Spain. The *terra incognita* thus became a domesticated Spanish territory.

These two instances show the prayerfulness of "magic," and the magic of prayer. Väinämöinen's chant was also prayerful, for it was grounded in submission to foundational realities and mysteries. The very need for comprehensive accuracy in the wording of the myth recital obviously signifies the necessity of complete obedience to a sacred and powerful reality that is formal in nature. Of course, faith in this chant is also faith in those divinities named in it, who made iron and who, by transmitting the chant, created it. And, for his part, Columbus followed archetypal forms in his petition to the sacred beings who made the entire world and this new land as well, and he even transformed the entire service into a kind of legal statement of territorial appropriation, so that personal prayer followed the logic of a deeper impersonal and "magical" transubstantiation of the land. Like Väinämöinen, he overcame anomaly through a cosmological recitation. Such reflections show the emptiness of distinctions between religious and magical rituals and, even more importantly, alert us to the two basic modes of the sacred, impersonal archetypal form and personal sacred presence. Archetypal form consists of cosmological structures that shape a divine order and may be renewed through ritual reenactments. [*See* Archetypes.] Sacred beings must be ritually invoked and acknowledged. As the instances of Väinämöinen and Columbus show, the two modes of the sacred often occur together in the same rite and can inspire the same sense of awe and personal submission.

The symbolic integrations of ritual. Religious ritual is evidently not a simple or infantile manifestation but is based on a kind of final summing-up of, acknowledgement of, and submission to reality. Ritual engages all levels of experience and weaves them together. It has often been noted, for example, that ritual symbolisms often center on such elementary acts as eating and sex. From this strong emphasis, in fact, Freudian psychoanalysis was able to draw evidence for its hypothesis that religion consists of sublimated or projected sexual hungers and symbols. Other theorists (in the modern period, most notably those emphasizing totemism and the Myth and Ritual school) deduced from the importance of food and eating in ritual that rituals were economic in origin and concerned with magical or proto-scientific control of the food supply. However, not only in the areas of sexuality and eating (two of the most rudimentary of bodily experiences), but also elsewhere, ritual makes use of activities that are familiar and deeply intimate, that when engaged in involve the body very strongly, or that have been repeated so often that they take on a habitual, automatic nature. The power that ritual has to make these acts conscious and, simultaneously, to bring them into relationship with central religious realities is a major part of its attraction and fascination. In effect, ritual sacramentalizes the sensory-motor sphere by lifting it into the sphere of the ultimate, while the energy of elemental awareness is reshaped and drawn into the support of the structures of clear consciousness and ultimate concerns. The secular is transformed by the sacred. [*See* Sacrament.]

The process can be observed in terms of particular ritual symbols. Each symbol is multivalent: it refers to many things, which may not be clearly present to consciousness but which exist in a kind of preconscious halo around it. Victor Turner, in a number of richly detailed studies, has emphasized a bipolar structure to this multivalency of ritual symbols: they are often drawn from sensory experience and passion (the "orectic" pole) and are made to represent social ideals (the "ideological" pole). So, as he shows, initiation rituals among the Ndembu of Zambia are structured around ideologically defined natural symbols (colors, plant species, etc.), which in the course of traumatic ordeals work deeply into the consciousness of candidates, reshaping their self-conception and view of the world and society. In the same way, Ndembu "cults of affliction" turn painfully destructive impulses and social tension, and even mental and physical illness, into affirmative communal experiences. We can elaborate this analysis further: a single symbol can draw on orectic *sensual* urges; can implicitly relate to a larger cognitive and *dispositional* structure that organizes all sensory experience into a coherent perception of the natural world; can be part of a ritual used by a participant to advance his own *ego-centered* utilitarian aims; can embody the *social* values of the actual group and perhaps even indicate the group identity; can be seen to point to wider *sociocultural and ideological* issues; and, finally, can be directed to *transcendental* spiritual beings or cosmological structures. This sixfold layering of symbolic meaning may be generally characterized as relating to the body's organic world, the social world, and the cosmological or transcendental realm. The ego's concerns connect the first and second, while ideological and broadly ecological issues connect the second and third, producing five levels of general symbolic significance that are unified in ritual enactments.

A Multidisciplinary Approach to Ritual. The various levels of symbolic reference in ritual help us to understand the applicability of many disciplines and theories to ritual. These can be seen as applying to one or another aspect or level of ritual action, although obviously this applicability also suggests that any one theory or discipline in itself cannot claim sole truth and must be supplemented and corrected by other approaches. For example, Freudian theory has helped us to see the relevance of organic processes in the development of personality, from infancy to the organization of behavior in adults. Freud was the first to show in detail just how, through sublimation, repression, projection, and other transformations, bodily symbolisms can be expanded in dreams, art, language, and ritual into entire cosmological dramas. Freud also showed how each organic symbolism organizes increasingly wider ranges of experience within it. This expansive tendency of each symbol, which we can call its imperialistic tendency to organize all experience around itself, brings it into competition with other symbols and even with conscious thought. However, as Volney Gay has recently shown, Freud's own restriction of meaningfulness to this organic level alone, and even solely to sexual complexes, and his general antipathy to religion, led him to suggest that religion and ritual are infantile and to equate the latter with regressive neurotic compulsions.

The operations by which bodily symbols are organized into coherent general dispositional structures of perception have been illuminated by the work of such psychologists as Jean Piaget, Heinz Werner and Bernard Kaplan, and C. G. Jung, each in his own way enlarging our understanding. Ernst Cassirer's philosophically sophisticated analysis of how cognition comes to organize space, time, and identity, enacting paradigms of these in ritual, may almost be taken as a philosophical phenomenology supplementing Mircea Eliade's researches and detailed demonstrations. Such studies enhance but also correct the often highly speculative approach of Jungian psychology to ritual symbolism. Of great importance is the work of structuralist anthropology, a field founded by Claude Lévi-Strauss and dedicated to the analysis of cognitive organization in cultural creations. According to this theory, rituals, myths, and other aspects of culture are structured cognitively by processes resembling binary computer operations. These mental operations lie finally outside of all meaning and simply reflect an autonomous cognitive drive toward order. Lévi-Strauss suggests in some of his works that each culture works out a tight and utterly consistent logic in its rituals and myths; elsewhere that coherence can only be found on a regional and even a global scale, particular cultures exemplifying only partial and unconscious cognitive unifications. It must be added that Lévi-Strauss (1979) finds ritual far more incoherent than myth, due largely to ritual's explicitly religious and emotive focus. However, other structural anthropologists have shown astonishingly coherent organizations of symbols in even the slightest details of ritual; action becomes a coded text or hidden language conveying information about the social and cultural universe of the performers. The actual meaning of the ritual to the actors may be considered irrelevant.

Critics of this approach have suggested that ritual may not be concerned after all with the cognitive classification of things but may instead relate to others of the six levels we have distinguished in ritual symbolic reference. Fredrick Barth points out that, as the media of social interaction, relatively unsystematic and incoherent symbolic networks may be sufficient or even especially desirable. He describes a Melanesian culture in which ritual symbols have only loose chains of analogical associations, varying from individual to individual and only imperfectly worked together. Since these metaphors and symbols by their very looseness underlie at some point or another every participant's experience, they can be variously meaningful to all and serve to bring them together. More generally, a purely cognitive approach ignores the possibility that ritual may be concerned above all with the cultivation of a basic stance on life, involving the recentering that I have earlier discussed. As Gilbert Lewis has suggested, rituals may even emphasize precisely the illogic and incoherence of symbols in an effort to capture the paradox, mystery, and transcendental reality of the sacred. Even more basically, if possible, the multivalence of symbols necessarily insures their ultimate formal incoherence, since the relational meanings often accrete to a symbol by experienced conjunction, not logic, and the "imperialism" of symbols makes each incompatible at some points with others. Particular rituals may achieve a unified meaning by making one symbolism dominant, using the rich though submerged associations of subordinate symbols simply to contribute to the sense of depth and authenticity of the rite.

The value of ritual to the ego world of rational calculation and social manipulation and interaction has been emphasized by a number of theorists. Some cultures and religions make such an approach easier than others; for example, as Emily Ahern has emphasized, in Chinese religions the heavenly spirits and gods are ranked in a bureaucratic hierarchy that is a transcendental continuation of earthly Chinese society and government. Prayers, offerings, and modes of address can therefore be interpreted in an almost wholly social and manipulative mode, if one is so inclined. Much of the debate about the "rationality" of ritual among anthropologists, referred to earlier, applies to this level of ritual meaning as well. These discussions have revived the viewpoints of E. B. Tylor, James G. Frazer, and others from the end of the nineteenth and beginning of the twentieth century that ritual was in its origins a pragmatic attempt to control nature, a rational even if scientifically ill-founded activity. Such theorists as Adolf Jensen and Robin Horton go on to make a distinction between "expressive" and "instrumental," or manipulative, aspects of ritual; the former relates to faith and is authentically religious, while the latter is said to be materialistic, pragmatic, and inauthentic. But such viewpoints not only ignore the recentering process underlying even the most utilitarian ritual; they have difficulty accounting for the fact that in many religions it is precisely the pragmatic application of cult that directly expresses the faith that the springs of reality flow forth in the actualities of human existence and that reality is benevolently concerned with human needs. There is no separation of spirit and flesh in such religions, and the aim of religion is to sanctify life. Still, in the multileveled significance of ritual symbolisms, rational ego-oriented calculations have a role.

So do social and political calculations, conscious or otherwise, for these act as a necessary check on a population of competing egos and permit a community to exist. The recentering that ritual forces on the ego, as in initiations, provides an intersubjective, social confirmation of reality necessary even for the individual ego, if it is to participate in a world it cannot wholly control. Inner structures of awareness are thus shared with others, and a community is created that has legitimacy to the degree that it is anchored in transcendental cosmological realities. Thus we find that in all religions ritual has enormous social value. Society can enhance itself by fusing transcendental symbolisms with its own norms, and ritual can be quite functional in overcoming tensions and divisions in the community (in this way sublimating violence).

This was quite powerfully brought out by the French sociologist Émile Durkheim in *The Elementary Forms of the Religious Life* (1912). Societies image themselves in their ritual symbols, he maintained; the "sacred" is the essential social idea. Religion is not for Durkheim (as it was for Otto) about abnormal personal states, but about normal social and natural life: the rainfall, the crops, good hunting, good health, children, and social continuity. Even relationships to particular spiritual beings are cast in terms of this deeper, more normative, structural and cosmological orientation. In effect, Durkheim brought to the attention of researchers a mode of the sacred they had ignored until then, the structural and cosmological mode. But he saw it chiefly in terms of social groupings and values; even individual spiritual beings symbolized the group or its relations with other groups. The community is re-created at times of initiation and festival.

Such ideas were developed into "functionalist" anthropology in the Anglo-Saxon countries under the leadership of A. R. Radcliffe-Brown and Bronislaw Malinowski. The organic interconnections between social values and rituals were demonstrated by this approach in many striking studies. Taboos, for example, do not so much arise from individual fears or longings as they do from the social purpose of identifying to participants the proper sentiments to feel in particular situations. Groups are identified by the rites they practice, roles within the group are differentiated (a special necessity in small-scale societies, in which roles overlap and daily interaction may be filled with personal antipathies and preferences), and tensions resolved by the community feeling engendered by the rites. The functionalists taught their contemporaries that even the most bizarre or apparently harmful practices (e.g., witchcraft and sorcery, painful initiatory ordeals, ritual head-hunting) might be socially constructive. But the genuinely needed tolerance that characterizes their work has recently been criticized as static, ahistorical, *a priori,* and Panglossian.

That ritual symbolisms may correspond to a society's economic and political forces and relate to historical changes in these forces as well has been a theme of recent Marxist anthropology. Whereas functionalists tended to limit their concern to the ideological structures elaborated by particular societies and often more or less consciously recognized by participants, Marxist analysis locates itself at a more comparative and materialistic level: the more extreme theorists, for example, argue in the vein of Enlightenment critics of religion that ritual consists of systematic falsehoods designed by ruling circles to justify their exploitation of the underprivileged (e.g., see Bloch, 1977). In any case, ritual is about political power or economic forces.

Recent studies have extended our insight into the integrative power of ritual to include a culture's relationship to its larger natural environment. One of the most striking demonstrations of this ecological function of ritual, in which ritual acts as a central control on a wide range of forces, is Roy A. Rappaport's description of the pig festival of the Tsembaga of Papua New Guinea (Rappaport, in Lessa and Vogt, 1979). Warfare, human fertility rates, land-occupation densities, protein supply during crises, wild pig marauders, and many other factors are kept in balance by this festival, truly bringing the Tsembaga into harmony with the ecological forces affecting their lives and even their survival. Once again, and from an unexpected perspective, we find a multiform unity between self and other, expressive and instrumental elements in ritual.

The Types of Ritual. Two basic approaches to the classification of ritual may be found in the literature on the subject, which we may call the functional-enumerative and the structural-analytical. The first has the attraction of seeming inductive, empirically firm, and precise: one simply notes down each kind of ritual behavior as one finds it, defining it by its function or explicit use. The result is usually a long and imposing list. Each item on the list is a special case to be explained separately. It is usually not noticed that rituals of different levels of generality are mixed together. For example, Crawford Howell Toy, in his *Introduction to the History of Religion* (1913), in an admittedly "not exhaustive list," presents the principal forms of early ceremonies as follows: emotional and dramatic (religious dances and plays, processions, circumambulations); decorative and curative; economic (hunting and farming rites, dietary rules, rainmaking); apotropaic (averting or expelling evil spirits or influences); puberty and initiation; marriage, birth, burial, purification and consecration; and periodic and seasonal. In a separate chapter he considers "totemism" (a supposed cult belonging to a specific cultural-historical epoch) and taboo (a universal ritual type), and in a third chapter "magic" (a general way of using rites) and divination (a specific kind of ritual). Toy's approach is often informative, but haphazard.

More systematic is the functional classification offered by Anthony F. C. Wallace (1966). He distinguishes between technological rituals aimed at the control of nonhuman nature (divination, "intensification" rites to increase food supply, protective rites to avert misfortune); therapy and antitherapy rituals affecting humans (curing rites and rites with injurious ends, like witchcraft and sorcery); ideology rituals directed to the control of social groups and values (passage rites of the life cycle and territorial movement, "social intensification" rites to renew group solidarity, like Sunday services, arbitrary ceremonial obligations, like taboos, and rebellion rites, which allow catharsis); salvation rituals enabling individuals to cope with personal difficulties (possession rites, shamanic rites, mystic rites, and expiation rites); and, finally, revitalization rituals designed to cure societal difficulties and identity crises, such as millenarian movements.

This classification system is clearly much more useful. However, its functional precision is not entirely adequate, since a single ritual may in actual performance belong to several or even all of these classes: for instance, Easter in a medieval Polish village was a technological ritual (as a spring festival and as a protective rite); offered therapy to ill believers and antitherapy to nonparticipants, like Jews; was an ideology ritual that renewed group solidarity and included arbitrary ceremonial obligations; and was a salvation and, on occasion, even a revitalization ritual.

Such overlap is almost impossible to avoid in classifications of ritual, due to the integrative thrust and multileveled nature of ritual. The main criterion in distinguishing rituals should perhaps be the overall intention or emphasis of the performers: thus we can say that Easter has in a general way moved historically from a revitalization ritual to a salvation ritual in the early church, and thereafter to a technological and therapy ritual in the Middle Ages, and finally to an ideology ritual at the present time. But if that is so, the external forms of the ritual do not necessarily help us to classify it, nor do they always correspond to a specific function. To put the matter a little differently, function is at base a structural matter and depends on context.

We may supplement Wallace's classification, then, with a structural one. Two of the founding classics of the modern study of religion suggest a starting point. Émile Durkheim, in his study of religion mentioned above, divided all rites into positive and negative kinds. By negative rituals he meant taboos, whose purpose, he said, was to separate the sacred from the profane, preserving the transcendence of the former and the everyday normality of the latter. Positive rituals chiefly included sacrificial rites, in the course of which the sacred and profane realms were brought together and the ordinary life of performers was infused with the ideal and the normative. The cultic life of religion moves continually between these two phases, maintaining and regenerating the stable universal order.

Sigmund Freud also distinguished similar basic types of ritual in his *Totem and Taboo* (1913). By "totem" Freud referred to the totemic sacrifice that, according to him, reenacted the primordial parricide.

Generalizing from these two classics, we may say that all rituals may be divided into those whose purpose is to maintain distinctions within a divine order and those whose purpose is to bridge divisions and effect transformations, renewing that order when it is threatened by internal or external change. These two traits, of structure maintenance and transformation, must exist in any system if it is to endure in a stable fashion, integrating change into itself without altering its basic form. Although both Durkheim and Freud saw structure maintenance in a negative light and in terms of taboos, it is evident that positive injunctions are also important and, indeed, that negative prohibitions often have a very positive intention. I shall therefore call rituals of this kind "confirmatory rituals," for in them the basic boundaries and internal spaces of the divine order are confirmed without change, while rituals that bridge divisions and regenerate the structure I shall call "transformatory rituals."

Confirmatory rituals. Both confirmatory and transformatory rituals act by centering the will in transcendental sources, that is, they anchor the immediate order in a realm that transcends it. As we shall see, these orders may nest hierarchically within each other: reverence to clan ancestors helps to establish the clan within the cosmos, but larger human groupings may need to center themselves in more inclusive realities. This suggests that the order that is being affirmed is to a certain degree situational and relative, and that it therefore may contain a certain amount of overlap, incoherence, and contradiction. These are existential realities, not logical postulates, as we have seen, although certain religions do indeed work out their inner structures with remarkable clarity.

Confirmatory rituals do not include only taboos, although this is the category that has been most thoroughly discussed. Positive injunctions are merely the other side of taboos, so that in some cases stress on one or the other aspect is merely a matter of temperament. Greetings of a religious nature, blessings, prayers of affirmation, and rituals of meditation that stress the sustained perception of transcendental meanings present in ordinary experience are further instances of confirmatory rituals. For example, observant Jews have traditionally been accustomed to recite blessings focused on God on every occasion of everyday life, from the time of rising in the morning to going to bed at night, on meeting strangers, friends, wise persons or individuals remarkable in any way, witnessing or hearing of strange occurrences, encountering good news or bad, seeing a beautiful tree or tasting a new fruit, and so forth. As religious Jews come to see all of life as an opportunity to dwell in God's presence, so do Buddhist monks discover the void within all events, analyzing every perception, thought, and event in terms of yogic categories and *śūnyatā*. Such practices ritualize consciousness, and are especially important for mystical groups of almost all world religions.

Such practices express a more general attribute of ritual: it acts as a frame to awareness. Recognizing within the fluid continuum of ordinary occurrences a specific way of directing one's behavior immediately removes one from a complete immersion in mere activity. It creates self-conscious choice of behavior, so that one chooses this way, not that; actions referring to a larger meaning or presence, not actions merely referring to self. As George Albert Coe remarked in *The Psychology of Religion* (Chicago, 1917), prayer "is a way of getting one's self together, of mobilizing and concentrating one's dispersed capacities, of begetting the confidence that tends toward victory over difficulties. It produces in a distracted mind the repose that is power. It freshens a mind deadened by routine. It reveals new truth, because the mind is made more elastic and more capable of sustained attention" (pp. 312–313). This power of confirmatory rituals is shared with transformatory rituals. However, confirmatory rituals tend to be more abbreviated, because their aim is to direct the performer into the world in a certain way and not simply to transform the performer. If such rites were drawn out and emphasized in themselves, they would have a contrary effect: the symbolic references within the rituals themselves would become the subject of concentration, replacing the focus on the ordinary field of activity. The internal nesting of symbols would displace banal realities, isolate the performers, and reveal a world of transcendental truths outside of common experience. This is what transformatory rituals do. Thus such rituals as taboo and sacrifice are closely related to each other, varying modes of the experience of liminality.

The framing power of ritual acts to shape consciousness itself and in confirmatory rituals sustains that modified consciousness as an enduring thing, producing the specific kind of self-consciousness and worldview aimed at by the particular religion. This power of ritual over consciousness creates cultural realities and so even from an empirical viewpoint actually produces changes in the environment. Godfrey Lienhardt (1961) has shown how such processes operate in detail among the Dinka of the southern Sudan: when a tardy herdsman, hurrying home before the sun falls, stops to tie a knot in a tuft of grass, he not only concentrates his mind but he actually modifies his reality, and this action as a whole has objective results. No Dinka supposes that commonsense efforts are actually replaced by such acts; such efforts are still needed, but a "slant" or framework of reality has been generated that facilitates activity. As Clifford Geertz has put it, ritual is both a "model of" and a "model for" reality (Geertz, in Lessa and Vogt, 1979), or, to use Martin Heidegger's term, ritual defines a "project," a way of entering into existence and bodily seizing it. Sherry Ortner (1978) has shown how key symbols operate ritually in this way among the Buddhist Sherpas of Nepal, sustaining pervasive moods or dispositional orientations to life and generating characteristic choices of behavior among the performers.

Striking advances have been made in recent years in our understanding of taboos. Decades ago it was common to regard taboos as superstitious, even infantile fear responses designed to ward off the sacred or perhaps lacking even that semirational goal. [*See* Taboo.] As recently as 1958, Jean Cazeneuve argued at length that taboos and purifications are intended to reject the sacred and to create an autonomous human sphere in which transcendence is an "impurity." With this view, Cazeneuve was building on Durkheim's important insight that taboos act to distinguish and thus to preserve both the sacred and the profane. However, more recent studies lead one to question whether there is any really profane sphere bereft of sacred quality and significance in most premodern religious systems. As Steiner showed, the profane was not to be understood as the "secular" in those systems, but simply as the common and everyday, as distinguished from the special quality of specifically transcendental things. Thus the profane could have sacred value. It is striking that the word *qadosh* ("holy") and its derivatives, such as *lehitqadesh* ("to make holy, to sanctify"), are used much more often in the Pentateuch about activities and things in this world and even the human sphere than they are about God. The first use of the root in the Bible is in regard to God making the Sabbath day holy (*Gn.* 2:3). The taboos of biblical Judaism describe ways of dwelling with God and not of keeping away from him: "You shall be holy, for I the Lord your God am holy" (*Lv.* 19:2). In effect, the taboos permit the sacred to be diffused in a controlled way through the entire world, building up a divine order rather than destroying it, as would occur if the shattering holiness of God were totally unveiled. (This important meaning of *qadosh* was entirely overlooked by Rudolf Otto in his *The Idea of the Holy*, leading to an unfortunate disregard for the cosmological and structural aspect of the sacred and a considerable distortion of the spirituality of the religions he described.)

Taboos not only surround sacred persons, places, and times, so as to preserve the intensity and specialness of these against the encroaching banality of ordinary life, but they also delineate the shifting frameworks of holiness that follow a person through life, at one time defining the sacred path for one to walk as a youth, at another time the path of the newly initiated, the married person, the elder, and so on. Different things are "sacred" to a person as he or she passes through the stages of life, and different things are "profane." Arnold van Gennep (1960) called this the "pivoting of the sacred" and concluded from it that the sacred is not an absolute quality, but a relative one. Taboos mark out these stages and confine the individual in them. For example, among the Aborigines of the northern Flinders Range in southern Australia, women and uninitiated males are not permitted to approach the areas set aside for men's initiations. These areas, I was told, were sacred and therefore taboo to women and young boys. But as novices the boys are led to those grounds, and henceforth they are allowed to go there: the taboo is lifted.

Taboos also define the enduring gradations in a continuum of sacrality. Among the Adnjamathanha people just mentioned, for example, anyone could go to the burial grounds, but certain things had to be done before entering them, and the only time that people could visit was in the late afternoon. As was mentioned, the men's sacred grounds were more taboo, with women and uninitiated men forbidden at all times; however, these grounds were divided into two parts, one near to the ordinary camp (which women could approach) and another in a remote part of the bush that was tabooed even to initiated men, except at times of special ceremonies. Taboos on food, noise, and even the things one carried differed according to which place one wished to visit. Taboos therefore can distinguish the more sacred from the less sacred. A striking account of the social impact of such taboos for Hindu society and caste was made by Edward B. Harper (1964): caste hierarchies are preserved by strict taboos governing personal relations, eating habits, marriage, and much else. These taboos are phrased in terms of purity and pollution. A brahman priest, after careful purifications, may serve the divinity in the temple, washing the divine image, changing its clothes, and offering food and flowers. The priest may thus "take the dirt" of the divinity, eating the offered food, carrying off the "dirty" clothes, and so on. Other castes are renewed by "taking the dirt" of the priest, and the process continues down to the outcastes who sweep, launder, and do other "impure" tasks for everyone. In this way the divine energy flows through the entire caste system, sustaining all of its gradations. The specific taboos thus have as their basic aim the preservation of the entire divine order, which is tacitly present at each observance. By keeping ten paces from the priest, one sustains the world.

Taboos also distinguish different species of the sacred from each other. Among the Adnjamathanha, as among most Australian Aboriginal peoples, the entire society was divided into totemic clans and divisions. Each clan had certain taboos to observe in regard to their own totem, which were not obligatory for other totems. For example, a clan would not hunt their own totem even though there was no taboo on eating it as there was among some other tribes. The entire society was symbolically divided in half, and each moiety had its own totems and its own special taboos. These taboos also controlled relationships between the two moieties, that is, they were not only directed to the natural world but structured the social world as well.

Finally, taboos act to distinguish fundamentally different modes of the sacred from each other, such as male sacrality and female sacrality, each gender having its own food prohibitions, its own tabooed activities, its special ceremonial centers tabooed to the other, and so on. The "pure" and the "impure" is another such pair of opposing modes. The "impure" often has the dangerous quality of being formless or anomalous and therefore threatening to the structures of the divine order. Death, for example, is often considered "impure" for this reason, even though it is also a form of the sacred, and so will be surrounded by taboos. What may be called positive and negative sacrality (e.g., "good" and "evil") are also distinguished by taboo. Positive liminality builds up the divine order, while negative liminality destroys it.

To summarize, confirmatory rituals such as taboos serve as framing devices that (1) bring the transcendental and ordinary realms into relationship while preserving each, (2) define and create, through the pivoting of the taboos and other rites, the transitory grades, stages, and roles of life, (3) fix the enduring gradations and divisions of social space (as in the caste system) and physical space (as in the various grounds and areas of the Adnjamathanha region), (4) distinguish the various species of the sacred from each other (as in Australian Aboriginal totemism), and (5) contrast the polar modes of the sacred (male-female, pure-impure, positive-negative).

Transformatory rituals. If confirmatory rituals sanctify the distinctions and boundaries that structure the cosmos (and therefore cluster especially around liminal points to preserve and define differences), transformatory rituals serve to bridge the various departments and divisions thus established, regenerating the cosmos in whole or in part when it is threatened by change. These rituals arise in response to anomaly, fault, disequilibrium, and decay, and they have as their aim the restoration of harmony and ideal patterns. Re-centering is their essential dynamic. They all accomplish this in basically the same way, in accordance with a sacrificial logic: (1) the disturbing element is disconnected from its surroundings, by literal spatial dislocation, if possible; (2) it is brought directly into contact with the transcendental source or master in the sacred, which dissolves it and reforms it—this is the time of flux, outside of ordinary structures; and (3) the reshaped element is relocated in the divine order. These rites often separate out from the disturbing element or situation those positive potentially integrative factors that can be reshaped into a constructive part of the divine order and the negative disintegrative factors that must be located in some peripheral and bounded part of the cosmos, where they belong.

We may further loosely distinguish between transitional rituals, which place the disturbing element in a new location in the divine order (e.g., through initiation, the child enters the adult sphere; in funerals the living person is acknowledged as fully dead, perhaps as an ancestor, etc.), and restorative rituals, which return the regenerated element to its previous place in the whole. Examples of transitional rituals include "rites of passage" (birth, initiation, marriage, mortuary rites), calendrical rites (seasonal and other regularly enacted rites, sometimes called rites of intensification), consecration rituals (founding a new village, accepting a stranger into the community, sanctifying a house, etc.), and conversionary rituals (penitential practices, rituals inducing radical personal change or ecstasy, and conversions as such). Restorative rituals include purifications, healing rites (which generally attempt to reintegrate the ailing organ or patient into a state of harmony with the body or community), divination, and crisis rites. Millenarian or revitalization movements exhibit both restorative and transitional features in different proportions in different movements, often combining themes from life cycle, calendrical, and conversionary rituals, and from all forms of restorative rituals as well. This is not surprising, since in these movements the struggle for a divine order becomes all-embracing and desperate. Depending on the emphasis, then, the rites common to these movements may be put in either the restorative or the transitional categories, as intensified forms of conversionary rites, or as vaster crisis rites.

In any case, we can only speak of general emphasis rather than sharp distinctions between the two subcategories of transformative rites. In most religions, for example, when New Year or harvest ceremonies are celebrated they both renew the annual cycle and restore the primordial form of things. Theodor H. Gaster (1961) has suggested that the seasonal rites of ancient Near Eastern religions sustained a "topocosm," the world as an organic whole. Reviving the world when it decayed, these renewals reenacted the ideal forms of the creation myths, so that their transitions were essentially restorative.

The liminal phase. Arnold van Gennep (1960), in his classic study of "rites of passage" (even the terms are his), emphasized that the crucial phase of these rites is the middle, liminal, or threshold phase, during which one is outside of ordinary life and exposed more directly to the sacred. The transcendental and transformative power of the liminal is indicated ritually in many characteristic symbolisms. Often we find "rituals of reversal," in which ordinary behavior is turned upside down: people might don the clothes of the other sex or indulge obligatorily in orgiastic or "mad" behavior (although ordinary life may be very restrained—thus the Carnival in several Mediterranean societies); the powerful may be humiliated and the weak may purge resentments. (The king of the Swazi was ritually slapped and the people acted out rebellious behavior during their harvest festivals; ordinarily modest and retiring Hindu women douse men with ochred water during the riotous Holī festival; children in the guise of monster beings threaten adults and extort sweets from them during American celebrations of Halloween). There is a certain sense of *communitas,* as Victor Turner (1969) puts it: the participants feel joined together in a unity that lies outside of ordinary social structures and that expresses the prior flux and even formlessness out of which those structures have emerged. Yet the exaggerated reversal of roles and behaviors serves to emphasize the goodness of social structures, which are returned to with a sense of refreshment after the liminal period; in the liminal rites themselves, as many anthropological studies have stressed, we may find the ideal roles of a society and the ideal patterns of the universe enacted with particular emphasis and clarity, although these patterns and roles may have become obscured by the personal interactions, forgetfulness, and above all the confusion of overlapping roles that occur in small-scale communities. However, in sectarian movements or otherworldly religions in more complex civilizations, this *communitas* and its contrast to ordinary life can be understood as access to an antithetical realm of the spirit denied to those in general society. In any case, the liminal period is "betwixt and between" and is appropriately the time for the triumph of monstrous and anomalous things, for inverted and extreme behaviors, for ecstasies, paradoxes, and the abnormal. The increased closeness to the primordial flux may be represented in masked dances, initiative rituals centering on devouring monsters, and the entry of transcendental beings and forces into the sacred area. The ritual follows the archetypal patterns laid down when these things were first done in the beginning by the ancestors and gods, or it obeys the teachings then given by the divine beings. For all is not formless and utter flux: there is a sacred form that *communitas* takes, which is that of the pristine dynamic that defines and sustains reality. Participants are unified by this common form, even if they each have different roles within its hierarchies.

The triumph of liminality is also demonstrated by distortions of ordinary sensory things. The body image is altered, for example: decorations cover the body, scarifications are made, distinctive clothes are worn, movement is severely restricted or is contorted, parts of the body are removed, or things are stuck into the flesh in painful ordeals. Distinctive treatment of the hair is a common indication of liminal status. Operations are also performed on nonhuman things (animals, plants, newly consecrated houses, sacred rocks, etc.) to indicate the dominance in them of spiritual meaning over perceptual or physical facticity. The self-sustaining integrity of merely perceptual experience is shattered, to be transformed by the authentic realities of the "ideal." The ability of the self to define reality on its own terms is thereby shaken, and it is forced to submit to the central and defining force of the transcendental other. Even the self is defined by the other, sustained by it, and required to acknowledge it. This is the essential point of sacrifice as such, the enactment of which takes so many forms in transformatory rituals.

Sacrifice. A great deal has been written about sacrifice, and often there has been an attempt to explain all forms of it in terms of one application or use of it (gifts given to a deity so as to obligate him to the giver, communion, etc.). [*See* Sacrifice.] Long lists of types of sacrifice based on their uses have been compiled. However, almost every actual instance can be shown to involve many of these functions. E. E. Evans-Pritchard (1956), in a celebrated analysis of sacrifice among the Nuer of the southern Sudan, was able to list no less than fourteen different ideas simultaneously present in those rites: communion, gift, apotropaic rite, bargain, exchange, ransom, elimination, expulsion, purification, expiation, propitiation, substitution, abnegation, and homage. He asserted, nevertheless, that the central meaning was substitution: all that is oneself already belongs to the transcendental presences and powers, which is explicitly acknowledged in the sacrifice by giving back to the divine some part of what defines the self or symbolizes it. Phenomenological studies of religion agree with this anthropological analysis or extend it further, stating that one offers back to the divine what is thus acknowledged as already belonging to it, including the entire world one uses and dwells in. All of these views confirm that sacrifice consists above all in actively re-centering the self and its entire world and renouncing personal autonomy. One is experientially and cognitively placed in a divine order, in which the merely physical or perceptual sensual connections of phenomena are broken and the transcendentally centered meaning is made to dominate.

The French sociologists Henri Hubert and Marcel Mauss showed that sacrifice served to bring into a mediated relationship a human group and the sacred powers that affected it, via manipulation of a victim who through consecration or general usage symbolically embodied or substituted for the group or some aspect of it (e.g., the scapegoat above all embodies the sins or flaws of the group, which are then expelled with him). By the conclusion of the rites, the victim might be taken up entirely into the sacred realm, or returned to the human group and shared among them. The first option, removal of the mediatory victim, desacralizes the community, expelling a surplus of perhaps baleful sacred power from the group and in any case preserving the separation of sacred and profane, while the second option, return of the now-transformed victim to the group, exemplifies the tendency to sacralize the community and establishes a mediated continuity with the divine. Luc de Heusch has called these the "conjunctive" and "disjunctive" powers of sacrifice.

However, as Kristensen (1961) has shown, the victim often symbolizes the god who receives it rather than the group that offers it. Water was sacrificed to Osiris, who was the Nile; wild animals were offered to Artemis, Mistress of the Wild; dogs were given to Hecate, for both were of the underworld. And even enemies of the divinity may be sacrificed to the god, demonstrating his power over everything. Everything is made to center on the sacred pivot of life.

J. H. M. Beattie (1980) notes that some theories of sacrifice emphasize the power and divinity of the recipient of sacrificial offerings (as in the gift theory of E. B. Tylor), while others emphasize the dynamic interchange of energies involved and even underline impersonal structures (as in the approach of James G. Frazer). Beattie classifies all sacrifices into four basic types, derived from the aim or focus of the participants: (1) sacrifice to maintain or gain close contact with spiritual beings, (2) sacrifice to separate the sacrificers from those beings, (3) sacrifice to gain access to or control of dynamic impersonal modes of liminality, and (4) sacrifice to separate such forces from the sacrificer or the person for whom the sacrifice is enacted. Such a schema can be applied only very loosely, however: impersonal and personal elements usually coexist, as, for example, in the Roman Catholic Mass, where personal prayers are part of the essential sacramental transformations that are effective regardless of personal intentions. Similarly, conjunctive and disjunctive motifs usually occur together. For example, in Hebrew sacrifice certain parts of the victim's body, including its blood, were removed and given to God before the flesh could be shared among the communicants and eaten. It would not be correct to assume from this that the blood was a form of negative liminality, to be expelled from the community in a purgative rite; quite simply, the essence of everything, in this case the blood or "life," belongs to God. Kristensen again helps us in distinguishing predominantly positive sacrificial rites of sanctification from sacrifices with the predominantly negative aim of causing a misfortune to cease.

Sacrifice is often literally present in transformatory rituals, but it need not be. It may be symbolically enacted in other ways. W. E. H. Stanner (1966) has shown in a detailed structural analysis of the initiation rites of the Murinbata Aborigines of northern Australia that the treatment of the novice precisely follows the dynamic of sacrifice—although this community, like almost all Australian Aboriginal societies, has no explicitly sacrificial rituals. Similar parallels to sacrifice have been noted in the treatment of the death and replacement of divine kings in Africa. Some religions do without literal sacrifice altogether, having sublimated the notion into the entire ritual system. Thus the rabbis consoled themselves after the fall of the Temple in 70 CE that prayer, charity, and good deeds would fully replace the sacrifices offered there; so too Protestant Christianity has generally abandoned sacrifices.

In any case, the essential dynamic of sacrifice is symbolical and spiritual. It operates within a world in which everything is a metaphor for the divine life. As a result, even religions with a great stress on sacrifice need not make use of bloody immolations (with which sacrifices seem to be associated in the common mind). The favored offerings in Hinduism are clarified butter and flowers. The Nuer are quite content to symbolize cattle with cucumbers in their sacrifices.

Cross-cultural and Historical Variations. Religions can clearly differ significantly in their reliance on ritual, the kinds of ritual preferred, and the purposes of ritual in general. The major variations are still being vigorously debated. Maurice Bloch (1977), arguing from a Marxist anthropological perspective, claims that the more institutionalized hierarchies a society has, the more ritual there is, especially of the "eternal return" type, which repeats past events. This is because rituals are highly limited codes of information that can be easily manipulated by the holders of power to falsify the sense of reality of the exploited classes; therefore ritual legitimates social inequality and must be greatest in those societies that are the most politically differentiated. However, American society, for example, is highly differentiated politically but tends to be antiritualistic and has little ritualism, whereas the Australian Aborigines devote a great deal of their time to ritual reenactments of events in the ancestral Dreaming. Max Gluckman (1965), on the other hand, has suggested that rituals are necessary in relatively undifferentiated societies to distinguish roles that tend to blur and overlap in everyday life, while in more complex societies role specialization is so advanced that ritual definitions of social structure are no longer needed. Ritual is therefore reduced to temple and priestly cult, while the rest of society is increasingly secularized. [*See* Secularization.]

A more ambitious and detailed historical schema is offered by Robert Bellah, an American sociologist (see his essay in Lessa and Vogt, 1972). He distinguishes a "primitive" stage of religion (erroneously identified with the Australian Aborigines) in which ritual is the continual reenactment of ancestral deeds, with all things supposedly so fused that no external or self-conscious perspective is possible; an "archaic" stage (found among most native cultures) in which worship, prayer, and sacrifice first appear, the result of a widening gap between humanity and divinity; a "historic" stage in which for the first time the gap between the sacred and profane is so great and society so complex that rituals stress salvation from the world rather than inclusion in it, and in which a religious elite emerges separate from the political elite to administer the otherworldly rites and specialize in or embody religious ideals; and finally, "early modern" and "modern" stages of religion (identified with Western culture) in which salvation is democratized and ritual is extended into the whole of life, made subjective, and finally dissolved in secularism (cf. Bellah's article, reprinted in Lessa and Vogt, 1972). Although instructive, such vast generalizations suggest that due caution is required.

Mary Douglas (1970) has tried to characterize the variations that can be found within religions at almost any level of complexity, without essaying sweeping historical syntheses. Cosmologies vary according to whether they tend to stress clear-cut rules and principles underlying the universe and society or the absence of such rules; they also vary in the identification of true being as located in a group or in the individual person apart from the group. These two polarities combine to produce four basic cosmologies. (1) Groups with a strong sense of rules ("grid") and of group identity tend to be highly ritualized, with fairly elaborate rites to demarcate the various sectors of the cosmology and with rich and dense symbolisms that thus define sin and sacramental salvation. These religions see the material and spiritual worlds as interfused. (2) Groups with very weak "grid" and weak sense of group identity, on the other hand, tend to have quite abstract ritual symbols, and indeed little use for ritual as such; here, what ritual exists is oriented toward personal states of ecstasy or aesthetic display. An instance might be contemporary counterculture communities. (3) Societies with weak "grid" but strong group identity tend to see salvation as obtained by belonging to the group; ritual stresses "we-them" polarities, which, because not rationalized in any coherent structure of principles or rules, tend toward strongly emotive fear of the "them" as evil persons or groups outside of any comprehensible order. Ritual is often used for self-purgation or for counter-witchcraft, and within the group ritual is used to stress ecstatic subjective states of *communitas* and to reenact the formation of the group. There may be an otherwordly, salvation-oriented type of cult, as in early Christianity. Sectarian movements are not uncommonly of this type. (4) Cultures or individuals with a strong sense of "grid" but weak on group identity characteristically produce ritual that services personal goals. In many Melanesian societies of this sort, ritual is used mainly to increase personal powers and to defeat personal enemies, to make one's own fields prosper, and so on. If the "grid" is understood in a moral sense, one may have a stoic outlook—cool, impersonal, and indifferent to society, but at the same time personally demanding. Variations of these four basic types can be found on every level of cultural complexity, and this is not a historical scheme as is Bellah's.

The use of ritual in modern cultures varies considerably. However, we can make a number of paradoxical assertions. First, antiritualism is quite strong in many circles, due to a number of factors. Ritual is oriented toward equilibrium and stability, but the modern period is a time of rapid change even in religious institutions. Ritual draws upon shared bodily experiences, which it uses to delineate a common cosmos; however, life experiences are highly varied today, and there is little agreement on the larger cosmos either. Religious institutions as such "do" very little in a scientistic, secularized world. Subjective and private experience is considered the realm of the spiritual, but it is often asserted that the sacred has never been so remote from actual human life. Yet the search for authentic realities continues, and when these are found, rituals reassert themselves. Industrialized Western societies spontaneously generate ritual and so do militantly antiritualistic Communist societies.

Much of the current debate about the impact of secularism on religion is really about the forms, intensity, and purpose of ritual in modern life. We cannot review the literature on secularism here. But it can be said that this literature has shown that the extent of ritual practice in Western and communist societies is much greater and more diverse than statistics on church attendance might suggest. Especially when we take into account the structural or cosmological focus of much religious ritual, it becomes evident that many community and national festivities are genuinely religious in nature.

W. Lloyd Warner's study of community ritual in "Yankee City," mentioned earlier, bears this out. In recent decades much has been written about "civil religion" in the United States and elsewhere. Robert Bocock, in a study of ritual in modern England (1973), has suggested that another form of ritualism in modern life can be termed "aesthetic" ritual. It is found in dance halls, art galleries, and sports stadiums, and its purpose is to orchestrate sensual and aesthetic experience of a personal nature. However, more obviously religious are ritual practices derived from new religious movements and personal cults, which offer the individual spiritual enhancement or attunement to the world: meditational practices, theosophical study groups, even many of the personal therapy groups that have assumed cultic form.

Within the Communist world, ritualism in the traditional religions has generally been condemned, yet new rituals have evolved to integrate people into the Marxist society and worldview. As Christel Lane (1981) and Christopher A. P. Binns (1979–1980) have documented, most aspects of life are now ritualized by the Soviet state. Within Communist China, where the desire to create a new world has taken, if anything, an even more intense form than in the Soviet Union, there has evolved a ritual of personal transformation and self-purgation, the "struggle sessions," whose aim is that of "revolutionary immortality" (the terms are Robert Jay Lifton's): the penitent seeks to strip away all personal willfulness or self-centered thinking and to merge his or her will with the "will of the People," which is synonymous with the inexorable, impersonal will of the universe. We see here a form of the ritual barter of immortalities no less intense than that called for by the classical Brahmanic sacrifice.

[*For discussion of specific forms of ritual, see* Worship and Cultic Life; Seasonal Ceremonies; *and* Rites of Passage.]

BIBLIOGRAPHY

References

Ahern, Emily M. *Chinese Ritual and Politics.* Cambridge, 1981.

Barth, Fredrick. *Ritual and Knowledge among the Baktaman of New Guinea.* New Haven, 1975.

Beattie, J. H. M. "On Understanding Sacrifice." In *Sacrifice,* edited by M. F. C. Bourdillon and Meyer Fortes. New York, 1980.

Binns, Christopher A. P. "The Changing Face of Power: Revolution and Accommodation in the Development of the Soviet Ceremonial System." *Man,* n.s. 14 (December 1979): 585–606; n.s. 15 (March 1980): 170–187.

Bloch, Maurice. "The Past and Present in the Present." *Man,* n.s. 12 (August 1977): 278–292.

Bocock, Robert. *Ritual in Industrial Society: A Sociological Analysis of Ritualism in Modern England.* London, 1973.

Cassirer, Ernst. *The Philosophy of Symbolic Forms*, vol. 2, *Mythical Thought*. New Haven, 1955.
Cazeneuve, Jean. *Les rites et la condition humaine*. Paris, 1958.
Douglas, Mary. *Purity and Danger*. New York, 1966.
Douglas, Mary. *Natural Symbols*. New York, 1970.
Durkheim, Émile. *The Elementary Forms of the Religious Life* (1915). New York, 1965.
Eliade, Mircea. *Cosmos and History: The Myth of the Eternal Return*. New York, 1954.
Eliade, Mircea. *The Sacred and the Profane*. New York, 1959.
Evans-Pritchard, E. E. *Nuer Religion*. Oxford, 1956.
Fernandez, James W. *Bwiti: An Ethnography of the Religious Imagination in Africa*. Princeton, N.J., 1982.
Freud, Sigmund. *Totem and Taboo*. New York, 1918.
Gaster, Theodor H. *Thespis*. New York, 1950.
Gay, Volney Patrick. *Freud on Ritual*. Missoula, Mont., 1979.
Gennep, Arnold van. *The Rites of Passage*. Chicago, 1960.
Girard, René. *Violence and the Sacred*. Baltimore, 1977.
Gluckman, Max. "Les rites de passage." In *Essays on the Ritual of Social Relations*, edited by Max Gluckman, pp. 1–52. Manchester, 1962.
Gluckman, Max. *Politics, Law and Ritual in Tribal Society*. Chicago, 1965.
Harper, Edward B. "Ritual Pollution as an Integrator of Caste and Religion." In *Religion in South Asia*, edited by Edward B. Harper. Seattle, 1964.
Horton, Robin. "A Definition of Religion, and Its Uses." *Journal of the Royal Anthropological Institute* 90 (1960): 201–226.
Horton, Robin. "African Traditional Thought and Western Science." In *Rationality*, edited by Bryan Wilson. Oxford, 1970.
Hubert, Henri, and Marcel Mauss. *Sacrifice: Its Nature and Function*. Chicago, 1964.
Jenson, Adolf E. *Myth and Cult among Primitive Peoples*. Chicago, 1963.
Kapferer, Bruce. *A Celebration of Demons*. Bloomington, Ind., 1983.
Kristensen, W. Brede. *The Meaning of Religion*. The Hague, 1960.
Lane, Christel. *The Rites of Rulers: Ritual in Industrial Society: The Soviet Case*. Cambridge, 1981.
Leach, Edmund R. "Ritual." In *International Encyclopaedia of the Social Sciences*, edited by David L. Sills, vol. 13. New York, 1968.
Leeuw, Gerardus van der. *Religion in Essence and Manifestation*. London, 1938.
Leinhardt, Godfrey. *Divinity and Experience: The Religion of the Dinka*. Oxford, 1961.
Lessa, William A., and Evon Z. Vogt, eds. *Reader in Comparative Religion*. 4 eds. to date. New York, 1958, 1965, 1972, 1979.
Lévi-Strauss, Claude. *The Savage Mind*. London, 1966.
Lévi-Strauss, Claude. *The Origin of Table Manners*. New York, 1979.
Lewis, Gilbert. *Day of Shining Red: An Essay on Understanding Ritual*. Cambridge, 1980.
Lifton, Robert Jay. *Revolutionary Immortality*. New York, 1968.
Needham, Rodney, ed. *Right and Left: Essays on Dual Symbolic Classification*. Chicago, 1973.
Ortner, Sherry. *Sherpas through Their Rituals*. Cambridge, 1978.
Otto, Rudolf. *The Idea of the Holy*. Baltimore, 1959.
Stanner, W. E. H. *On Aboriginal Religion*. Sydney, 1964.
Steiner, Franz. *Taboo*. New York, 1956.
Tambiah, Stanley J. *Buddhism and the Spirit Cults in North-east Thailand*. Cambridge, 1970.
Toy, Crawford Howell. *Introduction to the History of Religions*. Boston, 1913.
Turner, Victor. *The Forest of Symbols*. Ithaca, 1967.
Turner, Victor. *The Drums of Affliction*. London, 1968.
Turner, Victor. *The Ritual Process*. Ithaca, 1969.
Turner, Victor. *Dramas, Fields and Metaphors*. Ithaca, 1974.
Wallace, Anthony F. C. *Religion: An Anthropological View*. New York, 1966.
Warner, W. Lloyd. *The Living and the Dead; A Study of the Symbolic Life of Americans*. New Haven, 1959.
Zuesse, Evan M. "Meditation on Ritual." *Journal of the American Academy of Religion* 43 (September 1975): 517–530.
Zuesse, Evan M. *Ritual Cosmos*. Athens, Ohio, 1979.

General Works. Most good introductions to cultural anthropology have one or more chapters devoted to ritual and religion. An excellent one-hundred page overview unusual in that it draws upon both anthropological and religious studies is by W. Richard Comstock in a volume edited by him, *Religion and Man: An Introduction* (New York, 1971). The overview is separately printed as *The Study of Religion and Primitive Religions* (New York, 1972); the bibliography is very useful. The various editions of *Reader in Comparative Religion*, edited by William A. Lessa and Evon Z. Vogt (see "References" above) provide a continuously updated anthology and survey of anthropological research on ritual. The bibliographies are especially full, and one of them offers an annotated listing of the best monographs on the religions of particular native cultures. Also very useful are the three volumes edited by John Middleton anthologizing anthropological articles: *Gods and Rituals* (Garden City, N.Y., 1967), *Myth and Cosmos* (Garden City, N.Y., 1967), and finally *Magic, Witchcraft and Curing* (Garden City, N.Y., 1967).

For a historical survey of theories about religion and ritual since classical antiquity, especially strong on the nineteenth century and European schools, see Jan de Vries's *The Study of Religion: A Historical Approach* (New York, 1967). Robert Lowie's *The History of Ethnological Theory* (New York, 1937) and E. E. Evans-Pritchard's *Theories of Primitive Religion* (Oxford, 1965) are among the more penetrating anthropological accounts.

I have emphasized anthropology thus far. A good instance of how Freudian psychology can treat ritual structures in an illuminating way is Géza Róheim's *The Eternal Ones of the Dream* (New York, 1945). The work deals with central Australian Aboriginal rituals. Erik Erikson's psychoanalytic *Childhood and Society* (New York, 1950) shows the connection between ritual and games. Jean Piaget has reflected on the role and meaning of games in the psychological development of children in numerous books, such as his *Plays, Dreams, and Imitation in Childhood* (New York, 1961); many of his observations have a bearing on ritual. However, the classic study of this fascinating topic is Johann Huizinga's *Homo Ludens* (London, 1949), written not from a psychological but a humanistic perspective.

A synthetic, multidisciplinary approach to ritual, making use of the contributions of specialists in a variety of natural and social sciences within the context of a single theory of human development, is *The Spectrum of Ritual: A Bio-Genetic Structural Analysis*, edited by Eugene G. d'Aquili (New York, 1979).

The study of ritual in terms of its explicitly religious significance remains the province of scholars in the history and phenomenology of religions, for example, Mircea Eliade, Theodor H. Gaster, W. Brede Kristensen, and Gerardus van der Leeuw (see "References").

Major contributions to the general understanding of ritual are to be found in studies from within specific religious traditions, or in works devoted to their classic sources on ritual. As examples, I should mention from the Jewish tradition Gersion Appel's *A Philosophy of Mizvot* (New York, 1975) and Max Kadushin's *The Rabbinic Mind*, 2d ed. (New York, 1965); from the Catholic tradition Louis Bouyer's *Rite and Man* (Notre Dame, Ind., 1963) and Roger Grainger's *The Language of the Rite* (London, 1974); and from the Confucian tradition the classic *Li Chi* (The Book of Rites), translated by James Legge and edited by Ch'u Chai and Winberg Chai (New York, 1967)—the James Legge translation first appeared in "Sacred Books of the East," vols. 27 and 28 (London, 1885)—and the philosophic commentary by Herbert Fingarette, *Confucius: the Secular as Sacred* (New York, 1972). Reference has been made in the essay to some classic works on Hindu ritual; these are available in English translation. Arthur Berriedale Keith's *The Karma-Mīmāṃsā* (Calcutta, 1921) gives a general introduction to this school of philosophy, while Raj Bali Pandey's *Hindu Saṃskāras*, 2d ed. (Delhi, 1969), gives a good insight into the traditional understanding of personal rituals.

Ritual provides a way of dealing not only with the positive sides of the human condition but also its negative sides. A recent study has approached even the cultural phenomenon of the "feud" in terms of ritual theory: Jacob Black-Michaud's *Cohesive Force: Feud in the Mediterranean and the Middle East* (New York, 1975). One of the major ways of controlling violence is through the ritualization of it; a penetrating examination of the implications of this is René Girard's *Violence and the Sacred*, listed in the "References" above. Also see Ernest Becker's *Escape from Evil* (New York, 1975) and Eli Sagan's *Cannibalism: Human Aggression and Cultural Form* (New York, 1974), although both of these works tend to generalize overhastily—for example, recent research casts doubt on almost every European report of "savage cannibalism."

An overall bibliographic survey of study on ritual is available by Ronald L. Grimes, entitled "Sources for the Study of Ritual," *Religious Studies Review* 10 (April 1984): 134–145.

EVAN M. ZUESSE

RITUAL STUDIES began to emerge as a distinct field within the discipline of religious studies in 1977, at which time a consultation on ritual studies was called by the American Academy of Religion. By 1982 the consultation had attained official status and was named the Ritual Studies Group. Meanwhile, the *Religious Studies Review* had begun to classify reviews under the heading "Ritual Studies." Prior to that time articles on ritual would have been either listed under the rubric "Religion and the Arts," subsumed under specific traditions in the history of religions, or simply put in the category "Liturgy and Worship."

The study of ritual is not new. Theologians and anthropologists, as well as phenomenologists and historians of religion, have included it as one of their concerns. What is new about ritual studies is the deliberate attempt to consolidate a field of inquiry reaching across disciplinary boundaries and coordinating the normative interests of theology and liturgics, the descriptive ones of the history and phenomenology of religions, and the analytical ones of anthropology. As a result of this goal, the discipline of ritual studies is less a method one applies than a field one cultivates.

The contours of the field are shaped as much by scholarly history as by the goals of ritual studies. Between 1880 and 1920 the comparative study of religion and critical study of the Bible led to the creation of a discipline independent of Christian theological education. Subsequently, during the 1960s there was a rapid movement to include nonsectarian religious studies in the curricula of secular public institutions. These two developments differentiated the study of religion from religious practice and from its extension, theological education.

Though ritual studies—like religious studies in general—still show signs of their genealogy, they are not identical with liturgics, which is the study of Christian ritual from the point of view of systematic theology or church history in order to enhance worship. But the theological heritage is still evident insofar as ritologists often treat religious ritual—in contrast to, say, secular ceremony—as the classical or most fully developed form of ritual. The normative interests of ritual studies also manifest themselves in definitions of ritual that consider it to be "paradigmatic action." Ritual studies differ from liturgics by their insistence that no single religious tradition ought to be used as a standard for ritual criticism. Like literary criticism, ritual criticism may wish to recognize a rite as "classic," but this should be a comparative judgment, not a religious one; the criteria should be "actional" rather than theological. Furthermore, scholars of ritual studies insist that overt action—and not reflection on it or the social context for it—be the central consideration. As Theodore W. Jennings (1982) has noted, action itself is a way of both knowing and criticizing; it is not merely the handmaiden of theological reflection or social structure.

Ritual studies fall between liturgics and anthropology. The anthropology of ritual is not generally engaged in ritual criticism. In theory at least, anthropologists eschew making normative judgments, being ritually initiated, or appropriating the rites analyzed. Like liturgics, the study of ritual affirms the importance of attending to the scholar's own practices and responses, but like anthropology, it denies that they have a privileged position. In other words, ritual studies do not presuppose as rigid a distinction between the practice and the study of ritual as anthropologists sometimes do.

Between theological education and religious studies fall a number of bridging disciplines. Among them is one that is variously named "theology and literature," "religion and the arts," and "cultural theology." From the outset, ritual studies were influenced as much by this discipline's religio-aesthetic questions as by the more anthropologically oriented ones posed by historians and sociologists of religion. This accounts for the keen interest in linking ritual to its first cousins, drama and dance. Since theology itself has been very textually oriented, "religion and the arts" is sometimes reduced in practice to "theology and literature." Theologians and philosophers of religion have been slow to attend to nonverbal, nontextual phenomena. Ritual studies represent a movement away from the dominance of these verbally oriented conceptions of religion. Religion is also performance, not just language or text.

As soon as ritual is defined as a mode of action, the Christian theological temptation, particularly the Protestant one, might be to consider ritual a variant of ethics. Both ritual and ethics focus on action and consequently sometimes overlap. The difference, however, is that ethical action arises more from principles and maxims than from iconic images, sacred places, and concrete objects. Decision and choice mark an ethical act, whereas response, imitation, and embodiment distinguish a ritual one. A primary task—as yet unfinished—of ritual studies is theoretically to differentiate between ritual, dramatic, and ethical acts while showing the connections between these different kinds of action.

Besides this theoretical need, the study of ritual has a taxonomic one. The classifications of neither anthropologists nor liturgists suffice. Anthropologists sometimes use *ritual* as a synonym for the whole of a religion, while many liturgists use *magic* for other people's practices and *worship* for their own. Much work is needed to redefine terms in less prejudicial ways and to identify themes and processes that link one kind of ritual to another. Little thought has been given in religious studies to the relation of formal religious liturgies to ritualization behavior among animals. Even though some attention has been paid recently to "civil religion," little has been done to clarify the connections between its popular ceremonies and the elevated liturgies of synagogues, churches, and temples. Ritologists are trying to offset the theological predilection to perceive only the "high" end of ritual performance, since this bias blinds us to less differentiated interaction rituals. In doing so, they sometimes follow the lead of sociologist Erving Goffman, anthropologist Victor Turner, or ethologist Julian Huxley.

Current research on the "low," nonliturgical end of the ritual scale includes studies of rodeos, gambling, drug use, wrestling, storytelling, and gender display. An effort to link this research to more traditional liturgical scholarship might, for instance, inquire whether it is possible to distinguish what is "Jewish" from what is "masculine" or, say, "Southern" in the gestures of a male rabbi from New Orleans. Or one might try to specify the differences between gestures of ritual cleanliness in a hospital and those of ritual purity in Muslim funerary rites.

The development of ritual studies parallels that of performance studies. Though the former are housed in religion departments and the latter in drama departments, both emphasize the primacy of the human body and call attention to its capacity to enact social roles and body forth cultural meanings. Ritual and drama are manifestations of "environmental theater," to borrow Richard Schechner's term; they are attempts to construct temporary theaters of action with symbiotic relations to specially demarcated places, times, and objects. Schechner's definition (1977) of performance as "ritualized behavior conditioned/permeated by play" (p. 52) is applicable to some religious performances, particularly celebrations and perhaps even liturgies, which we usually think of as "serious" or "believed in" without giving due attention to the acting that goes on in them.

Just as important as the dramatic idea of acting, or serious play, is the psychological notion of "acting out." Psychologically defined, acting out is what happens when family members, especially adolescents, embody the unconscious contradictions of their family structures. In ritual studies, acting out might be redefined to refer to a ritual's displaying its tacit values, as opposed to its explicitly espoused values. Acting out, we could say, consists of messages unwittingly transmitted alongside those deliberately enacted. As a theoretical construct, the idea of acting out implies an observer who sees "through" or "below" the intentions of ritualists. An exemplary study that treats the acting out of youths in Western culture as a form of stylized ritual behavior is Bernice Martin's "The Sacralization of Disorder: Symbolism in Rock Music" (*Sociological Analysis* 40, 1979, pp. 87–124).

Freud's critique of ritual treated it as a collective version of the personal neurosis that he labeled "obsessive compulsion." Some psychologists of religion have turned their attention away from mysticism and religious experience to ritual and Freud's critique of it. As a result, ritologists are less prone than social anthropologists or psychologists to rule personal ritual out of order on principle. Ritologists, under the influence of psychologically oriented religionists, seriously entertain the possibility of nonpathological, private ritualizing.

Psychology of religion is still often linked to its theological counterpart, clinical pastoral education, so it has therapeutic and not just research-oriented motives. Similarly, ritual studies have in turn inherited an interest in therapeutic uses of ritual. Under the influence of both the clinic and the field (once considered the purview of therapists and anthropologists), ritual studies are developing a style of integrating participation, observation, and reflection. As clinicians and fieldworkers, religionists must maintain a balance between performing as insiders and watching as outsiders. Whereas history of religion (which typically studies ritual in Asia and Africa and more recently the Americas) has sometimes stressed scientific rigor, ritual studies have favored a more participatory style, one that fosters the interpenetration of cultural and religious horizons. Ritologists aim at explicating, rather than bracketing or denying, their involvement in the rituals they study. This is another respect in which they fall between the liturgical theologians and symbolic anthropologists. Whereas anthropologists and psychologists are likely to reduce ritual to its social covariants or its developmental consequences, theologians are more likely to elevate it to a norm or identify its meaning with what practitioners can offer as exposition of it. Ritologists attempt to mediate this split by taking the system of acts themselves as the proper context for interpreting a specific gesture or other symbol.

Two bridges between ritual studies and sociology are Robert Bellah's notion of civil religion and Erving Goffman's idea of interaction ritual. By way of the former, ritologists examine ceremonies (political, often conflictual, rites) and inquire into their interface with liturgies. Sociologist Richard Fenn (1982), for example, has studied "performative utterance," that is, the ritual efficacy of language in the court proceedings concerning Karen Ann Quinlan's right to die and in the trial of the Catonsville Nine for burning draft files. Samuel Heilman's discussion of gossip in *Synagogue Life: A Study in Symbolic Interaction* (1976) is another social scientific study that has encouraged ritual studies to attend to tacit dimensions of ritual.

That ritual studies cannot ignore the field of kinesics is obvious from the fact that ritual actions often take the form of carefully framed gestures; they are neither empty nor ordinary, but elevated. In ordinary interaction only a few gestures have such explicit, conventionalized meanings, and fewer still are pregnant with the significance of a hierophany. For the most part, ordinary gestural meaning is highly dependent on context. Although the study of ritual will probably not go as far as kinesics into the technicalities of structural linguistics, it can profit from kinesics-style film study and dance-annotation analysis, neither of which has been well explored in ritual studies, whose theory of gesture thus remains in a rudimentary stage.

On the scale of formality, interaction ritual generally falls below liturgy and ceremony. At the bottom of the scale is ritualization. Narrowly defined, this concept—central to ethology and closely associated with the name of Sir Julian Huxley—refers to the stylized aggressive and mating behavior of animals. The concept is crucial to ritual studies for two reasons: (1) people sometimes imitate such behavior in totemic rites, and (2) human aggression and gender display, like those of animals, are hedged with stylization, symbolization, and repetitiveness. An important question in ritual studies is whether human habituation is adaptive, and if so, in what environments. Human beings performing liturgies and aspiring to things divine are habitually rooted in the ecosystem and psychosomatic reality, both of which are ignored at the risk of self-destruction. Biogenetic research suggests that ritual mediates between genetic codes and ecological adaptation. If ritual in fact has survival value and is not reducible to a symptom or disease liability, there is an important link between "high" liturgical aspirations to ultimacy and the "low" biorhythms of ritualization behavior. If the findings of ethologists and biogeneticists are absorbed into ritual studies, religion can no longer be defined monothetically as, for instance, "the feeling of absolute dependence" (Schleiermacher) or "ultimate concern" (Tillich), but instead must be understood as a system of interacting processes—mythic, ritualistic, ethical, theological, and so on. In short, ritual studies can be thought of in at least three ways: as an interdisciplinary task, as a subfield of religious studies, or as a fundamental reconceptualization—in action-oriented terms—of religion itself.

[*For related discussion, see* Anthropology, Ethnology, and Religion. *Entries treating the materials studied by ritologists include* Ceremony; Drama, *article on* Performance and Ritual; Liturgy; Rites of Passage; Ritual; *and* Worship and Cultic Life. *See also the biography of Turner.*]

BIBLIOGRAPHY

Rites and Symbols of Initiation (New York, 1958) is an accessible example of Mircea Eliade's approach to the study of ritual. A good critique of Eliade, as well as an alternative definition of ritual, can be found in chapters 4, 5, 6, and 13 of Jonathan Z. Smith's *Map Is Not Territory* (Leiden, 1978) and in chapters 3, 4, and 6 of his *Imagining Religion: From Babylon to Jonestown* (Chicago, 1982). Two articles that provide reliable, basic orientation for the idea of ritual are Theodore W. Jennings's essay "On Ritual Knowledge," *Journal of Religion* 62 (April 1982): 111–127, and Roland A. Delattre's "Ritual Resourcefulness and Cultural Pluralism," *Soundings* 61 (Fall 1978): 281–301. A book-length treatment of basic issues is my *Beginnings in Ritual Studies* (Lanham, Md., 1982).

Volney Patrick Gay's *Freud on Ritual* (Missoula, Mont., 1979) is a rebuttal of the view that Freud considered ritual repressive. *Celebrations*, edited by Victor Turner (Washington, D.C., 1982), and *Ritual, Play, and Performance*, edited by Richard Schechner and Mady Schuman (New York, 1976), are useful collections of essays from a variety of disciplines. Turner's *From Ritual to Theatre: The Human Seriousness of Play* (New York, 1982) and Schechner's *Essays on Performance Theory, 1970–1976* (New York, 1977) contain the essentials for a theory capable of relating ritual to performance. Gregor Goethals's *The TV Ritual: Worship at the Video Altar* (Boston, 1981) combines an interest in visual iconography and popular culture with ritual studies.

A book that explores the relation of liturgy to other forms of ritual is George S. Worgul's *From Magic to Metaphor: A Validation of the Christian Sacraments* (New York, 1980); see also Ninian Smart's *The Concept of Worship* (New York, 1972). Roy A. Rappaport's *Ecology, Meaning, and Religion* (Richmond, Calif., 1979) helps bridge the gap between anthropology, ecology, and liturgy. *The Spectrum of Ritual: A Biogenetic Structural Analysis* (New York, 1979) by Eugene G. d'Aquili and others includes ground-breaking essays by scientists as well as theologians on the genetic foundations of ritual.

Erving Goffman's *Interaction Ritual* (Garden City, N.Y., and Chicago, 1967) and *The Presentation of Self in Everyday Life* (Garden City, N.Y., 1959) are the most accessible of his works on the ritualistic and dramatic qualities of social decorum. The crucial ethological essays on ritualization among animals and humans are those collected by Julian Huxley for *Philosophical Transactions of the Royal Society of London*, series B, 251 (1966): 247–524. Sociologist Richard K. Fenn's *Liturgies and Trials* (New York, 1982) uses speech-act theory to examine the conflicts between liturgical and legal uses of language.

RONALD L. GRIMES

RIVERS. Among the Native American Yurok people, who live along the Yurok River in northern California, orientation in the world was not provided by the four cardinal directions, but by the river itself: upstream and downstream. To these salmon fishermen, dependent upon the river for livelihood, the river alone was the primary axis of orientation.

In ancient times too, there were great civilizations whose life was so oriented toward one major river that they have come to be called river civilizations: Mesopotamia along the Tigris and Euphrates, Egypt along the Nile, the Indus Valley civilization along the Indus. In all these it is not surprising that the river itself should function as a fundamental means of world orientation and become associated with yearly inundation, fertility, and with life in its fullest sense.

Ancient Mesopotamian civilization made a distinction between Tiamat, the great mother of the salt waters of chaos and creation, and Apsu, the lord who ruled the "sweet waters" under the earth that fill the rivers and the springs. Ea was a descendent of Apsu, and Ea's offspring included Marduk, who was "born within the holy Apsu," associated with rivers, and called in one hymn the creator of the Tigris and Euphrates. Among his other creative tasks, Marduk "has opened the fountains [and] has apportioned waters in abundance" (Heidel, 1942, p. 56). Tammuz, too, is called a "son of the deep" and is the corn spirit who comes to life each year with the fertilizing waters of the rivers.

Ancient Egyptian civilization also saw fresh waters as springing from the abyss beneath the earth. There were said to be two rivers called the Nile, however, one that flowed on earth and one that flowed across the sky in heaven. This vision of the heavenly river, identified with the Milky Way, is also part of the mythology of the river Ganges in India. In ancient Egypt the Nile was so central that many of the great gods and goddesses are associated with the river in some way. The river itself is often depicted as the male god Hapi, with two full breasts, from which the northern and southern branches of the Nile spring; he holds two vases, which represent in another fashion the northern and southern Nile. The goddesses Anuket and Isis are both identified with the Nile as she inundates the land and fertilizes the fields. Khnemu (Khnum), the water deity with four rams' heads, is seen to represent the four sources of the Nile. Osiris, the dying and rising god, is also identified with the Nile as it sinks and rises again.

Although there is no systematic mythology available from the Indus Valley civilization to clarify how the inhabitants regarded the river itself, there is surely evidence in the large bathing pool of Mohenjo-Daro and in the elaborate drainage systems of both Harappa and Mohenjo-Daro that the inhabitants cared greatly for the cleansing properties of running water. Later Indian civilization, preserving this emphasis on running water and purification, has developed a full range of mythological and ritual traditions concerning sacred rivers.

During the Vedic period, sacred rivers are mentioned, often numbering seven: the five rivers of the Punjab, plus the Indus and the mysterious Sarasvatī. Later on, with the movement of the center of Aryan civilization into the Ganges Valley, the river Ganges (Skt., Gaṅgā) becomes preeminent among rivers. As a female divinity in the form of a heavenly river, Gaṅgā agreed in her mercy to flow upon the earth, falling first upon the head of Śiva, who broke the force of her cascade from heaven. It is said in the Hindu epics and Purāṇas, which tell the tale of Gaṅgā's descent and which contain descriptions of the world's mythic geography, that Gaṅgā actually split into four streams when she fell. From Mount Meru, the cosmic mountain in the form of a lotus flower at the center of the world, Gaṅgā flowed north, south, east, and west—watering the whole world with the waters of life. The southern branch became the Ganges of India. [*See also* Ganges River.]

The importance of the Ganges as the paradigmatic river—holy, cleansing, and life-giving—is further seen in its widespread duplication in other rivers. Today, India counts seven sacred rivers, often called the Seven Gaṅgās, that are thought to supply the whole of India with sacred waters. In addition to the Ganges, there are the Indus, also called Sindhu; the Sarasvatī, said to have disappeared from earth and to flow underground; the Yamunā, which flows from the Himalayas, through North India, past Kṛṣṇa's birthplace at Mathurā, and on to its confluence with the Ganges at Prayāga, the modern Allahabad; the Narmadā, which flows west across central India from its source in Amarakaṇṭaka to the Arabian Sea; the Godāvarī, which flows eastward from its sacred source above the temple of Tryambaka in Maharashtra; and the Kāverī, which flows eastward across southern India from its source at Talai Kāverī in Coorg country.

The ritual treatment of such rivers in India confirms their sanctity. The Narmadā, for instance, is circumambulated in a long pilgrimage that takes several years to complete. The confluence of rivers, like that at Prayāga where the Ganges, Yamunā, and Sarasvatī are said to meet, is an especially holy place and often becomes the site of special pilgrimage observances like the great Kumbha Melā held every twelve years. Along the banks of the Ganges, or at the source of the Narmadā or Kāverī, one may see the tall multiwicked lamps of the evening *ārati*, a ritual prayer performed for the very waters of the river itself.

River Gods and Deities. For Hindus, the Ganges is not only a sacred river but a liquid form of the divine. She is called "liquid *śakti*," or female energy, and is said to be Śakti, the female counterpart of the great lord Śiva, in the form of a river. Gaṅgā as a goddess is depicted as utterly auspicious, holding a lotus and a water pot while riding a crocodile. She is often addressed as Gaṅgā Mātā, Mother Ganges; the other seven rivers are similarly depicted as goddesses and addressed as "Mother."

Among many African peoples, rivers and streams are considered the homes of water spirits. The feminine names of rivers often signify a direct connection between flowing waters, fecundity, and the female. Some rivers are themselves seen as goddesses. The goddess Yemoja of the Yoruba, for instance, is said to have turned into the river Ogun and is symbolized by riverworn stones through which offerings are made to Yemọja. Yemọja's son was Ṣango, whose many wives were rivers. The most important among them was the faithful Ọya, who became the river Niger.

The personification of rivers and their identification with spirits was also prominent in ancient Syria, where the *baalim* had seats on the banks of streams and springs, as well as in ancient Greece, where Homer speaks of altars built upon river banks and of bulls sacrificed to the river. Native Americans have also identified rivers as spirits. In the Southwest, the Colorado River was traditionally thought of as female, and the San Juan River as male. The confluence of the two near Navajo Mountain in Utah was traditionally called the "nuptial bed," where numerous "water children" of springs, clouds, and rains were born.

Living Waters. We have noted that Hindu cosmology views the heavenly river Gaṅgā as flowing in four, or sometimes seven, streams into the four quarters of the earth. The waters of the Ganges, identified with the milk of mother cows, are truly life-giving waters, and are called "mother" as they are sipped by devout Hindus. The vision of Eden presented briefly in *Genesis* 2 also evokes a river issuing forth from the garden and splitting into four streams. Of the four, the Tigris and Euphrates are named and well known, but concerning the Pishon and the Gihon there is disagreement, although some speculation identified the Pishon with the Indus and the Gihon with the Nile. Josephus Flavius in the first century CE, Eusebius in the third century, and others after them identified the Pishon with the sacred Ganges, which by that time had become well known in the ancient world. The notion that such divine waters issue forth from Paradise is also present in the Sumerian myth of the land of Dilmun, where the living waters are associated with Tammuz. The Egyptian Nile, with its four sources, has also been identified with Osiris and Isis, both of whom are associated with the notion of the river as "living waters."

In one of the prophet Ezekiel's visions (*Ez.* 47), he sees a stream of water issuing from beneath the main door of the Temple in Jerusalem, flowing from the Holy of Holies itself. At first it is ankle-deep. Gradually it becomes a great river, deep enough to swim in. Its waters are the waters of life; even the salt waters become sweet and living waters once this sacred river flows into them. Along the banks of the river, on both sides, are trees of all kinds, bearing fresh fruit and healing leaves.

This vision is repeated in the *Revelation to John* in the New Testament (*Rv.* 22). An angel shows John the heavenly Jerusalem: there is no temple, but the Christ, the Light, the Lord alone, sits enthroned at the center. From "the throne of God and of the Lamb" flows the river of the waters of life. "Bright as crystal," it flows through the city and produces on either side the tree of life, bearing twelve kinds of fruits and yielding leaves for "the healing of the nations."

Purification and Rebirth. Living waters are purifying waters. [*See* Water.] The running water of rivers is often used ritually for purification, or where it is not available, the pouring of water may accomplish the same aim. The Hindu ritual tradition makes it clear that water used in purification must not be standing water, but flowing, living water. Lustrations with such water prepare one ritually for worship, or for eating, and remove the impurity associated with childbirth or with death. Bathing in the Gange is said to purify not only the sins of this birth but also those of many previous births.

Such use of running water, which is homologized to river water, is common elsewhere as well. Greek ritual prescribed bathing in a river or spring after an expiatory sacrifice. As recorded by Fray Bernardino de Sahagún, the Aztec prayer over a newborn child asks, "May this water purify and whiten thy heart: may it wash away all that is evil." Similar rites of baptism, in the Isis tradition as well as in the Christian tradition, use the symbolic power of living water to wash away the sins of the past. [*See* Baptism.]

Rites of healing are a form of rites of purification. The rivers of biblical Syria, Abana, and Pharpar were famous for healing. So it was with indignation that Naaman, the commander of the army of the king of Syria, received word from the prophet Elisha that he should bathe in the river Jordan seven times in order to be cleansed of his leprosy (*2 Kgs.* 5). To the present day the Jordan retains its reputation for healing, but especially so among Christians. The source of the Euphrates River was also famous for healing, and a bath there in the springtime was said to keep one free of disease all year long. The healing properties of the river Ganges are also well known, and pilgrims bring small sealed bottles of Ganges water home for medicinal use. Among the Hindus of Bali, the springs of Tampak Siring are filled with healing waters.

Rivers of Death. Crossing the river at the time of death, as part of the journey to another world, is a common part of the symbolic passage that people have seen as part of one's journey after death. In the *Epic of Gilgamesh,* the hero encounters a boatman who ferries him across the waters of death as he seeks the secret of immortality. [*See also* Boats.] The river Styx of Greek mythology is well known as the chief river of Hades, said to flow nine times around its borders. Styx is married to the Titan Pallas and according to Hesiod counts as her children Rivalry, Victory, Power, and Force. The power of the Styx is evidenced in the fact that Achilles gained his invulnerability by being dipped in the river as a baby held by his heel, the only part of his body thereafter vulnerable to mortal wounds. In addition, the most inviolable oath of the gods is sworn with a jug of water from the Styx, poured out while the oath is being uttered.

In Hindu mythology, the river Vaitaraṇī marks the boundary between the living and the dead; in the Aztec journey, the river Mictlan must be crossed on the way to the underworld; in Japan, rivers are part of certain landscapes designated as realms of the dead in both the Shintō and Buddhist traditions. The Sanzunokawa, for example, is said to divide the realms of the living and the dead. The dry riverbed of Sainokawara is said to be the destination of dead children.

The far shore of the river of life and death, or birth and death, thus becomes an important symbol for the destination of one's spiritual journey in many religious traditions. In the Buddhist tradition, *nirvāṇa* is referred to as the "far shore." In the Hindu tradition, holy places are called *tīrtha*s ("fords") because they enable one to make that crossing safely. Riverbank *tīrtha*s, such as Banaras and Prayāga, are thought to be especially good places to die. In the Christian tradition, crossing over the Jordan has come to have a similar symbolism. On the far shore is not only the promised land, but the spiritual promised land of heaven. Home is on the far shore. As the black American spiritual puts it:

> I look'd over Jordan and what did I see?
> Comin' for to carry me home.
> A band of angels comin' after me.
> Comin' for to carry me home.

BIBLIOGRAPHY

Darian, Steven G. *The Ganges in Myth and History.* Honolulu, 1978. A study of mythology, symbolism, sculpture, and history of the Ganges River.

Eck, Diana. "Gaṅgā: The Goddess in Hindu Sacred Geography." In *The Divine Consort: Rādhā and the Goddesses of India,* edited by John Stratton Hawley and Donna M. Wulff. Berkeley, 1982. A study of the mythology, ritual, and theology associated with the river Gaṅgā in the Hindu tradition.

Eliade, Mircea. *Patterns in Comparative Religion.* New York, 1958. An investigation of the nature of religion through the classification of hierophanies. See especially chapter 5, "The Waters and Water Symbolism."

Glueck, Nelson. *The River Jordan.* New York, 1968. An exploration of the geography, the archaeology, and the history of the valley of the Jordan.

Heidel, Alexander. *The Babylonian Genesis.* Chicago, 1942. A translation of the published cuneiform tablets of various Babylonian creation myths.

Hopkins, E. Washburn. "The Sacred Rivers of India." In *Studies in the History of Religions Presented to Crawford Howell Toy,* edited by D. G. Lyon and George Foot Moore, pp. 213–229. New York, 1912. An overview in short compass of India's sacred rivers.

Zahan, Dominique. *The Religion, Spirituality, and Thought of Traditional Africa.* Translated by Kate Ezra martin and Lawrence M. Martin. Chicago, 1979. See especially the chapter "The Elementary 'Cathedrals,' Worship and Sacrifice," which discusses natural manifestations of divinity in Africa, including the places associated with water.

DIANA L. ECK

ROBERTSON SMITH, WILLIAM. *See* Smith, W. Robertson.

ROHDE, ERWIN (1845–1898), German philologist. Rohde served as professor of classical philology at several universities; appointed to a chair at Kiel in 1872, he moved to Jena four years later and to Tübingen in 1878, followed by a very short stay in Leipzig in 1886, from where he went to Heidelberg.

Rohde's major study on the Greek novel, *Der griechische Roman und seine Vorläufer,* appeared in 1876. Its second edition (1900), prepared by Fritz Scholl, contains as an appendix an address given by Rohde in 1875, in which he suggests the desirability of further study of the book's tentative thesis: that the animal fables and many other tales from India and other parts of Asia originated in Greece and, much later, found their way back to the West, where speculations about their Asian origin began. A third edition of this work was published in 1914, prepared by Wilhelm Schmidt, and a fourth was released in 1961, reflecting an ongoing interest in the study.

Rohde's name, however, is associated primarily with *Psyche, Seelencult und Unsterblichkeitsglaube der Griechen* (1890–1894). In 1897 the author completed his preparations for the second edition of this work, which went through several later editions and was translated into English as *Psyche: The Cult of Souls and Belief in Immortality among the Greeks* (1925). The author stresses that the cult of the souls, discussed in part 1 of the book, is a notion clearly distinct from and to some extent in contrast with belief in immortality, to which the second part is devoted. The most succinct formulation of this distinction is found in chapter 8: "The continued life of the soul, such as was implied in and guaranteed by the cult of souls, was entirely bound up with the remembrance of the survivors upon earth, and upon the care, the cult, which they might offer to the soul of their departed ancestors." Belief in the immortality of the soul, in contrast, sees the soul as "in its essential nature like God," a notion in radical conflict with "the first principle of the Greek people," namely that of an absolute gulf between humanity and divinity (pp. 253–254).

Tracing the belief in the divinity and immortality of the soul back to its Thracian context, Rohde elaborates his thesis of the formative impact on Greek life and thought of, on the one hand, the religion of paramount gods of the Homeric poems and, on the other hand, the worship of Dionysos, a Thracian deity whose cult was "thoroughly orgiastic in nature." These two forces explain the two opposing features of the Greeks, an "extravagance of emotion combined with a fast-bound and regulated equilibrium." (p. 255). His description of "the awe-inspiring darkness of the night, the music of the Phrygian flute . . . , the vertiginous whirl of the dance," which could lead people to a state of possessedness, conveys vividly his own vision of the cult. "Hellenized and humanized," the Thracian Dionysos found his place beside the other Olympian gods, and continued to inspire, not least in the field of the arts: "the drama, that supreme achievement of Greek poetry, arose out of the choruses of the Dionysiac festival" (p. 285).

Much of Rohde's language has been adopted by later researchers. At the scholarly level, his thesis of the Dionysian origin of the Greek belief in immortality is now widely rejected, following the criticism of, among others, Martin P. Nilsson, and his interpretation of *psuchē* was largely abandoned after Walter F. Otto's study of 1923. But whatever criticisms have been raised, there is still widespread agreement that Rohde's *Psyche* is one of the most significant books in the field because of its remarkable erudition, the clarity of its methodology, and the tremendous impact it has had in circles beyond those professionally engaged in the study of the classical Greek world. The work is in its own right a "classical" expression of the belief in "the imperishable spirit of Hellas."

BIBLIOGRAPHY

In addition to works cited in the text of the article, Rohde's *Kleine Schriften*, 2 vols. (Tübingen, 1901), bears mention. Biographical resources on Rohde include Otto Crusius's *Ein biographischer Versuch* (Tübingen, 1902) and Friedrich Nietzsche's posthumously published *Friedrich Nietzsches Briefwechsel mit Erwin Rohde*, edited by Elizabeth Forster-Nietzsche and Fritz Scholl (Leipzig, 1923).

WILLEM A. BIJLEFELD

ROMAN CATHOLICISM. The first question in defining the scope of Roman Catholicism has to do with the term itself. There are Catholics who object to the adjective *Roman* because the community encompassed by the designation "Roman Catholicism" includes those who do not regard themselves as Roman. These are the so-called Uniate Catholics, the name given to former Eastern Christian or Orthodox churches that have been received under the jurisdiction of the church of Rome and retain their own ritual, practice, and canon law. They are the Melchite Catholics, the Maronites, the Ruthenians, the Copts, and the Malabars, among which there are six liturgical rites: Chaldean, Syrian, Maronite, Coptic, Armenian, and Byzantine.

There are, on the other hand, Christians who consider themselves Catholic but who do not accept the primatial authority of the bishop of Rome. This group insists that the churches in communion with the see of Rome should call themselves Roman Catholic to distinguish them from those Catholic churches (Anglican, Orthodox, Oriental, and some Protestant) not in communion with Rome. For some Protestants in this group, the Roman Catholic church did not begin as a church until the time of the Reformation. Indeed, in their eyes, Roman Catholicism is no less a denomination than Presbyterianism or Methodism, for example.

Protestantism is usually defined negatively, as the form of Western Christianity that rejects obedience to the Roman papacy. But this definition encounters the same difficulty described above. There are also non-Roman Christians who reject the papacy but who consider themselves Catholic rather than Protestant. For that reason alone it would be inadequate to define Catholicism by its adherence to papal authority.

Roman Catholicism refers both to a church (or, more accurately, a college of churches that together constitute the universal Catholic church) and to a tradition. If one understands the body of Christ as the whole collectivity of Christian churches, then the Roman Catholic church is a church within the universal church. And if one understands Christian tradition to embrace the full range and pluralism of doctrinal, liturgical, theological, canonical, and spiritual traditions, then the Roman Catholic tradition is a tradition within the one Christian tradition. For Roman Catholicism, however, the Catholic church and the Catholic tradition are normative for other Christian churches and traditions (as expressed in the Dogmatic Constitution on the Church, no. 14, issued by the Second Vatican Council).

As a church, Roman Catholicism exists at both the local level and the universal level. In the canon law of the Roman Catholic church, the term "local church" (more often rendered as "particular church") applies primarily to a diocese and secondarily to a parish. The term "local church" has a wider meaning in Catholic theology than in canon law. It may apply to provinces (regional clusters of dioceses within a country) and to national churches (all the dioceses within a country), as well as to parishes and individual dioceses. A diocese is a local church constituted by a union, or college, of other local churches known as parishes. Each diocese is presided over by a bishop, and each parish by a pastor. The universal Roman Catholic church, on the other hand, is constituted by a union, or college, of all the local Catholic churches throughout the world. There are more than one-half billion Catholics worldwide, by far the largest body of Christians. Apart from other important doctrinal, liturgical, theological, canonical, and spiritual links, what holds these various churches and individual members in solidarity is the bond each has with the diocese of Rome and with its bishop, the pope. [*See* Papacy *and* Church.]

As a tradition Roman Catholicism is marked by several different doctrinal and theological emphases. These are its radically positive estimation of the created order, because everything comes from the hand of God, is providentially sustained by God, and is continually transformed and elevated by God's active presence within it; its concern for history, because God acts within history and is continually revealed through it; its respect for rationality, because faith must be consonant with reason and reason itself, fallen and redeemed, is a gift of God; its stress on mediation, because God, who is at once the First Cause and totally spiritual, can have an effect on us only by working through secondary causes and material instruments, for example, the humanity of Jesus Christ, the church, the sacraments, the things of the earth, other people; and, finally, its affirmation of the communal dimension of salvation and of every religious relationship with God, because God has created us a people, because we have fallen as a people, because we have been redeemed as a people, and because we are destined for eternal glory as a people.

The very word *catholic* means "universal." What is most directly opposed to Catholicism, therefore, is not Protestantism (which, in any case, has many Catholic elements within it) but sectarianism, the movement within Christianity that holds that the church is a community of true believers, a precinct of righteousness within and over against the unredeemed world of sin, pronouncing judgment upon it and calling it to repentance but never entering into dialogue with it, much less collaboration on matters of common social, political, or religious concern. For the sectarian, dialogue and collaboration are invitations to compromise.

The contrast between Catholicism and sectarianism is nowhere more sharply defined than in their respective approaches to the so-called social question. Catholic social doctrine acknowledges the presence and power of sin in the world, but insists that grace is stronger. Catholic social doctrine underlines the doctrines of creation, providence, the incarnation, redemption, and sanctification through the Holy Spirit. Christians are called to collaborate with God in Christ, through the power of the Holy Spirit, to bring the entire fallen and redeemed world to the perfection of the kingdom of God, "a kingdom of truth and life, of holiness and grace, of justice, love and peace" (Vatican Council II, Pastoral Constitution on the Church in the Modern World, no. 39).

History. What are the origins of Roman Catholicism? What events and personalities have shaped it? How is it presently being transformed?

Peter and the Petrine ministry. If one insists that Roman Catholicism is not a denomination within Christianity but is its original expression, one faces at the outset the historical fact that the earliest community of disciples gathered in Jerusalem and therefore was Palestinian rather than Roman. Indeed, the see, or diocese, of Rome did not exist at the very beginning, nor did the Roman primacy.

If, on the other hand, one holds that the adjective *Roman* obscures rather than defines the reality of Catholicism, Catholicism does begin at the beginning, that is, with Jesus' gathering of his disciples and with his eventual commissioning, probably following the resurrection, of Peter to be the chief shepherd and foundation of the church. Therefore, it is not the Roman primacy that gives Catholicism its distinctive identity within the community of Christian churches but the Petrine primacy. [*See* Jesus *and the biography of Peter the Apostle. See also* Apostles *and* Biblical Literature, *article on* New Testament.]

Peter is listed first among the Twelve (*Mk.* 3:16–19, *Mt.* 10:1–4, *Lk.* 6:12–16) and is frequently their spokesman (*Mk.* 8:29, *Mt.* 18:21, *Lk.* 12:41, *Jn.* 6:67–69); he is the first apostolic witness of the risen Christ (*1 Cor.* 15:5, *Lk.* 24:34); he is prominent in the original Jerusalem community and is well known to many other churches (*Acts* 1:15–26, 2:14–40, 3:1–26, 4:8, 5:1–11, 5:29, 8:18–25, 9:32–43, 10:5, 12:17, *1 Pt.* 2:11, 5:13). Peter's activities after the council of Jerusalem are not reported, but there is increasing agreement that he did go to Rome and was martyred there. Whether he actually served the church of Rome as bishop cannot be known with certainty from the evidence at hand.

For the Catholic tradition, the classic primacy texts are *Matthew* 16:13–19, *Luke* 22:31–32, and *John* 21:15–19. The fact that Jesus' naming of Peter as the Rock occurs in different contexts in these three gospels does raise a question about the original setting of the incident. Did it occur before the resurrection, or was it a postresurrection event, subsequently "retrojected" into the accounts of Jesus' earthly ministry? In any case, the conferral of the power of the keys clearly suggests an imposing measure of authority, given the symbolism of the keys as instruments for opening and shutting the gates of the kingdom of heaven. On the other hand, special authority over others is not clearly attested, and indeed Peter is presented in the *Acts of the Apostles* as consulting with the other apostles and even being sent by them (8:14), and he and John act almost as a team (3:1–11, 4:1–22, 8:14).

But there seems to be a trajectory of images relating to Peter and his ministry that sets him apart within the original company of disciples and explains his ascendancy and that of his successors throughout the early history of the church. He is portrayed as the fisherman (*Lk.* 5:10, *Jn.* 21:1–14), as the shepherd of the sheep of Christ (*Jn.* 21:15–17), as an elder who addresses other elders (*1 Pt.* 5:1), as proclaimer of faith in Jesus, the Son of God (*Mt.* 16:16–17), as receiver of a special revelation (*Acts* 1:9–16), as one who can correct others for doctrinal misunderstanding (*2 Pt.* 3:15–16), and as the rock on which the church is to be built (*Mt.* 16:18).

The question to be posed on the basis of recent investigations of the New Testament is therefore whether the subsequent, postbiblical development of the Petrine office is consistent with the thrust of the New Testament. The Catholic church says "Yes." Some other Christian churches are beginning to say "Perhaps."

The biblical images concerning Peter continued in the life of the early church and were enriched by additional ones: missionary preacher, great visionary, destroyer of heretics, receiver of the new law, gatekeeper of heaven, helmsman of the ship of the church, co-teacher and co-martyr with Paul. By the latter half of the second century, the church had accommodated itself to the culture of the Greco-Roman world, particularly the organizational and administrative patterns that prevailed in areas of its missionary activity. Accordingly, the church adopted the organizational grid of the Roman empire: localities, dioceses, provinces. It also identified its own center with that of the empire, Rome. Moreover, there was attached to this city the tradition that Peter had founded the church there and that he and Paul were martyred and buried there.

In the controversy with gnosticism, defenders of orthodoxy appealed to the faith of sees (local churches) founded by the apostles, and especially to the faith of the Roman church, which was so clearly associated with Peter and Paul. During the first five centuries, the church of Rome gradually assumed preeminence among all the churches. It intervened in the life of distant churches, took sides in theological controversies, was consulted by other bishops on doctrinal and moral questions, and sent delegates to distant councils. The see of Rome came to be regarded as a kind of final court of appeal as well as a focus of unity for the worldwide communion of churches. The correlation between Peter and the bishop of Rome became fully explicit during the pontificate of Leo I (440–461), who claimed that Peter continued to speak to the whole church through the bishop of Rome.

Constantine and Constantinian Catholicism. One of the major events during this early period was the conversion of the Roman emperor Constantine I (306–337) in the year 312. Constantine subsequently pursued a vigorous campaign against pagan practices and lavished money and monuments upon the church. Roman law was modified to reflect Christian values more faithfully, and the clergy were accorded privileged status. For some, the conversion of Constantine provided the church with extraordinary opportunities for proclaiming the gospel to all nations and for bringing necessary order into the church's doctrinal and liturgical life. It also allowed the church to be less defensive about pagan culture and to learn from it and be enriched by it. For others, however, the event marked a dangerous turning point in the history of the church. For the first time, the church enjoyed a favored place in society. Christian commitment would no longer be tested by persecution, much less by death. The community of disciples was on the verge of being swallowed up by the secular, and therefore anti-Christian, values of the state and the society, which now embraced the church. Indeed, there is no word of greater opprobrium laid upon Catholic Christians by sectarian Christians than "Constantinian." [*See* Constantinianism.]

Monasticism. The first protest against Constantinianism, however, came not from sectarians but from Catholic monks. The new monastic movement had an almost immediate impact upon the church. Bishops were recruited from among those with some monastic training. For example, Athanasius (d. 373) was a disciple of Antony of Egypt (d. 355), generally regarded as the founder of monasticism. One historian has argued that the strong missionary impetus, the remarkable development of pastoral care, the effort to christianize the Roman state, and above all the theological work of the great councils of the fourth and fifth centuries would have been inconceivable without monasticism. On the other hand, when monks were appointed bishops they tended to bring with them some of their monastic mores, particularly celibacy and a certain reserve toward ordinary human experiences. As a result, there developed a separation between pastoral leaders and the laity, based not only upon the exercise of power and jurisdiction but also upon a diversity in spiritualities.

Imported into the West from the East, monasticism reached its high point in the middle of the sixth century with the founding of Monte Cassino by Benedict of Nursia (d. 547). Monks were directly involved in the missionary expansion of the church in Ireland, Scotland, Gaul, and England between the fifth and the seventh century. This missionary enterprise was so successful that, in the eighth century, English missionaries had a prominent role in evangelizing the more pagan parts of Europe.

In spite of its simple purposes of work and prayer, Western monasticism would serve as the principal carrier of Western civilization during the Middle Ages. No other movement or institution had such social or intellectual influence. With the restoration of some political stability to Europe by the middle of the eleventh century, monks tended to withdraw from temporal and ecclesiastical affairs to return to their monasteries, and a renewal of monasticism followed. The foundings of the Franciscans, Dominicans, Cistercians, and Jesuits were among the major effects of this renewal, as were the rich theological and spiritual writings that emerged from these communities by, for example, Thomas Aquinas (d. 1274) and Bonaventure (d. 1274). [*See* Monasticism, *article on* Christian Monasticism; Christian Spirituality; Religious Communities, *article on* Christian Religious Orders; Franciscans; Dominicans; Cistercians; Jesuits; *and* Missions, *article on* Christian Missions.]

Doctrinal controversies. At the heart of the Catholic faith, as at the heart of every orthodox expression of Christian faith, is Jesus Christ. In the fourth and fifth centuries there was a preoccupation with dogmatic controversies about the relationship between the one God, the creator of all things, and Jesus Christ, the Son of God and redeemer of humankind, and then about the relationship of the Holy Spirit to both. Arianism (Christ was only a creature, greater than humans but less than God) was opposed by the Council of Nicaea (325); Apollinarianism (Christ had no human soul), by the First Council of Constantinople (381); Nestorianism (the man Jesus was separate from the divine Word, or Logos; the two were not united in one person), by the Council of Ephesus (431); and monophysitism (Christ's human nature was completely absorbed by the one divine person), by the Council of Chalcedon (451). Jesus is at once divine and human. The divine and the human are united in one person, "without confusion or change, without division or separation" (the definition of the Council of Chalcedon). This stress on theological and doctrinal balance has been an abiding feature of the Catholic tradition.

The same balance was preserved in the great Western debate about nature and grace. Pelagianism had argued that salvation is achieved through human effort alone. Augustine of Hippo (d. 430) insisted on the priority of grace, without prejudice to human responsibility. Indeed, the church would later condemn quietism, Pelagianism's opposite, in the constitution *Caelestis pastor* of Innocent XI (d. 1689). Moral effort *is* essential to the spiritual life, although such effort is always prompted and sustained by grace. Grace, in turn, builds on nature, as the Scholastics would put it. [*See* Heresy, *article on* Christian Concepts; *separate entries on particular heresies; and* Councils, *article on* Christian Councils. *For discussion of Christology, see* Jesus.]

Structure and law. By the beginning of the fifth century, German tribes began migrating through Europe without effective control. This movement has been called, somewhat inaccurately, the barbarian invasions. It was to last some six hundred years and was to change the institutional character of Catholicism from a largely Greco-Roman religion to a broader European religion. The strongly militaristic and feudal character of Germanic culture influenced Catholic devotion, spirituality, and organizational structure. Christ was portrayed as the most powerful of kings. The place of worship was described as God's fortress. Monks were perceived as warriors of Christ. The profession of faith was understood as an oath of fidelity to a kind of feudal lord. Church office became more political than pastoral. Eventually a dispute arose about the appointment of such officers. Should they be appointed by the church or by the state? This led to the so-called investiture struggle, which was resolved in favor of the church through the leadership of Gregory VII (d. 1085).

When, at the beginning of the eighth century, the Eastern emperor proved incapable of aiding the papacy against the Lombards in northern Italy, the pope turned for help to the Franks. This new alliance led eventually to the creation of the Holy Roman Empire, climaxed in 800 with the crowning of Charlemagne (d. 814). The line between church and state, already blurred by Constantine's Edict of Milan some five hundred years earlier, was now practically erased. When the Carolingian empire collapsed, however, the papacy was left at the mercy of an essentially corrupt Roman nobility. The tenth and part of the eleventh centuries were its dark ages. Only with the reform of Gregory VII was the papacy's luster restored. Gregory attacked three major abuses: simony (the selling of spiritual goods), the alienation of church property (allowing it to pass from ecclesiastical hands to private hands), and lay investiture (granting the power of church appointment to secular authorities). Papal prestige was even more firmly enhanced during the pontificate of Innocent III (1198–1216), who fully exploited the Gregorian teaching that the pope has supreme, even absolute, power over the whole church.

Canon law was codified to support the new network of papal authority. The church became increasingly legalistic in its theology, moral life, and administration of the sacraments, especially marriage, which was regarded more as a contract than as a covenant based on mutual love. [*See* Scholasticism.] By the middle of the thirteenth century the classical papal-hierarchical concept of the church had been securely established. Newly elected popes were crowned like emperors, a practice observed for centuries until suddenly discontinued by John Paul I (d. 1978). Emphasis on the juridical aspects of the church did not subside until the Second Vatican Council (1962–1965), which declared that the church is first and foremost the people of God and a mystery (i.e., a reality imbued with the hidden presence of God) before it is a hierarchical institution. Indeed, that principle must be kept firmly in mind, lest this historical overview be read only from the top down. The story of the Catholic church always remains the story of Catholic people.

Divisions in the church. Through a series of unfortunate and complicated political and diplomatic maneuvers, the historical bond between the church of Rome and the church of Constantinople came apart. In 1054 the patriarch of Constantinople, Michael Cerularios (d. 1058), was excommunicated by papal legates, but it was the Fourth Crusade (1202–1204) and the sack of Constantinople by Western knights that dealt the crucial blow to East-West unity. [*See* Schism, *article on* Christian Schism.]

By the beginning of the fourteenth century, other events had introduced a period of further disintegration, reaching a climax in the Protestant Reformation of the sixteenth century. First, there was the confrontation between Boniface VIII (d. 1303) and Philip the Fair (d. 1314) over the latter's power to tax the church. The pope issued two bulls asserting his own final authority: *Clericis laicos* (1296) and *Unam sanctam* (1302), the latter having been described as the most theocratic doctrine ever formulated. But Philip arrested Boniface, and the pope died a prisoner.

Then there was the proliferation of financial abuses during the subsequent "Babylonian Captivity" of the papacy at Avignon, France (1309–1378). There followed a rise in nationalism and anticlericalism in reaction to papal taxes. Theological challenges mounted against the recent canonical justifications of papal power, especially in the advocacy by Marsilius of Padua (d. 1343) of a conciliar rather than a monarchical concept of the church. The Western schism of 1378–1417—not to be confused with the East-West schism involving Rome and Constantinople—saw at one point three different claimants to the papal throne. Finally, the Council of Constance (1414) turned to the principle of conciliarism (i.e., a general council of the church, not the pope, is the highest ecclesiastical authority) and brought the schism to an end. The three claimants were set aside (one was deposed, a second resigned, and a third eventually died), and Martin V (d. 1431) was elected on Saint Martin's Day, 11 November 1417.

There were, of course, more immediate causes of the Reformation: the corruption of the Renaissance papacy of the fifteenth century; the divorce of piety from theology, and of theology from its biblical and patristic roots; the debilitating effects of the Western schism; the rise of the national state; the too-close connection between Western Catholicism and Western civilization; and the vision, experiences, and personalities of Luther (d. 1546), Zwingli (d. 1531), and Calvin (d. 1564).

The Reformation itself took different forms: on the right, it retained essential Catholic doctrine but changed certain canonical and structural forms (Lutheranism and Anglicanism); on the left, it repudiated much Catholic doctrine and sacramental life (Zwinglianism and the Anabaptist movement); nearer to the center, it modified both Catholic doctrine and practice but retained much of the old (Calvinism). [*See* Reformation.]

The Council of Trent and post-Tridentine Catholicism. The Catholic response was belated but vigorous. Known as the Counter-Reformation, it began at the Council of Trent (1545–1563) and was conducted especially under the leadership of Paul III (1534–1549). The council, which was perhaps the single most important factor in the shaping of Catholicism from the time of the Reformation until the Second Vatican Council, a period of some four centuries, articulated Catholic doctrine on nature and grace, following a middle course concerning doctrines of salvation between Pelagianism, which emphasizes human effort, and Protestantism, which emphasizes God's initiative. The council also defined the seven sacraments, created the Index of Forbidden Books, and established seminaries for the education and formation of future priests. At the heart of the Catholic Counter-Reformation was the Society of Jesus (Jesuits), the strongest single force in helping the church regain its lost initiative on the missionary, educational, and pastoral fronts. [*See* Trent, Council of, *and* Humanism.]

By and large, the post-Tridentine Catholic church continued to emphasize those doctrines, devotions, and institutions that were most vehemently attacked by the Protestants: veneration of the saints, Marian piety, eucharistic adoration, the authority of the hierarchy, and the essential role of priests in the sacramental life of the church. Other important elements received less emphasis, perhaps because they were perceived as part of the Protestant agenda: the centrality of Christ in theology and spirituality, the communal nature of the Eucharist, and the responsibility of the laity in the life and mission of the church.

With the Reformation, Catholic missionary activity was reduced in those countries where Protestant churches began to flourish, but Catholicism was carried abroad by Spain and Portugal, who ruled the seas. New gains were sought to offset losses in Europe. Dominicans, Franciscans, and the newly formed Jesuits brought the Catholic faith to India, China, Japan, Africa, and the Americas. The Congregation for the Propagation of the Faith was founded in 1622 to supervise these new missionary enterprises.

By the beginning of the seventeenth century, the Catholic church faced yet another challenge from within: Jansenism, a movement in France that drew much of its inspiration from Augustine. Augustine had always stressed the priority of grace over nature, but Jansenism seemed to take his emphasis many steps further, portraying nature as totally corrupt and promoting a theory of predestination. From such principles there emerged a form of Catholic life that was exceedingly rigorous and even puritanical. When Rome moved against Jansenism, many in the French church saw Rome's action as a threat to the independence of French Catholicism. Gallicanism thus emerged as an essentially nationalistic rather than theological movement, asserting that a general council, not the pope, has supreme authority in the church. Consequently, all papal decrees would be subject to the consent of the entire church, as represented in a general council. Gallicanism was condemned by the First Vatican Council (1869–1870), which declared that infallible teachings of the pope are irreformable, that is, not subject to the consent of any higher ecclesiastical body or authority. [*See* Gallicanism.]

The Enlightenment. One cannot easily underestimate the impact of the Enlightenment on modern Catholicism, although it influenced Protestantism sooner and much more profoundly. Characterized by a supreme confidence in the power of reason, an optimistic view of human nature, and an almost inordinate reverence for freedom, the Enlightenment exhibited a correspondingly hostile attitude toward the supernatural, the notion of revelation, and authority of every kind, except that of reason itself. The Enlightenment affected Catholicism primarily in the Catholic states of Germany, where it stimulated advances in historical and exegetical methods, improvements in the education of the clergy, the struggle against superstition, liturgical and catechetical reform, and the promotion of popular education. However, much Catholic theology before the Second Vatican Council remained largely untouched by the Enlightenment.

The French Revolution. If the Enlightenment marked the beginning of the end of unhistorical, classicist Catholic theology, the French Revolution (1789) marked the definitive end of medieval Catholicism. The feudal, hierarchical society that had been so much a part of medieval Catholicism disappeared, but the French Revolution had other effects as well. It was so extreme that it provoked counterreaction among some European intellectuals, who returned with new enthusiasm to the basic principles of Catholicism (see "Romanticism," below). The Revolution also destroyed Gallicanism by uprooting the clerical system upon which it had been based. The clergy were compelled to look to Rome and the papacy for support and direction. Finally, the French Revolution gave the Catholic church the "grace of destitution." It no longer had much to lose, and so it was free once again to pursue the mission for which it was originally founded.

Romanticism. In France and Germany the French Revolution generated an opposite phenomenon, romanticism, which extolled Catholicism as the mother of art and the guardian of patriotism. Thousands who had been alienated from the Catholic church returned. With the notable exception of Cardinal John Henry Newman (d. 1890), theology at this time was restorative rather than progressive. What was restored, however, was not the witness and wisdom of sacred scripture and the ancient Christian writers but the literal content of a renewed scholastic philosophy and theology. There developed in France a rigid traditionalism, characterized by integralism and fideism, which was distrustful of all rational speculation and critical thinking in theology. The practitioners of such theology looked "beyond the mountains," the Alps, to Rome for papal direction (thus, the movement's name, ultramontanism). The popes of this day, Gregory XVI (d. 1846) and Pius IX (d. 1878), set themselves stubbornly against the winds of change and modernity. Nowhere was their defiant attitude more sharply formulated than in Pius's *Syllabus of Errors* (1864), which proclaimed that the pope "cannot and should not be reconciled and come to terms with progress, liberalism, and modern civilization." [*See* Ultramontanism.]

Although Pius IX successfully persuaded the First Vatican Council to define papal primacy and papal infallibility, he lost the Papal States (September 1870) and with them his remaining political power. Not until the Lateran Treaty of 1929 (renegotiated in 1983) were the pope's temporal rights to the Vatican territory acknowledged.

Catholic social doctrine. The nineteenth century also witnessed the rapid development of industrialism, and with it a host of new social problems, not least of which was the worsening condition of workers. Marxism stepped into the gap. The workers found themselves alienated not only from the fruits of their labor but from their Catholic heritage as well. The Catholic church responded, albeit belatedly, in 1891 with Leo XIII's encyclical *Rerum novarum,* which defended the right of workers to unionize and to enjoy humane working conditions and a just wage.

Catholic social doctrine was further refined by Pius XI (d. 1939) in his *Quadragesimo anno* (1931); by Pius XII (d. 1958) in his various Christmas, Easter, and Pentecost messages; by John XXIII (d. 1963), in his *Mater et magistra* (1961) and *Pacem in terris* (1963); by the Second Vatican Council's Pastoral Constitution on the Church in the Modern World, known also as *Gaudium et spes* (1965); by Paul VI (d. 1978), in his *Populorum progressio* (1967) and *Octagesima adveniens* (1971); by the *Iustitia in mundo* (1971) of the Third International Synod of Bishops; and by John Paul II's *Redemptor hominis* (1979) and *Laborem exercens* (1981). The twin pillars of Catholic social doctrine, as articulated in these documents, are the infinite dignity of each and every human person, and the responsibilities all persons, agencies, and nations have to the common good.

Modernism. Just as the Catholic church could not ignore various social, economic, and political developments initiated in the nineteenth century, neither could it ignore corresponding intellectual developments. As these developments began to make some impact on Catholic scholars, there emerged a new ecclesiastical phenomenon known as modernism. Modernism was not a single movement but a complex of movements. It assumed many different forms, some orthodox and some unorthodox. But distinctions were rarely made, and the term *modernist* was usually employed in early-twentieth-century discussions as one of opprobrium.

Modernists were those who refused to adopt a safely conservative standpoint on all debatable matters pertaining to doctrine and theology. Modernism was condemned by Pius X (d. 1914) through the Holy Office decree *Lamentabili* (1907) and the encyclical *Pascendi* (1907). Much of pre–Vatican II twentieth-century Catholic theology was written under the shadow of modernism. Deviations from the main lines of neoscholastic theology during this period were regarded as reductively modernist. Theologians, pastors, and others were required to swear to an antimodernist oath.

Some of the positions once denounced as modernist, however, were later reflected in the teachings of Vatican II and even in certain decrees of the Curia Romana, for example, regarding the historical truth of sacred scripture and the development of dogma. The modernists had argued that dogmatic truths, as well as truths contained in sacred scripture, are not absolute and unchanging but are affected by historical conditions and circumstances. Official Catholic teaching at first condemned this view but gradually accommodated itself to it, particularly in the Congregation for the Doctrine of the Faith's *Mysterium ecclesiae* (1973), which noted that "even though the truths which the Church intends to teach through her dogmatic formulas are distinct from the changeable conceptions of a given epoch and can be expressed without them, nevertheless it can sometimes happen that these truths may be enunciated by the Sacred Magisterium in terms that bear traces of such conceptions." [*See* Modernism, *article on* Christian Modernism, *and* Vatican Councils, *article on* Vatican II.]

Between the World Wars (1918–1939). The period before Vatican II was not without its progressive movements (otherwise Vatican II itself would be inexplicable). The liturgical movement bridged the gap between altar and congregation by emphasizing the nature of worship and by stressing the Thomistic principle that sacraments are signs of grace as well as causes of grace. As signs, sacraments must be understandable, in terms of both language and ritual. The biblical movement carried forward the work of critical interpretation without provoking additional papal condemnations. But Catholic biblical scholars labored under a cloud until Pius XII issued the so-called Magna Carta of Catholic biblical scholarship, *Divino afflante Spiritu* (1943). The social action movement continued to apply the teachings of the social encyclicals, particularly in support of the labor union movement. The lay apostolate movement under Pius XI and Pius XII sought to involve larger numbers of laity in the work of the church (a movement also known as Catholic Action). The ecumenical movement had a more difficult path, given the negative tone of Pius XI's encyclical *Mortalium animos* (1927), but pioneers like Yves Congar were preparing the way for Vatican II. Meanwhile, the missionary movement, which had experienced a major revival in the nineteenth century, with as many as 8 million converts, was increasingly liberated from undue colonial and European influence. Both Pius XI and Pius XII stressed the importance of establishing native clergies and native hierarchies in mission lands.

Pope John XXIII and the Second Vatican Council. No other persons or events have had so profound an impact on modern Catholicism as John XXIII and the Second Vatican Council he convoked. When elected in 1958, John insisted that his was "a very humble office of shepherd" and that he intended to pattern his ministry after that of Joseph in the Old Testament story, who greeted the brothers who had sold him into slavery with the compassionate and forgiving words, "I am Joseph, your brother." When the new pope ceremonially took possession of the Lateran Basilica in Rome, he reminded the congregation, which included cardinals, archbishops, bishops, and assorted ecclesiastical dignitaries, that he was not a prince surrounded by the outward signs of power but "a priest, a father, a shepherd." He visited the sick in the Roman hospitals, the elderly in old-age homes, the convicts at Regina Coeli prison.

John XXIII first announced his council on 25 January 1959 and officially convoked it on 25 December 1961. In his address at the council's solemn opening on 11 October 1962, he revealed again his spirit of fundamental hope. He complained openly about some of his closest advisers, who "though burning with zeal, are not endowed with much sense of discretion or measure. In these modern times they can see nothing but prevarication and ruin." He called them "prophets of gloom, who are always forecasting disaster, as though the end of the world were at hand." He believed instead that "Divine Providence is leading us to a new order of human relations." He had not called the council to preserve doctrine. "The substance of the ancient doctrine

. . . is one thing, and the way in which it is presented is another." This was not the time for negativism. The most effective way for the church to combat error would be by "demonstrating the validity of her teaching rather than by condemnations." The purpose of the council, therefore, would be the promotion of "concord, just peace and the brotherly unity of all."

Although John XXIII died between the first two sessions of the council, his successor, Paul VI, carried his program to fulfillment:

1. Vatican II taught that the church is the people of God, a community of disciples. The hierarchy is part of the people of God, not separate from it. Authority is for service, not for domination. Bishops are not merely the delegates of the pope, and laity are not merely instruments of their bishops. (See the Dogmatic Constitution on the Church.)
2. The church must read the signs of the times and interpret them in the light of the gospel. The church is part of the world, and its mission is to serve the whole human family in order to make the history of the human race more human. (See the Pastoral Constitution on the Church in the Modern World.)
3. Christian unity requires renewal and reform. Both sides were to blame for the divisions of the Reformation; therefore both sides have to be open to change. The body of Christ embraces more than Catholics (Roman or otherwise). (See the Decree on Ecumenism.)
4. The word of God is communicated through sacred scripture, sacred tradition, and the teaching authority of the church, all linked together and guided by the Holy Spirit. The sacred realities are always open in principle to a growth in understanding. (See the Dogmatic Constitution on Divine Revelation.)
5. The church proclaims the gospel not only in word but also in sacrament. Since the whole people of God must actively participate in this worship, the signs, that is, language and rituals, must be intelligible. (See the Constitution on the Sacred Liturgy.)
6. No one is to be forced in any way to embrace the Christian or the Catholic faith. This principle is rooted in human dignity and the freedom of the act of faith. (See the Declaration on Religious Freedom.)
7. God speaks also through other religions. The church should engage in dialogue and other collaborative efforts with them. The Jews have a special relationship to the church. They cannot be blamed as a people for the death of Jesus. (See the Declaration on the Relationship of the Church to Non-Christian Religions.)

After four sessions the Second Vatican Council adjourned in December 1965. The story of Catholicism since the council—through the pontificates of Paul VI (1963–1978), John Paul I (1978), and John Paul II (1978–)—has been shaped largely, if not entirely, by the church's efforts to come to terms with the various challenges and opportunities which that council presented: specifically, how can the church remain faithful to its distinctively Catholic heritage even as it continues to affirm and assimilate such modern values as ecumenism, pluralism, and secularity?

Catholic Vision and Catholic Values. Catholicism is not an isolated reality. The word *Catholic* is not only a noun but also an adjective. As an adjective, it modifies the noun *Christian.* The word *Christian,* too, is both a noun and an adjective. As an adjective, it modifies *religious.* The word *religious* also functions as an adjective and a noun. As an adjective, it modifies the word *human.* Thus the Catholic church is a community of persons (the fundamentally *human* foundation of Catholic identity) who believe in and are committed to the reality of God and who shape their lives according to that belief and in fidelity to that commitment (the *religious* component of Catholicism). The church's belief in and commitment to the reality of God is focused in its fundamental attitude toward Jesus Christ (the *Christian* core). For Catholics, as for every Christian, the old order has passed away, and they are a "new creation" in Christ, for God has "reconciled us to himself through Christ" (*2 Cor.* 5:17, 5:19). "Catholic," therefore, is a qualification of "Christian," of "religious," and of the human. To be Catholic is to be a kind of human being, a kind of religious person, and a kind of Christian.

To be Catholic is, before all else, to be human. Catholicism is an understanding and affirmation of human existence before it is a corporate conviction about the pope, or the seven sacraments, or even about Jesus Christ. But Catholicism is also more than a corporate understanding and affirmation of what it means to be human. Catholicism answers the question of meaning in terms of ultimacy. With Dietrich Bonhoeffer (d. 1945), Catholicism confirms that there is more to life than meets the eye, that there is "a beyond in our midst." With Paul Tillich (d. 1975), Catholicism affirms that there is a ground of all being which is being itself. With Thomas Aquinas, Catholicism affirms that all reality is rooted in the creative, loving power of that which is most real *(ens realissimum).* Catholicism answers the question of meaning in terms of the reality of God. In brief, Catholicism is a religious perspective, and not simply a philosophical or anthropological one.

But Catholicism is not some undifferentiated religious view. Catholicism's view of and commitment to God is radically shaped by its view of and commitment to Jesus Christ. For the Christian, the ultimate dimension of human experience is a triune God: a God who creates and sustains, a God who draws near to and identifies with the human historical condition, and a God who empowers people to live according to the vocation to which they have been called. More specifically, the God of Christians is the God of Jesus Christ.

But just as Jesus Christ gives access to God, so, for the Catholic, the church gives access to Jesus Christ. However, the church itself is composed of many churches, as noted above. The church universal is the communion of local churches, and the body of Christ is composed of denominations (for want of a better term). Thus the noun "church" is always modified: the Catholic church, the Methodist church, the Orthodox church, the Lutheran church, and so forth. Moreover, even those modifiers can themselves be modified: the Lutheran Church–Missouri Synod, the Lutheran Church of America, the American Lutheran Church, and so forth.

There are many churches, but one body of Christ. Within the community of churches, however, there is one church that alone embodies and manifests all the institutional elements necessary for the integrity of the whole body. In Catholic doctrine and theology, that one church is the Catholic church. As ecumenical as the Second Vatican Council certainly was, it did not retreat from this fundamental Catholic conviction:

> They are fully incorporated into the society of the Church who, possessing the Spirit of Christ, accept her entire system and all the means of salvation given to her, and through union with her visible structure are joined to Christ, who rules her through the Supreme Pontiff and the Bishops. This joining is effected by the bonds of professed faith, of the sacraments, of ecclesiastical government, and of communion.
> (Dogmatic Constitution on the Church, no. 14)

Since Vatican II, however, much has happened to suggest that the traditional lines of distinction have been blurred. It is more evident now that, in spite of the distinctiveness of the Catholic claims for the papal office, Catholic identity is rooted in much broader and richer theological values. Specifically, there is a configuration of characteristics within Catholicism that is not duplicated anywhere else in the community of Christian churches. This configuration of characteristics is expressed in Catholicism's systematic theology; its body of doctrines; its liturgical life, especially its Eucharist; its variety of spiritualities; its religious congregations and lay apostolates; its official teachings on justice, peace, and human rights; its exercise of collegiality; and, to be sure, its Petrine ministry.

Roman Catholicism is distinguished from other Christian traditions and churches in its understanding of, commitment to, and exercise of the principles of sacramentality, mediation, and communion. Differences between Catholic and non-Catholic (especially Protestant) approaches become clearer when measured according to these three principles.

Sacramentality. In its classical (Augustinian) meaning, a sacrament is a visible sign of an invisible grace. Paul VI provided a more contemporary definition: "a reality imbued with the hidden presence of God." A sacramental perspective is one that "sees" the divine in the human, the infinite in the finite, the spiritual in the material, the transcendent in the immanent, the eternal in the historical. Over against this sacramental vision is the view, strengthened by memories of past excesses in the sacramental vision, that God is so "totally other" that the divine reality can never be identified with the human, the transcendent with the immanent, the eternal with the historical, and so forth. The abiding Protestant fear is that Catholics take the sacramental principle to a point just short of, if not fully immersed in, idolatry.

The Catholic sacramental vision "sees" God in and through all things: other people, communities, movements, events, places, objects, the world at large, the whole cosmos. The visible, the tangible, the finite, the historical—all these are actual or potential carriers of the divine presence. Indeed, for the Catholic, it is only in and through these material realities that we can even encounter the invisible God. The great sacrament of our encounter with God, and of God's encounter with us, is Jesus Christ. The church, in turn, is the key sacrament of our encounter with Christ, and of Christ with us; and the sacraments, in turn, are the signs and instruments by which that ecclesial encounter with Christ is expressed, celebrated, and made effective for the glory of God and the salvation of men and women.

The Catholic, therefore, insists that grace (the divine presence) actually enters into and transforms nature (human life in its fullest context). The dichotomy between nature and grace is eliminated. Human existence is already graced existence. There is no merely natural end of human existence, with a supernatural end imposed from above. Human existence in its natural, historical condition is radically oriented toward God. The history of the world is, at the same time, the history of salvation.

This means, for the Catholic, that authentic human progress and the struggle for justice, peace, freedom, human rights, and so forth, is part of the movement of and toward the kingdom of God (Vatican Council II, Pastoral Constitution on the Church in the Modern World, no. 39). The Catholic, unlike Luther, espouses no doctrine of the two kingdoms. The vast body of Catholic social doctrine, from Leo XIII in 1891 to John Paul II a century later, is as characteristic of Catholic Christianity as any element can be. In virtue of the sacramental principle, Catholics affirm that God is indeed present to all human life and to history. To be involved in the transformation of the world is to be collaboratively involved in God's own revolutionary and transforming activity.

For the Catholic, the world is essentially good, though fallen, because it comes from the creative hand of God. And for the Catholic, the world, although fallen, is redeemable because of the redemptive work of God in Jesus Christ. And for the Catholic, the world, although fractured and fragmented, is capable of ultimate unity because of the abiding presence of the Holy Spirit, who is the "first fruits" of the final kingdom of God.

Mediation. A kind of corollary of the principle of sacramentality is the principle of mediation. A sacrament not only signifies; it also causes what it signifies. Indeed, as the Council of Trent officially taught, sacraments cause grace precisely insofar as they signify it. If the church, therefore, is not a credible sign of God's and Christ's presence in the world, if the church is not obviously the "temple of the Holy Spirit," it cannot achieve its missionary purposes. It "causes" grace (i.e., effectively moves the world toward its final destiny in the kingdom of God) to the extent that it signifies the reality toward which it presumes to direct the world.

On the other hand, sacraments are not only signs of faith, as Protestants affirmed at the time of the Reformation. For the Catholic, God is not only present in the sacramental action; God actually achieves something in and through that action. Thus, created realities not only contain, reflect, or embody the presence of God, they also make that presence effective for those who avail themselves of these realities. Encounter with God does not occur solely in the inwardness of conscience or in the inner recesses of consciousness. Catholicism holds, on the contrary, that the encounter with God is a mediated experience, rooted in the historical and affirmed as real by the critical judgment that God is truly present and active here or there, in this event or that, in this person or that, in this object or that.

Again, the Protestant raises a word of caution. Just as the principle of sacramentality edges close to the brink of idolatry, so the principle of mediation moves one along the path toward magic. Just as there has been evidence of idolatry in some Roman Catholic piety, so there has been evidence of a magical view of the divine-human encounter in certain forms of Catholic devotional life. Some Catholics have assumed that if a certain practice were performed a given number of times in an unbroken sequence, their salvation would be guaranteed. A magical worldview, of course, is not a solely Catholic problem, but it is an inherent risk in Catholicism's constant stress on the principle of mediation.

Catholicism's commitment to the principle of mediation is evident, for example, in the importance it has always placed on the ordained ministry of the priest. God's dealings with us are not arbitrary or haphazard. God is present to all and works on behalf of all, but there are also moments and actions wherein God's presence is specially focused. The function of the priest, as mediator, is not to limit the encounter between God and the human person but to focus it more clearly for the sake of the person, and ultimately for the community at large. [*See* Priesthood, *article on* Christian Priesthood, *and* Ministry.]

The principle of mediation also explains Catholicism's historic emphasis on the place of Mary, the mother of Jesus Christ. The Catholic accepts the role of Mary in salvation on the same ground that the Catholic accepts the role of Jesus Christ. God is present in, and redemptively works through, the humanity of Jesus. This is the principle of mediation in its classic expression. The Catholic understands that the invisible, spiritual God is present and available to us through the visible and the material, and that these are made holy by reason of that divine presence. The Catholic, therefore, readily engages in the veneration (not worship) of Mary, not because Catholicism perceives Mary as some kind of goddess or supercreature or rival of the Lord himself, but because she is a symbol or image of God. It is the God who is present in her and who fills her whole being that the Catholic grasps in the act of venerating yet another "sacrament" of the divine. [*See* Mary.]

Communion. Finally, Catholicism affirms the principle of communion: the human way to God, and God's way to humankind, is not only a mediated but a communal way. Even when the divine-human encounter is most personal and individual, it is still communal, in that the encounter is made possible by the mediation of a community of faith. Thus there is not simply an individual personal relationship with God or Jesus Christ that is established and sustained by meditative reflection on sacred scripture, for the Bible itself is the church's book and the testimony of the church's original faith. There is no relationship with God, however intense, profound, or unique, that dispenses entirely with the communal context of every relationship with God.

And this is why, for Catholicism, the mystery of the church has always had so significant a place in its theology, doctrine, pastoral practice, moral vision, and devotion. Catholics have always emphasized the place of the church as the sacrament of Christ, which mediates salvation through sacraments, ministries, and other institutional elements and forms, and as the communion of saints and the people of God. It is here, at the point of Catholicism's understanding of itself as church, that one comes to the heart of the distinctively Catholic understanding and practice of Christian faith. For here, in Catholic ecclesiology, one finds the convergence of those three principles that have always been so characteristic of Catholicism: sacramentality, mediation, and communion.

The Protestant again raises a word of caution. If one emphasizes too much the principle of communion, do we not endanger the freedom of individuals? If sacramentality can lead to idolatry, and mediation to magic, the principle of communion can lead to a collectivism that suppresses individuality, and an authoritarianism that suppresses freedom of thought.

But stress on the individual also has its inherent weakness, just as there are inherent weaknesses in the historic Protestant insistences on the otherness of God (over against the Catholic sacramental principle) and on the immediacy of the divine-human encounter (over against the Catholic principle of mediation). Some important Protestant theologians like Paul Tillich and Langdon Gilkey have come to acknowledge these inherent problems in Protestantism and the corresponding truth of the Catholic sacramental vision. According to Gilkey, the Catholic principle of symbol or sacramentality "may provide the best entrance into a new synthesis of the Christian tradition with the vitalities as well as the relativities of contemporary existence" (Gilkey, 1975, p. 22).

Theology and Doctrine. The principles of sacramentality, mediation, and communion frame Catholic thinking and teaching about every significant theological question. The following is not an exhaustive list, and some overlapping with the above discussion is inevitable.

Revelation and faith. Catholics share with other Christians the conviction that God has somehow communicated with humankind in the history of Israel; supremely in Jesus Christ, the Son of God; then through the apostles and evangelists; and, in a different way, through nature, human events, and personal relationships. Some Roman Catholics have tended to restrict revelation to the teachings of the church, just as some Protestants have tended to limit revelation to the Bible. But fundamentally, all Christians, conservative and liberal alike, are united in the belief that Jesus Christ, as both person and event, provides the fullest disclosure of God. Christian faith is the acceptance of Jesus Christ as the Lord and Savior of the world and as the great sacrament of God's presence among us.

Roman Catholics, however, have always been insistent that such faith is reasonable, not arbitrary or blind. The First Vatican Council (1869–1870) taught that faith is "consonant with reason." Roman Catholics, therefore, exclude fideism, on the one hand, and rationalism, on the other. Faith is neither beyond intellectual support nor fully open to intellectual scrutiny. It is neither rational nor irrational. It is reasonable. That is, we can identify solid motives for believing, and we can show that one need not surrender intellectual integrity in order to be a Christian.

The most celebrated Roman Catholic exponent and practitioner of this view has been Thomas Aquinas. For centuries Thomism and Catholicism have been identified in many minds. Accordingly, some Protestants have thought that Catholics are too analytical and too rational about their faith. And some Catholics have assumed that the "truth" of Roman Catholic claims is so demonstrably clear that any open-minded person would have to accept them once he or she examined the "evidence."

While Roman Catholic apologetics has moved away from its earlier rational, almost rationalistic, orientation, it remains committed to the notion that Christian faith does have a "content," that it is, for example, more than the personal acceptance of Jesus Christ or a feeling of absolute dependence upon God.

Creation and original sin. Roman Catholics adhere to the ancient Christian creeds, which professed their belief in one God, the Almighty Creator, who made the heavens and the earth, and all things visible and invisible. [*See* Creeds, *article on* Christian Creeds.] And they adhere as well to the later councils of the church, which added that God freely created the world from nothing at the beginning of time in order to share his own goodness, to manifest his own glory, and to sanctify humankind. Jesus Christ is not only the head of the whole human race but also is himself the summit of all creation. He is the Second Adam through whom all else came into being (*Col.* 1:15). Because of their understanding of creation, Roman Catholics have always had an essentially positive attitude toward the world.

But the specific origins of men and women have posed a more thorny problem. The councils of the church (specifically Lateran IV in 1215 and Vatican I in 1869–1870) had taught that all people owe their existence to the creative action of God. Although humankind was specially favored by God in the beginning, we sinned and thereby suffered both physical and spiritual losses (Council of Trent, 1545–1563). But how exactly did this original sin occur, and who "committed" it? Present Catholic scholarship, both biblical and theological, argues that there is no necessary connection between monogenism (the theory that the whole human race sprang from one set of parents) and the integrity of Catholic doctrine. What is clearly maintained is that humankind comes from the creative hand of God. This creative action, however, could have been an evolutionary process just as likely as a one-time event. And so, too, the entrance of human sin could have been evolutionary in character. Some would argue, therefore, that sin gradually spread through the human race until it became truly universal in the sin that was the rejection of Christ. But there are problems with this view, and many Catholic theologians continue to insist that the original sin be traced to a primal fault that immediately affected the entire race.

Nonetheless, original sin has a meaning that goes beyond the personal decisions of Adam and Eve. It is the state in which all people are born precisely because they are members of the human race. As such, we are situated in a sinful history that affects our capacity to love God above all and to become the kind of people God destined us to be. What is important to remember, Catholics insist, is that we came forth from the hand of God essentially good, not essentially evil. Sin has rendered our condition ambiguous, at best and at worst. Unlike some Protestants, Roman Catholics have been less inclined to paint the human scene in dark and ominous colors, several examples to the contrary notwithstanding. Humankind is redeemable because men and women are radically good. [*For discussion of sin and related issues in broad religious perspective, see* Fall, The; Death; Evil; Sin and Guilt; Redemption; *and* Incarnation.]

Nature and grace. The question of grace raises one of the sharpest issues that have historically divided Protestant from Roman Catholic. How is humankind justified and eventually saved? By our own efforts? By God's alone? Or by a combination of both? Appearances to the contrary, Roman Catholics have never endorsed the view that people are saved by their own power. That position, known as Pelagianism, has been condemned consistently by the councils of the church, especially by Trent, and by Augustine in particular. Catholics, however, regard the second view as equally objectionable, namely, that human beings contribute nothing at all to salvation, because it is so totally the work of God. Such a belief, Catholics have always argued, undermines human freedom and human responsibility and encourages a passive, quietist approach to the Christian life. We are saved neither by faith alone nor by works alone, but by a living faith that overflows in works befitting a "new creature" in Christ (*Gal.* 6:15).

To be in the state of grace means to be open to the presence of God, and of the Holy Spirit in particular. This indwelling of the Spirit really transforms us. Our sins are not merely "covered over." They are obliterated by an act of divine forgiveness and generosity, on the sole condition that we are truly sorry for having offended God in the first place. The graced person is still liable to sin, of course, and so in this sense he or she may be said to be both just and sinful *(simul iustus et peccator)*. But that gives a different meaning to the expression than some of the reformers assigned it. They would have been less prepared than Catholics to stress the internal transformation by grace. [*See* Grace *and* Merit, *article on* Christian Concepts.]

Jesus Christ and redemption. Roman Catholics share with other Christians the central conviction of Christian faith that Jesus of Nazareth is the Lord of history (*Phil.* 2:5–11), that he was crucified for our sins, was raised from the dead on the third day, was exalted as Lord of all, is present to history now in and through the church.

Jesus Christ is both human and divine in nature, yet one person. "Born of a woman" (*Gal.* 4:4), he is like us in all things save sin (*Heb.* 4:15). At the same time, he is of the very being of God, Son of the Father, the light of God in the world. He is, in the words of the Second Vatican Council, "the key, the focal point, and the goal of all human history" (Pastoral Constitution on the Church in the Modern World, no. 10).

While Roman Catholic piety has often emphasized the divinity of Christ at the expense of the humanity ("God" died on the cross; "God" dwells in the tabernacle, etc.), Roman Catholics have sometimes suspected some Protestants of reversing the emphasis in favor of Jesus' humanity. Whatever the exaggerations on either side of the Reformation divide, official Roman Catholic doctrine has always maintained a balance, without confusion, between the human and divine natures.

Roman Catholics believe, of course, in the centrality and absolute necessity of Jesus Christ for personal salvation and the salvation of all the world, but they do not believe that one must be an explicit Christian, confessing the lordship of Jesus, before one can be saved. People of good will who lead exemplary lives are just as likely to enter the heavenly banquet as professed Christians. Catholics have called this "baptism by desire." Conversely, Roman Catholics also acknowledge that professed Christians can be damned, their fervent appeal to the lordship of Jesus notwithstanding. "Not everyone who says to me, 'Lord, Lord,' shall enter the kingdom of heaven, but he who does the will of my Father who is in heaven" (*Mt.* 7:21).

Neither do Roman Catholics readily identify with the evangelical Protestant stress on the propitiatory nature of the crucifixion of Jesus, even though this view has durable roots in history, particularly in the writings of Anselm of Canterbury (d. 1109). Jesus did not die in order to pay off a debt coldly demanded by his Father. He was executed because his person and his message were threatening to the political and religious establishments of his day. By accepting death, he demonstrated that love and freedom are more powerful than apathy and fear. The crucifixion was the will of God in the sense that God wills the personal fulfillment of every man and woman, and specifically God willed that Jesus should confront and challenge the network of sin in human society even though such a confrontation and challenge would surely polarize all the forces of sin against him.

In any case, for Catholics the redemption was accomplished by the whole paschal mystery, that is, Christ's passing over to his Father through a life of suffering servanthood, his obedient death on the cross, and his resurrection, ascension, and exaltation at the right hand of God. The redemptive act is not limited to the crucifixion alone. [*See* Salvation *and* Atonement.]

Holy Spirit and Trinity. The Holy Spirit is God's self-communication as love and as the power of healing, reconciliation, and new life. The divinity of the Holy Spirit was defined by the First Council of Constantinople in 381. The Spirit has the same divine essence as the Father and the Son and yet is distinct from them both. Within the Trinity, the Spirit proceeds from the Father *through* the Son. Despite the bitter East-West dispute on this point, the Council of Ferrara-Florence (1438–1440) did allow for the preposition "through" as a legitimate alternative to the preferred conjunction "and." The God who created us, who sustains us, who will judge us, and who will give us eternal life is not a God infinitely removed from us (i.e., God the Father). On the contrary, God is a God of absolute proximity: a God who is communicated truly in the flesh, in history, within the human family (i.e., God the Son), and a God who is present in the spiritual depths of human existence as well as in the core of unfolding human history, as the source of enlightenment and community (i.e., God the Holy Spirit). The mystery and doctrine of the Trinity is the beginning, the end, and the center of all Christian and, therefore, all Catholic theology. [*See* Trinity.]

Mary. Whatever the popular exaggerations in the past, Roman Catholic doctrine does not say that Mary is coequal with Christ. However, she is the mother of Jesus, and her motherhood is what roots Christ in our humanity. Indeed, Mary's name was involved in the earliest christological controversies. If Jesus was not divine, then of course it would have been wrong to call her the Mother of God. But the Council of Ephesus condemned the Nestorians in 431, and Mary was proclaimed *theotokos* (Mother of God)—which effectively meant that Jesus was proclaimed as true God as well as true man.

Controversy has continued to surround Mary, especially since the middle of the nineteenth century: first in 1854 with the promulgation of the dogma of the Immaculate Conception (that she was conceived without original sin), then in 1950 with the dogma of the Assumption (that she was taken up bodily into heaven after her death). Mary has also been called the Mediatrix of all graces (i.e., by the will of Christ, all the grace he earned for us is channeled through her), co-Redemptrix (i.e., she shares somehow in the redemptive work of her Son, without prejudice to the supreme saving power of his own death and resurrection), and Mother of the church (i.e., she has a certain priority in the church, as chief among the saints, and is the prototype of the church, a sign of the church's call to obedience and fidelity to God's word). Controversy has been rekindled, too, in the matter of the Virgin Birth (i.e., Mary conceived Jesus by the power of the Holy Spirit alone, without benefit of a human partner), while reports of Marian appearances in Guadalupe (1531), Lourdes (1858), and Fatima (1917) have generated both skepticism and fervor.

Devotion to Mary is a characteristically Catholic phenomenon in that it expresses the three fundamental principles of Catholic theology and practice:

1. The principle of sacramentality, which affirms that the invisible and spiritual God is present through the visible and the material, and that these are in turn made holy by that presence. This includes Mary, in whom God is very specially present.
2. The principle of mediation, which affirms that grace is a mediated reality, first through Christ and secondarily through the church and other human instruments, including Mary.
3. The principle of communion, which affirms that the saving encounter with God occurs not only personally and individually but also corporately and ecclesially. To be in the church, that is, to be in communion with other Christians, is to be in and with Christ. Mary is the preeminent member of this communion of saints. Our unity with her is an expression of our unity in and with Christ.

Church, kingdom of God, and sacraments. For the Catholic, the church is the whole body, or congregation, of persons who are called by God the Father to acknowledge the lordship of Jesus, the Son, in word, in sacrament, in witness, and in service, and, through the power of the Holy Spirit, to collaborate with Jesus' historic mission for the sake of the kingdom of God. The mission of the church, as also Jesus' mission, is focused on the kingdom of God. By kingdom of God is meant the redemptive presence of God actualized through the power of God's reconciling Spirit. Literally, the kingdom of God is the reign, or rule, of God. The kingdom happens whenever and wherever the will of God is fulfilled, for God rules where God's will is at work. And since God's will is applicable to the cosmos, to nature, to objects, to history, to institutions, to groups as well as to individuals, the kingdom of God is as broad and as overarching as the claims and scope of the divine will itself.

The mission of the church is unintelligible apart from the kingdom of God. The church is called, first, to proclaim in word and in sacrament the definitive arrival of the kingdom of God in Jesus of Nazareth; second, to offer itself as a test case or sign of its own proclamation, that is, to be a people transformed by the Holy Spirit into a community of faith, hope, love, freedom, and truthfulness; and third, to enable and facilitate the coming of the reign of God through service within the community of faith and in the world at large. [*See* Kingdom of God.]

For the Catholic, the church does God's work because God is present and at work within it. To speak of the church as the presence and instrument of God is to speak of it sacramentally. Just as Christ is the sacrament of God, so the church is the sacrament of Christ. Because the church is a sacrament, it acts sacramentally. In the course of its history, the Catholic church has identified seven specific acts as sacraments in the strictest sense of the term: baptism, confirmation, and Eucharist (which together constitute the rite of Christian initiation), and marriage, holy orders, reconciliation (or penance), and the anointing of the sick. The sacraments, individually and collectively, are signs of faith, causes of grace, acts of worship, and signs and instruments of the unity of the church and of Christ's presence in the world.

The relationship between sign and cause, however, has provoked the most serious sacramental controversy, particularly at the time of the Reformation. The Council of Trent rejected two extreme notions of causality: the one that reduced sacraments to magical actions, and the other that robbed sacraments of their inner spiritual reality and efficacy. The sacraments cause grace, not because of the faith of the recipient but because of the working of God within the sacraments themselves *(ex opere operato)*. On the other hand, God does not force the human will. Faithfully reflecting the teaching of Thomas Aquinas, the Council of Trent recognized that the recipient must have the right disposition if the sacrament is to be spiritually fruitful: interior conversion, faith, and devotion. Finally, the validity of a sacrament does not depend on the holiness of the minister, although some sacraments can be validly celebrated only by certain authorized ministers (bishops in the case of holy orders; bishops and delegated priests in the case of confirmation; priests in the case of the Eucharist, the anointing of the sick, and penance; priests and deacons in the case of the sacrament of marriage, which the couple themselves administer to each other; and a priest or deacon in the case of baptism, although in principle anyone can administer baptism. [*See* Sacraments, *article on* Christian Sacraments, *and* Eucharist. *See also* Baptism.]

Catholic morality. For Catholicism, morality is a matter of thinking and acting in accordance with the person and the community one has become in Christ. It is therefore a matter not only of obeying the rules but also of being faithful to the spirit as well as to the letter of the gospel. Since human agents are free to accept or reject Christ and his gospel, Catholicism contends with the reality of sin. But the church's moral vision and its approach to the moral demands of Christian life are qualified always by its confidence in the power of grace and by its readiness to expect and understand the weaknesses and failures rooted in original sin. And so Catholicism is a moral universe of laws but also dispensations, of rules but also exceptions, of respect for authority but also freedom of conscience, of high ideals but also minimal requirements, of penalties but also indulgences, of censures and excommunications but also absolution and reconciliation.

Catholic morality, therefore, is characterized by a both/and rather than an either/or approach. It is not nature *or* grace, but graced nature; not reason *or* faith, but reason illumined by faith; not law *or* gospel, but law inspired by the gospel; not scripture *or* tradition, but normative tradition within scripture; not faith *or* works, but faith issuing in works and works as expressions of faith; not authority *or* freedom, but authority in the service of freedom; not the past *versus* the present, but the present in continuity with the past; not stability *or* change, but change in fidelity to stable principle, and principle fashioned and refined in response to change; not unity *or* diversity, but unity in diversity, and diversity that prevents uniformity, the antithesis of unity.

This both/and approach to morality also explains the so-called seamless-garment approach of U.S. Catholic bishops to contemporary issues such as nuclear warfare, capital punishment, aid to the handicapped, abortion, human rights, and the like. And the Catholic church's beliefs about the universality of grace and the capacity of all persons, Catholic or not, to come to an understanding of the law of God written in every human heart (*Rom.* 2:15) explains its conviction that Catholic moral teachings about such matters as nuclear warfare and abortion are also universally applicable, and not restricted to Catholics alone. [*See* Christian Ethics.]

The last things. Catholic teaching and belief about life after death applies to individuals, the church, and the human community as a whole. Everyone and everything is destined for the kingdom of God, but there is no guarantee of universal salvation. The separation of the sheep and the goats (*Mt.* 25) will occur at both the general judgment (i.e., at the end of human history) and at the particular judgment (i.e., at the end of each individual's life). Some will join God forever in heaven; some may be separated eternally from God in hell; others may find themselves in a state of merely natural happiness in limbo; and others will suffer in purgatory some temporary "punishment" still required of sins that have already been forgiven. Such "punishments" can be partially or fully remitted through the application of indulgences.

Each individual is destined for the beatific vision (heaven, eternal life) and the resurrection of the body. Purgatory is an intermediate state between heaven and hell, reserved for those who, at the moment of death, are not yet ready to see God "face to face" (*1 Cor.* 13:12). Catholic tradition holds that it is possible for the living (the church militant) spiritually to aid "the souls in purgatory" (the church suffering). All members of the church, living and dead, are bound together as a communion of saints. Just as the prayers of the living may benefit those in purgatory, so the prayers of the saints in heaven (the church triumphant) may benefit those on earth who make intercession to them.

Although the church has defined that certain persons are in heaven (canonized saints), it has never defined that anyone is actually in hell. Thus, a Catholic is required to believe in hell as a real possibility for those who utterly reject the grace of God, but the Catholic is not required to believe that anyone has actually been consigned to hell. The destiny of the unbaptized infant or young child, on the other hand, has, since the Middle Ages, been linked with a state called limbo, a condition of "natural happiness," where the individual is free of punishment but deprived of the vision of God. However, belief in limbo and teaching about limbo has declined as the hope of universal salvation has gradually increased since the Second Vatican Council.

Polity. According to its own official teachings, the Roman Catholic church is neither a monarchy nor an oligarchy nor a democracy. Its governance is of a unique kind because the church has a "unique essence" (Rahner and Ratzinger, *The Episcopate and the Primacy*, 1962, p. 33). The universal church is a college of local churches. The supreme jurisdictional power of this universal church is vested at one and the same time in the pope and in an ecumenical council, over which the pope presides and of which he too is a member. Indeed, the universal church is itself a kind of ecumenical council convoked by some human agent (today the pope, in the past popes and emperors alike). The papacy is the highest pastoral office in the Roman Catholic church because of the pope's status as bishop of the diocese of Rome. As such, he is head of the college of bishops, and is called the Vicar of Christ (more accurately, the Vicar of Peter) and pastor of the universal church on earth.

According to the legal tradition of the Roman Catholic church, however, the church seems closer to an absolute monarchy. The Code of Canon Law accords the pope "supreme, full, immediate and universal ordinary power in the Church, which he can always freely exercise" (canon 331). Therefore, there is "neither appeal nor recourse against a decision or decree of the Roman Pontiff" (canon 333, no. 3). The only way a pope can lose such authority is through death or resignation.

Just as the universal church is composed of an international college of local churches, so the universality of the church is expressed through the collegial relationship of the bishops, one to another. The bishop of Rome serves as the head and center of this collegial network. Even the Code of Canon Law of the Roman Catholic church acknowledges that the church is not a strict monarchy, for the college of bishops, which always includes the pope, "is also the subject of supreme and full power over the universal Church" (canon 336), a power that it exercises solemnly in an ecumenical council. Bishops also participate in the governance of the church through synods. A synod of bishops is a group of bishops who have been chosen from the different regions of the world to discuss matters of general interest to the church and to make recommendations for pastoral action. Since the Second Vatican Council, international synods of bishops have met in Rome every two, and then every three, years. An extraordinary synod of bishops was called by John Paul II in 1985.

The college of cardinals constitutes a special college of bishops within the larger episcopal college. There were lay cardinals until 1918, when the Code of Canon Law specified that all cardinals must be priests. Pope John XXIII decreed in 1962 that all cardinals must be bishops. The responsibility of the college of cardinals is to provide for the election of a new pope and to advise the pope when and if he seeks its counsel on matters pertaining to the governance of the universal church. In its present form, the college of cardinals dates from the twelfth century. Earlier the title had been bestowed on deacons and priests of the leading churches of Rome and on bishops of neighboring dioceses. The title was limited, however, to members of the college in 1567. The number of cardinals was set at seventy in 1586 by Sixtus V, and that limit remained in force until the pontificate of John XXIII, who gradually increased it. Paul VI limited the number of cardinals eligible to vote in papal elections to 120.

The Curia Romana is the administrative arm of the papacy. It consists of the Secretariat of State, the Council for the Public Affairs of the Church, and various congregations, tribunals, and other institutions, whose structure and competency are defined in special law. There are ten congregations (Doctrine of the Faith, Oriental Churches, Bishops, Discipline of the Sacraments, Divine Worship, Causes of Saints, Clergy, Religious and Secular Institutes, Catholic Education, and the Evangelization of Peoples, or Propagation of the Faith); three tribunals (Sacred Apostolic Penitentiary, Apostolic Signatura, and the Sacred Roman Rota); three secretariats (one for Christian Unity, one for Non-Christians, and one for Non-Believers); and a complex of commissions, councils, and offices, which administer church affairs at the central executive level (e.g., Theological Commission, Council of the Laity, and Central Statistics Office). The terms *apostolic see* or *holy see* apply not only to the pope but also to the Secretariat of State, the Council for the Public Affairs of the Church, and other institutions of the Curia.

The Code of Canon Law also stipulates that the pope "possesses the innate and independent right to nominate, send, transfer and recall his own legates to particular churches in various nations or regions, to states and to public authorities; the norms of international law are to be observed concerning the sending and the recalling of legates appointed to states" (canon 362). These legates are usually called nuncios and have ambassadorial rank. Those without full ambassadorial rank are called apostolic delegates.

The polity of the Roman Catholic church is not limited to the organizational structure and operation of its Rome base. In Eastern-rite churches that are in union with the Holy See, there are patriarchs and patriarchates that have "existed in the Church from the earliest times and [were] recognized by the first ecumenical synods" (Vatican Council II, Decree on Eastern Catholic Churches, no. 7). A patriarch is a bishop who has jurisdiction over all bishops, clergy, and people of his own territory or rite. "The Patriarchs with their synods constitute the superior authority for all affairs of the patriarchate, including the right to establish new eparchies [dioceses] and to nominate bishops of their rite within the territorial bounds of the patriarchate, without prejudice to the inalienable right of the Roman Pontiff to intervene in individual cases" (no. 9).

At the diocesan level there are bishops, auxiliary bishops, vicars general, chancellors, marriage courts, diocesan pastoral councils, and the like. At the parish level there are pastors, associate pastors, pastoral ministers, extraordinary ministers of the Eucharist, parish councils, and the like. The Second Vatican Council substantially expanded the participation of the laity in the governance of the church, particularly through its teaching that the church is the people of God (Dogmatic Constitution on the Church, nos. 30–33). [*For further discussion, see* Canon Law *and* Church, *article on* Church Polity.]

Spirituality and Ethos. As the name itself suggests, Catholicism is characterized by a radical openness to all truth and to every authentic human and spiritual value. One finds in it, in varying degrees, all the theological, doctrinal, spiritual, liturgical, canonical, structural, and social diversity and richness that are constitutive of Christianity as a whole. Catholicism is the very antithesis of a sect, and it is not inextricably linked with the culture of a particular nation or region of the world. It is in principle as Asian as it is European, as Slavic as it is Latin, as Mexican as it is Nigerian, as Irish as it is Polish.

There is no list of Catholic fathers or mothers that does not include the great figures of the period before as well as after the division of East and West and the divisions within the West. Gregory of Nyssa is as much a Catholic father as is Augustine or Thomas Aquinas. Nor are there schools of theology that Catholicism excludes. Catholicism embraces Ignatius of Antioch and Clement of Alexandria, Athanasius and Cyril of Jerusalem, Gregory of Nazianzus and Augustine of Hippo, Anselm of Canterbury and Bernard of Clairvaux, Abelard and Hugh of Saint Victor, Thomas Aquinas and Bonaventure, Roberto Bellarmino and Johann Adam Möhler, Karl Rahner and Charles Journet, as well as John and Luke, Peter and Paul. Nor are there spiritualities that Catholicism excludes. It is open to *The Cloud of Unknowing* and the *Introduction to the Devout Life*, to the way of Francis of Assisi and that of Antony of Egypt, to Ignatius Loyola and John of the Cross, to Abbott Marmion and Thomas Merton, to Catherine of Siena and Dorothy Day, to Teresa of Ávila and Mother Teresa.

Catholicism is not just a collection of beliefs and practices but a community of persons. Catholicism is, and has been, composed of martyrs and ascetics, pilgrims and warriors, mystics and theologians, artists and humanists, activists and outsiders, pastors and saints. Catholicism is in Dante Alighieri, Michelangelo Buonarroti, Blaise Pascal, Erasmus, Joan of Arc, Julian of Norwich, Thomas More, Thérèse of Lisieux, and many others. "The splendour of saints, the glory of cathedrals, the courage of reformers, the strangeness of myth and marvel, the soaring ecstasies of mystics and the sorrows of the poor—all these are the home of the Catholic enterprise" (Haughton, 1979, p. 249).

[*See also* Basilica, Cathedral, and Church; Iconography, *article on* Christian Iconography; *and* Music, *especially article on* Religious Music in the West. *For discussion of Christian worship, see* Worship and Cultic Life, *article on* Christian Worship; Christian Liturgical Year; Pilgrimage, *articles on* Roman Catholic Pilgrimage in Europe *and* Roman Catholic Pilgrimage in the New World; *and* Cult of Saints. *For discussion of the dispersion of Roman Catholicism, see regional surveys under* Christianity. *See also the biographies of religious leaders mentioned herein.*]

BIBLIOGRAPHY

Adam, Karl. *Das Wesen des Katholizismus.* Tübingen, 1924. Translated by Justin McCann as *The Spirit of Catholicism* (New York, 1954). Translated into many languages, including Chinese and Japanese, this work represents the best of pre–Vatican II Catholic theology, formulated in reaction to a prevailing neoscholasticism that tended to reduce Catholicism to a system of doctrines and laws. On the other hand, the text does reflect the exegetical, ecumenical, and ecclesiological limitations of its time.

Cunningham, Lawrence S. *The Catholic Heritage.* New York, 1983. Conveys the heart of Catholicism through certain ideal types, for example, martyrs, mystics, humanists, including "outsiders" like James Joyce and Simone Weil.

Delaney, John, ed. *Why Catholic?* Garden City, N.Y., 1979. A collection of essays by various American Catholic figures on their understanding of the meaning of Catholicism and on their own personal appropriation of that meaning. Contributors include Andrew Greeley, Abigail McCarthy, and Archbishop Fulton Sheen.

Gilkey, Langdon. *Catholicism Confronts Modernity: A Protestant View.* New York, 1975. Chapter 1, "The Nature of the Crisis," is particularly useful because it identifies what the author regards as the essentially positive characteristics of Catholicism: sacramentality, rationality, tradition, and peoplehood.

Happel, Stephen, and David Tracy. *A Catholic Vision.* Philadelphia, 1984. The approach is historical and the thesis is that Catholicism emerges progressively and processively as it encounters new forms of life that it constantly attempts to understand and transform. Jointly authored, the book may lack the necessary clarity and coherence that a less sophisticated inquirer would require.

Haughton, Rosemary. *The Catholic Thing.* Springfield, Ill., 1979. An original approach that portrays Catholicism as a reality shaped by an enduring conflict between what the author calls "Mother Church" (the more traditional, institutional side) and "Sophia" (the more unpredictable, communal side). In this regard, the book is similar to Cunningham's (above).

Hellwig, Monika K. *Understanding Catholicism.* New York, 1981. Covers some of the doctrinal and theological territory treated in my more comprehensive *Catholicism* (below), but without so much attention to historical and documentary detail.

Lubac, Henri de. *Catholicisme.* Paris, 1938. Translated by Lancelot C. Sheppard as *Catholicism: A Study of the Corporate Destiny of Mankind* (New York, 1958). As its English subtitle suggests, the book underlines the essentially social nature of Catholicism—in its creeds and doctrines, in its sacramental life, and in its vision of history. It draws heavily on patristic and medieval sources, excerpts of which are provided in an appendix.

McBrien, Richard P. *Catholicism.* Rev. ed. 2 vols. in 1. Minneapolis, 1981. The most comprehensive, up-to-date exposition of Catholic history, theology, and doctrine available. Its main lines are reflected in this article.

Rahner, Karl, and Joseph Ratzinger. *Episkopat und Primat.* Freiburg im Bresgau, 1962. Translated by Kenneth Barker and others as *The Episcopate and the Primacy* (New York, 1962). An important corrective to exaggerated notions of papal authority, and at the same time a significant contribution to the literature on the meaning of collegiality. Its ideas, written before Vatican II, were essentially adopted by the council.

RICHARD P. MCBRIEN

ROMAN RELIGION. [*This entry consists of two articles.* The Early Period *treats Roman religion from its origins to 100* BCE; The Imperial Period *covers the following centuries to 400* CE.]

The Early Period

Prior to the Roman unification, the Italian peninsula contained many different ethnic groups. Their influence on religious civilization varies from one to another. In this context a historian tends to highlight three great centers of culture: the Etruscans, established mainly to the north of the right bank of the Tiber; the Greeks of Magna Graecia, located to the south of the Volturno River; and the Latins, located to the south of the lower course of the Tiber up to the confines of Magna Graecia. These borders, however, are only approximate, since they fluctuated in reaction to historical changes.

Here the discussion will concern only the Latins and Rome, since they constitute the essential element of the Indo-European presence on the peninsula. Yet it is necessary to indicate the existence in Campania of the Oscans, who left behind important documents of juridical and religious interest (the *tabula Bantina* of the city of Bantia; the *cippus Abellanus* concerning the towns of

Abella and Nola; and the bronze plaque of Agnone with its precepts from sacred law). We should also not forget that the poet Ennius (239–169 BCE) stated that he had three souls, since he knew Greek, Oscan, and Latin (Aulus Gellius, *Noctes Atticae* 17.17). As for the Umbrians, located to the east of Etruria, they left an even richer legacy. Thanks to discovered inscriptions, and above all to the impressive document of the Eugubine Plaques, we are able to know their formulas of prayer as well as the names of their divinities. We now know about the liturgy required for the consecration of the city, about the prescriptions for the lustration of the people, about the sacrifices to be offered according to different places and divinities invoked, about divination by the observation of birds, and about prescriptions for the inauguration of the *templum* or the *pomerium* (religious boundary). One can see that the Osco-Umbrian documentation will sometimes provide valuable comparisons with the Latin data.

Let us return to the domain of the Latins and describe its expansion. At the beginning of the first millennium BCE (between the end of the Bronze Age and the beginning of the Iron Age) these people inhabited Latium Vetus (Old Latium), which extended to the south of the lower course of the Tiber up to the Pontine plain (*Pomptinus ager:* Livy, 6.5.2). This territory was bordered on the northwest by the Tiber and the land of the Etruscans and on the northeast by the Sabine area. On the east it was bounded by the Alban chain from the mountains of Palombara, Tivoli (Tibur), Palestrina (Praeneste), and Cori (Cora) as far as Terracina (Anxur) and Circeo (Circei), and to the west was the shore of the Tyrrhenian Sea. Within this area are the hills that served as habitats, such as Alba Longa, regarded as the most ancient Latin city, or Monte Cavo (Mons Albanus), which was the seat of a federal cult of Jupiter Latiaris.

This Latium Vetus, or Latium Antiquum, was augmented later on by the Latium Adiectum, or Latium Novum (New Latium), formed by the territories won by the Romans of the historical epoch (starting with the sixth century BCE) from the Volsci, the Aequi, the Hernici, and the Aurunci (see Pliny the Elder, *Historia naturalis* 3.68–70). Traditionally the Latins are called *populi Latini* ("Latin peoples") or by the collective noun *nomen Latinum* ("Latin nation"). They occupied the hills, which were easier to defend, in autonomous groups more or less bound to one another, a system termed *vicatim* ("by small villages"). These territorial associations were based essentially on religious bonds. Thus a feeling of community was created that was carried over into the historical epoch by the development of federations based on common cults: those around the sanctuary of Jupiter Latiaris on Mons Albanus, for example, or around the sanctuary of Diana Aricina located in "the sacred grove" of Aricia (Nemus Dianae). Another federal cult would play an exceptional role in history, because it held privileged ties with the Romans. It was centered at Lavinium, which Varro (*De lingua Latina* 5.144) identifies as the religious metropolis of Rome: ". . . Lavinium: . . . ibi di Penates nostri" ("Lavinium: there are our household gods"). Recent excavations have uncovered the site, which includes a necropolis going back to the tenth century BCE. There are also ruins of ramparts dating from the sixth century, the vestiges of a house of worship flanked by thirteen altars, and a mausoleum (it could be a *hērōion* in memory of Aeneas) that houses an archaic tomb from the seventh century BCE.

In the archaic period, the cradle of the future Rome was no more than one village among others. Various stages occurred before the official foundation of the Urbs ("city"), on 21 April 753 BCE (feast day of the Parilia, dedicated to shepherds and flocks) at the summit of what is now the Palatine. The *regio Palatina* ("Palatine region") was subdivided into three knolls, the most important of which was the Palatium, the other two being Cermalus and the Velia. (Regarding the concept of *Roma quadrata,* the expression appears already in Ennius's *Annals* 123 as a "city in four parts", it seems to constitute a projection into the past of the principle of orthogonal division that the Romans later applied in their urban design.)

We have evidence of a second phase, thanks to the topographical grid that corresponds to the feast of the Septimontium, celebrated on 11 December. The three knolls of the Palatine region (Palatium, Cermalus, Velia) are joined with the three knolls of the Esquiline group (Fagutal, Oppius, Cispius) along with the Subura (the Caelius was added later to this list of seven names). These are the stages of the procession that the abridger Sextus Pompeius Festus outlines for this feast, but in a different order probably in line with the liturgical itinerary. The list is borrowed, as is known, from the scholar M. Verrius Flaccus: Palatium, Velia, Fagutal, Subura, Cermalus, Oppius, Caelius, Cispius.

In the third stage of topographical development the city was divided into four regions: Palatina, Esquilina, Suburana, and Collina, the last comprising the Quirinal and the Viminal. Surrounding walls were constructed. Tradition attributes these initiatives to the next to last king, Servius Tullius. This has been confirmed, in that recent archaeological discoveries have verified a notable territorial extension of the city during the sixth century. As for the ramparts, if the date of the wall made by Servius in *opus quadratum* should be advanced to the fourth century, after the burning of Rome by the Gauls, the existence of walls in the sixth century is nonetheless established by the vestiges of an *agger* found on the Quirinal. The discovery at Lavinium of a rampart in *opus quadratum* dating from the sixth century leads, analogously to the Roman situation, to the same conclusion.

These, then, were the stages of the city's formation. Nevertheless, the Romans of the classical period preferred a simpler scheme in the form of a diptych: the "providential" passage from the "savage" state to the "civilized" state. The narrative by Cicero follows this form (*De republica* 2.4). He first evokes the divine origin of the twins Romulus and Remus (born of the god Mars and the Vestal Virgin Rhea Silvia), who were left exposed on the banks of the Tiber by their granduncle Amulius, king of Alba Longa, but were then miraculously saved by the intervention of a nursing wolf. The author then draws a contrast between the pastoral phase, which saw the assertion of the authority of Romulus (the elimination of Remus is passed over in silence), and the civilizing phase of the city's founder. During this period (from the eighth to the seventh century) Rome did not yet impose itself upon the Latin world, which contained several remarkable centers, *clara oppida* (Pliny the Elder, *Historia naturalis* 3.68). We can mention in passing the ones that archaeology has brought to light: Satricum, Antium (Anzio), Ardea, Lavinium (Pratica di Mare), Politorium (perhaps Castel di Decima), Ficana, and Praeneste (Palestrina).

It is possible to give some detail of the conditions of life in these population centers. They drew their sustenance mainly from animal husbandry and from the exploitation of natural resources (salt, fruit, and game). Their inhabitants progressively took up agriculture in pace with the clearing of the woods and the draining of the marshes, at the same time making pottery and iron tools. Their language belonged to the Indo-European family. The first document in the Latin language may be the inscription on the golden brooch of Praeneste, dated at the end of the seventh century: "manios med fhefhaked numasioi" (in classical Latin: "Manius me fecit Numerio," "Manius made me for Numerius.") However, the authenticity of this inscription has recently been strongly contested. (see M. Guarducci, *La cosidetta Fibula Prenestina,* Rome, 1980). As regards their rites, it was believed for a long time that the Indo-European invaders practicing cremation could be contrasted with the aborigines practicing burial, with the latter chronologically preceding the former. This picture no longer corresponds to the facts. Archaeology has revealed that the practice of cremation (end of the Bronze Age and beginning of the Iron Age) almost always preceded burial (late Iron Age: eighth to seventh century), with no ethnic significance attached to these usages.

In this community of Latins, Rome became progressively preponderant, once it had established its political and religious foundations. Tradition ascribes this growth on a shared basis to the first two kings, Romulus and Numa Pompilius. This preponderance was extended by the destruction of Alba Longa under the third king, Tullus Hostilius, and by the conquest of the coastal regions as far as Ostia, at the mouth of the Tiber. In the course of these operations, centers such as Tellenae, Ficana, and Politorium were wiped out. If it is true that Politorium corresponds to the modern city of Castel di Decima, the recent excavations in that locality would confirm tradition; indeed, they have brought to light a necropolis containing tombs dating from the eighth century into the end of the seventh—the *terminus* indicated by Livy (1.33.3) for the destruction of Politorium by the fourth king, Ancus Marcius.

Yet, once she became the mistress of Latium, Rome herself was subjected by the Etruscans. The last three kings, Tarquin the Elder (Tarquinius Priscus), Servius Tullius, and Tarquin the Proud (Tarquinius Superbus) are all presumed to be of Etruscan origin. After the expulsion of the last Etruscan king (in 509 BCE), Roman power wasted no time in consolidating itself, thanks to the victory gained (in 499 or 496) over the Latins at Lake Regillus. This was followed in 493 by the establishment of an alliance of "eternal peace" between the two parties, namely, the treaty of Spurius Cassius. The establishment of a federal cult of the Latin Diana on the Aventine no doubt falls within this same period of time. From then on, all Italy was destined sooner or later to acknowledge Roman law. One last revolt by Latins who took up arms during the first Samnite war (343–341 BCE) was put down with finality. The Latin league was dissolved in 338 BCE, and the Latins were incorporated into the Roman community.

Divinities of the Archaic Period. The Latin word designating divinity has an Indo-European origin. *Deus,* which phonetically comes from the ancient *deivos* (just as *dea* comes from *deiva*), means "heavenly being." In line with this etymology, *deus* and *dea* represent for the Latins powers in relation to the luminous sky *(divum),* in opposition to man *(homo),* who is bound to the earth *(humus), homo* itself being a derivative of an Indo-European word meaning "earth." One immediate consequence of this is the fact that the Latin noun is distinguished from its Greek homologue *theos,* which takes its meaning from a different etymology: *theos* probably is connected with the prototype **thesos,* which refers to the sphere of the sacred (Benveniste), though no one has been able to specify the limits of its meaning. We note, however, that this difference of vocabulary between the Latin and the Greek in naming the divinity fades at the level of the supreme god: *Iuppiter* (**Iou-pater,* with **Iou-* deriving from **dyeu-*) and *Zeus (*dyeus)* both go back to the same Indo-European root.

It also follows that the Latins represented the divinity as an individual and personal being. This linguistic fact at once discredits the "animist" notion that would postulate a pre-deist phase in Rome that would have preceded the advent of the personal divinity. The erroneous utilization of the word *numen,* arbitrarily confused with the Melanesian term *mana,* has fizzled out, as shown by Georges Dumézil.

How did Romans depict their gods? A remark by Varro (quoted by Augustine, *De civitate Dei* 4.31) deserves attention: "For more than 170 years, the Romans worshiped their gods without statues. If this custom had prevailed, the gods would be honored in a purer fashion." This reference to a lost state of purity *(castitas)* is an indirect criticism of the Hellenic anthropomorphism that attributed human passions and vices to the gods, as in Homer's *Iliad* or in Hesiod's *Theogony.*

Indeed, the native Roman divinities lack the embellishments of a mythology that is more or less abundant with picturesque variations. They were mainly defined by their specific competence, far from any tie with the human condition. (Georg Wissowa, 1912, had already observed that there was no marriage or union between gods and goddesses at Rome.) This fact is particularly verified by the existence of many divinized abstractions, such as Fides, the goddess of good faith, who received each year the common homage of three major priests. They would come in an open chariot to her chapel to ask her to preserve harmonious relations within the city. Also, Ceres, the etymology of whose name places her in charge of growth (especially of grains), appears as the background to the feast of the Cerialia, which was celebrated annually on 19 April. These, then, are not minor divinities, nor is Consus, the god of grain storage (*condere,* "to store"), who was celebrated at the time of the Consualia on 21 August, as well as at the time of the Opiconsiva on 25 August, when he was in association with Ops, the goddess who watched over abundance. As for Janus, god of beginnings and of passages, and Vesta, the goddess of the sacred fire, their importance in the Roman liturgy was such, as reported by Cicero (*De natura deorum* 2.67), that the former shared in the beginning of every religious ceremony, while the latter was invoked at the end.

Did this tendency toward divinized abstraction lend itself to excesses? One readily cites the example of the minor specialist gods that assisted Ceres in her functions, according to Fabius Pictor (quoted by Servius Danielis, *Ad Georgica* 1.21): Vervactor (for the plowing of fallow land), Reparator (for the renewal of cultivation), Imporcitor (for marking out the furrows), Insitor (for sowing), Obarator (for plowing the surface), Occator (for harrowing), Sarritor (for weeding), Subruncinator (for hoeing), Messor (for harvesting), Convector (for carting the harvest), Conditor (for storage), Promitor (for distribution). Another group of minor divinities gave Augustine (*De civitate Dei* 6.9.264–265) occasion for sarcastic comments in detailing its list. This group included lesser divine entities who were regarded as aiding the husband on his wedding night: Virginensis (to loosen the belt of the young virgin), Subigus (to subdue her), and Prema (to embrace her). "And what is the goddess Pertunda [from *pertundere,* "to penetrate"] doing here? Let her blush, let her flee! Let her leave the husband something to do! It is really a disgrace that someone else besides himself is fulfilling the duty that this goddess's name embodies."

What can be said about all this? Whatever the merit of these lists of specialized divinities (the first one, transmitted by Servius, is guaranteed by the quality of the source: Fabius Pictor, the author of books on pontifical law, contemporary with Cato the Elder), one can observe that they name only secondary entities that are served by no particular priest (even though the Roman institution recognized the *flamines minores,* the "lesser priests"). Nor did they appear in the liturgical calendar. Moreover, these entities moved in the wake of top-level divinities. This trait is expressly brought out by the list of lesser specialists who gravitate toward Ceres: the *flamen* (priest) of this goddess invokes them when he offers, during the Cerialia, the sacrifice to Tellus ("earth") and to Ceres. Everything indicates that the same applies to the list drawn up by Augustine: all those names fit easily within the circle of Juno Pronuba, protectress of marriages. Also, one can grant that these lesser gods constitute an inferior category of *di humiliores.* Most of the time they fall under the banner of the greatest among them, after the manner of clients who place themselves under the protection of a *patronus.* In this sense they share, as Georges Dumézil puts it, in the "*familia* of a great god." In any case, they demonstrate the analytic abilities of pontifical experts and their concern for accompanying each phase of an activity with a religious factor. Finally, this tendency to divine miniaturization corresponds to a kind of luxuriant manifestation of the inclination of Roman pontiffs toward abstract analysis.

These divine abstractions exist in both masculine and

feminine forms, without any interference between the two. The apparent exceptions are only illusory. Thus it is that Faunus has no feminine counterpart. (His name's meaning is uncertain; it has sometimes been compared by the ancients with *fari,* "to talk," as in Varro, *De lingua Latina* 7.36, and sometimes with *favere,* "to be favorable," as in Servius Danielis, *Ad Georgica* 1.10; this god had been assimilated to the Greek Pan, as is confirmed by the location of his temple, erected in 194 BCE on the Isle of the Tiber, i.e., in the extrapomerial zone.) Indeed, Fauna seems to be an artificial construction of syncretic casuistry that attempted to associate her with Faunus as either wife or sister or daughter (Wissowa, 1912). Her name was later confused with Fatua and with Bona Dea (an appellation also used in turn by Damia, a goddess originating in Tarentum).

The same holds true for Pales, the goddess whose feast, the Parilia, occurred on 21 April, the anniversary of the foundation of Rome. (In contrast, two Pales appear on the date of 7 July on the pre-Julian calendar of the town of Antium. Nothing prevents us from considering these as two goddesses liable for distinct tasks, the protection of different categories of animals: small and large livestock.) The god Pales, mentioned by Varro (quoted by Servius, *Ad Georgica* 3.1), belongs to the Etruscan pantheon and has no liturgical place in Rome.

How then is one to understand the expression "sive deus sive dea" ("whether god or goddess"), which is found in many prayers? It does not reflect uncertainty about the gender of a possibly epicene divinity but rather uncertainty about the identity of the divinity that one is addressing. In Cato's example the peasant, careful not to make a mistake in the form of address when pruning a *lucus* ("sacred grove"), where he does not know the protective divinity, envisions the two possibilities: he thus invokes either a god or a goddess.

The same prudence is evident in the precautionary formula inserted by the pontiffs, cited by Servius (*Ad Aeneidem* 2.351): "Et pontifices ita precabantur: Jupiter Optime Maxime, sive quo alio nomine te appellari volueris" ("And the pontiffs uttered this prayer: Jupiter, Best and Greatest, or whatever be the name by which you choose to be called"). This formula is all the more instructive in that it provides for the case in which Jupiter, while well identified by his Capitoline titles, might by chance desire some other name.

Since a Roman divinity is essentially defined by its action, even a single manifestation of this action suffices for the existence of the divinity to be acknowledged. Such would be an exceptional, but significant, case. In vain a voice once called out on the Via Nova in the silence of the night to announce the approach of the Gauls. The Romans later reproached themselves for their culpable negligence and erected a sanctuary to the voice under the name of Aius Locutius ("he who talks, he who tells"; Livy, 5.32.6; 50.5; 52.11). Similarly, a *fanum* (shrine) was constructed outside of the Porta Capena to the god Rediculus. This was because Hannibal in his march on Rome had retreated, overcome by apparitions, from that place.

All the divinities of autochthonous background had a privilege: their sanctuaries were allowed within the pomerial zone. What was this pomerium? According to Varro (*De lingua Latina* 5.143), it was a circle within the surrounding wall marked by stones and describing the limit inside of which urban auspices had to be taken. Rome included sectors outside the pomerial zone that were still part of the city: the Aventine Hill, which had been outside the city of the four regions (its incorporation into the city was attributed by tradition sometimes to Romulus and sometimes to Ancus Marcius), remained outside the pomerial zone until the time of Claudius (first century CE) even though it was surrounded by what was called "Servius's wall."

The same extrapomerial status held true for the Field of Mars, which owed its name to the military exercises that were conducted on its esplanade. Yet here there occurs a further practice that lies at the root of Roman law. On this emplacement there was an altar consecrated to Mars from time immemorial. It is mentioned by the "royal" law of Numa in relation to the distribution of the *spolia opima,* spoils taken from an enemy's general slain by one's own army commander, and was completed later on by the erection of a temple (in 138 BCE). The assemblies of military centuries *(comitia centuriata)* were also held there. In addition, every five years the purification of the people *(lustrum)* was celebrated there by the sacrifice of the *suovetaurilia,* the set of three victims—boar, ram, and bull—that had been paraded beforehand around the assembly of citizens. The presence of the old Mars outside the *pomerium* (similarly, another temple of Mars, constructed in 338 BCE to the south of Rome outside the Porta Capena, was also outside the pomerial zone) was in strict conformity with the distinction established between the *imperium domi,* the jurisdiction of civil power circumscribed by the pomerial zone, and the *imperium militiae* that could not show itself except outside this zone. This is why it was necessary to take other auspices when one wanted to go from one zone to another. If one failed to do so, every official act was nullified. This misfortune befell the father of the Gracchi, T. Sempronius Gracchus, during his presidency of the *comitia centuriata.* While going back and forth between the Senate and the Field of Mars, he forgot to take the military auspices again; as a result, the election of consuls that took place in the midst of the assemblies when he returned was rejected by the Senate (see Cicero, *De divinatione* 1.33 and 2.11). The delimitation of Roman sacral space by the pomerial line explains the distribution of the sanctuaries. Vesta, the goddess of the public hearth, could only be situated at the heart of the city within the pomerium, whereas a new arrival, such as Juno Regina, originating in Veii, was received, as an outsider, in a temple built on the Aventine (in 392 BCE).

Does this territorial distribution of the sanctuaries into zones *intra* and *extra pomerium* correspond in any way to the distinction made by the ancients between *di indigetes* and *di novensiles?* These expressions appear (though in reverse order) within the old formula of the *devotio* (quoted by Livy, 8.9.6) by which a Roman general "devoted himself"—in other words, consecrated himself, and the enemy army as well, to the *di manes* (the underworld gods) cited at the end of a list of other divinities. The meaning of these two terms is debated. It appears that many ancients and some moderns (among them Wissowa) yielded to a semantic slip by confusing *indigetes* with *indigenae,* thus interpreting the *di indigetes* as the "indigenous" gods, as opposed to more recent divinities. Although this confusion is philologically unacceptable, it still conveys a contrast that seems real. It seems likely that *novensiles* (*-siles* coming from *-sides,* just as *lacrima* comes from *dacrima,* as attested in Livius Andronicus) can be explained as deriving from *novus* and *insidere* in order to designate the "newly-resident" gods. As for the *indigetes,* I would connect the term with *indigitare* ("to recite ritually") and *indigitamenta* ("collection of litanies"). Thus the expression would designate the divinities invoked since time immemorial by preference. The Vergilian formula *di patrii indigetes* (*Georgics* 1.498) would thus be explained: far from being an idle repetition with *patrii, indigetes* adds a note of confidence drawn forth in permanent fervor.

Among the archaic divinities there were some who were split off, so to speak, in the course of time, so that their identity was not preserved except in the name of the feast that honored them. Even this element often remains obscure if no light is shed on it from elsewhere. This is where Indo-European comparative studies have shown themselves to be especially fruitful, thanks to the labors of Georges Dumézil. A few examples will suffice.

Roman calendars mark the date of 21 December as the feast of the Divalia, directed toward a goddess Angerona, about whom not much is known. A breakthrough was achieved by Theodor Mommsen, in his work *Römisches Staatsrecht* (1871–1888), when he underscored the coincidence of the feast with the winter solstice (an account of the calendar of Praeneste, successfully restored by that scholar, justified the celebration of the feast by the coming of the solar year). Georges Dumézil (1974) attempted to go further in explaining the name of the goddess by referring to the *angusti dies* of the solstice, a time when the light is *angusta,* or "restricted" (Macrobius, *Saturnalia* 1.21.15). He thus seeks to clarify its action (in conformity with the dynamic of divinized abstractions) as directed toward easing the passage through these *angustiae,* "a sadly brief period of time." As for the goddess herself, he remarked that she appeared with "her mouth gagged and sealed, a finger on her lips, in a gesture that commands silence." He understands this gesture of silence, advised in India and in Scandinavian mythology, as a means of concentration for gaining magical efficacy. In the mythologies, silence is placed at the service of the threatened sun.

The second example is even more suggestive, to the extent that it brings out the meaning of a liturgy that had become incomprehensible to the Romans of the classical period. It deals with the Matralia on 11 June in honor of Mater Matuta. Here again, the name of the divinity, however transparent (she is identified with the goddess Aurora by Lucretius 5.656), and the nearness of her feast to the summer solstice have not prevented certain scholars from forgetting these data and from seeing in Mater Matuta anything more than a simple mother goddess or benevolent mother. It is true that the liturgy of her feast could appear as mysterious as one wished.

On 11 June Roman matrons gathered in the goddess's temple. (This sanctuary, built in 396 BCE by M. Furius Camillus, replaced an earlier structure. According to tradition as reported by Livy [5.19.6], it took the place of a temple constructed by Servius Tullius. Recent excavations have uncovered two temples in the northern part of the Forum Boarium. One is attributed to Mater Matuta and the other to Fortuna, dating from the fifth to the fourth century. One of them contains an older stratum, datable to the end of the sixth century, the time of Servius Tullius.) During the ceremony, the matrons would carry in their arms not their own children but the children of their sisters. Having already sent a servant girl into the temple ahead of time, they now began to beat her with switches before casting her outside. These rites could not but appear strange in the absence of an explanatory ideology. Now, as Georges Dumézil has observed, the goddess Aurora is one of the most striking figures of the *Ṛgveda,* where she appears nursing and licking a child, who is either "both her own and that of her sister, the Night" (India is not embarrassed by such contradictory conceptions) or "of the latter alone."

All this occurs as if Rome had done nothing but retain

the most logical form of the mythologem: Aurora cherishing the child of her sister, the Night. But the myth has disappeared here; only the rite has survived. Once a year, the matrons perform actions inspired by some kind of sympathetic magic that Aurora is supposed to do every day. They throw a slave out of the temple; in the *Ṛgveda,* Aurora "chases away the black formlessness . . . the shadows." The matrons carry their nephews and nieces but not their own children; the Vedic Aurora accepts with an affectionate eagerness the child of her sister, Night.

This ceremony occurs on 11 June, and

> the nearness of the summer solstice is not happenstance. It is at the point when the days, as if weary, reduce to nearly nothing their growth and soon set about declining, that the goddess Aurora becomes most interesting for the people, just as, at the end of the disturbing process of shortening at the winter solstice, it is Angerona who arouses interest, the goddess who lengthens at last the days that become *angusti.*"
>
> (Dumézil, 1974, p. 344)

The example of the Matralia shows in a significant way that in Rome a rite could be preserved in spite of the loss of its underlying myth. In this connection, it is interesting to take note of the "theologian" Ovid's reaction to this exegetical problem. Given his and his contemporaries' ignorance of this Indo-European mythologem, he could only search through the skein of Greek mythology. Thanks to syncretism, he was able to settle on a comparison of Mater Matuta with the Greek goddess Ino/Leukothea. In search of a fable adaptable to the liturgical plan of 11 June, he chanced upon a matching outline. Indeed, Ino/Leukothea, who proved to be a kindly nurse for her nephew Bacchus (son of her sister Semele), was a malicious mother toward her own children. Ovid thus "justified" the liturgy of the Matralia by means of this parallel in addressing this exhortation to the mothers of Latium: "Let the mothers piously invoke the goddess not for their own offspring, for she did not bring any luck as a mother. Let them rather plead with her for the children of others, since she was of more service to her nephew Bacchus than to her own children" (*Fasti* 6.559–562).

Thus the archaic divinities, who survived only by virtue of the Romans' liturgical conservatism, have recovered their true identity thanks to Indo-European comparative studies. Nor is this the only benefit that can be credited to these studies, whose decisive contribution concerns the fundamental structures of religious heritage. Wissowa (1912) had already brought out the importance in Roman religion of the triad of Jupiter-Mars-Quirinus, who appears at the point of convergence of several factors and proceeds from the ancient priestly hierarchy as transmitted by Festus, who set down the following hierarchy: the king, the *flamen Dialis,* the *flamen Martialis,* the *flamen Quirinalis,* the *pontifex maximus.* Framed by the king and the grand pontiff, the three major *flamines* (the *flamines maiores*) bring into relief the gods to which they are respectively attached: Jupiter, Mars, and Quirinus. Their close union is emphasized by the ritual in which, once a year, they would go together to the chapel of Fides, to venerate the goddess of good faith. [*See* Flamen *and* Pontifex.]

The same triad is manifest in the interior arrangement of the Regia, or "king's house," which under the republic became the official seat of the pontifical college. Indeed, this building housed three different cults in addition to the cults of Janus and Juno, who were honored respectively as ushers of the year and of the month: the cult of Jupiter, associated with all the *nundinae* ("market days"); that of Mars, in the *sacrarium Martis;* and, in another chapel, the cult of Ops Consiva (abundance personified) in conjunction with Consus, the god of the storage *(condere)* of grains. This last goddess belongs to the group of agrarian divinities headed by Quirinus (whose *flamen* could substitute for any absent priest from within the whole of the jurisdiction of Quirinus: thus, in Ovid's *Fasti* 4.910 we learn that the *flamen Quirinalis* officiated in the ceremonies of Robigus, or Robigo, the divinity invoked against mildew in grains).

The same triad of Jupiter, Mars, and Quirinus is found after Janus, the god of passage, and before the divinities invoked by reason of particular circumstances in the old hymn of the *devotio* (Livy, 8.9.6) that a Roman general uttered in order to consecrate himself, at the same time as the enemy army, to the *di manes.*

The triad also appears in the regulations provided by the ancient royal law of Numa Pompilius for the distribution of the *spolia opima.* The first of these spoils were offered to Jupiter Feretrius, the second to Mars, the third to Janus Quirinus. The ternary scheme is clearly supported by the document, despite some difficulties of interpretation. The meaning of *Feretrius* (derived from *ferire* ("to smile") or from *ferre* ("to carry") is not certain. As for the expression *Janus Quirinus,* I have offered the explanation that the presence of Janus comes from his role as the initiator of the peacemaking function of Quirinus in opposition to the fury of Mars Gradivus. The tertiary scheme appears finally in the threefold patronage of the college of Salian priests ("who are under the protection of Jupiter, Mars and Quirinus"; Servius, *Ad Aeneidem* 8.663).

This cluster of Roman elements is confirmed by a parallel structure in the Umbrian pantheon: in the town of Iguvium, as in Rome, there existed a grouping of three gods—Iou, Mart, Vofiono—all bearing the common epithet Grabovio (its meaning obscure). This similarity between the two pantheons is all the more apparent since *Vofiono* is the exact linguistic equivalent of *Quirinus,* even to its adjectival form *-no-,* derived from a nominal root.

Let us return to the arrangement of this triad that, in Rome as in Iguvium, constituted a fundamental base for the archaic pantheon. The remarkable part is that it presents an order of three gods that correspond, in the Indo-European world, to three diversified functions. Jupiter embodies sovereignty in its magical and juridical aspects, which in Vedic India belong respectively to Varuna and Mithra; Mars embodies power (his physical and military attributes are similar to Indra in India); Quirinus (**Couirio-no,* the god of the community of citizens in time of peace) is connected with fruitfulness and with prosperity in its pastoral and agrarian forms. As Dumézil has demonstrated, this triad shows the survival of the characteristic tripartite ideology of the Indo-European world, which considered the hierarchical structuring of these three complementary functions to be indispensable for the prosperity of society. Despite a later evolution that would progressively fossilize their offices as the pantheon was opened to new gods, the three major *flamines* would remain the unimpeachable witnesses of this Indo-European heritage in Rome.

If, thanks to Roman conservatism and to comparative analysis, we can go back to some extent into prehistory, it is nonetheless true that Rome did not delay—indeed, it moved sooner than one would have thought until recently—in entering into history. The political event placed by tradition toward the end of the sixth century BCE, namely, the presence of the three kings who were of Etruscan origin (Tarquin the Elder, Servius Tullius, and Tarquin the Proud), involved a religious repercussion. The ancient masculine triad was replaced by a new triad in which Jupiter's masculine associates were replaced by two goddesses, Juno and Minerva. It is significant that goddesses replaced gods: Etruscan society accorded to women a more important social status than did Indo-European society. That these goddesses were none other than Juno and Minerva can be explained not only by the fact that their Etruscan homologues Uni and Mernva held respectable places in their pantheon but perhaps also by their meeting a two-sided need: to renew without destroying.

In a certain sense, did they not renew things with the abilities of their predecessors? Juno, the patroness of *iuniores* (especially of youth available for battle), succeeded Mars, the god of war; Minerva, the protectress of artisans and crafts, succeeded Quirinus, the god overseeing economic activity. The keystone of the triad remained immovable, even though Jupiter took on the traits of Tinia, as illustrated by the Etruscan artist Vulca of Veii.

Indeed, theological novelty brought about innovation at the levels of statuary and urban design: the era of aniconic divinities, mourned by Varro, was definitively over. Terra-cotta statues now came to be used by the believers, divine figures that remained within residences. One point is worthy of note: the temple built on the Capitoline Hill in honor of the new triad of Jupiter, Juno, and Minerva likewise marked the transition from the royal to the republican period. According to tradition, the construction of the Capitoline temple (the sanctuary of Jupiter, the Best, the Greatest) was begun under the Tarquins, while the dedication was performed by the consul M. Horatius Pulvillus in the first year of the republic (509 BCE). Jupiter Optimus Maximus sits on his throne in the central *cella* (shrine), flanked by Minerva on his right and by Juno on his left.

The Republican Period. A new era began with the expulsion of the last king, Tarquin the Proud, and with the institution of the republic. One comment is immediately required: the political change did not provoke any religious upheaval, and this contrast is indicative of the Roman mentality. In fact, the Capitoline triad was not called into question, in spite of its strong Etruscan connotation. Moreover, the title of king was maintained on the religious level. On that account, the official designation from then on was *rex sacrorum* or *rex sacrificulus;* in other words, a king limited to his liturgical functions but stripped of his political privileges. This point of prudence is explained by observing the care that the Romans took to avoid irritating their gods with untimely interventions in the realm of the sacred.

This care lies at the very root of their attitude toward the gods, and it is admirably expressed in the word *religio.* If the modern languages of the Western world (both Romance and Germanic) have failed to translate this word and have settled on a simple copy thereof *(religion, religione),* the reason lies in the fact that this idiom is untranslatable. Indeed, in the ancient world there was no Greek equivalent. All the expressions that one can bring to mind by analogy—*sethas* (respect for the gods), *proskunāsis* (adoration), *peulasthea* (reverential fear), *thrāskea* (cult)—are far from filling the semantic range of *religio.* Careful examination shows that the Latins, who were not concerned with philological rigor, connected *religio* more with the verb *religare* ("to tie"), alluding to the bonds between gods and men, than with the verb *relegere* ("to take up again with care"). Such as it is, *religio* expresses a fundamental preoccupation manifested in two complementary ways: the care to avoid divine wrath; the desire to win the benevolence and favor of the gods. It was the Romans' inner conviction that, without the accord of the gods, they could not succeed in their endeavors. This explains the solemn declaration of a Cicero (*De natura deorum* 2.3) proclaiming the Roman people to be "the most religious in the world."

This preoccupation is evident throughout Livy's history. Roman accomplishments rise and fall in complete rhythm with the disfavor or favor evinced by the gods. A revealing example is furnished in the episode of the Romans' desperation following upon the sack of Rome by the Gauls (in 390 BCE). Overwhelmed, they were nearly resolved to abandon the ruins of their city, at the instigation of their tribunes, in order to emigrate to Veii. It was then that M. Furius Camillus, the predestined leader—*dux fatalis*—and dictator who conquered Veii (in 396), and now the restorer of the situation in Rome (in 390), lit upon the decisive argument that inspired the mood reversal of the assembly: to abandon Rome, many times endowed with heavenly blessings since its origins, would be to commit sacrilege. In the course of his address, Camillus had called to mind this permanent lesson for the benefit of his listeners: "For consider the events of these last years, whether successes or reversals. You will find that everything succeeded when we followed the gods, and everything failed when we scorned them" (Livy, 5.51.4).

Under these conditions, it was essential for the Roman state authorities to know the divine will and to be able to consult it whenever necessary. To this end, there existed an indigenous institution especially charged with this mission: augury. [*See* Divination.] *Augur* (derived from an old neuter root **augus,* which Dumézil translates as "the fullness of mystical power" and which yields the noun *augurium* as well as the adjective *augustus*) designates the priest in charge of obtaining the *augurium,* or sign of supernatural manifestation, by performing the *auspicium,* the observation *(specere)* of birds *(aves).* Everyone knows that Rome was founded as a consequence of the *auspicium* of Romulus, who had benefited from the sight of twelve vultures. The augur during the historical epoch was a specialist in the interpretation of signs sent by Jupiter. The god was to assist the magistrate, the sole possessor of the right to take the auspices.

Later on, Rome did not hesitate to resort to other techniques, borrowed from its neighbors in Etruria or Magna Graecia: the *haruspicinae disciplina* ("lore of the haruspex"), the consultation of the Sibylline Books. This accumulation is explained simply: the desire to benefit from new techniques, all the more seductive the more they appeared to be fruitful. Let us focus on this point. The traditional augur could do nothing more than *constat,* verify the presence or absence of favorable auspices. The Etruscan soothsayer, in contrast, boasted of being able to foretell the future, either by examining the entrails of sacrificed animals or by observing lightning or by interpreting marvels. To this end, he would use respectively the *libri haruspicini,* the *libri fulgurales,* and the *libri rituales.* The first method, divining by examination of entrails, was especially in vogue. It featured, among the *exta* ("entrails") used, the liver, which was considered a microcosm of the macrocosm that was the world. Every lesion detected in some part of the former allowed an inference on the fate of the latter. One celebrated example of entrail-reading is narrated by Livy (8.9.1s) at the time of the battle of Veseris, launched in 340 BCE against the Latins: the soothsayer announced a happy result for the consul Manlius, but an unhappy one for the consul Decius.

The Sibylline Books, which had been introduced, according to tradition, under Tarquin the Proud, purported to contain prophetic verses. [*See* Sibylline Oracles.] These books, kept in the temple of Jupiter Capitoline (later, they would be transferred by Augustus to the sanctuary of Apollo Palatine) could be consulted, upon order of the Senate, by the priests specialized in that office, the *viri sacris faciundis.* The measures advocated by these priests (often the introduction of new divinities) were submitted to the evaluation of the senate, which would make the final decision. The sibyl was far from enjoying a liberty comparable to that of the oracle of Delphi: her responses were always subject to senatorial censorship. There is no need to stress further the benefit that the Romans hoped to gain from these techniques of foreign origin. This cluster of methods is moreover instructive to the extent that it reveals a fundamental trait of Roman polytheism. Founded upon a conservative tradition, it was perpetually open to enrichment and renewal. This double character made it resemble Janus Bifrons ("Janus the two-faced"), one face turned toward the past and the other to the future.

Therefore it is possible to recognize in the Roman pantheon different levels that were formed under the influence of different factors. Certain cults staked out, so to speak, the city's topographical development. Others reflected the struggle for influence within Roman society. Still others corresponded to the expansion of the Roman republic within and beyond the Italian peninsula.

One major cleavage allows us to identify very ancient cults that were linked to the territorial expansion of Rome. The first, the Lupercalia, celebrated on 15 February, delimited the very cradle of the city. On that date "the old Palatine stronghold ringed by a human flock" (Varro, *De lingua Latina*), was purified by naked Luperci (a variety of wolf-men, dressed in loincloths), who, armed with whips, would flog the public. Everything about this ceremony—the "savage" rite (see Cicero, *Pro Caelio* 26) and the territorial circumscription—demonstrates its extreme archaism.

The feast of Septimontium on 11 December designated, as its name suggested, a more extended territory. It involved no one except the inhabitants of the *montes* ("mountains"). These seven mountains (which are not to be confused with the seven hills of the future Rome) are the following: the knolls of the Palatium, the Germalus, the Velia (which together would make up the Palatine), the Fagutal, the Oppius, the Cespius (which three would be absorbed by the Esquiline), and the Caelius (S. Pompeius Festus, while still asserting the number of seven *montes*, adds the Subura to this list). This amounted, then, to an intermediary stage between the primitive nucleus and the organized city. One will note the use of the word *mons* to designate these knolls, as opposed to *collis*, which would be reserved for referring to the northern hills.

The feast of the Argei, which required two separate rituals at two different times (on 16 and 17 March and on 14 May), marks the last stage. It involved a procession in March in which mannequins made of rushes (Ovid, *Fasti* 5.621) were carried around to the twenty-seven chapels prepared for this purpose. On 14 May they were taken out of the chapels in order to be cast into the Tiber from the top of a bridge, the Pons Sublicius, in the presence of the pontiff and the Vestal Virgins. There are different opinions on the meaning of the ceremony. Wissowa saw in it a ritual of substitution taking the place of human sacrifices. (A note by Varro, *De lingua Latina* 7.44, specifies that these mannequins were human in shape.) However, Kurt Latte prefers to compare these mannequins of rushes to *oscilla* (figurines or small masks that were hung from trees), which absorbed the impurities that were to be purged from the city. The itinerary of the procession shows that it corresponds to the final stage of the city's development, the Rome of the *quattuor regiones* ("four regions"). Varro outlined the procession as follows: it proceeded through the heights of the Caelius, the Esquiline, the Viminal, the Quirinal, and the Palatine, and encircled the Forum—henceforth located in the heart of the city.

Other cults reflect, so to speak, the specific aspirations of the two classes that formed the basis of Roman society, the patricians and the plebeians. One observes an antagonism between the two classes that is evident not only on economic, social, and political levels but also on the religious level. We can recall that up until 300 BCE only the patricians were allowed to discharge as an official function the great traditional priesthoods, such as the pontificate and the augury. At that date a kind of religious equality was established by a law (the Lex Ogulnia), which, in providing members for these two colleges, reserved a good half of the seats for plebeians. Nevertheless, the patricians kept for themselves the privilege of admittance to the archaic priesthoods: the *rex sacrorum*, the three major *flamines*, and the Salii.

This rivalry between the two classes explains diverse cult initiatives that are nonetheless not necessarily mutually exclusive. In the critical phases of the city's history, they were able to coexist in a way that was satisfactory to both parties. A particularly convincing example comes to us from the beginning of the fifth century, when one individual strove to balance the two tendencies. It was the time when, according to Livy (2.18.3), "a coalition of thirty tribes" was formed against Rome. The situation induced the Romans to name a dictator, Aulus Postumius, who was vested with full powers, in place of the two consuls.

He had two problems to resolve: to stabilize the food supply, which had been disrupted by the state of war, and to confront the enemy in decisive combat. He successfully accomplished his twofold mission. The victory he won over the Latins (in 499 BCE) near Lake Regillus is celebrated in the annals. This battle entered a critical phase when the infantry failed to hold its ground. On that account, the dictator decided to send in the Roman cavalry and, at the same time, made a vow to build a temple dedicated to Castor. He thus combined, according to Livy's expression, "human and divine" means. He did so because this god, of Greek origin, was the patron of horsemen, by virtue of an old Indo-European tradition that associated him with the art of horsemanship. Before going into the campaign, the dictator took another step toward easing the difficulties surrounding the food supply: he made a vow to build a temple to the Roman triad of Ceres-Liber-Libera, the names of which barely disguised the Greek divinities Demeter-Dionysos-Kore.

The victory enabled Castor to become a Roman god and to acquire a temple above the Forum: the Aedes Castoris (dedicated in 484 by the dictator's son; Pollux was not to join his brother until the beginning of the empire, and even then the name Aedes Castorum recalled the original primacy of Castor). Since the harvests were abundant, Aulus Postumius also fulfilled his vow to the triad of Ceres-Liber-Libera by dedicating a sanctuary. This was a source of great satisfaction for the plebeians, for the sanctuary was entrusted to their charge and served as a meeting place for *aediles* (plebeian officials).

Thus, circumstances had moved Aulus Postumius to achieve a skillful balance by the concomitant foundation of a patrician cult and a plebeian cult. Only the placement of the sanctuaries revealed a difference of status: Castor was installed inside the pomerium, in the heart of the Forum, while Ceres and her associates had to be located outside of the pomerium, near the Circus Maximus.

Lastly, other cults owed their introduction to the expansion of Rome beyond its frontiers. In this connection, it helps to distinguish the cults of federal character from the isolated cults. Since time immemorial, there existed in Italy liturgical celebrations that united several cities. These ceremonies were presided over by cities that owed this honor to their prestige at the time. In the course of events, all concluded by bowing to Roman authority. Nevertheless, the ascendancy of the Urbs (Rome) was not always achieved in the same way or under the same conditions. The Romans' capacity for adaptation to different circumstances is evident here in an especially remarkable way, as illustrated by the following three cases.

One of the most ancient federal cults presupposes the original preeminence of the ancient city of Alba Longa: the *Feriae Latinae* ("Latin holidays") were celebrated at the summit of the Alban Hills in honor of Jupiter Latiaris. In earlier times, the Latins had been granted equal footing in sharing in the sacrifice, which consisted of a white bull (this detail, coming from Arnobius in *Adversus nationes* 2.68, would show that the ordinary rule, which provided a castrated victim for Jupiter, did not apply here). Once the consecrated entrails *(exta)* were offered to the god, all in attendance would share the meat, demonstrating thus their bonds of community. After the destruction of Alba Longa, Rome quite naturally picked up the thread of tradition by incorporating the Feriae Latinae as a movable feast in its liturgical calendar. Still, the attitude of the Romans was selective: even though they transferred the entire Alban population to Rome itself, they kept the Alban celebrations in their usual locations. They simply built a temple to Jupiter Latiaris where previously there was only a *lucus,* a sacred grove. During the historical epoch, the Roman consuls, accompanied by representatives of the state, would make their way to the federal sanctuary shortly after assuming their responsibilities and would preside there over the ceremonies. The Feriae Latinae had come under Roman control.

The conduct of the Romans was very different with regard to the federal cult of Diana. Tradition places this cult at Aricia near Lake Nemi, which is known as the *speculum Dianae,* "mirror of Diana" (Servius, *Ad Aeneidem* 7.515). An archaic rite determined that the priest of Diana's sacred grove, called the *rex nemorensis,* could hold office there until he was killed by his successor in single combat. During the historical period, this odd priesthood attracted only fugitive slaves. The federal altar had been consecrated to Diana by the Latin dictator Egerius Laevius, a native of Tusculum. Tusculum was the center of a federation of Latin towns (established perhaps after the disappearance of Alba Longa). When the cult came under Roman authority, it was transferred into the city on the extrapomerial hill of the Aventine. It had nothing there at first except an altar, then a temple that Varro acknowledges as having federal status: *commune Latinorum templum.* Yet this status was only one of appearance, since no assembly of Latin cities is recorded as ever having occurred on the Aventine during the Roman period, any more than at Aricia. Another point is significant: the anniversary of the temple fell on the ides of August and bore the name *Dies Servorum* ("slaves' day"). Whatever interpretation one gives to this designation, the fact remains that the cult of Diana was not of concern either on the Aventine or in Aricia. This time Rome had reduced a federal cult to a suitable level. In contrast with Jupiter Latiaris, Diana, whose name is a semantic homologue of *Jupiter* (since both names were formed from the root **diu;* she signified nocturnal light, just as he signified the light of day), was doomed to fade gradually away. Identified with Artemis, she would be invoked in Horace's *Carmen saeculare* as the sister of Apollo.

The relations that Rome held with Lavinium were very different. In the Roman mind, Lavinium had the same resonance as the Alban Hills, judging from the discourse that Livy attributes to the dictator Camillus. Camillus did not hesitate to put these two high places on the same level: "Our ancestors entrusted to us the celebration of religious ceremonies on Mount Alban and in Lavinium." In reality, the latter ranked higher than the former. Varro (*De lingua Latina* 5.144) specifies it as the source of Roman lineage and the cradle of the Roman *penates:* Lavinium benefited from a continual deference on the part of the Romans after the treaty that tradition traced back to the time of T. Tatius (Livy, 1.14.2). This deference was evident in the ritual processions of higher magistrates to the *penates* and to Vesta as they entered their office and as they left it. The deference was likewise evident in the annual pilgrimages by the pontiffs and the consuls to the sanctuary of Aeneas Indiges, which Ascanius is reputed to have built for his divinized father. If one considers that Lavinium was also the cradle of the religion of Venus, who was understood according to Trojan legend to be the *Aeneadum genetrix* ("mother of the descendants of Aeneas"), one can imagine that this exceptional site exerted in every way a great attraction for the Romans. Archaeology has recently made an important contribution concerning the territory of Lavinium by bringing to light, among other things, a *hērōin* (temple) from the fourth century BCE, constructed upon an archaic tomb (which its discoverer, Pado Sommella, identifies as the mausoleum of Aeneas) and a set of thirteen altars, of which twelve were in use in the middle of the fourth century. They may have served a new Latin federation presided over by Rome. Indeed, Rome did not stop at destroying the Latin confederation in 338 BCE, but also reinforced the privileges of Lavinium. For Lavinium, as Livy points out (8.11.15), had added to its titles the merit of loyalty by refusing to join the Latin revolt. It brought even more renown upon itself as a pilgrimage center. Thus Rome's attitude toward federal cults was definitively shown under three very different aspects: sometimes she assumed one (Alba Longa), sometimes she restricted one (Aricia), and sometimes she exalted one (Lavinium).

Just as varied was the Romans' behavior toward the divinities that they intended to introduce into their pantheon. By definition, polytheism lent itself to this sort of openness, when the traditional gods proved to be inadequate in a critical situation. Here again circumstances inspired the Romans' attitude. An early example is demonstrated by the entry of Castor into Rome, as related above. One recalls that the dictator Aulus Postumius, alarmed by the weakness of his infantry, had turned to the patron god of horsemen at the same time that he sent his cavalry into battle. He had made a vow to erect a temple to the god. The exceptional feature of this *votum* ("vow") was that Castor became installed right in the Forum, thus within the pomerial zone. He was exempted from the rule that located the residence of new divinities outside this area. Perhaps one of the reasons for this exception was the long-standing acclimatization of Castor to Latium (a dedication engraved on a bronze plaque dating from the sixth century BCE, found in Lavinium, mentions Castor and Pollux). Another reason was the importance of the occasion (it would have been the end of the young Roman republic had the Romans fallen at Lake Regillus to the Latins, who were emboldened by the exiled king, Tarquin). In any event, Castor, the god of a class (the *equites*), became the god of a nation (the Romans).

There were also other ways for foreign gods to be introduced into the Roman pantheon. When the Romans had trouble with an enemy city, they had the *evocatio* at their disposal. It consisted of a kind of abduction of divine power at the adversary's expense and to Rome's benefit. A famous case (and also unique in the annals) is seen in the siege of Veii (in 396 BCE). The war against that Etruscan city seemed endless. It was to last ten years, as long as the Trojan war. Struck by marvels ("Lake Alban had risen to an unaccustomed level without rain or any other cause"; Livy, 5.15.2), the Romans named M. Furius Camillus as dictator. In addition to his military successes, he achieved fame by addressing directly the city's protective divinity, Uni (the Etruscan homologue of Juno): "Juno Regina, who resides now in Veii, I pray that you will follow us after our victory into our city, which will soon be yours; you will there have a temple worthy of your majesty" (Livy, 5.21.3). In this way Juno Regina acquired a temple on the Aventine, as a divinity of outside origin, while still continuing to sit, as a national divinity, on the Capitolium at the side of Jupiter.

Finally, there was one other procedure: the capture, pure and simple, of a foreign divinity. *A priori*, this arrogant attitude can seem strange on the part of a people imbued with "religious" respect toward the supernatural world (by way of explaining the *evocatio*, Macrobius in *Saturnalia* 3.9.2 had advanced precisely this reason: "Quod . . . nefas aestimarent deos habere captivos," "They regarded it as sacrilege to make prisoners of the gods"). However, the seizure of Falerii in 241 BCE resulted in captivity for its goddess, who was then given a small shrine in Rome at the foot of the slope of Caelius, under the name of Minerva Capta (Ovid, *Fasti* 3.837). Apparently Rome no longer thought it necessary to treat the vanquished with caution, whether men or gods. She was adopting to her own advantage the *vae victis* formerly pronounced against her by a Gaulish chief.

Influences of Hellenism. The Greek influence played very quickly upon Rome both indirectly and directly. Indirectly, by means of the Etruscans, to the extent that the Etruscan pantheon was itself hellenized, with allowance made for its own specificity. Directly, by the nearness of Magna Graecia, while contact was taking place with continental Greece and Asia Minor. This influence contributed to anthropomorphism in conceiving the divine, above all once syncretism had established a table of equivalences between Greek and Italic divinities. How is *syncretism* defined? As a consequence of a mistaken etymology that confused *sugkrētismos* ("federation") with *sugkrēsis* ("mixture"), as Stig Wikander has shown, the term came to mean a "mixture of myths and religions." In this way the parallel connection between the Greek triad Demeter-Dionysos-Kore and the Latin triad Ceres-Liber-Libera (explained above) is ascribable to syncretist interpretation. Instead of remaining an abstract concept of "creative" force *(creare)*, Ceres was more or less identified with a Demeter in human form and enhanced by a moving legend (Demeter in search of her daughter Kore, abducted by Pluto). This "new" Ceres was made into a statue which, according to Pliny the Elder, was "the first bronze statue made in

Rome." Consequently, she gained a "house," the temple built in 493 BCE to the triad near the Circus Maximus. The temple was decorated with the painting and sculptures of Damophilos and Gorgasos, two celebrated Greek artists. In this instance, hellenization had consisted in overlaying an Italic abstraction with an image and a legend. There is only a hellenization by contamination between homologous divinities. [*See* Syncretism.]

Yet some Greek gods came into Rome outside of any process of contamination. This fact has already been examined in the case of Castor. The same held true for Apollo. His introduction was due to an epidemic. Indeed it was not the god of the Muses, nor the sun god, nor the prophet god who would later be the patron of the Sibylline Books (these titles would appear in the *Carmen saeculare* by Horace during the time of Augustus) and to whom the Romans had appealed for aid at the beginning of the fifth century; rather, this Apollo was the healing god. His temple, dedicated in 433 "pro valetudine populi" ("for the people's health"), was dedicated in 431 in the Flaminian Meadows at the southwest of the Capitol, within a sector that already bore the name Apollinare ("Apollo's enclosure"; Livy, 4.25.3, 40.51.4). The oldest invocation used in the prayers of the Vestals were directed to the "physician": Apollo Medice, Apollo Paean (Macrobius, *Saturnalia* 1.17.15).

This introduction had been recommended by the Sibylline Books that were consulted upon orders of the Senate by the *viri sacris faciundis.* The striking thing in the cases of Castor and Apollo lies in the circumstances surrounding their manifestations. In both instances there was an imperative necessity: for the former, the essential situation was in a crucial battle; for the latter, it was an alarming pestilence. In contrast with Castor, who was introduced by the lone initiative of the dictator Aulus Postumius, Apollo entered Rome as a consequence of a consultation with the Sibylline Books. This procedure would be put to use more and more, and, as a result, the Romans became familiar with a new form of devotion, the *lectisternia,* which had more significance on the emotional level than was usual in Roman worship. This worship consisted essentially in a canonical prayer followed by the offering of consecrated entrails (the *exta*) to the divinity (the distinction between *exta*—comprising the lungs, the heart, the liver, the gall bladder, and the peritoneum—and the *viscera,* flesh given over for profane consumption, is fundamental in Roman liturgy). The sacrificial ceremony was celebrated by qualified magistrates and priests around the altar, placed in front of the temple. On the contrary, in the *ritus Graecus* statues of the deities reposing on cushions *(pulvinaria)* were exposed within the temples on ceremonial beds *(lectisternia).* Men, women, and children could approach them and offer them food and prayers in a fervent supplication (see Livy, 24.10.13; 32.1.14) often presided over by the *viri sacris faciundis* (cf. Livy, 4.21.5).

The first *lectisternium* was celebrated in 399 BCE at the injunction of the Sibylline Books that had been consulted by the *viri sacris faciundis* upon order of the Senate, which was worried about a persistent epidemic in Rome. It joined in heterogeneous pairs Apollo and Latona, Hercules and Diana, Mercury and Neptune (Livy, 5.13.4–6). Outwardly, half of the names were of purely Greek origin (Apollo, Latona, Hercules) and the other half of Latin origin. In reality, even these last names applied to Hellenic divinities: Diana/Artemis, Mercury/Hermes, Neptune/Poseidon. The healing god Apollo, accompanied by his mother Latona, was at the head of the list during this period of epidemic.

Much more dramatic circumstances—Hannibal at the walls of Rome—instigated in 217 BCE the last and most celebrated *lectisternium* in the history of the republic (Livy, 22.10.9). On this occasion, the Romans for the first time adopted the Greek plan of a set of twelve deities divided into six couples in the following order: Jupiter and Juno, Neptune and Minerva, Mars and Venus, Apollo and Diana, Vulcan and Vesta, Mercury and Ceres. This ceremony would remain unique (one cannot regard as a parallel the merry parody organized by Augustus during a *cena* where the twelve dinner companions disguised themselves as gods and goddesses (see Suetonius, *Augustus* 70). Without a doubt, the Greek inspiration is evident in this list, presenting couples of gods and goddesses (the idea of grouping twelve principal deities would be repeated later by the installation of gilded bronze statues of the *di consentes* in the niches located below the Portico at the foot of the Capitolium).

Yet it is necessary to avoid misunderstanding the meaning of the coupling here. The Greek model appeared in outline after the first four couples: Zeus-Hera, Poseidon-Athena, Ares-Aphrodite, Apollo-Artemis. It could suggest a conjugal meaning for Jupiter and Juno and an erotic meaning for Mars and Venus, but nothing of the kind would apply for the association of Neptune and Minerva (which evokes the rivalry of Poseidon and Athena in giving a name to Athens), nor for Apollo and Diana/Artemis, who were brother and sister. One can also wonder if the Romans were not still more heedful of the representative value of these divine pairs. Only a functional bond makes sense for the two last couples, in Rome as well as in Greece: fire for Vulcan and Vesta, economic activity (commerce and grain) for Mercury and Ceres. As for the couples that seemed most to bear the stamp of Hellenism, they were explained perfectly in accord with Roman norms. Thus Jupiter and Juno were associated here, just as they had been in the Capitoline cult since the sixth century. Nor did Venus and Mars form a couple in Rome in the strict sense of the term. Mars, father of Romulus, is the old Italic god, while Venus, mother of Aeneas, appeared as the protectress of the Romans-Aeneades. In a word, Rome knew how to utilize the Greek plan to her own ends without in turn submitting to it. She joined together the two essential personages of her history: Aeneas, the founder of the nation, and Romulus, founder of the city.

This example makes manifest a constant attitude. Nothing is more significant in this connection than the introduction of the cult of Venus Erycina. Once again the circumstantial cause was the imperative need for supplementary divine aid. It was during the Second Punic War (218–210), after the disaster of Trasimene in 217 BCE. Named as dictator, Q. Fabius Maximus (who would bear the surname *Cunctator*, or "delayer") obtained from the Senate a consultation with the Sibylline Books, which prescribed, among other measures, a promise to provide a temple dedicated to Venus Erycina (Livy, 22.9.7–11). This choice becomes clear when one recalls that, at the time of the First Punic War, the consul Lucius Junius had "recognized" Venus, the mother of Aeneas, in the Aphrodite of Mount Eryx, which he had succeeded in occupying from the start (248 BCE) up till the victorious finish. Thus the dictator who was struggling with the same enemy (the Carthaginians) as before, ought to vow to the same goddess—as a pledge of victory—a temple, which was dedicated in 215 on the Capitolium. It was the "Trojan light" that earned for Venus Erycina, "mother of the Aeneades," this majestic entry to the summit of the Capitolium, which was included at that date within the pomerial zone.

Some ten years later, the oriental goddess Cybele was introduced on the same basis. Once more, marvels had impressed religious awareness: "two suns were seen; intermittent flashes had streaked through the night; a trail of fire reached from east to west. . ." (Livy, 29.14.3). An oracle drawn from the Sibylline Books had predicted "the day when an enemy of foreign race would bring war to Italian soil, he could be defeated and banished from Italy, if the Mater Idaea were carried from Pessinus to Rome" (Livy, 29.10.5). In this way the Magna Mater (alias Cybele), honored as a "Trojan" ancestor despite her primitive nature (she was represented by a black sacred stone), was solemnly received in Rome in 204 BCE and was installed on the Palatine. Until the building of her own temple, which was dedicated in 191 BCE, she was provisionally lodged in the temple of Victoria.

The entry of these two goddesses, understood in terms of the "Trojan light," is instructive on another account as well. In spite of the considerable honors that she accorded them (far from treating them as outsiders, she installed them on the prestigious hills of the Capitoline and the Palatine), Rome did not neglect to subject their cults to discreet censorship. She treated Venus Erycina in two ways: in the temple on the Capitoline (dedicated in 215) she venerated her as a Roman goddess. However, in the extrapomerial temple, built later outside of the Porta Collina and dedicated in 181, she considered her to be a foreign goddess, covered by the statute of the *peregrina sacra* ("foreign rites") which allowed for tolerance of certain original customs. The temple of Venus Erycina outside the Porta Collina admitted, as an extension of the one on Mount Eryx, the presence of prostitutes in imitation of the sacred courtesans on the Sicilian mountain. The restraints were even stricter for the Magna Mater Idaea. Her cult could be practiced only by the Galli, the eunuch-priests, to the exclusion of Roman citizens. It was placed under the police surveillance of the urban praetor.

The affair of the Bacchanals in 186 BCE can be explained in similar fashion. Rome's action was not directed against the god Bacchus when in 186 BCE she forbade the Bacchanalia by a Senate decree. (Engraved on a bronze plaque, this valuable document, found in 1640 in the Abruzzi region, is kept in the Vienna Museum; it is illuminated by the ample report in Livy, 39.8–18.) Bacchus was present not only in Magna Graecia (at Cumae, an inscription dating from the first half of the fifth century establishes the existence of a burial ground reserved for Bacchants) but also in Etruria, where he was rendered as Fufluns, and in Latium, where he was rendered as Liber, the god celebrated in the Liberalia of 17 March. Following a denunciation, alarm had been created by the secret gatherings (Livy, 39.8.3) that reeked of scandals involving both men and women. The Bacchants were accused of taking part in criminal orgies in a milieu marked by "the groans of victims amid debaucheries and murders." The prohibition was dictated out of a concern for public order, the best proof of which is the fact that the Senate decree did not abolish the authorized celebration of the mysteries of Bacchus (for a limited—no more than five—number of participants) on condition of being subject to the permission and control of the officials. In conformity with Roman traditions, the distinction was made between *coniuratio* ("conspiracy") and *religio*.

Public Worship. The aim of public worship (the *sacra publica*) was to assure or to restore the "benevolence and grace of the gods," which the Romans considered indispensable for the state's well-being. To that end, the calendar days were divided into profane days *(dies profesti)* and days reserved for the gods (*dies festi* or *feriae*), and thus for liturgical celebrations. [*See* Fasti.] However, if one looks at a Roman calendar, one observes that the list of days contains some other signs. When the days are profane, they are marked by the letter *F (fasti);* when they pertain to the gods, by *N (nefasti).* This presentation does not call in question the division of "profane" and "sacred" times. It simply changes the perspective as to when "divine" becomes "human." Indeed, for the Romans, the day is *fastus* when it is *fas* ("religiously licit") to engage in profane occupations, *nefastus* when it is *nefas* ("religiously prohibited") to do so, since the day belongs to the gods. (In reality, the analytical spirit of the pontiffs came up with yet a third category of *C* days *(comitiales),* which, while profane, lent themselves in addition to the *comitia,* or "assemblies." Further, there are other rarely used letters, such as the three *dies fissi* (half *nefasti,* half *fasti*). The *dies religiosi* (or *atri*) are outside these categories: they are dates that commemorate public misfortunes, such as 18 July, the Dies Alliensis (commemorating the disaster of the battle of Allia in 390 BCE).

The republican calendar (called *fasti*) divided the ferial days over the course of twelve months. Each month was marked by the *calendae* (the first day), the *nonae,* and the *idus* (the last two fell respectively on the fifth or seventh, and the thirteenth or the fifteenth, according to whether they were ordinary months or March, May, July, or October). The feasts were fixed *(stativae)* or movable *(conceptivae)* or organized around some particular circumstance. The letters *(N, F, C)* of the different days, as well as the forty-five most important feasts that stand out in capital letters in the stone calendars, go back to the most ancient period, that of the institution of the lunar-solar calendar attributed to Numa.

The Roman liturgy developed in line with an order of feasts consecrated to particular deities. An overlap was therefore possible: since the ides, "days of full light," were always dedicated to Jupiter, the sacrifice of the Equus October ("horse of October") on 15 December coincided with them. This liturgy was punctuated by the rhythm of seasons for the agrarian celebrations (especially in April and in July-August) and by the schedule of training for military campaigns. Thus it is interesting to note that the month of March contained nearly all the feasts marking the opening of martial activities, just as in the month of October the feasts marked their closing. In March there was registered on the calends a sacrifice to the god Mars; the blessing of horses on the Equirria on 27 February and 14 March; and the blessing of arms on the Quinquatrus and of trumpets on the Tubilustrium on 19 March. In addition, there was the Agonium Martiale on 17 March. The month of October displayed a comparable list. On 1 October, a rite of purification was performed for the Tigillum Sororium; on the ides, the sacrifice of the Equus October offered to Mars; and on 19 October, the Armilustrium, or purification of arms. In both March and October the Salii, carrying lances *(hastae)* and shields *(ancilia)* roamed the city performing martial dances.

The feasts of archaic character continued to be celebrated, while at the same time, the *ritus graecus* produced a more emotional liturgy. The *supplicatio* (organized in 207 BCE, following upon a miracle) in honor of Juno Regina of the Aventine make a particularly memorable impression with an innovation: twenty-seven girls sang a hymn composed especially for the occasion by the poet Livius Andronicus (Livy, 27.37.7–15).

Besides the liturgical feasts, it is also necessary to cite the *ludi,* games consisting essentially of chariot races. They went back to an old tradition represented by the Equirria. The new *ludi* replaced the *bigae,* teams of two horses, with the *quadrigae,* teams of four, for the races in the Circus Maximus and included various performances: riders leaping from one horse to another, fights with wrestlers and boxers. (The gladiator fights, which were Etruscan in origin, appeared in 264 BCE for private funeral feasts, but they did not become part of the public games until the end of the second century BCE.) These competitions were soon complemented by other spectacles: pantomimes and dances accompanied by the flute. The principal ones were the Ludi Magni or Ludi Romani, celebrated from the fifteenth through the eighteenth of September after the ides that coincided with the anniversary of the temple of Jupiter Capitoline. (It is known that an interval, *dies postriduanus*—the fourteenth of September in this instance—had to separate the ides from another feast day.) Considered to have been instituted by Tarquin the Elder (Livy, 1.35.9), they became annual events starting in 367 BCE, which is the date that saw the creation of the curule magistracy *(aediles curules).* The Ludi Plebei, a kind of plebeian reply to preceding games, were instituted later: they are mentioned for the first time in 216 BCE (Livy, 23.30.17). They took place in the Circus Flaminius, involved the same kind of games as the Ludi Romani, and were celebrated around the time of the ides of November. It is also noteworthy that the Ludi Romani and the Ludi Plebei were both held around the ides (of September or November) and dedicated to Jupiter, to whom a sacrificial meal, the Epulum Jovis, was offered. The public worship was conducted by a corps of specialized priests. While the *rex sacrorum* and the three major *flamines* appeared more and more as archaic characters, the *pontifex maximus* (the last of the ancient *ordo sacer-*

dotum) became the first in importance under the republic. He was the one to preside over the pontifical college in the Regia, or "king's house" of times past. He was the one to name the *rex sacrorum*, the *flamines maiores*, and the Vestal Virgins. He was attended by a college of pontiffs that grew from three to nine members (the Lex Ogulnia of 300 BCE), then to fifteen (the Lex Cornelia of 82 BCE), and finally to sixteen (the Lex Julia of 46 BCE). He had the upper hand in respect to the calendar, the public rites, and the temple laws.

As for the Vestal Virgins, residing near the Regia in the Atrium Vestae under the direction of a *virgo maxima*, their essential mission was to maintain the public hearth in the Aedes Vestae. They were six in number. Their service lasted thirty years and enjoyed great prestige (Cicero, *Pro Fonteio* 48). Their liturgical importance is confirmed by two significant points. Once a year, they would make their way to the king in order to ask him: "Are you vigilant, king? Be vigilant!" On another solemn occasion, the *virgo maxima* mounted the Capitolium in the company of the *pontifex maximus* (Horace, *Carmina* 3.30.8).

The Augures ("augurs") made up the second college. Their official title served as a clear definition: "The augurs of the state are the interpreters of the almighty Jupiter." In having recourse to the *auspicium*, divination by means of the observation of birds, they discerned the *augurium* (the presence of the heavenly blessing), specifically of the **augus* ("fullness of mystical power" in Georges Dumézil's translation). It also fell upon them to inaugurate both persons (the *rex sacrorum* and the three *flamines maiores*) and buildings *(templa)*. Their college's structure evolved like that of the pontifical college: beginning with three, the number of augurs grew to six, to nine (in 300 BCE), then to fifteen (under Sulla), and finally to sixteen (under Julius Caesar).

The *viri sacris faciundis*, "men in charge of the celebration of sacrifices," were responsible for safeguarding and for consulting the Sibylline Books by order of the Senate. There were at first two of them, then ten (beginning in 367 BCE), and finally fifteen. The Epulones were created in 196 BCE in order to relieve the pontiffs of some of their obligations. In particular, it was their duty to organize the sacrificial supper, the Epulum Jovis, at the Ludi Romani and the Ludi Plebei. They numbered three at first, then seven, and finally ten.

The plebeians' access to these four kinds of priesthoods was acquired gradually. The Lex Licinia Sextiae of 367 BCE assigned to them half of the ten seats of the *viri sacris faciundis*. In 300 BCE the Lex Ogulnia admitted the plebeians to a half-share in the colleges of the pontiffs and the augurs. In 103 BCE the Lex Domitia de Sacerdotiis established the principle of election of these priests by seventeen tribes chosen by lot, using a list of candidates presented by each college involved. From then on this method of recruitment was used (instead of co-optation) for the *sacerdotum quattuor amplissima collegia*.

In addition to the four *collegia*, it is worth mentioning the fraternities that, for their part, confirm the liking in Rome for priestly specialization. The twenty Fetiales saw to the protection of Rome in her foreign relations, especially with regard to declarations of war and conclusion of peace treaties. The twenty-four Salii (twelve Salii Palatini and twelve Salii Collini) were the dancer-priests who opened the season of war in March and closed it in October. The twenty-four Luperci (twelve Fabiani and twelve Quinctiales) acted only in the rites of the Lupercalia on 15 February. The twelve Arval Brothers were in charge of the blessing of the fields *(arva)*. They disappeared before the end of the republic but were restored by Augustus. (In their *Acta* they recorded the ancient liturgical chant, known as the *Carmen Arvale*.) [*See* Arval Brothers.]

Private Worship. The expression *Populus Romanus Quiritium* ("the citizens of Rome") attests in itself to the power of collective bonds: the individual does not exist except as a member of the community. The best proof of it is that the Latin grammarians have insisted on only one instance in which *Quirites* had a singular form: when the citizen left the community through death. Then, "a herald declared in the funeral notice: this Quiris has passed away."

Within this community there were smaller groups such as the *curia*, the *gens*, and the *familia*. It was within the bosom of the family, placed under the authority of the *pater familias*, that the first private forms of worship were celebrated. The day of birth *(dies natalis)* and the day of purification (*dies lustricus:* the ninth day for boys, the eighth for girls, when the infant received its name) were the family feasts. In the atrium of the family home, the infant would acquire the habit of honoring the household gods (the *lar familiaris* and the *di penates*). The allusion made in the *Aulularia* (v. 24s) by Plautus to the young daughter, who every day would bring "some gift such as incense, wine, or garlands" to the *lar familiaris*, shows that personal devotion was not unknown in Rome. Livy (26.19.5) cites a more illustrious example of this kind about P. Cornelius Scipio, the future conqueror of Hannibal. "After he received the *toga virilis*, he undertook no action, whether public or private, without going right away to the Capitolium. Once he reached the sanctuary, he remained there in contemplation, normally all alone in private for some time" (it is true that a rumor attributed divine ancestry to Scipio, something he very carefully neither confirmed nor denied). [*See* Lares.]

The taking of the *toga virilis,* or *pura* (as opposed to the *toga praetexta,* bordered with a purple ribbon and worn by children), generally took place at age seventeen during the feast of the Liberalia on 17 March. Before this point, the *puer* ("boy") had offered his *bulla* (a golden amulet) to the *lar familiaris* (under the republic, the plural *lares familiares* often designated, by way of extension, the group of divinities in the home: Lar, *penates,* Vesta. From then on, he was a *iuvenis.* He would go up to the Capitolium to offer a sacrifice and leave an offering in the sanctuary of the goddess Iuventas. Another family feast occurred on the birthday of the father of the family in honor of his genius. A warm atmosphere brought together the whole family (including the servants) at least twice a year. On 1 March, the feast of the Matronalia, the mothers of families would make their way up the Esquiline to the temple of Juno Lucina, whose anniversary it was. Together with their husbands they prayed "for the safeguarding of their union" and received presents. They themselves then prepared dinner for their slaves. Macrobius (*Saturnalia* 1.12.7), who mentions this custom, adds that on 17 December, the feast of the Saturnalia, it was the masters' turn to serve their slaves, unless they preferred to share dinner with them (*Saturnalia* 1.7.37).

At the end of life, the Feria Denecales (*denecales* or *deni-,* no doubt from *de nece,* "following death") were matched by the Feriae Natales. Their purpose was to purify the family in mourning. For the deceased was regarded as having defiled his family, which thus became *funesta* ("defiled by death"). To this end, a *novemdiale sacrum* was offered on the ninth day after burial. As for the deceased, his body, or a finger thereof kept aside *(os resectum)* in the case of cremation, was buried in a place that become inviolable *(religiosus).* The burial was indispensable in order to assure the repose of the deceased, who from then on was venerated among the *di parentes* (later the *di manes*). (If there were no burial, he risked becoming one of the mischievous spirits, the *lemures,* which the father of the family would expel at midnight on the Lemuria of 9, 11, and 13 May.)

During the Dies Parentales, from the thirteenth to the twenty-first of February, the family would go to the tomb of their dead in order to bring them gifts. [*See* Parentalia.] Since the period of time ended on 21 February with a public feast, the Feralia, the next day, 22 February, reverted to a private feast, the Caristia or Cara Cognatio; the members of the family gathered and comforted one another around a banquet. This explains the compelling need in an old family for legitimate offspring (either by bloodline or by adoption). In their turn, the duty of the descendants was to carry on the family worship and to calm the souls of their ancestors.

BIBLIOGRAPHY

Bayet, Jean. *Histoire politique et psychologique de la religion romaine.* 2d ed. Paris, 1969.

Castagnoli, Ferdinando. *Lavinium.* Vol. 1, *Topografia generale, fonti et storia delle richerche.* Rome, 1972.

Castagnoli, Ferdinando, et al., eds. *Lavinium.* Vol. 2, *Le tredici are.* Rome, 1975.

Catalano, Pierangelo. *Contributi allo studio del diritto augurale.* Vol. 1. Torino, 1960.

Connor, W. R. *Roman Augury and Etruscan Divination.* Salem, N.Y., 1976.

Conway, Robert S. *The Italic Dialects.* 2 vols. Cambridge, 1897. On the Tabula Agnonensis, see pages 191–193. On the Tabula Bantina, see pages 22–29.

Crawford, Michael. *The Roman Republic.* Cambridge, Mass., 1982.

Dumézil, Georges. *Rituels indo-européens à Rome.* Paris, 1954.

Dumézil, Georges. *Déesses latines et mythes védiques.* Brussels, 1956.

Dumézil, Georges. *Idées romaines.* Paris, 1969.

Dumézil, Georges. *La religion romaine archaïque.* 2d ed. Paris, 1974. Translated from the first edition by Philip Krapp as *Archaic Roman Religion,* 2 vols. (Chicago, 1970).

Dumézil, Georges. *Camillus: A Study of Indo-European Religion as Roman History.* Edited by Udo Strutynski and translated by Annette Aronowicz et al. Berkeley, 1980.

Fowler, W. Warde. *The Roman Festivals of the Period of the Republic* (1899). Port Washington, N.Y., 1969.

Fowler, W. Warde. *Religious Experience of the Roman People: From Earliest Times to the Age of Augustus* (1911). Totowa, N.J., 1971.

Latte, Kurt. *Römische Religionsgeschichte.* Munich, 1960.

Marquardt, Joachim. *Le culte chez les Romains.* 2 vols. Paris, 1889–1890.

Michels, Agnes K. *The Calendar of the Roman Republic.* Princeton, 1967.

Mommsen, Theodor. *Römisches Staatsrecht* (1871–1888). 3 vols. Basel, 1952.

Schilling, Robert. *Rites, cultes, dieux de Rome.* Paris, 1979.

Schilling, Robert. "Rome: Les dieux." In *Dictionnaire des mythologies et des religions,* vol. 2. Paris, 1981.

Schilling, Robert. *La religion romaine de Vénus, depuis les origines jusqu'au temps d'Auguste.* 2d ed. Paris, 1982.

Wikander, Stig. "Les '-ismes' dans la terminologie historico-religieuse." In *Les syncrétismes dans les religions grecque et romaine,* pp. 9–14. Paris, 1973.

Wissowa, Georg. *Religion und Kultus der Romer.* 2d ed. Munich, 1912.

ROBERT SCHILLING
Translated from French by Paul C. Duggan

The Imperial Period

The Roman state's extraordinary and unexpected transformation from one that had hegemony over the greater part of Italy into a world state in the second and first centuries BCE had implications for Roman religion which are not easy to grasp. After all, Christianity, a religion wholly "foreign" in its origins, arose from this period of Roman ascendancy. To begin, then, to understand the religious system of imperial Rome, it is best to confine ourselves to three elementary and obviously related facts.

The first is that the old Roman practice of inviting the chief gods of their enemies to become gods of Rome *(evocatio)* played little or no part in the new stage of imperialism. *Evocatio* does not seem to have had any role in the wars in Spain, Gaul, and the East; it is mentioned only, and on dubious evidence (Servius, *Ad Aeneidem* 12.841), in relation to Rome's conquest of Carthage.

The second fact is that while it was conquering the Hellenistic world Rome was involved in a massive absorption of Greek language, literature, and religion, with the consequence that the Roman gods became victorious over Greece at precisely the time that they came to be identified with Greek gods. As the gods were expected to take sides and to favor their own worshipers, this must have created some problems.

The third fact is that the conquest of Africa, Spain, and, ultimately, Gaul produced the opposite phenomenon of a large, though by no means systematic, identification of Punic, Iberian, and Celtic gods with Roman gods. This, in turn, is connected with two opposite aspects of the Roman conquest of the West. On the one hand, the Romans had little sympathy and understanding for the religion of their Western subjects. Although occasionally guilty of human sacrifice, they found the various forms of human sacrifices which were practiced more frequently in Africa, Spain, and Gaul repugnant (hence their later efforts to eliminate the druids in Gaul and in Britain). On the other hand, northern Africa, outside Egypt, and western Europe were deeply latinized in language and romanized in institutions, thereby creating the conditions for the assimilation of native gods to Roman gods.

Yet the Mars, the Mercurius, and even the Jupiter and the Diana we meet so frequently in Gaul under the Romans are not exactly the same as in Rome. The individuality of the Celtic equivalent of Mercurius has already been neatly noted by Caesar. Some Roman gods, such as Janus and Quirinus, do not seem to have penetrated Gaul. Similarly, in Africa, Saturnus preserved much of the Baal Hammon with whom he was identified. There, Juno Caelestis (or simply Caelestis, destined to considerable veneration outside Africa) is Tanit (Tinnit), the female companion of Baal Hammon. The assimilation of the native god is often revealed by an accompanying adjective (in Gaul, Mars Lenus, Mercurius Dumiatis, etc.,). An analogous phenomenon had occurred in the East under the Hellenistic monarchies: native, especially Semitic, gods were assimilated to Greek gods, especially to Zeus and Apollo. The Eastern assimilation went on under Roman rule (as seen, for example, with Zeus Panamaros in Caria).

Roman soldiers, becoming increasingly professional and living among natives for long periods of time, played a part in these syncretic tendencies. A further consequence of imperialism was the emphasis on Victory and on certain gods of Greek origin (such as Herakles and Apollo) as gods of victory. Victoria was already recognized as a goddess during the Samnite Wars; she was later associated with various leaders, from Scipio Africanus to Sulla and Pompey. Roman emperors used an elaborate religious language in their discussions of Victory. Among Christians, Augustine of Hippo depicted Victory as God's angel (*City of God* 4.17).

The Romans also turned certain gods of Greek origin into gods of victory. As early as 145 BCE L. Mummius dedicated a temple to Hercules Victor after his triumph over Greece. After a victory, generals often offered 10 percent of their booty to Hercules, and Hercules Invictus was a favorite god of Pompey. Apollo was connected with Victory as early as 212 BCE. Caesar boosted her ancestress Venus in the form of Venus Victrix. But it was Apollo who helped Octavian, the future Augustus, to win the Battle of Actium in September of 31 BCE.

Imperial Attitudes toward and Uses of Religion. Augustus and his contemporaries thought, or perhaps in some cases wanted other people to think, that the preceding age (roughly the period from the Gracchi to Caesar) had seen a decline in the ancient Roman care for gods. Augustus himself stated in the autobiographical record known as the *Res gestae* that he and his friends had restored eighty-two temples. He revived cults and religious associations, such as the Arval Brothers and the fraternity of the Titii, and appointed a *flamen dialis*, a priestly office that had been left vacant since 87 BCE. This revivalist feeling was not entirely new: it was behind the enormous collection of evidence concerning ancient Roman cults, the "divine antiquities," which Varro had dedicated to Caesar about 47 BCE in his *Antiquitatum rerum humanarum et divinarum libri*; the rest of the work, the "human antiquities," was devoted to Roman political institutions and customs. Varro's work became as much a codification of Roman religion for succeeding generations as existed, and as such it was used for polemical purposes by Christian apologists; it was, however, never a guide for ordinary worshipers.

For us, inevitably, it is difficult to do justice at the same time to the mood of the Augustan restoration and to the unquestionable seriousness with which the political and military leaders of the previous century tried to support their unusual adventures by unusual religious attitudes. Marius, a devotee of the Magna Mater (Cybele), was accompanied in his campaigns by a Syrian prophetess. Sulla apparently brought from Cappadocia the goddess Ma, soon identified with Bellona, whose orgiastic and prophetic cult had wide appeal. Furthermore, he developed a personal devotion to Venus and Fortuna and set an example for Caesar, who claimed Venus as the ancestress of the *gens Julia*. As *pontifex maximus* for twenty years, Caesar reformed not only individual cults but also the calendar, which had great religious significance. He tried to support his claim to dictatorial powers by collecting religious honors which, though obscure in detail and debated by modern scholars, anticipate later imperial cult.

Unusual religious attitudes were not confined to leaders. A Roman senator, Nigidius Figulus, made religious combinations of his own both in his writings and in his practice: magic, astrology, and Pythagoreanism were some of the ingredients. Cicero, above all, epitomized the search of educated men of the first century BCE for the right balance between respect for the ancestral cults and the requirements of philosophy. Cicero could no longer believe in traditional divination. When his daughter died in 45 BCE he embarked briefly on a project for making her divine. This was no less typical of the age than the attempt by Clodius in 62 BCE to desecrate the festival of Bona Dea, reserved to women, in order to contact Caesar's wife; he escaped punishment.

The imperial age was inclined to distinctions and to compromises. The Roman *pontifex maximus* Q. Mucius Scaevola is credited with the popularization of the distinction, originally Greek, between the gods of the poets as represented in myths, the gods of ordinary people to be found in cults and sacred laws, and finally the gods of the philosophers, confined to books and private discussion. It was the distinction underlying the thought of Varro and Cicero. No wonder, therefore, that in that atmosphere of civil wars and personal hatreds, cultic rules and practices were exploited ruthlessly to embarrass enemies while no one could publicly challenge the ultimate validity of traditional practices.

The Augustan restoration discouraged philosophical speculation about the nature of the gods: Lucretius's *De rerum natura* remains characteristic of the age of Caesar. Augustan poets (Horace, Tibullus, Propertius, and Ovid) evoked obsolescent rites and emphasized piety. Vergil interpreted the Roman past in religious terms. Nevertheless, the combined effect of the initiatives of Caesar and Augustus amounted to a new religious situation.

For centuries the aristocracy in Rome had controlled what was called *ius sacrum* ("sacred law"), the religious aspect of Roman life, but the association of priesthood with political magistracy, though frequent and obviously convenient, had never been institutionalized. In 27 BCE the assumption by Octavian of the permanent title *augustus* implied, though not very clearly, permanent approval of the gods (*augustus* may connote a holder of permanent favorable auspices). In 12 BCE Augustus assumed the position of *pontifex maximus*, which became permanently associated with the figure of the emperor *(imperator)*, the new head for life of the Roman state. Augustus's new role resulted in an identification of religious with political power, which had not existed in Rome since at least the end of the monarchy. Furthermore, the divinization of Caesar after his death had made Augustus, as his adoptive son, the son of a *divus*. In turn Augustus was officially divinized *(apotheosis)* after his death by the Roman Senate. Divinization after death did not become automatic for his successors (Tiberius, Gaius, and Nero were not divinized); nevertheless, Augustus's divinization created a presumption that there was a divine component in an ordinary emperor who had not misbehaved in his lifetime. [*See* Augustus.] It also reinforced the trend toward the cult of the living emperor, which had been most obvious during Augustus's life. With the Flavian dynasty and later with the Antonines, it was normal for the head of the Roman state to be both the head of the state religion and a potential, or even actual, god.

As the head of Roman religion, the Roman emperor was therefore in the paradoxical situation of being responsible not only for relations between the Roman state and the gods but also for a fair assessment of his own qualifications to be considered a god, if not after his life, at least while he was alive. This situation, however, must not be assumed to have applied universally. Much of the religious life in individual towns was in the hands of local authorities or simply left to private initiative. The financial support for public cults was in any case very complex, too complex to be discussed here. It will be enough to mention that the Roman state granted or confirmed to certain gods in certain sanctuaries the right to receive legacies (Ulpian, *Regulae* 22.6). In providing money for a local shrine an emperor implied no more than benevolence toward the city or group involved.

Within the city of Rome, however, the emperor was in virtual control of the public cults. As a Greek god,

Apollo had been kept outside of the *pomerium* since his introduction into Rome: his temple was in the Campus Martius. Under Augustus, however, Apollo received a temple inside the *pomerium* on the Palatine in recognition of the special protection he had offered to Octavian. The Sibylline Books, an ancient collection of prophecies that had been previously preserved on the Capitol, were now transferred to the new temple. Later, Augustus demonstrated his preference for Mars as a family god, and a temple to Mars Ultor (the avenger of Caesar's murder) was built. It was no doubt on the direct initiative of Hadrian that the cult of Rome as a goddess (in association with Venus) was finally introduced into the city centuries after the cult had spread outside of Italy. A temple to the Sun (Sol), a cult popular in the empire at large, and not without some roots in the archaic religion of Rome, had to wait until the emperor Aurelian in 274 CE, if one discounts the cult of the Ba'al of Emesa, a sun god, which came and went with the emperor Elagabalus in 220–221. Another example of these changes inside Rome is the full romanization of the Etruscan haruspices performed by the emperor Claudius in 47 CE (Tacitus, *Annals* 11.15).

A further step in the admission of Oriental gods to the official religion of Rome was the building of a temple to Isis under Gaius. The cult of Isis had been contested and ultimately confined outside the *pomerium,* associated as it was with memories of Cleopatra, the Egyptian enemy of Augustus. Jupiter Dolichenus, an Oriental god popular among soldiers, was probably given a temple on the Aventine in the second century CE.

We have some evidence that the Roman priestly colleges intervened in the cults of *municipia* and *coloniae,* but on the whole we cannot expect the cults of Rome herself to remain exemplary for Roman citizens living elsewhere. For example, Vitruvius, who dedicated his work on architecture to Octavian before the latter became Augustus in 27, assumes that in an Italian city there should be a temple to Isis and Sarapis (*De architectura* 1.7.1); Isis, we know, was kept out of Rome in those years. Caracalla, however, presented his grant of Roman citizenship to the provincials in 212 CE in hope of contributing to religious unification (*Papyrus Giessen* 40). Although the cult of the Capitoline triad appears in Egypt, the results of this grant were modest in religious terms.

Coins and medals, insofar as they were issued under the control of the central government, provide some indication of imperial preferences in the matter of gods and cults. They allow us to say when and how certain Oriental cults (such as that of Isis, as reflected on coins of Vespasian) or certain attributes of a specific god were considered helpful to the empire and altogether suitable for the man in the street who used coins. But since as a rule it avoided references to cults of rulers, coinage can be misleading if taken alone. Imperial cult and Oriental cults are, in fact, two of the most important features of Roman religion in the imperial period. But we also have to take into consideration popular, not easily definable trends; the religious beliefs or disbeliefs of the intellectuals; the greater participation of women in religious and in intellectual life generally; and, finally, the peculiar problems presented by the persecution of Christianity.

The Imperial Cult. Imperial cult was many things to many people. The emperor never became a complete god, even if he was considered a god, because he was not requested to produce miracles, even for supposed deliverance from peril. Vespasian performed miracles in Alexandria soon after his proclamation as emperor, but these had no precise connection to his potential divine status; he remained an exception in any case. Hadrian never performed miracles, but his young lover Antinoüs, who was divinized after death, is known to have performed some (F. K. Dörner, *Denkschriften der Wiener Akademie* 75, 1952, p. 40, no. 78).

Apotheosis, decided by the Senate, was the only official form of deification valid for everyone in the empire and was occasionally extended to members of the imperial family (Drusilla, the sister of Gaius, received apotheosis in 38 CE.) It had its precedent, of course, in the apotheosis of Romulus. [*See also* Apotheosis.] Ultimately, the cult of the living emperor mattered more. [*See* Emperor's Cult.] It was the result of a mixture of spontaneous initiative by provincial and local councils (and even by private individuals) and promptings from provincial governors and the emperor himself. It had precedents not only in the Hellenistic ruler cult but also in the more or less spontaneous worship of Roman generals and governors, especially in the hellenized East. Cicero, for example, had to decline such worship when he was a provincial governor (*Ad Atticum* 5.21.7).

The cult of Roman provincial governors disappeared with Augustus, to the exclusive benefit of the emperor and his family. When he did not directly encourage the ruler cult, the emperor still had to approve, limit, and occasionally to refuse it. Although he had to be worshiped, he also had to remain a man in order to live on social terms with the Roman aristocracy, of which he was supposed to be the *princeps*. It was a delicate balancing act. It is probably fair to say that during his lifetime the emperor was a god more in proportion to his remoteness, rather than his proximity, and that the success (for success it was) of the imperial cult in the provinces was due to the presence it endowed to an absent and alien sovereign. His statues, his temples, and his priests, as well as the games, sacrifices, and other ceremonial acts, helped make the emperor present; they also helped people to express their interest in the preservation of the world in which they lived.

The imperial cult was not universally accepted and liked. Seneca ridiculed the cult of Claudius, and Tacitus spoke of the cult in general as Greek adulation. In the third century the historian Dio Cassius attributed to Augustus's friend Maecenas a total condemnation of the imperial cult. Jews and Christians objected to it on principle, and the acts of the Christian martyrs remind us that there was an element of brutal imposition in the imperial cult. [*See* Persecution, *article on* Christian Experience.] But its controversial nature in certain circles may well have been another factor of the cult's success: conflicts help any cause. There is even some vague evidence (Pleket, 1965, p. 331) that some groups treated the imperial cult as a mystery religion in which priests revealed some secrets about the emperors.

Schematically it can be said that in Rome and Italy Augustus favored the association of the cult of his life spirit *(genius)* with the old cult of the public *lares* of the crossroads *(lares compitales):* such a combined cult was in the hands of humble people. Similar associations (Augustales) developed along various lines in Italy and gave respectability to the freedmen who ran them. Augustus's birthday was considered a public holiday. His *genius* was included in public oaths between Jupiter Optimus Maximus and the *penates.* In Augustus's last years Tiberius dedicated an altar to the *numen Augusti* in Rome; the four great priestly colleges had to make yearly sacrifices at it. *Numen,* in an obscure way, implied divine will.

In the West, central initiative created the altar of Roma and Augustus in Lyons, to be administered by the Council of the Gauls (12 BCE). A similar altar was built at Oppidum Ubiorum (Cologne). Later temples to Augustus (by then officially divinized) were erected in Western provinces. In the East, temples to Roma and Divus Julius and to Roma and Augustus were erected as early as 29 BCE. There, as in the West, provincial assemblies took a leading part in the establishment of the cult. Individual cities were also active: priests of Augustus are found in thirty-four different cities of Asia Minor. The organization of the cult varied locally. There was no collective provincial cult of the emperor in Egypt, though there was a cult in Alexandria. And any poet, indeed any man, could have his own idea about the divine nature of the emperor. Horace, for example, suggested that Augustus might be Mercurius.

Augustus's successors tended to be worshiped either individually, without the addition of Roma, or collectively with past emperors. In Asia Minor the last individual emperor known to have received a personal priesthood or temple is Caracalla. In this province—though not necessarily elsewhere—the imperial cult petered out at the end of the third century. Nevertheless, Constantine, in the fourth century, authorized the building of a temple for the *gens Flavia* (his own family) in Italy at Hispellum, but without "contagion of superstition"—whatever he may have meant by this (*Corpus inscriptionum Latinarum,* Berlin, 1863, vol. 11, no. 5265).

It is difficult to say how much the ceremonial of the imperial court reflected divinization of the emperors. We hear, however, that Domitian wanted to be called "dominus et deus" (Suetonius, *Domitian* 13.2). In the third century a specific identification of the living emperor with a known god seems to be more frequent (for instance, Septimius Severus and his wife, Julia Domna, with Jupiter and Juno). When the imperial cult died out, the emperor had to be justified as the choice of god; he became emperor by the grace of god. Thus Diocletian and Maximian, the persecutors of Christianity, present themselves not as Jupiter and Hercules but as Jovius and Herculius, that is, the protégés of Jupiter and Hercules. It must be added that during the first centuries of the empire the divinization of the emperor was accompanied by a multiplication of divinizations of private individuals, in the West often of humble origin. Such divinization took the form of identifying the dead, and occasionally the living, with a known hero or god. Sometimes the divinization was nothing more than an expression of affection by relatives or friends. But it indicated a tendency to reduce the distance between men and gods, which helped the fortunes of the imperial cult. We need to know more about private divinizations (but see Henning Wrede, *Consecratio in formam deorum,* Mainz, 1981).

Oriental Influences. Oriental cults penetrated the Roman empire at various dates, in different circumstances, and with varying appeal, although on the whole they seem to have supplemented religious needs in the Latin West more than in the hellenized East. They tended, though not in equal measure, to present themselves as mystery cults: they often required initiation and, perhaps more often, some religious instruction.

Cybele, the first Oriental divinity to be found acceptable in Rome since the end of the third century BCE, was long an oddity in the city. As the Magna Mater ("great mother"), she had been imported by governmental decision, she had a temple within the *pomerium,* and she was under the protection of members of the highest Roman aristocracy. Yet her professional priests, singing in Greek and living by their temple, were considered alien fanatics even in imperial times. What is worse, the goddess also had servants, the Galli, who had castrated themselves to express their devotion to her. [*See also* Cybele.]

Under the emperor Claudius, Roman citizens were probably allowed some priestly functions, though the matter is very obscure. Even more obscure is the way in which Attis, who is practically absent from the republican written evidence concerning Cybele, became Cybele's major partner. A new festival, from 15 to 27 March, apparently put special emphasis on the resurrection of Attis. Concurrently, the cult of Cybele became associated with the ritual of the slaying of the sacred bull *(taurobolium)*, which Prudentius (*Peristephanon* 10. 1006–1050) interpreted as a baptism of blood. The ritual was performed for the prosperity of the emperor or of the empire and, more frequently, for the benefit of private individuals. Normally it was considered valid for twenty years, which makes it questionable whether it was meant to confer immortality on the baptized.

Although Isis appealed to men as well as to women—and indeed her priests were male—it seems clear that her prestige as a goddess was due to the unusual powers she was supposed to have as a woman. The so-called aretalogies (description of the powers) of Isis insist on this. Thus the earliest aretalogy, found at Maroneia in Macedonia, tells of Isis as legislator and as protector of the respect of children for their parents (Merkelbach, 1976, p. 234). The Kyme text declares that she compelled husbands to love their wives (H. Engelmann, ed., *Kyme* 1.97), and the Oxyrhynchus hymn in her honor explicitly states that she made the power of women equal to that of men (*Oxyrhynchus Papyri* 11.1380). No god or goddess of Greece and Rome had achievements comparable with those of Isis. The girlfriends of the Augustan poets Tibullus and Propertius were captivated by her. In association with Osiris or Sarapis, Isis seems to have become the object of a mystery cult in the first century CE; as such she appears in Apuleius's *Metamorphoses*. [*See also* Isis.]

Late in the first century CE, Mithraism began to spread throughout the Roman empire, especially in the Danubian countries and in Italy (in particular, as far as we know, in Ostia and Rome). A developed mystery cult, it had ranks of initiation and leadership and was, to the best of our present knowledge, reserved to men—a clear difference from the cult of Isis. It was practiced in subterranean chapels rather than in temples, although his identification with the sun god gave Mithra some temples. The environment of the Mithraic cult, as revealed in numerous extant chapels, was one of darkness, secrecy, dramatic lighting effects, and magic.

What promise Mithra held for his devotees we do not know for certain. The cult seems to have encouraged soldierly qualities, including sexual abstinence. It certainly presented some correspondence between the degrees of initiation and the levels of the celestial spheres, which may or may not imply an ascent of the soul to these spheres. The killing of the bull (in itself different from the *taurobolium* and perhaps without any implication of baptism) was apparently felt to be a sacrifice performed not for the god but by the god. The initiates reenacted this sacrifice and shared sacred meals in a sort of communal life. Tertullian considered Mithraism a devilish imitation of Christianity, but the Neoplatonist Porphyry found in it allegorical depths. [*See also* Mithra; Mithraism; *and* Mystery Religions.]

The cult of Sabazios may have been originally Phrygian. Sabazios appears in Athens in the fifth century BCE as an orgiastic god. He was known to Aristophanes, and later the orator Aeschines became his priest. There is evidence of mysteries of Sabazios in Lydia dating from the fourth century BCE. In Rome the cult was already known in 139 BCE. It may at that time have been confused with Judaism, but Sabazios was often identified with Jupiter or Zeus, and there seems to be no clear evidence of syncretism between Sabazios and Yahveh. Sabazios was most popular in the second century CE, especially in the Danubian region. [*See* Sabazios.] In Rome his cult left a particularly curious document in the tomb of Vincentius, located in the catacomb of Praetextatus; it includes scenes of banquets and of judgment after death. Whether this is evidence of mystery ceremonies or of Christian influence remains uncertain. (See Erwin R. Goodenough, *Jewish Symbols in the Greco-Roman Period,* vol. 2, 1953, p. 45, for a description.) The tomb of Vincentius appears to belong to the third century, when, judging by the epigraphic evidence, there seems to have been a decline of the cult of Sabazios and, indeed, of all mystery cults. Although a shortage of inscriptions does not necessarily imply a shortage of adepts, one has the impression that by then Christianity was seriously interfering with the popularity of Oriental cults.

Another popular Oriental god occupies a place by himself. This is Jupiter Dolichenus, who emerged from Doliche in Commagene in the first century CE and for whom we have about six hundred monuments. Of the Oriental gods, he seems to have been the least sophisticated and to have disappeared earliest (in the third century). He was ignored by Christian polemicists. While he circulated in the empire, he preserved his native attributes: he is depicted as a warrior with Phrygian cap, double ax, and lightning bolt, standing erect over a bull. He was often accompanied by a goddess, called Juno Regina in the Roman interpretation. Twins, identified with the Castores, followed him; their lower parts were unshaped, and they were probably demons. Soldiers seem to have loved the cult of Jupiter Dolichenus. Its priests were not professional, and the adepts called each other brother. Admission to the cult presupposed instruction, if not initiation.

Extent of Syncretism. We are in constant danger of either overrating or underrating the influence of these Oriental cults on the fabric of the Roman empire. If, for instance, Mithraists knew of the Zoroastrian deity Angra Mainyu, what did he mean to them? How did this knowledge affect the larger society? At a superficial level we can take these cults as an antidote to the imperial cult, an attempt to retreat from the public sphere of political allegiance to the private sphere of small, free associations. The need for small loyalties was widely felt during the imperial peace. Distinctions between social, charitable, and religious purposes in these multiform associations are impossible. Tavern keepers devoted to their wine god and poor people meeting regularly in burial clubs are examples of such associations *(collegia)*. Ritualization of ordinary life emerged from their activities. Nor is it surprising that what to one was religion was superstition to another (to use two Latin terms which ordinary Latin speakers would have been hard-pressed to define). Although allegiance to the local gods (and respect for them, if one happened to be a visitor) was deeply rooted, people were experimenting with new private gods and finding satisfaction in them. Concern with magic and astrology, with dreams and demons, seems ubiquitous. Conviviality was part of religion. Aelius Aristides has good things to say about Sarapis as patron of the *symposium*. Pilgrimages to sanctuaries were made easier by relative social stability. Several gods, not only Asclepius (Gr., Asklepios), offered healing to the sick. (Here again we have Aelius Aristides as chief witness for the second century.) Hence miracles, duly registered in inscriptions; hence also single individuals, perhaps cranks, attaching themselves to temples and living in their precincts.

The real difficulties in understanding the atmosphere of paganism in the Roman empire perhaps lie elsewhere. It remains a puzzle how, and how much, ordinary people were supposed to know about official Roman religion. The same problem exists concerning the Greeks in relation to the religions of individual Greek cities. But in Greek cities the collective education of adolescents, as *epheboi*, implied participation in religious activities (for instance, singing hymns in festivals) which were a form of religious education. In the Latin-speaking world, however, there is no indication of generalized practices of this kind. People who tell us something about their own education, for example, Cicero, Horace, and Ovid, do not imply that it included a religious side. The situation does not seem to have changed in later times, as illustrated, for instance, in Tacitus's life of Agricola. Children at school no doubt absorbed a great deal from classical authors, but whether they read Homer or Vergil, they did not absorb the religion of their own city. Temples carried inscriptions explaining what was expected from worshipers as well as the qualities of the relevant god. Cultic performances, often in a theater adjoining the temple, helped to explain what the god was capable of. We cannot, however, draw a distinguishing line between cultic performances, perhaps with an element of initiation, and simple entertainment.

Another element difficult to evaluate is the continuous, and perhaps increased, appeal of impersonal gods within Roman religion. There is no indication that Faith (Fides) and Hope (Spes) increased their appeal. (They came to play a different part in Christianity by combining with Jewish and Greek ideas.) At best, Fides gained prestige as a symbol of return to loyalty and good faith during the reign of Augustus. But Fortuna, Tutela, and Virtus were popular; the typology of Virtus on coins seems to be identical with that of Roma. Genius was generalized to indicate the spirit of a place or of a corporation. Strangely, an old Latin god of the woods, Silvanus, whose name does not appear in the Roman calendar, became important, partly because of his identification with the Greek Pan and with a Pannonian god but above all because of his equation with Genius: we find the god protector of Roman barracks called Genius Castrorum or Silvanus Castrorum or Fortuna Castrorum. Victoria, too, was often connected with individual emperors and individual victories (Victoria Augusti, Ludi Victoriae Claudi, etc.).

A third element of complication is what is called syncretism, by which we really mean two different things. One is the positive identification of two or more gods; the other is the tendency to mix different cults by using symbols of other gods in the sanctuary of one god, with the result that the presence of Sarapis, Juno, and even Isis was implied in the shrine of Jupiter Dolichenus on the Aventine in Rome. In either form, syncretism may have encouraged the idea that all gods are aspects, or manifestations, of one god. [*See* Syncretism.]

Vaguely monotheistic attitudes were in any case encouraged by philosophical reflection, quite apart from suggestions coming from Judaism, Christianity, and Zoroastrianism. It is therefore legitimate to consider the cult of Sol Invictus, patronized by Aurelian, as a monotheistic or henotheistic predecessor of Christianity. But believers had to visualize the relation between the one and the many. This relation was complicated by the admission of intermediate demons, either occupying zones between god or gods and men or going about the earth and perhaps more capable of evil than of good. Even those who could think through, in some depth, the idea of one god (such as Plutarch) were still interested in Zeus or Isis or Dionysos, whatever their relation to the god beyond the gods. Those educated people who in late antiquity liked to collect priesthoods and initiations to several gods, in pointed contrast with Christianity, evidently did so because they did not look upon the gods concerned as one god only. The classic example of such a person is given by the inscription concerning Vettius Agorius Praetextatus dated 385 CE (*Corpus inscriptionum Latinarum,* Berlin, 1863, vol. 6, no. 1779).

This is not to deny the convergence of certain beliefs and experiences. To quote only an extreme case, a mystical experience like ascension to heaven was shared by Paul, Jewish rabbis, gnostics such as the author of the *Gospel of Truth,* and Plotinus.

Role of Women. Women seem to have taken a more active, and perhaps a more creative, part in the religious life of the imperial period. This was connected with the considerable freedom of movement and of administration of one's own estate which women, and especially wealthy women, had in the Roman empire. Roman empresses of Oriental origin (Julia Domna, wife of Septimius Severus, and Julia Mamaea, mother of Severus Alexander) contributed to the diffusion outside Africa of the cult of Caelestis, who received a temple on the Capitol in Rome. The wife of a Roman consul, Pompeia Agrippinilla, managed to put together a private association of about four hundred devotees of Liber-Dionysos in the Roman Campagna in the middle of the second century CE. (See the inscription published by Achille Vogliano in the *American Journal of Archaeology* 37, 1933, p. 215.) Women could be asked to act as *theologoi,* that is, to preach about gods in ceremonies even of a mystery nature. We have seen that Isis appealed to, and was supported by, women. It is revealing that Marcus Aurelius declared himself grateful to his mother for teaching him veneration of the gods.

The intellectual and religious achievements of women become more conspicuous in the fourth century. Women such as Sosipatra, described in Eunapius's account of the lives of the Sophists, and Hypatia of Alexandria are the counterparts (though apparently more broadly educated and more independent in their social actions) of Christian women such as Macrina, sister of Gregory of Nyssa (who wrote her biography), and the followers of Jerome. We are not surprised to find in the city of Thasos during the late Roman empire a woman with a resounding Latin name, Flavia Vibia Sabina, honored by the local Senate "as a most noteworthy high priestess . . . the only woman, first in all times to have honours equal to those of the senators" (H. W. Pleket, *Texts on the Social History of the Greek World,* 1969, no. 29).

Dedications of religious and philosophical books by men to women appear in the imperial period. Plutarch dedicated his treatise on Isis and Osiris to Clea, a priestess of Delphi; Diogenes Laertius dedicated his book on Greek philosophers (which has anti-Christian implications) to a female Platonist. Philostratus claims that Julia Domna encouraged him to write the life of Apollonius of Tyana. What is more, Bishop Hippolytos apparently wrote a book on resurrection dedicated to the pagan Julia Mamaea. We know from Eusebius that this same woman invited Origen to visit her in Antioch, obviously to discuss Christianity.

Literary Evidence. Epigraphy and archaeology have taught us much, but the religion of the Roman empire survives mainly through writings in Latin, Greek, Syriac, and Coptic (not to speak of other languages): biographies, philosophical disputations, epic poems, antiquarian books, exchanges of letters, novels, and specific religious books. Most of the authors speak only for themselves. But taken together, they convey an atmosphere of sophisticated cross-questioning which would have prevented minds from shutting out alternatives or concentrating solely on ritual. We can only give examples. The Stoic Lucan in his *Pharsalia,* a poem on the civil wars, excludes the gods but admits fate and fortune, magic and divination. Two generations later, Silius Italicus wrote an optimistic poem, turning on Scipio as a Roman Herakles supported by his father, Jupiter. More or less at the same time, Plutarch was reflecting on new and old cults, on the delays in divine justice, and (if the work in question is indeed his) on superstition.

In the second part of the second century Lucian passed from the caricature of an assembly of gods and from attacks against oracles to a sympathetic description of the cult of Dea Syria; he abused such religious fanatics as Peregrinus, as well as Alexander of Abonuteichos, the author of a cult, whom he considered to be an impostor. Perhaps what Lucian wanted to give is, in fact, what we get from him—the impression of a mind that refuses to be imposed upon. Fronto's correspondence with Marcus Aurelius confirms what we deduce from other texts (such as Aelius Aristides' speeches): preoccupation with one's own health was a source of intense religious experience in the second century CE. Apuleius, in *De magia,* gives a glimpse of a small African community in which suspicion of magic practices can upset the town (as well as the author). In *Metamorphoses,* also known as *The Golden Ass,* Apuleius offers an account of the mysteries of Isis which may be based on personal experiences. But Apuleius's *Golden Ass* is only one of the many novels which were fashionable in the Roman empire. The appeal of such novels probably resided in their ability to offer readers vicarious experiences of love, magic, and mystery ritual.

The variety of moods and experiences conveyed by these texts, from the skeptical to the mystical, from the egotistic to the political in the old Greek sense, gives us an approximate notion of the thoughts of educated people on religious subjects. These books provide the background for an understanding of the Christian apologists who wrote for the pagan upper class. Conversely, we are compelled to ask how much of pagan religious thinking was conditioned by the presence of Jews and, even more, of Christians in the neighborhood. The anti-Jewish attitudes of a Tacitus or of a Juvenal offer no special problem: they are explicit. The same can be said about the anti-Christian polemics of Celsus; here the problem, if any, is that the text is lost and we are compelled to make inferences from the reply given in changed circumstances by the Christian Origen. But there are far more writers who seldom or never refer to Christianity yet can hardly have formulated their thoughts without implicit reference to it.

How much Lucian or Philostratus (in his life of Apollonius of Tyana) was trying to put across pagan points of view in answer to the Christian message is an old question. The biography of Philostratus was translated into Latin by a pagan leader, Nicomachus Flavianus, in the late fourth century. Another author who may be suspected of knowing more about Christianity than his silence about it would indicate is Diogenes Laertius. In his lives of philosophers, he pointedly refuses to admit non-Greek wisdom and enumerates all the Greek schools, from Plato to Epicurus, as worthy of study and admiration. With the renascence of Neoplatonic thought in the third and fourth centuries and the combination of Platonism with mystical and magical practices (the so-called theurgy) in the circles to which Julian the Apostate belonged, the attempt to erect a barrier to Christianity is patent but, even then, not necessarily explicit.

The most problematic texts are perhaps those which try to formulate explicit religious beliefs. Even a simple military religious calendar (such as the third-century Feriale Duranum, copied for the benefit of the garrison of Dura-Europos) raises the question of its purpose and validity: how many of these old-fashioned Roman festivals were still respected? When we come to such books as the *Chaldean Oracles* (late second century?) or the Hermetic texts, composed in Greek at various dates in Egypt (and clearly showing the influence of Jewish ideas), it is difficult to decide who believed in them and to what extent. Such texts present themselves as revealed: they speak of man's soul imprisoned in the body, of fate, and of demonic power with only a minimum of coherence. They are distantly related to what modern scholars call gnosticism, a creed with many variants which was supposed to be a deviation from Christianity and, as such, was fought by early Christian apologists. We now know much more about gnostics, thanks to the discovery of the Nag Hammadi library, which supplemented, indeed dwarfed, previous discoveries of Coptic gnostic texts. Assembled in the fourth century from books mainly translated from Greek, the Nag Hammadi library represents an isolated survival. It points to a previous, more central movement thriving in the exchange of ideas. Can we assess the impact of the gnostic sects when they placed themselves between pagans and Christians (and Jews) in the first centuries of the empire? [*See* Gnosticism *and* Hermetism.]

State Repression and Persecution. The Roman state had always interfered with the freedom to teach and worship. In republican times astrologers, magicians, philosophers, and even rhetoricians, not to speak of adepts of certain religious groups, had been victims of such intrusion. Under which precise legal category this interference was exercised remains a question, except perhaps in cases of sacrilege. From Tacitus we know that Augustus considered adultery in his own family a crime of *laesa religio* (*Annals* 3.24). Whatever the legal details, there was persecution of druidic cults and circles in Gaul and Britain in the first century. Augustus prohibited Roman citizens from participating in druidic cults, and Claudius prohibited the cult of the druids altogether. Details are not clear, and consequences not obvious, though one hears little of the druids from this time on. Abhorrence of druidic human sacrifices no doubt counted for much. But Augustus also did not like the practice of foretelling the future, for which the druids were conspicuous, and he is credited with the destruction of two thousand *fatidici libri* (Suetonius, *Augustus* 31). The druids were also known to be magicians, and Claudius condemned to death a Roman knight who had brought to court a druidic magic egg (Pliny, *Natural History* 29.54). [*See also* Druids.]

This being said, we must emphasize how unusual it was for the Roman government to come to such decisions. Existing cults might or might not be encouraged, but they were seldom persecuted. Even Jews and Egyptians were ordinarily protected in their cults, although there were exceptions. The long-standing conflict between the Christians and the Roman state—even taking into account that persecution was desultory—remains unique for several reasons which depended more on Christian than on imperial behavior. First, the Christians obviously did not yield or retreat, as did the druids. Second, the Christians hardly ever became outright enemies of, or rebels against, the Roman state. The providential character of the Roman state was a basic assumption of Christianity. The workings of providence were shown, for Christians, by the fact that Jesus was born under Roman rule, while the Roman state had destroyed the Temple of Jerusalem and dispersed the Jews, thus making the church the heiress to the Temple. Third, the Christians were interested in what we may call classical culture. Their debate with the pagans became, increasingly, a debate within the terms of reference of classical culture; the Jews, however, soon lost their contact with classical thought and even with such men as Philo, who had represented them in the dialogue with classical culture. Fourth, Christianity and its ecclesiastical organization provided what could alternatively be either a rival or a subsidiary structure to the imperial government; the choice was left to the Roman government, which under Constantine chose the church as a subsidiary institution (without quite knowing on what conditions). [*See* Constantinianism.].

The novelty of the conflict explains the novelty of the solution—not tolerance but conversion. The emperor had to become Christian and to accept the implications of his conversion. It took about eighty years to turn the pagan state into a Christian state. The process took the form of a series of decisions about public non-Christian acts of worship. The first prohibition of pagan sacrifices seems to have been enacted in 341 (*Codex Theodosianus* 16.10.2). Closing of the pagan temples and prohibition of sacrifices in public places under penalty of death was stated or restated at an uncertain date between 346 and 354 (ibid., 16.10.4).

Even leaving aside the reaction of Julian, these measures cannot have been effective. The emperor remained *pontifex maximus* until Gratian gave up the position in 379 (Zosimus, 4.36.5). Gratian was the emperor who removed the altar of Victoria from the Roman Senate and provoked the controversy between Symmachus and Bishop Ambrose, the most important controversy about the relative merits of tolerance and conversion in late antiquity. Then, in 391, Theodosius forbade even the private pagan cult (*Codex Theodosianus* 16.10.12). In the same year, following riots provoked by a special law against pagan cults in Egypt, the Serapeum of Alexandria was destroyed, an act whose significance was felt worldwide. The brief pagan revival of 393, initiated by the usurper Eugenius, a nominal Christian who sympathized with the pagans, was soon followed by other antipagan laws. Pagan priests were deprived of their privileges in 396 (ibid., 16.10.4). Pagan temples in the country (not in towns) were ordered to be destroyed in 399 (ibid., 16.10.16). But in the same year festivals which appear pagan to us were allowed (ibid., 16.10.17).

No doubt the Christians knew how and where they could proceed to direct action. The economic independence and traditional prestige of local pagan aristocrats, especially in Rome, allowed them to survive for a time and to go on elaborating pagan thought, as we can see from Macrobius's *Saturnalia* and even from Boethius's *The Consolation of Philosophy*, although Boethius was technically a Christian who knew his Christian texts. The Neoplatonists of Athens had to be expelled by Justinian in 529. But in Africa Synesius became the first Neoplatonist to be baptized in the early fifth century (c. 403–410).

Hopes that the pagan gods would come back excited the Eastern provinces during the rebellion against the emperor Zeno in about 483, in which the pagan rhetorician and poet Pampremius had a prominent part (Zacharias of Mitylene, *Vita Severi*, in *Patrologia Orient.* 2.1.40; M. A. Kugener, ed., Paris, 1903). The peasants *(rustici)*, about whom Bishop Martin of Bracara in Spain had so many complaints, gave more trouble to the ecclesiastical authorities than did the philosophers and the aristocrats of the cities. Sacrifices, just because they were generally recognized as efficient ways of persuading the gods to act, were at the center of Christian suspicion. According to a widespread opinion shared by the apostle Paul (but not by all the church fathers) pagan gods existed—as demons.

BIBLIOGRAPHY

Georg Wissowa's *Religion und Kultus der Römer,* 2d ed. (Munich, 1912), and Kurt Latte's *Römische Religionsgeschichte* (Munich, 1960) are basic reading on the topic. They are supplemented by Martin P. Nilsson's *Geschichte der griechischen Religion,* vol. 2, 3d ed. (Munich, 1974), for the eastern side of the Roman empire. Jean Bayet's *Histoire politique et psychologique de la religion romaine* (Paris, 1957) proposes an alternative approach and is improved in the Italian translation, *La religione romana: Storia politica e psicologica* (Turin, 1959). All the publications by Franz Cumont and Arthur Darby Nock remain enormously valuable and influential. See, for instance, Cumont's *Astrology and Religion among the Greeks and Romans* (New York, 1912), *After Life in Roman Paganism* (New Haven, 1922), *Les religions orientales dans le paganisme romain,* 4th ed. (Paris, 1929), *Recherches sur le symbolisme funéraire des Romains* (Paris, 1942), and *Lux Perpetua* (Paris, 1949); see also Nock's *Conversion: The Old and the New in Religion from Alexander the Great to Augustine of Hippo* (Oxford, 1933) and his essays in *The Cambridge Ancient History,* vol. 10 (Cambridge, 1934) and vol. 12 (Cambridge, 1939), and in *Essays on Religion and the Ancient World,* 2 vols., edited by Zeph Stewart (Cambridge, Mass., 1972). The scattered contributions by

Louis Robert on epigraphic evidence are also indispensable; see, for instance, his *Hellenica*, 13 vols. (Limoges and Paris, 1940–1965).

Among more recent general books are J. H. W. G. Liebeschuetz's *Continuity and Change in Roman Religion* (Oxford, 1979), Ramsay MacMullen's *Paganism in the Roman Empire* (New Haven, 1981), Alan Wardman's *Religion and Statecraft among the Romans* (London, 1982), and John Scheid's *Religion et piété à Rome* (Paris, 1985). Volumes 2.16, 2.17, and 2.23 of *Aufstieg und Niedergang der römischen Welt* (Berlin and New York, 1978–1984) are mostly devoted to Roman imperial paganism and are of great importance. Ramsay MacMullen's *Christianizing the Roman Empire, A.D. 100–400* (New Haven, 1984) supplements his previous book from the Christian side.

Numerous monographs have been published on various topics. Here I can indicate only a few.

On the basic changes in Roman religion: Arthur Bernard Cook, *Zeus: A Study in Ancient Religion*, 3 vols. (Cambridge, 1914–1940); Johannes Geffcken, *Der Ausgang des griechisch-römischen Heidentums* (Heidelberg, 1920); Bernhard Kötting, *Peregrinatio religiosa: Wallfahrten in der Antike und das Pilgerwesen in der alten Kirche* (Münster, 1950); Frederick H. Cramer, *Astrology in Roman Law and Politics* (Philadelphia, 1954); Arnaldo Momigliano, ed., *The Conflict between Paganism and Christianity in the Fourth Century* (Oxford, 1963); E. R. Dodds, *Pagan and Christian in an Age of Anxiety* (Cambridge, 1965); Clara Gallini, *Protesta e integrazione nella Roma antica* (Bari, 1970); Peter Brown, *Religion and Society in the Age of Saint Augustine* (London, 1972); Javier Teixidor, *The Pagan God: Popular Religion in the Greco-Roman Near East* (Princeton, 1977); Sabine G. MacCormack, *Art and Ceremony in Late Antiquity* (Berkeley, 1981); Peter Brown, *Society and the Holy in Late Antiquity* (Berkeley, 1982). See also Morton Smith's article "Prolegomena to a Discussion of Aretalogies, Divine Men, the Gospels and Jesus," *Journal of Biblical Literature* 90 (June 1971): 174–199.

On the imperial cult: Christian Habicht, *Gottmenschentum und griechische Städte*, 2d ed. (Munich, 1970); Stefan Weinstock, *Divus Julius* (Oxford, 1971); Elias J. Bickerman et al., eds., *Le culte des souverains dans l'empire romain* (Geneva, 1973); J. Rufus Fears, *Princeps a diis electus: The Divine Election of the Emperor as a Political Concept at Rome* (Rome, 1977); S. R. F. Price, *Rituals and Power: The Roman Imperial Cult in Asia Minor* (Cambridge, 1984). Price's book should be supplemented by his article "Gods and Emperors: The Greek Language of the Roman Imperial Cult," *Journal of Hellenic Studies* 94 (1984): 79–95. See also H. W. Pleket's "An Aspect of the Emperor Cult: Imperial Mysteries," *Harvard Theological Review* 58 (October 1965): 331–347; Lellia Cracco Ruggini's "Apoteosi e politica senatoria nel IV sec. d.C.," *Rivista storica italiana* (1977): 425–489; and Keith Hopkins's *Conquerors and Slaves* (Cambridge, 1978), pp. 197–242.

On specific periods or individual gods: Jean Beaujeu, *La religion romaine à l'apogée de l'empire*, vol. 1, *La politique religieuse des Antonins, 96–192* (Paris, 1955); Marcel Leglay, *Saturne africaine* (Paris, 1966); R. E. Witt, *Isis in the Graeco-Roman World* (London, 1971); Robert Turcan, *Mithras Platonicus: Recherches sur l'hellénisation philosophique de Mithra* (Leiden, 1975); Maarten J. Vermaseren, *Cybele and Attis* (London, 1977); Friedrich Solmsen, *Isis among the Greeks and Romans* (Cambridge, Mass., 1979); Reinhold Merkelbach, *Mithras* (Königstein, West Germany, 1984). See also Merkelbach's article "Zum neuen Isistext aus Maroneia," *Zeitschrift für Papyrologie und Epigraphik* 23 (1976): 234–235.

On Roman sacrifice (not yet studied so thoroughly as Greek practices), see *Le sacrifice dans l'antiquité*, "Entretiens Fondation Hardt," no. 27 (Geneva, 1981), and for a theory of the mystery cult in the novels, see Reinhold Merkelbach's *Roman und Mysterium in der Antike* (Munich, 1962). Kurt Rudolph's *Gnosis: The Nature and History of Gnosticism* (San Francisco, 1983) and Giovanni Filoramo's *L'attesa della fine: Storia della gnosi* (Bari, 1983) are the best introductions to the subject, while *Gnosis und Gnostizismus*, edited by Rudolph (Darmstadt, 1975), provides a retrospective anthology of opinions. The collective volumes *Die orientalischen Religionen im Römerreich*, edited by Maarten J. Vermaseren (Leiden, 1981), and *La soteriologia dei culti orientali*, edited by Ugo Bianchi and Vermaseren (Leiden, 1982), provide further guidance in current research on various topics. Noteworthy also are the seminal essays in *Jewish and Christian Self-definition*, vol. 3, *Self-definition in the Graeco-Roman World*, edited by B. F. Meyer and E. P. Sanders (London, 1982).

For the transition from paganism to Christianity, the work of Lellia Cracco Ruggini is essential. See, for example, her "Simboli di battaglia ideologica nel tardo ellenismo," in *Studi storici in onore di Ottorino Bertolini* (Pisa, 1972), pp. 117–300; *Il paganesimo romano tra religione e politica, 384–394 d.C.*, "Memorie della classe di scienze morali, Accademia Nazionale dei Lincei," 8.23.1 (Rome, 1979); and "Pagani, ebrei e cristiani: Odio sociologico e odio teologico nel mondo antico," *Gli ebrei nell'Alto Medioevo* (Spoleto) 26 (1980): 13–101.

ARNALDO MOMIGLIANO

ROSENZWEIG, FRANZ (1886–1929), German-Jewish philosophical theologian, writer, translator of Jewish classical literature, and influential Jewish educational activist. Generally regarded as the most important Jewish philosophical theologian of this century, Rosenzweig also became a model of what the Jewish personality in the twentieth-century West might be.

He was born into an old, affluent, and highly acculturated German-Jewish family in Kassel, in which the sense of Jewishness, though lively, had shrunk to a matter of upper middle-class formalities. He studied at several German universities, ranging over multiple disciplines, and finished as a student of Friedrich Meinecke, the important German political and cultural historian. During those years he also had intense conversations on religion in the modern world, especially with close relatives and friends, several of whom had converted to Christianity. Having already adopted a strong German nationalist outlook, Rosenzweig also tried to sort out his own religious convictions at the very time that he was writing his Ph.D. dissertation (on Schelling and Hegel) and his first important book (*Hegel und der Staat,* 2 vols., 1920). In a night-long conversation on 7 July 1913 with his cousin, the physiologist Rudolf Ehrenberg (who had become a Christian theologian), and his distant relative Eugen Rosenstock-Huessy (later the influential Protestant theologian, also a convert), Rosenzweig decided that he, too, ought to become a Christian; however, he would take this step "as a Jew," not "as a pagan," and he would, therefore, briefly return to the synagogue. His experience there during the High Holy Days that year, however, changed Rosenzweig's mind completely: he would instead turn himself from a nominal into a substantial Jew, and he would devote his life to Jewish values. He studied with and became a close friend to the Neo-Kantian philosopher Hermann Cohen, who was then living in Berlin in retirement but was still very active with Jewish writing and teaching. Rosenzweig immediately began to write on Jewish subjects.

During World War I, Rosenzweig served in various, mainly military, capacities. He continued, however, to correspond with Rosenstock-Huessy on theological matters (Rosenstock-Huessy, *Judaism despite Christianity,* Alabama, 1968) and with Cohen and others on Jewish matters. He also wrote and published essays on historical, political, military, and educational subjects. Assigned to eastern Europe and the Balkans, he experienced some of the full-blooded life of the Jewish communities there. Above all, he began on postcards to his mother the composition that he finished on returning home from the war—his magnum opus, *Der Stern der Erlösung* (The Star of Redemption, Frankfurt, 1921). An injury he sustained during the war may have been the cause of his severe and eventually fatal postwar illness.

The Star of Redemption is a complex, difficult, and ambitious work, in some ways comparable to Hegel's *Phenomenology of Spirit.* The introduction to the first part argues that the fundamental and ineluctably individualistic fact of human death breaks up all philosophy *qua* monism, idealistic or materialistic, into the three realities of human experience: man, God, and the world. (Metaphysical empiricism is thus an apt name for what Rosenzweig also calls "the new thinking.") In the first part, he philosophically "constructs" these three realities very much in the manner of the later Schelling, as logico-mathematical and metaphysical entities. In this condition man, God, and the world constitute the "pagan" universe: they exist without interrelationships, as three unconnected points.

In the second part, the three realities enter into relationships with one another through "revelation," that is, by continuously revealing themselves to each other. God reveals his love to man and thus becomes available to human prayer, and the world is revealed as divine creation, available to human transformation. Speech is the operative force in this dimension of the world. Three points have formed a triangle. The final part of the book establishes the second triangle of the "star of redemption" when the individual relations between man, God, and the world are transformed into collective, historical forces, specifically, Judaism and Christianity. (Two interlocking triangles form the hexagram that is the Magen David, the Star of David, symbol of redemption.) Judaism is "the fire in the star"; that is, Israel is "with God/the truth," outside of history, in eternity. Christianity is the rays from the star on pilgrimage through the world and history toward God/the truth, in order to conquer the kingdom of God's eventual universal realm. In this dimension of the world, collective speech—liturgy and hymn—is the operative force. Judaism and Christianity are the two valid covenants—Sinai for Jews and Calvary for the rest of mankind, to be unified only when the road to truth has brought the Christian world to the Jewish domicile in truth. In the meantime loving acts of believers are to "verify" the love of revelation and prepare the eschatological verity of God as "the all in all." (Truth is thus Hegelian-existentialist "subjectivity," and the three parts of *The Star* explicate the basic theological triad of creation, revelation, and redemption.)

After the war Rosenzweig wanted to translate his beliefs and his pronounced educational interests into action. He settled in Frankfurt, where he entered into close relationships with Nehemiah Nobel, the Orthodox rabbi of the community; with Martin Buber; with a younger generation of German Jews; and with eastern European Jews on their way west. He founded what became famous as the Free Jewish House of Learning (Lehrhaus), in which teachers and students together sought out classic Jewish sources and, translating and publishing them, tried them out on the modern world. Rosenzweig and Buber were joined as teachers by well-known chemists, physicians, sociologists, and activists, and such influential contemporary Jewish scholars as S. D. Goitein, Ernst Simon, Gershom Scholem, Hans Kohn, Erich Fromm, and Nahum N. Glatzer.

Rosenzweig married in 1920 and fathered a son just before coming down with a disease so grave that he was expected to die within months. Instead he lived for six years, so paralyzed, however, that ultimately he could communicate only by blinking an eyelid to the recitation of the alphabet. Nevertheless his associates flocked to his side and spread his influence. Rosenzweig continued to write philosophical and religious essays and conducted a large correspondence. He edited the *Jüdische Schriften* (Jewish Writings) of Hermann Cohen (3 vols., Berlin, 1924) and, in an extensive introduction, reinterpreted Cohen's posthumous philosophical theology as having laid the basis for a proto-existentialist doctrine. He continued to study Jewish sources. He translated, among other things, the Hebrew poetry of Yehudah ha-Levi and supplied it with extensive commentaries. In 1924 he joined with Martin Buber to produce a new German translation of the Hebrew Bible, and in the process the two also developed a sophisticated theory of translation, language, and textuality. Their position was that the full meaning of a text develops through what has since come to be called "reception history." Thus the Bible is divinely revealed not as a matter of Orthodox dogma or in opposition to Bible-critical history but in terms of its effects over time. Translation must not adjust the text to a new culture but must confront the new culture with the text's own authenticity. This confrontation takes place on the ground of the universal, Adamite human speech embedded in the literary forms of both languages. When Rosenzweig died at the age of forty-three, the Bible translation had progressed to *Isaiah.* (Buber finished it in the 1950s.)

Rosenzweig's basic tenets led to some new and promising positions in modern Jewish life. Between the Orthodox belief in the Sinaitic revelation and the Liberal critical historicism regarding the Bible, his "postmodernist" view made it possible to take all of Torah with revelatory seriousness and punctiliousness, while neither rejecting modern scholarship nor committing oneself to a fideistic view. This coincided with and influenced the biblical work of such scholars as Buber, Benno Jacob, Yeḥezkel Kaufmann, and Umberto Cassuto. It also laid the basis for much subsequent renewed Jewish traditionalism among the acculturated in Germany and elsewhere. Rosenzweig's outlook, beyond the established fronts of Orthodoxy and Liberalism, also offered help with respect to Jewish law (*halakhah*). In opposition to Buber's subjectivistic, pietistic antinomianism, Rosenzweig called for an open-minded, receptive confrontation with Jewish law to embrace it "as much as I can" in terms of one's own preparation and honesty. His "two-covenant doctrine" serves as a strong foundation for Jewish-Christian dialogue, although it can easily be abused in an "indifferentist" spirit and although it suffers inherently from Rosenzweig's pervasive europocentrism (e.g., his total blindness to Islam) and his antihistoricism (cf. Hegel's "absolute spirit" after "the end of history"). Unlike his friend Buber, Rosenzweig rejected the notion of a Jewish state (which would bring Israel back into history); on the other hand, he naturally preferred Jewish self-reauthentification in language, ethnicity, culture, and religion to liberalistic acculturation in gentile societies. With the rise of Nazism, Rosenzweig's educational ideology, along with that of Buber, spoke to German Jewry so aptly and powerfully that the Lehrhaus pattern of highly cultured and acculturated teachers and students in community spread throughout the country and produced an "Indian summer" of German-Jewish creativity of a high order in the 1930s.

The impact of Rosenzweig's thought continues to be strong, philosophically and religiously. The interconnections between him and Martin Heidegger, whom Rosenzweig praises in his last essay ("Vertauschte Fronte," 1929; in *Gesammelte Schriften,* vol. 3, pp. 235–237), are increasingly being crystallized. Heideggerian existentialist phenomenologism, with Jewish-Rosenzweigian modifications, has further left its significant marks on diverse movements of thought—the Frankfurt School (of Hegelian neo-Marxists) on the one hand, and Emmanuel Levinas, who goes beyond Heidegger and Husserl in philosophy and takes Buberian-Rosenzweigian dialogism yet closer to historical Judaism, on the other. Rosenzweig's sophisticated traditionalism comprises ethnicity, language, and religion (though still without "land") and shows the way back from European high culture to Jewish self-definition.

BIBLIOGRAPHY

The most extensive collection of Rosenzweig's writing and study of his life is *Franz Rosenzweig, der Mensch und sein Werk: Gesammelte Schriften,* 6 vols. (Dordrecht, 1976–1984). In English, see *Franz Rosenzweig: His Life and Thought,* 2d rev. ed., edited by Nahum N. Glatzer (New York, 1961), and my *Franz Rosenzweig, 1886–1929: Guide of Reversioners* (London, 1961).

Rosenzweig's *magnum opus, The Star of Redemption,* has been translated by William W. Hallo (New York, 1971). It is discussed in Else-Rahel Freund's *Franz Rosenzweig's Philosophy of Existence: An Analysis of The Star of Redemption,* translated by Stephen L. Weinstein and Robert Israel and edited by Paul R. Mendes-Flohr (The Hague and Boston, 1979); it is also the subject of my book review in *The Thomist* (October 1971): 728–737.

STEVEN S. SCHWARZSCHILD

RO'SH HA-SHANAH AND YOM KIPPUR, holy days prominent in the Jewish religious calendar, mark the beginning of the new year and set off the special period traditionally designated for self-scrutiny and repentance. They are referred to as Yamim Nora'im ("days of awe"), the time when the numinous aspect of Judaism comes into its own.

Ro'sh ha-Shanah. Ro'sh ha-Shanah ("head of the year," i.e., New Year) is the name given in postbiblical times to the biblical festival of the first day of the seventh month (counting from the spring month of the Exodus from Egypt) and described (*Lv.* 23:23–25, *Nm.* 19:1–6) as a day of blowing the horn. The postbiblical name is based on Talmudic teachings that on this day all mankind is judged for its fortunes in the coming year. For this reason Ro'sh ha-Shanah is also called Yom ha-Din ("day of judgment"). Biblical scholars, exploring the origins of the festival, have noted the parallels with ancient Near Eastern agricultural festivities in the autumn and the enthronement ceremonies of the king as the representative of the god Baal or Marduk. According to the critical view, references to the festival occur in sections of the Pentateuch known as the Priestly code, which is postexilic and hence could well have been influenced by Babylonian practices. Such theories remain, however, conjectural. In *Nehemiah* 8:1–8 there is a vivid description of the dramatic occasion when the Israelites who had returned from Babylonian captivity renewed their covenant with God. Ezra read from the Torah on this first day of the seventh month; the people, conscious of their shortcomings, were distressed at hearing the demands of the Law, but Nehemiah reassured them: "Go your way, eat the fat, and drink the sweet and send portions unto him for whom nothing is prepared; for this day is holy unto our Lord; neither be ye grieved, for the joy of the Lord is your strength" (*Neh.* 8:10). These are the antecedents of the festival as it later developed (held on the first and second days of the autumnal month of Tishri), a day of both joy and solemnity. The day also became known as Yom ha-Zikkaron ("day of remembrance") because on it God remembers his creatures.

The themes of God as king and judge of the universe and the need for repentance all feature prominently in the Ro'sh ha-Shanah liturgy. The special additional prayer consists of three groups of verses and prayers: (1) *malkhuyyot* ("sovereignties," in which God is hailed as king), (2) *zikhronot* ("remembrances," in which God is said to remember his creatures), (3) *shofarot* ("trumpet sounds," which refer to the blowing of the horn). A popular medieval interpretation of these three is that they represent the three cardinal principles of the Jewish faith: belief in God, in reward and punishment (God "remembers" man's deeds), and in revelation (the horn was sounded when the Law was given at Sinai, as stated in *Exodus* 19:16). Another prayer of the day looks forward to the messianic age, when the kingdom of heaven will be established and all wickedness will vanish from the earth. In a hymn recited on both Ro'sh ha-Shanah and Yom Kippur, continuing with the judgment theme, God is spoken of as the great shepherd tending his flock. He decides on Ro'sh ha-Shanah, and sets the seal on Yom Kippur, "who shall live and who shall die; who shall suffer and who shall be tranquil; who shall be rich and who poor; who shall be cast down and who elevated." At various stages in the liturgy of Ro'sh ha-Shanah and Yom Kippur there are prayers to be inscribed in the Book of Life, based on a Talmudic passage stating that the average person whose fate is in the balance has the opportunity during the period from Ro'sh ha-Shanah to Yom Kippur to avert the "evil decree" by repentance, prayer, and charity. These days, including Ro'sh ha-Shanah and Yom Kippur, are consequently known as the Ten Days of Penitence, the period for turning to God and for special strictness in religious observances. The verse "Seek ye the Lord while he may be found" (*Is.* 55:6) is applied especially to this time of the year.

The central ritual of the Ro'sh ha-Shanah festival is the ceremony of blowing the shofar. Although the shofar may be fashioned from the horn of several kosher animals, a ram's horn, reminiscent of the ram sacrificed by Abraham in place of Isaac, is preferred. Many attempts have been made to explain the significance of the rite; Maimonides' is typical:

> Although it is a divine decree that we blow the shofar on Ro'sh ha-Shanah, a hint of the following idea is contained in the command. It is as if to say: "Awake from your slumbers, you who have fallen asleep in life, and reflect on your deeds. Remember your Creator. Be not of those who miss reality in the pursuit of shadows, who waste their years seeking vain things that neither profit nor deliver. Look well to your souls, and improve your actions. Let each of you forsake his evil ways and thoughts." (*Code of Law*, Repentance 3.4)

The shofar is sounded a number of times during the synagogue service. The three basic notes are *teqi'ah* (a long, drawn-out note, signifying hope and triumph), *shevarim* (a broken set of short notes), and *teru'ah* (a set of even shorter notes that, like *shevarim*, represents weeping). First, the *teqi'ah* suggesting firm commitment to God's laws is sounded followed by the two weeping sounds as man reflects on his sins and failings, and finally a second *teqi'ah* is blown signifying confidence in God's pardon where there is sincere repentance.

At the festive meal on Ro'sh ha-Shanah it is customary to dip bread in honey and to eat other sweet things while praying for "a good and sweet year." In some places the celebrants eat fish to symbolize the good deeds they hope will proliferate like fish in the sea in the year ahead. An ancient custom is to go to the seaside or riverside on the afternoon of the first day of Ro'sh ha-Shanah, there to cast away the sins of the previous year. This is based on *Micah* 7:19, a verse that speaks of God casting away the sins of the people into the depths of the sea.

Yom Kippur. Yom Kippur ("day of atonement") is the culmination of the penitential season, the day of repentance and reconciliation between man and God and between man and his neighbor. It is the most hallowed day in the Jewish year and is still observed by the majority of Jews, even those who are otherwise lax in religious practices. In Temple times, elaborate sacrificial and purgatory rites, described in *Leviticus* 16, were carried out. The high priest entered the Holy of Holies in the Temple, where no other person was allowed to enter under pain of death, to make atonement for his people. A whole tractate of the Mishnah *(Yoma')* describes in greater detail the Temple service on Yom Kippur. The Mishnah was compiled over one hundred and fifty years after the destruction of the Second Temple, but at least some of the material does represent the actual practice in the Second Temple period. After the destruction of the Temple in 70 CE, the day became one of prayer and worship. The reference to "afflicting the soul" (*Lv.* 16:29) on this day is understood as an injunction to fast. No food or drink is taken from sunset on the ninth of Tishri until nightfall on the tenth. Other "afflictions" practiced are abstaining from marital relations, from wearing leather shoes, and from bathing.

The ninth of Tishri, the day before Yom Kippur, is devoted to preparation for the fast. On this day, festive meals are eaten both for the purpose of gaining strength for the fast and to celebrate the pardon Yom Kippur brings. In Talmudic teaching, Yom Kippur does not bring atonement for offenses against other human beings unless the victims have pardoned the offenders. It is the practice, consequently, for people to ask forgiveness of one another on the day before the fast. The custom of *kapparot* ("atonements") is carried out in the morning. The procedure is to take a cockerel, wave it around the head three times, and recite "This shall be instead of me," after which the cockerel is slaughtered and eaten. Many medieval authorities disapproved of the practice as a pagan superstition, but it is still followed by some Jews. Others prefer to use money instead of a cockerel, and then to distribute it to the poor. Another custom still observed by some is that of *malqot* ("flagellation"), in which the beadle in the synagogue administers a token beating with a strap as atonement for sin. Many pious Jews, in preparation for the fast, immerse themselves in a *miqveh* (ritual bath) as a purification rite. Before leaving for the synagogue, as the fast begins, parents bless their children.

In the majority of synagogues, services are several hours long on Yom Kippur night, and continue without pause during the day from early morning until the termination of the fast. The evening service begins with the Kol Nidrei ("all vows"), a declaration in Aramaic to the effect that all religious promises that will be undertaken in the year ahead are hereby declared null and void. This was introduced as a means of discouraging such vows since a promise made to God had dire consequences if broken. Throughout the day hymns and religious poems composed over many centuries are chanted. These consist of praises, supplications, martyrologies, and, especially, confessions of sin. A prominent feature of the additional service (Musaf) is the remembering of the Temple service on Yom Kippur. At the stage that relates how the high priest would utter the divine name and the people would then fall on their faces, the members of the congregation kneel and then prostrate themselves. This is the only occasion nowadays when there is prostration in the synagogue. At the late-afternoon service, *Jonah* is read as a lesson that none can escape God's call and that he has mercy even on the most wicked if they sincerely repent. The day ends with Ne'ilah ("closing"), a special service signifying that the gates of heaven, open to prayer all day, are about to close. At this particularly solemn time of the day, the worshipers make an urgent effort to be close to God, many standing upright for the hour or so of this service. As the sun sets, the congregation cries out aloud seven times: "The Lord he is God." Then the shofar is sounded to mark the termination of the fast.

White, the color of purity and mercy, is used on Yom Kippur for the vestments of the scrolls of the Torah and the ark in which the scrolls are kept as well as for the coverings in the synagogue. Traditional Jews wear white robes; in fact, these are shrouds to remind man of his mortality. This tradition serves a main theme of Yom Kippur: human life is frail and uncertain, but one can place trust in God and share in God's goodness forever. Since the festival of Sukkot falls a few days after Yom Kippur, it is advised that as soon as the worshipers return home from the synagogue and before breaking the fast, they should make some small preparation for the erection of the Sukkot booths and so proceed immediately after the day of pardon to do a good deed.

[*See also* Atonement, *article on* Jewish Concepts.]

BIBLIOGRAPHY

Norman H. Snaith's *The Jewish New Year Festival* (London, 1947) considers the views of the myth and ritual school that Ro'sh ha-Shanah had its origin in enthronement ceremonies. Two useful little books of my own are *A Guide to Rosh Ha-Shanah* (London, 1959) and *A Guide to Yom Kippur* (London, 1957). A good survey of the liturgical themes of Ro'sh ha-Shanah and Yom Kippur is Max Arzt's *Justice and Mercy* (New

York, 1963). The anthology by S. Y. Agnon has been translated into English as *Days of Awe* (New York, 1948). Two anthologies with comprehensive bibliographies are Philip Goodman's *The Rosh Hashanah Anthology* (Philadelphia, 1970) and *The Yom Kippur Anthology* (Philadelphia, 1971).

LOUIS JACOBS

ROSICRUCIANS. Although the secrecy pledged by members necessarily limits knowledge of Rosicrucian fraternities and their legendary founder, Christian Rosencreutz (whose surname means "rose cross"), documents published in the early seventeenth century and specific historical allusions to the Rosicrucians from that time on both provide basic information on these fraternities and adumbrate their significance within the esoteric traditions that arose in early modern Europe. The story of Christian Rosencreutz was promulgated through the publications *Fama Fraternitatis* (1614) and *Confessio Fraternitatis* (1615), which recounted his life and teachings and described the fraternity he founded. A third document, the *Chymische Hochzeit Christiani Rosencreutz* (Chemical Wedding; 1616), portrayed an alchemistic initiatory process, the representation of which was based in part on the actual wedding of Frederick V, Elector Palatine, and Princess Elizabeth, daughter of James I of England.

History. According to the story recounted in these documents, Christian Rosencreutz was a German scholar born in 1378. He lived to be 106. One hundred and twenty years after his death, his followers, obeying his instructions, opened his tomb; they heralded this event as the "opening" of a new era in Europe. The tomb purportedly contained Rosencreutz's uncorrupted body, various artifacts, and texts summarizing his teachings. In his quest for wisdom, Rosencreutz had traveled to the Holy Land, Egypt, Morocco, and Spain; his teachings reflected the influences of alchemy, Alexandrian Hermetism, Christian gnosticism, Jewish mysticism (Qabbalah), and the Paracelsian medical tradition. Following his own preparation and study, Rosencreutz, with three companions, established the Society of the Rose Cross. This fraternity was to have no other profession than (in the manner of Paracelsus) to attend to the sick for free. [*See the biography of Paracelsus.*] Members were also required to travel in order to gain and to disseminate knowledge, to report yearly by letter or in person to the center Rosencreutz had founded (called the Home of the Holy Spirit), to wear no distinctive garb, to seek worldly successors, and to employ the rose cross as their seal and symbol.

Significantly, both the publication of the aforementioned Rosicrucian documents and the purported opening of Rosencreutz's tomb occured in the early seventeenth century, thus placing Rosicrucianism directly in the context of Reformation and Counter-Reformation currents. Further, the documents originally appeared in Bohemia, which at the time was a haven for alchemists, freethinkers, millenarians, and adherents of diverse religious traditions. The authorship of the three key texts has been attributed to Johann Valentin Andreae (1586–1654), a Lutheran theologian and mystic. Andreae later described the history of the Rosicrucians up to his time as pure fabrication; at their publication, however, his texts met with a receptive and enthusiastic audience. With the collapse in 1620 of the brief reign in Bohemia of Frederick and Elizabeth and the onset of the Thirty Years War, Rosicrucianism became associated with Protestantism and "heretical teachings." As part of their campaign against Rosicrucianism, the Jesuits even penned their own Rosicrucian-style document, the *Rosa Jesuitica* (c. 1620).

During the seventeenth century, Rosicrucian figures such as the "Great Hermeticist" Michael Maier (1568–1622) and the physician Robert Fludd (1574–1637) were instrumental in the spread of Rosicrucian thought and influence on the European continent and in England, respectively. The antiquarian Elias Ashmole (1617–1692) is believed to have brought the Rosicrucian current into speculative Freemasonry. [*See* Freemasons.] What linked these writers, as well as numerous minor figures, was less an identifiable Rosicrucian brotherhood than an adherence to Rosicrucian beliefs. The claims of Descartes and Leibniz—that, the secrecy of the Rosicrucian order notwithstanding, their efforts to meet a live Rosicrucian were in vain—support the contention that Rosicrucianism existed mainly as a religious and intellectual approach to life rather than as an actual association. In this connection, the question of whether Francis Bacon was a Rosicrucian is unimportant, for he certainly was influenced by, and a participant in, the Rosicrucian trends affecting European intellectual life.

Following a period of relative quiescence in the eighteenth and early nineteenth centuries, Rosicrucianism was revived. The Societa Rosicruciana in Anglia, founded in the latter part of the nineteenth century by Robert Wentworth Little (d. 1878), played an important role in the renewal and spread of Rosicrucianism. This was not, however, the only strain. Here, polemic concerns of divers Rosicrucian groups obscure the already uncertain history of interactions among European currents and the introduction of Rosicrucianism into America. In the mid-1980s, two major Rosicrucian societies exist in the United States: the Society of Rosicrucians, or Societas Rosicruciana in America, founded in New York City and presently located in Kingston, New

York, and the Ancient and Mystical Order of Rosae Crucis, based in San Jose, California. The Societas Rosicruciana publishes the *Mercury* quarterly; the first issue appeared in 1916. The Ancient and Mystical Order issues the *Rosicrucian Digest,* which began publication as the *Triangle* in 1921.

In addition to the establishment of Rosicrucian organizations, the late nineteenth century witnessed Rosicrucianism's strong influence upon Western esotericism. Rosicrucian traditions took form in the Order of the Golden Dawn, a Hermetic society whose initiates practiced a spiritual discipline that they claimed was based upon principles of occult science and the magic of Hermes Trismegistos. At various times, the order numbered William Butler Yeats and Aleister Crowley among its members. Rosicrucianism's influence was also felt in the artworks of an idealist renaissance fostered by the occult aestheticism of Joséphin Peladan's Salons de la Rose + Croix in Paris and in the work of Rudolf Steiner and the Anthroposophical Society. [*See* Anthroposophy *and the biography of Steiner.*]

Doctrines. From its beginnings, Rosicrucianism spread a message of general reformation, preached a new enlightenment, promised a new Paradise, and taught a combination of religious illumination, evangelical piety, and magic. Rosicrucian "science" comprised a system of mathematics and mechanics for the lower world, celestial mathematics for the higher world, and angelic conjuration for the supercelestial world. In principle, the angelic sphere could be penetrated by the use of Rosicrucian technique, and, thus, the essence of all reality was graspable. The initiates were offered insight into the nature of all life. The Hermetic axiom "As above, so below," typical of Rosicrucian teaching, had a profound effect on early modern scientific thought, and Rosicrucianism—like other occult paths—has been credited with having helped to prepare the way for the rise of modern science.

The *Chymische Hochzeit* depicts the initiatory aspects of Rosicrucianism. Echoing themes of the *Fama* and the *Confessio,* its story recounts Christian Rosencreutz's participation in the celebration of a royal wedding. Called on the eve of Easter from his preparation for Communion, Rosencreutz journeys to a magical castle full of treasures. There he joins the wedding party, and over the course of the Christian Holy Week he views many marvels and becomes initiated into chivalric orders. This romance stands as a spiritual allegory both of Rosencreutz's inner transformation and of the transformation of the Rosicrucian elect.

The esoteric dimension of the transformation is rendered in alchemical symbols. Union of bride and bridegroom represents a mystical marriage of the soul, and this spiritual image is bound to an alchemic metaphor of elemental fusion. Likewise, the theme of spiritual death and rebirth is tied to the alchemy of elemental transmutation. The symbolic components of the rose cross may further evidence the importance of the alchemical tradition to Rosicrucian spiritual discipline: within the alchemical lexicon, *ros,* or dew, is the solvent of gold, and *crux,* the cross, is the equivalent of light.

The emblem, however, clearly draws on other symbolic traditions as well. Rosicrucianism's roots in chivalric traditions are revealed in certain aspects of the rose cross. The "chemical wedding" leads to Christian Rosencreutz's initiation as a Red Cross knight, and the initiation he experiences in the allegorical tale is similar to that actually undergone by Frederick V (at the time of his marriage) into the English Order of the Garter, whose heraldric symbol is the Red Cross of Saint George.

The symbol of the rose and the cross also evokes mystical images of the rose of the Virgin and the death of Christ. (Coincidentally, the rose cross was one of Luther's emblems.) For contemporary Rosicrucians, the interpretation of the rose cross centers in the maxim "No cross, no crown," that is, the belief that one comes to the rose (signifying the divine) through mortal suffering.

BIBLIOGRAPHY

Arthur E. Waite's *Real History of the Rosicrucians* (London, 1887) is the standard account of Rosicrucianism. *The Secret Doctrine of the Rosicrucians* (Chicago, 1918), by Magus Incognito (pseudonym for Clifford Edward Brooksmith), is a partisan study of teachings and symbols. The best recent account, particularly of the cultural, intellectual, and political milieu in which Rosicrucianism emerged, is Frances A. Yates's *The Rosicrucian Enlightenment* (London, 1972). This book draws upon the full range of recent scholarship. *A Christian Rosenkreutz Anthology,* edited by Paul M. Allen and Carlo Pietzner (Blauvelt, N.Y., 1968), offers a useful compilation of traditional texts as well as essays by Rudolf Steiner and others associated with Anthroposophy. Francis King's *Magic* (London, 1975) explores Rosicrucian influences on Western magic.

HARRY WELLS FOGARTY

ROUSSEAU, JEAN-JACQUES

ROUSSEAU, JEAN-JACQUES (1712–1778), Geneva-born author, social and educational theorist, and advocate of a nondogmatic religion of nature. Rousseau was a prolific writer; however, his mature religious thought is encapsulated in a comparatively short section, "The Profession of Faith of the Savoyard Vicar," of *Émile* (1762), his treatise in support of experientially based educational methods. The straightforward, somewhat serene tone of this famous statement stands in marked contrast to the complex, turbulent pattern of its author's life history.

Amid the natural beauties of the Alps, Rousseau's vicar, a simple, unpretentious country priest, recounts his efforts to resolve his doubts, stemming from the diversity of competing beliefs. Dissatisfied with the philosophers, of whom he says he is not one, he has found a basis for certitude and optimism in his own experience. This has convinced him, ultimately, of the presence of order in the universe, which is only explicable by the existence of a powerful, intelligent, and beneficent God. He further asserts the immortality of the immaterial soul and the natural goodness of human beings. Evil stems from ignoring the "heavenly voice" of conscience, which teaches a sociable sympathy for others and rejects self-interest as the basis of right conduct. The vicar concludes that the adherent of natural religion may in good conscience follow the prescribed religious customs of the jurisdiction in which he or she happens to live, as he himself does in Roman Catholic Savoy.

The vicar's views are unquestionably Rousseau's own. Of equal importance with his positive beliefs is his rejection of, as unanswerable and, practically speaking, unimportant, many of the traditional central questions of metaphysics and theology, such as the meaning of "creation," the alleged eternal punishment of the wicked, and the status of "revelation." Although Rousseau, an admirer of the scriptural Jesus, considered himself a Christian, he refused, consistently with his natural religion, to endorse claims that Jesus' alleged miracles were proof of his divinity.

These religious views were central to Rousseau's entire outlook. In his autobiographical *Confessions* (completed in 1770 but published posthumously, in two parts, in 1782 and 1789) and elsewhere, he speaks rather positively of his early moral upbringing in Calvinist Geneva, although he had left there at the age of sixteen in search of wider horizons. Within a brief time, he had declared himself a convert to Catholicism in Turin. He next established some reputation as a music teacher and theorist, traveling to various Swiss and French cities before settling in Paris. There he made the acquaintance of Thérèse Levasseur, a working-class woman who became his lifelong companion, and of the social circle surrounding the *philosophes*, notably Diderot. He eventually contributed to their *Encyclopedia*.

An incident in the autumn of 1749, known as "the illumination of Vincennes," shaped Rousseau's subsequent career. Stopping along the road to rest, he glanced at a journal announcement of a prize essay contest on the question of whether the renaissance of the sciences and arts had contributed to the purification of morals. The insight that, on the contrary, civilization and progress had brought about degeneration from the more natural earlier state of humanity struck him forcefully. His *Discourse on the Sciences and Arts* (1750), which elaborates on the consequences of this degeneration, won the prize. In his *Discourse on the Origins of Inequality* (1755), he imaginatively reconstructs humanity's development from a happy but unenlightened early state of nature through successive stages leading to the establishment of private property, government, and ultimately despotism. But he also insists that an attempt to return to the primitive state would be unrealistic. His *Social Contract*, published in the same year (1762) as *Émile*, aims to show how a free community structured in accordance with the general will of its citizens could claim moral legitimacy. It concludes with the chapter "On Civil Religion," in which Rousseau proposes to combine the principles of natural religion with the state's need for religious reinforcement: a new doctrine affirming the "sacredness of the social contract and the laws" is the result.

Rousseau's work of 1762, particularly the "Profession of Faith," was attacked by Catholics, Protestants, and *philosophes* alike. He was forced to flee France to avoid arrest and was also condemned by the authorities of Geneva, whose citizenship and religion he had proudly readopted eight years earlier. Subsequent forced displacements and isolation led him to suspect the existence of a large conspiracy against him. But by the time of his death, Rousseau's ideas—especially, perhaps, as popularized in his romantic novel, *The New Heloise* (1761)—had won many adherents. His name later came to be associated with the French Revolution; Robespierre was a great admirer of Rousseau's, as was Kant, who took Rousseau's ideal of societal self-government—obedience to a law that one has prescribed for oneself—as his formula for moral autonomy.

Subsequent uses and interpretations of Rousseau's thought have been equally disparate. Was he a rationalist or a proponent of the purest sentimentality? A totalitarian or a democrat? A conservative or a protosocialist? A sympathetic portrayer of female heroines or a blatant sexist? A Pelagian, a Deist in spite of himself, or a consistent exponent of the fundamental ideas of the Reformation? Textual evidence exists for these and many other incompatible, ardently defended interpretations of Rousseau. What is correct in any case is that Rousseau had a keen sense for dialectical paradoxes in the human condition, and that he was a pioneer in exploring the complex tensions and ambivalences of the human psyche, beginning with his own.

BIBLIOGRAPHY

One complete English translation of *Émile* in current circulation is Barbara Foxley's (1903; reprint, London, 1966), and there is another of the *Profession of Faith of the Savoyard Vicar*, translated by Arthur H. Beattie as *Creed of a Priest of Savoy* (New York, 1956). Multiple translations of other major Rousseauean writings exist, the most numerous being those of *The Social Contract*. Particularly distinguished, in terms of scholarship, is Roger D. Masters and Judith R. Masters edition of *The First and Second Discourses* (New York, 1964). Ronald Grimsley has edited a collection entitled *Religious Writings* (Oxford, 1970). Among the numerous secondary works, Grimsley's *Rousseau and the Religious Quest* (Oxford, 1968) is perhaps the most useful introduction to this topic in English, although it cannot compare in comprehensiveness to Pierre Maurice Masson's *La Religion de Jean-Jacques Rousseau*, 3 vols. in 1 (1916; reprint, Geneva, 1970). Among more general English-language studies, Charles Hendel's two-volume *Jean-Jacques Rousseau, Moralist* (1934; reprint, New York, 1962), remains an especially lively and readable classic.

WILLIAM LEON MCBRIDE

ROY, RAM MOHAN (1772–1833), important early nineteenth-century reformer of Indian religion and society, founder of the Brāhmo Samāj. Roy's lasting influence has earned him the epithet "father of modern India."

Ram Mohan Roy was born into an orthodox Hindu brahman family on 22 May 1772 in Radhanagar, a small town in modern West Bengal. He was sent at an early age to Patna, then a center of Islamic learning, to study Persian and Arabic, the languages of social and political advancement at that time. At Patna, Roy became acquainted with Islamic thought, particularly Islamic monotheism and views on Hindu image worship, which was to have a lasting influence on his own religious beliefs. His new ideas and subsequent criticism of Hinduism caused such conflict with his parents that he left their home to travel around northern India, perhaps venturing as far as Tibet, to study the religions of those areas firsthand. Encouraged by his mother, he then settled down in Banaras (Varanasi) for a few years to study Sanskrit and the Hindu scriptures. At this time he also began to study English, which eventually enabled him to secure an appointment in Bengal under the East India Company in 1803.

Success as an administrator and an assured income from landed estates permitted Roy to retire at the age of forty-two and settle permanently in Calcutta, then the political and intellectual capital of India. There he launched an active career calling for reforms in Indian religion and society. There too he began to develop close ties with the Unitarian missionaries of Calcutta. Roy was attracted to the Unitarian doctrine of divine unity, and for a time (1824–1828) he regularly attended Unitarian services and considered himself a "Hindu Unitarian." Later, he and his followers rejected Unitarianism as unsuited to their views and principles; in 1828 they founded their own movement, which came to be known as the Brāhmo Samāj, a society organized to provide for the proper worship of *brahman*, whom Roy considered to be the one true God of the Hindu scriptures. In 1830 he set sail for England to realize a long-held dream of visiting Europe, the land of the scientific rationalism to which he had become so attracted. He was, unfortunately, never to return to India, for his life was cut short by a serious illness; he died at Bristol on 22 September 1833.

Roy's first work of major importance was the *Tuḥfat al-muwāḥḥidīn* (A Gift for the Monotheists). This work, written in Persian and Arabic at an early date but not published until 1804, argues that, by natural reason, all human beings believe in one being who is the source and governor of creation, but by habit and training at the hands of deceitful religious leaders, they stray from this virtuous belief. In 1815 Roy published a major study of Hindu Vedānta, *Vedāntagrantha* (also abridged as *Vedāntasāra*), and from 1816 to 1819 he published translations of five major Upaniṣads in both Bengali and English. He hoped to show by these efforts that the belief in and worship of the one *brahman* was the only sensible religious practice for Hindus. Roy published *The Precepts of Jesus* in 1820, which presented Christianity as a simple, virtuous moral code, avoiding mention of miracles and opposing the doctrine of the Trinity in favor of the unity of God. This publication upset both the orthodox Hindu community and the Baptist missionaries of Calcutta.

The two primary tenets of Roy's religious reform were the establishment of a Hindu monotheism and the abolishment of what he called Hindu "idolatry." He wrote in his English introduction to the *Vedāntasāra*:

> My constant reflections on the inconvenient or, rather, injurious rites introduced by the peculiar practice of Hindoo idolatry, which, more than any other pagan worship destroys the texture of society, together with compassion for my countrymen, have compelled me to use every possible effort to awaken them from their dream of error; and by making them acquainted with their scriptures, enable them to contemplate, with true devotion, the unity and omnipresence of nature's God. (de Bary, 1958, p. 575)

Roy believed that the pure Hinduism of an earlier age had become encrusted with degrading customs, of which it had to be purged. Although his appreciation of monotheism began with his exposure to Islamic thought and was strengthened by Christian Unitarianism, Roy was born a Hindu and would not be satisfied until he had found approval for his monotheistic ideas in the Hindu scriptures. He found this confirmation in his study of Vedantic thought, particularly that of the Upaniṣads. The Upaniṣadic *brahman*, according to Roy, is not a static absolute but rather the sole "author and governor of the universe." As for Hindu image worship, he contended that the scriptures recommend it only for the feebleminded and he therefore declared it inferior and unworthy of practice.

Much of what Roy criticized in Hinduism was precisely what was condemned by the Christian missionaries in Calcutta. His reform program had two essential purposes: to convince the Hindus that many of their beliefs and practices were not sanctioned by their own scriptures and to demonstrate both to the adherents of other religions and to the British rulers that, contrary to common understanding, the Hindu scriptures did not advocate polytheism and idolatry but in fact contained a lofty and rational message. These efforts, of course, caused deep resentment and outrage among many orthodox Hindus.

Roy also campaigned vigorously for certain social reforms. He promoted modern education and struggled ceaselessly for women's rights. Roy's influence was particularly conspicuous in the official British proscription of *satī* (the self-immolation of a widow on her husband's funeral pyre) in 1829.

Many scholars place Roy at the head of a reformation of Indian religion and society that was to change Indian culture significantly in the nineteenth and twentieth centuries. The most important and lasting event in his career was the establishment of the Brāhmo Samāj. Through this religious society, which nurtured such figures as Rabindranath Tagore and Keshab Chandra Sen, Roy's continuing influence was assured. Roy shaped the Brāhmo Samāj with his ideas, and many scholars will argue that it was the Brāhmo Samāj that shaped modern Indian culture.

[*See also* Brāhmo Samāj.]

BIBLIOGRAPHY

A reliable source for the life of Ram Mohan Roy is the first chapter of Sivanath Sastri's *History of the Brahmo Samaj*, 2d ed. (Calcutta, 1974). Two recent biographies are B. N. Dasgupta's *The Life and Times of Rajah Rammohun Roy* (New Delhi, 1980) and M. C. Kotnala's *Raja Ram Mohun Roy and Indian Awakening* (New Delhi, 1975). *The English Works of Raja Rammohun Roy*, 6 vols., edited by Kalidas Nag and Debajyoti Burman (Calcutta, 1945–1951), is the sourcebook of Roy's works for the English reader. A good study of Roy's religious ideas is Ajit Kumar Ray's *The Religious Ideas of Rammohun Roy* (New Delhi, 1976). For the lasting influence of Ram Mohan Roy and the Brāhmo Samāj, see David Kopf's *The Brahmo Samaj and the Shaping of the Modern Indian Mind* (Princeton, 1979).

Extracts from Roy's introduction to the *Vedāntasāra*, including the quotation that appears above, can be found in *Sources of the Indian Tradition*, edited by Wm. Theodore de Bary (New York, 1958), pp. 573–575.

David L. Haberman

ṚTA (Skt., "cosmic order") represents the Vedic notion of an impersonal and powerful force upon which the ethical and physical worlds are based, through which they are inextricably united, and by which they are maintained. *Ṛta* is the universal truth that gives effective strength to Vedic ritual practices, that serves as the foundation for proper social organization, and that preexists even the Vedic gods themselves, who find in it the very source and essence of their power. In many ways, *ṛta* stands as the Vedic antecedent for the notion of *dharma* (the established order of things, proper behavior, fitting truth), a concept of central importance not only to the various forms of Hinduism but also to the teachings of Buddhism, Jainism, and other South Asian religious systems.

The term *ṛta* is based on the Sanskrit verbal root *ṛ* ("go, move"), which itself reflects the Indo-European verbal root **ar* ("fit together properly"). Thus *ṛta* signifies the cosmic law that allows the universe to run smoothly, the dynamic structure in which every object and all actions have their proper place and in which all parts support and strengthen the whole in a flowing symbiosis. The word is related through **ar* to the Greek *harmos*, from which the English *harmony* derives, and to the Latin *ars* ("skill, craft"), the source of the English *art* and *artist*. Accordingly, the term *ṛta* connotes the experience of a "finely tuned" universe whose laws can give creative power to those gods and cultic specialists who understand its structures.

The *Ṛgveda* (c. 1200 BCE) commonly assigns to the gods such epithets as "he who possesses *ṛta*," "he who grows according to *ṛta*," or "he who is born of *ṛta*," descriptions representing the Vedic notion that the gods derive their strength from their adherence to cosmic law. If they—or humans, for that matter—were to go against the structures of *ṛta*, they would then be said to be *anṛta*, a common synonym for *vṛjina* ("crooked, wrong") and even *asatya* ("untrue"). Thus even the gods must obey the laws of *ṛta*. The principles of *ṛta* (like those of the Zand Avestan *asha*, a Zoroastrian notion to which *ṛta* is linguistically and conceptually related) function in eternal opposition to any principle of disjunctive or disintegrative power *(druh;* Av., *druj)* as well as to those personal demons and humans who seek to disrupt impersonal cosmic order by means of harmful magical practices *(yātu)*.

Throughout the Vedic period *ṛta* was understood to be an impersonal law and was never personified or hypostatized into a deity. Characteristically, the primary agent or guardian of the laws of *ṛta* is the god Varuṇa, who—in Vedic times at least—was an ethical sky god whose omniscient judgment the Vedic cult admired and feared.

As the impersonal source of cosmic and ethical order, *ṛta* includes important creative aspects. The gods find their ability to create the world precisely in their ability to recognize the principles of *ṛta*. These creative dimensions appear frequently in Vedic salutatory depictions of natural processes. Thus the wonderful facts that the sun rises in the east every morning and that water runs downhill are trustworthy cosmic events because they reflect the truth of cosmic harmony (see *Ṛgveda* 1.105.12). Furthermore, Vedic tradition held that the very structures of *ṛta* allow the human community access to the powers that drive the universe itself. This is most apparent in the performance of the ritual: since proper cultic activity embodies the structures and processes of cosmic law, the incorrect performance of the ritual would signal the collapse of cosmic order and would be as devastating to the Vedic community as it would be if the sun were not to rise or rivers not to flow.

[*For discussion of cosmic and religious order in later Hinduism, see* Dharma, *article on* Hindu Dharma.]

BIBLIOGRAPHY

The most complete study of *ṛta* continues to be Heinrich Lüders's *Varuṇa*, vol. 2, *Varuṇa und das Ṛta* (Göttingen, 1959). Shorter discussions may be found in Hermann Oldenberg's *Die Religion des Veda* (Berlin, 1894), pp. 195–221; Edward Washburn Hopkins's *Ethics of India* (New Haven, 1924), pp. 2ff., 40–44; and F. Max Müller's *Lectures on the Origin and Growth of Religion* (London, 1879), pp. 237–250.

WILLIAM K. MAHONY

RUDRA is a Vedic god and precursor of the great Hindu divinity Śiva. The name *Rudra* derives from the verbal root *rud* ("to howl, to roar"), from which he takes the epithet "the howler." The root *rud* also connotes "red" (as in English *ruddy*), suggesting that the earliest concept of the divinity was inspired by red storm clouds or the sound of thunder. Rudra has no correlates in other Indo-European mythologies.

Some scholars believe that the earliest prototype of Rudra may be traced to an Indus Valley seal in which four animals surround a seated figure. This seal, and some Vedic texts, suggest Rudra's connection with animals. As the Lord of Animals (Paśupati), he is their protector as well as their destroyer, an ambivalence common in many mythologies. The animal most frequently associated with Rudra is the bull, a symbol of rain and fertility. Typically, the figure in the Indus Valley seals is seated in a posture later associated with yogic meditation, leading some to postulate a non-Aryan origin of his post-Vedic role as the ascetic mendicant *par excellence*.

Rudra's wife is Pṛśni, whose name denotes a leather water bag, clearly an association with rainwater. This association is strengthened by references in the *Ṛgveda* to Rudra as the bringer of fertilizing rain. Rudra is invoked in only four hymns of the *Ṛgveda*, although he also figures in the later Saṃhitās and in the Brāhmaṇas. The Ṛgvedic hymns describe him as a well-dressed god riding in a chariot, carrying a bow and arrows. These hymns seek to avert the wrath of a fearsome and destructive god who hurls his lethal arrows at random upon men and beasts. In addition to the wind gods, Vāyu-Vātāḥ, Rudra's Vedic associates are the Rudras and the Maruts, who share his benign and chthonic traits respectively. The word *marut*, derived from the root *mṛ* ("to die"), seems to signify a spirit of the dead. Cultic worship of Rudra also confirms his close connection with Yama, the god of death, with spirits of the dead, and with the dark goddess Nirṛti. His oblations and the venue and manner of offering them are characteristic of a chthonic god. Rudra's later Vedic consort was Rudrāṇī, or Mīḍhuṣī. The latter, like Pṛśni, signifies Rudra's function as the "pourer," and indirectly connects him with fertility, a trait incipient from the Indus Valley period. This perhaps explains the worship of Rudra in the phallic emblem, which later almost completely replaced his anthropomorphic representation.

In the Vedic literature Rudra is intimately connected with Agni and Soma. Indeed, in his power, brilliance, and destructive capacity he is almost an alter ego of Agni. Like Soma, he dwells on a mountaintop, especially Mount Mūjavat, the abode of Soma in later literature. But from the *Yajurveda* onward, a syncretism begins in which the Ṛgvedic Rudra merges with other gods evidently of indigenous origin, reflecting the fusion of Aryan and non-Aryan peoples. In that text Rudra is invoked as the god of burglars, highwaymen, night rovers, and cheats. His benign characteristics persist, but dark and malevolent traits now appear, and his chthonic character is henceforth established. In later Vedic literature Rudra assumes such new names as Bhava, Śarva, Ugra, Mahādeva, and Śiva. Some of these figures are clearly of regional origin, while others are still unspecified but may be indigenous gods of non-

Vedic origin. Both the *Yajurveda* and the Brāhmaṇas record the progress of Rudra's syncretism with other gods until he finally merges into Śiva, his mythological successor. The complex "Rudra-Siva" is thus often used by students of the tradition to designate the mythological and cultic fusion of Śiva and his Vedic precursor.

Because of the fairly early syncretism with other indigenous regional and tribal gods, Rudra becomes a conglomerate of disparate traits. His evident ambivalence toward the sacrifice bears testimony to this. In the subsequent Śaiva mythological cycle, the sacrifice flees from him, or he is denied a share in Dakṣa's sacrifice. Infuriated, he destroys the sacrifice, killing men and injuring gods. These anti-Vedic traits continue to multiply until the Ṛgvedic god who granted boons, forgave sins, and blessed his devotees assumes a dual personality combining benign and malevolent traits.

[*See also* Śiva.]

BIBLIOGRAPHY

Agarwala, Vasudeva S. *Śiva Mahādeva, the Great God.* Varanasi, 1966.

Bhandari, V. S. "Rudra as the Supreme God in the Yajurveda." *Nagpur University Journal* 16 (October 1965): 37–42.

Bhattacharji, Sukumari. *Indian Theogony: A Comparative Study of Indian Mythology from the Vedas to the Puranas.* Cambridge and New York, 1970. Includes chapters on Rudra-Śiva.

Dange, Sadashiv Ambadas. "Tryambaka." *Journal of the Oriental Institute* (University of Baroda) 19 (1969): 223–227.

Machek, Václav. "Origin of the Gods Rudra and Pūṣan." *Archiv orientalni* 22 (1954): 544–562. A perceptive article.

Mayrhofer, Manfred. "Der Gottesname Rudra." *Zeitschrift der Deutschen Morgenländischen Gesellschaft* 103 (1953): 140–150. An original article on the import of the god's name.

O'Flaherty, Wendy Doniger. *Ascetism and Eroticism in the Mythology of Śiva.* London, 1973.

Pisani, Vittore. "Und dennoch Rudra 'Der Rote.'" *Zeitschrift der Deutschen Morgenländischen Gesellschaft* 104 (1954): 136–139. Seeks to trace the god's identity from the derivation of his name.

SUKUMARI BHATTACHARJI

RŪMĪ, JALĀL AL-DĪN

(AH 604–672/1207–1273 CE), Muslim mystic and poet. No Ṣūfī poet has exerted a vaster influence on Muslim East and Christian West than Jalāl al-Dīn, called Mawlānā, or Mawlawī, "our master." His Persian works are considered the most eloquent expression of Islamic mystical thought, and his long mystico-didactic poem, the *Mathnavī*, has been called "the Qur'ān in the Persian tongue" by the great fifteenth-century poet Jāmī of Herat.

Life. Muḥammad Jalāl al-Dīn was born in Balkh, now Afghanistan; the Afghans therefore prefer to call him "Balkhī," not "Rūmī," as he became known after settling in Anatolia, or Rūm. Although the date of his birth seems well established, he may have been born some years earlier. His father, Bahā' al-Dīn Walad, a noted mystical theologian, left the city some time before the Mongol invasion of 1220 and took his family via Iran to Syria, where Jalāl al-Dīn studied Arabic history and literature. They then proceeded to Anatolia, an area that had not yet been reached by the Mongol hordes and thus offered shelter to numerous mystics and scholars from the eastern lands of Islam. They enjoyed the liberal patronage of the Seljuk sultan ʿAlā' al-Dīn Kaykōbād. After Bahā' al-Dīn's family settled in Laranda (now Karaman), Jalāl al-Dīn married, and in 1226 his first son, Sulṭān Walad, was born. The aged Bahā' al-Dīn was invited to Konya (ancient Iconium), the capital of the Anatolian Seljuks, to teach in one of the city's numerous theological colleges. After his death in early 1231, Jalāl al-Dīn succeeded him in the chair.

A disciple of Rūmī's father, Burhān al-Dīn Muḥaqqiq, reached Konya in the early 1230s and introduced Jalāl al-Dīn into the mystical life and to the ideas of his father, whose *Ma'ārif*, a collection of sermons and a spiritual diary, were later to form an important source of inspiration for Rūmī. He also studied the Persian poetry of Ḥakīm Sanā'ī of Ghazna (d. 1131), the first poet to use the form of *mathnavī*, "rhyming couplets," for mystical instruction. Rūmī may have visited Syria in the 1230s, but nothing definite is known. His teacher later left Konya for Kayseri (Caesarea), where he died about 1242.

Shams al-Dīn. After ʿAlā' al-Dīn's death in 1236, the Mongols invaded Anatolia, and the internal situation deteriorated owing to the incompetence of his successors. In the midst of the upheavals and troubles in eastern and central Anatolia Jalāl al-Dīn underwent an experience that transformed him into a mystical poet. In October 1244 he met the wandering dervish Shams al-Dīn, "Sun of Religion," of Tabriz, and, if we believe the sources, the two mystics spent days and weeks together without eating, drinking, or experiencing any bodily needs. The discussions of Rūmī and Shams, who must have been about the same age, led Jalāl al-Dīn into the depths of mystical love but also caused anger and jealousy among his students and his family. Shams left Konya, and in the pangs of separation, Mawlānā suddenly turned into a poet who sang of his love and longing while whirling around to the sound of music. He himself could not understand the secret of this transformation and expressed his feelings in ever-new verses, declaring that it was the spirit of the beloved that made him sing, not his own will. There was no question of seeking a fitting rhyme or meter—they came to him spontaneously, triggered by a casual sound, a word, or a sight. The poems of this early period, which excel in their daring paradoxes and sometimes eccentric imagery, do not mention the name of the beloved but allude to it with frequent mention of the sun, which became Rūmī's favorite symbol to express the beautiful and destructive but always transforming power of love. In addition to classical Persian, he sometimes used the Turkish or Greek vernacular as it was spoken in Konya.

When news reached Konya that Shams al-Dīn had been seen in Damascus, Mawlānā's elder son, Sulṭān Walad, traveled there and succeeded in bringing his father's friend back. As Sulṭān Walad says in his poetical account of his father's life, "They fell at each other's feet, and no one knew who was the lover and who the beloved." This time, Shams stayed in Mawlānā's home, married to one of the young women there, and the intense spiritual conversation between the two mystics continued. Again jealousy built up, and Shams disappeared in December 1248. It seems certain that he was assassinated with the connivance of Mawlānā's younger son. Rūmī knew what had happened but refused to believe it; his poetry expressed the certitude that "the sun cannot die," and he even went to Syria to seek the lost friend. But eventually he "found him in himself, radiant as the moon," as Sulṭān Walad says, and most of his lyrical poetry came to be written in the name of Shams al-Dīn.

Friends and disciples. After reaching complete annihilation *(fanā')* in Shams, who had claimed to have attained the stage of being "the Beloved" and who appeared as the true interpreter of the secrets of the Prophet, Mawlānā found spiritual peace in his friendship with Ṣalāḥ al-Dīn, an illiterate goldsmith with whom he had long-standing relations through his own spiritual teacher, Burhān al-Dīn. Ṣalāḥ al-Dīn became, as it were, Rūmī's mirror; in his pure simplicity he understood the friend without questioning. To cement the relationship, Mawlānā married Sulṭān Walad to Ṣalāḥ al-Dīn's daughter, and his letters to his beloved daughter-in-law are beautiful proofs of his humanity.

The number of disciples that gathered around Rūmī grew steadily. They came from different layers of society, for he was a friend of some of the powerful ministers who, for all practical purposes, ruled the country; but there were also greengrocers and craftsmen among them. A number of women belonged to his circle, some of whom arranged musical sessions for him in their homes. Outstanding in piety and obedience among his disciples was the youthful Ḥusām al-Dīn Chelebī, who now became Rūmī's third source of inspiration.

A poem dated November 1256 reveals the moment when Ḥusām al-Dīn first assumed his new role. About that time, he had asked the master to compose a mystical *mathnavī* for the benefit of his students so that they would no longer need to go back to the epics of Sanā'ī and 'Aṭṭār. Rūmī began by reciting the famous "Song of the Reed," the eighteen introductory verses of the *Mathnavī,* which express the soul's longing for home, and from that time Ḥusām al-Dīn wrote down whatever inspirational teaching came from the master. The composition of the *Mathnavī* was interrupted in 1258 when Ṣalāḥ al-Dīn died after a protracted illness and Ḥusām al-Dīn lost his wife; the poems attributed to the next four years are usually didactic in character though lyrical in form. The dictation of the *Mathnavī* resumed in 1262, when Ḥusām al-Dīn was designated as Rūmī's spiritual successor *(khalīfah),* and continued almost to the master's death on 17 December 1273. His death was lamented not only by the Muslims but also by the numerous Christians and Jews of Konya, for he had friendly relations with all of them (and his verse at times shows a remarkable awareness of Christian thought and ritual).

Ḥusām al-Dīn, his first successor, died in 1284; then Sulṭān Walad, the obedient son, assumed the leadership of the disciples and shaped them into a Ṣūfī fraternity proper. He institutionalized the mystical dance, *samā',* in the form that has remained current through the centuries. By the time he died in 1312, the Mevlevi order (called Whirling Dervishes in the West) was firmly established and continued to exert great influence on Turkish culture, particularly music and poetry. The order was abolished, like all mystical fraternities, in 1925 by Kemal Atatürk; but since 1954 the anniversary of Rūmī's death is again being celebrated in Konya, and the performers of the *samā'* have toured Western countries under the label of a "tourist attraction."

Works. Mawlānā's writings can be divided into two distinct parts: the lyrical poetry that was born out of his encounter with Shams and is collected in the more than thirty-six thousand verses of the so-called *Dīvān-i Shams-i Tabrīz,* and the didactic *Mathnavī-yi ma'navī* with about twenty-six thousand verses, written in a simple meter that had already been used for similar purposes by 'Aṭṭār. Mawlānā's "table talks" have been collected under the title *Fīhi mā fīhi;* these prose pieces sometimes supplement the poetry, since the same stories are used at times in both works. More than a hundred letters, written to dignitaries and family members, have also survived; they show that Mawlānā was also practically-minded and looked well after those who entrusted themselves to him.

Dīvān-i Shams. The *Dīvān* is a remarkable piece of literature in that it translates the author's ecstatic experiences directly into poetry. The form is the traditional *ghazal* with its monorhyme. The rhythm is strong, and often the verses invite scanning by stress rather than by the rules of quantitative classical Persian prosody, although Rūmī uses the traditional meters most skillfully. He is also a master of rhetorical plays, puns, and unexpected ambiguities, and his allusions show that he had mastered Arabic and Persian classical literatures and history as well as religious writings completely. In some poems one can almost follow the flow of inspiration: beginning from a seemingly trivial event, such as a strange sight in the street, the mystic is carried away by the music of the words and the strength of his rapture until, at least in some longish poems, the inspiration tapers off even though the rhyme continues to carry him through some more (not too good) verses.

Mathnavī. As the *Dīvān* was largely born out of an ecstatic experience that was expressed in unusual and extremely rich imagery, it is difficult to analyze. The *Mathnavī* is somewhat more accessible, and it has been a source for mystical instruction ever since it was written. For the Western reader, the book is still not easy to understand, for stories grow out of stories to lead to a mystical adage or a highly lyrical passage, and after long digressions the poet may return to the original anecdote only to be carried away by a verbal association or, as we may surmise, by the interruption of a listener who set him on a different train of thought. The *Mathnavī* is a storehouse not only of Ṣūfī lore but also of folklore, proverbs, and sometimes very crude, even obscene stories that, again, turn into surprising symbols of spiritual experiences. The book contains so little technical terminology of the Ṣūfīs and so few theoretical discussions of "stages," "states," and so forth that some listeners objected to the master's simple "storytelling," as becomes evident from scattered remarks in the *Mathnavī* itself.

Content. The subject of Mawlānā's work is always love, the true moving power in life. Those verses in the *Dīvān* that can be assigned with some certainty to the early years (c. 1245–1250) use especially strong images to describe the mystery of love, the encounter between lover and beloved, the secrets of seeking and finding, of happiness in despair. They carry the reader away even though the logical sequence is not always very clear. Love is personified under different guises—Rūmī sees it as a police officer who enacts confiscation of man's goods or as a carpenter who builds a ladder to heaven, as a ragpicker who carries away everything old from the house of the heart, or as a loving mother, as a dragon or a unicorn, as an ocean of fire or a white falcon, to mention only a few of the images of this strongest power of life. God's preeternal address to the not-yet-created souls, "Alastu bi-rabbikum" ("Am I not your Lord?" Qur'ān 7:171), is interpreted as the first music, which caused creation to dance out of not-being and to unfold in flowers, trees, and stars. Everything created participates in the eternal dance, of which the Mevlevi ritual is only a "branch." In this ritual, the true mystery of love, namely "to die before dying," of sacrificing oneself in order to acquire a new spiritual life, is symbolized by the dervishes casting off their black gowns to emerge in their white dancing dresses, symbols of the luminous "body of resurrection." For the idea of suffering and dying for the sake of transformation permeates all of Rūmī's work, and he expresses it in ever-new images: not only the moth that casts itself into the candle, or the snow that melts when the sun enters the sign of Aries, but even the chickpeas that are boiled in order to be eaten, and thus to reach a higher level of existence in becoming part of the human body, speak of this mystery of transformation, as does the image of the treasure that can only be found in ruins; for the heart must be broken in order to find in itself the "hidden treasure," which is God.

Most interpreters, including the leading European expert, Reynold A. Nicholson, have understood Rūmī's work almost exclusively in the light of Ibn al-ʿArabī's theosophy. Although on friendly terms with Ibn al-ʿArabī's stepson and foremost interpreter, Ṣadr al-Dīn Qūnawī, Mawlānā was not fond of the "great master's" theoretical approach and his ingenious systematization. To explain everything in the *Mathnavī* in the light of *waḥdat al-wujūd,* "unity of being," as systematized by Ibn al-ʿArabī, would be wrong. Of course, Rūmī was deeply convinced, as is every true Muslim, that the multiplicity of phenomena is a veil before the absolute Divine Unity: God's creative command, "Kun!" ("Be!"), with its two letters *(kn),* is like a two-colored rope that makes people forget the unity of God who created it. The end of the ascending ladder of manifestations through which the creatures have to pass in their constant attempt to return to their beginning (symbolized by the reed bed out of which the complaining flute was once cut) lies in *ʿadam,* "positive nothingness," the divine essence that is absolutely hidden and beyond any qualifications. But Rūmī's experience of unity is not based on mere speculations of a gnostic approach to life; rather, it develops out of the experience of love, for the lover believes that everything he sees, hears, or feels merely points to the one Beloved with whom he experiences an ever-growing proximity until his own "I" has been burned away in the fire of separation, and he feels that only the Friend exists, who has taught him that "there is no room for two I's in the house."

This loving relationship is also expressed in prayer. Among all Muslim mystics, Rūmī has expressed the mystery of prayer most eloquently: prayer is the language of the soul, and the poor shepherd's prayer in which he offers his beloved God "to sweep his little room, to comb his hair, to pick his lice, and to bring him a little bit of milk" is more acceptable to God than learned words uttered without feeling or with pride, for it is the expression of true love. More importantly, prayer is a gift of God: the man who called "God" ever so long and was finally seduced by Satan to refrain from calling is informed by God himself that "in every 'O God' of yours there are a hundred 'Here am I' of mine." Without divine grace, people would not be able to pray—how could a rose grow out of mere dust?

It was out of this life of constant prayer that Mawlānā was able to teach and to inspire later generations. But one must not forget that he was well aware of this world, even though he considered it "like the dream of a sleeping person." Yet, the actions that occur in this dreaming life will be interpreted in the "morning light of eternity," and Mawlānā never tired of teaching his disciples that, as the Prophet had stated, "this world is the seedbed of the other world," for each action—rather, each thought—brings its fruits for spiritual development. Death, therefore, is the true mirror that will show everyone his real face.

This awareness of the world makes Rūmī's poetry especially powerful. There is nothing abstract in his verse, and he does not shun to mention the lowliest manifestations of life, since for him everything turns into a symbol of some higher reality. Spring is the time of resurrection, when the frozen material world suddenly becomes a paradise thanks to the thunder's "trumpet of Isrāfīl," and the trees, donning green paradisical garments, dance in the spring breeze of eternal love. Animals and plants, the arts and crafts of the citizens of Konya (sewing, weaving, calligraphy, pottery, and the like), and the skills of gypsy rope dancers inspired him as much as the legends of the Ṣūfī saints of yore, or the traditions of the Prophet. Allusions to and quotations from the Qur'ān form the warp and woof of his work. Just as the sun, according to Eastern folklore, is able to transform pebbles into rubies, so too Rūmī, touched by the "Sun of Tabrīz," who was for him the locus of manifestation of the divine sun of love, was able to transform everything into a poetical symbol. It goes without saying that not all his verse is on the same level, but the spirit is the same everywhere. Even though Rūmī, in a moment of anger, claimed that he thoroughly disliked poetry, he knew that he was forced by the mystical Friend:

> I think of rhymes, but my Beloved says:
> "Don't think of anything but of my face!"

The allusions to philosophical problems in some of the later lyrics, and especially in the fourth book of the *Mathnavī*, show that during the mid-1260s Rūmī developed some interest in more theoretical aspects of Sufism, but this period apparently did not last long.

Mawlānā's life can be seen as the ideal model of the mystic's progress: after the experience of the love of Shams, which, like a high-rising flame, burned him to complete annihilation, there followed a period of comparative quietude in his relationship with the goldsmith, a time of finding his transformed self. Finally, in the descending semicircle of his life, he returned to the world and its creatures by teaching Ḥusām al-Dīn the mysteries he had experienced through the medium of the *Mathnavī*. This sequence explains the stylistic differences between the *Dīvān* and the *Mathnavī;* it also explains why the *Mathnavī* became the centerpiece of mystical education wherever Persian was understood, from Ottoman Turkey to the borders of Bengal.

Legacy. In the East, the *Mathnavī* has been translated into many languages, and hundreds of commentaries have been composed; it has been a source of inspiration for mystics and kings alike. In the West, Rūmī's work was studied from about 1800 onward and inspired poets such as Rückert in Germany, whose free adaptations of some *ghazal*s are still the best introduction to Rūmī's style and thought. Through Rückert, Hegel learned of "the excellent Rūmī," in whom he saw a distant forerunner of his own thought. Numerous partial translations of Mawlānā's lyrics exist, but to do full justice to him is next to impossible because of the multicolored imagery of his verse, and the innumerable allusions would require a running commentary. Simple prose translations, again, cannot convey the delight that the reader feels when carried away by the rhythmical flow of these poems, which mark the high point of mystical verse in Islam.

BIBLIOGRAPHY

The most important Rūmī scholarship in the West has been carried out by Reynold A. Nicholson, whose *Selected Poems from the Dīvān-i Shams-i Tabriz* (1898; reprint, Cambridge, 1952) is the first major study of the *Dīvān* with useful notes, even though the tendency toward a Neoplatonic interpretation is somewhat too strong. Nicholson edited and translated *The Mathnawi of Jalālu'ddīn Rumi* (London, 1925–1940) in six volumes with two additional volumes of a most welcome commentary.

The *Dīvān*, which has been published often in the East, was critically edited in ten volumes by Badīʿ al-Zamān Furūzānfar (1957; reprint, Tehran, 1977). *Fīhi mā fīhi*, Mawlānā's prose work, is likewise available in several Eastern editions and in a translation by A. J. Arberry as *Discourses of Rumi* (London, 1961). Arberry has published other translations of Rūmī's work, including *Tales from the Masnavi* (London, 1961) and *Mystical Poems of Rumi* (Chicago, 1968, selections 1–200; Boulder, 1975, selections 201–400). Earlier translations of parts of the *Mathnavī* by James W. Redhouse, *The Mesnevi* (London, 1881), and E. H. Whinfield, *Masnavi i ma'navi* (1887; reprint, London, 1973), may be used for reference.

Afzal Iqbāl's *The Life and Thought of Mohammad Jalalud-Din Rumi* (Lahore, 1956), enlarged in later editions, provides an introduction to Rūmī's life and work, as does William Chittick's excellent book *The Sufi Path of Love* (Albany, N.Y., 1983). Most valuable are the studies of the Turkish scholar Abdülbâki Gölpınarlı, who has not only written a fine biography of Rūmī, *Mevlânâ Celâlettin, hayatı, felsefesi, eserlerinden seçmeleri* (Istanbul, 1952), and a history of the Mevlevi order, *Mevlânâ'dan sonra Mevelivîlik* (Istanbul, 1953), but has also translated the *Dīvān* (*Divan-i kebir*, 7 vols., Istanbul, 1957–1960) and the letters (*Mevlânâ'nın mektupları*, Istanbul, 1963) into Turkish. For a general survey, with emphasis on the poetical aspects of Rūmī's work, see my study *The Triumphal Sun* (London and The Hague, 1978), with extensive bibliography.

One of the oldest biographies of Mawlānā, his friends, and his family, Shams al-Dīn Aḥmad Aflākī's two-volume *Manāqib al-ʿārifīn*, was published in the Persian original by Tahsin Yazıcı (Ankara, 1959–1961) and translated by him into Turkish (*Âriflerin menkibeleri*, Ankara, 1964). The French version by Clément Huart, *Les saints des derviches tourneurs* (Paris, 1918–1922), is not very reliable.

There is a considerable literature on Rūmī, and (partly very free) translations of his poems, in German, the latest ones being *Aus dem Diwan* (Stuttgart, 1963) and *Rumi: Ich bin Wind und du bist Feuer* (Cologne, 1982) by me and *Licht und Reigen* (Bern, 1974) by J. Christoph Bürgel. Important for the serious scholar are Helmut Ritter's numerous studies, including "Philologika XI: Maulānā Ğalāladdīn Rūmī und sein Kreis," *Der Islam* 26 (1942): 116–158, 221–249, and "Neuere Literatur über Maulānā Calāluddīn Rūmī und seinen Orden," *Oriens* 13–14 (1960–1961).

Annemarie Schimmel

RUNES. The modern English word *rune* (Dan., *rune;* Swed., *runa;* Icel. pl., *rúnar;* Ger., *Rune*) signifies any character in the ancient Germanic, and especially Scandinavian, alphabet. The word is seemingly derived from a hypothetical Germanic form, **rūno-*, meaning "secret" (cf. modern Ger. *raunen*, "whisper"; Icel. *rýna*, "speak confidentially"; Goth. *rûna*, "secret"; AS *rún*, "rune, secret whispering"). The Finnish word *runo*, meaning "song," is an early borrowing from Germanic.

Comprising the earliest known form of writing in any Germanic tongue, runic inscriptions can be documented for as early as 200 CE. What is known of cultural, and especially linguistic, development in general leads to the supposition that runes must have been in existence for some generations by the time the earliest preserved inscriptions were carved. Numerous theories concern the date of their creation, the tribal identity of their inventors, and the models by which they were inspired. Much discussed also is the original purpose or purposes of the runes: were they invented and used initially to serve religious (and magical) ends or were they primarily conceived of as a mode of communication? It is attested that during the period of their employment—for a millennium and longer—they served both these purposes. (See figure 1 for a rendering, in normalized form, of the early runes.)

The geographical distribution of the earliest brief inscriptions points strongly to early Denmark as the primary center for the first important use of runes. From Denmark the loci of early Germanic inscriptions radiate outward to southern Norway and Sweden, to northern Germany, Poland (Rozwadów), and the Ukraine (Kowel), and ultimately to Hungary (Szabadbattyán) and Romania (Pietroassa). Later the runes spread to England, undergoing in time characteristic modifications

Figure 1. *Sample of Early Runes, in Normalized Form*

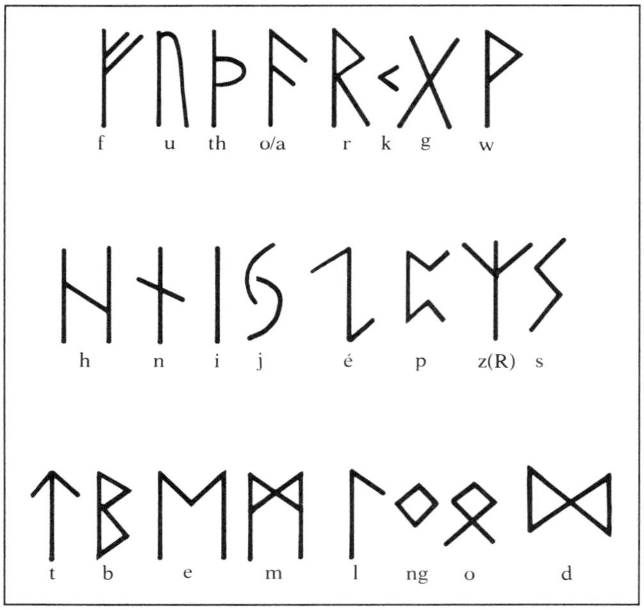

and additions and eventually awakening the interest of monks and bishops.

The geographical evidence for a centralized origin of the runes is reinforced by a linguistic consideration. From the outset, as evidenced by all known examples, there was no faltering or sign of experimentation: whether created by an individual genius or by a group, the runes were made full-blown, not only in their graphic and phonetic values but in their unique order and arrangement. Made up of twenty-four characters divided into three groups of eight, the runic "alphabet" is now known, after its first six characters, as the *futhark*. During the Viking age, commencing around 800, and through a second act of decisive linguistic creativeness, the Scandinavian *futhark* was shortened to sixteen characters, still arranged in three groups. This took place first in Denmark, then in Norway and Sweden. (See figure 2 for a sample of this younger *futhark*, taken from the runes of Rök, Sweden.)

The earliest inscriptions, from 200 CE or so, appear on small objects such as spearheads, buckles, amulets, and horns, apparently as marks of ownership. Their angular shape indicates the practice of carving onto wooden tablets. By the fourth century they were being chiseled into stone, particularly in Norway where rocks are plentiful. With that step, the runes acquired additional scope and permanence, chiefly as memorial inscriptions, which frequently have historical value of note. The oldest of this new type, dating from 350–400, is the brief inscription of Einang, Norway, reading "[I, Go-]dagastiz painted the rune" (i.e., carved the inscription). The longest inscription (720 runes) is that of Rök, which is partly versified and is filled with mythological and semihistorical allusions. The westernmost, and northernmost, inscription is the fourteenth-century carving from Kingiktorsoaq, Greenland, far above the Arctic circle.

FIGURE 2. *Sample of the Younger Futhark*

Of five thousand known inscriptions, more than three thousand are Swedish, most of which were carved before 1100. Lacking a cursive form and hence unhandy for manuscript use, and imperiled after 1100 by the spread of Latin letters, the runes nevertheless persisted, especially in Sweden, for several centuries. Ultimately, they fell into disuse save as an occasional pastime or for such limited purposes as marking the calendar or, recapitulating their earliest use, indicating ownership. In Sweden a form of runic shorthand enjoyed a limited vogue.

Conflicting theories derive the runes, via some early Germanic-speaking tribe, from the Greek alphabet, the Roman alphabet, or from North Italic (Etruscan); even Celtic influence has been posited. Suggested intermediaries are the Goths around the Black Sea and the Marcomanni, who were resident in Bohemia until their destruction at Vercellae in 18 CE. But the Gothic alphabet of Bishop Ulfilas (fourth century) itself shows runic influence, and the Marcomanni or their fellow Germans would simply have adopted the Latin alphabet entirely. The greatest number of similarities is between runic and Latin, and that accords well with the intense early relations between Rome and (pre-Danish) Jutland, "the long-time heartland of Germania" (Haugen, 1976).

Some early rune masters, however, had no doubt of the origin of the runes. It is explicitly stated on the Noleby Stone (Sweden, 450 CE), on the Sparlösa Stone (Sweden, 800), and in the Old Norse *Hávamál* (st. 80; cf. ss. 138–144) that the runes derived from the gods. Whether or not the runes were originally created for religio-magical purposes, they were certainly no less adaptable to such use than were the classical alphabets that preceded and coexisted with them. Early inscriptions repeatedly contain the word *alu*, meaning "protection, magic, taboo"; on the Stone of Nordhuglo (Norway, 425) the rune master proudly refers to himself as the *gudija* (priest) "protected against magic."

In time, Christian notions succeeded traditional Germanic conceptions. Inscriptions in the younger *futhark*, often carved within traditional serpentine patterns, came to be decorated with Christian crosses as well; the serpents were retained partly out of tradition and convenience as line markers and occasionally out of residual resentment or defiance of the "new faith." But as Christianity gained sway in the north, runic incantations, maledictions, and appeals to the Germanic gods yielded to such phrases as "So-and-so made this thing (e.g., built this bridge) for his soul." Late inscriptions are sometimes mixed with Latin phrases; the hammer of Þórr (Thor) is paired with a Christian cross; the Virgin Mary is mentioned.

In the British Isles runes were adroitly drawn into the service of the church. One of the finest examples of this is the splendid Ruthwell Cross (Dumfriesshire, c. 800), adorned with evangelical pictures and containing portions of *The Dream of the Rood.* The tenth-century Jelling Stone (No. 2), that huge royal Danish monument erected by King Harald Bluetooth in honor of his parents and himself, is aggressively Christian; on it, Harald claims credit for having christianized the Danes. Many rune stones have been transported to churchyards and even immured in church walls, as a rule with the inscribed face obscured, a practice that points rather to economic than to religious considerations.

In the sixteenth century the study of runes became a learned preoccupation in Sweden, whence it spread to Denmark, and by the nineteenth century the subject was being pursued to some effect in Germany and Great Britain. In the twentieth century much energy has been devoted to such topics as runic cryptography, speculative theories of Germanic uniqueness, and efforts to derive the runes from early conceptual signs *(Begriffszeichen).* Little of this has borne fruit, but the systematic study of runology during the past hundred years or so has brought forth works of great distinction.

BIBLIOGRAPHY

The important task of photographing, systematizing, and interpreting the great corpus of inscriptions is going forward in several countries. Notable names in modern runological research are, for Denmark, Ludvig Wimmer, Lis Jacobsen, Erik Moltke, and Karl-Martin Nielsen; for Iceland, (the Dane) Anders Baeksted; for Norway, Sophus Bugge, Magnus Olsen, Carl J. S. Marstrander, and Aslak Liestøl; for Sweden, Sven Söderberg, Erik Brate, Otto von Friesen, Elias Wessén, Elisabeth Svärdström, and Sven B. F. Jansson; for Finland, Magnus Hammarström; for Germany, Wilhelm Krause, Helmut Arntz, Hans Zeiss, and Hertha Marquardt; and for Great Britain, R. W. V. Elliott and R. I. Page. Excellent orientations and bibliographies can be found in the following works.

Derolez, R. *Runica Manuscripta: The English Tradition.* Ghent, 1954.

Düwel, Klaus. *Runenkunde.* Stuttgart, 1968.

Elliott, R. W. V. *Runes: An Introduction.* New York, 1959.

Haugen, Einar. *The Scandinavian Languages.* Cambridge, Mass., 1976.

Jansson, Sven B. F. *The Runes of Sweden.* Stockholm, 1962.

Musset, Lucien. *Introduction à la runologie.* Paris, 1965.

Page, R. I. *An Introduction to English Runes.* London and New York, 1973.

Erik Wahlgren

RUSSIAN ORTHODOX CHURCH.

Vladimir I, grand prince of Kiev, was baptized in 988. Having sent ambassadors to investigate the religions of his day, Vladimir was persuaded to embrace Greek Christianity when, according to the Russian *Primary Chronicle,* his envoys reported that at the liturgy in Constantinople they did not know whether they were in heaven or on earth. Vladimir's marriage to the Byzantine princess Anna and his economic dealings with the empire also played a significant part in his decision to align his principality with the imperial church of Byzantium.

Kievan Christianity. After the baptism of the Kievan peoples, Orthodox Christianity flourished in the lands of Rus'. Before the Tatar devastations in the thirteenth century, Kiev was a cosmopolitan city with commercial and cultural ties with Europe and the East. Its spiritual center was the Kievan Monastery of the Caves founded by Anthony of Kiev (d. 1072) and Theodosius (d. 1074). Now a museum, the monastery provided for the first literary and historical, as well as religious, writings in the Russian lands; for centuries it served as the theological and spiritual center of Ukrainian church life. In the early years of Christian Kiev, several remarkable churches were constructed, such as the Cathedral of Holy Wisdom (Hagia Sophia); these churches conformed to Byzantine patterns of architecture, iconography, and mosaic decoration. The leader of church life was the bishop of Kiev, often a Greek by nationality, who had the title of metropolitan.

The city-republics of Novgorod and Pskov to the north also developed vibrant Christian societies after their conversions, boasting wonderful architectural and iconographic achievements that very early began to show independence and originality. Spared attacks by the Tatars, these areas were threatened by crusading Christians from the West who desired to enforce Latin Christianity in the region. The Grand Prince Alexander Nevskii (d. 1263) led the Russians in their defeat of the invading Swedes (1240) and the Teutonic Knights (1242), thus preserving the Orthodox faith. He also managed to maintain peace with the Tatars through skillful diplomacy accomplished by extensive visits to the khans to whom he paid homage and tribute.

Muscovite Christianity. After the devastation of Kiev by the Tatars in 1240, the center of Russian political and ecclesiastical life shifted to Moscow in the wooded northeast. The Muscovite princes succeeded in bringing the rival cities of the region into submission, and with the final defeat of the Tatars by Grand Prince Dmitri Donskoi in 1380, their city reigned supreme among the Russians. The ascendancy of Moscow could not have occurred without the efforts of church leaders, particularly the metropolitans such as Alexis (d. 1378), who for a time served as governing regent, and the abbot Sergii of Radonezh (d. 1392).

Sergii is considered by many to be Russia's greatest saint and the "builder" of the nation. A simple monk who became famous for his ascetic labors and mystical gifts, he was appointed abbot of the Saint Sergius Trinity Monastery, which he founded in the wilderness north of Moscow (in present-day Zagorsk). The monastery soon became the center of social and economic as well as religious and spiritual life in the region. Its members and their disciples provided Russia over the centuries with hundreds of bishops, abbots, missionaries, thinkers, artists, and secular leaders, many of whom were canonized saints of the church. One such figure was the monk-iconographer Andrei Rublev, whose painting of the Trinity in the form of three angels who visited Abraham remains among the great masterpieces of Russian art. Closed after the 1917 revolution, the monastery was reopened after World War II, attracting thousands of pilgrims annually and housing the Moscow Theological Academy and Seminary, one of the three religious educational institutions, with those of Leningrad and Odessa, now operating in the U.S.S.R.

The Imperial Period. In the fifteenth century, with the fall of Constantinople to the Turks (1453), the theory developed that Moscow was the "third Rome," the last center of true Christianity on earth. Job, the metropolitan of Moscow, was named patriarch by Jeremias II of Constantinople in 1589, thus giving the Russian church a status of self-governance and honor equal to that of the ancient patriarchates of the Christian empire: Rome, Constantinople, Alexandria, Antioch, and Jerusalem. The patriarchate existed in Russia until the time of Peter the Great, who in 1721 issued the Ecclesiastical Regulation, which created a synodical form of church government patterned after that of the Protestant churches of Europe. The patriarchate was restored to the Russian church only in 1918, when the All-Russian Church Council, the first such assembly allowed since before Peter's rule, elected Tikhon Belavin (d. 1925), a former archbishop of the North American mission, to the office.

In the seventeenth century Patriarch Nikon (d. 1681) attempted to reform the Russian church according to the practices of the church of Constantinople. He corrected the liturgical service books and instituted Greek forms of ritual such as the practice of making the sign of the cross with three fingers instead of two, as was the practice among the Russians. Nikon's reform was taken as an assault on the "third Rome" theory since it radically questioned any special calling of the Russian church and nation. Its result was not only the resignation of the unyielding patriarch, but the schism of great numbers of "old ritualists" from the established church.

During the time of the westernization of Russia under Peter the Great and subsequent tsars, the Russian church became the virtual captive of the state. The patriarchate was abolished and replaced by the Holy Synod, consisting of bishops, presbyters, and laymen. Church councils were forbidden, ecclesiastical properties were appropriated and secularized, and church schools began to teach in Latin and to propagate Roman Catholic and Protestant doctrines (depending on the persuasion of those in authority). The clergy were alienated from the people, particularly the intellectuals, and the church structure was bureaucratized, with the lay government official for ecclesiastical affairs, the Oberprocuror of the Holy Synod, at its head.

Latinization in the Ukraine. From the end of the fifteenth century, the church in the Kievan area, by now a part of the Polish-Lithuanian kingdom, was canonically attached to the patriarchate of Constantinople and not to Moscow. In 1596, in Brest-Litovsk, the metropolitan of Kiev signed an act of union with the church of Rome, a move opposed by some bishops and most leading laypeople. Great numbers of believers in the territories of these bishops became Uniates at this time and, over the centuries, developed into strongly committed members of the Roman Catholic church. Until today the Ukrainian and Ruthenian Eastern Rite churches, both in the U.S.S.R. and abroad, remain staunchly anti-Russian and anticommunist, though in recent years somewhat less anti-Orthodox. [*See* Uniate Churches.]

The defense of Eastern Orthodoxy during this period was led by the Orthodox metropolitan of Kiev, Petr Moghila (d. 1647). Though violently anti-Catholic, Petr was himself trained in the West and became responsible for bringing many Latin doctrines and liturgical practices into the Orthodox church through his publications and the school that he founded in Kiev, which influenced not only the whole Russian church but the entire Orthodox world. In addition to the theological school in Kiev, higher faculties of theological study specializing in preparing missionaries for the Eastern regions were established in Moscow, Saint Petersburg (Leningrad after the Revolution), and Kazan.

Russian Missionary Activity. In the eighteenth and nineteenth centuries the missionary efforts of the Russian church were extensive. The scriptures and services of the church were translated into many Siberian languages and Alaskan dialects as the Eastern regions of the empire were settled and evangelized. Russian missionaries reached the Aleutian Islands in Alaska in 1794, thus beginning the history of Russian Orthodoxy in the New World. The monk Herman (d. 1830), a member of the original missionary party, was canonized a saint of the church in 1970 by both the Russian church and the Orthodox Church in America. The latter, formerly the Russian missionary diocese in North America, was recognized in the same year by the Moscow patriarchate as the fifteenth autocephalous (self-governing) Orthodox church in the world.

Joining Herman in the Orthodox calendar of saints were two other great missionaries. Innokentii Veniaminov (d. 1879) was a young married priest who traveled extensively through Siberia and North America, reaching as far as San Francisco. He created several Alaskan alphabets, translated many texts, wrote many books, and converted countless people before becoming head of the Russian church as metropolitan of Moscow, which post he occupied until his death. Nikolai Kasatkin (d. 1912) was the first Orthodox archbishop of Tokyo, and the founder of the now autonomous Orthodox Church of Japan. In addition to contributing to the conversion of thousands, he translated scriptures and services into Japanese and built the cathedral of Nikolai-Do in Tokyo.

Spiritual Revival. The eighteenth and nineteenth centuries also saw a revival of traditional Orthodox ascetical and mystical life uninfluenced by the westernizing tendencies of the ecclesiastical institutions. Paisii Velichkovskii (d. 1794) brought the hesychast method of mystical prayer, rooted in the invocation of the name of Jesus, into the Ukraine and Russia from Mount Athos, an important monastic center in northern Greece. He translated into Church Slavonic many ancient texts, including the anthology of writings on the spiritual life by the church fathers called the *Philokalia (Dobrotoliubie)*. (Church Slavonic, the language created for the Slavs by the Greek brothers Cyril and Methodius in the ninth century, is still used liturgically in the Russian church.) Bishop Feofan Govorov (d. 1894) translated into modern Russian many of the same works, including several contemporary Greek and Latin spiritual classics. Govorov also wrote many treatises on the spiritual life that continue to exercise wide influence in the Orthodox church. He accomplished this task after retiring as bishop and spending twenty-five years as a monastic recluse. Another retired bishop canonized for his ascetic life and spiritual writings was Tikhon of Zadonsk (d. 1783), who inspired the Russian novelist Dostoevskii to create a character with his name in *The Possessed.*

During this same period a tradition of spiritual eldership *(starchestvo)* emerged in Russia, the most famous center of which was the hermitage of Optina, where such elders *(startsy)* as Leonid, Macarius, and Ambrose spent several hours each day instructing and counseling people of all classes, including many philosophers, intellectuals, and statesmen, among whom were Tolstoi, Dostoevskii, Solov'ev, and Leont'ev.

The most famous saint of the time, however, was an elder from the Sarov monastery, the priest-monk Serafim (d. 1833), whose teachings on the Christian life understood as the "acquisition of the Holy Spirit" still have great influence among the Orthodox. Ioann of Kronstadt (d. 1908), a parish priest from the port town of Kronstadt near Saint Petersburg (Leningrad), also was acclaimed at this time throughout the nation as "all-Russian pastor." He is glorified in the church as a man of prayer and preaching who called the people to spiritual and sacramental renewal on the eve of the great revolution that both he and Serafim had in many ways predicted.

The turn of the century also saw a revival of patristic studies and a recapturing of the authentic Orthodox theological and liturgical tradition in the ecclesiastical schools, as well as a religious renaissance on the part of a significant number of Russian intellectuals, many of whom either perished in Stalin's prison camps, like Pavel Florenskii, or who were exiled to the West. Among the latter were such people as the philosopher Nikolai Berdiaev (d. 1948) and the theologian Sergei Bulgakov (d. 1944) who served as dean of the émigré Russian Orthodox Theological Institute of Saint Serge in Paris. The institute educated scores of pastors and church workers, and sent such scholars as George Fedotov (d. 1951), Georges Florovsky (d. 1979), and Alexander Schmemann (d. 1983) to Saint Vladimir's Seminary in New York.

Russian Orthodoxy Today. In the late 1980s the Russian Orthodox Church in the U.S.S.R. has the legal right to hold church services in buildings authorized by the state for such purposes. A council of twenty laypeople is needed to petition for the use of a church. Since very few churches and monasteries are functioning at this time, church services are normally very crowded. The church has no right to teach, preach, or pray outside of such buildings because "religious propaganda" is expressly forbidden by Soviet law. Admission to the three operating theological schools is strictly monitored by the state. There are no church schools for children and laypeople, who receive daily instruction in Marxist-Leninist doctrines, with the accompanying antireligious propaganda that is legally supported and officially enacted by the state.

The chief bishop of the Russian Orthodox Church in the U.S.S.R. is the patriarch of Moscow, who is elected by the All-Russian Church Council and confirmed by the government. In 1970 Patriarch Pimen Izvekov succeeded Aleksei Simanskii, who had been chosen to replace Sergei Stragorodskii in 1945. Sergei, who took the leadership of the church after Patriarch Tikhon Belavin died in prison in 1925, was officially elected patriarch only in 1943, when Stalin was moved to give concessions to the church to gain its support in the war effort against the Germans. At that time only four bishops were publicly functioning in the U.S.S.R.

The Moscow patriarchate cooperates with the Soviet government in national and political affairs in order to win concessions in ecclesiastical matters, such as the opening of churches and monasteries and the limited publication of Bibles, service books, and ecclesiastical journals. The policy of cooperation is often criticized by Orthodox believers both within and without the U.S.S.R.—believers such as the imprisoned priest Gleb Yakunin and the exiled writer Alexander Solzhenitsyn, who call for greater independence and resistance on the part of the official church leadership.

The Russian Orthodox church exists outside the U.S.S.R. in several parts of the world. In 1950 the so-called Russian Orthodox Church Outside Russia (also known as the "Synodal" Church) established its headquarters in New York. Unrecognized canonically by other Orthodox churches, this small monarchist group presents itself as the true Russian Orthodox church in opposition to the church in the U.S.S.R. The original Russian Orthodox missionary diocese in North America became the self-governing Orthodox Church in America in 1970. At this writing there are estimated to be about fifty million Russian Orthodox in the world who openly practice their faith, and untold numbers of others who are forced to believe in secret.

[*See also the biographies of the Russian Orthodox leaders mentioned herein.*]

BIBLIOGRAPHY

Arseniev, Nicholas. *Russian Piety*. 2d ed. Crestwood, N.Y., 1975.

Fedotov, G. P. *The Russian Religious Mind*, vol. 1, *Kievan Christianity: The Tenth to the Thirteenth Centuries;* vol. 2, *The Middle Ages: The Thirteenth to the Fifteenth Centuries* (1946–1966). Reprint, Belmont, Mass., 1975.

Fedotov, G. P. *A Treasury of Russian Spirituality* (1950). Reprint, Belmont, Mass., 1975.

Kovalevsky, Pierre. *Saint Sergius and Russian Spirituality.* Crestwood, N.Y., 1976.

Struve, Nikita. *Christians in Contemporary Russia.* New York, 1967.

Zernov, Nicolas. *The Russian Religious Renaissance of the Twentieth Century.* New York, 1963. Contains extensive bibliographical material on the Russian Orthodox church.

Zernov, Nicolas. *The Russians and Their Church.* New York, 1964.

THOMAS HOPKO

RUTH AND NAOMI.

RUTH AND NAOMI. In Hebrew scriptures, Ruth and Naomi are major characters in the *Book of Ruth.* The meaning of the word *ruth* (Heb., *rut*) is not clear. An old tradition falsely etymologizes it from a Semitic root that can convey the notion "friendship." Some Semiticists claim it derives from the root *rwṯ,* which permits the meaning "fertilized one."

Ruth's story is told in four chapters, each of which recounts an episode. The story covers a period of about two months and involves four major characters: Ruth, Naomi, Boaz, and an unnamed kinsman of Naomi's husband. Chapter 1 focuses on Ruth and Naomi; chapters 2–4 relate the circumstances leading to the marriage of Ruth and Boaz, an influential man of Bethlehem. The plot may be summarized as follows.

- *Chapter 1.* Elimelech and Naomi had been driven by famine from Bethlehem in Judah to Moabite territory. Their two sons, Mahlon and Chilion, had married Moabite women, Ruth and Orpah. Elimelech had died, as had, later, Mahlon and Chilion. Naomi then decides to return to Bethlehem to seek protection. She implores her daughters-in-law to stay in Moab. Orpah does so, but Ruth binds herself to Naomi's fate and accompanies her, at harvesttime, to a Bethlehem now blessed with plenty.
- *Chapter 2.* A woman in a man's world, a childless widow without hope for the future, a foreigner *(nokhriyyah)* in a clan-structured society, Ruth seeks and obtains clan protection as a maidservant *(shifḥah)* from Boaz, a distant relative of Elimelech.
- *Chapter 3.* Having celebrated the harvest, Boaz sleeps at the threshing floor. Spurred on by Naomi, Ruth approaches him. When he wakes, she asks to become his handmaid *(amah),* that is, to enter his private household. She also asks that he redeem Naomi's (i.e., Elimelech's) land, thus providing for Naomi's old age. Boaz insists on making her his wife *(eshet ḥayil,* "wife of a notable") and promises to try to acquire the right of redemption *(ge'ullah)* from the kinsman with prior rights. He praises her loyalty and gives her grain.

- *Chapter 4.* Before witnesses, Boaz asks his kinsman if he claims Elimelech's estate. The man affirms it. Boaz informs him that on the day he claims the land, he (Boaz) will claim Ruth, the widow of Mahlon, Elimelech and Naomi's son, in order to "perpetuate the memory of the dead upon his estate." Learning of Boaz's intention, the kinsman gives up his right to claim the land. Boaz then declares himself ready to accept Ruth as wife and to produce an heir to the land, invoking a tradition that "one may not permit the memory of a deceased to be blotted" from Israel. Boaz thus redeems Elimelech's land and marries Ruth. She bears him a son, Obed, who is to be the father of Jesse, the father of David.

The *Book of Ruth* is a superbly drawn folk tale. The heroine, Ruth, resolves the lacks experienced by two widows: hunger and childlessness. Its plot revolves around Ruth's becoming the wife of a notable, Boaz, while retaining her loving relationship with her former mother-in-law, Naomi. Boaz himself displays brilliant maneuvering to acquire the rights needed to fulfill Ruth's desire.

Despite its frequent recourse to God's name, the *Book of Ruth* provides little information on cultic and ritual acts. But its very presence in Hebrew scriptures endows it with a theologically pregnant situation wherein ordinary folk unwittingly achieve uncommon ends. The story has been regarded by some as a vehicle proclaiming Israel's postexilic theological universalism, but this interpretation is doubtful unless it can be shown that the narrative was propagated outside Hebrew circles. The tale of Ruth cannot be dated to a specific period of Israelite history. A date just before the exile to Babylon is plausible, but if, as some maintain, the story of Ruth circulated orally prior to its final written version, then the search for an exact date of its origin is hopeless.

The relationship of Ruth and Naomi has had enduring appeal, to layman and scholar alike. In *Ruth* 1, Naomi bitterly bemoans her fate, in which husband and sons died in a foreign land. She asks to be called not Naomi but Mara, thus offering a contrastive pair of names. In Hebrew, *na'omi* may mean "the pleasant one," while *mara'* may mean "the bitter one." Because this pair of names is also known as an epithet of Anat, a Canaanite goddess, some scholars have detected mythological motifs behind Naomi's words. Most prominently explored have been comparisons with the Greek myths of Demeter and Kore and with the Egyptian myths regarding Isis.

That Ruth was the ancestress of David the king (and hence of the Messiah), that she voluntarily accepted the Hebrew God, and that she represented the best in human dignity and kindness have endeared her to both Jewish and Christian readers. During Shavu'ot (Pentecost), her book is read with celebration and rejoicing. [*See* Shavu'ot.]

BIBLIOGRAPHY

The foregoing version of Ruth's story is presented in full in my book *Ruth: A New Translation with a Philological Commentary and a Formalist-Folklorist Interpretation* (Baltimore, 1979). Other understandings of the plot, with complications arising from considerations of leviratic marriage, are exemplified by Edward F. Campbell's *Ruth*, vol. 7 of the Anchor Bible (Garden City, N.Y., 1975).

JACK M. SASSON

RUUSBROEC, JAN VAN (1293–1381), Flemish Christian mystic, known as "the Admirable." Born in Ruusbroec, near (or in) Brussels, he was educated for the priesthood in both lower and higher studies under the care of his kinsman Jan Hinckaert, canon of Saint Gudule collegial church in Brussels. He was ordained a priest at age twenty-four and became influential in the theological and spiritual currents of the church and of the tradition of Middle Netherlandic (Netherlandic-Rhenish) mysticism. He led a devout life in the circle of friends around Hinckaert and Vrank van Coudenberch. Aware of the need to bring doctrinal teaching to the people in their own language, Ruusbroec wrote in the Brabant vernacular.

In 1343, impelled by a longing for silence and a richer spiritual life, Ruusbroec and his companions withdrew to the solitude of Groenendael, near Brussels. A few years later their association developed into a monastery of canons regular under the Augustinian rule of order. His gentleness gained him the epithet "the good prior," and his spiritual wisdom earned him the title "Doctor Admirabilis." He wrote four extensive treatises and seven shorter works; only seven of his letters have been preserved. His reputation for holiness was ratified when the church declared him "blessed" on 2 December 1908.

In Ruusbroec's doctrine, human being is fundamentally oriented toward the triune God. He sees God as at once indivisibly one and threefold, in constant tension between activity and essence. Essence enjoys itself quietly in modelessness. Activity is fecund. The Father, in knowing himself, creates relationships; he brings forth and expresses himself in his Son, the Word of God. In the reciprocal beholding of Father and Son, the Holy Spirit flows forth as the mutual bond of active love. Turning inward in essential love, they enjoy the unity of essence, which drives them afresh toward activity.

In turning outward, God creates according to the image of his Son and in the power of the Holy Spirit. The human creature in its selfhood is irrevocably distinct from the transcendent God. At the same time, however, the creature is in relation with and directed toward God because human being is created in the unity of God's likeness and image.

Ruusbroec sees humanity as structured in a threefold way, according to three interacting unities. The body and the lower faculties of the soul are under the heart and form the unity of the heart. The higher faculties of the soul, oriented to the highest human powers, form the unity of spirit, which in activity is receptive to God's essence. In these two lower unities, by the grace of God, the creature attains likeness to God in active (outer) life and in inner life ("unity by means"). According to the third unity, the creature attains its oneness with God's image in the contemplative life ("unity without means," or "unity without difference").

In Christ (the God-man) humanness is realized in the fullness of likeness and unity-of-image in himself, and this fullness is communicated to and in humankind. The ascent in likeness and unity is realized in Christ and in human beings: on earth, characterized by mortality, in the likeness of grace; in heaven, characterized by immortality and irradiated by the *lumen gloriae,* in the likeness of glory. Ruusbroec's grandiose view provides a balanced synthesis of God's outflowing transcendent love and of humankind's potentiality for harmonious ascent to union with God.

BIBLIOGRAPHY

Works by Ruusbroec

Ruusbroec, Jan van. *Werken.* 2d ed. 4 vols. Antwerp, 1944–1948. In original Dutch.

Wiseman, J. A., ed. *John Ruusbroec: The Spiritual Espousals and Other Works.* New York, 1985.

Works about Ruusbroec

Ampe, Albert. *Kernproblemen uit de leer van Ruusbroec.* 4 vols. Tielt, 1950–1957.

Ampe, Albert. "Jean Ruusbroec." In *Dictionnaire de spiritualité,* vol. 8. Paris, 1974.

Dupré, Louis. *The Common Life: The Origins of Trinitarian Mysticism and Its Development by Jan Ruusbroec.* New York, 1984.

Mommaers, Paul. *The Land Within: The Process of Possessing and Being Possessed by God according to the Mystic Jan van Ruysbroeck.* Chicago, 1975.

Mommaers, Paul, and Norbert de Paepe, eds. *Jan van Ruusbroec: The Sources, Content and Sequels of His Mysticism.* Louvain, 1984.

ALBERT AMPE, S.J.

S

SA'ADYAH GAON (882–942), properly Sa'adyah ben Yosef al-Fayyumī; Jewish theologian, jurist, scholar, and gaon ("head, eminence") of the rabbinic academy at Sura, Babylonia. Sa'adyah was born in Dilaẓ (modern Abu Suwayr) in the Faiyūm district of Upper Egypt. Virtually nothing is known about his family and early education. By age twenty-three, however, he had corresponded with the noted Jewish Neoplatonist Yitsḥaq Israeli (c. 855–955), published the first Hebrew dictionary *(Sefer ha-agron),* and composed a polemic against the Karaite schismatic 'Anan ben David (fl. 760). After leaving Egypt, Sa'adyah spent time in both Palestine and Syria but eventually, in 921 or 922, settled in Babylonia. There he championed the cause of the Babylonian rabbis in a dispute with Palestinian authorities over fixing the religious calendar and published his views in two treatises, *Sefer ha-zikkaron* and *Sefer ha-mo'adim.* Recognizing his ability, the exilarch, or hereditary leader of the Jewish community, awarded Sa'adyah with an academic appointment in 922 and subsequently elevated him to the gaonate of Sura. Soon afterward, in 930, a legal dispute between the two developed into a bitter political struggle in which each deposed the other from office. Sa'adyah was driven into formal retirement in Baghdad, but, ultimately, reconciliation led to his reinstatement in 937.

A versatile and prolific author, Sa'adyah pioneered in many areas of Jewish scholarship. He translated the Hebrew Bible into Arabic, wrote commentaries on most of its books, assembled the first authorized *siddur,* or Jewish prayerbook, and composed numerous other works in the fields of jurisprudence, grammar, lexicography, liturgical poetry, and theology. His most famous work, *Sefer emunot ve-de'ot* (The Book of Beliefs and Opinions, 933), was the first systematic exposition and defense of the tenets of Judaism and contains a detailed account of his views.

The Book of Beliefs and Opinions reflects both the cosmopolitanism and the sectarian rivalries characteristic of tenth-century Baghdad. Sa'adyah indicates that the intense competition between adherents of the various religious and philosophical creeds had produced an atmosphere of spiritual confusion in which believers were either mistaken or in doubt about the inherited doctrines of their religion, whereas unbelievers boasted of their unbelief. Seeking to dispel such doubt and establish a common basis for achieving religious certainty, Sa'adyah adopted the methods of *kalām* (Islamic speculative theology) current in his day. He aimed to defend the doctrines of his faith and to refute errors by using rational arguments that could convince any reasonable man. Thus, from mere acceptance of traditional doctrines, itself always open to doubt, the reader would arrive at rationally established beliefs or convictions, just as the book's title suggests.

To facilitate this transition, Sa'adyah begins by identifying the causes of error and doubt. He then analyzes three sources of truth and certainty and illustrates their proper use: (1) sense perception, (2) rational intuition of self-evident principles, and (3) valid inference. To these he adds a fourth source based on the other three, reliable tradition, which is both indispensable to civilized life and the medium in which God's revelation to the prophets is transmitted. While Sa'adyah confidently believes human speculation can arrive at the truth of everything disclosed in prophecy, revelation is still necessary to teach the truth to those incapable of speculation and to guide the fallible inquiries of those who are capable, since only God's knowledge is complete. Because verification of revealed truths confirms faith, Sa'adyah considers such verification a religious obligation.

Sa'adyah's organization of the rest of the treatise likewise reflects *kalām,* especially the preoccupation of the Mu'tazilī school with establishing God's unity and justice. To prove the existence of the one God, Sa'adyah employs four standard *kalām* arguments showing that the world was created and must therefore have a creator.

1. Since the world is spatially finite, the power within it that maintains it in existence must also be finite. But then the world's existence over time must likewise be finite, indicating that it was created.
2. Everything composite is created by some cause. Since the whole world displays skillful composition, it must have been created.
3. All bodies in the world are inseparably linked to accidental characteristics that are created in time. But whatever is inseparably linked to something created is itself created.
4. If the world were eternal, an infinite period of time would have to have elapsed for the present to be reached. But since an infinity cannot be traversed and we have reached the present, the world must have existed for only a finite period after being created.

Sa'adyah offers further arguments to show that the world could only have been created out of nothing and by a single deity.

Sa'adyah's discussion of God's nature and attributes traces the implications of his being a creator. For God to have created a world such as ours at a point in the past, he must be alive, powerful, and wise. But insofar as God is creator and not creature, he cannot possess the characteristics of creatures. Hence, he must be incorporeal and absolutely simple in nature. Moreover, the essential attributes of life, power, and wisdom should not be understood as separate features of God's nature but as identical with it. Only a deficiency of language necessitates speaking about distinct attributes. Similarly, reason dictates that whenever scripture depicts God with creaturely characteristics, these terms should be understood metaphorically.

In accounting for God's relation to his creatures, Sa'adyah takes up various questions about divine justice. By creating the world out of nothing, God wished to endow creatures with the gift of existence. He further sought to provide them with the means for attaining perfect bliss by giving them the commandments of the Torah. By thus requiring human effort to attain happiness rather than bestowing it by grace, God assured that such happiness would be all the greater. The commandments themselves fall into two classes: rational commandments, such as the prohibitions against murder and theft, and traditional commandments, such as the dietary and Sabbath laws. The authority of the former lies in reason itself, while that of the latter lies in the will of the commander. God revealed both types of law, because without revelation not even perfectly rational men would agree on the precise application of the rational laws, much less discover the traditional laws, on both of which their salvation depends.

For Sa'adyah, the fact of revelation is confirmed by the occurrence of publicly witnessed miracles, announced in advance, that could have been performed only by God's omnipotence. They are to be accepted as proof of the authenticity of the revelation, unless the revealed teaching is contrary to reason.

Once God holds man responsible for fulfilling his commandments, justice requires that people be able to choose to obey or disobey. Sa'adyah argues that sense experience attests to this ability in us and that reason shows that God does not interfere with its exercise. While God foreknows exactly what we shall choose, his knowledge in no way causes our choice. We can always choose otherwise, although he would foreknow that choice too.

Rewards and punishments are determined according to the majority of one's actions, and for Sa'adyah the suffering of the righteous and the prosperity of the wicked also conform to this rule. For either such experiences represent immediate retribution in this world for the minority of one's evil or good actions (with eternal reward or punishment for the rest to follow in the world to come), or they are temporary trials whereby God may increase one's reward in the hereafter. These latter are "sufferings of love," and bearing them bravely counts as a righteous act deserving reward. Indeed, Sa'adyah's commentary on *Job* interprets it as a debate designed to show that undeserved suffering really is a trial. For Job erroneously thought that God's justice consists simply in doing as he wishes, a position reminiscent of the rival Ash'arī school of *kalām,* while the friends mistakenly supposed all suffering is a penalty. Only Elihu claims that Job's afflictions are a trial that divine justice will repay, and God confirms this by reasserting his providence over all creation and restoring Job's material fortunes prior to rewarding his soul in the hereafter.

Sa'adyah defines the soul as a pure, luminous substance that can act only through the body. Because the body and the soul are jointly responsible for our behavior, God's justice requires that retribution affect both together. Accordingly, he will resurrect the bodies of Israel's righteous from the dust with the same power he used to create them *ex nihilo.* This event heralds Israel's messianic age and universal peace. It occurs either when all Israel repents or when God's foreordained end arrives, whichever is first. However, when God finishes creating the appointed number of souls, there will be a general resurrection and judgment, and a new heaven and earth. In this final retribution, the righteous will bask, and the wicked will burn, in the light of a miraculous divine radiance.

Sa'adyah concludes the treatise by describing the kind of conduct worthy of reward. Since man is a composite creature with many conflicting tendencies, he should not devote himself to one above all others. Rather, he should strive for a balance and blending of preoccupations determined by reason and Torah.

Aside from offering the first systematic exposition of Judaism in rational terms, Sa'adyah laid the foundation for all later medieval Jewish philosophy by asserting the complete accord of reason and revelation. Although Sa'adyah was far more confident than his successors about what reason could prove, his commitment to investigation and proof in all areas of Jewish scholarship gave rationalism a legitimacy in Judaism that it might not otherwise have enjoyed. He is rightly recalled as "the first of those who speak reason in every area."

BIBLIOGRAPHY

Still the best general survey of Sa'adyah's life and oeuvre is Henry Malter's *Saadia Gaon: His Life and Works* (1921; reprint, Philadelphia, 1978). The only complete English translation of Sa'adyah's main theological work is Samuel Rosenblatt's *Saadia Gaon: The Book of Beliefs and Opinions* (New Haven, 1948), with an analytical table of contents and a useful index. An abridged translation of the same work with an excellent introduction and notes is Alexander Altmann's *Saadia Gaon: Book of Doctrines and Beliefs,* available in *Three Jewish Philosophers,* edited by Hans Lewy et al. (New York, 1960). The most comprehensive discussion in English of Sa'adyah's entire worldview is Israel I. Efros's "The Philosophy of Saadia Gaon," in his *Studies in Medieval Jewish Philosophy* (New York, 1974), since it draws from a variety of Sa'adyah's works. A shorter but still valuable discussion remains Julius Guttmann's "Saadia Gaon," in *Philosophies of Judaism* (New York, 1964). A basic resource for understanding Sa'adyah's relation to *kalām* is Harry A. Wolfson's *The Repercussions of the Kalam in Jewish Philosophy* (Cambridge, Mass., 1979). Useful individual studies of Sa'adyah's communal activities as well as different aspects of his literary, scholarly, and theological work may still be found in the *Saadia Anniversary Volume,* edited by Boaz Cohen for the American Academy for Jewish Research (New York, 1943); Abraham Neuman and Solomon Zeitlin's *Saadia Studies* (Philadelphia, 1943); and Steven T. Katz's *Saadiah Gaon* (New York, 1980).

BARRY S. KOGAN

SAAMI RELIGION. The Saami (Lapps) are popularly called "a people with four countries" because they make up an ethnic unit under the jurisdiction of four states: Norway, Sweden, Finland, and the Soviet Union. The Saami languages belong to the Finno-Ugric group, and viewed linguistically the Saami are thus related to many peoples to the east (e.g., Finns, Karelians, Estonians, and others), but physically and anthropologically they are unique. This has given rise to a lively but not yet concluded scholarly debate as to the location of their original home. Today we can speak of three different Saami languages—East, Central, and South Saami—which share the same basic structure but are otherwise quite distinct.

The East Saami were converted by the Greek Orthodox Church in the sixteenth century, while those in the west accepted Lutheranism in the seventeenth and eighteenth centuries. The written texts that deal with the non-Christian conceptions of the Saami derive from the seventeenth and eighteenth centuries, and in the main they deal with the beliefs of the nomadic reindeer breeders of Finland and Scandinavia. The texts are written by clergymen and missionaries and are often formed as "confessions of heathenism." From the Saami of the east we have notes, written by ethnographers and linguists of the nineteenth and twentieth centuries, when the native religion had already become "the old custom" or "memories" and no one believed in the old gods. However, we have cause to believe that there exists a common basic structure in the religion of the whole Saami area, in which shamanism and sacrifices to the life-giving powers are dominant factors.

Relations between Men and Animals. As among other peoples of the subpolar region, the earliest economy of the Saami was based on hunting. Consequently, their most important rites revolved around animals and the killing of animals. We find an elaborate conceptual world in which animal spirits and divinities, that is, supernatural beings who have taken their forms from the animal kingdom, figure prominently.

The Finnish Saami called these spirits or "rulers" *haldi* (from the Finnish *haltija,* derived from an old Germanic word meaning "to own, to control, to protect"). They considered that all animals, places, and lakes had their own *haldi* that protected the animals of a particular species or area and that man was obliged to show his respect for the spirits through such tokens as sacrificial offerings.

The bear was, above all others, the sacred animal throughout the subpolar region, and the rites connected with the bear hunt clearly reflect the reverence men felt for animals and for all living things around them. Certain appointed ceremonies were observed from the very beginning of a hunt. The man who found the bear in the hibernating den led the group; "the drummer" went immediately after him, followed in a predetermined order by those whose duty it was to kill the bear. When the animal had been downed, the hunters sang songs of thanks both to the quarry and to Leibolmai ("alder-tree man"), who is variously described as the god of the hunt or the lord of the animals, but was, most importantly, the lord of the bears.

In their songs the hunters assured the bear that they had not intended to cause him any suffering; indeed, they also tried to divert attention from themselves and put the blame on others. In certain songs it was said that "men from Sweden, Germany, England, and all foreign lands" had caused the bear's death, and the women welcomed the hunters home as "men from all foreign lands." The meat was prepared by the men in a special place and brought into the *kota* ("tent" or "hut") through *boassio-raikie,* the holy back door situated opposite the ordinary door; arrayed in festive dress, the women sat waiting inside and spit chewed alder bark at the men as the meat was carried in. This custom should probably be regarded as a purification rite. Once the meat was eaten, all bones were buried in the order they are found in the body, so that the bear was given a proper funeral. The individual bear was probably regarded as a supernatural representative of its species; by showing it due respect the hunters secured the good will of all bears, and this was to their advantage during the next hunt. Some scholars have proposed that such solemn ceremonies were performed so that a particular slain bear could arise from the dead and be hunted down again, but this has not been established.

The skeletons of other animals were occasionally treated with the same reverence; at certain times of the year, for example, all the bones of a reindeer were placed before the holy image at the place of sacrifice after the assembled men had eaten the meat. The idol was smeared with blood and grease of the sacrificial animal. The women were permitted to participate in the holy meal only on special occasions. The sources report that the god to whom the reindeer was offered would then resurrect the animal in his kingdom and derive benefit from it there.

Idols. The word *seite,* or *siei'di,* identifies a central phenomenon in Saami religion. The word occurs only in the northern Saami languages, but in scholarly usage it has become a standard term for designating a phenomenon found throughout the Saami area. A *seite* was a stone formed by nature and standing on a place that was regarded as *passe* ("sacred," "holy") and to which sacrifices were made. An unusual cliff could have the same function, and a whole mountain could be regarded as a *seite.* Although we do not know its exact symbolism, we do know that *seite*-places were situated at certain points along the migration routes between different territories and that people laid sacrificial offerings there as they passed to bring them luck with their reindeer. There were also *seite*-stones on the shores of many lakes, and presumably sacrifices were made there to ensure good fishing.

Soul-Beliefs and Shamanism. The notion that animals have guardian beings that must be respected by man is based on the idea that every living being has at least two souls—a corporeal soul and a "free" soul. The free soul can manifest itself outside the body and is regarded as a guardian spirit and a double. Animals are men's equals and are treated as such. In dreams or in trancelike states such as ecstasy, the human free soul can leave the body and assume a concrete form.

Occasionally a malicious being captures a soul, posing a mortal threat to the bearer. It was believed, for example, that when a person fell seriously ill, it was because someone, perhaps a dead relative who wanted to summon him or her to the realm of the dead, had captured the soul of the afflicted. In such cases the *noaidie* ("shaman") intervened to help. Having gone through a long and painful period of apprenticeship, and possessing extraordinary psychic powers, the *noaidie* could enter a state of ecstasy and, under this trance, send his soul to the home of the dead, Jabme-aimo, to negotiate with the dead or the goddess of the dead (called Jabme-akka in certain places) about the return of the soul. Sometimes the soul could be recovered through the promise of a sacrifice, in which case the sick person got well. Among the other peoples of the subpolar region we also find the belief that the dead influenced the life of the living, with the shaman cast in a similar redemptive role.

The *noaidie,* however, could not undertake such a journey unassisted, and during his apprenticeship he had come into contact with supernatural beings that could aid him when necessary. Paramount among these helpers were the sacred animals: birds, fish (or snakes), and bull reindeer. The *noaidie* recruited his assistants from Sájva-ájmuo, the dwelling place of the holy spirits. (Sájva-ájmuo corresponds to Bâsse-Passevare, the sacred mountains in the northern Saami territory.) Other spirits could also help the *noaidie* in the performance of his office; a deceased *noaidie,* for example, could give the new *noaidie* advice or provide other assistance.

The *noaidie*'s ability to go into ecstasy made him a

general intermediary between human beings, who lived in the middle world, and supernatural beings in the other (upper and nether) worlds. This belief in the triadic division of the universe was shared with some of the peoples of northern Siberia. The *noaidie* regulated relations between people in the middle world and divinities and spirits in the other worlds, as well as between people and the powers of nature.

Deities. There is no doubt that the Saami were not only aware of their dependence upon the rulers of places and animals, but that they also worshiped heavenly and atmospheric divinities. These superterrestrial beings had no part in immediate everyday concerns, but they were powers to be reckoned with and were given sacrifices on special occasions. Among the eastern Saami, there was the divinity Tiermes, who manifested himself in thunder and has been linked to the Ob-Ugric god of the sky, Num-Turem, and to the Samoyed god of the sky, Num. Among the western Saami, Radien/Rariet ("the ruler"), in some places also called Vearalden Olmai ("man of the world, or cosmos") and Mailman Radien ("the ruler of the world"), headed the gods. The cult dedicated to him was meant mainly to further reindeer breeding, but he was also the god who sustained the world. This was symbolized by a pillar, known among some of the Saami as the world's *stytto,* which was erected beside the ruler's idol at the sacrificial site. It was believed that the North Star was attached to the uppermost point of the pillar.

The mighty thunder god Horagalles (also known as Attjie, "father," and Bajjan, "he who is above") could demolish the mountains with his hammer and scatter and injure the reindeer; sacrifices to him were thus meant to appease. The sun, Beivie, was vital to plant life, and sacrifices were made to ensure good grazing for the reindeer and rich vegetation in general. One observer writes that offerings to Beivie were burned to symbolize the heat of the sun. Beivie also helped to cure mental illness. The moon, Aske or Manno, also received sacrifices, particularly during midwinter. Bjiegg-Olmai ("wind man"), also known as Ilmaris, controlled the winds and weather and was worshiped throughout the Saami region.

Women were under the special protection of the goddess Madder-Akka ("old woman of the tribe") and her three daughters, Sarakka, Ugsakka, and Juksakka. These goddesses were thought to be intimately connected with the domicile. [*See* Akkah.]

BIBLIOGRAPHY

Source materials on Lapland and the Saami traditions begin to become abundant as early as the mid-seventeenth century, when priests and missionaries engaged in extensive christianizing in the area and reported to their superiors on all aspects of Saami culture, including religion and folklore. Some of these materials, exclusively from Swedish Lapland, were published by Johannes Scheffer in his *Lapponia* (Frankfurt, 1673). Scheffer was a Dutch scholar who had been commissioned to spread information about the Saami (Lapps) throughout Europe. The work was immediately translated into other languages, including English (*The History of Lapland,* Oxford, 1694). Another translation appeared in 1736.

Eighteenth-century missionary reports contain greater detail on the religious beliefs of the Scandinavian Saami, but few of them are available in a major language. Exceptions are Pehr Högström's *Beschreibung des der crone Schweden gehörenden Lapplanders* (Copenhagen and Leipzig, 1748) and Knud Leem's *Beskrivelse over Finmarkens Lapper, deres tungemaal, Levemaade og forrige Afgudsdyrkelse* (A Description of the Finnmark Lapps, Their Language, Customs, and Former Idolatry; Copenhagen, 1767).

The best sources that deal with the Saami of Finland and Russia, however, are much more recent. In his introduction to *Wörterbuch der Kola-lappischen Dialekte nebst Sprachproben* (Helsinki, 1891), Arvid Genetz provides a survey of traditional religion among the Russian Saami, and Toivo Immanuel Itkonen's *Heidnische Religion und späterer Aberglaube bei den finnischen Lappen* (Helsinki, 1946) is a collection of accounts of earlier beliefs among the Saami of Finland. Nickolai Kharuzin's *Russkie Lopari* (Moscow, 1890) contains extensive materials on myths, but the cult he describes derives largely from the materials of Scheffer and Högström—that is, from Scandinavia.

The Saami religion has, understandably, mainly attracted Scandinavian scholars, and the first surveys were published in one or another of the Nordic languages. Such scholars as Uno Holmberg (Harva after 1927), in *Lappalaisten uskonto* (Porvoo, 1915), and Rafael Karsten, in *The Religion of the Samek* (Leiden, 1955), were strongly influenced by the evolutionism popular at the time, which they supplemented with theories on borrowings. Holmberg's later survey of Finno-Ugric and Siberian mythology in *The Mythology of All Races,* vol. 4 (Boston, 1927), is methodologically much more modern. The most recent survey is Åke Hultkrantz's "Die Religion der Lappen," in *Die Religionen Nordeurasiens und der amerikanischen Arktis,* edited by Ivar Paulson et al. (Stuttgart, 1962).

There are some eighty preserved shaman drums, the oldest dating from the mid-seventeenth century. These have been described in detail by Ernst Mauritz Manker in *Die lappische Zaubertrommel,* vols. 1–2 (Stockholm, 1938–1950).

Various aspects of Saami religion, such as the bear ceremony, sacrifices, the shaman, rites of the dead, conceptions of the soul, the sun cult, the notion of the lord of animals, and the origin of the Saami, have also received extensive scholarly treatment.

LOUISE BÄCKMAN

SABAZIOS, a god of the Thracians and the Phrygians, is also known from Greek and Latin sources as Sabadios, Sauazios, Saazios, Sabos, Sebazios, Sabadius, and Sebadius. His name is related to the Macedonian word *sauâdai*, or *saûdoi*, meaning "satyrs" (Detschew, 1957, p. 427). According to some scholars (e.g., Lozovan, 1968), he was a Thracian mountain god whose cult was carried by Phrygian emigrants from Thrace to Anatolia.

Greek sources from the fifth century BCE onward mention Sabazios as a Thracian or Phrygian god. In Athens, his cult's initiation ceremonies took place by night, and the adepts were purified by being rubbed with mud. A sacramental drink was also involved. The identification of Sabazios with Dionysos, which occurs regularly in Hellenistic sources, is unquestionable. However, Phrygian inscriptions relate him to Zeus, and in North Africa, where his cult is attested as early as the fourth century BCE, he might have had the features of a heavenly god; hence he was later identified with the Semitic god Baal, both of them receiving the Greek epithet *hupsistos* ("highest, supreme"). He was probably worshiped in Thrace under other local names, such as Athyparenos, Arsilenos, Batalde Ouenos, Eleneites, Mytorgenos, Ouerzel(enos), and Tasibastenus.

Sabazios's name has been connected with the Indo-European **swo-*, meaning "[his] own," and with the idea of freedom, which occurs frequently among the epithets of Dionysos. Franz Cumont has suggested a relationship with the Illyrian *sabaia*, or *sabaium*, identifying a beer extracted from cereals (see Russu, 1969, p. 241). More recently, Gheorghe Muşu has translated *Sabazios* as "sap god," from the Indo-European roots **sap-* ("taste, perceive") and **sab-* ("juice, fluid"). This translation corresponds well to the pattern of Dionysos/Sabazios, who was the divinity of humidity and as such was connected with both vegetation and intoxication (see Muşu, in Vulpe, 1980, pp. 333–336).

The Jews of Syria and Anatolia identified Sabazios with Sabaoth. Under the Roman rulers Sabazios was worshiped in Thrace, where he was more often known as Sebazios or, in Latin, Sabazius, Sabadius, or Sebadius and where he received such epithets as *epēkoos* ("benevolent"), *kurios* ("lord"), *megistos* ("greatest"), and so forth. In Crimea, probably under Jewish-Anatolian influence, he was called *hupsistos*. He was constantly identified with both Zeus and the sun. Motifs of hands making the votive gesture of *benedictio Latina* are among the distinctive features of his cult. According to several Christian writers (Clement of Alexandria, Arnobius, and Firmicus Maternus), the most impressive rite of initiation into the mysteries of Sabazios consisted of the adept's contact with a snake *(aureus coluber)* that was first put over his breast *(per sinum ducunt)* and then pulled down to his genitals.

No less enigmatic than Zalmoxis, Sabazios was worshiped as early as the fourth century BCE both as a chthonic and as a heavenly god. Scholars have too often tried to solve this riddle by supposing a borrowing from Jewish religion, but Jewish influence was not relevant in Anatolia before the third century BCE. One should rather consider that chthonic features determined the character of the Thracian Sabazios, whereas the Phrygian Sabazios was probably connected with the sky.

BIBLIOGRAPHY

Bianchi, Ugo, and Maarten J. Vermaseren, eds. *La soteriologia dei culti orientali nell'impero romano*. Leiden, 1982. See the index, s.v. *Sabazios*.

Detschew, Dimiter. *Die thrakischen Sprachreste*. Vienna, 1957.

Lozovan, Eugen. "Dacia Sacra." *History of Religions* 7 (February 1968): 209–243.

Russu, I. I. *Ilirii istoria, limba şi onomastica romanizarea*. Bucharest, 1969.

Vulpe, Radu, ed. *Actes du Deuxième Congrès International de Thracologie*, vol. 3, *Linguistique, ethnologie, anthropologie*. Bucharest, 1980.

IOAN PETRU CULIANU and CICERONE POGHIRC

SABBATEANISM. *See the biography of* Shabbetai Tsevi.

SABBATH, JEWISH. *See* Shabbat.

SACRAMENT. [*This entry consists of two articles:* An Overview *and* Christian Sacraments. *The overview article discusses the notion of sacrament and presents a survey of sanctifying rites in various religious traditions.* Christian Sacraments *provides a history and the theology of those rites that are central to Christian salvation.*]

An Overview

The meaning of the term *sacrament* is heavily determined by Christian usage. This circumstance presents both important opportunities and certain difficulties for the scientific study of religion. On the one hand, the familiarity of the term and of the rituals to which it refers in Christianity makes possible, at least for the Western student of religion, progression from the known to the less known with the aid of developed categories used for comparative purposes. On the other hand, there is the danger that the derivation of the category of sacrament from Christianity will result in a distortion of other religions, unduly emphasizing cognates or analogies while ignoring or dismissing distinctive features of other traditions.

In order to both make good on the comparative opportunities provided by the term and to overcome the limitations of too heavy a reliance upon the perspective that has determined its customary meaning, this article will first indicate some of the antecedents to the standard Christian view of sacrament. A consideration of parallels or cognates to Christian sacraments will be followed by a brief consideration of the possibility of a more strictly formal definition of the category.

Hellenistic Sacraments. While classical Christian usage has largely determined the understanding of *sacrament* that the student of comparative religion employs in the study of religion, it is important to have some awareness of the pre-Christian understanding of *sacrament* and its Greek antecedent, *mustērion.* Three antecedents to the classical use of the term will be considered: the mystery cults, the apocalyptic mystery, and the mystical, or gnostic, tradition.

The mystery cults. The Greek *mustērion* is of uncertain etymology but is most probably associated with *muein,* meaning "to close" (the mouth), and thus "to keep secret." Certainly it was this connotation of secrecy that dominated the technical usage of the term to designate the Hellenistic cults, especially those associated with Eleusis, which are accordingly known as "mystery cults" or simply as "mysteries" *(mustēria).* The term *mustērion* designates the sharp dividing line between initiates, for whom the secret history of the god (his birth, marriage, or death and rebirth, depending on the cult) is dramatically reenacted, thus binding their fate to the god's, and noninitiates, who cannot participate in this kind of salvation. [*See* Mystery Religions.]

If the term were to be employed in this, its earliest technical religious sense, for phenomenological and comparative purposes, its application would necessarily be restricted to esoteric initiation rites of cult societies such as those found among the indigenous peoples of the Americas (for example, the Snake and Antelope societies of the Hopi). A somewhat more flexible usage might include those rites of passage that stress the esoteric character of the knowledge imparted.

Such usage, however, would be unwieldy for two reasons: (1) it would exclude many rituals for which the term *sacrament* has become standard—Christian and Hindu rituals in particular—and (2) it would duplicate existing terminology of initiatory rituals and rites of passage.

Apocalyptic usage. In the New Testament, *mustērion* is used in a way that is grounded in apocalyptic rather than cultic sensibility. Here *mustērion* refers to the disclosure of God's ultimate, or eschatological, intention. The term is used quite widely to designate anything that prefigures the final consummation of the divine will or plan. Thus Christian proclamation, biblical typology, and the inclusion of Jew and gentile in divine election could all be referred to as *mustērion* (which becomes *sacramentum* in Latin). Significantly, the term was not used in a specifically cultic sense at all in this period.

If this sense of the term, derived from late Jewish and early Christian apocalyptic writings, were to be decisive for phenomenological or comparative approaches to the study of religion, then the term's application would be restricted to those groups that have a strong orientation to future fulfillment. The Ghost Dance of the indigenous peoples of the North American Plains and the elaborate baptismal rites of the African independent churches are illustrations of ritual enactments of such eschatological expectations.

Gnostic usage. Deriving from the theory and practice of the mystery cults, certain mystical and especially gnostic philosophical traditions of the Hellenistic world used *mustērion* to apply to the quest for transcendental insight. While they dispensed with outward forms of ritual or cult, they nevertheless sought by knowledge a saving union with the divine. [*See* Gnosticism.] The religious tradition that best exemplifies this sense of *mustērion*/sacrament is the Hinduism of the Upaniṣads and of yoga. While these movements do not reject the ritual or cult but seek to give it a more pure, interior, and "noetic" significance, other reform movements—most notably Buddhism—reject this connection to the Vedic rites in the quest for ultimate insight. In the Western Christian tradition examples of sacramental mysticism often approximate the pattern of the yogic or gnostic transformation of external ritual into interior discipline. While these parallel phenomena demonstrate the way in which the bodily action of ritual may become paradigms for an interior praxis, it is with sacrament as a species of bodily action that the phenomenology of religion must be most concerned.

Emergence of the Classical Perspective. The Latin *sacramentum* was generally employed as a technical term for a military oath, the vow of a soldier. The initiatory function of this vow understood in relation to the vow of secrecy associated with the Greek mysteries made possible the appropriation of the term *sacramentum* for those activities (especially baptism) in which the Christian confession of faith (which, like the vow of soldiers, placed one in mortal danger) played an important role. Thus, despite the typically exoteric character of Christian doctrine and practice, ideas and practice associated with the Greek mysteries were used to interpret Christian rituals. *Sacramentum* gradually lost its wider, apocalyptic meaning, was increasingly used to refer to baptism and eucharist, and then was extended by analogy to apply to related ritual actions including confession and penance, confirmation, marriage, ordination, and unction. The earlier Latin sense of "vow" can still be discerned in baptism, confirmation, marriage, and ordination, but the oldest Greek associations with cultic participation in salvation predominate. Thus sacrament comes to be exclusively identified with a set of ritual actions that are understood to be both necessary to and efficacious for salvation.

Cognate Sacraments. Since the scientific study of religion is a discipline that has arisen within the culture most heavily influenced by Christianity, it is natural that much of its terminology is borrowed from Christianity. (Just as, *mutatis mutandis,* Christianity has borrowed its terminology from the cultures in which it has taken root.)

If sacrament is defined ostensively, by reference to the set of rituals that bear that name in Christianity, then we are confronted with the question of whether to restrict ourselves to the two sacraments accepted by most Protestants (baptism and eucharist) or to include the additional five sacraments (confirmation, penance, marriage, ordination, and extreme unction) accepted by Catholics. Clearly, eucharist and baptism have a place of singular importance in all Christian traditions; a phenomenological approach, however, will seek the widest possible range of data and so provisionally accept the more inclusive enumeration.

There are two sorts of such sacraments, those that deal with transitional moments and so are not repeated and those that are regularly repeated.

Sacraments of transition. The earliest and most important of the transitional sacraments is baptism. In early Christianity this ritual signified the movement from the worldly to the eschatological reality, or, under influence from the Greek mysteries, from the profane to the cultic sphere of participation in the fate of the god. This type of transitional rite is analogous to the initiation into cult societies of, for example, the indigenous peoples of the North American Plains. It is also characteristic of the African independent churches of central and southern Africa.

As Christianity became more or less coextensive with culture and society, the transition came more and more to be identified with birth or early infancy (a development contingent upon the understanding of penance and eucharist as supplementing the forgiveness of sins and transformation of life originally associated with baptism). As a ritual associated with infancy, it took the place of the Jewish rite of circumcision, except that it applied equally to female infants. It is thus similar in function to the Hindu sacrament of Nāmakaraṇa, in which the child receives a name.

As baptism became "infant baptism," the catechetical aspect of the ritual that inaugurated persons into full membership in the cult society became fixed in the form of confirmation. Insofar as confirmation is associated with adolescence, it could enter into homology with rites of tribal initiation—a species of ritual that is exceedingly widespread and well developed among the indigenous peoples of the Americas, Africa, and Australia [*see* Initiation]. In Africa and Australia the sacrament of initiation takes the form of segregating a cohort of adolescent males and placing them under great stress (often including circumcision) so that distinctions among them are erased. The loss of social identity and the violation of bodily integrity is accompanied by esoteric instruction and rites of great emotional force that frequently involve symbolism of death and birth. A significant number of groups, for example, the Bemba of Africa, have initiation rites (Chisungu) of similar intensity for adolescent females. Among North American aboriginal peoples, the young males (and, rarely, females) undertake the highly individualized dream or vision quest, which may entail a rigorous journey, fasting, and other ordeals. This individualized initiation contrasts sharply with the corporate initiation of African and other groups.

A further extension of transitional sacrament occurs with the development of extreme unction, the anointing of the sick. This sacrament may assume the form of a viaticum, by means of which the recipient is enabled to make the transition from this life to the world beyond. Insofar as the Christian sacrament of unction has the intention of healing (as in the anointing of the sick), it becomes repeatable and homologous to the healing rites found in virtually all religious traditions. Collections of incantations for this same purpose constitute the Egyptian *Book of Going Forth by Day,* and in ancient Iran the whispering of formulas to the dying person was accompanied by the administration of *haoma,* the sacred beverage.

Unlike baptism, confirmation, and unction, which traditionally have been required of all Christians, two other sacraments of transition, ordination and marriage (traditionally thought of as mutually exclusive), have developed. Rites of ordination are found in virtually all societies in which a priestly caste is drawn from the society as a whole. (In a number of societies the priesthood is hereditary, and rites associated with accession to cultic authority may be coterminous with accession to adulthood. This appears to be largely true of the brahmanic class of Hinduism, for example.) Marriage rites are obviously quite widespread although only those that have a clearly sacred or religious character are directly comparable. Often these have the added dimension of rites to ensure fertility.

Perhaps the most highly developed system of sacraments of transition is to be found in Hinduism. The term *saṃskāra,* which generally translated as "sacrament," refers to any rite of transition, of which several hundred may have been performed. In modern Hinduism the number is reduced (to between ten and eighteen). These sacraments begin with conception *(Garbhādhāna)* and continue through pregnancy (Puṃsavana, Sīmanta, Jātakarman). In addition to the naming ceremony (Nāmakaraṇa), which occurs a few days after birth, there are sacraments to mark the first appearance of the infant outside the home, the child's first solid food, the tonsure, and the piercing of the child's ears. Sacraments that mark the progress of the male child's education include Upanayana and Vedārambha. The completion of these studies requires a further sacrament (Samāvartana). Marriage (Vivāha) is the only sacrament permitted to *śūdras* or lower castes. The final transition of death is marked by the sacramental rites of Antyeṣṭi.

These sacraments generally involve sacrifices, ceremonies of fire and water, ritual washings, recitation of appropriate mantras and prayers, and so on. Both individually and collectively these Hindu sacraments are far more elaborate than the comparable set of Christian rituals and so may provide the student of religion with a more adequate set of categories for studying sacraments of transition.

Repeatable sacraments. While sacraments of transition are in principle nonrepeatable (with the possible and limited exceptions of marriage and extreme unction), two sacraments of great importance in traditional Christianity, penance and eucharist, do require repeated performance.

In the Christian tradition penance is related to baptism as the restoration of baptismal purity and to the Eucharist as the necessary preparation for participation. The confession of sin has a place of central importance in the religion of Handsome Lake practiced by contemporary Iroquois in the United States and Canada. Individual confession to a priest was of great importance in Central and South America, among the Inca and Maya, as is confession to a shaman among, for example, the Inuit (Eskimo).

The ritual that is most often associated with sacramentality is the Eucharist, Mass, or Communion of the Christian community. The selection of comparable rituals from the history of religions will depend upon the degree of emphasis placed upon one of three aspects: thanks giving or offering, communal meal, or sacrifice of the divine victim.

Certainly for much of Western history the last aspect has been especially emphasized. The most dramatic instances are the human sacrifices, which include the Greek *pharmakos,* a number of African rites, and practices belonging to the high civilizations of the Americas, especially the Aztec. [*See* Human Sacrifice.] Among the latter the sun god, Tezcatlipoca, was impersonated by the prisoner of war most honored for beauty and bravery, who received homage for a full year before being sacrificed. Many of the human sacrifices, including those to Huitzilopochtli, the god of war, were subsequently eaten as a form of ritual cannibalism.

Substitutions for the flesh of the divine victim are also found, including the eating of a dough image of Huitzilopochtli, which first was shot with an arrow, and a similar ritual involving the dough image of the tree god, Xocotl.

The communal meal is a common feature of many sacrifices. A vegetable, animal, or cereal offering is presented to the god and is subsequently shared by all participants, much as in the Christian Communion the bread and wine is first offered in thanksgiving and then shared by the participants. Where these rites are associated with first-fruits festivals or with harvest, the element of thanksgiving (eucharist) is especially pronounced. These rites are found not only in agrarian societies. Common among hunters and gatherers are rituals involving a communal meal in which the sacralized game animal is both praised and eaten. An example from the Pacific coast of North America is the ritual surrounding the first salmon catch. Among circumpolar peoples such rites are performed after successful bear hunts.

Here too should be mentioned the preparation of sacred substances whose consumption makes for unity with the divine. The *haoma* of Iran, the *soma* of India, and the hallucinogenic substances so important to the indigenous peoples of the Americas are illustrations. Members of the Native American Church, which includes many of the aboriginal peoples of North America, use peyote as a sacramental element within a liturgical setting in order to acquire union with the divine.

Formal Definitions of Sacrament. The procedure that has just been illustrated, of finding material cognates to the sacraments of the Christian tradition in the field of religious studies, while illuminating in certain respects, may tie the term too closely to the Christian tradition to be genuinely serviceable for phenomenological purposes. Accordingly, we may attempt to acquire a more formal definition of *sacrament,* one that can be employed for comparative purposes.

Since Christian theology has devoted considerable energy to the development of such a formal definition, we may look first to the theological definitions. When this is attempted, however, it becomes clear that these are either of such an *ad hoc* nature that they devolve to disguised ostensive definitions or are so broad as to identify virtually any ritual action. If, for example, *sacrament* is defined in accordance with the principle of *ex opere operatum* ("what the action signifies it also accomplishes"), any ritual thought by its practitioners to be efficacious (including, of course, all forms of magic) will be covered. If, on the other hand, only those ritual actions positively commanded by Jesus are said to be sacraments, this proves to be an ostensive definition (which, moreover, is usually applied in an arbitrary manner—so as to exclude ritual foot washing, for example). The same is true of definitions of *sacrament* that insist on the conjunction of matter and form. According to this view, *form* designates the crucial pronouncement whereas *matter* may refer, for example, to the water of baptism, the oil of unction, or the bread and wine of the Eucharist. Moreover, this notion of matter may be arbitrarily extended to apply also to the sacraments of penance (the sin of the believer) and marriage (the love between spouses).

If a formal definition is required, it appears that theology will not be of much help. It does seem possible, however, to propose a more strictly phenomenological definition. On this basis *sacrament* may be defined as "a ritual that enacts, focuses, and concentrates the distinctive beliefs, attitudes, and actions of any religious tradition." While any ritual may perform this function to some degree, it will usually be possible to discriminate within the ritual complex of a tradition as a whole that ritual (or group of rituals) that functions as a paradigm for other ritual action and so may be said to have a privileged and normative relationship to the articulated system as a whole. Usually these sacraments will be found within the prescribed corporate ritual or liturgy.

In this definition the initiation rites of the mystery religions, the Christian Eucharist, the Ghost Dance and peyote ritual of the North American Indians, and many other rituals already mentioned would be included. But the principle of inclusion is not their resemblance to specific Christian rituals but their location and function within the religious tradition of which they are a part.

In addition, rituals that are not material cognates to Christian sacraments and so are necessarily overlooked on the basis of an ostensive definition of sacrament now acquire a sacramental character. Thus the Shalako ceremony of the Zuni Indians of New Mexico, which displays the vigor and values of the Zuni while inviting the participation and blessings of the gods, is a sacrament in the form of a dance (to which there are no Christian but many other religious cognates). While regular occasions for prayer do not have a sacramental character in Christianity, they may well have this character in Islam, which is generally suspicious of ritual and of Christian sacraments in particular. Finally, the Buddhist practice of *zazen*, which consists of periods of sitting and breathing punctuated by periods of walking, may have a place of importance and function similar to the Christian Eucharist.

The further refinement of a phenomenological definition of *sacrament* in tandem with its use in the analysis of the place and function of particular rituals within the wider ritual complex of which they are a part is an important agenda for the study of religion.

BIBLIOGRAPHY

For concise historical background, see the article on *mustērion* by Günther Bornkaum in *Theological Dictionary of the New Testament*, edited by Gerhard Kittel and Gerhard Friedrich (Grand Rapids, 1964–1976), and the article "Mystery," in the *Encyclopedia of Theology*, edited by Karl Rahner (New York, 1975).

The classic treatment of rites analogous to sacraments of transition is Arnold van Gennep's *Les rites de passage* (Paris, 1909), translated by Monika B. Vizedom and Gabrielle L. Caffee as *The Rites of Passage* (Chicago, 1960). Victor Turner's *The Ritual Process* (Chicago, 1969) is a major contribution to the understanding of these rituals. A useful source for the Hindu sacraments is Raj Bali Pandey's *Hindu Saṁskāras: A Socio-Religious Study of the Hindu Sacraments*, 2d rev. ed. (Delhi, 1969). Åke Hultkrantz's *Religions of the American Indians*, translated by Monica Setterwall (Los Angeles, 1979), contains important information and an excellent bibliography. Ronald L. Grimes's *Beginnings in Ritual Studies* (Washington, D.C., 1982) suggests the relationship between *zazen* and the Eucharist.

THEODORE W. JENNINGS, JR.

Christian Sacraments

In the Christian community sacraments are acts of worship that are understood by the worshipers to give access to an intimate union with the divine and to be efficacious for salvation. The term *sacraments* is sometimes used in a very broad sense for places, persons, things, ceremonies, and events that mediate, or are intended to mediate, the presence and power of the divine. In this broad sense, Christians acknowledge sacraments in other religious traditions and also in the particular circumstances of the lives of individuals and groups. A simple illustrative story in the Hebrew scriptures (the Old Testament of Christians) is that of Jacob setting up a stone in the desert and calling the place Bethel, house of God (*Gn*. 28:10–22).

More usually the term *sacraments* refers to a limited number of ancient rituals understood to be the acts of Jesus Christ carried out through the continuing ministry of the church. The Eastern Christian and Roman

Catholic churches enumerate these rituals as seven: baptism, confirmation (or chrismation), eucharist, penance (sacrament of reconciliation), matrimony, ordination (or holy orders), and the anointing of the sick (extreme unction). Protestant churches usually enumerate the sacraments (in the narrower sense of the term) as only two, namely, baptism and eucharist, because these two are clearly identified in the New Testament.

The word *sacrament* derives from Latin *sacramentum,* meaning "oath," "pledge," or "bond." As a Christian term applied to rituals of worship, it is found no earlier than the third century, when it came into use in Western churches as a translation of the Greek term *mustērion,* which had the religious connotation of effecting union with the divine, even before Christians used the term in that sense. When the word *sacrament* is used in the singular without contextual specification, it may be assumed to mean the Eucharist.

Jewish Roots. At the time of Jesus of Nazareth the people of Israel, the Jewish community, enjoyed a rich accumulation of symbolism and ritual. Jesus and his early followers participated in that heritage and followed the observances. Characteristically, Christian rituals were shaped not only out of the immediate experience of the early Christian community but also out of the stories, imagery, and ritual observances of their Jewish tradition. This influence can be seen in Christian perceptions of sacred space and sacred time, and it also appears in the configuration of sacred actions. [*See* Rites of Passage, *article on* Jewish Rites.]

The core of the Christian sacramental system is the Eucharist, also known as the Divine Liturgy, the Lord's Supper, the Communion service, and the Mass. The ritual is based directly on the table grace of Jewish observance as solemnized in the Passover Seder. There are several common elements: the community is gathered to respond to God's call and to fulfill a commandment; the gathering is at a ritual meal at which prescribed foods are blessed, shared, and consumed; the accompanying prayers and ceremonies ritually reenact a past saving event so that the present worshipers become part of that past event and it becomes present in their experience; the doing of this anticipates a fulfillment that still lies in the future; the ritual (though not it alone) constitutes the participants as God's holy people. In the Jewish understanding and also in the Christian, the ritual is not effective in isolation from the community's daily life; on the contrary, it is effective precisely in its reshaping of the imagination and sense of identity of the worshipers, bringing about a transformation of individual and social life. [*See* Passover.]

Other sacramental rites that have clear antecedents in Jewish observances are baptism in water as a ritual of spiritual regeneration, the imposition of hands in blessing, and the action of anointing to confer an office or mission. Beyond the direct influence of ritual actions of Jewish life, there is the much more extensive and pervasive indirect influence of stories, prayers, and symbols from the Hebrew scriptures. Thus, baptism is not easily understood without knowledge of the Hebrew stories of creation and sin, of the Deluge, and of the passing through the waters of the Red Sea at the Exodus and through the waters of the Jordan River as Israel took possession of the Promised Land. Similarly, confirmation (chrismation) is not readily understood without reference to the theme of the breath of God, which runs through the Hebrew scriptures. [*See* Worship and Cultic Life, *article on* Jewish Worship.]

Early History. Although there are references to sacramental activity in the New Testament, and these are accompanied by a sacramental theology (e.g., *1 Cor.*), little is known about the form of early Christian ritual except through late second-century sources. By the fourth century most of the rituals were elaborate and well established in the patterns that were to endure, though they were not numbered explicitly as seven until the twelfth century in the West and the seventeenth century in the East.

Early Christian rites. The central sacrament has always been the Eucharist. From early times it has consisted of a ritual meal of small amounts of bread and wine, commemorating the farewell supper of Jesus before his death and extending the presence and friendship of Jesus to his followers through the ages. The celebration begins with readings from the Bible, prayers, usually a sermon on the biblical texts read, and sometimes, hymns. Then follows a great prayer of praise and thanksgiving, recited by the one who presides over the ritual; in this context the story of the farewell supper is recited and reenacted. The bread and wine are consecrated, the bread is broken and distributed to the worshipers, who consume it immediately, and the wine is likewise consumed. This eating and drinking is known as "communion." [*See* Eucharist.]

Admission to the community formed around the Eucharist is by baptism and confirmation. In the early centuries baptism was by total immersion of the candidate, preferably in running water, accompanied by a formula of profession of faith. This going through the water symbolizes a death and a spiritual rebirth. Baptism was surrounded by lesser ritual elements: a divesting of old clothes and donning of a new white robe (which was worn for about one week), an anointing, and the receiving of a lighted candle. The ritual was generally preceded by a fast of some days and an all-night vigil. A further step of the initiation into the community was a confirmation of the baptism by the bishop (the leader of the local church) with a laying on of hands, a further anointing, and a prayer that the Holy Spirit (the breath of God that was in Jesus) might descend upon the candidate. [*See* Baptism.]

In the early centuries, there were also many reconciliation (penance, repentance) rituals: the recitation of the Lord's Prayer was one. However, there was also a more formal ritual of reconciliation, later modified radically, that applied to those excommunicated from the Eucharist and the company of the faithful for some grave offense. A period of exclusion, accompanied by the wearing of a special garb and the performance of prescribed works of repentance that were supported by the prayers of the community, was concluded by a ceremony in which the bishop led the penitents back into the worship assembly to readmit them to the Eucharist.

The custom was established in the early centuries of the laying on of hands not only in confirmation but also in the designation of persons to certain ministries or offices in the life and worship of the community. Such laying on of hands symbolized the passing on of authorization understood to come in a continuous line from Jesus and his earliest followers. It was performed in the context of a worship assembly and was accompanied by prayers and solemnity. [*See also* Priesthood, *article on* Christian Priesthood, *and* Ministry.]

From the fourth century onward there is evidence of the blessing of marriages, at least in certain cases, by bishops, although the ritual of marriage was otherwise performed according to local civil custom. Of the anointing of the sick there is, despite the injunction found in the New Testament (*Jas.* 5:14), no clear evidence from the early centuries of the church.

Theology of the rites. Christian sacraments are based on the understanding that human existence in the world as human beings experience it is not as it is intended by God, its creator; hence we stand in need of salvation (redemption, rescue, healing). If all were in the harmony of God's creation, all things would speak to us of God and would serve our communion with God. However, because of a complex legacy of the misuse of human freedom (a legacy known as original sin), the things of creation and the structures of human society tend to betray us, turning us away from our own true good. Jesus Christ is seen as the savior (redeemer and healer) in his life, actions, teachings, death, and resurrection. The sacraments are understood as continuing his presence and redeeming power.

In the New Testament and the other writings extant from the earliest period of Christian history, known as the patristic period, the community dimension of the sacraments is inseparable from the communion with God that they offer. Sacraments are redemptive because they draw people into the fellowship in which salvation is found. Baptism is the outreach of God through Jesus in his community whereby it is possible for a person to turn (convert) from the ways and society of a world gone astray to the ways and society of the community of the faithful. That this is the meaning of baptism is evident in the New Testament in the early chapters of the *Acts of the Apostles* and in the instructions given in the early community, for instance, in the *Didache*. Similarly, the Eucharist is seen as fashioning worshipers into "one body" with Jesus Christ, which has far-reaching consequences for their lives and their relationships (as the apostle Paul explains in *1 Corinthians*, chapters 11–13).

In the patristic period, the theology of the sacraments was more inclusive and less specific than it later became, because the terms *mustērion*, among Greek writers, and *sacramentum*, among Latin writers, were being used rather generally for all Christian rituals, symbols, and elements of worship. But the emphasis is clearly on the Eucharist and the initiation into the fellowship of the Eucharist, with the understanding that it constitutes a dynamic in history. Not only does it commemorate the past event of the death and resurrection of Jesus, and put the worshiper in intimate communion with that event, but it anticipates a glorious fulfillment of all the biblical promises and hopes in the future, and puts the worshiper into intimate communion with that future, thereby transforming the quality of life and action within the historical present. [*See also* Atonement; Grace; *and* Justification.]

Sacraments in the Orthodox Christian Tradition. The sacramental practice and theology of the Orthodox churches is in direct continuity with the Greek patristic writings, emphasizing wonder and reverence in the presence of the holy.

Orthodox rites. Besides the seven sacraments enumerated above, Eastern Christianity recognizes a wide range of ritual considered sacramental in a broader sense: the anointing of a king; the rite of monastic profession; burial rites; blessing of water on the feast of the Epiphany; and blessings of homes, fields, harvested crops, and artifacts. These are not, however, all of equal importance.

Although, since the seventeenth century, the Orthodox churches have accepted the Western enumeration of seven rites, the manner of celebration of Orthodox sacraments does not correspond closely to the Western celebrations. The first sacramental participation of an Orthodox Christian is that of initiation, usually in infancy. The children are baptized by total triple immersion with an accompanying formula invoking the triune

God. This is followed immediately by the chrismation (anointing) of forehead, eyes, nostrils, mouth, ears, breast, hands, and feet, with words proclaiming the seal of the gift of the Holy Spirit. As soon as possible thereafter, the infant is given Communion (either a small taste of the wine, or both bread and wine). This initiation is performed by a bishop or a priest.

The Eucharist, also known as the Divine Liturgy, is ordinarily celebrated daily, though the community as a whole is more likely to participate on Sundays, special feasts, and weekdays of Lent. It is performed in a highly elaborated way with processions, candles and incense, congregational singing, and the wearing of special vestments by the celebrating clergy.

The ordinary ritual of repentance and reconciliation is not a public ceremony as in the early church but a private conversation between a Christian and a priest who acts in the name of the church. The penitent, the person seeking forgiveness and reconciliation through the ministry of the church, ordinarily stands or sits before a cross, an icon (sacred image) of Jesus Christ, or the book of the Gospels. The priest, who stands to one side, admonishes the penitent to confess his or her sins to Christ, because he, the priest, is only a witness. Having heard the confession, and having perhaps given advice, the priest lays his stole (a type of scarf used as a ritual vestment) on the head of the penitent, lays his hand on it and pronounces a prayer of forgiveness. Besides this ritual of repentance, which can be repeated many times by the same person, the anointing of the sick is available to all who are ill, whether or not they are in danger of death. Anointing of the sick has the double purpose of prayer for healing from illness and forgiveness of sin.

The Orthodox churches ordain men only to their ministries, as bishops, priests, deacons, subdeacons, and readers. Ordinations are performed by a bishop during the Liturgy, and the consecration of a bishop is normally performed by three bishops. Essentially the rite is that of imposition of hands, but this is preceded by an acclamation of the congregation in which the faithful approve the candidate and consent to his ordination. The candidate is then brought to the altar to kiss its four corners and the hands of the bishop. The bishop lays hands on the candidate with a prayer invoking God's blessing.

The Orthodox marriage ceremony, celebrated by a priest, has two parts, the Office of Betrothal and the Office of Crowning, and includes the blessing and exchange of rings, the crowning of the bride and groom, and the sharing of a cup of wine by the couple.

Theology of the rites. Orthodox liturgy is concerned with making the beauty of the spiritual an element of experience, even a haunting element of experience. Liturgy is "heaven on earth," an anticipation of the glorious future. The fundamental sacramental principle is that in Jesus Christ a process of divinization has begun that continues in the sacramental mysteries and draws the worshipers in. Christ himself is the first sacramental mystery, continuing to live in the church, whose sacred actions reach forward to a glorious fulfillment in the future. The sacramental actions are the realization or becoming of the church as heavenly and earthly community. Therefore, they establish communion with the redemptive events of the past, communion among persons, and communion with the heavenly realm.

In the theology of the Orthodox church there is a strong sense of the organic wholeness, continuity, and pervasive presence of the redemption in the world, and therefore an unwillingness to draw some of the sharp distinctions that the West has been willing to draw concerning the sacramental mysteries.

Western Developments up to the Sixteenth Century. In the West, the sacraments underwent more change than in the East. This was caused by many factors, such as the large-scale conversions of European peoples, the cultural discontinuity resulting from the dissolution of the Roman empire, the problem of the difference in languages, a poorly educated clergy in the medieval period, and some other characteristics of Western traditions in church organization and theology.

Western rites. In the practice of the sacraments as received from the early church, there were some modifications. In the initiation, which was almost always conferred on children in the medieval period, baptism, confirmation, and first participation in the Eucharist were separated. The custom grew up of baptizing not by immersion but by pouring water over the forehead of the child. Confirmation, being the prerogative of the bishop, might be considerably delayed, and Communion was delayed out of a sense that infants might "desecrate" the holy.

The Eucharist became something that the priest did; the people had little part in it and little understanding of it. Its symbolism had become rather obscure and overlaid with additions and the Latin language, which had been adopted because it was the vernacular in the West in earlier centuries, was retained long after ordinary people no longer understood it. Communion by the laity became rare at this time, and even then it was restricted to the bread alone, the priest being the only one who received from the cup. Many ordinary Christians sought their real inspiration and forms of worship outside the liturgy of the Eucharist and the sacraments, and thus a great variety of other devotional practices arose.

As in the East, the old solemn and public form of reconciliation gave way to a far more private one embodied in a conversation between penitent and priest. This had originated in a tradition of voluntary individual spiritual guidance given by a wise and spiritual person who was not necessarily a priest. However, by the thirteenth century it had become obligatory for all people to confess, at least once a year, "all their grave sins" to their own parish priest, and the ceremony was constructed rather like a judicial procedure. By a subtle shift of usage in the twelfth century, the prayer that God might forgive had become a declaration that the priest forgave by the power the church had vested in him.

There were also some changes in the other sacraments. The anointing of the sick became, in effect, the sacrament of the dying. Ordination was restricted not only to men, but to celibate men, and the consent of the faithful was not sought, even as a ritual formality. Effectively, the ranks of the clergy were reduced to two: bishop and priest. Men were ordained to the other ranks (deacon, subdeacon, minor orders) only as an intermediate step to the priesthood.

There seems to have been no obligatory religious ritual for a marriage until the eleventh century, although there was a custom of celebrating a Eucharist at which a canopy was placed over the bride and groom and a special blessing was pronounced. After the eleventh century, weddings were performed at the church door with the priest as witness and were followed by a Eucharist at which the marriage was blessed. Essential to the ceremony was the exchange of consent by the couple. A ring was blessed and given to the bride.

Theology of the sacraments. The Western theology of the sacraments is heavily indebted to Augustine, bishop of Hippo (d. 430), though the Scholastic theology of the West in the Middle Ages elaborated Augustine's teachings much more. Key ideas in Scholastic teaching are concerned with the validity, the necessity, and the efficacy or causality of the sacraments.

Validity is a legal concept, and this gave a different direction to Western sacramental theology from that of the East. Sacraments are valid if the rite is duly performed by a duly authorized minister, quite independently of the spiritual goodness or worthiness of that minister, because essentially they are the acts of Christ performed through the mediation of his church. Therefore a Eucharist correctly celebrated by someone who has gone into schism from the church or who is wicked would nevertheless be a true Eucharist.

According to the Scholastics, the necessity of baptism, and of sacraments in general, for salvation is grounded in the universal involvement of the human race in the heritage of sinfulness and disorientation. This led to much speculation in medieval times concerning the fate of people who were not baptized because the opportunity had not been presented to them. The Scholastics found an acceptable compromise in postulating, besides the "baptism of blood" of martyred converts who had not yet been initiated, a "baptism of desire" granted to those who lived in good faith by the light that God had given them.

There was strong emphasis in this theology on the efficacy of the sacraments because they were the acts of Christ. Their efficacy is to bestow grace, that is, an elevation of human existence to a privileged intimacy with God leading to salvation. Augustine's teaching tended to emphasize the gratuity of God's gifts so strongly that it gave the impression to some that the human response of faith and surrender was not a constituent of the sacramental encounter. Augustine and the medieval theologians taught that the salvific effect of (or the grace bestowed by) a sacrament was not dependent on the virtue of the one who administered the sacrament. Unfortunately, this was sometimes popularly understood as meaning that sacraments are also not dependent for their efficacy on finding faith in the recipient.

Sacraments in Post-Reformation Roman Catholic Tradition. The Council of Trent (1545–1563), while correcting many abuses, substantially reaffirmed both the practice and the theology of the sacraments as they had been received from the medieval period. It was not until the twentieth century, and particularly until the Second Vatican Council (1962–1965), that substantive developments occurred.

Roman Catholic rites. The most significant and pervasive changes in the sacramental rites following Vatican II were the restoration of a more extensive and careful use of scripture and of preaching on the biblical readings; a reconstruction of rites to emphasize the communal character of the sacraments and the full and active participation of the laity; and a simplification and clarification of the symbolism of the rites, effected by stripping away accretions and rediscovering the classic forms from the heritage of the early church, and also by introducing some cautious and modest contemporary adaptations.

In the case of adults, initiation has been restored to its ancient form with some adaptations. As in the primitive church, the culminating ceremonies are placed at the conclusion of a leisurely time of preparation known as *catechumenate*. In the case of infants, baptism has been simplified and made more clearly a community action and commitment.

The Eucharist, like the other sacraments, is now celebrated in the vernacular. Even in large congregations, the presiding priest now faces the community across the altar rather than facing away from the people. More people now have active roles in the ceremony. It is usual, not exceptional, for all to communicate, that is, to partake of the bread, and, on special occasions, also of the wine. The whole community at every Eucharist, not only the clergy on certain solemn occasions, exchanges a ritual "kiss of peace" (which is actually more usually a handshake).

The anointing has been reinstated as a sacrament of the sick rather than the dying. But perhaps the greatest changes have occurred in the structures for the sacrament of reconciliation, which now has not only an individual rite, but also a communal one and a mixed one. The individual form remains much as before but is enriched by scripture readings, while the focus of the rite has shifted from the judicial function to spiritual guidance in a progressive Christian conversion. The communal form consists of an assembly in which scripture is read; a sermon is preached; there are hymns and prayers including a common, generic confession of sin and repentance; and a general absolution, given in the name of the church. In the mixed form a similar service is held, but a pause is made during which individuals can go aside to make a personal and specific confession of sins to a priest out of earshot of the congregation, and an individual absolution is given.

The significant change in holy orders is not in the ceremony but in the fact that the Catholic church once again ordains permanent deacons (thereby restoring a third rank of clergy), who, moreover, may be married men. Marriages are more usually celebrated with an exchange of rings, rather than a ring for the bride only, and both partners receive the nuptial blessing. It is still understood that the partners themselves confer the sacrament on each other; the priest serves as witness.

Theology of the sacraments. The Catholic theology of the sacraments after Vatican II has returned to closer affinity with the patristic and Eastern understanding. The fundamental sacrament is Jesus Christ, who is made present in the sacrament of the church, which in turn is realized as a sacrament in its own sacramental actions and assemblies. But sacramentality is pervasive in Christian experience and not restricted to the seven special moments. The liturgy (especially that of the Eucharist) is the peak or summit of Christian life in that everything should lead to it and everything should flow from it. That is to say, life for the Christian community should be progressively transformed in the grace of Christ, in lifestyle, in relationships, and in community structures and values by the repeated immersion of the community in the eucharistic moment.

A distinct but related aspect of the renewed theology of the sacraments after Vatican II is the rediscovery of the link that was seen so clearly in the early church between Christian sacraments and social justice. The very ceremonies and symbols of the sacraments are seen as presenting a radical challenge to many of the existing structures of the world. Under the influence of biblical renewal and patristic scholarship, there is a consistent effort in contemporary Catholic sacramental theology to correct a former bias by constant remembrance that the sacraments are not simply acts of Christ but also of the community, are not only channels of grace but also acts of faith and worship.

Sacraments in the Protestant Tradition. Although Protestant churches cannot simply be taken as a unity when discussing the sacraments, they do have one factor in common: they define themselves by their discontinuity with the medieval church tradition. Positively they also define themselves by a special emphasis on scripture and on personal faith.

Protestant rites. In general, the Protestant churches acknowledge as sacraments, in the strict sense of the term, only baptism and the Lord's Supper. Although other rites are celebrated, they are ordinarily not called sacraments because Protestants generally find no evidence of their institution by Jesus Christ. Some Christian groups of the Western church that are traditionally grouped with Protestants do not acknowledge sacraments at all; examples are the Society of Friends (Quakers), Unitarians, and Christian Scientists.

Among those Protestant churches that practice baptism, some insist on the "believer's baptism" and therefore will not baptize infants because they are not capable of a response of faith. Such, for instance, are the Baptists, the Disciples of Christ, and the Mennonites. These groups practice baptism by immersion. Most Protestant groups, however, do baptize infants and consider the pouring (sometimes the sprinkling) of water over the head as sufficient, accompanied by the recital of a formula usually invoking the triune God.

Protestant churches in general do not celebrate the Eucharist (Lord's Supper) as frequently as do the Catholic and Orthodox churches. Even a weekly celebration is not customary in most cases, though a monthly Communion service is quite usual. Although there is a variety of rites in the various churches, the central elements remain: the blessing and breaking of bread and its distribution to the worshipers to eat, accompanied by the biblical words of and about Jesus at his farewell supper; the blessing and distribution of the cup of wine (in some cases nonalcoholic grape juice) to be drunk by the worshipers, also accompanied by the appropriate biblical formula; biblical readings and meditation; and some expression of fellowship in the community. In general the Eucharist as celebrated by the Protestant churches is marked by a certain austerity of ritual expression and elaboration when compared with the celebrations of the Catholic and Orthodox churches.

Most Protestant churches celebrate some or all of the other rites that the Catholic and Orthodox churches enumerate as sacraments, although Protestants do not accord the rites that designation. There is a variety of rites of reconciliation, ranging from private confession of specific sins to an ordained minister, through such other forms as mutual confession between laypersons or stylized, generic formulas in which the whole congregation acknowledges sinfulness and need of forgiveness, to the characteristic Mennonite rite of foot washing (commemorating the action of Jesus related in the *Gospel of John* 13:2–10).

Anointing of the sick and other anointings have traditionally been practiced in some churches and have become far more common under the influence of the charismatic and Pentecostal movements. Marriages are commonly celebrated with some religious ceremony that includes bestowal of a ring or exchange of rings, exchange of marriage vows, and an exhortation in the context of community worship. Although most Protestant churches have some type of ordination of ministers, the ceremonies for such conferral reflect the different ways in which ministry and the role and status of the minister are understood.

Theology of the rites. Common to the Protestant churches is the insistence on the primacy of the Bible and on faith in salvation. Generally the efficacy of sacraments is not emphasized, while the role of the faith of the individual participant is stressed. This emphasis, combined with a strong sense of the priesthood of all believers, means that there is less concern over the "validity" of sacraments, and especially over the "validity of orders" of presiding ministers than in the Catholic and Orthodox traditions.

A major concern in celebrating the two great sacraments is obedience to the command of Jesus to do so, as that command is read in the New Testament. However, a significant difference exists between the Lutheran and the Calvinist understanding. In the former an act of God in the sacrament is effective when it encounters faith in the participant. In the latter a sacrament is a sign of God's grace but does not confer that grace.

Ecumenical Issues. The sacraments raise some ecumenical questions among Christians of different churches. One of these is the question of "intercommunion," that is, whether Christians of one church may receive communion at the Eucharist of another. Most churches allow this practice, at least in some circumstances. Another question is whether Christians transferring from one church tradition to another should be baptized again. With some exceptions, the churches do not confer baptism a second time, because they consider the first baptism valid. The question of accepting the ordination to ministry of other churches has proved far more controversial.

[*For discussion of related issues in broad religious perspective, see* Ablutions; Anointing; Confession of Sins; Hands; Healing; Initiation; Marriage; Ordination; Repentance; Rites of Passage; *and* Water.]

BIBLIOGRAPHY

The most inclusive single-volume introduction to sacraments in the Western tradition is Joseph Martos's *Doors to the Sacred* (New York, 1981). The biblical themes that underlie the symbolism of the sacraments are discussed briefly in my book *The Meaning of the Sacraments* (Dayton, Ohio, 1972). A detailed account of the historical development of the symbolism is given in Jean Daniélou's *The Bible and the Liturgy* (Notre Dame, Ind., 1966). What is known of the origins of the Christian rites in apostolic times is summarized in Ferdinand Hahn's *The Worship of the Early Church* (Philadelphia, 1973). The development of the rites through the patristic period is described in Josef A. Jungmann's *The Early Liturgy to the Time of Gregory the Great* (Notre Dame, Ind., 1959). The rites of the Orthodox tradition and their theological explanations are described in part 2 of Timothy Ware's *The Orthodox Church* (Baltimore, Md., 1963). A further presentation of contemporary Orthodox sacramental theology is available in Alexander Schmemann's *Sacraments and Orthodoxy* (New York, 1965). A Protestant discussion of the rites and their theology, written from a Reform perspective but discussing the Lutheran tradition also, is G. C. Berkouwer's *The Sacraments,* translated from the Dutch by Hugo Bekker (Grand Rapids, Mich., 1969). Another Protestant account, written from the perspective of the Disciples of Christ, is J. Daniel Joyce's *The Place of the Sacraments in Worship* (Saint Louis, 1967). A detailed history of the rites from the point of view of the Episcopal church is Marion J. Hatchett's *Sanctifying Life, Time and Space: An Introduction to Liturgical Study* (New York, 1976). The Catholic theological understanding of the sacraments prior to Vatican II is succinctly presented in Bernard Piault's *What Is a Sacrament?* (New York, 1963). The Catholic understanding of the sacraments in the light of Vatican II is very clearly presented in Bernard Cooke's *Sacraments and Sacramentality* (Mystic, Conn., 1983). Karl Rahner's *The Church and the Sacraments* (London, 1963) is a short but highly technical reformulation of the older Roman Catholic sacramental theology in the light of a renewed ecclesiology. Edward Schillebeeckx's *Christ: The Sacrament of the Encounter with God* (Mission, Kans., 1963), an epoch-making book in its time, is a similar reformulation linking traditional sacramental theology to a renewed Christology. Bernard Cooke's *Ministry to Word and Sacraments: History and Theology* (Philadelphia, 1976) is a lengthy study showing the historical development of the sacraments in relation to changing perceptions of priesthood. A series of essays on the ecumenical questions relating to the sacraments is collected in *The Sacraments: An Ecumenical Dilemma,* edited by Hans Küng (New York, 1967), and *The Sacraments in General: A New Perspective,* edited by Edward Schillebeeckx and Boniface Willems (New York, 1968). Technical and detailed bibliographies are given in each of these volumes.

MONIKA K. HELLWIG

SACRED AND THE PROFANE, THE. When referring to the sacred and the profane and distinguishing between them, the languages of modern scholarship are indebted to Latin, even though they may have equivalent or synonymous terms for both that have been derived from their own linguistic traditions. To the Roman, *sacrum* meant what belonged to the gods or was in their power; yet when referring to *sacrum* one was not obliged to mention a god's name, for it was clear that one was thinking of cult ritual and its location, or was primarily concerned with the temple and the rites performed in and around it. *Profanum* was what was "in front of the temple precinct"; in its earlier usage, the term was always applied solely to places. Originally, *profanare* meant "to bring out" the offering "before the temple precinct (the *fanum*)," in which a sacrifice was performed. *Sacer* and *profanus* were therefore linked to specific and quite distinct locations; one of these, a spot referred to as *sacer,* was either walled off or otherwise set apart—that is to say, *sanctum*—within the other, surrounding space available for profane use. This purely spatial connotation adheres to the two terms to this day, and implies that it represents a definition of them, or at least of their more important features. It makes sense wherever the church still stands next to the town hall, the cult site alongside the village council chamber, and wherever an assembly of Buddhists or Muslims is something other than an assembly of professional economists or athletes.

If we cling to the spatial aspect of these terms, however, and attempt to use it as a means of distinguishing not only between the two of them but also between religion and nonreligion, we are led astray. This occurs if one posits the sacred as a special category of religion in the way that the correct or the true has been made a category of cognition theory, the good a category of ethics, and the beautiful a category of aesthetics. The sacred is then what gives birth to religion, in that man "encounters" it; or it functions as the essence, the focus, the all-important element in religion. Of course it is possible to define the sacred in such a way if one determines that a single attribute is sufficient for an all-encompassing statement about religion. But when one is forced to find attributes that suggest religion's links to altogether different concepts, aside from those having to do with the quality of lying beyond a specific boundary, one discovers that the attribute of sacrality is no longer enough, even if one views its original spatial aspect as a transcendental or metaphysical one. And today, confronted as we are with definitions advanced by critics of ideology, sociologists, psychoanalysts, and others, we are indeed forced to find such attributes. Any definitions, even simple descriptions of the sacred and the profane, are affected by these as well; they also depend, in turn, on the manifold factors one has to muster when identifying the concept of religion.

Yet it is not necessary to discard the ancient Roman distinction between *sacer* and *profanus,* for the idea that they exist side by side represents a fundamental paradigm for making distinctions in general. It therefore has a certain heuristic value, though admittedly only that and nothing more.

The relationship between the sacred and the profane can be understood either abstractly, as a mutual exclusion of spheres of reality, or cognitively, as a way of distinguishing between two aspects of that reality. The former approach necessarily presupposes that such exclusion is recognizable; the latter, that one is dealing with ontic factuality. Even if one assumes a transsubjective reality, the boundary between the two spheres may prove to be movable or even fictitious, and even if one confines oneself to the fact of subjectivity, one may at times conclude that transcendence conditions the individual psychologically. Thus, when asking whether the sacred and the profane "exist," and how man "experiences" them, one encounters even greater difficulties than when inquiring after being and its various modes. Even though this article contains primarily the most important information about the various ways in which the sacred has been perceived in the history of religions, these difficulties of meaning must be borne in mind. It is necessary to suppress one's own conclusions about how and in what dimensions the sacred might exist, and about what it "is," in favor of the numerous theories that have been advanced on the question; according to these, conclusions may only be drawn case by case, in the light of the data and the theoretical arguments presented, and may well come out differently in every instance. Only with such reservations in mind can we consider the nature of the sacred and the profane.

Means of Identification

In selecting evidence of the sacred and its relationship to the profane we must be limited to two approaches: either it is tacitly perceived as something real, or it assumes some kind of symbolic form. In order to establish tacit perception, we require proofs that silence is maintained for the sake of the sacred. These proofs suffice not only for the mystic, for example, who could speak but prefers to maintain silence, but also for persons who have spoken, but whose language we do not know: namely, the people of prehistory and early historical times.

Symbolic forms may be specifically linguistic or of a broader cultural nature. If they are linguistic, the historian of religions must distinguish between the language spoken by the people who are the objects of study ("object language") and the one spoken by the scholar, though naturally the two will have shadings and terms in common. One can best make this distinction by keeping one's own definition of what is sacred or profane separate from the definition that is given by the culture under scrutiny itself ("self-definition"). Each definition naturally identifies the sacred and profane in a different way. The self-definition is part of those languages in which religious and nonreligious documents have come down to us; in terms of methodology, these are the same as object languages. The definitions the historian develops must arise not only out of the categories of language, but also out of those of modern sociology, psychology, aesthetics, and possibly other disciplines as well, categories employed in an attempt to understand the sacred and profane without resorting to the concepts one customarily translates with *sacred* and *profane;* in terms of methodology, this amounts to a metalanguage.

If the symbolic forms are not of a linguistic nature, there is no self-definition at all. The definitions given from outside to which one must restrict oneself, in this case to relate to language, are not *meta*linguistic in nature, for the object area is not expressed merely in language, but rather through social behavior, anthropological data, or works of art.

Whether considered a linguistic or a nonlinguistic expression, the definition given from outside can assume an affirmative character, and in so doing turn into the self-definition of the scholar who identifies himself with a given artifact, be it in a text, a specific event, a psychic configuration, or a work of art. The researcher compiling a definition can thus identify himself with both its sacredness and profaneness.

As a rule, one should give neither of these means of identification precedence over the other. It is for purely practical reasons that we now turn our attention first to those methods relying on linguistic evidence.

Philological Methods. It is an axiom in the logic of criticism that one can declare the use of a concept of sacredness in a source to be false. However, the conclusions of the modern scholar, no matter how subtly they might not only deny phenomena of sacredness within religions but also manage to demonstrate them outside of religions, are constantly in need of correction by object-language traditions.

Seen in terms of the history of scholarship, the first object-language tradition to contain the terms for *sacred* and *profane* (upon which the terminology of the medieval precursors of modern scholarly languages was based) was the Latin of the Roman classical writers and church fathers, including, among the texts of the latter, the Vulgate and the harmony of its gospel texts represented by Tatian's *Diatessaron* in the Codex Fuldensis. Equating words resulted in the double presentation of terms in the vernacular, as we can still see from various contextual, interlinear, and marginal glosses, and in the translations of the *Abrogans,* an alphabetical dictionary of synonyms, and the *Vocabularius Sancti Galli,* in which the terms are arranged by subject. Bilingualism, resulting from the rechristianization of Spain, was also responsible for the earliest translation of the Qur'ān by Robertus Ketenensis and Hermannus Dalmata, for the unfinished *Glossarium Latino-Arabicum,* and for some important translations from Hebrew, which not only reflect the Jews' skill as translators throughout the Diaspora, but also represent active endeavors on the part of the medieval mission among the Jews. Terms for the sacred and its opposites could thus be translated into the vernaculars directly out of Hebrew, Latin, and Catalan, and out of the Arabic by way of Latin. They also became available from Greek, once the early humanists, the forerunners of the modern scholars, had rediscovered the Greek classics through the Latin ones, and the original text of the New Testament and the Septuagint by way of the Vulgate. At the Council of Vienne, in 1311–1312, it was decided to appoint two teachers each of Greek, Arabic, Hebrew, and Chaldean at each of five universities; thenceforth Latin emerged once and for all as a metalanguage with respect to the terminologies of these languages (including Latin itself, now considered as an object language), and in so doing came to stand fundamentally on the same footing as the European vernaculars.

In order to avoid short-circuiting self-confirmations within the terminology of sacredness, it is best to consider this complex as an independent one transmitted to modern scholarship not from the Middle Arabic of the Islamic traditionalists, nor from the Middle Hebrew of the Talmudists, but solely from the Middle Latin of the Christian scholars. It must be distinguished from a later complex that resulted from the use of the European vernaculars in missionary work and in colonization. These were able to reproduce certain word meanings from the native languages, but more often led to interpretations dependent on the terminology of sacredness from the former complex, rather than congenial translation. Moreover, true bilingualism was only present in the work of a few explorers and missionaries. More recently, of course, translation has been accomplished increasingly in accordance with methods taken from the study of the early oriental languages, of Indo-European, and of comparative philology, as well as from linguistic ethnology; only in the twentieth century have all of these achieved independence from interpretations provided by classical antiquity and by Judeo-Christian-Islamic tradition.

Philologia classica sive sacra. The relationship between *sacer* and *profanus* can be called a contradictory opposition, if one understands *sacer* as the object-language expression of something true and *profanus* as its logical negation. In the rich cultic vocabulary of Latin *sacer* is of prime importance. Rites such as those of the *ver sacrum*—the sacrifice of all animals born in the spring and the expulsion from the community and cult congregation of all grown men about to establish their own domestic state (for the purpose of securing the support of Mars, who worked outside communal boundaries)—or the *devotio*—the offering of an individual life as a stand-in for an enemy army, so that Mars will destroy it as well—serve as prime examples of the characteristic relationship between the *sacrum*'s liability and certain kinds of human behavior. It follows that all cult objects and sites included in ritual acts can also be *sacra*. This meaning gives rise to derivations such as *sacrare, sacrificare, sancire, sacramentum, sacerdos*. Of these, *sancire* ("to set aside as *sacer*"; later also "to designate as being *sacer*," or, even more generally, "to establish with ceremony") is the most fertile, for its participle *sanctus* would ultimately come to characterize everything appropriate to the *sacrum*. *Sanctus* could thus assume a multitude of meanings, including those of cult infallibility and moral purity. Accordingly, it was an ideal translation for the Greek *hagios* of the New Testament and the Septuagint, and, by way of the latter, for the Hebrew *qadosh* as well. When used in such a Judeo-Christian context, *sacer* was then restricted in meaning to "consecrated," and this tended to fix a change in meaning that had begun already in the Latin of the writers of the Silver Age, as *sacrum* ceased to have an almost innate quality and came to depend on the act of consecration to a deity. A new formation such as *sacrosanctus* ("rendered *sanctum* by way of a *sacrum*") attests to this difference, as well as to the continuing similarity between the two meanings.

The basic meaning of *profanus* may also be discovered within the context of human actions, for the spatial connotation, which is always at its root, doubtless first derived from the use made of the area outside the *sacrum*. Originally, perhaps, this space may even have been used for rites, for the fact that even here we are dealing not with banal functions but with special ones is shown by legal arguments about how assets owned by a god or in the estate of a deceased citizen can be used "profanely."

Along with *profanus*, there is also another concept that is the opposite of *sacer*, namely that of *fas*. This designates, in a purely negative way, the sphere in which human affairs may take place. *Fas est* means that one *may* do something without any religious scruples, but not that one *must* do so. It first appears as a qualifier for a permitted act, then for a condition as well, and accordingly was used through all of the literature of the Roman republic only as a predicate concept. Livy, who also used the term *sacrosanctus* with some frequency, was the first to employ the concept as a subject as well. Specific times came to be distinguished by the activities appropriate to them. *Dies fasti* were days on which civil, political, commercial, or forensic activities were *fas*, or permitted by the religious institutions; *dies nefasti* were those on which such activities were *nefas*, that is, not permitted, or sacrilegious.

The meaning of *fas* does not accord with that of *fanum*, then—nor are they related etymologically; *fas* is related to *fatum*—as though *fas* is "what is appropriate to the *fanum*." Here it is rather the profane sphere that is the positive starting point. *Fas* is the utterance (from *fari*, "speak") of the responsible secular praetor who permits something; *nefas* is that which the priest responsible in the *fanum* finds unutterable, which constitutes sacrilege on those days over which his institution has control. When one recognizes that what is here accepted as natural and immutable passes over into what has been fixed by man and is therefore subject to change, and which can be objectively false just as its opposite can, then one can speak of the opposition between *fanum/sacer* and *fas* as a contrary one.

Sacer thus has a contradictory opposite *(profanus)* and a contrary one *(fas)*. In addition, finally, there is a dialectical opposition contained within the concept of *sacer* itself. This comes from the ambivalence produced when, as with *fas*, the extrasacral sphere is assumed as the positive starting point in one's appraisal. *Sacer* is thus what is venerated, to be sure, but also something sinister; or, to put it another way, it is both holy and accursed. Consecration to a god is perceived by humans as a blessing, whereas being possessed by a god is perceived as a misfortune. One must not make this dialectical contrast into an actual one by construing possession and misfortune as a fatal consecration to an underworld deity inimical to humans, for in so doing one destroys an ambiguity that is part of the basic structure of every religious experience. Positively, *sacer esto* simply means that a person is handed over to a deity; negatively, it implies that he is excluded from the community. The negative side of the dialectic may extend as far as demonization. If damnation or demonization is manifest on the historical level, then one is dealing with something other than profanation, and, outside the holy, still another sphere is revealed in addition to the profane. The dialectical relationship with this sphere comes about only through man's limited capacity for experience, and must not be enhanced by philologically setting up some finding related to *sacer;* that is, it must not be turned into an essential contrary working inside the nature of a *numen* or a deity.

The types of contrasts between the terms designating the sacred and the profane are less fundamental in Greek than in Latin, even though elements of ambivalent background experience may also be recognized in *hagios* and *hieros.* For the most part, the expressions have the character of a primary positing dependent on premises other than those relating to the differences between inclusion in or exclusion from a given precinct, or between ritual and nonritual behavior. As a rule, the antithesis was only created belatedly, through the use of the alpha privative, as in *anhieros, anosios, amuētos,* or *asebēs;* the only term that appears to relate to an original negative concept, namely the opposite of *hieros,* is *bebēlos,* which can be translated as "profane," while *koinos* can function as the opposite of practically all the concepts of sacredness. In our survey of the latter, then, the contrary concepts may be easily imagined, even though not specifically named.

From Mycenaean times on, the decisive concept is that designated as *hieros.* Behind it, most likely, is a sense of force altogether lacking in the early Roman term. *Hieros* functions almost exclusively as a predicate, both of things and of persons: offerings, sacrificial animals, temples, altars, votive gifts (even including money), the road leading to Eleusis, the wars engaged in by the Delphic amphictyony, and priests, initiates in the mysteries, and temple slaves. Only very rarely did anyone go so far as to call a god or a goddess *hieros;* Greek-speaking Jews and Christians were forced to resort to the term *hagios.* Traces of some experiential ambivalence are apparent when a *hieros logos,* or cult legend, is regarded as *arrēton* ("unspeakable") and a shrine as *aduton* or *abaton* ("unapproachable"). It is nonetheless striking that in Homer and the older Greek literature a whole range of things may be called *hieros:* cities, walls, hecatombs, altars, temples, palaces, valleys, rivers, the day and the night, the threshing floor, bread and the olive tree, barley and olives, chariots, guard and army units, individual personality traits, mountains, letters, bones, stones used in board games. Here it is rare to find *hieros* used with any connection to the gods, as when grain and the threshing floor, for example, are spoken of as the gifts of Demeter. On the whole it is tempting to speak of a certain profanation due to literary redundancy, though in fact a complete reversal of meaning is never produced.

Hagnos, which also encompasses what is pure in the cultic sense, is even more profound in its meaning than *hieros;* it relates to *hazesthai* ("to avoid in awe, to fear, to venerate") in the same way that *semnos* ("solemn, sublime, holy"—i.e., lacking the component of purity) relates to *sebesthai* ("to be afraid, to perceive as holy"). *Hagnos* is more frequently used than *hieros* when referring to the gods (Demeter, Kore, Persephone, Zeus, Apollo, Artemis), but in that they are elements that can purify, water and fire can also be *hagnos,* as can sky, light, and ether. Because of this connotation, *hagnos* can be used not only for things and persons in the same way as *hieros,* but may also designate rites and festivals or the conditions of sexual purity and of freedom from the contamination of blood and death, as, for example, when applied to bloodless offerings *(hagna thumata). Hagnos* can even extend to the whole conduct of one's life outside the cult, though the connotation "sacred" never entirely disappears; it is only in Hellenistic Greek that it comes to mean "purity of character." Whether one is justified in calling this a profane use or not depends upon one's judgment of the nature of postclassical religiosity in general. In any case, the only clearly contradictory opposite of *hagnos* is *miaros* ("polluted, disgusting").

From the root *hag-,* from which *hagnos* derives, the adjective *hagios* was also created. This does not limit, but rather emphasizes (hence, too, its superlative *hagiōtatos*), and is used especially of temples, festivals, and rites, though only rarely of the reverent attitudes of men. In classical Greek and the pagan Greek of Hellenistic times it is used only relatively rarely. Precisely for this reason its clear religious connotation was preserved, and this is what recommended the term to Hellenistic Jewry as a virtually equivalent translation for the Hebrew *qadosh,* whereas from the *hieros* group of words one finds only *hiereus* as a possible rendering of the Hebrew *kohen* ("priest"), and *hieron* to designate a pagan shrine. The New Testament develops even further the sense given to *hagios* in the Septuagint—though unlike the Septuagint it can also use *hieron* when referring to the Temple in Jerusalem—and thereby transmits this sense to the Greek of the church fathers and the Byzantine church. Secular modern Greek continues to use *hagios* as the standard term for "sacred" to this day.

The word *hosios* designates behavior that conforms to the demands of the gods. Accordingly, it can be applied to human justice just as properly as to a correctly performed cult ritual. Both are carried out on the profane level. Though one cannot translate *hosios* with "profane," one must think of it as a contrary opposite of *hieros:* if money belonging to the gods is *hieron,* that means one cannot touch it, but the rest, which is *hosion,* may be freely used. The Septuagint never uses *hosios* as a translation for *qadosh* but generally does for *ḥasid* ("pious"). The Vulgate, however, renders *hosios* unaffectedly with *sanctus,* whether applied to man or to God.

Sebesthai ("to shrink back from a thing, to be awestruck") has no parallel in the Semitic languages, and hence the word is important solely in the classical Greek tradition. The related adjective *semnos* implies exaltedness or sublimity when used of gods; when applied to speeches, actions, or objects (a royal throne, for example) it suggests that they command respect. It appears only infrequently in the Greek Bible for various terms, just as does the important classical concept *eusebēs,* which is chosen in a few instances to render *tsaddiq* ("the just one"), which in turn may also be translated with *dikaios.* The Vulgate has difficulty with both adjectives, and makes do with approximations or circumlocutions.

In the Hebrew Bible the all-important concept is *qadosh.* If its root is in fact *qd* ("to set apart"), its fundamental meaning is not unlike the Roman *sacer.* But it is also possible that its root is *qdsh,* as in the Akkadian *qadashu* ("to become pure"), which would point to a cultic connection. Nothing is *qadosh* by nature, however; things only become *qadosh* by being declared so for, or by, Yahveh Elohim. All of creation is potentially eligible: persons, especially priests; places, especially the city of Jerusalem; festivals, especially the Sabbath; buildings, especially the Temple; adornments, especially the priest's crown and robe; bodies of water; plants; and animals, especially sacrificial ones. The prophets—assisted by a trend that emerged from the reading of God's law at the Israelite feast of covenantal renewal and culminated in the establishment of the Holiness Code (*Lv.* 17–26)—managed to transfer the attribute "holy" almost exclusively to Yahveh Elohim. As a result, only a very few of the above-mentioned categories of objects and activities continued to be accorded the attribute of holiness in the actual target language of Hebrew. In large part, reference to holy places, times, actions, and objects is metalanguage interpretation. It is not factually wrong, for even a holiness accorded by God on the basis of his own holiness is deserving of the name. Nevertheless, one must be aware of the special quality of having been created by him that is typical of such holiness; this is in distinct contrast, for example, to the Greek concept of nature. And it affects the designation of what is profane in Israel. An important thesis of secularization theory asserts that the desacralization of the world, especially of nature and its wonders as it was accomplished in the Israelite theology of holiness, and later transmitted by Christianity, was one of the fundamental preconditions for the worldliness of the modern era. If one does not regard this basic precondition as a *conditio sine qua non,* it is doubtless correctly identified. It would be possible to view the realm of created things in the Israelite concept of the world as profane, just as one might view secularity as a legitimizing criterion for what constitutes the modern era, but that profaneness would be altogether different in kind from that of Rome or Greece. Given this situation, it is understandable that in the Old Testament languages (Hebrew and Septuagint/Vulgate translations) the "profanity" of the world is expressed in quite dissimilar fashion and only fragmentarily, depending upon whether it is mentioned in the cult context of pure and impure or in prophetic preaching about obedience and sin. As a clear contradiction to *qadosh* we thus find, in only a few instances, the adjective *ḥol,* which is rendered by the Septuagint with *bebēlos* and by the Vulgate with *profanus* (*ṭame',* "impure," becomes *akathartos* and *pollutus,* respectively; *ṭaher,* "pure," becomes *katharos* and *mundus*). *Ḥol* designates only something that is accessible and usable without ritual, while the verb *ḥalal* suggests a genuine desecration by means of an abomination.

The grateful use of created things, which God makes holy, by men who are likewise holy because God is, is not the same thing as the Greeks' and Romans' removal of things from profane use. The closest parallel to the latter in Israel is the practice of bans. Translated etymologically, *ḥerem* ("the banned object") means what has been set apart. The difference not only between this practice and profane use of a holy object but also between it and the sacrifice of an object lies in the fact that the purpose for the setting apart is the object's destruction. The Septuagint quite correctly expresses the term's identity with the idea of damnation by using *ana(te)thema(tismenos),* while the Vulgate makes do with *consecratum* or *votum.*

In Arabic, at least since the appearance of the Qur'ān, words with the root *ḥrm* take on the central importance that *qdsh* and its derivatives have in Hebrew. At the same time, the Arabic *qds* and its offshoots (*muqaddas,* "holy") continue to survive with more general meaning. This switch in the relative values of the two may have occurred simply because all of the concepts of sacredness having to do with rites and sacrifices were concentrated on a specific precinct. It is as though the Israelite concept of holiness, bound as it was to the ideas of sacrifice and consecration, were multiplied by the Roman concept, with its original link to a well-defined location. The city of Mecca is a *ḥarīm*, a circumscribed, inviolable spot. The strip of land that surrounds and protects it is known as *al-ḥaram*. In the city's center lies *al-masjid al-ḥarām*, the "forbidden mosque," so named because it may not be entered by those who have not performed an *iḥrām*, or consecrated themselves. In the center of its inner courtyard, *al-ḥaram al-sharīf* (the "noble precinct"), lies the *aedes sacra*, the Kaʿbah, *al-bayt al-ḥarām* (the "forbidden house"). Everything outside this complex is known as *ḥill*, where, just as in the *profanum*, except during a period of three months, everything is *ḥalāl* ("permitted") that is prohibited in the sacred sites. The Arabic *ḥalāl* is thus close in meaning to the Hebrew *ḥol*, but quite different from *ḥalāl*.

Linguistica externa. Regarding the problem of "the holy," a number of groups of terminologies have to be located between the Latin/Greek/Hebrew/Arabic ensemble and the modern scholarly languages influenced by them, terminologies that can suggest things similar to those existing in the gap between those object languages and these metalanguages. Semantic antinomies that can remain unrecognized in the latter should certainly not influence this terminology. There are three ways of attempting to establish meanings here: through etymological "translation," through synonyms, and through analysis of the context and its cultural background. The first of these, especially favored in the case of the Indo-European and Semitic languages, is altogether worthless. Reliable checks are only provided by context analysis. In this way one can discover "synonyms"—though not always synonyms in the strict sense—which more or less approximate what the metalanguages define as sacred/holy and profane.

The Sanskrit term *iṣira* has the same root as the Greek *hieros*, but contextually it means "strong, robust, impetuous." Sanskrit does not even have a separate word for "holy," though there are numerous adjectives applied to objects and persons in the religious sphere, such as *puṇya* for a geographical location, *tīrthaka* for a ford, or the crossing or passageway to a pilgrimage shrine, or substantives such as *muni* for a seer or an ascetic. Related etymologically to the Greek *hazesthai*/*hagios* are the Sanskrit *yaj* and Avestan *yaz*. These two also mean "to hold in awe," but their usage is limited to the sense of "bestow, present," as when one brings a gift to a deity (Skt. *ijyā*, Av. *yasna*, "the offering"), and there is no connotation, as in the Greek *hagios*, of an otherworldly essence from which the earthly is thought to have derived. For this latter sense Avestan has the word *spenta*, to which are related the Slavic *svętu* and Lithuanian *šventas*. These latter two are used in Christian contexts for *sacer*, but their root meaning originally lay somewhere between "supernaturally powerful" and "especially favorable, extremely useful." Pahlavi translations render *spenta* with *abzōnīg* ("overflowing, bursting with power"). The cultural background is the world of plants and animals, which in its abundant energy has the miraculous ability to bring forth new life and set it to work in its own cause.

The Germans have translated *spenta* with *heilwirkend* ("producing well-being" or "prosperity") employing a root that means "whole, sound, intact," and that gave rise to the German *heilig* ("holy"). Gothic *hails* meant "healthy"; Old Icelandic and Old High German *heil* is "a good omen" or "good fortune." Runic *hailag* means roughly "gifted with good fortune [by a god]," but also, conversely, "consecrated [to a god]." This becomes equal to the Gothic adjective *weihs* and its related active verb *weihan*, medial verb *weihnan*, and abstract noun *weihitha*, which appear in the Gothic translation of the Bible in place of the Greek *hagios*, *hagiazein*, *hagiazesthai*, and *hagiasmos*, respectively. All in all, the German *heil-* words connote a physical integrity with distinct religious significance. Possession of such integrity is a boon that can be given. The god who bestows it thereby becomes one to whom one gives veneration (Ger., *weiht*). Accordingly, even in Gothic the two concepts *weihs* and *hails* (which can also develop to *hailigs*) are interchangeable, and the situation in other Germanic languages is similar.

In general the synonyms in the Indo-European languages for what the metalanguages imply with their contrast between profane and sacred boil down to a qualitative exaggeration, intensification, or concentration of aspects of nature.

Among the ancient peoples of Asia Minor, to whose ideas the mythology of the Hittites in part attests, there appears to have been no special word for mysteries, such as the amazing magnetic force of stones or the destruction of creation by the creator himself. Yet a Hittite adjective, *parkui*, refers to the state of purity required in preparation for contact with the gods, and another, *shuppi*, designates such contact itself. Among the Sumerians, for reasons whose elaboration would go beyond the scope of this article, one must assume from earliest times a well-defined pantheon that predated all ritual. The basic polytheistic structure is of a more general character than anything that has been defined to demonstrate a consistent background world beyond the differentiations into socially and functionally limited deities. Yet even the world of the gods is permeated by a single, unifying element that one can only call "the divine." This is the *me,* which is met with in compounds like *melam* ("divine radiance, divine majesty"). Mythical men and kings can also exhibit it, in which case they are god-men. The gods pronounce *me* and exclude it from the framework of fate, which they in fact subordinate to the *me.* Man is required to bring himself into conformity with this *me* so as to be able to realize it in the world. There are numerous adjectival terms corresponding to this concept, the most important being *kug, mah,* and *zid.* In Babylonian, *kug* is translated with *ellu* ("[ritually] pure, bright, free"), *mah* with *siru* ("first-rank, exalted"), and *zid* with *imnu* ("right-hand") or *kanu* ("to be firm"). Alternatives to *ellu* in Babylonian spells are the terms *namru* ("clear, radiant") and *quddushu* ("purified, [made] perfect"), the latter having the same root as the Hebrew *qdsh.* Moreover, the Babylonian creation epic *Enuma elish* attests to a primordial cosmogony in a preexistent world. For the relationship between what the metalanguages call the sacred and the profane we find *analogies* in the relationship between human and animal forms of deities, as well as between their constructive activity (including Marduk's creation of the world) and the social organization of gods and human beings.

In Egypt, whose language became accessible to us by way of Greek (through the Rosetta Stone), temples and necropolises especially were set apart from the everyday world, and, in connection with them, so were gods and specific objects. This sense of being separate did not have to be concentrated in a specific term, but from the first to twentieth dynasties this was frequently done with the word *dsr. Dsr* means, first of all, a kind of vibrating motion, but it can also designate a defense against a rush of attackers or, more generally, a clearing resulting from the settling of a whirlwind. These have in common a sense of thrusting away that amounts to the establishment of distance. The word came to be used, in an increasingly abstract sense, for such distance when an appropriate attribute was required to describe the location of a cult statue in a necropolis, a shrine, the eternal body of the god Re, the space in which bulls were sacrificed, the realm of the gods, and the underworld paths reserved for the dead once they had become Osiris. It is simplest to conceive of the relationship of such places and objects to the everyday world as the subsequent removal of the distance at which they have been placed. Something of this sort happens when texts used in the context of religious institutions become the models for secular literature; the most important ancient Egyptian narrative, the *Story of Sinuhe,* for example, poses as a copy of an autobiographical tomb inscription.

Our knowledge of the Chinese and Japanese languages is due in general to the presence of Jesuit missionaries in China and Japan in the sixteenth century. Our deeper understanding of the vocabulary of East Asian religions comes most of all from Chinese translations of Buddhist texts originally written in Indian dialects, and already known to us through other channels; and, later, from the study of Japanese renderings of the better-known Chinese. The first bilingual (i.e., Chinese- or Japanese-European) dictionaries finally appeared in the nineteenth century. Whether or not there are precise equivalents for *sacred* and *profane* is largely a matter of each individual lexicographer's interpretation. The Chinese *shen-sheng,* which some gloss as meaning "holy," is held by others to mean, roughly, "extremely right," "highly exalted," or "doubtless as it must be." Of course, it is possible to interpret an ecstatic act such as submersion into the totality of the Tao as the attainment of holiness; however, the foundation in physical nature that is discovered to be a basic principle of the mystical experience is so much more magical here than in other religions that a difference in quality results. The relationship between the sacred and the profane would thus be roughly the same as that between alchemy and hygiene, both of which are practiced within Taoism as a means of attaining "not-dying."

The Shintō concept of nature is doubtless both more spiritual and more mythological. The *kami,* or nature and ancestral deities, are profane or sacred to the precise degree in which they do or do not belong organically to the everyday world of the living. The monks *(shidosō)* and wandering *hijiri* who carried the rites and concepts of the popular and even more magical esoteric Buddhism out into the provinces, and thereby contributed greatly to its fusion with Shintō, can rightly be called "holy men"—whatever that may imply about the charismatic leaders of new religions in the present day, who take them as their models.

The metalanguage expressions *sacred* and *profane* and their equivalents are only synonyms for all of the views derived from the various terminologies discussed here. If one proceeds from the roots of their subject matter and not from an all-inclusive hermeneutics, they are not complete synonyms but only partial ones, of a conceptual rather than a stylistic nature.

Metalanguage meanings. The modern scholarly languages for the most part presuppose the changes of meaning that the classical vocabulary ultimately experienced as a result of being put to Christian use, in part after certain non-Christian usages that prepared the way. These changes of meaning are characterized by the fact that a clear distinction exists between the quality of God in the beyond and the quality of creation in the here and now; and the terms are distributed accordingly. This distinction must not be thought of as static, however, for it can be suspended in either direction, that is to say, both by God's communication with man and by man's consecration of things to God.

In the first sense, the Latin term *sanctus* had ultimately come to mean a primarily divine quality; and consequently we now have the French *saint* and the Italian and Spanish *santo.* The Germanic languages, on the other hand, perpetuate the root that in the language's earliest stages had meant "intact, healthy, whole," represented by the English *holy* (related to *whole;* synonyms: *godly, divine*), by the German and Dutch *heilig,* and by the Swedish *helig.* And the Slavic languages preserve a root that had meant "efficacious" in the early stage of the language: the Russian *sviatoi,* for example, or Polish *święty.*

In the second sense, that is, for the quality attained by dedication to God, Latin had preserved the term *sacer,* which was linked to places, objects, and situations. Later, though relatively early, *sacer* existed alongside *sanctus,* which, confusingly enough, could also be used to refer to this mode of transformation. *Sacer* could be exchanged for the clearer form *sacratus,* and it is from this that the French *(con)sacré,* the Italian *sacro* (synonym: *benedetto*), and the Spanish *(con)sagrado* derive. For this meaning English employs the Romance word *sacred,* while German and Dutch make use of the ancient root **ueik-* (possibly a homonym; "to set apart" or "to oppose oneself to someone") with the forms *geweiht* and *gewijd.* In addition, German also substitutes for this a form from the former word group, using *geheiligt* in the sense of *geweiht,* a situation that gives rise to constant misunderstanding. This misunderstanding had been prepared for by the double direction of Gothic *weihs/hailigs,* and it was strengthened by imitating the biblical wording. For the sake of clarity, some careful speakers therefore prefer the form *dargeheiligt* to mean "consecrated." This substitution also occurs in Swedish, which uses only *vigd* and *helgad.* In the scholarly Slavic language ambiguity is avoided through incorporation of the simple form into a composite, as in the case of the Russian *sviaschchennyi* and the Polish *świątobliwy.*

In Latin, *profanus* had continued to be the opposite of both *sanctus* and *sacer,* the latter in its broader, classical Roman sense as well as its more limited Judeo-Christian meaning. Accordingly, the Romance languages and Romance-influenced English still use the term, while the strictly Germanic languages have it only as a loan word. In all of them there are synonyms with the meaning "secular," or something similar. Synonyms of this type have completely replaced the Latin form in the Slavic languages; Russian has *svetskii* or *zemnoi,* Polish *świecki* or *światowy.*

It is most important to notice the metalanguage nature of these terms as they are used to translate expressions from the linguistic complex Latin/Greek/Hebrew/Arabic, as well as from other languages. Scholars have frequently failed to do so, and this has led to a great number of semantic antinomies that were not recognized as such and therefore became, often enough, the cause of premature or totally false identifications.

Sociological Methods. For the examination of symbolic forms of a nonlinguistic nature, the methods of sociology are the most effective. Of such nonlinguistic forms, the most important are, of course, rites. Much would suggest that rites were in fact the very earliest forms of religious expression. I shall here assume stereotypings to be next in importance, forms that are even more hypothetical and that serve, among other things, as the rationale for institutionalizations. The two scholars who have analyzed these forms most profoundly are Émile Durkheim and Max Weber, and I shall draw on their findings. In so doing I accept their identifications, by and large, though not their theories regarding the ultimate origin of religion(s).

Neither Durkheim's nor Weber's method is correct in itself, but together they may well be so. Durkheim's idea that, in contrast to individual reality, society is of the nature of a thing, and Weber's idea that social reality is made up of continuous human action, inclusive of theorizing, are complementary. It is true of both, as for most of the other sociological approaches, that they strive to work with pure designations, but that these are also more or less stamped by metalanguage usage and by concepts from classical and church tradition. This often tends to compromise the accuracy of translation from native languages; but, on the other hand, this is what permits at least an approximate understanding of unfamiliar terms.

The nature of the sacred and profane in the objectivity of social reality. In *The Elementary Forms of the Religious Life* (New York, 1915), Émile Durkheim points out that all religious beliefs share one characteristic in common. They presuppose, he notes,

> a classification of all things, real and ideal, of which men think, into two classes or opposed groups, generally designated by two distinct terms which are translated well enough by the words *profane* and *sacred (profane, sacré)*. . . . By sacred things one must not understand simply those personal beings which are called gods or spirits; a rock, a tree, a spring, a pebble, a piece of wood, a house, in a word, anything can be sacred. A rite can have this character; in fact, the rite does not exist which does not have it to a certain degree. . . . The circle of sacred objects cannot be determined, then, once for all. Its extent varies infinitely, according to the different religions. . . . We must now show by what general characteristics they are to be distinguished from

> profane things. One might be tempted, first of all, to define them by the place they are generally assigned in the hierarchy of things. They are naturally considered superior in dignity and power to profane things. . . . It is not enough that one thing be subordinated to another for the second to be sacred in regard to the first. . . . On the other hand, it must not be lost to view that there are sacred things of every degree. . . . But if a purely hierarchic distinction is a criterium at once too general and too imprecise, there is nothing left with which to characterize the sacred in its relation to the profane except their heterogeneity. However, this heterogeneity is sufficient to characterize this classification of things and to distinguish it from all others, because it is very particular: *it is absolute.* In all the history of human thought there exists no other example of two categories of things so profoundly differentiated or so radically opposed to one another. The traditional opposition of good and bad is nothing beside this. . . . In different religions, this opposition has been conceived in different ways. Here, to separate these two sorts of things, it has seemed sufficient to localize them in different parts of the physical universe; there, the first have been put into an ideal and transcendental world, while the material world is left in possession of the others. But howsoever much the forms of the contrast may vary, the fact of contrast is universal. (pp. 52–54)

These words express the most strictly sociological theory of all those that have been advanced regarding the concept of the sacred and the profane. Durkheim argues that it is society that continuously creates sacred things. The things in which it chooses to discover its principal aspirations, by which it is moved, and the means employed to satisfy such aspirations—these it sets apart and deifies, be they men, objects, or ideas. If an idea is unanimously shared by a people, it cannot be negated or disputed. This very prohibition proves that one stands in the presence of something sacred. With prohibitions of this kind, cast in the form of negative rites, man rids himself of certain things that thereby become profane, and approaches the sacred. By means of ritual deprivations such as fasts, wakes, seclusion, and silence, one attains the same results as those brought about through anointings, propitiatory sacrifice, and consecrations. The moment the sacred detaches itself from the profane in this way, religion is born. The most primitive system of sacred things is totemism. But the totem is not the only thing that is sacred; all things that are classified in the clan have the same quality, inasmuch as they belong to the same type. The classifications that link them to other things in the universe allot them their place in the religious system. The idea of class is construed by men themselves as an instrument of thought; for again it was society that furnished the basic pattern logical thought has employed. Nonetheless, totemism is not merely some crude, mistaken prereligious science, as James G. Frazer supposed; for the basic distinction that is of supreme importance is that between sacred and profane, and it is accomplished with the aid of the totem, which is a collective symbol of a religious nature, as well as a sacred thing in itself. Nor does a thing become sacred by virtue of its links through classification to the universe; a world of profane things is still profane even though it is spatially and temporally infinite. A thing becomes sacred when humans remove it from ordinary use; the negative cult in which this happens leads to taboo. A man becomes sacred through initiation. Certain foodstuffs can be forbidden to the person who is still profane because they are sacred, and others can be forbidden to the holy man because they are profane. Violation of such taboos amounts to desecration, or profanation, of the foodstuffs in the one case, of the person in the other, and profanation of this kind can result in sickness and death. In the holy ones—that is to say, both the creatures of the totem species and the members of the clan—a society venerates itself.

The meaning of* sacred *and* profane *in the context of subjective religious action. Max Weber states in *Wirtschaft und Gesellschaft* (Tübingen, 1922) that the focus for sociology is the "meaning context" of an act. In order to interpret an act with understanding, the sociologist

> has to view [social] structures as simply the consequences and connections of specific action on the part of *individual* persons, since for us these are the only representatives of meaningful action we can comprehend. . . . Interpretation of any action has to take notice of the fundamentally important fact that [the] collective structures . . . belonging to everyday thought are *conceptions* of something in part existing, in part desired to be true in the minds of actual persons . . . conceptions on which they *base* their actions; and that as such they have a most powerful, often virtually dominating causal significance for the manner in which actual persons conduct themselves. (pp. 6–7)

The same also applies to religiously (or magically) motivated communal action, which can only be comprehended from the point of view of the subjective experiences, conceptions, and goals of the individual, that is, from the point of view of its meaning. According to Weber, such action is at bottom oriented to the here and now. It gradually attains a wealth of meanings, ultimately even symbolic ones. Trial and adherence to what has been tried are of particular importance, since deviation can render an action ineffective. For this reason, religions are more tolerant of opposing dogmatic concepts than they are of innovations in their symbolism, which could endanger the magical effect of their actions or rouse the anger of the ancestral soul or the god. Hence we encounter in all cultures religious stereotyping, in rites, in art, in gestures, dance, music, and writing, in exorcism and medicine. The sacred thus becomes specifically what is unchangeable. By virtue of it, religious concepts also tend to force stereotypes upon behavior and economics. Any actions intended to introduce change have to be correspondingly binding. The ones most likely to fulfill this requirement are specific contracts. The Roman civil marriage in the form of *coemtio* was, for example, a profanation of the sacramental *confarreatio*.

Anthropological Methods. At times man reveals himself in situations that appear to be of a different quality than ordinary ones. The latter form the basis for comparison either as the sum of his normal behavior or as a social cross section. For the moment, comparisons demonstrating the specific differences between a possibly sacred condition and a profane one, or showing social appraisal of a specific human type as sacred in contrast to the profane average person, are best relegated to categories of a historical anthropology, for as yet no historical psychology exists that might penetrate still further. A culture may choose to identify any number of unusual individual conditions or situations as sacred or profane. The most important of these warrant closer examination.

Ecstasy and trance. Even in terms of ethology, one could probably establish a similarity between men and animals in the way they concentrate on an opponent, holding their breath in silence and maintaining a tense calm from which they can instantly switch into motion. Presumably this has its roots in the moment when the first hunter found himself confronting his prey. As far as humans are concerned, the perpetuation and further development of this primeval behavior is a history of self-interpretations that presuppose continuously changing social contexts. This was probably first apparent in shamanism, and continues to be so wherever it persists. Contributing to the Greek concept of *ekstasis* was the idea that man is capable of "standing outside himself." Specifically, from the fifth century BCE on, it was believed that one could physically step out of one's normal state; and from the first century BCE, that one's essential being, the soul, the self or perceiving organ, could take leave of the body. The notion of ecstasy is found throughout the history of the human psyche and human culture. It may seize a person for no apparent reason or be induced through meditation, autohypnosis, fasting, drugs, fixing the eyes on specific objects, or extended ritual repetition of certain words or motions. Ecstasy is not necessarily sacred; it can also be profane, though quite often specific manifestations, such as intoxication, glossolalia, receptivity to visions and voices, hyperesthesia, anesthesia, or paresthesia, are identical. In technologically poor cultures, profane ecstasies may accompany initiations, rites of passage, and preparation for war, or may be reactions to specific defeats or social setbacks. Examples of profane ecstasies in literary cultures are those of the Corybantes and Maenads of Greece, of the dancers and flagellants who appeared in the wake of the Black Death in the fourteenth century, of Shakers and Quakers, of individual psychopaths, and of social outcasts. Ecstasy is only sacred in the context of historical religion and is never the primal germ of any religion. Nevertheless, ecstasy can be experienced within a religion as the basic source of its particular variety of mysticism.

It then passes over into trance, of which possession has already been recognized as the hyperkinetic primal form. When the being by which one is possessed, or—to put it more mildly—inspired, is held to be a god who has replaced the extinguished consciousness, classical Greek already spoke of *enthousiasmos*. By definition, such possession is sacred. Profane trances, on the other hand, are those accompanied by visions of distant events, or past or future ones.

Sexuality and asceticism. Sex, especially female sexuality, is considered sacred. It stands as the positive condition contrary to both infertility and asexuality. If a woman was infertile, it probably meant above all that she was malnourished, and starvation is always profane when not undertaken in deliberate fasts as a means of conquering the physical self. (The sacredness of the mother must certainly have been enhanced when, in the Neolithic period, agriculture was first developed—a new science made possible by Mother Earth.)

Sexuality, especially active sex, is also held to be the contrary of asexuality, the profane sign either of the normal condition of both sexes as the result of danger, cold, or constant labor, or of the lesser capacity for frequent orgasm on the part of the male.

The importance in archaic societies of dominant goddesses, especially mother goddesses, is solely dependent on the sacredness of their sexuality and is not a result of their given character as either the otherworldly representatives of matriarchal societies or the polar referents in patriarchal ones. From the role of a great goddess alone it is impossible to draw any conclusions about a given social order. Such goddesses are frequently of a dual nature, both helpful and cruel, both givers and destroyers of life, and this ambiguity is altogether a part of their sacredness.

Asceticism is not the profanation of sexuality but rather a transcendence over man's normal condition into a perfection that lies in the opposite direction. The ascetic practices self-denial with regard to all aspects of life, including eating and drinking. In suppressing his sexuality, he is to a certain extent both acknowledging its sacred dimension and claiming that sacredness for himself.

Innocence and wisdom. Since Vergil's fourth *Eclogue,* perhaps since the prophecies of Isaiah, or even earlier, the innocence of the messianic child has been seen as sacred. Mere babbling childishness, on the other hand, is profane. Yet one can hardly conclude from the innocence of the messianic child how sinful or jaded the society that hopes for him actually considers itself.

Wisdom can be the sacredness of old age, as in the case of the Hindu guru, the mystagogue of late antiquity, or the *tsaddiq* in Jewish Hasidism, who only after long experience is able, through his own example, to help his fellow men find communion with God. Feebleness on the part of the elderly is widely considered to be profane, and when it poses a burden on the young they tend to segregate themselves from it socially. In extreme cases the old are sent off into the wilderness, as in some cultures of ancient India, or are left behind in an abandoned campsite, a practice of some nomadic peoples. The aged exile only avoids being profane by seeking his own salvation, and that of the others, through a curse, rather than through wisdom.

Charismatic and magical gifts. The relationship between these is complex, especially since subsequent explanation of a magical or miraculous act frequently shifts the accent or undertakes to reevaluate it, and since modern interpretation is bound to suspect an element of trickery in the majority of miracles.

A miracle worker was often thought of as a sacred person, as were Origen's pupil Gregory Theodoros of Sykeon and others who were given the epithet *Thaumaturgus.* But not all of the figures canonized as saints by the Catholic church, for example, were miracle workers—unless, of course, one considers it miraculous that anyone could have fulfilled absolutely the commandment to love God, his neighbor, and his enemy. Conversely, it is also possible for a miracle worker *not* to be recognized as a saint or be held to have been so according to religious scholarship—as were Jean-Baptiste-Marie Vianney and Giovanni Melchior Bosco—and still not count as a charlatan like Cagliostro or Rasputin (who were, in fact, probably neither totally profane nor demonic). Here profaneness is easier to define: that person is profane who is simply incapable of controlling sicknesses, natural forces, or his own feelings of animosity. We also hear of "false prophets," as, for example, in ancient Israel or in Lucian's satire on the pseudoprophet Alexander—though we cannot know whether these were simply instances of certain holy men winning out over others. In late antiquity it was possible for charismatic persons to rise to "sainthood," for better or for worse, by taking over the control of cities or towns in which the elected administration or leading landholders had been rendered powerless by social or religious upheavals (see Brown, 1982). Similarly, magic can be either sacred or profane, as we can see if we examine it from the perspective of history.

Sacred and Profane in History

Related to the anthropological approach is the historical. In terms of history, qualities of objects, modes of conduct, events, relationships, and persons in part define themselves as sacred or profane, and insofar as they do we may either accept them or criticize them. In part, however, it is up to us to establish and define them. In either case it is quite possible that the sacred is truly metaphysical, eternal, and transhistorical and manifests itself only fragmentarily and partially in a continuing succession of historical objects. It is equally possible in either case that the sacred is constantly forming itself anew out of certain symbol-making forces inherent in the historical processes, by transcending even the objectifications of such forces.

In the history of religions there are numerous examples of belated creation of the sacred out of the profane. The sacred may initially have been only a catch-all concept for specific desires and may have later become genuine; or it may have come into being by means of true consecration, or sanctification, in both senses of the term, as I have identified them. One thinks, for example, of the sanctification of actions that were originally only ethical, of the evolution of the gift (Marcel Mauss's term) into the offering, of the emergence of gods from men by way of the intermediate stage of the hero, and so forth.

Related to this is the problem of whether we are to view the sacred and profane as having come into being simultaneously, or one before the other. All three possible theories have been advanced. Unfortunately, however, the findings of religious phenomenology and the history of religions permit no sure pronouncements about the very earliest religious manifestations. Even the basic assumption that religion came into being along with the appearance of man, though most likely correct, provides us with no solution to the problem of priority. For even if one makes such an assumption, one still cannot know whether religion once encompassed the whole of life, or whether there was not from the very beginning a profane worldview alongside the religious one, with its knowledge of the sacred.

Origins. The sacred may be an integral part of religion, but when studying its history it is necessary to treat it as quite independent. According to one possible view, the sacred and the profane came into being simultaneously. Another theory has it that the sacred was a later elevation of the profane. Still a third presupposes a kind of primal pansacrality, claiming that the sacred was once a totality that encompassed or unified the entire world. Even the magical was not yet detached from it. And the profane, whether magical or not, only gradually developed through a kind of primal secularization.

The primal polarity and homogeneity of the sacred and profane. For this thesis one can point to caves and grottoes from the middle Paleolithic (the Drachenloch and the Wildenmannlisloch in the Swiss canton of Saint Gall; Petershöhle in Middle Franconia, in Germany), others from the late Paleolithic (Altamira, Lascaux, Trois Frères, Rouffignac), and numerous Neolithic ones. Their special nature fulfills only the two criteria for holiness: *(a)* spatial detachment from the settings of everyday life and *(b)* unusualness; but these are sufficient to justify calling them sanctuaries. These caves are difficult to reach, they are located either at a great height or far below the surface, access to them is either narrow or hard to find, and they are too low or too dark for everyday activities. They contain artworks sequestered away from day-to-day viewing as well as deposits of bones and skulls that cannot be merely the remains of meals. These facts indicate that here, in addition to the profane area (namely, the sitting, sleeping, and eating space near the cave entrance), there was also a sacred room. The question of whether the deposits were offerings or not, and whether they were meant for a single god or several, remains unanswered. But it is virtually certain that the caves were used for sacred activities, in many cases for initiation rites. Entering them, one proceeded out of the *profanum* into the *sacrum.* It is not known what other relationships may have been maintained between these two, but it is clear that they did exist side by side. It is then altogether probable that each had come into being as distinct from the other, and that at no earlier date did the two occupy a single space that was predominantly only one or the other. [*For more on this, see* Sacred Space.]

The priority and homogeneity of the profane and subsequent appearance and heterogeneity of the sacred. This thesis accords with the one that supposes that there was once a time when mankind was as yet without religion. It is based primarily on ethnological theories, and in part also on psychoanalytical ones. It claims, with James G. Frazer, that magic as a prescientific science proved wanting, and man therefore had to seek refuge in religion.

In the formula of dogmatic Marxism, primeval man's social existence was so primitive that his consciousness was wholly absorbed with practical matters and was incapable of giving birth to religious abstractions. Only when magic became necessary to assist in the attainment of food through hunting and agriculture did religion evolve along with it, and its function was then further bolstered by the appearance of hierarchical social structures.

According to Wilhelm Wundt and others, the sacred had its origins in notions of impurity. Taboo, the instilling of a reluctance to touch, was common to both (and still continues to be so), whereas the everyday sphere is profane and pure. At some point this reluctance entered the religious sphere and split into awe in the presence of the sacred and loathing for the demonic; everything that was displeasing to the sacred deity was now held to be impure, that is, profane, and the sacred was pure. Gradually, the impure has come to function as the opposite of the sacred, and between the two lie the pure and the ordinary—now seen as profane, that is, as the realm of what is permissible. [*See* Purification.]

In Freud's view, the central taboo is the one against incest; it derives from the will of the primal father. After he has been killed, one's relationship to him becomes ambivalent and finds its synthesis in the idea of sacredness. The reason behind his murder is the primal father's castration of his sons, which is replaced symbolically by circumcision. It is the circumcision performed on the male progeny of Israel, for example, that represents the actual sanctification of that people.

René Girard argues that the sacred arose out of sacrifice, which, as the ultimate form of killing and bloodletting, brings to an end the chain of force and counterforce that constitutes the profane history of mankind. Since the ultimate use of force that cancels out everything can no longer be arbitrary, it comes to be circumscribed and restrained through rituals. Once the resultant sacred act is correctly identified as such and distinguished from profane action, the roles of the sacred and profane in society are truly segregated. If the sacred and the profane come to be indistinguishable, a sacrificial crisis ensues; this is at the same time a confusion of roles and brings on a social crisis. The force required to restore stability is applied both by individuals and by the collective: by individuals in the form of asceticism, self-discipline, and other actions against the self, through which they attain sacredness; and by the collective, through deflection onto a scapegoat, which protects society from the threat that groups within it will destroy each other. (See Girard, [1972] 1977.)

Some of these theses can point to changes that have actually occurred in the relationship between the sacred and profane through the course of history, and even Freud's theory, though otherwise impossible, contains an element of truth in the fact that the exercise of religion can actually become a compulsive act. Girard's thesis is doubtless the most realistic in its incorporation of the nature of man, and the nature of his socialization, within the primary constitution of sacrifice (to the extent to which the latter exists at all). But none of this is of any use toward a valid reconstruction of prehistory.

The priority and homogeneity of the sacred and heterogeneity of the profane. All of the things that we now distinguish as religion, magic, and science; as religious worship, sorcery, and medicine; as prophecy, law-giving, and ethics; and as priests, kings, and shamans were once united in a sacral unity. Such is the widespread, fundamental view derived from the thesis of a primal monotheism, as propounded by thinkers from Andrew Lang to Wilhelm Schmidt; derived, too, from the theologoumena of a primal revelation advanced by Johann Tobias Beck and Adolf Schlatter, the elements of E. B. Tylor's animism theory, the *mana-orenda* identification from the period between R. H. Codrington and Gerardus van der Leeuw, and the preanimism or dynamism theory promulgated from R. R. Marett to Konrad T. Preuss. One can say that the profane becoming independent is the result of a process of differentiation out of primal sacrality only if one ignores the synonymity between the very definition of the sacred and the naming of the phenomena on which these theories are based. [*For more on this, see* Secularization.]

Temporal Existence. Since it is impossible to verify any theory of origins or development, it is advisable to do without one altogether, and to adopt the approach of Mircea Eliade, who for historical consideration sees the sacred as an element in the structure of consciousness, rather than as a stage in the history of its development. Regardless of the similarity of religious phenomena throughout cultures, it is the cultural-historical context that at the same time lends an immeasurable novelty to their various manifestations. As for the phenomena of the sacred and the profane, the following temporal aspects are of fundamental importance.

Unchangeableness. The sacred is absolutely unchangeable only if one has extrahistorical reasons for treating it as a metaphysical, eternal, or transhistorical reality. As understood by Max Weber, it is not unchangeable. On the historical plane, unchangeableness and constancy are evident to the degree that in everything that the religious phenomenologies identify as sacred—persons, communities, actions, writings, manifestations of nature, manufactured objects, periods, places, numbers, and formulas—not only are situations, motive, and conditions expressed, but an ancient type remains operative, or makes a reappearance. Once delineated, such types can reappear at any moment, and they persist through great periods of time. Notwithstanding, genuine changes also take place.

Metamorphoses. These appear as either transcendence over the profane or secularization—now no longer considered primary, as it was above—of the sacred. The former occurs in initiations, sacraments, and baptisms, in the use of stones for shrines or of animals as offerings, in the blessing of an object, an act, or a person. The latter is evident on a large scale in world-historical processes. On a small scale it is present whenever a sacred function is simulated, when a myth is transformed from the fact that it *is* into a reporting of facts, when a sacred text is read for entertainment, or whenever someone's behavior swerves from his vows to God, without his actually sinning. The ultimate form of secularization is the destruction of the sacred while the profane continues to exist; the greatest possible transcendence is the restitution of the sacred together with a fundamental skepticism regarding the profane.

Destruction. The destruction of religion is not the same thing as the destruction of the sacred. The destruction of a religion occurs most clearly when it is confined to institutions, as these can simply be abolished. It is less apparent when a religion ceases to have its original function, but this too can finally be ascertained. The sacred, on the other hand, increasingly tends, in industrial society, to be transformed from the active element it once was into a kind of unexpressed potentiality. It then decays in social intercourse and such intercourse becomes wholly profane. Nevertheless, its archetype persists in the human spirit, and is always capable of restoring the religious feeling to consciousness, if conditions are favorable.

Just what sort of conditions these have to be, no one can say. It may be that they are altogether unfavorable when a civil religion is established of the type envisioned by Jean-Jacques Rousseau at the end of his *Social Contract;* it may also be that they are indeed favorable when no organized religion continues to play any role.

Restoration. It is possible to try to secure once more the place for the sacred in society that it lost thanks to the disappearance of the distinction between it and the profane that once existed. This is what motivates the scholarship of the Collège de Sociologie. Every community that is intact and wishes to remain so requires a notion of the sacred as *a priori.* Archaic societies that provided sufficient room for the sacred kept it socially viable in secret fraternities or through magicians or shamans. Modern societies can achieve the same by means of public events such as festivals, which generate social strength, or by the establishment of monastic, elitist orders, or the creation of new centers of authority.

Determining the Relationships

The relationships between the sacred and the profane occur both on the level of their expression in language and on a (or *the*) level of existence that is characterized by various different ontological qualities. The relationships between these two levels themselves are of a more fundamental nature. Since only the *homo religiosus* is capable of bearing witness to the manner of such existence, and not the scholar, we can speak of it only in formal categories that reveal both the conditions of our possible perception of the sacred and the transcendental prerequisites of its mode of being.

The Epistemological Approach. Non-Kantian religious thinkers and scholars have always restricted themselves to their inner experience. What they have found there could easily be rediscovered in history. The experiential method, which tends toward psychology, was therefore always superbly compatible with the historical-genetic method. On the other hand, it is also possible to apply a logical, analytical, transcendental method, and in fact this can be used in investigating the possibilities of both inner experience and historical perception. Heretofore, discussion of these alternatives has been most productive toward determining the position of the philosophy of religion, and therefore religion itself, within the overall scheme of culture and scholarship. At the same time, it has tended to curtail any elucidation of the religious phenomenon in general and the phenomenon of the sacred and its relation to the profane in particular. Perhaps one could take it further.

A priori and a posteriori. In his book *Kantisch-Fries'sche Religionsphilosophie und ihre Anwendung auf die Theologie* (Tübingen, 1909), Rudolf Otto took a rational approach to the *a priori* concept and applied it to the idea of God. God is not an object alongside or superior to other objects, and he cannot be placed in one of the various standard relationships. He is able to transcend space and time as well as every particular relationship. Accordingly, it must be possible to imagine the sacred as standing in a transcendental primal relationship to things. One way or the other, the *a priori* concept is rational.

Rationality and irrationality. When writing *Das Heilige* (1917), Otto abandoned his transcendental philosophical position. He did not give up the *a priori* concept, however, but rather reinterpreted it with a psychological slant. In this way, the transcendentality of the rational applied to the *a priori* concept becomes the capacity of thought to be rational. This capacity can then be opposed to the irrational. The rational concepts of absoluteness, necessity, and essential quality, as well as the idea of the good, which expresses an objective and binding value, have to be traced back to whatever lies in pure reason, independent of experience, whereas the irrational element of the sacred must be traced back to the pure ideas of the divine or the numinous. Here, from the point of view of irrationality, "pure" becomes the attribute of something psychically given, and the *a priori* becomes emotional.

On the other hand, as Anders Nygren argues, just as one questions the validity of perception, using the *a priori* of cognition theory, it becomes necessary to question the validity of religion, using the religious *a priori* concept. Further, Nygren and Friedrich Karl Feigel suggest, it becomes necessary to comprehend the sacred as a complex category *a priori*, not so as to be able to experience it in itself, but rather so as to identify the sacred in experience and cognition, even in the course of history.

The Ontological Approach. Links exist not only between the sacred and the profane, each of which has its own complexity, but also between the sacred and the demonic, the profane and the evil, the profane and the demonic, and the sacred and the evil. The first and second links have ontological implications, the third and fourth have ethical ones, and the fifth has both. We obscure the demonic aspect when we ask the question whether we can have an ethic that can deal with the awesome potential powers at modern man's disposal without restoring the category of the sacred, which was thoroughly destroyed by the Enlightenment. In Hans Jonas's view, these powers continue to accumulate in secret and impel humankind to use them, and only respectful awe in the face of the sacred can transcend our calculations of earthly terror. But it is not the task of this article to enter into a discussion of ethical implications; we must be content to consider the ontological ones.

Ambivalence. Otto described the positive aspect of the sacred by using the numinous factor *fascinans* and various subordinate factors of the numinous factor *tremendum.* He characterized its negative aspect by way of a subordinate factor of the latter that he called "the awesome." [*See* Holy, Idea of the.] In so doing he provided countless studies with the suggestion of an ambivalence that truly exists and is not to be confused with the dialectic of the hierophanies. However, Otto was referring primarily to the essence of the sacred in itself. Such an approach is logically possible only if one begins consistently and exclusively from "above." Since Otto declares both aspects to be factors of the same numinousness, his methodological starting point becomes, *de facto,* if not intentionally, Judeo-Christian theocentricity. This is certainly extremely productive, but it also exhibits one of the limits of scholarly study of religion: namely its continual orientation, only seeming to overcome the theological *a priori,* at the starting point of historical scholarship, namely recognition of the ambivalence in the ancient Roman notion of the *sacrum.*

Dialectics. Eliade has concentrated the links between the complexes of the sacred and the profane on the plane of appearances, introducing the inspired concept of hierophany. A hierophany exposes the sacred in the profane. [*See* Hierophany.] Since there are numerous hierophanies (though the same ones do not always appear everywhere), he sets up a dialectic of hierophanies to explain why an object or an occurrence may be sacred at one moment but not at another. [*See also* Sacred Time.] Such an approach makes it possible to examine every historical datum and identify it as sacred or profane—and in so doing to write a new history of religions within profane history. In addition, one can draw conclusions about the objectivity of the sacred, which is satiated with being and therefore has the power, functioning through the hierophanies (including even their profane element), to become apparent. Eliade does both. The former demonstrates a historical phenomenology, and points toward an as yet unrealized historical psychology of religion. The latter is subject to the same criticism as the ontological proof of God.

Ideogrammatics and Hermeneutics

The sacred remains closely bound to the modalities of its names. One cannot do without the testimony revealed in language, but one must not restrict the sacred to the terms language provides. In addition to such testimony, one has to discover the sacred in experience. The sum of linguistic testimony and descriptions of such experience can serve both as a check on each other and as mutual confirmation.

Deciphering the Sacred. Using this approach, one can only speak of the sacred ideogrammatically. Classical phenomenology of religion is content to present the sacred as revealed in so-called phenomena that corroborate each other within a larger context. However, this kind of evidence obscures the ambivalence that permits one to experience a sacred phenomenon simultaneously with a profane one. Therefore, one can only understand the phenomenon of the sacred, whether evidenced with the aid of language or writing or not, as something like the Greek *idea,* and accordingly regard the forms of the sacred accessible to description and investigation as its ideograms. However, these can also be understood as "tautograms," that is, as designations that withhold immanence, but at the same time one cannot call them profane merely because they lack the connotation of transcendence into the sacred. Otto's book on the holy was already in large part an ideogrammatics of the sacred.

Understanding the Sacred. At the heart of the findings from the study of synonyms that have given us reasons for speaking of both the sacred and the profane in the singular are certain basic attributes, such as separateness, power, intensity, remoteness, and otherness. Cognition theory has less difficulty identifying the sacred when it examines larger systems, within which such fundamental attributes are mutually complementary. In doing so, one can not only recognize the ideograms of the sacred in texts but also treat the sacred as though it were explained. Eliade's work represents just such a hermeneutics of the sacred as distinguished from the profane.

BIBLIOGRAPHY

The most influential modern book on the subject is Rudolf Otto's *Das Heilige* (Breslau, 1917; often reprinted), translated by John W. Harvey as *The Idea of the Holy* (Oxford, 1923). The most important earlier contributions (Wilhelm Windelband, Wilhelm Wundt, Nathan Söderblom), subsequent ones (Joseph Geyser, Friedrich Karl Feigel, Walter Baetke, et al.), and various specific philological studies are collected in *Die Diskussion um das Heilige,* edited by Carsten Colpe (Darmstadt, 1977). A new epoch began with the work of Mircea Eliade, and one could cite a great number of monographs by him. As the most relevant, one might single out his *Traité d'histoire des religions* (Paris, 1949), translated by Rosemary Sheed as *Patterns in Comparative Religion* (New York, 1958), and *Das Heilige und das Profane* (Hamburg, 1957), translated by Willard R. Trask as *The Sacred and the Profane* (New York, 1959).

Hans Joachim Greschat has provided a new study of the classical late nineteenth-century theme in his *Mana und Tapu* (Berlin, 1980). Examples from an African people are provided by Peter Fuchs in *Kult und Autorität: Die Religion der Hadjerai* (Berlin, 1970) and by Jeanne-Françoise Vincent in *Le pouvoir et le sacré chez les Hadjeray du Tchad* (Paris, 1975). Exemplary philological investigation of linguistic usage and concepts among the Greeks, Romans, Jews, and early Christians is found in the article "Heilig" by Albrecht Dihle in the *Reallexikon für Antike und Christentum,* vol. 13 (Stuttgart, 1987); similar study of late antiquity appears in Peter Brown's *Society and the Holy in Late Antiquity* (London, 1982). The same subject matter, expanded to include the ancient Orient and India, is found in the important work edited by Julien Ries et al., *L'expression du sacré dans les grandes religions,* 3 vols., (Louvain, 1978-1986), for which there is a separate introduction by Julien Ries, *Le sacré comme approche de Dieu et comme ressource de l'homme* (Louvain, 1983). Supplementing this with respect to Egypt is James Karl Hoffmeier's *"Sacred" in the Vocabulary of Ancient Egypt: The Term ḎSR, with Special Reference to Dynasties I–XX* (Freiburg, 1985).

Theoretical implications are investigated by Ansgar Paus in *Religiöser Erkenntnisgrund: Herkunft und Wesen der Apriori-Theorie Rudolf Ottos* (Leiden, 1966) and by Georg Schmid in *Interessant und Heilig: Auf dem Wege zur integralen Religionswissenschaft* (Zurich, 1971). Important sociological investigation of ritual is found in Jean Cazeneuve's *Sociologie du rite* (Paris, 1971) and of the history of force, counterforce, and sacrifice in René Girard's *La violence et le sacré* (Paris, 1972), translated by Patrick Gregory as *Violence and the Sacred* (Baltimore, 1977). Additional ethical implications are considered by Bernhard Häring in *Das Heilige und das Gute, Religion und Sittlichkeit in ihrem gegenseitigen Bezug* (Krailling vor München, 1950). On the disappearance of the sacred through secularization and its reappearance in times of crisis, see Enrico Castelli's *Il tempo inqualificabile: Contributi all'ermeneutica della secolarizzazione* (Padua, 1975) and Franco Ferrarotti and others' *Forme del sacro in un'epoca di crisi* (Naples, 1978). Summaries from various points of view include Roger Caillois's *L'homme et le sacré* (1939; 3d ed., Paris, 1963), translated by Meyer Barash as *Man and the Sacred* (Glencoe, Ill., 1959); Jacques Grand'Maison's *Le monde et le sacré*, 2 vols. (Paris, 1966–1968); and Enrico Castelli and others' *Il sacro* (Padua, 1974).

CARSTEN COLPE
Translated from German by Russell M. Stockman

SACRED SPACE. A sacred place is first of all a defined place, a space distinguished from other spaces. The rituals that a people either practice at a place or direct toward it mark its sacredness and differentiate it from other defined spaces. To understand the character of such places, Jonathan Z. Smith has suggested the helpful metaphor of sacred space as a "focusing lens." A sacred place focuses attention on the forms, objects, and actions in it and reveals them as bearers of religious meaning. These symbols describe the fundamental constituents of reality as a religious community perceives them, defines a life in accordance with that view, and provides a means of access between the human world and divine realities.

As meaningful space, sacred space encompasses a wide variety of very different kinds of places. [*See also* Geography.] It includes places that are constructed for religious purposes, such as temples or *temenoi*, and places that are religiously interpreted, such as mountains or rivers. It includes spaces that can be entered physically, as the outer geography of a holy land, imaginatively, as the inner geography of the body in Tantric yoga, or visually, as the space of a *maṇḍala*. Sacred space does not even exclude nonsacred space, for the same place may be both sacred and nonsacred in different respects or circumstances. In traditional Maori culture, for example, the latrine marks the boundary between the world of the living and that of the dead. As such, it is the ritual place at which an unwanted spirit can be expelled or the help of the spirits obtained. Therefore, it is sacred. And it is still a latrine. Similarly, a house is a functional space, but in its construction, its design, or the rites within it, it may be endowed with religious meaning. A shrine that is the focus of religious activity on certain occasions may be ignored at other times. In short, a sacred place comes into being when it is interpreted as a sacred place.

This view of sacred space as a lens for meaning implies that places are sacred because they perform a religious function, not because they have peculiar physical or aesthetic qualities. The tradition articulated by Friedrich Schleiermacher and developed by Rudolf Otto links the perception of holiness to religious emotion. Originally or authentically, therefore, sacred places ought to have had the power to evoke an affective response. And many sacred places do precisely that: the sacred mountains of China, the Gothic cathedrals of Europe, and the sources and the estuaries of India's holy rivers have a beauty and a power that are elements of their religious dimension. But such qualities of place are not inevitable. Many sacred places, even places that are central in the religious life of the community, are unimpressive to someone outside the tradition. The form of the place, without a knowledge of what and how it signifies, may not convey any religious sense whatever. Ṛddhipur, for example, is the principal pilgrimage place of the Mahānubhāvs, a Kṛṣṇaite Maharashtrian sect. It is the place where God lived in the incarnate form of Guṇḍam Rāül, where he deposited divine power, and where he performed acts that revealed his divine nature. It is the place visited by another divine incarnation, Cakradhar, who founded the Mahānubhāv community. But Ṛddhipur itself is completely unexceptional, and the places where Guṇḍam Rāül performed his deeds are indicated only by small stone markers. There is nothing there that gives rise to a sense of awe or mystery, and yet the village is revered and protected by religious restrictions. The place is not aesthetically profound, but it is nonetheless religiously powerful.

Establishment of Sacred Space. Both the distinctiveness of sacred space and its reference to the ultimate context of a culture are often expressed in the conviction that sacred space is not arbitrary. Objectively, and not only subjectively, a sacred place is different from the surrounding area, for it is not a place of wholly human creation or choice. Rather, its significance is grounded in its unique character, a character that no purely human action can confer on it.

In traditional societies, the whole land of a culture is normally sacred, and this sacredness is often communicated in the narratives of its foundation. Sometimes the land is uniquely created. The *Kojiki* and *Nihongi* record the traditions of the age of the *kami* when Japan and its way of life were established. According to these texts, the divine pair, Izanagi and Izanami, looked down upon the waters of the yet unformed earth and dipped a jeweled spear into the ocean. From the brine that dripped from the spear the first island of Japan was formed. The divine couple later gave birth to other deities, among them the sun goddess, Amaterasu, whose descendants rule over Japan. Thus, Japan is different from all other places: it is the first land, and the land whose way of life is established by the gods. Or a land may become sacred because it is given by a god, like the land of Israel. Or again, a land may be established by ritual. According to an early Indian tradition in the *Śatapatha Brāhmaṇa,* the land lying to the east of the Sadānīrā River was unfit for habitation by brahmans. It became fit when the sacrificial fire was carried across the river and established in the land.

Similarly, a sacred structure or place within a holy land possesses something—a character, a significance, or an object—that sets it apart. The traditions of the greater Hindu temples and pilgrimage places declare that they are intrinsically, not ascriptively, sacred. The holiest images of the Śaiva tradition are the *svayambhū-liṅga*s, images of Śiva that are not human creations but self-manifestations of the god. Similarly, the holiest places of the goddess are the *pīṭha*s, the places where the parts of her body fell after her suicide and dismemberment. In other cases, not an object but the very ground itself fixes the worship of a divinity to a particular spot. According to the traditions of the temple at Śrīraṅgam, the shrine originated in heaven. From there it was brought to earth, to the city of Rāma. Rāma then gave it to a pious demon, who wished to take it with him to his home in Sri Lanka. On the way, however, he put it down near a ford on the Kāverī (Cauvery) River, and when he tried to pick it up again he could not move it. The god of the temple then appeared to him and told him that the river had performed austerities to keep the shrine within her bounds and that the god intended to stay there (Shulman, 1980, p. 49). The current location of the temple is therefore where the god, not any demon or human, chose it to be.

The gods may also communicate the special sanctity of a place through signs. Animals often serve as messengers of divine choice. So, for example, the Aztec city of Tenochtitlán was founded at the place where an eagle landed on a blooming cactus, and Aeneas followed a pregnant sow to the place where it farrowed and there founded Alba Longa. The search for such signs could develop into a science of divination. Chinese geomancy is just such an attempt to sort out the objective qualities of a place by studying the contours of the land and the balance of waters, winds, and other elements. [*See* Geomancy.]

In other cases, a location becomes holy because of religiously significant events that have occurred there. From the time of Muḥammad, Jerusalem has been a holy place for Islam. Although various traditions were attached to the city, it was above all the Prophet's journey there that established its sanctity. One night Muḥammad was brought to Jerusalem and to the rock on the Temple mount, and from there he ascended through the heavens to the very presence of God. The mosque of the Dome of the Rock and the establishment of Jerusalem as a place of pilgrimage both expressed and intensified the sanctity of the city. That sanctity was heightened by the discovery of tokens of Muḥammad's journey: his footprints on the rock, the imprint made by his saddle, and even the place where the angel Gabriel flattened the rock before the Prophet's ascent. And it was further intensified by bringing other religiously significant events into connection with it. The stories of Abraham and Isaac, of Melchizedek, king of Salem, and of Jacob's ladder were among the other biblical and nonbiblical narratives set there. As this example illustrates, a sacred place can draw a variety of traditions to itself and thereby become even more powerfully sacred.

Places may also be made sacred through the relics of holy beings. [*See* Relics.] A grave may sanctify a place, for the tomb marks not only the separation of the living from the dead but also the point of contact between them. In early Christianity, for example, tombs of martyrs became places of communion with the holiness of the deceased. Later, beginning about the sixth century, the deposition of relics became the center of rites for the consecration of a church. These sanctified the church and, within the church, the sanctuary where they were installed.

Finally, the form of a place may give it meaning and holiness. In different cultures, various kinds of places suggest the presence of deities. As we have seen, the land of Japan is holy because it is created and protected by the *kami.* Within Japan there are particular places where the *kami* are manifestly present: mountains, from Mount Fuji to the hills of local shrines, for example, may be tokens of the presence of the *kami.* In India, rivers and confluences are sacred, for purifying waters and meeting streams suggest places where gods are present and approachable. In these cases, the shape of the land suggests meanings to which the sacredness of the place draws attention.

At the beginning of this section, I stated that sacred

places are typically not arbitrary. But there are places of religious activity that are meaningful precisely because they are arbitrary. If the tendency to institute sacred places is universal, so also is the tendency to deny the localization of divinity. The Indian devotional tradition, like other religious traditions, is pulled in two directions: one toward divinities located in specific places, the other toward the denial that divinity should be sought in any place other than within. "Why bow and bow in the mosque, and trudge to Mecca to see God? Does Khuda live in the mosque? Is Ram in idols and holy ground?" asks Kabīr (Hess and Singh, 1983, p. 74).

Mosque architecture shows the tension between the sanctification of a place and the denial of any localization of divine presence. The mosque carries values typical of other sacred places. The interior is oriented toward a holy center: the *miḥrāb* (prayer niche) directs worship toward the sacred city of Mecca. The space of the mosque is differentiated from other kinds of spaces: persons must leave their shoes at the entrance. Within the area of the mosque, the holiest area, the sanctuary *(ḥaram)*, is clearly marked from the courtyard *(ṣaḥn)*. Some mosques are pilgrimage places because they are burial sites of holy men or women who endow them with spiritual power. The most prominent of these is the mosque at Medina built over the tomb of the Prophet.

At the same time, the architecture can be read quite differently as the meaningful negation of sacred space. The primary function of the mosque is to serve as a space for common prayer. It has significance in Islam because the community gathers and worships there, not because of the character of the place. "All the world is a *masjid*," a place of prayer, says one tradition (cf. Kuban, 1974, p. 1). In Islamic lands the mosque often does not stand out from secondary buildings or call attention to itself as a holy place. Even the dome, which typically surmounts it and which recalls the arch of heaven, has a generalized meaning of power or place of assembly and does not necessarily designate a sacred place. Neither is that symbolism of the sky pursued within the mosque, nor does it have liturgical significance. While the sanctuary is oriented toward Mecca, the remaining parts of the building do not have any inherent directional or axial structure. Even the *miḥrāb*, which might be a place of particular holiness, is kept empty, emphasizing that the deity worshiped is not to be located there or anywhere. All this accords with the Islamic view that while God is the creator of the world, he is above it, not within it. The mosque is sacred space according to our definition of sacred space as a place of ritual and a place of meaning. But it is expressive, meaningful space because it denies the typical values of sacred places. [*See also* Mosque, *article on* Architectural Aspects.]

Similar negations of localization occur in Protestant architecture, particularly in the Protestant "plain style." During the Reformation in Holland, for example, larger Gothic churches were not destroyed but were recreated into places of community prayer and preaching. Sculptural ornament was removed, clear glass was substituted for stained glass, the high altar was removed, and the chancel was filled with seats. In short, all the visible signs of the sacredness of a specific location were eliminated. The architecture made positive statements as well, but statements that again located sanctity elsewhere than in place. A high pulpit was centrally situated and became a focal point, but the pulpit was not itself a place of divine power or presence. Rather it pointed to the holiness of the word of God, which was read and preached there. Again, these churches are sacred places by being visible denials that the holiness of divinity is mediated through the symbolism of space. [*See also* Architecture.]

Functions of Sacred Space. The symbols that give a place meaning typically refer to the religious context in which a people lives. This section examines the ways in which sacred space acts to fix this context and to create interaction between the divine and human worlds. Three roles of sacred space are especially significant, for they are widely attested in religious systems and fundamental to their purposes. First, sacred space is a means of communication with the gods and about the gods. Second, it is a place of divine power. And third, it serves as a visible icon of the world and thereby imparts a form to it and an organization to its inhabitants.

Places of communication. First, sacred spaces are places of communication with divinity, places where people go to meet the gods. This function is often indicated by symbols that represent a link between the world of humans and transcendent realms. Such symbols might be vertical objects that reach from earth toward heaven, such as mountains, trees, ropes, pillars, and poles. North Indian temples, for example, connect the realm of heaven, symbolized by the *amṛtakalaśa* ("jar of the elixir of deathlessness") atop the temple, with the plane of earth. The spires of these temples are also architectural recapitulations of mountains, which are the dwelling places of the gods. The Kailāsa temple, for example, bears not only the name of the mountain on which Śiva dwells, but even its profile. But symbols that express the intersection of realms can be of other forms as well. In Byzantine churches, to walk from the entrance toward the altar is to move from the world of humans toward that of divinity. The doorway between these realms is the iconostasis, the screen between the chancel and sanctuary. As they pass through the doors of the iconostasis, priests become angels moving between realms. The icons themselves provide visual access to heaven. In general, "the iconostasis is not a 'symbol' or an 'object of devotion'; it is the gate through which this world is bound to the other" (Galavaris, 1981, p. 7).

Another way of joining gods and humans is through symbols of the gods. A sacred place may include images of the gods or other tokens that make their presence manifest. A Hindu temple is a place of meeting because it contains a form in which the god has graciously consented to dwell. The Ark of the Covenant in the Holy of Holies of the Temple in Jerusalem was the throne of Yahveh, a visible sign of his presence or of the presence of his name. Shintō shrines are dwelling places for the *kami,* whose material form is a sacred object called a "divine body" or "august-spirit substitute." It is housed within the innermost chamber of the shrine, kept from sight by doors or a bamboo curtain, but its presence invests the shrine with the presence of divinity. Similarly, a Japanese home becomes a sacred place when it has a *kamidana,* which enshrines symbols of the *kami,* and a *butsudan,* an altar that holds both Buddha images and ancestor tablets.

Even without explicit symbols of communication or tokens of the gods, a place may be understood as a point of contact between gods and humans. Islam strongly resists localization or visible symbols of divinity. Although the Ka'bah is the center toward which worship is directed, it does not house an image of God, nor is it the dwelling place of God. Nonetheless, Islamic interpretation occasionally characterizes it as a place of particular access to divinity. A medieval tradition describes the Black Stone embedded in the Ka'bah as God's right hand, "which he extends to his servants (who kiss it), as a man shakes hands with his neighbors," and a 1971 newspaper article urges: "When you touch the black stone and kiss it—you place your love and your yearnings in it and turn it into a mailbox from which your love is delivered to the creator of this world whom eyes cannot see" (Lazarus-Yafeh, 1981, pp. 120, 123). As these cases suggest, the deity is not exactly present, yet the Ka'bah does become the point of communication between God and humanity.

As a place of communication with divinity, a sacred space is typically a place of purity because purity enables people to come in contact with the gods. There, the imperfections and deficiencies, the "messiness" of normal life, are reduced. The sacred place reveals the ideal order of things, which is associated with the perfect realm of divinity, with life and vitality among humans, or with the values to which people should aspire. The Shintō shrine is a place of purity, for it is a place of the *kami* and it is a place that excludes pollution, for pollution is decay and death. The shrine's purity is expressed in the rites of approach to it. Traditionally, an open pavilion with a stone basin provides water for rinsing the hands and mouth, and three streams spanned by bridges lead to a shrine, so that worshipers purify themselves as they cross these streams. Its purity also is expressed in clarity of definition. *Torii* (Shintō gateways), fences, enclosed spaces, and bridges mark distinct areas and signal the approach to the deity. Other sacred places mark the movement from a zone of impurity to one of purity by defining an intermediate space for rites of purification. Some churches, synagogues, and mosques have such an area at the entrance to the principal space of the sacred precincts.

A sacred place can be a place of communication not only with divinity but also about divinity. For example, a central paradox of religion is that if divinity is everywhere, then it must be somewhere. Even if the whole world is "full of God's glory," that glory must be manifest in some place. This paradox is reflected in the Temple at Jerusalem, which contained the Ark of the Covenant, symbolizing the throne of Yahveh, but which enshrined no image of Yahveh. Similarly, in Deuteronomic theology, Yahveh has made his name but not his person to be present at the Temple. In their different ways, therefore, both the Temple and the text sought to mediate the paradox of the simultaneous localization and universality of Yahveh. Larger Hindu temples, on the other hand, normally have a variety of images of deities. Typically, worshipers will see other gods and goddesses or other forms of the central divinity of the shrine, or they will worship at shrines to other divinities in prepration for their approach to the central deity. A Hindu temple thus reflects Indian views of a divine hierarchy, which culminates in a particular divine being. Or, again, in Renaissance churches architectural balance and harmony reflect divine beauty and perfection. In all these instances, the form of the place expresses the nature of the deity worshiped there.

Places of divine power. Because it is a place of communication with divine beings, the sacred place is also a locus for divine power, which can transform human life. The nature of this transformation varies according to the religious tradition and reputation of the sacred space. According to a Hindu tradition, pilgrimage places provide *bhukti* ("benefit") and *mukti* ("salvation"). Typically, one benefit is healing. In medieval Christianity, for example, many pilgrimages were inspired by a desire to witness or to experience miraculous cures. Pilgrimage was so closely associated with healing, in fact, that a young man of Warbleton refused to go to Canterbury, "for I am neither dumb nor lame and my health is perfectly sound." Another person argued, "I am in excellent health. What need have I of St. Thomas?" (Sumption, 1972, p. 78). Lourdes remains a place of pilgrimage for millions seeking miraculous cures, though the Catholic church has certified few healings as true miracles. A place may even specialize in its cures. As the location of a manifestation of the god Śiva, the mountain Arunācala heals especially lung disease and barrenness, and two Ṣūfī shrines in the Punjab help leprosy and leukoderma (Bharati, 1963). The power of divinity encountered at sacred places may also secure more general goals of physical and material well-being. Success in business or in school, the birth of children, or simply the blessing of the deity may all be reasons to visit a sacred place.

Salvation can also be attained at sacred places. According to various Hindu traditions, to die at Banaras, to be cremated there, or to disperse the ashes of the dead in the Ganges at Banaras assures salvation for the deceased. Often salvation is directly related to the purity of a sacred place and its ability to purify those within it. An English reformer, Hugh Latimer, lamented that the sight of the blood of Christ at Hailes was convincing pilgrims that "they be in clean life and in state of salvation without spot of sin" (Sumption, 1972, p. 289). The sacred place as an access to divinity thus also becomes a way to the perfection of human life.

Places as icons of the world. Sacred space is often a visual metaphor for a religious world. The connection between the ordering of space and the ordering of human life is a natural one. A life without purpose or meaning is often expressed in spatial metaphors: it is to be "lost," "disoriented," and "without direction." Because they are defined spaces, sacred places are natural maps that provide direction to life and a shape to the world. They order space—often geographic space, always existential space—and by ordering space, they order all that exists within it. The Lakota sweat lodge provides a good example of the ordering of space in the image of a sacred place. The outer perimeter of the lodge is a circle. Its frame is created by bending twelve to sixteen young willows from one quadrant of the circle across to the opposite quadrant. According to Black Elk, "the willows are set up in such a way that they mark the four quarters of the universe; thus the whole lodge is the universe in an image, and the two-legged, four-legged, and winged peoples, and all the things of the world are contained in it." A round hole, which will hold heated rocks for making steam, is dug in the center of the lodge. This center "is the center of the universe, in which dwells Wakantanka [the Great Spirit], with his power which is the fire" (Brown, 1971, p. 32). The center belongs to Wakantanka, for he is the summation of all divine powers. The sweat lodge, therefore, encompasses physical space and draws the other realities of the Lakota world into its form. Its center becomes an ultimate point of reference in which space, all beings, and all powers finally converge.

Another spatial metaphor closely connected with sacred places is orientation. The sacred place focuses attention on a symbolically significant region by being itself turned, or turning those within it, toward that region. [*See* Orientation.] Sacred places show a variety of orientations and values of direction. First Coptic and Eastern churches, and later Western churches, were oriented toward the rising sun, which was the symbol of the resurrected Christ. Hindu temples face various directions for various reasons. For example, the temple of Taraknātha at Tarakeswar faces north. The head of the monastic community at the temple has explained that north is particularly auspicious, first, because it is the opposite of south, the direction of the world of the dead; second, because it is the direction of Mount Kailāsa, the home of Śiva; and third, because by beginning in the north, circumambulation of the inner shrine first proceeds east, the direction of the sun and of the light of knowledge (Morinis, 1984, p. 291). The abbot's explanations show the restless logic of sacred space, which finds significance in its every facet. In other traditions, the cardinal directions are not the basis for orientation: synagogues traditionally are oriented toward Jerusalem, and mosques toward Mecca. These places are similar not because they express similar systems of orientation but because they all make direction meaningful.

Sacred places also create actual and functional divisions of geographic space, divisions that are at the same time metaphors for different ways of life. In ordering the world, they may be not only centers on which the world converges but they may also mark boundaries between realms. These may include both boundaries between visible and invisible realities and geographic boundaries. The Maori latrine mentioned above formed the border between the world of humans and that of the dead, which was associated with excrement. But the world of the dead was also the world of the gods. A ritual of biting the latrine beam opened up communication across this boundary. Those who wished to expel an unfriendly spirit bit the beam to send the spirit back to its realm. Those who wished to obtain the help of the gods bit it in order to establish contact with the gods. The border formed by the latrine was thus open in both directions.

Boundaries created by sacred spaces can also define the limits of the visible world or create distinctive spaces within it. In a northern Thai tradition, for example, a series of twelve pilgrimage shrines created a system of nested spaces. Beginning from the innermost and smallest area, this system encompassed successively larger concentric areas and defined the successively broader communities to which the people at the center belonged (see figure 1). These communities were seen from the perspective of the Ping River valley, in which four of the twelve shrines were located. These four shrines and four other shrines associated with the major northern Thai principalities outside the Ping River valley defined the second community, that of the Lanna Thai people. The third community included all adherents of northern Thai and Lao Buddhism, which were perceived as closely related. This community was defined through the addition of a shrine in northeastern Thailand sacred to the Lao peoples of Thailand and Laos. Fourth, the addition of the Shwe Dagon shrine in Rangoon, Burma, identified Thai Buddhism with that of the peoples of lower Burma, to whom the Shwe Dagon shrine was especially sacred. Fifth, the shrine at Bodh Gayā, where the Buddha gained enlightenment, joined Northern Thai and Burmese Buddhism to the community of all Buddhists. The last shrine was in the Heaven of the Thirty-three Gods. This location is still within the sphere of the worlds governed by *karman,* and thus it defines the community of all sentient beings in heaven and earth who are subject to death and rebirth. In this way, the sacred shrines both distinguished and integrated the various spaces and beings of the world to which the people of the Ping River valley were related.

Similarly, in South Asia the traditional pattern of city planning created a series of concentric spaces around a central temple in the urban heart of a region. This pattern occurs, for example, in Katmandu. The city is surrounded by twenty-four shrines of the Mātṛkās, the eight mother goddesses. A ritual of sequential worship at these shrines arranges them into three sets of eight, which form three concentric circles around Katmandu.

FIGURE 1. *Sacred Topography Defined by the Twelve Shrines*

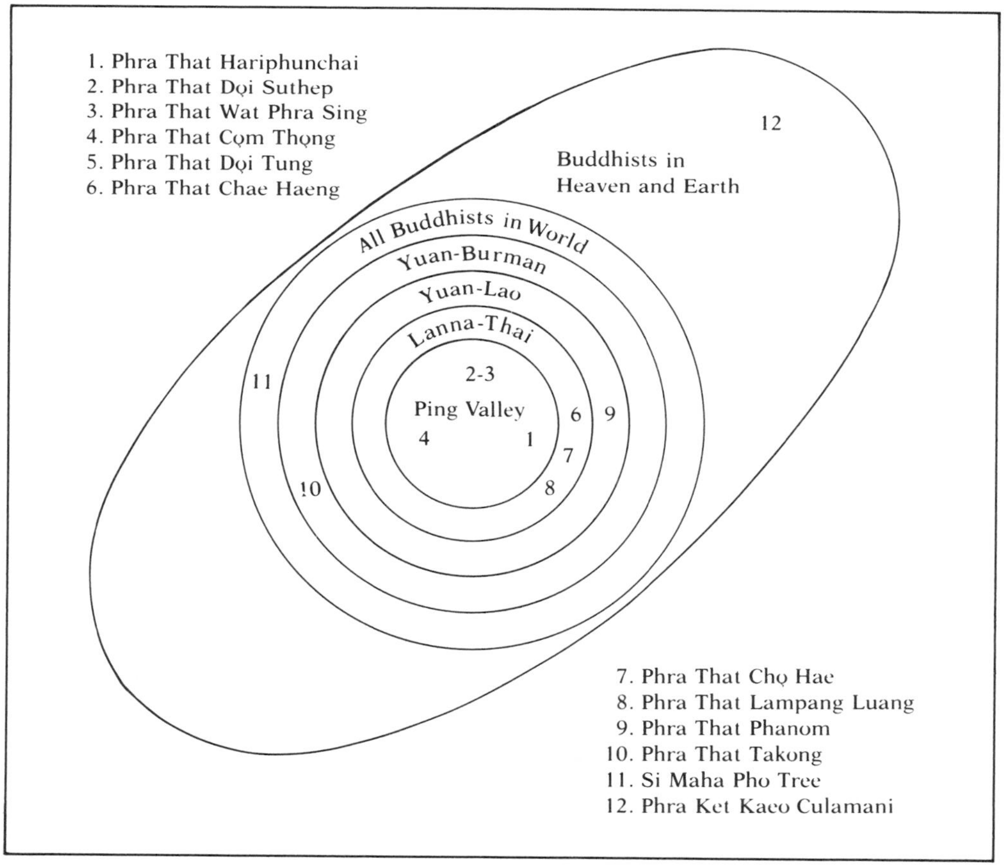

SOURCE: Charles F. Keyes, "Buddhist Pilgrimage Centers and the Twelve-Year Cycle," *History of Religions* 15 (1975): 86.

The widest circle encompasses the area traditionally under the kings of Katmandu. The second encloses the valley of Katmandu, which includes surrounding villages and areas familiar to the urban population. The third defines the city itself. The central part of the city was laid out in twelve rectangular wards centered on the temple to Taleju, a goddess closely connected with the Malla kings. The geometric clarity of the city distinguished it from the surrounding areas and marked it as the most sacred area in which the realization of divine order was most perfectly articulated. In this way, the shrines define different levels of sanctity extending from the sacred center of the city to the entire kingdom.

Encoding of Sacred Space. The functions of sacred space are, in their different ways, aspects of its essential function: to identify the fundamental symbols that create the patterns of life in a culture. This section will sketch some of the symbolic systems that make sacred space meaningful. These systems are superimposed on the structure of a place and thereby joined to one another and to the manifest form of that place. A space can encompass, among many other things, the human body, the cosmos, the stages in the creation of the cosmos, the divisions of time, the sacred narratives of a tradition, and the various spheres of human life. The more central a place is in the religious life of a culture, the more numerous the systems to which it refers.

Body. The human body is a primary system—if not *the* primary system—through which people order and interpret the world. [*See* Human Body.] It is itself a space, sometimes even a sacred space—as in forms of Tantric yoga, in which the body becomes the field for the transformations effected by yoga. It also can be a correlate of external spaces, to which it imparts a shape and character. In many instances that correlation between body and place is explicit. The horizontal plan of Gothic churches represented not only Christ on the cross but the human form more generally. In the symbolism of the Byzantine church, the nave represented the human body, the chancel the soul, and the altar the spirit. In South Asian culture areas, body symbolism of sacred places is pervasive. Hindu temples, for example, are explicitly recapitulations of the body. The symbolic blueprint of a temple is the Vāstupuruṣa Maṇḍala, a diagram drawn on its future site. This diagram incorporates the directions, the lunar mansions, the planets, the gods, and the human body and symbolically transmits their forms to the temple rising above it. Indian architectural manuals explicitly liken the temple to the body: the door is the mouth; the dome above the spire is the head. Just as the human skull has a suture, from which the soul at death departs to heaven, so also the dome is pierced with a finial; and the inner sanctum of the temple is the place of the soul within the human body. "The temple," summarizes the *Śilparatna*, "should be worshiped as the cosmic man" (cf. Kramrisch 1976, vol. 2, p. 359).

A variety of meanings is invested in such correspondence of place and body. Both the Gothic church and the Hindu temple are images of the cosmos as well as the body, and thereby both portray the sympathy and parallelism between microcosm and macrocosm. The Gothic church signifies the body of Christ, who is the whole Christian church, who is the incarnate deity, and upon whom the world and history center. The correspondence of the church and the body of Christ thus gives visible expression to the centrality of Christ in the world and his presence in the life of the community. Because the Hindu temple represents a human body, the journey into the temple is also a journey within oneself. Contact with the image of divinity in the heart of the temple is the symbolic replication of the meeting of divinity within the center of one's being. Thus, while the shape of the body generally imparts meaning to space, the specific meaning is developed in the context of individual religious traditions.

Cosmos. Sacred space often imparts form to the world by taking the form of the world. According to Mircea Eliade's paradigm of sacred space, the major vertical divisions of the world intersect at the sacred place and are represented in it. [*See* Cosmology.] These divisions are frequently the upperworld, the earth, and the underworld. David D. Shulman has found this pattern in the temples of Tamil Nadu, which contain not only symbols that rise from earth upward but also symbols of a *biladvāra*, a doorway to the underworld. Other structures express more unique cosmological conceptions. At Wat Haripuñjaya in Thailand, for example, the *ceitya*, which is the central structure of the sacred complex, vertically encompasses the three fundamental realms of the Buddhist world: the sensuous, the formed, and the formless. The *ceitya* not only represents these different spheres but also the possibility of ascent to full enlightenment.

Sacred places may represent not only the vertical realms of the world but one or another of its layers. As noted, the sacred place is often the place where humans enter the realm of the gods or, conversely, the place where the gods are among humans. In either case, it becomes the place of the presence of divinity and therefore an image of the realm of divinity. Through its use of simple geometric forms, proportionality, and light, for example, the Gothic cathedral was imagined as the image of the heavenly city. The holy cities of Jerusalem and Banaras have heavenly prototypes, according to Christian and Hindu traditions, and hence they are the forms of heaven.

Heaven may be not only the realm of the gods but also the exemplar of divine order and regular progression. The sacred place may be a heaven on earth, which transposes the eternal and sanctified order of heaven onto the plane of earth. At the founding of cities within the Roman world, for instance, the augur drew a circle quartered by lines running east-west and north-south. This diagram replicated the heavenly order and thereby established it on earth. Through ritual formulas, the diagram was then projected onto the whole tract of land to be encompassed by the city, so that the periphery of the city reproduced the boundary of the universe. The east-west line represented the course of the sun; the north-south line, the axis of the sky. The augur and the city thus stood at the crossing point of these two lines and hence immovably and harmoniously at the center of the universe.

Cosmogony. Sacred space may also reproduce the successive steps through which the world came into being. Again, according to Eliade's paradigm, because the sacred place is the center around which the world is ordered and the point of intersection with the realm of the divine, it is also the point of origin. [*See* Center of the World.] Creation began there and from there it extended. That symbolism is apparent in the architecture of the Hindu temple. In the innermost shrine of the temple is the dark center from which emerge the forms of the world, portrayed on the walls or gateways of larger temples. The naturalness of this symbolism can be illustrated by its secondary attachment to places whose primary meaning lies elsewhere. According to *Midrash Tanḥuma'*, Qedoshim 10, for example, Jerusalem and the Temple are holy because the Holy Land is the center of space and the Temple is the center of the Holy Land: "Just as the navel is found at the center of a human being, so the Land of Israel is found at the center of the world . . . and it is the foundation of the world. Jerusalem is at the center of the Land of Israel. The Temple is at the center of Jerusalem. The Holy of Holies is at the center of the Temple. The ark is at the center of the Holy of Holies, and the Foundation Stone is in front of the ark, which spot is the foundation of the world." Such symbolism conveys the primacy of the place, for what is first in time is naturally first in significance.

Time. The divisions of time may also be represented in the sacred space, especially when time is ordered or governed by the rites performed there. For example, the sides of the *ming-t'ang*, the Chinese calendar house, represented the seasons. Each side was further divided into three positions representing the months of one season. The rituals enacted at the place guaranteed the orderly progression of these cycles of time. They also guaranteed that the movement of time, and thus the fate of all living beings, depended upon the emperor, who carried out these rites. A different kind of temporal symbolism was connected with the brick altars created in particular Vedic rites. The layers and bricks of the altar represented the seasons, the months, the days and nights, and finally the year, which was the symbol of the totality of time. The completion of the rite was the consolidation of time and ultimately the attainment of immortality for the sacrificer. [*See also* Sacred Time.]

Sacred narratives. Sacred space may not only bear the imprint of the natural world but also of sacred narratives. A particular place may be a reminder of events said to have occurred there, or it may contain tokens or depictions of sacred narratives which recall them to memory and reflection. At Wat Haripuñjaya in Thailand, the walls of the *vihāra* (monastic compound) are adorned with illustrations that tell the lives of the Buddha in his earlier incarnations and express the basic moral values of Buddhism. Similarly, Christian churches of both the East and the West contain paintings and sculptures depicting the history of salvation. In Eastern churches, for example, the upper part of the iconostasis contains depictions of the twelve great events in the life of Jesus, which are celebrated in the great feasts of the Christian year. Other icons might depict scenes from the Bible or from the lives of saints and martyrs, all of which recall the history of God's work in the world. Or again, the rites of the *ḥajj* move within a space that reminds the pilgrim of two critical moments in Islamic sacred history: the time of Abraham, who built the Ka'bah and who established monotheistic worship there, and the time of the Prophet, whose final pilgrimage is recalled in rites at the plain of Arafat. In this last instance, the sacred place not only recalls an event but is also the location of the event, for the Prophet gave his last sermon during his farewell pilgrimage at Arafat. The place removes the physical distance between the worshiper and the event, and in doing so, it also mitigates the temporal distance between the time of the Prophet and the present. By thus collapsing space and time, it endows the event with an imposing reality.

Spheres of human life. In their form or function, sacred places organize human life and activity. Grounding the precarious and fluid structures of social organization in these places imparts to them a sense of conformity to a system that is not arbitrary but intrinsic to the very nature of things. The sacred place often creates a vivid parallelism between the objective order of the universe, the eternal realm of the gods, and the constructs of human relationships.

This aspect of the sacred place has been investigated in an extraordinary work by Paul Wheatley, *The Pivot of the Four Quarters.* In it, Wheatley discusses the ceremonial complexes that were the seed and integrating center of ancient urbanism. These ceremonial centers "were instruments for the creation of political, social, economic, and sacred space, at the same time they were symbols of cosmic, social, and moral order" (Wheatley, 1971, p. 225).

In Wheatley's description, the ancient Chinese city functioned in just this way to anchor the human order in the divine. The city was laid out as an image of the universe: it possessed cardinal orientation and a major north-south axis corresponding to the celestial meridian. The center of the city was the most sacred spot, corresponding to the polestar, the axis around which the sky turned. And in the center was the royal palace. The city, therefore, recreated the celestial order on earth and its pivot in the ruler. As the heavens eternally moved around the polestar, so the state revolved around the emperor. The political order was firmly established in the objective order of the universe, which was made plain in the sacred images of space.

The ceremonial complex as cosmic center also helped make it an economic center. In Mesopotamia, for example, agricultural labor was apparently under the centralized control of the temple officials. The preeminent economic function of the ceremonial center lay in its role as an instrument of redistribution. This could imply either storage and reapportionment of goods or merely rights of disposal. The ancient cities of Sumer, the temple cities of Cambodia, and Tenochtitlán, the capital of the Aztec empire, are all examples of cities whose sacredness confirmed the economic control they exercised.

A sacred area may also project the image of the social order. The villages of the Boróro of Mato Grosso, Brazil, for example, were laid out in a cosmological image. The houses formed a rough circle around the men's house, and this circle was divided into quarters by axes running north-south and east-west. But these divisions also governed the social life of the village and its systems of kinship and intermarriage (cf. Lévi-Strauss, 1973, pp. 227ff.). A sacred space may be the center of a system of social prestige that divides and structures society. In the South Indian temple town of Śrīraṅgam, the two innermost ring roads closest to the temple are inhabited almost exclusively by brahmans. Other, less prestigious, castes live farther toward the periphery.

In one way or another, sacred space orders space in a socially meaningful way. Because a sacred place is both visible and comprehensible, it lends concreteness to the less visible systems of human relationships and creates an identifiable center of social and political organization.

Conclusion. We began with the assumption that if a place is the location of ritual activity or its object, then it is sacred. To designate a place as sacred imposes no limit on its form or its meaning. It implies no particular aesthetic or religious response. But if sacred places lack a common content, they have a common role. To call a place sacred asserts that a place, its structure, and its symbols express fundamental cultural values and principles. By giving these visible form, the sacred place makes tangible the corporate identity of a people and their world.

[*See also* Orientation; *for discussion of specific kinds of sacred spaces, see* Basilica, Cathedral, and Church; Caves; Mountains; Rivers; *and* Temple.]

BIBLIOGRAPHY

For recent scholarship, the agenda for the study of sacred space has been largely set by Mircea Eliade. His paradigm of the form and meaning of sacred space is presented in a number of his works, especially *The Sacred and the Profane: The Nature of Religion* (New York, 1959), pp. 20–67; *Patterns in Comparative Religion* (New York, 1958), pp. 367–387; and "Centre du monde, temple, maison," in *Le symbolisme cosmique des monuments religieux,* edited by Giuseppe Tucci (Rome, 1957), pp. 57–82.

A number of scholars have made significant contributions to the discussion of the symbolism of space by opening up or refashioning elements of Eliade's paradigm. Among the most thoughtful are Jonathan Z. Smith's *Map Is Not Territory: Studies in the History of Religions* (Leiden, 1978), esp. pp. 88–146, and *Imagining Religion: From Babylon to Jonestown* (Chicago, 1982), esp. pp. 53–65. The final chapter in Paul Wheatley's *The Pivot of the Four Quarters: A Preliminary Enquiry into the Origins and Character of the Ancient Chinese City* (Chicago, 1971), entitled "The Ancient Chinese City as a Cosmomagical Symbol," pp. 411–476; Davíd Carrasco's "Templo Mayor: The Aztec Vision of Place," *Religion* 11 (July 1981): 275–297; Benjamin Ray's "Sacred Space and Royal Shrines in Buganda," *History of Religions* 16 (May 1977): 363–373; and Kees W. Bolle's "Speaking of a Place," in *Myths and Symbols: Studies in Honor of Mircea Eliade,* edited by Joseph M. Kitagawa and Charles H. Long (Chicago, 1969), pp. 127–139, are case studies that also advance the discussion of sacred space in this general line.

For other approaches to the meaning of architectural space, see the essays in *Traditional Concepts of Ritual Space in India: Studies in Architectural Anthropology,* edited by Jan Pieper, "Art and Archaeology Research Papers," no. 17 (London, 1980), and *Shelter, Sign, and Symbol,* edited by Paul Oliver (London, 1975). Kent C. Bloomer and Charles W. Moore's *Body, Memory, and Architecture* (New Haven, 1977) is an especially clear introduction to meaning in architecture and the role of the body in establishing meaning.

Studies of the religious significance of urban space include Joseph Rykwert's *The Idea of a Town: The Anthropology of Urban Form in Rome, Italy and the Ancient World* (Princeton, 1976); Diana L. Eck's *Banaras: City of Light* (New York, 1982); and the previously cited work by Wheatley. This essay also utilized Niels Gutschow's "Ritual as Mediator of Space: Kāthmāndu," *Ekistics* 44 (December 1977): 309–312, and Jan Pieper's "Three Cities of Nepal," in Paul Oliver's *Shelter, Sign, and Symbol* (cited above), pp. 52–69.

For pilgrimage places and the religious definition of space, see E. Alan Morinis's *Pilgrimage in the Hindu Tradition: A Case Study of West Bengal* (Oxford, 1984); Jonathan Sumption's *Pilgrimage: An Image of Mediaeval Religion* (London, 1972); Charles F. Keyes's "Buddhist Pilgrimage Centers and the Twelve-Year Cycle: Northern Thai Moral Orders in Space and Time," *History of Religions* 15 (1975): 71–89; Agehananda Bharati's "Pilgrimage in the Indian Tradition," *History of Religions* 3 (Summer 1963): 135–167; Anne Feldhaus's *The Deeds of God in Ṛddhipur* (Oxford, 1984); and Hava Lazarus-Yafeh's *Some Religious Aspects of Islam: A Collection of Articles* (Leiden, 1981). The last has three excellent essays on both popular and classical traditions concering Jerusalem, the *ḥajj*, and the Ka'bah.

Study of the places of worship is an engaging entry into the subject of sacred space and into history of religions generally. For Hinduism, the fundamental work has long been Stella Kramrisch's *The Hindu Temple*, 2 vols. (Calcutta, 1946). The temple is analyzed from the ground up and placed within the tradition of Brahmanic thought. David D. Shulman's *Tamil Temple Myths: Sacrifice and Divine Marriage in the South Indian Śaiva Tradition* (Princeton, 1980) draws on localized traditions that explain the origins and power of shrines.

In Buddhism, one of the most richly symbolic structures is Borobudut in central Java, and the classic study is Paul Mus's *Barabuḍur: Esquisse d'une histoire du bouddhisme fondée sur la critique archéologique des textes*, 2 vols. (Hanoi, 1935). For more recent interpretation, see *Barabuḍur: History and Significance of a Buddhist Monument*, edited by Luis O. Gómez and Hiram W. Woodward, Jr. (Berkeley, 1981). Borobudur is both a *maṇḍala* and a stupa. For the former, see Giuseppe Tucci's *The Theory and Practice of the Maṇḍala*, translated by Alan H. Brodrick (London, 1969), and for the latter, *The Stupa: Its Religious, Historical and Architectural Significance*, edited by Anna Libera Dallapiccola, "Beiträge zur Südasienforschung Südasien-Institut Universität Heidelberg," vol. 55 (Wiesbaden, 1980). Donald K. Swearer's *Wat Haripuñjaya: A Study of the Royal Temple of the Buddha's Relic, Lamphun, Thailand* (Missoula, Mont., 1976) shows the expression of the moral, spiritual, cosmic, and social orders in the symbol systems of a Buddhist religious complex.

For the interpretation of Islamic architecture, Doğan Kuban's *Muslim Religious Architecture: The Mosque and Its Early Development* (Leiden, 1974) provides a brief introduction and a useful bibliography. See also *Architecture of the Islamic World: Its History and Social Meaning*, edited by George Michell (London, 1978).

The Gothic cathedral illustrates one expression of Christianity in architecture, and its symbolism has been luminously explored in Otto von Simson's *The Gothic Cathedral: Origins of Gothic Architecture and the Medieval Concept of Order* (New York, 1956). Harold W. Turner's *From Temple to Meeting House: The Phenomenology and Theology of Places of Worship* (The Hague, 1979) interprets the history of church architecture as the tension between buildings that localize the presence of divinity and those that serve for congregational worship. The sanctity of Eastern Christian churches is communicated largely through its icons. See, for example, George Galavaris's *The Icon in the Life of the Church: Doctrine, Liturgy, Devotion* (Leiden, 1981).

The interpretation of the Maori latrine presented in this essay follows F. Allan Hanson's "Method in Semiotic Anthropology, or How the Maori Latrine Means," in his edited volume, *Studies in Symbolism and Cultural Communication*, "University of Kansas Publications in Anthropology," no. 14 (Lawrence, Kans., 1982), pp. 74–89. For Black Elk's description of Lakota rites and places, see *The Sacred Pipe: Black Elk's Account of the Seven Rites of the Oglala Sioux*, edited by Joseph Epes Brown (1953; Baltimore, 1971). The analysis of the Boróro village is found in Claude Lévi-Strauss's *Tristes tropiques*, translated by John Weightman and Doreen Weightman (New York, 1973).

Kabīr is only one of the many saints of various traditions who had little use for the sacred places. For Kabīr as iconoclast, see *The Bījak of Kabīr*, translated by Linda Hess and Shukdev Singh, edited by Linda Hess (San Francisco, 1983).

JOEL P. BRERETON

SACRED TIME. Time is the context and content of reality, at once the eternal, unchanging environment of our being and its momentary, ever-changing mode of expression. Conceived absolutely, it is timeless; perceived relatively, it is timely. And it is the paradoxical relation of these two that is a significant focus of much of the world's religions. Not only, along with science, does religion seek to mark such stages of relative time as it can denote, but religion goes beyond science in attempting to understand the translogical connection of relative temporal stages to timeless eternity itself. [*See* Eternity.] Beginning and ending with the absolute (the eternal), religion tries to perceive the particular and relative (the moment and history) in its light. [*See* Myth, *article on* Myth and History.]

Both in the scope of its interest and in its attempt to conjoin the absolute with the relative, religion's approach to time is fundamentally different from that of science. In seeking to comprehend all aspects of reality, as does philosophy, religion's path diverges to the extent that it remains aware of the limits of comprehension. It is reality itself, not ideas about reality, that the religious want to approach and merge into. Therefore religious life does not end with thinking or even comprehending but with apprehending, doing, and being. Worship, prayer, revelation, and enlightenment are often, for the world's religions, activities and events most highly esteemed insofar as they transcend the limitations of thinking's duality, its subject-object opposition, freeing people from their isolation as onlookers to what religions believe is their fulfillment as united participants.

Our actual involvement in time is so complete and inescapable that difficulties in achieving the distance required for its comprehension immediately arise. In his *Confessions,* Augustine lamented, "What is time? If nobody asks me, I know, but if I want to explain it to someone, then I do not know" (11.14.17). Many feel the same way on first reflection. Reasoning further even the notion that time is somehow understandable, though inexpressible, fades before the realization that time is a concomitant of consciousness, inalienable from the very process of thinking. People cannot stop time or step aside from it, even for a moment, to contemplate its nature. In actuality, time's immanence is experienced as overwhelming.

In theory, time can be considered abstractly as the measure of change, the principle of duration, the medium of movement, the order of events—even as a primary category in itself, undefinable in terms of any other. But again, time's boundaries (or lack of them) are problematic. While experienced time is too close, too immanent to be examined, theoretical time is too grand and too transcendent; hidden in the depths of all its abstractions are the implications of time's radical independence. Time is the cause of change, duration, movement, and the order of events; it causes all of them. But what causes time?

Experience of Time in Religion. Religions approach the question in two ways. Those that conceive of time as infinite conclude it is uncaused. On the other hand, those that think time is finite and caused go further, wondering what was before its beginning and what will be after its end. They inquire about the context in which such time currently passes and, like the others, finally find the answer in the idea of infinite time, the timeless time of eternity. Thus even when timely time is thought to be finite, its ground in eternity is not, and the problem of comprehension remains. As we cannot step aside from the timely, we find we cannot step outside of the timeless. On the contrary, echoing the early Hindu declaration that *brahman* (the Absolute) is not what the mind can know but that whereby the mind can know (*Kena Upaniṣad* 1.5), religions are led to a perception not of time as an abstraction of our temporal being but of our temporal being as an expression of time.

Those who ponder the nature of time conclude with this final paradox: not only is temporal being dependent on time, but the time on which it is dependent appears in its most profound nature as infinite, unchanging, and eternal. Time breaks through the logic we seek to impose on it; it transcends the timely and reveals itself as timeless.

Temporal and Absolute Reality. For religions that consider reality in primarily temporal (as contrasted with spatial or ontological) terms, this eternally timeless time is conceived of as absolute reality itself—as God. Later Zoroastrianism is perhaps the most well-known exemplar of such faith, finding in Zurwān ("time") the ultimate resolution of the oppositions of Ahura Mazdā (light, goodness, spirit) and Angra Mainyu (darkness, evil, matter). Thought by many to be heretical in terms of Zarathushtra's insistence on fundamental dualism, Zurvanism was nonetheless the dominant form of his religion in its later stages in the Sasanid empire (224–651 CE). Beyond the oppositions of good and evil, Zurwān was worshiped as the eternal father of all distinctions, the source and controller of every being.

This affirmation of the Absolute's overcoming of all temporal oppositions is basic to religions, even those that do not describe it in primarily temporal terms. Most of these other religions choose ontological, not temporal, categories as the most fundamental: they describe the ground of all being and not-being and of their growth out of and decay into one another as "Being-Itself" or "Not-Being-Itself." Insofar as there is nothing that this absolute source is not, it seems to many religions to deserve the ultimately positive titles of "Being-Itself," "the All," "the One," or "God"; for those religions it is eternal. Insofar as the absolute source transcends all internal distinctions within itself, it seems appropriate for other religions to employ negative terminology and call it "Not-Being-Itself," "No-thing," "the Void," or "Chaos"; for those religions it is timeless. Religions in both camps agree that their names for ultimate reality are misleading. Descriptive language depends on oppositions, contrasts, and distinctions in order to proceed, and for that reason it is ineffective for comprehending the mystery of an absolute that transcends them. So whether they use positive or negative words to describe the Absolute, religions assert that both aspects of relative reality are subsumed within it: "Being-Itself" and "Not-Being-Itself" each include being and not-being.

And whether time or being or even space is chosen as the primary characterization of the Absolute, religions agree that it is timelessly eternal, eternally timeless. For religions like Jainism and Buddhism, which refuse any notion of creation and thus reject the distinct actuality of timely time and relative being, this absolute reality is all that exists. [*See* Nirvāṇa.] Jinasena, a ninth-century CE Jain teacher of the Digambara sect, portrays such reality in positive terms as eternal: "Know that the world is uncreated, as time itself is, without beginning and end. . . . Uncreated and indestructible, it endures under the compulsion of its own nature" (*Mahāpurāṇa,* 4.38–40). The Buddha, on the other hand, describes this reality in negative terms as timeless. For him the temporal worlds of form—the realms of Brahmā and of radiance—perpetually evolve out of one another in such a manner that their inhabitants are led falsely to believe in their reality. Yet both of these temporal spheres are essentially unstable; in fact, they are so ephemeral and empty that neither can be thought truly to exist. Only not-being, absolute timelessness, really is real (see *Dīgha Nikāya* 3.28).

Though religions diverge on how seriously the separate reality of the timely world ought to be taken, even those that posit a radical creation agree that it stems from the timelessly eternal. For them the Absolute is the source not only of temporal being and not-being but of manifest time as well. Religions favoring mythological rather than strictly philosophical descriptions often portray this absolute reality eternally existing in uncontrasted (though sometimes dynamic) unity before the beginning of temporality. They envisage its first act as the creation of finite being and time, as in this description from the *Book of Genesis:* "In the beginning God created the heavens and the earth. The earth was without form and void, and darkness was on the face of the deep; and the spirit of God was moving over the face of the waters. And God said, 'Let there be light,' and there was light. And God saw that the light was good; and God separated the light from the darkness. God called the light Day and the the darkness he called Night. And there was evening and there was morning, one day" (*Gn.* 1:1–5).

Some religions envision a more gradual process of creation and describe a period of preexistence before the temporal world actually began. In this timeless period, the forms of relative reality exist innately, embryonically, or ideally in not yet manifest form. The Aranda people of central Australia, for instance, say that images of creatures existed in the timeless dreams of the ancestor Karora, finally bursting forth into timeless reality from his navel and armpits as wishes and dreams for them flashed through his mind. And the Witóto of Colombia proclaim that before the beginning there was nothing but appearance; creation required the efforts of the god Nainema to give the phantasm substance. Many North American Indian traditions believe that creatures live in the sky or underground before the commencement of earthly existence.

Distinctions between the timeless and the timely are difficult to make in such religions. When the creation of the world (like the creation of human beings) is envisaged as a long and complex process involving multiple stages of gestation, it becomes particularly hard to decide exactly which is the determining stage. For some religions, even though the forms of being may develop gradually, the inauguration of relative time is a sudden and seemingly key event. The Hawaiian creation chant portrays eternal timelessness as endless darkness. While the evolution of all forms of being occurs in that darkness, it is only when they are completed that daylight dawns and individual development is ready to begin. The creation chant of the Tuamotu Islanders emphasizes the timelessness of the period of preexistence and formative events. Although it dramatizes the creator's acts sequentially (and thus could seem to suggest time's passing), it repeatedly punctuates their telling with the reminder that "still it is night." Only when the god Kiho is finished creating does the day of timely time commence. Unrelieved darkness is almost always the symbol used by religions to describe the timelessness before timeliness. The Melanesians of the Banks Islands, however, depict eternity differently—in terms of uncontrasted light. Rather than having to produce daylight, as is usually the first task of creator deities bent on beginning relative time, the god Qat's problem concerns the establishment of night. One myth relates how Qat sailed out over the sea to the far edge of the sky where Night itself touched him over the eyes and gave him black eyebrows and taught him to sleep. Only with night active in the world could the creation be finished and time begun. The early Zoroastrians also envisaged timelessness in terms of homogeneous light, and for them, too, timely reality commenced with the creation of darkness.

Time and Being. For other religions, metaphors relating to being rather than time seem the crucial indicators of creation's completion. Creatures are portrayed as existing but not yet fully formed physically or psychically. Rather than inhabiting the sky or underworld, they often live on the earth in a special place where they exist in timeless harmony, sometimes even in a partnership of sorts, with their creator. Basic acts of creation—naming, ordering, fashioning—continue until individuation occurs when the creator leaves (as in African and Australian religions) or when man is expelled (as in biblical faiths). The temporal status of this Dreaming, as the Australian Aborigines call it, is ambiguous. Occurring technically in timely time, it is nonetheless formative of temporal events and is treated as timeless. The principles employed in the establishment of being and time during this period are understood as archetypical and perpetually fundamental; within time at least, they are always and thus presently relevant. While scholars of religion commonly notice this phenomenon as a feature of "nonhistorical" religions, particularly those of Australia, an analogous presumption is apparent in the "historical" religions as well. In telling the story of Adam and Eve and in calling their sin "original," biblical religions, for example, do not simply refer to an error passed along through time to subsequent generations. Adam is for them not only the first man but the essential one: the sin committed in that time of beginning is perceived as formal and archetypical, timelessly part of the human condition.

The indissoluable connection of time and being is thus made evident throughout the world's religions. Not only do they assert it in their understanding of absolute reality and reaffirm it in their descriptions of the process of creation, they also conjoin the temporal and ontological aspects of reality in their analyses of its relative form. Often this is accomplished by deifying finite time and being in a single symbol. In the Hindu Brāhmaṇas, for instance, creation takes the form of Prajāpati—temporal being personified—who is both a generator of finite beings and the time period of their existence. "Prajāpati is the year," proclaims the *Śatapatha Brāhmaṇa* (11.1.6) in describing the inauguration of temporal existence.

Gods Associated with Time. Some religions, however, respond to the awesome nature of relative reality and its dependence on the Absolute by stressing one or the other of its aspects. Those that emphasize ontology deify personifications of *timely existence.* Those that accentuate the temporal aspect of finite reality, on the other hand, deify personifications of *existent time* and often worship these lords of temporality along with gods representing other great powers evident in the relative world. The ancient Maya probably carried such worship to its furthest extent in the rituals attending their adoration of *kin* ("time, day, sun"). Like other religions that stress the temporal, they particularly honored the events in which time noticeably manifested itself, granting divine status even to relatively short time periods and celebrating them with involved rituals.

Insofar as it is impossible to determine the precise functions of many of the gods in complex traditions, it is difficult to be certain of the full scope of the worship of timely time. Divine roles merge as seamlessly as the realities they symbolize interrelate with each other. Just as *kin* betokened for the Maya the sun and day as well as time, gods in other religions best known for their typification of the sun or day may also have served to represent aspects of time to their adherents. Religions overtly worshiping fate or destiny can also be included among those possibly honoring aspects of relative time. (At least the reverse is often true.) Fatalism was a notable element in later Zoroastrianism's belief in Zurwān's control of all beings, and it also seems to have been a popular feature in much pre-Islamic Arab religion, where time was thought to be the cause of all earthly happiness and misery. Although limited evidence reveals only one North African group (the Banū Bakr ibn Wā'il) overtly worshiping time as a deity (under the name of Aud), esteem for the power of time was sufficiently widespread in the Arab world to lead Muḥammad (570–632 CE) to complain of the unbelievers' notion that "it is time that destroys us" (Qur'ān, surah 14:23). A carryover into Islam of the recognition of time's import may be found in the figure of Manāt, one of the three "daughters" of Allāh; her name seems to have stemmed from a word meaning "apportioning," a reference to the amount of time allotted to a person.

In all such worship of temporal time lie presumptions of how it manifests itself. And to the extent that time is the context of being, these presumptions of its manner of manifestation reveal religions' conceptions of the purpose of being. Attitudes toward time reflect attitudes about the meaning of existence.

Views of Time. One of the major indications of fundamental religious outlook in this regard is the determination of time's direction. Many religions think of time linearly, as a sequence of moments, and seek to characterize the relation of moments to one another in light of the whole. [*See* History.] Some religions see this relation as progressive, others find it circular and essentially static, and still others find it degenerative. [*See* Ages of the World.] Each of these determinations is internally complex, and all are further complicated by religion's perpetual and profound interest in the relation not just of temporal moments to one another and to the whole of timely time but to the timelessly eternal as well.

Judaism. Perhaps the Bible speaks most powerfully of temporal time, of history, as progressive. Conceived by God at the creation as the medium for the complete realization of being and thus for the salvation of man, history is meaningful. It moves purposefully from its divine origin in the beginning to its divine culmination in the end. And along the way, God is thought to be continually active in time through the covenant with his people. The biblical God both transcends and is immanent in temporal time, and history overall is profoundly understood as a manifestation of his divine will. Given human freedom, however, the Bible more commonly experiences the day-to-day continuum of history in terms of its disharmony with that will. Although it is Judaism's faith that at the end of finite time the purpose of being will be fulfilled and the mistakes of history overcome by the Messiah, within time these failures seem glaring. Nevertheless, biblical pessimism regarding the sins of humankind finally must be evaluated in the context of the Bible's optimism regarding people's essential, if unrealized, goodness; their failure to progress equally along with time, to be fully as God intended, is grievous only in light of that very progress and intention. None of these temporary failures detract from the belief that temporality is real and important. In fact, as Jacob Neusner (1975) has shown, beginning with the era common to Christianity, Judaism increasingly shifted emphasis from its messianic expectation for the future to an estimation of history as itself an expression of present eternity. In changing focus from the eternal God's transcendence to his immanence, Jewish thinkers argue that within each moment of time, even in the most seemingly mundane events of history, lies the possibility of being's realization.

Christianity. Christianity also carries within its estimation of temporality this complex understanding of the relation of time to eternity. Like Judaism, it believes timely time to be grounded in and established by the eternal. While this faith is reflected in Judaism by dating history from the presumed date of creation, in Christianity it is expressed by dating events from the birth of Christ. Christians structure all history around what they perceive to be a manifestation of the eternal in the temporal. They understand time as divided into three periods (before, during, and after Christ's physical presence on earth) and see history moving progressively through these stages to its completion in Christ's final return. Not only do Christian thinkers find eternity manifest in history, but like the Jews they also proclaim it evinced in the moment. The *Gospel of John* records the paradoxical message that eternal, absolute reality is always present, here and now, in the timely. Portrayed in that gospel as the beginning, end, and centerpoint of time, Christ announces "I am" (*Jn.* 13:19). And when his credibility is challenged by those wondering how he could have seen the patriarch Abraham hundreds of years before, Christ further explains, "Before Abraham was born, I am" (*Jn.* 8:58). The point is emphatically made here that absolute reality is eternal and therefore always present, and for those of the faithful who identify with the timelessly existing reality within their temporal selves, merely timely significance is transcended and eternal meaning is realized.

Islam. Islam similarly finds time purposeful in both its relative and particular aspects. Like other religions "of the Book," it conceives the temporal to be established, continually sustained, and given direction by the eternal; and, like Christianity in particular, it demonstrates this understanding by dating history from the event it values as the most determining breakthrough of the absolute into relative duration—the Hijra, the emigration of Muḥammad from Mecca to Medina in 662 CE. Not only does Islam describe history itself as meaningful in its movement from the creation through the "time of ignorance" *(Jāhilīyah)* and the present period of Qur'anic revelation to the final day of judgment; at least some Muslim scholars also perceive each moment within time as the direct creation of the eternally active God. For thinkers such as al-Ashʿarī (874–935 CE), God is the only real cause of events; none other really produces effects. For them, creation is discontinuous and only appears otherwise because of God's merciful consistency. The eternal God is thus revealed both in the overall span of time and in its constituent moments—a perception that led the thirteenth-century Ṣūfī poet ʿIrāqī to write the following lines: "Hidden, manifest, / both at once: / You are not this, not that— / yet both at once" (*Fakhruddin Iraqi: Divine Flashes*, trans. William C. Chittick and Peter Wilson, New York, 1982).

Hinduism, Buddhism, and Jainism. The notion of the timeless within time is affirmed as well by the Hindus, Buddhists, and Jains. According to most Eastern religions, enlightenment may only occur within the moment. Although individuals may experience history as progressive, in such faiths it is understood in terms of the universe as essentially static. Temporal time is portrayed in the Hindu Purāṇas, the epics, and the writings of Indian astronomers (c. 200 BCE–500 CE) as complexly cyclical. Four *yuga*s, or universal epochs, form part of a calendar that organizes temporal time from an instant ("an eye-blink") to the lifespan of the god Brahmā. Alternating with related periods of darkness, the *yuga*s are of degenerating duration and moral purity. Each *yuga* is associated with a virtue: the *kṛtayuga* of 4,800 divine *(deva)* years with self-discipline, the *tretāyuga* of 3,600 divine years with wisdom, the *dvāparayuga* of 2,400 divine years with sacrifice, and the *kaliyuga* of 1,200 divine years with generosity. The time periods encompassed here are enormous. One day in the life of Brahmā is the equivalent of 4,320,000,000 human years; one year in the life of Brahmā equals 360 Brahmā days or 1,555,200,000,000 human years; and one lifetime of Brahmā is one hundred times longer than that. After one lifetime of Brahmā, the world of manifest temporal reality dissolves into potentiality for a period of equal duration only to reemerge and eventually dissolve again, alternating between relative being and not-being forever. (Hindu astronomers defined the present point of time within this infinitely pointless scheme as the last *kaliyuga* in the first day of the second half of Brahmā's current life.)

Endlessly cyclical, temporal time has no meaning for such faiths. Its sequences, so carefully calibrated, are finally devoid of real significance, and yet within them and within the context of an individual's life or lives, some progress toward realizing absolute reality and meaning may be made. Though history itself contains no promise of fulfillment, through it and in spite of it such fulfillment may be found. For Hinduism, this task is molded by the concept of *dharma*, or duty; temporal existence is seen as an opportunity to work through and learn the lessons of each of life's four stages (student, householder, forest dweller, and wandering ascetic) until a level of self-understanding is reached whereby temporality itself can be transcended and the eternal dimension of self *(ātman)* freed. This same principle operates in Jainism and Buddhism: although these religions differ in their characterization of the timeless aspect of reality, they agree that its final realization liberates the enlightened one (the "conqueror" of relativity) from the cycles of temporality and the wheel of birth and death. For these religions, the conception of time as relative and historical—and the consideration of that time as truly meaningful—is the essence of delusion. By contrast, the conception of time as particular—as timeless instants continually expressing the eternal—is the essence of enlightenment.

Tribal religions. Traditional religions consider the relation of the eternal to the timely (and to its relative and particular aspects) somewhat differently. In *African Religions and Philosophies*, John S. Mbiti (1969) describes sub-Saharan perceptions of time as experientially based. Rather than understanding time as an abstract phenomenon, traditional African religions speak of it as ontological and actual, tied to real events. Occurences in the present or relevant to it belong to *sasa*, a "now" period that includes the implied future and the remembered past as well as the momentary present; those in the distant or mythic past, not immediately relevant to the present but serving as its foundation and context, belong to *zamani*. These time periods are neither mathematically precise nor exactly linearly related. An old person's *sasa* is greater than a child's and the community's is greater still. Moreover, certain notable events from long ago may still be in *sasa*, while other more recent but less relevant occurences exist only in *zamani*.

In that time must be experienced to be real, according to this view, the abstract future is nonexistent. Whereas Westerners tend to depict manifest time as an abstract line along which they move toward fixed points in the future, traditional Africans portray their living representatives always standing in the present while time flows by them into the past; they envisage no time line stretching toward future dates. Time becomes real only in the present or in a near future conceived as its extension. A farmer sowing seed in his fields can think of their growth and harvest because these developments are inherent in the present. More long-term or abstract future events, however, are thought of as ones which will occur in the present or past of the community experiencing them; the farmer knows that when he dies and moves through *sasa* to *zamani*, he will be considered a reality of the past by his surviving relatives. This is the perspective on his future that he adopts, for the determining centerpoint of the traditional African experience of temporality is the perpetual, vital present. Timely time becomes manifest there and it is from that point that it moves "backward" into the past. The resulting accretion of time carries the living community farther and farther away from the original experience of God in the creation. In this view, history can be understood as degenerative—a steady fall away from the initial divine presence. Yet within such religion the notion of individual progress toward God exists. As the buildup of time renders the community increasingly distant from God, it carries individuals closer. The farmer who ages, dies, and becomes a member of the "living dead" (a personally remembered ancestor) and, finally, one of the community of spirits, accrues being and time in that process. Compared to those still living, he gains ontological superiority through being in time and is recognized as an intermediary between beings who are temporally alive and being-itself, which is eternally so.

In addition to this emphasis on the transcendent aspects of the timeless god, traditional African religion also takes note of its timely immanence. Not only is the source of reality in the depths of *zamani*, it is endlessly realized in the actuality of *sasa*. God is once and always active in this belief system; he is both the source and sustainer, everywhere evident in the created reality of the perpetual present.

If traditional religion in Africa tends to stress the transcendence of the eternal, at least some forms of traditional religion in North America focus on its immanence. Benjamin Lee Whorf (in Tedlock and Tedlock, 1975) points out that Hopi Indians have no notion of temporal time as a smooth continuum flowing out of a future, through a present, and into a past. Their language in fact has no words, grammatical constructions, or expressions that refer to such temporality. Rather, the Hopi envisage two separate realms of reality: the objective manifested world, which includes all that is or has been valid to the senses; and the subjective, manifesting realm, which incorporates everything we call "future" as well as the mental or emotional aspect of each thing and of the cosmos as a whole. This latter mode is the dynamic, though unmoving, condition of thought thinking its way into manifestation. It is not advancing toward people from some future but exists already in mental form in hope, evolving from the subjective to the objective. Within the objective realm, as manifestations of the subjective extend out beyond the observer into the remote past in time and the distant place in space, they blur together and finally become one in the beginnings of time. Recounted in myths, these beginnings are experienced once again as subjective and mental.

The Hopi's sense of the development of present reality includes a description of four successive worlds—Tokpela, Tokpa, Kuskurza, and this world, Túwaqachi. Like the "four ages of man" described by the Greek poet Hesiod (eighth century BCE), these worlds are portrayed in descending order, and the present one is not as beautiful and easy as preceding ones. Nevertheless, Túwaqachi is still a realm of potential fulfillment.

Rather than considering such history abstractly, the Hopi experience it in personal terms. On the evening of the new year, after all the fires of the community have been extinguished, the Hopi initiates climb down a ladder into a kiva to hear their people's story. They hear how their forefathers were fashioned by Spider Woman and Sótuknang and were told to maintain wisdom, harmony, and respect for the love of the creator, Taiowa, at all times. They listen to the tale of how most of those first people eventually forgot their purpose, how their world was destroyed by fire, and how the few faithful survived beneath the ground and finally emerged to the second world. They learn how eventually most of these survivors also forgot their purpose and were destroyed by ice and how those who still remembered took refuge again within the earth and endured to emerge into the third world. And as the night of their initiation continues, the young Hopi hear how even the people of the third world sinned, how that world was destroyed by water, and how the few faithful ones remaining survived in hollow reeds. Finally, as the night is ending, they hear about this fourth and present world. They attend once again to the commandments given to its people—to them: to have wisdom, to live in harmony, and to respect the love of Taiowa, the creator. As the dawn breaks and they climb out of the kiva, these young Hopi emerge into a new day, a new year—their own new world of ever-present possibility. The timeless immanence of the eternal in time is thus once again underscored.

Religious and Secular Views. In this emphasis on the relation of relative time (both momentary and historical) to the eternal, religious thought profoundly distinguishes itself from what is nonreligious. Secular approaches to time are concerned only with the interdependence of time periods, determining how one day, year, or age pertains to another. Such thinking about time presumes creation yet stops short of considering its consequences. Time is conceived as finite (and thus dependent) and yet is treated as if it were interdependent. Once established in this manner, it is dissected in terms of its constituent parts. Periods of time are understood to emanate directly out of their predecessors and are thereby judged "profane" or ordinary. No question is raised as to the dependence of finite time overall or in any of its momentary instances.

In contrast, religions endlessly question the nature of reality. Conceiving the temporal as finite (if real at all), they accept the consequences of its limits and push on to explore how it is grounded in the infinite and eternal. They assert that temporal reality is dependent not only overall but in each of its parts. Religions celebrate as "sacred" the connection of each manifestation with the eternal. This remains their central interest, regardless of how variously they conceive of time's periodicity. The intention of this view of time is frequently misperceived by analysts as an attempt to escape the requirements of the timely, and, as Mircea Eliade (1959) notes, it is sometimes even misunderstood as such by religious people. But escape is not the goal of religions here: on the contrary, rather than avoid the consequences of the moment, religions take them most seriously, seeking to perceive in the depths of the timely an expression of the eternal.

With that common predisposition uniting them, religions describe the ages of time in numerous and different ways. Not all religions agree on the overall limits of temporality itself. Those, like some forms of the Eastern religions that hold it to be without beginning and end, consider proclamations of its relative reality, and hence of its sacrality, as illusory. Others that consider temporality to have a long or even endless series of beginnings and endings also temper their assumption of its overall meaningfulness. Faiths like those of the Zoroastrians, Hindus, Buddhists, Jains, ancient Greeks, Hopi, Maya, Aztec, and Maori posit distinct periods of being—disconnected worlds—existing after one another and often separated by equally long periods of not-being. For these religions, there are in effect many histories, and how seriously they understand sacrality in connection with this present one in the series depends on how distinct from the others they believe it to be. Still other religions, like Judaism, Christianity, and Islam, conceive of definite and unique limits to temporality. For them this present history is the only emanation of the eternal, and, as a result, they find it fully sacred in its import. The difference between religions on this issue is not based on what they agree is the profound relation of timely time to the timeless, but rather on what they conceive are the dimensions of the timely.

Beyond the determination of the span of finite time overall, religions also distinguish smaller but equally significant forms of periodicity in which the same pattern of creation of the temporal out of the eternal is revealed. The aeon, century, year, month, week, day, hour, minute, instant, and their equivalents in other cultures all serve to mark specific periods of temporal time, and, in considering their relation to timelessness, religions proclaim them sacred and for that reason especially celebrate their beginnings and ends.

Of course, many such designations of time periods are arbitrary. Millennia, centuries, decades, weeks, hours, and minutes often depend more on methods of counting than on natural phenomena, and religions relying on different mathematical systems figure time's periodicity in various ways. The Maya calibrations, for instance, result in nine major time periods: twenty *kins*, or days, make one *uinal;* eighteen *uinal*s make one *tun* (about one solar year); twenty *tuns* make one *katun,* and so on through *baktuns*, *pictuns*, *calabtuns*, and *kinchiltuns*. Combining sacred and civil schemes of reckoning, the Maya and other Mesoamericans who followed their lead concluded that each total period of actual manifest time lasts fifty-two years—a complete Calendar Round, or *xiuhmolpilli* (Nahuatl, "year bundle"). Other religions focus on different intervals of long duration as significant and especially sacred.

Even in fixing shorter intervals there is no complete agreement on abstract time periods. While for biblical faiths the week is considered a distinct entity and is marked off by celebration of the sabbath, for others seven-day spans of time are of no particular significance: a week does not exist as a thing in itself and alternate time periods are honored instead. Religions are consistent in their approach to the arbitrarily determined forms of time's periodicity only in that they all make such determinations and, when they do, consider the resultant time periods sacred in terms of their dependence on the eternal.

Rites and Rituals. While religions disagree over the duration of such abstract epochs, they agree on the sacrality of time periods more directly evidenced by the world—the day, month, and year. Daily prayers and rituals regularly mark the faith of religions' avid adherents, and prescriptions for them can be found in most sacred books.

Underlying these practices there remains the perception that temporality is not only initially but perpetually contingent on the eternal, and must be renewed or even re-created continuously if it is not to disintegrate into not-being. The ancient Egyptians dramatized this understanding in their myth of the solar deity Re's nightly conquest over the powers of the underworld, and other religions envisage similarly divine interventions.

Monthly and seasonal rituals reflect the same concept. Again, a particular time period is over and the dependence of being requires divine activity to initiate the next. Analyzing the pattern of the religious response to such transitions, Theodor Gaster (1950) writes that the function of such rituals is to enact simultaneously on the temporal plane what the myths reveal to be the activities of divine forces on the durative. Ritual imitation of the combat between life and death, for instance, commonly takes place in spring. The Iroquois Indians staged a fight between men dressed as Teharonhaiwagon (the life god) and Tawiskaron (the power of winter). Among the Yakut people of northeastern Siberia, a person representing spring and riding on a white horse would encounter another on a red horse personifying winter. In his *Teutonic Mythology* (1835), Jakob Grimm described the survival of such rituals in popular Germanic folk religion where two people disguised as summer and winter (one clothed in ivy, the other in straw or moss) would fight with each other until summer won.

Mock combats are only one part of seasonal religious activities, however. Gaster describes the basic features of the overall seasonal pattern in the ancient Near East as fivefold: (1) a demonstration of the end of the former temporal world (the king, as a symbol of the spirit of that world, is slain or deposed), (2) an interval of non-time, a vacant period of chaos (customary activities are suspended or reversed; a temporary king is appointed), (3) the symbolic purgation of evil from the world (the king is purified or confesses sins), (4) the initiation of new vitality and the inauguration of the new time period, the new world (the king engages in mock combat, undergoes a sacred marriage and is reinstated or inducted), and (5) celebration (a communal feast is held).

Annual rituals are of course the most universal expression of religions' recognition of the contingency of temporality, and the pattern of the creation of temporal being out of timeless Being-Itself (or Not-Being-Itself) is demonstrated most forcefully in New Year ceremonies. Mircea Eliade (1954) describes annual rituals as involving a return to the beginning of time, a repetition of sacred events which took place in the time of the creation, and a consequent renewal of the world.

The particular significance of annual rites stems from the widespread conception of the year as a full and complete unit of timely time. In some religions, the year and temporal being itself are simply defined as the same, as they are in the brahmanic Hindus' description of Prajāpati or the Maya notion of *kin*. In other faiths, the belief that the era of creation lasts only one year is explained more subtly and is revealed clearly only in annual ceremonies. For religions that take this perception most seriously, annual rituals may celebrate entirely new creations. The Ngaju people of South Borneo, for example, think temporality begins with the appearance of the constellation Orion and with the commencement of work in the fields, lasting through the harvest. After that, and before the beginning of the next creation, the world undergoes a time of chaos—the nontemporal period of *helat nyelo*. Social distinctions in force during the calendar year are dissolved; social regulations are lifted. People return from the fields, gather together to offer sacrifices, and combine socially and sexually into one symbolic being to be born again from the tree of life. Creation occurs and is enacted when representatives of Jata (the god of the underworld) and Mahatala (the god of the upperworld) rise up from the waters and descend from the mountain to unite.

Similar religious practices are followed in cultures around the world. In ancient times, the Babylonians fasted during the first week of Teshrit, the first month of the new year; in Greece, the festival of Thesmophoria was marked by abstention from food; and in the Attis cult in Asia the annual resurrection of the fertility spirit followed a lenten period. Traditional American Indians, among them the Cherokee, Choctaw, Comanchee, and Natchez, also observe periods of austerity and sacrifice before the new year. Seen in connection with other annual ceremonies of purgation and mortification, these rituals indicate pervasive belief in the yearly dissolution and re-creation of the world.

For other religions, the annual rituals imply no radical break in the continued existence of worldly reality and serve only as an occasion to recall time's perpetual dependence on the eternal. The difference here is one of degree, not kind. Judaism annually retells the sacred history of its people; Christianity celebrates yearly the birth, life, death, and resurrection of Jesus Christ; and Islam perennially repeats its periods of fasting in the month of Ramaḍān and calls the faithful to pilgrimage in Mecca. But the formative events these activities celebrate are not treated only in terms of their temporal nature. In each instance, the truths originally revealed in these occurrences are perceived as archetypical and always true, not merely prototypical and once true. Jews continue to feast at Passover not just because God once brought their ancestors out of Egyptian bondage but because it is their faith that all people can always be freed from any bondage with God's help. The Christian church announces the miracle of the resurrection not by stating that "Christ rose two thousand years ago" but by proclaiming on Easter morning, "Alleluia, Christ is risen!" Even in these most history-conscious faiths, connection to the eternal remains the focus at annual rites.

Time and the Individual. In a similar way, religions emphasize the dependence of individual, temporal lives on the eternal. Ultimately created out of timeless Being-Itself (or Not-Being-Itself), each creature is understood as perpetually sustained by its maker, and, on the occasion of a person's transition from one period of life to another, religions regularly honor his or her connection to the absolute.

Consensus among religions on the periodicity of individual lives is as hard to achieve as it is on the periodicity of the world's life. Some see existence as a category larger than life; others view it as coterminous with life; and still others think it lesser than life. Those faiths that affirm reincarnation and believe that an individual's existence spans many lifetimes understand birth and death as transitional rather than completely determining events. Conversely, those religions that take very seriously the movement from one life stage to another (the transition from childhood to adolescence, for instance) regularly include in their initiation rites enactments of ritual deaths and rebirths, renamings, and other indications that new creations of temporal being out of the eternal are thought to have occurred. The difference between these views and practices are not essential, however, as religions agree in their belief that the temporality of life is profoundly meaningful only in relation to eternity.

Twenty days after a child's birth, the Hopi mother passes a piece of corn (symbolizing the maize mother or the power of the earth) over her newborn's body, naming him and wishing for him a long and healthy life. Walking toward the east, she raises him up to the sun (representative of the creator Taiowa) and announces, "Father Sun, this is your child." Again she wishes that he will grow old. In the adolescent initiation ceremony of the Aborigines of eastern Australia, boys pass over to the sky-world (symbolized by specially marked trees on the initiation ground) and return new men; when they die, their burial grounds are similarly marked to indicate they have returned again to the realm of timelessness. Among the Ngaju people, all transition rites replicate the drama of creation. In marriage the bride and groom undergo ritual death by substitution (a slave is sacrificed or a coconut is speared) and are born anew as a couple. In ancient Egypt, the soul of the dead journeyed through the underworld like the sun god Re to be born again into eternity. These and countless other rituals demonstrate the belief that temporal being is continuously sustained and re-created out of the eternal. In contrast to the secular view that generations simply give birth to one another and that people simply grow up and die, religions persistently recall the origin of all temporal being in the timeless and see the sacred nature of that connection perpetually expressed and re-expressed in the moments and events of life.

Organized religions presume that the demands of daily life so engage people in thinking secularly that they become myopic in their self-understanding and blind to their dependence on the Absolute. Recognition of the contingent nature of their finite being (and of all finite time and being) is commonly forgotten, sublimated into fear of death or other threats to temporal existence, or rendered so abstract a thought as to be irrelevant to lived life. Religions celebrate specific times as sacred in order to teach or remind people to think of reality—their own and the world's—in a more profound manner. They proclaim that what is absolute in the universe must also be of ultimate value in people's lives if they are to be truly happy and successful, in harmony with reality. This, they claim, requires a shift in perspective. Religions reject the possibility of completely understanding people or events or any timely thing including the temporal world itself only in terms of other timely things, arguing that each thing's relation to timeless reality is what is essentially defining. They urge their followers to think beyond self-perceptions that are merely temporally relevant to those that are eternally significant.

Although religions define specific times in the life of the world or individuals as sacred, the new perspective gained in their celebration reveals the even more transforming realization that all times are sacred. Each moment, each "eye-blink" of time, is understood by those who have undergone this transformation to be a vehicle for the eternally timeless. Thus in religions around the world, fervent believers greet every day as "God's day" and consider every stage of life right and sacred. To them, the biblical God says of himself, "I am"; Allāh is felt nearer than the jugular vein; and the timelessly eternal is revealed always in the now. To these enlightened ones, the meaning of time only temporally understood seems illusory, while its meaning considered eternally seems absolutely real. To such seers of the religious view, people are not just products of their time but creatures of timeless eternity itself.

[*See also* Calendars; Chronology; New Year Festivals; *and* Seasonal Ceremonies.]

BIBLIOGRAPHY

Interdisciplinary studies of the nature of time can be found in several collections of essays edited by J. T. Fraser: *The Voices of Time* (New York, 1966) and *The Study of Time*, 2 vols. (New York, 1972). The religious attitude toward time is considered in the following works: S. G. F. Brandon's *History, Time, and Deity* (Manchester, 1965); *Man and Time*, vol. 3 of *Papers from the Eranos Yearbooks*, edited by Joseph Campbell (New York, 1957); Mircea Eliade's *Cosmos and History: The Myth of the Eternal Return* (New York, 1954); Eliade's *The Sacred and the Profane* (New York, 1959); Theodor H. Gaster's *Thespis* (New York, 1959); Philip Rahv's "The Myth and the Powerhouse," in his *Literature and the Sixth Sense* (Boston, 1969); and my *Primal Myths* (San Francisco, 1979). Studies of attitudes toward time in specific religions include Vine Deloria, Jr.'s *God Is Red* (New York, 1973); Henry Corbin's *Cyclical Time and Ismāʿīlī Gnosis* (London, 1983); Douglas R. Given's *An Analysis of Navaho Temporality* (Washington, D.C., 1977); John S. Mbiti's *African Religions and Philosophies* (New York, 1969); Joseph Needham's *Time and Eastern Man* (London, 1965); Jacob Neusner's *Between Time and Eternity: The Essentials of Judaism* (Encino, Calif., 1975); Stanley J. Samartha's *The Hindu View of History* (Bangalore, 1959); and Benjamin Lee Whorf's "An American Indian Model of the Universe," in *Teachings from the American Earth*, edited by Dennis Tedlock and Barbara Tedlock (New York, 1975).

BARBARA C. SPROUL

SACRIFICE. The term *sacrifice*, from the Latin *sacrificium* (*sacer*, "holy"; *facere*, "to make"), carries the connotation of the religious act in the highest, or fullest sense; it can also be understood as the act of sanctifying or consecrating an object. *Offering* is used as a synonym (or as a more inclusive category of which sacrifice is a subdivision) and means the presentation of a gift. (The word *offering* is from the Latin *offerre*, "to offer, present"; the verb yields the noun *oblatio*.) The Romance languages contain words derived from both the Latin words. The German *Opfer* is generally taken as derived from *offerre*, but some derive it from the Latin *operari* ("to perform, accomplish"), thus evoking once again the idea of sacred action.

Distinctions between sacrifice and offering are variously drawn, as for example, that of Jan van Baal: "I call an offering every act of presenting something to a supernatural being, a sacrifice an offering accompanied by the ritual killing of the object of the offering" (van Baal, 1976, p. 161). The latter definition is too narrow, however, since "killing" can be applied only to living beings, human or animal, and thus does not cover the whole range of objects used in sacrifice as attested by the history of religions. A truly essential element, on the other hand, is that the recipient of the gift be a supernatural being (that is, one endowed with supernatural power), with whom the giver seeks to enter into or remain in communion. Destruction, which can apply even to inanimate objects, is also regarded as essential by some authors but not by all; thus, according to the *Encyclopaedia Britannica,* a sacrifice is "a cultic act in which objects were set apart or consecrated and offered to a god or some other supernatural power" (1977, vol. 16, p. 128b). On the other hand, it is indeed essential to the concept that the human offerer remove something from his own disposal and transfer it to a supernatural recipient. The difference between the broad concept of offering and the narrower concept of sacrifice may be said to reside in the fact that a rite, a more or less solemn external form, is part of sacrifice.

Sacrifice differs from other cultic actions. The external elements of prayer are simply words and gestures (bodily attitudes), not external objects comparable to the gifts of sacrifice. Eliminatory rites, though they may include the slaying of a living being or the destruction of an inanimate object, are not directed to a personal recipient and thus should not be described as sacrifices. [*See* Scapegoat.] The same is true of ritual slayings in which there is no supernatural being as recipient, as in slayings by which companions are provided for the dead (joint burials) or that are part of the dramatic representation of an event in primordial time.

According to some theories, the conception of sacrifice as gift-giving is the result of a secondary development or even of a misunderstanding of rites that originally had a different meaning. (On this point, see "Theories of the Origin of Sacrifice," below.)

Morphology (Typology) of Sacrifice

The various forms of sacrifice show some common elements that respond to the following questions: (1) Who offers the sacrifice? (2) What is offered? (3) What external forms belong to the act of offering? (4) In what places and at what times are sacrifices offered? (5) Who is the recipient of the sacrifice? (6) For what reasons are sacrifices offered? The classifications implied by these questions often overlap (e.g., the type of material used for the sacrifice may determine the rite).

The Sacrificer. Most religions allow not only sacrifices offered by a group or community but also individual sacrifices for entirely personal reasons; in unstratified societies, therefore, everyone is in principle able to offer sacrifices. In fact, however, such purely personal sacrifices are rare, and as soon as sacrifices become connected with a group, however small, not every member of the group but only a representative may offer them. The sacrificer may be the head of a family or clan, an elder, or the leader of a band of hunters; in matrilinear societies, the sacrificer may be a woman. This is true especially of hunting and food-gathering cultures as well as nomadic pastoral cultures; even when these include individuals with specific ritual functions (medicine men, sorcerers, soothsayers, shamans), the function of offering sacrifice is not reserved to them. (In pastoral cultures we can sometimes see that only at a secondary stage do shamans replace family heads for certain sacrifices.) Food-planting cultures, on the other hand, commonly have cultic functionaries to whom the offering of sacrifice is reserved (e.g., the "earth-chiefs" in West African cultures). In sacrifices occasioned by some public endeavor or concern (e.g., an epidemic, or before or after a military campaign) the head of the tribe or larger group is the natural offerer of sacrifice. In archaic high cultures the function often goes with the kingly office; frequently, however, it decreases in importance in the course of further development and is then discernible only in vestigial form.

The more fully articulated the divisions in a society, the more often there is a class of cultic ministers to whom the offering of sacrifice is reserved. In this situation, tensions and changing relations of power can arise between king and priests, as in ancient Egypt. When a special priestly class exists, membership is either hereditary or must be earned through a consecration that is often preceded by lengthy training, or both may be required: descent from a certain family, class, or caste and training that leads to consecration. The consecrated functionary who is an offerer of sacrifice often must then submit to further special preparation (through purificatory rites, etc.) before exercising his office. A priest may have other cultic or magical functions in addition to that of offering sacrifice; he may, for example, act as oracle, exorcist, healer, or rainmaker, he may be a source of tradition and knowledge, and he may have noncultic functions as well.

Myths sometimes speak of the gods themselves as offering sacrifice. Sacrifice by human beings is then simply an imitation of the primal sacrifice that played a role in the establishment of the cosmic order.

Material of the Oblation. Scholars often generalize, as for example: "If we look about in the history of religion, we find there are very few things that have not, at some time or in some place, served as offering" (van Baaren, 1964, p. 7). Others will say that everything which has a value for human beings can be the material of sacrifice; the value may be symbolic and not necessarily inherent (as seen, for example, in the firstlings sacrifices of food-gatherers). Perhaps we may say that originally what was sacrificed was either something living or an element or symbol of life; in other words, it was not primarily food that was surrendered, but life itself. Yet inanimate things were also included in the material for sacrifice. (But do not archaic cultures regard a great deal as living that to the modern scientific mind is inanimate? Some scholars emphasize not the life but the power of the object.) Only by including inanimate objects is it possible to establish a certain classification of sacrificial objects, as for example, on the one hand, plants and inanimate objects (bloodless offerings), and, on the other, human beings and animals (blood offerings). But such a division is not exhaustive, since a comprehensive concept of sacrifice must include, for example, a bloodless consecration of human beings and animals.

Bloodless offerings. Bloodless offerings include, in the first place, vegetative materials. Thus food-gatherers offer a (symbolic) portion of the foodstuffs they have collected. Cultivators offer to higher beings (whom they may regard as in need of nourishment) sacrifices of food and drink: fruits, tubers, grains, and the foods that are made from these plants (meal, baked goods, oil), along with drinks, especially beer and other alcoholic beverages, that are poured out as libations. Among herders milk and milk products (e.g., koumiss, a drink derived from milk and slightly fermented, used in Inner Asia) play a similar role, especially in firstlings sacrifices (see below). In the ritual pouring (and especially in other ritual uses) of water, the intention is often not sacrifice but either some other type of rite (lustration, purification, or expiation) or sympathetic magic (e.g., pouring water in order to bring on rain). The offering of flowers or of a sweet fragrance otherwise produced (as in the widespread use of incense, or, among the American Indians, of tobacco smoke) also serves to please the gods or other higher beings.

Inanimate objects used in sacrifice include clothing, jewelry, weapons, precious stones and precious metals, sacrificial vessels made of metal, and, in more advanced civilizations, coins (especially as substitutes). Also used in sacrifice are all sorts of objects that are offered as votive gifts and are kept in a sanctuary, though it is possible that sympathetic magic also plays a role here, as for instance when one seeks deliverance from illnesses by depositing likenesses of the diseased organs.

Blood offerings. When animals or human beings serve as the sacrificial gift, the shedding of blood may become an essential part of the sacrificial action. Thus *ritual* slaying makes its appearance among cultivators and herders. (The practice is generally not found in hunting cultures, where a small but symbolically important part of the animal slain during the hunt is offered; thus the slaying is not part of the sacrificial action but precedes it. The slaying by the Ainu of a bear raised for the purpose is perhaps not really a sacrifice but a "dismissal" rite.)

The most extensive development of ritual slaying is found among cultivators. Here blood plays a significant role as a power-laden substance that brings fertility; it is sprinkled on the fields in order to promote crop yield. [*See* Blood.] Head-hunting, cannibalism, and human sacrifice belong to the same complex of ideas and rites; human sacrifice is also seen as a means of maintaining the cosmic order. [*See* Cannibalism *and* Human Sacrifice.] The combination of blood rites with magical conceptions of fertility is found more among tuber cultivators than among grain cultivators (but it is also found among maize growers, as in Mesoamerica). The assumption that all blood sacrifices originated among food cultivators and then were adopted at a later stage by nomadic herders is one-sided; ritual slaying probably made its appearance independently among the latter.

Blood sacrifices consist primarily of domesticated animals: among cultivators, sheep, goats, cattle, pigs, fowl; among nomads, also reindeer, horses, and camels (whereas pigs are regarded as unclean animals and not used, while fowl would not usually be kept). Dogs too may serve as sacrificial animals; they are especially sacrificed to provide companions for the dead. The offering of fish, birds other than domesticated fowl or doves, and wild animals is rarer. The characteristics of the sacrificial animal are often determined by the recipient; thus brightly colored animals are offered to the divinities of the sky, black animals to the divinities of the underworld and the dead or to feared demonic beings.

Sacrificial animals are not always killed by the shedding of their blood; they are sometimes throttled (especially in Inner Asia) or drowned in water or a bog. Furthermore, there is also the bloodless consecration of an animal, in which the animal is not killed but transferred alive into the possession of the divinity or other higher being, after which it often lives out its life in a sacred enclosure. Such animals can best be described as offerings, not as victims.

Substitutes. Blood sacrifices, especially those in which human beings were offered, were often replaced at a later stage by other sacrificial gifts, as, for example, "part-for-the-whole" sacrifices, like the offering of fingers, hair, or blood drawn through self-inflicted wounds. Some authors would thus classify so-called chastity sacrifices and include under this heading very disparate and sometimes even opposed practices such as, on the one hand, sexual abandon (sacral prostitution) and, on the other, sexual renunciation, castration, and circumcision.

Animal sacrifices can replace human sacrifices, as seen in well-known examples from Greek myth, epic, and history and in the Hebrew scriptures (Old Testament; *Gn.* 22:1–19). This shift may also be due to the suppression of an older religion (e.g., of the Bon religion of Tibet by Buddhism) or to measures taken by a colonial regime (e.g., the British rule in India) against human sacrifice. Substitute gifts for human beings or animals may also be of a vegetative kind (e.g., sacrificial cakes) or may consist of payments of money. Another form of substitution is that by representations, such as the clay figure substitutes for human beings that were buried with a high-ranking dead person and sent into the next world with him. Such figurines accompanying the dead are known from ancient Egypt and China; however, it is not certain that the practice was preceded by actual human sacrifices in these countries or that these practices are best described as sacrifices. Other kinds of pictorial representations have also been used, including objects cut from paper. Many votive offerings should probably be listed under this heading.

That human sacrifices were replaced by other kinds of sacrifices is certain in many instances, as in the late stage of Punic religion, when under Roman rule human sacrifices were replaced by other gifts (for example, lambs), as is attested by votive inscriptions; in other instances it is simply a hypothesis that certain rites replaced human sacrifice. Thus the so-called hair sacrifice is often a rite of initiation, sacralization, or desacralization (a rite of passage) in which the hair is not really a sacrificial gift and need not have replaced any human sacrifice. Sacral prostitution may also be understood as a magical rite of fertility or as a symbolic act of union with a divinity, rather than as a substitute for human sacrifice.

Divine offerings. In the examples given under the previous heading, a sacrificial gift is replaced by another of lesser value. The opposite occurs when the sacrificial gift itself is regarded as divine. This divine status may result from the idea that the sacrificial action repeats a mythical primordial sacrifice in which a god sacrificed either himself or some other god to yet a third god. In other cases the sacrificial object becomes divinized in the sacrificial action itself or in the preparation of the gifts. Thus among the Aztec the prisoner of war who was sacrificed was identified with the recipient of the sacrifice, the god Tezcatlipoca; moreover images of dough, kneaded with the blood of the sacrificed human, were identified with the sun god Huitzilopochtli and ritually eaten. In the Vedic religion divinity was assigned to the intoxicating drink *soma,* and in Iranian religion to the corresponding drink *haoma* or to the plant from which it was derived. For Christians who regard the celebration of the Eucharist as a rendering present of Christ's death on the cross, Christ himself is both offerer and sacrificial gift.

Rite (Manner and Method) of Sacrifice. Sacrifice involves not only a visible gift but an action or gesture that expresses the offering. This may consist of a simple deposition or a lifting up of the gift, without any change being effected in the object. The external form of the offering is already determined in many cases by the material of sacrifice; in the case of fluids, for example, the natural manner of offering them is to pour them out (libation), which is a kind of destruction. If the gift is a living being (animal or human), the destruction takes the form of killing. It is doubtful, however, whether destruction can be regarded as an essential element of any and every sacrificial rite. It is true that in many sacrifices the offering is in the form of slaughter or ritual killing; in others, however, the slaughter is only a necessary presupposition or technical requirement for the act of offering as such. Thus, among the Israelites, Levitical law prescribed that the slaughtering not be done by the priest; the latter's role began only after the slaughtering and included the pouring of sacrificial blood on the altar.

When food as such is in principle the real object offered, slaughter is a necessary first step if the animal sacrificed is to be in a form in which it can be eaten. When it is thought that the divinity (or, more generally, the recipient) does not eat material food but simply receives the soul or life of the sacrificial animal, burning may be used as a way of letting the soul rise up in the form of smoke ("the odor of sacrifice"; see also, on the burning of incense, below). When blood in particular is regarded as the vehicle of life, the pouring out of the blood, or the lifting up of bleeding parts of the victim, or even the flow of blood in the slaughtering may be the real act of offering. Another category of blood rites serves to apply the power in the blood to the offerers, their relatives, and the sphere in which they live their life (dwelling, property); this application may take the form of, for example, smearing.

The conception that the offerers have of the recipient and of his or her location also helps determine the form of the rite. If the recipient is thought to dwell in heaven, then the smoke that rises from a burning object becomes an especially appropriate symbol. The offerers will prefer the open air and will choose high places, whether natural (mountains, hills) or artificial (roofs, temple towers), or else they will hang the sacrificial gift on a tree or stake. Sacrifices to chthonic or underworld beings are buried, or the blood is allowed to flow into a hole. For water divinities or spirits the sacrifice is lowered into springs, wells, streams, or other bodies of water (although the interpretation of prehistoric burials in bogs as "immersion sacrifices" is not undisputed), or the offerers fill miniature boats with sacrificial gifts. Sacrifices offered to the dead are placed on the graves of the latter, or the blood of the victims is poured onto these graves.

Finally, the intention of the offerers or the function of the sacrifice also influences the form of the rite. If the sacrifice establishes or renews a covenant or, more generally, if it promotes the communion or community of recipient and offerer, then a sacrificial meal is usually an indispensable part of the rite. This meal can be understood as sharing a meal with the god or, the recipient, or more rarely, as ingesting the god; in this second case, the communion has a mystical character. In the first case, acceptance by the recipient removes the sacrificial gift from the profane sphere and sanctifies it; the recipient now becomes a host and celebrates a banquet with the offerer, who thereby receives back the sacrificial gift (or at least a part of it) as a vehicle now laden with higher powers. Thus understood, the sacrificial meal can be called a sacrament. The meal also establishes or strengthens the communion of the offerers with one another when it is a group that makes the offering. More rarely, people have believed that they eat the god himself in the flesh of the sacrificial animal (as in some Greek mysteries) or in images of dough (which were sometimes mixed with the blood of sacrificed human beings, as among the Aztec). (For the Christian conception of the Eucharist as a sacrificial meal, see below.)

Other rituals also express communion. For example, part of the sacrificial blood is poured on the altar, while the participants are sprinkled with the rest (as in the making of the covenant at Sinai, according to *Ex.* 24: 3–8). Or a person walks between the pieces of a sacrificial animal that has been cut in half.

In other cases the victim is completely destroyed, as in a burnt offering, or holocaust, which may express homage or complete submission to the divinity on which the offerers consider themselves dependent. Total destruction often also characterizes an expiatory sacrifice, in which a sacrificial meal is antecedently excluded by the fact that the sacrificial animal becomes the vehicle of sin or other uncleanness and must therefore be eliminated or destroyed (e.g., by being burned outside the camp).

The ritual of sacrifice can take very complicated forms, especially when professionals (priests) do the offering; part of their training is then the acquisition of a precise knowledge of the ritual. The sacrificial action is in stages: the sacrificial animal is often chosen some time in advance, marked, and set aside; before the sacrificial act proper, it is ritually purified and adorned; next comes the slaughter of the animal, then the offering proper or consecration or transfer from the profane to the sacred sphere or condition. At times, signs are heeded that are thought to show acceptance of the gift by the recipient. The division of the sacrificed animal can take various forms: an uncontrolled tearing apart of the victim by the participants, in imitation of a dismemberment reported in myth, or a careful dissection, as when the condition of specific organs yields omens (divination). In some sacrifices the bones may not be broken. A special form of division is cutting in two, which is practiced not only in sacrifices proper but also in rites of purification and expiation. (See Henninger, 1981, pp. 275–285.) A sacrificial meal may conclude the sacrifice, but there may also be special concluding rites for releasing the participants from the realm of the sacred. It is sometimes also prescribed that nothing is to be left of the sacrificial gift and nothing carried away from the sphere of the sacred; any remnants must be buried or burned (though this last action is not the same as a burnt offering).

Place and Time of Sacrifice. The place of offering is not always an altar set aside for the purpose. Thus sacrifices to the dead are often offered at their graves, and sacrifices to the spirits of nature are made beside trees or bushes, in caves, at springs, and so on. Artificial altars in the form of tables are relatively rare; they become the normal site of sacrifice only in the higher civilizations, where they are usually located in a temple or its forecourt and are sometimes specially outfitted, as for example with channels to carry away the sacrificial blood. Far more frequently, natural stones or heaps of stones or earthen mounds serve as altars. A perpendicular stone is often regarded as the seat of a divinity, and sacrifice is then offered in front of the stone, not on it. Flat roofs and thresholds can also be preferred locations for sacrifice.

With regard to time, a distinction must be made between regular and extraordinary (occasional or special) sacrifices. The time for regular sacrifices is determined by the astronomical or vegetative year; thus there will be daily, weekly, and monthly sacrifices (especially in higher cultures in which service in the temple is organized like service at a royal court). Sowing and harvest and the transition from one season to the next are widely recognized occasions for sacrifice; in nomadic cultures this is true especially of spring, the season of birth among animals and of abundance of milk. The harvest season is often marked by first-fruits sacrifices that are conceived as a necessary condition for the desacralization of the new harvest, which may only then be put to profane use. The date of the New Year feast is often established not astronomically but in terms of the vegetative year. [*See* New Year Festivals.] In the life of the individual, birth, puberty, marriage, and death are frequently occasions for sacrifices. The annual commemoration of a historical event may also become a set part of the calendar and thus an occasion for sacrifice. [*See* Seasonal Ceremonies.]

Extraordinary occasions for sacrifice are provided by

special occurrences in the life of the community or the individual. These occurrences may be joyous, as, for example, the erection of a building (especially a temple), the accession of a new ruler, the successful termination of a military campaign or other undertaking, or any event that is interpreted as a manifestation of divine favor. Even more frequently, however, it is critical situations that occasion extraordinary sacrifices: illnesses (especially epidemics or livestock diseases) and droughts or other natural disasters. Many expiatory sacrifices also have their place in this context, whether offered for individuals or the community (see below).

Van Baal (1976, pp. 168–178) distinguishes between low-intensity and high-intensity rites; the former occur in normal situations, the latter in disasters and misfortunes, which are taken as signs that relations with higher beings have been disturbed. This division is to a great extent the same as that between regular and extraordinary sacrifices, but it pays insufficient heed to the fact that joyous occasions may also lead to extraordinary sacrifices.

Recipient of Sacrifice. Many definitions of sacrifice specify divine beings (in either a monotheistic or a polytheistic context) as the recipients of sacrifice, but this is too narrow a view. All the many kinds of beings to whom humans pay religious veneration, or even those whom they fear, can be recipients of sacrifice. Such recipients can thus be spirits, demonic beings, and even humans, although sacrifice in the proper sense is offered to humans only when they have died and are considered to possess a superhuman power. The dead to whom sacrifice is offered include especially the ancestors to whom is attributed (as in Africa and Oceania) a decisive influence on human beings. Care for the dead (e.g., by gifts of food and drink) need not always indicate a cult of the dead; a cult exists only when the dead are regarded not as helpless and in need (as they were in ancient Mesopotamia), but rather as possessing superhuman power.

Intentions of Sacrifice. Theologians usually distinguish four intentions of sacrifice: praise (acknowledgment, homage), thanksgiving, supplication, and expiation; but several or even all four of these intentions may be combined in a single sacrifice. From the standpoint of the history of religions this schema must be expanded somewhat, especially with regard to the third and fourth categories.

Praise (homage). Pure sacrifices of praise that express nothing but homage and veneration and involve no other intention are rarely found. They occur chiefly where a regular sacrificial cult is practiced that resembles in large measure the ceremonial of a royal court.

Thanksgiving. Sacrifices of thanksgiving are more frequent. According to the best explanation of firstlings sacrifices, these, in the diverse forms they have taken in various cultures, belong to this category. (For divergent interpretations, see "Theories of the Origin of Sacrifice," below.) Votive sacrifices likewise belong here, insofar as the fulfillment of the vow is an act of thanksgiving for the favor granted.

Supplication. Yet more commonly found are sacrifices of supplication. The object of the petition can range from purely material goods to the highest spiritual blessings (forgiveness of sins, divine grace). The line of demarcation between these sacrifices and sacrifices of expiation and propitiation is often blurred.

Sacrifices of supplication include all those sacrifices that, in addition to establishing or consolidating the link with the world of the sacred (which is a function of every sacrifice), are intended to have some special effect. Such effects include the maintenance of the cosmic order; the strengthening of the powers on which this order depends (e.g., by the gift of blood, as in the human sacrifices of the Aztec); and the sacralization or consecration of places, objects, and buildings (construction sacrifices, dedication of boundary stones, idols, temples), of individual human beings, and of human communities and their relationships (ratification of treaties). Construction activities are often thought to be an intrusion into the sphere of superhuman beings (spirits of earth and water, or divinities of earth and water) who may resent them; for this reason, scholars speak in this context of sacrifices intended to appease or placate. These come close to being expiatory sacrifices (in the broadest sense of the term), insofar as the offerers intend to forestall the anger of these higher beings by a preventive, apotropaic action (protective sacrifices).

Sacrifices are also offered for highly specialized purposes, for example, in order to foretell the future by examining the entrails of the sacrificial animal.

Expiation. In the narrow sense, expiatory sacrifices presuppose consciousness of a moral fault that can be punished by a higher being who must therefore be placated by suitable acts on the part of the human beings involved. [*See* Atonement.] But the concept of expiation (purification, lustration) is often used in a broader sense to mean the removal or prevention of every kind of evil and misfortune. Many authors assume that the ethical concept of sin was a late development and therefore consider rites of purification and elimination for the removal of all evils (in which no relation to higher personal beings plays a part) to be the earliest form of expiation. Furthermore, when there is a human relationship to personal beings, a distinction must be made. These beings (spirits, demons, etc.) may be regarded as indifferent to ethical considerations, unpredictable, and capricious, or even malicious, envious, cruel, and bloodthirsty. In this case expiation means simply the removal of what has roused (or might rouse) the anger of these beings, so that they will leave humans in peace; no relationship of goodwill or friendship is created or sought. On the other hand, the higher beings may be regarded as inherently benevolent, so that any disturbance of a good relationship with them is attributed to a human fault; the normal good relationship must therefore be restored by an expiatory sacrifice or other human action; in these cases we speak of atonement, conciliation, or propitiation. The human fault in question may be moral, but it may also be purely ritual, unintentional, or even unconscious.

Certain facts, however, render questionable the overly schematic idea of a unilinear development from a nonethical to an ethical conception that is connected with general theories on the evolution of religion. Even very "primitive" peoples have ideas of higher beings that approve and keep watch over moral behavior. Furthermore, not only in the high cultures but in primitive religions as well, expiatory sacrifice is often accompanied by a confession of sins. A more highly developed form of the ideas underlying expiatory sacrifice may be linked to the concept of representation or substitution, especially when the role of substitute is freely accepted (self-sacrifice). This, however, is not the proper context for speculative theories (developed especially by James G. Frazer and those inspired by him) on the ritual slaying of the king, who may be replaced by a substitute; Frazer is speaking of the magical influence of the king in his prime on the general welfare of the community, and not of disturbances of the communal order by faults for which amends must be made.

Theories of the Origin of Sacrifice

Very different answers have been given to the question of which of the various forms of sacrifice presented above is to be regarded as the oldest and the one out of which the others emerged either by development to a higher level or by degeneration. In each case, theories of sacrifice have been heavily influenced by their authors' conceptions of the origin and development of religion. Scholars today generally approach all these explanations with some skepticism. A brief review of the various theories is nonetheless appropriate, since each emphasizes certain aspects of the phenomenon and thus contributes to an understanding of it.

Sacrifice as Gift. Before the history of religions became an independent discipline, the conception of sacrifice as gift was already current among theologians; it was therefore natural that the history of religions should initially make use of this concept. [*See* Gift Giving.] In this discipline, however, the conception acquired two completely different applications: the sacrificial gift as bribe and the sacrificial gift as act of homage.

The gift as bribe. The gift theory proposed by E. B. Tylor (1871) supposes that higher forms of religion, including monotheism, gradually developed out of animism as the earliest form. Since the spirits resident in nature are indifferent to moral considerations and have but a limited sphere of power, they can be enriched by gifts and thereby influenced; in other words, they can be bribed. Sacrifice was therefore originally a simple business transaction of *do ut des* ("I give so that you will give in return"), an activity without moral significance. Sacrifice as homage and as abnegation or renunciation developed only gradually out of sacrifice as bribe; but even when it did, the *do ut des* idea continued to be operative for a long time in the later stages of religion, especially wherever sacrifice was conceived as supplying the recipient with food.

Critics of this view have stressed that in archaic cultures the giving of a gift, even between human beings, is not a purely external transaction but at the same time establishes a personal relation between giver and recipient. According to some scholars, the giving of a gift also involves a transfer of magical power for which, in a very generalized sense, they often use the term *mana.* This personal relation is even more important when a gift is presented to superhuman beings. Thus it is understandable that sacrificial gifts of little material value can be quite acceptable; such gifts need not be interpreted as efforts to circumvent the higher beings and their influence. In light of this consideration, later theories of sacrifice gave the *do ut des* formula a deeper meaning and regarded the commercial understanding of it as a degenerate version.

The gift as homage. Wilhelm Schmidt (1912–1955, 1922) understood the sacrificial gift in a way completely different from Tylor. He took as his point of departure the principle that the original meaning of sacrifice can be seen most clearly in the firstlings sacrifices of primitive hunters and food-gatherers. These are sacrifices of homage and thanksgiving to the supreme being to whom everything belongs and who therefore cannot be enriched by gifts—sacrifices to the giver of foods that human beings do not produce but simply appropriate for themselves through hunting and gathering. These sacrifices consist in the offering of a portion of food that is often quantitatively small but symbolically important. In nomadic herding cultures this sacrifice of homage and thanksgiving takes the form of an offering of the firstlings of the flocks (young animals) or of the products of the flocks (e.g., milk). In food-growing cultures the fertility of the soil is often attributed to the dead, especially the ancestors; they, therefore, become the recipients of the first-fruits sacrifice. When this happens, however, the character of the sacrifice is altered, since the recipients now have need of the gifts (as food) and can therefore be influenced. According to Anton Vorbichler (1956), what is offered in firstlings sacrifices is not food but life itself, but since life is seen as deriving from the supreme being as creator, the basic attitude of homage and thanksgiving remains unchanged.

Schmidt's historical reconstruction, according to which firstlings sacrifices are the earliest form of sacrifice, has not been sufficiently demonstrated. From the phenomenological standpoint, however, this kind of sacrifice, in which the gift has symbolic rather than real value and is inspired by a consciousness of dependence and thanksgiving, does exist and must therefore be taken into account in any general definition of sacrifice.

Sacrifice as a (Totemic) Communal Meal. W. Robertson Smith (1889) developed a theory of sacrifice for the Semitic world that he regarded as universally applicable. He saw the weakness of Tylor's theory, which paid insufficient heed to the sacral element and to the function of establishing or maintaining a community. Under the influence of J. F. McLennan, who had done pioneer work in the study of totemism, Smith proposed a theory of sacrifice whereby the earliest form of religion (among the Semites and elsewhere) was belief in a theriomorphic tribal divinity with which the tribe had a blood relationship. Under ordinary circumstances, this totem animal was not to be killed, but there were rituals in which it was slain and eaten in order to renew the community. In this rite, recipient, offerer, and victim were all of the same nature; sacrifice was thus originally a meal in which the offerers entered into communion with the totem. As a vivid example of such a ceremony, Smith cites a story told by Nilus of a camel sacrifice offered by the bedouin of the Sinai. It was the transition to a sedentary way of life and the social changes effected by this transition that gave rise to the conception of sacrifice as a gift comparable to the tribute paid to a sovereign, the latter relationship being taken as model for the relation to the divinity. The burnt offering, or holocaust, was likewise a late development.

Smith's theory is valuable for its criticism of the grossly mechanistic theory of Tylor and for its emphasis on the communion (community) aspect of sacrifice; as a whole, however, it is unacceptable for a number of reasons. First, the idea of sacrifice as gift is already present in the firstlings sacrifices offered in the egalitarian societies of primitive hunters and food-gatherers; it does not, therefore, presuppose the model of the offering of tribute to a sovereign. Second, it is doubtful that totemism existed among the Semites; furthermore, totemism does not occur universally as a stage in the history of human development, as was initially supposed in the nineteenth century when the phenomenon was first discovered, but is rather a specialized development. Third, the *intichiuma* ceremonies (increase ceremonies) of central Australian tribes are magical rites aimed at multiplying the totem animal species. They were used by early theorists of totemism, but they do not in fact match the original model of sacrifice postulated by Smith. Finally, the supposed account by Nilus is not a reliable report from a hermit living in the Sinai Peninsula but a fiction whose author is unknown; it shares with the late Greek novel certain clichés used in depicting barbarians and cannot be regarded as a reliable historical source (see Henninger, 1955). Smith's theory of sacrifice also contributed to Freud's conception of the slaying of the primal father, which Freud saw as the origin of sacrifice and other institutions, especially the incest taboo; this conception is therefore subject to the same criticisms.

As Link between the Profane and Sacral Worlds. Henri Hubert and Marcel Mauss (1899) rejected Tylor's theory because of its mechanistic character. They also rejected Smith's theory because it arbitrarily chose totemism as a universally applicable point of departure and reconstructed the development of the forms of sacrifice solely by analogy and without adequate historical basis and, further, because offering is an essential element in the concept of sacrifice. Hubert and Mauss themselves begin with an analysis of the Vedic and Hebraic rituals of sacrifice and, in light of this, define sacrifice as "a religious act which, by the consecration of a victim, modifies the condition of the moral person who accomplishes it, or that of certain objects with which he is concerned" (*Encyclopaedia Britannica*, 1977, vol. 16, p. 129a). The victim is not holy by nature (as it is in Smith's theory); the consecration is effected by destruction, and the connection with the sacral world is completed by a sacred meal. Implied here is the view (which goes back to Émile Durkheim) of the French sociological school that the sacral world is simply a projection of society. "Gods are representations of communities, they are societies thought of ideally and imaginatively. . . . Sacrifice is an act of abnegation by which the individual recognizes society; it recalls to particular consciences the presence of collective forces, represented by their gods" (Evans-Pritchard, 1965, p. 70).

The objection was raised against this explanation that conclusions universally valid for the understanding of sacrifice as such, especially in "primitive" societies, cannot be drawn from an analysis of two highly developed forms of sacrifice, even if the two differ among themselves. Thus E. E. Evans-Pritchard, having called the work of Hubert and Mauss "a masterly analysis of

Vedic and Hebrew sacrifice," immediately adds: "But masterly though it was, its conclusions are an unconvincing piece of sociologistic metaphysics. . . . They are conclusions not deriving from, but posited on a brilliant analysis of the mechanism of sacrifice, or perhaps one should say of its logical structure, or even of its grammar" (Evans-Pritchard, 1965, pp. 70–71).

Sacrifice as Magic. Hubert and Mauss considered the recipient of sacrifice to be simply a hypostatization of society itself. Other authors have gone even further, regarding the idea of a recipient as not essential to the concept of sacrifice. They more or less explicitly presuppose that the idea of an impersonal force or power, to which the name *mana* is given more frequently than any other, is older than the idea of soul or spirit as understood in animism. For this reason, the idea of sacrifice as a purely objective magical action (the triggering of a magical force that is thought to be concentrated especially in the blood), accomplished by destruction of a sacrificial gift (e.g., the slaying of an animal), must be the basic form, or at least one of the basic forms, of sacrifice. Sacrifices of this kind are said to be "predeistic." Expressions such as this, which imply a temporal succession, are also used by phenomenologists, who claim in principle to be simply describing phenomena and not asserting any kind of development. In this view the concept of sacrifice as gift is a secondary development in which gifts to the dead played an important role (Loisy, 1920). According to Gerardus van der Leeuw (1920–1921), sacrifice conceived as gift constitutes a transfer of magical force; the *do ut des* formula describes not a commercial transaction but the release of a current of force (*do ut possis dare,* "I give power to you so that you can give it back to me"). The recipient is strengthened by the gift; the two participants, deity and human beings, are simultaneously givers and receivers, but the central role belongs to the gift itself and to the current of force that it sets in motion. This theory, then, combines to some extent the gift theory and the communion theory, but it does so from the standpoint of magic.

There do in fact exist rituals of slaying and destruction in which no personal recipient is involved and that are regarded as operating automatically; there is no evidence, however, that such rituals are older than sacrifice in the sense described earlier. The examples constantly adduced come to a very great extent from high cultures (e.g., Roman religion). An especially typical form occurs in Brahmanic speculation, where sacrifice is looked upon as a force that ensures the continuation of a cosmic process to which even the gods are subject. Other examples come from food-growing peoples. When human beings contribute by their own activity to the production of food, their consciousness of dependence on higher powers is less than in an economy based on the appropriation of goods not produced by humans. Thus it is easier to adopt the idea that the higher powers can be influenced and even coerced by sacrifices and other rites. For this reason, the firstlings sacrifices of hunters and food-gatherers do not fit in with speculations that give priority to magic, nor do such speculations take account of such sacrifices, and thus the full extent of the phenomenon of sacrifice is lost from view. Sacrifice and magic should rather be considered as phenomena that differ in nature; they have indeed influenced each other in many ways, but neither can be derived from the other. The personal relation that is established by a gift is fully intelligible without bringing in an element of magic (see van Baal, 1976, pp. 163–164, 167, 177–178). [*See* Magic.]

Sacrifice as Reenactment of Primordial Events. According to Adolf E. Jensen (1951), sacrifice cannot be understood as gift; its original meaning is rather to be derived from certain myths found in the cultures of cultivators, especially in Indonesia and Oceania. These myths maintain that in primordial time there were as yet no mortal human beings but only divine or semidivine beings (*dema* beings); this state ended with the killing of a *dema* divinity from whose body came the plants useful to humans. The ritual slaying of humans and animals, headhunting, cannibalism, and other blood rites are ceremonial repetitions of that killing in primordial time; they affirm and guarantee the present world order, with its continuous destruction and re-creation, which would otherwise be unable to function. Once the myth had been largely forgotten or was no longer seen to be connected with ritual, rites involving slaying were reinterpreted as a giving of a gift to divinities (who originally played no role in these rites, because the primordial divine being had been slain); blood sacrifices thus became "meaningless survivals" of the "meaningful rituals of killing" of the earlier food-growing cultures. Magical actions are likewise degenerate fragments of the originally meaningful whole formed by the mythically based rituals of killing.

This theory has some points in common with Freud's theory of the murder of the primal father and with the theory according to which sacrifice originated in the self-sacrifice of a divine being in the primordial time of myth. The common weakness of all these theories is that they take account only of blood sacrifices. These, however, developed only in food-growing and even later cultures, whereas in the firstlings sacrifices of hunters and food-gatherers there is no ritual killing, and bloodless offerings are widespread in many other cultures as well.

Sacrifice as Anxiety Reaction. In the theories discussed thus far, except for the theory of sacrifice as a gift in homage, firstlings sacrifices receive either inadequate attention or none at all. Vittorio Lanternari (1976), on the other hand, provides a formal discussion of these, but gives an interpretation of them that is completely different from that of Schmidt. Lanternari's point of departure is the analysis of a certain form of neurosis provided by some psychologists; according to this analysis, this kind of neurosis finds expression in the undoing of successes earlier achieved and is at the basis of certain religious delusions. Lanternari maintains that a similar psychic crisis occurs among "primitives" when they are confronted with success (hunters after a successful hunt, food cultivators after the harvest) and that this crisis leads them to undertake an at least symbolic destruction of what they had gained. For Lanternari, then, a firstlings sacrifice is the result of anxiety, whereas for Schmidt it is an expression of gratitude. Hunters feel the slaying of the animal to be a sacrilege, which explains the rites of Siberian peoples that seek a reconciliation with the slain animal and a repudiation of the killing. For cultivators the sacrilege consists in the violation of the earth, which is the dwelling of the dead, by the cultivation of the soil; they feel anxiety at the thought of the dead and worry about future fertility, even if the harvest is a good one. It is a secondary matter whether the symbolic destruction of the gain is accomplished by offering food to a higher being or by simply doing away with a portion of it.

Critics of the psychopathological explanation have pointed out the essential differences between the behavior of neurotics and the religious behavior exhibited in firstlings sacrifices. In the psychically ill (those who are defeated by success), efforts at liberation are purely individual; they are not part of a historical tradition, are not organically integrated into a cultural setting, and do not lead to inner deliverance. In religious life, on the contrary, efforts to surmount a crisis are organically inserted into tradition and culture, tend to restore psychic balance, and in fact achieve such a balance. For this reason the "primitive" peoples in question are not defeated by life, as neurotics are; on the contrary, their way of life has stood the test of ages. Whatever judgment one may pass on the value or nonvalue of the underlying religious views and modes of behavior of these peoples, one cannot characterize them as pathological; for this reason a psychopathological explanation of sacrifice must also be rejected. This is not to deny that fear or anxiety plays a significant part in certain forms of sacrifice; such feelings result primarily from the ideas of the offerers about the character of the recipient in question (see Henninger, 1968, pp. 176–180).

Sacrifice as a Mechanism for Diverting Violence. Whereas Jensen derived rituals involving killing, which were subsequently reinterpreted as "sacrifices," from certain myths of food-growing cultures, René Girard (1977, 1978) has proposed a more comprehensive theory that explains not only sacrifice but the sacred itself as resulting from a focusing of violent impulses upon a substitute object, a scapegoat. According to Girard, the peaceful coexistence of human beings cannot be taken for granted; when the desires of humans fasten upon the same object, rivalries arise and with them a tendency toward violence that endangers the existing order and its norms. This tendency can be neutralized, however, if the reciprocal aggressions are focused on a marginal object, a scapegoat. The scapegoat is thereby rendered sacred: it is seen as accursed but also as bringing salvation. Thus the focusing of violence on an object gives rise to the sacred and all that results from it (taboos, a new social order). Whereas the violence was originally focused on a randomly chosen object, in sacrifice the concentration takes a strict ritual form; as a result, internecine aggressions are constantly being diverted to the outside and cannot operate destructively within the community. At bottom, therefore, sacrifice lacks any moral character. Eventually it was eliminated by the critique of sacrifice that began in the Hebrew scriptures and, most fully, by the fact that Jesus freely made himself a "scapegoat" and in so doing transcended the whole realm of sacrifice. Girard supports his thesis by appealing to the phenomenon of blood sacrifice, which (especially in the form of human sacrifice) is a constant in the history of religions, and by citing the evidence of rivalry and violence, leading even to fratricide, that is supplied by the mythical traditions (especially myths of the origin of things) and also by history (persecution of minorities as scapegoats, etc.).

A critique of this theory can in part repeat the arguments already advanced against Jensen. Apart from the fact that it does not distinguish between sacrifice and eliminatory rites, Girard's concept of sacrifice is too narrow, for he supports it by reference solely to stratified societies and high cultures. It could at most explain blood sacrifices involving killing, but not sacrifice as such and certainly not the sacred as such, since the idea of the sacred exists even among peoples (e.g., in Australia) who do not practice sacrifice. As was pointed out earlier, firstlings sacrifices (of which Girard does not speak) have intellectual and emotional presuppositions far removed from Girard's key concepts of "primal murder" and "scapegoat mechanism."

The value of the theories here reviewed is that each of them highlights a certain aspect of sacrifice. It is unlikely that we will ever have a sure answer to the question of whether there was a single original form of sacrifice or whether, on the contrary, various forms developed independently.

Sacrifice in History

It will never be possible to write a complete history of sacrifice. In any case, sacrifice is found in most of the religions known to us. The extent to which the human mind has taken the phenomenon of sacrifice for granted is clear, for example, from the role it plays in many myths dealing with primordial time. Probably to be grouped with these sacrifices is the sacrifice that Utanapishtim, the hero of the Mesopotamian flood story, offers after the flood, as well as the one that Noah offers in the biblical flood story (*Gn.* 9:20–21). Even earlier, the Bible tells of the sacrifices offered by Cain the farmer and Abel the shepherd (*Gn.* 4:3–5); these are expressly said to be firstlings sacrifices. Aristotle, too, was of the opinion that the sacrifice of firstlings (of field and flock) is the oldest form of sacrifice. As we know today, these sacrifices were also performed by peoples—hunters and food-gatherers—whose economy was of a purely appropriative kind.

Archaic Cultures. Scholars disagree on whether there are unambiguous indications of sacrifice in the Paleolithic period. On the basis of a comparison with the practices of more recent hunting peoples, various authors have interpreted the burial of the skulls and long bones of cave bears as part of firstling sacrifices; this view, however, has met with strong criticism. Nonetheless, Hermann Müller-Karpe (1966, pp. 224–229) insists that there is clear evidence of sacrifice in the early Paleolithic period. There is undisputed evidence of sacrifice in the Neolithic period (Müller-Karpe, 1968, pp. 334–348; see also pp. 348–371 on the treatment of the dead).

Sacrifice is also found in all the types of nonliterate cultures made known to us by ethnologists. It is not detectable, however, among some primitive hunters and food-gatherers, for example, in Australia; whether it was present there at an earlier time is uncertain. On the other hand, it is amply attested among nomadic shepherds in both Asia and Africa, and among food-growing peoples, from primitive tuber cultivators down to the most highly developed grain growers, who themselves mark a transition to the high cultures (as for instance the ancient rice-growing cultures of Japan and China). It is typical of many food-growing cultures (e.g., in Africa) that, while they believe in a supreme creator god, they assign him hardly any role in cult. Sacrifices are offered primarily or even exclusively to lesser divinities, spirits of nature, and ancestors who in some instances are regarded as mediators and intercessors with the supreme creator god.

Historical High Cultures. In Shintō, the ancient nature religion of Japan, sacrifices were offered to the divinities of nature and to the dead; these were in part regularly recurring sacrifices determined by the rhythm of the agricultural year and in part sacrifices of supplication or sacrifices in fulfillment of vows made under extraordinary circumstances. While originally offered simply by individuals, sacrifice eventually became the concern of the community and was therefore offered by the emperor or by priests commissioned by him. Human sacrifices also occurred.

In China the sacrifice that the emperor offered to heaven and earth at the time of the winter solstice had an important function. In addition to sacrifices determined by the agricultural year, sacrifices especially to the ancestors played a large part in the life of the people. These were offered at the graves of the dead, in the clan's hall of the ancestors, or before the family's ancestral tablets. The emperor sacrificed to his ancestors in temples erected especially in their honor.

For ancient Egypt, the archaeological, epigraphical, and literary evidence points to a strictly ritualized sacrificial cult, administered by a highly organized priesthood and including daily sacrifices in the temples, where the divinity was treated like a sovereign in his palace.

The same was true of ancient Mesopotamia, where the Sumerians already had a professional priesthood and a rather full calendar of feasts with accompanying obligatory sacrifices. Both priesthood and calendar were to a very large extent taken over and developed still further by the invading Semites. The ritual and therefore the sacrificial cult of the Hittites were strongly influenced by the pre-Indo-European population of Anatolia (whose language also continued to be largely used in ritual), but were also influenced by Mesopotamia. Mythological and ritual texts from Ugarit give evidence of a sacrificial cult that in part was influenced by Mesopotamia and in part showed peculiarly Canaanite characteristics; some of the terms connected with sacrifice are related to Hebrew terms.

The evidence for the other Semites is sketchy. In the high cultures of southern Arabia, which are known to us from inscriptions dating from as far back as the first millennium BCE, the sacrificial cult was administered by a professional priesthood and was offered mainly to the three major astral divinities (Sun, Moon, Venus). Documentation for northern and central Arabia begins at a later time; apart from rock inscriptions containing scattered details about religion, the chief sources are literary, mostly from the Islamic period, and provide rather sparse information about pilgrimages to the shrines of local divinities and the sacrifices offered there.

In Vedic and later Hindu religion, sacrifice, which was controlled by the brahmans, was ritualized down to the smallest detail and given a comprehensive speculative theological explanation. In the horse sacrifice (the Aśvamedha) and in other cultic practices, as, for example, the sacrifice of butter and of the sacred intoxicating drink *soma,* there are elements common to the Indo-Iranian world, but after the immigration of the Aryans into India, these were to some extent amalgamated there with pre-Aryan rites. Buddhism, on the other hand, rejected sacrifice in principle; tendencies to a spiritualization of sacrifice and its replacement by asceticism are also found in some currents of Hinduism.

Animal sacrifices were also practiced in the oldest form of Iranian religion, where they were inherited from the Indo-Iranian period. During his reform, Zarathushtra (Zoroaster) abolished these practices. In later times such sacrifices again made their appearance to some extent; they were offered, however, not to Ahura Mazdā but to subordinate heavenly beings. Bloodless sacrifices, involving especially the sacred intoxicating drink *haoma,* remained especially important.

Historical Greek religion combined the religion of the Indo-European invaders with that of the pre-Indo-European population; the same combination marked the sacrificial cult. There were bloodless sacrifices of food and drink. In blood sacrifices a distinction was made, as far as objects and ritual were concerned, between those offered to the ouranic gods *(hiereia, thusiai),* which culminated in a sacrificial meal, and those offered to the chthonic gods *(sphagia),* in which there was no sacrificial meal and the victim was often completely cremated or buried (sacrifices of destruction). Pigs and cattle were sacrificed to the ouranic gods, while inedible animals (horses, asses, dogs) were the chief offerings to the chthonic gods. Human sacrifice was later replaced by other sacrifices. The sacrificer was the ruler in the earliest period; later on there were professional priests.

In its earliest form, before intensive contact with Greek religion, Roman religion was pronouncedly agrarian. Occasions for sacrifices were therefore determined primarily by the agricultural year, and only later by special occasions in civic life. Etruscan influence shows in the divination *(haruspicia)* that was connected with sacrifice; the animals sacrificed were chiefly pigs, sheep, and cattle *(suovetaurilia).* Like Roman religion generally, the sacrificial cult had a marked juridical character.

The sacrifices known from the Hebrew scriptures (Old Testament) are, in their external form, largely the same as those found in the surrounding world, especially among the Canaanites. As far as ritual was concerned, a distinction was made chiefly between the burnt offering, or holocaust *(ʿolah),* in which the sacrificial animal was completely burned up, and the sacrifice of salvation or peace *(zevaḥ shelamim).* In the latter, only certain parts of the sacrificial animal were burned; the blood, regarded as the vehicle of life and therefore not to be consumed by humans, was poured out (in many sacrifices it was smeared on the altar), and the rite ended with a sacrificial meal. Expiatory sacrifices constituted a special category comprising *asham,* "guilt sacrifice," and *ḥaṭʾaṭ,* "sacrifice for sin," the distinction between which is not entirely clear. In these sacrifices the animal had to be burned up, probably because it had become the vehicle of impurity. *Minḥah* meant a bloodless sacrifice (of vegetables), but the term was also used in a broader sense. There were, in addition, incense sacrifices and libations. The sacrificial cult was ritualized in great detail, especially in the period after the Babylonian exile. In this ritual the three major feasts, those involving a prescribed pilgrimage to the central sanctuary, were marked by extensive sacrifices. In addition, there were daily sacrifices in the temple. There were also individual occasions for sacrifice, some of them prescribed, others inspired by freely made vows. After the destruction of the Second Temple in 70 CE, the sacrificial cult ceased and was replaced by other religious activities.

Islam is in principle opposed to sacrifice. "It is not their flesh and blood [i.e., that of sacrificial animals] that reaches God but the piety of your heart" (Qurʾān, surah 22:38). Sacrifice thus has no place in official worship. Pre-Islamic blood sacrifices live on, in external form, in the great slaughters that take place as part of the pilgrimage ritual at Mount Arafat near Mecca, and similarly in almost all the countries of the Islamic world, on the tenth day of the month Dhū al-Ḥijjah. These are interpreted, however, as commemorations of the sacrifice of Abraham and as almsgiving, inasmuch as the flesh is given to the poor or to anyone who wants it. Blood sacrifices (and bloodless ones as well) are also part of popular piety, especially of veneration of the saints; but these are not sanctioned by orthodox Islam.

According to New Testament teaching, which is developed especially in the letter to the Hebrews, the sacrifices of the Old Testament were only provisional and had to cease under the new covenant. The self-giving of Jesus in his death on the cross is understood as the definitive and perfect sacrifice that has the power in itself to effect expiation and redemption and that therefore makes all earlier sacrifices superfluous. In the Roman Catholic church and the Eastern churches the celebration of the Eucharist is regarded as a rendering present (not a repetition) of the sacrifice of the cross, and therefore itself constitutes a real sacrifice in which Jesus

Christ the high priest, using the ministry of the ordained priests who represent him, offers himself as the perfect sacrificial gift. The sixteenth-century reformers rejected the official priesthood and the sacrificial dimension of the Eucharist (Calvin took the most radical position on this point); the celebration of the Lord's Supper thus became simply a commemoration of Jesus and, though a sacrament, had no sacrificial character. In recent times, there has been a tendency in the Lutheran church to confer to some degree a sacrificial character on the Lord's Supper. Even more explicit however is the emphasis placed on the sacrificial character of the Lord's Supper by the Anglican church. In Protestantism generally the term *sacrifice* refers to a purely interior attitude.

Conclusion

In the course of its history, which can be traced through several millennia, sacrifice has undergone many changes, and this in all its aspects: changes in the material of sacrifice (occasioned by economic changes but also by ethical considerations, e.g., in the suppression of human sacrifice); changes with regard to place and time (centralization of cult, regulation of feasts and thereby of the occasions for sacrifice); changes in the offerer (the rise of classes of official sacrificers); and changes in ritual and motivation. These developments do not, however, reflect a one-directional "advance." Egoistic and magical motives were not always eliminated by higher motives; in fact, they often asserted themselves even more strongly in connection with manifestations of religious degeneration. In the same context a quantitative increase in sacrifices is also often to be seen; thus in some late cultures the number of human sacrifices became especially extensive (e.g., among the Punics and the Aztec).

Disapproval and criticism of sacrifice might spring from a skeptical, antireligious attitude that condemned sacrifice as meaningless waste. However, it could also be motivated by a more profound reflection on the meaning of sacrifice in the light of religious interiority, leading to an emphasis on inner conviction, the self-giving of the human being to the divinity, which finds symbolic expression in sacrifice, and without which the external rite has no religious value. This cast of mind could lead to the complete abolition of the external rite, but also to a consciously established accord between external action and interior attitude.

Tendencies to the spiritualization and ethicization of sacrifice were already present in Indian religion, where they produced a mysticism of sacrifice; in the philosophers of classical antiquity, who regarded ethical behavior as of highest value; and above all in the biblical religions. Early in the Hebrew scriptures the idea was expressed that obedience to God's commandments is better than sacrifice (*1 Sm.* 15:22), and the prophetic criticism of sacrifice was directed at an outward cult unaccompanied by interior dispositions and ethical behavior. The wisdom literature, too, repeatedly stresses the superior value of religious dispositions and moral behavior. This outlook became even more pronounced in postbiblical Judaism, once the destruction of the Second Temple in 70 CE had put an end to the sacrificial cult. From the beginning, Christianity emphasized not only the continuance of cultic sacrifice in the celebration of the Eucharist but also the necessity of a self-surrender that finds external expression in other ways as well; thus, even in the New Testament, prayers, hymns of praise, good works, and especially love of neighbor are described as "sacrifices." These tendencies became particularly strong in Protestantism, which no longer acknowledged the Eucharist to be a sacrifice.

Finally, the idea of renunciation, which is connected with the offering of a gift, was especially emphasized in Christianity, so that every kind of asceticism and self-abnegation came to be called sacrifice (there is a similar development in Buddhism). A one-sided emphasis on this aspect led finally to a very broad and metaphorical use of the term *sacrifice.* Thus an abandonment of possessions and a personal commitment to an idea or to the attainment of certain goals, especially if this commitment demands costly effort, is described as sacrifice in the active sense of the term. We also speak of the victims of wars, epidemics, natural disasters, and so on with a sense that they are, in a passive sense, sacrificial victims. Thus the word *sacrifice* ultimately became very much a secular term in common usage; yet the origins of sacrifice in the religious sphere remain evident.

BIBLIOGRAPHY

Baal, Jan van. "Offering, Sacrifice and Gift." *Numen* 23 (December 1976): 161–178.

Baaren, Th. P. van. "Theoretical Speculations on Sacrifice." *Numen* 11 (January 1964): 1–12.

Bertholet, Alfred. *Der Sinn des kultischen Opfers.* Berlin, 1942.

Closs, Alois. "Das Opfer in Ost und West." *Kairos* 3 (1961): 153–161.

Evans-Pritchard, E. E. *Theories of Primitive Religion.* Oxford, 1965.

Faherty, Robert L. "Sacrifice." In *Encyclopaedia Britannica.* 15th ed. Chicago, 1974.

Girard, René. *Violence and the Sacred.* Translated by Patrick Gregory. Baltimore, 1977.

Girard, René. *Des choses cachées depuis la fondation du monde.* Paris, 1978.

Gray, Louis H., et al. "Expiation and Atonement." In *Encyclo-*

paedia of Religion and Ethics, edited by James Hastings, vol. 5. Edinburgh, 1912.

Heiler, Friedrich. *Erscheinungsformen und Wesen der Religion.* Vol. 1 of *Die Religionen der Menschheit.* Stuttgart, 1961.

Henninger, Joseph. "Ist der sogenannte Nilus-Bericht eine brauchbare religionsgeschichtliche Quelle?" *Anthropos* 50 (1955): 81–148.

Henninger, Joseph. "Primitialopfer und Neujahrsfest." In *Anthropica.* Studia Instituti Anthropos, vol. 21. Sankt Augustin, West Germany, 1968.

Henninger, Joseph. *Les fêtes de printemps chez les Sémites et la Pâque israélite.* Paris, 1975.

Henninger, Joseph. *Arabica Sacra: Aufsätze zur Religionsgeschichte Arabiens und seiner Randgebiete.* Fribourg, 1981.

Hubert, Henri, and Marcel Mauss. "Essai sur la nature et la fonction du sacrifice." *L'année sociologique* 2 (1899): 29–138. An English translation was published in 1964 (Chicago): *Sacrifice: Its Nature and Function.*

James, E. O. *Sacrifice and Sacrament.* London, 1962.

James, E. O., et al. "Sacrifice." In *Encyclopaedia of Religion and Ethics,* edited by James Hastings, vol. 11. Edinburgh, 1920.

Jensen, Adolf E. *Myth and Cult among Primitive Peoples.* Translated by Marianna Tax Choldin and Wolfgang Weissleder. Chicago, 1963.

Kerr, C. M., et al. "Propitiation." In *Encyclopaedia of Religion and Ethics,* edited by James Hastings, vol. 10. Edinburgh, 1918.

Lanternari, Vittorio. *'La Grande Festa': Vita rituale e sistemi di produzione nelle società tradizionali.* 2d ed. Bari, 1976.

Leeuw, Gerardus van der. "Die *do-ut-des*-Formel in der Opfertheorie." *Archiv für Religionswissenschaft* 20 (1920–1921): 241–253.

Leeuw, Gerardus van der. *Religion in Essence and Manifestation* (1938). 2 vols. Translated by J. E. Turner. Gloucester, Mass., 1967.

Loisy, Alfred. *Essai historique sur le sacrifice.* Paris, 1920.

Müller-Karpe, Hermann. *Handbuch der Vorgeschichte.* 2 vols. Munich, 1966–1968.

Le sacrifice, I–V. Nos. 2–6 of *Systèmes de pensée en Afrique noire.* Ivry, France, 1976–1983.

Schmidt, Wilhelm. *Der Ursprung der Gottesidee.* 12 vols. Münster, 1912–1955. See especially volume 6, pages 274–281, 444–455; volume 8, pages 595–633; and volume 12, pages 389–441, 826–836, and 845–847.

Schmidt, Wilhelm. "Ethnologische Bemerkungen zu theologischen Opfertheorien." In *Jahrbuch des Missionshauses St. Gabriel,* vol. 1. Mödling, 1922.

Smith, W. Robertson. *Lectures on the Religion of the Semites: The Fundamental Institutions* (1889). 3d ed. Reprint, New York, 1969.

Tylor, E. B. *Primitive Culture* (1871). 2 vols. Reprint, New York, 1970.

Vorbichler, Anton. *Das Opfer auf den uns heute noch erreichbaren ältesten Stufen der Menschheitsgeschichte: Eine Begriffsstudie.* Mödling, 1956.

Widengren, Geo. *Religionsphänomenologie.* Berlin, 1969.

Additional literature is found in the works cited in the article, especially those by Hubert and Mauss, Loisy, Schmidt, Bertholet, van der Leeuw, Henninger, Lanternari, Heiler, James, and Widengren, as well as in *Le sacrifice,* especially volume 1.

JOSEPH HENNINGER
Translated from German by Matthew J. O'Connell

SACRILEGE. Most dictionaries define *sacrilege* as a "violation of what is sacred," and such an act is commonly interpreted as an offense against religion. A Latin dictionary would further explain that *sacrilegium* is primarily a theft from a holy place, and thus implies profanation. This is clear from the word iteself, which derives from *sacer* ("holy") and *lego* ("gather," i.e., "steal").

Obviously the history of religions is scarcely concerned with temple or church robbery as such. Sacrilege becomes an object of investigation only insofar as it exhibits specific religious patterns that, although perhaps deriving from actual facts, are no longer essentially connected with them. For the historian of religions, sacrilege becomes interesting primarily when it is identified as an element in some movement that is intended either to reverse or to reform an established religion—for example, in some sort of antinomian activity. Needless to say, this kind of "sacrilege" is impious and criminal only for one of the parties involved, the one that has an interest in presenting the facts in such a way as to show that they are intended to subvert accepted religious and social norms. In most cases of what appears to be an interreligious conflict, the incriminated party is not actually guilty of any sacrilegious intentions. These are attributed to it only because it behaves according to a different religious and moral code. Taoist circles were persecuted by the Confucian authorities as being immoral and pernicious, and their practices ruinous to the health; for the Romans, Christians were impious criminals; while the Christians regarded as sacrilegious Jews, gnostics, Manichaeans, Cathari, Waldensians, and witches, as well as many other actual or alleged "infidels" and "heretics." [*See* Heresy.]

Antinomianism. Before one starts analyzing the patterns of sacrilege in those cultures and social environments in which they are the most obvious, one should try to describe another important religious phenomenon, namely, antinomianism.

Antinomianism is subversion of a religious or moral code. The degree of tolerance shown toward antinomianism by established religions varies. To some extent antinomianism is accepted, and even encouraged, as being a distinctive feature of exceptionally gifted personalities (shamans, initiates, mystics, saints). There are religions in which antinomianism is fully codified and belongs to a certain pattern of collective or individual initiation. There are other religions in which antinomianism is fully accepted as the characteristic of a special school, such as Ch'an Buddhism in China or Zen Buddhism in Japan. Other religions, by contrast, never clearly distinguish antinomianism from heresy. It thus becomes a matter of historical importance to establish whether certain antinomian manifestations still fall within the borders of the licit, or are to be considered heretical. In such cases, heresy is fully codified, antinomianism is not. Finally, there are religious systems in which no antinomianism is overtly tolerated, though historical circumstances may call for caution in the prosecution of antinomian circles. It is obvious, of course, that Taoist ethics and practices are antinomian from the point of view of Confucianism. The latter succeeded in ridding itself of the most licentious of these, but the Taoist mentality was never uprooted altogether. When Taoist practices were overtly or covertly revived by the imperial court, the Confucian administration was compelled to live with them.

Antinomianism was actively practiced in Tantrism, whether Buddhist or Śaiva, and it is obvious that the Vajrayāna, the Kāpālikas, and other ascetic schools were described in demonic terms by those outside their circles. Tantric literature itself, however, emphasizes the superhuman freedom enjoyed by the adept: as a subversion of mundane values, antinomianism enables man to take part in the divine freedom.

It is not my purpose to proceed further in the description of the multifarious phenomenon of antinomianism. As far as the present article is concerned, the following general distinction is sufficient: antinomianism may be either the effect of an interreligious contact or strictly an intrareligious phenomenon. In the first case, the values of a certain religion (e.g., Taoism) are antinomian from the point of view of another religion (e.g., Confucianism). In its propaganda, the latter will employ all means, including plain slander, whether invented for the purpose or based on genuine misunderstanding, in order to show that the former religion is sacrilegious. In the second case (as for instance in the case of the gnostics with regard to the Jewish religion, or the Protestants in relation to the Roman Catholic church) an antinomian movement arises within the orthodox circles of a certain religion, aiming at its reform, which is possible either by a subversion of values that have been proved to be false (e.g., gnosticism), or by a return to the purity of a genuine, "primitive" message or situation (e.g., Protestantism). Such movements are literally heretical, that is, they are intrareligious trends that tend to subvert an established religion *ab intra.* In both cases, the reaction of the orthodox is more or less the same, namely, to spread the word that the antinomian movement is sacrilegious, and to declare it heretical. The distinction between inter- and intrareligious conflicts is not always clear, certainly not in the eyes of those called upon to diagnose heresy.

The European Pattern. It is not my purpose to provide the reader with a map of all the cases in which the interaction of religions resulted in accusations of sacrilege. Such interactions, or inner developments, involve many issues, not only religious issues but also social, juridical, and other kinds. In the following pages, I will restrict my discussion to an analysis of such issues as they become involved in a single pattern of sacrilege, that found in European civilization from late antiquity to the end of the seventeenth century. Even though the accusations found here remained essentially the same, the social environment was in a state of constant change, and the issues involved, both conscious and unconscious, changed as well.

The history of heresy, inquisition, and witchcraft in the Christian church has been the subject of an enormous body of scholarship. The picture presented here is far from complete, and the reader should be on guard against easy or fashionable generalizations. In the history of the concept and pattern of sacrilege in Europe, one is confronted with striking paradoxes: it is often the case that sacrilege was neither invented nor spread by those one would have at first suspected. Sometimes the very forces that were responsible for the prosecution of sacrilege were the ones that prevented such prosecution from being effective. If trials for sacrilege finally came to an end, this did not happen according to any known law of human progress. A thorough investigation of this phenomenon, as of any other phenomenon in history, will show that whenever human consciousness, reflection, and intentionality are involved, things are far from being simple.

The Roman empire. In the Roman empire, sacrilege was considered to be a crime carrying the penalty of death, and torture was sometimes used to extort confession. The persecution of Christians in particular was justified by a pattern of defamation: besides their sacrilegious practices, the Christians were represented as murderers of infants and as engaged in promiscuous sexual intercourse.

This basic pattern of defamation, analyzed historically by Norman R. C. Cohn in his influential book *Europe's Inner Demons* (1975), was then taken over by the victorious church and applied to several of its enemies, both external and internal. The revival of Roman criminal law in the eleventh century provided the legal procedures for the conduct of the Christian Inquisition.

These procedures were in turn copied by the lay authorities of Europe at the time of the witch craze of the sixteenth and seventeenth centuries. We shall see that by this time the Inquisition itself adopted a skeptical attitude that in some cases prevented abuses by the secular powers. [*See* Inquisition, The.]

The eleventh to thirteenth century. The revival of Roman criminal law in the eleventh century seems to have been accompanied by a revival of the ancient Roman pattern of the defamation of Christians, used this time, however, by the Christians themselves against enemies of their own. This was not entirely new. Augustine had used these tactics against the Manichaeans, and John of Odzun had used them against the Armenian Adoptionists in 719. Now the target was the heretics of Orleans (1022), who were said to recite a litany of demons, renounce Christ, spit upon his image, engage in sexual orgies, sacrifice children, and practice cannibalism. At the end of the century (1076–1096), the priest Alberic of Brittany had been convicted of sacrilege for having smeared the crucifix with excrement and poured animal blood upon the altar. He was further accused of selling this blood to the people as relics.

By 1150–1160, a group of heretics in Germany had been accused of offering solemn sacrifices to the Devil, practicing incestuous intercourse, and ridiculing the celebration of the Nativity on Christmas Eve when, in mockery of the Christian kiss of peace, their priest allegedly uncovered his backside to be kissed by the congregation. This is perhaps the earliest testimony concerning the *osculum infame* ("kiss of infamy"). In 1182, Walter Map mentioned the kiss of infamy as being practiced upon the backside, the genitals, or the paw of a huge cat. Down to the mid-fifteenth century, the new conventicles of the alleged worshipers of Satan were called synagogues (later *sabbat*, a term also used in reference to witches), a clear reference to a group to whom sacrilegious activities of the most extreme kind were attributed, namely the Jews. Sexual intercourse with the Devil is mentioned for the first time in 1275, when a woman in Carcassonne was burned at the stake for this sacrilege. Let us now examine the progress of canon and criminal law up to that time.

Inquisitorial and criminal procedure to the fourteenth century. The relationship between ecclesiastic and criminal justice forms one of the most fascinating chapters in the history of European civilization. Without some knowledge of this relationship, it is impossible to understand such a fundamental phenomenon as the witch craze. It is important to establish two facts: first, that this relationship underwent constant changes; and second, that it varied from country to country.

In the early Middle Ages, religious offenses in Germany were prosecuted by the secular authorities. The accusation had to be proved, and thus the accuser risked greater damages than the accused. In Spain under the Visigoths, by contrast, religious offenses were, according to the juridical formula, *mixti fori*, that is, they belonged both to the ecclesiastical and to the lay authorities. In Italy, according to Langobardic law, the crime of *maleficium* fell under secular jurisdiction. In northern Italy, under French influence, the episcopal inquisition was in place after 800. Indeed, in the Frankish empire, justice in religious matters was assured by episcopal visitation and inquisition (Lat., *inquisitio*, "investigation"), the bishop being supported by the landlord as *defensor ecclesiae* (this is the oldest form of local justice, the *justice seigneuriale*). After the fall of the Frankish empire, however, the institution of royal justice became increasingly important, having been taken as a model by the local landlords.

The procedures of the episcopal inquisition were introduced by the church in 1184. A further step was taken by Gregory IX (1227–1241), who created the papal Inquisition as a central institution staffed by the Dominicans and the Franciscans and directed from Rome. Torture, sporadically employed since the eleventh century, was expressly recommended for inquisitorial procedures against heretics by Innocent IV in 1252. The death penalty, in accordance with Roman law, had been applied since the eleventh century in the French and German territories, but not in southern Europe. Starting in 1197, the death penalty for heretics upon relapse was decreed in Aragon, France, Lombardy, Sicily, and Germany. In 1232, it became effective for the entire Holy Roman Empire. In 1198, Innocent III had recommended execution upon relapse in instances when excommunication had proved ineffective. By the fifteenth century, witches were burned as heretics upon first conviction rather than after a relapse.

The trial of the Templars. By the end of the thirteenth century, the pattern of alleged sacrilege ascribed to heretical conventicles needed only a finishing touch to be complete. Most of the scattered elements that form its structure were already in place: synagogues of Satan; flight through the air; the kiss of infamy on the backside of the Devil (sometimes in the form of a cat, a toad, etc.); sexual intercourse with the Devil; promiscuous sexual intercourse; sodomy; infanticide; renouncing the faith, church, and sacraments, and profanation of the latter; obscene gestures; spitting upon the cross; eucharistic wafers of a horrible composition; and so forth. Combined in the fourteenth and fifteenth centuries, these elements came to form the picture of the "heresy of the witches."

In the famous trial of the Templars, Philip IV, of

France, and his counselor, Guillaume de Nogaret, used some of these elements, which already enjoyed great popularity, to discredit and destroy a rich military-religious order. In this political trial of the early fourteenth century, Philip IV employed many of the same techniques that were to become famous in the twentieth century through the Nazi and Communist tribunals.

During the trial, which started on 13 October 1307 and came to an end on 22 March 1312, when the order was suppressed, several Templars, including Grand Master Jacques de Molay and Visitor Hugues de Pairaud, confessed their guilt, then retracted, reconfessed, and retracted again. Though outstanding scholars like Jeffrey Burton Russell believe that the Templars' confessions may have been genuine, at least in part, the general impression is that they were carefully staged by the royal keeper of the seals, Guillaume de Nogaret, along with other agents and jailers of the king, using torture, moral pressure, and false promises, not to mention the help of several traitors among the French Templars. The Templars were accused of having a sacrilegious ritual of initiation, of renouncing Christ as a false prophet, and of spitting on the cross and giving the kiss of infamy, either on the backside of their preceptor or on the statue of a cat. They were also charged with homosexual practices.

During the trial, a conflict of authority developed between the king and Pope Clement V, who resided first in Poitiers and later in Avignon, outside the French territories. It appears that the French inquisitor took orders from Philip rather than from the pope, while the king's power was considerably limited by the papal legislation on heresy and by the ability of the pope to suspend any inquisitorial activity. Moreover, when, in 1308, the king consulted the masters of theology of the University of Paris, their answer went against his cause: in matters of heresy, only the church may have the leading role; secular authorities are entitled to take the initiative only upon papal approval.

The witch craze. The sacrilegious actions attributed to the sect of the witches had multiplied by the middle of the fifteenth century. [*See* Witchcraft.] Witches were now believed to make eucharistic wafers out of excrement, trample the cross or the consecrated bread, renounce the Christian faith, God, church, Christ, and so on. The desecration of the cross or sacraments was said to be ceremonially performed by the whole "synagogue" or enjoined upon a proselyte. Witches were said to trample, spit, and defecate on the cross. In 1437, the heretic Jubertus was accused of spitting on the statues of the Virgin. According to the inquisition at Lyon, witches retained the Host in their mouths after a mass, took it home and used it in *maleficium,* insulted it at the assembly, or desecrated it by mixing it with excrement. A witch was said to have defecated in the nave of the church and urinated into the holy water font. In Artois, witches were believed to pour holy water onto the floor and stamp on it. A Jewish sorcerer was said to burn statues of Christ and the Virgin and to insult Christ, the Lamb of God, by crucifying a lamb and giving it to the dogs to eat.

All the requisites for a "black mass" were thus already present by the mid-fifteenth century. The first known black mass took place in Brescia in 1480, as a parody of the Christian sacrament. Rather than being a mere invention of the French occultists of the nineteenth century, as several scholars think, black masses were actually performed in Paris at the end of the witch-craze period. During the short-lived popularity of black masses, the inventiveness of blasphemers reached new heights. Besides the numerous obscene and repulsive ways to desecrate the Host, copulation with statues of Christ and of the Virgin was practiced. Traces of a perversion called "Mariolatry" are preserved by a record of the Paris police from 1765 that mentions two monks from the Crépy monastery who entered an inn and requested a bed for three, their companion being a statue of the Virgin.

The sect of the witches. Did the persons to whom the above-mentioned practices were ascribed really exist? There are two leading theories on this subject: that of Norman R. C. Cohn, who maintains that no such activities were actually performed and that they were an ancient invention ready to be used against all sorts of threatening social groups; and that of Jeffrey Burton Russell, who is prone to accept most of what was attributed to the witches as evidence for the existence of a vast antinomian movement in Europe. Joseph Hansen has already noted that the Alps were the cradle of beliefs about witches and argued that popular belief tends to be stronger and more persistent in mountainous zones. Hansen also believed that the pattern of witchcraft was a creation of late medieval scholasticism. He was thus obliged to add that folk belief in the Alps was strangely akin to scholastic demonology. As a matter of fact, there was little that was new about scholastic demonology, which developed along the lines of theories of the Hellenistic era and late antiquity that became very influential in late Neoplatonic circles.

Russell argued, against Hansen, that it was not Alpine folk belief combined with scholasticism that produced the phenomenon of witchcraft, but late medieval heresy, which had found in the Alps the only safe refuge against prosecution. This antionomian movement would then have spread further, into the economically most developed zones of Europe: Lombardy, France, the Rhineland, and the Netherlands.

Who prosecuted witchcraft? If we admit that the first sign of the witch craze was the papal bull *Summis desiderantes affectibus* of 1484, followed shortly after (1486) by the manual of inquisitorial prosecution by the inquisitors Henry Institoris (Kraemer) and Jacob Sprenger, then it is legitimate to assume that it was the papal inquisition that started the great trials. In France, however, witchcraft was prosecuted by the secular authorities, and by the seventeenth century the Inquisition had ceased its activities there. In the mid-sixteenth century, jurists like the Dutch Jodocus Damhouder, who wrote *Praxis rerum criminalium* (1540), pleaded for the transfer of witchcraft trials to the secular courts, and as a consequence the Inquisition withdrew from Germany in the following century. It remained active in Italy and Spain, however, which is a rather strange fact, since the prosecution of witches was unusually mild in southern Italy. Moreover, the studies of Julio Caro Baroja have shown that the Spanish Inquisition was by no means zealous in prosecuting witchcraft in the sixteenth and seventeenth centuries. In Spain, too, the responsibility for trials lay with the local authorities acting under pressure from the public. We are forced to conclude that, even though the papal Inquisition started the whole affair, by the end of the sixteenth century it was secular justice that played the leading role in all the countries involved.

As Hansen noted, Protestantism did not bring about any revolutionary reversal in the prosecution of witches, which continued steadily in Protestant countries. Both in France and in England, however, Calvinism helped promote the skepticism concerning the existence of witchcraft that was later to prevail. It was the unique achievement of one of the greatest of Renaissance scholars, D. P. Walker, to have shown the extent to which liberal English Protestantism contributed to changing the ancient beliefs in demons.

The social project of the church. Paradoxically, it was a serious reading of one of the most terrible documents ever written, the *Malleus maleficarum* (The Hammer of Witches) by Institoris and Sprenger, that gave Amand Danet the opportunity to analyze the unconscious bases of the social project of the church at the end of the fifteenth century. In this document, published in 1486, the church is represented as operating in a disorderly environment *(une conjoncture de désordre)*. Disorder is attributed to several external and internal factors: the disturbing presence of unbelievers on the borders of Christendom; adverse climatic factors; terrible maladies; and, most of all, the vices produced in men and especially, in women by the violation of religious prescriptions. All these troubles are in turn laid at the door of the sacrilegious practices of the sect of the witches. Furthermore, the *Malleus* adds dramatically, if the world is wretched, its end must be near. The church must employ all means to ensure that men have a maternal, protective place of refuge. But this space must be purified of disorderly elements, and purification is accomplished through fire: the fire of the stakes upon which the sinful witches, as representatives of Satan, are to be burned alive.

The *Malleus* was the basic text of the inquisitors during the witch craze. Interestingly enough for the position of the Inquisition in the countries where inquisitorial procedures continued into the eighteenth century, the *Malleus* defines witchcraft as a *delictum mixtum,* a "mixed offense," not *mere ecclesiasticum,* "exclusively ecclesiastical." Responsibilities for penalty and torture belonged to secular justice. As we shall see, in the seventeenth century the Inquisition was to try in vain to restrain the process that it had set in motion so successfully at the end of the fifteenth century.

The end of prosecution. Why did the prosecution of witches come to an end? Mainly it was due to a change in mentality, but this change itself had multiple causes and took various forms in the main territories involved.

France deserves special attention, not because the witch craze was stopped there earlier than in other countries, but because it was the territory studied by Robert Mandrou in his great work, *Magistrats et sorciers en France au dix-huitième siècle* (1968). Mandrou was the first to undertake a thorough study of the causes of the change in mentality that took place in France in the course of the eighteenth century. The end point of this process of change was marked by the famous *ordonnance royale* issued by Louis XIV in 1682, which simply bracketed witchcraft as irrelevant to justice itself, stating that cases of "alleged magic" *(prétendue magie)* were to be prosecuted only insofar as they involved criminal prosecution for such things as murder by poisoning.

Mandrou discovered that, by the middle of the seventeenth century, there were two main groups that were loath to recognize the reality of witchcraft: the judges of the Paris parliament, and the physicians who attended local authorities during the great witchcraft trials and possession cases. As for the parliaments of the great cities, some would automatically align themselves with the skeptical position of the Paris parliament (e.g., the parliament of Burgundy, at Dijon), while others remained more traditional in attitude (e.g., the parliament of Normandy at Rouen, or that of Provence at

Aix). The most zealous prosecutors of witches were the representatives of local justice, whose capital sentences were systematically, though not universally, commuted by the Paris parliament upon appeal, at least if local justice complied with the requirements of witchcraft trials, which automatically involved appeal. Abuses of power by lower judges were frequent. After 1670, the minister Colbert began conscientiously to punish such abuses, and this undoubtedly restrained the enthusiasm of the lower judges considerably.

Mandrou left aside the important issue of the French cases of diabolic possession in the eighteenth century, an issue later taken up by Walker (1980). From his analysis of several cases of possession in France and England, Walker came to the conclusion that the situation in the two countries was completely different. In France, exorcism was practiced by the Roman Catholic church in order to show the effective results of transubstantiation and the miraculous power of the Host upon demons. In all the French cases considered by Walker (Laon, 1566; Soissons, 1582; Marthe Brossier, 1599), the unclean spirits recognized the magic power of the Host. The fact that such a demonstration was performed at all suggests the presence of a group that challenged the doctrine of transubstantiation. And indeed such a group existed: the sacramentarian Protestants, represented by the Calvinist Huguenots, regarded the Catholic Mass as an idolatrous magical ceremony. The above-mentioned cases of possession occurred in France before the Edict of Nantes, in force from 1598 to 1685, and were thus meant to demonstrate, by public exorcism, the superiority of the Catholics over the Calvinists. During the period when Huguenots were free to practice, the royal authorities would prevent such forms of demonstrative exorcism from being performed. By 1685, when persecution of Huguenots revived, possession was out of fashion in France. Indeed, since possession implied possession by demons, it was automatically ranged among cases of witchcraft. After the *ordonnance* of 1682, witchcraft was no more punishable as such, and thus possession became less of an issue.

In comparison with the rest of Europe, England is a special case. According to the Witchcraft Act of 1563, the conjuring of spirits was punishable by death upon first offense, while witchcraft not involving murder was only lightly punished (one year's imprisonment and the pillory). This made the practice of exorcism dangerous for the exorcists themselves, who risked being put to death as conjurers. However, some exorcisms were performed in secret by Roman Catholics and, without excessive secrecy, by the puritan John Darrel, who tried to drive spirits away by the force of prayer. This led to a very interesting controversy between Darrel and the Anglican authorities. The Anglicans maintained that the exorcists and Darrel were trying to perform miracles, and miracles, though still possible in the apostolic age, were considered to have been ever since impossible. The doctrine of the cessation of miracles in the postapostolic age, held firmly by the Anglicans (and also cautiously put forward by Calvin), was certainly not favorable for either witch-hunting or conjuring spirits.

Spain, like Italy, was a territory of the Inquisition. Analyzing an action against witchcraft that took place in the district of Logroño (diocese of Pamplona), between 1609 and 1614, and which involved no fewer than 1,802 convicts, Baroja (1970) came to a spectacular conclusion. Among the authorities involved, there were two distinct groups: those who believed in witchcraft, and those who were quite skeptical about it. The first group consisted of the local inquisitors, the local secular authorities, the local clerics, and the inhabitants of a region, who threatened to take justice into their own hands. Skepticism, on the other hand, which eventually prevailed over the impassioned opinions of the prosecutors, was shown by the commissioner of the Inquisition (in this case, the unusually skeptical Don Alonso de Salazar y Frías), the council of the Inquisition, the great inquisitor himself, representatives of the Jesuits, the local bishops, and the royal justice. Since the actual proceedings were not made public, later generations continued to believe that it was always the Inquisition that sent witches to the stake, whereas in reality, the skepticism of the Spanish Inquisition in the sixteenth and seventeenth centuries stood in opposition to the local authorities and the local inhabitants. From the questionnaires concerning witches sent to the inquisitor, one could even reach the conclusion that the prevailing hypothesis of the council was quite modern: witches, it was suggested, extracted drugs from plants and acted while intoxicated, and thus were mentally incapacitated.

In Italy, with the exception of the northern regions influenced by France, the prosecution of witches was comparatively mild. If in France royal justice put an end to the witch craze, if in England the doctrine of the cessation of miracles clearly inhibited the expansion of witch trials, if in Spain the skepticism of the Inquisition itself prevailed over the belief of the masses, then in Italy witchcraft was primarily a problem of doctrine, and it was through a bizarre development of doctrine that, by the end of the seventeenth century, some consequential changes had been introduced into the concept of sacrilege.

In broad outline, the then current doctrine of demonology was as follows: all demons, including the incubus and the succubus, were diabolic beings. Trade with demons was sacrilegious insofar as it involved the archenemy of religion and mankind, the Devil. Under these circumstances, the learned Franciscan Lodovico Maria Sinistrari (1622–1701), Consultor of the Supreme Tribunal of the Most Holy Inquisition in Rome, wrote a treatise on demons that, though unpublished until 1875, reflects an important change in the doctrine held by the church. Sinistrari did not deny that most demons were satanic creatures. But at least the incubus and the succubus, he argued, do not mean any harm against religion, and thus commerce with them is only a carnal sin; it is not sacrilegious. The incubus and the succubus are not interested in religious matters; they belong to a subtle folk of rational creatures that may take human form and are tremendously lustful. Their approaching men and women is not a sacrilege, it is only a sin *contra castitatem*, against chastity.

Sinistrari was well aware of the explosive consequences of this position; that is why he proceeded very cautiously in presenting the matter, taking care not to contradict the greatest authorities on the subject. However, according to his doctrine, an important part of human imagination, namely the erotic imagination, was rescued from the vengeful arm of religion.

By the end of the seventeenth century, for several reasons and in various ways, the ancient belief concerning sacrilege had collapsed. This gave way to a world in which there was less and less room for any supernatural intervention. The world, to use Max Weber's famous term, has ever since been "dis-enchanted" *(entzaubert)*.

[*See also* Blasphemy.]

BIBLIOGRAPHY

For a brief attempt to summarize the distinctive features of antinomianism as a historico-religious phenomenon, see my article, "La religione come strumento del potere," in *Iter in silvis*, vol. 1 (Messina, 1981), pp. 109–128.

Legislation on sacrilege, witchcraft, and heresy in the early Middle Ages is discussed in Joseph Hansen's excellent work *Zauberwahn Inquisition und Hexenprozess im Mittelalter und die Entstehung der grossen Hexenverfolgung* (Munich, 1900), which has now been supplemented by Jeffrey Burton Russell's *Witchcraft in the Middle Ages* (Ithaca, N.Y., 1972). A different view of sacrilege, up to the end of the fifteenth century, is presented by Norman R. C. Cohn in his *Europe's Inner Demons* (New York, 1975). An excellent book on the trial of the Templars is Malcolm Barber's *The Trial of the Templars* (Cambridge, 1978).

An excellent work on the evolution of the witch trials in France is Robert Mandrou's *Magistrats et sorciers en France au dix-septième siècle: Une analyse de psychologie historique* (Paris, 1968). The principal texts used by Mandrou for his demonstration are collected in his *Possession et sorcellerie au dix-septième siècle: Textes inédits* (Paris, 1979). Mandrou's important thesis is supported by the observations made in D. P. Walker's *Unclean Spirits: Possession and Exorcism in France and England in the Late Sixteenth and Early Seventeenth Centuries* (Philadelphia, 1980). On the skeptical stand of the Spanish Inquisition in the witch trials during the sixteenth and seventeenth centuries, see Julio Caro Baroja's *Inquisición, brujería y criptojudaísmo* (Barcelona, 1970).

One of the best available translations of the *Malleus maleficarum* is the French translation by Amand Danet; preceded by Danet's excellent introduction, it can be found in Henry Institoris (Kraemer) and Jacob Sprenger's *Le marteau des sorcières*, translated and edited by Amand Danet (Paris, 1973). An English translation of Sinistrari's *De daemonialitate* by Montague Summers is included in R. E. L. Masters's *Eros and Evil: The Sexual Psychopathology of Witchcraft* (New York, 1962).

IOAN PETRU CULIANU

SADDUCEES. The Sadducees (Heb., Tseduqim) were proponents of one of the three schools of thought of Judaism that flourished in Palestine from the time of the Hasmonean Revolt until after the destruction of the Temple in Jerusalem in 70 CE. According to Josephus Flavius (*Jewish Antiquities* 13.297), the Sadducees taught that only those laws written in the Pentateuch were to be regarded as binding, while those laws that had not been written down were not to be observed. This principled commitment to the written law brought the Sadducees into violent conflict with the Pharisees, who taught that God had given both the written and oral law.

The Sadducees also came into conflict with the Pharisees over the issues of the role of fate in human affairs, and the immortality of the soul and the resurrection of the body. The Sadducees, in opposition to the Pharisees, "do away with Fate, holding that there is no such thing and that human actions are not achieved with her decree, but that all things lie within our own power, so that we ourselves are responsible for our well-being, while we suffer misfortune through our own thoughtlessness" (ibid., 13.173). So, too, the Sadducees rejected the Pharisaic belief in the immortality of the soul and the resurrection of the body and held to the literal promises in the Pentateuch that all rewards and punishments would be meted out by God in this world (cf. Josephus, *Jewish War* 2.162–165, *Antiquities* 18.12–17, *Mk.* 12:18–25, *Mt.* 22:23–33, *Lk.* 20:27–40, *Acts* 23:6–10).

Although the Sadducees were persistent in their teachings until the destruction of the Temple in 70 CE, their following was said to be limited to a small minority of people drawn almost exclusively from the aristocratic priestly families of a bygone era when the Aaronic system was in full flower and as yet uncontested by the Pharisees.

Josephus first mentions the Sadducees obliquely: he

says that they were well established in the time of Jonathan the Hasmonean. We may therefore surmise that the Sadducees emerged, along with the other groups, sometime during the Hasmonean Revolt (166–142 BCE) and that they came to be called Sadducees (Tseduqim) because they claimed that only a direct descendant of Zadok (Heb., Tsadoq) the high priest in Solomon's Temple, could serve as high priest. This claim was voiced in opposition to the establishment of a Hasmonean line of high priests, which the Sadducees claimed to be in violation of the high priestly succession from Aaron to Eleazar to Phinehas and their direct descendants as explicitly set forth in the written law. By this opposition the Sadducees differentiated themselves from the Pharisees, who recognized the legitimacy of the Hasmonean high priestly line on the basis of the oral law. Indeed, it is possible that it was this opposition that impelled the supporters of the Zadokite line to denounce the teachers of the twofold law as "separatists," or "heretics" (Heb., *perushim;* Gr., *pharisaioi;* Eng., Pharisees).

As opponents of the early Hasmoneans, the Sadducees had influence with neither the masses of the people nor the first Hasmonean high priests, Jonathan and Simon (142–134 BCE). During the high priesthood of John Hyrcanus (134–104 BCE), however, they struck a deal whereby they were willing to recognize John as high priest if he, in turn, would abrogate the oral law of the Pharisees and reinstate the exclusive authority of the written law. This *modus vivendi,* however, was bitterly resisted by the masses, who rose up in violent revolt against John's son, Alexander Yannai (103–76 BCE). So fierce was the opposition that when Alexander died, his widow, Salome Alexandra (76–67 BCE.), on ascending the throne restored the Pharisees to power and reinstituted the oral law (*Antiquities* 13.405–417).

It is likely that the Sadducees, faced with the reality of their relative impotence, made peace with the situation and the Pharisees. For their part, the Sadducees agreed to carry out their priestly duties in the Temple in accordance with the prescriptions of the Pharisees, while the Pharisees agreed to allow the Sadducees to serve as priests in the Temple (cf. *Antiquities* 18.12–17). Henceforth, differences between the Sadducees and the Pharisees were limited to verbal clashes and spirited debate (*Yad.* 4.6, 4.8, 7).

Although during the period of the procurators several Sadducees were appointed high priest (one of whom was Caiaphas, who is said to have judged Jesus, in *Antiquities* 18.35), their power was political and not religious in nature, since all public worship was in accordance with the unwritten laws of the Pharisees (*Antiquities* 18.12–17).

With the destruction of the Temple in 70 CE, the Sadducees no longer had any institutional *raison d'être,* and they gradually faded out of existence.

BIBLIOGRAPHY

Bentzen, Aage. "Zur Geschichte der Zakokiden." *Zeitschrift fuer die Alttestamentliche Wissenschaft* 51 (1933):173–176.

Lightley, J. W. *Jewish Sects and Parties in the Time of Jesus.* London, 1925.

Manson, T. W. "Sadducee and Pharisee: The Origin and Significance of the Names." *Bulletin of the John Rylands Library,* no. 22 (1938): 144–159.

Rivkin, Ellis. *The Shaping of Jewish History: A Radical New Interpretation.* New York, 1971.

Rivkin, Ellis. "Ben Sira: The Bridge between the Aaronide and Pharisaic Revolutions." *Eretz-Israel* 12 (1975): 95–103.

Smith, Morton. "Palestinian Judaism in the First Century." In *Israel: Its Role in Civilization,* edited by Moshe Davis. 1956; New York, 1977.

Zeitlin, Solomon. *Religious and Secular Leadership.* Philadelphia, 1943.

ELLIS RIVKIN

SAʿDĪ (AH 597?–690/1200?–1291 CE), pen name of Abū ʿAbd Allāh Musharrif (al-Dīn) ibn Muṣliḥ al-Dīn Saʿdī-yi Shīrāzī, Islamic Persian belletrist, panegyrist, and popularizer of mystically colored poetry. His exact name (other than the universally used *nom de plume*) and his precise birth and death dates have been much disputed, and he has often been credited with longevity of well over a century. He was born and died in the south Iranian capital of Shiraz, but allegedly spent some half of his life elsewhere, partly perhaps to escape the Mongol invasions and the constant petty warfare within Iran itself. His wanderings fall into three categories: study, most importantly at Baghdad; pilgrimages to the holy cities of Islam (Mecca and Medina); and general drifting, as he claims, all over the Islamic world and beyond.

At one point, so he relates, he was a prisoner of war of the Crusaders and was set to hard labor until ransomed into an unfortunate marriage. Some time around the second and major Mongol invasion of the Middle East in the late 1250s, he seems finally to have retired to his native city—Shiraz was somewhat off the beaten track for the Mongols, as it proved—and established himself as a man of letters and a sort of court-holding sage. The detailed facts of Saʿdī's life are almost as much disputed as his full name and dates, for most of the information derives from, or depends heavily on, his own avowedly "poeticized" writings. However, along with his acknowledged stature as a writer, certain features of his career are hardly open to doubt: his hard-won erudition, his urbane and even cynical world experience, and his familiarity with all aspects of the dervish way of life, both practical and theoretical.

Sa'dī's writings, most of which are poetry, fall into various categories and are often published in one large volume as *Kullīyāt* (Collected Works). Once again, there is much controversy as to the period of his life to which some items belong, but the two longest and most significant can be fairly specifically dated. These are the *Būstān* (Herb Garden), completed at some time in late autumn of 1257, and the *Gulistān* (Rose Garden), published in the spring of 1258. In the few months between these two dates there occurred one of the most traumatic events, at least from the psychoreligious point of view, in the history of Islamic society: the sacking of the capital city of Baghdad and the extinction of the venerable Abbasid caliphate. Yet if the onrushing storm is nowhere presaged in the former work, its aftermath—at only some eight hundred kilometers' distance—is equally passed over in silence in the latter. There could be several plausible reasons to account for this idyllic detachment on the part of one of Iran's great commentators on life: one is that (other arguments notwithstanding) Sa'dī might have been a Shī'ī, and no sorrier than Naṣīr al-Dīn Ṭūsī to see the symbol of perceived Sunnī usurpation so drastically defaced. Certainly, despite one or two brief and formal elegies elsewhere on the passing of the old order, he would soon come to offer panegyrics to the new rulers.

The *Būstān* is a work of some 4,100 lengthy couplets, divided into ten unequal sections, the rich content of which is only approximately indicated by such general titles as "On Humility," "On Contentment," and so forth. Though clearly grounded in a rather humane, mystically tinged Islamic, and even pre-Islamic, tradition, it is ethical, moralistic, and edifying rather than religious in any strict sense. An element of entertainment, rarely missing from such works in Persian at any time, is provided by frequent variation of matter, style, and pace, and by the inclusion of some 160 illustrative stories (some quite short and not designated as such). At the same time, the poem is not merely exhortatory, but reflective and in places almost ecstatic. Yet if it achieves a beneficial moral effect, it does so primarily through its incomparable style and narrative power: at virtually all points throughout its lengthy sweep, it is fluent, elegant, graphic, colorful, witty, paradoxical, and above all epigrammatic.

The *Gulistān,* Sa'dī would have us believe, is a hasty compound of material left over from the *Būstān.* Superficially, it is certainly quite similar in subject matter, but it is much more obviously a work of art and light entertainment. Arranged in eight main sections, again of considerable vagueness as to central theme, it is primarily a collection of stories, told in exemplary (often rhyming) Persian prose with verse embellishments in both Persian and Arabic. The general tone is much less lofty than that of the *Būstān;* indeed, it is frequently quite worldly, even cynical and flippant. Despite this, it has always been the more popular of the two in both East and West, though manuscripts and editions of both have been reproduced beyond counting, so quintessentially Persian are they held to be.

Apart from a few prose essays, the rest of Sa'dī's writings consists largely of monorhyming poems of two kinds: the long *qaṣīdah* (some forty double lines or more) and the shorter, more lyrical *ghazal* (of a dozen double lines or so). These poems are usually classified in various arbitrary ways having little or nothing to do with their essential character. Quite a few are circumstantial and panegyric, and some (not included in most editions) are downright obscene. Excepting a few in Arabic, nearly all of them are in Sa'dī's native Persian, and the great majority anticipate Ḥāfiẓ (d. 1389?) in ambiguously using the language of earthly love for mystical statement or vice versa. Sa'dī was a complex character, clearly vain of his own literary skill and disingenuous about his loyalties, and his allegedly religious utterances, however sublime, can rarely be taken at simple face value. Indeed, he often warns his readers against taking any of his words too literally. His supreme achievement was to speak with the voice of his age and his culture, and his writings are religious only in the sense that the age was (and the culture still is) deeply permeated by the matter of religion.

BIBLIOGRAPHY

The literature on Sa'dī is enormous, but most of it (apart from articles in the standard histories of Persian literature and similar reference works) is still not available in Western languages, and nearly all of it is long out of print. The standard monograph, which reviews virtually everything worthwhile prior to its own date, is Henri Massé's *Essai sur le poète Saadi* (Paris, 1919).

Editions of Sa'dī's works in Persian are countless; practically none of them are in any sense critical. As to translations, few of the individual poems have been satisfactorily rendered into any Western languages. There are, however, reliable and recent English renderings of the two major works: the *Būstān,* which I have translated with an introduction and notes as *Morals Pointed and Tales Adorned* (Toronto, 1974), and *The Gulistān or Rose Garden of Sa'dī,* translated by Edward Rehatsek (1888), which I have revised with an introduction (New York, 1965). Both of these contain further bibliographical information.

G. M. WICKENS

ṢADR AL-DĪN SHĪRĀZĪ. *See* Mullā Ṣadrā.

SAGAS. From the late twelfth century onward, nearly two hundred years after the introduction of Christianity, an extensive saga literature was produced in Iceland. The Icelandic sagas are prose works in narrative form, including novels and tales, biographies of famous men, and accounts of events in Iceland. From a literary point of view, the most important group is that of the Family Sagas, dealing with people and events in the early period of the settlement of Iceland (late ninth and tenth centuries). These are partly based on oral tradition, but events and legends are interpreted by their authors, as in a historical novel. They vary greatly in length and quality, and the finest of them are recognized as literary masterpieces, the most outstanding of which is the *Brennu-Njálssaga* (Saga of Burnt Njall). A second group is the Sagas of the Bishops, lives of the early bishops of Iceland, which were among the earliest sagas to be written. A third is the Sagas of the Kings, accounts of the lives of the rulers of Norway from legendary times, of which the best known is the collection making up the *Heimskringla* of Snorri Sturluson. A fourth is a small group of contemporary sagas under the title *Sturlungasaga,* partly written by Snorri's nephew Sturla Thórðarson, and telling of events in which he played a part. Finally there are the Sagas of Old Times, sometimes known as "Lying Sagas," which make no pretense of accurate recording of the past. These are tales of fantastic adventures, the exploits of kings and heroes in the legendary past, battles with monsters and supernatural beings, and experiences of travelers in strange lands north or east of Scandinavia.

After Christianity was accepted in 1000 CE, records began to be kept in writing, and before long, written literature was produced, first in Latin and then in Icelandic. Schools were set up to teach the new learning, and Icelanders went abroad to study, bringing new literary influences to Iceland when they returned. Already possessed of a rich oral literature—for storytelling had flourished there from the time of settlement—the Icelandic people took great pride in preserving their family traditions. Under the influence of new ideas, they composed written sagas in their own language, some as a record of history, some as serious literary works based on traditions of the past, others primarily for entertainment. But viewed through the eyes of Christian writers, the picture of the religious past may be based on vague memories and popular tradition, deliberate antiquarian reconstruction, or the writer's own suppositions as to what the old religion was like, based on the Hebrew scriptures or Vergil. The sagas express little direct hostility to the worship of the traditional gods, except possibly in the sagas of early Christian kings or those describing the conversion. On the other hand, religion tends to remain in the background in these works, since the main interest lies in struggles for power, family relationships, the rise of outstanding men, and tragic deaths as the result of feuds or local conflicts.

The sagas thus form a complex body of material. They do not offer an eyewitness view of pagan Iceland, although the narrative art of the saga writers is such that they may sometimes give that impression. They contain some material, however, of considerable interest to the historian of religion. The *Eyrbyggjasaga* (Saga of the Eyre Dwellers), for instance, chronicles the arrival from Norway of Thorolf, a devoted worshiper of the god Þórr (Thor) who came to settle in western Iceland. He is shown choosing his land at the prompting of the god, setting up pillars brought from Þórr's shrine in Norway, marking out his land with fire, and building a new temple near his home. Although the elaborate description of this temple and its resemblance to a Christian church may be misleading, the association of Þórr with the land, with the choice of a sacred field for the Law Assembly and the taking of oaths on a sacred ring, is on the whole convincing. Moreover, Thorolf took as a holy place a little rocky hill known as Helgafell, an outstanding landmark visible from many miles away, shaped like a large burial mound. We are told of a belief that men of Thorolf's family entered the hill after death and that sounds of feasting could be heard there. This is in keeping with what is known of the Germanic cult of the ancestors, linked with the great burial mounds of Scandinavia, and it seems to be based on local traditions independent of literary influences. Similarly, in the *Víga-Glumssaga* the hero's family are worshipers of the god Freyr, the chief of Vanir deities of fertility, and are responsible for a holy field that is renowned for its crops. In time of trouble, the young hero deserts Freyr's cult for that of the warrior god Óðinn (Odin), bringing down Freyr's wrath upon himself when he slays a man in the sacred field. Such glimpses of the place of religion in men's lives, the close relationship between the gods and the land, and their association with law offer a valuable addition to the literary presentation of the gods in the Eddas.

The sagas tell of the swearing of oaths of vengeance, of sacrificial feasts, divination practices, and the favor of the *landvættir* ("land spirits") toward certain men, bringing luck in farming and fishing. They present Þórr as a protector against storms and bad weather at sea and as the god who supports order in the community; Freyr appears as the bringer of good harvests, and Óðinn is the god who causes strife among men but who also endows poets and orators with power over words. They emphasize the importance of the "luck" of a king or a family, which may be handed on from one man to another, and which is sometimes personified as a female guardian spirit. They include tales of shape changing, where men take on animal form in dreams or in the excitement of battle. [*See* Shape Shifting.] Such information is scattered through the sagas and must always be treated with caution. For instance, the arresting account in the *Hrafnkelssaga* of a sacred horse shared by the hero with the god Freyr, on which he swore that no man should ride on pain of death, is now generally recognized to be a late and fictitious presentation of heathen beliefs and practices unlikely to have been part of the early tradition in Iceland.

Apart from the sagas that are recognized as impressive creative works of literature, there are fragments or badly preserved sagas telling of religious practices. Some appear in the *Landnámabók* (Book of the Land-Takings), a composite account of the settling of Iceland. The earliest surviving version of this was written in the late thirteenth century, and some of its tales come from oral sagas or from lost written ones. The sagas as a whole contain much folklore, stories of the return of the dead and of witchcraft in particular, which may represent beliefs and popular tales at the time when they were written. Much folklore is also associated with the sagas of the early Christian kings of Norway, Olaf I Tryggvason and Olaf II Haraldsson, who are represented as outdoing heathen wizards with their Christian magic. More interesting for our knowledge of the Germanic gods is the legendary history of the early kings in the *Ynglingasaga.* Here the Swedish royal family is presented as the descendants of Freyr and as worshipers of Óðinn. Some of the myths included are not found elsewhere, like that of the war between the Æsir and the Vanir, the two groups of gods.

The sagas and stories produced primarily for entertainment, like those added to the later Sagas of the Kings, form a body of work of mixed quality. There are many lively, humorous tales, some mocking heathen practice, particularly of the Swedes, who kept up the worship of the old gods longer than Norwegians and Danes. There is, for instance, a tale of a young Norwegian who joined the priestess of Freyr in her journey around the farms to bring men good seasons, and who impersonated Freyr with outstanding success. This may have been suggested by foreign tales of the impersonation of the gods of the ancient world, but the comedy depends on the fact that such practices were thought to take place as part of the Vanic cult, and evidence outside the sagas confirms this.

Some of the Sagas of Old Times include stories about the gods. In the *Gautrekssaga* we have the tale of Starkaðr the Old, a famous warrior renowned for his courage and ruthlessness as a follower of Óðinn. His mother dedicated him to the god before birth in return for help in a brewing contest, and when he grew to manhood, Óðinn compelled him to commit unforgivable treachery and bring about the sacrificial death of the king he served, causing him to be hanged and stabbed in accordance with the rites of the Germanic Wōdan. The tale of Sarkaðr went back to earlier times in the North; the tale of another popular hero, Sigurd the Volsung—in particular his dragon slaying and tragic death—seems to go back to the tenth century, when it was depicted on memorial stones in Scandinavia and northern England. On the other hand, the story of Sigurd's father, Sigmund, another follower of Óðinn, who received his famous sword from the god, may go back to early Germanic heroic tradition. Other heroes of the past, such as Ragnar Lodbrok, said to have been put to death in a snake pit, and the Danish king Hrólfr Kraki, who fell with his warriors in a blazing hall in Sweden, seem to have been heroic figures of the Viking age. Such heroic legends may be distinguished from comic tales that mock the gods, like the *Sǫrla Þáttr* (Tale of Sorli), in which Óðinn employs Loki to steal Freyja's necklace so that he can compel her to do what he wants. Even this, however, is linked with an earlier heroic tradition, that of the quarrel of Hedin and Hogni and their everlasting battle in the otherworld.

Thus the sagas are a rich mine of traditions about northern and Germanic heroes, tales of Óðinn's famous warriors, information concerning religious practices, folklore, and later material introduced from foreign sources to make a good story. Evidence about early Germanic religion is consequently difficult to extract and varies greatly in value.

Because Iceland was a new colony, established on a virtually empty island in the late ninth century, the saga writers were cut off from their homeland and the religious traditions linked with holy places and burial grounds there. They had no established priesthood to keep up the old traditions, and the *goðar,* who organized the religious feasts, were men of power and authority in the various districts rather than religious leaders. On the other hand, we can see in the sagas the attempts made by the early settlers to fill the gap, establishing new places of sanctity, particularly the impressive sacred site at Thingvellir where the general assembly (Þing) met once a year. They made offerings to the spirits of the new land, who may be seen as the equivalents of the mythic Vanir. Many Icelanders claimed descent from royal families in Norway and Denmark and set out to record early traditions from these countries. In the twelfth century there was a revival of interest in the heroic past with its tales of gods and heroes. Traces of this can be seen in the sagas, and the new outburst of creative activity inspired by interest in the past may deceive us into thinking that we are dealing with firsthand sources when they are nothing of the kind. It is precisely because of the richness and artistry of the sagas that they must be viewed with caution as reliable sources for early religion in the North.

BIBLIOGRAPHY

Many of the lesser-known Icelandic sagas have not been translated, but a number of the Family Sagas are obtainable in English in inexpensive editions. There are good modern translations by Gwyn Jones, Hermann Pálsson, and others. *The Saga of Gisli,* translated by George Johnston (Toronto, 1973), includes an essay by Peter Foote that gives a brief account of saga literature. General works on the saga are Theodore M. Andersson's *The Problem of Icelandic Saga Origins* (New York, 1964) and Peter Hallberg's *The Icelandic Saga,* translated by Paul Schach (Lincoln, Nebr., 1962). The problems of saga sources and conflicting theories are discussed in detail by Lars Lönnroth in *Njáls Saga: A Critical Introduction* (Berkeley, 1976). For the particular problem of the *Hrafnkelssaga,* see *Hrafnkels Saga Freysgoða: A Study by Sigurdur Nordal,* translated by R. George Thomas (Cardiff, 1958).

The Sagas of the Kings in Snorri Sturluson's *Heimskringla* have been translated by Lee M. Hollander (Austin, 1967); and the Olaf Sagas have been translated by Samuel Laing in *The Olaf Sagas,* part 1 of *Heimskringla by Snorri Sturluson,* 2 vols., with introduction and notes by Jacqueline Simpson (London, 1964). A number of the Sagas of Old Times have been translated individually; some will be found in Nora Kershaw's *Stories and Ballads of the Far Past* (Cambridge, 1921) and others in Jacqueline Simpson's *The Northmen Talk* (London 1965), which has a useful introduction. An anthropological approach to the attitude toward magic and religion expressed in the sagas and in the poems will be found in Rosalie H. Wax's *Magic, Fate and History: The Changing Ethos of the Vikings* (Lawrence, Kans., 1969).

HILDA R. ELLIS DAVIDSON

SAHAK PARTHEV, chief bishop of Armenia from circa 387 to 439. Sahak, son of Nersēs the Great, is surnamed Parthev, or Part'ew ("the Parthian"), because of his descent from Gregory the Illuminator and the Armeno-Parthian Arsacid dynasty. There is very little information about his early years and the first two decades of his pontificate. The fifth-century Armenian historians Koriwn and Lazar of P'arpi speak for the most part about his role in the cultural movement at the time of the invention of the Armenian alphabet in AD 404. Sahak, who presided over the Persian sector of Armenia, patronized the educational, missionary, religious, and literary activities of Mesrop Mashtotsʿ, the inventor of the Armenian alphabet. Sahak was instrumental in the spread of literacy in the royal central provinces of Armenia; he personally revised the Armenian version of the scriptures on the basis of the Septuagint and translated several works of the Fathers from Greek, a language in which he was proficient.

In 420 Sahak went to the Persian court in Ctesiphon (near present-day Baghdad), where he intervened on behalf of the Persian Christians who were being persecuted. In 428, when the Sasanids put an end to the Arsacid dynasty of Armenia, Sahak was removed from office, since he was of Arsacid lineage. He was replaced by southern and Syriac bishops, but evidently continued to exercise authority in spiritual matters.

Sahak is well known for his correspondence with Patriarch Proclus of Constantinople (434–446) and Bishop Acacius of Melitene concerning the "heretical" teachings of Theodore of Mopsuestia. Contact with these bishops led Sahak to banish Theodore's works from Armenia. A part of Sahak's letter to Proclus was officially read during one of the sessions of the Second Council of Constantinople in 553.

In the mid-430s, while Sahak was still alive, the canons of the councils of Nicaea and Ephesus were brought to Armenia and translated into Armenian, probably by Sahak himself. There are also canons attributed to Sahak that are probably not authentic that are from a later period predating the eighth century.

Koriwn states that Sahak translated and adapted the Greek liturgical texts for practical use. The exact nature of his influence on the present-day liturgical books has still not been carefully studied. There are also hymns ascribed to him that bear the stylistic marks of later centuries. The earliest translations of the Fathers, however, were made under his supervision, according to the trustworthy testimony of Koriwn.

Sahak died on 7 September 439, and was buried in Ashtishat. Soon thereafter a martyrium was built over his grave, and he was venerated as a saint. In his youth he had married and fathered a daughter, who became the mother of Vardan Mamikonian, the commander-in-chief of the Armenian army. Sahak was the last of the bishops of Armenia who were of the lineage of Gregory the Illuminator. He is greatly venerated by the Armenians as a saint and honored, with Mesrop Mashtotsʿ, as the cofounder of the Armenian literary tradition.

BIBLIOGRAPHY

Conybeare, F. C. "The Armenian Canons of Saint Sahak Catholicos of Armenia." *American Journal of Theology* 2 (1898): 828–848.

Garitte, Gérard, ed. *La narratio de rebus Armeniae.* Louvain, 1952.

Koriwn. *Vark' Mashtots'i.* Yerevan, 1941. Translated into English by Bedros Norehad as *Koriun: The Life of Mashtots* (New York, 1964).

Lazar of P'arpi. *Patmut'iwn Hayots* (1763). Tbilisi, 1904. Translated into French by P. S. Ghésarian as "Lazare de Pharbe, Histoire d'Arménie," in *Collection des Historiens de l'Arménie,* edited by Victor Langlois, vol. 2 (Paris, 1869).

Tallon, Maurice. *Livre des lettres.* Beirut, 1955.

KRIKOR H. MAKSOUDIAN

SAICHŌ (767–822), also known by his posthumous title Dengyō Daishi; founder of Japanese Tendai, a sect derived from the teachings and practices of the Chinese T'ien-t'ai school.

Life. Saichō was born into a family of devout Buddhists. At the age of twelve he went to study at the provincial temple in Ōmi. There he studied under Gyōhyō (722–797), a disciple of Tao-hsüan (702–760), the Chinese monk who had brought Northern School Ch'an, Kegon (Chin., Hua-yen) teachings, and the *Fan wang* precepts to Japan in 736. Saichō's studies of meditation and Kegon "one-vehicle" (Skt., *ekayāna;* Jpn., *ichijō*) doctrines during this period influenced his lifelong doctrinal predilections. Shortly after he was ordained in 785, he decided to climb Mount Hiei. He remained there for approximately a decade to meditate and study. During his retreat, Saichō read about Chinese T'ien-t'ai meditation practice in Kegon texts and managed to obtain several T'ien-t'ai texts that had been brought to Japan by Chien-chen (Ganjin, 688–763) in 754 but had subsequently been ignored by Japanese monks.

The capital of Japan was moved from Nara to Nagaoka in 784, and then to Kyoto in 795. Mount Hiei was located to the northeast of Kyoto, a direction considered dangerous by geomancers, but Saichō's presence on the mountain protected the new capital and brought him to the attention of the court. In addition, the court was interested in reforming Buddhism by patronizing serious monks without political aspirations and by supporting those teachings that would bridge the traditional rivalry between the Hossō (Yogācāra) and Sanron (Mādhyamika) schools. Soon various court nobles, especially those of the Wake clan, began to show an interest in Saichō. With court support, Saichō traveled to China in 804 to obtain T'ien-t'ai texts and to study with Chinese teachers. During his eight months there, he received initiations into a variety of Buddhist traditions, including the T'ien-t'ai school, Ox-head Ch'an, the *Fan wang* precepts (a set of fifty-eight Mahāyāna disciplinary rules), and Esoteric Buddhism.

Upon his return to Japan in 805, Saichō discovered that his brief studies of Esoteric Buddhism attracted more attention than his mastery of Tendai teachings. Saichō's major patron, Emperor Kammu (r. 781–806), was ill, and Saichō used Esoteric rituals in an attempt to restore Kammu's health. Shortly before Kammu died the court awarded Saichō two yearly ordinands, one in Tendai and one in Esoteric Buddhism. This event marked the formal establishment of the Tendai school.

Saichō spent the next few years studying Esoteric Buddhism, but his efforts were overshadowed by the return of Kūkai (774–835) from China in 806. Kūkai's knowledge of Esoteric Buddhist practice and doctrine was clearly superior to that of Saichō. Although Saichō and some of his disciples went to study with Kūkai and borrowed Esoteric texts from him, by 816 irreconcilable differences on doctrinal issues, a dispute over the loan of certain Esoteric texts, and the defection of Taihan (778–858?), one of Saichō's most able disciples, ended Saichō's hopes of mastering Esoteric Buddhism.

During the years that Saichō studied Esoteric Buddhism, more than half of the Tendai yearly ordinands left Mount Hiei. Many of them defected to the Hossō school; others departed in order to study Esoteric Buddhism with Kūkai or to support their ailing mothers. It became clear that if Tendai were to survive, Saichō would have to retain many more of his students on Mount Hiei. During the last five or six years of his life, Saichō strove to secure the place of Tendai within Japanese Buddhism, and in the process composed almost all of his major works.

Saichō's activities during this period can be divided into two categories. First, he defended Tendai doctrines and meditation practices against attacks by the Hossō monk Tokuitsu (d. 841?). Saichō argued that everyone could attain Buddhahood and that many could do so in their present lifetime through Tendai and Esoteric practices. He firmly rejected the Hossō argument that the attainment of Buddhahood required aeons of practice and that some people would never be able to attain it. Second, Saichō proposed major reforms in the Tendai educational system, in monastic discipline, and in the ordination system. Saichō suggested that Tendai monks be ordained on Mount Hiei, where they would be required to remain for the next twelve years without venturing outside the monastery's boundaries. Ordinations were to be supervised by lay administrators *(zoku bettō)* who also held important positions at court.

In addition, Saichō criticized the *Ssu fen lü (Dharmaguptaka Vinaya)* precepts, which traditionally had been conferred at ordination in China and Japan. He argued that the *Ssu fen lü* were Hīnayānist rules that would cause the recipient to retrogress, not progress, in his religious practice. The *Ssu fen lü* precepts were to be replaced with the *Fan wang* precepts, a set of Mahāyāna precepts traditionally used in East Asia to inculcate Mahāyāna attitudes in monks, nuns, and lay believers, but not to ordain laypeople as monks or nuns. The adoption of the *Fan wang* precepts was intended to strengthen monastic discipline on Mount Hiei by providing the monks with a more relevant guide to conduct than the *Ssu fen lü* precepts. After the yearly ordinands had completed their twelve years on Mount Hiei, many of them were to receive official appointments as administrators of monastic affairs in the provinces. During their terms, they were to devote much of their time to projects that would benefit the populace. Saichō expected these activities to contribute to the spread of Tendai influence.

Saichō's proposals were vehemently opposed by the Hossō and other Nara schools because their approval would have entailed implicit recognition of Saichō's criticisms of Hossō doctrine and practice. In addition, the proposals would have removed Tendai monks from the supervision of the Office of Monastic Affairs (Sōgō). The court, not wishing to become involved in disputes between schools, hesitated to act on Saichō's proposals. As a result, Saichō died without seeing his reforms approved; however, one week after Saichō's death the court approved the proposals as a posthumous tribute.

Thought. Most of Saichō's works were polemical and designed either to prove that Tendai doctrine and practice were superior to that of any of the other schools of Japanese Buddhism or to argue that the Tendai school should be free of any supervision by other schools. In his defense of Tendai interests, Saichō discussed a number of issues that played important roles in later Japanese religious history.

Saichō had an acute sense of the flow of Buddhist history. The teachings of the *Lotus Sutra,* the text that contained the Buddha's ultimate teaching according to the Tendai school, had been composed in India and then transmitted to China. Japan, Saichō believed, would be the next site for the rise of the "one-vehicle" teachings propagated by Tendai. Saichō was conversant with theories on the decline of Buddhism and believed that he was living at the end of the Period of Counterfeit Dharma *(zōmatsu),* described as an era in which many monks would be corrupt and covetous.

Although Saichō believed major changes were needed in Japanese Buddhism, he did not use theories on the decline of Buddhism to justify doctrinal innovations, as did some of the founders of the Kamakura schools. Rather, Saichō argued that because Buddhism in the capital had declined, monks should retreat to the mountains to practice assiduously. [*See also* Mappō.]

Many of Saichō's doctrinal innovations were based on his belief that the religious aptitude of the Japanese people as a whole had matured to the point where they no longer needed any form of Buddhism other than the "perfect teachings" *(engyō)* of the Tendai school. Earlier Buddhist thinkers had also been interested in the manner in which the religious faculties of people matured, but had usually discussed the process in terms of individuals rather than whole peoples.

Religious training for people with "perfect faculties" (*enki,* i.e., those whose religious faculties respond to the "perfect teachings") was based on the threefold study *(sangaku)* of morality, meditation, and doctrine. Saichō believed that T'ien-t'ai teachings on meditation and doctrine were adequate, although they could be supplemented by Esoteric Buddhism. However, he was dissatisfied with the traditional T'ien-t'ai position on morality, which maintained that a monk could follow the *Ssu fen lü* precepts with a Mahāyāna mind. Saichō argued that adherence to the *Ssu fen lü* would cause a monk to retrogress toward Hīnayāna goals. Tendai practices could be realized only by using the Mahāyāna *Fan wang* precepts for ordinations and monastic discipline.

Chinese T'ien-t'ai had been a syncretistic tradition, particularly at the T'ien-t'ai Yü-ch'üan monastery. Chinese monks had been interested in Ch'an and Esoteric Buddhism as well as in the *Ssu fen lü* and *Fan wang* precepts. Saichō inherited this tradition, but developed certain aspects of it in innovative ways. For example, Saichō considered Esoteric Buddhism to be essentially the same as Tendai *(enmitsu itchi)* and thus awarded Esoteric Buddhism a more central place in the Tendai tradition than it had been given by most Chinese monks. Like Kūkai, Saichō emphasized the importance of striving for enlightenment as an immediate goal to be attained in this existence *(sokushin jōbutsu).* Tendai and Esoteric practices, he felt, provided a direct path *(jikidō)* to enlightenment, whereas the teachings of the Nara schools required aeons to bring the practitioner to enlightenment.

The Chinese T'ien-t'ai systems for classifying teachings *(kyōhan)* developed by Chih-i (538–597) had been designed to demonstrate how the "perfect teachings" of the *Lotus Sutra* revealed the ultimate meaning of all other Buddhist traditions and could be used to unify and interpret various Buddhist doctrines. Later, as the competition between T'ien-t'ai and other schools intensified, T'ien-t'ai scholars such as Chan-jan (711–782) developed classification systems that demonstrated the complete superiority of the *Lotus Sutra* over other teachings. Saichō's rejection of Hossō doctrine and the *Ssu fen lü* precepts was based on the later T'ien-t'ai classification systems. Saichō also developed his own systems, which emphasized the importance of relying on the Buddha's words from such texts as the *Lotus Sutra,* rather than on the commentaries (*śāstra*s) used by the Hossō and Sanron schools. In addition, he stressed the importance of matching teachings to the faculties of the religious practitioner so that enlightenment could be rapidly attained.

[*See also* Tendaishū; Shingonshū; *and the biographies of Chih-i and Kūkai.*]

BIBLIOGRAPHY

Saichō's works have been collected in *Dengyō Daishi zenshū,* 5 vols. (1926; reprint, Tokyo, 1975). Important collections of Japanese scholarship are *Dengyō Daishi kenkyū,* 5 vols. (Tokyo, 1973–1980), and Shioiri Ryōdō's *Saichō* (Tokyo, 1982). For a study of Saichō in English, see my book *Saichō and the Establishment of the Japanese Tendai School* (Berkeley, 1984).

PAUL GRONER